THE OXFORD HANDBOOK OF
THE DISNEY MUSICAL

THE OXFORD HANDBOOK OF

THE DISNEY MUSICAL

Edited by
DOMINIC BROOMFIELD-MCHUGH
and
COLLEEN MONTGOMERY

OXFORD
UNIVERSITY PRESS

Oxford University Press is a department of the University of Oxford.
It furthers the University's objective of excellence in research, scholarship,
and education by publishing worldwide. Oxford is a registered trade mark of
Oxford University Press in the UK and certain other countries.

Published in the United States of America by Oxford University Press
198 Madison Avenue, New York, NY 10016, United States of America.

© Oxford University Press 2025

All rights reserved. No part of this publication may be reproduced, stored in a retrieval system, transmitted, used for text and data mining, or used for training artificial intelligence, in any form or by any means, without the prior permission in writing of Oxford University Press, or as expressly permitted by law, by license or under terms agreed with the appropriate reprographics rights organization. Inquiries concerning reproduction outside the scope of the above should be sent to the Rights Department, Oxford University Press, at the address above.

You must not circulate this work in any other form
and you must impose this same condition on any acquirer

Library of Congress Cataloging-in-Publication Data
Names: Broomfield-McHugh, Dominic, editor. | Montgomery, Colleen, editor.
Title: The Oxford Handbook of the Disney Musical / Edited by
Dominic Broomfield-McHugh, Colleen Montgomery.
Description: New York : Oxford University Press, 2025. |
Series: Oxford handbooks series | Includes bibliographical references and index.
Identifiers: LCCN 2024058889 | ISBN 9780197633496 (hardback) |
ISBN 9780197633519 (epub) | ISBN 9780197633526
Subjects: LCSH: Walt Disney Company. | Musical films—United
States—History and criticism. | Animated films—United States—History
and criticism. | Musicals—United States—History and criticism.
Classification: LCC PN1999.W27 O94 2025 | DDC 791.43/6—dc23/eng/20250118
LC record available at https://lccn.loc.gov/2024058889

DOI: 10.1093/oxfordhb/9780197633496.001.0001

Printed by Marquis Book Printing, Canada

Contents

Acknowledgments ix
List of Contributors xi
Introduction xix
    Dominic Broomfield-McHugh and Colleen Montgomery

PART I. THE CLASSICAL PERIOD

1. Act One: The Beginnings of the Disney Musical   3
   J. B. Kaufman

2. Music, Nature, and Materiality in *Bambi*   20
   Daniel Batchelder

3. Musical Evocation, Intertextuality, and Accompaniment in Early Disney Cartoons   40
   Malcolm Cook

4. "Whistle while You Work...": *Snow White and the Seven Dwarfs*, Disney's Fairy-Tale Musicals, and the American Dream   62
   Tracey Mollet

5. Hall Johnson, the Hall Johnson Choir, and Disney: 1941–1955   77
   Julianne Lindberg

PART II. ADAPTATION

6. New Agrabah, Same Old Disney Orientalism: Commodity Racism and Western Effacement of the "Middle East"   101
   Michelle Anya Anjirbag

7. Mutating Stitch: Shifting Approaches to Vocal Performance and Language in the *Lilo & Stitch* Franchise   125
   Rayna Denison

8. From Victoriana to Vaudeville: Alice's Adventures in Musical Adaptation 149
   Dominic Broomfield-McHugh

9. Fidelity-fiduciary-expialidocious: *Mary Poppins*'s Returns 172
   Sean Griffin

10. "Come On, Song! I'm Reflecting!": Reinterpretations of the Musical in Disney's Contemporary Sequels and Remakes 187
    Eve Benhamou

11. Haven't I Seen This Somewhere Before? *The Little Mermaid Live!*, Content Cannibalization, and Disney's Television Legacy 209
    Kelly Kessler

PART III. SOUND, MUSIC, AND TECHNOLOGY

12. Lady and the Transcription: Peggy Lee's Legal Battle with Disney 231
    Colleen Montgomery

13. Singing Mice and Grunting Reindeer: Musical Representations of the Nonhuman and Relating to Animals in Disney Animated Musicals 255
    Kate Galloway

14. The Original Film and Its Broadway Sequel: *Epic Mickey* and *Epic Mickey 2* 277
    Lisa Scoggin

15. The *Jungle Book* Vultures and Generational Listening 297
    Elizabeth Randell Upton

16. That's Integration! Digital VFX Technologies and the Disney Renaissance Musicals (1989–1999) 315
    Christopher Holliday

PART IV. CULTURE AND IDENTITY

17. "The Doors of Perception": Animated Color, Surrealism, and the Latin American Disney Musicals 347
    Kirsten Moana Thompson

18. Disney Divas 375
DEBORAH PAREDEZ AND STACY WOLF

19. Negotiable Diversity: How the *Frozen* Franchise Disneyfied Sámi Music and Culture 406
MIHAELA MIHAILOVA

20. Television Girlhoods, the Musical: Diversity, Imperfection, and Embedded Fan Practices in Disney Channel's *Descendants* 427
MORGAN GENEVIEVE BLUE

21. Imagineering *con Sabrosura*: Cultural Imagineering and Latinidad in the Twenty-First-Century Disney Musical 450
JACQUELINE AVILA AND JUAN FERNANDO VELÁSQUEZ OSPINA

PART V. DISNEY THEATRICAL

22. Before *The Beast*: Entertainment Conglomerates on Broadway in the 1980s 477
ELIZABETH L. WOLLMAN

23. Branding, Demographics, and the Disney Broadway Playbook 498
DEAN ADAMS

24. We're All in This Together: Disney Theatrical in Partnership 520
AMY S. OSATINSKI

25. An Ethnographic and Critical Approach to Disney Musicals in US K–12 Schools 542
SAMMY GROB AND STACY WOLF

26. "There May Be Something There That Wasn't There Before": New Songs in Disney's Broadway Musicals 571
ALEX BÁDUE

27. *Finding Nemo: The Musical*: When Theater Is a Theme-Park Attraction 591
JENNIFER A. KOKAI AND TOM ROBSON

Index 613

Acknowledgments

This book would not have been possible without the unwavering support, guidance, and dedication of many collaborators. We are deeply appreciative of our contributors whose fine scholarship we are privileged to showcase in this collection. Thanks are equally due to our reviewers for their generous and immensely insightful feedback. We are also enormously grateful to Norm Hirschy, who enthusiastically championed the project, as well as to Lauralee Yeary, Rachel Ruisard, and the entire Oxford University Press team for patiently shepherding the book through publication. Last but certainly not least, we are thankful to our families for their unfailing love and encouragement.

Contributors

Dean Adams is a Professor in the Department of Theatre and Senior Associate Dean of Performing Arts at the University of North Carolina at Charlotte. From 1989 to 2011, he was the Artistic Director of the Connecticut Theater Festival in Simsbury, Connecticut. As a producer and director, Adams has presented or co-produced productions with Hartford Stage, Parsons Dance Company, MOMIX, Pilobolus, Cirque de la Symphonie, Hartford Symphony, and Hubbard Street Dance Chicago. He directed and designed a touring production of *Once upon a Mattress*, the first musical ever to tour the People's Republic of China (chronicled in the PBS documentary *Beyond the Wall*), in 1987. Dean holds an MFA in Directing from Florida State University, an MA in Communications and Theatre from the University of Maryland, and a BA in Drama and English from Tufts University. He is a member of the Stage Directors and Choreographers Society and Actors' Equity Association.

Michelle Anya Anjirbag is an affiliated researcher at the University of Antwerp, where she completed a postdoctoral fellowship with the Constructing Age for Young Readers project. Her research interests include adaptation; fairy tales and folklore; Disney; magical libraries; fantasy through sociological lenses; the intersection of literature, media, and culture; representations of gender and age; and cross-period approaches to narrative transmission across cultures and societies. Her work has appeared in a variety of journals and edited collections.

Jacqueline Avila is an Associate Professor of Musicology at the University of Texas, Austin. Her research examines film music and the intersections of identity, tradition, and modernity in the Hollywood and Mexican film industries. She is the author of *Cinesonidos: Film Music and National Identity during Mexico's Época de Oro*, published by Oxford University Press in its Music/Media Series. Additional publications have appeared in *Latin American Music Review*, *Opera Quarterly*, and *American Music*.

Alex Bádue is an Assistant Professor of Music at Hamilton College. He is the author of *Why Aren't They Talking? The Sung-Through Musical from the 1980s to the 2010s* (2022). He has conducted research on the compositional process, musical structure, reception, and social impact of musicals by Jason Robert Brown, William Finn, Michael John LaChiusa, Jonathan Larson, and Jeanine Tesori, as well as Disney Broadway musicals. He also researches the interactions between Latin American and US American popular-music industries in the 1940s and 1950s. He received his PhD in Musicology from the University of Cincinnati's College–Conservatory of Music.

Daniel Batchelder is a musicologist based in the San Francisco Bay Area. His research and teaching have focused primarily on stage and film musicals, with a particular emphasis on the animated musicals of the Walt Disney Studios. His work has appeared in publications from Routledge and Oxford University Press, and he was the guest editor for a special edition of *American Music* on music and sound in Disney media. His review of *Walt Disney's Snow White and the Seven Dwarfs: Master Score* was awarded the Eva Judd O'Meara Award for best review in the journal *Notes*.

Eve Benhamou is a Teaching Fellow in Film Studies at the Université Paul-Valéry Montpellier 3 (France). Prior to this, she taught at the University of the West of England's School of Animation, Swansea University, and the University of Bristol (UK). Her research explores the multifaceted relationship between animation and contemporary live-action cinema, with a focus on aesthetics, film genres, and representations of gender. She published her first monograph in 2022, *Contemporary Disney Animation: Genre, Gender and Hollywood*, and is contributing chapters to *Feminine/Masculine: On Gender in English-Language Cinema and Television* (2024) and *The Routledge Companion to Animation Studies* (forthcoming). Her work is also featured in the *Animation Practice, Process & Production* journal and the *Animation Studies 2.0* and *Fantasy/Animation* blogs.

Morgan Genevieve Blue is an independent scholar and owner of BLUE Indexing & Editorial Services, where she supports scholars throughout the publishing process. In 2024, she joined the executive board of Console-ing Passions International Conference on Television, Audio, Video, New Media, and Feminism. She holds a PhD in Radio-TV-Film from the University of Texas at Austin. She is the author of *Girlhood on Disney Channel: Branding, Celebrity, and Femininity* (2017) and co-editor of the second volume of *Mediated Girlhoods* (2018). Her work also appears in the edited collections *Fleeting Images* (2013), *Voicing Girlhood in Popular Music* (2019), and *The Television Genre Book*, 4th ed. (2023), as well as in the following journals: *Feminist Media Studies*; *Film, Fashion and Consumption*; *Journal of Children and Media*; and *Red Feather Journal*.

Dominic Broomfield-McHugh is a Professor of Music at the University of Sheffield and a Visiting Professor of Film and Theatre Music at the historic Gresham College in London. His scholarship focuses on the American musical on stage and screen, and his books include *Loverly: The Life and Times of "My Fair Lady"* (2012), *The Complete Lyrics of Alan Jay Lerner* (2018), *Adapting "The Wizard of Oz"* (2018), *The Oxford Handbook of Musical Theatre Screen Adaptations* (2019), *The Letters of Cole Porter* (2019), *The Big Parade: Meredith Willson's Musicals from "The Music Man" to "1491"* (2021), and *The Oxford Handbook of the Hollywood Musical* (2022). He is Associate Producer of the PBS documentary *Meredith Willson: America's Music Man*, for which he was awarded an Emmy, and has appeared on all the main BBC television and radio stations as well as NPR in America. He has given talks and lectures at the Sydney Opera House, New York City Center, the Library of Congress, the British Film Institute, New York Public Library, Sadler's Wells, and Lincoln Center, among many others. He was Reviews Editor of

Studies in Musical Theatre for seven years and is Series Editor of *Oxford Guides to Film Musicals*.

Malcolm Cook is an Associate Professor of Film at the University of Southampton, UK. His monograph *Early British Animation: From Page and Stage to Cinema Screens* was published in 2018 and was runner-up for the 2019 Norman McLaren/Evelyn Lambart Award for Best Scholarly Book in Animation from the Society for Animation Studies. He is currently researching useful animation, especially within advertising, and he has written several chapters on this topic, which appear in *The Animation Studies Reader* (2018) and *Aardman Animations: Beyond Stop-Motion* (2020). He has also co-edited (with Kirsten Moana Thompson) the collection *Animation and Advertising* (2019) and contributed a chapter to it on Disney and automobile advertising. The collection received an Honourable Mention for Best Edited Collection in the British Association of Film, Television and Screen Studies Awards 2021 and was runner-up for the 2021 SAS McLaren/Lambart award.

Rayna Denison is a Professor of Film and Digital Arts at the University of Bristol, UK. She does research and teaching around contemporary Japanese and American animation, with a particular focus on animation franchising and industrial history. Denison has written the monographs *Anime: An Industrial History* (2015) and *Studio Ghibli: An Industrial History* (2023), edited a collection titled *Princess Mononoke: Understanding Studio Ghibli's Monster Princess* (2018), and co-edited the Eisner Award–nominated collection *Superheroes on World Screens* (2015). Her research can also be found in a wide range of journals including the *Journal of Cinema and Media Studies*, *Japan Forum*, the *International Journal of Cultural Studies*, and *Animation: An Interdisciplinary Journal*.

Kate Galloway is an Assistant Professor of Ethnomusicology, Sound Studies, and Games at Rensselaer Polytechnic Institute. Her research addresses how and why contemporary artists remix and recycle sounds, music, and texts encoded with environmental knowledge and the creative and social phenomena of internet music communities and practices of listening to the internet. With Paula Harper and Steven Gamble, she co-organized the Music and the Internet Conference (2023), and with Harper and Christa Bentley, she is co-organizer of the first multiday Taylor Swift conference, Taylor Swift Study Day: Eras, Narrative, Digital Music and Media (2021). With Harper and Bentley, she is co-editing the forthcoming collection *Taylor Swift: The Star, the Songs, the Fans*. With Elizabeth Hambleton, she is co-editor of the collection *Music and Sonic Environments in Video Games: Listening to and Performing Ludic Soundscapes*.

Sean Griffin is a Professor of Film and Media Arts in the Meadows School of the Arts at Southern Methodist University. He is the author of *Tinker Belles and Evil Queens: The Walt Disney Company from the Inside Out* and *Free and Easy: A Defining History of the American Musical Film*, and coauthor of *America on Film: Race, Class, Gender and Sexuality at the Movies* and *Queer Images: A History of Lesbian and Gay Film in America*. He has also edited a number of anthologies and contributed a number of articles on the musical genre and Disney to journals and other anthologies. Before becoming a professor, Griffin helped produce television ad campaigns for Disney and Touchstone motion pictures.

Sammy Grob is a teacher, music director, composer, arranger/orchestrator, and performer based in Washington, DC. He teaches vocal music and theater at the Charles E. Smith Jewish Day School and serves as adjunct faculty at American University and George Washington University. Previously, he was an assistant conductor with the National Children's Chorus, founded and directed the Brooklyn Music School's Community Choir, and served as a teaching artist with several arts education organizations in New York City. He holds a BA in Psychology and Education from Yale University; his chapter in this volume is a partial adaptation of his award-winning undergraduate thesis on critical education as applied to school musicals. Additionally, he sings with an award-winning choir.

Christopher Holliday is a Lecturer in Liberal Arts and Visual Cultures Education at King's College London, specializing in Hollywood cinema, animation history, and contemporary digital media. His research is concerned with digital technologies and forms of computer animation in contemporary moving-image culture, and his work on animation and visual effects has appeared in *Animation Practice, Process & Production*; *Animation: An Interdisciplinary Journal*; *Convergence: The International Journal of Research into New Media Technologies*; *Early Popular Visual Culture*; *Journal of British Cinema and Television*; *Journal of Cinema and Media Studies*; *Journal of Popular Film and Television*; and *The London Journal*. Holliday is the author of *The Computer-Animated Film: Industry, Style and Genre* (2018) and co-editor of the anthologies *Fantasy/Animation: Connections between Media, Mediums and Genres* (2018) and *Snow White and the Seven Dwarfs: New Perspectives on Production, Reception, Legacy* (2021), as well as the creator and curator of the website/blog/podcast www.fantasy-animation.org.

J. B. Kaufman is an author and film historian who has published and lectured extensively on Disney animation, American silent film history, and related topics. His books include *The Fairest One of All*, *South of the Border with Disney*, and *Pinocchio: The Making of the Disney Epic*. He is also coauthor, with Russell Merritt, of *Walt Disney's Silly Symphonies: A Companion to the Classic Cartoon Series* and the award-winning *Walt in Wonderland: The Silent Films of Walt Disney* and collaborated with David Gerstein on two major Taschen histories of Mickey Mouse and Donald Duck. Kaufman has also written numerous articles on aspects of American silent film and has presented programs at festivals including the TCM Classic Film Festival, the San Francisco Silent Film Festival, and Le Giornate del Cinema Muto in Pordenone, Italy, where he was a 2020 recipient of the Jean Mitry Award.

Kelly Kessler is a Professor of Media and Popular Culture at DePaul University and the author of *Destabilizing the Hollywood Musical: Music, Masculinity, and Mayhem* (2010) and *Broadway in the Box: Television's Lasting Love Affair with the Musical* (2020), as well as the editor of *Gender, Sex, and Sexuality in Musical Theatre: He/She/They Could Have*

Danced All Night (2022). Kessler also served as the editor of a special issue of *Studies in Musical Theatre* focused on unpacking the iconic image of the musical diva. A selection of her work on exploring gender and genre in American film and television can be found in *Cinema Journal, Television and New Media, Feminism at the Movies,* and *Televising Queer Women,* and her public scholarship has appeared on sites such as *Primetimer, The Advocate,* and *Wired*.

Jennifer A. Kokai is, with Tom Robson, the co-editor of *Performance and the Disney Theme Park Experience: The Tourist as Actor* (2019, 2nd ed. forthcoming) and the coauthor of the monograph *Disney Parks and the Construction of American Identity: Tourism, Performance, Collaboration* (2024). With Robson, she has contributed essays about Disney theme parks to the *Journal of Themed Experience and Attractions Studies* and *Virtual Interiorities*, as well as the forthcoming *Enveloping Worlds: Toward a Discourse of Immersivity and Participatory Performance*. She has published a monograph, *Swim Pretty: Aquatic Spectacles and the Performance of Race, Gender, and Nature* (2017), and articles in *Theatre Topics, Theatre History Studies,* the *Journal of Dramatic Theory and Criticism*, the *Journal of American Drama and Theatre*, and *Review: The LMDA Journal*, as well as numerous anthologies. She is also an internationally produced playwright. She is currently the Director of the School of Theatre and Dance and the Endowed Chair of the Holloway and the Brit at the University of South Florida.

Julianne Lindberg is an Associate Professor of Musicology at the University of Nevada, Reno. Her research interests include American musical theater, musical modernism, and children's musical cultures, with a focus on musical and theatrical articulations of gender, race, age, and class in musicals of the pre–World War II era. Her book, *Pal Joey: The History of a Heel* (2020), traces the genesis and cultural significance of Rodgers and Hart's classic musical comedy, *Pal Joey*. Lindberg's current projects include an examination of representations of childhood and adolescence in American musicals of the 1930s and an edited collection, with Nicholas Gebhardt, on vaudeville's impact on stage and screen musicals. Her recent and forthcoming publications can be found in *American Music, Studies in Musical Theatre, The Routledge Companion to Jazz Studies, Rodgers and Hammerstein in Context, The Cambridge Companion to Sinatra,* and *The Oxford Handbook of Musical Theatre Screen Adaptations*.

Mihaela Mihailova is an Assistant Professor in the School of Cinema at San Francisco State University. She is the editor of *Coraline: A Closer Look at Studio LAIKA's Stop-Motion Witchcraft* (2021). She has published in the *Journal of Cinema and Media Studies, The Velvet Light Trap, Convergence: The International Journal of Research into New Media Technologies, Feminist Media Studies, Animation: An Interdisciplinary Journal, Studies in Russian and Soviet Cinema, [In]Transition, Flow,* and *Kino Kultura*. She has also contributed chapters to *Animating Film Theory* (with John MacKay), *Animated Landscapes: History, Form, and Function, The Animation Studies Reader,* and *Drawn from Life: Issues and Themes in Animated Documentary Cinema*. Mihailova is the co-editor of the open-access journal *Animation Studies* (https://journal.animationstud

ies.org/) and the co-president of the Society for Animation Studies. Her current book project, *Synthetic Creativity: Deepfakes in Contemporary Media*, was recently awarded a National Endowment for the Humanities grant.

Tracey Mollet is an Associate Professor in Media and Communication at the University of Leeds, UK. She is the author of *Cartoons in Hard Times: The Animated Shorts of Disney and Warner Brothers in Depression and War 1932–1945* (2017) and *A Cultural History of the Disney Fairy Tale: Once upon an American Dream* (2020). She has published widely on the Walt Disney Company's contributions to popular culture and their wider relationship to fairy-tale narratives and the American dream.

Colleen Montgomery is an Associate Professor in the Department of Radio, Television, and Film at Rowan University. She is a film and media scholar whose research centers on animation, film sound/music, and vocal performance. She is currently completing a monograph on vocal performance in Disney and Pixar animation. She is also co-editing *The Oxford Handbook of Media and Vocality* with Lisa Coulthard and Katherine Spring. Her work is published in journals including *American Music, Animation Studies, the Journal of Cinema and Media Studies, Media Industries*, and *Music Sound and the Moving Image*, as well as in several edited collections.

Amy S. Osatinski is an Associate Professor of Theatre History and Head of the BA in Theatre Innovation and Entrepreneurship in the School of Theatre at Oklahoma City University, where she teaches courses in theater history and dramaturgy and serves as a director, intimacy director, and dramaturg for the production season. She is also a scholar focusing on musical theater, contemporary theater, and intersections with popular culture and technology. Osatinski's monographs are *Disney Theatrical Productions: Producing Broadway Musicals the Disney Way* (2019) and *20 Seasons: Broadway Musicals of the 21st Century* (2024). Her scholarship can also be found in *The Routledge Companion to Musical Theatre, IBroadway, The Palgrave Handbook of Musical Theatre Producers, Studies in Musical Theatre, Theatre Topics*, and the *Texas Theatre Journal*.

Deborah Paredez is the author of *Selenidad: Selena, Latinos, and the Performance of Memory* (2009) and *American Diva* (2024) and of the poetry collections *This Side of Skin* (2002) and *Year of the Dog* (2020). She is the Chair of the Creative Writing Program at Columbia University and the cofounder of CantoMundo, a national organization dedicated to Latinx poets and poetry.

Tom Robson is the co-editor, with Jennifer A. Kokai, of *Performance and the Disney Theme Park Experience: The Tourist as Actor* (2019; 2nd ed. forthcoming) and the coauthor of the monograph *Disney Parks and the Construction of American Identity: Tourism, Performance, Collaboration* (2024). Together, he and Kokai have contributed essays on Disney parks and immersive theater to the *Journal of Themed Experience and Attractions Studies*, the edited collection *Virtual Interiorities*, and the forthcoming *Enveloping Worlds: Toward a Discourse of Immersivity and Participatory Performance*. Individually,

Robson has contributed essays to the collections *Fan Phenomena: Disney* and *Working in the Wings: New Perspectives on Theatre History and Labor*, as well as the journals *Theatre History Studies*, *Ecumenica*, and *Jump Cut*. He is currently a clinical assistant teaching professor in Purdue University's Cornerstone Integrated Liberal Arts program.

Lisa Scoggin completed her PhD in Musicology at Boston University and received degrees from Oberlin College and the University of Wisconsin–Madison. Her musicological interests include (but are by no means restricted to) music in film, television, animation, and video games. She has written, presented, and published on various topics in these areas, including work on *Mulan* (1998), United Productions of America, early American television animation, and *Song of the Sea* (2014); a book on the television show *Animaniacs* (1993–1998); and the edited collection *The Intersection of Animation, Video Games, and Music: Making Movement Sing*, in which she was a contributor and co-editor (with Dana Plank).

Kirsten Moana Thompson, Professor and Chair of the Film and Media Program at Seattle University, teaches and writes on animation and color studies, as well as Pacific and American studies. Recent work has focused on the animated "useful" film, intersectional animated surfaces in *Moana*, the material color history of Disney 2D animation and the ink and paint department, and Ludwig von Drake and the Disney promotional film. She is the coauthor of the award-winning *Animation and Advertising* (2019), the first book to examine the relationship of animation with nontheatrical media. She has also published *Apocalyptic Dread: American Cinema at the Turn of the Millennium* (2007) and *Crime Films: Investigating the Scene* (2007), and, with Terri Ginsberg, she coedited *Perspectives on German Cinema* (1996). She is currently working on several new books: *Color, American Animation and Visual Culture, 1890–1960* and *Animated America: Intermedial Promotion, from Times Square to Walt Disney*.

Elizabeth Randell Upton is an Associate Professor in the Musicology Department at the University of California–Los Angeles, where she teaches classes on European music before 1600, musical revivals, medievalism, nostalgia, and the Beatles. Her research centers on songs and the meanings that listeners derive from songs. Her book *Music and Performance in the Later Middle Ages* (2013) examined the circumstances of song performance and listening experiences for late-fourteenth- and early-fifteenth-century music, especially the songs of Guillaume Du Fay (1397–1474). She is on the editorial boards of *Postmedieval: A Journal of Medieval Cultural Studies* and the new *International Journal of Disney Studies*. Her current book project situates the early music "authenticity wars" of the 1980s in the experiences of listeners to classical and popular music. Her previous research on Disney includes articles on singing in *Snow White* (1937) and nostalgic futurism in Disneyland's *Main Street Electrical Parade* (1972).

Juan Fernando Velásquez Ospina is the Chair of Graduate Programs in the School of Arts and Researcher of the Grupo de Investigación en Músicas Regionales at the Universidad de Antioquia in Medellín, Colombia. His research intersects cultural history, urban history, decoloniality, and sound studies to explore the relationships and networks connecting urban modernization, social formation processes, and sound in nineteenth- and twentieth-century Latin America. His articles and essays have appeared in journals such as *Latin American Music Review, Americas: A Hemispheric Music Journal*, and the *Boletín de Música de Casa de las Américas*. His forthcoming book is *Inscribing Sounds: Music Technologies and Aural Culture in Late-Nineteenth- and Early-Twentieth-Century Colombia*.

Stacy Wolf is Professor of Theater and Music Theater and American Studies at Princeton University. She is the author of *A Problem Like Maria: Gender and Sexuality in the American Musical* (2002), *Changed for Good: A Feminist History of the Broadway Musical* (2011), and *Beyond Broadway: The Pleasure and Promise of Musical Theatre across America*, which was a finalist for the Association for Theatre in Higher Education's 2020 Outstanding Book Award. Wolf co-edited *The Oxford Handbook of the American Musical* and "Sondheim from the Side," a special issue of *Studies in Musical Theatre* that brings together personal reflections on Sondheim's musicals by women, queers, Jews, people of color, and others. Wolf has published articles on *Hamilton* and gender and on college student productions of Sondheim's musicals in the age of #MeToo. Current projects include an article about the composer Jeanine Tesori and a cowritten book, *Feminist Approaches to Musical Theatre*.

Elizabeth L. Wollman is Professor of Music at Baruch College, City University of New York, and a member of the Doctoral Faculty in Theatre at the CUNY Graduate Center. She researches and writes about the relationship between the industry and aesthetics of contemporary American stage musicals. She is the author or editor of many articles, chapters, and books about musicals, including *The Theater Will Rock: A History of the Rock Musical, from* Hair *to* Hedwig (2006), *Hard Times: The Adult Musical in 1970s New York City* (2013), and *A Critical Companion to the American Stage Musical* (2017). With Jessica Sternfeld, she was co-editor of *The Routledge Companion to the Contemporary Musical* (2020) and currently co-edits the journal *Studies in Musical Theatre*.

Introduction

DOMINIC BROOMFIELD-MCHUGH AND COLLEEN MONTGOMERY

THE *Oxford Handbook of the Disney Musical* brings together scholars from a range of disciplines to interrogate an enduringly popular and influential cultural phenomenon. It's clear by now that the Disney canon—and especially the musicals—is a fruitful site of critical discovery, and this book builds on a considerable heritage of scholarship. Film studies has particularly shown the potential of the Disney musical, joined in more recent years by contributions from musicology, with key scholarship including the monographs *Understanding Disney: The Manufacture of Fantasy* (Janet Wasko, 2020), *Demystifying Disney: A History of Disney Feature Animation* (Chris Pallant, 2011), and *Music in Disney's Animated Features:* Snow White and the Seven Dwarfs *to* The Jungle Book (James Bohn, 2017); the edited collections *Drawn to Sound: Animation Film Music and Sonicity* (Rebecca Coyle, 2010) and *Disney Discourse: Producing the Magic Kingdom* (Eric Smoodin, 1994); and a special issue of *American Music* (Spring 2021). Whether examining animation, technology, music, or the commercial sphere, these and other studies have repeatedly shown why Disney has continued to dominate the world of entertainment a century after the launch of the Disney Brothers Cartoon Studio, which became the Walt Disney Company.

Broadening the purview of extant scholarship while also reflecting its methodological multiplicity, this collection takes an expansive approach to the Disney musical. By representing the perspectives of scholars from film, theater, television, musicology, children's literature, and cultural studies, we aimed to create a multidisciplinary resource on the subject as a whole. From animated musical shorts to Disney video games, the *Handbook* acknowledges that Disney uses the musical across a range of media and explores what that means culturally, commercially, and technologically. These insights into key ideas of the critical discourse around different aspects of Disney's output are favored over a comprehensive or exhaustive account of the company's work. Thus, some famous movies or activities are not mentioned at all—not because we consider them unimportant but because this is a handbook of studies rather than an encyclopedic guide to the history of the subject.

Reflecting this, the collection groups essays thematically under five broad headings. Part I examines Disney's short- and feature-film musicals of the classical period, from the 1920s to the 1950s. In particular, J. B. Kaufman and Malcolm Cook consider how and why Disney started making musical films and how they work. Tracey Mollet's chapter on *Snow White* and Daniel Batchelder's on *Bambi* present readings and contexts for these well-loved early classics. Bringing the section into the 1950s, Julianne Lindberg draws on archival materials to examine choir leader Hall Johnson's contributions to Disney musicals.

Complementing this, Part II presents a special focus on adaptation. Disney has relied not only on adapting preexisting material for many of its classic animated films (e.g., Dominic Broomfield-McHugh explores how the studio adapted *Alice in Wonderland*) but also on readapting its own properties (a priority outlined by Eve Benhamou), whether for live-action reimaginings (as discussed by Michelle Anya Anjirbag on *Aladdin* and Sean Griffin on *Mary Poppins's Returns*) or video games (as Lisa Scoggin examines). Kelly Kessler's chapter on Disney on television—focusing in particular on *The Little Mermaid Live!*—and Rayna Denison's on the global *Lilo & Stitch* franchise add meaningful insights into how the company has adapted its work for different media and audiences.

Part III explores the interconnected themes of sound, music, and technology. Colleen Montgomery's chapter on Peggy Lee's legal fight for remuneration for her voice work for *Lady and the Tramp* uses archival materials to shed light on important aspects of the studio's history. Complementing these, Kate Galloway's chapter considers the human sounds and music associated with Disney's anthropomorphizing of nonhuman animals in a swath of films from *Snow White* to *Cinderella* to *The Little Mermaid* and *Frozen*, while Elizabeth Randell Upton examines the impact of the Beatles on the score for *The Jungle Book*. The "Disney Renaissance" musicals (1989–1999) come under scrutiny in Christopher Holliday's chapter, which explores the importance of technological hybridity to the creation of musical numbers in this period.

Part IV of the book presents a special focus on representation and identity in the Disney musical. Bridging the previous section's interest in technology and this section's investment in culture and identity, Kirsten Moana's chapter looks at the ways Technicolor shaped the depiction of Latin America in Disney's "Good Neighbor" musicals. Turning to the gendered dimensions of the company's representational politics, Stacy Wolf and Deborah Paredez map the musical characteristics of the Disney diva, while Morgan Genevieve Blue parses constructions of girlhood in Disney television musicals. As several authors in this part highlight, Disney's representational practices with respect to race, culture, and ethnicity have long been fraught. Mihaela Mihailova unpacks Disney's attempts to offer "authentic" constructions of Indigeneity in *Frozen II*, while Jacqueline Avila and Juan Fernando Velásquez Ospina trace the evolution of the Disney musical's representation of Latinidad across the twenty-first century.

Part V of the collection addresses Disney's unexpected but largely successful move to presenting its work onstage through Disney Theatrical Productions. Elizabeth Wollman investigates the context in which Disney entered the theatrical domain, and

Dean Adams considers how changing audience demographics have explained the ways in which Disney Theatrical have developed since 2000. Alex Bádue dives into the process of putting popular Disney animations on Broadway, with a special focus on the addition of songs to the original movie scores to match the longer running time of stage musicals, while Jennifer Kokai and Tom Robson analyze the process by which the animated *Finding Nemo* found new life as a theme-park attraction. Two final chapters acknowledge the importance of places and audiences beyond Broadway in the reception and success of Disney's stage musicals. Stacy Wolf and Sammy Grob look at how adaptations of Disney's work have become important for the development of personal identity in schools, and Amy S. Osatinski presents a global perspective on Disney Theatrical activities.

The Walt Disney Company's recent centennial provides an apt opportunity to reflect on the importance of the musical to the conglomerate's evolution in diverse segments of the media industries. As Malcolm Cook comments, "It's hard to imagine the studio enjoying such longevity without its strong musical legacy."[1] Our hope is that the collection's interdisciplinary, multimethodological approach makes it not only of general interest but a particularly useful pedagogical text, accessible to a range of scholars working in different disciplinary contexts. The book combines innovative original research, analyses of previously unexamined archival documents, case studies, topical discussions, and critiques of current knowledge and existing scholarship to give voice to new perspectives on this important topic.

NOTE

1. https://theconversation.com/disney-films-have-always-been-musical-even-in-the-silent-era-214936.

PART I
THE CLASSICAL PERIOD

CHAPTER 1

ACT ONE: THE BEGINNINGS OF THE DISNEY MUSICAL

J. B. KAUFMAN

It has long been a truism—because it was so unmistakably obvious—that music was, from the beginning, an essential part of the classic Disney animated films. Walt Disney's first sound film, the 1928 milestone *Steamboat Willie*, makes the point inescapable, not only featuring soundtrack music from beginning to end but also focusing half its footage on Mickey and Minnie's delightfully improvised rendition of "Turkey in the Straw." Subsequent cartoons built on that precedent. Throughout the early 1930s, Mickey Mouse was rarely far from a piano or other instrument, and the Mickey series was quickly supplemented by another Disney series whose very title, Silly Symphonies, suggested its emphasis on music. That primacy continued throughout the 1930s and was irrevocably baked into the Disney animated world by the time of *Snow White and the Seven Dwarfs* and the other classic feature-length films.

But observing the importance of *music* in the Disney oeuvre is one thing; considering individual films as *musicals* is another. This chapter uses as its definition animated films of the 1920s and '30s that correspond roughly to stage or film musicals of the same period: shows focused on *performances*, by one or more characters, of song and/or dance numbers.

FINDING A MUSICAL VOICE

Even by this loose definition, it's clear that the roots of the Disney musical go back to the beginning. The aforementioned *Steamboat Willie*, Disney's very first venture into sound, may be said to qualify by virtue of that impromptu performance of "Turkey in the Straw." The brilliant innovation of *Steamboat Willie* was not merely that it boasted a soundtrack—other sound cartoons had already been produced by rival studios—but also the *way* it used sound. Thanks to a system devised by Walt, Wilfred Jackson, and

Ub Iwerks, the sound in their cartoons could be precisely synchronized with the picture with pinpoint accuracy. As a result, Mickey, Minnie, and the other characters in *Steamboat Willie* really did appear to be producing the sounds on the soundtrack. This was an effect that no other cartoon studio could duplicate at the time, and audiences responded enthusiastically.

Not only that, but this system was used to construct witty gags that were specifically built on music. Perhaps the most celebrated moment in *Steamboat Willie* occurs at the beginning of the "Turkey in the Straw" sequence: a goat, spying Minnie's sheet music lying unprotected on the deck, eats it. Minnie is dismayed, but Mickey bends the goat's tail into the shape of a crank, effectively transforming the goat into a living music box. When Minnie turns the crank, the goat, having "digested" the music, plays it back through his open mouth. It's an ingenious conceit, founded on cartoon logic, and music is not simply an ornament to the gag but is integral to it. Here's a gag, the film seems to tell us, that could not exist *without* sound and music. (In fact, however, the same gag had appeared in practically identical form in a silent Disney cartoon earlier in 1928: *Rival Romeos*, starring Oswald the Lucky Rabbit. Seen today in hindsight, this moment in *Rival Romeos* seems almost a deliberate dry run for the gag's fuller realization in *Steamboat Willie*.)

This is the beginning of a precedent. Mickey and Minnie's unorthodox rendition of "Turkey in the Straw" in their first sound film—wringing music from farm animals, kitchen utensils, and other unlikely "instruments"—qualifies on some level as a performance, effectively planting the seed of the Disney musical. And more conventional performances are not far behind; *The Opry House*, the fifth Mickey Mouse, continues to point the way. *The Opry House* is explicitly set in the eponymous venue ("opera house" being understood, from the nineteenth century on, as a euphemism for any kind of entertainment hall), with a series of musical vaudeville acts performed for an audience.

But for the purist, seeking a more formally traditional performance to mark the true birth of the Disney musical, another milestone in the summer of 1929 will make a convenient starting point. *The Skeleton Dance* inaugurates Walt's parallel cartoon series, the Silly Symphonies, and is almost entirely constructed around an extended dance number.

The film opens in a graveyard, at the stroke of midnight, where—after some spooky introductory atmospherics—four skeletons emerge from their graves and face the camera. From this point on, the film is nothing more or less than a showcase for their performance. The musical score, by Disney's first musical director, Carl Stalling, is formally organized into distinct movements (one of them appropriating Edvard Grieg's "March of the Dwarfs"), each movement introducing a new phase of the dance. Playing directly to the audience, the skeletons begin with a jaunty vaudeville chorus line, then progress to rounds and other dance forms, with individual moves borrowed from ballet and from the Charleston. Lending variety to these steps are interpolated rhythmic whimsies: one skeleton turns another upside down and uses it as a pogo stick; one skeleton uses another's ribcage as a xylophone. The skeletons are self-assured performers, their deadpan expressions (no pun intended) conveying a cool panache as they caper and twirl. Their revels are brought to an end by the cock's crow, at which they break ranks and scamper to return to their graves—or, rather, to one large common grave—before sunrise.

Having produced a dance number, the Disney studio rounded out its musical bona fides with a song number. Mickey Mouse had made his initial mark in sound cartoons but had never actually spoken dialogue on the screen until Walt made a point of introducing dialogue in the Mickey short *The Karnival Kid*, released in the summer of 1929. Over the objections of his distributor, who feared that English dialogue would handicap the cartoons' appeal to overseas audiences, Walt pressed on. In the next cartoon, Mickey would not only speak but *sing*. Walt's letters to his distributor capture his excitement over this idea.[1] He pictured a cartoon built around Mickey's efforts to write a song, culminating in a performance of the new number, and suggested the working title "Mickey's Theme Song."

The film, completed in late August as *Mickey's Follies*, dispenses with the songwriting scenes. Instead, as the title suggests, it's framed as an extended performance by Mickey and his troupe for a barnyard audience. The new song is given what will become a familiar type of showcase in feature-length movie musicals for decades afterward: played as an "overture" under the main title, teased with a modest performance (instrumental in this case) in an opening scene, then—after an interlude in which the supporting acts (a chorus line of saucy ducks, an Apache dance by chickens, an operatic pig) provide a suitable buildup—performed in all its glory by the star of the show.

The song itself, "Minnie's Yoo Hoo," is something of a Disney milestone. Composed by Stalling, it's based on an idea Walt had suggested in his letters:[2] a playful recital of the noises produced by the other barnyard animals, all of which "sound like the dickens" by comparison with "Minnie's Yoo Hoo!" Mickey "sells" the song in an enthusiastic vocal performance marked by wildly exaggerated animation, then performs another verse and chorus on a variety of instruments, then tops *that* off with a soft-shoe dance that literally brings down the house.

Modest though it may be, "Minnie's Yoo Hoo" was the Disney studio's first original song, and Walt promoted it enthusiastically. It was published in sheet-music form by the music publisher Villa Morét and was promoted in the Mickey Mouse newspaper comic strip.[3] As Walt had suggested, it did become Mickey's theme song, played under the main title of each new Mickey Mouse cartoon as late as 1933.[4] It was also used as the theme song of the burgeoning new Mickey Mouse Clubs, which attracted crowds of youngsters to Saturday matinees at their local theaters across the country and overseas. Using animation recycled from *Mickey's Follies*, the studio supplied a four-minute sing-along trailer to the theaters that hosted those club chapters. Thereafter, club meetings were marked by group vocal renditions of "Minnie's Yoo Hoo," belted out lustily by young club members and led by Mickey himself.

By the end of 1929, then, the foundations of the Disney musical had been laid. And for a time, that was where the matter rested. After a decade of struggle, Walt Disney had finally found a secure foothold in the competitive film business and was beginning to thrive. He and his artists were laser-focused on producing the best one-reel animated cartoons they could manage, and it seems reasonable to assume that at this time, they had no thought of launching a tradition of "Disney musicals."

To be sure, there still was plenty of musical content in the Disney cartoons. *The Skeleton Dance* and *Mickey's Follies* were quickly followed by a succession of other shorts that featured heavy doses of singing and, in particular, dancing. Disney scholar Russell Merritt has commented on the importance of dance in the early Silly Symphonies: "From *The Skeleton Dance* through *The Clock Store* [1931], comic dances will define Silly Symphonies. During the first two and a half years, in fact, they—more than anything else—are what Symphony characters do."[5] Mickey, too, continued to indulge his musical proclivities and occasionally appeared in another short featuring a full-blown performance: *Fiddling Around*, *The Barnyard Concert* (both 1930), *Blue Rhythm* (1931).

But none of these efforts moved the studio any closer to what we might recognize as a musical. Notably, there was a dearth of original songs. Walt's pride in "Minnie's Yoo Hoo" notwithstanding, it remained the studio's one original song for several years. Its composer, Stalling, left the studio a few months afterward in January 1930. He would go on to a long and distinguished career at other cartoon studios, particularly Schlesinger/Warner Bros. His immediate replacement as musical director at the Disney studio was Bert Lewis, who supplied serviceable, workmanlike musical scores but few if any original tunes. Stalling, a former theater organist, had drawn heavily on the classical repertoire in his cartoon scores (a practice he would continue at other studios). Lewis followed this lead in his incidental scoring, but the songs in Disney shorts of this period tend toward preexisting numbers: "In the Good Old Summertime" in *The Picnic*, Irving Berlin's "All Alone" in *The Gorilla Mystery*.

New Talent and a Breakthrough

The musical content of the Disney films took a dramatic upward turn in the early 1930s with the hiring of two new staff composers. The first of these was Frank Churchill, a largely self-taught musician who performed regularly in nightclubs and on the radio.[6] By all accounts, Churchill was originally brought to the studio simply as a session pianist for a cartoon soundtrack and immediately made a strong impression on everyone present. Animator Ed Benedict remembered wandering into the recording session on his lunch hour and being impressed with the newcomer's natural talent: "He was absolutely superb. He was a superb piano player! Oh, my God, was he good."[7]

Churchill was quickly added to the studio staff, and in addition to his facility as a pianist, he demonstrated a knack for improvising appealing melodies. By the spring of 1931, his scores were beginning to alternate with Lewis's scores in Disney cartoons. Director Wilfred Jackson recalled that working with Churchill on a new score was an exhilarating experience: "Frank could give a director so many satisfactory tunes to choose from, and could make each one of them sound so good as he romped through it on the piano, that it was often quite difficult to decide which one *not* to use with the action."[8]

Now, gradually at first, the musical range of the studio's shorts began to expand. This development corresponded to a parallel development in the narrative content of the films, particularly the Silly Symphonies. As the novelty value of dancing creatures synchronized with music, which had distinguished the Symphonies at first, began to wear thin, the films displayed stronger plots. And now when a story seemed to call for a vocal interlude, Churchill could be counted on to provide one with seemingly effortless ease. The Silly Symphony *Santa's Workshop* (1932) amounts to a miniature cartoon operetta, with exchanges between Santa and his elves (or "gnomes") couched in passages of rhymed dialogue nimbly alternating with fragments of song. In *Building a Building* (1932), with Mickey Mouse as a construction worker, Minnie arrives at the construction site selling box lunches. Churchill supplies her with a charming little song, "Who'll Buy a Box Lunch?," in which she advertises her wares: "Baloney! And macaroni! And a huckleberry pie!" Musical moments like these enriched audiences' experience of the Disney cartoons and verged on the simultaneously developing world of movie musicals.

But the real milestone came in the spring of 1933, with the release of *Three Little Pigs*. The astounding national and worldwide success of this cartoon in 1933—often attributed to its effectiveness as a cheerful antidote to the Depression—has been documented elsewhere.[9] Of particular interest to us here is the corresponding success of the song at the center of the film, Churchill's "Who's Afraid of the Big Bad Wolf?," which became an unexpected hit in its own right. The song was published, this time by Irving Berlin Inc. (and with added lyrics by Ann Ronell, leading to an erroneous latter-day impression that Ronell was actually a co-composer of the original song).[10] It was also widely recorded, in renditions ranging from "Variations," by the piano duo of Jacques Fray and Mario Braggiotti, to jazzy performances by Ben Bernie and Ethel Shutta. The song's impact on popular culture was reflected in the movies as well, as interpolated fragments turned up in films as diverse as the Marx Brothers' *Duck Soup* (1933) and Frank Capra's *It Happened One Night* (1934). By the spring of 1934, *Time* was referring to "Who's Afraid" as "the tune by which 1933 will be remembered."[11]

The film that introduced this hit song to the world, besides being itself a hit, was—in terms of the one-reel animated cartoon—unquestionably a musical. And structurally, it was a rather sophisticated musical at that. Ross Care has pointed out that "the song...is never rendered intact during the entire film, being fragmented, forestalled or interrupted by the narrative (and thus giving the action roughly the ABACADA structure of a musical rondo)."[12] The first chorus, rendered saucily by Fiddler Pig and Fifer Pig, is cut short when the two pigs suddenly find themselves face to face with the Wolf, are very much afraid, and take to their heels to the accompaniment of frantic chase music. This pattern recurs throughout the film: each time the pigs reach a place of temporary security, they celebrate with a chorus of "Who's Afraid," which is interrupted afresh by some new tactic of the Wolf's. In addition, Care observes, "song, rhymed speech, and traditional background scoring were seamlessly wedded to musical gags, e.g., when the wolf, to foil the two gullible pigs, pretends to give up the pursuit of them (to the accompaniment of a charmingly bland 'wolf-trot'), or when the Practical Pig executes an imposing piano cadenza a la Rachmaninoff as the wolf literally blows himself blue in the face while vainly attempting to blow down the door of the brick house."[13]

The record-breaking success of *Three Little Pigs* and "Who's Afraid" was not lost on Walt, and more of these little musicals—cartoons built around performances of original songs—began to appear on the studio's release schedule. One notable example came just a few months later in 1933. In *Puppy Love*, Mickey Mouse and Pluto pay a romantic call on, respectively, Minnie and her pet Pekingese, Fifi. The short charts the parallel courses of the two couples as they make romance, experience misunderstandings, quarrel, and ultimately make up and reunite. Churchill's musical score includes two vocal numbers, one of which, the title song "Puppy Love," is performed as a duet by Minnie and Mickey—not simply tossed off but given a featured showcase. Minnie, displaying the sheet music, announces that she has found "the cutest song," and Mickey accompanies her on piano as she takes a star turn, performing the vocal. Minnie then joins Mickey at the keyboard, and the two of them jam on a hot jazz performance of the song. (This time, the film even affords Churchill a kind of screen credit. As the song sheet sits on Minnie's music rack, we see that one page is headed "Puppy Love," while the facing page—in very small letters but plainly visible in a 35mm print or a high-definition video transfer—announces, "by Frank Churchill.")

By the time *Puppy Love* was released in September 1933, the success of "Who's Afraid" had already had its effect on Disney promotional efforts, and the studio had established a regular music-publishing arrangement with Irving Berlin Inc. "Puppy Love" was hardly the blockbuster hit that "Who's Afraid" had been, but, like other contemporary Disney songs, it was published and recorded and found its way into the popular-music market.

THE SILLY SYMPHONIES GROW UP

In the meantime, another notable composer had joined the Disney staff. Leigh Harline was hired in December 1932, roughly two years after Churchill, and quickly began to bring his own brand of musical brilliance to the Disney cartoons. In some ways, the two musicians were direct opposites. Where Churchill was largely self-taught, Harline was classically trained. Where Churchill was (to outward appearances) carefree and happy-go-lucky, Harline was quiet and studious.[14] Their respective styles complemented each other: Churchill could be counted on for catchy, appealing melodies, Harline for sophisticated musical textures. On the one hand, Harline's thoughtful, erudite approach was essential in constructing the complex musical structures of shorts such as *The Band Concert* or *Music Land* (both 1935). On the other hand, writer Bill Cottrell recalled that Harline, originally assigned to another 1935 short, *Three Orphan Kittens*, was replaced by Churchill because the director wanted an improvisation on Zez Confrey's "Kitten on the Keys" for a sequence in which the kittens were literally walking on a piano keyboard. Of the two composers, Churchill was the one who could take part in story conferences and spontaneously, intuitively adapt Confrey's original to the planned action of the cartoon kittens on the keys.[15]

When the runaway success of *Three Little Pigs* and "Who's Afraid" in 1933 sparked a taste for further animated musicals, Harline demonstrated that he, too, could turn out appealing original songs. At least two notable Disney musicals appeared in 1934 featuring Harline originals: *Grasshopper and the Ants*, with the Grasshopper's theme song "The World Owes Me a Living," and *The Wise Little Hen*, in which the title character approaches her lazy neighbors with recurring refrains of her signature tune. Clearly, Churchill and Harline were emerging as a collective musical powerhouse at the Disney studio in the mid-1930s. Occasionally, they were called on to collaborate on a score, and at least two of these joint compositions qualified loosely as musicals: *Lullaby Land* (1933) and *Funny Little Bunnies* (1934). Each of these shorts followed the same pattern: Churchill contributed a title song which was showcased in the film, while Harline composed the additional cues that made up the balance of the score.

In order to appreciate the developments that were appearing in these miniature Disney musicals in the mid-'30s, it's important to understand the contemporaneous changes taking place on the stage and in live-action films. The "book musical," as many of us understand it today, was still in an evolutionary state in the 1930s. Similarly, movie musicals were in a state of flux. After the talking-picture revolution of the late 1920s and following a period of slavish imitation of the stage, the film musical had begun to find its way. A few imaginative filmmakers discovered ways to use the inherent properties of the medium to construct a unique cinematic aesthetic of the musical. Here again, production numbers were the centerpiece of the medium at first, and they ranged from solo or duet performances to large-scale chorus numbers. The years 1933–1935 saw the apex of the screen extravaganzas of Busby Berkeley, which took the basic convention of the dance number and supercharged it with fantastic camera angles, kaleidoscopic formations of dancers, and visual effects far beyond the reach of any theater stage.

The vogue for Berkeley's numbers passed quickly, however, and in its place a subtler, more sophisticated approach began to appear. As early as 1932–1933, two landmark film musicals, *Love Me Tonight* and *Hallelujah, I'm a Bum*, featured innovative song scores by no less than Richard Rodgers and Lorenz Hart. The films are models of story construction, moving seamlessly from dialogue to rhymed dialogue to song and back again. During 1934–1935, the legendary pairing of Fred Astaire and Ginger Rogers was also being established, and the team behind their films offered an alternative approach of their own—still centered on production numbers (custom-tailored to the immense talents of Astaire and Rogers), still featuring paper-thin plots, but integrating the songs with the script and taking full advantage of the intimacy afforded by the camera.

We can see the idea of the "integrated" musical at work in Harline's successes of 1934. *The Wise Little Hen* follows the model of *Three Little Pigs* and many other contemporary Silly Symphonies: starting with a traditional tale—in this case, the children's story of "The Little Red Hen"—and fleshing it out with entertaining characters and an engaging musical structure. The centerpiece of Harline's score is a recurring title theme, identified on the cue sheet simply as "The Wise Little Hen." In practice, however, this melody has multiple uses: not only is it an instrumental theme that underscores the hen's scenes, but it also serves as a musical narration, sung by an off-screen male trio that introduces the story in the opening sequence, then returns periodically to comment on the plot as it continues. The song's chorus doubles as a recurring vocal number for the hen herself, voiced by Florence Gill, as she appeals to her lazy neighbors (Peter Pig and, in his screen debut, Donald Duck) for help. We hear it first as "Help Me Plant My Corn," then, later, after her field has produced an abundant crop, as "Help Me Harvest Corn," and each time, the two idlers offer no help at all. (When the time comes to *eat* the corn, they seem much more willing to help, but by that time, the hen has seen through their excuses and has a surprise in store for them.) These musical passages are pleasing in themselves and also help to advance the story; in effect, they *are* the story. *The Wise Little Hen* is a delight on several levels, and much of its charm stems from the satisfying symmetry of its musical program.

Similarly, *Grasshopper and the Ants* begins with the essence of the Aesopian original but builds on it with engaging personalities and a catchy song. Aesop's grasshopper (as the story has been passed down to us) is female, has spent the summer singing instead of storing food, and, pitilessly rejected by the ants, is sent away to starve at the tale's end.[16] Disney's Grasshopper is a happy-go-lucky male and is carefree and irresponsible as the story demands but essentially sympathetic. Story development of the film started in September 1933, while *Three Little Pigs* was still enjoying its historic success in theaters, and the Grasshopper's theme song was clearly designed with an eye on the popularity of "Who's Afraid of the Big Bad Wolf?"

Harline's contribution in this film, "The World Owes Me a Living"—a line that was already a popular catchphrase in the early 1930s—is an irresistibly appealing tune, introduced in the opening summertime sequence as the Grasshopper plays it on his fiddle. Observing with great amusement the industry of the ant community as they store food for the winter, the Grasshopper advances the plot by singing the song to one young ant ("Andy" in internal production papers), who happily embraces the song's hedonistic philosophy—until the Queen Ant catches him shirking his duties. Andy races back to his work, while the Grasshopper sings a second chorus to the Queen herself. In a slight variation on the song's official title,[17] the Grasshopper sings the hook line to both Andy and the Queen as "The world owes *us* a living." At film's end, granted a reprieve by the Queen—allowed to stay and share the ants' warm winter quarters and food supply as long as he provides music for the community—the Grasshopper demonstrates that he has learned his lesson by reversing the terms of the chorus: "I owe the world a living!"

"The World Owes Me a Living" was not destined to repeat the universal popular-music success of "Who's Afraid," but it did carve a niche of its own, published and widely heard on radio and records. (In particular, it was heard on soundtrack recordings and other retellings of the film story.) And, like its predecessor, it found a distinctive afterlife in the movies. Not only was it heard in features as dissimilar as *Now and Forever* (1934, in which it was sung by a very young Shirley Temple) and John Ford's *The Whole Town's Talking* (1935), but it also came in for extensive reuse by the Disney studio itself. The Grasshopper's voice in *Grasshopper and the Ants* had been supplied by story artist

Pinto Colvig, who was also speaking in an identical voice for the emerging character that we know today as Goofy. Now, in a kind of extended in-joke, "The World Owes Me a Living" became a recurring theme song for Goofy—sometimes played as an instrumental motif under Goofy's scenes, sometimes warbled on the screen by the Goof himself. Beginning with *On Ice* (1935), a dozen later Disney cartoons kept Harline's melody alive in this unusual way.[18]

These two examples are not isolated cases. Following these entries, the Disney release schedule for 1935 blossomed with further cartoons that qualified as musicals by any definition. *The Robber Kitten* tells of an imaginative kitten who runs away from home to become a swashbuckling bandit—until he has a sobering encounter with a real highwayman. The notorious outlaw, a bulldog named Dirty Bill, introduces himself in a self-titled theme song by Churchill: "I never took a bath and I never will!" *The Cookie Carnival* pictures a beauty contest in Cookie Town, in which an outcast cookie girl is unexpectedly crowned queen and is then courted by a succession of amorous pastries. The pageant parade, the girl's beautification, and the vaudeville turns by her would-be suitors are all narrated in a sprightly Harline song score. *Who Killed Cock Robin?*, which incorporates multiple layers of satiric comedy and emerges as one of the most brilliant of all Silly Symphonies, begins with Robin's assassination by an unknown assailant and proceeds to recast the traditional nursery rhyme as a courtroom murder trial with a cast of birds. Churchill's musical score occasionally veers into operetta, largely because the jury is deliberately conceived as a Gilbert and Sullivan chorus.[19] But Churchill also inserts two songs grounded in the world of contemporary popular music. In the opening sequence, Robin serenades Jenny Wren with a song identified on the cue sheet as "Will You Love Me Tonight"[20] but represented on the soundtrack by the lyric "Boo-boo-boo-boo-boo-boo," sung in an unmistakable imitation of Bing Crosby. Even more devastating is Jenny herself, rendered on the screen as an avian caricature of Mae West, who struts into the courtroom crooning "Somebody Rubbed Out My Robin," a wickedly accurate sendup of the songs in West's own musical features.

(We might also note a short that was planned as a musical but retooled before completion: *The Tortoise and the Hare*, the Academy Award winner of 1934. Churchill's score for this cartoon originally included a song, "Slow but Sure," that was intended as a vocal number for Toby Tortoise.[21] This idea was abandoned during production. "Slow but Sure" is heard in the finished film, not as a song number but simply as an instrumental theme underscoring Toby's scenes.)

It's important to remember that Churchill and Harline were not the only composers on Disney's staff during the mid-1930s. Lewis, the musician who had stepped into the breach when Carl Stalling first departed the studio in 1930, remained on board into the summer of 1935.[22] Lewis contributed a healthy share of instrumental scores to Disney cartoons during those years but remains incidental to our story because his output did not include song numbers. *The Flying Mouse* (1934), for example, is underscored by a full program of instrumental cues written by both Lewis and Churchill, but the vocal songs—"If I Were a Bird" and, notably, "You're Nothin' but a Nothin'"—are both Churchill's work. Another name of note was Al Malotte, who joined the Disney staff in

1935, just about the time Lewis was leaving.[23] Malotte was better known in the music world as Albert Hay Malotte, composer of a celebrated musical setting of "The Lord's Prayer." His Disney work did include a few cartoons that could be classified as musicals, such as *Broken Toys* (1935), with a cast of castoff toys and dolls in a city dump. Rallying his fellow toys to fix themselves up and march to a nearby orphanage to cheer up the children at Christmastime, a sailor doll sings Malotte's "We're Gonna Get Out of the Dumps."

For the most part, however, Churchill and Harline were recognized—at the time and by later generations—as Disney's star composers during the 1930s, and for their achievements during that key period, they have been justly lionized. However, Larry Morey, the talented lyricist who worked with them both, is overlooked far too often in discussions of the Disney classics of these years. This is unjust, not only because of the abundance of clever lyrics Morey supplied (for most of the songs mentioned here, among others) but also because he played a unique role in the studio's films. He was actually employed in the story department, and his dual responsibilities—contributing to story construction and also providing lyrics for the songs—amounted to a tacit acknowledgment that the studio, like the rest of the film industry, was moving in the general direction of integrated musicals. Charged with crafting both plot mechanics and song lyrics, Morey was in a position to weave them together in a more or less seamless form of musical storytelling.

This was very much in keeping with Walt Disney's own tendency during these years toward ever greater maturity of craftsmanship in his films. In story construction, refinements to character animation, camera technique, the painting department's color palette, the "Rembrandt look" of the studio's background paintings—in every area of production—we see Walt moving toward an increased level of sophistication during the mid- to late 1930s. So pronounced was his perfectionist mania that he adopted what now seems an unnecessarily harsh attitude toward his own earlier films. Mickey Mouse and Silly Symphony shorts of only a few years before are acknowledged today as classics, but the Walt of the late 1930s professed only embarrassment at the sight of them.[24] However this attitude may strike us today, it indicates a mindset that was fully in sympathy with the creators of stage and film musicals who sought to assimilate songs and music into their narratives with subtlety.

The Flowering of the Disney Musical: *Snow White and the Seven Dwarfs*

There was a good reason, beyond fundamental artistic principles, for Walt's increased interest in sophisticated technique during these years. Alongside production of his celebrated short cartoons—secretly at first, then more and more openly—Walt and his artists were working on a sensational new endeavor: a feature-length animated film. The film that would become *Snow White and the Seven Dwarfs* began to take shape in Walt's mind as early as 1933,[25] and during the succeeding years, in month after month of story conferences, it came increasingly into focus. As the outside world waited in anticipation to find out just what magical innovation Walt Disney had up his sleeve this time, Walt himself, along with his artists and writers, shaped this raw idea into a detailed plan for a fresh new experience in film entertainment. By the spring of 1936, their plan had taken such concrete form that experimental animation could begin, and by year's end, the film was in full production. The finished picture would be unveiled to the world in December 1937.

From the earliest story conferences on, it was established without question: *Snow White* would be framed as a musical. During the early stages of its development, the success of *Three Little Pigs*, *Grasshopper and the Ants*, and other musical cartoons was still fresh in the studio's collective memory, as was the parallel success of their original songs in the popular-music market. The point was demonstrated again and again during the mid-1930s: the use of song numbers added an undeniable measure of appeal to Disney cartoons. Now, embarking on his first feature-length picture—an enormous gamble under the best circumstances—Walt needed every advantage he could muster. He was not about to waste the opportunity to add that element of appeal to his film.

Like everything else in the feature, the creation of the musical numbers in *Snow White* built on the foundation of experience. The earliest surviving story notes for the film include lists of song possibilities that might be spotted throughout the narrative.[26] By November 1934, Churchill was at work composing the songs, notably "Some Day My Prince Will Come," one of the most renowned songs in the score.[27] His work would continue through the next three years as the film took shape. Ultimately, the team of Churchill and Morey would produce the full song score, while the film's incidental score was assembled from the combined efforts of Churchill, Harline, and another up-and-coming composer at the Disney studio: Paul J. Smith.

If the foundations of the Disney musical were laid in 1929 with *The Skeleton Dance* and *Mickey's Follies*, and *Three Little Pigs* in 1933 represented a milestone in establishment of the form, then *Snow White and the Seven Dwarfs* was the final breakthrough. Here is a film that is undeniably a musical by any standard. Delightful as earlier Disney efforts had been, we can consider them as musicals only if we take into account the brevity of the one-reel format and the consequent need to compress the story arc, the song numbers, and everything else into a tightly restricted running time. *Snow White*, a ten-reel feature, requires no such allowances: like any other classic musical of the period, it relates an extended narrative, supported by and built around a full program of song numbers. And in fact, it introduces a refinement that had been missing from earlier Disney efforts. "Who's Afraid of the Big Bad Wolf?," "The World Owes Me a Living," and other previous original songs had achieved widespread popularity, but all had fallen into the category of "novelty" songs. *Snow White* has its share of novelty numbers, but it also boasts at least two bona fide love songs—the type of number that formed the mainstay of most other musicals and the lifeblood of the popular-music business. "Some Day My Prince

Will Come," in particular, would sustain its popularity long after the film's release and would go on to take its place among the standards in American popular music. To hear such a lovely romantic ballad issuing from the lips of an animated cartoon character was only one of the startling revelations *Snow White* brought to audiences in 1937–1938.

Nor was "Some Day" the only hit song to emerge from *Snow White*. Novelty numbers such as "Heigh Ho" and "Whistle while You Work" exerted an immediate appeal and are still familiar today. Other songs that were not specifically romantic ballads were not exactly classifiable as novelties, either. "With a Smile and a Song," sung by Snow White to cheer herself up after her terrifying experience in the woods, was a close cousin to the morale-building songs that had flourished in America during the early years of the Depression. (The reader may notice the heavy concentration of the word "Song" in the film's song titles, further underlining the centrality of music in *Snow White*.)

The film that introduced this collection of musical gems was purposefully constructed along the lines of "integrated" musicals. With few exceptions, the songs were not simply performance numbers but served to illuminate character or advance the plot. Walt was never one to issue a lengthy manifesto on his theories of filmmaking practice, but history does record a comment that reveals his attitude toward musicals at the time. During a story conference on the film's party sequence, in which the Seven Dwarfs sang "The Silly Song"—a song that *was* a performance number, inserted just for fun—Walt acknowledged his enthusiasm for the number but added: "It isn't really clever, you know. It's still that influence from the musicals they have been doing for years. Really, we should set a new pattern ... a new way to use music; weave it into the story so somebody doesn't just bust into song."[28]

Morey's distinctive role at the studio, observed earlier—his dual responsibility for both songwriting and story construction—was a key ingredient in planning this musical structure in *Snow White*. From the earliest recorded story conferences for the feature in autumn 1934, Morey was one of the core members of the story team. As development continued over the next two years, numerous conference transcripts—for both musical and nonmusical sequences in the story—attest to Morey's heavy involvement in plot structure. This effort did not go unnoticed; as Walt wrote to Roy Disney after the film's release, "Larry's lyrics were only a small part of what he contributed to *Snow White*."[29]

In the finished film, this careful planning is manifested in a plot structure that is compelling in itself and also functions as a setting for a jewel-like song score by Morey and Churchill. The interlocking of story and music is apparent from the very opening of the film: after the main titles and a brief dialogue passage that establishes the Queen's character, Snow White herself is introduced in song. We see her in rags in the castle garden, standing by the wishing well and singing her opening song, "I'm Wishing." As she sings the chorus, her reflection in the well joins in, her echoed voice singing counterpoint, then harmony. This was a long-standing cartoon conceit, the character whose shadow or reflection takes on an independent life of its own, here cast in a sweetly romantic light.

The song's verse predicts that an echo from the well will signal the wish's fulfillment; now, on cue, the Prince rides by, hears the lovely voice in the garden, and hops over the wall to join Snow White in the closing strains of the chorus. Startled, Snow White runs inside the castle, but she stops to listen as the Prince's words of reassurance blend into the verse of *his* opening number, "One Song." She ventures shyly onto the balcony as he serenades her with the chorus. After this the Prince promptly disappears, not to be seen again until the film's end, but in the space of only a few minutes, this opening sequence has introduced the two characters and established their romance. A key piece of exposition has been conveyed simply, directly, but with an ineffable charm that could be accomplished only through music.

As the film unfolds, this tight bonding of story and song continues. Over and over, a passage of rhymed dialogue segues almost imperceptibly into the verse of a song. Snow White, discovering the dwarfs' cottage and finding it badly in need of cleaning, muses aloud to her animal friends about who the inhabitants could be. She issues the animals their assignments: "Now you wash the dishes / You tidy up the room. / You clean the fireplace / And I'll use the broom!"—and suddenly, "Whistle while You Work" is under way, moving the story forward with a delightful blend of music and comedy. Later, after the dwarfs have welcomed Snow White into their home, they prevail on her to tell them a story. She obliges by relating the story of her own romance. Their questions and her answers form a rhythmic pattern, and before we know it, we're hearing a verse that flows into the film's landmark romantic ballad, "Some Day My Prince Will Come."

And *Snow White*'s musical refinements don't end there. The deceptive simplicity of the film's storybook style conceals a wealth of sophisticated technique, not least in the musical score. As we've seen, "Some Day My Prince Will Come" was one of the first songs composed for the film, late in 1934. The verse ends with a yearning five-note phrase to the words "He was so romantic . . ." By contrast, Snow White's introductory song in the garden, "I'm Wishing," was one of the last songs written for the score, composed in the spring of 1937. Here Churchill deliberately reuses that five-note phrase, twice, at the beginning of the verse—"Want to know a secret? Promise not to tell?"—then resolves it in the next line: "We are standing by a wishing well." This device goes largely unnoticed by most viewers, but it provides a subtle, almost subliminal unifying link between the two songs.

As for Morey, his efforts on behalf of the *Snow White* songs continued even after the soundtrack recordings were finished. An important part of the film's marketing campaign was publication of the songs in sheet-music form, and Morey devised alternative lyrics, suitable to the generic world of popular music, for publication. In November 1937, a good nine months after "Some Day" had been recorded for the film, Morey wrote to the music publisher: "I am still not satisfied with the lyric on 'Some Day My Prince Will Come' although I have sent you a couple of copies. . . . I shall finish the song up this week and will send the new lyric to this number as well as a finished copy of the 'Wishing' song."[30] The published songs did differ significantly from the versions heard in the film, and not only because of the variant lyrics. Following standard practice, only the chorus of each song was sung in the film, while the published song sheet also included a verse. There was an additional Morey-Churchill song, titled simply "Snow White," which was not heard in the film at all but was published as part of the film's promotional campaign.[31]

PINOCCHIO

In the meantime, Leigh Harline was embarking on what would become a landmark achievement of his own, the studio's second feature. Disney's *Pinocchio* would be released in 1940 and, again, would be a musical. If anything, Harline's accomplishment would be even more extraordinary than Churchill's: every cue in the picture, both the songs and the incidental score, would be either composed or co-composed by Harline.

Characteristically for the Disney studio in its peak years, *Pinocchio* is not simply a rehash of past glories but is, in fact, utterly unlike *Snow White*. It boasts a graphic style uniquely its own, its storyline is much darker than that of the earlier film (and in some ways darker than that of the source novel), and, as a musical, it follows a pattern markedly dissimilar to that of its predecessor. One might argue that it leans away from the integrated style of *Snow White*, in that it features more out-and-out performance numbers: Pinocchio's song in the puppet show ("I've Got No Strings"), Jiminy Cricket's showy number in the workshop ("Give a Little Whistle").

But these numbers are hardly gratuitous insertions; each is integral to the plot. Pinocchio's performance in Stromboli's puppet show is an important and fateful turning point in the story, and his performance of the song, starting as a nervous beginner, gaining confidence as he goes, and ultimately embracing what he thinks is his destiny as a performer, conveys a wealth of exposition in a subtle and sophisticated way. "Give a Little Whistle," too, occurs at a key moment in the plot: Jiminy Cricket has just been appointed Pinocchio's conscience, and he promises in song his availability whenever Pinocchio faces a moral dilemma. Also, as Jiminy Cricket belts out the song in best showbiz tradition, he implicitly acknowledges the Cricket's singing voice, Cliff Edwards, who had already enjoyed a successful career in vaudeville and early film musicals. Edwards was a familiar presence to movie audiences in 1940, and as Jiminy Cricket "sells" his big number in the workshop, he evokes associations with an earlier tradition of musicals.

Among the other points of divergence between *Snow White* and *Pinocchio* is the distribution of song numbers within the body of the film. *Pinocchio* boasts a rich song score, but the songs occur in the early sequences of the film; the majority of them are concentrated in the first four reels. Thereafter, they turn up at lengthier intervals. After Pinocchio arrives in the sinister environs of Pleasure Island, the story takes a particularly dark and dangerous turn, and from that point on—until a quick end-title reprise in the closing moments—nobody in the movie is in a singing mood. This is an important point: Walt and his artists embrace the musical genre but are bound by no particular formal requirements. The musical conventions must serve the needs of the story.

Perhaps most notably, *Pinocchio*, having no conventional boy-girl romance, has no "evergreen" romantic ballad to compare with "Some Day My Prince Will Come" in *Snow White*. What it does have is no less enduring: "When You Wish upon a Star," one of the most celebrated tunes in the Disney canon. Once again, the film's standout song was composed early in story development. Its original purpose was modest: the writers simply wanted a song that linked to the idea of Geppetto's wish for a son. But from the moment Harline and lyricist Ned Washington unveiled "When You Wish upon a Star" in autumn 1938, the number was recognized as something special. The story crew immediately earmarked it to underscore the credit titles at the film's opening. Walt admired the way this would work in context: "We don't have to stop the picture for a song like that, and yet it plants the whole atmosphere. So when the old man makes his wish, it's right in line."[32] In the finished film, that opening off-screen performance (by Edwards) does indeed cast a subliminal spell over the rest of the story. In addition, the melody is woven into the incidental score at key moments, chiefly in scenes featuring the Blue Fairy, who has been summoned by Geppetto's wish.

As with *Snow White*, the songs of *Pinocchio* figured heavily in the film's promotional campaign. In fact, some of the *Pinocchio* songs took on a separate life of their own, entirely apart from their use in the film. "Turn On the Old Music Box," heard only as an instrumental theme in the film's underscoring, was actually written and published as a vocal number, complete with lyrics. "Three Cheers for Anything," written for the delinquent boys to sing on their way to Pleasure Island, was cut from the film before completion but was published anyway, along with the rest of the film's songs. And whereas the *Snow White* campaign had included a song written only for marketing purposes, Washington and Harline supplied six "exploitation songs" for promotional use only, celebrating the film's major characters (including two for Pinocchio himself). Three of these nondiegetic songs were published, and in a musical in-joke, some of them were heard in the film after all, subtly integrated into the incidental score. Of the millions of viewers who have enjoyed *Pinocchio* over the years, few have noticed this cunning detail.

These marketing efforts paid off handsomely; like the *Snow White* song score—and, indeed, like other Disney songs going back to "Who's Afraid of the Big Bad Wolf?" a scant seven years earlier—the *Pinocchio* songs established a separate success. "When You Wish upon a Star," in particular, was instantly and widely popular. Hundreds of artists recorded it (beginning with Edwards, who recorded a side for Decca shortly before the film's release), and it received the Academy Award for the year's best song.[33] The song's lasting success in the music business at large was mirrored inside the studio, where "When You Wish" would be adopted fourteen years later as the theme song of the *Disneyland* television program and, arguably, the theme of the Disney brand itself.

Taken together, *Snow White and the Seven Dwarfs* and *Pinocchio* can be seen as the zenith of the "first phase" of the Disney musical, a grand summation of a phenomenon that had begun on such modest terms, scarcely a decade earlier. They also stand as a kind of triumphant valedictory by, respectively, Churchill and Harline. To be sure, both would be heard from again. Harline's prodigious output included several Disney shorts that were still in the production pipeline in 1940 and would be released at later dates. Churchill, still a fountain of appealing melodies, produced a rich assortment of them that would be heard in the later features *Dumbo* and *Bambi*.

But by the summer of 1942, when *Bambi* was released, both these musical giants had departed the Disney studio. Churchill had died, by his own hand, in May of that year.[34]

Harline had left the studio in September 1941, following the infamous Disney strike but also following the unaccountable (in this writer's opinion) failure of the press to recognize the brilliance of his *Pinocchio* score, his brace of Oscars notwithstanding. (He would continue to turn out exceptional scores for other studios for years afterward.) Collectively, these composers—along with Carl Stalling and a few others—left behind an indelible legacy. Their body of work not only established the foundation of the Disney musical but produced some of its all-time classics.

Notes

1. Letters, Walt Disney to Charles Giegerich (in the Powers office, New York), May 3 and May 27, 1929 (Walt Disney Archives, hereafter WDA).
2. Letter, Disney to Giegerich, May 3, 1929 (WDA).
3. Performances of "Minnie's Yoo Hoo" in the Mickey Mouse strip usually consisted of short snippets that turned up unexpectedly. In the daily strip for October 28, 1930, a few words of the verse can be seen emanating from a radio, but most of the instances occurred in the color Sunday Mickey Mouse strips, which were launched in 1932. In the Sunday page for October 16 of that year, Mickey sings the entire chorus—in sections, at intervals, pausing in between to deal with his mischievous nephews.
4. The main title of *Jungle Rhythm*, delivered in November 1929, is underscored by the verse of the song. Subsequent Mickeys used the song's chorus as their main title music. The music was newly recorded for each film and sometimes featured appropriate adaptations; for example, in *Touchdown Mickey*, a 1932 football comedy, the cue ends with a rousing collegiate cheer. By 1933, the practice of using this song was beginning to be abandoned in favor of original main-title music for each short. *Mickey's Gala Premier* (1933) opens with an original theme, but when the action moves to a theatrical showing of a Mickey film-within-the-film, the titles are underscored with the familiar chorus of "Minnie's Yoo Hoo."
5. Russell Merritt and J. B. Kaufman, *Walt Disney's Silly Symphonies: A Companion to the Classic Cartoon Series*, 2nd ed. (New York: Disney Editions, 2016), 7.
6. For a good biographical sketch of Churchill, see James Bohn, *Music in Disney's Animated Features* (Jackson: University Press of Mississippi, 2017), 58–61.
7. Ed Benedict to author, June 11, 1983.
8. Ross Care, "Symphonists for the Sillies," *Funnyworld*, no. 18, Summer 1978, 44.
9. See J. B. Kaufman, "*Three Little Pigs*: Big Little Picture," *American Cinematographer*, November 1988, 38–44.
10. This writer has no wish to embarrass present-day authors who have perpetuated this mistake, but it's worth noting that Churchill bristled at the misattribution as early as 1933, when the song sheet was first published. James Bohn quotes Walt Disney in a later interview: "It was damn near a calamity.... I can't remember the incident in any detail, but it was a very unpleasant thing. Churchill was terrifically disturbed, and we were never consulted by Berlin or Bourne when the music was put out." Quoted in Bohn, *Music in Disney's Animated Features*, 48; in turn quoting Tighe Zimmers, *Tin Pan Alley Girl: A Biography of Ann Ronell* (Jefferson, NC: McFarland, 2009), 126.
11. *Time*, April 23, 1934.
12. Care, "Symphonists for the Sillies," 42.

13. Ibid.
14. For a good biographical sketch of Harline, see Bohn, *Music in Disney's Animated Features*, 79–83.
15. Bill Cottrell to author, November 15, 1987.
16. See D. L. Ashliman, ed., *Aesop's Fables* (New York: Barnes & Noble Classics, 2003), 146. The versions of the fables in this edition are based on the translations of V. S. Vernon Jones, published in 1912 by W. Heinemann (London), here slightly revised by Ashliman.
17. Actually, the film's cue sheet gives the song title as "Oh, the World Owes Me a Living." *Grasshopper and the Ants* cue sheet (WDA).
18. For the record, all these cartoons were preceded by another in-joke: *Mickey's Garden* (1935), in which a brief instrumental snippet of the song is heard underscoring the appearance of a grasshopper.
19. Joe Grant (one of the film's writers) to author, November 18, 1995.
20. *Who Killed Cock Robin?* cue sheet (WDA).
21. The song was published separately, complete with the original lyric by Larry Morey. "Slow but Sure" song sheet (WDA).
22. Bert Lewis personnel card, Disney Studio (WDA).
23. Al Malotte personnel card (WDA).
24. "Believe it or not, Riley, they used to laugh at this.... That was quite the stuff at that time." Walt Disney to Riley Thomson while screening *Wild Waves* (1929) in a meeting on a proposed revue of Mickey Mouse shorts, June 27, 1939 (WDA).
25. Walt's earliest thoughts about producing a feature were sparsely documented, but by mid-1933, some Disney artists were excitedly reporting on his comments in letters to friends and family. See J. B. Kaufman, *The Fairest One of All: The Making of Walt Disney's* Snow White and the Seven Dwarfs (San Francisco: Walt Disney Family Foundation Press), 31–32.
26. "Possible Songs," manuscript story treatment, August 9, 1934 (WDA). This is the earliest surviving written treatment for the film.
27. In 1941, Churchill testified in a copyright-infringement lawsuit that he had composed the melody of "Some Day My Prince Will Come" "on or about" November 1934. Case summary, *Allen v. Walt Disney Productions*, June 27, 1941, www.lexis.com.
28. Walt Disney in story conference on *Snow White*, sequence 8A, February 16, 1937 (WDA).
29. Memo, Walt Disney to Roy Disney, September 17, 1938, Re: Music Royalties to Larry Morey (WDA).
30. Letter, Larry Morey to Saul H. Bernstein (Irving Berlin Inc.), November 8, 1937 (WDA).
31. One instance was in *Souvenir Album: Words and Music of All the Songs from the World's Greatest Picture: Walt Disney's* Snow White and the Seven Dwarfs (New York: Bourne, 1938), 45–48.
32. Walt Disney in story conference on *Pinocchio*, sequence 1E (later renumbered 1.6), September 27, 1938 (WDA).
33. This was not *Pinocchio*'s only Oscar; the Academy also recognized the film's incidental score.
34. See "Frank Churchill Kills Himself," *Hollywood Reporter*, May 15, 1942, 11.

CHAPTER 2

MUSIC, NATURE, AND MATERIALITY IN *BAMBI*

DANIEL BATCHELDER

The opening shot of *Bambi* (1942) counts, I believe, among the most beautiful sequences of animation ever created. The film's first minute and a half consists of a long, slow sweep through a lush forest landscape devoid of characters but replete with sumptuous dark colors and exquisite details. Interspersed between thick growths of trees and shrubbery lie glimpses of a magnificent waterfall whose waters lead first to a stream, then to a babbling brook. This journey unfolds against the sound of an off-screen wordless chorus singing the melody of Frank Churchill and Larry Morey's "Love Is a Song" on "ah" and "ooh" syllables over gentle oscillating string figures. The music crescendoes, then blossoms into a new key just as we see the sun break over the waterfall. Birds chirp, water glimmers, and the orchestra soars as the audience is left in awe of the scene's spellbinding beauty.

This lengthy, placid shot stands among the Walt Disney studio's most elaborate and expensive scenes of its golden age, a period of tremendous technological and artistic flourishing spanning from the animation studio's first sound short, *Steamboat Willie* (1928), through its first forays into feature-length animated films, from *Snow White and the Seven Dwarfs* (1937) to *Bambi*. Even before the shooting of this opening scene could begin, hours upon hours of labor went into inking, painting, and lighting the verdant scenery to convincingly represent a dense glade with glimmers of sunlight. The entire creative process was subjected to endless planning and revision; only then could the laborious photographic process begin. Using multiplane camera technology, the studio photographed multiple layered panes of painted glass that would be moved at varying speeds and rephotographed—at a rate of twenty-four frames per second, thus requiring more than two thousand individual shots—in order to provide an illusion of three-dimensional depth. The resulting footage simulates a camera tracking both rightward and forward, revealing the horizontal landscape while simultaneously entering it.[1]

What is most impressive about this shot, however, is that the finished product appears absolutely effortless. The viewer's tranquil entry into the forest—and, by extension, into the world of *Bambi*—betrays nothing of the time, energy, and labor (and, most likely, heartbreak and frustration) that went into its creation. Though in reality every detail of the shot down to the very smallest iota was planned, this meticulousness disappears into a sequence that seems totally unforced and spontaneous—even natural.

This ironic dissonance between process and result in an animated film provides the basis of this chapter, wherein I locate *Bambi* in a broad discourse of aesthetic critical theory. Although this dialogue appears in writings about a variety of dramatic media, ranging from opera to live-action film to animation, they all reach a remarkably similar conclusion about the illusory qualities of the medium they regard. Positioning *Bambi* as an extreme, boundary-defining example, I contend that Disney's early animated musicals can be read to replace evidence of labor, effort, and technology with images of pleasure, naturalism, and magic. The causes and implications of this procedure are far too vast for this present project. Yet while this process of magical erasure is not unique to the musical genre, or to the medium of animation, or even to the Disney studio, investigating the role of music and song in this special kind of transformation allows us to touch upon several issues in orbit around the studio. This line of inquiry thus provides vital insight into the communicative potential of the animated musical and the ways in which Disney mobilized these properties. I end by fanning out to examine Disney's golden age animated musicals collectively. All told, this chapter explores a key aspect of how animated musicals interface between their creators and their audiences.

Bambi and Disney's Golden Age

Before diving too deeply into discussions of the animated musical writ large, it is important to locate *Bambi* in its immediate aesthetic and historic contexts.[2] The creative talent within the Disney studio during its golden age was undeniable, and this era saw the production of wildly ambitious films that expanded the technological, artistic, and expressive possibilities of the animated medium. The studio's earliest industrial achievements centered around music and sound. First deployed in the Mickey Mouse short *Steamboat Willie*, Disney's bar-sheet and exposure-sheet systems worked in tandem to graphically align sonic and visual events, thereby allowing the film and its soundtrack to be recorded with a heretofore unheard-of degree of accuracy of synchronization. "Because of this precise pre-planning of music and images," I have argued, "*Steamboat Willie* presents an animated world in which *everything*—from the characters and props to scenery that bounces and sways—moves in time to a constant stream of steadily paced music."[3] Film-music scholars have long described the close, explicit synchronization between musical and visual gestures in live-action film as "mickey-mousing," betraying a clear connection to Disney's use of the technique. Yet I submit that in the studio's early sound films, "the persistent, symbiotic affirmation of sonic and visible gestures ... flaunts the cartoon's impossible audiovisual space, affording sounds both with and without an apparent visual source a phenomenological equivalence that markedly breaks with classical Hollywood sound-design traditions."[4]

Disney continued to utilize and refine this technique in its parallel Mickey Mouse and Silly Symphonies cartoon short series, exploring the new comedic and dramatic possibilities enabled by the tight match between music and animated film. As rival animation studios began incorporating sound, however, Disney endeavored to distinguish itself by continually pursuing technical and aesthetic advancements in the still-novel medium. Disney artists were enrolled in compulsory life-drawing classes at the Chouinard Art Institute, where they learned to represent forms and movements with lifelike precision.

> Throughout the 1930s, Disney productions increasingly avoided the loony, illogical free-for-all that defined other studios' cartoons and instead pursued a brand of fantasy that relied ever more heavily on generous doses of plausibility. Disney's Depression-era adjustments—the infusion of markedly human personalities, the addition of colour, the simulation of [three-dimensional] depth, and the convincing alignment of sound and animated image—may thus be understood as steps away from cartoonish zaniness and towards a prioritization of verisimilitude.[5]

These movements toward an animation style grounded in realism helped Disney make the nearly unfathomable transition from cartoon shorts to feature-length animated films, beginning triumphantly with the lauded *Snow White and the Seven Dwarfs*. By tempering the film's fantastical fairy-tale elements with lush landscapes, realistic movements, and characters with recognizably lifelike traits, the studio presented skeptical audiences and critics with a film that far exceeded expectations for the animated medium. *Snow White* likewise exploited the studio's continuous mickey-mousing technique to help usher in and legitimize the nascent genre of the animated feature musical:

> With the creation of *Snow White* ... Disney laid the musicodramatic groundwork for a film genre that has persisted triumphantly to the present day.... Disney's deployment of music and sound helped to align *Snow White* with contemporary expectations for "artistic integrity" in film, a volatile term that nevertheless held great importance at the time. The perception of integrity encouraged audiences and critics to see the film as more than a mere novelty and instead receive it as a respectable cinematic achievement, thereby legitimizing the feature-length animated musical as a viable form of dramatic expression.[6]

Despite *Snow White*'s popular and critical success, the remainder of Disney's golden age was plagued by uncertainty and instability. Originally slated as the studio's second feature, *Bambi* proved immensely challenging to produce, and its release was subjected to continuous delays. In the meantime, Disney faced mounting financial concerns. While *Snow White*'s budget ran far over original estimates, the film, along with its copious related merchandise, turned a substantial profit. Much of this income went toward building a new studio location. *Pinocchio* (1940) likewise exceeded its initial budget, though it failed to produce a profit comparable to its predecessor.[7]

Released in late 1940, Disney's third full-length offering, the experimental "concert feature" *Fantasia*, proved financially disastrous. With the help of Leopold Stokowski and a team of audio engineers, Walt Disney chose to intensify the viewing experience by screening the film in the newly invented Fantasound system, an early form of surround sound that allowed for dramatic, multidimensional audio including panning effects. While this system made for a vivid moviegoing experience, it also required each theater exhibiting the film to install expensive new speakers around its auditorium. Still recovering from the Great Depression and with war growing overseas, this proved to be a cost that few American theater owners, and virtually none in Europe, were willing to bear. Despite a moderately successful road show, Disney pulled *Fantasia* from release, and a great deal of Fantasound equipment was sold for scrap.[8]

With financial burdens from overspending, a dwindling overseas market, and *Bambi* still not ready for release, the Disney studio called a Hail Mary. Walt Disney had acquired the rights to an unpublished children's story about a flying circus elephant in 1939 with the intent to develop it into a short film. Facing bankruptcy, however, the studio decided to expand the film into a feature. Created on a shoestring budget in less than a year and clocking in with a mere sixty-four-minute running time, *Dumbo* (1941) is as heartwarming as it is compact. This eminently likable, feel-good little film about a triumphant underdog proved an antidote to *Fantasia*'s perceived pompousness and grandeur.[9]

While *Dumbo*'s financial and critical success buoyed the financially weak studio, this proved to be little more than a temporary stopgap, for Disney was also plagued by internal troubles at this time. Though the studio's industrialized division of labor allowed it to produce high-quality films with efficiency, it also had the adverse effect of devaluing and demoralizing its workers, who acted like cogs in a great machine. As the workshop grew, Walt Disney became ever more imperious toward and detached from his staff. What's more, as Michael Barrier writes, "in keeping with his intensely personal management of the studio, Disney had always dispensed money in an essentially arbitrary way, passing out substantial raises on the spot when he liked someone's work."[10] Under this disorganized pay structure, two animators with equally heavy workloads could earn very different salaries.

By 1940, the Screen Cartoonists Guild, formed two years earlier, had unionized most of Hollywood's major animation studios, with the exception of Disney. In December of that year, however, certain key animators—including Art Babbitt, who had been in the studio since the early 1930s and had contributed crucial character and directorial work to all its extant feature films—felt the sting of Disney's imbalanced system of labor and joined the guild. The studio founder reacted poorly; feeling that his employees should be grateful and blindly loyal to him, he refused to recognize the organization. Tensions escalated until May 28, 1941, when Walt Disney sent a letter of termination to Babbitt. The very next day, more than two hundred studio staff members went on strike. Workers picketed for five weeks, and by the end of this time, Disney had lost nearly half of its employees, dealing the studio a crippling blow and forcing it to finish *Bambi* significantly short-handed.[11]

Global history likewise proved disastrous for the studio's final golden age feature. Premiering in August 1942, *Bambi* was an insular, isolationist film inadvertently released during wartime. As David Whitley writes, "though *Bambi* is not in any obvious sense about war, its feeling for a pure, natural world that is a retreat from aggressive and predatory human instincts links strongly with the isolationist, non-intervention policies that held sway in American politics up till 1942."[12] Critics particularly denounced the vilification of Man, the film's off-screen but powerfully destructive antagonist, in a post–Pearl Harbor world. The *Cincinnati Enquirer*'s review of the film, for instance, includes both a warning from critic E. B. Radcliffe and haunting added commentary from the paper's editor:

> With most of us feeling that Man is a pretty good kid, despite his faults, some will protest at finding him cast in the role of a killer and destroyer. And that's his role in the picture. [Ed. note: Which is presented at a time when man is waging universal war against his fellowman.][13]

"The emotional charge of a charming film about innocent and peaceful nature," Whitley summarizes, "had perhaps lost its historical moment, as the American people geared themselves up for commitment to the harsh realities of the war effort."[14] *Bambi* failed to recoup its production costs at the box office, and Disney only narrowly avoided bankruptcy by the grace of the US Office of War Information, which commissioned a series of wartime propaganda films from the studio.[15]

Although *Bambi* proved to be the death knell for the golden age of Disney animation, considered on its own the film represents an undeniable achievement in the medium. Scholars frequently celebrate—and criticize—*Bambi* as the film in which Disney engages most closely with reality. This film was to be the de facto culmination of the animators' requisite life-drawing classes at the Chouinard school. Walt Disney famously kept a small menagerie of live animals, including two fawns, in the studio, while animator Maurice "Jake" Day traveled to Maine to study the visual effects of light in the forest at various times and seasons.[16] This high degree of meticulousness resulted in an exquisitely detailed film that places a heavy premium on realistically representing the natural world.

Several critics have commented on this commitment to verisimilitude, and not always in positive terms. Barrier writes that "most of the drawing and animation in *Bambi* is unfailingly expert, but there is in the way that *Bambi*'s animals look and move no caricature at all—only mere prettiness of the kind brought by giving them graceful movements and large, liquid eyes."[17] Paul Wells points to *Bambi* as the pinnacle of Disney's hyperrealist agenda, while Robin Allan writes of the film's "uneasy blend of cartoon and realism."[18]

Other scholars have nuanced their discussion of realism by asserting that *Bambi* represents a utopic version of nature. In his compelling monograph on nature in Disney animation, Whitley concedes that the film's plot "is relayed to the viewer within animated frames that strive for new heights of realism; indeed, the degree of realism within *Bambi* disturbed a number of early viewers of the film, who felt that this had pushed beyond the aesthetic boundaries appropriate for animation."[19] Still, although *Bambi* deals heavily with verisimilitude, "the film is capable of engaging with our feelings powerfully because it is also, at a deeper level, a version of the Eden myth."[20] Whitley underscores this claim with a quotation from Disney biographer Marc Eliot, who describes *Bambi* as "the purest evocation yet of Disney's vision of a perfect world."[21] None of these commentators, however, has investigated the vital role that music plays in fabricating this hyperrealist world.

"What Can Compare with Your Beautiful Sound?": *Bambi*'s Musical Diegesis

I have elsewhere argued that the first third of *Snow White and the Seven Dwarfs* rallies the expressive potential of closely matched musical and visual gestures by creating a utopic space that seems to be governed by the logic of musical rhetoric.[22] Yet while *Snow White* largely limits its use of the continuous mickey-mousing paradigm to the first third of its running time, studio composers Frank Churchill and Edward Plumb's detailed score to *Bambi* hardly ever departs from this approach. The orchestral underscoring, for instance, explicitly mirrors even the subtlest affective shifts. In sequence 4.1, "Dawn on the Meadow," the placid pastoral music that accompanies Bambi and his mother approaching the meadow (take 1) switches to a nervous *misterioso* chromatic figure over sustained string harmonics (take 2) as Mother checks for danger. A sudden chaotic fanfare sounds (take 3) when Bambi carelessly rushes into the clearing. Mother stops him and advises him to be cautious over a tense silence; the *misterioso* then returns as she apprehensively approaches the field (takes 4–7). A flourish of strings and woodwinds (take 8) marks the arrival of a flock of birds; their presence signals safety, as does a heartening resolution to E-flat major that makes way for a reassuring oboe solo.[23] The entire process takes less than two minutes.

Though impressive, this close illustration of affect is hardly different from the commonplace dramatic function of classical Hollywood scoring practices. Far more intricate, and far more specific to the animated medium, are *Bambi*'s constant musical affirmations of visual gestures. Over the entirety of the film, hardly a footfall goes by without mickey-mousing. In the sequence described above, Plumb's scoring accompanies Mother's cautious steps onto the meadow after Bambi's naive charge (take 4). Her irregular, tentative movements—which clearly demonstrate the Disney artists' close study of the gaits of live deer—necessitate awkward metric shifts between 4/4, 7/4, and 6/4 in the conductor's score. Bitonal flute and clarinet chords on each downbeat mark the falls of her front legs, while descending half-step figures in the English horn and stopped French horn demonstrate the lifts and replacements of her hind legs. As Mother suddenly snaps to attention at a possible sound (inaudible to the audience), Plumb inserts a pizzicato tone cluster, followed by a tense 5/4 measure of silence (take 5). The incredibly detailed musical mirroring of Mother's steps returns as she continues on; the camera then cuts to young Bambi, who nervously shrinks backward and downward into the surrounding thicket as a solo violin plays a chromatic descent, mimicking his trajectory (take 6).[24]

Instances of this sort of hypervigilant audiovisual synchronization abound throughout *Bambi*. In a particularly famous example, the use of mickey-mousing permits slippage between plotted narrative and musical number. As Bambi and his mother lie down to sleep, accompanied by silence on the soundtrack, a lone clarinet note mickey-mouses a single raindrop. Another drop follows and then another; the score continues to link these to the solo clarinet, which repeats its first pitch before dropping down a fourth. As more drops fall, more instruments enter, and the clarinet's figure becomes a repeating 1-5-1 oom-pah accompaniment. As the camera cuts to a new shot, an off-screen chorus picks up on this background foundation and begins to sing the song "Little April Shower." In a few short seconds, the film transitions from a complete lack of underscoring to a full-fledged song through a mickey-moused link.

As in *Snow White*, this approach to scoring allows music to infiltrate the diegesis in a way that does not seem awkward or forced but rather creates an aestheticized space that sublimates all sonic and visual elements into a cooperative, interdependent totality.[25] The very fabric of the world of *Bambi*, the film suggests, is woven through and through with music. Arguably, many of the film's primary pleasures lie in this intimate intertwining of orchestral scoring, sound, mood, and movement, creating a version (or vision) of the natural world in which art and beauty reign supreme—even in the face of tragedy, given the scoring of *Bambi*'s heartbreaking death scene and climactic forest fire.

Bambi's insistence upon a diegetic world that conflates art and nature does not end with the implications of the continuous mickey-mousing paradigm. Music and song here work in other ways to create this special utopic landscape. Studio lyricist Morey's lyrics for "Love Is a Song," for example, make explicit connections between life, love, and music, declaring that "hope may die yet love's beautiful music / comes each day like the dawn." If *Snow White*'s cheer-up songs, with their promise that "life flows along / with a smile and a song," conflate music with a Pollyanna spirit of good-natured optimism, *Bambi*'s opening number suggests that tragedy may be counteracted by a metaphorical amalgam of "love's sweet music." As the film's theme song, and the event that precedes even the opening shot, "Love Is a Song" sets a decisive tone for the kind of world *Bambi* represents: one in which music and nature are continuous.

This mode of conflation also adds a new dimension to the clarinet mickey-mousing at the opening of "Little April Shower" discussed above. Following this synesthetic link into song, the off-screen voices once again compare a natural phenomenon to music by delivering a celebratory paean to the *sound* of rain "beating a tune" as it falls, eventually asking, "what can compare to your beautiful sound?" Evidently, *Bambi*'s magical conflation of life and nature with art and music extend beyond mickey-mousing. Rather, this peculiar alignment appears to be an explicit project, directly and repeatedly expressed through the film's lyrics.

Ross Care's thoughtful analysis points to another way in which *Bambi* links music with nature:

> At times heard en masse, at others fragmented into separate sections or even soloists ... the choral voices project both song lyrics ... and the purely phonetic sounds (similar in effect to the mythic, pantheistic orchestra-choral textures of Ravel's *Daphnis and Cloe* [sic] and Ralph Vaughan Williams's *Flos Champi* [sic]) heard during the opening multiplane pan, the autumn and winter montages, and at various points throughout the film.[26]

Throughout the score, Churchill and Plumb make heavy use of a wordless mixed chorus, often performing choral arrangements by Charles Henderson. Acting like an extension of the orchestra, the choir adds colorful "oohs" and "ahs" to the heavily impressionistic score. Yet music's constant close interaction with the film's diegesis means that these interjections add more than timbral variety.

Henderson's arrangement of "I Bring You a Song" sets the opening lines for alternating baritone and soprano soloists, obliquely suggesting a dialogue between Bambi and Faline. As the soloists deliver these lines, the chorus sings a countermelody on the syllable "ooh." The conductor's score includes the phrase "ZEPHYR EFFECT" above the chorus staves—and indeed, this instruction corresponds to a shot of a breeze blowing through tall grass.[27] Although the choir soon changes from vocables to lyrics in the bridge section, here it serves both as harmonic support to a musical number and, at the same time, as the sound of wind in a hypermusical diegesis.

The wordless chorus fulfills these dual roles several times throughout the film, suggesting wind sounds that are continuous with the harmonic, rhythmic, and melodic demands of the continuous orchestral scoring. This method of blurring the lines between sound and music occurs not only during songs but also in moments clearly removed from the spaces of musical numbers. Consider, for example, the transition between the film's autumn and winter sequences, wherein choral "ahs" join whirling flute and violin figures to accompany footage of fallen leaves swirling through the air. Such musical effects contribute to *Bambi*'s arsenal of techniques for creating an inextricable link between music and nature.

Bambi as a Musical

In previous discussions of animated musicals, I reasoned that the utopic musicalized landscapes generated by the continuous mickey-mousing paradigm create a valuable slipperiness between the registers of speech and song. In the context of a diegesis thoroughly imbued with the rhetoric of musical logic, a character can burst into song at the slightest provocation without risking the potential jarring effects that this shift can entail in other settings.[28] In addition to significantly minimizing the dissonant fissure between speech and song, this special diegetic construction allows characters who participate in song to display an essential symbiotic harmony with the universe that contains them:

> By allowing a character to engage in song, Disney explicitly mobilizes the animated medium's ability to transform and redirect sound through artificial sources. In the hyperrealist and hypermusical diegesis of *Snow White*'s opening scenes, the chirping of a forest bird provides a rhythmically and tonally conventional counter-melody to the singing of a human character, simultaneously recognizing and modifying real-world distinctions between seemingly random, natural birdsong and deliberately crafted human song. Singing allows Snow White to channel the music that appears to govern everything around her, erasing the distinctions between her body and every other form in the surrounding diegesis.[29]

Following this logic, characters in *Bambi* could easily harness the expressive potential of their own world, using song to convey their emotions in a way that seemed contextually organic and natural—and yet this is not the case.

With the exception of diegetic birdsong, none of *Bambi*'s onscreen characters is made to sing. Indeed, although the film contains four distinct musical numbers, it is difficult to neatly classify *Bambi* as a musical. Care writes:

> As is readily apparent in viewing the film, *Bambi* (unlike *Snow White* and *Pinocchio*) boasts no "star turn" numbers, opting instead for emphasizing the background score which weaves songs and incidental music cunningly together to the virtual exclusion of the character solo. The resulting construct is a seamless musical tapestry which envelops the tenuously plotted story in a delirious, lyrical haze of piquant melodies and complexly modernistic, programmatic background scoring.[30]

Crucially, off-screen voices carry all four of Churchill and Morey's songs. The songs these voices sing do not directly express the emotions of the on-screen characters; in fact, most of these musical numbers, such as they are, do not even correspond to specific linear events. Rather, they take the form of montages, highlighting a series of loosely related images centered around a single event. "Little April Shower," for example, depicts the effects of a rainstorm on the forest and its animal inhabitants, while "Let's Sing a Gay Little Spring Song" accompanies jubilant birds as they nuzzle and coo in flirtatious couples. "Looking for Romance (I Bring You a Song)" underscores Bambi and Faline's own courtship ritual, suggested visually by the couple galloping through an impressionistic, richly colored landscape and kicking up swirling gusts of leaves and petals (as the pair are "deflowered"?). The remaining number, the Academy Award–nominated "Love Is a Song," departs from this pattern slightly. First heard in full over the opening credits (featuring Donald Novis, an uncredited tenor soloist), the song acts as a sort of refrain for the entire film, bookending its depiction of the life cycle from birth to death to rebirth with the promise that "Love is a song that never ends."[31]

This prominent use of off-screen voices marks a distinction between how *Bambi* and *Snow White* operate as musicals. Due to the nature of her surroundings, Snow White's singing represents an exceptionally powerful mode of expression. By engaging in song, a character in the context of continuous mickey-mousing appears to tap into the music that saturates the diegesis, thereby situating herself as an organic extension of her universe. Singing erases the boundaries between Snow White's body and all the forms that surround her—which are already animated, quite literally, to the music that pervades the filmic space, anyway—and allows her to harness this life force for the purposes of self-expression.[32] In the case of *Bambi*, however, a lack of singing characters essentially cuts out the middleman. If songs in *Snow White* flowed from the core of the musical diegesis through its characters, then the sound of an off-screen chorus—an extension of the unseen but always heard orchestra that synesthetically renders visual gestures audible—appears to well up directly from nature itself. Care comes to a similar conclusion, stating that off-screen song "becomes, in *Bambi*, the veritable voice of nature."[33]

Ordinarily, the act of bursting into song in a musical lends the diegesis a malleable relationship to realism; this slipperiness permits viewers to suspend their disbelief and perceive the resulting musical number as a direct expression of the singing character's ideas or feelings. Yet *Bambi* directs its delocalized songs not through individual characters but rather through the entirety of the film's diegesis. Songs that appear to spring from the fabric of the universe thus do not serve as expressions of individuals but rather as a manifestation of the universe itself. The notion that the universe might be able to express itself in the form of a song represents a powerfully utopic vision of the world, backing up Whitley's claim that in *Bambi*, "the forest is conjured with a kind of joyful and lyrical delight appropriate for the representation of unfallen nature within paradise."[34] This ability to give voice to nature proves to be an immensely valuable tool in Disney's creation of a continuous "reality" inextricably imbued with music.

The relentless insistence on situating music as a part of nature carries broad dramatic implications. By weaving music into the fabric of a cohesive symbiotic film world, *Bambi* places music on the same plane of reality as the characters and landscape that seem to be innately attuned to its sounds. The version of the world presented in this film effaces the boundaries that separate sound, image, and movement, resulting in a diegesis in which aesthetic concerns become synonymous with life itself. In this utopic space, the entire hermetically sealed universe can communicate in the legible and structurally predictable form of a popular song, with its familiar patterns of formal repetition and harmonic fulfillment. This phenomenon operates in full force from the very opening of the film, with its meticulously crafted yet seemingly effortless first shot: in drawing its audience's attention toward an absorptive alternative reality, Disney simultaneously pulls focus from the materiality of the film. Although viewers may be aware that every color, every gesture, and every sound represents the overdetermined result of painstaking labor on behalf of the studio, *Bambi* counteracts this recognition by creating the assimilative illusion of an organic universe governed by art and aesthetics.

Effacing Technology

The construction of an airtight universe that privileges art and music carries profound implications. Once *Bambi* adjusts its viewers to its primary logical conditions, the film remains largely consistent in its adherence to its central visual, sonic, and dramatic conceits. Slight moments of deviation do occur, primarily in the film's springtime sequences. As Flower and Thumper successively fall victim to "twitterpation" (the film's euphemistic nickname for sexual attraction) upon meeting females of their respective species, both characters display blatantly cartoonish double takes, more redolent of Warner Bros.' Tex Avery than of Disney. Moments later, Bambi receives a kiss from Faline, and as he grins dopily, the forest setting changes into a landscape of clouds that the two deer frolic around weightlessly. Shortly thereafter, the title character encounters a rival male; as the stags battle over Faline's affection, the film presents the fight scene with expressionistic shadows and bold, dark colors. These moments take advantage of animation's ability to express subjective states, mobilizing the medium's fluidity to represent the characters' feelings.

Yet these sequences serve as the exceptions that prove the rule. By briefly deviating from *Bambi*'s established mode of quasi-naturalistic representation for the sake of subjectivity, the remainder of the film, despite its logically unrealistic music and anthropomorphism, appears all the more objective and natural by contrast. In short, *Bambi* works to maintain a cohesive construction of the world that remains largely consistent over the film's running time. This adherence to its own rules allows the film's diegesis to appear self-contained and organic. In so doing, *Bambi* effaces evidence of its status as a hypercontrolled product of labor.

In many ways, *Bambi*'s promotion of a worldview that links music, nature, and life is a quintessentially Romantic one. The film's close connections between visual and musical gestures, all contained under the aegis of a largely naturalistic world, suggest an aesthetic version of spontaneous generation, wherein the content of plot and action dictate—and largely subsume—the form of creative artistic and musical decisions. In one sense, this evocation of nineteenth-century aesthetic ideals falls in line with Disney's long-term grasps toward artistic respectability. If *Snow White* counteracted critical skepticism about the cultural value of animation and film musicals by engaging with Wagnerian ideals of organicism and synthesis, then *Bambi* represents the apotheosis of this project.[35] And while *Fantasia* generally stands as a more transparent bid toward artistic integrity, that film largely concerned itself with draping images upon existing symphonic documents of "high art" culture, essentially elevating the artistry of animation by a process of association. *Bambi*, however, discloses an entire self-contained universe that operates according to a Romantic aesthetic paradigm, not in prolonged bursts, as in *Snow White*, but from start to finish.

In his study of the *Gesamtkunstwerk*'s impact on Western culture, Matthew Wilson Smith highlights an essential contradiction that informs understandings of the total work of art:

> The history of the *Gesamtkunstwerk* is, to a large degree, the history of un-reconciled dialectical struggles performed under the sign of aesthetic totality.... While the iconic *Gesamtkunstwerk* seeks to bury all outward signs of mechanical production, it nevertheless relies heavily upon mechanization for its pseudo-organic effects.[36]

Smith contextualizes this paradox within incongruent nineteenth-century attitudes about art's relationship to industrialization. Wagner's *Festspielhaus*, for instance, ironically "combined an unprecedented reliance upon stage technology with an unprecedented attempt to hide the means of its own production."[37]

Yet this reading extends beyond the nineteenth century. Bertolt Brecht, for instance, famously reacted against Wagnerian synthesis, disdaining that dramatic approach's reliance on manipulative illusion. Brecht particularly felt that music, when used as a device to smooth over the unreality of performed drama, encouraged a dangerous indifference in its audiences that blinded them to the work's political and ideological implications. "A single glance at the audiences who attend concerts," he wrote, "is enough to show how impossible it is to make any political or philosophical use of music that produces such effects. We see entire rows of human beings transported into a peculiar doped state, wholly passive, sunk without trace, seemingly in the grip of a severe poisoning attack."[38] Brecht's Epic Theater emerged as an antidote to this apathy via cohesion: by embracing elements of fracture and incongruity in what he called the *Verfremdungseffekt*, usually translated as "distancing effect" or "alienation effect," Brecht's theatrical works shocked audiences out of a state of passive assimilation.[39]

This brings us back to *Bambi*. The intensive positioning of ostensibly unrealistic elements—especially music—as part of a cohesive construction of naturalism places the film only a short theoretical distance from the *Gesamtkunstwerk*, particularly as received by prewar American critical circles. Following the lead of Smith and Brecht (and numerous of the latter's other contemporary cultural theorists, as I discuss below), it becomes possible to tease out an essential illusory project in *Bambi*, one that seeks to conceal its foundation in technology and labor and lulls audiences into accepting the film's own cohesive system of representation as natural and organic. I do not wish to claim that the Disney studio was engaging deliberately in this project. However, this mode of criticism provides an extremely useful analytical framework that will allow us to probe further the dramatic function of music in its early features and to examine resonances between the animated musical and a variety of other media.

To observe the role of music and sound in *Bambi*'s deletion of industry in favor of naturalizing artistry, we may return to the film's opening multiplane shot. Following the exciting modulation by third at the reveal of a waterfall, the faint sounds of chirping birds appear on the soundtrack. These warbles could pass as field recordings, the call of a lark or a whippoorwill captured in its natural habitat. Their lack of an obvious tonal or rhythmic relationship to the underscoring locates these bird calls as something other than music, suggesting that the sounds of nature exist on a separate ontological plane from the sound of the orchestra. This dissonance occurs *before* any characters appear on-screen, and thus before the score has had a chance to mickey-mouse any gestures beyond the coincidence of a modulation with the appearance of the waterfall.

Once characters do begin to populate the screen, however, these relationships shift. In a veritable manifesto of personality animation, a bevy of forest animals wake from their slumber and undertake a series of anthropomorphized morning ablutions. A squirrel stretches and groggily rubs its eyes, revealing a chipmunk using its fluffy tail as a blanket; a mouse washes its face with a drop of dew. Unsurprisingly, every one of these motions finds a correlation in the accompanying music; the moment the field mouse touches the droplet, for example, Churchill's score (here orchestrated by Charles Wolcott) introduces a celesta figure to suggest the tiny shimmering of the water.[40] Following the first appearance of a rabbit (Thumper, we will later discover) to a *rubato* violin solo, a bird enters frenetically into the sonic and visual space of the film, waking up the forest animals. The song it sings, however, is now musical. Its jaunty 2/4 melody in F major—which, as James Bohn notes, bears a striking similarity to the main motif in George Gershwin's *An American in Paris*—is doubled in the off-screen orchestra by violins and xylophone.[41] While the opening bird sounds were dissonant with the underscoring, these birdsongs are now continuous with it.

Bambi thus uses birdsong as an extremely subtle bridge into the hyperrealistic "reality" of the film. The transition from lifelike bird sounds to utopic musical whistling seems to gently nudge the audience to gradually suspend its disbelief, preparing them for and ultimately culminating in the essential fantastical device of talking animals. These shifting conceits subtly and gradually assimilate viewers to the sonic world of the filmic forest, just as the opening shot welcomes viewers visually. By this same token, as we are pulled into this world, we are simultaneously pulled out of the real world. Devices such as these bird calls thus seal in the universe of *Bambi* from the outside, constructing a set of logical conditions that largely remain unbroken through the film's running time.

Of course, none of these bird sounds was provided by actual birds; rather, they were provided by Marion Darlington, an American actress who specialized in imitating birdsong. Darlington was a Disney studio regular who lent her talent to the soundtracks of several early shorts and features, including *Flowers and Trees* (1932), *Snow White and the Seven Dwarfs*, *Pinocchio*, and *Cinderella* (1950).[42] Yet the film absorbs her into its diegesis, obfuscating her identity as a human actress and transforming her vocal presence into that of a bird. While this transformation from voice actor to cartoon character is essentially not different from any other animated text, the hermetic seal that encloses *Bambi*'s version of nature seems to completely obliterate any recognition that Darlington—or any other live human—had a hand in the film's creation.

Other scholars have pointed to this erasure of labor and industry in the animated medium, particularly as it was handled by Disney. In *Understanding Animation*, Paul Wells writes that "the early development of the cartoon form," with its frequent commingling of live-action and animated characters, "was characterized by an overtly signified tension between animation and its relationship to live-action."[43] Yet "with the emergence of the industrial cel-animation process," he continues, "the role and presence of the artist was essentially removed and, consequently, cartoons/orthodox animation prioritized narrative, character, and style, rarely privileging the signification of their creation, unless as a system to create jokes."[44] This prioritization resulted in what Wells terms a fundamental "absence of artist" in traditional animated texts.[45] He reiterates a similar point in a later monograph with a specific focus on the Disney studio's corporate policies, positing "[Walt] Disney's model of creating animation through an industrial and commercial process which readily denied the specific artistic credibilities of individual creators and was predicated upon the 'branding' of the animated film in his own name."[46]

Wells's critique reveals a powerful skepticism about traditional animation. The industrialization of the industry—a process spearheaded by Walt Disney and his factory-like studio—meant that cartoons could be churned out quickly and efficiently. This increased industriousness, however, was counteracted by an aesthetic shift that privileged storytelling and beauty over clever explorations of animation's labile relationship with reality. Wells argues that this trend toward stylistic consistency in American studios effaced evidence of individual labor, changing cartoons from thrilling expressions of creative liberty to mass-produced corporate commodities.

Wells's focus on branding resonates with similar claims about the configuration of the author in dramatic media that relies, either explicitly or implicitly, on Wagnerian ideals of synthesis. James Bradley Rogers has highlighted essential similarities between diverse forms of music drama that touted principles of cohesion and unity, particularly the *Gesamtkunstwerk* and the integrated musical. By emphasizing these qualities in *Oklahoma!* (1943), released only one year after *Bambi*, creators such as Richard Rodgers, Oscar Hammerstein II, and Rouben Mamoulian diverted critical attention away from the unpredictable exigencies of live theater and redirected it toward the formal properties of the work itself. This rhetorical strategy minimized the role of the performers and instead celebrated the apparent sovereignty of a text that could not be altered without doing damage to its essential integrity. This approach, in turn, asserted the works' creators as hegemonic geniuses who were to be celebrated for their ingenuity.[47]

Jane Feuer makes strikingly similar claims to those of Wells and Rogers in her groundbreaking study of film musicals. Proposing that "the Platonic ideal of a Hollywood film is one in which the audience perceives even the celluloid stock as the stuff of magic and the story as transcending its origin in light and shadow," Feuer explains that the film musical genre threatens to alienate its audience in two major ways.[48] First, the technological mediation of film causes the medium to lose the sparkling immediacy of live performance. Second, as objects of mass reproduction, film musicals can seem impersonal and artificial, reducing viewers to consumers. In order to minimize this distance, she posits, Hollywood musicals work carefully to recreate a sense of liveness and spontaneity, constructing an elaborate system of fantasy that masks any sense of predetermination from the audience. Writing initially of rehearsal scenes in backstage musicals but quickly stepping back to make important claims about the entire genre, Feuer submits the following:

> The dances and the practicing of them are shown in such a way as to efface their own origins in labor (dancing and choreography) and in technology (filming). The process of creation and cancellation in turn renders transparent the creation of the Hollywood musicals themselves. *An illusion of spontaneity* ultimately serves to cancel out the place musicals occupy in the history of entertainment as mass art becomes folk art. We are never allowed to realize that musical entertainment is an industrial product and that putting on a show (or putting on a Hollywood musical) is a matter of labor for producing a product for consumption.[49]

To this end, Feuer centrally declares that "the Hollywood musical becomes a mass art which aspires to the condition of a folk art, produced and consumed by the same integrated community."[50]

Disney's golden age musicals similarly work to create this "illusion of spontaneity." Because these films exploit the combination of animation and music to fabricate the illusion of self-generated, autonomous worlds, it follows that musical numbers stand as the sites in which this project of concealment operates at its fullest force. The smoke and mirrors of sung expression can distract viewers from implicit biases with catchy tunes, clever lyrics, and flashy animated choreography. These films significantly minimize both the artificiality of their medium and the dissonance resulting from shifting registers between speech and song. With its commitment to realism and its naturalization of music, *Bambi* can therefore be said to represent the pinnacle of this illusory project. Wells's, Rogers's, and Feuer's resonant arguments thereby implicate the film as an exercise in manipulation. By presenting itself (falsely) as a mode of organic, transparent expression, *Bambi* erases evidence of its origins as a mass-produced, overdetermined corporate commodity. Purging specific indicators of the work of individual animators, composers, inkers, actors, and so forth, the film coalesces all its labor into a single, undifferentiated mass bearing the monolithic stamp of a single name: Walt Disney.

Toward a Conclusion

Although I have only begun to skim the surface of the vast and important issue of representational strategies in Disney animation, I will take this opportunity to switch gears somewhat and end my discussion on a more positive note. As an animated musical that privileges a coherent and absorptive diegesis, *Bambi* erases signs of deliberateness in favor of an illusion of spontaneity and naturalness. The film's utopic construction of the world transforms numerous aspects of the human experience into flattened, reductive shadows of their real-life counterparts. Bucolic forest scenes replace war, love replaces sex, and humankind is kept safely out of sight. A great deal of this transformative work is carried out in the spaces of songs. The Disney studio thus appears to take advantage of the slippery logical conditions of musical performances in a hypermusical animated diegesis to transform reality into a system of discrete, consumable codes.

By now, it should be abundantly clear that the study of the Disney studio's aesthetic priorities is riddled with contradictions. Throughout its golden age, for instance, the studio maintained a deeply ambivalent relationship to the idea of reality. Although mandated life-drawing classes and detailed renderings of nature reveal a concentrated interest in verisimilitude, the presence of anthropomorphic characters, fantastical settings, and magic threatened to undermine semblances of realism. What's more, while the studio developed crucial technical advancements for the animation industry, the films that resulted from these improvements frequently worked to sublimate the presence of these apparatuses.

Walt Disney himself—or, at least, the iconographic version of him in public consciousness—embodied several of his namesake studio's contradictory views. While he publicly declared disinterest in the cultural value of his work, this attitude is difficult to reconcile alongside artistically ambitious projects such as *Fantasia* and *Bambi*. To the press, Walt Disney variously represented an artist, an entertainer, a technical wizard, a powerful business leader, and a humble all-American guy.[51] This inconsistent public image, Eric Smoodin writes, enabled the press to mythologize Disney's films in by-now-familiar ways:

> Constructing cartoons as marvels of technology on the one hand and as the handiwork of an individual genius on the other, the journals endorsed one of the paradoxes of capitalist mythology: industry becomes a wonderland and turns into fun, while at the same time workers disappear and the product seems to spring fully formed from the head of the gifted individual.[52]

At the same time, though, Walt Disney's construction of a multifaceted and ambivalent persona allowed him to "[bridge] gaps between areas that were—and still are—often perceived as unbridgeable: art and commerce, high art and low art, immediate acceptance and trailblazing the future."[53]

Steven Watts attempts to reconcile the Disney studio's golden age contradictions by proposing a unifying aesthetic paradigm: "Disney's balancing of these varied elements ultimately produced an attractive aesthetic hybrid that can be described as 'sentimental modernism.' He created an overarching framework in which visual verisimilitude and a free-flowing modernist sensibility supported each other with a kind of tensile strength."[54] Watts goes on to enumerate several key elements of this artistic mode:

> First, it blended the real and the unreal, naturalism and fantasy, and manipulated each in an attempt to illuminate the other. Second, it secured nonlinear, irrational, quasi-abstract modernist explorations comfortably on the cultural map by utilizing certain tropes from the Victorian past—an exaggerated sentimentality clearly defined moralism, disarming cuteness—as familiar artistic signposts.[55]

Watts claims that sentimental modernism allowed Disney's golden age films to bridge the cultural and aesthetic priorities of the nineteenth century with those of the machine age. These films embraced technology while simultaneously using it as a means to an aesthetic end, explored modernist dream states without shying away from sentimentality, and boldly straddled the space between mass production and artistic integrity. "Never explicitly articulated but nonetheless powerful," Watts concludes, "an attempt to return magic, wonder, and irrationality to the modern world was central to Disney's work."[56]

This line of analysis is compelling. Sentimental modernism accounts for the studio's inconsistent aesthetic priorities while simultaneously locating these in their specific cultural moment. Yet this unifying theory seems somewhat incomplete to me. While I have strongly advocated for historical specificity in this and other analyses of Disney media, grounding these films in the first half of the twentieth century does not explain why so many people still care so strongly about them. How is it, for example, that *Snow White and the Seven Dwarfs* continues to engage and entertain people of all ages in the ninth decade of its existence? What are the pleasures of Disney's golden age animated musicals?

Disney's golden age bookended a trying time in American history: *Steamboat Willie* premiered less than a year before the 1929 stock market crash, while *Bambi* arrived just late enough to see the United States enter World War II. Throughout the protracted Great Depression that spanned these events, the cinema represented an important escape for many Americans. Applying the concept of escapism to evaluate an artwork's worth threatens to damn the work to charges of vacuousness. After all, if its ultimate goal is to help people turn off their brains for an hour or two, wouldn't any semblance of substance simply stand in the way?

Of course, this argument against depth is not the case. Although escapist entertainment provides an important outlet for troubled audiences, it does not simply ignore real-life issues; rather, it transforms and works through these issues, guiding viewers along the way. As we have seen, Disney's films maintain complex and ambivalent relationships with reality—or, at least, something resembling reality. While other American animation studios comfortably used the limitless expressive boundaries of the medium to show audiences things that could only exist in a cartoon, Disney was hesitant to adopt this approach. Instead, the studio used its films to negotiate tensions between fantastic and realistic modes of representation. And it is in this very process of negotiation, I argue, that we find pleasure in the animated musical.

This mediation was, and still is, facilitated by the cooperation of animation and music. Both media serve as fundamental indexes of fantasy, inasmuch as orchestral underscoring and anthropomorphic animal friends are discontinuous with what it is like to be a person in the real world. And yet the interactions of these expressive agents represent the very essence of the types of worlds created by Disney. By exploring and experimenting with the creative possibilities of a musical animated synthesis, the studio discovered a brand-new way to communicate. Further, the dual registers of speech and song gave the studio's musicals access to another dimension in which they could exploit the friction between the real and the fantastic.

Consequently, we may put aside attempts to reconcile the studio's many contradictions and instead embrace its films' delicious dissonances. Disney's golden age musicals present joy and sadness, comedy and tragedy, life and death. They take us to fantastical worlds that could only exist in an animated film, only to populate these worlds with characters we recognize from our daily lives. They are all at the same time quintessential documents of their precise historical moment—they could hardly have come from any other time, any other place—and enduring heirlooms that continue to engage and entertain viewers to this day.

Notes

1. Michael Barrier, *Hollywood Cartoons: American Animation in Its Golden Age* (New York: Oxford University Press, 2000), 262.
2. I have written at length about Disney's golden age aesthetics, and to avoid unwarranted repetition, I briefly gesture here toward what I have elsewhere explored in depth. Although this chapter should stand on its own, it relies significantly on discussions and theoretical frameworks laid out in these previous publications.
3. Daniel Batchelder, "Disney's Musical Landscapes," in *The Oxford Handbook of Children's Film*, ed. Noel Brown (New York: Oxford University Press, 2022), 345.
4. Ibid., 347.
5. Ibid., 351–352.
6. Daniel Batchelder, "*Snow White* and the Seventh Art: Sound, Song, and Respectability in Disney's First Feature," *American Music* 39, no. 2 (Summer 2021): 139.
7. See Barrier, *Hollywood Cartoons*, 229, 272.
8. After several regular rereleases, it was not until 1969, when the film was accompanied by a psychedelic ad campaign that appealed to young adults experimenting with mind-altering drugs, that *Fantasia* recouped its initial losses. See John Culhane, *Walt Disney's* Fantasia (New York: Abradale Press, 1983), 31; for more details on *Fantasia*'s release, see pp. 8–32; Barrier, *Hollywood Cartoons*, 245–280; Steven Watts, *The Magic Kingdom: Walt Disney and the American Way of Life* (Columbia: University of Missouri Press, 1997), 113–119.
9. Barrier, *Hollywood Cartoons*, 271–274, 309–314.
10. Ibid., 282.
11. Ibid., 284–285, 306–308; Watts, *The Magic Kingdom*, 203–214.
12. David Whitley, *The Idea of Nature in Disney Animation* (Aldershot: Ashgate, 2008), 74.
13. E. B. Radcliffe, *Cincinnati Enquirer*, August 22, 1942, 20.
14. Whitley, *The Idea of Nature*, 74.
15. Barrier, *Hollywood Cartoons*, 368 et pass.
16. Leonard Maltin, *The Disney Films*, 4th ed. (New York: Disney Editions, 1995), 55.
17. Barrier, *Hollywood Cartoons*, 317.
18. Paul Wells, *Understanding Animation* (Abingdon: Routledge, 1998), 25; Robin Allan, *Walt Disney and Europe* (Bloomington: Indiana University Press, 1999), 184.
19. Whitley, *The Idea of Nature*, 61.
20. Ibid., 61.

21. Marc Eliot, *Walt Disney: Hollywood's Dark Prince* (London: Birch Lane, 1993), 177.
22. See Batchelder, "Disney's Musical Landscapes," 356–358; Batchelder, "*Snow White*," 145–148. (Portions of this section have appeared in Batchelder, "Disney's Musical Landscapes.")
23. Frank Churchill and Edward Plumb, *Bambi* score (1942), Library of Congress item 168, sequence 04.1, 1–6.
24. Ibid., 4–5.
25. See Batchelder, "Disney's Musical Landscapes," 348–356; Batchelder, "*Snow White*," 148–152.
26. Care, "Threads of Melody: The Evolution of a Major Film Score—Walt Disney's *Bambi*," in *Wonderful Inventions: Motion Pictures, Broadcasting, and Recorded Sound at the Library of Congress*, ed. Iris Newsom (Washington, DC: Library of Congress, 1985), 90–91.
27. Churchill and Plumb, *Bambi* score, sequence 11.0, 2.
28. See Batchelder, "Disney's Musical Landscapes," 356–360; Batchelder, "*Snow White*," 148–152.
29. See Batchelder, "Disney's Musical Landscapes," 357–358.
30. Care, "Threads of Melody," 90.
31. Thomas S. Hischak and Mark A. Robinson, *The Disney Song Encyclopedia*, updated ed. (Lanham, MD: Taylor Trade Publishing, 2013), 135.
32. See Batchelder, "*Snow White*," 149–150.
33. Care, "Threads of Melody," 90.
34. Whitley, *The Idea of Nature*, 61–62.
35. See Batchelder, "*Snow White*," 148–152.
36. Matthew Wilson Smith, *The Total Work of Art: From Bayreuth to Cyberspace* (New York: Routledge, 2007), 3.
37. Ibid., 4.
38. Bertolt Brecht, *Brecht on Theater: The Development of an Aesthetic*, ed. and trans. John Willett (New York: Hill and Wang, 1992), 89.
39. See Ibid., 91–99 (especially 94–96), 136–147 (especially 143–145). Sergei Eisenstein's theory of montage carried out a similar project in film.
40. Churchill and Plumb, *Bambi* score, sequence 01.1, 2.
41. James Bohn, *Music in Disney's Animated Features* (Jackson: University Press of Mississippi, 2017), 108.
42. Maltin, *The Disney Films*, 26.
43. Wells, *Understanding Animation*, 38.
44. Ibid., 38.
45. Ibid., 38.
46. Paul Wells, *Animation and America* (New Brunswick, NJ: Rutgers University Press, 2002), 9–10.
47. See James Bradley Rogers, "Integration and the American Musical: From Musical Theatre to Performance Studies," PhD diss., University of California–Berkeley, 2010, 38–50.
48. Jane Feuer, *The Hollywood Musical*, 2nd ed. (Bloomington: Indiana University Press, 1993), 36.
49. Ibid., 13; emphasis added.
50. Ibid., 3.
51. See Eric Smoodin, *Animating Culture: Hollywood Cartoons from the Sound Era* (New Brunswick, NJ: Rutgers University Press, 1993), 96–101; Watts, *The Magic Kingdom*, 164–182.

52. Smoodin, *Animating Culture*, 96.
53. Ibid., 100.
54. Watts, *The Magic Kingdom*, 104.
55. Ibid.
56. Ibid., 107.

Bibliography

Allan, Robin. *Walt Disney and Europe*. Bloomington: Indiana University Press, 1999.
Barrier, Michael. *Hollywood Cartoons: American Animation in Its Golden Age*. New York: Oxford University Press, 2000.
Batchelder, Daniel. "Disney's Musical Landscapes." In *The Oxford Handbook of Children's Film*, edited by Noel Brown, 342–364. New York: Oxford University Press, 2022.
Batchelder, Daniel. "*Snow White* and the Seventh Art: Sound, Song, and Respectability in Disney's First Feature." *American Music* 39, no. 2 (Summer 2021): 138–153.
Bohn, James. *Music in Disney's Animated Features*. Jackson: University Press of Mississippi, 2017.
Brecht, Bertolt. *Brecht on Theater: The Development of an Aesthetic*. Edited and translated by John Willett. New York: Hill and Wang, 1992.
Care, Ross. "Threads of Melody: The Evolution of a Major Film Score—Walt Disney's *Bambi*." In *Wonderful Inventions: Motion Pictures, Broadcasting, and Recorded Sound at the Library of Congress*, edited by Iris Newsom, 81–116. Washington, DC: Library of Congress, 1985.
Culhane, John. *Walt Disney's* Fantasia. New York: Abradale Press, 1983.
Eliot, Marc. *Walt Disney: Hollywood's Dark Prince*. London: Birch Lane, 1993.
Feuer, Jane. *The Hollywood Musical*. 2nd ed. Bloomington: Indiana University Press, 1993.
Hischak, Thomas S., and Mark A. Robinson. *The Disney Song Encyclopedia*. Updated ed. Lanham, MD: Taylor Trade Publishing, 2013.
Maltin, Leonard. *The Disney Films*. 4th ed. New York: Disney Editions, 1995.
Rogers, James Bradley. "Integration and the American Musical: From Musical Theatre to Performance Studies." PhD diss., University of California–Berkeley, 2010.
Smith, Matthew Wilson. *The Total Work of Art: From Bayreuth to Cyberspace*. New York: Routledge, 2007.
Smoodin, Eric. *Animating Culture: Hollywood Cartoons from the Sound Era*. New Brunswick, NJ: Rutgers University Press, 1993.
Watts, Steven. *The Magic Kingdom: Walt Disney and the American Way of Life*. Columbia: University of Missouri Press, 1997.
Wells, Paul. *Animation and America*. New Brunswick, NJ: Rutgers University Press, 2002.
Wells, Paul. *Understanding Animation*. Abingdon: Routledge, 1998.
Whitley, David. *The Idea of Nature in Disney Animation*. Aldershot: Ashgate, 2008.

CHAPTER 3

MUSICAL EVOCATION, INTERTEXTUALITY, AND ACCOMPANIMENT IN EARLY DISNEY CARTOONS

MALCOLM COOK

MUSICALITY was an integral part of the aesthetic construction and reception of early Disney cartoons, even in the so-called silent era. The extant Alice Comedies and Oswald the Lucky Rabbit cartoons often evoke music through the depiction of musical notes, instruments, and singing. Their gags and plot lines frequently revolve around musical scenarios, and they make direct intertextual reference to specific popular songs or theatrical traditions. Furthermore, live accompaniment practices in exhibition venues would have been directed by these on-screen cues, resulting in a heightening of their comedic effect, even if this varied from cinema to cinema. This chapter demonstrates that musical evocation, intertextuality, and accompaniment were key to Disney films from the outset, indicating both the continuities and the developments that occurred in the studio's first decade.

As this *Handbook* makes clear, the Disney studio has become synonymous with music, but this history is only rarely extended to its early work. Walt Disney's famous and often-repeated pronouncement "It was all started by a mouse" on the 1954 television episode "The Disneyland Story" not only posited Mickey Mouse as the origin of all that came later but implicitly tied the studio to the innovations in sound that Mickey was associated with. The incorporation of synchronized sound in *Steamboat Willie* (1928) is one of the most famous and canonic in animation history, widely recorded as a break from earlier practices, both for the Disney studio and for animation in general. While this may be true in technological or economic terms, in aesthetic and cultural terms the silent-era cartoons were deeply musical in ways that alternately were a harbinger of what would follow or they reflected distinctive sound practices in the silent era. The cartoons discussed in this chapter aren't musicals, properly speaking, as they don't adhere to the classical patterns of that genre. Nevertheless, they clearly have a strong connection with Disney's later work in this field, such as the intermedial connections with the theatrical and musical industries and the privileging of music as a primary structuring element.

A number of scholars have explored the relationship between silent- and sound-era Disney cartoons. For Lea Jacobs, the "mickey-mousing" in Disney sound cartoons of the 1930s "represented a surprising innovation" for audiences accustomed to silent-era practices.[1] Jacobs is primarily concerned with 1930s sound cartoons and the way the close visual synchronization with sound or music affected the audience experience of these films. For Jacobs, these were effects only achievable through mechanically reproduced sound and therefore constitute a distinct break from the earlier period. Conversely, for Daniel Goldmark, "*Willie* neither gave birth to the sound age nor did it kill the silent form."[2] Goldmark's focus is on industry-wide silent-era examples, and he finds continuity in practices, such as the intertextual references to popular music, that are evident in silent and sound cartoons equally. Donald Crafton similarly explores the shifts between the two periods across a range of cartoon series. He recognizes the importance of musical evocation in silent-era cartoons, such as the "hieroglyphic" use of musical notation.[3] However, he puts forward that there was a "distinct break in the conceptual framework of animation, away from a lexigraphic mode and toward a mode exploiting the compulsive-obsessive application of, and passionate appreciation of music, the melomanic."[4] This bears comparison with Norman Klein's account of early cartoons being a "graphic narrative," derived from intermedial connections with comic strips and graphic art, although Crafton sees the influence in less deterministic terms.[5] For Klein, synchronized sound again "divides epochs" in animation and "alters graphic narrative," even to the extent that alternately watching the Mickey Mouse cartoon *Plane Crazy* (1928) with and without its soundtrack impacts the experience of the film in profound ways.[6] While these nuanced accounts are not in simple opposition, they indicate the need for further investigation and consideration of the ways sound and music were at play in early Disney cartoons and the continuities and differences with other series (synchronically) and over time (diachronically).

A trade-press advertisement that launched the Oswald the Lucky Rabbit series (figure 3.1) encapsulates the three characteristics of sound in silent-era Disney cartoons that are explored here and that structure this chapter: evocation, intertextuality, and accompaniment.[7]

It was printed in the promotional *Universal Weekly* in June 1927 at the time of the Oswald series being released and therefore would serve to introduce exhibitors to the character, and it is very revealing of the musicality of this series.[8] First, and most obvious, Oswald is shown singing with musical notes rising above his open mouth. This was, of course, a common graphic notation used in comic strips, indicating the continued intermedial inheritance of animated cartoons in this era, as discussed by Crafton and by Klein. Nevertheless, it also clearly positions Oswald as a musical character, and this evocation of sound through musical notes or written words was a commonplace element of all the early Disney films. The image accurately conveys a musical characteristic exhibitors and viewers were familiar with and could expect from this new series.

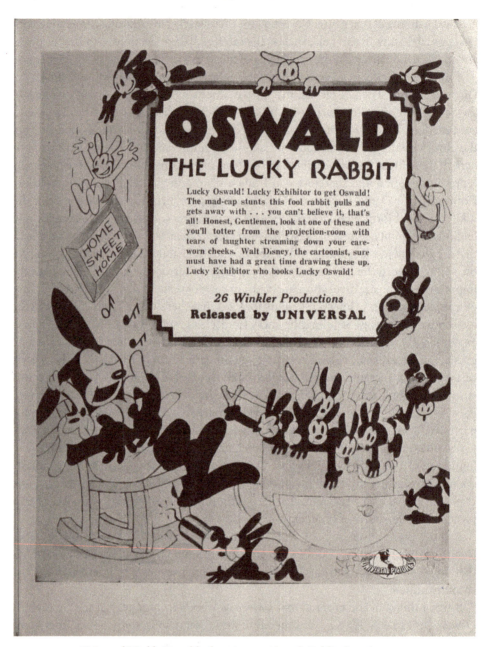

FIGURE 3.1. *Universal Weekly* Oswald advertisement (1927). Public domain.

Second, those musical notes rise upward from Oswald's open mouth and draw the reader's eye to a sign reading "Home Sweet Home." This phrase is still in use today, but its musical origins are commonly forgotten. However, in 1927, it would immediately remind readers of the 1823 song by Henry Bishop, adapted from a John Howard Payne opera, which originated and popularized the phrase and became a widely reproduced and recorded composition. Intertextual references to specific compositions, or to musical and theatrical traditions, regularly appear in the early Disney cartoons, engaging the audience through their prior musical knowledge.

Third, and finally, that "Home Sweet Home" sign is indicative of the ways silent-era cartoons could cue accompanists in exhibition venues to guide their musical enhancement of the films and even incorporate the audience into the soundscape of these films. While other more prestigious films might have purpose-written scores, cue sheets, or musical suggestions published in film trade press, shorts rarely justified such activity, and accompanists were commonly left to their own devices. This trade-press advertisement, like the on-screen intertextual references mentioned above, would direct cinema musicians to play the given song, especially something as familiar as "Home Sweet Home." Furthermore, this could contribute to the comedic effect of the film. In this example, "Home Sweet Home" was a sentimental ballad and in most cases was honestly and sincerely delivered and received. Yet here it is clearly evoked as an ironic commentary on the scenario Oswald finds himself in. The ad shows him surrounded by a multitude of child rabbits mischievously playing or misbehaving, one even literally disrupting the "Home Sweet Home" by knocking that sign onto Oswald's head. Rather than the longing for a faraway home that the original song's lyrics evoke, Oswald is more likely to be wishing to be anywhere but home when the pending calamities strike him. The ad thus indicates how the musical accompaniment of cartoons could add further layers to the comedy and twist the meaning of otherwise sincere music. Playing music that would create this kind of ironic dissonance with the image on-screen was known variously as kidding, funning, or burlesquing.

"Home Sweet Home" was also specifically associated with the community-singing movement and therefore with active audience participation in the soundscape of the cinema. The reference in the Oswald advertisement might easily have cued the accompanist to use this song and encourage the audience to participate in a sing-along with it. Although accompaniment practices in the silent era were heterogeneous, there is sufficient evidence to indicate the ways it would have contributed to the audience's musical experience of, and even involvement in, these early Disney cartoons.

Musical Evocation

A retrospective view of silent films might assume that they would avoid drawing attention to sound; however, on the contrary, early Disney cartoons actively played upon and foregrounded music. The 1922 film *The Four Musicians of Bremen* was made for the Newman's Laugh-O-Grams series while Walt Disney was still in Kansas City. It not only indicates Walt Disney's tendency to adapt established fairy tales, but it also adapts one in which music is central to the narrative. The film opens with the titular musicians in peril, clearly identified by the instruments they carry. Their musical abilities quickly come to their aid in the story, as they play music together to charm fish out of the sea for their dinner, with musical notes graphically evoking their playing. Likewise, the first Alice Comedy, *Alice's Wonderland* (1923), also produced in Kansas City, features a three-piece cat band playing for Alice with musical notes rising from their instruments, while two other cats dance to the music. Numerous other Alice Comedies open with a first scene depicting characters playing music, including *Alice Gets in Dutch* (1924), *Alice Helps the Romance* (1926), *Alice's Circus Daze* (1927), and *Alice the Whaler* (1927). The first Oswald cartoon produced, although only released later, was *Poor Papa* (1927), which similarly features several musical sequences, with graphical notes signifying the presence of music. Other Oswald cartoons open with him singing or whistling, including *Oh, What a Knight* (1928) and *Tall Timber* (1928). The depiction of musical situations is a constant in these early Disney cartoon series, often foregrounded by being part of the establishing scene, with graphical musical notes a recurring feature.

Despite this consistency, there are some breaks and developments in the evocation of sound elements over the period addressed here, most notably in the use of intertitles and speech balloons. The early Alice Comedies included substantial live-action footage of Alice and her gang, and it is therefore not surprising that they also adopted the use of intertitles, which were common in many films of this period. In some cases, these served as a form of narration and subtitle, setting up the scenario of the subsequent sequence.[9] In *Alice's Mysterious Mystery* (1926) a card introduces Alice and her cat Julius as "A Couple of Sherlocks on the Trail of the Missing Link." In most cases, however, intertitles in the Alice Comedies were used to communicate spoken language and thus were a part of the soundscape of the cartoons. In *Alice Gets in Dutch*, intertitles are used equally for dialogue in a live-action sequence in Alice's school classroom and within the cartoonland when Alice instructs her animal friends for a battle. Yet this latter scene also includes speech balloons for Alice's dialogue ("Company Fall In"). Speech bubbles were exclusively used to communicate spoken language. We might assume that the decision to choose between intertitles and balloons for speech was largely dictated by practical production choices, such as the longer phrases afforded by title cards or additions made during editing, but the choice often seems arbitrary in the finished films. Significantly, both intertitles and speech balloons declined in use as the Alice series progressed, and neither is found in the Oswald the Lucky Rabbit series.

Dialogue was also included in both series through brief phrases written out onscreen but without a surrounding balloon. A very common example is the depiction of characters laughing with "ha ha" written above them. This can be seen in films including *Alice Gets in Dutch*, *Alice the Peacemaker* (1924), *Alice Gets Stung* (1925), *Alice Solves the Puzzle* (1925), *Alice the Jailbird* (1925), *Sky Scrappers* (1928), *The Fox Chase* (1928), and *Hungry Hoboes* (1928). Other text, such as "help" or "stop," similarly feature regularly in both series. These brief moments of on-screen speech might be considered out of the scope of this chapter, as they are linguistic in nature, or "lexigraphic," as Crafton describes them.[10] However, they do contribute to the graphical soundscape of the cartoons as they are clearly meant to be understood as verbalized language, accompanied by the characters' jabbering mouths. Occasionally, it is even possible to lip-read what is being expressed; for example, in *Hungry Hoboes*, Oswald orders a chicken to lay an egg, and his count of "one, two, three" is easily recognized. These brief moments of speech are thus distinct from other icons or hieroglyphs, such as question marks or exclamation points, which communicate a reaction rather than sound. Furthermore, these on-screen words are very commonly onomatopoeic sounds that have only very limited linguistic meaning and are primarily intended to evoke the sounds of actions.

Common examples include a "zzz" indicating the snoring of sleeping characters (seen in *Alice in the Jungle* [1925], *Alice Gets Stung*, *Alice the Fire Fighter* [1926], *The Mechanical Cow* [1927], and *The Ocean Hop* [1927]), a "kiss" or "smack" directed between amorous lovers (seen in *Alice in the Jungle*, *Alice's Mysterious Mystery*, *Alice the Fire Fighter*, and *Oh, What a Knight*), or the "ouch," "yow," or "eee" of characters being hit (seen in *Four Musicians of Bremen*, *Alice's Wonderland*, *Alice the Peacemaker*, *All Wet* [1927], *Rival Romeos* [1928], *Ozzie of the Mounted* [1928], and *Hungry Hoboes*). These are complemented by similar graphic-word phrases emitted by inanimate objects where the source has no capacity for language and the word is clearly intended as an evocation of a pure sound. Repeated examples of this include the "clang clang" or "toot toot" of a train (seen in *Alice's Wonderland* and *Trolley Troubles* [1927]), the "honk honk" of an automobile horn (seen in *Alice's Brown Derby* [1926], *Oh Teacher* [1927], and *Rival Romeos*), the "ding dong" of bells ringing (seen in *Alice's Mysterious Mystery*, *Alice the Fire Fighter*, and *Great Guns* [1927]), or the "pop" or "bang" of guns (seen in *Alice's Balloon Race* [1926], *Africa before Dark* [1928], and *The Fox Chase*). As discussed below, these would all serve as clear cues for accompanists to use music or effects to echo the given sound. However, they also invite the audience to imagine the soundscape of the world they are watching, and they contribute to the musicality of these cartoons in more advanced ways.

These on-screen graphic signifiers of music are very commonly used as parts of the gags in these cartoons. They are not simply an embellishment or practical instruction to accompanists but become the purpose of many of the silent-era Disney cartoons. The ubiquity of musical notes as icon or hieroglyph, noted above, means they are commonly used in self-reflexive gags or plots. In *Alice Gets in Dutch*, a musical note becomes stuck in a saxophone and has to be physically pulled out, and later a musical note transforms into a stick person who dances on a staff. In *Alice the Whaler*, a parrot eats the rising musical notes as if they were grapes, while in *Alice the Fire Fighter*, a pianist saves someone from a burning building by playing their instrument, with the rising music notes forming a stairway for the victim to escape. *Alice the Piper* (1924) structures the whole narrative of the cartoon around music, starting with a group of mice dancing to a radio, from which musical notes and staffs float. Alice and her cat Julius take on the role of the pipers of the title to get rid of the mice by luring them with their own musical performances, although they finally succeed by using a vacuum cleaner to suck up all the mice.

The Oswald series likewise incorporated these kinds of musical gags and narratives, the most elaborate of which are seen in *Rival Romeos*. As the title suggests, the plot revolves around Oswald and a rival suitor attempting to woo the affections of "Juliet," who is situated on a balcony, continuing the Shakespeare allusions. Oswald's approaches are musical, as he arrives with a banjo and attempts to serenade his love but is thwarted in a series of music-related gags. Oswald provides an exaggerated performance, including an extreme high-angled close-up in which the whole screen is taken up by his flapping tongue. However, the rising musical notes he is producing turn into stick people who begin to fight. Oswald inspects his sheet music and realizes it has been altered by a black fly, misleading him into playing discordant notes. This gag works in immediate terms to produce laughter through a surreal unhinging of expectations, but it also astutely comments on the translation between the visual and the musical at stake in a silent cartoon that evokes sound. Oswald, as a sight-reading musician, translates the visual sheet music into the auditory, but the silent cartoon must translate that back into a visual form for the audience to understand it, in this case musical notes rising that then become anthropomorphized and start fighting to communicate musical dissonance. Moreover, this gag, in a film in production in late 1927 and released in 1928 when the coming of sound in Hollywood was a prominent industry concern, can also be read as a commentary on mechanical reproduction of sound. That a trained musician might mistake a fly on their sheet music as a note and play it unthinkingly is faintly ludicrous and is part of the comedy. Significantly, it also serves as commentary on mechanically reproduced sound where automation means such errors could easily occur, such as an unintended hole in a player-piano roll or a scratched gramophone record or, indeed, a fly on the optical soundtrack of a film print.

A second gag in *Rival Romeos* likewise plays upon the mechanical reproduction of sound and the translation between visual and auditory forms. Unbeknownst to Oswald, a goat starts to eat his sheet music and then his banjo, preventing Oswald from any further serenading. Oswald alternately berates, begs, and physically attacks the goat before realizing musical notes are coming out of its mouth, at which point he manipulates the goat's tail as if it is a barrel organ and proceeds to grind the music out of him. Like the prior gag discussed above, this plays upon the idea of mechanically reproduced sound, suggesting that printed sheet music could be directly and automatically translated into its musical referent without any skill or interpretation. Observant readers will note that a nearly identical gag was used in *Steamboat Willie*, made less than a year later. The unoriginal repetition, of course, reflects the industrial logic of the factory production line of animated cartoons at this time, but we can also see this musical gag as an indication of the many continuities between silent-era and early sound cartoons that belie the idea that *Steamboat Willie* was an absolute break from past practices.

This sequence from *Rival Romeos* also demonstrates another key element of the musicality of early Disney cartoons in its spatial construction. Sound and music, whether in the form of onomatopoeic words or musical notes, are frequently used to establish spatial continuity across cuts and orient the viewer. In *Rival Romeos*, Oswald is located below a balcony when he begins to play, recalling the famous *Romeo and Juliet* scene alluded to by the cartoon's title. As he begins to play and sing, musical notes rise on the left-hand side of the screen. We then cut to a separate shot at the level of the balcony, with the musical notes again rising on the left, providing a clear connection with the prior space and orienting the viewer in relation to it. A similar spatial orientation occurs later in the cartoon when Oswald turns the goat's tail like a barrel organ, and musical notes are emitted in a left-to-right, top-to-bottom direction. The film cuts to a previously unseen bedroom space and a new character, which could be disorientating, except that the continuation of the musical notes and their direction of travel construct a clear set of spatial and aural relationships for the spectator (figure 3.2).

Similar situations, in which visualized sound carries between shots, occur in many of the early Disney cartoons, including the earlier Alice Comedies series. It is fitting that *Alice the Fire Fighter* includes several vivid examples, given that firefighter films have been an important site for the development and discussion of film narrative and grammar.[11] An external shot of a fire station with "zzz" coming from the window indicates that its unseen inhabitants are asleep, which is followed by a cut to a row of beds that signal the source, while the "clang clang" of the fire bell drifts through the window, providing a clear and efficient spatial relationship and orientation. Later in the film, a female victim trapped in a burning building calls out "help," and the word carries over a cut into a separate shot where Alice "hears" it and is thereby able to call for help and enact a rescue. Similar uses of visualized sound as part of spatial construction and continuity editing are seen in cartoons including *Alice's Spooky Adventure* (1924), *Alice the Peacemaker*, *All Wet*, *Ozzie of the Mounted*, and *Tall Timber*. It is important to note that this effect is by no means unique to Disney cartoons and is evident in other silent-era series that predated or coexisted with them. For example, the 1919 cartoon *Charley on the Farm*, made by Pat Sullivan and Otto Messmer before they created Felix the Cat, includes a similar scene in which sound from outside drifts into a window and disturbs their Charlie Chaplin caricature. Likewise, Felix the Cat cartoons such as *Felix Strikes It Rich* from 1923 and *Uncle Tom's Crabbin'* from 1927 feature similar uses of visualized sound to link spaces across cuts.

These examples indicate that early Disney cartoons did not simply represent music but were musical in their very construction. This can also be seen in the use of animation cycles. As Nicholas Sammond, Scott Bukatman, and others have noted, the

FIGURE 3.2. *Rival Romeos*, spatial construction through visualized sound. Screenshot by author.

development of animation as a regular part of film programs in the 1910s and 1920s was predicated on the industrialization of the laborious production process.[12] Numerous techniques were developed to enable this, including the Bray/Hurd patents and how-to instructional guides, but the use of cycles (repetitions of short sequences of animation) was an especially visible one.[13] Run, walk, and dance cycles are frequently used to extend the screen time of the cartoons without the need for additional drawing. It is notable that these are especially common for the musical moments in the early Disney cartoons. In the very first Alice film, *Alice's Wonderland*, she encounters a set of cats, three playing instruments while two others dance. Each of the cats has a small number of different frames/poses that are cycled multiple times to create an extended sequence. Similarly, in the first produced Oswald the Lucky Rabbit cartoon, *Poor Papa*, Oswald is overrun by his progeny, who dance and play musical instruments; in each case, a cycle of a few frames is repeated multiple times to create the intended effect.

Poor Papa was not released until much later, despite being the first in the series produced. Russell Merritt and J. B. Kaufman indicate that it was rejected by distributors Charles Mintz and Universal because there was "too much repetition of action" and because of "there being not even a thread of story throughout its whole length."[14] This is an interesting critique that goes beyond simple production values. Walt Disney and the Disney studio have been widely credited with, and heralded for, the implementation of story and character in animated cartoons, culminating in the shift to feature-length stories starting with *Snow White and the Seven Dwarfs* in 1937. Yet here it is external distributors and producers who advocated for these qualities and drove the studio to adopt them, with similar discussions also occurring during production of the earlier Alice Comedies, with pioneering female producer Margaret Winkler advocating for changes to Disney's work.[15] Moreover, and especially important to the discussion of sound in this chapter, the disputed aesthetic patterns evident in the first Oswald cartoon are distinctly musical: repetition, circularity, rhythm. The very structure of these early Disney cartoons was closer to popular music than it was to narrative cinema. Alice and Oswald were born musical.

Musical Intertextuality

The previous section demonstrated that early Disney cartoons consistently evoked music in general terms through graphic visualization of sound, gags, and narratives. Likewise, there was an inherent structural musicality in their spatial construction and nonlinear patterning. However, the connections with the Grimms' fairy tales, Lewis Carroll's *Alice's Adventures in Wonderland*, and William Shakespeare's *Romeo and Juliet* indicate the regular adaptation, imitation, and referencing of intermedial sources, among which are compelling links with music in these silent-era cartoons. Like the "Home, Sweet Home" example described in the introduction, intertextual references to music, especially popular music of the period, are a regular part of the early Disney cartoons and further enhanced the audience's sense of them as deeply imbricated with musical culture.

Poor Papa not only includes music as part of its gags and storyline but is itself an unofficial adaptation of a song (figure 3.3). "Poor Papa (He's Got Nothin' at All)" was written by Billy Rose and Harry Woods in 1926, released a year before the film was made, and performed or recorded by a number of artists, including a popular version by Whispering Jack Smith.[16] The song's setup is closely aligned with the narrative of Oswald's debut in which the "Poor Papa" of the title is overburdened with children. The song's lyrics describe, in somewhat misogynistic tones, the "sixteen kids ... all lined up and cried ... you should have heard them bawl." The lyrics even call them "happy hooligans," a reference to Frederick Burr Opper's newspaper comic strip which had also been adapted as an animated cartoon series from 1916 to 1921.[17] This reference makes an explicit link between the song and cartooning that indicates the caricatured nature of the situation it depicts, highlighting its suitability as a scenario. While there is no evidence that the song was licensed or officially adapted, the shared title and unmistakable similarity between the song's lyrics and the cartoon are sufficient to support a case that it inspired the Disney studio to loosely adapt the lyrics.

Similar direct references to other popular songs are evident in other Oswald cartoons, such as *Rival Romeos*. In the sequence discussed earlier in which a goat eats Oswald's sheet music, the song titles are clearly and intentionally presented. The first, "Hot Lips,"

FIGURE 3.3. "Poor Papa" sheet music. Left: York University Libraries, Clara Thomas Archives & Special Collections, John Arpin Collection, JAC001731. Right: sheet music from 1926. Public domain.

was a 1922 "blue fox trot" written by Henry Busse, Henry Lange, and Lou Davis.[18] Busse was the cornetist with the famous Paul Whiteman jazz band who recorded the song with great success.[19] The second music sheet the goat eats is labeled "Hot Mama." This is presumably a shortened reference to "Red Hot Mamma" from 1924, written by Gilbert Wells, Bud Cooper, and Fred Rose.[20] The song was especially associated with vaudeville performer Sophie Tucker, who was later billed as the "last of the red hot mammas" following the title of a song featured in a 1929 Vitaphone synchronized sound film.[21] In both cases, the song titles would be sufficiently familiar to many audience members to provoke recognition, especially if the accompanist took their musical cues from the on-screen events, as discussed further in the next section. Moreover, the song titles are clearly intended to add to the comedic effect of the gags occurring on-screen. The "Hot Lips" reference appears when the goat is drooling and licking its lips at the prospect of eating, creating a humorous reinterpretation of the title away from its original overt description of a "hot" jazz player (or covert sexual innuendo) toward the goat. Likewise, when the "Hot Mama" sheet becomes visible, the film cuts to a closer iris shot allowing us to see a provocatively posed female figure on the music sheet, and the goat proceeds to lasciviously peel the title of the song off the page to eat it, then uses its tongue in a suggestive manner to lick and slurp the lines off the cover as if it were spaghetti. The gags in this sequence are thus enhanced by the intertextual musical references by creating incongruity between the potentially sexual implications of the hot jazz and the farmyard animal consuming the sheet music.

As the latter example indicates, such references tend to be scattershot and are not always discernible to a present-day audience unfamiliar with the early-twentieth-century popular-music context of the cartoons. The title of the Oswald cartoon *Oh Teacher* might evoke the 1922 song "Oh Teacher Teacher: Let Me Do the Teaching Awhile" by Guy Stoddard and Dick Quayle, although the plot of the cartoon bears little resemblance to the song lyrics.[22] In several Alice Comedies (*Alice and Three Bears* [1924], *Alice in the Wooly West* [1926]), the heroine exclaims "My Hero" to her cat Julius when the plot is resolved. This was a common phrase but was especially associated with a musical number from *The Chocolate Soldier*, an operetta by Oscar Straus from 1908, which was still in regular circulation in the 1920s.[23] Iris Ethel Vining, whose column is discussed further in the next section, proposed Straus's piece for the accompaniment of a Felix the Cat cartoon at the moment he wins a boxing fight, indicating its common usage and recognition in the context of cartoons.[24] Early in *Alice's Egg Plant* (1925), musical notes and the lyrics "He's a mean papa" drift out of a building marked "Hen's Dormitory," indicating that the inhabitants are singing, angering Julius the cat, who serves in this cartoon as their manager. This seems likely to be a reference to "Mean Papa, Turn in Your Key (You Don't Live Here No More)," written by Bob Miller and Cal DeVoll, copyright 1923.[25] A recording of the song by Clara Smith was released in August 1924, six months before the production of the Disney cartoon was completed.[26] Individually, these examples are inconclusive, but collectively, they indicate a pattern of intertextual referencing to specific musical works and to the tropes and genres of popular music more generally.

"Mean Papa" also draws attention to a further form of musical intermedial referencing that occurs in these cartoons. The recording of the Miller and DeVoll composition by Smith was listed in the trade press under "Negro Records," indicating that it fell into the blues or "race music" idiom, raising questions about the race of the characters in early Disney cartoons and the musical implications of this.[27] Crafton and Sammond have both explored in detail the inheritance from vaudeville blackface minstrelsy of cartoons from this period, including directly identifying Oswald as a key example.[28] As these authors demonstrate, early animation inherited significant elements of blackface minstrelsy in iconography and plot scenarios, and this also included a substantial musical inheritance. The most overt example of this is, again, *Rival Romeos*, in which Oswald plays a banjo to accompany his singing, the instrument strongly associated with Black musicians and minstrelsy.[29] This became an archetypal image of Oswald, for example, being used in a merchandising set sold to the public to promote Oswald.[30] Similarly, in the earlier Alice Comedy *Alice Helps the Romance*, Julius the cat's rival opens the cartoon playing a banjo, contributing to the minstrel iconography in his design and serving as rapid characterization for his trickster persona.

Beyond the specific influence of minstrelsy, other racialized musical references played a role in early Disney, serving as shorthand methods for characterization or scene setting. Returning to the use of "Mean Papa" in *Alice's Egg Plant*, this song establishes in the first scene a power dynamic that plays out in the rest of the cartoon, as the hens go on strike and reject enforced labor and control. Margaret Bohanon has argued that the performances of African American women blues singers in this period, including Smith, provided a space for working-class resistance, and the use of one of these songs to introduce the hens would seem to draw on this heritage.[31] The visual design of the hens here retains a strong, if cartoony, resemblance to real chickens, with no obvious racialized element. This is in contrast to Julius the cat, whose design adheres closely to the minstrel iconography that Sammond identifies, and he is heavily anthropomorphized, with few feline features. However, the singing of "Mean Papa" figures the hens as Black women, with Julius playing the role of overseer and Alice as the master of the "egg plant." Julius even removes his tail and uses it as a whip to impel the hens to work. While the laboring white male animators of the Disney studio may have felt some solidarity with the overworked hens in this cartoon, it would be disingenuous to suggest that the film offers any genuinely subversive or progressive political views on race or class. The intertextual and intermedial musical references here are best understood as a rapid means to establish a scenario, seen in countless plantation stories, in order to provide the basis for a series of gags.

The same can be said for several other racialized allusions to music in these early Disney cartoons. Both *Alice's Circus Daze* and the Oswald cartoon *Bright Lights* (1928) include scenes in which a dancer, accompanied by on-screen musicians, performs an exotic dance, perhaps styled after jazz age star Josephine Baker or, as Crafton argues, a more generic "cooch" dancer.[32] In *Alice Chops the Suey* (1925), a "Chinese" rat whistles to signal his colleagues, with the visualized musical notes in this instance rendered in a calligraphic typeface implying an accented form of oriental music. In each case, the effect of these sequences would in part depend on the choices made by the accompanists. If they played popular jazz or ethnically coded music, such as the generic "Chinese Music" by J. S. Zamecnik, it would heighten and reinforce the stereotyped caricatures presented on-screen.[33] The variability of practice at the time and the inaccessibility of historical live performances for present-day research mean it is difficult to be certain about such matters. However, firsthand accounts and industry discourses in primary materials provide sufficient evidence that accompaniment was an important part of the musical reception and understanding of these cartoons.

Musical Accompaniment

The previous discussion has already alluded to a number of ways the live accompaniment in exhibition venues in the silent era would have contributed to the musical experience of early Disney cartoons and enhanced their comedic and dramatic effects. Graphic visualization would not only evoke sound and music in the imagination of the audience but could also serve as cues to the accompanist to play appropriate effects and melodies. Direct intertextual references to specific songs, such as "Poor Papa," provided more precise guidance about the suitable music to play. Moreover, music could go beyond reinforcing what was seen on-screen to enhance and embellish it, by playing with sound/image relationships or even inviting audience participation.

Silent-film music and accompaniment practices have received some attention from film historians and musicologists in the wake of the renewed interest in early and silent film that followed the 1978 International Federation of Film Archives (FIAF) meeting in Brighton.[34] However, musical practices in this period were especially heterogeneous, and it is vital to pay heed to Rick Altman's call for the "recognition of regional, generic and chronological variation."[35] Cartoon accompaniment is a case in point, as it differed considerably from the typical practices of the time. In his extensive study *Silent Film Sound*, Altman demonstrates that by the 1920s, accompaniment practices for narrative feature films had become circumscribed by a set of trade-press discourses and industry guidelines that sought to limit the creative, and sometimes disruptive, contribution of the accompanist to the picture being shown.[36] Short-film accompaniment, including cartoons, has received far less attention from academic scholars, replicating their undervaluation at the time. However, there is sufficient primary evidence to indicate that the dominant practices Altman describes were not applicable to cartoons and even that they were intentionally reversed for comedic effect.

Trade-press music columns, music handbooks, and how-to guides served as key publications and therefore provide valuable insight into otherwise lost live-performance practices. While some of these ignored comedies, under which cartoons were often subsumed, writers including Iris Ethel Vining, first organist at the Granada Theatre in San Francisco, and Harry Wagner, organist at the Empress Theatre in Chicago, showed attention and sensitivity to the value of fitting music to cartoons. In 1925, Wagner decried the custom in some houses to have "the organist take his rest during the comedy, leaving the audience in silence," arguing instead that among shorts, "cartoon comics come next in line of importance in musical background," second only to newsreels.[37] Likewise, Vining argued that "playing comedies is the most difficult of all picture accompaniments."[38] Vining repeated this assertion in an extended column describing how she accompanied a Felix the Cat cartoon that "fell rather flat" and was "sagging" on first presentation, until she developed appropriate techniques, which are also those advocated by other sources of the period.[39]

The first cartoon accompaniment technique is effective use of sounds and effects, enabled either by the versatile organs that were increasingly in use in the 1920s or through specific traps and sound devices advertised in the trade press. For example, Vining identifies a boxing scene in the Felix cartoon as a moment to "ring the gong."[40] This bears close similarity to a sequence in the first Alice Comedy, where the Disney cartoonists whom Alice visits are watching two cartoon cat pugilists. After a few seconds of fighting, one of the cartoonists looks at his watch, then taps a hammer against a jar of pens and brushes to signal the end of the round, his action overlaid with a graphic "clang." Vining's column indicates that this would have served as a visual cue for an accompanist to reinforce the on-screen visualized sound. Wagner makes similar comments in general terms, suggesting that it is "great sport to mimic" cartoon pictures using "numerous traps and mechanical effects" resulting in a "squeal, wheeze, groan, glissando, cry, crash etc. etc.," terms that are similar to, or even match, the sound words often seen in the Disney cartoons discussed earlier.[41] Edith Lang and George West in their handbook *Musical Accompaniment of Moving Pictures* likewise advocated that "a battery of traps and other accessories are really needed to emphasize in a comic manner the action on the screen."[42] Such an approach was not universally advocated. For example, Erno Rapee in his *Encyclopaedia of Music for Pictures* sounds a "word of warning" against effects for comedy films, "which, if not carried out with taste and judgement will kill the laughter of your audience."[43] Besides indicating again the fundamental heterogeneity of practices in this period, this also reflects Rapee's bias toward orchestral, rather than organ, accompaniment. In another column, Vining notes that "we organists have an advantage over the orchestra leader ... it is impossible for an orchestra to accompany a picture as an organist can, for the organist is working with one pair of eyes, one pair of hands, one intelligence, all coordinated."[44] Whereas an orchestra required careful rehearsal, which was justified for feature films but not subsidiary shorts, a skilled organist could improvise using the faculties of musical technology. This enabled the organist to make the organ "talk, sing, whistle, growl, snarl, snore, sneeze, laugh, cough, cry, bark, roar, meow and yell for help," Vining's list again closely matching the on-screen cues seen in the cartoons discussed here.[45]

The use of popular, recognizable music is also highlighted by advice columns and handbooks and played an important role in the reception of cartoons. Lang and West argue that cartoons and comedies are "admirably adapted to the introduction of all sorts of popular songs and dances" and that accompanists should "keep in touch with the publications of popular music houses ... [and] the latest phonograph records," as these will provide a strong draw for the audience as "people like to hear their favourite tunes."[46] Rapee likewise advocates for "popular hits of the day" or "well known or old time songs" in his discussion of comedy.[47] Beyond the general appeal of playing popular and recognizable music to accompany the cartoons, music columns and handbooks indicate that they could often enhance the comedy in them through musical punning, matching the lyrics or title of a song with the scenario in the cartoon. Conventional good practice for accompanying dramatic films had largely outlawed "kidders" who "spoof" the film, with George Beynon in 1921 describing such practices as "offensive" and "buffoonery."[48] In contrast, this type of accompaniment was encouraged for comedic effect for short films. Most commonly described as "burlesquing," it could also be called "funning," "punning," or "kidding."[49] Vining gives the example of the use of the song "All Alone," which is "rather sad as written, but it can be twisted to be downright funny," as she uses it as a fox trot "with Felix the cat marooned on a back fence."[50]

Vining's column-length account of accompanying a Felix the Cat cartoon provides the most extensive insight into the way such musical-accompaniment practices could play a role in the reception of cartoons. The cartoon described was almost certainly *Felix Outwits Cupid* (1925), which played at Vining's workplace, the San Francisco Granada Theatre, in July 1925, the month before the article was published.[51] Unfortunately, no copy of the film is known to exist. She suggests that "just a line of the music is necessary to give the audience the idea of the title," which can then create an "incongruous, clever, silly or a burlesque" relationship with the images on-screen. Examples include Felix running away from a dog accompanied by "Runnin' Wild," Felix firing arrows at a tree which justifies "In the Shade of the Old Apple Tree," and the appearance of flowers after a successful fight warranting "Where the Daffodils Grow." Clearly, such an approach is as much about linguistic punning as it is truly musical in nature. Nevertheless, it depended on the audience's deep musical knowledge to recognize the melodies and skilled playing by the organist to synchronize effectively with the cartoon and integrate different musical styles and keys into a seamless flow. Returning to examples of intertextual referencing in early Disney cartoons described above, it is clear that they would serve as cues to an accompanist to achieve similar effects, such as the incongruity of playing "Home Sweet Home" during *Poor Papa* while Oswald struggles with his innumerable offspring or the use of "Hot Lips" to accompany the goat in *Rival Romeos*. The familiarity and associations of the songs chosen could, in some cases, even prompt singing as well as laughter from the audience.

As I have written about elsewhere, and as Esther Morgan-Ellis, Dave Russell, and others have explored, community singing became a popular activity in the United States during the World War I, and similar movements were seen in Britain, Australia, and elsewhere in the postwar period.[52] Large public gatherings were led by a musical director in shared singing for the purpose of musical, patriotic, or civic betterment, and these commonly took place in cinemas, either as part of a wider film program or as standalone events. "Home Sweet Home" was a staple of community singing, as indicated by its inclusion in multiple community-singing handbooks that instructed musical directors.[53] These movements had a very small repertoire by necessity, as the songs needed to be simple and familiar enough to allow groups of hundreds or thousands of people to participate effectively. Sing-along films with the lyrics to "Home Sweet Home" had been distributed in 1914 and 1924, the first as part of the Animated Songs series from Imperial and the latter from the Sing Them Again series from Educational.[54] In some presentations, especially when actively encouraged by the organist or musical director, the use of a song like "Home Sweet Home" could promote the audience singing.

In a similar example, during *Alice's Wild West Show* (1924), three cowboys are shown singing in harmony, accompanied by on-screen accordion and piano, the familiar musical notes rising to reinforce the musical moment. A close-up then shows the three singers with their words written out: "Sweet Ad-Uh-Line." This is a reference to "(You're the Flower of My Heart,) Sweet Adeline," a 1903 song by Harry Armstrong and Richard H. Gerard.[55] This was a staple within the small repertoire of the community-singing movement, having been featured in musical handbooks, and was especially recommended in "'Close-Harmony' Songs for Men," matching the scenario of the Alice Comedy.[56] Most recently, in 1923, it had featured in the Sing Them Again sing-along film series which promoted community singing in cinemas.[57] The use of this song might well have provoked audience participation in some circumstances.

Caution is needed for such a reading. Musical practice would have varied among different exhibition venues, and Vining's account is undoubtedly an exceptional example intended as a model of best practice rather than an account of typical accompaniment. Nevertheless, it indicates the role live performance played for silent-era cartoons that is easily forgotten or assumed inaccessible in present-day reception. Goldmark indicates one way this practice did filter into later animation production and reception, through the career of Carl Stalling, the famed composer and arranger of scores for Disney and Warner Bros. cartoons. Stalling started his career as a live accompanist during the silent era, and Goldmark argues the "film-funner" approach he learned there carried over into his use of popular music in later sound cartoons, replicating the knowing referentiality described above.[58] Sing-alongs would be a significant part of later Disney presentations, from the Mickey Mouse Clubs in the early 1930s up to present-day sing-along versions of musical films on the Disney+ streaming service and in theme parks.[59] In this respect, at least, an inheritance and continuity between silent-era and sound cartoons is clearly evident.

Conclusion

As the discussion here has demonstrated, music and sound were very much a part of silent-era Disney cartoons, and this was often multifaceted and refined, drawing on the rich musical context of the 1920s. It is beyond the scope of this chapter to comprehensively or conclusively consider the degree to which the coming of sound constituted a distinct break or merely an evolution of sound in Disney cartoons, but a few brief remarks are necessary.

Crafton notes that there was a clear and swift decline in the use of "hieroglyphic conventions" of visualized sound in the switch to synchronized sound, amply demonstrated through a comparison of the Oswald cartoon *Bright Lights* with the early Mickey Mouse vehicle *The Opry House* (1929), which straddle the technological change.[60] In the latter, written speech and sounds are largely absent, and musical notes make far less frequent appearance even in the very early sound cartoons. This is hardly surprising given the new opportunities available. In some cases, the same effects could be achieved by transposing graphic references into musical allusions. A comparison of *Poor Papa* with *Mickey's Nightmare* (1932) is indicative here, aided by the latter strongly echoing the plot of the earlier silent film. For *Poor Papa*, as suggested above, the paratextual material and accompaniment practices of the period might well have resulted in "Home Sweet Home" being used to interpret the on-screen musical notes and comment on the scenes. In contrast, early scenes in *Mickey's Nightmare* are accompanied by the 1927 song "My Blue Heaven" to very similar effect. The method may have changed, but the outcome is similar.

In other aspects, however, the early sound Disney cartoons initially lose some of the facility of the visualized sound in silent-era cartoons. As described earlier, visualized sound was commonly used in the Alice Comedies and Oswald cartoons to link spaces through a graphic form of continuity editing and allowing the audience to see one thing and "hear" another, contributing to character and plot development. It is significant that this sophisticated formal construction is not evident in the first Disney sync-sound cartoon *Steamboat Willie*, where sound is more firmly anchored by image and vice versa. Background music, such as the main melodies of the songs "Steamboat Bill" and "Turkey in the Straw," does carry across cuts; however, sound effects and singing are always secured to a visible source. Despite the intricacy of Disney's landmark debut of Mickey Mouse, its handling of sound is simplified in spatial terms compared with the preceding silent cartoons: we only ever hear what we can also see. Of course, later Disney cartoons and films would develop increasingly nuanced uses of sound and music that surpassed those seen in the silent era. However, this example suggests that this was not a case of unbroken linear progression and that further work is needed to track the ebbs and flows, the continuities and discontinuities, between silent- and sound-era practices.

Notes

1. Lea Jacobs, *Film Rhythm after Sound: Technology, Music, and Performance* (Berkeley: University of California Press, 2015), 65.
2. Daniel Goldmark, "Before *Willie*: Reconsidering Music and the Animated Cartoon of the 1920s," in *Beyond the Soundtrack: Representing Music in Cinema*, ed. Daniel Goldmark, Lawrence Kramer, and Richard Leppert (Berkeley: University of California Press, 2007), 240.
3. Donald Crafton, "From the Lexigraphic to the Melomanic: Accommodations to Sound in Studio Animation," in *Aesthetics of Early Sound Film*, ed. Daniel J. Wiegand (Amsterdam: Amsterdam University Press, 2023), 67–68.

4. Ibid., 68.
5. Norman M. Klein, *Seven Minutes: The Life and Death of the American Animated Cartoon* (London: Verso, 1993), 3.
6. Ibid., 3, 8.
7. *Universal Weekly*, June 25, 1927, 40.
8. The first released Oswald cartoon, *Trolley Troubles*, was premiered in July 1927; *Exhibitors Herald*, July 30, 1927, 25. See also Russell Merritt and J. B. Kaufman, *Walt in Wonderland: The Silent Films of Walt Disney* (Pordenone: Le Giornate del Cinema Muto, 1993), 150.
9. For more discussion of different types of title cards, see André Gaudreault and Timothy Barnard, "Titles, Subtitles, and Intertitles: Factors of Autonomy, Factors of Concatenation," *Film History* 25, nos. 1–2 (2013).
10. Crafton, "From the Lexigraphic to the Melomanic," 67–68.
11. André Gaudreault, "Detours in Film Narrative: The Development of Cross-Cutting," *Cinema Journal* 19, no. 1 (1979); Charles Musser, *Before the Nickelodeon: Edwin S. Porter and the Edison Manufacturing Company* (Berkeley: University of California Press, 1991), 212–235.
12. Scott Bukatman, *The Poetics of Slumberland: Animated Spirits and the Animating Spirit* (Berkeley: University of California Press, 2012), 107–108; Nicholas Sammond, *Birth of an Industry: Blackface Minstrelsy and the Rise of American Animation* (Durham, NC: Duke University Press, 2015), 91–99.
13. John Randolph Bray and Earl Hurd, "Bray-Hurd: The Key Animation Patents," *Film History* 2, no. 3 (September–October 1988); Edwin George Lutz, *Animated Cartoons. How They Are Made, Their Origin and Development* (London: Chapman & Hall, 1920).
14. Merritt and Kaufman, *Walt in Wonderland*, 87.
15. Malcolm Cook, "Margaret J. Winkler," in *Women Film Pioneers Project*, ed. Jane Gaines, Radha Vatsal, and Monica Dall'Asta (New York: Columbia University Libraries, 2020).
16. Billy Rose and Harry Woods, "Poor Papa (He's Got Nothin' at All)" (New York: Irving Berlin, 1926).
17. *Motion Picture News*, April 6, 1918, 2034; Denis Gifford, *American Animated Films: The Silent Era, 1897–1929* (Jefferson, NC: McFarland, 1990), 62–64.
18. Henry Busse, Henry Lange, and Lou Davis, "Hot Lips" (New York: Leo Feist, 1922).
19. *Variety*, July 21, 1922, 17.
20. Gilbert Wells, Bud Cooper, and Fred Rose, "Red Hot Mamma" (New York: Rainbow, 1924).
21. *Variety*, February 7, 1924, 31; *Billboard*, October 20, 1928, 21; *Kinematograph Weekly*, September 12, 1929, 39.
22. Guy Stoddard and Dick Quayle, "Oh Teacher Teacher: Let Me Do the Teaching Awhile" (St. Louis: Stark, 1922).
23. *1922 Catalogue of Victor Records* (Camden, NJ: Victor, 1922).
24. *Exhibitors Herald*, August 15, 1925, 25.
25. Bob Miller and Cal DeVoll, "Mean Papa, Turn in Your Key (You Don't Live Here No More)" (Chicago: Harold Rossiter, 1923).
26. *Talking Machine World*, July 15, 1924, 158; Merritt and Kaufman, *Walt in Wonderland*, 137.
27. *Talking Machine World*, July 15, 1924, 158.
28. Donald Crafton, *Shadow of a Mouse: Performance, Belief, and World-Making in Animation* (Berkeley: University of California Press, 2013), 119–127; Sammond, *Birth of an Industry*.
29. Robert B. Winans, "Banjo," in *The New Encyclopedia of Southern Culture*, Vol. 12: *Music*, ed. Bill C. Malone (Chapel Hill: University of North Carolina Press, 2008), 174.

30. *Universal Weekly*, April 21, 1928, 22.
31. Margaret Bohanon, "'Wild Women Don't Have the Blues': African-American Women Blues Singers and Working Class Resistance," PhD diss., Case Western Reserve University, 2001.
32. Crafton, *Shadow of a Mouse*, 124.
33. J. S. Zamecnik, *Sam Fox Moving Picture Music* (Cleveland: Sam Fox, 1923).
34. Thomas Elsaesser, "General Introduction," in *Early Cinema : Space–Frame–Narrative*, ed. Thomas Elsaesser and Adam Barker (London: BFI, 1990), 5; James Chapman, Mark Glancy, and Sue Harper, "Introduction," in *The New Film History: Sources, Methods, Approaches*, ed. James Chapman, Mark Glancy, and Sue Harper (Basingstoke: Palgrave Macmillan, 2007), 5–6.
35. Rick Altman, "The Sounds of the Silents in Britain, ed. by Julie Brown, Annette Davison (Review)," *Music, Sound, and the Moving Image* 8, no. 1 (2014): 94.
36. Rick Altman, *Silent Film Sound* (New York: Columbia University Press, 2004), 246.
37. *Exhibitors Herald*, December 5, 1925, 14, 38.
38. *Exhibitors Herald*, February 28, 1925, 10.
39. *Exhibitors Herald*, August 15, 1925, 14.
40. Ibid.
41. *Exhibitors Herald*, December 5, 1925, 14.
42. Edith Lang and George West, *Musical Accompaniment of Moving Pictures: A Practical Manual for Pianists and Organists* (Boston: Boston Music, 1920), 36.
43. Erno Rapee, *Encyclopaedia of Music for Pictures* (New York: Belwin, 1925), 16.
44. *Exhibitors Herald*, May 23, 1925, 24.
45. *Exhibitors Herald*, May 23, 1925, 15.
46. Lang and West, *Musical Accompaniment*, 37.
47. Rapee, *Encyclopaedia of Music*, 16.
48. George W. Beynon, *Musical Presentation of Motion Pictures* (New York: G. Schirmer, 1921), 57.
49. Altman, *Silent Film Sound*, 342, 84–85; Daniel Goldmark, *Tunes for 'Toons: Music and the Hollywood Cartoon* (Berkeley: University of California Press, 2005), 15.
50. *Exhibitors Herald*, August 15, 1925, 14.
51. *Motion Picture News*, July 25, 1925, 439.
52. Dave Russell, "Abiding Memories: The Community Singing Movement and English Social Life in the 1920s," *Popular Music* 27, no. 1 (2008); Esther M. Morgan-Ellis, *Everybody Sing! Community Singing in the American Picture Palace* (Athens: University of Georgia Press, 2018); Malcolm Cook, "Animating the Audience: Singalong Films in Britain in the 1920s," in *The Sounds of the Silents in Britain: Voice, Music and Sound in Early Cinema Exhibition*, ed. Annette Davison and Julie Brown (Oxford: Oxford University Press, 2012); Kay Norton and Esther Morgan-Ellis, eds., *The Oxford Handbook of Community Singing* (Oxford: Oxford University Press, 2024).
53. Peter W. Dykema, ed., *18 Songs for Community Singing* (Boston: C. C. Birchard, 1913); *Community Music: Suggestions for Developing Community Singing, Choruses, Orchestras and Other Forms of Community Music* (New York: Community Service, 1920); *Community Music: A Practical Guide for the Conduct of Community Music Activities* (Boston: C. C. Birchard, 1926).

54. Malcolm Cook, "Sing Them Again: Audience Singing in Silent Film," in *Music in Silent Film: From the Nickelodeon to The Artist*, ed. Ruth Barton and Simon Trezise (Abingdon: Routledge, 2018), 63, 67.
55. Harry Armstrong and Richard H. Gerard, "(You're the Flower of My Heart,) Sweet Adeline" (New York: M. Witmark, 1903).
56. *Community Music: Suggestions for Developing Community Singing*, 74–75.
57. *Moving Picture World*, September 8, 1923, 100; Cook, "Sing Them Again."
58. Goldmark, *Tunes for 'Toons*, 10–43.
59. Cook, "Sing Them Again"; Malcolm Cook, "Selling with Singalongs: Community Singing as Advertising in Cinema, Radio and Television," in *The Oxford Handbook of Community Singing*, ed. Kay Norton and E. M. Morgan-Ellis (Oxford: Oxford University Press, 2024), 38.
60. Crafton, "From the Lexigraphic to the Melomanic," 75–76.

Bibliography

Altman, Rick. *Silent Film Sound*. New York: Columbia University Press, 2004.

Altman, Rick. "*The Sounds of the Silents in Britain*, ed. by Julie Brown, Annette Davison (Review)." *Music, Sound, and the Moving Image* 8, no. 1 (2014): 93–95.

Armstrong, Harry, and Richard H. Gerard. "(You're the Flower of My Heart,) Sweet Adeline." New York: M. Witmark, 1903.

Beynon, George W. *Musical Presentation of Motion Pictures*. New York: G. Schirmer, 1921.

Bohanon, Margaret. "'Wild Women Don't Have the Blues': African-American Women Blues Singers and Working Class Resistance." PhD diss., Case Western Reserve University, 2001.

Bray, John Randolph, and Earl Hurd. "Bray-Hurd: The Key Animation Patents." *Film History* 2, no. 3 (September–October 1988): 229–266.

Bukatman, Scott. *The Poetics of Slumberland: Animated Spirits and the Animating Spirit*. Berkeley: University of California Press, 2012.

Busse, Henry, Henry Lange, and Lou Davis. "Hot Lips." New York: Leo Feist, 1922.

Chapman, James, Mark Glancy, and Sue Harper. "Introduction." In *The New Film History: Sources, Methods, Approaches*, edited by James Chapman, Mark Glancy, and Sue Harper, 1–26. Basingstoke: Palgrave Macmillan, 2007.

Community Music: A Practical Guide for the Conduct of Community Music Activities. Boston: C. C. Birchard, 1926.

Community Music: Suggestions for Developing Community Singing, Choruses, Orchestras and Other Forms of Community Music. New York: Community Service, 1920.

Cook, Malcolm. "Animating the Audience: Singalong Films in Britain in the 1920s." In *The Sounds of the Silents in Britain: Voice, Music and Sound in Early Cinema Exhibition*, edited by Annette Davison and Julie Brown, 222–240. Oxford: Oxford University Press, 2012.

Cook, Malcolm. "Margaret J. Winkler." In *Women Film Pioneers Project*, edited by Jane Gaines, Radha Vatsal, and Monica Dall'Asta. New York: Columbia University Libraries, 2020. https://wfpp.columbia.edu/pioneer/margaret-j-winkler/

Cook, Malcolm. "Selling with Singalongs: Community Singing as Advertising in Cinema, Radio and Television." In *The Oxford Handbook of Community Singing*, edited by Kay Norton and E. M. Morgan-Ellis, 29–49. Oxford: Oxford University Press, 2024.

Cook, Malcolm. "Sing Them Again: Audience Singing in Silent Film." In *Music in Silent Film: From the Nickelodeon to The Artist*, edited by Ruth Barton and Simon Trezise, 61–75. Abingdon: Routledge, 2018.

Crafton, Donald. "From the Lexigraphic to the Melomanic: Accommodations to Sound in Studio Animation." In *Aesthetics of Early Sound Film*, edited by Daniel J. Wiegand, 67–85. Amsterdam: Amsterdam University Press, 2023.

Crafton, Donald. *Shadow of a Mouse: Performance, Belief, and World-Making in Animation*. Berkeley: University of California Press, 2013.

Dykema, Peter W., ed. *18 Songs for Community Singing*. Boston: C. C. Birchard, 1913.

Elsaesser, Thomas. "General Introduction." In *Early Cinema: Space–Frame–Narrative*, edited by Thomas Elsaesser and Adam Barker, 1–8. London: BFI, 1990.

Gaudreault, André. "Detours in Film Narrative: The Development of Cross-Cutting." *Cinema Journal* 19, no. 1 (1979): 39–59.

Gaudreault, André, and Timothy Barnard. "Titles, Subtitles, and Intertitles: Factors of Autonomy, Factors of Concatenation." *Film History* 25, nos. 1–2 (2013): 81–94.

Gifford, Denis. *American Animated Films: The Silent Era, 1897–1929*. Jefferson, NC: McFarland, 1990.

Goldmark, Daniel. "Before *Willie*: Reconsidering Music and the Animated Cartoon of the 1920s." In *Beyond the Soundtrack: Representing Music in Cinema*, edited by Daniel Goldmark, Lawrence Kramer, and Richard Leppert, 225–245. Berkeley: University of California Press, 2007.

Goldmark, Daniel. *Tunes for 'Toons: Music and the Hollywood Cartoon*. Berkeley: University of California Press, 2005.

Jacobs, Lea. *Film Rhythm after Sound: Technology, Music, and Performance*. Berkeley: University of California Press, 2015.

Klein, Norman M. *Seven Minutes: The Life and Death of the American Animated Cartoon*. London: Verso, 1993.

Lang, Edith, and George West. *Musical Accompaniment of Moving Pictures: A Practical Manual for Pianists and Organists*. Boston: Boston Music, 1920.

Lutz, Edwin George. *Animated Cartoons: How They Are Made, Their Origin and Development*. London: Chapman & Hall, 1920.

Merritt, Russell, and J. B. Kaufman. *Walt in Wonderland: The Silent Films of Walt Disney*. Pordenone: Le Giornate del Cinema Muto, 1993.

Miller, Bob, and Cal DeVoll. "Mean Papa, Turn in Your Key (You Don't Live Here No More)." Chicago: Harold Rossiter, 1923.

Morgan-Ellis, Esther M. *Everybody Sing! Community Singing in the American Picture Palace*. Athens: University of Georgia Press, 2018.

Musser, Charles. *Before the Nickelodeon: Edwin S. Porter and the Edison Manufacturing Company*. Berkeley: University of California Press, 1991.

1922 Catalogue of Victor Records. Camden, NJ: Victor, 1922.

Norton, Kay, and Esther Morgan-Ellis, eds. *The Oxford Handbook of Community Singing*. Oxford: Oxford University Press, 2024.

Rapee, Erno. *Encyclopaedia of Music for Pictures*. New York: Belwin, 1925.

Rose, Billy, and Harry Woods. "Poor Papa (He's Got Nothin' at All)." New York: Irving Berlin, 1926.

Russell, Dave. "Abiding Memories: The Community Singing Movement and English Social Life in the 1920s." *Popular Music* 27, no. 1 (2008): 117–133.

Sammond, Nicholas. *Birth of an Industry: Blackface Minstrelsy and the Rise of American Animation*. Durham, NC: Duke University Press, 2015.

Stoddard, Guy, and Dick Quayle. "Oh Teacher Teacher: Let Me Do the Teaching Awhile." St. Louis: Stark, 1922.

Wells, Gilbert, Bud Cooper, and Fred Rose. "Red Hot Mamma." New York: Rainbow, 1924.

Winans, Robert B. "Banjo." In *The New Encyclopedia of Southern Culture*, Vol. 12: *Music*, edited by Bill C. Malone, 174–175. Chapel Hill: University of North Carolina Press, 2008.

Zamecnik, J. S. *Sam Fox Moving Picture Music*. Cleveland: Sam Fox, 1923.

CHAPTER 4

"WHISTLE WHILE YOU WORK...": *SNOW WHITE AND THE SEVEN DWARFS*, DISNEY'S FAIRY-TALE MUSICALS, AND THE AMERICAN DREAM

TRACEY MOLLET

Snow White and the Seven Dwarfs[1] is widely regarded as one of the most successful and innovative feature films of all time. Costing $1.5 million to make, the story of the young princess and the seven little men was "*Variety*'s top grossing film of 1938 and set a record rental take of $8.5 million at the conclusion of its first theatrical release."[2] While scholars such as Chris Pallant, Christopher Holliday, and Janet Wasko have underlined the film's status as an "emblematic Disney product" or "Classic Disney,"[3] *Snow White*'s status as the world's first feature-length animated *musical* is often overlooked. The film itself was always envisaged as a musical, with story notes as far back as 1934 detailing the development of the narrative through song. As noted by biographer Bob Thomas, Walt Disney wanted to "set a new pattern, a new way to use music, [to] weave it into the story."[4] Indeed, Sadeen Elyas has detailed that *Snow White* can be understood as the first fully integrated film musical, as Disney believed that "music could be an integral part of storytelling in a film ... to deliver exposition, develop characters and situations and most importantly, as a tool to advance the plot."[5] The film thus stands out for Disney scholars as a blueprint of sorts, a foundation upon which all future Disney musical productions would be built. What is of particular interest in this regard, however, is the way in which *Snow White and the Seven Dwarfs* sits within a crucial historical moment: the 1930s. Not only was this the period when Hollywood was transitioning to sound and when musicals such as *Gold Diggers of 1933*, *The Merry Widow*, and *Swing Time* experienced extraordinary popularity, but it was also the decade in which America's national fairy tale, the American dream, was born.[6]

Coined by James Truslow Adams in 1931 in his work *The Epic of America*, the first written iteration of the American dream underlined that success was attainable for every individual in America, regardless of their status or position in life.[7] Following the Wall Street Crash of 1929, breadlines, foreclosures, and high unemployment were a defining feature of everyday life for many, and as a result, such an ideal was hugely comforting. Lawrence Levine notes that during the 1920s, Americans' conceptions of their national myth were "intricately equated with material growth and material expansion,"[8] and thus the onset of the Depression had a significant impact on the American psyche, which needed significant redefinition in order to ensure its survival. The myth acted as a fairy tale for the American people, making their time of hardship seem temporary and their happily-ever-after all but guaranteed. The hope and optimism infused within the ideology of the American dream were also at the heart of the defining presidency of the decade: the tenure of Franklin Delano Roosevelt.

When Roosevelt ascended to the presidency in 1933, central to his first hundred days in office was the restoration of confidence in the nation's key institutions. Through the Emergency Banking Act of 1933, the president and the secretary of the Treasury were granted regulatory authority over America's banking system. The Federal Deposit Insurance Corporation protected people's cash deposits, while the Federal Emergency Relief Administration supplied states with $500 million of federal relief money to help the unemployed.[9] These measures built a new sense of nationalism in the United States, founded upon the union of the American people with their government, and specifically with their president. During a fireside chat delivered on May 7, 1933, Roosevelt underlined that "in the present spirit of mutual confidence and mutual encouragement, we go forward."[10] Lawrence R. Samuel notes that in the 1930s, FDR's political ideologies were "infused ... with communitarian values."[11] Much of Roosevelt's policies and rhetoric were centered around collective action and optimism as the key tenets of success for Americans. However, most important, such an ideal (or a fairy tale's happily-ever-after) had to be *earned* through hard work rather than simply inherited. Nowhere was this sentiment more evident than in the musical genre of the 1930s.

While Hollywood studios began making musicals in the late 1920s with productions such as *The Jazz Singer* and *The Broadway Melody*, it was not until the 1930s that the feature-film musical really began to take shape.[12] Harvey Cohen has highlighted that Hollywood "slowly learned that the old rules of Broadway did not apply to film musicals" and that perhaps "American audiences needed a more uniquely American reinterpretation of the musical, reflecting the spirit of the times."[13] The Warner Bros. "backstage" musicals of the early 1930s directly situate their characters within the financial turmoil of the decade, as their working-class protagonists forge a path to success and happiness by working together and by undergoing a journey of social mobility. While feature-film operettas and the RKO Fred Astaire–Ginger Rogers romantic comedies such as *The Gay Divorcée* and *Top Hat* were undoubtedly more escapist fare for audiences, their narratives are still of interest as they embody something "lost or desired"[14] or, as

Richard Dyer articulates, "something we want deeply that our day to day lives don't provide."[15] This "wanting" is absolutely central to a reading of Disney's first fairy tale amid the turmoil of 1930s America. Much like *Snow White*, all of these films are comforting fairy tales of a sort, with narratives that echo the classical Hollywood narrative template put forward by David Bordwell, Janet Staiger, and Kristin Thompson.[16] Their plots are driven by their protagonists' desires and dreams, they place a strong focus on coupling, and they conclude with an "idealized, utopian view of life."[17] Nowhere were these fairy tales more durable than within Hollywood itself. These films brought fame to young directors, producers, and actors who had achieved success through the very same hard work and perseverance promoted in their movies.[18]

Walt Disney was portrayed as a "living demonstration of the American Dream," widely seen as a Horatio Alger type of figure—an example of the ordinary man who had experienced the "rags to riches" fairy tale and lived happily ever after in Hollywood.[19] It is worth noting that Walt Disney's preoccupation with fairy-tale narratives began not with *Snow White* in 1937 but in the 1920s, with the Laugh-O-Gram Studio producing spoofs of "Cinderella," "Puss in Boots," and "Jack and the Beanstalk." Much like the musical genre, however, Disney's adaptations of such stories didn't begin to reach their full potential until the 1930s, when the Walt Disney Company's embrace of fully synchronized sound and three-strip Technicolor combined to create fantastical short subjects such as *Three Little Pigs* and *The Ugly Duckling* in their musical series, the Silly Symphonies.[20] It is well documented that the success of the former production kickstarted Walt Disney's desire to make a full-length animated-feature fairy tale with *Snow White and the Seven Dwarfs*.[21] The release of *Three Little Pigs* was especially important in bringing together fantasy and reality within the Disney musical genre. The short's signature song, "Who's Afraid of the Big Bad Wolf?," was received with gusto by the American people, becoming a rallying cry for the country's battle with the Depression. "The Wolf" is even mentioned as being at the door of the chorines in *Gold Diggers of 1933* and in the musical number "Never Gonna Dance" in *Swing Time*, proving its cultural resonance.[22] It was the first time that parallels had been drawn between people's daily struggles and the obstacles encountered by fairy-tale characters of Disney's creation. With *Three Little Pigs*, the Walt Disney Studios created models for social action, and this is continued in Disney's adaptation of *Snow White*.

This chapter argues that, much like other Depression musicals of the era, *Snow White and the Seven Dwarfs* strongly evokes the context of its release in two significant ways. First, it focuses on a "Cinderella" narrative for the dreaming young princess at the story's center and emphasizes kindness and optimism. Second, the film embraces the ideals of community and togetherness. These ideals are epitomized by the dwarfs as a unit, as well as within the sense of family evoked among Snow White, the dwarfs, and the animals of the forest. Closely linked to its veneration of the community is the film's villainization of the evil queen who rejects Roosevelt's values and embraces materialism and vanity for individual status and personal gain. For each of these values, echoing significant traits of the musical genre, *Snow White and the Seven Dwarfs* offers singing and dancing as a specific outlet through which these values are integrated into the film's narrative. In this fairy-tale world, musical performance is both the manner through which these ideologies are channeled and a way in which they can be accessed. The latter feature was particularly common in films of the 1930s, in which Depression musicals "mobilized a physical response to the social paralysis of the decade":[23] characters literally danced their troubles away. It has been convincingly argued that in the 1930s, the "very act of bursting into song is a performance of being American" and that when characters in musicals express their "fairy tale ... deep desires" through "I want" songs such as *The Wizard of Oz*'s "Over the Rainbow" or, in *Snow White*, "I'm Wishing" and "Some Day My Prince Will Come," they are presenting an "American Dream of wish fulfillment that is expansive."[24] In these key ways, *Snow White and the Seven Dwarfs* crystallizes the relationship between the Disney fairy-tale musical narrative and the American dream: an ideological preoccupation that permeates throughout Disney's considerable stable of animated fairy-tale musicals in the twentieth and twenty-first centuries.

"I'm Wishing...": Snow White and Her Musical Fairy-Tale Journey

A central trait of Snow White's narrative journey is her transformation from "rags to riches"—the journey of social mobility at the heart of the American dream. Snow White, as the protagonist of the story, is portrayed as a model for social action. Her "riches" are achieved through her embrace of hard work and optimism: Roosevelt's key sociopolitical values. When considering the film's position as a musical, it is notable that Walt Disney even described the dialogue in the film poetically, noting that it "[should] have meter, and at the right time, tie in with the music, so the whole thing has musical pattern ... phrasing and fitting the mood to get away from straight dialogue."[25] Thus, these values underpin both Snow White's musically delivered dialogue and the lyrics of every song the young princess sings in the film. "Some Day My Prince Will Come" and "Whistle while You Work" are considered to be some of the Walt Disney Company's most cherished musical outputs, representing "some of the most decisive indices in which the Disney ideology is most securely embedded."[26] In *Snow White*, these songs, and the characters who perform them, underline the importance of a positive attitude and an industrious mindset.

Our first shot of the young princess in Disney's fairy-tale musical highlights her humility. Much like the young chorines in Warner Bros. backstage musicals, Snow White is immediately cast into a "Cinderella" narrative. We see her dressed in rags and scrubbing the castle floor, enslaved in the castle she used to call home, and closely watched over by the evil queen. Despite her situation, Snow White remains kind, productive, and hopeful. The bestselling nonfiction book of the 1930s, Dale Carnegie's *How to Win Friends and Influence People*, highlighted the importance of values and behavior to success.[27] Indeed, in the absence of material riches, it seemed more important than ever that an "ordinary" person could experience extraordinary success. The narrative in the film reads that "rags cannot hide her gentle grace," suggesting that Snow White's character is her most valuable asset.[28] Indeed, it is her character, expressed through song, that draws the prince to her in the film's opening scenes. Its power resonates deeply and fuels his later desire to "search far and wide" for his princess, until they are reunited in their happily-ever-after.[29] Her innocence also protects her from the huntsman, as he breaks down in tears, unable to follow through with the evil queen's request to kill Snow White.

One prominent reviewer labeled *Snow White and the Seven Dwarfs* a "fairy tale for adults" offering a "tonic for disillusion."[30] The feature acts as a comforting distraction for those suffering under the scarcities of the Depression era and reassures those who embrace Roosevelt's confidence that all will be well. This underlines a central tenet of the Disney fairy-tale musical. The journey that the heroes and heroines must take in order to go from rags to riches must be inspired by hard work and optimism, which underpinned Roosevelt's policies in the 1930s and forms the basis of the American dream in that era. Their desire for "riches" cannot be a desire for material wealth (although this is often granted regardless). It has to be simply a desire for happiness; it is a state of mind, a psychological transformation. While many characters in the Astaire–Rogers stable of 1930s musicals are already situated within a world of opulence, this psychological transformation is key to their narrative journey. In most of these films, Astaire's character has his life outlook transformed by falling in love with Rogers's character. He learns the importance of hard work, teamwork, and kindness in these narratives and is thus granted his happily-ever-after. In *Snow White and the Seven Dwarfs*, Snow White shares her deepest desires for a happy ending with the dwarfs. The young princess sings, "Some day my prince will come / Some day we'll meet again / And away to his castle we'll go / To be happy forever I know."[31] However, as she embraces the ideology of the 1930s, she is wishing for love and happiness, rather than wishing for riches or for the throne to which she is entitled. Indeed, Snow White's certainty in her happily-ever-after ("we'll be happy forever I know") serves to reassure and comfort working-class Americans that perhaps their struggles are only temporary and that, eventually, success will come.

What is of interest here is not only the values that underpin the music but the function of music itself within the film's narrative and the way in which this contributes to the overall tone of the film. Within both stage and screen musicals, the act of song and dance has a higher significance. Rick Altman argues that music stands for "personal and communal joy."[32] *Snow White* is not alone among musicals of the 1930s in offering songs as solutions to characters' problems. While 1920s stage musicals also used this musicodramatic device, it was particularly common in Depression musicals. The characters in Warner Bros. backstage musicals take particular note of their economic circumstances, and this is explicitly cited as the reason they're engaging in musical performance. However, in the Astaire–Rogers musicals of the decade, characters do not even mention the Depression, as musical performance itself becomes a way of dealing with narrative obstacles. Indeed, the protagonists in films such as *Top Hat* and *Follow the Fleet* often sing through or about their problems, finding temporary or lasting happiness in the act of musical expression itself.[33] In *Top Hat*, Jerry Travers and Dale Tremont (played by Astaire and Rogers, respectively) become caught in bad weather and sing through their plight, finding happiness in song and dance: "The weather is frightening / The thunder and lightning / Seem to be having their way / But as far as I'm concerned, it's a lovely day."[34] *Follow the Fleet*'s Bake Baker addresses the uncertainty of his circumstances during the famous number "Let's Face the Music and Dance," in which the heavy burden of his "trouble ahead" is alleviated through the power of musical performance.[35]

Against the background of personal strife, Snow White manages to find joy through singing. When the huntsman refuses to carry out the queen's orders and murder the princess, Snow White runs into the woods and comes face to face with all manner of frightening creatures. When she emerges from her plight, she engages with the animals in the forest, imagining that all that is needed to restore her happiness is music. She sings, "With a smile and a song / Life is just a bright shiny day / Your cares fade away / And your heart is young."[36] These lyrics underscore the proposition that in the musical, "characters are able to satisfy their desire, or at least to feel better, by singing and dancing."[37] Songs are also offered as musical aids when undergoing unpleasant tasks. "Whistle while You Work," the song that accompanies Snow White's cleaning of the dwarfs' cottage, highlights the centrality of music to succeeding in the task at hand ("It won't take long when there's a song").[38]

As the young princess's positive outlook, dreams, and wishes are rewarded by the end of the film with her happily-ever-after, the narrative clearly endorses the traits of optimism and hard work—central to Roosevelt's New Deal. Such values also surface in subsequent Disney musicals, confirming *Snow White and the Seven Dwarfs*' status as an ideological blueprint of sorts. *Cinderella*'s "A Dream Is a Wish Your Heart Makes" and *Sleeping Beauty*'s "Once upon a Dream" both contain references to remaining positive and being true of heart.[39] While later Disney musicals do still retain these values, they also expand the scope of their princesses' dreams. Belle in *Beauty and the Beast* dreams of "adventure in the great wide somewhere," while *The Princess and the Frog*'s Tiana works "real hard each and every day" and embraces Snow White's certainty of future happiness ("Things for sure are going my way").[40] Through the utopian world of the musical, these ideals are shown to be intrinsic to the Disney happily-ever-after. Their roots in *Snow White and the Seven Dwarfs* surface as a 1930s idealization of the American dream in all subsequent Disney fairy-tale musicals.

"Off to Work *We* Go": Collectivism in the Disney Musical

Many scholars of the Hollywood musical have noted the prevalence of "group effort and success" in films of this genre during the 1930s.[41] The Warner Bros. backstage musicals released in 1933 all ride the wave of optimism that accompanied FDR's inauguration and the early New Deal reforms. Agencies such as the Civil Works Administration and the Works Progress Administration provided jobs for the unemployed, putting millions of Americans back to work.[42] *Gold Diggers of 1933*, for example, charts the struggles of three chorines, Polly, Carol, and Trixie, as the financial hardships of the Depression shut down the production they are performing in. The three live together, sharing food and clothing, *and* they work together on the show that is going to secure their personal and financial futures. As Bruce Babington and Peter William Evans have stated, the film "underlines the communal energy and pulling together that will defeat the Depression."[43] While not as explicitly tied to sociopolitical context as in these films, this emphasis on collective action is at the heart of Disney's *Snow White and the Seven Dwarfs*.

The most obvious display of community in this fairy-tale musical is in the dynamic of the dwarfs themselves. As I have argued elsewhere, these characters exemplify the community spirit roused by Roosevelt's New Deal.[44] Their work in the mines is not carried out for individual pursuit of wealth. This is showcased in the lyrics of their famous work song, "Heigh Ho," as they sing, "We dig up diamonds by the score / ... / And we don't know what we dig 'em for."[45] They live humbly in their cottage in the forest, sharing a bedroom; such was the plight of many traveling workers throughout America during the years of the Great Depression.[46] Despite their lack of material motivation, associated with a culture of abundance in the 1920s, the dwarfs are meticulous, productive, and thorough in their execution of their work.

Besides working together, the dwarfs operate as a very successful unit throughout the narrative of *Snow White and the Seven Dwarfs*. They showcase synchronicity when marching to and from work, when washing for dinner, and in musical performance when they play their instruments and dance for and with Snow White during her first night at the cottage. Walt Disney was particularly keen on the "togetherness" of the dwarfs in the latter sequence, exclaiming upon listening to the demo track, "Yeah, that's a happy song ... a happy group!"[47] Yet the dwarfs are all individual characters with very specific identifying characteristics, showcasing men of all temperaments and all walks of life. The ability of the everyday American to thrive and achieve success, in spite of all odds, was central to the American dream, with Adams underlining that "each man and each woman shall be able to attain to the fullest stature of which that are innately capable."[48] Disney's fairy-tale musicals often celebrate the triumph of the underdog, seen in later productions such as *The Little Mermaid* and *Aladdin* and even in outlaw Flynn Ryder's narrative journey in *Tangled*.[49]

The dwarfs are also of interest in terms of overall character positioning in the film's plot. It is the collective of all seven of the dwarfs, and not the individual prince, who ultimately save Snow White from the evil queen, chasing the queen from the cottage and up the mountain, where she meets her eventual demise. This indicates that it is within the collective that success can be found, rather than through the actions of one individual. In other ways, too, *Snow White and the Seven Dwarfs* champions a communitarian ethos. From the moment of her escape into the woods, Snow White bonds with the animals through song, forming a kind of family. In the "Whistle while You Work" sequence, the young princess and her woodland friends work *together* to clean up the dwarfs' cottage, and later they help her to bake a pie for Grumpy. They also play a central role in the film's narrative by warning the dwarfs that Snow White has been tricked by the evil queen into biting the poisonous apple. And in the final sequence of the film, when Snow White is woken from her sleep by the prince, the animals are an intrinsic part of the princess's farewell to the dwarfs, a key part of the treasured family she leaves behind. All subsequent Disney musicals place emphasis on the power of togetherness and family. From Sebastian the crab's celebration of life, "Under the Sea," to the communal energy of hospitality in *Beauty and the Beast*'s "Be Our Guest" to *High School Musical*'s theme song, "We're All in This Together," these films all explore the central importance of "social cohesion [in the] community."[50]

Contrarily, the evil queen in Snow White embodies individualism, vanity, and greed. The culture of the 1920s, which many held responsible for the Wall Street Crash, was characterized by abundance and materialism.[51] While *Gold Diggers* does not have an antagonist figure like the evil queen, another one of the chorines, Faye, displays some of the characteristics of the fairy-tale villain. In one of the film's first scenes, the gold diggers are in sleepwear, with no makeup on, and Faye bursts into their apartment wearing a fancy dress, sun hat, and sunglasses, bragging that she looks "much better in clothes than any of [them]."[52] While this may seem a minor observation on her character's disposition, it is certainly of interest that Faye is the only one of the group who is not granted her happily-ever-after by the end of the film.

Unlike Snow White, who is industrious and conscientious, the villainess in Disney's tale rejects hard work in favor of admiring herself in the mirror. Dressed in lavish, regal black and gold dresses and cloaks, and sitting upon a gold-embellished throne, she has not been seen to *earn* her privilege, which makes her character unworthy of a happily-ever-after. As I have written elsewhere, the queen recalls the "negative representation of robber barons of the Gilded Age,"[53] with her vast wealth and heartless greed. The positioning of Snow White in rags at the beginning of the film also accentuates their differences. The evil queen not only places value on appearances but also desires Snow White's wealth (and therefore power and influence). As has been intrinsic to fairy tales since their inception, the evil queen is fueled by jealousy as an overriding motivation for her actions in the narrative. She wants more than she is entitled to. It is also of interest that the evil queen, unlike Snow White, lacks authenticity and honesty. Transforming her "true" appearance to conceal her identity, she manipulates Snow White into eating the apple when she visits the cottage toward the film's end. She promises that it is a "magic, wishing apple" and thus will provide a quick and easy road to her happily-ever-after.[54] This embrace of manipulation in the service of vanity is true of most villains in Disney's fairy-tale musicals. Figures such as Lady Tremaine in *Cinderella*, Ursula in *The Little Mermaid*, and Mother Gothel in *Tangled* all exploit situations for their own individual gain. For example, Ursula the sea witch is prepared to use black magic in order to provide a quick road to the happily-ever-after, while Mother Gothel craves the power of Rapunzel's magical hair in order to grant herself the beauty of eternal youth. In embracing individual vanity at the expense of hard work and authenticity, these characters reject the central ethos of Roosevelt's presidency and of the American dream in the 1930s, which placed emphasis on working hard together in order to achieve success.

Conclusion

Snow White and the Seven Dwarfs, the Depression musical, and the American dream were all born in the 1930s, and thus Disney's first feature film serves as a foundation upon which all future Disney fairy tales were built. These fairy-tale musicals all feature an intrinsic connection to the ideology of the American dream—as it was realized in the 1930s. They all have heroines who dream for *more* but find their happiness in the adventure of the journey itself and in the day-to-day act of dreaming. This act, combined with hard work and optimism, is often enough to propel their journey of social mobility, as they go from rags to riches, achieving their happily-ever-after by the narrative's end. For example, Ariel in *The Little Mermaid* dreams of a life on the land, Belle from *Beauty and the Beast* seeks adventure, and Anna in *Frozen* seeks freedom from the confines of the castle walls.[55] These desires are most fervently articulated through song, as in *Snow White and the Seven Dwarfs*. All of Disney's fairy tales also celebrate the triumph of the underdog and the importance of community spirit, exemplified most ardently by the "I've Got a Dream" musical number in *Tangled*.[56] The ruffian characters in the Snuggly Duckling represent people of all backgrounds and all walks of life, much like *Snow White*'s dwarfs, and due to their incredible teamwork, they are permitted to have their dreams come true by the end of the film. As Desirée Garcia notes of musicals in the 1930s, these narratives "suggest that the happiest and most contented people are those who appreciate and dedicate themselves to home, family and the community," and these messages "provide a buffer against the unsettling forces of change brought about through … the self interest promoted by capitalist society,"[57] the heart of the ideology that was responsible for the Wall Street Crash.

Disney's fairy-tale story of the lost princess who finds home through her optimistic outlook, embrace of community spirit, and song *is* the story of the American people during the 1930s. Millions lost their jobs, their homes, and their sense of purpose but were able to rediscover their faith in the American dream through the sense of hope infused in Depression musicals like *Snow White and the Seven Dwarfs*. Disney's fairy-tale musicals thus uphold the essential tenets at the heart of the American dream, providing audiences with models for social action through which their happily-ever-after could be ensured. These films thus bind America's national and cultural myth to the magical fantasies of the fairy tale but also to the colorful, utopian world of the musical, fusing these narratives together, elevating one simple conclusion: in the Disney fairy-tale musical, America is the only possible site of the happily-ever-after.

Notes

1. David Hand et al., dirs., *Snow White and the Seven Dwarfs* (Walt Disney Productions, 1937).
2. Iwan Morgan, "Introduction: Hollywood and the Great Depression," in *Hollywood and the Great Depression: American Film, Politics and Society in the 1930s*, ed. Ivan Morgan and Philip John Davies (Edinburgh: Edinburgh University Press, 2016), 7.
3. Christopher Holliday and Chris Pallant, "Introduction: Into the Burning Coals," in *Snow White and the Seven Dwarfs: New Perspectives on Production, Reception, Legacy*, ed. Christopher Holliday and Chris Pallant (New York: Bloomsbury Academic, 2021), 1; Janet Wasko, *Understanding Disney: The Manufacture of Fantasy* (Cambridge: Polity Press, 2001), 113.
4. Bob Thomas, *Walt Disney: An American Original* (New York: Hyperion, 1994), 136.
5. Sadeen Elyas, "With a Smile and a Song: *Snow White and the Seven Dwarfs* as the First Integrated Musical," in *Snow White and the Seven Dwarfs: New Perspectives on Production, Reception, Legacy*, ed. Christopher Holliday and Chris Pallant (New York: Bloomsbury Academic, 2021), 120.
6. Mervyn LeRoy, dir., *Gold Diggers of 1933* (Warner Bros., 1933); Ernst Lubitsch, dir., *The Merry Widow* (Metro-Goldwyn-Mayer, 1934); George Stevens, dir., *Swing Time* (RKO Radio Pictures, 1936).
7. James Truslow Adams, *The Epic of America* (New York: Simon Publications, 1931).
8. Lawrence Levine, *The Unpredictable Past: Explorations in American Cultural History* (New York: Oxford University Press, 1993), 209.
9. David M. Kennedy, *Freedom from Fear: The American People in Depression and War 1929–1945* (Oxford: Oxford University Press, 1999), 134.
10. Franklin Delano Roosevelt, "Fireside Chat 2: On Progress in the First Two Months," May 7, 1933, https://millercenter.org/the-presidency/presidential-speeches/may-7-1933-fireside-chat-2-progress-during-first-two-months.
11. Lawrence R. Samuel, *The American Dream: A Cultural History* (Syracuse, NY: Syracuse University Press, 2012), 20.
12. Alan Crosland, dir., *The Jazz Singer* (Warner Bros. Pictures, 1927); Harry Beaumont, dir., *The Broadway Melody* (Metro-Goldwyn-Mayer, 1929).
13. Harvey Cohen, *Who's in the Money: The Great Depression Musicals and Hollywood's New Deal* (Edinburgh, Edinburgh University Press, 2018), 41.
14. Mark Sandrich, dir., *The Gay Divorcee* (RKO Radio Pictures, 1934); Mark Sandrich, dir., *Top Hat* (RKO Radio Pictures, 1935); Andrew Bergman, *We're in the Money: Depression America and Its Films* (London: Harper & Row, 1972), xiii.
15. Richard Dyer, "Entertainment and Utopia," in *Hollywood Musicals: The Film Reader*, ed. Steven Cohan (London: Routledge, 2002), 20.
16. David Bordwell, Janet Staiger, and Kristin Thompson, *The Classical Hollywood Cinema: Film Style and Mode of Production to 1960* (New York: Columbia University Press, 1986).
17. Bruce Babington and Peter William Evans, *Blue Skies and Silver Linings: Aspects of the Hollywood Musical* (Manchester, UK: Manchester University Press, 1985), 3.
18. Martin Halliwell, *American Culture in the 1930s* (Edinburgh: Edinburgh University Press, 2007).
19. Richard Schickel, *The Disney Version: The Life, Times, Art and Commerce of Walt Disney* (New York: Simon & Schuster, 1986), 11.

20. Burt Gillett, dir., *Three Little Pigs* (Walt Disney Productions, 1933); Jack Cutting and Clyde Geronimi, dirs., *The Ugly Duckling* (Walt Disney Productions, 1939).
21. See, for example, Michael Barrier, *Hollywood Cartoons: American Animation in Its Golden Age* (Oxford: Oxford University Press, 1999), 124; Leonard Maltin, *Of Mice and Magic: A History of American Animated Cartoons* (New York: NAL Books, 1980), 53.
22. LeRoy, *Gold Diggers of 1933*, 00:07:47–00:07:49; Dorothy Fields and Jerome Kern, "Never Gonna Dance," *Swing Time Official Motion Picture Soundtrack* (Brunswick, 1936).
23. Giuliana Muscio, *Hollywood's New Deal* (Philadelphia: Temple University Press, 1997), 72.
24. Mervyn LeRoy, dir., *The Wizard of Oz* (Metro-Goldwyn-Mayer, 1939); Ryan Bunch, *Oz and the Musical: Performing the American Fairy Tale* (New York: Oxford University Press, 2022), 9.
25. Neal Gabler, *Walt Disney: The Biography* (London: Aurum 2006), 254.
26. Eleanor Byrne and Martin McQuillan, *Deconstructing Disney* (London: Pluto Press, 1999), 8.
27. Dale Carnegie, *How to Win Friends and Influence People* (New York: Simon & Schuster, 1937).
28. Hand et al., *Snow White*, 00:03:06–00:03:09.
29. Ibid., 01:19:14–01:19:24.
30. Frank Nugent, "One Touch of Disney," *New York Times*, January 23, 1938, 157. https://timesmachine.nytimes.com/timesmachine/1938/01/23/issue.html.
31. Frank Churchill and Larry Morey, "Some Day My Prince Will Come," *Songs from Snow White and the Seven Dwarfs* (Victor Records, 1937).
32. Rick Altman, *The American Film Musical* (Bloomington: Indiana University Press, 1987), 109.
33. Mark Sandrich, dir., *Follow the Fleet* (RKO Radio Productions, 1936).
34. Irving Berlin, "Isn't This a Lovely Day," *Top Hat: Original Motion Picture Soundtrack* (Brunswick, 1935).
35. Irving Berlin, "Let's Face the Music and Dance," *Follow the Fleet: Original Motion Picture Soundtrack* (Brunswick, 1936).
36. Frank Churchill and Larry Morey, "With a Smile and a Song," *Songs from Snow White and the Seven Dwarfs* (Victor Records, 1937).
37. Barry Keith Grant, *The Hollywood Film Musical* (Oxford: Blackwell, 2012), 46.
38. Frank Churchill and Larry Morey, "Whistle while You Work," *Songs from Snow White and the Seven Dwarfs* (Victor Records, 1937).
39. Clyde Geronimi, Wilfred Jackson, and Hamilton Luske, dirs., *Cinderella* (Walt Disney Productions, 1950); Mack David, Al Hoffman, and Jerry Livingston, "A Dream Is a Wish Your Heart Makes," *Cinderella: Original Motion Picture Soundtrack* (Victor Records, 1950); Clyde Geronimi, Les Clark, Eric Larson, and Wolfgang Reitherman, dirs., *Sleeping Beauty* (Walt Disney Productions, 1959); Jack Lawrence and Sammy Fain, "Once upon a Dream," *Songs from Sleeping Beauty* (Walt Disney Music Company, 1959).
40. Howard Ashman and Alan Menken, "Belle: Reprise," *Beauty and the Beast Official Motion Picture Soundtrack* (Walt Disney Records, 1991); Randy Newman, "Almost There," *The Princess and the Frog Official Motion Picture Soundtrack* (Walt Disney Records, 2009).
41. Grant, *The Hollywood Film Musical*, 16.
42. Kennedy, *Freedom from Fear*, 134.
43. Babington and Evans, *Blue Skies and Silver Linings*, 64.

44. Tracey Mollet, "With a Smile and a Song: Walt Disney and the Birth of the American Fairy Tale," *Marvels and Tales* 27, no. 1 (2013): 118.
45. Frank Churchill and Larry Morey, "Heigh Ho," *Songs from Snow White and the Seven Dwarfs* (Victor Records, 1937).
46. Walter J. Stein, *California and the Dust Bowl Migration* (Westport, CT: Greenwood Press, 1973).
47. Gabler, *Walt Disney*, 254.
48. Adams, *The Epic of America*, 214.
49. Jack Zipes, "Breaking the Disney Spell," in *From Mouse to Mermaid: The Politics of Film, Gender and Culture*, ed. Elizabeth Bell, Lynda Haas, and Laura Sells (Bloomington: Indiana University Press, 1995), 21–42; Ron Clements and John Musker, dirs., *The Little Mermaid* (Walt Disney Pictures, 1989); Ron Clements and John Musker, dirs., *Aladdin* (Walt Disney Pictures, 1992); Nathan Greno and Byron Howard, dirs., *Tangled* (Walt Disney Pictures, 2010).
50. Howard Ashman and Alan Menken, "Under the Sea," *The Little Mermaid Official Motion Picture Soundtrack* (Walt Disney Records, 1989); Howard Ashman and Alan Menken, "Be Our Guest," *The Little Mermaid Official Motion Picture Soundtrack* (Walt Disney Records, 1989); Matthew Gerrard and Robbie Nevil, "We're All in This Together," *High School Musical Official Motion Picture Soundtrack* (Walt Disney Records, 2006); Steven Cohan, "How Do You Solve a Problem Like the Film Musical?," in *The Sound of Musicals*, ed. Steven Cohan (London: BFI, 2010), 9.
51. Warren Susman, *Culture as History: The Transformation of American Society in the Twentieth Century* (New York: Smithsonian Books, 1984), 179.
52. LeRoy, *Gold Diggers of 1933*, 00:09:09–00:09:11.
53. Mollet, "With a Smile and a Song," 117.
54. Hand et al., *Snow White*, 01:12:54–01:12:57.
55. Chris Buck and Jennifer Lee, dirs., *Frozen* (Walt Disney Pictures, 2013).
56. Glenn Slater and Alan Menken, "I've Got a Dream," *Tangled: Original Motion Picture Soundtrack* (Walt Disney Records, 2010).
57. Desirée Garcia, *The Migration of Musical Film: From Ethnic Margins to American Mainstream* (New Brunswick, NJ: Rutgers University Press, 2014), 4.

Bibliography

Adams, James Truslow. *The Epic of America*. New York: Simon Publications, 1931.
Altman, Rick. *The American Film Musical*. Bloomington: Indiana University Press, 1987.
Ashman, Howard, and Alan Menken. "Be Our Guest." *Beauty and the Beast Official Motion Picture Soundtrack*. Walt Disney Records, 1991.
Ashman, Howard, and Alan Menken. "Belle: Reprise." *Beauty and the Beast Official Motion Picture Soundtrack*. Walt Disney Records, 1991.
Ashman, Howard, and Alan Menken. "Under the Sea." *The Little Mermaid Official Motion Picture Soundtrack*. Walt Disney Records, 1989.
Babington, Bruce, and Peter William Evans. *Blue Skies and Silver Linings: Aspects of the Hollywood Musical*. Manchester, UK: Manchester University Press, 1985.
Barrier, Michael. *Hollywood Cartoons: American Animation in Its Golden Age*. Oxford: Oxford University Press, 1999.

Beaumont, Harry, dir. *The Broadway Melody*. Metro-Goldwyn-Mayer, 1929.

Bergman, Andrew. *We're in the Money: Depression America and Its Films*. London: Harper & Row, 1972.

Berlin, Irving. "Isn't This a Lovely Day?" *Top Hat: Original Motion Picture Soundtrack*. Brunswick, 1935.

Berlin, Irving. "Let's Face the Music and Dance." *Follow the Fleet: Original Motion Picture Soundtrack*. Brunswick, 1936.

Bordwell, David, Janet Staiger, and Kristin Thompson. *The Classical Hollywood Cinema: Film Style and Mode of Production to 1960*. New York: Columbia University Press, 1986.

Buck, Chris, and Jennifer Lee, dirs. *Frozen*. Walt Disney Pictures, 2013.

Bunch, Ryan. *Oz and the Musical: Performing the American Fairy Tale*. New York: Oxford University Press, 2022.

Byrne, Eleanor, and Martin McQuillan. *Deconstructing Disney*. London: Pluto Press, 1999.

Carnegie, Dale. *How to Win Friends and Influence People*. New York: Simon & Schuster, 1937.

Churchill, Frank, and Larry Morey. "Heigh Ho." *Songs from Snow White and the Seven Dwarfs*. Victor Records, 1937.

Churchill, Frank, and Larry Morey. "Some Day My Prince Will Come." *Songs from Snow White and the Seven Dwarfs*. Victor Records, 1937.

Churchill, Frank, and Larry Morey. "Whistle while You Work." *Songs from Snow White and the Seven Dwarfs*. Victor Records, 1937.

Churchill, Frank, and Larry Morey. "With a Smile and a Song." *Songs from Snow White and the Seven Dwarfs*. Victor Records, 1937.

Clements, Ron, and John Musker, dirs. *Aladdin*. Walt Disney Pictures, 1992.

Clements, Ron, and John Musker, dirs. *The Little Mermaid*. Walt Disney Pictures, 1989.

Cohan, Steven. "How Do You Solve a Problem Like the Film Musical?" In *The Sound of Musicals*, edited by Stephen Cohan, 1–18. London: BFI Publishing, 2010.

Cohen, Harvey. *Who's in the Money: The Great Depression Musicals and Hollywood's New Deal*. Edinburgh: Edinburgh University Press, 2018.

Crosland, Alan, dir. *The Jazz Singer*. Warner Bros. Pictures, 1927.

Cutting, Jack, and Clyde Geronimi, dirs. *The Ugly Duckling*. Walt Disney Productions, 1939.

David, Mack, Al Hoffman, and Jerry Livingston. "A Dream Is a Wish Your Heart Makes." *Cinderella: Original Motion Picture Soundtrack*. Victor Records, 1950.

Dyer, Richard. "Entertainment and Utopia." In *Hollywood Musicals: The Film Reader*, edited by Steven Cohan, 19–30. London, Routledge, 2002.

Elyas, Sadeen. "With a Smile and a Song: *Snow White and the Seven Dwarfs* as the First Integrated Musical." In *Snow White and the Seven Dwarfs: New Perspectives on Production, Reception, Legacy*, edited by Christopher Holliday and Chris Pallant, 117–132. New York: Bloomsbury Academic, 2021.

Fields, Dorothy, and Jerome Kern. "Never Gonna Dance." *Swing Time Original Motion Picture Soundtrack*. Brunswick, 1936.

Gabler, Neal. *Walt Disney: The Biography*. London: Aurum, 2006.

Garcia, Desirée. *The Migration of Musical Film: From Ethnic Margins to American Mainstream*. New Brunswick, NJ: Rutgers University Press, 2014.

Geronimi, Clyde, Les Clark, Eric Larson, and Wolfgang Reitherman, dirs. *Sleeping Beauty*. Walt Disney Productions, 1959.

Geronimi, Clyde, Wilfred Jackson, and Hamilton Luske, dirs. *Cinderella*. Walt Disney Productions, 1950.

Gerrard, Matthew, and Robbie Nevil. "We're All in This Together." *High School Musical Official Motion Picture Soundtrack*. Walt Disney Records, 2006.

Gillett, Burt, dir. *Three Little Pigs*. Walt Disney Productions, 1933.

Grant, Barry Keith. *The Hollywood Film Musical*. Oxford: Blackwell, 2012.

Greno, Nathan, and Byron Howard, dirs. *Tangled*. Walt Disney Pictures, 2010.

Halliwell, Martin. *American Culture in the 1930s*. Edinburgh: Edinburgh University Press, 2007.

Hand, David, Wilfred Jackson, Larry Morey, Perce Pearce, Ben Sharpsteen, and William Cottrell, dirs. *Snow White and the Seven Dwarfs*. Walt Disney Pictures, 1937.

Holliday, Christopher, and Chris Pallant, eds. *Snow White and the Seven Dwarfs: New Perspectives on Production, Reception, Legacy*. New York: Bloomsbury Academic, 2021.

Kennedy, David M. *Freedom from Fear: The American People in Depression and War 1929–1945*. Oxford: Oxford University Press, 1999.

Lawrence, Jack, and Sammy Fain. "Once upon a Dream." *Songs from Sleeping Beauty*. Walt Disney Music Company, 1959.

LeRoy, Mervyn, dir. *Gold Diggers of 1933*. Warner Bros., 1933.

LeRoy, Mervyn, dir. *The Wizard of Oz*. Metro-Goldwyn-Mayer, 1939.

Levine, Lawrence. *The Unpredictable Past: Explorations in American Cultural History*. New York: Oxford University Press, 1993.

Lubitsch, Ernst, dir. *The Merry Widow*. Metro-Goldwyn-Mayer, 1934.

Maltin, Leonard. *Of Mice and Magic: A History of American Animated Cartoons*. New York: NAL Books, 1980.

Mollet, Tracey L. *A Cultural History of the Disney Fairy Tale: Once upon an American Dream*. London: Palgrave Macmillan, 2020.

Mollet, Tracey. "With a Smile and a Song: Walt Disney and the Birth of the American Fairy Tale." *Marvels and Tales* 27, no. 1 (2013): 109–124.

Morgan, Iwan. "Introduction: Hollywood and the Great Depression." In *Hollywood and the Great Depression: American Film, Politics and Society in the 1930s*, edited by Iwan Morgan and Philip John Davies, 1–28. Edinburgh: Edinburgh University Press, 2016.

Muscio, Giuliana. *Hollywood's New Deal*. Philadelphia: Temple University Press, 1997.

Newman, Randy. "Almost There." *The Princess and the Frog Official Motion Picture Soundtrack*. Walt Disney Records, 2009.

Nugent, Frank. "One Touch of Disney." *New York Times*, January 23, 1938.

Roosevelt, Franklin Delano. "Fireside Chat 2: On Progress in the First Two Months," May 7, 1933. https://millercenter.org/the-presidency/presidential-speeches/may-7-1933-fireside-chat-2-progress-during-first-two-months.

Samuel, Lawrence R. *The American Dream: A Cultural History*. Syracuse, NY: Syracuse University Press, 2012.

Sandrich, Mark, dir. *Follow the Fleet*. RKO Radio Pictures, 1936.

Sandrich, Mark, dir. *The Gay Divorcee*. RKO Radio Pictures, 1934.

Sandrich, Mark, dir. *Top Hat*. RKO Radio Pictures, 1935.

Schickel, Richard. *The Disney Version: The Life, Times, Art and Commerce of Walt Disney*. New York: Simon & Schuster, 1986.

Slater, Glenn, and Alan Menken. "I've Got a Dream." *Tangled: Original Motion Picture Soundtrack*. Walt Disney Records, 2010.

Stein, Walter J. *California and the Dust Bowl Migration*. Westport, CT: Greenwood Press, 1973.

Stevens, George, dir. *Swing Time*. RKO Radio Pictures, 1936.

Susman, Warren. *Culture as History: The Transformation of American Society in the Twentieth Century*. New York: Smithsonian Books, 1984.

Thomas, Bob. *Walt Disney: An American Original*. New York: Hyperion, 1994.

Wasko, Janet. *Understanding Disney: The Manufacture of Fantasy*. Cambridge: Polity Press, 2001.

Zipes, Jack. "Breaking the Disney Spell." In *From Mouse to Mermaid: The Politics of Film, Gender and Culture*, edited by Elizabeth Bell, Lynda Haas, and Laura Sells, 21–42. Bloomington: Indiana University Press, 1995.

CHAPTER 5

HALL JOHNSON, THE HALL JOHNSON CHOIR, AND DISNEY: 1941–1955

JULIANNE LINDBERG

> The Hall Johnson Choir was the only choir in the history of the American cinema to become a movie star.[1]

HALL Johnson (1888–1970)—musician, composer, arranger, and director of one of the first professional Black choirs in the US—made a significant mark on the sound and function of the choir in American stage, film, and television works.[2] His life spanned Reconstruction, segregation on and off-Broadway, the economic Depression of the 1930s, the rise and fall of publicly funded theater and choral programs, and later reintegration efforts on stage and screen. As vocalist and biographer Eugene Thamon Simpson has noted, it is extraordinary that Johnson was able to support himself throughout his career without being affiliated with a church or a university; his activity was entirely professional, and thus, he had to navigate a changing landscape—in terms of racial politics, choral aesthetics, and business practices—on Broadway and in Hollywood.[3] Much of Johnson's legacy rests on his many choral arrangements of spirituals: his choir—professionally known as the Hall Johnson Choir—performed these pieces in tours across the US and Europe, and it is difficult to overstate Johnson's role in "the appreciation, the acceptance, and the performance of Black vocal music" in the United States.[4] His arrangements were and are regularly programmed by choral societies, universities, and churches. He worked with the best-known theater and film directors of the day, the most high-profile film studios, and the biggest producers, including Walt Disney.

Johnson's contributions to the Disney legacy have been overlooked, largely because the films in which the choir were featured are now considered some of Disney's most racist productions and have subsequently been either reworked or left in the Disney vault. Both the minstrel stereotypes represented by the crows in *Dumbo* (1941) and the romanticized narrative of plantation life in *Song of the South* (1946)—two productions with the Hall Johnson Choir—have been heavily critiqued by activists, film critics, and scholars. Johnson's dealings with Disney between 1941 and 1955, however, illuminate several important issues facing Black artists and their experiences with both Disney and the larger entertainment industry at mid-century: the changing currency of "authentic" Black sound in film and stage productions, the differences between WPA-era work models and those operating in Hollywood, and the significance of growing civil-rights movements to how Black artists—and the sound of the Negro spiritual—were perceived on-screen.[5] Johnson both created and resisted commercial depictions of sonic Blackness and was thus always interacting with that fraught nexus between agency and exploitation.

THE HALL JOHNSON CHOIR

The Hall Johnson Choir itself, which started out as sixteen singers in its debut concert in 1926 and swelled to five hundred by the 1946 performance of Johnson's cantata *Son of Man*, existed in many different configurations depending on the needs of the production.[6] The original eight members of the group, which Johnson doubled for the choir's debut, included Marguerite Avery and J. Mitchell (sopranos), Consuela Carr and Ruthena Matson (altos), Mack Reeves and Morris Caver (tenors), and George McClean and Service Bell (basses). By 1930, the choir had a regular core of 150 mixed voices, split between a concert choir, a Broadway choir for *Green Pastures* (for Marc Connelly's Pulitzer Prize–winning play), and a reserve choir.[7] Simpson also notes that there were a handful of smaller units, including the Swanee Six, the Whispering Trio, and the Over Jordan Sextet. After the choir's debut, it was quickly engaged at high-profile venues, including the newly opened Roxy Theatre (where it was in residence for two weeks), a concert organized by the wealthy patron Cobina Wright (honoring Maurice Ravel and attended by Deems Taylor, Walter Damrosch, and others), Pythian Temple, New York's famed Town Hall, and Lewisohn Stadium. Critics lauded the singers' "ebullient energy," "individual quality," "phenomenal sense of rhythm," and "uncannily clear" diction.[8] Damrosch remarked that the choir sang "with fine precision, beautiful tone quality, and above all, with a deep inner emotion which fairly sweeps the listeners along."[9] Most critics attributed the choir's musical and performative excellence to something inborn, essentializing along the lines of race. In a *Musical Courier* review, for instance, a critic remarked:

> There is little or no evidence of either vocal or cultural training in the singing.... The conductor, Hall Johnson, is evidently an educated negro with musical training, but he does not allow that training to color his understanding of the picturesque charm

of negro music as it is.... So far as one can judge, Mr. Johnson does no more than keep his forces together.... The result is extraordinarily fine, and an example of how negro folk music should be sung.[10]

The idea that Johnson did "no more than keep his forces together" grates tremendously against the firsthand accounts of choir members, who remember Johnson as a conductor who was "fanatical about details" and who "let nothing go by. He took his time and worked diligently to get exactly what he wanted."[11] William Warfield remembered that Johnson was "a stickler about having his arrangements performed exactly as he wrote them."[12] The thousands of hours in rehearsal and hard work on the part of Johnson and his choir were often reduced to an idealized notion of inborn musicality associated with Blackness; this quality is what made critics remark upon their "authenticity." A perceived authenticity was valued by theater and film writers and producers hungry for music that provided a naturalistic quality to their often-romanticized Southern pastorals.[13]

Johnson himself was invested in the idea of authenticity but to very different ends. What constituted Black cultural authenticity was heavily contested in Black communities in the US during Johnson's lifetime. The New Negro movement expressed one of the most prominent positions in this debate and one that Johnson, as an educated son of a professor who attended Atlanta University and Juilliard, identified with early on. Johnson's significant role in arranging Negro spirituals was praised by Alain Locke, a leading figure of the New Negro movement, who believed, as Johnson did, that spirituals should be performed in a choral context to embody the communal aspect of their original setting.[14] Johnson's group, however, was often sought out by white creative teams on Broadway to satisfy an "authentic" idea of Blackness during a time when the US was searching for an "American sound." As Micah Wittmer has said, "the performance of choral and musical theater works by Hall Johnson provides a means of understanding the urgency Johnson felt to portray Negro folk culture authentically during a time when African American culture was being considered by white artists as a crucial element of American national culture."[15] The complicated legacy of how the choir was used by mostly white producers and directors should be understood alongside the significant contributions made by Johnson and his group.

The choir's work on Connelly's award-winning Broadway play *The Green Pastures* (1930) catapulted it to fame. The show was critically praised by the mainstream press, critiqued by the Black press, and ran for 640 performances; the story is a classic white vision of Black culture, using stories from the Bible and depicting what a Black heaven might look like, complete with a fish fry; the character "The Lord" was played by Richard B. Harrison (the 1936 film later changed the character's name to "De Lawd"). Johnson directed the choir and provided arrangements for the film, with the choir singing traditional spirituals throughout, including "In Bright Mansions Above" (one of the first spirituals he had ever arranged), "Go Down Moses," and "Hallelujah, King Jesus!," the last of which was an original composition by Johnson. The choir both sang and acted in the play.

After the choir's spectacular and widely lauded performance in Connelly's play, Johnson decided to write his own choral-centered play about African American spirituality. In 1933, *Run, Little Chillun* premiered on Broadway; Johnson wrote the script, songs, and arrangements and directed the choir for what he called a "music-drama" (often referred to as a "folk opera").[16] As Simpson notes, the show didn't have a backer (especially difficult during the lean years of the Depression), so Johnson worked to raise money by organizing a transcontinental concert tour featuring twenty of his best singers.[17] *Run, Little Chillun* ran for 126 performances and was remounted in a WPA-funded production that ran for two years in Los Angeles. As composer, director, arranger, sometimes scriptwriter, and touring musician, Johnson led his choir to fame and notoriety. For more than two decades (1930–1951), the choir was the premier professional choir in the US.

THE HALL JOHNSON CHOIR ON FILM

While the choir had earned its fame via high-profile concert engagements and Broadway productions, its legacy also rests on the large body of work it produced in Hollywood. By 1939, a critic for the *Pittsburg Press* commented that Johnson, whose choir he characterized as "internationally famous, hailed by critics the world over," had "become a sort of overlord of one phase of film activity."[18] The critic went on to say:

> Almost from the day of his arrival [in Hollywood] Johnson's counsel has been sought by producers engaged in making pictures that dealt with the South. Although the producers pay when they use the choir, Johnson gives his advice free because he wants pictures about the South and the Negro to be true to life. "It works out splendidly," said Johnson on his free advice policy. "I don't like to see jarring notes in pictures any more than I like to hear them in music."[19]

This comment captures a number of realities that affected the life and career of Johnson during his time in Hollywood: the assumption that the "Negro spiritual" was a sonic representation of the American South, the certainty that Johnson's "free advice" was given to producers who then went on to monetize that advice, and the fact that the advocacy for the Negro spiritual seen in Johnson's work was still foundational during his time in Hollywood.

Before working with Disney, Johnson and the Hall Johnson Choir had already made a huge mark on film soundtracks, eventually recording for at least twenty-four films between 1929 and 1947.[20] Their earliest films—including the shorts *St. Louis Blues* (1929), featuring Bessie Smith, and *Black and Tan* (1929), featuring Duke Ellington and Fredi Washington—weren't expressly tied to a religious context, although the use of the choir in these secular settings certainly heightened the spiritual affect and drama of the scenes it was featured in. Most Hollywood film producers, however, utilized spirituals either written or arranged by Johnson to signal sonic Blackness within the context of the South or even the antebellum South.

By the time the choir began its relationship with Disney, it had worked with the most high-profile studios of the day and was respected as one of the most significant choirs in the US and certainly in Hollywood. It is not surprising, then, that Disney engaged the choir for its films. As with other producers, the choir was used primarily by Disney to capture an essentialized American Blackness,rooted in the South.[21]

DUMBO (1941)

The Hall Johnson Choir's first involvement with Disney was on the award-winning animated film *Dumbo* (1941), which chronicles a baby circus elephant's journey from ostracized outsider to entertainment star. Dumbo's ears (which led to his insulting nickname, replacing "Jumbo Jr.," the name his mother gave him), his young age, and the fact that he doesn't speak a single word over the course of the film mark him as separate from the world he inhabits, the classic outsider. The idea of difference and the relationship between the othered character and the society that forces him "outside" have made this film an interesting example in disability studies.[22] The film has also been discussed in terms of race, specifically Blackness, and has been critiqued for the minstrel stereotypes present in the Black-coded crows' musical number and the stereotype of Black manual laborers as "happy-hearted" and financially irresponsible in the "Song of the Roustabouts" sequence.[23]

Disney was in financial trouble prior to the release of *Dumbo*; the now-classic films *Pinocchio* (1940) and *Fantasia* (1940), which each cost more than $2 million to produce, were not initially box-office successes, and Disney struggled to recoup costs while also dealing with the loss of its overseas markets during the war. *Dumbo* was thus Disney's attempt to produce a more cheaply made film that would draw an audience and help pull the company out of the hole it found itself in. While nearly all the voice actors on the film were uncredited and scant records survive, a small group of male voice actors and members of the Hall Johnson Choir were involved in the production and featured on the song and scene surrounding "When I See an Elephant Fly," a pivotal moment late in the film. Potentially due to the company's financial troubles, it leaned into the small-vocal-group aesthetic, abandoning the full-studio-choir sound of *Snow White* and *Pinocchio*. Other small vocal groups, both white, in the film included the King's Men, a vocal quartet popular in the 1930s–1950s who sang "Song of the Roustabouts," and the Sportsmen Quartet, featured on "Look Out for Mr. Stork," "Casey Junior," and "Pink Elephants on Parade." The songs in *Dumbo* were written by Frank Churchill (who had also worked with Disney on *Snow White and the Seven Dwarfs* and later *Bambi* and *Peter Pan*) and Oliver Wallace (*Cinderella, Alice in Wonderland, Peter Pan, Lady and the Tramp*), with lyrics by Ned Washington, who famously wrote the lyrics for "When You Wish upon a Star."

"When I See an Elephant Fly," one of the best-known songs from *Dumbo*, features five voices playing the parts of the crows. The crows happen upon Dumbo and Timothy Q. Mouse, Dumbo's only friend, the morning after they accidentally get drunk on a barrel of champagne and thereafter hallucinate the famous "pink elephants" sequence. Timothy is surprised to find that he and Dumbo are sleeping their hangovers off in a tree; Timothy exclaims that Dumbo must have flown up there. The crows mock them roundly. The five singing crows are led by Jim Crow, his name an obvious nod to the best-known blackface minstrel archetype (the *Dumbo* character's name was later changed to Dandy Crow).

The main animator for the crow sequence was Ward Kimball, one of Disney's "nine old men," the core group of animators responsible for Disney's first golden age. As Todd James Pierce notes, Kimball had a special interest in jazz and worked on a number of shorts that made him a clear fit for this sequence: in the 1937 Disney short *Woodland Café* (one of the Silly Symphonies), Kimball was responsible for animating insects and arachnoids to resemble jazz musicians (one cricket was a clear parody of Cab Calloway); in the 1938 Disney short *Mother Goose Goes to Hollywood*, which included caricatures of entertainment figures from Laurel and Hardy to Katharine Hepburn, Kimball was responsible for animating the caricatures of Fats Waller and, again, Calloway, this time in human form.[24] Both shorts reveal Kimball's interest in connecting the feel of jazz—syncopation, swing, and the kinetic energy of jazz dance—to the visual plane; the characters bop, shake, and shimmy in an energetic caricature of their real-life counterparts. The two shorts reveal that Kimball's approach to animating Black characters was rooted in blackface minstrelsy: the highly exaggerated lips and rolling eyes of the crickets in *Woodland Café* appear on the Calloway character and all of his Black-coded insect bandmates, and the same device is used for the Black humans in the *Mother Goose* short (especially the anonymous Black background characters).[25]

Kimball's crow sequence was purportedly inspired by African American dance. In several interviews and features preceding the release of *Dumbo*, Kimball recounted how he was guided by his Black cook, Teka:

> Kimball obtained some initial guidance into body rhythm by watching the actions of his Negro cook, Teka. Teka likes hot music, prefers it, in fact, to anything in the swing school. She is expert at singing while she works, and Kimball followed her around making sketches. He even had a piano moved into her kitchen and sat by while Teka's boy friend came over each Thursday and Saturday to bang out some fancy tunes while the evening dinner was being either prepared or cleared away.[26]

This article, in the *Brooklyn Daily Eagle*, also explains that Kimball researched jazz dance by attending, sketchbook in hand, Harlem's Savoy Ballroom, where he "had [the dancers] perform in front of [his] box. They repeated the Harlem Conga, Jitteroo and went back to the Lindy Hop for some of the hotter numbers."[27] Both of these sources show that Kimball and, by extension, Disney were concerned with visual movement that they deemed authentically Black. As in Southern pastoral films, which idealized

Blackness in the service of a safe, romanticized vision of the past, Kimball used this ethnographic approach to jazz and jazz dance to lend authenticity to his depiction of Blackness in the film (and potentially to ward off any critiques related to racial representation).[28] This concern with naturalistic movement led Disney to hire a pair of dancers—an African American vaudeville duo called the Jackson Brothers—to act as models for the crow sequence. Eugene Jackson remembers that "the making of *Dumbo* wasn't easy for us as dancers. We didn't have all of the modern technology of today. When it wasn't right, we had to dance over and over again."[29] Like dance, the music used in "When I See an Elephant Fly" is rooted in African American vernacular though parodied for the purpose of the song sequence.

Sonically, this song was a departure for the Hall Johnson Choir; rather than utilize Johnson's full-bodied arrangements of spirituals, it trades in the sound of vaudeville-adjacent jazz acts of the era, including groups such as Cab Calloway and His Orchestra. Jim Crow was voiced by Cliff Edwards, the white singer and actor who had previously worked with Disney as the voice of Jiminy Cricket in *Pinocchio* and who had a long career as the novelty singer Ukulele Ike, initially playing blackface roles. The other crows are usually credited as the Hall Johnson Choir, although other sources cite voice actors including Jim Carmichael, Nick Stewart (of *Amos 'n' Andy* fame), and James Baskett (who would later play Uncle Remus in *Song of the South*) as the voices of the crows, with the members of the choir singing in the background.[30]

The choir functions as part of the rhythm section, "comping" in the way of a jazz piano, vocalizing on "ahh" or "ooh" vowels, accentuating the syncopations and both supporting and playing off the melody carried by Edwards as Jim Crow. The choir singers' presence in the song adds a richness and a theatrical quality well suited to the animated fantasy that wouldn't be present with only a standard rhythm section. The choir moves to the foreground toward the end of the song, where full-voiced, wide harmonies bring the song to a dramatic close. The drama of the ending is reinforced by the visuals; it's the first time in the sequence when all five crows come together, highlighting the choral quality heard in the song.

There is very little extant information about the actual recording of the song, except for information gleaned from interviews with Kimball, Dick Huemer (another animator who worked on the screenplay for *Dumbo*), and Ben Sharpsteen (the supervising director of the film). Kimball remembers that the Hall Johnson Choir recorded with Edwards, observed by Kimball, Huemer, Sharpsteen, composer Wallace, lyricist Washington, and sound mixer Sam Slyfield (at the least). Huemer remembers that the choir members "hugely enjoyed doing it. They even offered suggestions, and we used some of their ideas—lines of dialogue, little touches. Happens all the time when you're making a picture."[31] While it is difficult to ascertain what exactly these "lines of dialogue" and "little touches" were, this sense of collaboration was echoed by Sharpsteen. He remembers that Washington was "greatly upset" after "the singers suggested a change in the lyrics that seemed to be in character and to fit what we were trying to do," and he went on to defend the input of the choir.[32] It appears that these suggestions came directly from Johnson himself and potentially had to do with an unfavorable representation of race via the crows; as animation historian Michael Barrier notes, the original transcript of *Dumbo* includes a note by Sharpsteen that states, with no further elaboration, that the "black singers' leader 'opposed some of the lyrics in it.'"[33] Knowing Johnson's outspoken feelings about race and representation (first seen in essays including his critique of *Porgy and Bess* for *Opportunity* in 1936), it is possible, even probable, that Johnson was critical of Washington's original lyrics along the lines of racial representation.[34]

The lyrics, at least as they now exist, are less objectionable than the performance of Jim Crow by Edwards. Edwards sings the lead vocal line throughout while scatting (and at one point imitating a muted trumpet) and deliberately dropping consonants throughout. The last line of the chorus—"but I be done seen about everything / when I see an elephant fly"—is inflected in such a stereotypically "jive talk" manner that it's difficult not to hear it as a parody of Blackness. His manner of speech and the delivery are clearly meant to exude a kind of hipness associated with jazz and jazz subcultures.[35] None of the other crows—all voiced by Black singers—affects the same manner of speech.

SONG OF THE SOUTH (1946)

While there are plenty of contemporary critiques of the crows and the song "When I See an Elephant Fly," those in 1941 were not nearly as full-throated as would be the criticisms of *Song of the South*. One of the only feature-length films by Disney to remain continually in the Disney "vault," *Song of the South*, which saw its last theatrical screening in 1986, is by far Disney's most controversial film. It was Disney's third attempt at mixing live-action and animated sequences in a feature-length film (after *Saludos Amigos* [1942] and *The Three Caballeros* [1944]). Disney had long been interested in adapting the Uncle Remus stories written by Joel Chandler Harris, a white journalist from Georgia who loosely based them on African American folklore he had purportedly heard recounted by slaves at a plantation in Eatonton, Georgia, where he was working as a printer's apprentice in the years leading up to the Civil War. The Uncle Remus stories feature the trickster Brer Rabbit, his friends and foes (including Brer Fox and Brer Bear), and his many exploits and ensuing moral lessons.

Disney's film fashions a live-action world alongside the animated Brer Rabbit stories. The live-action story is set during Reconstruction and centers around the emotional world of Johnny, a seven-year-old boy who is visiting his visiting his grandmother's Georgia plantation with his mother. The rocky relationship between his mother and father upsets Johnny (the first scene reveals that his parents are planning to split up); because of this, he attempts to run away. While trying to leave, Johnny is noticed by Uncle Remus, a grandfatherly Black man who is telling one of his stories to a young Black boy named Toby. Uncle Remus quickly takes Johnny under his wing, which vexes his mother. Johnny's mother's response implies that Uncle Remus's stories—famously told via animated sequences—are filling Johnny's head with nonsense and getting him into trouble.

Indeed, a paternalistic attitude toward Uncle Remus is present throughout. After a series of incidents, Johnny's mother tells Uncle Remus that he is no longer allowed to be anywhere near Johnny. This leads Uncle Remus to pack up to leave; Johnny chases after him and is intercepted by a bull and seriously injured. Back at the big house, the Black plantation workers gather outside the home while the white residents are inside gathered around Johnny's bedside (this scene is scored with a choral lament). Johnny calls for Uncle Remus, who resumes his storytelling, miraculously pulling Johnny back from the brink and saving the day.

The Hall Johnson Choir is credited with three songs in the film, including "Uncle Remus Said," "Let the Rain Pour Down," and "All I Want." "Uncle Remus Said"—with words and music by Johnny Lange, Hy Heath, and Eliot Daniel—is an upbeat folk tune sung around a campfire, and it fades in as young Johnny is creeping through the woods surrounding his grandmother's plantation, attempting to run away. The song recounts the folklore behind certain creation stories, successively describing how "the leopard got its spots," how "the camel got those humps," and how "the pig got a curly tail." Using a call-and-response format, the choir sings the chorus ("That's what Uncle Remus said / That's what Uncle Remus said / Listen now to what I say / That's how the critters got that way") while soloists perform the verses. The visual here is significant: the large group of singers, played on-screen by members of the Hall Johnson Choir, are shown in shadow and from a distance, perhaps mimicking how Johnny sees them, and are thus seen not as individuals but as a group without differentiation. As the film progresses, this remains the case; the only Black characters afforded any individuality are Uncle Remus (James Baskett), Aunt Tempy (Hattie McDaniel), and young Toby (Glenn Leedy). Every other Black character is treated as a set piece.

"Let the Rain Pour Down" is first performed as an uptempo work song, sung during a transition from one scene to the next. Again, the plantation workers—men, women, and children—are seen from a distance as they walk down a dirt road alongside draft animals while carrying farm tools. The song includes, like many of Johnson's arrangements, lively choral counterpoint as the low voices sing the melody against percussive choral interjections by the high voices. Many critics of the film were particularly upset by the cheerful attitude of these laborers, especially in the context of a Southern plantation. The text reinforced the upbeat affect of the music: "Wake up early in the mornin' / when the dong-dong ring, look up / Goin' down to the kitchen room, / It's the same ol' thing." The quality of smiling servitude here, the way the Black characters function to move the white characters' narrative forward, and the pastoral plantation setting amount to a decidedly antebellum atmosphere, despite when the film was set.

The reprise of "Let the Rain Pour Down" is distinctly less cheerful. After Johnny's mother bans Uncle Remus from spending time with her son, both the boy and the older man are heartbroken. The choir sings a downtempo version of the song under a monologue by Uncle Remus, and the lyrics are altered to reflect Uncle Remus's mood: "When you're achin' with the mis'ry, / and you're old and gray, / Then you'd better be thankful / that He let you stay." It is difficult to watch the scene where Uncle Remus decides to leave the plantation; he remarks that "this here's the only home I knows," reminding one of displacement, of the poor treatment of Uncle Remus by his employers (which also reads as "masters"), *and*, if viewing this scene from the perspective of the NAACP and other civil-rights groups and activists of the time, of his poor treatment by the film. The servile attitude with which he approaches conflict with the daughter of his employer—a character who does not read as sympathetic—is a feature of the plantation genre in film. Cedric Robinson reminds us, in a discussion of the "racial regimes" of golden age film, that plantation genre films often critique individuals rather than systems of oppression.[36]

The final song attributed to the Hall Johnson Choir is the traditional spiritual "All I Want." The song was arranged by Ken Darby and featured in the climactic scene at the end of the film when the injured Johnny is unconscious in bed. The Black plantation workers gather around the big house, heads bowed and hats off. The choir begins on a low hum and moves in and out of the foreground as the action unfolds on-screen. This is a song of supplication; the choral texture alternates between soloist and full choir, pleading for mercy on behalf of Johnny, with the full choir singing the refrain "more and more faith in Him." The attitude of supplication, read as a prayer on behalf of Johnny, shows the precise function of the choir in this film: it is there to further the narrative arc of the white characters and to lend pathos and sentimentality to the film.

While the Hall Johnson Choir sometimes performed the compositions of others (their work on *Dumbo* is, of course, an example of this), it is curious that none of these songs, ostensibly all imitating Negro folk songs or spirituals, was arranged by Johnson, the most visible arranger of Negro folk songs and spirituals in the country. "Let the Rain Pour Down" and "All I Want" were composed and arranged, respectively, by Darby. Darby was a choral director, composer, and vocalist who had performed with the King's Men on *Dumbo* (singing "The Song of the Roustabouts") and whose relationship with Walt Disney Studios lasted from 1941 to 1948. Beyond *Song of the South*, he "wrote songs, coached singers, sang, arranged, and conducted units that became part of cartoon/live action feature-length films," including *Make Mine Music, Pinocchio, Dumbo, Fun and Fancy Free, Melody Time*, and *So Dear to My Heart*.[37] In addition to composing and arranging for *Song of the South*, he is also credited as the vocal director. There is no clear evidence about what songs he directed, but it is unlikely that he directed the Hall Johnson Choir, as Johnson had many assistant directors among his choir's ranks.

Many critics of the film were quite forceful in their negative critiques, even if positive about the artistic merits of the film. Walter White's widely circulated critique, made on behalf of the NAACP, stated that "the production helps to perpetuate a dangerously glorified picture of slavery. Making use of the beautiful Uncle Remus folklore, 'Song of the South' unfortunately gives the impression of an idyllic master-slave relationship which is a distortion of the facts." John T. Lane, president of the NAACP's New York branch, remarked that "in portraying our people as happy and docile under the rotten system of slavery a grave injustice is done us."[38] Lane laments particularly that this is a children's film, as "millions of children ... will get their impression of colored people in this unsavory light."[39] Bosley Crowther of the *New York Times* had similar concerns, stating sardonically that "Old Uncle Remus (James Baskett) is just the sweetest and most wistful darky slave that ever stepped out of a sublimely unreconstructed fancy of the Old South."[40] Crowther went on to say, in perhaps the most-quoted critique of the film, that Disney

> committed a peculiarly gauche offense in putting out such a story in this troubled day and age. For no matter how much one argues that it's all childish fiction, anyhow, the master-and-slave relation is so lovingly regarded in your yarn, with the Negroes bowing and scraping and singing spirituals in the night, that one might almost imagine that you figure Abe Lincoln made a mistake. Put down that mint julep, Mr. Disney! It doesn't become your youthful face.[41]

All of the above critics allude to the idea that the characters depicted on-screen were slaves. Supporters of the film (then and now) usually respond by saying that the film was set during Reconstruction and thus that these critics are "confused about the time of the story."[42] Even the Production Code Office advised Disney to "be certain that the frontispiece of the book mentioned in the bottom paragraph on this page establish the date in the 1870s."[43] This explanation, however, doesn't address the representation of Blackness as servile and certainly doesn't consider the widespread practice of peonage during Reconstruction and in the Jim Crow South.

It shouldn't have been any surprise to Disney and the creators of *Song of the South* that there would be a negative reaction to the film. In fact, it seems that they (Walt Disney in particular) deliberated ignored these concerns. In addition to the heightened and highly visible civil-rights activities during World War II, Disney had also been directly warned, in a series of correspondence by the Production Code Administration (PCA), that his script could be received unfavorably. As early as August 1944, Joseph Breen, head of the PCA office, had suggested to Disney that

> before proceeding much further with the development of this story, you secure the services of a competent person to advise you concerning the over-all, as well as the detailed acceptability, of this story from the standpoint of the American negroes. These good people, in recent months, have become most critical regarding the portrayal on the motion picture screen of the members of their race, and it will be well for you to take counsel with some responsible leaders among the negroes concerning this particular story.[44]

Breen's comment that "in recent months" Black critics had been more forceful in their critique of negative images of African Americans on-screen is indirectly referencing the general efforts of civil-rights organizations, as well as the specific activities of the NAACP's involvement with the War Activities Committee of the motion-picture industry, newly formed in 1942. The committee was responsible for screening films for "anti-American" and antiwar messages during World War II; the office also distributed several propaganda films. Most important for our purposes, the committee was actively working with the NAACP to address negative stereotypes of African Americans in film.

The War Activities Committee and Breen's office were naturally in contact. Breen went so far as to secure the services of Francis Harmon, former executive assistant at the PCA office and current executive vice chairman of the War Activities Committee. Breen asked Harmon to write a memo for Disney from the perspective of the committee. His comments specifically referenced the singing in the film:

> Pages 67, 112 and 116: These scenes show Negro groups singing happily. It is the characterization of the individuals in these groups to which certain types of Negro leaders are most likely to take exception. It is recommended, therefore, that these groups not be played for comedy, that their clothes be plain and reasonably clean, rather than having them dressed in rags, and that the scenes depend upon the singing of the groups to hold audience interest, rather than funny business which is certain to be resented by some negroes.[45]

It does seem that Disney heeded these particular warnings (at least in reference to the clothing of the Black singers and the elimination of comic bits by the choir), but Breen's overall worry that "this particular story" (a Southern pastoral released just as the early civil-rights movement was gaining momentum) could be objectionable was dismissed. After receiving a revised script, Breen warned Disney again that a consultant or input from a Black organization would be prudent. As late as December 13, 1944, Breen wrote:

> May I suggest again the advisability of your taking counsel with some responsible negro authorities concerning the overall acceptability, from the standpoint of the negroes, of this story. As I have already presumed to suggest to you, our negro friends appear to be a bit critical of all motion picture stories which treat of their people, and it may be that they will find in this story some material which may not be acceptable to them.[46]

This was the last time Breen would make such a suggestion, and his other comments on the film were highly complimentary. He did, however, anticipate the backlash that accompanied the film's premiere, which took place in Atlanta. Baskett and McDaniel were notably absent.

There is no evidence that Disney ever hired a consultant, but it would seem likely that Johnson, who, after all, is credited with the choral singing, would have contributed his thoughts on the film (as early as 1939, it was remarked that "Johnson's counsel has been sought by producers engaged in making pictures that dealt with the South").[47] Even this, however, can be debated. In fact, Johnson's involvement in the entire production is shrouded in some degree of mystery, due largely to an extant letter written in 1960 by Johnson to the Walt Disney Company. Disney had released a soundtrack for the film in September 1959 (DQ 1205), some pressings of which include attribution to "The Hall Johnson Choir" directly on the record, and Johnson apparently had recently acquired a copy of the album. In his letter to the company, Johnson claims that he never worked on the production and found the performance of the choir in the film antithetical to his life's work:

> There is a beautiful melody in the W.D. album called "All I Want"—listed "Traditional." I never heard it before—but it is just the kind of Negro folk song we specialize in. As recorded, the arrangement is not at all in the racial style (how could they be expected to know?) but, worse than that, the diction is atrocious—simply for lack of consonants. Pure phonetics and clear articulation have always been our "pride and joy," and no singer who has ever been in three of my rehearsals could possibly turn out such sloppy words. Imagine how I feel to have the name of our choir signed to such singing. True, in "show business," good diction is desirable, but not too important. The opening chorus, "Song of the South," by the Studio Choir is a case in point. This would be quite effective—if you could only understand the words without straining the ears! At that, it is as good as the average movie chorus—but for me, the "average" is not good enough![48]

He goes on to say that "as long as one single 'Uncle Remus' recording is still available anywhere, it constitutes an effective and absolute refutation of everything I have always preached (racially and musically) in every class, lecture, rehearsal, or performance."[49] This strongly stated letter is further confused by Disney's response (officially signed "Walt Disney Music Company"), which confirms after "going into old records" that the record is indeed the original soundtrack and provides details of the 1945–1946 session(s), including the number of singers used (forty), the location (Goldwyn Studios), the casting agency (Goldwyn Casting Department), how the choir referred to itself in the contract ("The Hall Johnson Choir"), and that Johnson himself, while working on a Mickey Mouse Club feature in 1955, "remembered very well the same Disney people who worked on the film in 1945–46."[50] The letter doesn't engage with Johnson's objections, instead simply and directly claiming that the choir did, in fact, work on the film.

As far as the available records show, Johnson never responded to this letter, and he suffered a stroke just three months later. Simpson asserts that the most likely explanation for these contradicting letters is that Disney had contracted a "counterfeit Hall Johnson Choir" without realizing it, potentially made up of Hall Johnson Choir singers without Johnson's knowledge.[51] After all, "[b]y 1945, Los Angeles was teeming with Hall Johnson singers," and it is possible that "one of his ambitious assistants contracted a group of local Hall Johnson singers to do this film."[52] This does seem likely; we know that the choir, as far back as 1930, had multiple units operating at the same time under assistant directors. Some of Johnson's former singers—particularly Jester Hairston and Leonard De Paur but also Juanita Hall and others—became high-profile directors in their own right. If Johnson did not work on the film, as seems to be the case, the "Hall Johnson Choir" likely did, and his influence was nevertheless felt through these singers.

Johnson's claim that the singing on the film "constitutes an effective and absolute refutation of everything I have always preached (racially and musically)" is particularly interesting. We know that he had worked on Southern pastoral films before, and we know that he was a stickler for musical precision, particularly in terms of articulation.

Johnson's interpretation of the singing on *Song of the South* is in line with his uncompromising attitude toward performance. The idea that Johnson found *Song of the South* racially problematic stems, potentially, from the time the film was released and the concentrated attention groups such as the NAACP paid to Hollywood films and racial representation. Regardless of his involvement on the film, by 1946, Johnson's choral sound was associated with romanticized plantation films and their regressive politics; this was the last film the Hall Johnson Choir was associated with.

The Sprites and Sprouts and the Mickey Mouse Club

Johnson's final involvement with Disney was in the mid-1950s, when he was asked to prepare a choir for a newly launched television program, *The Mickey Mouse Club* (*MMC*). In 1955, Johnson was contacted by Hal Adelquist, producer for the *MMC*, and asked to put together a choir of Black children who would occasionally perform on the show. While the core members of the *MMC* were white—including Annette Funicello as one of the original Mouseketeers and featuring Jimmie Dodd as emcee—performers of color were sometimes part of their "Talent Roundup," a segment with specialty acts including ice skaters, magicians, singers, family acts, comedians, and acrobats. Johnson referred to the group as the Sprites and Sprouts and enlisted the help of singer Wathea Sims Jones, whom Johnson described as a "specialist in child-training."[53] According to Johnson, he was contacted by Disney prior to the launch of the *MMC*; he subsequently put together a group that by 1956 had been "in regular rehearsal for [a] year."[54] The group performed in concert as well as on the *MMC*.[55] While Johnson alludes to "several T.V. appearances" with the *MMC*, I have only been able to identify one performance, on October 14, 1955, where the children's choir performed in one of the show's "Talent Roundup" features.

Johnson was not paid to retain and rehearse this children's choir—in fact, it appears that Johnson did much of the legwork in advance of signing a clear contract. Simpson calls Johnson's approach to choosing and rehearsing the Sprites and Sprouts an example of Johnson's "old-fashioned" approaches to business: instead of assembling an ad hoc group of vocalists to satisfy the studio, he did what he had always done, which was to create a choir that he thought he could keep active for Disney projects as well as other purposes (Simpson cites this as an example of Johnson's "personal goals" continually superseding that of the studio he was working for). This is potentially one of the reasons Johnson was destitute toward the end of his life; he didn't work in the professional studio manner and at the quick pace of his contemporaries (including his former students such as Hairston), which would dictate that a choral director and/or contractor hire singers drawn from a curated list of Los Angeles professionals, who would then rehearse according to a short, contracted period before recording.[56] Johnson had never worked this way; dating back to his work for the WPA, Johnson was used to having months of rehearsal and was able to both teach by rote and employ singers who weren't necessarily studio-ready. This approach created a strong community of singers who were proud to be associated with Johnson and his legacy. Johnson's way of working also got him into some trouble and lost him more than a few opportunities.[57] Johnson's work with the Sprouts and Sprites was the last time he would work for Disney. In fact, opportunities to work in general stopped trickling in. For an artist without a secure position (whether in a church or a university, or otherwise), this was devastating.

Conclusion

The Hall Johnson Choir's involvement with Disney is just one side of its varied and shifting role on the stage and in film. Johnson's career did not survive the changes taking place in Hollywood (or on Broadway) when time was considered money and there was no way for a choir to rehearse for months at a time in advance of a studio engagement. The sound of Johnson's choir, especially in the context of films set in the South, was increasingly understood as a remnant of a less enlightened era. And while Johnson is responsible, more than any other one person, for the performance, dissemination, and appreciation of Black vocal music, and particularly the Negro spiritual, in the US, his choir and his career didn't survive in any substantial form beyond the early 1950s. Like many of the other films that the Hall Johnson Choir is credited with working on, Johnson and the choir's work with Disney is typically dismissed as dated at best and racist at worst. By the 1950s, Hollywood and Broadway both dealt with the very real charges of racism, bigotry, and limited, stereotyped roles for Black people in the entertainment industry by simply not casting Black talent as frequently. The trends on Broadway, for instance, were dismal; after a postwar push toward integration on the stage, roles for Black actors dropped off significantly in the 1950s.[58] Lena Horne commented on this situation in 1958:

> We have discontinued the use of the stereotype, but we have opened up nothing else. I think that a good role, whether it's a maid or a laundress, is to be desired if it's a good role. But in the past they have never varied the stereotype, so by cutting it out completely it has hurt the Negro performer economically. You have the desire to play other things beyond the stereotype, but you can't even play that anymore.[59]

Hollywood followed a similar logic, with significant exceptions, and Walt Disney Studios wouldn't animate another significant Black human character in a feature film until 2001, when they released *Atlantis: The Lost Empire* featuring the character of Dr. Joshua Strongbear Sweet (identified as both African American and Native American and whose animation was supervised by Ron Husband). In the end, Johnson and his choir's interaction with the Walt Disney Company reflected the changing currency of Black voices and ideas about Black authenticity in Hollywood. And while Disney has kept Johnson's contributions in the proverbial (and actual) vault, the leagues of singers whose lives he touched are perhaps a better barometer of his legacy.

Notes

1. Eugene Thamon Simpson, *Hall Johnson: His Life, His Spirit, and His Music* (Lanham, MD: Scarecrow, 2008), 107.
2. Historians have wrestled over the criteria by which choirs are deemed "professional," but most agree that an independent organization—free from associations with a church or a university and thus indicative of a shift in the history of Black choirs in the US—is a central feature. This typically means that the Fisk Jubilee Singers, tied as they were (and are) to Fisk University, are seen in a different category from the professional Black choirs, including Hall Johnson's and Eva Jessye's, of the 1920s. For an in-depth look at the development of professional Black choirs, see Isaiah R. McGee, "The Origin and Historical Development of Prominent Professional Black Choirs in the United States," PhD diss., Florida State University, 2007.
3. Simpson, *Hall Johnson*, 57.
4. Ibid., 91.
5. I am deliberately using "Negro spiritual," as this is the term that Johnson himself used to describe the musical genre in which he was most prolific. See Hall Johnson, "Notes on the Negro Spiritual," in *Readings in Black American Music*, ed. Eileen Southern, 2nd ed. (New York: W.W. Norton, 1983).
6. Simpson, *Hall Johnson*, 5.
7. Ibid., 11.
8. W. J. Henderson, "Negro Choir at Pythian Temple," *New York Sun*, March 1, 1928; M.W., "Johnson's Negro Choir Pleases Concert Audience," *Herald Tribune*, March 1, 1928.
9. Walter Damrosch, New York Public Library, Hall Johnson Negro Choir Clippings, folder 2.
10. "Reports of New York Concerts," *Musical Courier*, March 29, 1928; New York Public Library, Hall Johnson Negro Choir Clippings, folder 2.
11. Arthur Bryant and Louvenia Pointer, in Simpson, *Hall Johnson*, 330–331.
12. William Warfield, in ibid., 335.
13. This can be seen in several Broadway plays from the 1920s and 1930s, including Dorothy and DuBose Heyward's *Porgy* (1927), Marc Connelly's *The Green Pastures* (1930), and George Abbott's *Sweet River* (1936).
14. For more on Johnson's understanding of and approach to "authenticity" in Negro spirituals and folk songs, see Micah Wittmer, "Performing Negro Folk Culture, Performing America: Hall Johnson's Choral and Dramatic Works (1925–1939)," PhD diss., Harvard University, 2016, 14–16. Wittmer also discusses differing perspectives, including that of Zora Neale Hurston, who was a critic of Johnson.
15. Wittmer, "Performing Negro Folk Culture," 4.
16. As many, including Wittmer, have noted, George Gershwin's *Porgy and Bess* was far from the first attempt to write an African American–focused "folk opera"; Johnson's *Run, Little Chillun* was an important precedent.
17. Johnson left the rest of the choir to rehearse under the direction of his assistant conductor, Juanita Hall, who would go on to become an able choir director and Broadway star in her own right (she would lead the choir in George Abbot's *Sweet River* [1936]).

18. This article was written during the period when the choir was recording for the Stephen Foster biopic *Swanee River*. Alexander Kahn, "Negro Choir Leader Wins Screen Fame," *Pittsburg Press*, October 16, 1939.
19. Ibid.
20. The precise number of films the Hall Johnson Choir worked on is difficult to fix, as studios were "haphazard" in how singers and choirs were credited (as will be discussed later in this chapter). Robynn Stilwell, "Black Voices, White Women's Tears, and the Civil War in Classical Hollywood Movies," *19th-Century Music* 40, no. 1 (Summer 2016): 68n10.
21. Several sources, including the finding aid at the Library of Congress, claim that the Hall Johnson Choir performed on the soundtrack for *Snow White and the Seven Dwarfs* (1937). As of this writing, however, I have not been able to confirm its involvement. While the choir first came to Hollywood in 1936, recording for the film version of *The Green Pastures* and a slate of other films including Frank Capra's *Lost Horizon*, it seems exceedingly unlikely that it was used by Disney to capture the fairy-tale choral sound in *Snow White*. For one, Hollywood had only ever used the choir in a racialized way. The only director and composer to use the choir without any reference to the idea of sonic Blackness were Capra and Dmitri Tiomkin on the films *Lost Horizon* (1936) and *Meet John Doe* (1941); even so, *Lost Horizon* used the choir to evoke the sound of the distant Himalayas and the exoticized inhabitants of the fictional Shangri-La, where the bulk of the film takes place. In *Lost Horizon*, the choir is also seen on-screen as the inhabitants of Shangri-La; both films credit the choir in either the opening or closing titles. Tiomkin purportedly heard the choir in concert (soon after its arrival in Los Angeles to record for the film version of *The Green Pastures*) and, according to Jester Hairston, "went crazy for the sound." Bette Yarbrough Cox, *Central Avenue: Its Rise and Fall (1980–c. 1955), Including the Musical Renaissance of Black Los Angeles* (Los Angeles: BEEM, 1996), 171.
22. See, for instance, Nicholas Sammond, "Dumbo, Disney, and Difference: Walt Disney Productions and Film as Children's Literature," in *The Oxford Handbook of Children's Literature*, ed. Julia Mickenberg and Lynne Vollone (New York: Oxford University Press, 2011), 147.
23. A 1960s-era critique of *Dumbo* by film scholar Richard Schickel, for instance, characterized the crows as "too obviously negro caricatures." Richard Schickel, *The Disney Version: The Life, Times, Art and Commerce of Walt Disney* (New York: Simon & Schuster, 1968), 265. More recent critiques take note of the crows' place in the larger, destructive history of blackface minstrelsy in animated features. See, for instance, Nicholas Sammond, "Race, Resistance and Violence in Cartoons," in *The Animation Studies Reader*, ed. Nichola Dobson et al. (New York: Bloomsbury Academic, 2019), 229. Disney itself has recently acknowledged this history. If you view the film on Disney+, for instance, it is preceded by a title card with a content warning that reads, in part: "This program includes negative depictions and/or mistreatment of people or cultures. These stereotypes were wrong then and are wrong now."
24. Todd James Pierce, *The Life and Times of Ward Kimball: Maverick of Disney Animation* (Jackson: University Press of Mississippi, 2019), 32.
25. For more on the prolific characterizations of Black people and characters in animated films and shorts by Disney and other studios, see Henry T. Sampson, *That's Enough Folks: Black Images in Animated Cartoons, 1900–1960* (Lanham, MD: Scarecrow, 1998); Christopher P. Lehman, *The Colored Cartoon: Black Representation in American Animated Short Films, 1907–1954* (Amherst: University of Massachusetts Press, 2009).

26. "Disney Models Scene on Hot Savoy Ballroom," *Brooklyn Daily Eagle*, October 10, 1941.
27. Ibid. Pierce notes that it is unlikely, given Kimball's schedule, that he actually went to New York to visit the Savoy; it was more likely that Kimball saw a performance of Whitey's Lindy Hoppers—who started out at the Savoy—in Los Angeles (the professional dance group was regularly featured in film, including in an unbelievably athletic scene in the film adaptation of *Hellzapoppin'* from 1941). Pierce, *The Life and Times of Ward Kimball*, 76.
28. Pierce notes that Kimball was "really worried about how the crows would be accepted" and attributes the numerous interviews and press releases about the origins of the crows' dance to a desire to "ascribe a type of racial respect to both this sequence and the dance depicted." Pierce, *The Life and Times of Ward Kimball*, 94.
29. Jackson also remembers being brought into the studio decades later, in 1995, for an interview for a series of books "giving credit to African American dancers for their part in helping create the foundation for the Disney film animation. No mention of sharing this film's royalties with me was ever discussed, but that's show biz." Eugene W. Jackson, *Eugene "Pineapple" Jackson: His Own Story* (Jefferson, NC: McFarland, 1999), 59. Footage of the Jackson Brothers is extant and can be seen in the bonus material for the seventieth-anniversary Blu-ray release of the film.
30. Michael R. Pitts, *RKO Radio Pictures: Horror, Science Fiction and Fantasy Films, 1929–1956* (Jefferson, NC: McFarland, 2015), 90; Thomas S. Hischak, *100 Greatest American and British Animated Films* (Lanham, MD: Rowman & Littlefield, 2018), 89.
31. Didier Ghez, ed., *Walt's People*, Vol. 4 (Orlando: Theme Park, 2015), 54.
32. Don Peri, ed., *Working with Walt: Interviews with Disney Artists* (Jackson: University Press of Mississippi, 2008), 18–19.
33. Michael Barrier, "'What's New' Archives: Cliff Edwards, Ward Kimball, Jack Kinney, and the Crows," January 14, 2010, http://www.michaelbarrier.com/WhatsNewArchives/2010/WhatsNewArchivesJan10.html#cliffedwards.
34. While generally positive, Johnson critiques Gershwin for not being sufficiently informed to produce "authentic Negro musical language … sung and acted in a characteristic Negro style." He goes on to say, "The informing spirit of Negro music is not to be caught and understood merely by listening to the tunes and Mr. Gershwin's much-publicized visits to Charleston for local color do not amount even to a matriculation in the preparatory-school that he needed for his work." Hall Johnson, "Porgy and Bess—A Folk Opera," *Opportunity*, January 1936, 25.
35. For explorations of the idea of "hipness" and its intersection with race, desire, and appropriation, see Ingrid Monson, "The Problem with White Hipness: Race, Gender, and Cultural Conceptions in Jazz Historical Discourse," *Journal of the American Musicological Society* 48, no. 3 (Autumn 1995); Phil Ford, *Dig: Sound and Music in Hip Culture* (New York: Oxford University Press, 2013).
36. Cedric Robinson, *Forgeries of Memory and Meaning: Blacks and the Regimes of Race in American Theatre and Film before World War II* (Chapel Hill: University of North Carolina Press, 2007), 272–380.
37. Ken Darby and J. E. Wallace Sterling, *Hollywood Holyland: The Filming and Scoring of* The Greatest Story Ever Told (London: Scarecrow, 1992), xix.
38. "Negro Citizenry Picket Theatre with Walt Disney Film," *New York Age*, January 11, 1947.
39. Ibid.
40. Bosley Crowther, "Spanking Disney: Walt Is Chastised for 'Song of the South,'" *New York Times*, December 8, 1946.

41. Ibid.
42. See, for instance, Jim Korkis, *Who's Afraid of the Song of the South? And Other Forbidden Disney Stories* (Orlando: Theme Park, 2012), 68.
43. Francis Harmon, memo requested by Joseph Breen to accompany Production Code Administration (PCA) response to Walt Disney, July 31, 1944 (PCA files, Academy of Motion Picture archives).
44. Letter, Joseph Breen to Walt Disney, August 1, 1944 (PCA files, Academy of Motion Picture archives).
45. Harmon, memo.
46. Letter, Joseph Breen to Walt Disney, December 13, 1944 (PCA files, Academy of Motion Picture archives).
47. Kahn, "Negro Choir Leader Wins Screen Fame."
48. Letter, Hall Johnson to the Walt Disney Company, December 4, 1960 (in Simpson, *Hall Johnson*, 284).
49. Ibid.
50. Letter, Walt Disney Music Company to Hall Johnson, March 3, 1961 (in Simpson, *Hall Johnson*, 285).
51. Simpson, *Hall Johnson*, 286.
52. Ibid.
53. Simpson, *Hall Johnson*, 49.
54. Ibid., 125.
55. The group performed, for instance, at the Wesley Methodist Church in Los Angeles for a "Negro History Week" event partially sponsored by the Greater Los Angeles Music Alliance. Also on the program was a song written and performed by Mrs. A. C. Harris Bilbrew about the death of Emmett Till. "Mrs. Bilbrew to Sing Till Song in History Week," *California Eagle*, February 2, 1956.
56. As Simpson states regarding the 1962 Grammy Award–winning record of *Porgy and Bess* that he recorded on (featuring William Warfield and Leontyne Price), "the recording took perhaps three recording sessions, with a single hour rehearsal for the chorus before each session. The modern professional chorus consists not only of professional voices, but of singers who are professional musicians and are prepared to give a stylistic reading of most standard repertoire with little or no rehearsal." Simpson, *Hall Johnson*, 278.
57. A particularly detrimental incident occurred during an otherwise triumphant German tour that the Hall Johnson Choir took in 1951. On the day of a concert at "New Theater" in Nuremberg, Johnson kept the choir late in rehearsal; because of this, the concert was delayed and didn't start until an hour after the advertised time. While the reviews were glowing, word of this event reached the State Department and other industry professionals. According to Simpson, this cost Johnson State Department funding for a festival in Paris (which the group could not otherwise afford and thus did not attend) and his chance to conduct the European tour of *Porgy and Bess* in 1952. Simpson, *Hall Johnson*, 28–29.
58. In the 1951–1952 season, Frederick O'Neal, an African American actor working on behalf of the Actors' Equity Association, found that only thirteen Black actors had parts on Broadway (and only three of those were supporting roles; the rest were bit parts or extras); compare this to the 1946 season, when more than 250 Black actors were working in Broadway shows. This is discussed in Allen Woll, *Black Musical Theatre: From* Coontown *to* Dreamgirls (Baton Rouge: Louisiana State University Press, 1989), 216–217.
59. "Interview—Lena Horne," *Equity* 43, April 1958.

Bibliography

Barrier, Michael. "'What's New' Archives: Cliff Edwards, Ward Kimball, Jack Kinney, and the Crows," January 14, 2010, http://www.michaelbarrier.com/WhatsNewArchives/2010/WhatsNewArchivesJan10.html#cliffedwards.

Cox, Bette Yarbrough. *Central Avenue: Its Rise and Fall (1980–c. 1955), Including the Musical Renaissance of Black Los Angeles.* Los Angeles: BEEM Publications, 1996.

Darby, Ken, and J. E. Wallace Sterling. *Hollywood Holyland: The Filming and Scoring of* The Greatest Story Ever Told. London: Scarecrow, 1992.

Ford, Phil. *Dig: Sound and Music in Hip Culture.* New York: Oxford University Press, 2013.

Ghez, Didier, ed. *Walt's People*, Vol. 4. Orlando: Theme Park, 2015.

Hischak, Thomas S. *100 Greatest American and British Animated Films.* Lanham, MD: Rowman & Littlefield, 2018.

"Interview—Lena Horne." *Equity* 43, April 1958.

Jackson, Eugene W. *Eugene "Pineapple" Jackson: His Own Story.* Jefferson, NC: McFarland, 1999.

Johnson, Hall. "Notes on the Negro Spiritual." In *Readings in Black American Music*, edited by Eileen Southern, 268–275. 2nd ed. New York: W. W. Norton, 1983.

Johnson, Hall. "Porgy and Bess—A Folk Opera." *Opportunity*, January 1936, 25.

Korkis, Jim. *Who's Afraid of the Song of the South? And Other Forbidden Disney Stories.* Orlando: Theme Park, 2012.

Lehman, Christopher P. *The Colored Cartoon: Black Representation in American Animated Short Films, 1907–1954.* Amherst: University of Massachusetts Press, 2009.

McGee, Isaiah R. "The Origin and Historical Development of Prominent Professional Black Choirs in the United States." PhD diss., Florida State University, 2007.

Monson, Ingrid. "The Problem with White Hipness: Race, Gender, and Cultural Conceptions in Jazz Historical Discourse." *Journal of the American Musicological Society* 48, no. 3 (Autumn 1995): 396–422.

Peri, Don, ed. *Working with Walt: Interviews with Disney Artists.* Jackson: University Press of Mississippi, 2008.

Pierce, Todd James. *The Life and Times of Ward Kimball: Maverick of Disney Animation.* Jackson: University Press of Mississippi, 2019.

Pitts, Michael R. *RKO Radio Pictures: Horror, Science Fiction and Fantasy Films, 1929–1956.* Jefferson, NC: McFarland, 2015.

Robinson, Cedric. *Forgeries of Memory and Meaning: Blacks and the Regimes of Race in American Theatre and Film before World War II.* Chapel Hill: University of North Carolina Press, 2007.

Sammond, Nicholas. "Dumbo, Disney, and Difference: Walt Disney Productions and Film as Children's Literature." In *The Oxford Handbook of Children's Literature*, edited by Julia Mickenberg and Lynne Vollone, 146–166. New York: Oxford University Press, 2011.

Sammond, Nicholas. "Race, Resistance and Violence in Cartoons." In *The Animation Studies Reader*, edited by Nichola Dobson, Annabelle Honess Roe, Amy Ratelle, and Caroline Ruddell, 217–234. New York: Bloomsbury Academic, 2019.

Sampson, Henry T. *That's Enough Folks: Black Images in Animated Cartoons, 1900–1960.* Lanham, MD: Scarecrow, 1998.

Schickel, Richard. *The Disney Version: The Life, Times, Art and Commerce of Walt Disney.* New York: Simon & Schuster, 1968.

Simpson, Eugene Thamon. *Hall Johnson: His Life, His Spirit, and His Music*. Lanham, MD: Scarecrow, 2008.

Stilwell, Robynn J. "Black Voices, White Women's Tears, and the Civil War in Classical Hollywood Movies." *19th-Century Music* 40, no. 1 (Summer 2016): 56–78.

Wittmer, Micah. "Performing Negro Folk Culture, Performing America: Hall Johnson's Choral and Dramatic Works (1925–1939)." PhD diss., Harvard University, 2016.

Woll, Allen. *Black Musical Theatre: From* Coontown *to* Dreamgirls. Baton Rouge: Louisiana State University Press, 1989.

PART II
ADAPTATION

CHAPTER 6

NEW AGRABAH, SAME OLD DISNEY ORIENTALISM: COMMODITY RACISM AND WESTERN EFFACEMENT OF THE "MIDDLE EAST"

MICHELLE ANYA ANJIRBAG

IN 1992, Disney released the animated film *Aladdin*, cementing with *The Little Mermaid* (1989) and *The Lion King* (1994) the multicultural push of what would come to be known as the "Disney Renaissance." The film was critically and commercially successful and helped to reform the perception of Disney as a leading brand in family entertainment; however, it was not without its critics, both from academic quarters and from the community it purported to represent. *Aladdin*'s reliance on orientalism and orientalist stereotypes in its construction of the Middle East—or, in the case of the 2019 live-action remediation,[1] the Middle East, South Asia, and the Silk Road—is something that needs to be grappled with as a no-longer-acceptable form of narrative creation. This chapter explores the controversies with both screen adaptations of *Aladdin* by Disney and identifies how the production approaches almost thirty years apart both mark problematic attempts at expanding on-screen representation by Disney. When looking at Disney's productions of the Aladdin story from 1992 through 2019, what is abundantly clear is that even while playing with the idea of a bigger, vaster, "whole new world," the corporation in fact managed to flatten that world, if not erase large swaths of it through misrepresentation.

Aladdin's Animated Legacy, Orientalism, and Commodity Racism

Disney's multicultural projects of its Renaissance period, *Aladdin* included, participate in "commodity racism." According to C. Richard King, Carmen Lugo-Lugo, and Mary K. Bloodsworth-Lugo, commodity racism is a primary mediator in a global, postindustrial order, where the legacies and realities of racism make the system functional, meaningful, and profitable. But the presence of commodity racism must always involve a process of erasure by which difference is both desired and demonized and in which too often alternatives to established norms become absorbed as fads or fashions, readily accessible for co-optation and commodification rather than being oppositional problems.[2] Commodity racism explains Disney's focus on image over a deeper deconstruction of "racial structures and their unspoken center—whiteness,"[3] as it offers "positive images that stress humanness and inclusion as they celebrate diversity and singularity,"[4] and as such has contributed to as well as "converged with the fragmentation of the consuming public into niche markets,"[5] reflecting a desire to cultivate "ethnic" markets."[6] Although these problems are not limited to the various *Aladdin* productions, Disney's animated *Aladdin* and the remediation exemplify this strategy, making "a dual move in an era marked by multiculturalism," "simultaneously [hailing] a broad, purportedly raceless audience and [targeting] ethnic consumers, thus reinforcing racialized differences and their entanglements with power."[7] This strategy is also one that echoes through the productions of other films in different ways, including other Disney Renaissance films such as *Hercules* (1997) and *Mulan* (1998) or even more recent films such as *The Princess and the Frog* (2009) and *Moana* (2016), and is part of a larger problematic pattern. But by looking at the versions of *Aladdin* produced in 1992 and 2019, we can highlight the problems of nonauthentic representation in a very particular way.

The 1992 animated film, though commercially and critically successful, faced significant criticism from the American-Arab Anti-Discrimination Committee (ADC) regarding the use of "stereotype and misrepresentation"[8] in the film. Preferring "fantasies of an exotic and alien generic Arabia as a backdrop for a formulaic romance to a culturally accurate and historically anchored story in an actual time and place,"[9] *Aladdin* reiterates orientalisms and relies on visual stereotypes to indicate moral positioning in that the heroes are light-skinned, and the rest are dark-skinned, swarthy, accented, and with exaggerated features. While the visual stereotypes were not addressed, ADC criticism did result in the removal of the most egregious stereotypes from the opening song, "Arabian Nights." In retrospect, this was at best, as King, Lugo-Lugo, and Bloodsworth-Lugo describe it, a "half-measure," as it maintained the reference to barbarism and therefore the incorporation of Arabs into the Disney universe as its barbaric others but "without the overt and violent overtones"[10] and while also making oblique public commitments to diversity.

The existence of *Aladdin* as a Disney production cannot be disentangled from its historical positioning at the time of its production, which has been thoroughly explored by scholars including Christopher Wise, Dianne Sachko Macleod, and Eleanor Byrne and Martin McQuillan. Wise writes about the Islamophobia at the heart of the thematic racism of the animated *Aladdin* in the context of the Gulf War, noting that "the cavalier insensitivity of films like *Aladdin* has directly contributed to the culture of misunderstanding that now prevails in the United States, and has prevailed in the year that led 'us' to the controversies in which 'we' and 'our' children are now embroiled."[11] Wise writes from a both post–Gulf War and post–September 11, 2001, point of view. The controversies he alludes to are those in which Arab people and culture—US misunderstandings of what it projected as sharia law—were habitually othered as the counterpoint to Western European and North American (WENA)[12] or, more specifically, US concepts of freedom. Wise's argument rests on the point that in *Aladdin*, the vague construct of arcane and ancient laws is what is ultimately problematic and what is stopping the American-coded heroes Aladdin, Jasmine, and the Genie from ultimately finding the various freedoms they seek. He asserts that "the film functions as a symbolic resolution of the contradiction (for Westerners mainly, especially Americans) of the persistence of Islamic theocratic government in the era of former president George Bush's '[whole] new world order.' "[13] Put another way by Byrne and McQuillan, "*Aladdin* on a superficial level is the story of an evil Islamic dictator who aspires to rule the world but is brought low by an Americanised youth, his Western-friendly allies, and advanced military technology."[14] Macleod directly connects the successes of *Aladdin* to the "televised staging of the Gulf War that was taking place while the film was in production at Disney Studios. Mirroring and magnifying popular stereotypes of Arab culture, *Aladdin* played to an audience already primed by the media."[15] This is important to consider, because it means that neither the characterizations of the heroic characters nor those of the villains can be separated from racialized identities surrounding the us-versus-them constructions of the United States/West versus the "Middle East" in the 1990s through the 2000s.

In addition to orientalist tropes deployed throughout the film and the references to barbarianism, Macleod draws a direct line between the vilifying of the image of Jafar and political cartoons of both Ayatollah Khomeini and Saddam Hussein:

> Like Hussein, Jafar is mustachioed and dark skinned, but his appearance also owes a debt to political cartoons that reduced Khomeini to a turbaned and robed silhouette. In both cases the stereotype of the evil Orientalist Other has been collapsed into the enemy image.... The fictional villain is a devious plotter and untrustworthy ally who pretends loyalty to his benevolent master while scheming to seize his possessions. It was this personification of Hussein-the-betrayer that was beamed from satellite dishes around the world in 1990–1991.[16]

Essentially, the idea of orientalized evil as both implicit and cartoonish was drawn not only from fictional representations but also from contemporary realistic images that were pertinent to the news media landscape at the time. Macleod connects this manipulation of contemporary image to the orientalist artists of the nineteenth century, including the impetus to "rely on the illusion of innocence,"[17] to mask the deeper problems with the propagated images, such as the adoption of "hypnotic attention to detail to signal the 'truthfulness' of their depictions of this locale."[18] It is interesting, too, that this is enacted simultaneously with another kind of orientalizing: the characterization of the effeminate oriental male villain. Jafar's gender bending is visible in his physical similarity (tall and thin) to female Disney villains, such as the Evil Queen and Maleficent. He is also presented as not wearing the same distinguishing trousers as the other male characters in the film, wearing eye makeup, and exhibiting "prissy and preening" behavior.[19] Jafar's characterization was further deliberately conceived of and influenced through a queer lens by openly gay lead animator Andreas Deja, who "conceiv[ed] of the character as a gay man 'to give him his theatrical quality, his elegance.'"[20] The characterization remains in the *Aladdin* sequels and television programming, and it both does and does not evolve in the live-action film. As such, it lends itself toward a consideration of the orientalist geography of the film itself: what and where is the "Middle East" versus other locations of the "not West" or the "Orient" after all?

Relocating *Aladdin* and Agrabah from Animation to Broadway Stage

Despite these criticisms, Disney's theater division also remediated the film into a stage production in 2014 following the success of similar transformations of Disney Renaissance–era films from screen to stage such as *Beauty and the Beast* in 1994 and *The Lion King* in 1997, and even despite the less successful *The Little Mermaid* in 2008–2009.[21] Sam Baltimore meticulously traces the shift from the animated film back toward Howard Ashman's original treatment in the stage musical, identifying specifically how it was "developed within a tradition of queer Orientalism" that was excised from the film after development on the film continued following Ashman's death in 1991.[22] He highlights the return to both queerness and "the musical restoration of Blackness"[23] in the stage musical, while also specifically observing that the "Arabian Nights" number expresses what Alan Menken described as "Middle Eastern style" through "jingling bells, gapped scales, arabesque ornamentation in vocal and woodwind lines, all staples of the 1940s Orientalist films Menken used as a model."[24] According to Baltimore's reading, what Ashman seems to have intended as satire for an insider audience instead arguably becomes a musical codification of performed orientalist attitudes for a new audience, reiterating in some ways the "orientalist fantasy" that Emily Clark and colleagues identify as having lived on in US popular theater since the 1880s and that even for Disney in particular resurfaced in the 2013 stage production of *The Jungle Book*.[25] In the context of this history and critical reception, the announcement that the studio would be remediating *Aladdin* in live action to be released in the late 2010s was provocative, as the stage version did not make clear that Disney had learned to better negotiate the racial politics of an ever-changing world in which the corporation's claims to functioning as an authoritative arbiter of cultural identity were being more vocally and more consistently challenged.

Returning to the Screen: Steps Forward into a Whole New World

All of this is not to say that there was no new ground broken in the film; however, I maintain that the problematic "mishmash" approach overpowers *Aladdin*'s potential. This was the first live-action remediation to have a solely nonwhite primary cast, which is important in and of itself, and the casting of Will Smith as the Genie is especially significant. Not only did the studio pass Robin Williams's legacy on to a member of an underrepresented demographic, but it opened the door to two particularly powerful moments. The first, the opening-frame tale where Smith as a character is the human parent of two apparently mixed-race children on a ship, telling them a tale that becomes the story of "Aladdin and the Lamp." Images of Black fatherhood are starkly absent in Disney films, especially where Blackness is given shape in a human body. The only other example occurs ten years earlier in the opening scenes of *The Princess and the Frog*. Tiana's father is subsequently dead for narrative purposes, a slight change from the "eighty-six the mother" pattern of Disney animated film.[26] Smith as the Genie is depicted as a kind, sincere suitor. His interactions with the handmaiden Dahlia (Nasim Pedrad) are without a sense of masculine bravado, and he serves as a friend, adviser, confidant, and all-around positive male role model to Mena Massoud's Aladdin. Positive, sensitive men who do not project hypermasculinity are relatively absent from the Disney transmedia universe and offer opportunities for scholarship on these themes. Nevertheless, making one of the few examples of this representation also a Black, African American man, played by an actor known for playing characters who complicate the image of Blackness in American popular culture, was quite accidentally subversive.

The second powerful moment occurs in a scene after Aladdin tricks the Genie into getting them all out of the Cave of Wonders without using a wish. Aladdin asks the Genie what he would wish for, after the Genie has proven he can look "totally normal" by losing the blue skin in favor of Smith's natural Black skin. The Genie takes a bite from an apple he conjured, returns that apple to the ether, and responds, "Hm, no one's really asked me that before. It's an easy one though, I'd wish to be free." (As he says this line, he taps the ornate gold bangles on his wrists that in both this film and the animated film signaled his bondage as chains, before zapping into different versions of his blue-Genie-self waiting to serve new masters.) As he returns to being a Black man instead of a blue-toned fantastic creature, he continues, "freedom. I'd wish to be, to be human."

For a company that has dealt with Blackness before this with stereotype and obfuscation meant to cater to the white gaze, this line is incredibly poignant. In a US-produced film for "family audiences," which Paul Wells locates as predominately representing or speaking to a "particular aesthetic and ideological orthodoxy of quasi-Republican, tradition-directed stability,"[27] a Black man talking about the need to be free constitutes a disruption to Disney's status quo. Smith's personhood cannot be disentangled from this moment in the film, nor can it be disentangled from the current political moment or the legacy of slavery in the United States. Nevertheless, it is a single line in the film, and the most significant, humanized part for a Black man in the Disney fairy-tale universe still sees him placed into slavery and needing someone non-Black to free him. But if moments such as this could persist, it would be a potential way to draw attention to the wider contexts in which Disney as a corporation exists, rather than trying to keep its fairy-tale world separate from the everyday concerns of politics, sociocultural unrest, and negative historical legacies.

Just as the Genie's characterization was made more complicated, so, too, was Jafar's by making him pursue not just an oblique sense of power but geopolitical power through invasion of specific neighboring countries. The camp element in his character remains,[28] along with his penchant for wearing robes, carrying a snake staff, and wearing eyeliner. However, his voice is notably pitched much higher and softer than in the animated feature. Just as Jasmine's and Aladdin's mothers are revived (to an extent) in this film, Jafar is also given a backstory: he's a former thief who crawled his way out of the same position Aladdin inhabits to become one of the most powerful people in Agrabah. This still plays on the tropes of villainous Arab peoples and the regional tensions that have persisted since the Gulf Wars and contextually defined the animation. Nevertheless, this backstory also makes Jafar, if not more understandable or sympathetic, more than a caricature of Middle Eastern bogeymen waiting to take down "the West." This innovation in backstory is not of this film's invention, as a version of it had already been explored by the wider corporation in the ABC-produced television show *Once Upon a Time*; in both cases, this move steps away from the over-the-top, almost gender-bending villainy of the animation. However, racist caricature continues to proliferate in the character of Jafar in the wider context of the Disney corporation, especially in the *Descendants* transmedia, as in that narrative space, Jafar has come to embody the stereotypical salesman of the animated opening while also being a notorious thief who cares more about what his children steal for him to con unsuspecting others with than creating a supportive family environment.[29]

The most deliberate, overt evidence of a "cleaned-up palimpsest" created between the animation and the remediation is in the characterization of Jasmine. She is a stronger character within the confines of this fantasyscape. Instead of just wanting to leave the palace for freedom's sake, Jasmine aspires to rule her people after her father. She is portrayed as thoughtful, well read, and curious about the wider world. Her dismissal of a situation where she was being bartered as a prize for some prince in a convenient alliance through marriage is a holdover from the animation. However, this Jasmine is far more direct about the commercial nature of how her marriage is being arranged, directly asking what "Prince Ali" hopes "to buy" with the gifts he has brought and ridiculing Prince Anders, a white character added to this iteration, who proves himself less than her equal in their meeting. Animated Jasmine rejects suitors because she wants to marry for love; this Jasmine believes that her duty to her people transcends any legal restrictions on her life and choices—such as the one that states she must marry a prince—or other practices that keep her from ruling.

Jasmine's newly created agency in this version, which is in dialogue with Disney's revised gender politics around what it means to be a princess since the 2010s and *Tangled*, *Brave*, and *Frozen*, is best displayed in a scene after Jafar has used his first wish to make himself sultan and is attempting to persuade the palace guards to his side, using the law as the reason for them to abandon their posts and swear loyalty to him as sultan: the law states that the palace guards protect the title, not the person who may have held it. Jasmine is being removed from the room by guards when she begins to sing "Speechless (Part 2)," the solo added for her character in the remediation. This song, in both parts, is about Jasmine feeling silenced in her position and finding her voice. After the song, Jasmine pulls away from the guards and addresses Hakim, the captain of the guard. She speaks to his history with her family, how he grew from the son of a groundskeeper to this trusted post, and how she knows him "to be both loyal and just." She goes on to tell him that he has a choice to make and that "duty isn't always honor. Our greatest honor isn't speaking up against our enemies, but defying those whose approval we seek the most. Jafar is not worthy of your admiration nor your sacrifice." When Jafar asserts that he is doing what he is doing for the glory of Agrabah, she responds, "No. You seek glory for yourself. And you would win it off the backs of my people!" She continues to Hakim, "these men, they will follow where you lead but it's up to you. Will you stand silent while Jafar destroys our beloved kingdom or will you do what is right and stand with the people of Agrabah?" She wins Hakim back to her side; he acknowledges her as "my princess" before bowing to her father, saying, "my sultan." This scene allows Jasmine to realize her potential and in the eyes of those who have been responsible for protecting her—the guards and her father—prove that she is capable of protecting not only them but the rest of the kingdom. She speaks against Jafar's evil when no one else does and acts without waiting for some kind of rescue. Thus, Jasmine represents progress in terms of depicting female agency, recalling a key figure of the Disney Renaissance without reproducing the oversexualized damsel-in-distress trope of the first iteration.

After Jafar is defeated and Aladdin wishes the Genie free, the Sultan pulls Jasmine aside. He names her the sultan after him, acknowledging that he kept her trapped in the palace out of a fear of losing her as he had lost her mother. This is also new ground for Disney—another example of a positive depiction of fatherhood and an acknowledgement that little girls cannot play princess forever; little girls grow up to do more, achieve their potential, even rule kingdoms. The remediation disrupts the ending of the animation further; the Sultan does not change the law. He leaves that power in Jasmine's hands, saying, "As sultan, you may change the law; he is a good man," disrupting the idea that Aladdin would inherit the kingdom, as implied at the end of the animation. As Jasmine follows Aladdin out of the palace, she commands him to stop as "his sultan," making her marriage firmly not only her choice but executed through her agency.

Nevertheless, Jasmine's interactions are still bound by the idea that women in certain cultures are bound by bad laws that they need to transcend through the exertion of personal agency to claim personal freedoms they are being denied. Some of this comes to bear in the lyrics of the new song written for the character, "Speechless." Some of the lines reflect things said to Jasmine by Jafar about what her place in the kingdom should be, but references to rules "written in stone" that are "centuries old" still recall the deployment of oblique references to sharia law and Islamic or Arabic culture in the animated version. This song is to some degree the parallel to Aladdin's "One Jump Ahead"/ "One Jump Ahead (reprise)," and the female "I want" song in this film, which was absent in the animation. Unfortunately, the potential for this song and its placement as an extradiegetic portion of the narrative are never fully realized, as director Guy Ritchie and his team play with temporality in how "Speechless (Part 2)" is shot. While Part 1 is simply a monologue by Jasmine after a negative encounter with Jafar, Part 2 is shown as a moment out of time, meant to place viewers inside Jasmine's head as events around her are paused. The effect is limited, as the song itself is out of step with the original score and book, more a power ballad than something arising naturally from the soundscape created for the rest of the film. Jasmine might look like a princess from a hybridized fairy-tale world, but when singing this song, she embodies WENA notions of feminism that are constructed as directly oppositional to the culture and the laws restricting her freedom, agency, and voice. Because of this implicit cultural binary again being drawn out—much like the emphasis on Mulan's individualism in the face of a restrictive and backward culture in the 1998 animation—viewers are reminded of their position as outsiders to this world and also that what Jasmine wants most is to be more like them, to share in their values and truly achieve self-realization.

Another Arabian Night: Rebuilding Agrabah Again for the Contemporary Imagination

It is in this total context that I consider the 2019 live-action film, especially the worldbuilding executed in which to stage the narrative. The given location and the geography of *Aladdin*—the fictional city of Agrabah, located in "a place where 'winds from the East' meet 'sands from the West' "[30]—even in lyric form "calls attention to the spatial [and conceptual] relativity of the Middle East."[31] This is a story that already has a complicated history and geography. "Aladdin and the Magic Lamp" is famously associated with the Arabian Nights, but it is a Chinese story rather than an Arabic one, which became incorporated into the region's oral tradition by the fifteenth century and later appeared in textual translations in Paris in the eighteenth century,[32] and it is further set "in the

Persia of Arabian legend."[33] Aladdin has a fraught history in the so-called West through pantomime and theatrical productions, which cannot be disentangled from the Disney permutations of telling this story, whether thinking about the animated film, the stage production, television shows, the characters' presence in the parks, the live-action film, or the narrative's afterlives in the wider Disney corporate context. The Disney performance, both as animation and as live action, becomes complicit in the same orientalizing of the fifteenth and even the eighteenth centuries, relocating and rebuilding many foreign spaces into a single exoticized imaginary construction.

Spatiality discourses can contribute to a better understanding of the intersection of real-world orientalization in Disney's *Aladdin* media and fantasy world-building and the sense of "place" attributed to Agrabah. Robert T. Tally Jr. writes, "The act of writing itself might be considered a form of mapping ... even one who operates in such nonrealistic modes as myth or fantasy, must determine the degree to which a given representation of a place refers to any 'real' place in the geographical world."[34] While Tally is addressing literary constructs of space and place, this observation becomes even more poignant when it comes to not only a sense of mapping space through literary representation of physical space, real or imagined, but rather visually and aurally representing such space for audiences via stage musical, television, or film productions. Drawing from Yi-Fu Tuan's observations on how space becomes "place" once it is observed long or deeply enough to give it a particular meaning,[35] Tally continues to observe that works become "infused with the places that [they] explor[e]" and that "often, the story and the places are inextricably bound together."[36] Such observation holds no less true for Disney's many reincarnations or fantasies of Agrabah and the narratives that take place within that particular place. Arguably, with it being a constructed "world within a work of fantasy, the [viewer] is encouraged to think of these spaces as being very much real."[37] Agrabah is a construction, but also, in order to fall into the flow of song, spectacle, and narrative, to believe the so-called Disney magic spell being woven, audiences have to believe in the place as if it is as real as the proto-European fairy-tale constructions where other Disney classics are located, such as Belle's pre-Revolutionary France in *Beauty and the Beast* or, more recently, the Scandinavian-esque construction of Arendelle that shapes the *Frozen* narratives.

Phrasing such as "the Persia of Arabian legend"[38] describes a notion of geographical and historical specificity abandoned by Disney, which is not in itself necessarily a bad thing. However, it also points to a depth and nuance in construction of identity that Disney has made more difficult to contend with for those who embody such an identity because of how exactly they have abandoned that geographical and historical specificity. Just as other Disney films depict reimaginings of imaginings of other periods fleshed out with historicizing detail, so, too, does this film, albeit not as a US-centric imagining of a fantasist's Persia in the Arab imaginary but rather in the US-imperial visual language of orientalized barbarism that serves as a stand-in for nuanced representation of the various peoples who call that region of the world their home. The temporal constructions of Westernized history demand a Eurocentric point of view that positions everything in relative geospatial temporalities to Europe, and later, the anglophone world. Such construction has also flattened and merged the specific regional histories of Iran/Persia, Iraq, Kuwait, Syria, and India. Discussions about the animated *Aladdin* move between vague descriptors of "Middle Eastern" cultural representation and more firm standpoints of "the Arab world," revealing a lack of recognition that these are both generalizations that are then broadly applied to the diverse peoples and cultures of that region. It seems almost accidental that this derivation of a story from the Arabian Nights, located in a derivation of Baghdad, does pick up on one of the threads inherent in the original source—"the culture of medieval Baghdad"[39]—though it does not deploy anything further in terms of tapping into the rich material of the underlying source narrative.

This remains a problem in the live-action remediation. Disney's *Aladdin*, in all its iterations, fails to use the same historicism that marks its European-rooted medievalist fairy-tale and folkloresque narratives. Historicity left its mark on the quasi-medievalist spaces of *Beauty and the Beast*, *Maleficent*, and *Cinderella*, and those same medievalist impulses need to be considered in terms of both iterations of *Aladdin*. What I explore here is how specific historicizing details—whether building shapes and architecture, names, or landscape—were deployed to evoke not a realistic depiction of a medieval-era Middle Eastern kingdom but what Disney's target audience would find believable in such a geographically and temporally located imaginary space. The distinction between realistic and believable is an important component of Disney's fantasy-building and world-making ethos. In the Disney+ documentary series following the making of *Frozen II*, the co-head of effects animation Marlon West frames the discussions that inform animation detail decisions by saying, "We don't do realism here, we do believability."[40] Such a statement begs the question, believable to whom? Disney's foray into more diverse storytelling via what bell hooks termed "the commodification of Otherness"[41] as a way of maintaining its hegemonic power and positioning needs to be directly understood as undergirding its construction of other worlds, of depicting the other; the company's *Aladdin* productions' deployment of varying types of orientalism are normative in Disney's place-making strategy, not the exception.

Considering the widely publicized use of the Oceanic Story Trust in the making and marketing of *Moana*, it is interesting that the remediation of the animated film that first generated a political response in the Disney Renaissance period was handled with the same apparent level of research that was invested in the 1998 animated *Mulan*, which is to say, a token level. In the promotional material surrounding *Mulan*, the producers and animators emphasize research trips to China to inform the making of the film but never really go beyond the idea of what an authentic ancient China might look like to a Western or specifically US-based audience. Similarly, the live-action *Aladdin* trades strongly on ideas of what WENA or US-centric audiences will read as authentic, rather than building a true sense of culture into the landscape of its reinvention of Agrabah. But Ritchie's presentation at best corrupts the narrative by attempting to root something set in the Middle East while drawing poorly from both Bollywood theatrical aesthetics and Moroccan architectural aesthetics. In the process, the live-action *Aladdin* also turns to brownface for extras. The use of brownface exhibits how weak the WENA imagination is when it comes to any sensibility of the vastness of the worlds it tries to compress into a limited understanding of the Middle East in which it effaces all brown people from a vast region through equivalency.

Effacement is different from erasure, which Disney is certainly guilty of as well. Instead of simply not representing a group of people or erasing them from the consciousness of its productions, effacement limits and defines how individuals of various backgrounds might be interpreted and classified by those who would largely only encounter them through media. I use the term "effacement" to refer to a thinning out or a disappearing of something here, not by not representing it but by forcing pluralities of identities and experiences to fit a singular representation or belong in a singular space. Effacement thus describes what Disney has done to the Middle East, North Africa, and the Indian subcontinent, in the particular kind of orientalizing and exoticizing present in both *Aladdin* film productions and other related media. Despite burgeoning and growing film industries in India, Iran, and across the Middle East and North African (MENA) countries, all of which have had their own successes with building fantasyscapes full of influences from across the old paths of the Silk Road, the 2019 live-action remediation of *Aladdin* instead chose to build a medievalized, orientalized fantasyscape whose moves toward alleged better representation instead promulgate the same old problematic stereotypes and results yet again in a faux "Middle East" once again poorly constructed by "the West."

The live-action *Aladdin* is more re-creation than reimagining, but in such a way that could be best thought of as what Pete Kunze has referred to as a "cleaned-up palimpsest."[42] From its opening frame to its attempted course correction in the characterization of Jasmine and attempts to apparently walk back the whitewashing of the animated film in the casting of the narrative's heroes, Disney has attempted surface-level fixes to the problems flagged in the animation both at its release and in criticism in the intervening years, while still sticking as closely as possible to scene-by-scene replication of iconic moments with some additions to the narrative. However, in looking at the world-building, the musical numbers, and some of the casting controversies, it becomes more apparent that the attempt to deconstruct the orientalism of the previous iteration, despite some progress, does not quite hit the mark.

From the opening, this is not the *Aladdin* of 1992. Smith is a merchant about to tell two children on a ship the story of "Aladdin and the Lamp." From that introductory frame tale, mirroring the merchant gambit performed by Williams in 1992, the song "Arabian Nights" begins. This version is drastically changed in lyrics, with the opening stanza reading, "Oh, imagine a land, it's a faraway place / Where the caravan camels roam / Where you wander among every culture and tongue / It's chaotic, but, hey, it's home."[43] The lyrics continue with references to flying carpets, bazaars, spices, silks, dreams, and trade roads, even framing a plot point of the narrative itself with the added stanza "There's a road that may lead you / To good or greed through / The power your wishing commands," before referencing darkness, the potential for finding fortune, the idea that one's destiny is one's to control, and then also making reference to what Jafar is looking for at the beginning of the film: a "diamond in the rough" to open the Cave of Wonders.

This runs at a different meter from the rest of the song as a bridge before returning to the recognizable refrain that sets the heavily orientalized and exoticized scene.

Despite the addition of the harbor to recast Agrabah as a multicultural stop on a Silk Road–esque trading route, which could also be used to explain the magpie approach to cultural appropriation deployed in the film, the net effect is an amalgamation of the Middle East and South Asia that ultimately feels more like the orientalized pantomime of the eighteenth century. The Middle East and South Asia have been folded together beyond the animation, transplanting a Taj Mahal–inspired castle out of Agra, India, and into an Iraq-like desert. This is made apparent through the various paratextual materials released by Disney, including interviews with those working on the film. The Walt Disney Studios promotional video "World of Aladdin" includes sound bites describing a "team of cultural advisers" per director Ritchie, shooting in Wadi Rum, Jordan, and production designer Gemma Jackson's multiple influences incorporated into the set building of Agrabah. Producer Dan Lin describes the decision to shoot "on location" as a step taken to make sure the studio was "as authentic as possible," but the clip ends there, never clarifying exactly what the film is being authentic to. Lin says that "our world of Agrabah is truly a global trading port, heavily influenced by Arabia, but also influenced by other neighboring cultures as well."[44]

The historicism of Disney's medievalist remediations of the proto-European fairy tales was signaled by details corresponding to specific historical periods. Historicizing details here are tied to implications of geography rather than time, because in the invented kingdom of Agrabah, time, or temporal location within a specific flow of history, matters less than the indication of "where." This is the orientalism of *Aladdin* narratives fully realized in the contemporary. The invented, exotic location is not one that can be fully reconciled with WENA constructions of temporality because it breaks the magic of the exoticized construction, which must exist out of time for it to remain believable to a part of the world that cannot and does not grapple well with the real region's more complex history, and to do so would unseat its own concept of its own supremacy. Agrabah is constructed based on stereotype, with "authentic" details chosen to address the gaze of WENA cultures, even while it effaces genuine representation through the construction of an imaginary region, separate from its other temporally located fantasies that, if being truly historical, would exist in a parallel temporality.

The geographically situated historicism comes to bear in the construction of the sets, which were predominantly built on soundstages in the UK, as well as the backlot of Longcross Studios.[45] These draw influences from souks in Marrakech and Burmese monasteries, as well as historically orientalized depictions that signal "Persia" or "India," layered together. Jackson has spoken about the vastness and depth of the sets made to aid in the construction of the story's worldbuilding across several interviews and about the decision by the film ultimately not to film on location in Morocco or use a "real" location for the fictional city. Her statements on the matter include: "In the end, I think it's great that we didn't because I think I was freer just to pull things from where I wanted them, I didn't just have to be Moroccan, I could go anywhere I liked in my imagination"; "I loved Iznik ceramics, I love Turkish and Persian miniatures ... there's the Orientalist paintings that I used, a lot of the Victorians used to go on those wonderful journeys and do these fabulous paintings stuffed full of detail"; and "the reference that I had was a real mishmash—obviously you can't lift anything directly or you'll get done by everyone right, left, and center so you have to steal a bit of this, a bit of that and a bit of the other, and mix it up and make it your own."[46]

There is a lot to unpack in those statements from people at the production level of the film who are responsible for film and narrative as concept and realizing it for the viewer. On the surface, this is another iteration of the Disney marketing pattern: signaling research done without defining what exactly is "authentic" about the film or the narrative told. There is also the question of what it means to be "influenced by Arabia." The term "Arabia" properly refers to a geopolitical designation of the Arabian Peninsula, made up of the countries of Saudi Arabia, Oman, Qatar, Kuwait, Yemen, and the United Arab Emirates, and it also includes Bahrain, the Socotra Archipelago, and several other islands. To use such a nonspecific geopolitical designation as the root of the film's inspiration displays the deployment of orientalism rather than research-driven improvement in world-building. Most concerning, in some ways, is Jackson's lack of reflexivity over her statements regarding her influences and how these statements alone demonstrate a certain centering of the construction of otherness from the perspective of someone who exercises control over the shaping of culture on a global stage. Jackson's sources seem to be primarily her imagination or elements of a mixture of cultures, regardless of whether these influences are geographically or culturally aligned with producer Lin's statement about being inspired by "Arabia." The elision of Turkish ceramics (Iznik ceramics) with "Turkish and Persian" miniatures, along with "Orientalist paintings" and "Victorian paintings," speaks more to how this part of the world is constructed in this production designer's perception than to research that would have yielded, perhaps, a different texture to the world-building of the film. Pulling details from already orientalized depictions and folding together South Asian, Persian, and Arab cultures does not provide more broad and accessible representation but rather does not let any of these cultures see a recognizable reflection of itself.

The goal, then, for Disney is neither historical accuracy nor cultural accuracy but rather to capture what Martha Bayless refers to in her discussion of the Disney castle as a marker of historicity as a "history-flavored Otherworld,"[47] with a slightly different "flavor" from its usual fare, or believability over realism, with no further thought given to who, in fact, "authenticates" that "flavor" for the masses. The historicism of specific details that ratify the expression of the Disney fairy-tale mode becomes more complex and complicated when also dealing in postcolonial temporalities, and the WENA positionality of the corporation cannot be overlooked or understated. Such elision might not matter when presenting this othered world-building to Disney's core audience base; however, as the corporation has gone even more global in terms of both its target audiences and the kinds of materials it produces, such acts are far more noticeable. There is also a lack of reflexivity in Jackson's statement that she could not "just lift anything directly" without realizing that the "mishmash" she describes is still appropriative and still decontextualizes cultural elements by placing them outside their proper contexts. This is perhaps most disappointing because while this is Disney's first attempt at a live-action depiction of this narrative and WENA film and theater are peppered with orientalized versions of this story, there do exist other versions of this kind of fantasy space from Bollywood and other film industries from the part of the world Disney is struggling to depict, and plenty of experts know how to do this "authentically"; they just seem to have not been employed here. The disconnect between "research" and cultural knowledge becomes almost hypervisible in the musical sequences.

The "A Whole New World" end-title duet and the "Friend Like Me" reprise, along with the other musical sequences, further complicate the pastiche of research. In 1992, a version of "A Whole New World" by Peabo Bryson and Regina Belle was featured as the end title. This version, known as "Aladdin's Theme" on the film album, topped the US charts in 1993 and went on to win several awards. The song took on a life outside the confines of the film itself, becoming a love ballad in its own right, with covers produced both by Disney properties and by fans. In the 2019 remediation, "A Whole New World (End Title)" is sung by British-Pakistani former One Direction boy-band member Zayn Malik and a relatively unknown singer, Zhavia Ward. The song itself was updated to reflect a twenty-five-year shift in pop music, but it also includes instrumentation at the beginning and end of the track to audibly orientalize what was a solidly American Broadway musical genre piece of music, even considering the end-credit version performed by Bryson and Belle. Tapping Malik as the male voice of the ballad, an internationally recognizable "diverse" face, is in line with other casting decisions for the film. However, when considering the co-casting of Ward, things become complicated. Ward was born Carisa Zhavia Vercetti, and she is, at face value, a white woman from California who sports blond dreadlocks and engages in significant cultural appropriation and apparent Blackfishing.[48]

It seems a misstep to put so much energy into promoting the "authenticity" of the remediation of *Aladdin* and then not follow through on all the details, especially when there is an established talent industry in the region that Disney is claiming to be honoring in this film. This is emblematic of a surface response to how diversity or multiculturalism is conceived of in the film—and more widely by Disney. In this presentation of otherness, Disney thought through the process part of the way in tapping Malik but did not think of the full effect of the rest of the choice. In a similar vein, where the remediation dropped the uses of "Allah" peppered throughout the animated film, the "Friend Like Me" reprise that is used as the end credit includes a Bollywood-esque dance number in which many characters take their bows, and Smith and DJ Khaled instead pepper this number with "Habibi," a term of endearment used across the Arabic-speaking world.

The "Friend Like Me" reprise is also one of three musical numbers that include what looks somewhat like a Bollywood dance. It is one of four dance-themed numbers: "Friend Like Me" in the Cave of Wonders when Aladdin releases the Genie from the lamp, the "Prince Ali" sequence, the dance shared by Jasmine and Aladdin at the palace, and the end-credit dance sequence. "Friend Like Me" is a theatrical showstopper, true to the film's Disney and Hollywood heritage. The other three musical numbers, however, engage in a decontextualization of Bollywood theatrical elements, specifically in terms of their costuming and choreography. Bollywood itself is a "homogenized label ... imposed on Indian films by western critics in an example of cultural relativism."[49] Bollywood is a space where in a globalized world, a part of the Indian diasporic community can locate this particular film industry as a "form of cultural resistance to the imperialist dominance of Hollywood on a global scale,"[50] even as the term itself "denies the diversity of film genres that are made in the subcontinent in a range of languages, and instead privileges the formulaic, Hindi film-musical."[51] It is that formula that Disney's 2019 *Aladdin* plays with, blending it with the American musical-theater understanding more central to its own playbook. However, Disney doesn't quite mediate the differences between the two, depending on particular choreography that has become more recognizable in WENA countries thanks to productions such as *Slumdog Millionaire* and its "Jai Ho" sequence and performances on series such as *So You Think You Can Dance*. Two of the most obvious signals of the commodified construct of "India as a fetishized commodity"[52] deployed in *Aladdin* are the use of belly dance and a particular kind of movement known as "tutting," the articulated use of the limbs in geometric and angled shapes reminiscent of the forms seen in hieroglyphics, which have become emblematic of performing "Bollywood" in the West—something that Proma Khosla notes "only gained popularity in the last century."[53]

Khosla also notes that beyond the choreography itself, which "whittle[d] these art forms down to what the West already recognizes of them" and "repackaged only the most harsh, angular movements," the staging of the musical numbers is out of place, "shot so that the dancers move faster than most human being are physically capable of doing" while still being "shockingly low-energy, with the most offensive choice being to not fill the frame within an inch of its life."[54] This is most apparent in the "Prince Ali" sequence, where the wide shots of the market from above highlight the empty space rather than filling the screen. A similar technique is used in the scene where Jasmine and Aladdin dance at the party hosted by the Sultan in the palace, which utilizes social belly dance. But despite the opportunity to draw from a range of Middle Eastern, East African, or Indian folk dances that are done in circular formations, such as *dabke*, *līwa*, or *garba*, the scene fails to do so,[55] nor does it use the choreography itself to build chemistry between the two leads. Through these sequences, Disney enacts the performance of "what the West recognizes" as being "Bollywood" as a hallmark of Indianness or South Asian culture. In that reproduction, the claim to authentic representation becomes more stilted.

As a point of contrast, the Hindi version of this film included a song by artist Badshah titled "Sab Sahi Hai Bro," which loosely translates to "all right, bro," released on Disney India's television and online channels to promote the film. The music video for this song features scenes from the film cut together with those of the artist accompanied by backup dancers and has a completely different feel from the Bollywood-esque scenes in the film. In fact, it displays almost completely opposite sensibilities, trading Ritchie's wide shots, sped-up frame rates, and emphasis on harsh, angular, and inhuman choreography for much closer framings where the dancers and movement fill the screen.

While the choreography looks far simpler, it is impeccably articulated in unison and fits into the larger picture being created.[56] This video brings to light the very distinct differences between something being generated from within a particular culture and something being made to look like it came from a particular culture.

Bollywood as an identifier of Indianness is not limited to Disney's deployment or US cultural production. Daboo explores the "very simplistic equation in the UK," where India equals Bollywood, which can lead to an expectation from the hegemonic ideology of the mainstream theater audience and industry that if there is something onstage that comes under the heading of Asian/Indian, then this must mean an incorporation and presentation of Bollywood. Therefore the performance will be a piece of colorful entertainment, with high-energy song-and-dance numbers wrapped in an exotic masala-flavored theatrical experience.[57]

Accepting the assertion that "higher-profile shows create discourse at a national level ... which also shapes identity"[58] has implications for Disney's cultural positioning as an international corporation using a deployment of Bollywood-esque elements while engaging in simultaneous local, global, and glocal identity projection in a production like *Aladdin*. Rather than being a nostalgic space of diasporic identity formation, the use of Bollywood elements to cement the South Asian aspect of the Silk Road–inspired fantasyland of Agrabah becomes the method by which Disney meets hegemonic expectations for what a South Asian–inspired fantasy should look like. Simultaneously, such rooting allows the corporation to avoid more nuanced interweaving of otherness that might require more work on the part of the audience, sidestepping the problem of representing Arab culture as the root inspiration of Agrabah altogether.

Who Can Represent Whom? Racial Ambiguity and Casting Controversies

The film also courted casting controversies, namely, Naomi Scott's casting as Jasmine and alleged use of brownface for the extras. Jasmine is meant to be a Middle Eastern or Arab princess, but Scott herself is half South Asian, half Caucasian. Such casting raises concerns about that idea of effacement, that all brown people are somehow the same, and it also calls into question the idea of a US-corporation-produced "hybrid Middle Eastern–South Asian world."[59] Disney's vice president of multicultural engagement Julie Ann Crommett said of the decision to cast Scott:

> [T]here was a real intention for Agrabah to become the center of the Silk Road and reflect the diversity and movement of what we can loosely construe that time period to have been, which was a golden age as well for the region.... [T]here are South Asian individuals who associate with Aladdin and with Jasmine as well, and I think there was a sense of we should reflect some part of the community in the principal

cast so that we're actually being inclusive of who sees themselves and identifies with this text.[60]

Crommett displays the problem with Disney's continued reliance on racial and ethnic ambiguity in live-action casting, "where ethnic or racial differences are subsumed or represented as unimportant and inconsequential"[61]—in this case, using ambiguous brown bodies to stand in for all brown bodies of an ill-defined region, something that Angharad Valdivia identified as the "fourth stage of representation" or "ambiguous or hybrid representation," where "easily identifiable ethnicities are replaced by one or more ambiguous bodies that can sign in for more than one ethnicity."[62]

Ironically, or perhaps sadly, in the case of the live-action Jasmine, the reception illustrates the gap between corporate intention and real-world impact, where people who fundamentally do not understand what it is at stake when it comes to demands for better representation act as experts and try to find simple solutions that are easily read as surface-level pandering to multiple groups. People find themselves in productions because a twisted mirror is better than no mirror at all, but this has less to do with some universal appeal of the character of Jasmine and more to do with the lack of other options for people of other backgrounds to find themselves reflected in Disney's fantasy spaces and fairy-tale narratives. Crommett continued:

> What we've done intentionally with Naomi's character as part of the plot is that her mother is actually from a different land, and it's very clear in the movie that her mother is from a different land that's not Agrabah and that's drawing on a lot of her motivations in terms of how she sees the future of Agrabah as a welcoming place that embraces people from other places because her mother was from somewhere else. And we felt that was really important for so many reasons to speak to the idea of trade, intersectionality, intersectional identity, as part of the broader Arab experience and South Asian experience by extension ... that opens up a really beautiful conversation and I think nods to all the different audiences who possibly saw themselves in the original animated film.[63]

In such a statement, Crommett continues to reflect both a misunderstanding of why so many different audiences "possibly saw themselves" in the animated Aladdin and a very shallow understanding of the term "intersectionality" at a time when its use was rising in popular discourses without any of the context of legal framework that undergirded its coinage by Kimberlé Crenshaw[64]—perhaps reflecting the danger of concepts from critical race theory being embraced without proper education regarding their contexts in capitalist spaces. Intersectionality is not something that can be imposed; intersectional identities are inhabited and negotiated on a day-to-day basis and are not automatically projected through a mixed-race character who is still supposed to somehow serve as the only representative princess for an entire region with pluralities of cultures within it.

This is not the first time the broader corporation had cast an actress of South Asian heritage as Jasmine, as Karen David played her for the incorporation of Agrabah into

Once Upon a Time. However, the Walt Disney Studios paratextual material that was released accessibly to the public on YouTube did not itself specify exactly to what the world-building was being authentic. Instead, explicit references to things like "the Silk Road" and "hybrid Middle Eastern–South Asian" came in interviews for more tabloid-esque publications, resulting in a nonspecific glossing over of a very diverse part of the world. While on one hand people of diverse backgrounds might find themselves in this film in a way they had not found themselves in a Disney production before, it is still a construction of a part of the world for a specific audience, and it still performs an act of effacement. Crommett's commentary on the region, while being problematic in its unrooted deployment of the social-justice and Black feminism-driven language of intersectionality, also sidesteps the issues of Disney solely trying to redeem itself from the errors made in its prior iteration of the story in terms of how it depicted Arab culture. As Farid-ul-Haq notes regarding the blending of South Asian and Middle Eastern culture: "Why is Disney doing this to a movie which would have helped with Middle Eastern representation in Hollywood? ... [I]t was clear Disney wasn't interested in well-written Middle Eastern representation on the big screen."[65] A more rooted sense of particularly Middle Eastern representation, with a commitment to then expanding the worlds depicted by Disney, if there was truly a recognition that those of South Asian or South Asian diaspora backgrounds are also searching for positive representation of themselves, might have been a stronger step toward better pluralistic and multivocal representation. As such, casting a Middle Eastern female lead would have taken steps to redress the orientalizing construct that is still at the heart of this Agrabah and might have provided a solution that was less a one-size-fits-all approach to brownness in the Disney universe, no matter how much the fairy-tale aspect of the narrative, its location, or Jasmine's mother being from another land was emphasized.

This orientalizing most obviously reared its head when reports arose regarding the utilization of brownface with some extras, including extra Kaushal Odedra, who spoke to *The Sunday Times* about the experience of seeing other extras lined up to "have their skin tone changed" despite shooting in London adjacent to a vast South Asian diasporic community. For Odedra, even if Disney made an effort to hire diverse extras for most of the needed cast, still having people in brownface meant that "Disney are sending out a message that your skin colour, your identity, your life experiences amount to nothing that can't be powdered on and washed off."[66] Disney asserted that this was a method only utilized "in a handful of instances when it was a matter of specialty skills, safety and control,"[67] but Donatella Galella reminds us that "racialized representation can make the spectator of color painfully conscious of racism even in anticipation of a performance."[68] Odedra's commentary stands: to imply that the film has gone to extensive lengths in terms of casting, research on the setting, and investing time in culturally specific theatrical modes in order to be authentically diverse and then not devote budget to hiring the right people for various jobs creates a situation where the corporation still does not understand portrayal of diverse identities as beyond a surface-level problem.

A Modernized Story but Many of the Same Old Problems

As seen in the context of the missteps and the focus on the image rather than the various cultural and historical contexts surrounding both the Disney production and the history of the narrative itself, Disney's live-action *Aladdin* continues to trade in stereotypes and negative fantasies. Instead of drawing from a "real" culture or series of cultures and trying to lend a narrative authenticity, the film draws from a faux construction of many interwoven cultures, which creates a problem where Disney can rely on the construct of fantasy and turn to the point that Agrabah is not a real place to combat criticism instead of acknowledging the poor reflection. After all, people are not meant to "be" from Agrabah or the fictional lands that might touch its borders, because it is fictional. In terms of being a "cleaned-up palimpsest," the question remains, "cleaned up" for whom? In whose eyes could this be considered better, and how could the film that had the most opportunities and resources to hire experts in creating this kind of fantasy world in an authentically informed way have missed those opportunities so completely? The orientalism of the old and the orientalism of the new still exist in a way that does not disrupt the problem of historicity constructed in the other fairy-tale remediations.[69] This is still a construction of a time and a place one step removed from reality but with its world-building reinforced by specific details—in this case, predominately through art, costume, aesthetic, and choreography. It still holds the same implications of empire and US-centrism. It is unclear if there is necessarily a way for Disney to deconstruct these issues from its hegemonic positioning, though Disney's most recent films continue to try.

Notes

1. Guy Ritchie, dir., *Aladdin* (Walt Disney Pictures, 2019).
2. C. Richard King, Carmen Lugo-Lugo, and Mary K. Bloodsworth-Lugo, *Animating Difference: Race, Gender, and Sexuality in Contemporary Films for Children*. (Plymouth, UK: Rowman & Littlefield, 2011), 139–140.
3. Ibid., 140.
4. Ibid.
5. Ibid., 140–141.
6. Ibid., 141.
7. Ibid.
8. Ibid.
9. Ibid.
10. Ibid., 142.
11. Christopher Wise, "Notes from the *Aladdin* Industry: Or, Middle Eastern Folklore in the Era of Multinational Capitalism," in *The Emperor's Old Groove: Decolonizing Disney's Magic Kingdom*, ed. Brenda Ayres (New York: Peter Lang 2013 [2003]), 112.
12. Karl Sharro, April 2016, https://twitter.com/KarlreMarks/status/722404296785072128.

13. Wise, "Notes from the *Aladdin* Industry," 105–106.
14. Eleanor Byrne and Martin McQuillan, *Deconstructing Disney* (London: Pluto, 1999), 74.
15. Dianne Sachko Macleod, "The Politics of Vision: Disney, *Aladdin*, and the Gulf War," in *The Emperor's Old Groove: Decolonizing Disney's Magic Kingdom*, ed. Brenda Ayres (New York: Peter Lang, 2013 [2003]), 179.
16. Ibid., 186.
17. Ibid., 190.
18. Ibid., 182.
19. Amanda Putnam, "Mean Ladies: Transgendered Villains in Disney Films," in *Diversity in Disney Films: Critical Essays on Race, Ethnicity, Gender, Sexuality and Disability*, ed. Johnson Cheu (London: McFarland, 2013), 155–157.
20. Sean Griffin, *Tinker Belles and Evil Queens: The Walt Disney Company from the Inside Out* (London: New York University Press, 2000), 141–142.
21. Emily Clark et al., "'I Wanna Be Like You': Negotiating Race, Racism and Orientalism in *The Jungle Book* on Stage," in *The Disney Musical on Stage and Screen: Critical Approaches from 'Snow White' to 'Frozen,'* ed. George Rodosthenous (London: Bloomsbury Methuen Drama, 2017), 188.
22. Sam Baltimore, "Ashman's Aladdin Archive" in *The Disney Musical on Stage and Screen: Critical Approaches from 'Snow White' to 'Frozen,'* ed. George Rodosthenous (London: Bloomsbury Methuen Drama, 2017), 206.
23. Ibid., 215.
24. Ibid., 216.
25. Clark et al., "'I Wanna Be Like You,'" 185.
26. Lynda Haas, "'Eighty-Six the Mother': Murder, Matricide, and Good Mothers," in *From Mouse to Mermaid: The Politics of Film, Gender, and Culture*, ed. Elizabeth Bell, Lynda Haas, and Laura Sells (Bloomington: Indiana University Press, 1995).
27. Paul Wells, *Animation and America* (Edinburgh: Edinburgh University Press, 2002), 103.
28. Putnam, "Mean Ladies," 155–157.
29. Melissa De La Cruz, *The Isle of the Lost: A Descendants Novel* (New York: Disney Hyperion, 2017); Kenny Ortega, dir., *Descendants* (Disney Channel, 2015).
30. Byrne and McQuillan, *Deconstructing Disney*, 75.
31. Ibid., 75.
32. Macleod, "The Politics of Vision," 182; see also Jessica Tiffin, *Marvelous Geometry: Narrative and Metafiction in Modern Fairy Tale* (Detroit: Wayne State University Press, 2009), 212–218; Cristina Bacchilega, *Fairy Tales Transformed? Twenty-First-Century Adaptations and the Politics of Wonder* (Detroit: Wayne State University Press, 2013), chap. 4; Marina Warner, *Stranger Magic: Charmed States and the Arabian Nights* (London: Chatto & Windus, 2011).
33. Macleod, "The Politics of Vision," 182.
34. Robert T. Tally Jr., *Spatiality* (London: Routledge, 2013), 45.
35. Cited in ibid., 51.
36. Ibid., 51.
37. Ibid., 148.
38. Macleod, "The Politics of Vision," 182.
39. Warner, *Stranger Magic*, 8.
40. Marlon West, in "Big Changes," *Into the Unknown: Making Frozen II*, season 1, episode 4 (Disney, 2020), https://www.disneyplus.com/video/789ad3c5-d782-4814-94fa-4b9667fa44b0.

41. bell hooks, "Eating the Other," in *Black Looks: Race and Representation* (Boston: South End Press, 1992), 21.
42. I owe this phrase to a talk delivered by Pete Kunze at the University of Cambridge on May 27, 2020. Themes from that talk are reflected in Peter C. Kunze, "Revise and Resubmit: *Beauty and the Beast* (2017), Live-Action Remakes, and the Disney Princess Franchise," *Feminist Media Studies* 1 (2021): 121–136, https://doi.org/10.1080/14680777.2021.1944259.
43. Alan Menken, Benj Pasek, and Justin Paul, "Arabian Nights," *Aladdin: Original Motion Picture Soundtrack* (Walt Disney Records, 2019).
44. "Disney's Aladdin: 'World of Aladdin' Special Look," Walt Disney Studios, May 16, 2019, https://www.youtube.com/watch?v=-GUrDu_duuE.
45. Ra Moon, "Where Was Aladdin Filmed? The Magical City of Agrabah and the Desert of Wadi Rum," Atlas of Wonders, May 25, 2019, https://www.atlasofwonders.com/2019/05/aladdin-agrabah-filming-locations-wadi-rum.html.
46. Piya Sinha-Roy, "How Agrabah Was Brought to Life in Disney's Live-Action *Aladdin*," *Entertainment Weekly*, May 16, 2019, https://ew.com/movies/2019/05/16/aladdin-production-design-agrabah/.
47. Martha Bayless, "Disney's Castles and the Work of the Medieval in the Magic Kingdom," in *The Disney Middle Ages: A Fairy Tale and Fantasy Past*, ed. Tison Pugh and Susan Aronstein (New York: Palgrave Macmillan, 2012), 40.
48. "Blackfishing" is a term attributed to Wanna Thompson describing public figures altering their appearances to look Black or mixed-race. See Pippa Raga, "Newcomer Zhavia Ward Comes from a Family of Musicians and Influencers," Distractify, May 9, 2019, https://www.distractify.com/p/zhavia-ward-mom-bobbi-jo-black; Taylyn Washington-Harmon, "What Is Blackfishing and Why Some People Do It," Health.com, August 17, 2020, https://www.health.com/mind-body/what-is-blackfishing.
49. Jerri Daboo, "One under the Sun: Globalization, Culture and Utopia in Bombay Dreams," *Contemporary Theatre Review* 15, no. 3 (2006): 331.
50. Ibid.
51. Ibid.
52. Ibid., 332.
53. Proma Khosla, "The Dancing in 'Aladdin' Is an Excruciating Missed Opportunity," Mashable, May 27, 2019, https://mashable.com/article/aladdin-dancing/?europe=true.
54. Ibid.
55. Ibid.
56. See Jeva Lange, "Aladdin Tried, and Failed, to Bring Bollywood Magic to America," The Week, May 24, 2019, https://theweek.com/articles/842888/aladdin-tried-failed-bring-bollywood-magic-america; "Aladdin: Sab Sahi Hai Bro—Badshah," Disney India, May 20, 2019, https://www.youtube.com/watch?time_continue=169&v=l5X8Hb_aNI4&feature=emb_logo.
57. Jerri Daboo, *Staging British South Asian Culture: Bollywood and Bhangra in British Theatre* (London: Routledge, 2018), 4.
58. Ibid., 7.
59. Piya Sinha-Roy, "How Disney Handled the Casting and Cultural Authenticity of Live-Action *Aladdin*," *Entertainment Weekly*, December 21, 2018, https://ew.com/movies/2018/12/21/disney-aladdin-cultural-authenticity/.
60. Sinha-Roy, "How Disney Handled the Casting and Cultural Authenticity."

61. Diana Leon-Boys and Angharad Valdivia, "The Location of US Latinidad: *Stuck in the Middle*, Disney, and the In-Between Ethnicity," *Journal of Children and Media* 15, no. 2 (2021): 218–219.
62. Angharad Valdivia, "Mixed-Race on the Disney Channel: From Johnnie Tsunami through Lizzie McGuire and Ending with the Cheetah Girls," in *Mixed Race Hollywood*, ed. Mary Bettrán and Camilla Fojas (London: New York University Press, 2008), 272–273.
63. Sinha-Roy, "How Disney Handled the Casting and Cultural Authenticity."
64. Kimberlé Crenshaw, "Mapping the Margins: Intersectionality, Identity Politics, and Violence against Women of Color," *Stanford Law Review* 43, no. 6 (July 1991): 1241–1299.
65. Farid-ul-Haq, "'Aladdin' Trailer Released! Why Is a Middle Eastern Story a Bollywood Flick?" *The Geekiary*, March 12, 2019, https://thegeekiary.com/aladdin-trailer-bollywood/61837.
66. Andy Jones, "Genie, Brown Up Some Extras for Aladdin," *Sunday Times*, January 7, 2018, https://www.thetimes.co.uk/article/genie-brown-up-some-extras-for-aladdin-z9s922xb3?wgu=270525_54264_15920677915127_cc63b365f8.
67. "Aladdin: Disney Defends 'Making Up' White Actors to 'Blend In' during Crowd Scenes," BBC, January 8, 2018, http://www.bbc.co.uk/newsbeat/article/42601893/aladdin-disney-defends-making-up-white-actors-to-blend-in-during-crowd-scenes.
68. Donatella Galella, "Feeling Yellow: Responding to Contemporary Yellowface in Musical Performance," *Journal of Dramatic Theory and Criticism* 32, no. 2 (2018): 71.
69. See Michelle A. Anjirbag, "Enter the Castle: Reiterating Medievalism in the Framing of Disney's Fantasyscapes," *Children's Literature Association Quarterly* 45, no. 4 (Winter 2020).

Bibliography

"Aladdin: Disney Defends 'Making Up' White Actors to 'Blend In' during Crowd Scenes." BBC, January 8, 2018. http://www.bbc.co.uk/newsbeat/article/42601893/aladdin-disney-defends-making-up-white-actors-to-blend-in-during-crowd-scenes.

"Aladdin: Sab Sahi Hai Bro—Badshah." Disney India, May 20, 2019. https://www.youtube.com/watch?time_continue=169&v=l5X8Hb_aNI4&feature=emb_logo.

Allers, Roger, and Rob Minkoff, dirs. *The Lion King*. Walt Disney Animation Studios, 1994.

Anjirbag, Michelle A. "Enter the Castle: Reiterating Medievalism in the Framing of Disney's Fantasyscapes." *Children's Literature Association Quarterly* 45, no. 4 (Winter 2020): 346–363.

Bacchilega, Cristina. *Fairy Tales Transformed? Twenty-First-Century Adaptations and the Politics of Wonder*. Detroit: Wayne State University Press, 2013.

Baltimore, Sam. "Ashman's *Aladdin* Archive: Queer Orientalism in the Disney Renaissance." In *The Disney Musical on Stage and Screen: Critical Approaches from 'Snow White' to 'Frozen,'* edited by George Rodosthenous, 205–220. London: Bloomsbury Methuen Drama, 2017.

Bayless, Martha. "Disney's Castles and the Work of the Medieval in the Magic Kingdom." In *The Disney Middle Ages: A Fairy Tale and Fantasy Past*, edited by Tison Pugh and Susan Aronstein, 39–56. New York: Palgrave Macmillan, 2012.

"Big Changes." *Into the Unknown: Making Frozen II*, season 1, episode 4. Disney, 2020. https://www.disneyplus.com/video/789ad3c5-d782-4814-94fa-4b9667fa44b0.

Byrne, Eleanor, and Martin McQuillan. *Deconstructing Disney*. London: Pluto, 1999.

Clark, Emily, Donatella Galella, Stefanie. A Jones, and Catherine Young. "'I Wanna Be Like You': Negotiating Race, Racism and Orientalism in *The Jungle Book* on Stage." In *The Disney Musical on Stage and Screen: Critical Approaches from 'Snow White' to 'Frozen,'* edited by George Rodosthenous, 185–203. London: Bloomsbury Methuen Drama, 2017.

Clements, Ron, and John Musker, dirs. *Aladdin*. Walt Disney Animation Studios, 1992.

Clements, Ron, and John Musker, dirs. *The Little Mermaid*. Walt Disney Animation Studios, 1989.

Crenshaw, Kimberlé. "Mapping the Margins: Intersectionality, Identity Politics, and Violence against Women of Color." *Stanford Law Review* 43, no. 6 (July 1991): 1241–1299.

Daboo, Jerri. "One under the Sun: Globalization, Culture and Utopia in Bombay Dreams." *Contemporary Theatre Review* 15, no. 3 (2006): 330–337.

Daboo, Jerri. *Staging British South Asian Culture: Bollywood and Bhangra in British Theatre*. London: Routledge, 2018.

De la Cruz, Melissa. *The Isle of the Lost: A Descendants Novel*. New York: Disney Hyperion, 2017.

"Disney's Aladdin: 'World of Aladdin' Special Look." Walt Disney Studios, May 16, 2019. https://www.youtube.com/watch?v=-GUrDu_duuE.

Farid-ul-Haq. "'Aladdin' Trailer Released! Why Is a Middle Eastern Story a Bollywood Flick?" The Geekiary, March 12, 2019. https://thegeekiary.com/aladdin-trailer-bollywood/61837.

Galella, Donatella. "Feeling Yellow: Responding to Contemporary Yellowface in Musical Performance." *Journal of Dramatic Theory and Criticism* 32, no. 2 (2018): 67–77.

Griffin, Sean. *Tinker Belles and Evil Queens: The Walt Disney Company from the Inside Out*. London: New York University Press, 2000.

Haas, Lynda. "'Eighty-Six the Mother': Murder, Matricide, and Good Mothers." In *From Mouse to Mermaid: The Politics of Film, Gender, and Culture*, edited by Elizabeth Bell, Lynda Haas, and Laura Sells, 193–211. Bloomington: Indiana University Press, 1995.

hooks, bell. "Eating the Other: Desire and Resistance." In *Black Looks: Race and Representation*, 21–39. Boston: South End Press, 1992.

Jones, Andy. "Genie, Brown Up Some Extras for Aladdin." *Sunday Times*, January 7, 2018. https://www.thetimes.co.uk/article/genie-brown-up-some-extras-for-aladdin-z9s922xb3?wgu=270525_54264_15920677915127_cc63b365f8.

Khosla, Proma. "The Dancing in 'Aladdin' Is an Excruciating Missed Opportunity." Mashable, May 27, 2019. https://mashable.com/article/aladdin-dancing/?europe=true.

King, C. Richard, Carmen R. Lugo-Lugo, and Mary K. Bloodsworth-Lugo. *Animating Difference: Race, Gender, and Sexuality in Contemporary Films for Children*. Plymouth, UK: Rowman & Littlefield, 2011.

Kunze, Peter C. "Revise and Resubmit: *Beauty and the Beast* (2017), Live-Action Remakes, and the Disney Princess Franchise." *Feminist Media Studies* 1 (2021): 121–136. https/doi.org/10.1080/14680777.2021.1944259.

Kunze, Peter C. "Why Belle Loves Books: Industrial Approaches to Children's Culture." Lecture, Centre for Research in Children's Literature at Cambridge, May 27, 2020.

Lange, Jeva. "Aladdin Tried, and Failed, to Bring Bollywood Magic to America." The Week, May 24, 2019. https://theweek.com/articles/842888/aladdin-tried-failed-bring-bollywood-magic-america.

Leon-Boys, Diana, and Angharad N. Valdivia. "The Location of US Latinidad: *Stuck in the Middle*, Disney, and the In-Between Ethnicity." *Journal of Children and Media* 15, no. 2 (2021): 218–232. 10.1080/17482798.2020.1753790.

Macleod, Dianne Sachko. "The Politics of Vision: Disney, *Aladdin*, and the Gulf War." In *The Emperor's Old Groove: Decolonizing Disney's Magic Kingdom*, edited by Brenda Ayres, 179–192. New York: Peter Lang, 2013 [2003].

Menken, Alan, Benj Pasek, and Justin Paul. "Arabian Nights." *Aladdin: Original Motion Picture Soundtrack*. Walt Disney Records, 2019.

Moon, Ra. "Where Was Aladdin Filmed? The Magical City of Agrabah and the Desert of Wadi Rum." Atlas of Wonders, May 25, 2019, https://www.atlasofwonders.com/2019/05/aladdin-agrabah-filming-locations-wadi-rum.html.

Ortega, Kenny, dir. *Descendants*. Disney Channel, 2015.

Putnam, Amanda. "Mean Ladies: Transgendered Villains in Disney Films." In *Diversity in Disney Films: Critical Essays on Race, Ethnicity, Gender, Sexuality and Disability*, edited by Johnson Cheu, 147–162. London: McFarland, 2013.

Raga, Pippa. "Newcomer Zhavia Ward Comes from a Family of Musicians and Influencers." Distractify, May 9, 2019. https://www.distractify.com/p/zhavia-ward-mom-bobbi-jo-black.

Ritchie, Guy, dir. *Aladdin*. Walt Disney Pictures, 2019. Sinha-Roy, Piya. "How Agrabah Was Brought to Life in Disney's Live-Action *Aladdin*." *Entertainment Weekly*, May 16, 2019. https://ew.com/movies/2019/05/16/aladdin-production-design-agrabah/.

Sinha-Roy, Piya. "How Disney Handled the Casting and Cultural Authenticity of Live-Action *Aladdin*." *Entertainment Weekly*, December 21, 2018. https://ew.com/movies/2018/12/21/disney-aladdin-cultural-authenticity/.

Tally, Robert T. Jr. *Spatiality*. London: Routledge, 2013.

Tiffin, Jessica. *Marvelous Geometry: Narrative and Metafiction in Modern Fairy Tale*. Detroit: Wayne State University Press, 2009.

Valdivia, Angharad N. "Mixed Race on the Disney Channel: From Johnnie Tsunami through Lizzie McGuire and Ending with the Cheetah Girls." In *Mixed Race Hollywood*, edited by Mary Bettrán and Camilla Fojas, 269–289. London: New York University Press, 2008.

Warner, Marina. *Stranger Magic: Charmed States and the Arabian Nights*. London: Chatto & Windus, 2011.

Washington-Harmon, Taylyn. "What Is Blackfishing and Why Some People Do It." Health.com, August 17, 2020. https://www.health.com/mind-body/what-is-blackfishing.

Wells, Paul. *Animation and America*. Edinburgh: Edinburgh University Press, 2002.

Wise, Christopher. "Notes from the Aladdin Industry: Or, Middle Eastern Folklore in the Era of Multinational Capitalism." In *The Emperor's Old Groove: Decolonizing Disney's Magic Kingdom*, edited by Brenda Ayres, 105–114. New York: Peter Lang, 2013 [2003].

CHAPTER 7

MUTATING STITCH: SHIFTING APPROACHES TO VOCAL PERFORMANCE AND LANGUAGE IN THE *LILO & STITCH* FRANCHISE

RAYNA DENISON

CHRIS Sanders and Dean DeBlois's *Lilo & Stitch* (2002) was made at an interstitial moment in the history of the Walt Disney Company. The film sits within a period that Chris Pallant terms "Neo-Disney," which he describes as a five-year interregnum period that became "perhaps the most consistently experimental in the Studio's history, containing a package feature, feature-length science fiction animation, and a western parody."[1] *Lilo & Stitch* was part of this transitional Neo-Disney era—one of the animated science-fiction films in Pallant's analysis—and it was also a production positioned artfully between the newly emerging norm of computer animation and Disney's long tradition of hand-drawn animation.[2] Seen in this light, *Lilo & Stitch* is a film defined by experimentation. This is especially clear in the filmmakers' approach to language and the voice, which Sanders and DeBlois use to play games with their audiences. These vocal and linguistic variances have since become a hallmark of the wider Stitch-centered franchise.

Stitch, as a character, has become a central figure in the Walt Disney Company's attempts at international collaboration, especially in East Asia. Just as the alien Stitch has traveled between cultures and even worlds, in the two decades of the character's production history, Disney's Stitch-based franchising has taken advantage of fluctuations in the company's production landscape. In particular, the franchise has mutated to foster a transmedial, cross-cultural, and polyglot approach to language and vocal performance. This chapter considers how the initial experiments with language and voice acting in *Lilo & Stitch* have since expanded across a transcultural franchise that continues to mutate its central characters and their meanings in order to engage playfully with questions of synergy, alterity, and belonging. The popularity of Stitch as a character now means that the franchise's unruly protagonist has been repeatedly reimagined in a variety of cultural settings and types of texts. Unusually for Disney, many of the adaptations of *Lilo & Stitch* have taken place within an Asian animation landscape—in terms of both production and consumption. As Janet Wasko has argued, after Disney began to conglomerate in earnest across the 1980s and into the 1990s, the company became known as "masters at business cross-fertilization, and perhaps the quintessential masters of synergy."[3] Elsewhere, Wasko argues that 1984 marked an intensification in Disney's search for synergy, when Michael Eisner was hired in from Paramount to run Disney, along with what he termed Team Disney. Wasko asserts that Eisner's strategy "emphasized corporate partnerships, limited exposure in new investments, diversified expansion, and further developed [Disney's] corporate synergy."[4] However, despite the smooth growth implied in these accounts, Disney's search for synergy has been as reactive as it is proactive. Furthermore, long after the collapse of Team Disney, the Walt Disney Company has continued to seek out new opportunities for globalizing partnerships, collaborations, and licensing opportunities all over the world. Disney has found such relationships in everything from film and television production to video games and theme parks,[5] leading the studio to become established as one of the US's leading media conglomerates.[6] Responding to these debates, this chapter questions the extent to which Disney's characters are every truly global.

Through an analysis of the approach taken to language and vocal performance in the *Lilo & Stitch* franchise, this chapter examines the tensions inherent in Disney's globalizing synergistic practices. Japan has been a key collaborator for Disney in the Stitch franchise, offering a developed market for Disney's already popular character to be redeveloped. Global localization has been judged a hallmark of Japanese transnational industrial practice since the 1990s. Koichi Iwabuchi argues that glocalization is "articulated less in association with the symbolic and ideological domination by the powerful nation-state and more with local camouflaging which smooths the economic expansion of transnational corporations."[7] The tensions between global characters and their localization for new audiences meaningfully brings the transcultural adaptations of Stitch into touch with wider debates about Disney's problematic global reach and the limits of synergy in transcultural franchising. From arguments about cultural Disneyfication to those who have critiqued Disney's attempts at representing characters from around the world, Disney has received consistent and sustained approbrium for everything from its cultural imperialism to its inauthenticity and culturally tone-deaf adaptation practices.[8] All while seeking greater levels of global reach and increased synergy.

These attempts to create synergy can be read on the surface of Disney's productions across the past three decades, and perhaps especially so in its franchise expansion texts such as direct-to-television (and home video) films and television shows. Although this chapter begins with a consideration of vocal performance in the first *Lilo & Stitch* film, subsequent films and television shows from the wider *Lilo & Stitch* franchise will also be considered too, examining how performances have changed as the franchise has been taken up in new national production contexts.

The first film in the *Lilo & Stitch* franchise follows a young Hawaiian girl, Lilo Pelekai (originally voiced by Daveigh Chase), who is being raised by her sister Nani (Tia Carrere) after their parents' death in a car accident. To help Lilo deal with her grief, the sisters adopt a "dog," actually an alien named Experiment 626 (Chris Sanders), whom Lilo renames Stitch. Stitch has escaped from his "evil genius" scientist creator, Jumba Jookiba (David Ogden Stiers, using a Russian accent), and his captors, the Galactic Federation,[9] who are intent on recapturing Stitch throughout the first film's narrative. After focusing on Stitch's original vocal performance, later sections analyze how other characters and their voice performers were used to assert the authenticity of the film's version of Hawaiian language. Thereafter, the chapter investigates how these efforts changed in the wider direct-to-television sequels as well as in *Lilo & Stitch: The Series* (2003–2006) demonstrating a push towards the margins of Disney production as the franchise expanded. The final section then examines the impact of two spin-off television series, *Suticchi!* (*Stitch!*, 2008–2011) and the more recent *Ān líng yǔ shǐ dí qí* (*Stitch and Ai*, 2017). These shows resituate Stitch away from his first Earth family in Hawaii, placing him instead in Japan (possibly in an parallel universe) and China. These spin-off shows provide a counterpoint to the franchise's depictions of Hawaiian culture and language and are indicative of Disney's ongoing, glocalizing quest for ever greater and more naturalized forms of cross-cultural acceptance of Disney products. But in undertaking these new collaborative projects, Disney also cedes some control over content, which leads to new approaches to characters and their vocal performances that can undermine Disney's attempts at synergistic franchising.

Although comparison across languages would be potentially instructive, given that *Stitch and Ai* was first recorded in English before being redubbed into Mandarin Chinese and given that it was the English dub of *Stitch!* that circulated widely outside of Japan, the focus here mainly on the English versions of these shows. The English dubs have been selected for two additional reasons. First, English is the language to which the original film defaults as a shared language understood by both *Lilo & Stitch*'s human characters and its alien ones. This places 'Ōlelo Hawai'i (Hawaiian) in the position of a second language that the alien characters must learn along with facets of Hawaiian culture. A central question therefore is how the spin-off television shows featuring Stitch play with this relationship between language and culture. Comparing English-language versions of these television programs allows this chapter to consider the impact of shifting cultural perspectives and animation production cultures on the franchise overall. Second, I want to examine how Disney works to make the vocal landscape of franchises distinct *and* consistent as they cross between cultures and languages. Previous work on Disney Character Voices International (Disney's dubbing subsidiary) has tended to focus on how the company creates new dubs as films flow from an American production center out to the rest of the world.[10] In the case of the expanded Stitch franchise, however, Disney's collaborations with animation studios in Japan and China meant that the dubbing process was as much about localizing content for the US as the other way around. For these reasons, focusing on the casting and performances of US-voice dubs for *Stitch!* and *Stitch and Ai* provides insight into Disney's approach to cross-cultural synergy.

Stitch's Industrial Voice

Deep in space, the Galactic Council's court is in session. The Grand Councilwoman asks a blue-furred, six-limbed alien creature with sharp claws, pointed teeth, and a bad attitude to tell the assembled court if there is anything good in its nature. The monster clears its throat: "*Meega, nala kweesta!*" it shouts, full of mischievous glee. As the Grand Councilwoman gasps her response, "So naughty!" the aliens around her faint dramatically, become outraged, or even, in the case of one robot Council member, lean over the bench to vomit nuts and bolts. This untranslated vulgarity is the first phrase uttered by Stitch, and it is a good example of the playful approach to language that co-creators Sanders and DeBlois set out to take with the audiences for *Lilo & Stitch* in 2002. On one level, the filmmakers' use of an invented alien language signals the cultural alterity of Stitch's speech. On another, the reactions to the phrase position Stitch as an outsider even within the construct of this alien court, where the Council uses English.

More important in industrial terms, the filmmakers deploy Stitch's invented language at times when they want to push at the boundaries of permissible "family-friendly" content in *Lilo & Stitch*. In accordance with Catherine Lester's analysis of the "impossible" genre of children's horror film, Sanders and DeBlois adapt transgressive tropes from adult-oriented genres by subtly deviating from Disney norms or becoming, "'child-friendly' by excluding—or finding strategic ways to alleviate—... elements that might be thought to distress child viewers."[11] Stitch's use of untranslated vulgarity becomes a means of alleviating the risks inherent in his profane speech, making content "impossible" in a family film accessible to *Lilo & Stitch*.

Stitch is key to understanding the kinds of boundary-pushing experimentation undertaken in *Lilo & Stitch*. Throughout *Lilo & Stitch*, Sanders and DeBlois use Stitch as a cipher for the production process itself, and his voice is the clearest evidence of their approach. An example of this is found in Stitch's insistent connection with Elvis Presley. The use of Presley's music in the film forms a more complex aspect of characterization than initially implied by its ostensibly surface connection to *Lilo & Stitch*, notably Presley's Hawaii-based films like *Blue Hawaii* (Norma Taurog, 1961), which DeBlois cites as an influence for *Lilo & Stitch*.[12] Shortly after Lilo adopts Stitch from a dog pound, she demonstrates his weirdness to her sister Nani. Lilo wakes Nani up by dragging a record player and Stitch into Nani's bedroom. She then places Stitch's claw on a record player. Lilo opens Stitch's mouth by holding on to his nose, and a metallic creak repeatedly marks the hinging action of Stitch's jaw as Lilo opens and closes his mouth. As we hear the creak, Presley's "Suspicious Minds" begins to emanate from inside Stitch. Lilo briefly closes Stitch's mouth, and the music stops, starting up again with a creak as she reopens it. Presley's singing voice is uncannily re-embodied within Stitch in these moments. Although it could generate unease about Stitch's nature Presley's reassuringly familiar voice alleviates the potential for horror in this scene.

Lilo & Stitch uses Presley's music as a dominant soundtrack element, along with a score by Alan Silvestri that combines orchestral music with a song performed by a

Hawaiian children's choir and local musician Mark Keali'i Ho'omalu. Using Presley's music, which Disney does not own, was a departure from the studio's extensive history of using in-house or hired-in composers to pen the popular music that appears in its animated films. As James Bohn argues, even from its earliest decades, Disney animation was "created using a system that put music at the center of the filmmaking process," called prescoring, which afforded the studio's composers "nearly the entire time from early production planning to the final mixdown to compose, fine-tune, and perfect their work."[13] Where Silvestri's score is normally nondiegetic, adding affect to scenes, the use of Presley's music is differently integrated into Lilo & Stitch's soundtrack. Presley's songs continually shift from diegetic appearances, like the one described above in which Stitch becomes a record player's speaker system, to nondiegetic uses of Presley songs that comment on the content of specific scenes. In an instance of the latter, Stitch is required to become a "model citizen" by social worker Cobra Bubbles (Ving Rhames), and Lilo introduces Stitch to Presley as an exemplar of American citizenry. In an extended montage, Presley's "Devil in Disguise" plays as Stitch's attempts to impersonate Presley go awry, repeatedly ruining Nani's attempts to find a new job. The sequence culminates in a beach performance that takes the nondiegetic song and weaves it back into the diegesis. In the scene, Stitch plays a refrain from "Devil in Disguise" on a guitar while wearing an Presley wig and a rhinestone jumpsuit. Stitch's comparative inarticulateness means that he never sings Presley's songs in his own voice, miming instead or playing guitar along with them. Instead, the character's association with Presley's music becomes a way for the filmmakers to vocalize his alterity, while simultaneously giving voice to Stitch's inner thoughts and motivations. In this respect, Presley's preexisting songs become variants of the uses of musical tropes that defined the Disney Renaissance's Broadway-inspired musical dramas.[14] The alignment of Stitch with Presley's songs marks an experimental departure from the norms of the Disney musical in Lilo & Stitch but still layers a singable soundtrack with associative meanings as a significant aspect of Stitch's characterization.[15]

The use of music to articulate Stitch's feelings and behavior is indicative of a shifting verbal tapestry woven around the character. Sanders and DeBlois have stated that they originally intended Stitch to be a silent protagonist. When promoting the film, DeBlois stressed the connections between Stitch and Disney's tradition of "silent" animal stars, invoking the title characters of Dumbo (Ben Sharpsteen, 1941) and Bambi (David Hand, 1941) as Stitch's inspirations.[16] Stitch thereby functions as a callback to past Disney characters and traditional forms of American cartoon animation through his comparative *lack* of voice.

However, the need to voice Stitch became clear as the film entered production. Sanders recalls: "As we pitched the early storyboards, I would just give that character that voice. It's a voice that I would use to call people on the phone and annoy them. It was just this dumb voice I used from time to time when it felt right."[17] Sanders also remembers, "We thought, Oh my God, we can't get into a thing where we've got a real actor and we're like, 'No, could you just make a bunch of dumb noises?' You just know that suddenly Stitch would be making all these speeches."[18] With this in mind, DeBlois persuaded Sanders to continue to use his "annoying" Stitch voice in the finished film—a nasally inflected, higher-than-normal, back-of-throat pattern of speech that stands out in the film's diegesis as neither human, "ordinary" alien, nor animal. A. O. Scott of the *New York Times* noted in 2002 that Stitch "sounds like Donald Duck doing an impression of Toshiro Mifune."[19] Scott's observation about the mixing of vocal tones in the performance of Stitch forces attention back onto *Lilo & Stitch*'s interstitial position in Neo-Disney's animation, in this instance mashing together references to a classic Disney animated character with the voice of one of Japan's most famous actors in order to make sense of the inherent incongruity and cultural conflations at work in Sanders's vocal performance of Stitch, as well as within the film's wider diegesis.

But Sanders's performance as Stitch is also animalistic. The reframing of Stitch as a pet dog adopted by the Pelekai family limits the amount of spoken dialogue given to Stitch in Sanders and DeBlois's original film, despite how quickly the character picks up phrases in English and Pidgin Hawaiian once he crash lands in Hawaii. On meeting Lilo in the dog pound, Stitch attempts to copy Lilo's cheerful greeting, answering her with a stilted, elongated "ha'ai" before being told by Nani that dogs don't talk. Subsequently, Stitch reverts largely to animalistic noises, including a wide array of growls, mutters, chuckles, and faux barks spoken in front of human authority figures. However, Stitch's language changes when speaking with Lilo and other alien characters, interspersing these guttural noises with "alien" nonsense language and more short words and phrases in English and Pidgin Hawaiian.

A ready example of this hybrid approach to vocalization and multiple languages can be found toward the end of film, after Lilo is captured and taken into space by Galactic Federation representative Captain Gantu (Kevin Michael Richardson), who is trying to recapture Stitch. In the scene, Stitch has escaped, but Lilo remains in peril. Nani confronts Stitch about being an alien after he is recaptured by his creator Jumba Jookiba and "Earth expert" alien Agent Pleakley (Kevin McDonald). Nani sobs after being told Lilo is gone for good, and Stitch approaches her, repeating a refrain from the film that the sisters say to each other:

> Stitch (labored): *O'hana* means family. Family means . . .
> Nani: . . . nobody gets left behind.
> Stitch: Or forgotten. Yeah. . . . Hey! [Speech continues rapidly in alien without translation.]
> Jumba: What?! After all you put me through, you expect me to help you just like that? Just like that?!
> Stitch: 'e.
> Jumba: Fine.
> Pleakley: Fine? You're doing what he says?
> Jumba: Well, he's very persuasive.

The playfulness at work in Stitch's vocal performance is shown in these fast shifts in tone from Stitch's labored attempt to communicate with Nani to his short but rapid-fire speech to Jumba. The film's message is clearly relayed by Stitch and Nani, who come to an understanding through the repetition of Lilo's mantra about o'hana. Then, to shift tone and generate humor, Stitch's alien speech gains meaning and intelligibility only through Jumba's response to it. As becomes normal within the franchise, the meaning of Stitch's speech is revealed through the responses of other characters, mostly alien characters like Jumba, who act as interpreters for Stitch on behalf of the audience and other humans. More significantly, where Stitch has only limited communication abilities in English and Hawaiian, he is revealed to be far more articulate in his native language. In this, the performance by Sanders plays to issues of cultural understanding, reflecting upon the film's wider themes about finding home and family. The use of key phrases in Hawaiian exemplifies the way *Lilo & Stitch* finds authenticity in the local, exploring its core themes through indigenous Hawaiian culture.

ALTERITY AND ATTEMPTED HAWAIIAN AUTHENTICITY IN *LILO & STITCH*

Reflecting upon *Lilo & Stitch*'s themes of family creation and Hawaiian culture, Emily Cheng has argued that Stitch's transition from alien menace to

> object/dog to productive family member (the images during the credits show Stitch doing the family's household chores, such as cooking and laundry) signifies the trace of the other in both family and nation, as his role now resonates with histories of laboring alien bodies central to Hawai'i's development as a state.[20]

Stitch's domestication, in Cheng's reading, becomes emblematic of wider concerns she holds regarding the troubling representation of Polynesian people in *Lilo & Stitch*. Cheng connects the need to contain and "civilize" Stitch as a cipher for the "alien threat to the U.S. nation-state staged in the Pacific and as a threat to civilization itself."[21] As with Stitch's vocal performance, therefore, Sanders and DeBlois's attempts to consider a variety of otherness (a broken family, space aliens masquerading as human on Earth, the reliance of Hawaiian civil society on tourism, and the commodification, and even "Disneyfication," of Hawaiian culture)[22] reveal tensions between the mainland US culture and its connections to indigenous island cultures in Hawaii. The representation of Lilo's indigenous family is core to expressing these tensions, as Nani is shown working in various aspects of Hawaii's tourist and service industries. However, although *Lilo & Stitch* provides representation for aspects of Hawaiian culture from hula to surfing, it is through its embrace of Pidgin Hawaiian language that the film attempts to forge its deepest connections to this island state of the US, emphasizing local speech patterns and bringing in concepts such as *o'hana* as central storytelling elements. Colleen Montgomery has highlighted the problematic power differences within the French

Polynesian dubbing process for the more recent Disney film *Moana* (John Musker and Ron Clements, 2016).[23] As Montgomery has asserted, there is a wider tone-deafness to Disney's relationship with Polynesia. For instance, Disney's lack of consideration can be seen in the absence of a Hawaiian-language dub for *Lilo & Stitch*.

This is despite the filmmakers' repeatedly assertions about the importance of Hawaiian culture to *Lilo & Stitch*'s production. The production team spent time in Hawaii, and they talk about their desire to represent Hawaiian culture accurately and sensitively in the making-of videos for *Lilo & Stitch*. This was particularly the case for hula. In a report on the film's twentieth anniversary with Hawaiian-born voice star Carrere, Sanders attests:

> [S]ome people treat hula as this sort of silly thing. *Gilligan's Island* [1964–1967]. They'll dress up in hula skirts and do some sort of mockery of the hula—that's how Hollywood has treated it. What we learned very quickly from everybody we were consulting with is you don't do that.

Carrere adds, "Well, it's a storytelling device, and there are certain schools of hula from different *kumus*, the teachers that handed it down. It's very much a special and very particular art form."[24] Sanders and DeBlois relied heavily on this kind of local interlocution in the promotion for *Lilo & Stitch*, and Carrere repeatedly fulfilled this legitimizing function. On the level of Hawaiian cultural practices like hula, Carrere's commentary often works to add nuance to the explanations of indigenous Hawaiian culture provided by Sanders and DeBlois. In the exchange quoted above, for instance, Sanders argues that they were attempting to redress wider representational insensitivity enacted by past Hollywood films about Hawaii, while Carrere explained how a more authentic hula tradition might be presented.

Carrere's most significant contributions in this manner come in her comments about *Lilo & Stitch*'s voice-recording process. In the same anniversary interview, she states:

> When I first met with Chris and Dean, they said, "Well, you're from Hawaii. What do you think about the story?" I said, "Well, how do you feel about Pidgin?" It's such a particular cadence of speech. All the different ethnicities—Filipino, Chinese, Japanese, Portuguese, Hawaiian—all worked on the plantations together, and they couldn't speak each other's languages, so they put together Pidgin English, which is made up of broken words and phrases of all the different languages. Chris and Dean said, "How do you want to infuse it into the character?" I said, "Well, I wouldn't want it to be too strong where the viewer can't understand. Just a bit of Pidgin, to infuse that character with authenticity." I was so happy that they were open to that.[25]

Carrere's suggestion of using Pidgin Hawaiian to legitimize vocal performances raises darker aspects of Hawaiian history, without overtly referring to Hawaii's history of indentured immigrant labor or slavery.[26] Instead, Carrere sets up the distinctive commingling of languages that has come to define local Hawaiian dialect and language as a positive and inclusive way for the filmmakers to incorporate Hawaiian culture into *Lilo & Stitch*. However, she demurs about fully embracing Hawaiian language. Instead, the Pidgin Hawaiian that Carrere recommends sits at a nexus point between Hawaii's complex transcultural history and the language and culture of its native population. Carrere goes from star voice actor to cultural expert and adviser in this speech, though she is not ethnically Hawaiian. Carrere's lived understanding of Hawaiian culture and her instinct to introduce Pidgin Hawaiian commingle in her commentaries, providing a significant additive performance of Hawaiian culture to the film's promotion. Therefore, Carrere authenticates the film by adding local performance cadences as well as language elements to naturalize representations of local Hawaiian communities in *Lilo & Stitch*. But she does so as a means of gently redressing past representational errors, rather than providing an accurate or complete entry point into authentic Hawaiian culture.

This legitimating lens includes Carrere's performance of the famed Hawaiian song "Aloha 'Oe" ("Farewell to Thee") by Lili'uokalani, which Carrere-as-Nani sings when Cobra Bubbles threatens to separate the Pelekai sisters. Describing this sequence of events, Sanders remembers:

> So when Nani sings "Aloha Oe," she's saying goodbye to her sister, but she's not really facing up to it. That worked beautifully for the film. If it hadn't been for Tia, who was the right voice, who was Hawaiian, who was perfect for the role, and who helped to bring that into the whole story [sic]. A great actor, who is right for the role, will change the course of the film.[27]

Whether a convenient fiction to justify the inclusion of Hawaiian culture's most recognizable song or more sincerely meant, Sanders's version of *Lilo & Stitch*'s production history places Carrere at the heart of *Lilo & Stitch*'s creation. Hers becomes one of only three prominent Hawaiian voices in the film's promotion (the other two being costar Jason Scott Lee and musician and hula expert Mark Keali'i Ho'omalu), all of whom take on the burden of authenticating *Lilo & Stitch*'s version of Hawaii. In doing so, the promotional narrative around the film works to create an impression of depth and engagement with Hawaiian culture on the part of the filmmakers, playing an obfuscatory game that hides the limited participation available to local Hawaiian communities in the creation of *Lilo & Stitch*.

By comparison to Sanders and DeBlois's presentation of Stitch as a voice that comes directly out of the film's production culture, then, the inclusion of authentic Hawaiian language and voices in the film came comparatively late in the planning stages (though the original voice tracks were recorded early in the film's production). These differing approaches to language and voice in *Lilo & Stitch* can therefore be read as coming to illustrate the tensions between the local and the corporate, challenging both the filmmakers' and the Walt Disney Company's claims to be seeking out authentic forms of representation.

Mutating Approaches to Voice and Language as *Lilo & Stitch* Goes beyond Cinemas

Sanders and DeBlois only directed the first *Lilo & Stitch* film. When it was released, there was some question from the press about the film's economic potential. Russell Smith, reviewing the film for the *Austin Chronicle*, for example, wondered about *Lilo & Stitch*'s likelihood of success given that "[t]here's no trace of wearisome CGI wonders, no market-tested outrageousness, no hope whatsoever of the lucrative creative/marketing 'synergy' we've come to expect from the Disney juggernaut."[28] In contrast to expectations, however, when *Lilo & Stitch* proved to be one of the most successful films of the Neo-Disney era (earning more than $270 million on release), a franchise was quickly unspooled around it.[29]

In part, the surprise at *Lilo & Stitch*'s success is a reflection of the film's alterity within Disney's wider production culture. The film was created outside of Disney's usual animation production studio in Burbank, California. Instead, *Lilo & Stitch* was made at the short-lived Walt Disney Animation Florida, situated inside Disney's MGM Studios theme park, where (in the Florida studio's original building) visitors could watch animators at work as part of their theme-park experience.[30] Sanders and DeBlois made *Lilo & Stitch* after having scripted the hit film *Mulan* (Barry Cook and Tony Bancroft, 1998) at Walt Disney Animation Florida. In fact, the pair continued to work at Walt Disney Animation Florida even after *Lilo & Stitch*, starting their own production company, Stormcoast Pictures, to make live-action and animated films.[31] Sanders and DeBlois worked at Walt Disney Animation Florida until Disney closed the studio in the middle of their next film, *A Few Good Ghosts*, which has not subsequently been completed.[32] At Disney's Florida studio, *Lilo & Stitch* was always already at the margins of Disney animation, geographically and corporately. Perhaps as a consequence, *Lilo & Stitch* was also made with a more restricted budget than other Neo-Disney films[33] and with a visual aesthetic more in keeping with Sanders's personal character design style, rather than those associated with Disney.[34] This distance from the center of Disney's animation production in California has resulted in a long-term discourse about *Lilo & Stitch*'s separation from the norms of Disney production.[35] Further, the initial film's financial success ensured that Sanders and DeBlois's distinctive sound design and aesthetic would live on in the extended franchise.

With Sanders and DeBlois busy with their next film production, Disney looked to capitalize on the box-office success of *Lilo & Stitch* by creating a franchise using patterns similar to those of previous hits of the Disney Renaissance period. Despite sequels and franchising being common practice at the Walt Disney Company from the 1990s onward, Pallant remains one of the few to elucidate the relationship between Disney's tent-pole animated feature films and its direct-to-television (DTV) and direct-to-video (also described in the trade press as DTV) sequels. Pallant calls this Eisner's "spin-off strategy": "During Eisner's reign, it was common practice for at least one straight-to-video sequel to be produced following the success of a major animated feature," beginning with a sequel to the blockbuster *Aladdin*, called *Aladdin: The Return of Jafar* (Toby Shelton, Tad Stones, and Alan Zaslove) in 1994.[36] More recent work on Disney franchising has taken up this cause, comparing originals to their wider franchises, but this scholarship tends to analyze Disney's recent cycle of "live-action" remakes rather than attending to DTV sequels and television shows.[37]

Direct-to-television sequels and animated television shows, as Pallant notes, have played significant roles in extending the commercial and cultural presence of Disney's biggest animated blockbusters. Jason Scott's analysis of Disney's post-1984 home-video production practices explores how the corporation's Buena Vista Home Entertainment subsidiary has "served to Disneyize home entertainment, through appropriation, hybrid consumption, and branded experiences" of Disney home-video content.[38] Scott contends that shifting home-video technologies across the 1980s and 1990s allowed Disney to continually re-exploit its library of films, while also producing expansion texts that cemented audience preferences for "franchised" brands based on popular Disney animated films and characters. For *Lilo & Stitch*, Sanders and DeBlois stated that Disney had begun production of the sequel and a connected television show within months of the film's original release. In an interview in December 2002, Sanders said:

> There's a weekly TV series for Saturday morning, to be shown next year, and there's also a direct-to-video sequel. Both will take up where the film ended and continue the story, which is natural given the original film is almost a prequel to the rest of the characters' lives. We've brought this family to a point where they're going to hang together.... The spin-offs explore something we were never able to explore with our film.... We felt strongly that *Lilo and Stitch* [sic] could lend itself to other things, so we started working with the spin-off guys quite a bit before the film was released. In animation terms, this is coming out at blinding speed![39]

Sanders's sense of *Lilo & Stitch* as a starting point for a larger network of texts decenters his blockbuster film within its own emerging franchise. Sanders works to refine the core identity of *Lilo & Stitch* away from questions of local and indigenous representation in this statement. Additionally, the creators of the original were able to continue exerting control over aspects of the franchise's content, and even its performances by working with, as Sanders puts it, the "spin-off guys."

This control was exercised for at least *Lilo & Stitch*'s initial DTV sequels and spin-off television show. In addition, there has also been a separate DTV sequel, which more properly functions as a midquel. First into production was *Stitch!: The Movie* (Tony Craig and Bobs Gannaway, 2003), which functions as a feature-length pilot episode for *Lilo & Stitch: The Series* (2003–2006), the final feature-length story for which is a further DTV sequel titled *Leroy & Stitch* (Tony Craig and Bobs Gannaway, 2006). This first strand sequel production was made under the auspices of Tony Craig and Robert "Bobs"

Gannaway at Walt Disney Television Animation. The television program was developed by Gannaway with Craig and Jess Winfield for that same corporate division of Disney. This part of the franchise follows Lilo and Stich's continuing adventures in Hawaii, where they find, name, and rehabilitate Jumba's experiments after the aliens' dehydrated pods are accidentally released across the Hawaiian islands. In this, *Lilo & Stitch: The Series* shares much in common with other adventure-driven, girl-centered television animation of the period, although, as Katia Perea observes, the DTV franchising begins a trend in which "Disney reminds us that boys are supposed to be fans of Stitch not Lilo."[40] The series does so by focusing on Stitch's ever-widening family of "cousins," shifting focus toward the alien, rather than human, components of the franchise. It is also, however, worth noting that the franchise's merchandising has long favored Stitch over Lilo.

In terms of voice performances, the introduction of new alien experiments in the films and episodes of this first strand of *Lilo & Stitch* franchising resulted in new variants on Stitch's "alien" vocal performance. Some experiments, like Experiment 625 (named Reuben by Lilo in *Leroy and Stitch*, performed by Rob Paulson),[41] are able to speak English fluently, whereas others, like Angel (Tara Strong), who becomes Stitch's love interest, mirror Stitch's speech patterns. By comparison with these more complexly verbose aliens, others like Experiment 221/Sparky (Frank Welker)—the first alien experiment released in *Stitch!: The Movie*—speak only a few words. Sparky, for example, mostly communicates through hisses that align with his electrically charged nature and character design. This places the alien experiments at the core of the franchise's linguistic experimentation, as animators work to differentiate and vary characters across dozens of television episodes. In this regard, *Lilo & Stitch: The Series* has more in common with "collector"-style narratives like those found in *Transformers* (1984–1987) or *Pokémon* (1997–), rather than with other girls' adventure animation.[42]

The animators use a range of tools to achieve these goals. Sometimes they emphasize elements like character design gimmicks (for instance, Experiment 608/Slugger, whose tail is like a baseball bat, voiced by Frank Welker), sometimes they use sound effects (as with Experiment 032/Fibber, who make a buzzer-style noise when the characters around him lie), and sometimes human or alien voices are used to create a pantheon of likable aliens with active roles to fulfill in Hawaiian society. Focusing on these alien experiments generates animation experiments, too, wherein voices and animation add variety and scope to the world that Sanders and DeBlois originally built for *Lilo & Stitch*.

Sitting off to one side was a more direct midquel to the original film, which was called *Lilo & Stitch 2: Stitch Has a Glitch* (Michael LaBash and Tony Leondis, 2005). As this suggests, there were two separate production teams working near-simultaneously on the *Lilo & Stitch* franchise as it expanded. *Lilo & Stitch 2: Stitch Has a Glitch* was directed by Tony Leondis and Michael LaBash at DisneyToon Studios in Australia. This separation of sequel production across two international sites and studios has generated a loose approach to temporality within the franchise, bunching DTV film and television narratives into a compressed temporal period following the end of the original film. Neither straightforwardly serial production[43] nor preplanned transmedia storytelling,[44] therefore, the quickly expanding *Lilo & Stitch* universe might be more accurately thought of as a more complexly tiered or multistrand franchise.

Quoting Sharon Morrill, then president of DisneyToon Studios in Australia, commentator Joe Strike writes about how this division of labor in Disney's DTV sequel production has tended to produce confusion rather than synergy:

> The overlapping output from the TV group sometimes results in, if not dueling, then overlapping sequels. Case in point, "*Stitch Has a Glitch* is my movie, but it's not based on the TV series where Stitch has all the experiments," [Sharon] Morrill explains. "*Glitch* is really a sequel to the feature film."[45]

The idea of overlapping texts compressing sequel time is a hallmark of two aspects of Disney DTV franchising: first, how important the first film in a Disney franchise remains even as a corpus of new texts are created around it; and second, that franchising is a less tightly restricted aspect of Disney animation production than it might initially appear when viewed in the light of synergy. In situating *Lilo & Stitch 2: Stitch Has a Glitch* as the "true" sequel to the original film, Morrill also lays claim to prominence for her own studio within Disney's wider production firmament. Seen in this light, Morrill's assertion of official sequel status for *Lilo & Stitch 2: Stitch Has a Glitch* is indicative of the way Disney's canon building around blockbuster animated hits can become the subject of corporate retconning born of internal competition between divisions.

This intra-franchise competition for status adds further layers to the tensions between consistency and innovation in the *Lilo & Stitch* franchise, ones that can be heard in the vocal tracks of its texts. The *Lilo & Stitch* franchise is remarkably consistent in the retention of its original cast of voice actors across these differing strands of production. However, there are a couple of overt signs of conflict caused by overlapping productions. For example, for *Lilo & Stitch 2: Stitch Has a Glitch* in 2005, Daveigh Chase's Lilo was replaced by the voice of rising star Dakota Fanning, but only for that single film.

Chase reappeared in the franchise in 2006, performing Lilo once again in *Leroy & Stitch*. Otherwise, the only major absence in the regular franchise cast has been Jason Scott Lee, who only appears as the voice of Nani's would-be romantic partner, David Kawena, in *Lilo & Stitch* and *Lilo & Stitch 2: Stitch Has a Glitch*. Lee's absence from the larger part of the *Lilo & Stitch* franchise is significant in that the Hawaiian star actor was replaced by voice actor Dee Bradley Baker, rather than with another Hawaiian performer. Baker does an imitation of Lee's original vocal performance in his parts of the franchise, using similar lilting cadences. In doing so, Baker's imitation obscures the absence of Hawaiians in the first strand of the Stitch-based franchise.

Lee's absence aside, the main cast remains comparatively consistent, including the retention of prominent star cast members like Carrere but also Sanders, who has worked on other high-profile animation directing projects concurrently with his continuing vocal performances as Stitch. This voice cast committed not just to film and DTV films but also to *Lilo & Stitch: The Series*, which ran between 2003 and 2006. As the franchise shifted narrative format between film and serial television production, only Ving Rhames stepped away from his role as social worker and former CIA agent Cobra Bubbles. The intensity of *Lilo & Stitch* productions between 2002 and 2006 and the consistency in its voice-casting practices are significant for what these productions suggest about Disney's approach to franchising—not least, that when it comes to DTV sequels and television, aurally there is little internal hierarchy between media formats. This seems to be a consequence of placing the initial DTV sequels and *Lilo & Stitch: The Series* under the control the Walt Disney Television Animation unit, indicating that content for television was a driving force for Disney franchising practices in the mid-2000s. Moreover, Disney's retention of the original film's cast ensures both canonicity and quality markers in the face of tighter budgets and production schedules for television animation.

However, the need for long-form storytelling and extensions to the original narrative did alter the approach to language as the franchise developed. New erasures and experiments emerge in this franchising process. In one significant example, the end theme song for *Stitch!: The Movie*, "Aloha E Komo Mai," was composed and written by Mark Hammond, Danny Jacob, and Ali B. Olmo and performed by Stitch Sanders and the Christian pop group Jump5. Entirely non-Hawaiian in its creation, this theme song marks a departure from the initial blockbuster film's insistence on including local musical talent from Hawaii. Additionally, the song mixes Stitch's "alien" language with phrases in Hawaiian and English, which creates an equivalence between Hawaiian and alien languages for non-Hawaiian-speaking audiences. While English phrases in the song act as partial translations of the Hawaiian-language content, the admixture of Stitch's alien speech and Hawaiian muddies the waters of potential cultural comprehension.

Though problematic in terms of authentically representing Hawaiian culture, "Aloha E Komo Mai" reappears in truncated form as the opening theme song for *Lilo & Stitch: The Series*, where it plays at the beginning of every episode, making no distinction between Stitch's invented language and Hawaiian-language lyrics. The song even reoccurs in the last film in this part of the franchise, closing *Leroy & Stitch*. The repetition of "Aloha E Komo Mai" across the franchise becomes emblematic of a shift away from the discourses around inclusion heard from Carrere and others in relation to the first film. But more than this, the insistent repetition of "Aloha E Komo Mai" signals deliberate exoticization of Hawaiian language in later parts of the *Lilo & Stitch* franchising soundscape. Cheng argues that this accords with a touristic version of Hawaii in the *Lilo & Stitch* franchise that "rests on the exoticization but also the containment of difference as well as historical memory."[46] As with Carrere's softening of Hawaiian history around the first film, the use of music in the wider franchise suggests not just exoticization and containment of difference but additionally, and even more problematically, the conflation of Hawaii with the fantastic.

Where Hawaii becomes increasingly exoticized and commodified by turns in the *Lilo & Stitch* franchise, Stitch's alien language has become more codified. Repetition and constant need for interpellation and translation from other alien characters like Jumba and Pleakley have given linguistic structure to Sanders's originally improvised dialogue as the films and series have progressed. In a post on social-media site TikTok, Sanders recently revealed that it was *Lilo & Stitch: The Series* that gave Stitch's invented language a name, Tantalog, and that it was the television show that began to codify and regularize the language's uses and meanings. Sanders has refused, however, to translate Stitch's most famous phrase, "*Meega, nala kweesta!*" re-proclaiming its extremity, despite the fact that it has been regularly and repeatedly uttered by multiple characters across the franchise.[47]

This move toward intelligibility has the obvious benefit of helping to regularize and streamline performances (for example, allowing repeated use of previously recorded lines of dialogue). Making Stitch more comprehensible also lessens his (and other Tantalog-speaking villains') potential threat level, indicating that the show's demographic was skewing toward younger age groups as time went on. Giving Stitch's Tantalog a name and his words implied meanings is, therefore, a sign of the kinds of domestication that Cheng cites as problematic in relation to otherness, as it requires Stitch to conform to normalizing linguistic rules.

Lilo & Stitch 2: Stitch Has a Glitch offers a departure from these trends. The film reintroduces Hawaiian hula culture as a central theme, using the untranslated word *kumu* as an honorific for Lilo and Stitch's hula teacher. In addition, the film uses sound as well as animation's plasmatic potential to announce Stitch's titular "glitch." When his goodness levels drain away, Stitch's eyes turn luminous green, and his body rapidly and elastically pulls into alternative shapes and sizes. In these moments, Stitch's voice is reduced guttural noises. But these noises are sped up and slowed down intermittently, exaggerating Stitch's devolution to the animalistic and indicating his struggle to maintain control over his body. The film relates this vocal shift to Stitch's origins in Jumba's laboratory, as we are shown Stitch's creation in flashback.

In the laboratory, Stitch's origins are marked by cute whimpers, but these are quickly followed by more threatening growls and then Tantalog that Jumba does not translate. By taking Stitch back to these precivilized, less intelligible, and more "alien" utterances, the midquel becomes aurally distinctiveness within the wider franchise. Subsequent moments of glitching contrast between Stitch's "civilized" and glitching forms by contrasting uses of voice. When his normal self Stitch becomes more articulate in English, for example telling Lilo, "No, he's not" when Lilo thinks the spirit of Presley is telling them to do a hula dance about a chicken. A few moments earlier, in a laundromat where Presley once washed his underwear, Stitch glitches, voiced with a high-pitched, cackling laugh. In this way, the film separates Stitch's characterization into two performances, each with its own individual performance aesthetic, in which the aural is as significant as the visual. In these ways, *Lilo & Stitch 2: Stitch Has a Glitch* returns to an earlier moment in the franchise in order to rethink the central characters' storytelling potential and in doing so adds variety and scope to the vocal performance landscape of the franchise.

From Hawaii to Asia: Remaking *Lilo & Stitch*

After 2006, there was a break in the film and television franchising afforded to *Lilo & Stitch*. Although the franchise also took in theme-park rides and video games, the main franchise drew to a close with *Leroy & Stitch*. However, in the years that followed, Stitch returned in two non-Disney television series, *Stitch!* and *Stitch and Ai*. The former resituates Stitch in Japan, while the latter moves him to China. More than this, though, the productions were moved abroad, with *Stitch!* being animated by Japanese studios Toei Animation and Madhouse (and, later, Shin-Ei Animation)[48] and *Stitch and Ai* being produced in China by Anhui Xinhua Media and Panimation Hwakai Media. Both shows were made in the later part of the 2010s, and both focus on Stitch's adventures with new female friends in Asian countries. In Japan, Stitch joins Yuna Kamihara's household, and in China, he joins Ai Ling Wang's family. Besides stylistic shifts in the aesthetics of the franchise, which align more closely with Japanese anime and China's emergent three-dimensional CG productions (though *Stitch and Ai* remains largely two-dimensional), the major shift in the shows is the introduction of new local cultures.

One reason to focus on the English translations is that it becomes possible to see how these two later shows work to introduce and naturalize their distinctive cultural landscapes. The production of *Stitch!* offers an inherently transcultural and transindustrial interpretation of the *Lilo & Stitch* franchise. Made in Japan under the auspices of the newly formed Walt Disney Japan, forged out of the merger of multiple subsidiaries, *Stitch!* was Disney's first foray into collaborative production with Japan's thriving anime industry. On top of this, *Stitch!* has been proclaimed by Walt Disney Japan's then-president Paul Candland as a personal reflection on the time he had previously spent in Okinawa.

Candland argues that the show's catchphrase, "*Icharibachōdē*," was drawn from the time he spent working on the Okinawan island. Candland further contends that the use of Okinawa as a setting and this catchphrase, meaning "We are brothers when we meet," were intended to rehabilitate Okinawa's postwar reputation. Journalist Tomoko Ishizuka writes:

> Not just in Japan, but also in America, Okinawa has been remembered as a sad place where large numbers of American and Japanese soldiers died. However, he [Candland] realized after living there that it is a place filled with beautiful nature and populated by warm-hearted people.[49]

Stitch! tackles the delicate task of rehabilitation by introducing a pantheon of (mostly invented) *yōkai* characters whom Stitch and Yuna learn about and work with to improve their town's lot throughout the series.

Yōkai is a difficult term to define (making it an ideal corollary for the franchise's growing and varied alien creatures) but can be understood as a pantheon of what Michael Dylan Foster refers to as "ghosts etc.,"[50] often linked to the Shinto religion in Japan but more widely cited as folkloric creatures. In *Stitch!* Yuna and Stitch learn about these supernatural creatures from Yuna's grandmother, who frequently emphasizes the importance of balance between the local human culture and the forest surrounding their island community on Okinawa. The choice of Okinawa, as with Hawaii, thereby places the story world on the margins of Japanese culture and in a place with its own traditional culture separate from the rest of Japan.

Similarly, *Stitch and Ai* sees Stitch crash land in the mountainous Huangshan eastern region of Anhui in China after he is captured by an alien species called Jaboodies. The location once again separates Stitch from urban spaces, and a major threat in the show is Ai Ling's aunt's threats to remove Ai Ling from her sister's care (similar to Lilo and Nani's situation in the first film), taking Ai Ling away from her mountain home to the city. In another overt repetition of previous franchise content, *Stitch and Ai* sees Stitch having prophetic dreams, and in "The Scroll" (episode 4), he travels with Jumba, Pleakley and Ai Ling to a shrine where they receive ancient scrolls that depict monsters. Thereafter, Stitch has to avoid the villainous Jaboodies and Wollagongs, both of whom want to weaponize him, while attempting to follow the scrolls and solve their mysteries. In their differing ways, each of these shows works to introduce traditional aspects of their respective East Asian cultures, commingling these with space adventures to enhance the cross-cultural spectacle.

Each treats language in its own ways. In *Stitch!* Stitch becomes more articulate in English (and Japanese) than in previous texts in the franchise. This helps to ameliorate cultural differences being explained as the series unfolds while enhancing Stitch's aural presence in the show. The contrast is purposeful and grounded in the need to differentiate Stitch's alien presence from the indigenous *yōkai*. However, the character's increased levels of verbal fluency in English are also a product of anime's normal use of high levels of dialogue. The extensive dialogue in anime has emerged as a trope in the wake of cost-saving limited animation early in Japanese anime history.[51] By comparison, the Stitch of *Stitch and Ai* is less verbose and more prone to shifting between languages as he interacts with characters from differing backgrounds. Stitch speaks more English with Ai, for example, and more Tantalog with Pleakley and Jumba, as was the case in the earlier *Lilo & Stitch* television franchise. The Japanese *Stitch!* therefore acts as an outlier in the franchise, shifting Stitch closer to the norms of anime and away from Disney animation.

Tellingly, these later cross-cultural adaptations also marked the departures of the main voice cast. None of the stars who had performed in the earlier parts of the franchise returned for the Asian-produced sequel series, and were replaced by professional voice actors. For example, voice actor Ben Diskin steps into the role of Stitch in both *Stitch!* and *Stitch and Ai*. Diskin works across the US animation and video-game industries but, significantly in the case of *Stitch!*, has also performed high-profile roles in US dubs for anime, including *Blood+* (2007–2008) before *Stitch!* Diskin has also performed in a plethora of subsequent high-profile anime dubs, from the English dub for *Sailor Moon* (2014–2018) to Netflix and Sanrio's *Aggretsuko* (2018–2023). Diskin's hiring by Disney Character Voices International to appear as Stitch in both of these Asian series is indicative of the way Disney seeks to stabilize transcultural interpretations of its characters, even after their initial performers move on. The only character whose voice actor had a significant link to the preceding franchise was Jumba Jookiba, as Winfield continued as the character after appearing in both *Stitch!* and *Stitch and Ai*. Winfield seems to have taken on the role of Jumba in the wake of Stiers's ill health in the mid-2010s. In addition, Winfield had helped to write and develop *Lilo & Stitch: The Series* before stepping into this role, creating an industrial link back to the earlier part of the franchise.

Shifting toward professional voice actors, away from more star-studded casts, is an obvious cost-saving maneuver. But the shift in casting the two later television shows relating to Stitch is also suggestive of franchise maturity, inasmuch as the original voice performances had become so well known that soundalike performances would suffice for these spin-offs. Diskin and Winfield both, for example, use similar vocal tics, and even accents, to those of their franchise predecessors. Winfield's faux-Russian accent is the more contentious, suggesting a more generalized "speciesist" approach to characterizing the aliens in the wider Stitch-based franchise. Much as Thomas Lamarre argues (following John Dower) that animal characters have been used to propagandistic ends, there has been a "persistence of this racial consciousness and racial typology whenever human animals are depicted as nonhuman animals."[52] This persistence of typology begins in the franchise built around *Lilo & Stitch* with the performance of Jumba as a Russian-inflected "evil genius" scientist. Far from the franchise's opening claims to inclusivity, therefore, the lingering use of accents among antagonist characters in the wider Stitch-based franchise suggests that old political rivalries linger on in its aggressive alien forces. Moreover, these are not straightforwardly US antipathies, as the Antipodean-inspired Wollagongs from *Stitch and Ai* seem to reflect political rivalries nearer to the domestic Chinese market than the American one.

Conclusions

The recently announced "live-action" version of *Lilo & Stitch* has officially resecured Sanders's participation as Stitch.[53] In this manner, the *Lilo & Stitch* franchise has come full circle, placing the central character's performance back into the control and voice of its creator. With the production already struggling to assert its authenticity amid controversies surrounding actors and their connections to Hawaiian culture, Sanders's return to the franchise performs a steadying function, while also ensuring a continuity that belies the adaptive jumps this franchise has taken from feature animation to television-driven productions and back to feature (with CG animation) live-action performances.

The dominance of television animation in Disney's franchising practices for animation is, in no small part, a consequence of the Walt Disney Company's globalizing reliance on television broadcasting practices, seen first in satellite and cable Disney channels and now refracted through the streaming-platform lens of Disney+. One surprising consequence of Disney+ as a platform and consolidator of Disney animation franchising, however, is the inconsistent acknowledgment of Disney's cross-cultural search for ever-expanding possibilities of synergy. Depending on where you watch, the later cross-cultural Asian collaborations spinning off from *Lilo & Stitch* can vanish from sight. On Disney+ *Stitch!* and *Stitch and Ai* turn into ephemeral, ghostly franchise texts, in much the same way that they rely on local folklore for their fantastical, supernatural content.

Nevertheless, as represented to global audiences, the franchise lives on, however partially, as a dramatic reminder of Neo-Disney's experimental attempts to engage with peoples, languages, and cultures marginalized within their respective nations. These representations have subsequently been used as educative tools for wider English-speaking cultures, with whom games of recognition and obfuscation are played in order to familiarize global audiences with these non-English-speaking cultures.

Across the franchise, Stitch has been both remarkably experimental and yet unmutated as a result. Always an outsider and linguistically shifting to suit local animation industry requirements, Stitch is a useful signifier of glocalization. At the same time, however, Sanders's ongoing performance as Stitch in the main franchise has allowed the character a consistency. It has ensured that even the increasingly condensed variations on the original themes of *Lilo & Stitch* have remained coherent.

Where mutation has occurred within the franchise is in its wider cultural messaging, inclusive at one moment, culturally appropriating in the next. By examining the Stitch-based franchise's more recent texts, moreover, we can see how transnational adaptations of even Disney's films focused on America's margins can result in problematic representations of perceived cultural others. Language and vocal performance in the *Lilo & Stitch* franchise challenges us to examine approaches to character and performance diachronically, as shifting adaptation practices and transcultural interpretations can significantly mutate even Disney's most emphatically consistent characters.

Notes

1. Chris Pallant, *Demystifying Disney: A History of Disney Feature Animation* (London: Bloomsbury Academic, 2013), 125.
2. Famously, *Lilo & Stitch* makes use of Disney's tradition of watercolor background paintings, not seen since *Dumbo* (1941), but it also utilizes computer-generated animation, seen most clearly in the film's (and later franchise's) space vehicles.
3. Janet Wasko, *Understanding Disney: The Manufacture of Fantasy* (Cambridge: Polity, 2001), 36.
4. Janet Wasko, "The Walt Disney Company," in *Global Media Giants*, ed. Benjamin Birkinbine, Rodrigo Gomez, and Janet Wasko (New York: Routledge, 2016), 12.

5. Mike Budd and Max H. Kirsch, ed., *Rethinking Disney: Private Control, Public Dimensions* (Middletown, CT: Wesleyan University Press, 2005); Pallant, *Demystifying Disney*; Robert Alan Brookey, *Hollywood Gamers: Digital Convergence in the Film and Video Game Industries* (Bloomington: Indiana University Press, 2010), 89–109.
6. Wasko, "The Walt Disney Company," 11–25.
7. Koichi Iwabuchi, *Recentering Globalization: Popular Culture and Japanese Transnationalism* (Durham, NC: Duke University Press, 2002).
8. For examples, see Budd and Kirsch, *Rethinking Disney*.
9. Sometimes also referred to as the Galactic Alliance within the franchise, whose military arm is the Galactic Armada.
10. Colleen Montgomery, "From Moana to Vaiana: Voicing the French and Tahitian Dubbed Versions of Disney's *Moana*," *American Music* 39, no. 2 (Summer 2021).
11. Catherine Lester, "The Children's Horror Film: Characterizing an 'Impossible' Subgenre," *Velvet Light Trap* 78 (Fall 2016): 34.
12. Cited in Bilge Ebiri, "An Oral History of *Lilo & Stitch*," Vulture, October 19, 2022, https://www.vulture.com/2022/10/an-oral-history-of-lilo-and-stitch-a-hand-drawn-miracle.html.
13. James Bohn, *Music in Disney's Animated Features:* Snow White and the Seven Dwarfs *to* The Jungle Book (Jackson: University of Mississippi Press, 2019), 4.
14. Peter C. Kunze, *Staging a Comeback: Broadway, Hollywood, and the Disney Renaissance* (New Brunswick, NJ: Rutgers University Press, 2023).
15. For more on Disney musicals and their stage adaptations, see George Rodosthenous, ed., *The Disney Musical on Stage and Screen: Critical Approaches from* Snow White *to* Frozen (London: Bloomsbury, 2017).
16. Jerry Beck, "Disney's Magic Returns: *Lilo & Stitch*," Animation World, June 20, 2002, https://www.awn.com/animationworld/disneys-magic-returns-lilo-stitch.
17. Russell Subiono, "Celebrating 20 Years of 'Lilo & Stitch' in Hawai'i with Creator Chris Sanders," *The Conversation*, Hawai'i Public Radio, July 12, 2022, https://www.hawaiipublicradio.org/the-conversation/2022-07-12/celebrating-20-years-of-lilo-stitch-in-hawaii-with-creator-chris-sanders.
18. Ebiri, "An Oral History of *Lilo & Stitch*."
19. A. O. Scott, "Film Review: Escaping Deep-Space Exile and Making Friends in Hawaii," *New York Times*, June 21, 2002, https://www.nytimes.com/2002/06/21/movies/film-review-escaping-deep-space-exile-and-making-friends-in-hawaii.html.
20. Emily Cheng, "Family, Race and Citizenship in Disney's *Lilo & Stitch*," in *Monsters and the Monstrous: Myths and Metaphors of Enduring Evil*, ed. Niall Scott (New York: Brill, 2007), 130.
21. Ibid., 124.
22. Shunya Yoshimi, "Japan: America in Japan/Japan as Disneyfication: The Disney Image and the Transformation of 'America' in Contemporary Japan," in *Dazzled by Disney: The Global Disney Audiences Project*, ed. Janet Wasko, Mark Phillips, and Eileen R. Meehan (Leicester: Leicester University Press, 2001).
23. Montgomery, "From Moana to Vaiana."
24. Tia Carrere and Chris Sanders, in Ebiri, "An Oral History of *Lilo & Stitch*."
25. Carrere, in ibid.

26. For more, see, for example, Jessie G. Lutz, "Chinese Emigrants, Indentured Workers, and Christianity in the West Indies, British Guiana and Hawaii," *Caribbean Studies* 37, no. 2 (July–December 2009).
27. Sanders, in Ebiri, "An Oral History of *Lilo & Stitch*."
28. Russell Smith, "Lilo & Stitch," *Austin Chronicle*, June 21, 2002, https://www.austinchronicle.com/events/film/2002-06-21/142169/.
29. Recent reporting has made much of *Lilo & Stitch*'s $270 million plus global box office. See, for example, Zach Sharf, "'Lilo & Stitch' Director Got 'Frustrated' by 'Frozen' Praise: We Did Sisterhood over Romance First," *Variety*, June 22, 2022, https://variety.com/2022/film/news/lilo-stitch-director-frustrated-frozen-1235300612/.
30. Cole Delaney, "'Lilo & Stitch' at 20: Directors Chris Sanders and Dean DeBlois Reunite (Video Interview)," Cartoon Brew, June 22, 2022, https://www.cartoonbrew.com/interviews/lilo-stitch-20th-anniversary-deblois-sanders-218046.html.
31. Leigh Godfrey, "*Lilo & Stitch* Creators Launch Own Production Company," Animation World, November 27, 2002, https://www.awn.com/news/lilo-stitch-creators-launch-own-production-company.
32. Ebiri, "An Oral History of *Lilo & Stitch*."
33. Chris Pallant, "Neo-Disney: Recent Developments in Disney Feature Animation," *New Cinemas* 8, no. 2 (2010): 103–117.
34. Beck, "Disney's Magic Returns."
35. Andrew Osmond, "Lilo & Stitch Revisited: Part 1," Animation World News, December 31, 2002, https://www.awn.com/animationworld/lilo-stitch-revisited-part-i.
36. Pallant, *Demystifying Disney*, 83.
37. Peter C. Kunze, "Revise and Resubmit: *Beauty and the Beast* (2017), Live-Action Remakes, and the Disney Princess Franchise," *Feminist Media Studies* 23, no. 1 (2023).
38. Jason Scott, "Disneyizing Home Entertainment Distribution," in *DVD, Blu-Ray and Beyond: Navigating Formats and Platforms within Media Consumption*, ed. Jonathan Wroot and Andy Willis (London: Palgrave, 2017), 15.
39. Osmond, "Lilo & Stitch Revisited: Part 1."
40. Katia Perea, "Girl Cartoons Second Wave: Transforming the Genre," *Animation: An Interdisciplinary Journal* 10, no. 3 (2015): 198.
41. Strong, Frank Welker, and Tress MacNeille are credited with providing voices for the majority of the alien experiment characters in *Lilo & Stitch: The Series*. They are all professional voice actors who work across US animation, especially in television animation roles.
42. For more on the production of these toy- and computer-game-based franchises, see Derek Johnson, *Media Franchising: Creative License and Collaboration in the Culture Industries* (New York: New York University Press, 2013); Joseph Tobin, ed., *Pikachu's Global Adventure: The Rise and Fall of Pokémon* (Durham, NC: Duke University Press, 2004).
43. Constantine Verevis, *Movie Remakes* (Edinburgh: Edinburgh University Press, 2006).
44. Henry Jenkins, *Convergence Culture: When Old and New Media Collide* (New York: New York University Press, 2006).
45. Joe Strike, "Disney's Animation Cash Crop—Direct-to-Video Sequels," Animation World News, March 28, 2005, https://www.awn.com/animationworld/disney-s-animation-cash-crop-direct-video-sequels.
46. Cheng, "Family, Race and Citizenship," 127.

47. Chris Sanders, as Chrissandersart, TikTok post, September 2, 2022, https://www.tiktok.com/@chrissandersart/video/7062525036485299502.
48. Tomoko Ishizuka, "(Frontrunner) Paul Candland, Walt Disney Japan President: Planning and Producing an Anime 'From Okinawa'" ["(*Furontorannā*) *Woruto Dizunī Japan shachō Pōru Kyandorandosan: 'Okinawa-hatsu' anime o kikaku seisaku*"], *Asahi Shimbun*, March 15, 2008, B1–B2.
49. Ishizuka, "(Frontrunner) Paul Candland," B2.
50. Michael Dylan Foster, *Pandemonium and Parade: Japanese Monsters and the Culture of Yokai* (Berkeley: University of California Press, 2008).
51. Jonathan Clements, *Anime: A History* (London: BFI, 2012).
52. Thomas Lamarre, "Speciesism Part I: Translating Races into Animals in Wartime Animation," in *Mechademia 3*, ed. Thomas Lamarre, Christopher Bolton, and French Lunning (Minneapolis: University of Minnesota Press, 2008), 76.
53. Beatrice Verhoeven, "Chris Sanders in Final Talks to Return as the Voice of Stitch in Disney's Live-Action 'Lilo & Stitch' (Exclusive)," *Hollywood Reporter*, April 21, 2023, https://www.hollywoodreporter.com/movies/movie-news/chris-sanders-stitch-in-live-action-lilo-and-stitch-1235399164/.

Bibliography

Beck, Jerry. "Disney's Magic Returns: *Lilo & Stitch*." Animation World, June 20, 2002. https://www.awn.com/animationworld/disneys-magic-returns-lilo-stitch.

Bohn, James and Jeff Kurtti (contributor). *Music in Disney's Animated Features: Snow White and the Seven Dwarfs to The Jungle Book*. Jackson: University of Mississippi Press, 2019.

Brookey, Robert Alan. *Hollywood Gamers: Digital Convergence in the Film and Video Game Industries*. Bloomington: Indiana University Press, 2010.

Budd, Mike, and Max H. Kirsch, eds. *Rethinking Disney: Private Control, Public Dimensions*. Middletown, CT: Wesleyan University Press, 2005.

Cheng, Emily. "Family, Race and Citizenship in Disney's *Lilo & Stitch*." In *Monsters and the Monstrous: Myths and Metaphors of Enduring Evil*, edited by Niall Scott, 123–132. New York: Brill, 2007.

Clements, Jonathan. *Anime: A History*. London: BFI, 2012.

Delaney, Cole. "'Lilo & Stitch' at 20: Directors Chris Sanders and Dean DeBlois Reunite (Video Interview)." Cartoon Brew, June 22, 2022. https://www.cartoonbrew.com/interviews/lilo-stitch-20th-anniversary-deblois-sanders-218046.html.

Ebiri, Bilge. "An Oral History of *Lilo & Stitch*." Vulture, October 19, 2022. https://www.vulture.com/2022/10/an-oral-history-of-lilo-and-stitch-a-hand-drawn-miracle.html.

Foster, Michael Dylan. *Pandemonium and Parade: Japanese Monsters and the Culture of Yokai*. Berkeley: University of California Press, 2008.

Godfrey, Leigh. "*Lilo & Stitch* Creators Launch Own Production Company." Animation World, November 27, 2002, https://www.awn.com/news/lilo-stitch-creators-launch-own-production-company.

Ishizuka, Tomoko. "(Frontrunner) Paul Candland, Walt Disney Japan President: Planning and Producing an Anime 'From Okinawa'" ["(*Furontorannā*) *Woruto Dizunī Japan shachō Pōru Kyandorandosan: 'Okinawa-hatsu' anime o kikaku seisaku*"]. *Asahi Shimbun*, March 15, 2008, B1–B2.

Iwabuchi, Koichi. *Recentering Globalization: Popular Culture and Japanese Transnationalism.* Durham, NC: Duke University Press, 2002.

Jenkins, Henry. *Convergence Culture: When Old and New Media Collide.* New York: New York University Press, 2006.

Johnson, Derek. *Media Franchising: Creative License and Collaboration in the Culture Industries.* New York: New York University Press, 2013.

Kunze, Peter C. "Revise and Resubmit: *Beauty and the Beast* (2017), Live-Action Remakes, and the Disney Princess Franchise." *Feminist Media Studies* 23, no. 1 (2023): 121–136.

Kunze, Peter C. *Staging a Comeback: Broadway, Hollywood, and the Disney Renaissance.* New Brunswick, NJ: Rutgers University Press, 2023.

Lamarre, Thomas. "Speciesism Part I: Translating Races into Animals in Wartime Animation." In *Mechademia* 3, edited by Thomas Lamarre, Christopher Bolton, and French Lunning, 75–95. Minneapolis: University of Minnesota Press, 2008.

Lester, Catherine. "The Children's Horror Film: Characterizing an 'Impossible' Subgenre." *Velvet Light Trap* 78 (Fall 2016): 22–37.

Lutz, Jessie G. "Chinese Emigrants, Indentured Workers, and Christianity in the West Indies, British Guiana and Hawaii." *Caribbean Studies* 37, no. 2 (July–December 2009): 133–154.

Montgomery, Colleen. "From Moana to Vaiana: Voicing the French and Tahitian Dubbed Versions of Disney's *Moana*." *American Music* 39, no. 2 (Summer 2021): 237–251.

Osmond, Andrew. "Lilo & Stitch Revisited: Part 1." Animation World, December 31, 2002. https://www.awn.com/animationworld/lilo-stitch-revisited-part-i.

Pallant, Chris. *Demystifying Disney: A History of Disney Feature Animation.* London: Bloomsbury Academic, 2013.

Pallant, Chris. "Neo-Disney: Recent Developments in Disney Feature Animation." *New Cinemas: Journal of Contemporary Film* 8, no. 2 (2010): 103–117.

Perea, Katia. "Girl Cartoons Second Wave: Transforming the Genre." *Animation: An Interdisciplinary Journal* 10, no. 3 (2015): 189–204.

Rodosthenous, George, ed. *The Disney Musical on Stage and Screen: Critical Approaches from Snow White to Frozen.* London: Bloomsbury, 2017.

Sanders, Chris [as Chrissandersart]. TikTok post, September 2, 2022. https://www.tiktok.com/@chrissandersart/video/7062525036485299502.

Scott, A. O. "Film Review: Escaping Deep-Space Exile and Making Friends in Hawaii." *New York Times*, June 21, 2002. https://www.nytimes.com/2002/06/21/movies/film-review-escaping-deep-space-exile-and-making-friends-in-hawaii.html.

Scott, Jason. "Disneyizing Home Entertainment Distribution." In *DVD, Blu-Ray and Beyond: Navigating Formats and Platforms within Media Consumption*, edited by Jonathan Wroot and Andy Willis, 15–33. London: Palgrave, 2017.

Sharf, Zach. "'Lilo & Stitch' Director Got 'Frustrated' by 'Frozen' Praise: We Did Sisterhood over Romance First." *Variety*, June 22, 2022. https://variety.com/2022/film/news/lilo-stitch-director-frustrated-1235300612/.

Smith, Russell. "Lilo & Stitch." *Austin Chronicle*, June 21, 2022. https://www.austinchronicle.com/events/film/2002-06-21/142169/.

Strike, Joe. "Disney's Animation Cash Crop—Direct-to-Video Sequels." Animation World, March 28, 2005. https://www.awn.com/animationworld/disney-s-animation-cash-crop-direct-video-sequels.

Subiono, Russell. "Celebrating 20 Years of 'Lilo & Stitch' in Hawaiʻi with Creator Chris Sanders." *The Conversation*, Hawaiʻi Public Radio, July 12, 2022. https://www.hawaiipublicradio.org/the-conversation/2022-07-12/celebrating-20-years-of-lilo-stitch-in-hawaii-with-creator-chris-sanders.

Tobin, Joseph, ed. *Pikachu's Global Adventure: The Rise and Fall of Pokémon*. Durham, NC: Duke University Press, 2004.

Verevis, Constantine. *Movie Remakes*. Edinburgh: Edinburgh University Press, 2006.

Verhoeven, Beatrice. "Chris Sanders in Final Talks to Return as the Voice of Stitch in Disney's Live-Action 'Lilo & Stitch' (Exclusive)." *Hollywood Reporter*, April 21, 2023. https://www.hollywoodreporter.com/movies/movie-news/chris-sanders-stitch-in-live-action-lilo-and-stitch-1235399164/.

Wasko, Janet. *Understanding Disney: The Manufacture of Fantasy*. Cambridge: Polity, 2001.

Wasko, Janet. "The Walt Disney Company." In *Global Media Giants*, edited by Benjamin Birkinbine, Rodrigo Gomez, and Janet Wasko, 11–25. New York: Routledge, 2016.

Yoshimi, Shunya. "Japan: America in Japan/Japan as Disneyfication: The Disney Image and the Transformation of 'America' in Contemporary Japan." In *Dazzled by Disney: The Global Disney Audiences Project*, edited by Janet Wasko, Mark Phillips, and Eileen R. Meehan, 160–181. Leicester: Leicester University Press, 2001.

CHAPTER 8

FROM VICTORIANA TO VAUDEVILLE: ALICE'S ADVENTURES IN MUSICAL ADAPTATION

DOMINIC BROOMFIELD-MCHUGH

In a book about Disney's musicals, *Alice in Wonderland* (1951) has an essential place. Discounting reprises, the film contains fourteen songs compared with *Snow White*'s eight, *Pinocchio*'s five, *Dumbo*'s seven, *Bambi*'s four, and *Cinderella*'s six. This speaks to the special status of song, narratively and aesthetically, in the film. Further, compared with most of Disney's feature-length animations, for which one or perhaps two songwriting teams would be hired (*Cinderella*'s original team was replaced by another, for example, but none of the original team's work was used), *Alice in Wonderland* involved at least five teams of songwriters, four of whose work was heard in part in the released film.

The first team to be hired was the combination of veteran Disney composer Frank Churchill (1901–1942), who composed music for *Snow White*, *Dumbo*, and *Bambi*, and lyricist Ted Osborne (1900–1968), who worked on a number of Disney shorts in the 1930s. Texts for several of Churchill's songs were also lifted directly from Lewis Carroll's original *Alice* books, in which characters regularly burst into rhyme or song. Churchill and Osborne's work was completed between 1938 and 1939 as part of a story reel led by storyboard artist Al Perkins and art director David S. Hall, and then abandoned after the onset of war.[1]

Between 1947 and 1949, three teams of Broadway/Tin Pan Alley songwriters came on board. In 1947, composer Gene de Paul (1919–1988), now best remembered for writing the score for MGM's *Seven Brides for Seven Brothers* (1954), joined forces with lyricist Don Raye (1909–1985), whose profile was significant in the 1940s thanks to his work for the Andrews Sisters, but of the three surviving songs credited to them, only the Cheshire Cat's song ("'Twas Brillig") was used. They were followed by the *Cinderella* songwriting team of Mack David (1912–1993), Jerry Livingston (1909–1987), and Al Hoffman (1902–1960), who wrote five songs, of which only "The Unbirthday Song" was retained. Their input was in 1948.

Then came composer Sammy Fain (1902–1989), who later worked on *Peter Pan* for Disney and *Calamity Jane* for Warner Bros., and lyricist Bob Hilliard (1918–1971), now remembered for the Frank Sinatra standard "In the Wee Small Hours of the Morning." Fain and Hilliard's numbers, which make up the bulk of the song score, were copyrighted in 1949, presumably the main year of their involvement. Lastly, English composer Oliver Wallace (1887–1963), who wrote much of the underscoring to the film, composed four short songs that were used in the final film, working with lyricists Ted Sears (1900–1958) and Cy Coben (1919–2006). It is likely that these were provided during the last period of the film's development in 1950–1951, when Wallace was working on the underscoring. Among these twelve songwriters—all of them men, in a film about the adventures of a seven-year-old girl—more than forty songs were written, most of them abandoned (see appendices).

This extraordinary process, product, and amount of labor speak both to the challenges of putting Carroll's stories on-screen and to the significance of the project at Disney. Walt's first engagement with Alice as a character was in 1923, with the silent short *Alice's Wonderland*, later releasing a further fifty-six shorts (1924–1927) about her—most of them unconnected to Carroll's stories but all strongly reinforcing the character—and first contemplating a feature-length version in 1932–1933. This was abandoned when Paramount released a version of the story in 1933.[2] Significant attempts to bring the project to fruition were made in 1938–1939 (as noted above), 1944 (animators Bill Cottrell and T. Hee), 1945 (screenplay by Aldous Huxley, with Ginger Rogers rumored to star), and 1947, some of them potentially mixing live action with animation (Mary Pickford, Virginia Davis, and Margaret O'Brien are among the other actresses regularly mentioned in connection with the film), before its eventual release as a cartoon in 1951.

Alice in Wonderland is also significant for forming a pair with *Peter Pan*, in that both films are explicitly set in London and were released, two years apart, at a time of international tension in which the US and the UK were intensely linked through NATO during the Cold War and subsequently led to Disney's later gaze at Englishness in *Mary Poppins* and *Bedknobs and Broomsticks*. Further, *Alice* disengages from the princess trope of other classical Disney films, thus shedding the teleological pull of the salvation of a prince; although the film is highly gendered, from a structural point of view, this move away from the marriage-as-goal trope makes it distinctive. Yet the film was a commercial and critical disappointment on first release, only gaining a cult status much later on college campuses due to its psychedelic imagery and hookah-smoking Caterpillar.

This chapter uses adaptation theory to present a new evaluation of Disney's version of Carroll's stories. It exploits primary sources to consider how the different stages of the creative process took divergent approaches to the source material and argues that this disparity is reflected in an incoherence in the resultant film. The chapter considers different songs written for the same moment or scene, drawn from more than thirty studio scores submitted to the Library of Congress's copyright deposit between 1939 and 1951, as well as demo recordings released by Disney on laserdisc and Blu-ray editions of the movie. The latter official releases also offer insights into the storyboards for two aborted attempts to make the film, as well as for certain dropped sequences such as "Pig and Pepper." Overall, the chapter argues that Disney's repeated changes of direction during the making of the film led to an ambivalent relationship with the source material rather than an active adaptation of it with a distinctive point of view. While multi-author teams have a successful precedent in this period of American popular culture in the form of the musical theater revue (e.g., *The Band Wagon*, which opened on Broadway in 1931 to rave reviews), the way the film draws on vaudeville stylistically at various points is inconsistent and sometimes attenuates the progress of the story arc, and the use of fragments of twelve different songwriters' work for 1951's *Alice* may be a reflection of the studio's wider misunderstanding of Carroll's particular, unusual books.

Lewis Carroll's "Bits and Scraps"

In a special feature on the sixtieth-anniversary Blu-ray release of *Alice*, narrator Kathryn Beaumont (who provided the voice of the title character in the film) comments that the studio "found the episodic elements of the [Carroll] stories very difficult to adapt indeed."[3] Conversely, animation director Ward Kimball reported that this was a helpful aspect of the material in terms of the division of labor: "[B]ecause of the story's episodical nature, Walt could quickly assign different people to different sequences or characters without worrying too much about hook-ups between the sequences."[4] This diffuse focus of responsibility reflects Disney's need to push ahead with the film at a time when it was economically imperative to the studio, and his staff was clearly aware that an overarching vision for how the film was going to work had not been agreed on. Frank Thomas, another of the film's supervising animators, remarked in 1985: "Walt felt that there was something in this story that he dearly loved but he didn't know what to do with it and he kind of looked to the animators and the story people to give him something."[5]

In her *Theory of Adaptation*, Linda Hutcheon is keen to "tackle head-on the subtle and not so subtle denigration of adaptation in our (late-Romantic, capitalist) culture that still tends to value the 'original,' despite the ubiquity and longevity of adaptation as a mode of retelling our favorite stories."[6] While this defense of the value of adaptations of literary classics in popular culture is helpful to the current project in the sense that Disney's *Alice* is as valuable a work as Carroll's, it is easy for such a stance to overlook the fact that for the Disney animators and writers, the relationship between Carroll's novel and Disney's adaptation was mostly linear (allowing for the potential for some impact of Disney's Alice Comedies and other screen adaptations on the 1951 animation). Thus, it's useful to consider the relationship between Carroll's text and Disney's movie, not with the aim of valuing the "original" more than the adaptation but rather to help understand how the Disney team's troubled process of adapting the novel (hinted at in the above quotations) led to what is, with the best will in the world, an uneven film.

Although Carroll's *Alice* is a much-adapted text, it has to be acknowledged that this high Victorian work is more complicated than most children's stories to adapt. Charles Dodgson—the real-life Carroll—himself commented on the difficult nature of his two books, *Alice in Wonderland* (1865) and *Through the Looking-Glass* (1871). In one diary entry, he referred to the first book as "my interminable fairy-tale,"[7] hinting at its impenetrability and the feeling that it could go on and on. In 1887, he wrote an essay, "'Alice' on the Stage," in response to a theatrical adaptation of the book by Savile Clarke, referring to his stories as "airy nothings" and explaining that the first book "was written without the slightest idea that it would be so adapted." Most striking of all, he confessed that "'Alice' and the 'Looking-Glass' are made up almost wholly of bits and scraps, single ideas which came of themselves."[8] There was no overall plan, and it was never meant to be a dramatic story, Carroll explains, and this points to why it was complicated for Disney's artists to know what to do with the material.

There is a vast literature on the meanings of the *Alice* books, too much to summarize here, but it is enough to note for the purposes of this chapter the general agreement that these stories are (1) part of the literature of "nonsense" that flourished in the nineteenth century and (2) the product of an Oxford mathematician whose primary field was logic. Thus, the books can be (and have been) read as having no meaning at all but are structured as a series of debates as heated as that at any Oxford college. They may be absurd, but they are laid out with contexts and language that can certainly be understood. Hence, for example, the books are generally agreed to be amusing; *something* identifiable, therefore, is amusing, or there would be nothing to be amused by. (Or to bring it back to the books: "The Hatter's remark seemed to her to have no sort of meaning in it, and yet it was certainly English," Alice thinks at one point.) The puns with which the stories are stacked, and which scholars have picked over at length, show the importance of the semantic in the book's success: Edward Guiliano explains, "It delights us with characters and startling turns in an imaginary world that is not-so-unimaginarily ours."[9]

That's why, for example, the premise of *Through the Looking-Glass*—that because Alice has stepped into a mirror-image world, everything is backward—is so amusing. Carroll lays out a series of jokes based on this reverse logic, including reproducing the first stanza of "Jabberwocky" in mirror image on the page in chapter 1. And in *Alice in Wonderland*, the back-to-front logic of the Queen of Hearts' "sentence first—verdict afterwards" is even more powerful, because although the alarming logic to reversing the supposed process of making the sentence to a crime based on the verdict may tickle the reader, Carroll is clearly critiquing the injustices of the British penal system in the Victorian era. Throughout both books, Carroll makes reference to things that can be guessed—the Mock Turtle's allusion to his classics master at school teaching "Laughing and Grief" obviously signifies Latin and Greek, for example—and others that Carroll himself admitted he couldn't remember or didn't know the meaning of. In "'Alice' on the Stage," for example, he explains, "I have received courteous letters from strangers, begging to know whether 'The Hunting of the Snark' is an allegory, or contains some hidden moral, or is a political satire: and for all such questions I have but one answer: 'I don't know!'"[10] Therefore, the Disney studio was adapting a hyperlayered text, some of whose meanings were easy to surmise, some of whose meanings were hidden but deducible, and some of which was such nonsense that the author couldn't explain it.

The final aspect of the Carroll texts that made them particularly difficult to adapt was the narrative style of most of the chapters. Notwithstanding the drama of Alice falling down the rabbit hole or stepping through the looking glass, many of the chapters of both books take the form of a debate or deliberation between Alice and one or more other characters, with minimal action. The iconic status of the vivid and much-reproduced original illustrations (from the first editions of the novels) by John Tenniel makes it easy to forget that not much happens in most of the chapters. For example, in the Humpty Dumpty chapter from *Through the Looking-Glass*, Alice happens upon the egglike character on the wall and spends almost every page of the chapter in discussions such as the following:

> "I don't know what you mean by 'glory,'" Alice said.
>
> Humpty Dumpty smiled contemptuously. "Of course you don't—till I tell you. I meant 'there's a nice knock-down argument for you!'"
>
> "But 'glory' doesn't mean 'a nice knock-down argument,'" Alice objected.
>
> "When *I* use a word," Humpty Dumpty said, in rather a scornful tone, "it means just what I choose it to mean—neither more nor less."
>
> "The question is," said Alice, "whether you *can* make words mean so many different things."
>
> "The question is," said Humpty Dumpty, "which is to be master—that's all."[11]

This is a good example of what Hugh Haughton describes as *Alice in Wonderland*'s nature as "a philosophical jokebook, a mixture of genially grotesque pantomime and surreal Socratic dialogue."[12] Haughton also notes that "Alice is engaged in a quest to interpret and master the complex and strange phenomena of the largely adult world she encounters—there are no other *children* in her dream. What Alice knows, and how she interprets it, holds centre stage, giving her a paradoxical intellectual authority."[13] The Socratic method, in which Alice's "intellectual authority" is challenged by a range of characters—many of whom adopt a similarly antagonistic position despite assuming disparate forms and sizes—is at the heart of Carroll's approach. No wonder, then, that making Disney's adaptation was such a drawn-out process.

Finding Approaches to the "Falling down the Rabbit Hole" and "Mad Hatter's Tea Party" Episodes

With such a formidable and complex text, Disney's approach clearly needed to be creative rather than faithful. Hutcheon's comments on this are particularly helpful: comparing cultural adaptation to Darwin's theory of evolution, she explains that "[t]o think of narrative adaptation in terms of a story's fit and its process of mutation or adjustment, through adaptation, to a particular cultural environment is something I find suggestive.... [Stories] travel to different cultures and different media."[14] Finding that fit, to a new time, place, culture, and medium, was the challenge of Disney's *Alice in Wonderland* project. The multiple attempts to make it work are a reflection of this.

The 1939 storyboards of the version led by Hall and Perkins, reproduced on the laserdisc, offer an unusual insight into adaptation as process, in that they show a profound difference of approach from the familiar 1951 movie. Although brief aspects of this version are more passively faithful to the books, the overall adaptation finds Alice in a much more hostile and threatening Wonderland than Carroll's. This tone is set within the first few minutes. Alice falls down the rabbit hole and encounters a fiery ball, which turns out to be a jar of marmalade. The screenplay notes: "The falling drops of marmalade change into giant bats with gleaming eyes and scarlet wings.... As they swarm around Alice, the bats grab her and stop her from falling further as they shout: 'WHO ARE YOU ANYWAY? WHERE DO YOU THINK YOU'RE GOING? IT'S TERRIBLE DOWN DERE! DE QUEEN'LL KILL YOU! GO HOME WHILE YOU GOT THE CHANCE!' "[15] The apparent racialization of the bats, indicated by the use of dialect in this dialogue excerpt, is used to make them part of a nightmare vision of the rabbit hole, with the bats threatening Alice with death if she goes further. Wonderland is immediately framed as hostile. Disney himself realized that the approach wasn't working, complaining on January 14, 1939, that there was "nothing to promote laughter."[16] By the time of the 1943 version, this darker aspect of the story had been eradicated, and the fall down the rabbit hole more closely resembles the tone of the 1951 release, albeit with less atmosphere and character.

But the Mad Hatter's tea party is perhaps the most useful scene for demonstrating effective adaptation strategies. It's a vivid example in part because of the divergence of approach in 1951 compared with the 1939 and 1943 storyboards. For one thing, the position of the episode in the film is different: in 1951, it is just before the penultimate section of the film, leading via Tulgey Wood to the three-pronged Queen of Hearts sequence (painting of the roses, croquet game, and trial), but the 1939 version places it before longer scenes in the Rabbit's garden, the Duchess's house (the later unused "Pig and Pepper" sequence), and then the Queen's sequence, while the 1943 version makes it the third main episode in the film. Carroll's book places it seventh out of twelve chapters, but in moving it to a later spot in the 1951 film, Disney made a good choice; its vaudeville-like focus on slapstick, puns, and character make an ideal prelude to the action of the Queen's garden scenes.

Still, the biggest evolution was in the tone and focus of the adaptation of the tea party scene, not unlike the removal of the bats' section mentioned above. In the 1939 storyboards, Disney moves the party setting from the March Hare's house in Carroll ("[Alice] thought it must be the right house, because the chimneys were shaped like ears and the roof was thatched with fur") to a sinister imagining of the Mad Hatter's house. Disney's writers describe how Alice "peeps nervously in at the show window, and finds it filled with spooky dummies, all looking like the Mad Hatter." Their eyes follow her around as she enters, and "She is about to run away in terror" when she hears and then sees the Hare, the Hatter, and the Dormouse having tea in the garden. "They are complete maniacs," continues the text on the slide, "fugitives from an insane asylum."

Later, "Alice decides the screwballs are probably harmless," and the scene briefly proceeds as in the book, with the Hatter and the Hare telling Alice there is no room despite the table being long and there being many chairs. Unlike in the book, Alice then marches off, disgusted with the nonsense of the party. However, she unexpectedly encounters the Hare and the Hatter *again*, coming toward her and now friendly. They flatter her, then pick her up and walk her back to the tea table. (This, in particular, is contrary to the chapter in the book, where they ignore Alice when she decides to leave.)

The scene proceeds again a little more like the book now, with the Hatter and the Hare waking up the Dormouse, who is encouraged to tell a story but falls asleep in the middle of it. They dump the Dormouse into the teapot, which is what is happening as Alice leaves the table at the end of this chapter in the novel, but the 1939 Disney version continues with Alice climbing over the wall, then finding herself once more at the tea party—except "The attitude of the screwballs has changed again." They now sing the (ultimately unused) Churchill–Osborne song "It's Crazy to Be Sane" ("never ever use your brain / or you soon will find your mind / behaving like a hurricane") and then proceed to "mend" the White Rabbit's watch with different items of food (in the book, it's the Hatter's own watch). They realize that they can't mend it because it isn't broken, so the Hatter throws it over the wall to break it, whereupon it hits the Rabbit (who is not in the scene in the book); he joins the party but threatens them with vengeance from the Queen.

From here, the rest of the scene is entirely invented by the Disney artists and, as with the bats in the opening of this 1939 version, is sinister in mood. The Hare and the Hatter smear the Rabbit's shirt with jam, shampoo him with tea, and shave him with butter, using a jagged bread knife for a razor; they then throw him back over the wall. Now they turn on Alice and say that her hair needs cutting and that her legs are too long and need cutting too. They "close in on her, knives in hand," and Alice "ducks under the tablecloth, and runs for her life." This Gothic version of the scene is grounded in trauma narratives, from the ableist framing of the Hare and the Hatter as "fugitives from an insane asylum" through to the final "running for her life."

Disney was unhappy with the approach. As part of the January 14, 1939, story meeting mentioned above, he declared, "I think we're on the wrong track," and continued:

> Alice is the only logical one in the place, but they [i.e., the Hatter and the Hare] convince her in a screwball way that they are right. That is what your Mad Tea Party is to me. When they move around, there is a reason why they move around. I don't think Carroll ... is good at all. But he has a spirit there, a crazy Marx Brothers spirit. Yet even with the Marx Brothers, there is a purpose to what they are doing.... You've got to quit thinking of that book and quit trying to make that book on the screen. You must try to make a motion picture with the idea of *Alice in Wonderland* behind it.[17]

What's interesting about Disney's remarks here is that he offers almost a textbook—literally Hutcheon's textbook—definition of an effective, creative screen adaptation of a literary work. In the same comments, he suggests that the film must be funny to an American audience ("To hell with the English audiences or the people who love Carroll"), saying the material must be "modernised," as if Carroll were "writing it today with our technique in mind."

Initially, it's as if the staff had not really understood Walt's critique. The 1943 storyboards remove most of the violence from the 1939 version—the Rabbit and Alice are not physically threatened in the same way, though the Dormouse is still doused in the teapot—but the structure of the scene is broadly similar. However, the 1951 version took quite a different approach, with a key ingredient: Ed Wynn, who voiced the Mad Hatter. Wynn started out in vaudeville and later moved on to the *Ziegfeld Follies*, Broadway, and his own comedy show. It was noted above that Walt had been looking for a "Marx Brothers" approach in order to make the film funny; Wynn proved to be the solution.

Part of what he brought to the Mad Hatter's scene was unintentional. Disney commissioned a live-action version of the film, using the voice actors from the soundtrack, to give the animators something to work from. Mark Salisbury quotes animation director Kimball explaining how Wynn had trouble miming to his vocal track: "It drove him crazy. He said, 'I can't do it. Why don't you turn that darn voice track off and I'll remember roughly what I said.'"[18] Kimball goes on to explain how a single microphone was used to pick him up. "Well, the nonsense Ed ad-libbed on that sound-stage was a lot funnier than some of the recorded stuff we had carefully written out for him. When Walt saw the black-and-white test he said, 'Let's use that sound track! That's great!'" (Some of this footage can be seen on the Blu-ray of the movie.) Alongside comedian Jerry Colonna—a veteran of the Bob Hope–Bing Crosby *Road* films—as the Hare, Wynn was able to bring to the scene a sense of contemporary American entertainment through improvisation while still embodying the broadest ideas of Carroll's original.

Another aspect of this scene that works particularly well is "The Unbirthday Song," the only contribution to the score by David, Hoffman, and Livingston. In itself, the use of a different team's work for this unusual scene may partly be behind why it stands out (in a positive sense), and even if the significance of this different authorship is an illusion, there is no doubt that the calliope effect of the woodwind-heavy orchestration (marked in the piano-conductor score housed at the Library of Congress as a "gadget band"), with its ocarinas, bassoons, and tin whistles, creates a distinctive gesture of creepy weirdness, perhaps evoking a fairground carousel. It could be a variety act or something from the music hall, and this frames the scene much better than the less imaginative naming of the characters' madness in the 1939 song "It's Crazy to Be Sane" for the same scene, or indeed of the use in 1943 of another abandoned song, "Speak Roughly to Your Little Boy" (authorship unknown), which the Hare and the Hatter sing while stuffing the Dormouse into the teapot.

Instead, David, Hoffman, and Livingston repurpose an idea from the Humpty Dumpty chapter of *Through the Looking-Glass*, which is omitted from the final film (some Humpty Dumpty character sketches survive and are included on the laserdisc). Livingston recalls that Disney had asked them to get involved in providing a song for this scene "even though we weren't on the picture," which seems to underplay their wider work, given the five songs with which they are credited. He also recounts how "[f]inally, Mack David came up with the 'un-birthday' idea. Since there are 364 un-birthday days each year, it was a perfect reason for a mad tea party. And, it fit perfectly with the more-than-mad hatter."[19] In fact, it comes from the book: when Alice encounters Humpty Dumpty on the wall and compliments him on his "beautiful cravat," the egg explains that the White King and Queen gave it to him for an un-birthday present ("A present given when it isn't your birthday"). Hoffman's misremembering and miscrediting of the source of the idea behind "The Unbirthday Song" ironically takes away from its brilliance: Livingston was able to search in Carroll's books for the kernel of an idea in a different episode to bring the spirit of the tea party scene to life. This leap of the imagination is exactly the approach Walt was looking for and makes parts of the film outstanding.

Three Modes of Song: Musicalizing the Cheshire Cat, Tweedledum and Tweedledee, and the Garden of Live Flowers

One of the film's noticeable features—if not a consistently successful one—is the use of song to anchor each episode and/or character. Among the cleverest is the Cheshire Cat's song "'Twas Brillig," the only number by Raye and de Paul to make it into the picture. Like "The Unbirthday Song," its concept is actually taken from a completely different context in Carroll: Raye's lyrics are drawn from the "Jabberwocky" poem that Alice reads in a book in chapter 1 of *Through the Looking-Glass*. The requirements for the Cheshire Cat's song were particular. Unlike most of the other characters, he appears in several scenes as a unifying presence, sometimes guiding and sometimes misguiding Alice through the woods and causing chaos at her trial. The Cat has the ability to appear and disappear, his grotesque, toothy smile sometimes emerging before or fading after the rest of his body parts.

"'Twas Brillig" fits the bill brilliantly for the Cat to sing; it enhances his unfathomable nature by giving him nonsense to sing. As late as March 20, 1950,[20] the studio considered including the Jabberwock as a character in the Tulgey Wood sequence of the film, and Raye and de Paul actually used the poem "Jabberwocky" in another unused song, "Beware the Jabberwock," whose C minor tonality and rising sequences seem like slightly heavy-handed attempts to evoke a creepy character. Further, this earlier song comes in the form of a warning to scare Alice, not unlike the bats' dialogue about the dangers of Wonderland in the 1939 storyboards discussed above. Far more imaginative is the text's repackaging in a moderate swing tempo (Raye and de Paul's background in writing for the Andrews Sisters came to the fore) in C major, its minor seventh chords and chromatic melody giving "'Twas Brillig" a quirky air that depicts the Cat as uncanny without him naming himself as such.

The effectiveness of the Cat being *revealed* as peculiar rather than *described* as such becomes particularly obvious when comparing it with another song written for the same character. The copyright deposit copy of Fain and Hilliard's unused song "I'm Odd" is dated September 28, 1949, versus the date of January 15, 1951, for Raye and de Paul's "'Twas Brillig," which suggests (but does not confirm) that the latter team may have been asked to come back and rework "Beware the Jabberwock" (as a trunk song) into "'Twas Brillig" when "I'm Odd" didn't fit the bill. Whatever the chronology, it's clear why "I'm Odd" (a reconstruction of which can be heard on the Blu-ray; a piano-vocal score is in the songbook *Disney's Lost Chords*[21]) was dropped. As with "Beware the Jabberwock," C minor is used to denote a threatening presence, and a fast martial beat in cut common time similarly indicates threat without really *being* threatening. Likewise, the lyrics are a self-portrait of the Cat as a strange person—"My head begins to jingle 'most every time I nod, / 'cause obviously, quite obviously, I'm odd," he sings—but their imagery is not strange enough to have their intended effect. Raye's use of "Jabberwocky" for "'Twas Brillig" instead squarely places the Cat in the world of Carroll's nonsense. (A snippet is used later in the film when the Cat returns, reinforcing its status as his "emergence theme.")

In addition to the adaptive challenges described earlier in this chapter, the most awkward aspect of Carroll's two books from the point of view of a screen adaptation is the predilection of many of the characters to break into song and, in particular, to start telling a story (in ballad form) about other characters that aren't otherwise part of the books. On the page, this works well; it adds to the nonsense and entertains both Alice and the reader, if sometimes disconcertingly. But Walt Disney knew that his film was a different entity. "It was imperative that we create a plot structure," he said in an interview, "for Carroll had not had need for such a thing. We decided, of course, that Alice's curiosity was the only possible prime mover for our story and generator of the necessary suspense. The result is a basic chase pattern that culminates when Alice, after her strange adventures, returns to the world of reality."[22] Therefore, anything in the books that does not form part of the chase is a distraction.

Despite Walt himself having apparently understood the kind of adaptation that was needed, Disney's staff fell for this trap twice in the same scene in their version of *Alice*. The Tweedledum and Tweedledee sequence features three songs, and only the first aligns with the more effective strategies outlined above. "How Do You Do and Shake Hands" occurs at the opening of this episode of the film and matches the vaudevillian style of "The Unbirthday Song," its wacky instrumentation replacing the latter's ocarinas with car horns; it is the perfect ditty to depict the identical twins, whose individual identities are lost when they shake hands and bounce around. Here the use of a music-hall-style turn works well because it communicates character instantly. But as Alice tries to leave them and continue her journey through the woods, the twins detain her by telling her "the story of the curious oysters," better known as "The Walrus and the Carpenter." The four-minute song, in which the twins relate how the walrus and the carpenter capture and eat some gullible oysters from the sea, pauses the progress of the film while the twins shift to static narrator mode and the animators evoke the action that is being described. While the song is supposed to be a moral tale to warn Alice against being too inquisitive, it feels more like a mini-cartoon inside the main animation and does nothing to add to the "chase pattern" described by Disney in the interview cited above. Alice disappears, and nothing that is being described is actually happening to her. No wonder that when they start a further tangential narrative song, "Old Father William," Alice creeps away. Although all three songs in this sequence have the mood of the British music hall—Brian Sibley rightly identifies the influence of Lancashire-born entertainer George Formby in voice actor J. Pat O'Malley's performance in this scene— the second and third songs feel like sideshows, extraneous, and therefore difficult for the audience to invest in.[23]

On the face of it, the narrative status of "All in the Golden Afternoon" is similar to the "Walrus" and "William" songs in that the number is telegraphed as being a reported "tale" (about the magic garden of flowers), but there are crucial differences that make it much more effective. Fain and Hilliard cleverly use the evocative opening line of Carroll's poetic prelude to *Alice in Wonderland* (in which he explains the origins of the story that we're about to read) and combine it with images from different chapters of *Through the Looking-Glass* to describe a magical pastoral scene, perhaps the epitome of Wonderland. Alice observes "curious butterflies," and the Rose corrects her: "You mean bread-and-butter-flies" (they have slices of bread for wings). Similarly, Alice sees "A horsefly ... I mean, a rocking-horse-fly" (a rocking horse with wings), and the Rose endorses her interpretation of what she's seeing: "Naturally." The insects come from Carroll's "Looking-Glass Insects" chapter (chapter 3) and the flowers from the "Garden of Live Flowers" chapter (chapter 2), but Disney's artists synthesize them into a scene whose main purpose is the performance of a grand choral number.

The flowers argue over which song they should sing, with each genus proposing a song about them, but the Rose intervenes: "Girls, we shall sing 'Golden Afternoon'— that's about all of us." This dialogue frames the song as a diegetic number: Alice and the flowers know that they are singing, and in this respect, the number shares functional similarities with "The Walrus," which the on-screen characters also know is being narrated (if not necessarily sung). However, "All in the Golden Afternoon" is *about* the flowers and insects, and therefore Alice is part of the experience and is learning something. Indeed, she joins in near the end before her voice cracks when the tessitura becomes too high, and the animators go to town wittily drawing attention to the performative nature of the number: what look like poppy or cornflower buds thrash about to the sound of timpani and a rudbeckia loses its petals when a cymbal crash is heard, as if the flowers were instruments.

In the "Live Flowers" chapter of the book, the flowers are immediately at odds with Alice, but in Disney's version, they are initially much friendlier, understanding her to be a fellow flower, and the episode in the chapter is interrupted by the arrival of the

Red Queen, who takes Alice off. But for Disney, the garden itself is the focus, and it's noticeable not only that the space is gendered—the Rose refers to the other flowers as "girls"—but that Alice finds harmony, both literally and metaphorically, for the first time in the story in a feminized space. Yet when the song is over, a different spin is put on this gendered atmosphere. The scene becomes about English class tensions (specifically, middle-class snobbery, its feminization a misogynist framing), with the use of exaggerated accents (mostly British Received Pronunciation) matched with a discussion about whether Alice is a wildflower or a "common" weed. They push her away, and the sequence comes to an end.

Taken together, these three modes of song reveal the three main strategies for using song as the structural hook of a scene in the film. "'Twas Brillig" uses material from a different part of Carroll's text to reveal the essence of the Cat through nonsense; "The Walrus and the Carpenter" lifts Carroll's text more directly, maintaining its original "narrated" framing; and "All in the Golden Afternoon" combines ideas from different Carroll chapters to create a sequence that is more song than dialogue. An easy gloss of these strategies shows that the more liberal the approach, the more successful the outcome. The "Walrus" song retains Carroll's static, didactic original to its detriment, while the "Golden Afternoon" scene's use of different Carrollian images provides one of the film's most beautiful scenes but does not provide much focus narratively; the Cat's song is at once the most purposeful and the most nonsensical, and here the film strikes the ideal balance.

Conventions of the Musical: Introducing Alice and the Rabbit through Song

In other respects, the film's score maps onto well-established conventions of the Broadway and Hollywood musical. Fain and Hilliard in particular write with a solid sense of genre and function in many of their contributions. The opening scene of the film is wrapped around three of their songs, all of which contribute effectively to the diegesis precisely because of their sense of purpose in contributing to the adaptation, before the film changes tack. First comes the title song, which is heard over the opening titles. This serves the function of the typical Disney fairy-tale opening of "once upon a time," an omniscient chorus asking "How do you get to Wonderland?" and going on to ask a series of further questions on the same subject. The song acts as a useful framing device for the movie and is the kind of grand movie theme that Fain would go on to become famous for (e.g., "Love is a Many-Splendored Thing" and "April Love"). Jud Conlon's spectacular vocal arrangement, which sometimes breaks down the chorus into eight-part chords, draws attention to the sophisticated harmonic writing with its obvious chorale-like

European influences backed by a symphonic accompaniment. While having the punch of a barbershop performance, it is more like an art song, and the English setting of *Alice* makes this particularly appropriate. Ironically, the melody opens with a rising semitone on "Al-ice" that will be crucial to the Cheshire Cat's song ("Bril-lig") later in the film, despite the songs being by different composers; this link may not be accidental, because the version of "Alice in Wonderland" submitted for copyright in October 1950 set both syllables of "Al-ice" on the same pitch rather than on two, suggesting it may have been tweaked during the arrangement process to create that wider connection with other songs in the movie. But the main point here is that because the way the title song is used is conventional, we automatically understand what it is supposed to communicate.

Fain and Hilliard draw on another convention of the musical in the next song, Alice's "In a World of My Own." The "I Want" song, best exemplified in the earlier Disney catalog by Snow White's "Some Day My Prince Will Come," embodies a main character's desires, and in the case of *Alice*, both its content and its position within the first couple of minutes of action mean it's obvious to the audience that vital contextual information is being conveyed. Alice's nanny is trying to get her to engage with a book and dismisses her preference for picture books as "nonsense." This has the opposite of the intended effect, because Alice breaks into a reverie in which she describes to her cat Dinah what "a world of [her] own" would be like. The reverie aspect is key to making the number an "I Want" song; these are almost always about dreams and as such represent the aspect of the musical that most fundamentally ties the genre to the American dream (i.e., song facilitates the expression of personal aspiration). Here, though, it's much more crucial, because the sense of Alice sinking into a dream is what leads seamlessly to her adventures in Wonderland; both the audience and Alice find themselves in Alice's dream without her literally falling asleep ever being telegraphed to the audience.

The song—which, incidentally, again features a rising chromatic interval in its opening phrase (on "[Cats and] rab-bits") that ties it to the wider musical character of the film's score as a whole—feels a bit like a development of the main title song. Whereas the latter generally pondered how one gets to Wonderland, Alice's "In a World of My Own" describes what happens there, and as such it's an effective prelude to key aspects of the plot. Rabbits will reside in "fancy little houses and be dressed in shoes and hats and trousers," and the flowers will be able to "talk to [her] for hours," she sings; and of course, it later happens. Having two songs about different aspects of Wonderland within the first five minutes of the running time is hugely effective in setting the scene.

As with earlier examples in this chapter, the archival materials that reveal the process of writing "In a World of My Own" help us to understand why it is effective (because the discarded versions were not). Fain and Hilliard made a separate attempt to write a song for this spot, called "Beyond the Laughing Sky" (it can be heard as a special feature on the Blu-ray). Musically, it is perhaps too similarly languorous to the main title song, and the lyric also appears to duplicate the mood and diction of the title song with a question: "Why does the whispering wind sound like a lullaby?" it begins. As a romantic ballad, it is musically powerful—not for nothing would Fain reuse it in *Peter Pan* as "The Second Star to the Right"—but it did not satisfy the needs of its position in *Alice*. "In a World of My Own" is a little quirkier, is much more focused on Alice's vision of Wonderland (which facilitates this song being the vehicle for her shift into dream), and, in tandem with the title song, firmly embeds the fact that this will be a *musical* film, one in which songs will not only be heard but play a key part in the language of the film.

As if to prove this will be the case, Fain and Hilliard deliver a third song that practically segues out of "In a World of My Own" and tells the next part of the scene in song. If Alice's song is a projection of Wonderland, "I'm Late" conjures up one of its key inhabitants: the White Rabbit, who appears through the woods whistling a bouncy chromatic theme with woodwind and xylophone accompaniment that resembles something between a symphonic scherzo and a slapstick "cops and robbers" scene from a Mack Sennett Keystone Cops movie. The song introduces the broadly vaudevillian mood that will recur at most of the film's finest moments, the dramatic irony of the music functioning as a complement to Carrollian nonsense language to tell us not to take anything too seriously. As a character song, it also works superbly: the falling chromatic scales represent the Rabbit's neuroticism, as if to say that he's always on the go yet always running around in circles. The song is also effective as a kind of "travel" song, taking the Rabbit and, by extension, Alice and the audience, from the riverside setting of the "real" world to the rabbit hole down which her adventures will be found. Using song, and not just music, gives the scene energy, and whenever the Rabbit reappears in the film, "I'm Late" recurs as a leitmotif.

Problems of the Vaudevillian Impulse

While using vaudeville as a generic and stylistic reference point serves aspects of the film well, in other respects it is a hindrance. One egregious example has been given above: Fain and Hilliard's "Walrus" song is like a standalone music-hall turn and creates distance between the audience and Alice's journey. Sears and Wallace's "Old Father William" at the end of the same scene falls into the same category, and to this we can add another by the same team in the same musical style: "We'll Smoke the Blighter Out." This is more integrated narratively than the other two, because it is sung by the Dodo (voiced by Bill Thompson, now remembered for voicing Droopy for MGM) in response to the Rabbit's dilemma of how to get Alice out of his house when she has grown enormous and become stuck inside. The pompous Sullivanesque 6/8 march matches the Dodo's naval uniform and forced aristocratic English accent and charts the character's ruthless collection of the Rabbit's wooden items, which he throws into a heap, ready to set the house on fire. Although jaunty, the song's attempt to be witty is too forced, and its brevity means that it sets up the expectation of a bigger gesture without delivering a point or action (in the end, Alice eats a carrot and shrinks and runs away); it almost feels like a verse without a refrain, a fragment of *H.M.S. Pinafore* without a fully realized purpose.

The Dodo's earlier appearance in the film is also let down by undercooked musical strategies. He first emerges during Alice's early seconds in Wonderland when she floats in the bottle on the sea of her own tears, the bird coming into view to the sound of the traditional "Sailor's Hornpipe," which he briefly sings along to (again, the *Pinafore* reference is set up, perhaps in an attempt to situate the scene in the world of Carroll's Victorian musical contemporaries). It's a shame that Fain and Hilliard didn't provide the Dodo with an equivalent to "I'm Late" here; like that number, the "Hornpipe" serves as both a travel song and a character song, but because it is so short and a well-known folk tune, it does not really form part of the original musical fabric of the film. Instead, "Row, Row, Row Your Boat" is now heard briefly in the orchestra as a transition while Alice struggles to stay afloat, the use of another preexisting "musical borrowing" adding to the sense of the general and the generic, and it segues into "The Caucus Race," in which different birds march in a circle around the Dodo.

This is one of the biggest missteps of Disney's adaptation as a whole; it is too literal an adaptation of Carroll in one of his most explicit satires of Victorian society and yet misses the point. To the adult reader of the book, it's obvious that when Carroll has the animals march around and around in circles to dry off and then declare "everyone" the winner of the "caucus race," he's commenting on the circularity and competitiveness of the use of the caucus to deal with political situations in English society. Haughton explains: "Carroll self-mockingly portrays the Dodo as prone to political pomposity, no doubt learned at Oxford." He adds that because a caucus is supposed to be about using solidarity to create unified action, "The idea of a 'caucus race' undermines the whole idea of a caucus as well as that of a race."[24]

But because Disney's overall inclination was to reconceive the books for a modern American audience in vaudeville-type entertainment, the need to read this song as a satire of British Victorian society is too dense to land. Nor does Disney's version have the crucial debating before and after the "race" for even this subtextual meaning to be apparent; there is no declaration in the film, as in the book, by the Dodo that "*Everybody* has won, and *all* must have prizes."[25] It's tempting to blame Fain and Hilliard for missing the point of Carroll's episode, but the copyright deposit version of the song, dated March 30, 1949, reveals that they wrote a longer song with different lyrics that originally foregrounded the political satire. The original version of the refrain claimed that it "Makes no difference where you run as long as you don't stop" and added that at the end of the race, "no one ever seems to lose." The end of the song also featured the demand for prizes from the book and concluded: "Hail the caucus race where ev'rybody wins a prize." It seems, therefore, that the Disney artists stepped back from fully embracing the satire of Carroll's chapter that was augmented in Fain and Hilliard's original conception. Yet the studio chose to retain a decontextualized version of the race, hoping that the vaudevillian nonsense of the animals marching in circles to a jaunty tune would provide enough charm to carry the scene.

The third Wallace–Sears song in the film is another problematic addition with a sense of vaudeville. The Caterpillar's "A-E-I-O-U," written for character actor Richard Haydn, suffers from its orientalist musical characteristics, derived from both Carroll's description and Tenniel's drawing (unlike many of the characters, the Disney version of the Caterpillar strongly resembles Tenniel's). The main idea of the scene is cute in the abstract: when the Caterpillar speaks, letters from his speech emerge from his mouth as he smokes his hookah. This provides a great concept for the Disney animators to create something visually distinctive for this episode. But the image of the hookah, Haydn's accent, and the disdainful characterization combine to create a depiction of the Caterpillar entirely based on the othering tendencies of both Carroll's era and the vaudeville (in which yellowface performances were common).[26] Further, "A-E-I-O-U" is another example of Wallace and Sears providing an undeveloped song fragment rather than a complete song. As she approaches him, Alice hears the Caterpillar singing the vowels to a racially stereotyped chromatic melody, but nothing more comes of it. Instead of a song, Alice starts to recite Isaac Watts's 1715 poem "How Doth the Busy Little Bee" and is interrupted by the Caterpillar, who recites his own version ("How doth the little crocodile").[27] This is musically accompanied by the "A-E-I-O-U" theme, again framing the character as the product of an orientalist vision. Thus, the scene suffers twice: once from outdated cultural references and once from the absence of the kind of strong musical scenic structure that Fain and Hilliard provide in the opening scene of the film.

Song and Genre in the Final Sequences

Fain and Hilliard take over again for the final two scenes: the Tulgey Wood sequence, in which Alice becomes lost and sits reflecting on the perils of her curiosity, and the Queen's garden scene. The wood scene finds the Disney artists on some kind of home territory: the way Alice gets lost and encounters initially disconcerting but ultimately sympathetic animals strongly parallels *Snow White* and, to an extent, the visual world of *Bambi*. The primary difference here is that *Alice*'s animals are anthropomorphized objects (e.g., a bird made from a mirror, a dog in the form of a brush, frogs made from a cymbal and timpani, vultures made from umbrellas). At last, the film's chase is paused because Alice herself decides to give up, rather than because another character detains her, and her more active role in this decision makes it a powerful gesture. Once she has stopped, the visual element of the scene is also powerful: the "animals" perch listening to her soliloquy, and many of them start to shed tears, as does Alice.

The soliloquy itself comes in the form of Fain and Hilliard's song "Very Good Advice," and as with their work in the opening scene of the movie, their experience of writing for character in (other) musicals means they know how to use song to clinch a dramatic moment. Alice sobs her way through the song with sustained string chord accompaniment and, later, distant choral "oohs"; her sentiments could have been declaimed in speech, but the use of a thirty-two-bar song structure (melody plus accompaniment) heightens the expressivity to a more emotive level of storytelling. Here, at last, Alice moves from curiosity to vulnerability—perhaps too late, but it pulls the focus away from the nonsense characters she meets and toward Alice and her feelings.

From there, the Cheshire Cat returns to reveal a shortcut through a tree trunk to the Queen's garden, Alice's final destination in Wonderland. She hears and then sees a group of playing cards painting a white rose bush red to appease the Queen of Hearts, and Fain and Hilliard come up trumps with an appropriate song, "Painting the Roses Red." The Card Painters are voiced by the Mellomen, a male vocal quartet who contributed to several other major Disney features (*Peter Pan*, *Lady and the Tramp*, *The Jungle Book*). Here their song is a jaunty march, written out in a straight 4/4 meter in the copyright deposit version dated July 27, 1949, but performed in a bouncier 6/8 in the movie. When Alice happens upon them, the Cards are singing to accompany their activity, but Fain and Hilliard cleverly transition from this illustrative function to a more narrative one by having Alice interject to ask them what they're doing ("Oh pardon me / But Mister 3 / Why must you paint them red?"), using the same music. They then respond in song to explain that the Queen likes them red (and if they didn't change the color, "She'd raise a fuss / And each of us / Would quickly lose his head").

Thus, although the whimsical vamp, barbershop voicing, and melodic line (in other words, the musical surface) broadly fit with the vaudevillian aspects noted earlier in this chapter, the function of the song changes substantially as the music progresses (from vocal soundtrack to vocal dialogue). This is the strength of the Fain–Hilliard sophisticated "theater" approach in which song is used flexibly, familiar from operetta and Broadway musicals. There is another musical transformation in this sequence, too: the song's 6/8 vamp becomes the 4/4 "March of the Cards" which underscores much of the action around the croquet game. Fain revealed in an interview that it was Walt's idea to create this: "I had this two-bar intro, or 'vamp,' that I was using for another song [i.e., 'Painting the Roses Red'], and Walt heard it one day. He came over and said, 'Sammy, I like that. I think it would fit with the cards marching. Do you think you can do something with it?' "[28]

That forms the end of new music in the movie, but it is not the end of song gestures familiar from operetta and the musical. After the roses number, Alice plays croquet with the Queen, but the Cheshire Cat pops up and causes confusion. Alice is put on trial, again encountering the Hatter and the Hare, who reprise the "Unbirthday Song." She magically grows, then shrinks, and is pursued out of the court by the Queen and her subjects. Alice has now reached the climax of her dream, and as she retraces her steps through Wonderland, other songs are also reprised, including "The Caucus Race" and (without the lyrics) the Caterpillar's song when she meets the latter floating on the sea of tears. These reprises are interspersed with general mickey-mousing, but the decision to bring back songs in reprise-finale style keeps the film in the performance-oriented world of the musical genre and avoids the horror imagery of both the 1939 and 1943 storyboards: in the former, Alice is tied to a wooden board and looks with terror on a guillotine descending toward her; in the latter, she is chased more aggressively, up ropes and walls.

Conclusion

Two months before *Alice in Wonderland* was released to mixed reviews and a box-office loss, Walt Disney published an article in the magazine *Films in Review*, titled "How I Cartooned 'Alice.'"[29] It began: "The animation of *Alice in Wonderland* presented the most formidable problems we have ever faced in translating a literary classic into the cartoon medium. We became aware of these problems at the very first of our staff conferences." He identifies these problems as (1) Carroll's greater interest in "ideas and fantasy" than in "the rules of suspense and story structure," (2) the large number of Carroll's characters (more than eighty by Disney's calculation), and (3) the need to tell the story in a fraction of the time available to Carroll in his two books.

Yet Disney reveals nothing about the role of song, and the songwriters, in providing pathways to either a narrative structure or an overall style for the film. The primary sources and analysis in this chapter show that while the thirteen credited story artists and ten directing animators obviously led the daunting task of turning Carroll's *Alice* into Disney's, the songwriters were behind many of the ideas that made a *musical* adaptation not only possible but an effective way of translating the novels into animation. Thanks to Fain and Hilliard, the opening and closing minutes of the film use the language of song to establish character and advance the plot. It's true that the use of such a diffuse team of writers and songwriters overall resulted in a kaleidoscopic approach, where each sequence of the film has its own way of dealing with Carroll's episodic structure. The outcome may be uneven, but at the film's best, by using vaudevillian voice actors, musical techniques, and imagery, Disney and his artists evolve Victorian political jokes into contemporary American storytelling.

APPENDIX 1

SONGS BY SONGWRITING TEAMS IN *ALICE IN WONDERLAND*

Wallace, Sears, Coben, and Carroll	Churchill, Osborne, and Carroll	David, Hoffman, and Livingston	Fain and Hilliard	Raye and de Paul
"A-E-I-O-U" (The Caterpillar Song), with Sears	"Alice and Bottle," with Osborne (unused).	"Curiosity" (unused), LOC June 2, 1948	"Alice in Wonderland" (theme song), demo July 13, 1949	"Beautiful Soup" (set to Johann Strauss's "Blue Danube" waltz), written for the Mock Turtle (deleted character), demo August 5, 1947 (DVD lists composition date as July 16, 1947)
"How D'Ye Do and Shake Hands," with Coben	"Alice in Wonderland," (unused, m. only), LOC Aug. 14, 1939	"Dream Caravan" (unused), LOC Aug. 4, 1948, demo July 23, 1948	"All in the Golden Afternoon," LOC Sept. 28, 1949	"Beware the Jabberwock," LOC June 2, 1947, demo May 14, 1947
"Old Father William," with Carroll	"Garden Snips" (unused, m. only), LOC July 12, 1939	"Everything Has a Useness" (unused), June 28, 1948 (demo on DVD and LD, rec. July 22, 1948)	"Beyond the Laughing Sky" (unused; DVD says it was too similar to "Over the Rainbow" and risky to begin with a ballad; became "The Second Star to the Right"; replaced by "In a World of My Own"), demo Feb. 25, 1949, copyright deposit May 16, 1949	"'Twas Brillig," demo June 1, 1949

Wallace, Sears, Coben, and Carroll	Churchill, Osborne, and Carroll	David, Hoffman, and Livingston	Fain and Hilliard	Raye and de Paul
"We'll Smoke the Blighter Out," Sears and Winston Hibler	"It's Crazy to Be Sane," with Osborne) (unused), July 25, 1939	"If You'll Believe in Me (I'll Believe in You)" (unused; written for the Lion and the Unicorn, cut from final film), Aug. 4, 1948, songwriters' demo July 23, 1948	"The Caucus Race," demo March 11, 1949, copyright deposit May 2, 1949	
	"Lobster Quadrille" with Carroll (unused; became "Never Smile at a Crocodile" from *Peter Pan*), LOC June 6, 1939	"The Unbirthday Song," LOC 1948, demo Feb. 15, 1949	"I'm Late," demo March 11, 1949	
	"Mock Turtle Soup Song," with Carroll (unused), LOC June 15, 1939, demo July 13, 1949		"I'm Odd" (unused), Sept. 28, 1949	
	"Pepper Lullaby," with Carroll (unused), LOC July 27, 1939		"In a World of My Own," 1949, piano-only demo Feb. 3, 1949	
	"Sketch for Alice in Wonderland (Cater Pillar Tread)," Churchill (unused music)		"March of the Cards" (music only)	

Wallace, Sears, Coben, and Carroll	Churchill, Osborne, and Carroll	David, Hoffman, and Livingston	Fain and Hilliard	Raye and de Paul
			"Painting the Roses Red," 1951	
			"Very Good Advice," 1949	
			"The Walrus and the Carpenter," demo Aug. 10, 20, 1947, 22, 1947 (Blu-ray lists a second undated version)	
			"Where Is Wonderland?" (revised as "Alice in Wonderland"), LOC July 27, 1949	

APPENDIX 2

ADDITIONAL, UNATTRIBUTED, UNUSED SONGS CULLED FROM DVD AND LASERDISC RELEASES

"Alice and the Cheshire Cat," demo July 19, 1947
"Beautiful Soup" (different version)
"The Carpenter Is Sleeping," demo July 18, 1948
"Dance," demo July 18, 1948
"Entrance of the Executioner," demo July 18, 1948
"Entrance of the Walrus and the Carpenter," demo July 18, 1948
"Finale," demo July 18, 1948
"Gavotte of the Cards," demo July 18, 1948
"How Doth the Little Crocodile," demo Aug. 4, 1947
"Humpty Dumpty" (origin of "Unbirthday Song"), demo July 18, 1948
"The Jabberwocky Song" (lyrics from Carroll), demo Aug. 5, 1947
"The Lion and the Unicorn," demo Aug. 4, 1947
"So They Say," demo July 18, 1948
"Speak Roughly to Your Little Boy," demo July 18, 1948

"When the Wind Is in the East" (Mad Hatter's song), demo July 18, 1948

"Will You Join the Dance?" (a different version of "Lobster Quadrille"), demo Aug. 5, 1947

Notes

1. Mark Salisbury discusses the abandonment of the Perkins-Hall version on the grounds that "Hall's decision to stick close to [original Carroll illustrator John] Tenniel's creations made his designs difficult to animate." Mark Salisbury, *Walt Disney's "Alice in Wonderland": An Illustrated Journey through Time* (Los Angeles: Disney Editions, 2016), 54. The laserdisc release of the film also reveals that Perkins made a story analysis dated September 6, 1938. Aspects of the 1939 story reel are discussed later in this chapter.
2. Ibid., 46. The 1995 laserdisc release of the film also reveals that Technicolor film tests were shot with Mary Pickford at this point.
3. Part of the discussion leading up to the complete reconstruction of the Cheshire Cat's unused song, "I'm Odd."
4. David Tietyen, *The Musical World of Walt Disney* (Milwaukee: Hal Leonard, 1990), 93.
5. Frank Thomas interview, clip from "Reflections on Alice," Blu-ray release.
6. Linda Hutcheon, *A Theory of Adaptation*, 2nd ed. (Oxford: Routledge, 2013), xx.
7. Quoted by Hugh Haughton in his introduction to Lewis Carroll, *Alice's Adventures in Wonderland and Through the Looking-Glass* (London: Penguin, 1998), xxxiv.
8. Lewis Carroll, "'Alice' on the Stage," reproduced in ibid., 293–294.
9. Edward Guiliano, *Lewis Carroll: The Worlds of His Alices* (Brighton, UK: Edward Everett Root, 2019), 78.
10. Carroll, "'Alice' on the Stage," 295.
11. Carroll, *Alice's Adventures in Wonderland and Through the Looking-Glass*, 186.
12. Haughton, introduction, lviii.
13. Ibid., lvi.
14. Hutcheon, *A Theory of Adaptation*, 31.
15. *Alice in Wonderland*, 1995 laserdisc edition.
16. Daniel Koltenschulte, ed., *The Walt Disney Film Archives* (Cologne: Taschen, 2016), 430.
17. Koltenschulte, *The Walt Disney Film Archives*, 430.
18. Salisbury, *Walt Disney's "Alice in Wonderland,"* 76.
19. Tietyen, *The Musical World of Walt Disney*, 96.
20. The Blu-ray release of the film includes a special feature in which a synopsis of the scene with this date is shown.
21. Russell Schroeder, *Disney's Lost Chords* (Robbinsville, NC: Voigt Publications, 2007), 173–175.
22. Tietyen, *The Musical World of Walt Disney*, 93–94.
23. Brian Sibley, "In a World of Her Own," in Koltenschulte, *The Walt Disney Film Archives*, 413.
24. Haughton's editorial notes to his edition of Carroll, *Alice's Adventures in Wonderland and Through the Looking-Glass*, 305.
25. Carroll, *Alice's Adventures in Wonderland and Through the Looking-Glass*, 26.
26. For a useful overview of yellowface in North American theater and film, see Josephine Lee, "Yellowface Performance: Historical and Contemporary Contexts," in *Oxford Research Encyclopedia of Literature*, February 25, 2019, https://doi.org/10.1093/acrefore/9780190201098.013.834

27. Alice recites it early on in the book rather than in the Caterpillar chapter, Carroll's parody "crocodile" version coming unexpectedly out of her mouth.
28. Tietyen, *The Musical World of Walt Disney*, 96.
29. Walt Disney, "How I Cartooned 'Alice': Its Logical Nonsense Needed a Logical Sequence," *Films in Review* 2, no. 5 (May 1951): 7–11. Sibley, "In a World of Her Own," 413, questions whether Disney himself wrote the article.

CHAPTER 9

FIDELITY-FIDUCIARY-EXPIALIDOCIOUS: *MARY POPPINS*'S RETURNS

SEAN GRIFFIN

THE Walt Disney Company has produced many artistic contributions to the film-musical genre, such as its first feature film, *Snow White and the Seven Dwarfs* (1937), and its string of animated triumphs in the late 1980s and early 1990s, including *The Little Mermaid* (1989), *Beauty and the Beast* (1991), and *The Lion King* (1994). These motion-picture musicals received not only critical acclaim but also incredible financial gain and are arguably key to the international power the company now holds in the entertainment industry. As such, particularly with the more recent successes, Disney has worked to maximize their profit potential. Using strategies of synergy, these titles have become a form of "branded" entertainment that can be sold and resold in various ways. To provide one example, the success of *The Lion King* spurred a variety of merchandising tie-ins to the original animated feature: a soundtrack CD, action figures, Halloween costumes, coloring books, and so on—as well as the home-video release and its debut broadcast on the Disney Channel cable station. Straight-to-video sequels and a spin-off syndicated animated series based on supporting characters Timon and Pumbaa resulted, too. In 1997, Disney Theatrical converted the film musical into a live stage musical which is still running on Broadway, as is the 1999 London production. In 2019, the studio released a new screen version of the project, using CGI animation to make it look more as if actual animals were performing the roles (with star performers such as Donald Glover and Beyoncé as the voices). In this way, Disney has been able to continuously squeeze more returns out of this one property.

Mary Poppins (1964) is another landmark musical in the Disney canon and generally regarded as one of the best films ever made by the studio. Like the others mentioned above, the film exceeded box-office expectations, and, as will be discussed, it helped boost the company into a new era of expansion. Perhaps unsurprisingly, the Walt Disney Company sought to capitalize on that success. Yet, as this chapter examines, Disney's attempt to brand Mary Poppins as intellectual property for future ventures has not gone as smoothly or as profitably as the company had hoped. I argue that there is an internal tension structured within the original film around issues of capital gain that may have created a stumbling block for Disney to successfully deploy its usual modus operandi of synergy.

The Magic of Mary

The opening to *Mary Poppins* is perhaps surprisingly understated. A tremulous, reverent orchestra plays softly over a meticulously rendered painting of the London cityscape at twilight. Perhaps such a quiet opening lures the audience to "lean in" to the adventures that await, but such a humble beginning is nonetheless striking. Recall that the film was released in the middle of Hollywood's commitment to the big-budget blockbuster, as studios tried to draw viewers away from their TV sets through sheer size and spectacle. Julie Andrews, who would win a Best Actress Oscar for her portrayal of Mary Poppins, would go on to become identified with the musical-blockbuster trend of the 1960s (*The Sound of Music* [1965], *Thoroughly Modern Millie* [1967], *Star!* [1968], and *Darling Lili* [1970]).

The somewhat hushed start of *Mary Poppins* sets the audience up for what ultimately will be the key to the film's themes: it's the small things that matter, those tiny acts of human kindness that lead to happiness and fulfillment, more than material comfort. The song written by Richard M. and Robert B. Sherman that provides the opening strains of the overture precisely expresses that sentiment. "Feed the Birds" advises the listener to pay attention to the tattered old woman sitting on the steps of St. Paul's Cathedral asking passersby to pay "tuppence a bag" for seed to feed the pigeons (thus being charitable to her as well as the birds). Walt Disney reportedly loved this song and regularly asked the Shermans to come to his office and play it for him, and he supposedly teared up regularly during those performances.[1] The central narrative of the film shows Mr. Banks (David Tomlinson), a mid-level banker aspiring to a greater career in finance, learning that spending precious time with his two children, Jane (Karen Dotrice) and Michael (Matthew Garber), is ultimately more important than working constantly. Juxtaposed against the beauty of "Feed the Birds" is the humorous bombast of another song, "Fidelity Fiduciary Bank." Banks and his superiors sing *this* tune in an attempt to persuade Michael to give his tuppence to them to invest in bank shares rather than to buy seed for the birds of St. Paul's. Through the subtle machinations of the magical nanny Mary Poppins, Banks shifts his outlook from the attitude of "Fidelity Fiduciary Bank" to that of "Feed the Birds."

The opening scenes of the film center around Mr. Banks as he confidently rules the house—even though the home is plainly shown in various stages of chaos (of which he seems somewhat oblivious). Yet once Mary Poppins literally lands on his doorstep (flying down while holding her umbrella) to watch over the children, she largely shoves him off-screen for long portions of the film. His attempts to reassert his authority go blithely unheeded, and ultimately he must adjust to *her* authority. As Douglas Brode has observed in his survey of the Disney oeuvre and the 1960s counterculture, Banks is pleased to be a "raw capitalist" until "the intervention of that hippie-ish heroine, Mary Poppins."[2] Unlike Mr. Banks's petit bourgeois aspirations, Mary Poppins regularly is shown right at home with communities farther down on the class ladder: cavorting across rooftops with chimney sweeps, joining in performance with animated Cockney buskers, and being friends with Bert (Dick Van Dyke), who seems to shift from one low-paying type of work to another every day. In other moments, she smoothly participates in elements associated with higher social culture, but she upends them with aplomb—such as bursting in on a fox hunt while riding a freed carousel horse (and helping to save the fox from perdition) or pouring afternoon tea while those assembled float near the ceiling of the room. Her joyous ability to transcend and upend the British class structure is somehow connected to her talent for overcoming the laws of physics and even her triumph over the English language with the amalgamation of "supercalifragilisticexpialidocious," a "word you say when you don't know what to say."

"Supercalifragilisticexpialidocious" itself indicates the importance of the Sherman brothers as central creative voices in fashioning the adaptation of the books by P. L. Travers to the screen. Walt had been interested in making a movie about Mary Poppins for more than a decade, but various attempts at story treatments had not satisfied him. Walt also faced much resistance from Travers herself in transferring her beloved nanny to the silver screen. While the Shermans considered Travers as a foe, she nevertheless did approve of "Feed the Birds" and even eventually argued for keeping "Stay Awake" in the film, saying that the reverse psychology of the lyrics was exactly something her Mary Poppins would do.[3] Similarly, Walt appreciated how the songs the Shermans wrote helped shape the film's narrative. Their use of a particular tune displays the character arc that Mr. Banks goes through in his encounters with the nanny. The song "The Life I Lead" introduces Banks and describes his self-satisfied, well-ordered, patriarchal universe. The song is reprised about midway through the film as he attempts to take Mary Poppins to task for taking the children on adventures he finds questionable. Yet she appropriates the number, turns it to her own plan, and by the end has him agreeing to take charge of the children himself. Then, toward the emotional climax of the film, as Banks feels desolate and ruined, about to be fired from his position at the bank, the melody returns one more time ("A Man Has Dreams"). This sung conversation with Bert brings him to the realization that his devotion to work—"grind grind grind at that grindstone"—has been at the expense of quality time with his offspring: "and all too soon they've up and grown, and then they've flown, and it's too late for you to give." It is from this epiphany that Banks becomes a new man, indicated by his own ability to pronounce "supercalifragilisticexpialidocious," which he had been incapable of doing previously. His use of it to rebuke his superiors at the bank implicitly indicts the gobbledygook vernacular they speak in "Fidelity Fiduciary Bank." Banks leaves them so he can go fly a kite with his children. Her goal achieved, Mary Poppins departs the household into the clouds.

Mary Poppins's ability to continuously outmaneuver and overpower Mr. Banks is a somewhat stunning reversal of gender dynamics—certainly for the 1910s, the era in which the film is set, but even for 1964, the year the film was released. Granted, it can be argued that the film dismisses women's liberation in its portrayal of Mrs. Banks (Glynis Johns) and her involvement in the British suffragette movement.[4] Just as Mr. Banks is critiqued for ignoring the children in favor of his career, it is implied that Mrs. Banks's participation in protest marches keeps her from being present enough as a mother. Further, while she seems initially strident in her commitment, that fervor goes right out the window the second her husband comes home. Ultimately, to show that she, too, has learned the importance of spending time with her family, she offers up her "Votes for Women" sash to be the tail on Michael's kite, as the foursome happily run off to the park together at the end of the film. Nevertheless, Mary Poppins's presence counters that potential critique of feminism. Unlike Mrs. Banks's bourgeois dabbling in women's-rights protests, Poppins simply lives a life free from male domination and doesn't care who is put out by it. She not only expertly manipulates Mr. Banks but also smoothly elides any potential romantic entanglement with Bert—and flies off at the end of the film not heterosexually linked up with any man. Undoubtedly, the outlook of author Travers factors here, a strong, opinionated woman who became famous in studio folklore for how she faced off against Walt in maintaining her say over how her character would be portrayed.[5]

Consequently, *Mary Poppins* manages to walk an intriguing balance in its social outlook. It seems to regard first-wave feminism as humorous and yet provides a strong, independent female protagonist. It is a high-budget musical spectacle that seems to teach audiences that money isn't everything. (It should be noted here that once Mr. Banks himself learns this lesson, he manages to keep his job at the bank.) In providing magical special effects and cartoon characters, the movie appealed to children, but it provided enough dramatic heft to draw parents in as well. In its balance of traditional elements and more progressive ideas, the picture positioned itself perfectly for its time, with the postwar conventions of one generation just on the verge of giving way to more radical notions espoused by a younger generation and its counterculture.[6]

Further, for a film seeming to express that material gain is, well, immaterial, *Mary Poppins* would become the highest-grossing film in the studio's history to that point and the top-grossing film of 1964—beating out the lavish Warner Bros. adaptation of the Broadway hit *My Fair Lady* (which had made Andrews a stage star, but her role was given to Audrey Hepburn for the film version). In its original theatrical release, the picture grossed more than $31 million. It would result in such a financial mother lode that it would become the foundation for the company's plans to build a new theme park in Florida. Walt had created a separate entity devoted to research and development of technology for use at Disneyland back in 1953, called WED Enterprises (the moniker coming from Walt's initials, since he bankrolled the institution as a separate entity from the studio). Using the enormous profits of *Mary Poppins*, the company in 1965 formally incorporated WED Enterprises (buying out Walt's personal ownership) and built new facilities. Dubbed the Manufacturing and Production Organization, the division went by the initials MAPO, which was not coincidentally a portmanteau using the first two letters of Mary and Poppins (and employees of the division wore name tags emblazoned with a silhouette of Mary Poppins with umbrella and carpetbag).[7] Thus, the success of that delicate balance of elements in *Mary Poppins* would help carry the company through the loss of Walt in 1966 and help open Walt Disney World in 1971.

THE TROUBLES WITH TRAVERS

Such success led inevitably to thoughts of follow-ups. Evidence indicates that the studio began conceptualizing a sequel almost immediately. Such talks, though, went nowhere, in large part, from most reports, due to the intransigence of Travers, who reportedly was not terribly pleased with how the first film turned out.[8] Unable at this point to move forward, the studio instead produced a *Poppins* clone: *Bedknobs and Broomsticks* (1971). This project had been bandied about within the studio for a number of years as a backup in case negotiations with Travers on the first *Mary Poppins* ever collapsed.[9] Thus, the film carries many similarities to *Mary Poppins*: a single woman with magical powers taking children under her wing, with a lengthy animated sequence, a score by the Shermans (including "The Beautiful Briny Sea," a song originally written for *Poppins*), directed by Robert Stevenson, and even David Tomlinson returning as the leading male actor. The film was successful but nowhere near the level of box office as *Poppins*, bringing in just more than $17 million, about half of what the first film earned.[10] While thought of fondly by many, it still stands in the shadows of the 1964 film. One of the major differences between the two movies is what happens to the central female character. Whereas Mary Poppins remains independent and unattached as she flies off into the clouds, Eglantine Price (Angela Lansbury) gets domesticized. Not only does she become the children's permanent guardian, but she also gets romantically attached to Emelius Browne (Tomlinson). As will be shown, this would be only the first effort to redirect certain of the more ideologically transgressive aspects of the original *Mary Poppins*.

The desire to bring back Mary Poppins never completely ebbed. Conversations continued across the years, including Travers herself trying her hand at writing a sequel screenplay, with Brian Sibley. *Mary Poppins Comes Back* was in various forms of discussion in the early 1980s between Travers and Walt's nephew, Roy E. Disney—but again, nothing came of it, partially due to the changeover to a new executive board at Disney in 1984.[11] This was the dawn of Michael Eisner, Frank Wells, and Jeffrey Katzenberg, who dubbed themselves Team Disney. Together the triumvirate would bring the company out of the financial doldrums experienced in the wake of Walt's death and would propel it toward becoming a corporate juggernaut. Key to Team Disney's template was synergy, seeing how all of the company's intellectual property could be repurposed and resold across its many platforms—its theatrical films, its home-video department, its cable network, its merchandising division, its theme parks—and each sale simultaneously acting as marketing for sales on those other platforms. Once the new team was up and running, Katzenberg and Martin Kaplan (Vice President in Charge of Live-Action Production) approached Travers again about a sequel, but her terms (including not wanting Andrews) led to no agreement.[12] Another Team Disney stratagem—strongly maintaining ownership and control of Disney projects—likely did not help negotiations.

Team Disney's pursuit of synergistic potential led to its creation of Disney Theatrical Productions in 1993, and its multimillion-dollar investment in the renovation of the Times Square/Broadway district in New York City, including the purchase and refurbishment of the New Amsterdam Theater. While Disney Theatrical would fund some original productions, it has largely overseen the adaptation of some of its most successful motion-picture musicals to the stage, beginning with *Beauty and the Beast* (which first opened on Broadway in 1994). Most of these adaptations had to solve not only going from screen to stage but also the difficulty of going from animation to live-action. The studio's most successful live-action film musical was, of course, *Mary Poppins*, and thus, it would seem a natural selection to adapt. The problem was that Travers gave the rights to develop a theatrical version of her books not to Disney but to British impresario Sir Cameron Mackintosh, who had produced major hit stage musicals including *Cats*, *Les Misérables*, *The Phantom of the Opera*, and *Miss Saigon*. In a further attempt to stymie Disney's ability to capitalize on *Mary Poppins*, Travers's agreement with Mackintosh stipulated that all creative people involved had to be British and that no one involved with the 1964 film could work on whatever production was created.[13]

Under this stipulation, Mackintosh brought on a number of major British talents to craft a theatrical musical about Travers's magical nanny, including Sir Richard Eyre as director and Julian Fellowes as writer of the book. The songwriting team of George Stiles and Anthony Drewe was also retained. Yet Mackintosh ultimately realized that audiences would be disappointed if any stage musical did not include the well-loved songs written by the Shermans. After the passing of Travers in 1996, a collaboration with Disney Theatrical became more possible. Nevertheless, the stage property was not a full replica of the original film: some of the score by the Shermans was used, and the plot of the original movie functioned as a foundation, but a new storyline was fashioned. The creators of the live stage production also recognized the folly of attempting to replicate the special-effects magic possible on film (such as the audio-animatronic bird that Andrews sings with in "A Spoonful of Sugar" which was a forerunner to the attractions that would be developed at MAPO). Thus, new sequences were developed with park statues and the children's toys coming to life, as well as magical moments happening in the kitchen of the Banks home. The production opened in December 2004 in London's West End, and ran for more than three years. Its success ensured a transfer to the US and Broadway, which began in November 2006, and it ran for six years and 2,619 performances, closing to make way for the next Disney screen-to-stage adaptation, *Aladdin*.

While perhaps not as much of a runaway critical and financial juggernaut as the 1964 film, the stage version of *Mary Poppins* was still very successful. Of all the other attempts to revive the Disney Mary Poppins brand, it is the iteration as focused on critiquing the drive for money and economic position as the original film. Quite arguably, the stage version is the most class-conscious of all the productions surveyed in this chapter. Mr. Banks is not introduced as someone feeling blithely dominant over his household until Mary Poppins disrupts his equilibrium. Rather, he is portrayed as a man slaving at his job, desperate to maintain appearances as a comfortable middle-class banker with a home, a cook, and a nanny for the children, even though this all stretches his salary to the breaking point. As Sibley and Michael Lassell point out in their book about the making of the stage musical, writer Fellowes (who had already written the film *Gosford Park* [2001] and would go on to the award-winning television series *Downton Abbey* [2010–2015]) had a very "clear understanding of the social niceties of the English class system that prevailed in the Edwardian era."[14] As such, Banks is much more threatened by Mary Poppins—and, to the surprise of those familiar only with the original film, she decides to leave at the end of Act 1.

In Act 2, the woman who had been Banks's own nanny is hired—a tyrant named Miss Andrew (which, although the name is in the original books, is an ironic moniker in relation to Travers's attitude towards the original film). Mary Poppins returns to vanquish Miss Andrew, and Banks comes to the same realization as before, thus ensuring the requisite happy ending, with Mary Poppins flying away (this time up beyond the balcony seats via elaborate engineering in the theater). The appearance of Miss Andrew and the ongoing anxiety of Banks are among other elements in the stage production that make it much darker than the 1964 film. Jane and Michael are presented as very out-of-control children at the outset, and it seems they need to be "scared straight" by a couple of pretty terrifying sequences, including a nightmare scene in which their toys come to life, threatening to mishandle them the way Jane and Michael have always treated their playthings. The intensity of these darker moments led the West End production to ban anyone younger than three years old from attending performances, because the show was felt too scary for small children. Perhaps realizing the likely lost revenue, this nightmare sequence was revised in its transfer to the States and Broadway, even replacing the original song "Temper, Temper" with a new one titled "Playing the Game."

A number of factors may have influenced this darker tone. First, the influence of Travers over the stage version, even after her death, may have led to maintaining a more taciturn rendition of Mary Poppins and her environment. Tied to that, class division and dynamics have been traditionally more pronounced in British culture than in American society, and thus, the economic issues contained in the original film's narrative were brought out more in this British-based stage production. And lastly, at the time of the stage show's debut in 2004, the world was still grappling with the emotional trauma of the events of September 11, 2001, and the subsequent War on Terror—thus, global society *was* dark and scared. As I personally witnessed during the West End run, theater patrons often wept at the end as Mary Poppins glided away; things might be better for the Banks family, but the audience still felt they needed her to stay and take care of them. Such outpourings of emotion suggested that Mary Poppins still mattered to people—and Disney saw this as further indication that it needed to see what else she could do not only for audiences but for the company.

The Faltering in Franchising

The Mackintosh and Disney Theatrical co-production of the stage musical showed that Disney would have better success negotiating with the trustees of the Travers estate than they had with Travers herself when she was alive. By this time, Bob Iger had succeeded Eisner as CEO of the Walt Disney Company. Iger carried on and expanded the strategies of Team Disney that began in the late 1980s: to vigorously pursue tight ownership of intellectual property and then to synergistically exploit that intellectual property across multiple platforms and iterations—in other words, to invest heavily in projects that could become a dependable franchise. As such, Iger pursued the acquisition of a number of companies with lucrative franchises (buying already-fashioned franchises rather than creating new ones): Jim Henson's Muppets, Lucasfilm, Marvel, and eventually the entire 20th Century Fox studio. Every hit project was no longer judged just by its initial success with customers but was also judged by its potential to become a "brand." Such an outlook would factor into renewed interest in whether Mary Poppins could eke out any more tuppences.

The first chance to pursue a Poppins franchise was not a musical but a dramatic film about the making of the first movie. Screenwriters Kelly Marcel and Sue Smith had developed a script about Travers that centered around her contentious relationship with Walt Disney over adapting *Mary Poppins* to the big screen. They had developed the project as an independent film through BBC Films and Essential Media Entertainment. Yet when Disney was contacted about getting the rights to use material for this new motion picture, the studio bought up the rights to the property itself.[15] Walt Disney Studios chairman Alan Horn referred to the project as a "brand deposit."[16] Steve Jobs coined the term "brand deposit" to define how to add value to a company's (or a brand's) image and reputation. So, in regarding Mary Poppins as a brand within the Disney cache, the biopic *Saving Mr. Banks* (2013) would not only potentially bring critical and box-office acclaim to the company but also add luster to and interest in potential future Mary Poppins projects.

Certainly, Disney positioned *Saving Mr. Banks* as its prestige film project for the year. The film was given a much more lavish budget than had originally been envisioned as an independent film, including location shooting at a redressed Disneyland (to make it look as it did in 1964) and the casting of two Academy Award–winning stars for the leads: Tom Hanks as Walt Disney and Emma Thompson as Travers. The finished film hit theaters at the end of the year, when films are generally released for maximum consideration for Oscar nominations. A number of reviewers recognized how the movie functioned as hype for reviving the Mary Poppins brand. Geoffrey Macnab's review of the film for the British journal *The Independent* noted: "On the one hand, *Saving Mr. Banks* ... is a probing, insightful character study with a very dark undertow. On the other, it is a cheery, upbeat marketing exercise in which the Disney organization is re-promoting one of its most popular film characters."[17] Lou Lumenick's review for the *New York Post* was perhaps even more blunt: "*Saving Mr. Banks* is ultimately much less about magic than making the sale, in more ways than one."[18]

In the wake of the release of *Saving Mr. Banks*, Disney steamrolled ahead in producing a cinematic musical sequel. The Travers estate gave the approval for such a sequel, and in 2015, studio executives met with the team of Rob Marshall, John DeLuca, and Marc Tuton (who had just produced *Into the Woods* [2014] for the studio) to pitch the project to them.[19] *Mary Poppins Returns* would premiere on Christmas Day, 2018, with Marshall directing, a new raft of songs written by Marc Shaiman and Scott Wittman, and Emily Blunt replacing Andrews in the lead role. Plainly, from comments made by Marshall early in the film's release, the idea of a Mary Poppins franchise was in the air. Speaking at a BAFTA event in January 2019, he indicated that talks had happened about a third film, saying, "Listen, how many *Star Wars* films have there been, you know what I mean? Or James Bond films. If there's a great character and story to tell, why not?"[20]

The results of all this careful planning were not as good as hoped. Both films made money but nowhere near expectations. *Saving Mr. Banks* received only one Oscar nomination (for Thomas Newman's score), and Box Office Mojo reported that it came in fifth at the box office on its opening weekend.[21] While audiences largely ignored *Saving Mr. Banks*, another Disney movie which had opened three weeks prior (and which the studio seemed to be uncertain how to market) became a cultural phenomenon. Coming in at third place at the box office the week that *Banks* opened was the animated musical *Frozen* (2013), which would win two Oscars (for the song "Let It Go" and as Best Animated Feature), and the Internet Movie Database (IMDB) lists it as eventually earning $1.3 billion worldwide.[22] In comparison, *Banks* would bring in $118 million by the end of its international theatrical run.[23] *Mary Poppins Returns* did similarly respectable yet unremarkable business and garnered only lukewarm enthusiasm. Purported box-office projections for its five-day opening weekend were in the range of $49 million to $51 million; during that period, Box Office Mojo reported the film actually garnered $32.5 million.[24] IMDB lists a $130 million budget spent making the film and a gross of $172 million in the US and Canada.[25] In the years since Marshall made that comment about a third Mary Poppins film (or more), no further announcements have been made to suggest that more "brand deposits" are in the works.

So what happened? Why did the Disney synergistic "magic" not work? There are a variety of potential reasons, ranging from sociohistorical (*Mary Poppins* hit a sweet spot in American culture in the mid-1960s, but the national zeitgeist had shifted by 2018) to purely aesthetic (*Mary Poppins* is a well-made film, but *Mary Poppins Returns* is less so). Granted, the creative personnel involved in the sequel plainly attempted to honor what made the initial film work—in certain ways, almost slavishly. For example, songwriters Shaiman and Wittman penned practically perfect pastiches of the original score by the Shermans, and their placement within the structure of the sequel's narrative is an almost exact mapping of where the songs were placed in the first musical. "Can You Imagine That" replicates "A Spoonful of Sugar" as Mary Poppins engages in magic with the children in the nursery (albeit this time in their bathroom); "The Royal Doulton Music Hall" functions much like "Jolly Holiday" to introduce an animated adventure (with the animation drawn in the manner used by the studio in the 1960s); "A Cover Is Not the Book" mimics "Supercalifragilisticexpialidocious" in its music-hall style; "Turning Turtle" and its sequence with Cousin Topsy (Meryl Streep) duplicates the "I Love to Laugh" segment with Uncle Albert (Ed Wynn); "Trip a Little Light Fantastic" is a redo of "Step in Time" (but with lamplighters doing stunts with bicycles rather than chimney sweeps jumping around on rooftops); and "Nowhere to Go but Up" copies "Let's Go Fly a Kite" as a joyous final number (with balloons rather than kites). The Oscar-nominated song "The Place Where Lost Things Go" is obviously modeled on "Feed the Birds." As perhaps is apparent, the plot of the sequel also follows the path of the original film, with the Banks household again in disarray, a male parent needing guidance from Mary Poppins, and issues with the bank acting as a fulcrum. Perhaps the film did not match expectations precisely because it modeled itself too closely on the original film and thus felt like a pale copy—unlike the stage production, which went in its own direction in a number of ways.

Larger industrial factors could be considered as well. In 1964, Disney was still regarded as a relatively smaller Hollywood studio, and *Mary Poppins* was an attempt to "bat in the big leagues." Thus, the film had an underdog cache that helped it, particularly against Warner Bros. and *My Fair Lady*, which had decided to bypass Andrews. By the time *Mary Poppins Returns* was produced, Disney had become a global powerhouse that many regard almost as an evil empire. Just like the reviews cited earlier of *Saving Mr. Banks* that saw the film as a cold, calculated economic move rather than an artistic achievement, Christopher Orr's review of *Mary Poppins Returns* in *The Atlantic* was subtitled "Cunning Homage or Shameless Rip-Off?"[26] Such a viewpoint brings up another aspect: in attempting to fashion Mary Poppins as a franchise, both of these films attempt to "remold the brand" as well. This is perhaps most obvious in *Saving Mr. Banks*, which presents Travers giving in emotionally at points to the 1964 film when she watches it. Articles about *Saving Mr. Banks* pointed out a number of other historical revisions, such as creating more in-person interaction between Walt and Travers than had actually happened, which shows him explaining and wooing Travers toward his creative point of view—and supposedly partially succeeding.[27] More than that, the film suggests that Walt not only wins her (guarded) approval of the motion picture, but he also manages to help her work through her troubled memories of her alcoholic father (suggesting that the figure of Mr. Banks is her way of processing that traumatic relationship). Thus, rather than a strong, independent female forcing a businessman to rethink his priorities (as in *Mary Poppins*), *Saving Mr. Banks* shows a businessman helping a strong, independent female through her own dysfunctional past. The film's title highlights this dichotomy, upholding a male figure rather than naming the female author who is the actual protagonist of the story. Granted, publicity about the film made big mention of including reference to (but no on-screen representation of) Walt's chain-smoking, which would lead to his death from lung cancer only two years after the initial release of *Mary Poppins*.

But *Saving Mr. Banks* pretty nakedly attempts to burnish Walt's (and the studio's) reputation in order to "deposit" into the Mary Poppins brand. In refashioning the history so as to rein in Travers's rebellious independence, the movie also reverses a number of messages going on in the original film musical.

Similar attempts to harness and redirect what the Mary Poppins brand stands for occur within the musical sequel. It should be noted that a number of reviewers considered Blunt's rendition of Poppins "truer to the spirit of P. Travers's books" or closer to "Travers's original vision" than how she was written and how Andrews portrayed her back in 1964.[28] Yet, although it matches the original film's narrative structure and song placement, *Mary Poppins Returns* is also careful to endorse rather than bite the corporate philosophy that engendered it. Economic issues in the film are hard to ignore, since it begins with a title informing the audience that the story takes place during the "Slump" of the 1930s, the era commonly referred to in the United States as the Great Depression. Michael (Ben Wishaw) and Jane (Emily Mortimer) are now adults, and Michael is recently widowed and raising three children in the old Banks homestead. Although Michael works at the same bank as his father, he is only a clerk, and the house is in danger of being repossessed by the bank.

One can argue that the sequel is just as critical of high finance as the original film, presenting the bank's president, Mr. Wilkins (Colin Firth), as the central antagonist. He is a much more conventional and starkly drawn villain than any individual in the 1964 production, but that itself is important to recognize. The original film indicts a larger conceptual mindset shared by Mr. Banks and a number of executives for whom he works: a narrow focus on capital and investment. On the other hand, while Wilkins is clearly evil, most of the other people working at the bank seem to be empathetic to the Bankses' plight and eventually come to their aid. Some of these other employees are also people of color (something sorely lacking in the original film), further suggesting the institution as progressive and enlightened. Thus, Wilkins is positioned as "one bad apple" rather than representative of a larger system. The film actually upholds capitalism, arguing that it is capable of bringing justice and ethical resolution. First, it is revealed that Mr. Banks actually did take Michael's tuppence and invested it in bank shares, which saves the day and helps keep the home. This revelation absolutely contradicts the message of the first film, endorsing Banks's desire that Michael give the money to the bank rather than the bird woman. Second, when Wilkins attempts to disavow the certificate proving the ownership of those shares, Wilkins's uncle, Mr. Dawes Jr., sweeps in to overrule Wilkins. Adding to the sense of the "good" bank trustee riding to the rescue, Dawes is played by Dick Van Dyke in a carefully planned heartwarming cameo.[29]

Various other attempts to parallel aspects of the first film are reworked so as not to detract from the ultimate endorsement of big banking, perhaps unsurprising in an era when corporate venture capitalism and financial engineering dominate the entertainment industries.[30] Jane's involvement in union organizing acts as a parallel to her mother's involvement in the suffragette movement and is given perhaps even greater dismissive treatment. Mrs. Banks at least gets her own song, an anthem to first-wave feminism titled "Sister Suffragette." This is one of the only compositions without a match in the sequel, thus silencing any potential ode to the glories of unionization. Perhaps it is not surprising, then, that the other tune from the original film that has no comparative match in the sequel is "Fidelity Fiduciary Bank," which lampooned the celebration of capital investment. The only tangible benefit to Jane's support of the labor movement is that it helps create a potential romantic connection between her and Jack (Lin-Manuel Miranda), the lamplighter who effectively stands in for Bert of the original film.

A potentially larger parallel is the emotional repair needed within the Banks family, this time Michael and his children coming to grips with the loss of his wife and their mother. Mary Poppins seems there initially to provide a mother substitute, and "The Place Where Lost Things Go" is an attempt to help deal with the children's grief. "Feed the Birds" not only provides the opening strains to the first film but grounds the moral of that tale. "The Place Where Lost Things Go," on the other hand, is not as central to the sequel's narrative. None of songs of this film coheres or builds upon others in the ways the score from the first film does, as described earlier. Rather, the Shaiman and Wittman pastiche of a score is more concerned with linking up to individual songs from the previous picture.

The importance of "Feed the Birds" to *Mary Poppins* is emphasized by its use as underscore in the narrative climax, when Banks realizes the importance of spending time with his family rather than at the bank. In contrast, "Where the Lost Things Go" is not played during the sequel's climax, because the climax has nothing to do with processing the family's collective sorrow. In the largest break from the structure of the original film, *Mary Poppins Returns* inserts a race against time to get the certificate of shares to the bank before midnight. Thus, any larger emotional lesson is shoved aside in favor of old-fashioned melodramatic thrills. If anything, Mary Poppins flying off once again at the end of the sequel indicates not only that the Bankses no longer need her services but that they have let go of their need for the departed wife/mother—particularly now that Michael, Mr. Banks, and Mr. Dawes Jr. are able to set things right. Thus, just like *Saving Mr. Banks*, *Mary Poppins Returns* attempts to uphold both capitalism and patriarchy, plainly in an effort to bring added income to an international conglomerate that has succeeded handsomely via patriarchal capitalism.

Nonetheless, as evidenced by the underperformance of the sequel in its theatrical run, such attitudes literally were not bought by audiences. Viewers could simply choose to watch their home video of the original film (or stream it on Disney+) rather than see a warmed-over clone with ideologically altered DNA. The lack of the hoped-for spark may be emblematized in the sequel's final moments, as a balloon lady in the park helps all the characters go aloft singing "Nowhere to Go but Up." This character of the balloon lady was devised to provide a cameo for Andrews in the conclusion, but Dame Julie turned down the offer.[31] Thus, Angela Lansbury served as a substitute, much as she had done when she played a Mary Poppins manqué in *Bedknobs and Broomsticks*. While Lansbury's presence evinces a warmth of affection in many viewers, it holds nowhere the amount of emotional reaction that an appearance by Andrews would have generated. In trying to repackage and reorient the lessons taught in the original Mary Poppins film, Disney found that it had some learning to do itself.

Conclusion: Nowhere to Go but Up?

While Disney has expertly fashioned (or bought up) a number of franchises, the gambit did not seem to suit the character of Mary Poppins. In part, the effort was too obvious and soured potential customers. It seemed that Poppins would not shrink-wrap into easily repackaged products. Except for the arguable success of the stage musical co-produced with Mackintosh, Disney's attempts to duplicate the magic of the 1964 film did not materialize. What that production and the original movie have in common are a greater awareness of class and a skepticism about fulfillment via material wealth, an attitude that more recent franchise attempts tried to elide or erase. Ironically, then, the texts that are the least supportive of capitalism are the entries in the franchise that have done the best in the marketplace.

So what is the lesson to be learned from this attempt at creating a musical franchise? Perhaps it is that the alchemy that culminates in a successful musical text is chimeral and that it is precisely that delicate balance of factors that makes it special, magical, and not easily duplicated. That aura of uniqueness is a large part of what makes it valuable, both emotionally and financially. *Mary Poppins* was, in a number of ways, the culmination of everything Walt had learned about filmmaking, and it stands as a testament to his vision. But it is also due to the insightful creativity of the Sherman brothers, as well as Andrews being in the exact correct moment in her career to be cast in the lead role—and of course, the imagination of Travers. Those factors were beyond any individual's control and often in conflict with one another. That "supercalifragilisticexpialidocious" alchemy has seemed impervious to being reduced to a formula, particularly when people in charge tried to alter or improve things in order to bring Mary Poppins into line.

Back in the mid-1930s, the groundbreaking success of the cartoon short *The Three Little Pigs* (1933) helped the studio to expand its creative possibilities. In the wake of that success, a number of people (theater owners, customers, etc.) asked Walt to make more cartoons featuring the Three Little Pigs. Eventually, he capitulated, with *The Big Bad Wolf* (1934), *Three Little Wolves* (1936), and *The Practical Pig* (1939). None of these shorts got anywhere near the critical or box-office attention the first cartoon received. Walt himself had been ambivalent about doing follow-ups but felt pressured to do so. The lackluster results proved to him that, as he famously said, "You can't top pigs with pigs."[32] Walt felt that you needed to move on to the next project rather than trying to recapture lightning in a bottle. The new corporate Disney often seems to feel it has the formula for cloning lightning. Nevertheless, attempts to "top Poppins with Poppins" stumbled, and Mary slipped gracefully up into the skies out of reach. When she may return, who can say?

Notes

1. Robert B. Sherman and Richard M. Sherman, *Walt's Time: From Before to Beyond*, ed. Bruce Gordon, David Mumford, and Jeff Kurtti (Santa Clarita, CA: Camphor Tree, 1998), 49.
2. Douglas Brode, *From Walt to Woodstock: How Disney Created the Counterculture* (Austin: University of Texas Press, 2004), 93.
3. The History vs. Hollywood website contains a recording of Travers singing along to "Feed the Birds" with the Shermans: https://www.historyvshollywood.com/video/pl-travers-discusses-feed-the-birds/.
4. For a more extended critique of the film's representation of the suffrage movement, see Ana Stevenson, "'Cast Off the Shackles of Yesterday': Women's Suffrage in Walt Disney's *Mary Poppins*," *Camera Obscura* 33, no. 2 (2018): 69–103.
5. Neal Gabler, *Walt Disney: The Triumph of the American Imagination* (New York: Vintage), 596–598.
6. Leslie H. Abramson, *Mary Poppins: Radical Elevation in the 1960s* (London: Routledge, 2023); Chris Cuomo, "Spinsters in Sensible Shoes: *Mary Poppins* and *Bedknobs and Broomsticks*," in *From Mouse to Mermaid: The Politics of Film, Gender, and Culture*, ed. Elizabeth Bell, Lynda Haas, and Laura Sells (Bloomington: Indiana University Press, 1995), 212–223, also reads an intriguing lesbian subtext into the heroines of these two films.
7. "The Story of Imagineering," https://sites.disney.com/waltdisneyimagineering/our-story/.
8. Gabler, *Walt Disney*, 600.
9. David Koenig, *Mouse under Glass: Secrets of Disney Animation and Theme Parks* (Irving, CA: Bonaventure), 145–146.
10. https://www.the-numbers.com/movie/Bedknobs-and-Broomsticks#tab=box-office.
11. Vincent Dowd, "Mary Poppins: Brian Sibley's Sequel That Never Was," BBC News, October 20, 2013, https://www.bbc.com/news/entertainment-arts-24581937.
12. Benjamin Svetkey, "Making of 'Mary Poppins Returns': How Rob Marshall Returned Disney's 'Guarded Jewel' to the Big Screen," *Hollywood Reporter*, December 7, 2018, https://www.hollywoodreporter.com/movies/movie-features/mary-poppins-returns-how-rob-marshall-brought-it-big-screen-1166094/.
13. John Sibley and Michael Lassell, *Mary Poppins: Anything Can Happen if You Let It* (New York: Disney Editions: 2007), 348–349.
14. Ibid., 349.
15. Mike Fleming, "Disney Acquiring Black List Script 'Saving Mr. Banks,' on Making 'Mary Poppins,'" Deadline Hollywood, February 8, 2012, https://deadline.com/2012/02/disney-acquiring-black-list-script-saving-mr-banks-on-making-mary-poppins-227838/.
16. Pete Hammond, "CinemaCon: Disney's Vegas Act Includes Johnny Depp and 'Lone Ranger' Footage," Deadline Hollywood, April 17, 2013, https://deadline.com/2013/04/cinemacon-talk-of-star-wars-lone-ranger-monsters-u-and-the-tentpole-strategy-highlight-alan-horns-disney-vegas-act-477287/.
17. Geoffrey Macnab, "*Saving Mr. Banks*: Film review—A Sugar Coated, Disingenuous Marketing Exercise for Disney," *The Independent*, November 28, 2013, https://www.independent.co.uk/arts-entertainment/films/reviews/saving-mr-banks-film-review-a-sugar-coated-disingenuous-marketing-exercise-for-disney-8970986.html.
18. Lou Lumenick, "'Saving Mr. Banks' More Like 'Selling Mary Poppins,'" *New York Post*, December 10, 2013, https://nypost.com/2013/12/10/saving-mr-banks-more-like-selling-mary-poppins/.

19. Borys Kit, "New 'Mary Poppins' Movie in the Works from Disney," *Hollywood Reporter*, September 14, 2015, https://www.hollywoodreporter.com/news/general-news/new-mary-poppins-movie-works-823064/.
20. Dan Zinski, "Mary Poppins Returns Sequel Reportedly in Development," Screen Rant, January 10, 2019, https://screenrant.com/mary-poppins-3-rob-marshall-emily-blunt/.
21. https://www.boxofficemojo.com/date/2013-12-22/.
22. https://www.imdb.com/title/tt2294629/?ref_=nv_sr_srsg_0_tt_8_nm_0_in_0_q_Frozen.
23. https://www.imdb.com/title/tt2140373/?ref_=fn_al_tt_1.
24. Anthony D'Alessandro, "'Aquaman' darting to $120M+ in competitive Christmas 5-Day Corridor," Deadline Hollywood, December 18, 2018, https://deadline.com/2018/12/aquaman-bumblebee-mary-poppins-returns-jennifer-lopez-christmas-box-office-1202522277/; see also https://www.boxofficemojo.com/date/2018-12-23/.
25. https://www.imdb.com/title/tt5028340/?ref_=nv_sr_srsg_0.
26. Christopher Orr, "'Mary Poppins Returns': Cunning Homage or Shameless Rip-Off?," *The Atlantic*, December 15, 2018. https://www.theatlantic.com/entertainment/archive/2018/12/mary-poppins-returns-review-emily-blunt-sequel-disney/578410/
27. Caitlin Flanagan, "Becoming Mary Poppins," *The New Yorker*, December 19, 2005, https://www.newyorker.com/magazine/2005/12/19/becoming-mary-poppins; Margaret Lyons, "*Saving Mr. Banks* Left Out an Awful Lot about P. L. Travers," *New York*, December 26, 2013, https://www.vulture.com/2013/12/saving-mr-banks-pl-travers-fact-check-mary-poppins.html.
28. Orr, "'Mary Poppins Returns'"; Stephanie Zacharek, "Review: *Mary Poppins Returns* Honors the Spirit of Its Predecessor," *Time*, December 19, 2018, https://time.com/5484129/review-mary-poppins-returns-blunt/.
29. Matt Goldberg, "How 'Mary Poppins Returns' Misses the Spirit of the Original," Collider, December 26, 2018, makes a similar observation about the sequel flipping the moral of the first film; https://collider.com/mary-poppins-returns-ending-explained/#:~:text=At%20the%20climax%2C%20Mr.,George%20Banks%20at%20Fidelity%20Fiduciary.
30. For more on this shift in the entertainment industries, see Andrew deWaard, "Financialized Hollywood: Institutional Investment, Venture Capital, and Private Equity in the Film and Television Industry," *Journal of Cinema and Media Studies* 59, no. 4 (Summer 2020): 54–84.
31. Brent Malkin and Marc Lang, "'Mary Poppins Returns': Why Julie Andrews Turned Down a Cameo," *Variety*, November 30, 2018, https://variety.com/2018/film/awards/mary-poppins-returns-julie-andrews-1203065856/.
32. Gabler, *Walt Disney*, 415.

CHAPTER 10

"COME ON, SONG! I'M REFLECTING!": REINTERPRETATIONS OF THE MUSICAL IN DISNEY'S CONTEMPORARY SEQUELS AND REMAKES

EVE BENHAMOU

"LIFE isn't some cartoon musical where you sing a little song and all your insipid dreams magically come true. So let it go." This line from *Zootopia* (2016), uttered by pragmatic, cynical police officer Chief Bogo (Idris Elba) to naively optimistic young recruit Judy Hopps (Ginnifer Goodwin), self-reflexively mocks one of the core components of Disney animation: the musical. Within a film drawing on the cop-buddy genre as primary influence, this piece of dialogue distances *Zootopia* from the studio's past animated canon. Since the 2000s, Disney animation has indeed recurrently discarded musicals, from the experimental "Neo-Disney" phase of science-fiction and adventure animated features in the early 2000s up to Marvel adaptation *Big Hero 6* (2014) and films heavily drawing on the action mode, such as *Zootopia* and *Raya and the Last Dragon* (2021).[1] Yet, although Disney animated musicals have become a rarer occurrence, they remain extremely successful. Chief Bogo's line specifically references Disney's Oscar-awarded "Let It Go," the most famous song from *Frozen* (2013), a musical that became a blockbuster hit, was the highest-grossing animated film of all time upon its release, and was followed by multiple short films, a Broadway adaptation, and a sequel. This phenomenon also stands out when one considers the studio's contemporary remakes; it is notably *The Lion King* (2019) that has rivaled *Frozen* in terms of box-office records, confirming the enduring popularity of this genre within Disney animation.[2]

Beyond its intertextual and musical reference, *Zootopia*'s line also knowingly hints at wider perceptions of Disney's animated canon, which I refer to as the "Disney formula." As developed in previous work, I use the formula as a concept initially "characterizing the studio's 1930s hyperreal hand-drawn aesthetic and sentimental narratives" and which "gradually crystallized a limited set of tropes that had come to signify 'Disney'—tropes that were consolidated throughout films, critical discourses and an expanding synergistic machine."[3] By the 1990s, the formula had "become synonymous with hit fairy-tale musicals, sanitized literary adaptations and archaic constructions of gender."[4] Chief Bogo's cynical remark effectively captures the way Disney's formula has been satirized by competitors, such as DreamWorks' *Shrek* franchise (2001, 2004, 2007, 2010), and criticized in academic and popular accounts. The line refers to the perceived predictability and saccharine nature of Disney narratives, based on the seemingly unrealistic generic templates of the musical ("sing a little song") combined with the fairy tale ("your insipid dreams magically come true"). It is precisely this idea of Disney animated films, their familiar, cheerful optimism and sincere romanticism, that has been mocked, revised, and reclaimed in the studio's contemporary output—as illustrated in *Zootopia*—a phenomenon that was amplified in Disney's latest remakes and sequels.

Writing on sequels, Carolyn Jess-Cooke observes that they rely on "important registers of continuation, nostalgia, memory, difference, originality, revision and repetition";[5] Disney's reappropriation of its own iconic musical tropes is central in that regard. As the studio's first theatrically released animated sequel since *The Rescuers Down Under* (1990), *Ralph Breaks the Internet* (2018) does not solely develop further the characterizations, visuals, and generic tropes of *Wreck-It Ralph* (2012);[6] by integrating a highly self-reflexive, narratively pivotal musical sequence within its initial action-adventure framework, *Ralph Breaks the Internet* adds novelty to its franchise with an explicitly parodic angle. The film humorously foregrounds and reinterprets an iconic component of the Disney formula in a way that parallels another contemporary animated sequel with parodic musical elements, released the following year: *Frozen II* (2019). These animated sequels feature alongside numerous Disney properties similarly drawing on revision and repetition: live-action remakes. Since the 2010s, a great number of Disney animated films have been re-envisioned and reframed for new audiences. *Beauty and the Beast* (2017) and *Aladdin* (2019) were the first among these to nostalgically preserve the musical identity of their animated predecessors, while also including original songs. Drawing on *Ralph Breaks the Internet*, *Frozen II*, *Beauty and the Beast*, and *Aladdin* as case studies, this chapter explores how Disney reinterprets a core component of its generic formula, namely the musical sequence, throughout its contemporary output. More specifically, the chapter investigates how the studio's sequels and remakes repurpose such an iconic generic convention and to what extent they re-envision the Disney formula in the process.

The chapter is divided into two parts, corresponding to two singular musical tropes typically associated with Disney: the "I Want" song, as illustrated by "A Place Called Slaughter Race" in *Ralph Breaks the Internet* and "Speechless" in *Aladdin*, and the romantic song (or love duet), as exemplified by "Lost in the Woods" in *Frozen II*, "A Whole

New World" in *Aladdin*, and "Beauty and the Beast." Positioned at the intersection of the fairy tale and the musical, each sequence crystallizes core components of the Disney formula. This chapter analyzes how the latter is reinterpreted, from playful parody to nostalgic celebration, through the combined frameworks of genre studies and postfeminism. I approach this concept as a sensibility fusing "empowerment rhetoric with traditionalist identity paradigms," characterizing contemporary popular media and associated constructions of gender.[7] From a broader perspective, this chapter illuminates the contrasting ways in which animation and live-action filmmaking operate in relation to the studio's formula, delineating different yet complementary approaches that reflect Disney's wider strategies toward its own canon.

Restaging the Liberating Fantasy of the "I Want" Song

Richard Dyer describes musicals as "discourses of happiness"; musical set pieces offer solutions to or respite from the problems set up within the narrative.[8] In this sense, they are utopian: they express hopes, wishes, alternatives, "'something better' to escape into."[9]

The most iconic expression of this convention in Disney's musicals is the "I Want" song. Dramatically performed by the hero or heroine, the "I Want" song expresses yearning for "a better world beyond the confinements of [their] present situation."[10] In other words, in the "I Want" song, Disney protagonists express their overwhelming desire for another life, hoping for enlightenment, freedom, and adventure beyond the constraints of their "provincial town" ("Belle" in *Beauty and the Beast* [1991]) or "island" ("How Far I'll Go" in *Moana* [2016]). In some cases, the "I Want" song also conveys characters' longing for self-discovery ("Reflection" in *Mulan* [1998]) or acceptance by their peers ("Go the Distance" in *Hercules* [1997], "Out There" in *The Hunchback of Notre Dame* [1996]). In these examples, Disney protagonists wish for a place—literal or figurative—where they belong. In earlier Disney animated films, such a sense of belonging depends heavily on finding a romantic partner ("I'm Wishing" in *Snow White and the Seven Dwarfs* [1937], "I Wonder" in *Sleeping Beauty* [1959]). Whatever the wish expressed in the "I Want" song may be, the Disney musical will naturally conclude with its fulfillment. This outcome points to other tropes of the Disney formula, intrinsically linked to the genre of the musical itself: cheerfulness, optimism, idealism, and sometimes innocence and sentimentalism as conveyed by the female protagonists.

Ralph Breaks the Internet and the *Aladdin* remake both restage Disney's musical convention of the "I Want" song, preserving a familiar framework while subverting and renewing some of its core components. The music for both "A Place Called Slaughter Race" and "Speechless" was composed by Alan Menken, who worked on most Disney musicals from *The Little Mermaid* (1989) to *Tangled* (2010). These songs, performed by

Vanellope (Sarah Silverman) and Jasmine (Naomi Scott), respectively, play a pivotal narrative role, helping them articulate their feelings and desires. In both cases, the heroines initially feel trapped, whether in the predictable and childlike space of the video game "Sugar Rush" or in the palace of Agrabah and its "centuries-old," "unbending" rules. By the end of each song, the heroine will come to a decision concerning her own future: her actions, behavior, and resolve will consequently shift. Both musical sequences are also similar in their setup: these are fantasy sequences, taking place—partly or fully—in the character's mindscape. While few Disney animated musicals have relied on such fantasy sequences for the "I Want" song, they bring the liberating, exhilarating, and utopian potentials of this trope further. For example, in *The Princess and the Frog*'s (2009) "Almost There," the crumbling, dusty sugar mill that Tiana (Anika Noni Rose) is hoping to buy transforms into the elegant, stylish restaurant of her dreams, inspired by a stylized magazine illustration; her modest, practical yellow dress turns into a glamorous white gown, and she sings while confidently interacting with fictional staff, expertly cooking elaborate dishes, and welcoming numerous customers. Expectedly, the film concludes with the opening of the grand, highly popular restaurant. Beyond their pivotal narrative function, the fantasy "I Want" song is repurposed in different ways in "A Place Called Slaughter Race" and "Speechless." The former becomes a self-aware parodic tool to mock Disney's musical tropes, and the studio's wider generic formula in the process, while "Speechless" follows from more recent Disney musicals such as *Frozen* in their use of the "I Want" song as a dramatic, typically postfeminist display of female rebellion and empowerment.

In order to fully understand the parodic stance of "A Place Called Slaughter Race," it must be pointed out that *Ralph Breaks the Internet*, like the original *Wreck-It Ralph*, does not explicitly introduce itself as a musical; Vanellope's "I Want" song stands out as a singular original performance, apparently clashing within its generic milieu. By contrast, *The Princess and the Frog* directly opens with a song, functioning as a prologue, while *Frozen* and *Moana* include original songs as soon as the title credits start—"Vuelie" and "Tulou Tagaloa," respectively. Such musical openings function as generic reminders. Although a growing number of Disney animated films have distanced themselves from the musical since the 2000s, the latter has arguably been the most consistent and identifiable generic component of Disney animation throughout its history. Therefore, audiences have come to accept and expect the musical as a central—if not the primary—generic template for Disney animated films and its associated conventions, such as the "I Want" song and the romantic duet. Steve Neale's concept of generic "verisimilitude," involving different systems and forms of "plausibility, motivation and belief" which vary from genre to genre, is particularly useful in this context.[11] In musicals, characters *will* spontaneously and effortlessly burst into song, while others may join and dance in sync; they are all fully, genuinely, and harmoniously immersed in this utopian realm. Challenging this regime of verisimilitude subverts the foundations of the Disney musical and its wider formula; this is precisely what happens in *Ralph Breaks the Internet*.

Such a generic clash takes place when Vanellope meets the fourteen iconic Disney princesses and heroines inhabiting the "Oh My Disney" website. In this iteration, the leading ladies foreground a striking level of generic self-awareness, paving the way for "A Place Called Slaughter Race." They expertly and playfully list the formulaic traits of the Disney princess, from her propensity to talk to animals to her perceived reliance on patriarchal figures, and insist on a core characteristic of the Disney heroine: her musical abilities, as displayed by Ariel's spontaneous demonstration. Excited about her new outfit, inspired by Vanellope's casual attire, Ariel (Jodi Benson) expresses her happiness at wearing a "shirt," reprising the melody of "Part of Your World." Despite her genuine and passionate interpretation, her rendition of this "I Want" song lacks the dramatic, empowering, and liberating potential of the musical trope. While in *The Little Mermaid* the song describes Ariel's longing for the human world and its promise of freedom and knowledge, here it is fully dedicated to a simple piece of clothing. Vanellope's bafflement further challenges Ariel's musical performance: she points out the nondiegetic soundtrack, the "spotlight" over Ariel, and the princess's unexpected yet seamless transition from dialogue to song. Although the princesses casually explain that "that's what happens when a princess sings about her dreams," Vanellope does not share their regime of verisimilitude.

Her first attempt at an "I Want" song not only amplifies the initial generic clash taking place throughout the sequence but also further subverts the iconic musical trope. Encouraged by her peers ("What is it you really *want*? Sing about that!"), she relies on the melody of "Oh Christmas Tree," awkwardly copying and adapting its lyrics ("Oh, steering wheel / Oh, steering wheel / Oh, yes I want a steering wheel"). Her out-of-tune performance is accompanied by awkward dancing steps and abruptly concludes with scatting. Notably, this performance is also a cappella, as if no orchestral score could match Vanellope's catastrophic rendition. Her apparent lack of musical skills is shocking within the context of a Disney animated film—all the princesses look embarrassed for their peer. A beautiful singing voice is supposedly an innate quality for the Disney heroine: Princess Aurora receives "the gift of song" at birth from fairies; Snow White's and Ariel's mellifluous voices charm their respective Princes. Casting choice plays a pivotal role in this context. Jennifer Fleeger notes that 1930s and 1950s animated heroines were voiced by actresses with an operatic background, such as Adriana Caselotti for Snow White; since the 1990s, these have been replaced by Broadway performers, such as Benson (Ariel) and Rose (Tiana), and pop singers, such as Mandy Moore (*Tangled*'s Rapunzel).[12] By contrast, Silverman (Vaneloppe) is primarily known for her work in stand-up comedy and television; her musical performances and vocal talents are framed within the context of comedy, satire, and parody, a tone that is intertextually evoked, to some extent, through her voicing of Vaneloppe. The princesses' very pragmatic description of the formulaic process underlying the "I Want" song further mocks the extraordinary appeal of the singing princess: as Pocahontas (Irene Bedard) explains to Vanellope, the song should magically come to her if she stares at "a form of water" (examples include a "wishing well" for Snow White, the "ocean" for Moana, a "horse trough" for Mulan) and will convey her dream through a "metaphor." Self-reflexively detailing the recipe for a successful performance of the "I Want" song, this sequence playfully yet effectively demystifies Disney's musical formula—in the process, it draws on a specific strand of the musical genre, the "backstage musical."

Jane Feuer's description of the backstage musical shares similarities with *Ralph Breaks the Internet*'s self-aware take on the genre. Applying this label to a wide range of films, such as *Easter Parade* (1948) and *The Band Wagon* (1953), Feuer observes that these musicals take the audience to places they would not have access to, such as the wings, detailing the elaboration and practice of musical productions, in other words, the "backstage" world behind the performances.[13] The penchant of backstage musicals for revealing their "own inner gears" demystifies the "illusion" of the live performance; these films reveal the stage paraphernalia used to create the "magic" and show the performers out of character.[14] The overall effect is to reframe the production as "an act of extreme calculation" and as a routine, a mere "job."[15] To some extent, this is what happens in *Ralph Breaks the Internet*: the "inner gears" of the "I Want" song are revealed by the princesses while they are "off work," so to speak, relaxing in the wings of "Oh My Disney" (the princess room), and after having replaced their iconic costumes with comfortable loungewear. By drawing attention to the fact that these songs are elaborate performances requiring a specific setting and soundtrack, as well as vocal, dancing, and improvisational abilities, the film asks audiences to momentarily question the dominant regime of verisimilitude in the film and to laugh at the predictable conventions of Disney's musical formula.

The staging of "A Place Called Slaughter Race" initially draws on such a parodic, self-reflexive setup. Vanellope's "I Want" song ultimately comes to her at the gates of "Oh My Disney" after a phone call from Ralph (John C. Reilly). He has gathered enough money to buy a new steering wheel and save "Sugar Rush" so that they can all return to their respective games. Vanellope cannot articulate the reason for her malaise on hearing this positive news. Staring at a puddle—a "form of water"—her reflection is magically transported into Slaughter Race. Her fantasy musical performance begins, explicitly signified by a multitude of intertextual references to Disney's animated canon, from the mise en scène to the orchestration. The musical transition is conveyed through sparkling fairy dust over the puddle and an ethereal violin melody. Like Snow White and Aurora, Vanellope sings while interacting with a bird landing on her hand; when the pace of the song joyfully accelerates, she is greeted by all the characters of Slaughter Race, recalling the beginning of *Beauty and the Beast*'s "Belle." Menken's cheerful and upbeat score, reminiscent of his work on 1990s Disney fairy tales, added to Vanellope's childlike and high-pitched voice, comically contrasts with the threatening and dangerous surroundings of Slaughter Race.

Unlike the idyllic pastoral decor or breathtaking landscapes of Disney's musicals, from enchanted forests to majestic snowy mountains, Slaughter Race consists of a violent urban environment, including "fallen wires, dumpster fires, creepy clowns and burning tires." Unlike the cute anthropomorphic animals typically joining with a joyful tune, Vanellope's singing partners include a one-legged pigeon and a white shark. Such pairings are reminiscent of another self-aware restaging of the Disney musical, in a film that functions as a precursor to Disney's playful parody of its own wider fairy-tale and romantic tropes, while relying on the humorous contrasts between animation and live-action worlds: *Enchanted* (2007).[16] In the latter's "Happy Working Song," Princess Giselle (Amy Adams) delightedly sings to rats, flies, and pigeons—including a one-legged one. In "A Place Called Slaughter Race," all of these incongruous clashes are accompanied by the initial demystification of Disney's musical generic tropes: Vanellope urges her song to manifest ("Come on, song! I'm reflecting!"), she is blinded by the spotlight above her, and she explicitly points out that she is using metaphors and that she is "rhyming." As opposed to Giselle in *Enchanted* or Ariel in the sequence previously described, Vanellope consistently draws attention to the fact that she is appropriating the generic tropes of the Disney musical. Far from a spontaneous, effortless performance, it is a gradual, self-aware process.

Despite the unconventional, self-reflexive, and parodic staging of "A Place Called Slaughter Race," it ultimately transforms into a more familiar version of the "I Want" song. Once Vanellope effectively embraces its rules and adopts the regime of verisimilitude of the musical, she happily gives in to the performance. The spotlight, a prop that symbolizes the artificial and potentially nonsensical aspects of musical conventions for Vanellope—its source is not visible, seemingly coming from nowhere—correspondingly disappears when Vanellope sings "My spirits [are] climbing." As her solo "I Want" song becomes an ensemble song, with various characters from Slaughter Race joining her, she effortlessly harmonizes with them. As opposed to her awkward moves during her first singing attempt, her dance steps are smooth, in perfect sync with her partners. She is so immersed in the musical realm that her moves parallel the beat of the music, in perfect mickey-mousing fashion. Losing herself to the "I Want" song allows the latter to fulfill its primary function. Vanellope uses it to convey her longing for the exciting and unpredictable world of Slaughter Race, expressing a feeling she was not able to articulate otherwise. The initially self-aware parody transforms into a more sincere celebration of this iconic Disney musical trope. "A Place Called Slaughter Race" concludes with the expansive extravagance of Disney's fairy-tale ensemble performances, such as *The Little Mermaid*'s "Under the Sea." Its last shot is of a dreamy Vanellope, both happily and longingly repeating the last line—"A place called Slaughter Race ..." Such a tonal shift throughout the song is in line with the double strategy of the backstage musical; as Feuer points out, the initial demystification of the performance is "always followed by a new mystification, the celebration of the seamless final show."[17] In other words, by the end of the sequence, Vanellope is no longer performing in a self-aware, artificial manner; she has become a genuine, singing Disney princess.

Such musical progression crystallizes a wider trend throughout Disney's portrayals of animated heroines, drawing on postfeminist sensibilities. Relying on Stéphanie Genz's definition, these contemporary characters indicate "both a dependence on and independence from feminism."[18] More specifically, I argued in previous work that these heroines, such as *Tangled*'s Rapunzel or *Frozen*'s Anna, move across a postfeminist "spectrum."[19] They possess not only generically subversive and empowering qualities but also more traditionally gendered traits within the context of a Disney fairy-tale musical. They are introduced in a restrictive domestic space, subsequently thrive within an action-adventure environment while gradually gaining self-assurance, yet are ultimately framed within a romantic happy ending, marrying their true love. The very fact that Vanellope is revealed as a princess at the end of *Wreck-It Ralph*, in a film that does not rely on fairy-tale tropes, emphasizes the postfeminist duality of her characterization: she may be an intrepid and talented racer, discarding sparkling pink dresses, but she's also a cute little girl repeatedly described as "adorable," too young to be paired with a love interest. Correspondingly, in *Ralph Breaks the Internet*, she bonds both with Slaughter Race characters through her passion for cars and thrilling chases and with the other Disney princesses (initially) through her clothing choices. In song, she displays both self-awareness and a sense of innocence and wonder, as epitomized in "A Place Called Slaughter Race." Through such postfeminist framing, Disney both nostalgically draws on and revises the iconic figure of the singing Disney princess.

While *Ralph Breaks the Internet* reclaims the trope of the "I Want" song from a playfully parodic approach, such restaging takes a more serious, solemn turn in *Aladdin* with "Speechless," an original addition reflecting the wider revision of Jasmine's characterization. In the 1992 animated film, no solo is attributed to Jasmine (Linda Larkin); her only musical performance is as part of romantic duo in "A Whole New World" (sung by Lea Salonga). Considering Disney's musicals contemporary with *Aladdin*, such as *The Little Mermaid* and *Beauty and the Beast*, this choice is surprising. In the sequence in which Jasmine is introduced, she voices her frustration at the law forcing her to get married and at her wider lack of agency: she cannot leave the palace or make her own decisions. From a generic perspective, this is the ideal context for an "I Want" song, echoing Belle's and Ariel's yearning for freedom and wish to escape from patriarchal constraints in "Belle" and "Part of Your World." Of all the iconic Disney princesses and heroines, as featured in *Ralph Breaks the Internet*'s "Oh My Disney" sequence, Jasmine is the only one who does not perform her own song. Even other male-centered animated films include solos for female characters, such as Megara's "I Won't Say (I'm In Love)" in *Hercules*. Such a generic anomaly might point to the more subordinate, secondary nature of a princess who crystallized academic and popular criticisms regarding both Disney's representations of femininity and nonwhite women in the 1990s. For example, Amy Davis observes that "despite her strength and individuality," Jasmine is portrayed as "a reward for Aladdin."[20] Kellie Bean similarly points out that, like her animated contemporaries, Jasmine loses her "mildly feminist attitudes" once she is repositioned within a "conventional marriage scenario."[21] Clare Bradford draws another parallel between Jasmine and several other Disney heroines: like Ariel, Pocahontas, and Mulan, Jasmine is "powerless in the face of entrenched practices" and requires her "father's authority" to ultimately achieve her goals and marry the man of her choice.[22] Her subordinate position is emphasized through the exoticization of her body, an Arab princess whose "sexualized presence is privileged above all else," as noted by Celeste Lacroix.[23] Such a portrayal contrasts with Jasmine's subsequent live-action counterpart.

Attributing an "I Want" song to the 2019 Jasmine represents a pivotal generic move ultimately giving significantly more prominence to her character—a shift that was particularly emphasized throughout the paratexts of the film. Menken insisted in interviews that live-action Jasmine was "more" than a Disney princess: "a three-dimensional flesh and blood young woman who wants to be heard and respected."[24] This new perspective on the character echoes the distinctly postfeminist sensibilities influencing the portrayal of 2010s animated heroines underlined earlier and the wider revisions notable in Disney's live-action remakes. In remakes such as *Maleficent* (2014), *Cinderella* (2015), and *Beauty and the Beast*, subplots are expanded upon and character motivation developed. Most noticeably, constructions of gender and race are amended, facilitating what Tracey Mollet describes as "a considerable distance" between themselves and their "(now dated) animated counterparts."[25] It is in this context that "Speechless" can be approached.

Jasmine's first performance of "Speechless" arises from an argument between herself, the vizier Jafar (Marwan Kenzari), and her father, the Sultan (Navid Neghaban). While animated Jasmine's conflicts with these patriarchal figures of authority stem from romantic motives—she wants to marry for love and protect Aladdin—live-action Jasmine insists on political pursuits. After the disastrous visit of a suitor, Jasmine explains to her father that she wishes to lead the kingdom on her own. Yet her ambition is frustrated. Her father recalls that a woman cannot be a sultan ("it has never been done in the 1,000-year history of our kingdom"), while Jafar warns about her inexperience. Therefore, she must marry for Agrabah to have a ruler. In other words, the concept of marriage is reconfigured, not a sentimental fantasy but a governing imperative. Defeated and hurt, Jasmine leaves her father's office, only to be caught up by Jafar, who threateningly advises that her life would be easier if she were to accept the kingdom's traditions and were "to be seen and not heard." Holding her breath, she remains still and looks off-screen, while her tiger Rajah scares Jafar away as he attempts to get closer. She retreats to her bedroom, closing the door as the first guitar chords of "Speechless" can be heard. Her singing is quiet and soft, accompanied by a nondiegetic guitar and stringed instruments. The pace of the song is mirrored by her slow steps throughout her room. A sense of resignation and helplessness stands out from her performance, echoed by the lyrics ("Broken again, left with nothing to say / My voice drowned out in the thunder"). Although she expresses her ambition ("All I know is I won't go speechless"), she is still unsure and fragile ("I tremble when they try it"). She ends the first chorus on her balcony, collapsing on a bench. The whole song is shot in a long take, with the camera closely following Jasmine, heightening the feeling of entrapment that permeates the sequence. At this stage, "Speechless" evokes the typical "I Want" song, whose heroine is held by patriarchal constraints. The first occurrence of this song introduces Jasmine's main challenges: from a generic perspective, she must find a more confident musical voice and, correspondingly, her political voice.

The reprise of "Speechless" transforms the "I Want" song into a song of empowerment and self-assertion. It is reprised after Jafar, standing in front of the Sultan's throne, has successfully stolen Aladdin's lamp and become Sultan thanks to the Genie's powers. When he orders his guards to invade Shirabad, Jasmine's late mother's kingdom, the Sultan and Jasmine protest. Jafar quickly interrupts Jasmine, with words that parallel their earlier conversation: "I think we've heard enough from you, Princess. It's time you start doing what you should have done all along. Stay silent." While she is being removed by guards, Jafar's lines are repeated in voice-over ("understand it's better for you to be seen and not heard," "stay silent"). The echo of his words resonates while Jasmine walks toward the camera. She starts singing, seemingly in her own mindscape, as her performance does not elicit any reaction from the guards escorting her out of the room. This second verse of "Speechless" repeats, again, both her father's and Jafar's words, recalling "Every rule, every word / centuries old and unbending" and quoting "stay in your place," "better seen and not heard." These imposing constraints are reinforced by the guards physically leading her out of the palace room, where political decisions are made. A shift occurs with the chorus, and there is a cut to Jasmine, back to the camera, forcefully breaking free and turning around, singing, "I won't be silenced." From that moment, the guards disappear one by one, leaving a trail of dust behind them. These magical occurrences, with actors digitally erased, signal the start of the fantasy section of the "I Want" song.

This turning point highlights the contrast between this performance of "Speechless" and the one described earlier: while the former was characterized by helplessness and quiet despair, this reprise showcases Jasmine's newfound confidence, expressing freely her resentment and rebellion. This part of the song is shot in another long take, during which Jasmine finally voices her frustration and anger at the way she is treated. Her vocal performance is more energetic and louder, accompanied by an orchestra and drums setting a quicker pace; her movements are wider and free. This vigorous shift is reinforced by the quicker tracking shots keeping her at the center of the frame while she determinedly walks back into the palace room. When she sings "Let the storm in / I cannot be broken," the camera tracks around her so rapidly that the background becomes out of focus. As all other patriarchal figures of power disappear—all the guards, the Sultan, and finally Jafar—she ends up standing tall in front of the throne. This fantasy "I Want" song becomes a successful and liberating musical moment of empowerment, which motivates Jasmine's behavior in the rest of the sequence. After the last line of the song, Jasmine finds herself again outside the room, escorted by the guards, just before the fantasy shift. This time, however, she loudly calls Hakim, the man in charge of the guards, and manages to persuade him to defy Jafar in a heartfelt yet confident monologue on duty and leadership, during which she is only interrupted once by the vizier, no longer able to counter her arguments. It is precisely this *speech*, namely Jasmine's words and determination, that makes her father realize that she has the "courage and strength" to govern. He ultimately names her sultan at the end of the film, during a discussion accompanied by the musical theme of "Speechless"—concluding Jasmine's journey from powerless princess to empowered leader.

In many aspects, "Speechless" echoes the structure of *Frozen*'s most popular song, "Let It Go," pointing to the typically postfeminist limits to these songs of empowerment. Both "Speechless" and "Let It Go" start with a restless heroine frustratedly repeating the patriarchal rules imposed upon her (Elsa singing "Conceal, don't feel, don't let them know") before triumphantly rejecting them. Both heroines express their own power in new ways, whether figurative power (political influence for Jasmine) or literal power (magical abilities for Elsa). While digital animation is used in radically opposed ways in the two sequences, it similarly highlights the heroine's newfound control of her physical surroundings and her released emotions: Elsa can create elaborate designs and structures which get more and more impressive throughout the song, and Jasmine seems able to make her opponents disappear. Yet for both, these songs transform into temporary fantasies of empowerment. Elsa is trapped and captured by the villain Hans, helpless when he attempts to murder her.[26] Jasmine is forced to marry Jafar to protect her father; although she manages to escape with Aladdin, she becomes a passive observer, magically suspended in midair during Aladdin and Jafar's final confrontation—not unlike animated Jasmine, who is trapped in a giant hourglass. While Elsa is rescued by her sister, in a fairy tale that ultimately foregrounds both romance and sisterhood, Jasmine's first act as an empowered sultan is to marry the man of her choice, in a remake that presents a princess who can ultimately "have it all." Considering postfeminism as a spectrum, Jasmine's "I Want" song, or, rather, her "song of self-assertion," can be placed at the empowering end; this revised Disney musical trope crystallizes the revisions made to her character. However, the legacy of her animated counterpart subsists: the imperatives of marriage and heteronormativity also push this character, at times, toward the more traditionalist end of the spectrum. These moments are restaged in a particularly nostalgic light, through another typical trope of Disney's musical formula: the romantic song.

Reanimating the Romantic Disney Song

The romantic song is another iconic component of the Disney musical, revealing the sentimental core of the studio's formula. Either a duet sung by the protagonists, as in *Cinderella*'s (1950) "So This Is Love" and *Sleeping Beauty*'s "Once upon a Dream," or a solo performed by a secondary character while the couple is waltzing—"Beauty and the Beast", *The Princess and the Frog*'s "Ma Belle Evangeline"—it plays a central role in Disney films that involve romance. It is through the romantic song that the two leads realize, acknowledge, and share their feelings for each other. This function can be observed in numerous musicals: as Rick Altman notes, music "is the signifier *par excellence* of the value of the couple and of courtship," ultimately expressing "romantic triumph."[27] Harmonious dancing and singing symbolize the couple's compatibility. As with the "I Want" song, the successful performance and outcome of the romantic Disney song presuppose sincerity and enthusiasm—characters that are fully immersed within their generic milieu.

It is precisely such a sense of sincerity, reframed as naive innocence and sentimentalism, that is mocked in Disney's 2000s and 2010s musicals—as exemplified by *Ralph Breaks the Internet*'s Ariel, passionately singing about her new shirt. Within a romantic context, such questioning of generic tropes tends to be voiced by male characters. For example, *Enchanted* and *Tangled* rely on the male leads to deconstruct not only the musical nature of the Disney fairy tale but also its sentimental underpinnings. *Enchanted*'s Robert (Patrick Dempsey) is introduced as a cynical divorce lawyer, while Flynn Rider (Zachary Levi) behaves as an experienced, overconfident seducer in front of Rapunzel. Far from chivalrous and gallant Disney princes, they correspondingly pragmatically refuse to take part in musical performances and sincerely express their feelings. When thugs spontaneously burst into song to perform "I've Got a Dream" in *Tangled*, Flynn appears baffled, skeptically raising his eyebrows, and quickly bored. Moments later, he refuses to join them ("Sorry boys, I don't sing"), and when forced, he initially struggles to take part; his dance steps are at first awkward and clash with the others', and he talks rather than sings. Similarly, Robert is stunned at Giselle's spontaneous singing of "That's How You Know" in the middle of Central Park ("Don't sing, it's OK") and shocked when other New Yorkers join her in song and dance ("I've never heard this song"). He seems immune to Giselle's infectious cheerfulness, confusedly and grumpily following her ("I don't dance, and I really don't sing"). However, these self-aware, ironic instances are short-lived; these heroes end up embracing the core tenets of Disney's musical formula.

Both *Enchanted* and *Tangled* include romantic songs that fully restore the utopian, blissful, and sentimental scope of the studio's musical formula. In "I See the Light," Flynn's performance shifts from nondiegetic to diegetic and from solo to duo, in a particularly smooth manner. He effortlessly harmonizes with Rapunzel, becoming a conventional, one might say formulaic, Disney hero. During the song "So Close" in *Enchanted*, Robert is also able to waltz flawlessly with Giselle and softly sing to her. In both instances, the musical performance is no longer demystified; it is celebrated and restored as an appealing, iconic component of the Disney formula. Writing on *Enchanted*, Yvonne Tasker describes this configuration as typical of the "doubleness" of postfeminist sensibilities, the "contradictory play of ironic knowingness on one hand, and the seemingly sincere presentation of ideas of true love on the other."[28] While "So Close" and "I See the Light" represent conventional musical expressions of true love, on the traditionalist end of the postfeminist spectrum, such romantic songs are becoming rarer and rarer in an animated context. *Frozen*'s romantic duet "Love Is an Open Door" takes a sinister turn when Prince Hans is revealed as the villain, seducing Anna solely to access the throne. In retrospect, Anna's enthusiastic and innocent performance in "Love Is an Open Door" clashes with Hans's self-aware and calculated musical courtship.[29] Such a reversal— from romantic duet to villain song—contributes to *Frozen*'s wider re-envisioning of the Disney fairy tale. From the perspective of the musical, this reversal has significantly impacted the sentimental, authentic appeal of a trope that was central in the studio's canon. Disney's love songs were regularly awarded Oscars, becoming representative of their respective animated films—from "Beauty and the Beast" and "A Whole New World" to *The Lion King*'s "Can You Feel the Love Tonight." *Frozen II* reclaims this musical trope through its association with Anna's true love interest, Kristoff, a sincere romantic lead which *Frozen* already portrayed as a desirable alternative to falsely courteous and chivalric Hans. Kristoff's rendition of "Lost in the Woods" restores to some extent the sense of genuine enthusiasm and delight at the core of Disney's romantic songs while amplifying their more recent parodic and self-aware impulses. Such a postfeminist combination introduces a singular reinterpretation in the process.

"Lost in the Woods" is the only love song in *Frozen II*, standing out throughout Disney's musical canon as one of the very few romantic solos performed by a male character, expressing his feelings in the absence of the heroine; as such, it represents both a generic and a gendered departure. In addition to "I Want" songs, most male solos function as prologues ("When You Wish upon a Star" in *Pinocchio* [1940], *Aladdin*'s "Arabian Nights"), are scheming devices (*The Lion King*'s [1994] "Be Prepared," *Pocahontas*'s [1995] "Mine, Mine, Mine"), or are performed to facilitate a male-bonding experience (*Aladdin*'s "Friend Like Me," *Hercules*'s "One Last Hope"). *The Hunchback of Notre Dame* is a notable exception, including songs of innocent love (Quasimodo's "'Heaven's Light") and twisted lust (Frollo's "Hellfire"). In this context, "Lost in the Woods" is even more noteworthy. Performed by Kristoff (Jonathan Groff), a character introduced as introverted and awkward in *Frozen*, the song becomes a heartfelt, open declaration, expressing the scope of his feelings for Anna. Such a gender reversal echoes the reconfiguration of *Ralph Breaks the Internet*, in which Vanellope plays the role of the sarcastic Disney hero initially refusing to take part in a musical performance, as opposed to the naive, supposedly naturally gifted Disney princess. Through another reversal, Kristoff abandons sarcasm, typical of contemporary Disney male leads, for a sincere expression of his romantic feelings. Such a shift is mediated through a heavy dose of musical parody.

"Lost in the Woods" illustrates to some extent Tasker's concept of postfeminist "doubleness": the same song alternates between sincerity and excess, endearing emotion and humorous diversions. In a way, it combines the extravagance of *Enchanted*'s "How Does She Know" with the sense of genuineness of "So Close." It takes place after a misunderstanding between Anna and Kristoff: Anna believes he left her while he was trying to plan his proposal, and he realizes too late that she is gone, accompanying her sister Elsa to find the mysterious voice calling her. Lonely and defeated, Kristoff performs a reprise of *Frozen*'s "Reindeer(s) Are Better Than People," adding a question to his faithful reindeer Sven: "why is love so hard?" At that point, the musical sequence turns into a fantasy sequence, in a way that is strongly reminiscent of "A Place Called Slaughter Race." It starts, again, with the apparition of a spotlight (its source is not shown) surrounded by sparkling fairy dust and a change in the color scheme, from the misty grays and browns of the forest to purple and gold. Such a mise en scène highlights the artificial, constructed aspect of musical performances, as if Kristoff had magically landed on a stage; still, this is the only song in the film that is represented as such, all the other songs being seamlessly integrated within the diegesis. This self-aware shift is reinforced by the inclusion of a recurring Disney trope, occurring for the first time in the *Frozen* franchise. Sven, for whom Kristoff has provided the voice so far, starts singing on his own, becoming a truly anthropomorphic sidekick like *Cinderella*'s mice or *The Little Mermaid*'s Sebastian. The reindeer's unexpected new ability introduces a degree of both familiarity and incongruousness: animals can sing according to Disney's regime of verisimilitude, but not in *Frozen*'s diegetic world—until "Lost in the Woods."

This humorous, unexpected transition to a fantasy sequence is made even more explicit through Kristoff's reaction. Like Vanellope stepping into the musical version of Slaughter Race, Kristoff is dumbfounded, staring at Sven in wide-eyed amazement. However, like Vanellope, he decides to "let down [his] guard," with Sven's encouragement, and gives in to the musical performance. He stands up, looks around hesitatingly, and walks off-screen while the first notes of "Lost in the Woods" can be heard. Although he does not point it out, his song is composed of metaphors (like Vanellope's): without Anna, he feels "lost"; she represents his "true North," his "only landmark." He draws a parallel between the fact that they have taken different paths in the forest (literally) and the fact that they may be at different points in their relationship. He wants to propose to her, yet he repeatedly fails to do so, and Anna misinterprets his attempts ("Up till now the next step was a question of how / I never thought it was a question of whether"). He concludes with a heartfelt reaffirmation of his longing and sincere love for her.

Such a performance, both genuinely emotional and playfully theatrical in its mise en scène, gradually becomes more and more extravagant. Elements of framing, composition, and editing combine to further demystify the integrity of the Disney love song, transforming into a parodic music video, a hyperbolic version of a power ballad. While singing, Kristoff recurringly appears in different parts of the frame at the same time, and he is also shown in close-ups and extreme close-ups, in which he once breaks the fourth wall, staring at the (digitally simulated) camera. The second verse is illustrated by a love montage, consisting of flashbacks from *Frozen* representing pivotal moments of his romance with Anna, including their meet-cute and their first kiss. Neither the audience nor Kristoff has time to linger on these romantic snapshots; the love montage concludes with the shot of the first kiss dissolving into one of Kristoff, alone, embracing a disappearing Anna. She is repeatedly portrayed as a fleeting image walking at his side, sitting next to him. Kristoff even confuses her silhouette with a pile of rocks. As a result, although he expresses some genuine sadness and longing, such feelings are humorously subverted through his numerous mistakes. The reinterpretation of a romantic-comedy trope—the love montage—combined with the mise en scène and editing typical of music videos, creates comedy because of the perceived incongruousness, adding another dimension to the playful subversion of the Disney love song.

Integrating elements of contemporary live-action cinema and music videos into the diegesis of an animated fairy tale supposedly taking place in the mid-nineteenth century, "Lost in the Woods" builds on and amplifies a relatively minor trend in contemporary Disney musicals: the reliance on incongruous and anachronistic intertextual references. Sam Summers terms the latter "contra-diegetic intertexts," which became a staple of DreamWorks animation in the 2000s, alongside a self-reflexive sarcastic tone and a cartoonal mode, as exemplified by the *Shrek* franchise.[30] Such an approach aimed to mock the perceived datedness of Disney fairy tales while modernizing the genre. The use of music was central to this, as shown in two distinct yet complementary ways. The *Shrek* franchise included well-known pop songs in its soundtrack—as illustrated by Smash Mouth's "All Star" in its first installment—strikingly contrasting with "the Broadway-esque show tunes of Alan Menken and the lush original compositions of Elton John and Phil Collins" typical of 1990s Disney musicals.[31] When DreamWorks's fairy tales did showcase original songs, multiple references to twentieth-century American culture were included. For example, *Shrek 2*'s (2004) "Fairy Godmother Song" referenced the contemporary beauty-and-wellness industry, humorously weaving a sarcastic commentary on postfeminist constructions of femininity into a supposedly magical song of transformation ("Cellulite thighs will fade away," "Nip and tuck, here and there / To land that prince with the perfect hair / Lipstick, liners, shadows, blush!"). As Summers points out, mainstream animated musicals prior to DreamWorks', such as Disney's, almost entirely refrained from such contra-diegetic intertexts; these intrusions would "compromise the integrity of their meticulously constructed diegesis."[32] Furthermore, these would also demystify the magical aura of childlike innocence, sincerity, and timeless blissfulness intrinsic to Disney songs. Since the 2010s, some Disney musicals have started imitating DreamWorks' take in subtle ways: *Tangled*'s "I've Got a Dream" mentions "cupcakes" and "interior design," and *Frozen*'s "Love Is an Open Door" has its duo doing what resembles a robot dance. "Lost in the Woods," however, significantly magnifies and heightens these isolated attempts; arguably, the whole song is a contra-diegetic performance.

Positioned between Olaf's (Josh Gad) comical yet earnest song "When I'm Older" and Elsa's second spectacular solo "Show Yourself," Kristoff's "Lost in the Woods" operates a tonal shift, drawing on 1970s and 1980s American power ballads, music videos, and artists to convey his emotions. He is shown singing to a pine cone as if it were a microphone, eyes closed and hand to his ear, and performs the bridge with three reindeers in a configuration that imitates the music video of Queen's "Bohemian Rhapsody"—the three animals towering behind him, singing in front of a dark background. Queen is indeed quoted as an inspiration both by songwriter Kristen Anderson-Lopez and actor Groff for the band's theatricality, alongside performers such as Bryan Adams.[33] From the gradually expanding chorus of reindeers to Kristoff's unrestrained singing, throwing himself against a tree, staring at the camera, or tapping on his chest in sync with the rhythm of the song ("When did I become the one who's always chasing your heart?"), this musical fantasy sequence is undeniably marked by excess and extravagance. It stands out compared not only with *Frozen II*'s other songs but also with Disney's romantic solos and duets overall, notably the formulaically more reserved romantic interpretations of *Tangled*'s Flynn or *Enchanted*'s Robert. Groff explains: "Normally you're seeing the girl pining over the guy singing an emotional ballad.... Now it's giving the boys the opportunity to feel their feelings and sing about whatever is going on for them."[34] Admittedly, a male character "pining" for his love interest in song is not unprecedented in the context of the musical—Tony singing "Maria" in *West Side Story* (1961) is one of many examples—yet it is unprecedented in the context of *Disney* musicals, in which musical performances tend to follow, to some extent, a more traditionalist gender binary. Such a gender reversal is in line with the rest of the film, in which Anna and Elsa are fully involved in the action-adventure milieu and bring the narrative forward. Yet Kristoff's heartfelt performance is also consistently balanced with parody, contra-diegetic jokes, and theatrical excess. Therefore, *Frozen II* subverts and reinvents the romantic Disney song, revising its associated construction of gender while mediating this revision with a heavy dose of DreamWorks-style comedy, blending sincerity and knowingness in a typically postfeminist way.

Frozen II's reframing of the Disney romantic song markedly differs from that of the studio's live-action remakes. *Beauty and the Beast* and *Aladdin* not only maintain the presence of this central musical trope—unlike *Maleficent* and *Cinderella*—but also reverently restage it. Far from the humorous excess of their contemporary animated counterparts, the live-action iterations of "Beauty and the Beast" and "A Whole New World" draw on the sensibilities of their 1990s predecessors, with sincerity and sentimentalism. They function as nostalgic "bubbles," highly familiar re-enactments in the midst of wider aesthetic and narrative alterations. Mollet argues that such "iconic moments" are "emotionally significant" for the millennial audience, recalling childhood memories of watching and listening to these highly popular songs.[35] Nostalgia also plays a pivotal role in the context of romance. Writing on 1990s and 2000s romantic comedies, Michele Schreiber notes that they are characterized by "postfeminist nostalgia": "a relapse into an ostensibly outmoded desire for romantic fulfillment as a reassuring escape from the contradictions between feminist ideals and the realities of the labor and mating markets."[36] Illustrating the "doubleness" described by Tasker, Maria San Filippo adds that they preserve "the fantasy of women's fulfillment through heteronormative coupling ... while simultaneously displaying feminist revisionism."[37] Disney's live-action remakes proceed in a very similar way. While they attempt to update the portrayal of the princesses—live-action Belle reads Shakespeare and teaches other girls how to read, live-action Jasmine becomes sultan—they preserve more traditional, sentimental, heteronormative displays, which culminate with the romantic song. These musical sequences include several shots imitating the originals very closely—for example, Belle and the Beast walking down the stairs of the ballroom together, Aladdin giving his hand to Jasmine and asking her, "Do you trust me?" While live-action princesses wear a variety of costumes, sometimes only vaguely reminiscent of their animated counterparts, they don the recognizable princess outfits—blue top and bouffant trousers for Jasmine, yellow layered gown for Belle—in these musical sequences. In other words, they appear as the closest embodiment of their animated counterpart. Such a nostalgic framework is heightened through subtle changes, linked directly to the shift from hand-drawn animation to live-action and computer animation.

One of the most significant amendments in these live-action musical sequences is the downplaying, sometimes even erasure, of any element that would stand out as too humorous, caricatured, or exaggerated. In other words, the remakes primarily focus on the live-action characters and their romance, discarding any "animated" distraction. In the animated version of "Beauty and the Beast," there are regular cuts from the dancing couple to supporting anthropomorphic characters Lumière and Cogsworth. The candelabra and the clock closely watch and cheer the Beast's courting of Belle: Lumière nudges Cogsworth knowingly when the two start waltzing; they raise their "arms," wink, and give the Beast a "thumbs up" when Belle leans against his chest and he excitedly looks at them; Lumière even encourages another candelabra to dim its light at the end of the song, creating a more intimate atmosphere. Their presence suggests that Disney's romantic musical sequence, the epitome of authentic emotion and love, is also, to some extent, a performance that requires the proper setting, costumes, and soundtrack. It is notably Mrs. Potts, not the couple, who sings "Beauty and the Beast," a continuous commentary on their nascent feelings ("Barely even friends / Then somebody bends / Unexpectedly") and their predictable outcome ("Certain as the sun / Rising in the east"). The presence of these comic anthropomorphic sidekicks is heavily downplayed in the live-action remakes. Stylized and caricatured hand-drawn design is replaced by photo-realistic detail for these computer-animated characters; they become elaborate props, silent spectators in the corner of the frame, no longer interacting with the Beast. When the lighting is dimmed toward the end of the sequence, it seems to occur by magic. The focus is, instead, on Belle and the Beast and their elaborate choreography, with the Beast dipping and lifting Belle. Without the humorous distractions of anthropomorphic sidekicks, which hint at the formulaic structure of the romantic Disney song, this live-action reinterpretation highlights the romantic aspect of the sequence; Belle and the Beast only gaze at each other, seemingly lost in the dance. Showcasing the couple in such a way not only amplifies the sentimental sensibility of the sequence but also reinterprets its aesthetic and the implications of its medium, its animated nature.

Although animation still plays a pivotal role in both remakes, from the depiction of fantasy settings to the representation of otherworldly characters, it is used in a way that reflects the wider narrative strategies of the film, making potentially old-fashioned romantic displays believable and appealing to modern audiences—or, rather, remystifying Disney's formula. Bérénice Bonhomme notes that in Disney's remakes, the shift from animation to live action seems to unavoidably involve further explanation, justification, and development regarding plot and characterization.[38] Correspondingly, the lead couples share more time on-screen and provide further background information on their families. Such an approach directly impacts the musical sequences and, most significantly, the romantic songs.

While *Beauty and the Beast*'s "Be Our Guest" and *Aladdin*'s "Friend Like Me" preserve, to some extent, the extravagance and fantasy of their animated counterparts, being primarily performed by computer-animated characters, this is not the case for "A Whole New World" or "Beauty and the Beast." The magical potentials of a carpet ride or a waltz with an anthropomorphic beast are mediated through a photorealistic, rational lens. In the animated version of "A Whole New World," Aladdin and Jasmine fly over Egypt and Greece within a few minutes, catch bits of cloud in their hands, and always land back on the carpet, even though it loops high up in the sky. In other words, the hand-drawn animated sequence gleefully defies the laws of physics, challenging constructions of time and space as seen in live-action cinema. In the live-action remake, "A Whole New World" becomes a—paradoxically—plausible musical sequence, in which Aladdin and Jasmine remain in the proximity of Agrabah, tightly hold the carpet when it rapidly flies down a waterfall, and stay relatively close to the ground. Although both the carpet and the settings are computer-animated, they are seamlessly and credibly integrated on-screen. Lilly Husbands and Caroline Ruddell observe that the use of computer animation in contemporary mainstream live-action films "does not distract from our enjoyment of the scene because a certain 'realism' is achieved."[39] In the context of "A Whole New World," this means that the romantic musical performance of the actors, conveying the nascent feelings of the protagonists, can remain the primary focus of the sequence. The live-action remake of *Beauty and the Beast* relies on a complex mix of "motion-capture and CGI" to animate the Beast in order to similarly maintain a cohesive aesthetic;[40] motion capture precisely allows "physically accurate and convincing motion."[41] Therefore, the Beast's dance with Belle becomes as smooth and credible as if it was performed by two real actors. Such live-action reinterpretation transforms the Disney romantic song into a particularly enticing display. Far from outmoded, the studio's sentimental formula—along with its heteronormative ideals—becomes even more (aesthetically) believable and appealing.

Conclusion

This chapter explored how contemporary Disney films, and most particularly animated sequels and live-action remakes, rely on the musical sequence as a pivotal tool in order to re-envision the studio's generic formula. As illuminated through the analysis of *Ralph Breaks the Internet*'s "A Place Called Slaughter Race," *Frozen II*'s "Lost in the Woods," *Aladdin*'s "Speechless" and "A Whole New World," and *Beauty and the Beast*'s title song, these films adopt a dual strategy, both preserving and reinterpreting the core components of iconic musical tropes: the "I Want" song and the romantic song. In the process, they both revise and celebrate Disney's wider formula, subverting while reclaiming some of its aspects—in a typically postfeminist way. The tone and approach adopted contrast, however, depending on the medium. Self-aware parody, playful demystification, and contra-diegetic extravagance, introduced in the late 2000s with the live-action/animation hybrid *Enchanted*, seem firmly located within the animation milieu a decade later. More subversive elements are mediated by such a humorous lens: the gender reversal at work in "Lost in the Woods," the questioning of Disney's musical regime of verisimilitude in both that song and "A Place Called Slaughter Race." By contrast, a particularly reverent perspective is adopted in live action, whether the transformation of the "I Want" song into a song of self-assertion, as in "Speechless," or the sentimental restaging of old-fashioned romance, as in "A Whole New World" and "Beauty and the Beast." As animated sequels, *Ralph Breaks the Internet* and *Frozen II* amplify Disney's contemporary debunking of its own formula through comedy and satire, whereas live-action remakes crystallize the studio's reliance on nostalgia and the childlike appeals of fairy-tale fantasies in order to revive aspects of the very same formula. Illuminating how these seemingly opposed yet complementary strategies function throughout varying Disney films, this chapter examined the multiple ways in which the studio reappropriates and plays with the idea of the Disney formula. In the process, the studio undeniably aims to re-envision the boundaries between and the potentials of animated and live-action musicals.

Notes

1. For a detailed analysis of the "Neo Disney" period, see Chris Pallant, "Neo-Disney: Recent Developments in Disney Feature Animation," *New Cinemas* 8, no. 2 (2010): 103–117.
2. *Frozen* remained the highest-grossing animated film of all time ($1.3 billion gross worldwide) until 2019, when it was replaced by Disney's *The Lion King* remake (2019; $1.6 billion gross). See Noel Brown, *Contemporary Hollywood Animation: Style, Storytelling, Culture and Ideology since the 1990s* (Edinburgh: Edinburgh University Press, 2021), 15.
3. Eve Benhamou, *Contemporary Disney Animation: Genre, Gender and Hollywood* (Edinburgh: Edinburgh University Press, 2022), 46.
4. Ibid.
5. Carolyn Jess-Cooke, *Film Sequels: Theory and Practice from Hollywood to Bollywood* (Edinburgh: Edinburgh University Press, 2009), 2.
6. Although theatrically released animated sequels represent a very rare occurrence throughout the Disney canon, it is worth noting that the 2000s and 2010s were dominated by animated sequels from competing studios, from Blue Sky's *Ice Age* franchise (2002, 2006, 2009, 2012, 2016, 2022) to Illumination's *Despicable Me* (2010, 2013, 2015, 2017, 2022). The box-office success of Pixar's sequels, epitomized by the critically acclaimed *Toy Story* franchise (1995, 1999, 2010, 2019, 2022), may have informed Disney's recent return to theatrical sequels.
7. Diane Negra and Yvonne Tasker, "Introduction: Feminist Politics and Postfeminist Culture," in *Interrogating Postfeminism: Gender and the Politics of Popular Culture*, ed. Diana Negra and Yvonne Tasker (Durham, NC: Duke University Press, 2007), 18.
8. Richard Dyer, *In the Space of a Song: The Uses of Song in Film* (Abingdon: Routledge, 2012), 101.
9. Richard Dyer, "Entertainment and Utopia," in *Hollywood Musicals: The Film Reader*, ed. Steven Cohan (London: Routledge, 2002), 20.
10. Eleanor Byrne and Martin McQuillan, *Deconstructing Disney* (London: Pluto, 1999), 24.
11. Steve Neale, *Genre and Hollywood* (London: Routledge, 2000), 32.
12. Jennifer Fleeger, *Mismatched Women: The Siren's Song through the Machine* (New York: Oxford University Press, 2014), 108, 107–136 for further detail on the singing voices of Disney princesses.
13. Jane Feuer, *The Hollywood Musical* (Basingstoke: Macmillan, 1993), 44. For some authors, the backstage musical corresponds to an early trend of the wider Hollywood musical, including films such as *Gold Diggers of 1933* (1933) and *42nd Street* (1933), in which narrative and number are kept clearly separated: musical performances occur independently, onstage or in cabarets. See Dyer, "Entertainment and Utopia," 26.
14. Feuer, *The Hollywood Musical*, 44.
15. Ibid.
16. For an analysis of *Enchanted* from this specific perspective, see Benhamou, *Contemporary Disney Animation*, 43–46.
17. Feuer, *The Hollywood Musical*, 44.

18. Stéphanie Genz, "'I Am Not a housewife, but …': Postfeminism and the Revival of Domesticity," in *Feminism, Domesticity and Popular Culture*, ed. Stacy Gillis and Joanne Hollows (New York: Routledge, 2009), 50.
19. Benhamou, *Contemporary Disney Animation*, 16–17.
20. Amy M. Davis, *Good Girls and Wicked Witches: Women in Disney's Feature Animation* (New Barnet, UK: John Libbey, 2006), 189.
21. Kellie Bean, "Stripping Beauty: Disney's 'Feminist' Seduction," in *The Emperor's Old Groove: Decolonizing Disney's Magic Kingdom*, ed. Brenda Ayres (New York: P. Lang, 2003), 58–59.
22. Clare Bradford, "'Where Happily Ever After Happens Every Day': The Medievalisms of Disney's Princesses," in *The Disney Middle Ages: A Fairy-Tale and Fantasy Past*, ed. Susan Aronstein and Tison Pugh (Basingstoke: Palgrave Macmillan, 2012), 182.
23. Celeste Lacroix, "Images of Animated Others: The Orientalization of Disney's Cartoon Heroines from *The Little Mermaid* to *The Hunchback of Notre Dame*," *Popular Communication* 2 (2004): 222.
24. Angelique Jackson, "'Aladdin': Naomi Scott on Why Her Princess Jasmine Needed Nasim Pedrad's New Character," *Variety*, May 24, 2019, https://variety.com/2019/scene/news/naomi-scott-aladdin-jasmine-charlies-angels-1203225763/.
25. Tracey L. Mollet, *A Cultural History of the Disney Fairy Tale: Once upon an American Dream* (Cham: Palgrave Macmillan, 2020), 158.
26. For a more detailed analysis of "Let It Go" from this perspective, see Benhamou, *Contemporary Disney Animation*, 170–174.
27. Rick Altman, *The American Film Musical* (Bloomington: Indiana University Press, 1989), 109.
28. Yvonne Tasker, "*Enchanted* (2007) by Postfeminism: Gender, Irony, and the New Romantic Comedy," in *Feminism at the Movies: Understanding Gender in Contemporary Popular Cinema*, ed. Hilary Radner and Rebecca Stringer (London: Routledge, 2011), 68.
29. For further details on this musical sequence, see Catherine Lester, "Frozen Heart and Fixer Uppers: Villainy, Gender, and Female Companionship in Disney's *Frozen*," in *Discussing Disney*, ed. Amy Davis (New Barnet, UK: John Libbey, 2019), 198–199.
30. Sam Summers, *DreamWorks Animation: Intertextuality and Aesthetics in Shrek and Beyond* (Cham: Palgrave Macmillan, 2020), 9, 17.
31. Ibid., 67.
32. Ibid., 77.
33. Joanna Robinson, "*Frozen II*: The Story behind Jonathan Groff's Surprising '80s Ballad," *Vanity Fair*, November 15, 2019, https://www.vanityfair.com/hollywood/2019/11/jonathan-groff-song-frozen-2-lost-in-the-woods-making-of.
34. Ibid.
35. Mollet, *A Cultural History*, 155.
36. Michele Schreiber, "'Misty Water-Colored Memories of the Way We Were …': Postfeminist Nostalgia in Contemporary Romance Narratives," in *Reclaiming the Archive: Feminism and Film History*, ed. Vicki Callahan (Detroit: Wayne State University Press, 2010), 364–383.
37. Quoted in Maria San Filippo, "Introduction—Love Actually: Romantic Comedy since the Aughts," in *After "Happily Ever After": Romantic Comedy in the Post-Romantic Age*, ed. Maria San Filippo (Detroit: Wayne State University Press, 2021), 8.

38. Bérénice Bonhomme, "Disney, remakes et reprises," *Mise au Point* 10 (2018), https://doi.org/10.4000/map.2423.
39. Lilly Husbands and Caroline Ruddell, "Approaching Animation and Animation Studies," in *The Animation Studies Reader*, ed. Nichola Dobson et al. (New York: Bloomsbury Academic, 2019), 7.
40. Kate Erbland, "'Beauty and the Beast' Is a Technological Marvel, but for Its Actors, the Challenge Was Daunting," IndieWire, March 17, 2017, https://www.indiewire.com/2017/03/beauty-and-the-beast-technology-dan-stevens-guga-mbatha-raw-1201794115/.
41. Mihaela Mihailova, "Animation and Realism," in *The Animation Studies Reader*, ed. Nichola Dobson et al. (New York: Bloomsbury Academic, 2019), 54.

Bibliography

Altman, Rick. *The American Film Musical*. Bloomington: Indiana University Press, 1989.

Bean, Kellie. "Stripping Beauty: Disney's 'Feminist' Seduction." In *The Emperor's Old Groove: Decolonizing Disney's Magic Kingdom*, edited by Brenda Ayres, 53–64. New York: P. Lang, 2003.

Benhamou, Eve. *Contemporary Disney Animation: Genre, Gender and Hollywood*. Edinburgh: Edinburgh University Press, 2022.

Bonhomme, Bérénice. "Disney, remakes et reprises." *Mise au Point* 10 (2018). https://doi.org/10.4000/map.2423.

Bradford, Clare. "'Where Happily Ever After Happens Every Day': The Medievalisms of Disney's Princesses." In *The Disney Middle Ages: A Fairy-Tale and Fantasy Past*, edited by Susan Aronstein and Tison Pugh, 171–188. Basingstoke: Palgrave Macmillan, 2012.

Brown, Noel. *Contemporary Hollywood Animation: Style, Storytelling, Culture and Ideology since the 1990s*. Edinburgh: Edinburgh University Press, 2021.

Byrne, Eleanor, and Martin McQuillan. *Deconstructing Disney*. London: Pluto, 1999.

Davis, Amy M. *Good Girls and Wicked Witches: Women in Disney's Feature Animation*. New Barnet, UK: John Libbey, 2006.

Dyer, Richard. "Entertainment and Utopia." In *Hollywood Musicals: The Film Reader*, edited by Steven Cohan, 19–30. London: Routledge, 2002.

Dyer, Richard. *In the Space of a Song: The Uses of Song in Film*. Abingdon: Routledge, 2012.

Erbland, Kate. "'Beauty and the Beast' Is a Technological Marvel, but for Its Actors, the Challenge Was Daunting." IndieWire, March 17, 2017. https://www.indiewire.com/2017/03/beauty-and-the-beast-technology-dan-stevens-guga-mbatha-raw-1201794115/.

Feuer, Jane. *The Hollywood Musical*. Basingstoke: Macmillan, 1993.

Fleeger, Jennifer. *Mismatched Women: The Siren's Song through the Machine*. New York: Oxford University Press, 2014.

Genz, Stéphanie. "'I Am Not a Housewife, but …': Postfeminism and the Revival of Domesticity." In *Feminism, Domesticity and Popular Culture*, edited by Stacy Gillis and Joanne Hollows, 49–62. New York: Routledge, 2009.

Husbands, Lilly, and Caroline Ruddell. "Approaching Animation and Animation Studies." In *The Animation Studies Reader*, edited by Nichola Dobson, Annabelle Honess Roe, Amy Ratelle, and Caroline Ruddell, 5–15. New York: Bloomsbury Academic, 2019.

Jackson, Angelique. "'Aladdin': Naomi Scott on Why Her Princess Jasmine Needed Nasim Pedrad's New Character." *Variety*, May 24, 2019. https://variety.com/2019/scene/news/naomi-scott-aladdin-jasmine-charlies-angels-1203225763/.

Jess-Cooke, Carolyn. *Film Sequels: Theory and Practice from Hollywood to Bollywood.* Edinburgh: Edinburgh University Press, 2009.

Lacroix, Celeste. "Images of Animated Others: The Orientalization of Disney's Cartoon Heroines from *The Little Mermaid* to *The Hunchback of Notre Dame*." *Popular Communication* 2 (2004): 213–229.

Lester, Catherine, "Frozen Heart and Fixer Uppers: Villainy, Gender, and Female Companionship in Disney's *Frozen*." In *Discussing Disney*, edited by Amy Davis, 193–216. New Barnet, UK: John Libbey, 2019.

Mihailova, Mihaela. "Animation and Realism." In *The Animation Studies Reader*, edited by Nichola Dobson, Annabelle Honess Roe, Amy Ratelle, and Caroline Ruddell, 47–57. New York: Bloomsbury Academic, 2019.

Mollet, Tracey L. *A Cultural History of the Disney Fairy Tale: Once upon an American Dream.* Cham: Palgrave Macmillan, 2020.

Neale, Steve. *Genre and Hollywood.* London: Routledge, 2000.

Negra, Diane, and Yvonne Tasker. "Introduction: Feminist Politics and Postfeminist Culture." In *Interrogating Postfeminism: Gender and the Politics of Popular Culture*, edited by Diana Negra and Yvonne Tasker, 1–25. Durham, NC: Duke University Press, 2007.

Pallant, Chris. "Neo-Disney: Recent Developments in Disney Feature Animation." *New Cinemas* 8, no. 2 (2010): 103–117.

Robinson, Joanna. "*Frozen II*: The Story behind Jonathan Groff's Surprising '80s Ballad." *Vanity Fair*, November 15, 2019. https://www.vanityfair.com/hollywood/2019/11/jonathan-groff-song-frozen-2-lost-in-the-woods-making-of.

San Filippo, Maria. "Introduction—Love Actually: Romantic Comedy since the Aughts." In *After "Happily Ever After": Romantic Comedy in the Post-Romantic Age*, edited by Maria San Filippo, 1–24. Detroit: Wayne State University Press, 2021.

Summers, Sam. *DreamWorks Animation: Intertextuality and Aesthetics in Shrek and Beyond.* Cham: Palgrave Macmillan, 2020.

Tasker, Yvonne. "*Enchanted* (2007) by Postfeminism: Gender, Irony, and the New Romantic Comedy." In *Feminism at the Movies: Understanding Gender in Contemporary Popular Cinema*, edited by Hilary Radner and Rebecca Stringer, 67–79. London: Routledge, 2011.

CHAPTER 11

HAVEN'T I SEEN THIS SOMEWHERE BEFORE? *THE LITTLE MERMAID LIVE!*, CONTENT CANNIBALIZATION, AND DISNEY'S TELEVISION LEGACY

KELLY KESSLER

Mice on All of the Screens

It was a banner year for "the Mouse" in 2019. Crossing platforms, genres, and audiences, Disney was on point. The company's name was stamped on eight of the fifteen top-grossing movies of that year, with all five of the top slots tapping into presold audiences via Disney-owned franchises, sequels, or remakes: *Avengers: Endgame, The Lion King, Toy Story 4, Captain Marvel,* and *Frozen II*.[1] That same year saw the company launch its highly anticipated Disney+ into a tough market glutted with new streaming services, premiering within days of Apple TV+ and less than a year from HBO Max and Peacock. On the small screen, Disney's ABC network may have been struggling, but it was riding strong on the continued success of long-running shows such as *The Bachelor* (2002–), *Modern Family* (2009–2020), and *Grey's Anatomy* (2005–), all continuing to tap into the coveted 18–49 demographic.[2] Onstage, Disney Theatrical Productions introduced yet another big-screen-to-New-York-stage musical, with the Menken-Zippel-Horn-Diaz production of *Hercules* opening at the Delacorte Theatre as part of the Public Works program. Although this one would not find the level of popularity that others had, it drew a heavy-hitting cast, featuring Tony Award winner Roger Bart; Jelani Aladdin, Kristoff in Broadway's *Frozen*; and Upright Citizens Brigade alum and *Bloody Bloody Andrew Jackson*'s Jeff Hiller.

And then it happened. ABC and Disney threw their hats into the "live television musical" ring and tried to pull off a Frankenstein's monster of a mediated mishmash in the form of *The Little Mermaid Live!* As part of the relatively moribund *The Wonderful World of Disney* series, ABC brought the American broadcast-television audience a weird hybrid: part 1989 animated film, part 2008 Broadway musical, part television live spectacular, part puppet show, and part Cirque du Soleil–inspired aerial work. It was everything and nothing an audience could have dreamed of. But it was also not shocking, based on Disney's historical approach to television.

This chapter takes a look at *The Little Mermaid Live!* and explores how it differed stylistically from the earlier live television musicals of the 2010s and how its hybrid format was totally on-brand in the context of Disney's prior sixty years on the small screen. From its placement on the Disney-owned ABC network to its advertising spots to its hybrid format, *The Little Mermaid Live!* was classic Disney television. By looking back at Disney's decades-long relationship with the television industry, one that began when the motion-picture industry started to hit major bumps in the road, the choices made for the 2019 family spectacular not only become somewhat more coherent but also make sense in the grander scheme of Disney's business model. It may not have been the prettiest "live" television musical, but it was the Disney-est.

Stop Saying Live! The Shifting Form of the Twenty-First-Century Live Television Musical

In 2013, NBC launched the twenty-first-century resurgence of the live television musical with its production of *The Sound of Music*, dubbed *The Sound of Music Live!* Promotional materials harked back to the golden age of television, conjuring visions of NBC's 1955 live television presentation of *Peter Pan*, hot off its Tony Award–winning Broadway production and nestled comfortably in the network's prestige anthology series *Producers' Showcase*. Mary Martin's first televised appearance as the musical lost boy drew in 66.1 percent of the viewing audience.[3] The *Sound of Music Live!*'s producers Craig Zadan and Neil Meron hung their promotional hats on the nostalgia cultivated by many reairings of the show and a desire for families to once again gather around the television-shaped hearth to watch a live musical extravaganza, as folks had done with *Peter Pan* and hundreds of televised musicals in the years following.[4]

In 1955, almost all television was live. *Peter Pan* had been hailed by NBC's president Sylvester "Pat" Weaver as bringing Broadway into living rooms across the country.[5]

Regular TV viewers may not have been able to make it to see a Broadway show all the way from Kansas City, but they could surely see one from the comfort of their own sofas with the help of Mary Martin and NBC. In 2013, American broadcast television had a very different relationship with liveness. It had been half a century since the majority of television programming had turned away from broadcasting live. It had been more than a quarter of a century since cable television had started posing a major challenge to networks and poaching their viewers. And it was closing in on a decade since streaming services like Hulu, Netflix, and Amazon had brought time-shifting and user-driven programming selection to an entirely new level. The television broadcast networks—ABC, NBC, CBS, Fox, and the CW—were in major trouble. The most reliable sources of viewers for this once impenetrable wall of television broadcasting had become the types of programming for which time-shifting was simply impractical: sports and reality, two genres that relied heavily on immediacy and viewers watching synchronously. NBC took a shot with *The Sound of Music Live!* and found itself riding high, with 18.6 million viewers, a 4.6 rating, and 450,000 Tweets dedicated to viewers' love (or hate) of the television special.[6] What was clear by the next morning was that NBC had found a new way to attract solid numbers of family viewers to live television. So in came the new live musicals.

Between *The Sound of Music Live!* and *The Little Mermaid Live!*, Fox and NBC released a string of live (and live-ish) musicals, seemingly attempting to find that magic mix that would solidify the genre and usher in a devoted block of dedicated family viewers. After its first foray into the revitalized genre with *The Sound of Music Live!*, NBC aired *Peter Pan Live!* (2014), *The Wiz Live!* (2015), and *Hairspray Live!* (2016), and Fox hit it big with its smash hit *Grease Live!* (2016). All of these entries had one thing in common: the entire show was performed live for the television audience during the broadcast. After the first two musicals emerged in seemingly hermetically sealed worlds that made them look less theatrical and more like live movies, *The Wiz Live!*—once discussed as being a tryout for a new Broadway revival of the 1975 show—shifted to a more proscenium-style production, added projections, and added Cirque du Soleil performers and stunts to up the visual ante.[7]

Grease Live! revved things up with a much more intense social-media presence, both before and during the performance, and the inclusion of a live audience on-screen. As the cast rushed from one end of the Warner Bros. studio lot on golf carts, vaguely costumed audience members being used as extras cheered them on from the sidelines and the Rydell High gymnasium. *Hairspray Live!* took a cue from *Grease* with what director Alex Rudzinski described as a 360-degree interactive experience, with a side stage full of influencers posting to their rapt audiences across social-media platforms and an entire Facebook live second-screen experience bringing viewers behind-the-scenes looks, trivia tidbits, and commentary by *Glee* star Darren Criss. And then in 2018, NBC put on a rock-and-roll *Jesus Christ Superstar* starring pop stars John Legend and Sara Bareilles, with Broadway stalwart and Tony winner Brandon Victor Dixon (*Shuffle Along*, *The Scottsboro Boys*, *The Color Purple*) and shock rocker Alice Cooper. Less musical theater and more rock concert, the show was a numbers hit with the viewing audience and apparently a hit with the throngs of audience members screaming just off-stage as if they were at a Beatles concert. What liveness meant across these various musical extravaganzas shifted from year to year, but NBC and Fox were doing their best to drag time-shifting and streaming viewers into a regular prime-time television event.

Alongside these live musicals were a number of quasi-live television musical productions, with Fox's Easter spectacular *The Passion* (2016) blending a prerecorded passion play and live musical performances and a march through New Orleans with a giant cross. A few months later, Fox presented *The Rocky Horror Picture Show: Let's Do the Time Warp Again*, a prerecorded new production of the show starring Laverne Cox as Frank-n-Furter and screened in front of a live theatrical audience who intermittently screamed at the screen as if they were in the movie theater. And *Rent Live!* underdazzled audiences with its unplanned bait-and-switch. The special had been prepped as a live musical in the style of the other Fox and NBC offerings, but after one of the key actors broke his foot during a dress rehearsal, Fox ended up airing a taped dress rehearsal for a live studio audience forced to respond as if they were watching something live. This production proved that "the show must go on" was really just a suggestion in this case. So it was into this environment of shifting "live musicals" that *The Little Mermaid Live!* emerged in 2019. From its initial announcement, the idea had always been that the special would be some kind of live and recorded hybrid, but what would it look like?

Disney's first foray into the twenty-first-century trend looked nothing like any of the specials that had come before it in the preceding six years. Whereas all of the above musicals were "live" in one way or another, and in the more successful of them, performance was live throughout the duration of the show, Disney went another way with its entry. When it was first announced in May 2017, the planned production was described by the *Hollywood Reporter* as something that would "intertwine the beloved 1989 animated film with live musical-performances via cutting-edge technology." It would include celebrity performances that would be "woven seamlessly throughout the original film."[8] The press stylistically linked the upcoming televised special to new Hollywood Bowl productions which had embraced a blend of live performance and film screening. Just months later, the press announced that ABC would be dropping its plans for *The Little Mermaid Live!* and that the live television production had been "beached" without explanation.[9] By the time the project had been re-announced for an August 2019 air date, the Hollywood Bowl had already staged a thirtieth-anniversary hybrid celebration of *The Little Mermaid* as an "Immersive Live-to-Film" extravaganza starring Broadway crossover stars such as Lea Michele (*Glee*, *Spring Awakening*) as Ariel, Harvey Fierstein (Tony Award winner for *Hairspray* and *Torch Song Trilogy*) as Ursula, and Peter Gallagher (Drama Desk nominee for *Guys and Dolls* and loving patriarch on Fox's *The OC*) as King Triton.[10]

Enter *The Little Mermaid Live!* in the large dual shadows of the animated feature and *Grease Live!* Hamish Hamilton—awards show, Super Bowl halftime show, and music video director—chose not to lean into any of the three for this directorial foray. For the two hours *The Little Mermaid Live!* was on air, just more than half an hour of that time was taken up by actual live performance of the songs made popular by either the 1989

Disney animated classic—which had arguably single-handedly brought the animated blockbuster back to cinemas after a major hiatus—or the 2008 Broadway show. The rest of the on-air time was spent showing a reairing of the motion-picture classic on a screen hanging on the stage itself (figure 11.1). That way, the "live" theatrical audience could alternate between watching the musical numbers onstage and following along with at-home audience members as they watched the popular original animated feature on their TV screens.

This allowed "Part of Your World," "Kiss the Girl," and "Poor Unfortunate Souls" to emerge as somewhat flashy and at times puppet-filled musical numbers sung by the likes of Auli'i Cravalho (*Moana*), rapper Shaggy, and hip-hop icon Queen Latifah, while giving director Hamilton no reason to cast actors for any characters who didn't sing. If a character was not in a musical number, no need to send out a casting call for this special. Even seemingly integral characters like King Triton were ditched for this production. *USA Today* described Ariel's screen-bound father as "seemingly stuck in the prison of 1989 animation."[11] Luckily, those who created the hybrid adaptation for television brought over a couple of numbers from the Broadway production, so Prince Eric (Graham Phillips from Broadway's *13* and television's *The Good Wife*) could at least find his way to the live stage.

The much-heralded *Grease Live!* had done some similar combining of source material, blending the film and stage productions and integrating new numbers, such as "All I Need Is an Angel" written for Carly Rae Jepsen to sing as Frenchy. The other shows had largely stuck to their Broadway versions, allowing for minor adjustments, like *Peter Pan Live!* stripping out the overtly racist "Ugg-a-Wugg" for an only kind-of-racist "Indians." But *The Sound of Music Live!*, *Peter Pan Live!*, *The Wiz Live!*, *Grease Live!*, and *Hairspray*

FIGURE 11.1. The Little Mermaid Live! drops its movie screen onto the stage so the theatrical and at-home audiences can view the non-musical sections as one.

Live! all leaned in on their liveness. The only question was whether viewers saw some backstage action as well—quick changes, racing actors, shifting scenery, and so on. For all five of the aforementioned specials, the productions were wholly live for the viewers at home, even if they did have varying levels of telegraphed theatricality. Unfortunately, *The Little Mermaid Live!* was perhaps more *Rent: Live* (which I have previously written about as having delivered "failed experiential promises" and a classic bait-and-switch) than *Grease* or *Hairspray*. The *Hollywood Reporter* even dubbed the Disney special a "classic bait-and-switch" and questioned the very veracity of calling it "live" in the first place.[12]

Disney took its shot, hailing the gods of "special-event programming" and hoping to bring viewers to ABC in real time. Those who tuned in via their televisions, smartphones, tablets, or whatever devices could bring them an ABC network live feed found the show's Ariel, Prince Eric, and Chef Louie (John Stamos) decked out in costumes that resembled the screen versions of their characters. Zaldy, Emmy-winning costume designer from *RuPaul's Drag Race*, went all-out and full camp with Queen Latifah's grandiose Ursula costume: foot-tall white wig, black pleather octopus ballgown, and giant floating tentacles suspended by cables and moving as she sang. Shaggy's Sebastian costume looked more Michael Jackson's "Beat It" than "Kiss the Girl," with the singer clad in red leather pants and jacket and having ditched the originally designed crab claws preperformance. The human cast was joined by puppet versions of Ariel's fishy friend Flounder, Ursula's amorphous henchmen Flotsam and Jetsam, and other Muppet-like sea creatures. In addition to spicing things up with the puppets, the show included brief moments of aerial work to simulate swimming, and the live studio audience was intermittently given props like blue fabric to simulate waves or crab claws for "Under the Sea" to crank up the wow factor. (See figures 11.2, 11.3, and 11.4.)

FIGURE 11.2. Queen Latifah slays both literally and figuratively during the reveal of her spectacular Ursula costume in 'Poor Unfortunate Souls.'

FIGURE 11.3. Shaggy's refusal to wear his crab claws make the show's puppet-filled 'Under the Sea' number a bit more Michael Jackson than Sebastian.

FIGURE 11.4. The production's 'Fathoms Below' highlights Disney's blending of theatrical spectacle and audience participation, as the viewers at home see the stagebound ship surrounded by audience members waving blue strips of fabric to evoke the crashing waves.

The show's executive producer Raj Kapoor arguably saw these additions as Disney and ABC's way of upping the ante on the previous live productions. Per Kapoor, "We had this whole creative team that comes from a vast range of experiences, and everyone wanted to put their own spin on it because we see this as blending the theatrical version with the feature film version with a live awards show meeting elements of the Super Bowl."[13] Although reviews were mixed, ABC got what it was looking for that evening: 8.98 million tuned in that night to see the "live" production, with the special earning a 2.6 rating in the 18–49 demographic. The production had a higher rating than any of the previous twenty-first-century TV musicals since *Grease Live!* in 2016, and it was the top "entertainment" telecast since the series finale of *The Big Bang Theory* nearly six months prior.[14] Even this weird hybrid event gave Disney a hit.

It's All Part of the Disney Way: Disney Sells Itself on the Small Screen

But was this significant formal shift in the television musical remotely surprising? For those familiar with the history of the Walt Disney Company and specifically Walt Disney's relationship to television, the mix-and-match form of *The Little Mermaid Live!* was simply business as usual. Although Walt Disney Studios began as part of the motion-picture industry, its diversification into other areas was built by capitalizing on the recognizability, repackaging, and reselling of its existing properties across platforms, a process Walt Disney himself referred to as "total merchandising." In his book *Hollywood TV*, Christopher Anderson describes Disney as carpeting the market:

> Products aimed at baby boom families and stamped with the Disney imprint— movies, amusement park rides, books, comic books, clothing, toys, TV programs, and more—would weave a vast, commercial web, a tangle of advertising and entertainment in which each Disney product—from the movie *Snow White* to a ride on Disneyland's Matterhorn—promoted all Disney products.[15]

This economic strategy was in full bloom on November 5, 2019, when Disney's ABC aired the first of its twenty-first-century live television musicals.

The 1950s had been a time of major destabilization of and migration for the motion-picture studios. After the 1948 Paramount Decision had forced the big Hollywood studios to dismantle their oligopolistic structures and divest of their theater chains, big hitters like Warner Bros. began diversifying their investments by moving over into television production.[16] Paramount's divested theater chain United Paramount Theatres began buying television stations in the early 1950s and merged with the third-place television network ABC in 1953. As studios scrambled to find footing amid changes in the Hollywood landscape and in the burgeoning New York–based television industry, Walt Disney and his brother Roy were already a decade into figuring out how to diversify their products. One of the smaller studios and one that had struggled during the instability of the World War II era, Disney had already sought out alternative avenues for its products.[17] By 1943, "upward of 90 percent" of Disney's work was related to the war effort and subsidized by government funding. Disney's leading animated characters were not only supported by but also supporting the war effort.[18] Less than a decade later, Disney turned its sights to television, with its first television special airing on NBC in 1950, a Christmas party titled *An Hour in Wonderland* and featuring a sneak peek at the studio's upcoming animated feature *Alice in Wonderland* (1951). In less than three years, Disney would captivate the baby-boomer audience, raise ABC from the bottom of the network food chain, and revolutionize its own business model. It would also use that same *Alice in Wonderland* again, as economically viable, repurposed content for a first-season episode of its inaugural television series.

DISNEYLAND SELLS IT ALL

Although the musical was not always at the center of Walt Disney's television ventures, the business model that would come to define Disney's television success would later be used to reinvigorate Disney's marriage of musicals and the small screen. After shopping around their idea for a television series, Roy and Walt Disney struck a deal with ABC. The network committed $2 million for a fifty-two-week season, consisting of twenty new episodes, each of which would run twice during the year and twelve of which would run for a third time. This deal satisfied what ABC's president Leonard Goldenson had articulated as the network's desire to target young families and create a sense of consistency. Previously a lawyer for Paramount and tasked with reorganizing United Paramount Theatres, Goldenson has been quoted as saying, "The real strength and vitality of television is in your regular week-in and week-out programs. The strength of motion pictures was always the habit of going to motion pictures on a regular basis, and that habit was taken away from motion pictures by television."[19] Along with strengthening ABC's position within the television industry, Disney's deal with the network brought an added bonus for the studio and one that would foreshadow Disney's future grasp across entertainment outlets and leisure industries: as part of the deal, ABC agreed to invest $500,000 into the building of the Disneyland park, giving the network 35 percent ownership.[20] Without even a clear vision for what the television series would look like, the Disney company had sold itself based on its brand and captivation of a desirable and growing family demographic.

Walt Disney's Disneyland—named after the theme park that had yet to open—premiered on ABC on October 27, 1954. The anthology series presented an array of new and repurposed pieces of Disney programming under that series name and various others (e.g., *Walt Disney Presents*, *Walt Disney's Wonderful World of Color*, and *Walt Disney*) from 1954 to 1983, moving between ABC (1954–1961), NBC (1961–1981), and CBS (1981–1983), until the 1983 launch of Disney's flagship cable channel, the Disney Channel, arguably pushed the series off the air.[21] Nevertheless, for thirty years, Disney would be a nonstop part of the American television landscape. It was here that its pattern of repurposing, cross-promotion, and total merchandising really took hold on a level that surpassed its initial quarter-century within the motion-picture and military-propaganda industries. The very first episode of *Walt Disney's Disneyland*, "The Disneyland Story," exemplified the calculated strategy of using the new television series as a means to hawk the studio's new and existing products and prepare an eager generation of young television viewers—and their money-earning parents—to make the trek from Anywhere USA to a yet-unbuilt Disneyland theme park. This same strategy would be written all over *The Little Mermaid Live!* sixty-five years later in its form, advertising model, and location.

Episode 1 of *Disneyland* aired just seven months after the first rumors of the ABC–Disney deal and provided audiences a potpourri of Disney content and hullabaloo.[22] From the show's first moments on television, the larger Disney empire—particularly the musical—was at the center of the action. The voice of *Pinocchio*'s (1940) Jiminy Cricket crooned "When You Wish upon a Star" as the animated credit sequence began, and the voice-over informed audiences that each week would present material structured around one of four amazing "lands." Viewers and potential ticket buyers soon discovered that those lands would coincide with areas of the Disneyland theme park which was under construction at that very moment. As the opening touted Frontierland, Tomorrowland, Adventureland, and Fantasyland, *Peter Pan*'s (1953) Tinkerbell—who would become a sort of series mascot—brought familiarity and wonder to the series structure.

The first episode began with a flyover of the Disney studio, bringing excited viewers previously unseen sights of where the magic all happened. Workers hustled and bustled down the Disney studio thoroughfare as the show cut to a seemingly average day, with makeup artists preparing Kirk Douglas, Peter Lorre, and "Esmerelda" the seal for a day's work as the show provided behind-the-scenes glimpses of actors, creatures, and special effects for Disney's upcoming theatrical release *20,000 Leagues under the Sea* (1954), which would be released just two months later, in time for Christmas. After watching James Mason battle a forty-ton squid, the show cut to Disney cartoonists capturing Helene Stanley's dancing form for what the show erroneously dubbed the studio's "next" animated feature, *Sleeping Beauty* (1959), and the yet-unreleased number "Once upon a Dream." (*Lady and the Tramp* would actually beat the slumbering princess to the big screen, hitting theaters in 1955 and becoming Disney's first feature animated film during the *Disneyland* era.) From dancing Aurora, the show moved into the music studio, making viewers privy to the Disney magic of sound engineering, with makeshift instruments and bubble-driven keyboards producing the fantastical sounds familiar in Disney animation.

After establishing the general environment of and goings-on at the Walt Disney Studios, Walt himself made his premiere as the series' kindly host and introduced audiences to the Disneyland theme park via overhead drawings, maps, flyovers, and models. He told audiences that the land of "hopes and dreams, facts, and fancy" would be ready for visitors next year and that they, the television audience, would be part of the exciting process of the park's construction through this weekly television series. He showed glimpses of Disneyland's Main Street and the four aforementioned worlds from which the series would air. As he ruminated on Frontierland, he took viewers to Norman Foster, the director of show's upcoming *Davy Crockett* three-part series. Foster introduced Fess Parker, Disney's Crockett, singing the title song "The Legend of Davy Crockett." The inaugural episode of *Disneyland* went on to feature bits of animal documentary from Spain and the Galapagos and Falkland Islands, as producer Ben Sharpsteen told viewers about Disney's thirty documentary crews spread all around the globe filming content for the Adventureland portions of the series. From there, Disney introduced Tomorrowland through a discussion of collaborations between animators and scientists, with some musings about space flight and the planet Mars, nearly six years before Yuri Gagarin became the first man to journey into space. And finally, Fantasyland—the world of imagination where "hopes and dreams are all that matters"—brought viewers fleeting glimpses of clips from the studio's already iconic musicals *Peter Pan*, *Alice in Wonderland*, and *Cinderella* (1950), before introducing a five-minute excerpt of Brer Rabbit and his "laughing place" from *Song of the South*'s (1946) Uncle Remus.

Once Walt had introduced all of the park's new worlds, he returned to talk to viewers about one of his greatest "friendships." He told the viewing audience about when he "met" Mickey by showing the studio's first (but unreleased) Mickey Mouse short, *Plane Crazy* (1928). After reflecting on his mouse friend's incredibly successful career and Academy Award, Walt "introduced" viewers to Mickey's cadre of animated friends, showing Pluto in 1939's *The Pointer* and Goofy and Donald Duck in 1937's *Lonesome Ghosts*. He went on to chronicle the feature animation successes "Mickey" had created, showing drawings from the studio's first animated feature, *Snow White* (1937), as well as artwork from *Bambi* (1942) and *Dumbo* (1941). Walt closed the episode by heralding Mickey's "Broadway debut" of *Fantasia* (1940) at the Broadway Theater in New York City. After just a couple of minutes of *Fantasia*, Walt encouraged audiences to come back the following week and treated them to a three-minute preview of what would be the subsequent week's airing of the Disney animated musical *Alice in Wonderland*.

This first episode serves as an effective model not only for the following decades of the Disney TV series but for the Disney business writ large. According to Anderson, the *Disneyland* series took minimal financial outlay from the Disney studio.[23] Whereas most new series at the time required an agreement for thirty-nine new episodes per season, ABC agreed to only twenty for the new *Disneyland* series. As illustrated by the first episode, Disney relied heavily on two major elements to amass most of its weekly content: animation and documentary products from the Disney vaults and behind-the-scenes footage from and promotional clips for upcoming documentaries and live and animated features. This first season would also rely heavily on the park build to help manufacture a sufficient amount of anticipation for all of its baby-boomer viewers.

Season 1 also included "Operation Undersea," with Walt reflecting on his burgeoning interest in the undersea world as he prepared for *20,000 Leagues under the Sea* and some new and exciting filmmaking techniques the studio had devised in order to shoot the live-action Disney feature. That specific episode went on to win the Emmy Award for Best Individual Program of the Year. It also included ads for a joint *Disneyland*–Hudson auto dealership contest, offering a grand prize of a trip to Disneyland for three and a custom Hollywood Hudson V8, or trips to Disneyland and a Hudson Wasp or Hudson Rambler Wagon (just right for the family). The contest offered twenty-seven additional trips to Disneyland, and any kid who brought his or her mom and dad into a Hudson dealer showroom would receive an autographed picture of Parker, *Disneyland*'s Davy Crockett, and a free *Davy Crockett* comic book. The same episode included ads for Peter Pan peanut butter and the upcoming animated feature *Lady and the Tramp*, as well as previews of upcoming episodes, which would include behind-the-scenes footage of the soon-to-be-released and ultimately Academy Award–winning nature documentary feature *Vanishing Prairie* (1954) and the Academy Award–winning short subject *Seal Island* (1948), both produced by Sharpsteen, who introduced the studio's nature documentary units in episode 1.

Over the next year, the series would highlight the construction of the park, whetting the appetites of its viewers, and on July 17, 1955, ABC triumphantly aired *Dateline: Disneyland*, a ninety-minute, star-studded television special celebrating the opening of the park and featuring the likes of Walt Disney, Art Linkletter, Fess Parker, Buddy Ebsen, Ronald Reagan, Frank Sinatra, Sammy Davis Jr., Gale Storm, and actors who voiced such iconic Disney characters as Peter Pan (Bobby Driscoll) and *Alice*'s March Hare (Jerry Colonna). The *Disneyland* series would air self-promotional piece after piece, pulling out shorts and film clips from the Disney vaults and making sure audiences were in the know about everything newsworthy happening during Disney's park construction, at the film studio, and on location. It was one-stop shopping for Disney products, all from the comfort of America's living rooms.

By the end of season 1, the mark of Disney's victorious move to television had been made. The series became ABC's first to crack the Nielsen top ten and was being viewed weekly in nearly 40 percent of the nation's 26 million television-viewing households.[24] Between late 1954 and early 1955, *Disneyland* aired the three-part Davy Crockett miniseries, which then went on to spark a national coonskin-cap craze and three *Billboard*-charting versions of "The Ballad of Davy Crockett" (including Disney's Parker recording). In mid-1955, Disney's Buena Vista Film Distribution Company went on to repackage the three-part miniseries as a theatrical motion picture that grossed an additional $2.1 million for Disney, a move that foreshadowed the company's later capitalization on the economic potential of moving content from one platform to another and doing its best to maximize profits across them all. Roy and Walt Disney had taken their animation studio and turned it into a cross-market, cross-platform national phenomenon that sold and resold its products with new and nostalgic flair from audience to audience and generation to generation. And this was just the start. They still had multiple platforms to conquer, ones the studio would slather with new and repurposed musical content.

The Mouse Buys It All: Who Works for Whom?

Although the *Disneyland* series temporarily left network television in 1983, this by no means signaled that the studio was giving up on the power of television. The 1983 launch of the premium (or pay) cable channel the Disney Channel provided yet another way to repurpose existing content and carve out a new audience willing to pay to see Disney fare. The first Disney feature to appear on the cable channel was, yet again, *Alice in Wonderland*, just as it had been first on the *Disneyland* series. The studio's first original made-for-cable film, *Tiger Town* (1983), went on to win a CableACE Award that year.[25] Despite some forays into new programming, Disney continued to make the US Environmental Protection Agency's mantra of "Reduce, Reuse, Recycle" a lucrative business model. Their move into cable led to a string of original and popular musical franchises such as *Cheetah Girls 1, 2*, and *One World* (2003, 2006, 2008); *High School Musical 1, 2*, and *3* (2006, 2007, 2008); *Camp Rock 1* and *2* (2008, 2010); *Teen Beach Movie 1* and *2* (2013, 2015); and *Descendants 1, 2*, and *3* (2015, 2017, 2019), all premiering during the first two decades of the twenty-first century and launching a string of teen stars and a wide range of tie-in merchandising. Clearly, the emergence of the Disney Channel and the temporary disappearance of the flagship *Disneyland* series did not signal the decline of Disney's reign on television. The company just changed its game slightly while it wheedled its way into new broadcast avenues of participation and practices that would be further reflected in years to come when Disney dipped its toes into the live-television-musical arena.

In the years between the initial demise of the weekly *Disneyland* series/emergence of the Disney Channel and Disney ultimately merging with Capital Cities/ABC in 1996, Disney kept a strong presence on broadcast television, repurposing old content for new audiences. Between 1984 and 1996, Disney specials were all over the broadcast dial, relegated to no single network. And the union of Disney and music was often at the center of these specials. Dozens of Disney installments appeared on television during that decade, whether part of the on-again, off-again revamped version of *Disneyland* or as stand-alone specials. Specials such as *Disney's All Star Mother's Day Album* (1984, CBS), *Disney Goes to the Academy Awards* (1986, ABC), *Disney's Golden Anniversary of Snow White* (1987, NBC), *New Kids on the Block at Walt Disney World* (1991, ABC), *Disney's Greatest Hits on Ice* (1994, CBS), *Wonderful World of Disney: 40 Years of Television Magic* (1994, ABC), *Lion King: A Musical Journey* (1994, ABC), and the *Nancy Kerrigan Special: Dreams on Ice* (1995, CBS) all capitalized on Disney's early process of cross-marketing, repositioning existing product, and cultivating new audiences for old works. Then came the merger and Disney's renewed marriage with ABC.

Announced in 1995 and completed in early 1996, the $19.5 billion merger of Capital Cities/ABC and Disney made the already powerful Mouse even more dominant across media industries. No longer just the content creator for a growing network, Disney had switched roles with ABC, with the once-struggling animation studio now the owner of one of the major broadcast networks in the United States.[26] With this move, ABC became the home for Disney content airing on broadcast television. Shortly after the merger, ABC audiences saw a string of Disney-themed ice-skating specials, Disney's recent hit *Toy Story* (1995) airing under the *Wonderful World of Disney* brand, and "The Making of *The Hunchback of Notre Dame*" providing a bit of televised hullabaloo for Disney's most recent theatrical release, one that had hit the big screens just two weeks before. In addition to these repurposed, cross-promotional, and celebratory specials, ABC entered a new world of original television musicals, some harking back to Disney products and others providing Disney's entrance into other types of stories and franchises. These musicals provide insightful and simultaneous looks back at Disney's early television practices and forward at what would come with *The Little Mermaid Live!* two decades later.

Between 1997 and 2000, ABC and Disney, under *The Wonderful World of Disney* television umbrella, released three television musicals that brought old products to new audiences, all the while hawking ABC and Disney content, both old and new. The first was a new multiracial television production of *Rodgers and Hammerstein's Cinderella*, first produced for CBS television and starring Julie Andrews in 1957. The 1997 ABC reimagining sought a new and more diverse audience, and it starred Brandy, who had appeared on the short-lived ABC sitcom *Thea* between 1993 and 1994, cracked the *Billboard* US top twenty and US R&B top ten with her self-titled debut album in 1994, and was at the time of *Cinderella*'s airing appearing on her own UPN series, *Moesha* (1996–2001). The young singer appeared alongside such A-list stars as multiplatinum singer and burgeoning actress Whitney Houston (*The Bodyguard* [1992], *Waiting to Exhale* [1995], *The Preacher's Wife* [1996]), costar of NBC's hit *Seinfeld* (1989–1998) Jason Alexander; and comedian and Oscar winner for *Ghost* (1990) Whoopi Goldberg, in addition to Broadway stars Bernadette Peters and Victor Garber. Two years later, *The Wonderful World of Disney* aired a new production of *Annie*, starring newcomer Alicia Morton, Broadway bigwigs like Tony nominee and winners Garber, Kristin Chenoweth, and Audra McDonald, as well as Oscar winner Kathy Bates as the infamous Miss Hannigan. Only months later, ABC completed its hat trick of television musicals with *Geppetto*, a remake of the original *Pinocchio* book and including "I've Got No Strings" from the 1940 Disney animated classic, as well as new numbers written by the composer and lyricist of *Pippin* and *Godspell*, Stephen Schwartz. The *Pinocchio* reboot starred Drew Carey—then in his fifth season of ABC's *The Drew Carey Show* (1995–2004)—and R&B star and *Billboard* topper Usher, as well as television stars Julia Louis-Dreyfus (*Seinfeld* [1989–1998]), Brent Spiner (*Star Trek: The Next Generation* [1987–1994]), and René Auberjonois (*Benson* [1979–1986], *Star Trek: Deep Space Nine* [1993–1999]), providing a little bit of something across demographics.

The first of ABC/Disney's new television musicals aired just three years after Disney Theatrical opened its first Broadway adaptation of one of its animated classics, *Beauty and the Beast*, and the same year as the reopening of the Disney-renovated New

Amsterdam Theatre and premiere of the phenomenally successful Broadway adaptation of *The Lion King*. With Disney comfortably settled into ABC and the controlling entity of a multimedia conglomerate encompassing the worlds of television and film production and distribution, book and music publishing, theme parks, and so on, these new musicals reflected the various pies in which the parent company had its many fingers.

Commercials placed during the *Cinderella* airing included those for *The Little Mermaid*'s rerelease, *Beauty and the Beast*'s release on VHS, and an upcoming, brand-new *Wonderful World of Disney* production of *Oliver Twist* starring Elijah Wood and Oscar winner Richard Dreyfuss, who would soon be appearing in the Disney Touchstone Pictures/Disney Buena Vista Pictures *Krippendorf's Tribe* (1998). Disney took a similar route with *Annie*, taking advantage of the broadcast to advertise the *Annie* soundtrack and VHS and an Annie.Disney.com contest, as well as *Mickey's Once upon a Christmas* on VHS, *Winnie the Pooh* on VHS, and upcoming *Wonderful World of Disney* airings of *Space Jam* (1996) and *Geppetto*. *Geppetto* then went on to advertise its own VHS tapes and soundtrack, as well as a VHS release of Disney's *The Fox and the Hound* (1981). It also included a promo for *The Wonderful World of Disney*'s upcoming airing of *Mulan* (1998), as well as Disney's Saturday-morning kids' block "One Saturday Morning," Touchtone-produced/Buena Vista-distributed *Romy and Michele's High School Reunion* (1997), ABC's *The Drew Carey Show*, and an array of other ABC-distributed programs. Perhaps even more so than Disney's original plan of total merchandising, the position the company held within a both growing and narrowing mass-media industry allowed Mickey's white gloves to reach across an array of markets, forms, and audiences. This wasn't just about catching the growing boomer generation on the newest hot medium so Walt could bring them into the new park. At the turn of the millennium, Disney was everywhere and closing in on being everything.

BIG-SCREEN ARIEL ON THE SMALL SCREEN

Sixty-five years after the premiere of *Disneyland*; more than six decades after the opening of the first of twelve Disney parks spanning three continents; more than thirty years after the launch of the Disney Channel, Disney's Buena Vista Television, and Touchtone Films; just over a quarter-century after Disney Theatrical brought Disney to Broadway; two decades after the Capital Cities/ABC–Disney merger; and less than a decade after NBC and Fox brought the live musical back to American television, Disney and ABC brought *The Little Mermaid Live!* to American audiences in a way that bucked the trend established by those other networks but fully embraced six centuries of Disney television. It may have been weird, but it was on-brand. A look back at *The Little Mermaid Live!* through a lens of this television history brings into full view the industrial consistency of this media monolith, even if perhaps at the expense of actual entertainment for the viewing audience.

From stem to stern, the live underwater musical embraced the Disney way: repurposing old content to cut costs. This fully harked back to Walt and Roy's *Disneyland* method, one that relied heavily on repurposing material like the less-than-successful *Alice in Wonderland* over and over, airing Academy Award–winning nature documentaries, and pulling Disney shorts from the vaults to pepper the show's sixty-minute runtime. Unlike *Grease Live!* and *The Sound of Music Live!*, *The Little Mermaid* was already part of the roster of the network that aired it. More so even than the documentaries and shorts aired as part of the early *Disneyland* series, *The Little Mermaid* was intimately and financially linked to the owners of the ABC network itself. Rather than reaching out to a hot content creator, Disney reached right into its own back pocket for its first live television musical. In addition to relying on its own content, Disney bigwigs' or Hamilton's decision to bring to life only the musical portions of the classic animated feature and otherwise just present the film itself undoubtedly decreased the overall labor that would go into mounting the televised production, minimizing sets, cast, and rehearsal and build time.

Press accounts circulating around the productions of *Grease Live!* and *The Sound of Music Live!* often touched on their respective networks seeking to choose musical vehicles that might speak to family audiences.[27] *The Little Mermaid Live!* had the family audience in the bag, but clearly the driving force for content selection was one of existing rights. ABC was Disney, and Disney could use ABC to repopularize Ariel and her endless string of clothing, action figure, plush, game, music, and video tie-ins. Like scads of Disney specials that came before *The Little Mermaid Live!* (e.g., *The Donald Duck Story* [1954], *Disney's Greatest Villains* [1983], *Disney World's 20th Anniversary* [1991], *The Best of Disney Music* [1993], *Disney's Most Unlikely Heroes* [1996], etc.), the ABC live-musical venture attempted to tap into waves of nostalgia, through both the inclusion of the original animated film sequences and the choice of Jodi Benson, the film's original Ariel, to introduce the production at the start of the show. Similar nostalgic nods arguably went into casting choices, with Disney's Moana tapped to step into Ariel's fin.

Aside from following the Disney way with what was on the screen during the actual production, the show embraced the larger promotional techniques followed by Disney for decades. From the earliest episodes of *Disneyland* on through to the Disney television musicals of the late 1990s and early 2000s, advertising slots and bumpers had been used to hawk upcoming theatrical releases, next week's episodes, and tie-in merchandising. *The Little Mermaid Live!* was no exception. Although the special had originally been announced years before, its seemingly serendipitous return in 2019 placed it on the ABC broadcast schedule just one week prior to the launch of the parent company's new, much-hyped streaming service, Disney+. *The Little Mermaid Live!* broadcast included two Disney+ commercials: one general and one announcing the new live-action *Lady and the Tramp*. *The Little Mermaid Live!* and *The Little Mermaid* animated feature would both land on Disney+ just weeks after the television broadcast of the live(-ish) musical. In markets with ABC-owned and -operated stations, those ABC affiliates owned by Disney itself, advertising slots for the new streaming service were complemented with *Frozen II* (2019) co-branding that depicted *Frozen II*'s Anna, Elsa, Olaf, Kristoff, and

Sven alongside the ABC logo while announcing the film's upcoming November 22 release. No longer relegated to taking up showtime with Disney promotion, Disney could blend promotion with network branding itself to cross-promote the station and upcoming Disney releases. When Walt and Roy had been pitching *Disneyland* in hopes of finding outside funding for their park, could they have imagined the power their company would wield three-quarters of a century later? With no idea of how the media landscape would shift and sprawl, likely not.

And the Mouse Marches On

The continued sprawl, cannibalization, and repurposing of Disney media and the Disney landscape won't halt with the questionable form of ABC's *The Little Mermaid Live!* Three years later, they were at it again, blending the ABC network, a popular Disney property's anniversary, and live-event programming with *Beauty and the Beast: A 30th Celebration*. Again, the show was directed by Hamilton and co-executive-produced by Kapoor (as well as Hamilton, movie director Jon Chu, and others). Kapoor reiterated *The Little Mermaid Live!*'s goal that they "didn't want the at-home audience to feel like a spectator. [They] wanted them to feel as if they were a guest in the television special." Bringing in heavy hitters from Broadway (Joshua Henry), country (Shania Twain), R&B (H.E.R.), and pop (Josh Groban), as well as multiplatform stars (Rita Moreno, Martin Short, and David Alan Grier), Disney sought once again to draw in a multigenerational audience with promises of live performance and scads of nostalgia. It landed on Disney+ only one day later. In that same three-year span, Disney released additional live-action film versions of popular animated features, with *Mulan* premiering in 2020 and *Cruella* hitting screens in 2021, and Disney Theatrical announced its plans for a future Broadway production of *Coco* (2017). And just in case ABC did not foster enough *Little Mermaid* nostalgia for audiences, the company announced the 2023 live-action motion-picture version of the film prior to *The Little Mermaid Live!*'s airing, just to provide a little extra dose of anticipatory Ariel and Sebastian. Disney and the world-recognized Mouse will continue to bring music to an array of screens and stages, but audiences should likely plan to hear everything in various forms, on various stages, and behind an array of paywalls. Disney music and Disney musicals are truly the gift that keeps taking.

Notes

1. "Domestic Box Office for 2019," Box Office Mojo, https://www.boxofficemojo.com/year/2019/.
2. Michael Schneider, "100 Most-Watched TV Shows of 2019–20: Winners and Losers," *Variety*, May 21, 2020, https://variety.com/2020/tv/news/most-popular-tv-shows-highest-rated-2019-2020-season-masked-singer-last-dance-1234612885/.

3. Wayne Oliver, "Radio and Television Highlights," *Times Herald* (Port Huron, MI), March 10, 1955.
4. Meron and Zadan announced, "We're thrilled to be reteaming with NBC and Bob Greenblatt in bringing *Peter Pan* back to its roots as a live television event." Adam Hetrick, "*Peter Pan* Will Be NBC's Next Live Television Musial Event," *Playbill*, January 19, 2014, https://playbill.com/article/peter-pan-will-be-nbcs-next-live-television-musical-event-com-213913.
5. Wayne Oliver, "'$5.80 Ticket' for *Peter Pan*: TV of Broadway Play Set Tomorrow," *Chicago Daily Tribune*, March 6, 1955, NW12B.
6. Dawn C. Chmielewski, "'Sound of Music Live' among Twitter's Favorite Things," *Los Angeles Times*, December 9, 2013, https://www.latimes.com/entertainment/envelope/cotown/la-et-ct-sound-of-music-live-among-twitters-favorite-things-20131209-story.html; Josef Adalian, "*The Sound of Music Live*: A Huge Hit That Will Likely Mean More Big TV Events," Vulture, December 6, 2013, https://www.vulture.com/2013/12/sound-of-music-live-ratings-high.html.
7. The potential move to Broadway had been communicated through personal discussions with costume designer Paul Tazewell and confirmed in pieces like the 2016 *Playbill* article "*The Wiz Live!* Still Plans to Come to Broadway," *Playbill*, October 13, 2016, https://playbill.com/article/the-wiz-live-still-plans-to-come-to-broadway.
8. Kate Stanhope, "ABC Slates 'Little Mermaid' and Rolling Stone Live Musicals," *Hollywood Reporter*, May 16, 2017, https://www.hollywoodreporter.com/tv/tv-news/abc-little-mermaid-rolling-stone-live-musicals-1004221/.
9. Gary Levin, "ABC Drops Plans for 'Little Mermaid' Musical," *USA Today*, August 3, 2017, https://www.usatoday.com/story/life/tv/2017/08/03/abc-drops-plans-little-mermaid-musical/535299001/.
10. Nellie Andreeva, "'The Little Mermaid Live' Event a Go on ABC with Auli'i Cravalho as Ariel, Queen Latifah & Shaggy Co-Starring," Deadline, August 5, 2019, https://deadline.com/2019/08/little-mermaid-live-event-special-abc-with-aulii-cravalho-stars-ariel-queen-latifah-ursula-shaggy-sebastian-1202660483/; Andrew Gans, "Lea Michele and Harvey Fierstein Head Cast of Hollywood Bowl's Immersive 'The Little Mermaid,'" *Playbill*, May 17, 2019, https://www.playbill.com/article/lea-michele-and-harvey-fierstein-head-cast-of-hollywood-bowls-immersive-the-little-mermaid/.
11. Kelly Lawler, "ABC's Baffling 'Little Mermaid Live!' Sunk Straight to the Bottom of the Ocean," *USA Today*, November 5, 2019, https://www.usatoday.com/story/entertainment/tv/2019/11/05/little-mermaid-live-review-abc-terrible-musical-not-live-enough/4166621002/.
12. Kelly Kessler, "Failed Experiential Promises and the Bait-and-Switch of Fox's *Rent: Live*," FlowTV, March 24, 2019, https://www.flowjournal.org/2019/03/rent-live/; Robyn Bahr, "'The Little Mermaid Live!': TV Review," *Hollywood Reporter*, November 5, 2019, https://www.hollywoodreporter.com/tv/tv-reviews/little-mermaid-live-review-1252669/.
13. Danielle Turchiano, "'The Little Mermaid Live' Team Talks More Musical Numbers, Aerial Work and Understudies," *Variety*, November 5, 2019, https://variety.com/2019/tv/features/the-little-mermaid-live-aulii-cravalho-john-stamos-shaggy-graham-phillips-new-score-understudies-1203392411/.
14. Dino-Ray Ramos, "'The Little Mermaid Live!' Ratings Swim to the Top Tuesday," Deadline, November 6, 2019, https://deadline.com/2019/11/little-mermaid-live-ratings-abc-musical-1202779078/.
15. Christopher Anderson, *Hollywood TV* (Austin: University of Texas Press, 1994), 18.

16. For more on the Paramount Decision's impact on the motion-picture studios and the television industry, see Anderson, *Hollywood TV*; Douglas Gomery, "Failed Opportunities: The Integration of the U.S. Motion Picture and Television Industries," *Quarterly Review of Film Studies* 9, no. 3 (1984): 219–228.
17. Marilyn Chase, "How Disney Propaganda Shaped Life on the Front during WWII," *Smithsonian Magazine*, July 11, 2022, https://www.smithsonianmag.com/history/how-disney-propaganda-shaped-life-on-the-home-front-during-wwii-180979057/.
18. For more on Disney's World War II propaganda, see Tracey L. Mollet, *Cartoons in Hard Times: The Animated Shorts of Disney and Warner Brothers in Depression and War 1932–1945* (New York: Bloomsbury Academic, 2017); Ben Sharpsteen et al., dirs., *Walt Disney on the Front Lines: The War Years* (Buena Vista Home Entertainment, 2003).
19. Anderson, *Hollywood TV*, 140.
20. Ibid., 141.
21. The television series moved through various titles, forms, and networks: *Disneyland* (1954–1958, ABC), *Walt Disney Presents* (1958–1961, ABC), *Walt Disney's Wonderful World of Color* (1961–1969, NBC), *The Wonderful World of Disney* (1969–1979, NBC), *Disney's Wonderful World* (1979–1981, NBC), *Walt Disney* (1981–1983, CBS), *The Disney Sunday Movie* (1986–1988, ABC), *The Magical World of Disney* (1988–1990, NBC), *The Wonderful World of Disney* (1991–1997, CBS; 1997–, ABC).
22. Bill Cotter, *The Wonderful World of Disney Television: A Complete History* (New York: Hyperion, 1997), 59. Specifics about *Disneyland* episodes and Disney television movies, and the advertisements shown in them, were pulled from screenings of content at the Paley Center for Media in New York City.
23. Anderson, *Hollywood TV*, 142–143.
24. Ibid., 148.
25. The CableACE Awards were given by the National Cable Television Association from 1978 to 1997 to recognize excellence in cable TV programming.
26. ABC did not experience an easy transition into network ownership, slipping from number one in 1995 to being the third-place network in 1996 and dropping to number four in key demographics by 2002. ABC certainly saw bright points with highly rated reality competition shows such as *Who Wants to Be a Millionaire?* (1999–2002) and *The Bachelor*, well-received family sitcoms that leaned into diversity such as *Black-ish* (2014–2022) and *Modern Family*, and the powerful award-winning Shonda Rhimes's block of *Grey's Anatomy*, *Scandal* (2012–2018), and *How to Get Away with Murder* (2014–2020), but the Capital Cities/ABC–Disney merger was by no means a windfall for the media giant. Bill Carter, "Television: In a Ratings Reversal, ABC Slips to the Bottom of the Network's Wheel of Fortune," *New York Times*, March 4, 1996, D5; Sallie Hofmeister, Brian Lowry, and Richard Verrier, "No Happy Ever After for ABC in Disney Saga," *Los Angeles Times*, March 31, 2002, A1.
27. Adam Hetrick, "NBC to Broadcast Live Version of *The Sound of Music*; Neil Meron and Craig Zadan Will Produce," *Playbill*, June 29, 2012, https://playbill.com/article/nbc-to-broadcast-live-version-of-the-sound-of-music-neil-meron-and-craig-zadan-will-produce-com-195237; Kate Stanhope, "'Grease: Live' Team Promises to Pay 'Respect' to Film, Adds Stars Didi Conn and Barry Pearl," *Hollywood Reporter*, January 15, 2016, https://www.hollywoodreporter.com/tv/tv-news/grease-live-team-promises-pay-856349/.

PART III
SOUND, MUSIC, AND TECHNOLOGY

CHAPTER 12

LADY AND THE TRANSCRIPTION: PEGGY LEE'S LEGAL BATTLE WITH DISNEY

COLLEEN MONTGOMERY

SHORTLY after the release of the Marvel prequel *Black Widow* in July 2021, the film's star Scarlett Johansson made headlines when she filed suit against the Walt Disney Company for breach of contract and intentional interference with contractual relations. At issue in the "explosive lawsuit" was Disney's decision to simultaneously release the film in theaters and via its subscription video-on-demand (SVOD) service, Disney+.[1] This day-and-date release strategy, Johansson's legal team alleged, violated a clause in her contract that guaranteed a "wide theatrical release" for the film—a stipulation they claimed both parties understood to mean an *exclusive* theatrical release window of roughly three to four months. Her lawyers also argued that collapsing the theatrical and SVOD release windows for the film significantly reduced Johansson's compensation which was, per the filing, "based largely on 'box office' receipts generated by the Picture."[2] Ultimately, the suit contended that Disney expressly designed its rollout of the film to reduce Johansson's profit participation while simultaneously trading on her star power to lure new subscribers to Disney+ and thereby bolster the company's stock price. In response to the lawsuit, Disney issued an uncharacteristically scathing rebuke, calling the complaint "especially sad and distressing in its callous disregard for the horrific and prolonged global effects of the COVID-19 pandemic."[3] While the two parties eventually settled out of court for an undisclosed amount, the widely publicized legal dispute brought to the fore questions of whether and how actors should be remunerated for SVOD and secondary-market sales.

Johansson, however, was not the first star to engage in a public legal battle with Disney over the issue of a performer's right to share in profits generated in ancillary, nontheatrical markets. This chapter takes as its central case study a breach-of-contract lawsuit that singer, songwriter, and actress Peggy Lee filed against the Walt Disney Company in relation to her work on the 1955 animated feature film *Lady and the Tramp*. Lee's lawsuit in many ways parallels Johansson's complaint. Much like the *Black Widow* case, Lee's suit arrived at a moment when Disney's exploitation of new home-viewing technologies was ushering in significant changes to the company's long-standing film-distribution models. Whereas Johansson's claim centered on streaming for new releases, Lee's revolved around Disney's release of classic features from its "vault" on videocassette and laserdisc. Her suit alleged that the act of reproducing and distributing her performances for the film on VHS and laserdisc without her consent violated the terms of her original contract. Lee's case, however, was much more than a simple dispute between a star and a studio over a paycheck. Rather, much like Johansson's, Lee's suit emerged as part of a larger struggle over performers' compensation with respect to new industry approaches to monetizing film content. This chapter considers the legal and industrial dimensions of Lee's contractual relationship with Disney in the 1950s, the technological shifts that gave rise to her complaint in the 1980s, and the broader impact of the suit for Disney and other vocal performers in its classical-era animated features.

In so doing, I build on Emily Carman and Philip Drake's work on the history of Hollywood talent contracts, the legal frameworks that undergird these agreements, and performers' resistance to these regimes. As Carman and Drake argue, studios' contractual agreements—and, crucially, disagreements—with performers "reveal detailed information about the industrialisation of creative processes in Hollywood, highlight the balance of power in negotiating deals between parties and present us with important material through which to analyse the historical development of the Hollywood industry."[4] For a company like Disney that strictly limits scholars' access to its corporate archives, contractual disputes like Lee's—and the publicly available legal paper trail they generate—provide valuable insight into the studio's contractual agreements with performers. By closely examining Lee's breach-of-contract suit against Disney, this chapter aims to elucidate the legal, technological, and industrial frameworks that shaped her relationship with Disney as a vocal performer and composer for one of its classic animated musicals. To conduct this analysis, the chapter examines a range of primary materials, including the extensive case files for Lee's suit, archival materials in the Library of Congress that shed light on her contributions to the film, and contemporary reporting on her suit, its resultant jury trial, and numerous rounds of appeals.

I begin by laying out the provisions of Lee's 1952 contract with Disney and her various roles in the production. I then discuss the context within which her legal battle with the studio emerged in the 1980s. Drawing on Kate Fortmueller's work on the 1980 Screen Actors Guild (SAG) strike, I consider how Lee's suit was part of a larger labor struggle for residual compensation at the dawn of the VHS era. Finally, I address the impact of Lee's successful suit and its continued relevance in the contemporary landscape of media labor. Indeed, *Peggy Lee v. Walt Disney Productions* is a particularly timely case study in the wake of the recent SAG and Writers Guild of America strikes—labor disputes that also centered on the interrelated issues of fair compensation and studios' exploitation of new technologies and distribution channels.

While a range of scholarship has examined the Walt Disney Company's labor policies and practices across different facets of the conglomerate's diversified business—from its theme parks to animation and live-action film and television studios—little work has closely analyzed Disney's labor contracts and contractual disputes with performers. Although Lee's case has received some attention in the popular press, such accounts do not adequately unpack the industrial conditions that led to Lee's suit, the complexities of her four-year legal battle, and the impact of her lawsuit on other Disney performers.[5] Thus, by tracing the origins, outcomes, and implications of Lee's legal battle, this chapter also aims to understand better the history of Disney's labor relationships with contracted talent in its animated films.[6]

PEG: PEGGY LEE'S WORK ON *LADY AND THE TRAMP*

In the late 1930s, Disney story artist Joe Grant devised the initial concept art for what would ultimately become the animated musical romance *Lady and the Tramp*. The original story centered on an upper-class dog named Lady who finds herself pushed aside when her family welcomes a new baby. Through the early 1940s, artists, writers, and Walt Disney himself continued to refine the Lady story. Most notably, they introduced Tramp, a character inspired by the 1945 Ward Greene short story "Happy Dan, the Cynical Dog," to which Disney had acquired the rights. Development of the film stalled, however, during World War II as the animation studio shifted its resources toward servicing government and military contracts for training, public service, and propaganda films.[7]

It wasn't until the postwar period, when Disney ramped up active work on the film, that the studio began crafting songs for the picture. Disney engaged English composer Oliver Wallace, a longtime Disney employee who scored major Disney films such as *Dumbo* (1941), *Cinderella* (1950), *Alice in Wonderland* (1951), and *Peter Pan* (1953), to write the film's score. At the same time, as Russell Schroeder argues, several of the studio's "regular composing teams began developing possible song moments" for the film.[8] This included Wallace himself, who wrote two songs: a tune about lost love, "Had I Known," with lyrics by Gil George, and "Lady," written from the perspective of the dog's owners, with lyrics by Sidney Fine and Ed Penner. Additionally, the studio brought in Eliot Daniel and lyricist Ray Gilbert, who worked together on several Disney films in the 1940s, to craft a song for the Tramp character.[9] The resulting number, "I'm Free as the Breeze," is an upbeat theme written from the dog's carefree point of view.[10] Gilbert also wrote a song titled "Lady and the Tramp" with composer Allie Wrubel, who equally wrote music for several 1940s Disney pictures.[11] None of the above songs, however, was used in the film. Although, as Schroeder argues, "Lady and the Tramp," which essentially lays out the plot of the film, was perhaps intended as an exploitation song and not written for explicit use in the film, Disney seems not to have been satisfied with the other extant songs clearly written for use in the film. It was ultimately Peggy Lee's songs, co-written with Sonny Burke, that would become the film's iconic musical numbers.

Lee's work on *Lady and the Tramp* began in 1952, when she signed the first of two contractual agreements with Walt Disney Productions, both of which are included as exhibits in her lawsuit. Disney's signatory on both contracts was Gunther Lessing, vice president. According to case files from the suit, Lessing (who was also Disney's general counsel at the time) and Spencer Olin (assistant to general counsel) drafted the language of the contracts. The first employment agreement was executed in June 1952. This joint contract commissioned Lee and her co-songwriter Joseph F. "Sonny" Burke "as a song-writing team, to write original words and music" for the picture.[12] According to Lee's 1989 autobiography, it was Burke, whom she knew through his work as an artists and repertoire (A&R) man at her music label Decca Records, who invited her to participate in the Disney project.[13]

For their services, Lee and Burke received a flat fee of $1,000 to be split equally between them. The agreement also entitled the songwriters to receive royalties from the publication of their music: three cents for "each regular piano copy and/or orchestrations" sold in the US and Canada, and 33⅓ percent of the net proceeds of international sales outside of Canada. The songwriting contract further specified, however, that Lee and Burke were excluded from receiving any royalties generated "by virtue of grand rights, dramatic rights, television rights and other performance rights, including the use thereof in motion pictures, photoplays, books, merchandising, television, radio, and endeavors of the same or similar nature."[14]

As a part of their contracted work for Disney, Lee and Burke penned ten songs. These included six songs that were used in the film, several of which Lee performed: the opening song, "Peace on Earth," a choral piece that pairs original music and lyrics with the hummed melody of "Silent Night"; "What Is a Baby?," a song that relays Lady's confusion about the new member of her family; "La La Lu," a lullaby that Darling, whom Lee voiced, sings to her newborn infant; "The Siamese Cat Song," a duet for which Lee performed both parts; "He's a Tramp," a song performed within the diegesis by Peg, a character both inspired and voiced by Lee; and "Bella Notte," a romantic ballad that serves as the title characters' love theme. The pair wrote four additional songs that were not used in the film: "Jim Dear," a song written from Darling's point of view that expresses her love for her husband; "Old Trusty," a jazz ballad about Lady's eponymous bloodhound friend and neighbor; and two uptempo jazz tunes about Tramp and his carefree lifestyle, "Singing ('Cause He Wants to Sing)" and "That Fellow's a Friend Of Man."

While she was initially engaged only as a songwriter, according to Lee, Walt Disney asked her to voice characters after hearing demo tapes she recorded of the songs she and Burke penned.[15] She thus entered into a separate contract with Disney in October 1952 for her vocal performance work. Case files from the suit indicate that Lessing, Olin, and Jack Lavin, former casting director for Walt Disney Productions, participated in the negotiations for this contract. The agreement engaged Lee to render her "artistic services as a singer and in the recording of dialogue in and in connection with" the film. It stipulated that she would receive $3,500 for six days of work and an additional $250 per day should her work exceed six days.[16]

Crucially, this contract included a subclause (12b) indicating that the agreement did not grant Disney the right to "make phonograph recordings and/or transcriptions for sale to the public" of her work on the film.[17] Disney argued in court that this provision reflected the fact that Lee was under an exclusive one-year phonograph-recording contract with Decca Records at the time. The latter contract (dated April 2, 1952) granted Decca Lee's "exclusive personal services in connection with the production of phonograph records."[18] As a result, Decca produced the soundtrack album for *Lady and the Tramp*. At the time, Disney did not have an in-house record label, as Disneyland Records was not established until the year after *Lady and the Tramp*'s release in February 1956.[19]

Lee's vocal performance contract with Disney specified that her work would entail, among other things, performing the speaking and singing role of a character then named Mame. As Lee recounts, this character later became her namesake, Peg, at Walt Disney's request (supposedly to avoid giving the dog a name too similar to then–First Lady Mamie Eisenhower).[20] More than a mere namesake for the Pekingese, as animator Eric Larson recounts, Lee served as a partial model for the torch-singing Peg's personality and physicality (figure 12.1).[21] Lee would ultimately furnish the voices for three additional characters: Darling, one of Lady's owners, and the troublemaking Siamese cats Si and Am—figures whose visual design, accented speech, orientalist musical representation, and characterization are deeply steeped in racist tropes.[22]

FIGURE 12.1. "Peg" the Pekingese, a character inspired and voiced by Peggy Lee in *Lady and the Tramp*. Screenshot by author.

As Lee asserted in her suit, Disney widely promoted her contributions to the film. In her lawsuit, Lee repeatedly claimed that "Disney signed her to be the star and only 'name' performer" in the film.[23] Her multifaceted involvement in the project is undoubtedly foregrounded in both the film text and its attendant marketing paratexts. Following the company credits and title card at the film's outset, Lee is listed first among the credited cast (her October 1952 agreement guaranteed her screen credit) and then cited once more as co-songwriter for the film. Her songwriting, recording, and vocal performance work for *Lady and the Tramp* also figured into Disney's promotional campaign for the film. For example, the 1955 trailer includes segments of "Bella Notte," clips of Peg's song "He's a Tramp," and "The Siamese Cat Song." The pressbooks for the film's original release and subsequent rereleases also repeatedly deploy her star image and prominently emphasize both her creative roles in the project and critical accolades her work garnered.[24] Beyond these materials, Lee herself also actively participated in the marketing campaign. Perhaps most notably, she appeared in an episode of the *Disneyland* television show promoting the film.

The episode, titled "A Cavalcade of Songs," aired in February 1955, four months ahead of the film's release. It centers on the important role that music plays in Disney's animated features, and about half of its runtime is devoted specifically to *Lady and the Tramp*. As Walt Disney describes it in the episode, the *Lady and the Tramp* segment offers viewers a "behind-the-scenes" look at the construction of the film's songs "from their inception through their recording to their appearance" in the picture. The segment begins with a staged spotting session: Lee and Burke walk through the film's storyboard with writer and artist Joe Rinaldi and story unit director Erdman Penner to identify places to add songs and the types of songs best suited to each narrative moment. Subsequent scenes include a vignette representing Lee and Burke composing and performing a version of "The Siamese Cat Song" (figures 12.2 and 12.3), a Walt Disney-narrated overview of all of the songs Lee and Burke composed for the film, and finally a mock recording session for the film featuring Lee performing Peg's song "He's a Tramp" accompanied by singing quartet and frequent Disney collaborators the Mellomen, who provide the voices of the dogs Lady meets at the pound.

Although it initially received mixed critical reviews, *Lady and the Tramp* was a commercial success. It marked both Disney's first foray into making animated features in Cinemascope and its second-most-successful outing at the box office (after *Snow White and the Seven Dwarfs*) at the time of its release. In keeping with its then-standard practice for remonetizing features, the studio subsequently rereleased the film theatrically four times between 1962 and 1986. As Lee attested in a deposition for her lawsuit, at the studio's request, she participated in the publicity campaign for each of these rereleases.[25] Indeed, her lawyers went as far as to say that she "was held out by the Walt Disney Company as its principal public relations spokesperson for the movie" and that "[a]side from Walt Disney himself, no one is more closely identified with the motion picture and its success."[26] According to Lee, however, this promotional work was almost entirely unpaid.

FIGURE 12.2. Peggy Lee and Sonny Burke re-enact their songwriting process in the 1955 *Disneyland* episode "Cavalcade of Songs." Screenshot by author.

FIGURE 12.3. Peggy Lee performs "The Siamese Cat Song" in the 1955 *Disneyland* episode "Cavalcade of Songs." Screenshot by author.

The Struggle for Residual Compensation

In October 1987, Disney issued *Lady and the Tramp* on VHS and laserdisc as a part of its Walt Disney Classics home-video line. The film was the seventh title in the series. The release was a major success, overtaking *Top Gun* (the top domestic box-office release of 1986) to become the top-selling videocassette of 1987.[27] As Lee's legal counsel asserted in her suit, publicity materials for the release emphasized her multiple roles in the film and her star status. For example, her suit cites the following line from Disney's press release for the videocassette: "Legendary entertainer Peggy Lee not only composed five still popular songs for the film with Sonny Burke, but she also sang three of them and served as the voices of four characters ... Ms. Lee continues to dazzle standing-room-only audiences worldwide via countless shows and appearances featuring her songs from this film."[28]

As Lee recalls in her autobiography, the studio contacted her in November of that year to participate directly in promotional activities for the release. As she describes it, Disney engaged her to give live television interviews from the Disneyland park with twenty outlets in the US and Canada as well as record interviews from her home in Bel Air (including, for example, an appearance on *The Today Show*).[29] For her promotional efforts, she received an honorarium of $500, a sum that, according to biographer James Gavin, Lee deemed "insulting."[30] In fact, Gavin claims that the star was so "outraged" by the modest fee that she allegedly instructed her assistant at the time, John Saulle (whom Gavin interviewed for his book), to pull her original contract with Disney for her work on *Lady and the Tramp*. Upon reviewing the terms of her agreement, Lee reportedly concluded that by distributing the film on VHS without her consent, Disney may have violated a key provision in her contract—a discovery that prompted her to seek legal recourse. While the dramatic narrative of Lee pulling her contract in anger and demanding satisfaction may well be accurate, she did not file suit until a year after she completed the above-referenced promotional work.

Disney's honorarium may have been the spark that lit the fuse on Lee's suit, but the technological and industrial shifts that home-video ushered in had already become a powder keg in Hollywood. Lee's suit must be understood in relation to these broader struggles in the film and television industries in the 1980s over the issue of residual compensation for profits generated in television and home-video markets. In 1980, SAG and the American Federation of Television and Radio Artists (AFTRA), the unions representing film and television performers, commenced negotiations with the Association of Motion Picture and Television Producers (AMPTP) for a new labor contract. As Fortmueller details, although the home-video market was still "largely speculative" in 1980, the unions, wagering that these technologies would become important in the future, made VHS and videodisc a key issue in their negotiations.[31] When negotiations stalled, 67,000 union members walked out in July 1980 and remained on strike for nearly three months.[32]

As Fortmueller relays, residuals became a major sticking point in the strike. In the unions' negotiations with AMPTP, a central question became at what point a performer's residuals should kick in—in terms of the number of airings or the volume of video tapes or discs sold. When the unions reached a tentative deal with the studios, there was also conflict within the ranks of the membership over the proposed terms of compensation for pay TV and video residuals. A small but vocal faction opposed ratification of the deal on the grounds that it provided a "weak foundation" for future negotiations. Although their concerns arguably proved valid (as evidenced by the more recent SAG-AFTRA strike, which centered in part on low residual rates for supplementary markets), the dissenters did not win out. Roughly 83 percent of the membership voted to ratify the deal. In terms of home video, the contract secured for actors "4.5 percent of the producers' gross after the sale of 100,000 units (videocassettes and videodisks)."[33]

This agreement, however, did not apply to Lee's work on *Lady and the Tramp*. Although the 1960 joint Writers Guild of America (WGA) and SAG strikes (the last double strike of its kind prior to the 2023 labor action) established an important framework for residual compensation in Hollywood, as part of the deal, SAG agreed to forgo residuals for films made before 1960. Under the leadership of its then president Ronald Reagan, SAG had initially lobbied for residuals for films from 1948 forward, but after a month-long strike, the guild agreed to a compromise. The final contract provided actors with residual payments for films made from 1960 onward and a $2.5 million payment to the SAG pension and healthcare fund in lieu of residuals on earlier projects.[34]

Understandably, some Classical Hollywood performers whose work was largely excluded from this agreement did not receive the contract favorably, and continued to fight for compensation. Perhaps most notably, in 1981, Mickey Rooney mounted an unsuccessful legal challenge to this pre-1960 residuals issue. His case would become an important antecedent to Lee's. The suit was brought under antitrust laws against eight studios (Columbia, MGM, Paramount, RKO, 20th Century Fox, United Artists, Universal Studios, and Warner Bros) and listed as co-plaintiffs "several hundred" unnamed film performers. According to Rooney, among the actors supposedly joining the suit were Rock Hudson, Paul Newman, Shelley Winters, Barbara Stanwyck, and many others seeking recompense for the "hundreds of millions of dollars" their films had generated in "alternative markets" including home video.[35] The judge in Rooney's case, however, did not find his claim compelling and dismissed the complaint. In his ruling, Judge William Conner cited the "extremely broad rights" that the studio's talent contracts granted the defendants over the distribution and exhibition of the films in which the stars performed. The judge explicitly noted that the contracts were written

> plainly intending that such rights would be without limitation unless otherwise specified and further indicating that future technological advances in methods of reproduction, transmission and exhibition would inure to the benefit of defendants.

The contracts generally do not limit defendants' right to "exhibition" of the films, but also convey the rights of "recording," "reproducing," "transmitting," and "exploiting."[36]

In short, Lee was far from the only performer waging a battle against the studios for residual remuneration. Questions about whether and how performers should share in profits from home-video sales were pressing issues for Hollywood performers and their guilds in the 1980s. Unlike Rooney's contracts, however, Lee's agreement with Disney included the aforementioned clause that limited the studio's rights to reproduce her work. While Disney cited Rooney's case as a precedent that supported its position, Lee's lawyers argued that there were critical discrepancies between the broad language of Rooney's contracts and the more narrowly circumscribed allowances in Lee's *Lady and the Tramp* agreement. This language, as I examine below, formed the crux of her successful legal battle.

LEE V. THE WALT DISNEY COMPANY

Prior to taking formal legal action against Disney, Lee first had her lawyers contact the company to try to secure a settlement. Representing Lee in the matter were Alvin Deutsch, the attorney responsible for her music-publishing deals, and his partner David Blasband, a copyright law expert.[37] On June 17, 1988, Deutsch wrote directly to Disney's chairman and CEO, Michael Eisner. In his letter, he emphasized Lee's contributions to and continued involvement in publicizing the film, including "to help launch the audio-visual cassette version which, even before its release, garnered millions of orders." He then drew Eisner's attention to a specific subclause in Lee's October 1952 contract with the company for her "services 'as a singer and in the recording of dialogue,'" noting that it expressly states:

> (b) Anything herein to the contrary notwithstanding it is agreed that nothing in this agreement contained shall be construed as granting us the right to make phonograph recordings and/or transcriptions for sale to the public, wherein the results or proceeds of your services hereunder are used.[38]

In reference to this clause, Deutsch then asserted: "Based on common usage of the quoted language as supported by current case law. Sales of the videocassette version fall directly within the ambit of the proscriptive language." The letter concluded with a request that Eisner reply "within the week regarding an appropriate consideration for our client for covering such a use."[39] When no such reply arrived, Deutsch sent a second letter on July 12 cautioning Eisner that while it would "be in the interests of both parties to avoid litigating this issue and the attendant publicity, we have been authorized to serve the requisite pleadings in the event that we have not received a satisfactory response."[40]

In fact, Disney's vice president of business and legal affairs, John J. Reagan, had penned a reply on July 11, 1988, that would soon reach Deutsch. In his letter, Reagan disputed Deutsch's claims, arguing that Lee's contract granted Disney "all rights to the results and proceeds" of her work on *Lady and the Tramp*. "The sole reservation" to this agreement, Reagan argued, "was not to the grant of rights for videocassettes but to phonograph records and sheet music."[41] While subclause 12b did explicitly relate to phonograph recordings, Reagan's claim that it dealt with sheet music was, as Lee put it in a deposition, "mystifying."[42] It was Lee's separate songwriting contract with Disney, not the one referenced in Deutsch's letter, that covered sheet-music sales.

While Reagan's claims are rather puzzling, Disney's unyielding attitude in response to Lee's entreaty is not entirely surprising. Eisner's aggressive stance toward copyright and intellectual property is well known. It was during his tenure, for example, that Disney successfully lobbied for the enactment of the Copyright Extension Act in 1998 (often pejoratively called the Mickey Mouse Protection Act). Eisner's philosophy that "when it comes to intellectual property, you can't be too litigious" seems to have informed the company's approach to Lee's case.[43] Rather than quietly negotiate a settlement out of court and out of the public eye, Disney engaged in a four-year fight to protect its intellectual property rights.

The legal dogfight commenced on November 16, 1988, when Lee filed suit against Disney in the Superior Court of California for the County of Los Angeles. Representing Lee in the matter were Blasband and Los Angeles litigators Neil Papiano and Deborah Nesset, whom Blasband recruited. The complaint included two causes of action: breach of contract and unjust enrichment. With respect to the first cause of action, Lee's lawyers contended that by marketing videocassettes of *Lady and the Tramp* without her consent, Disney had violated subclause 12b of her agreement. On this count, they sought damages totaling $12.5 million. The second cause of action alleged that Disney had "realized substantial monetary profits from the unauthorized use of plaintiff's valuable and unique contribution to 'Lady and the Tramp' as a result of its sales of videocassettes of this work."[44] Lee's team sought an additional $12.5 million in damages for this alleged "unjust enrichment."

As Deutsch had cautioned, Lee and her lawyers courted significant "attendant publicity" for her suit. The day after her legal team filed, articles detailing her $25 million complaint appeared in publications including the *New York Times*, *Variety*, and the *Hollywood Reporter*. Whether intentionally or not, these pieces tended to frame Lee's plight rather sympathetically by pointing up the stark difference between the sum Lee earned for her work on the film ($4,500) and the $90 million the VHS tape alone had generated, according to Disney's own published figures. As the *Hollywood Reporter* article noted, having sold 3.5 million copies, *Lady and the Tramp* had, by that point, become the third-best-selling cassette to date.[45] Disney, the articles relayed, refused to comment on the suit "as a matter of policy." Lee, by contrast, had much to say and did not mince words. She told the *Hollywood Reporter* that while she was proud of her work on the film, "you can't eat pride. Eventually you have to make some money back and when something makes that much money and everyone else is making money, why shouldn't I?"[46] Similarly, the *New York Times* quoted her as saying, "I think it's shameful that artists can't share financially from the success of their work. That's the only way we can make our living."[47] The figures cited in the article accurately reflected the terms of her contract, but one might argue that Lee had, in fact, received some form of residual compensation for her songwriting and song performance work on the film. As Disney pointed out in court, between the film's release and the time of her suit, she received around "$162,000 in songwriting and artist's royalties."[48] Of course, this compensation was related not to sales of the film itself but to the sale or use of the music she wrote and performed for the film.

While press coverage of the case came swiftly after filing, the suit itself made very slow progress through the legal system. For a case that essentially hinged on a single word in a single sentence of a single subclause in a contract, the fight was incredibly protracted. In the spring of 1990, more than a year and a half after Lee lodged her complaint, the courts handed down a major decision in the case. On March 30 of that year, Roy Reardon, the litigator representing Disney, had filed a motion for summary judgment to dismiss the case. The motion was based on several key arguments. First, Disney's lawyers claimed that "the explicit language of the contract" in question "gave Disney the right to reproduce the movie, including Ms. Lee's voice, in any way Disney chose."[49] In support of this position, they pointed to clause 11, which sweepingly assigned Disney "all rights of every kind and character whatsoever in and to all recordations of [Lee's] voice and all instrumental, mechanical and other sound effects produced by [Lee]" and the "unlimited right to reproduce and/or transmit" these recordings. The clause not only covered currently available "reproducing and/or transmitting devices" but also "all other improvements and devices which are now or which hereafter may be used in connection with the production, exhibition and/or transmission of any present or future kind of motion picture productions."[50] Disney noted that the clause was "virtually identical" to language in Rooney's case, which the court had construed as granting studios the right to sell videocassettes without compensation.[51]

Second, Disney contended that whereas clause 11 referred to the movie itself and the reproduction thereof, clause 12 dealt with ancillary uses of Lee's voice. Subclause 12b simply carved out the right to make phonograph records of her voice, as she had already granted Decca that right. Thus, the company maintained that the broad rights in clause 11 were not "nullified" by "a single word" in 12b.[52] Third, and most important, whereas Lee's legal team maintained that the word "transcription" in 12b should be understood to mean "copy," Disney argued that the term referred specifically and *exclusively* to "a form of audio recording used in radio broadcasting."[53] More precisely, Disney alleged that when the contract was drafted in 1952, both parties understood the term "transcription" to mean an "electrical transcription," "a form of recording, usually a 16 inch 33 1/3 RPM disc, that was used to deliver programming to radio stations that were not part of a broadcast network."[54] Lee herself, they argued, had acknowledged that this was a common trade usage of the term "transcription" in a deposition for the case. To accept Lee's construction of her contractual rights, they argued, the court would have to find that Disney gave the performer the power to veto its ability to "sell *any copy of any kind of the movie.*"[55] This interpretation, they claimed, was nonsensical and clearly not the contract's intent.

Lee's team, however, filed a competing motion for summary adjudication, also on March 30. Fundamentally, their position was that the common definition of the term "transcription" is "copy" and that the word should be interpreted that way in the contract. Unlike Disney, which did not produce any witnesses to the drafting and negotiation of the contract, Lee's counsel was able to provide firsthand testimony on the intended meaning of subclause 12b. In a written declaration, Lee refuted Disney's position that in 1952, both she and the studio had understood "transcription" to mean a large disc used by radio stations. She dismissed such a notion as "pure speculation, without support from any person who participated in the negotiations" or drafting of the contract. Rather, she stated that when she reviewed her contract, she expressed concerns directly to Disney representatives about the rights she was "being asked to convey." In response, an unspecified party to the negotiations drew her attention to the language in 12b, which, she argued, "states in clear English that Disney must obtain my permission before it can sell copies of the movie or any part thereof to the public." She therefore understood the contract to mean that Disney would retain the rights to exhibit the movie in theaters and on television, and she "would be entitled to participate in the profits derived from sales to the public."[56]

Second, in her declaration, Lee asserted that she had an interest in protecting more than simply the right to phonograph recordings of her work. As she detailed, in the 1940s, she had worked on numerous "soundies," short films of musical performances projected on coin-operated visual jukebox machines known as Panorams. As such, she claimed, she understood well the importance of guarding rights to a range of "mediums where products embodying [her] services would be sold to the public."[57] Third, both Lee and her lawyers pointed up a logical issue with Disney's claim that 12b referred to electrical transcriptions for radio broadcasts: the discs were not sold to the public; in fact, due to their size, they could only be played on special radio-broadcasting equipment, not standard commercial phonographs.[58]

Finally, and most crucially, Lee's legal team cited Disney's successful 1969 lawsuit against the Alaska Television Network (ATN) for copyright infringement. The suit centered on ATN's production and distribution of videotape recordings of Disney films and television shows that were exhibited on cable television. In its argument, Disney directly quoted a passage from the 1909 Copyright Act that codified the copyright holder's exclusive right to "make or to procure the making of any transcription or record" of the material.[59] In other words, Disney had used the word "transcription" to refer specifically to a videotape copy in prior legal proceedings—a definition it was now trying to claim was invalid.

Ultimately, the judge found Lee's arguments concerning the provisions of subclause 12b convincing. In the first place, the judge agreed that the kinds of electrical transcriptions Disney claimed the clause referred to weren't sold to the public. Second, he found that "Disney itself has sought that the word 'transcriptions' include video cassettes."[60] The judge thus found Disney liable for breach of contract for selling videocassettes of *Lady and the Tramp* without Lee's permission. He ruled that she was entitled to a jury trial to determine the "monetary relief" she should be awarded for this violation. Although her lawyers successfully petitioned the court for an expedited trial (based on a provision in the California Code of Civil Procedure that grants preference to plaintiffs older than seventy), it would nonetheless be another year before Lee would have her day in court.

Lee's Trial by Jury

Lee's jury trial commenced on March 1, 1991, in the Superior Court of Los Angeles. Once more, the case attracted significant "attendant publicity," with press from "*Variety*, the *Hollywood Reporter*, the *Los Angeles Times*, and CNN" covering the courtroom proceedings.[61] Their accounts made much of Lee's physical condition, noting, for example, her use of an oxygen tank and a wheelchair. As the *Los Angeles Times* put it, "Sitting up in her wheelchair, frail and with failing eyesight, singer Peggy Lee hardly fits the image of a Hollywood giant killer."[62] This press coverage, Gavin argues, framed Lee sympathetically for the public. So, too, he claims, did evidence and testimony presented to the jury. As evidence of her contributions to the film, Lee's legal team screened both the full film and her segments on *Disneyland*'s "Cavalcade of Songs." In an interview with Gavin, Stephen Lachs, the presiding judge in the case, recalled, "It's a film that to this day will bring tears to my eyes. The jury was watching the film, which has wonderful music, and yeah—you became very sympathetic."[63]

Lee's lawyer, Blasband, described her performance in the witness box as equally compelling. Lee, who took the stand on March 7, was the first of the plaintiff's three witnesses. In her testimony, she highlighted both her well-known contributions to the film as a songwriter and vocal performer and ways in which she'd influenced the shape of the narrative. For instance, she relayed an anecdote she frequently repeated for the press: that Walt Disney had originally intended for Trusty, Lady's faithful bloodhound friend, to die, until Lee convinced him such a fate would be too sad. Stories like this aimed to illustrate not only the extent of her creative input on the film but also her close working relationship with Walt Disney. "Dear Walt," Lee argued, was a generous man who would not have wanted her to be treated with the kind of disrespect and disregard the company's current heads had shown her.[64] The second witness for the plaintiff was Disney's director of financial reporting, William Zulager. Zulager (who appeared as an adverse witness) attested to the revenue Disney had earned from the VHS tape: a reported $72 million worldwide gross. Lee's team used this testimony to lay the groundwork for their damages claims. Last to take the stand for the plaintiff was Lee's key "expert witness," entertainment lawyer Marc Bailin. Bailin's testimony was central to establishing the plaintiff's position that Lee should be entitled to whatever she could reasonably have negotiated for in 1987, had Disney abided by its contractual commitments.

Bailin argued that, based on "industry norms," Lee could plausibly have negotiated for at least 12.5 percent of *Lady and the Tramp*'s VHS gross, or roughly $12 million. His contention was that it was standard in the film industry for "royalty participants" like actors to "participate in a pool equal to 25% of the gross proceeds from sales of videos."[65]

He claimed that, because Disney had a contractual obligation to obtain Lee's permission to sell VHS "transcriptions" of the film, she would have been in a strong negotiating position had Disney not violated the terms of her agreement (as the first part of the court case had established). Disney thus would have either had to settle with Lee or refrain from releasing the film at all. The logic behind Bailin's monetary calculations, however, was unclear at best. Indeed, Disney's counsel pointedly questioned not only the basis for Bailin's figures but also his expertise on matters of compensation for vocal performers in animated films. Even Judge Lachs was notably unimpressed with Lee's expert, describing him in a courtroom conference with the attorneys as "the least credible expert I have heard ever."[66]

Nonetheless, Bailin's line of argumentation—that, had Disney acted lawfully, it would have had no choice but to pay Lee or refrain from releasing the film on VHS—became an important part of the plaintiff's case. Papiano put it perhaps most colorfully in the following lines of his closing statement:

> [T]he question remains, would Disney have balked and said, "No, I won't distribute this famous, great, best movie we have because we are not going to pay you, Peggy Lee, for rights that Walt Disney gave you, because we think Walt Disney was a crazy old man that didn't know what he was doing, and we are going to forget the whole thing." That is stretching the imagination much, much too far, I suggest to you.[67]

On March 13, Disney began mounting its defense. First among its witnesses was Ann Daly, senior vice president of marketing for North America for Buena Vista Home Video. Disney used Daly's testimony to begin to establish one of its core arguments in the trial: that Lee's involvement in the film was not central to the VHS tape's success. Daly testified that Disney spent an "unprecedented" $11 million on the VHS marketing campaign for *Lady and the Tramp* but that Lee was not the primary figure in this promotional effort. Rather, the campaign focused most heavily on the film's animated characters. She went on to assert that the target market for the VHS tape was "mothers of children between the ages of 5–12" and that therefore, "Buena Vista was aiming at a completely different audience than Miss Lee's fans."[68] Daly's claims about the target audience for the cassette are in keeping with the company's broader approach to marketing VHS tapes in this period. Nevertheless, that Disney actively recruited Lee to participate in the release's promotion and used her voice, image, and name in a variety of advertising paratexts belies Daly's claim about the performer's supposed irrelevance to the campaign. Daly went even further, however, by suggesting that it "would not have made a difference in the sales of the videocassettes if a voice other than Miss Lee's was heard on the videocassettes."[69]

Disney had hoped to build on Daly's bold contention by arguing that it could, in fact, have replaced Lee's voice in the VHS release "without harming the commercial value of the videocassettes."[70] More precisely, Disney sought to argue that, rather than pay Lee royalties, it could have dubbed over her vocal performances, as is common practice for translating vocal performances in non-English-language versions of Disney animated films. To prove this theory, Disney attempted to enter into evidence rerecorded excerpts of the VHS release with Lee's voice overdubbed. These dubbed versions were not intended for actual commercial release but created especially for the trial to illustrate Disney's point. The plaintiff objected to the introduction of this evidence on the grounds that it was purely hypothetical and raised questions beyond the jury's purview. For example, how could the jury determine whether replacing Lee's voice would indeed have had no impact on the sales of the VHS tape? Would the replacement voice have been a soundalike? An entirely new performance? How would audiences have reacted to either of these new voices? Did Lee's contract even grant Disney the legal right to replace her voice at all in the English-language version? Given these questions, Lachs ultimately upheld the plaintiff's objections and excluded both the tape and the line of argumentation as overly speculative.

With the dubbing avenue closed off, the defendant made a case as to the contemporary standard for Disney's voice-acting royalty payments for ancillary media sales. The first witness to give evidence about these norms was Katie O'Connell, vice president of business and legal affairs for Walt Disney Pictures and Television. At the time, O'Connell was responsible for negotiating all voice-talent contracts for Disney animated films. She testified that based on "her personal knowledge, her experience in the industry, and her review of prior Disney contracts, *no* performer in an animated film has ever been granted a percentage of the revenues from videocassette sales, other than as part of the general agreement with the Screen Actors Guild." This, she argued, was not only Disney's "firm policy" but also standard practice across the animation industry. She therefore concluded that had the 1980 SAG contract applied to pre-1960 work, Lee would have been entitled to $391,000 (4.5 percent of the producer's gross on sales over 100,000 units, as discussed above).[71] This, of course, was far less than Lee was requesting at trial.

To confirm these rates and practices, Disney then called two actors to the stand who had recently performed in Disney animated films. The first was Cheech Marin, who voiced the chihuahua, Tito, in the 1988 animated musical *Oliver & Company*. The second was Jodi Benson, who voiced the title character in *The Little Mermaid* (1989). Both performers testified that the only form of compensation they received from sales of videocassettes of their films was SAG-mandated residuals. Shoring up their testimony was casting agent Susan Edelman, who also testified that in her professional experience, vocal performers in animated films received only SAG residuals from videocassette sales.[72]

The final witness for the defense was arguably its highest-profile and certainly its highest-ranking executive: the vice chairman and chair of the Animation Department and Walt Disney's nephew, Roy E. Disney. He directly, and pointedly, countered many of Lee's claims. In particular, he challenged Lee's characterization of "dear Walt" as a generous employer who would have wanted her to receive compensation. Rather, Roy stressed that his uncle had a firm policy of paying vocal performers a flat fee precisely "so that his company could keep the profits."[73] Prior to the ratification of the 1960 SAG collective-bargaining agreement, no one, he emphasized, "received a percentage ownership of the proceeds of an animated film except the studio."[74] Much like Daly, he also contended that the real stars of Disney's animated features are its characters, not the performers who voice them. To illustrate this argument, he noted that the most iconic scene in *Lady and the Tramp*, in which the dogs share a plate of spaghetti, features no dialogue. Rather, he stated, "Everything comes from the drawings."[75] Disney's chosen example, however, is somewhat puzzling, as the scene is famously set to and derives much of its affective impact from a diegetic performance of the film's well-known song, "Bella Notte," which first plays during the film's opening credit sequence. Lee, who co-wrote the song with Burke, does not perform the song in the film, but this sequence nonetheless highlights her crucial contributions, which Roy's testimony sought to downplay. Having very recently watched the full film in the courtroom, the jury members would arguably have been aware of the significant role Lee's music plays in the scene.

With witness testimony concluded, counsel delivered closing statements, and jury deliberations subsequently began on March 18. In short, the jury was tasked with determining what amount Lee "would have gained if both sides had fully performed under the contract and "the reasonable value of what it would cost Buena Vista to obtain Lee's permission to distribute the videocassettes."[76] As instructed, the jury determined individual award amounts for four separate but related issues: Disney and its distribution arm Buena Vista Home Video's issuing of the videocassette without Lee's consent, its unlawful profiting from said release, its use of Lee's name and voice in the US promotion of this release, and its use of the same in the overseas marketing campaign. As stipulated in advance, however, Lee only received the largest of the four awards that the jury granted, not their combined sum. Each count was regarded as an "alternative theory of recovery" related to the same breach-of-contract damage, so only one award could be issued.[77] As such, on March 20, the jury awarded Lee a $2.3 million settlement—the sum they settled on for Disney/Buena Vista's distribution of the film on home video in violation of Lee's contract.[78]

The case, however, did not end there. Following the reading of the verdict, Lee's counsel filed a "motion to conform the judgement to the verdict." The reasoning was that the jury had not properly comprehended that Lee would only receive the highest of the four awards and that they had intended for her to receive the combined sum of $3.8 million. At the request of the plaintiff, each of the jurors submitted an affidavit attesting that they unanimously "understood and intended that their various awards be totalled."[79] Lee's counsel was, in fact, so convinced that Lee was entitled to the full amount that contemporary reports about the trial's verdict often list her award as $3.8 million based on statements that her attorneys made to the press. The court, however, denied this motion. It also denied the plaintiff's subsequent motion for a new trial. A third motion for attorney's fees and costs was submitted to a separate judge to referee. He rendered his decision in Lee's favor, but it took until December 1991 for that verdict to be determined.

For its part, Disney, which was also unsatisfied with the results of the trial, filed a formal appeal on May 23, 1991. In response, Lee's attorneys filed a cross appeal less than one month later, which not only countered the complaints in Disney's appeal but once more attempted to secure additional compensation for their client, primarily based on their position that the jury had intended to award Lee roughly $1.5 million more than the court's judgment. It took nearly a year and a half for these competing appeals to wend their way through the courts. Neither of them was successful. In one last effort, Disney attempted to take the case to the California Supreme Court, but this endeavor also failed. Thus, more than four years after it began, the case finally concluded in December 1992.[80] Ultimately, Disney was required to pay Lee roughly $3.3 million, including the original $2.3 million award along with about $1 million in legal expenses incurred throughout the lengthy court case.

CONCLUSION: IS THAT ALL THERE IS?

Lee was not the first vocal performer in a Disney animated musical to sue the company for residual compensation. Fifty years prior to Lee's case, Adriana Caselotti, the voice of Snow White, and her costar who voiced Prince Charming, Harry Stockwell, filed companion suits against Walt Disney Productions and RCA Victor (the label that released the film's soundtrack album) over the use of their voices on the record.[81] They claimed that when they recorded their performances for *Snow White*, they were not aware that their voices would be used in any capacity beyond the picture. For her work on the film, which included roughly forty-five recording sessions over a three-year period, Caselotti received approximately $970 total.[82] Stockwell received around $500 for his more minor contributions. By the time they brought suit in October 1938, Caselotti's rendition of "Some Day My Prince Will Come" had featured on *Billboard*'s top ten, and the film's soundtrack album had sold more than forty thousand copies. As *Variety* noted, the record's sales outpaced "by a huge margin the disc turnover of any other music out of Hollywood" at the time.[83] Caselotti and Stockwell, however, received no royalties for these sales and thus respectively sought $200,000 and $100,000 in damages.[84]

The crux of Caselotti and Stockwell's claim was that they had not granted Disney permission to reproduce their song performances from the film on its soundtrack album. Thus, much like Lee's case, their complaint hinged on the reproduction and dissemination of their vocal performances in a Disney animated film via ancillary media technologies or forms. Also like Lee's suit, the case ultimately rested on competing interpretations of talent contracts and the rights they purportedly reserved for the performer or granted to the studio. In a further parallel, the *Snow White* suit was a protracted affair that extended through 1943. A lower court judge initially found that the performers' contracts did indeed grant Disney "the right to reproduce in any manner whatsoever any recordings … of the plaintiff's voice."[85] The plaintiffs successfully appealed this ruling and brought the case to trial, but it ended in a hung jury. The performers ultimately reconciled with Disney (and Caselotti, as noted above, would go on to participate in promotional campaigns for *Snow White*'s rereleases), but neither she nor Stockwell received the residual compensation they sought.[86]

Thus, although Lee was reportedly disappointed with her settlement (much of which, she lamented, would go to the IRS and to her lawyers), her case set an important legal and historical precedent. While she did not receive the level of compensation she had hoped for, she nevertheless described her lawsuit as "a great moral victory" and opined that "it will at least show other artists that they should never be afraid, no matter how big the organization is," to fight for fair treatment.[87] Lee's words proved prescient. As commentators had predicted when news of her lawsuit first broke, her case opened the door for a string of subsequent claims and, following her victory, settlements.

In May 1989, Mary Costa, the voice of *Sleeping Beauty*'s (1959) titular princess, filed a $2 million suit against Disney in relation to the 1986 VHS release of the film.[88] After fighting the suit for more than two years, three months after the jury handed down Lee's verdict, Disney settled with Costa out of court for an undisclosed amount. In December 1990, Ilene Woods, who voiced Cinderella, sued Disney for the considerably larger sum of $20 million. Most notably, the language of her suit directly mirrored Lee's. Her counsel alleged that by distributing the 1988 VHS tape of *Cinderella* (1950) without her consent, the company had violated a clause in her contract that forbade it from "making transcriptions of the movie for sale to the public."[89] Disney also reached an out-of-court settlement with Woods.

Although the two Disney princess suits were understandably the highest-profile, they were not the only ones that drew on Lee's precedent. In 1992, for example, the Philadelphia Orchestra, which performed in Disney's *Fantasia* (1940) under the direction of conductor Leopold Stokowski, alleged in its suit that it was entitled to half of the $120 million in profits the VHS and laserdisc releases of the film had generated.[90] Subsequently, in 2000, Gia Prima, the widow of musician Louis Prima who voiced King Louie the ape in *The Jungle Book*, sued in relation to the VHS and DVD releases of the film.[91] Disney equally settled these claims out of court. In sum, Lee's suit provided a critical legal pathway for performers to share, at least in part, in the enormous profits Disney generated from its move into home video in the 1980s.

As the recent SAG and WGA strikes make clear, the interrelated issues of studios' exploitation of new technologies and distribution channels and fair residual compensation for ancillary market sales remain extremely relevant in the contemporary media industries. Unions, guilds, and their labor actions have obviously played a invaluable role in securing fair remuneration for performers, especially at key moments of technological change in the media industries. As this chapter suggests, however, contractual disputes have also played an important part in this struggle, particularly for performers like Lee whose work is in some way excluded from their guild's negotiated compensation agreements. Examining legal battles like Lee's and those to which it gave rise is thus critical to better understanding the history of labor relations in the media industries.

Notes

1. Tatiana Siegel, "Scarlett Johansson Opens Up about the Pain and Triumph of Disney Legal Battle over 'Black Widow' and Wes Anderson's 'Liberating' Cannes Film," *Variety*, May 9, 2023, https://variety.com/2023/film/features/scarlett-johansson-disney-lawsuit-child-actor-interview-1235605851/.

2. *Periwinkle Entertainment Inc., F/S/O Scarlett Johansson v. The Walt Disney Company*, no. 21STCV27831 (California Superior Court, July 29, 2021).
3. Brent Lang, "Disney Fires Back at Scarlett Johansson, Calls 'Black Widow' Lawsuit 'Sad and Distressing,'" *Variety*, July 29, 2021, https://variety.com/2021/film/news/disney-scarlett-johansson-black-widow-lawsuit-response-pandemic-1235030837/.
4. Emily Carman and Philip Drake, "Talent Contracts in Hollywood," in *Hollywood and the Law*, ed. Paul McDonald et al. (London: British Film Institute, 2015), 209.
5. See, for example, Brian Gabriel, "Lady and the Lawsuit: Peggy Lee's War with Disney," Cartoon Brew, September 4, 2015, http://www.cartoonbrew.com/disney/peggy-lee-war-disney-lady-and-the-tramp-113688.html.
6. See, for example, Jane Kuenz, "Working at the Rat," in *Inside the Mouse: Work and Play at Disney World*, ed. Jane Kuenz et al. (Durham, NC: Duke University Press, 1995), 110–162, https://doi.org/10.4324/9781315881201-16; Kit Johnson, "The Wonderful World of Disney Visas," *Florida Law Review* 63, no. 4 (2011): 915–958; Kirsten Moana Thompson, "'Quick–Like a Bunny!' The Ink and Paint Machine, Female Labor and Color Production," *Animation Studies* 9 (February 2014), http://journal.animationstudies.org/category/volume-9/kirsten-thompson-quick-like-a-bunny/; Christopher Chavez and Aleah Kiley, "Starlets, Subscribers and Beneficiaries: Disney, Latino Children and Television Labor," *International Journal of Communication* 10 (May 25, 2016): 2612–2636.
7. "Lady's Pedigree: The Making of *Lady and the Tramp*," *Lady and the Tramp*, DVD, disc 2, Platinum Edition (Walt Disney Studios Home Entertainment, 2006).
8. Russell Schroeder, *Disney's Lost Chords*, Vol. 3 (Robbinsville, NC: Voigt Publications, 2017), 189.
9. Gilbert worked as a lyricist on a number of Disney films, including *Dumbo* (1941), *The Three Caballeros* (1944), and, most notably, *Song of the South* (1946), for which he penned the popular "Zip-a-Dee-Doo-Dah." Daniel worked alongside Gilbert on several projects, including *Make Mine Music* (1946), *Melody Time* (1948), and *Song of the South*, and composed several additional songs for *Fun and Fancy Free* (1947) and *So Dear to My Heart* (1948).
10. Schroeder, *Disney's Lost Chords*, 190–192.
11. Wrubel's Disney credits include *Make Mine Music*, *Melody Time*, and, most notably, *Song of the South*, for which he composed the well-known song, "Zip-a-Dee-Doo-Dah."
12. *Lee v. The Walt Disney Company*, no. C705414 (State of California Superior Court, 1991) A147.
13. Peggy Lee, *Miss Peggy Lee: An Autobiography* (New York: Dutton, 1989), 147.
14. *Lee*, no. C705414, at A31–32.
15. Charles Solomon, "Peggy Lee Bangs Out Jazz in 'Lady and the Tramp,'" *Los Angeles Times*, December 26, 1986, https://www.latimes.com/archives/la-xpm-1986-12-26-ca-392-story.html.
16. *Lee*, no. C705414, at A8.
17. Ibid., at A11.
18. Ibid., at A36.
19. Disney acquired the rights to the Decca release soundtrack for *Lady and the Tramp* in 1975.
20. Lee, *Miss Peggy Lee*, 148.
21. Solomon, "Peggy Lee Bangs Out Jazz."
22. For analysis of racism, orientalism, and the Siamese cats, see Kimiko Akita and Rick Kenney, "A 'Vexing Implication': Siamese Cats and Orientalist Mischief-Making," in *Diversity in Disney Films: Critical Essays on Race, Ethnicity, Gender, Sexuality and*

Disability, ed. Johnson Cheu (Jefferson, NC: McFarland, 2013), 50–66; Thomas Solomon, "Music and Race in American Cartoons: Multimedia, Subject Position," in *Music and Minorities from around the World: Research, Documentation and Interdisciplinary Study*, ed. Ursula Hemetek, Essica Marks, and Adelaida Reyes (Newcastle upon Tyne: Cambridge Scholars, 2014), 142–166.

23. *Lee*, no. C705414, at A273.
24. The Library of Congress, National AudioVisual Conservation Center, *Lady and the Tramp* (Press Book, Box C-095).
25. Her involvement in these rereleases was not exceptional. Other performers, including Adriana Caselotti, the voice of Snow White, made similar public appearances over the years. Eric Hoyt, *Hollywood Vault: Film Libraries before Home Video* (Berkeley: University of California Press, 2014), 108.
26. *Lee*, no. C705414, at A344.
27. Sharon Bernstein, "The Lady and the Lawsuit: Trial: Singer Peggy Lee's Lawsuit against the Walt Disney Co. for Breach of Contract over the Videocassette Release of 'Lady and the Tramp' Will Be Heard Wednesday in Superior Court," *Los Angeles Times*, February 19, 1991, http://articles.latimes.com/1991-02-19/entertainment/ca-1596_1_peggy-lee.
28. *Lee v. The Walt Disney Company*, no. B058897 (State of California Second Appellate District, 1992).
29. Lee, *Miss Peggy Lee*, 149.
30. James Gavin, *Is That All There Is? The Strange Life of Peggy Lee* (New York: Simon & Schuster, 2014), 457.
31. Kate Fortmueller, *Below the Stars: How the Labor of Working Actors and Extras Shapes Media Production* (Austin: University of Texas Press, 2021), 114.
32. John Carmody, "Breakthrough on Key Issue in Actors' Strike," *Washington Post*, September 18, 1980, https://www.washingtonpost.com/archive/lifestyle/1980/09/18/breakthrough-on-key-issue-in-actors-strike/0eb17019-9a96-4d4d-93c5-347d2abe94d9/.
33. Fortmueller, *Below the Stars*, 115.
34. Thomas Doherty, "The Last Time Actors and Writers Both Went on Strike: How Hollywood Ended the 1960 Crisis," *Hollywood Reporter*, July 18, 2023, https://www.hollywoodreporter.com/business/business-news/sag-wga-1960-hollywood-strike-reagan-history-1235538551/.
35. "Rooney Sues on Sale of Films to TV," *New York Times*, June 25, 1981, Movies, https://www.nytimes.com/1981/06/25/movies/rooney-sues-on-sale-of-films-to-tv.html.
36. *Rooney v. Columbia Pictures Industries, Inc.*, 538 F. Supp. 211 (S.D.N.Y. 1982), 228.
37. Gavin, *Is That All There Is?*, 457.
38. *Lee*, no. C705414, at A467.
39. Ibid., at A468.
40. Ibid., at A467.
41. Ibid., at A470.
42. Ibid., at A143.
43. Gavin, *Is That All There Is?*, 459.
44. *Lee*, no. C705414, at A5.
45. James Ulmer, "Lee Lawsuit over Disney 'Lady' Vid May Set Precedent," *Hollywood Reporter*, November 17, 1988, 1, 4.
46. Ibid., 4.

47. Glenn Collins, "Peggy Lee Is Suing Disney," *New York Times*, November 17, 1988, C20, http://www.nytimes.com/1988/11/17/movies/peggy-lee-is-suing-disney.html.
48. *Lee*, no. C705414, at A103.
49. Ibid., at A118.
50. Ibid., at A11.
51. Ibid., at A120.
52. Ibid., at A117.
53. Ibid., at A125.
54. Ibid.
55. Ibid., at A118.
56. Ibid., at A140–141.
57. Ibid., at A145.
58. Ibid., at A277.
59. Ibid., at A193.
60. Ibid., at A744.
61. Gavin, *Is That All There Is?*, 478.
62. Bernstein, "The Lady and the Lawsuit."
63. Gavin, *Is That All There Is?*, 480.
64. Ibid.
65. *Lee*, no. C705414, at 74.
66. *Lee*, no. B058897.
67. Ibid., at 28.
68. Ibid., at 23.
69. Ibid.
70. Ibid., at 26.
71. Ibid., at 23–24.
72. Ibid., at 24.
73. Gavin, *Is That All There Is?*, 483.
74. *Lee*, no. B058897, at 25.
75. Ibid., at 24.
76. Ibid., at 74.
77. Gavin, *Is That All There Is?*, 484.
78. *Lee*, no. B058897, at 8.
79. Ibid., at 57.
80. Liz Smith, "$3 Million to Peggy Lee Stands for Singing on 'Lady ... Tramp,'" *The Sun*, December 22, 1992, 2D, https://www.proquest.com/docview/1976690772/abstract/C97B5157C0424BB4PQ/1.
81. "Pictures: Jury in N.Y. Disagrees on 300G 'Snow White' Suit," *Variety*, June 1943, 6.
82. *Caselotti v. Walt Disney Productions Ltd. and RCA Manufacturing Company* (NYS2d, 1939).
83. "'Snow White' Disc Sales Set All-Time Pic High at 450,000," *Variety*, September 1938, 4.
84. *Caselotti*, at 15.
85. Ibid.
86. Jon Burlingame, *Sound and Vision: 60 Years of Motion Picture Soundtracks* (New York: Watson-Guptill, 2000), 2.
87. Rebecca Freligh, "Peggy Lee Still Rates 'Miss Standing Ovation,'" *Cleveland Plain Dealer*, February 14, 1993.
88. David Conyers, "Sleeping Beauty Wins Round in Lawsuit Series," *St. Petersburg Times*, July 13, 1990, Tampa Bay and State.

89. Dan Boyle, "Woman Providing Voice of Cinderella Files Suit over Video," *Austin American-Statesman*, January 1, 1991, F11, Lifestyle.
90. Allan Kozinn, "'Fantasia' Orchestra Sues Disney," *New York Times*, May 7, 1992, C17, https://www.nytimes.com/1992/05/07/movies/fantasia-orchestra-sues-disney.html.
91. Ann O'Neill, "Disney Case Could Define 'Recording,'" *Los Angeles Times*, July 30, 2000, https://www.latimes.com/archives/la-xpm-2000-jul-30-me-61590-story.html.

Bibliography

Akita, Kimiko, and Rick Kenney. "A 'Vexing Implication': Siamese Cats and Orientalist Mischief-Making." In *Diversity in Disney Films: Critical Essays on Race, Ethnicity, Gender, Sexuality and Disability*, edited by Johnson Cheu, 50–66. Jefferson, NC: McFarland, 2013.

Bernstein, Sharon. "The Lady and the Lawsuit: Trial: Singer Peggy Lee's Lawsuit against the Walt Disney Co. for Breach of Contract over the Videocassette Release of 'Lady and the Tramp' Will Be Heard Wednesday in Superior Court." *Los Angeles Times*, February 19, 1991. http://articles.latimes.com/1991-02-19/entertainment/ca-1596_1_peggy-lee.

Boyle, Dan. "Woman Providing Voice of Cinderella Files Suit over Video." *Austin American-Statesman*, January 1, 1991, F11 Lifestyle.

Burlingame, Jon. *Sound and Vision: 60 Years of Motion Picture Soundtracks*. New York: Watson-Guptill, 2000.

Carman, Emily, and Philip Drake. "Talent Contracts in Hollywood." In *Hollywood and the Law*, edited by Paul McDonald, Eric Hoyt, Emily Carman, and Philip Drake, 209–234. London: British Film Institute, 2015.

Carmody, John. "Breakthrough on Key Issue in Actors' Strike." *Washington Post*, September 18, 1980. https://www.washingtonpost.com/archive/lifestyle/1980/09/18/breakthrough-on-key-issue-in-actors-strike/0eb17019-9a96-4d4d-93c5-347d2abe94d9/.

Caselotti v. Walt Disney Productions Ltd. and RCA Manufacturing Company. NYS2d, 1939.

Chavez, Christopher, and Aleah Kiley. "Starlets, Subscribers and Beneficiaries: Disney, Latino Children and Television Labor." *International Journal of Communication* 10 (May 25, 2016): 2612–2636.

Collins, Glenn. "Peggy Lee Is Suing Disney." *New York Times*, November 17, 1988, C20. http://www.nytimes.com/1988/11/17/movies/peggy-lee-is-suing-disney.html.Conyers, David. "Sleeping Beauty Wins Round in Lawsuit Series." *St. Petersburg Times*, July 13, 1990, Tampa Bay and State.

Doherty, Thomas. "The Last Time Actors and Writers Both Went on Strike: How Hollywood Ended the 1960 Crisis." *Hollywood Reporter*, July 18, 2023. https://www.hollywoodreporter.com/business/business-news/sag-wga-1960-hollywood-strike-reagan-history-1235538551/.

Fortmueller, Kate. *Below the Stars: How the Labor of Working Actors and Extras Shapes Media Production*. Austin: University of Texas Press, 2021.

Freligh, Rebecca. "Peggy Lee Still Rates 'Miss Standing Ovation.'" *Cleveland Plain Dealer*, February 14, 1993.

Gabriel, Brian. "Lady and the Lawsuit: Peggy Lee's War with Disney." Cartoon Brew, September 4, 2015. http://www.cartoonbrew.com/disney/peggy-lee-war-disney-lady-and-the-tramp-113688.html.

Gavin, James. *Is That All There Is? The Strange Life of Peggy Lee*. New York: Simon & Schuster, 2014.

Hoyt, Eric. *Hollywood Vault: Film Libraries before Home Video*. Berkeley: University of California Press, 2014.

Johnson, Kit. "The Wonderful World of Disney Visas." *Florida Law Review* 63, no. 4 (2011): 915–958.

Kozinn, Allan. "'Fantasia' Orchestra Sues Disney." *New York Times*, May 7, 1992, C17. https://www.nytimes.com/1992/05/07/movies/fantasia-orchestra-sues-disney.html.

Kuenz, Jane. "Working at the Rat." In *Inside the Mouse: Work and Play at Disney World*, edited by Jane Kuenz, Shelton Waldrep, Susan Willis, and Karen Klugman, 110–162. Durham, NC: Duke University Press, 1995. https://doi.org/10.4324/9781315881201-16.

"Lady's Pedigree: The Making of *Lady and the Tramp*." *Lady and the Tramp*. DVD, disc 2, Platinum Edition. Walt Disney Studios Home Entertainment, 2006.

Lang, Brent. "Disney Fires Back at Scarlett Johansson, Calls 'Black Widow' Lawsuit 'Sad and Distressing.'" *Variety*, July 29, 2021. https://variety.com/2021/film/news/disney-scarlett-johansson-black-widow-lawsuit-response-pandemic-1235030837/.

Lee, Peggy. *Miss Peggy Lee: An Autobiography*. New York: Dutton, 1989.

Lee v. The Walt Disney Company, no. B058897. State of California Second Appellate District, 1992.

Lee v. The Walt Disney Company, no. C705414. State of California Superior Court, 1991.

O'Neill, Ann. "Disney Case Could Define 'Recording.'" *Los Angeles Times*, July 30, 2000. https://www.latimes.com/archives/la-xpm-2000-jul-30-me-61590-story.html.

Periwinkle Entertainment, Inc., F/S/O Scarlett Johansson v. The Walt Disney Company, no. 21STCV27831. California Superior Court, July 29, 2021.

"Pictures: Jury in N.Y. Disagrees on 300G 'Snow White' Suit." *Variety*, June 1943, 6.

"Rooney Sues on Sale of Films to TV." *New York Times*, June 25, 1981, C13. https://www.nytimes.com/1981/06/25/movies/rooney-sues-on-sale-of-films-to-tv.html.

Schroeder, Russell. *Disney's Lost Chords*, Vol. 3. Robbinsville, NC: Voigt Publications, 2017.

Siegel, Tatiana. "Scarlett Johansson Opens Up about the Pain and Triumph of Disney Legal Battle over 'Black Widow' and Wes Anderson's 'Liberating' Cannes Film." *Variety*, May 9, 2023. https://variety.com/2023/film/features/scarlett-johansson-disney-lawsuit-child-actor-interview-1235605851/.

Smith, Liz. "$3 Million to Peggy Lee Stands for Singing on 'Lady … Tramp.'" *The Sun*, December 22, 1992, 2D. https://www.proquest.com/docview/1976690772/abstract/C97B5157C0424BB4PQ/1. "'Snow White' Disc Sales Set All-Time Pic High at 450,000." *Variety*, September 1938, 4.

Solomon, Charles. "Peggy Lee Bangs Out Jazz in 'Lady and the Tramp.'" *Los Angeles Times*, December 26, 1986. https://www.latimes.com/archives/la-xpm-1986-12-26-ca-392-story.html.Solomon, Thomas. "Music and Race in American Cartoons: Multimedia, Subject Position." In *Music and Minorities from around the World: Research, Documentation and Interdisciplinary Study*, edited by Ursula Hemetek, Essica Marks, and Adelaida Reyes, 142–166. Newcastle upon Tyne: Cambridge Scholars, 2014.

Thompson, Kirsten Moana. "'Quick—Like a Bunny!' The Ink and Paint Machine, Female Labor and Color Production." *Animation Studies* 9 (February 2014). http://journal.animationstudies.org/category/volume-9/kirsten-thompson-quick-like-a-bunny/.

Ulmer, James. "Lee Lawsuit over Disney 'Lady' Vid May Set Precedent." *Hollywood Reporter*, November 17, 1988, 1, 4.

CHAPTER 13

SINGING MICE AND GRUNTING REINDEER: MUSICAL REPRESENTATIONS OF THE NONHUMAN AND RELATING TO ANIMALS IN DISNEY ANIMATED MUSICALS

KATE GALLOWAY

THE Walt Disney Company positions itself as a socially responsible company actively engaged in environmentally sustainable practices that are geared toward protecting the planet and presenting a positive environmental legacy for young people and future generations. This environmental action and the aesthetics of sustainability are audibly present in the music and sound design of the company's animated features. The Disney studio has excelled at both music and animation, but a fascinating point of intersection concerns Disney's musical and sonic treatment of the animated nonhuman animal. Across Disney's musicals, human and human-like characters sing with the nonhuman world, continuing and extending Walt Disney's personal and aesthetic politics of conservationism which emphasized the connection of humanity with nonhuman nature and our collective responsibility to the environment and its living and nonliving things.

There is a long history of the Disneyfication of animals on-screen.[1] Animals are everywhere in Disney films. Their depictions are stereotypical, but they can also be species-specific: rats are frequently portrayed as villainous, shady, or shrewd; mice are small and have other species-specific traits that allow them to help out and do things that humans cannot; birds are virtuosic communicators with a musicality closely aligned with that of human singing; dogs are loyal and friendly, and they both howl and sing; cows and chickens serve agricultural purposes; and rabbits, deer, squirrels, and other woodland creatures are fuzzy, cute, and approachable in times of fear and in the face of the unknown. For Walt Disney and the animation division of the Disney studio, the animated medium was full of possibilities to imagine, interpret, and represent nature, the animal kingdom, and human–animal relations.

Humans have created and encountered the nonhuman as performers in multiple domains for centuries: viewed in zoo, marine park, and circus; choreographed by expert equestrians to complete a series of moves to music in dressage freestyle events that are built on technical training, rhythm, and communication between horse and rider; and trained and bet on as racers and fighters. In the words of Margo DeMello, "Americans love watching animals. We love watching them eat, play, interact with each other, and even sleep. We also love touching them and being as close as possible to them."[2]

While some nonhuman animals receive musical treatment, their singing, dancing, and speaking are performed by human voice actors. The mice in *Cinderella* (1950) who sing "The Work Song" while preparing Cinderella's dress for the ball and almost the entire nonhuman animal casts of *The Jungle Book* (1967) and *The Lion King* (1994) are voiced by human actors. Marion Darlington, who trained at the California School for Artistic Whistling founded by Agnes Woodward in 1909, provided bird sounds for many of Disney's early animated features, including *Cinderella*, *Bambi* (1942), *Pinocchio* (1940), and *Snow White and the Seven Dwarfs* (1937), but went uncredited for her nonhuman-animal musical performances.[3] However, her musical labor in the representation and voicing of human characters is credited in *Snow White*, where she is named as the whistling performer in "Whistle While You Work."

In other instances, such as *The Little Mermaid* (1989), instrumental music stands in for some of the animal sounds, as the species-specific characteristics such as how they produce sound or the materiality of their skin or shell are conflated with specific instrumental timbres (e.g., a string orchestra stands in for the stridulations of crickets), while other nonhuman animated characters such as Kristoff's reindeer companion Sven in *Frozen* (2013) primarily communicate in species-specific forms of acoustic communication. In the Disney animation studio's attempt to portray real-seeming animals to audiences in the medium of animation, these nonhuman characters seem to talk, through either the use of explicit speech or implied cross-species communication that is understood by both the human and nonhuman characters.[4] These portrayals of nonhuman voicing also illustrate to audiences that the human is inseparable from nature.

In this chapter, I examine a range of instances where human performers participate in the sonic representation of anthropomorphized and non-anthropomorphized nonhuman characters to illustrate how music and sonic design choices and approaches to "voicing" the nonhuman animal in Disney musical films highlight the importance of media narratives in shaping environmental attitudes, how nonhuman animals are represented, and the ways we relate to them and include them in our lives. I listen closely to the musical treatments and "voicing" of the nonhuman animal across a range of Disney animated musicals, including *Snow White and the Seven Dwarfs*, *Cinderella*, *The Little Mermaid*, and *Frozen*. "Voicing" the nonhuman animal is multivalent, and what a voice is and can be is exhaustively explored through portrayals of the nonhuman across audiovisual media.[5] I mean "voice" in the typical sense of the term, including spoken dialogue and the sung voice. I also use voice to examine representational strategies that "give voice to" nature and the nonhuman, granting beyond the human characters agency in the narrative and soundscape of the animated feature and encouraging audiences to connect and empathize with nature. The audioviewer must also be a part of nature if Cinderella, Snow White, and Kristoff can all hear nature and communicate across species boundaries. I refer to individual people and animals with the gender-neutral singular pronoun "they" instead of objectifying the nonhuman animal by using "it" or the sex-/gender-related "he" or "she" unless otherwise clearly stated in the characterization of the nonhuman animal on-screen. In some cases, the sex of the animal featured in Disney's films cannot be reliably identified, while in other instances, Disney relies on established gender tropes (e.g., dresses for female mice). By calling the animals depicted in Disney's animated features "they" or referring to them by name, I recognize the animals as individuals with narrative agency rather than objects.

Mediated Animal Sonorous Worlds

Since the 1970s and 1980s, scholarship embracing the study of human–animal relationships, considering animals as subjects, has proliferated across the disciplines, occupying a place in sociology, philosophy, literary and cultural studies, and history, to name a few. In the American Historical Association's blog, Dan Vandersommers announced the "animal turn" in history, writing that "over the last 30 years, nonhuman animals have crept slowly, but persistently, from the margins of history to its center."[6] In the past decade, musicologists have increasingly taken up questions of the animal and animality, frequently in conversation with ecomusicology. Rachel Mundy called for research into what she termed "the animanities," a study of living creatures that is not restricted to the human species."[7] Although animal-related music scholarship certainly predates Mundy's groundbreaking article, new research from established and developing scholars continues to ask challenging questions about animal musicality, the connections between humans and animals through music, and human understandings of animals in music making.

The ubiquity of animals in musical spheres is evidenced by articles in *Grove Music*, an authoritative encyclopedia, on "Animal Music," "Birdsong," and "Bird Instruments," to name a few.[8] Animals have long served as inspirations for, components of, and occasional participants in human musical creation: Josquin des Prez's "El Grillo," horsehair bows and gut strings, George Gershwin's "Walking the Dog," and the "chirp" and "thrush" songstresses of the swing era.[9] As such, the shift suggested here goes beyond the call for multinational listening, which involves diverse, inclusive listening across national, geographic, and cultural borders, and instead embraces "multinaturalism" that both relativizes and interrogates the constructions of nature and humans.[10] In *Exposed: Environmental Politics and Pleasures in Posthuman Times*, Stacy Alaimo calls for an integrative environmental stance in which we think, experience, feel, act, and perform as and with the nonhuman materiality of the world.[11] By extending the analysis of music in the Americas to nonhuman performers and musicality, music scholars can gain a better understanding of how listening across different kinds of sound cultures shapes how we listen to and represent others, how we listen to nonhuman aurality and aural culture, and how technology has contributed to the study of nonhuman and human musicality. This chapter contributes to the study of animal musicalities and the cultural meanings of sounds and movements of both human and nonhuman animals and the sonic relationships between humans and nonhuman animals, listening beyond the visual, discursive, symbolic, and tactile encounters between human and nonhuman animals.[12]

Conservation, Sound Design, and Early Disney Animals

In *The Great Animal Orchestra*, soundscape ecologist Bernie Krause speaks of the sonic splendor of the animal world, the inherent value in listening to the global soundscapes, and hearing human conceptions of musicality in the natural world.[13] Walt Disney's interest and involvement in progressive conservation movements that were gaining popularity across the United States found their way into the vivid and varied animation and sound design of the natural world in early Disney animated shorts and feature films. Like *The Great Animal Orchestra*, early Disney features such as *Bambi* and *Snow White and the Seven Dwarfs* foreground aesthetic and affective experiences of the sonic properties of the sonic environment in a plea for recognizing the impact of human behavior and preserving it. While Krause relies on rich narrative detail, time-lapsed field recordings, and spectrograms, films like *Bambi* and *Snow White* rely on the aesthetic and expressive priorities of music, song, rhyme, and human voice actors' mimetic interpretation of the musicality of animals (e.g., whistled birdsong) over the explicitness of sound effects and dialogue.[14]

In *Snow White and the Seven Dwarfs*, the forest animals are central characters and protagonists in the film's narrative, serving as protectors and helpers to the princess. Birds, rabbits, deer, chipmunks, squirrels, raccoons, quails, and even a turtle inhabit the forest. A number of sonic and musical moments emphasize an interconnectedness with and empathy for nature and its living and nonliving entities. Snow White has a unique connection to nonhuman nature, as she is the only character who has the ability to speak with the forest and its animal life.

The theme and depiction of wild nature were central to Disney's aesthetic when the studio first ventured into the animated feature film in 1937.[15] Disney sets out to establish the musicality of the natural world in the first half of *Snow White*, where animators use expressive and mimetic musical gestures, devices, and sound effects to draw attention to and sonify the movement and vitality of on-screen nature and animals and to portray nature as inherently musical. Breathing life into the on-screen landscapes of early animated films was informed by Walt Disney's interest in conservationism and his desire for audiences to empathize with nature and nonhuman animals.[16] The use of small- and large-scale audiovisual synchronicities had the creative potential to enhance the visual depiction of the wonder of nature and of the nonhuman and the sonorous soundscape of the everyday world.

Following a terrifying flight through the unknown depths of the forest and frightened by the unknown darkness and sounds of the wilderness, Snow White collapses in a puddle of tears on the ground cover in a clearing. As night clears and the sun begins to come up, its rays peeking through the dense forest foliage, the woodland creatures cautiously approach her to investigate this newcomer to their forest. Rabbits, squirrels, bluebirds, and deer crouch to the ground, scurry closer, sniffing and sensing Snow White's heaving, sobbing body. They approach her at different species-specific paces—the rabbits gently hop, while the squirrels scurry—and their movements do not share a rhythmic relationship with the nondiegetic score. Snow White appears to sense the furry softness of one brave rabbit. As she raises her head to see what belongs to that warm, furry pelt, she comes face to face with the rabbit and lets out a high-pitched exclamation of surprise to see she is surrounded by so many woodland animals. Her unanticipated strident vocalization startles the animals, and they quickly retreat into their hollows. Snow White begins speaking with the animals, pleading with them, "Please don't run away," while trying to signal to them that her presence is not a threat and that she won't harm them, because like the animals of the forest, she has also been the victim of human cruelty and was wrongly afraid of the unknown when she first fled into the forest. After apologizing to the animals for frightening them, Snow White sings to connect with them.

She explains that she was crying and upset because she was afraid of the forest and the unknown, but now she knows it is full of friendly, warm creatures who were concerned for her well-being. She asks them, "What do you do when things go wrong?" One of the bluebirds sings and warbles a short refrain in response to her question. Snow White interprets their musical response as their solution to her quandary: they sing a song when they are afraid. The three birds nod, confirming her interpretation and reaffirming that Snow White has the special ability to speak and sing with the animals of the forest and that they understand her and she understands them.

First, she sings a coloratura vocalize that imitates birdsong, before she begins to sing conventionally in the style of the Disney musical. She communicates with musical gestures that she and the woodland creatures mutually understand, and the animals understand her spoken and sung words as well, as she coaxes and soothes them and ultimately gains their trust through song. Snow White sings to the forest animals to lure them out of their hiding places and forge a unique human–nonhuman relationship where they rely on each other for safety, protection, and companionship. Some might say the forest animals serve merely as a foil, to make it appear as though Snow White is talking to someone and not just to herself. However, the animals' reactions to her speech and singing strongly imply that they are listening to her and entranced by her voice.

This musical number, "With a Smile and a Song," begins with a call-and-response between Snow White and the birds, as she sings a short melodic phrase in vocables and the birds respond in imitation in bird song (figure 13.1a). The speech-song style of Snow White's spoken voice and her vocal mimicry of birdsong blur the lines between "music" and "not music," leaving the audioviewer to question whether this is a song or an expression of the musicality of nature and its soundscape. This vocal exchange between Snow White and the bluebirds is passed back and forth three times, with the final and most virtuosic response sung only by the nestling bluebird, who is still perfecting their song, wincing when their response doesn't conclude on the same pitch that Snow White sang to them. It is at that point that the birds' vocal gestures and the movements of the woodland creatures gradually synchronize, signifying Snow White and the animals' mutually dependent ability to communicate and reciprocally relate. As Snow White continues to sing "With a Smile and a Song," the deer take a moment away from grazing, racoons look up from their watering hole, rabbits and raccoons bound over a log into the clearing, and a family of quails come out from thick ground cover to listen while the birds provide vocal backup. The woodland creatures gather around Snow White in the clearing, listening to her message about the affective capabilities of music to bring about positivity and perseverance when facing fear and trepidation. The squirrels and rabbits sit in her lap and at the hem of her dress, and a fawn nudges their body to be cradled under Snow White's arm (figure 13.1b). Snow White's song has brought both her and the animals comfort, mutual understanding, and companionship. Early Disney animated features like *Snow White* rely on expressive musical gestures that highlight music–image relationships to depict the realism of Disney's conservationist aesthetics of a wild nature undisturbed by humans but which humanity has the ability to appreciate and protect.

Cinderella's Mice and Nonhuman Vocal Effects

Norma Swank-Haviland, like many of the women in the ink and paint department of the Disney animation studios, was called upon to voice the animals.[17] However, it is difficult to say what voice-over parts were performed by whom due to crediting practices of the time.[18] While Swank-Haviland voiced the female mice in *Cinderella*, it was the veteran Disney sound effects artist and longtime voice of the iconic character Mickey Mouse, Jimmy MacDonald, who voiced the male mice. MacDonald went on to provide other animal noises and vocalizations that came to define the soundscape of early Disney films that featured prominent nonhuman protagonists, including the Dormouse in *Alice and Wonderland* (1951), the tick-tock of the clock-eating crocodile in *Peter Pan* (1953), *Lady and the Tramp*'s (1955) chorus of howling dogs, the buzzing bees for *Winnie the*

SINGING MICE AND GRUNTING REINDEER 261

FIGURE 13.1. Snow White soothes and summons the woodland creatures in "With a Smile and a Song." Screenshots by author.

Pooh and *Donald Duck* cartoons, and various animals across the animal kingdom of *The Jungle Book* (1967), as well as starring as Chip in the *Chip and Dale* shorts.[19] According to her interview in Mindy Johnson's popular history of the ink and paint department, Swank-Haviland also seems to have voiced Chip, although uncredited, in some shorts.[20]

Cinderella's mice are given a handful of key musical numbers that highlight nonhuman musicality, advance the narrative, and provide comic relief. But singing mice are not unusual. Mice, like birds, sing, particularly when mating; however, mouse song is beyond the range of human hearing, being too high-pitched.[21] Disney's sonic treatment of its mice brings their song into the range of human hearing for only certain human beings—secret princesses destined for greatness and a happy ending, like Cinderella. What is of note is that in order to make the human actors seem more mouse-like and place their songs in a higher, more appropriate vocal range correlating with their size and mannerisms, the human voice actors' performances were shifted up in pitch by increasing the tape recording's speed.

While many contemporary uses of autotune sound-processing technologies covertly treat, correct, and shape the voice out of the listener's sight, overt autotune can make human singers sound unnatural, or perhaps even nonhuman.[22] For example, in 1958, with "The Chipmunk Song" sung by Alvin and the Chipmunks, pitch shifting was used to mask the humanness of the voice actor and craft an anthropomorphized nonhuman vocality, which became known as the "'Donald Duck' or 'chipmunk' effect," as Jonathan Sterne and Mara Mills have shown.[23]

In "The Work Song (Cinderelly, Cinderelly)," we hear the timbral results of "time-compression listening"[24] and how it is used to characterize the mice and remove the humanness of the voice actors. Through "The Work Song," the mice have the opportunity to describe the abuse and exploitation inflicted on Cinderella by her stepmother and stepsisters, a privilege to complain that Cinderella doesn't have. The mice can mimic the stepsisters' "shrill," demanding voices that tear their "Cinderelly" in all directions, performing uncompensated physical and emotional labor, because their voices are not audible to the rest of the household. Only Cinderella can communicate with them.

An earlier version of *Cinderella* contained a deleted song, "The Mouse Song," in which Cinderella decides to repay the kindness the mice have bestowed on her by using her seamstress skills to make unique outfits for each of them. During the musical number, the mice reveal the outfits they have made for themselves. Although this song did not make it into the final version of Disney's 1950 film, the species-specific title signals the prominent position the mice hold in the film's narrative.[25]

The mice realize that with all the preparations for the stepsisters and the stepmother to attend the Prince's ball that evening, Cinderella will be unable to finish her own dress in time to go with them. They decide to help their friend and surprise Cinderella by completing her outfit. The mice alternate between singing and lilting speech as they decide who will cut the fabric and who will sew, driven by the collective desire to "make a lovely dress for Cinderelly" and provide her with the care she is unable to give herself. The birds lend a wing by reaching high locations to drape fabric, make measurements, and lay down ribbon trimmings as they tweet and sing—just a backup chorus, however, because they are not given anthropomorphic speech like the mice. While the audience cannot understand what the birds are saying and can only infer that they are on the same page as the mice because they, too, are helping Cinderella, the mice are able to communicate with the birds and across the boundaries between species.

SEBASTIAN'S GREAT ANIMAL ORCHESTRA

Even though earlier Disney animated features and shorts such as *Cinderella* and *Lady and the Tramp* featured singing, dancing, and speaking animals, the trope became crystallized in films of the "Disney Renaissance," a period of resurgence in Disney animation that began with 1989's *The Little Mermaid*. The film's story world is populated by anthropomorphized animal characters and employs nuanced music–image relationships to convey the musicality of the natural world. Sebastian the crab calls on nature's orchestra for "Kiss the Girl" in one last effort to help Ariel break the spell cast upon her by Ursula. There is only one more day left for Ariel to get Prince Eric to fall in love with her and kiss her so that she can remain human and regain her voice, which Ursula has taken. If she doesn't, she must return to the ocean voiceless and under Ursula's control. Sebastian the crab, Scuttle the seagull, and Flounder the flounder have come to Ariel's aid to play matchmaker.[26] As Eric and Ariel spend some time alone together in a rowboat on a tranquil lagoon, Sebastian and Scuttle try to establish a romantic atmosphere with some mood music. Scuttle declares that this is the time for some "vocal romantic stimulation." Forcing a group of songbirds from their branch, Scuttle puffs his chest and flexes his vocal muscles first, squawking off-key and unmusically the love theme of Pyotr Tchaikovsky's *Romeo and Juliet* overture. While Ariel winces at her friend's flawed performance, Eric, who is unable to communicate with and understand the animals the way Ariel can, hears Scuttle's song as painful. The seagull is not known for having a lyrical call, and even though birders note that seagulls have a rich repertoire of calls, their song is often described in field guides as a noisy squealing or squawking call of alarm. Sebastian quickly covers Scuttle's beak, dampening his unmusical vocality.

If anyone is going to conjure the musicality of the animal world, it is Sebastian, King Triton's adviser and distinguished court composer. "Kiss the Girl" features Sebastian crooning, supported by an animal orchestra which he conducts with the repurposed frond of a lagoon plant. To set the appropriate mood, he first needs percussion from the mallard ducks striking the undersides of turtles with their wings, followed by strings in the stridulations of crickets and winds in the long grasses and reeds (figure 13.2). While the instrumentation of the calypso love song "Kiss the Girl" is scored for percussion, strings, and woodwinds, the complex music–image relationship of the animation positions the nonhuman animals as possessing and expressing human musicality.

Only after nature has set the expressive tone for this romantic moment does Sebastian enter with the directness of the song's lyrics, crooning the words with a cattail microphone intimately into Eric's ear and accompanied by flamingos and a frog choir on the refrain. Through song, Sebastian suggests that Eric does want to kiss Ariel but is too shy to do so and that he should go ahead to see if she returns his affections. However,

FIGURE 13.2. Sebastian the crab conducts his animal orchestra in "Kiss the Girl." Screenshots by author.

FIGURE 13.2. Continued

the song ends just before Ariel and Eric are about to finally kiss, the boat they are in tips over, and they both fall into the water, much to the shock of Sebastian, Flounder, and Scuttle. Another opportunity to lift Ursula's spell has been thwarted.

On a number of occasions in *The Little Mermaid*, Sebastian relies on his aquatic orchestra of crustaceans, fish, amphibians, and aquatic fowl to change the course of Ariel's narrative and help influence her decisions. "Under the Sea," sung in a calypso style with a Jamaican accent by Sebastian, who is voiced by the African American actor and singer Samuel E. Writing, describes the beautiful, welcoming, joyous, vibrant, and carefree life and sensory experiences of the sea in an attempt to change Ariel's mind about the human world on land that she dreams of joining. The calypso style is reinforced by accompaniment performed on-screen by an exotic blue lobster. As he plays a group of clamshells of different sizes, they surprisingly resound with the varied metallic timbres of an orchestra of steel drums, a series of uniquely tuned percussion instruments recycled from oil drums, instead of the dull clack of shells. Although the deep-sea environment is inhospitable to human beings, it affords Ariel so much more in comparison with life on land. Up on the shore, humans and their value systems dominate, and Sebastian warns her that she could feel trapped in a fishbowl, because it is not an environment where sea creatures can thrive. Even worse, they could become dinner.

"Under the Sea" is Sebastian's musical plea for Ariel to remain in the ocean and resist the urge to become a human in order to spend the rest of her life with Eric. He warns her that "the seaweed is always greener" on the other side of the ocean and that she has yet to experience the messiness of the human world where she will face struggle and hardship, concerns that don't impact those who dwell on the ocean floor. Sebastian calls on the musical expertise of the newt on flute, the plaice on bass, the chub on the tub, and the carp on harp, among many other aquatic species, who provide instrumental accompaniment and join Sebastian in his celebratory message (figure 13.3). Sebastian's lyrics and

FIGURE 13.3. Sebastian and the lobster with their steel shell orchestra; the carp on the harp; the plaice on the bass; the chub on the tub. Screenshots by author.

SINGING MICE AND GRUNTING REINDEER 267

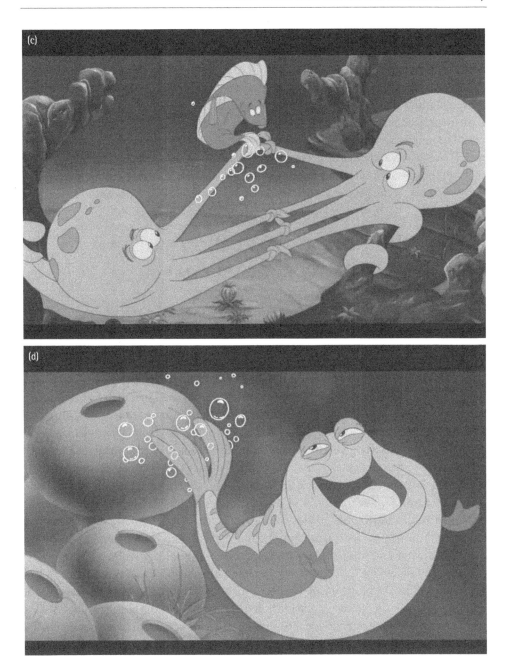

FIGURE 13.3. Continued

performance fail to convince Ariel that it's "better down where it's wetter." Sebastian is so wrapped up in his performance and the complex choreography of his crustacean band that he fails to notice Ariel sneaking off with the help of Flounder to pursue her dream of living on land.

"Under the Sea" also presents some of the most troubling ethnic and racial stereotyping in the film, as Sebastian's Jamaican-inflected accent combined with lyrics promoting life under the sea as stress-free ("Up on the shore they work all day / Out in the sun they slave away / While we devotin' / Full time to floatin'") conflates representations of Blackness with laziness as Sebastian ultimately implies that you don't have to get a job and contribute to society when you live under the sea.[27] This sonic representation of Sebastian made audible through the choice of accent, vocal cadence, vernacular language, and musical accompaniment others him and many other living things that call the ocean home, further reinforcing hierarchies of human–nonhuman difference as Disney "manages to tacitly transport racial earthly stereotypes to the water."[28]

"Reindeer(s) Are Better Than People" and *Frozen*

The Disney musical hit *Frozen*, which prominently features a playful reindeer named Sven, has been celebrated for its feminist message that challenges the historic portrayal of women, especially princesses, across Disney's animated features.[29] *Frozen* has been widely acknowledged for its departure from established tropes of the Disney animated musical. Of note, as Ryan Bunch addresses, are the ways in which *Frozen* deviates from the regressive and conservative gender politics prevalent across Disney animated features.[30] *Frozen* even parodies the clichéd tropes of earlier Disney princesses, as illustrated by Elsa's refusal to give Anna her blessing, flummoxed and outraged that her sister got engaged to marry Prince Hans, a man she had just met that day. *Frozen* was both celebrated and criticized for its use and erasure of Indigenous Sámi, and in the sequel *Frozen II* (2019), Disney increased its direct collaboration with Sámi culture bearers as consultants and contributors.[31] With *Frozen* and *Frozen II*, the Disney studios also made strides with respect to representation of culture, place, and ecology and by including a Sámi character and music by a Sámi composer.[32] The script describes the character of Kristoff as a Sámi ice harvester who was adopted at birth by a community of Nordic trolls, but unlike the Northuldra, Kristoff is not explicitly coded as Indigenous in the film. But since Kristoff grew up outside human civilization in the Nordic wilderness, he is coded as more connected to locality and the land through mutually dependent companionship with Sven, his pet reindeer and best friend since childhood.

Audiences have come to expect the speaking, singing, and dancing anthropomorphized animals that populate Disney's animated musicals. *Frozen*, however, is a stark departure in its sonic and musical treatment of nonhuman animal characters. *Frozen*, as Ryan Bunch explains, either replicates or revises the tropes that fit into the tradition of other animated Disney musicals and brings "their contradictions and complexities to the surface."[33] Earlier animated musicals such as *The Little Mermaid* feature full song-and-dance numbers by their nonhuman protagonists that serve an anthropomorphizing function, making the characters relatable to the audience and closing the "fantastical gap" in the narrative by providing opportunities for characters across different species to plausibly understand and relate to each other, thereby allowing the narrative to progress.[34] With *Frozen*, Disney revisits the conservationist aesthetics of early Disney animated shorts and feature films, such as the Silly Symphonies, *The Old Mill*, *Bambi*, and *Snow White and the Seven Dwarfs*, where human characters communicate and empathize with nonhuman nature across species boundaries through song and the implied musicality of nature and avoid anthropomorphic representations. In *Frozen*, the representational realism of reindeer in the character development and vocality of Sven is experienced alongside the whimsical singing and talking snowman Olaf. *Frozen* is a complicated on-screen world where environmental realism exists alongside the fantastical.

Although Kristoff and Sven's friendship is a secondary plot point in the film, it is an important portrayal in animated film of a companion-species relationship, a special kind of mutually dependent relationship between humans and certain kinds of nonhuman animals that Donna Haraway describes as she explores what humans can learn from nonhuman animals' relationships with their own kind.[35] Haraway writes, "an ethics and politics committed to the flourishing of significant otherness [might] be learned from taking dog-human relationships seriously; and ... how ... stories about dog-human worlds [might] finally convince ... people ... that history matters in naturecultures."[36] Even though Kristoff, like all of *Frozen*'s male characters, is secondary to the film's primary feminist message of the healing power of the love between sisters, *Frozen* conveys an unlikely yet rich friendship between Kristoff and Sven that implies a two-way dependency that is central to Haraway's companion-species model.

The contemporary animated musical has its own genre conventions, and realism is not one of them; however, Chris Buck and Jennifer Lee and their team of animators took the representation of Sven the reindeer seriously, balancing species-specific representation and character relatability. These species studies and modeling sessions represent a return to the representational techniques of early Disney animators who closely studied live animals for films like *Bambi* and *Dumbo*. Much attention is paid to the physical appearance of Disney's animated characters, including the large, lashed eyes and cinched-in waists of their princesses. *Frozen* did not escape such criticism. Despite the film's feminist narrative arc, the eyes of *Frozen*'s princesses were still disproportionately large and wide, and one of Kristoff's sidekicks is the talking and singing snowman Olaf voiced by comedian Josh Gad.[37]

The development of Sven's character was informed by several reindeer studies, which reduced the likelihood the animators would provide his character with excessive anthropocentric traits. In order to study reindeer for the development of this pivotal character, codirectors Buck and Lee first visited a reindeer management farm in Roros, Norway, owned and operated by members of the Sámi community. The animation team later brought reindeer into the studio to study their mannerisms, behavior, and movement to implement into their design of Sven's portrayal.[38] However, they found that real reindeer didn't have the range of physical motion or mannerisms that suited some of the interactions Sven's character would have with Kristoff, Olaf, and the other human characters. Reindeer can be aloof and skittish; however, Sven, who is a devoted companion to Kristoff, is not your typical reindeer. Sven's depiction was ultimately a multispecies fusion of real-life reindeer traits with the mannerisms of a dog.

The grunts, snorts, and snuffles Sven makes were performed and recorded by the voice actor Frank Welker, who is known for creative vocal effects that have brought many animals and creatures to life on film, mimicking the vocality of wild reindeer interspersed with expressive vocalizations that sound more like a loving and loyal household dog. Jonathan Groff, the voice actor for Kristoff, also lends his voice to Sven's vocality, translating Sven's plasmatic and expressive bodily gestures and species-specific vocalizations into English. While Olaf the snowman in *Frozen* and other nonhuman animals and creatures in Disney animated films have the ability to talk and sing, Sven does not. Groff said that the filmmakers had informed him when he began his work for the film that he would also provide a "reindeer voice," recording a duet with himself for the song "Reindeer(s) Are Better Than People."[39] He said that "a lot of people have weird pet voices for their pets," and according to Groff, he and the filmmakers were exploring the vocalizations of reindeer and the ways human owners manipulate their natural voices to create unique characters that give voices to their pets. He "tried a bunch of different voices" before settling on the one he used to translate Sven's species-specific vocality as performed by Welker.[40]

The short audience favorite "Reindeer(s) Are Better Than People" that Kristoff sings to and with Sven is instigated by a conflict with Oaken, the humble shopkeeper and owner of Wandering Oaken's Trading Post and Sauna, after Oaken demands that Kristoff pay more money for a pickaxe, rope, and some carrots for Sven than Kristoff thinks they are worth. He also doesn't have that kind of money on his person. Oaken is offended by Kristoff's accusation that he is trying to extort him and throws him out into the cold, forcing Kristoff to take shelter in the stable with Sven for the night.

"Reindeer(s) Are Better Than People" is a quasi-duet between Kristoff and Sven, although Sven is unable to speak or sing like a human.[41] Thus, Kristoff must use his voice to provide the lines that Sven would sing if he could. Kristoff begins by opining that reindeer are better than people because people will "beat you" and "cheat you," though people smell better than reindeer. Singing in duet with himself, he then ventriloquizes Sven's reply that both statements are true "For all except you."

Kristoff's voicing of Sven is similar to the phenomenon of the "pet voice" heard across social media. Human–pet ventriloquism in the form of the digital pet voice is a form of speaking with and through animals to convey our very human emotions and thoughts.[42] The communicative and aesthetic use of a pet voice is a persistent soundmark of the social-media soundscape, but it is not a novel communicative function exclusive to online culture. As historian Katherine Grier notes, as early as the nineteenth century, people exchanged letters to each other in the voices of their pet companions.[43] Groff, Kristoff's voice actor, alternates his natural voice with another version of his voice, one that is supposed to sound more like his reindeer, an anthropomorphized pet voice in his duet with himself.

Kristoff can understand what Sven is saying, which is why he sings in duet with himself as Sven, he does voice-overs for Sven, and they have full conversations together where Kristoff responds in English to Sven's grunts and snuffles (figure 13.4). It

SINGING MICE AND GRUNTING REINDEER   271

FIGURE 13.4. Kristoff singing in duet on "Reindeer(s) Are Better Than People," as himself and voicing Sven. Sven gazes at Kristoff in a loving way as Kristoff sings Sven's thoughts on the line "Every one of them's bad except you." Screenshots by author.

is clear from Sven's facial expressions, reactions, and vocalizations that he understands Kristoff and what he is singing and approves of his translation. At times, Sven's bodily movements share a discernible rhythmic relationship with the pacing of Kristoff's sung and spoken words and trace the same contours as Kristoff's vocal gestures. There are other moments throughout the film when Kristoff and Sven have the ability to understand each other. Sven often acts as Kristoff's conscience or voice of reason, the "voice" of Sven and the one in Kristoff's head that persuades him to continue accompanying Anna on her journey up the North Mountain so she won't freeze to death. In return, he might get a new sled to replace the one that crashed when they fled a pack of predatory wolves.

"Reindeer(s) Are Better Than People" addresses Kristoff's distrust of people and his preference for the company of reindeer, specifically Sven, his best friend and companion since childhood. Kristoff was raised by trolls apart from the human community rather than his biological Sámi parents, and this is where his wariness of humans originates. The song also illustrates Kristoff's unique relationship with Sven. While he is shy and isolated and takes time to warm up to people who come into his life like Anna, he is comfortable and at ease and can immediately be himself when he is with Sven and the other reindeer. This short musical number, intended for comic relief, is an important moment where the music–text relationship conveys a significant on-screen multispecies relationship and connections with the natural world.

Conclusion: Listening to Disney's Musical Animals

Animated musical features like *Snow White*, *Cinderella*, *The Little Mermaid*, and *Frozen* that feature singing and dancing animals or musical treatments of nature present audioviewers with audiovisual narrative contexts in which "anything [can] become endowed with a musicality of movement and expression all its own."[44] Musicking animals have attained a centrality in animated musical environments. The Disney animation studio's audiovisual representations of nonhuman animal musicking and sonic communication reveal that when we listen, perform, make, and share with the diverse musicalities of our nonhuman kin, we can nuance our understanding of our complex and entwined interspecies relations.

We listen to our sonic environments in order to understand them and how we sonically relate to others in these places, learning to attune ourselves to their large-scale and subtle changes. Human aesthetic ideals and the ways we sense the world around us shape practices of representing environments and their living and nonliving things. Practices of critically listening to sonic environments must extend into our digital environments of everyday life. It is not just a matter of how these animals are transmitted to human listeners but a matter of content and attuning our listening bodies to the strategies used to format, replay, manipulate, edit, score, and remix the nonhuman animal for audio-visual consumption.[45]

The animation division of the Disney studio mobilized the potential of music and sound in animation to convey the legacy of Walt's dedication to environmentalism and care for the nonhuman world to new generations of young people and Disney's intergenerational audience. Listening closely to the sonic and musical treatment of Disney's animals, cultural knowledge concerning screen-media representation can contribute new understanding of nonhuman musicking that is beyond the intentional control of human listeners and expand upon the current discourse addressing how human culture needs to listen to diverse auralities, and this expanded listening palette might involve using other sensory modes to hear the more-than-human world.

Notes

1. Rebecca Rose Stanton. *The Disneyfication of Animals* (New York: Palgrave Macmillan, 2021).
2. Margo DeMello, *Animals and Society: An Introduction to Human–Animal Studies* (New York: Columbia University Press, 2012), 39.
3. Craig Eley, "'A Birdlike Act': Sound Recording, Nature Imitation, and Performance Whistling," *Velvet Light Trap* 74 (2014): 4–15.
4. These real-seeming animal portrayals make up a genre of filmmaking that Marc Shell refers to as the "talking animal" genre. Marc Shell, "Animals That Talk," *Differences: A Journal of Feminist Cultural Studies* 15, no. 1 (2004): 84–107.
5. See also James Buhler and Hannah Lewis, eds., *Voicing the Cinema: Film Music and the Integrated Soundtrack* (Oxford: Oxford University Press, 2020).
6. Dan Vandersommers, "The 'Animal Turn' in History," AHA Today, November 3, 2016, https://www.historians.org/perspectives-article/the-animal-turn-in-history-november-2016/.
7. Rachel Mundy, "Evolutionary Categories and Musical Style from Adler to America," *Journal of the American Musicological Society* 67, no. 3 (2014): 761.
8. P. J. B. Slater and Emily Doolittle, "Animal Music," Oxford Music Online (2014); Maria Anna Harley, "Birdsong," Oxford Music Online (2001); Arthur W. J. G. Ord-Hume, "Bird Instruments," Oxford Music Online (2001).
9. Kathryn Lawson, "Canaries, Chirps, and Thrushes: Closer Hearings of the Jazz Aviary," paper presented at Locations and Dislocations: An Ecomusicological Conversation, Princeton, NJ, April 2016, and at Feminist Theory and Music, Madison, WI, August 2015. See also Kathryn Lawson, "Children's Bird Songs, the Rhetoric of Conservation, and Politics of the Voice in the United States, 1900–1930," in *Childhood and Pethood in Literature and Culture: New Perspectives in Childhood Studies and Animal Studies*, ed. Anna Feuerstein and Carmen Nolte-Odhiambo (New York: Routledge, 2018), 197–214.
10. Ana María Ochoa Gautier, "Acoustic Multinaturalism, the Value of Nature, and the Nature of Music in Ecomusicology," *Boundary 2* 43, no. 1 (2016): 107–141.
11. Stacey Alaimo, *Exposed: Environmental Politics and Pleasures in Posthuman Times* (Minneapolis: University of Minneapolis Press, 2016).

12. See, for example, Emily Doolittle, "Crickets in the Concert Hall: A History of Animals in Western Music," *Trans* 12 (2008), www.sibetrans.com/trans/articulo/94/crickets-in-the-concert-hall-a-history-of-animals-in-western-music; Sabine Feisst, "Animal Ecologies: Laurie Spiegel's Musical Explorations of Urban Wildlife," *Social Alternatives* 33, no. 1 (2014): 16–22; Jack Harrison, "Two Left Feet: A Study of Multispecies Musicality in British Women's Sport," PhD diss., University of Toronto, 2021; Rachel Mundy, *Animal Musicalities: Birds, Beasts, and Evolutionary Listening* (Middletown, CT: Wesleyan University Press, 2018); Rachel Mundy, "Museums of Sound: Audio Bird Guides and the Pleasures of Knowledge," *Sound Studies* 2, no. 1 (2016): 52–68; Tina Ramnarine, "Acoustemology, Indigeneity, and Joik in Valkeapää's Symphonic Activism: Views from Europe's Arctic Fringes for Environmental Ethnomusicology," *Ethnomusicology* 53, no. 2 (2009): 187–217; Helena Simonett, "Of Human and Non-Human Birds: Indigenous Music Making and Sentient Ecology in Northwestern Mexico," in *Current Directions in Ecomusicology: Music, Culture, Nature*, ed. Aaron S. Allen and Kevin Dawe (New York: Routledge: 2016), 107–116; Denise Von Glahn, *Music and the Skillful Listener: American Women Compose the Natural World* (Bloomington: Indiana University Press, 2013); Holly Watkins, "Music between Reaction and Response," *Eventual Aesthetics* 2, no. 2 (2013): 77–97.
13. Bernie Krause, *The Great Animal Orchestra: Finding the Origins of Music in the World's Wild Places*. Boston: Little, Brown, 2012.
14. Daniel Batchelder traces the early aesthetic development of music–image relationships in the animated shorts and feature films of the Walt Disney studio with a particular focus on their so-called golden age which featured productions such as *Snow White* and *Bambi*, tracing their musical landscapes to innovations heard in earlier Disney animated shorts (e.g., *Steamboat Willie*, *The Old Mill*). Daniel Batchelder, "Disney's Musical Landscapes," in *The Oxford Handbook of Children's Film*, ed. Noel Brown (Oxford: Oxford University Press, 2022): 342–364.
15. Although later animated features such as *Lady and the Tramp* (1951), *One Hundred and One Dalmatians* (1961), and *Oliver & Company* (1988) feature domesticated animals, these films still address the contrasts between good and evil, the "natural" and the "human," in their portrayal of character behavior and morality.
16. Batchelder writes of how mickey-mousing techniques "became an ever-more sophisticated expressive tool" and a dramatic mode" in the depiction of Disney's animated narrative environments. Batchelder, *Disney's Musical Landscapes*, 352–356. On Walt Disney's interest in and involvement with the American conservationism movement and how it influenced his aesthetic goals, see David Whitley, *The Idea of Nature in Disney Animation: From Snow White to WALL-E* (Farnham, UK: Ashgate, 2012), 1–18, 19–38, 61–78.
17. Mindy Johnson, *Ink & Paint: The Women of Walt Disney's Animation* (Los Angeles: Disney Editions, 2017). Also see https://www.mindyjohnsoncreative.com/single-post/a-farewell-to-the-woman-behind-walt-disneys-chip.
18. https://www.cartoonbrew.com/rip/norma-swank-haviland-chip-voice-actor-obituary-215830.html See also Tim Hollis and Greg Ehrbar, *Mouse Tracks: The Story of Walt Disney Records* (Jackson: University of Mississippi Press, 2023).
19. Marc Mancini, "Sound Thinking," *Film Comment* 19, no. 6 (November/December 1983): 40–43, 45–47.
20. Johnson, *Ink & Paint*.
21. See Rachel Feltman, "Mice Sing Just Like Birds, but We Can't Hear Them," *Washington Post*, April 1, 2015, https://www.washingtonpost.com/news/speaking-of-science/wp/2015/04/01/mice-sing-just-like-birds-but-we-cant-hear-them/.

22. Andy Kelleher Stuhl, Alexandra Hui, Alexander Russo, and Amy Skjerseth, "Sounds of Accompaniment: Transcript from an SCMS 2022 Panel on Music, Technology, and Labor," *Journal of Popular Music Studies* 34, no. 3 (2022): 6–29.
23. Jonathan Sterne and Mara Mills, "Second Rate: Tempo Regulation, Helium Speech, and 'Information Overload,'" Triple Canopy 26, October 1, 2020), https://www.canopycanopycanopy.com/issues/26/contents/second-rate.
24. Ibid. See also Mara Mills and Jonathan Sterne, "Aural Speed-Reading: Some Historical Bookmarks," *PMLA* 135, no. 2 (2020): 401–411.
25. Some online sources mistakenly identify "The Work Song" as the same musical number as "The Mouse Song" which was deleted from the final film. See https://disney.fandom.com/wiki/The_Mouse_Song.
26. In the 2023 live-action adaptation of *The Little Mermaid*, Scuttle (voiced by Awkwafina) is portrayed as a female northern gannet so that the character could be featured in underwater scenes with Flounder, Sebastian, and the other ocean animals.
27. Claudia Sackl, "Screening Blackness: Controversial Visibilities of Race in Disney's Fairy Tale Adaptations," in *On Disney: Deconstructing Images, Tropes and Narratives* (Berlin: Springer, 2022), 81–96.
28. Regina Bendix, "Seashell Bra and Happy End: Disney's Transformations of 'The Little Mermaid,'" *Fabula* 34, nos. 3–4 (1993): 280–290.
29. On voice, identity, and the representation of young women in film, see Robynn Stilwell, "Listen to the Mockingjay: Voice, Identity, and Agency in the Hunger Games Trilogy," in *Voicing Girlhood in Popular Music*, ed. Jacqueline Warwick and Allison Adrian (New York: Routledge, 2016), 258–280; Robynn J. Stilwell, "Girls' Voices, Boys' Stories, and Self-Determination in Animated Films since 2012," in *Voicing the Cinema: Film Music and the Integrated Soundtrack*, ed. James Buhler and Hannah Lewis (Oxford: Oxford University Press), 127–148; Auba Llompart and Lydia Brugué, "The Snow Queer? Female Characterization in Walt Disney's *Frozen*," *Adaptation* 13, no. 1 (2020): 98–112.
30. Ryan Bunch, "'Love Is an Open Door': Revising and Repeating Disney's Musical Tropes in *Frozen*," in *Contemporary Musical Film*, ed. K. J. Donnelly and Beth Carroll (Edinburgh: Edinburgh University Press, 2017), 89; see also Rick Altman, *The American Film Musical* (Bloomington: Indiana University Press, 1987), 16–58; Raymond Knapp, *The American Musical and the Formation of National Identity* (Princeton, NJ: Princeton University Press, 2005), 9.
31. Kelsey Fuller, "'Reindeer Are Better Than People': Indigenous Representation in Disney's Frozen," paper presented at the Rocky Mountain Music Scholars Conference, online, 2020; Kelsey A. Fuller, "Sounding Sápmi in Multimedia: Gender, Politics, and Indigenous Solidarity in Contemporary Sámi Music," PhD diss., University of Colorado–Boulder, 2020, 172–205.
32. Tina K. Ramnarine, "Frozen through Nordic Frames," *Musik-och Dansetnologisk Tidskrift/Journal for Ethnomusicology and Ethnochoreology* 1 (2016): 14, http://carkiv.musikverk.se/www/Puls_01_2016-04- 01.pdf#page = 13, Radheyan Simonpillai, "Disney Signed a Contract with Indigenous People before Making Frozen II," *Now Toronto*, November 19, 2019, https://nowtoronto.com/movies/news-features/disney-frozen-2-indigenous-culture-sami/. See also Fuller, "Sounding Sápmi in Multimedia, 172–205.
33. Bunch, "'Love Is an Open Door,'" 90.
34. Robynn J. Stilwell, "The Fantastical Gap between Diegetic and Nondiegetic." In *Beyond the Soundtrack: Representing Music in Cinema*, ed. Daniel Goldmark, Lawrence Kramer, and Richard Leppert (Oakland: University of California Press, 2007), 184–202.

35. Donna Haraway, *The Companion Species Manifesto: Dogs, People, and Significant Otherness* (Chicago: Prickly Paradigm, 2003).
36. Ibid., 3.
37. Philip N. Cohen, '"Help, My Eyeball Is Bigger Than My Wrist!": Gender Dimorphism in *Frozen*," Huffington Post, December 18, 2013, http://www.huffingtonpost.com/philip-n-cohen/gender-dimorphism-frozen_b_4467178.html; Kara Wahlgren, "For the Love of Olaf, Can We Stop Dissecting *Frozen*?" Huffington Post, March 4, 2014, http://www.huffingtonpost.com/kara-wahlgren/for-the-love-of-olaf-can-we-stop-dissecting-frozen_b_4893806.html.
38. Jonathan Berr, "Behind Norway's 'Frozen' Windfall from Disney," CBC News, June 6, 2014, https://www.cbsnews.com/news/behind-norways-frozen-windfall-from-disney/; Dan Sarto, "The Animation of Disney's 'Frozen': Striving to Capture the Performance," Animation World, October 11, 2013, https://www.awn.com/animationworld/animation-disneys-frozen-striving-capture-performance. The actor who adapted Sven to the stage for the Broadway production of *Frozen* underwent similar species studies in order to embody the reindeer. Michael Paulson, "The Secret Life of Sven," *New York Times*, June 26, 2018, https://www.nytimes.com/2018/06/26/theater/frozen-sven-reindeer-broadway.html.
39. Karen Benardello, "Roundtable Interview with Jonathan Groff," We Got This Covered, November 26, 2013, https://wegotthiscovered.com/movies/roundtable-interview-jonathan-groff-frozen/; Chuck Mirarchi, "Jonathan Groff Is as Cool as Kristoff in Disney's *Frozen*," Huffington Post, November 26, 2013, https://www.huffpost.com/entry/jonathan-groff-is-cool-as_b_4330084.
40. Terry Gross, "'Mindhunter' Actor Jonathan Groff on His Most Life-Altering Roles," NPR, August 16, 2019, https://www.npr.org/2019/08/16/751740114/mindhunter-actor-jonathan-groff-on-his-most-life-altering-roles.
41. In the 2019 sequel *Frozen II*, Sven has the ability to sing his own lines of the duet in a continuation of "Reindeer(s) Are Better Than People"; however, he doesn't retain this ability in the actual world. Sven can only sing because the musical number is taking place as a fantasy in Kristoff's imagination.
42. Jessica Maddox, "Pet Voice Isn't All about the LOLz," *Saturday Evening Post*, January 10, 2023, https://www.saturdayeveningpost.com/2023/01/pet-voice-isnt-all-about-the-lolz/.
43. Katherine C. Grier, *Pets in America: A History* (Durham, NC: University of North Carolina Press, 2015).
44. Susan Smith, "The Animated Film Musical," in *The Oxford Handbook of the American Musical*, ed. Raymond Knapp, Mitchell Morris, and Stacey Wolf (Oxford: Oxford University Press 2011), 169. See also Landon Palmer, "Everybody Wants to Be a Cat: Jazz Culture and Disney Animation in the 1960s," in *Musicals at the Margins: Genre, Boundaries, Canons*, ed. Julie Lobalzo Wright and Martha Shearer (London: Bloomsbury, 2021, 172–186.
45. Jody Berland, "Assembling the (Non)Human: The Animal as Medium," *Imaginations* 8, no. 3 (2017): 139–152.

CHAPTER 14

THE ORIGINAL FILM AND ITS BROADWAY SEQUEL: *EPIC MICKEY* AND *EPIC MICKEY 2*

LISA SCOGGIN

In the early twenty-first century, Disney was able to reacquire the rights to Oswald the Lucky Rabbit (which it lost in 1928) and was looking to introduce him again as part of its family of characters.[1] With the help of the highly acclaimed video-game maker and Disney fanatic Warren Spector, it did so in the game *Epic Mickey* (2010). Set in Wasteland—a world modeled after the original Disneyland but half broken and full of forgotten (as of 2010) Disney cartoon characters—the music regularly hints at the then-current Disneyland but twists it enough to emphasize the broken parts of Wasteland and, by extension, Mickey and Disneyland itself.[2] The game had considerable buzz and sold well—more than 2 million copies as of June 2011—despite having mixed reviews. Perhaps unsurprisingly, then, Spector and his colleagues created a sequel, *Epic Mickey 2: The Power of Two*, which was released in 2012.[3] This game features characters with voices throughout, as well as numerous songs, thus expanding from a game with a considerable amount of music to a game that Spector considered to be a full-fledged Broadway-style musical. This chapter examines how music is used in both of these games to reflect and comment on the Disney ethos, considering Disneyland specifically and Disney films in general.

DECONSTRUCTING DISNEYLAND: *EPIC MICKEY*

For much of its history, the Walt Disney Company has worked to represent idealized, clean-cut, conservative Middle American values.[4] For example, for several decades,

Disneyland and Walt Disney World "cast members" (i.e., public-facing employees) were not allowed to have facial hair, let alone visible tattoos or other similar forms of personal expression.[5] *The Parent Trap* encouraged a nuclear family with both a mother and a father rather than single-parent households. Even *Mulan*, set in "ancient" China, is adapted to reflect American values and expectations.[6] Starting in the late 2000s, however, postmodern influences crept into some of Disney's works, often with the result of creating a more complex scenario.[7] Disney continued this trend in the video game *Epic Mickey* (2010).[8] Through its plot, the player sees, as the *New York Times* notes, "a dystopian version of the Magic Kingdom" and a less-than-ideal Mickey Mouse and Oswald the Lucky Rabbit.[9] Visually, the parallels between the park and the game setting are obvious and, in fact, have been discussed in many articles and YouTube videos. The music also plays a vital part, however, in creating the dystopia that is Wasteland during the gameplay. Indeed, the musical interaction with the visuals of *Epic Mickey* work to create a world that, while still holding to Disney's roots, provides a complexity that was seldom seen in the company's twentieth-century, more traditional cartoons.

The opening cinematic provides a glimpse into the attitudes and overall structure of the game. Here the player sees that the narrator, a wizard named Yen Sid (Disney backward), who looks suspiciously like the one in *The Sorcerer's Apprentice*, has created a world for forgotten cartoons. Mickey, dressed in his red pants and thus designated as an early, more mischievous iteration of the character, has snuck into the room through a magic mirror and decides to use the magic paintbrush to create what is meant to be another mouse but rapidly turns into a monster similar to Chernabog (the evil character in the "Night on Bald Mountain" section of *Fantasia*).[10] (See figure 14.1.) Mickey tries to erase the monster but ultimately spills paint and thinner into the newly created world, making it, as Yen Sid calls it, a "Wasteland." Mickey escapes back home. Time passes, as seen on a calendar that shows stills of his successes, but ultimately the monster pulls Mickey (along with the brush) into the Wasteland.

From this sequence, the player may recognize that Mickey is more malleable here than in many other games (and cartoons), thus emphasizing the less black-and-white world compared with much traditional Disney fare. The idea of a broken or deconstructed Disneyland that may be changed using paint or thinner is also suggested, demonstrating not only game mechanics but also a basic setting and characters. Visual Disney references abound—including *Fantasia* (1940), *Through the Mirror* (1936), *Plane Crazy* (1928), and Disneyland, to name just a few—as well as a mix of original music and Disney-related musical references, most obviously "The Sorcerer's Apprentice" from *Fantasia* (thus foreshadowing both visual and aural approaches to the gameplay itself).

Once he is pulled into Wasteland, Mickey's primary goal is to get home. Luckily, he grabbed the magic paintbrush on his way in and is able to use it to progress. He may use paint to bring into being specific objects or to befriend enemies; he may also use thinner to make certain objects disappear or destroy enemies. This has an effect on various outcomes of the game. For instance, as game creator Spector notes, it will help determine whether Mickey gets a lot of help from friends but is perhaps weaker individually or whether he is a strong but solitary hero.[11] It also affects the orchestration of

FIGURE 14.1. Screenshot of Mickey Mouse and the Blot from the opening cinematic of *Epic Mickey*.

the music in certain settings: with more use of paint, the music sounds what composer James Dooley describes as "brighter," with more clarinets and flutes, while the use of paint thinner adds more "dark" instruments such as trombones and bassoons.[12]

Most of Mickey's journey takes him through various portions of Wasteland in the form of a three-dimensional action game. Since (according to the backstory) Oswald the Lucky Rabbit, the original inhabitant of this world, used ideas for Disneyland to fashion each setting, there are a fair number of similarities between Wasteland and Disneyland, but the two don't quite match. (See table 14.1 for details on the setup of each as seen in 2010.)[13] One of the bigger differences is that in Wasteland, characters go from area to area via projector screens, which, in terms of gameplay, translate into two-dimensional (i.e., flat-looking) platformers set in old Mickey Mouse or Oswald cartoons.[14] I'll get to those sections momentarily, but for now, let's look at some of the 3D settings in more detail—particularly how the music in each section relates to the corresponding visual surroundings.

Dark Beauty Castle is the first and the last portion of Wasteland that the player sees in the game. According to Austin Grossman in *The Art of Epic Mickey*, the castle is primarily based on Disneyland's Sleeping Beauty Castle but with parts of Walt Disney World's Cinderella Castle, the castle from *The Mad Doctor* (1933), and the castle from *Beauty and the Beast* (1991).[15] (Gameplay for this setting is almost entirely within the castle, which is considerably larger than the actual walkable space in the castle in Disneyland.) While

Table 14.1. The setup of Disneyland (2010) versus the setup of Wasteland.

Disneyland (California) Setup	Wasteland (*Epic Mickey*) Setup
Lands include Fantasyland (which includes Sleeping Beauty Castle and It's a Small World), Main Street, Adventureland, New Orleans Square, Toontown, Tomorrowland, Frontierland, and Critter Country.	Lands include Dark Beauty Castle, Gremlin Village, Mean Street, Ventureland, Bog Easy, Ostown, and Tomorrow City.
Transportation between areas is done via train and walking, with a monorail into and out of the park.	Transportation between areas is done via cartoons/projection screens.
Central hub is at the Walt & Mickey statue.	Central hub is at the Walt & Oswald statue.
Sleeping Beauty Castle is easily accessible from the hub.	Dark Beauty Castle is not easily accessible from the hub.
Disneyland in its initial form was created by Walt Disney and others.	Wasteland was created by Yen Sid, with help from Oswald, and then destroyed in part by Mickey.
The world is populated with current characters, humans, and animatronics.	The world is populated with forgotten characters, Beetleworx, and Blotlings.

the disparate influences work well together, the castle doesn't feel as if it would belong in an actual Disney park: few straight lines are to be found, the colors are dingy, and the doors to the hallway are not quite symmetrical (not to mention the emphasis on Oswald rather than Mickey or princesses in the stained glass and other artwork.)

The music for this and other playable portions is generally on a loop (with modifications, based on the aforementioned use of paint and thinner).[16] Much of the music here was composed originally for the game, but Dooley does weave a minor-key variant of a very well-known theme into it: "Once upon a Dream" from Disney's *Sleeping Beauty* (and from Pyotr Tchaikovsky, of course). The orchestration in particular is considerably different, occurring most noticeably on bells and a glockenspiel, which creates a tinny, hollow sound suggesting that it is a shadow of what it once was.[17] Indeed, the player hears a majestic swell complete with French horns that slowly dies away just prior to the bell section, helping to emphasize the implied decay. Overall, then, both the visual representation and the music suggest something familiar but not quite right, and so the music directly relates to both the actual Disneyland building and the sense of unease associated with the imitation.

The Gremlin Village represents the remainder of Fantasyland (including the Mad Tea Party and the Dumbo the Flying Elephant rides) but concentrates on the It's a Small World ride, taking a boat through Asia, Europe, and Africa settings. As with many other areas of the game, the creators do not make an exact replica but rather present a version of it that includes and often exaggerates various iconic elements and structures; while the flying carpets seem appropriate, for example, the scale of the *Epic Mickey* Eiffel Tower feels closer to the real thing than the one in the ride, and the tiny dragon kite in the Disneyland version is blown to gargantuan size in the game.[18]

In the final portion of this area, Mickey has a boss fight against the clock tower—an insane version of the facade of It's a Small World, with a newly crazed face, large blocklike arms, and huge mechanical fists acting as though its wires were literally crossed. As with Dark Beauty Castle, the composer chooses to base much of the music on a song directly related to the ride: the "It's a Small World" theme. Here, though, the music (as with the boss itself) is both considerably more menacing and a parody of itself. The melody is altered somewhat from its original form, often using a minor key and always slowed down to a more ponderous, hulking tempo. Thus, when the flutes play a portion of the theme, it comes across as a music box that isn't wound up enough. A cluster of French horns (often muted) play other segments of "It's a Small World," using close dissonances in the harmonies to add a touch of the sinister. A calliope, along with pitched and nonpitched percussion, adds to the character of clockworks gone awry through its constant pulsing and oompahs over the melody. This music clearly reflects the insane, mechanical nature of the boss as well as the twisted representation of the park. It could, however, also represent something else: the irritation many feel when the song gets stuck in their head after having been on the ride at Disneyland. Both in the game and in the park, the music seems to repeat over and over and over again, such that (at least for the author) the player is ready to move on aurally from this portion of the game when given the opportunity.

Not all of the music in the game is so directly related to the corresponding real-world ride. The mountain in Wasteland, for instance, has music corresponding not to Disneyland's Matterhorn ride (which has no music, only sounds of howling wind and yetis) but, rather, what surrounds Wasteland's mountain. In examining the setting, the player notices that the game version of the mountain consists almost entirely of piles of giant Mickey Mouse merchandise—hence the name "Mickeyjunk Mountain." (See figure 14.2.) However, Dooley avoids the obvious here, forgoing Alpine music or imitation wind sounds. Instead, he weaves a version of the *Mickey Mouse Club* (1955–1958) theme song into his score, using for it an orchestration that resembles a cheap toy piano.[19] The inherent implication in this is that through shows like *The Mickey Mouse Club*, Disney is pushing its merchandise—much more than they will ever need, and much of which will end up in the trash—to fans everywhere. If the music is taken out of context, however, as it is on the soundtrack, the connection is not quite as obvious; it just makes for another tie-in to the world of Disney.

Other areas contain music that is even less directly related to the music from the actual park yet is still reminiscent of it. In Tomorrow City, the Wasteland version of Tomorrowland, the music does not use a strongly recognizable theme as the ones mentioned previously do. This may be in part because Tomorrowland itself has changed so drastically over the years. Indeed, Tomorrow City contains several forgotten rides, including the Notilus (which is the *Finding Nemo* ride in real life as of this writing), the People Mover (currently defunct at Disneyland), the Great Big Tomorrow (the Carousel of Progress in real life, which has been changed to Innoventions and a *Star Wars* exhibit at Disneyland), the Sky Tram (no longer in evidence), and Space Voyage (the long-gone Moonliner at Disneyland).[20] Instead, the composer relies on orchestration to set the

FIGURE 14.2. Screenshot of the beginning of the Mickeyjunk Mountain area.

mood, throwing in laser sounds, theremin bits, and purposely synthesized-sounding material, all to simulate a "retro sci-fi" sound similar to what is used as background music when one walks around Tomorrowland today.

Mean Street, the Wasteland's equivalent of Main Street (and thus meant to emulate the center of an early-twentieth-century small town in Middle America), has many of the same buildings as the Disney version, including an Emporium, an ice cream parlor, a town hall, a movie theater (showing *Steamboat Oswald* instead of *Steamboat Willie*), and even Walt's apartment above the firehouse. The buildings, however, appear to have been built by somebody who did not own a straightedge; literally, they form a slightly twisted version of the park. As with Tomorrow City, the music for Mean Street relates to the setting through stylistic inference more than direct theme use. Dooley uses melodies similar to early-1900s popular song, particularly with his gentle ragtime syncopations in the sections using clarinet and flute. However, he does not include anything specifically recognizable as relating to Main Street or Disney overall. (This is perhaps because the songs used at the time on the actual Main Street, such as "Seventy-Six Trombones" or "Alexander's Ragtime Band," are not particularly associated with Disney unless one is at the park.) As with the other examples, the feeling of being at Disneyland comes across in the music, but the player always senses that something is not quite what it should be. Here, while the music is in F major and is pleasant enough, it simply lacks the energy and excitement of the real thing (which has an added energy for many as the first part of the park that people see).

The art and music in the 2D platforms (or transitional cartoons) work rather differently from the action spots. Spector has endeavored to make the player feel as if they are actually in a real cartoon, so while individual portions of the cartoon are placed in ways to make a good game, each part (as well as the setting as a whole) is drawn very much like the original film. Overall, there appears to be more reverence for the cartoons themselves than there is for the park, and this is noticeable in the music as well.

This is especially true in the *Sleeping Beauty*, *Steamboat Willie*, and *Fantasia* segments. *Sleeping Beauty* (complete with a castle in the background and a dragon to, in this case, avoid) occurs near the end of the storyline, soon after Mickey returns to Dark Beauty Castle. To match the style of the 1959 movie, the colors here are not only lush (as one would expect in a Disney cartoon of that era) but also bright and cheery for the most part, providing a stark contrast between it and the 3D castle setting on either end of it. The music matches the scenery, using an orchestration based on instruments such as the clarinet, flute, and violin. As with the Dark Beauty setting, the "Once upon a Dream" melody makes an appearance, but here it is much more obvious, and the style and melody much more closely match those of the original cartoon.

The *Steamboat Willie* segments, which occur near the beginning of the game during the Gremlin Village/It's a Small World section, include as their elements the boat, Pete, a few cranes, a cow, a goat or two, and visible musical notes.[21] Again, the color scheme matches the original 1928 cartoon, with black-and-white characters (with the exception of Mickey) and a setting in glorious grayscale. The music takes segments from the beginning of the cartoon, including "Steamboat Bill" (composed by Arthur Collins) on the clarinet and flute rather than whistled by Mickey in the original cartoon (as well as in producer/distributor segments used in numerous Disney projects in recent years).[22] Its strong association with Disney as a whole and Mickey specifically immediately places the player in that world (despite the song's existence prior to the film).

Perhaps the music that most strictly adheres to the original appears in the three 2D segments based on "The Sorcerer's Apprentice" from *Fantasia* (1940). These occur in the last portion of the storyline, when Mickey moves from tower to tower within Dark Beauty Castle. As is typical in these 2D platforms, elements of the original cartoon appear throughout; here those include magic brooms, barrels, and lots and lots of water. (See figure 14.3.) The music, though, doesn't just contain elements of "The Sorcerer's Apprentice"; it basically *is* "The Sorcerer's Apprentice." No other music makes an appearance, and the orchestration generally matches that of the original.[23] This section may be the closest to an actual Disney cartoon that the character comes to in the entire action portion of the game.

Not all of the 2D sequences match the original music and cartoon in the same way that these do, however. In the case of the Oswald cartoons that Mickey traverses, there was no original music to begin with, so that would not be possible. Take, for instance, *Oh What a Knight* (1928). The composer chooses to emulate an old theater organ, producing a theme similar to what one might have heard in movie theaters during the silent era. (It even includes bits of recognizable tunes—in this case, snippets of Richard Wagner's *Die Meistersinger*—just as organists of the time might have done.)[24] Of course, the music

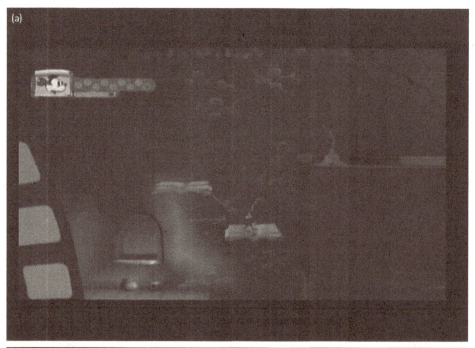

FIGURE 14.3. Screenshots of the "Sorcerer's Apprentice" transition cartoon.

here does not attempt to line up with the action in the way that actual cartoons might have, but since the action is random based on the player's action, this is not surprising.

Another sequence in which the two do not match is from Mickey's *Jungle Rhythm* (1929). As with the Oswald and other 2D portions, the visual elements and overall style conform to the original cartoon. Here Dooley refrains from using the original music at all, perhaps because it used a hodgepodge of light classics more in line with the Silly Symphonies. Instead, he bases his music on a particularly anachronistic melody: "Jolly Holiday" from *Mary Poppins* (1964). As with the Main Street and Tomorrow City settings, the composer relies on inference to connect the visuals and the music, expecting the player to relate the two through the similarities of what is on the screen in each film—in particular, the use of various animals in a fantasy environment. The combination of this implication and the changes in style and orchestration of the original melody allows the music to still feel true to the cartoon despite the anachronism.

So far, I have examined both the 3D and 2D action scenes—in other words, the playable portion of the game. However, as with most noncasual modern video games, *Epic Mickey* also uses cutscenes—small videos used to explain ideas or push along the story. Since these do not involve the player, the music may be synchronized closely to the action. Most of the cutscenes within the storyline are not as elaborate as the introduction, which lasts for more than four minutes and is shot in a 3D, cinematic style; in fact, other than the epilogue, all the other cutscenes are presented in a different style entirely. Spector uses two templates for these: the first is basically an extension of whatever setting Mickey is currently in and uses the same music as that setting; the second (also viewable as "extra content") is really designed more to act like stand-alone movies in the style of former Disney artist Mary Blair.[25] It is this style that I would like to examine in more detail by looking briefly at three examples: Mickey learning about the Blotling villains, Mickey learning about Oswald, and Mickey meeting Horace Horsecollar.[26]

Near the beginning of the game, Gus the Gremlin, Mickey's companion throughout, teaches Mickey about the Blotlings in a style reminiscent of the Disney educational cartoons of the 1970s—complete with chalkboard.[27] Gus appears wearing a mortarboard (complete with tassel) and carrying a pointer like an old-fashioned schoolteacher. As he explains how to fight the enemies, the characters appear (now as chalk sketches) on the chalkboard. (See figure 14.4.) Although there is only a little mickey-mousing, the accompanying music—a lively tune that weaves bits of the title theme and variations thereof—coordinates well with the action and helps portray the general idea, particularly through its use of orchestration and a mix of major-key (for examples of good results) and minor-key (for examples of bad results) melodic motives.

Later, when Mickey has just about reached the top of Mickeyjunk Mountain, he learns more about Oswald the Lucky Rabbit, who was a silent-film cartoon star for Disney before Mickey came onto the scene. The music in the background for this scene is Oswald's theme; that and Mickey's theme are the two pieces of music that Spector specifically asked Dooley to write. Each theme is designed to represent the nature of the respective character and appears in various places within the game. Mickey's theme, described by the composer as "something that can be fanfarish [sic], but also simple," is meant to show

FIGURE 14.4. Screenshot of Gus the Gremlin explaining how to fight in the Nintendo Wii version of *Epic Mickey*.

the character as the protagonist and ultimately the hero of the story.[28] Oswald's theme is a bit trickier, as the player does not know Oswald's intentions or story until later in the game. In addition, the original Oswald shorts were during the "silent" era and (as previously mentioned) did not have precomposed scores. Thus, Dooley notes that he chose to make it "more of the time period in which he was created."[29] In essence, this results in an uptempo, slightly jazzy melody with light syncopation to represent both the happy-go-lucky nature of Oswald in his films and the general attitude of the Roaring '20s. Here the music stays bright and cheery until Gus explains about the end of Oswald's career and the Thinner Disaster (i.e., what happened in the opening cutscene), at which point the tessitura of the music becomes lower, with the melody emphasizing half steps and a minor key to illustrate the textural change.

A different scene, shown once Mickey reaches Mean Street, occurs when he first meets Horace Horsecollar, who was a regular in Mickey Mouse cartoons during the 1930s. In *Epic Mickey*, Horace has a job as a not particularly good detective. Horace is eager to have Mickey remember him, though unfortunately, Mickey has no idea who he is—after all, he is a forgotten character.[30] Again, the music reflects the action, but in this case, extra meaning may be layered on top of it. It starts with a stereotypical "detective noir" sound (complete with muted trumpet chord) when Mickey and Gus first see Horace, both commenting on his job and his surroundings in general. Once he starts talking about his past, however, the music becomes an upbeat, old-fashioned dance, even including a little tap-dancing rhythm. Once Mickey admits not remembering Horace, though, the noir music returns, again reflecting on the reality of his situation: nobody else remembers him, either, and so he's stuck in Wasteland.

Now that we've examined some of the music and visual settings in *Epic Mickey*, what does this mean in terms of the atypically complex image of Mickey Mouse, Disneyland, and Disney in general that this game presents? Mickey, particularly in his 1930s design, harks back to the more mischievous creature that he was in cartoons such as *Steamboat Willie*, *Jungle Rhythm*, and *Fantasia*—all of which are vehicles in this game. Although the music is only somewhat supportive of this, the storyline of the game as well as the paint-and-thinner game dynamics confirm the change: Mickey is a living cartoon character, with an actual heart to boot.[31]

While Mickey gains more of a personality, and thus a more positive (though not always pleasant) spin, Disneyland's alter image presents a considerably less attractive view. Much of the music for the settings sounds as if it wants to suggest a pleasant environment but (purposely) fails miserably to do so. The visuals portray a dirtier, sloppier version of the park overall. Both the musical and visual details are similar enough to the original that the player can make the connection, but they are off-kilter enough that even the casual observer notices the problem. In other words, although this alternative Disneyland tries to be the happiest place on earth, it does not succeed—a view that, until relatively recently, the Disney corporation would not allow.

The actual Disney cartoons, however, are still loved and honored throughout this game. The cartoon elements in the 2D settings are presented in the original style without caricature or exaggeration. Musical elements in these same portions are also generally closer to the original, and those for which the original music was not used still have music that feels true to the cartoon. Even the cutscenes are designed as a sort of tribute to a well-loved former Disney artist.

Thus, the overall impression of Disney as seen through the looking glass of this video game is a mixed one. The main characters of Mickey and Oswald have their foibles, and the residents of Wasteland do the best they can with what they have, just as happens in the real world. Only in the fantasy-within-a-fantasy—the classic cartoons—does the world seem perfect.

The Power of Song: *Epic Mickey 2*

While *Epic Mickey* is a musical in that it's filled with music that relates not only to the setting but also to the characters and their nature (especially that of Mickey), it's not the traditional type of "characters breaking into song without warning" musical that is the hallmark of so many Disney musicals. This is in part because the only character who actually speaks is Yen Sid, the narrator, at the beginning and end of the game. All of the other characters get by with squeaks, sighs, and other similar utterances—what many gamers call "mumbles" or "mumble mode."[32] The animation and the accompanying closed captions do all of the heavy lifting. This type of structure creates smaller file sizes and a less region-specific approach, but it makes singing a challenge.

All of this changes in *Epic Mickey 2: The Power of Two*. The "forgotten" characters (re)introduced in the first game are now familiar faces but with fresh new voices for all of the characters. Numerous voice actors (including some who are well known in the voice-acting community, such as Frank Welker, Jim Cummings, and Tress MacNeille) bring those voices to life, and the spoken word is everywhere, both in cutscenes and during gameplay.

In addition, the focus of the game is different. Whereas the first *Epic Mickey* looks to Disneyland specifically, the second considers Disney as a whole. Music for the areas from the original game match its predecessor, but music for the new areas not seen in the original game for the most part don't obviously look to their Disneyland counterparts for musical inspiration in the same way. In fact, numerous areas of the game don't have visible counterparts at all.[33] Instead, the focus is on singing, which, for Spector, is part of what makes Disney animation Disney animation: "They're not interactive—in THIS game—but using songs as storytelling tools seemed necessary for a game that claims to honor Disney's creative history."[34] Dooley (composer for this game as well, in conjunction with lyricist Mike Himelstein) agrees, stating, "The storytelling actually happens in the songs, as it does in any other traditional movie-style musicals that Disney has a long history of."[35] In fact, Spector, Dooley, and Himelstein all go so far as to call this game a musical.[36]

While there is a considerable amount of singing, interestingly, almost all of it comes from one character: the Mad Doctor (or Doc for short).[37] Only twice do other characters sing, and both of these times are at the instigation of the Doc. (See table 14.2 for a list of songs/sung text.) Interestingly, the Doc's primary mode of communication is singing for almost all of the game, until the player gets near the climax. To my knowledge, there is no explanation on record for why Doc is almost exclusively *the* singer for the game,

Table 14.2. Sung sections in *Epic Mickey 2*.

Song Number	First Words	Graphic Style
1	Friends, friends, friends, I stand before you a changed man	3D
2	Mickey, you don't trust me	Mary Blair
3	Oswald, I'm on your frequency	3D
4	Oswald, Mickey, come to my lab	3D/In-game
5	It's so sad, so sad to say the least	Mary Blair
6	Hello, my friends, I have bad news	In-game
7	Prescott, dear Prescott	Mary Blair
8	Welcome, boys and girls, to the wonderful world of evil	In-game
9	Testing, testing. Dear Diary	Mary Blair/pop-up book
10	One more step	Mary Blair
11	What a gift	3D

and for so much of it. I do, however, have a few theories as to why this might be the case in terms of the storyline.[38] The Mad Doctor, as he notes in one of his songs, chose to become at least partially animatronic when working with the Blot in the first *Epic Mickey* game, and now those parts are breaking down. He desperately wants to be a toon again, which, in his mind, means Disney, which means Broadway-style songs. He sings in order to convince everyone around him (and himself) that he can and should be a part of the animation world again—not just a forgotten character but a character, period. By singing, he is playing the part that he believes a cartoon should play and working to get others to do the same. Indeed, the staging of several of his songs works to emphasize the stage, as if he were playing a part. For instance, at the end of the song where he sings about wanting to be a toon (song 5 in table 14.2), he reaches up to the sky in a way reminiscent of Tim Robbins–directed films, and the player sees that the ground underneath him is shaped like a semicircular stage, with flowers being thrown to him as if to indicate the end of a performance. (See figure 14.5.) Earlier, when first seeing Mickey, he sings about the danger in Wasteland (with an emphasis in B-flat minor to stress his concern) so convincingly that Oswald asks if he's OK. The music and the action stop, and the Doc gestures to Oswald, as if to say that he will answer only if Oswald joins him by singing his question (and thus behaving as a cartoon should). Finally, Oswald acquiesces, and the Doc claps and continues on with his song.

This is not to say that the Mad Doctor is a hero because he is singing, or even that he's trying to show that he's good rather than evil. As evidenced by other chapters in

FIGURE 14.5. Screenshot of the Mad Doctor singing about wanting to be a toon.

this volume, there's a lot of great music for Disney villains. But as Dooley indicates in a short promotional video for the game, the songs help indicate early on both that the Doc is trying to convince other Wasteland citizens of his newfound goodness *and* that he's actually evil to the player.[39] In the first song, for instance, the composer notes the use of modal mix combined with both sliding half steps down to emphasize the minor key ("Friends, friends, friends ...") and half steps up to emphasize the major key ("Help me, help you ...") as part of what does this, playing into the musical trope of minor for evil and major for good. We also hear muted horns as he sings about trouble, a timbral connection to the original game during which such sounds indicated both trouble and evil (and thus foreshadowing the Doc's true nature).

As the plot moves forward to the point where the Mad Doctor has garnered several others to his side but his motives are questionable, the players hear the one true ensemble piece. It seems that Prescott, another Gremlin, was the villain, and Mickey and Oswald are about to question him about his motives, when suddenly, the Doc, Daisy Duck (who is a TV reporter in the game), and Small Pete (who is the sheriff) appear. A Beetleworx camera hypnotizes Prescott before he can speak. The Doc immediately takes over, theatrically asking Prescott through song why he turned to evil and did all of these horrible things. Prescott, in his response, sings primarily on two single pitches, as if he has been programmed and cannot express his own emotion. Pete, for his part, seems to be happy to be working with the Doc and being a part of his plans, and so he takes part in the singing as well. Even Daisy sings her question to the Doc, although both she and Prescott end on the dominant rather than the tonic, as if to simply be a part of the Mad Doctor's charismatic force. While the reason for others joining is not completely clear, I suggest that since the player is at the point in the plot where they are made to think that Oswald is losing his grasp on Wasteland, having others sing instead of speaking further indicates the separation between him and his constituents. He continues to sing even when he obviously has evil intentions. For example, as Mickey and Oswald go through a projector on their way to the Mad Doctor's attic, they travel not through a normal cartoon but through a junkyard filled with mechanical trash and a giant Mad Doctor automaton. Appropriately, the music does not stem from a cartoon but is instead the Doc singing "The Wonderful World of Evil" (a play on "The Wonderful World of Disney"), in which he clearly states that he wants to take revenge on Wasteland and, in the process, become a toon again. He expands on this and explains it blatantly to Mickey and Oswald when they find his diary, a combination recording and pop-up book that explains in song and pictures what he has done, his reasoning behind it, and what will happen now, thus presenting his villainous monologue in literal musical pictures.

At the climax of the game, however, the Mad Doctor's modus operandi changes. In the scene just before the game's final boss battle, the Doc gives up any pretense of being good in front of Mickey and Oswald. He starts to sing (complete with theatrical hand movements): "One step more and your friends are ..." And then he speaks: "... history." His further exposition continues to be spoken, and his movements are considerably less theatrical. No longer is he trying to play the part of a good cartoon (or any cartoon, for that matter) in a Disney animated musical. Perhaps the animatronics in him have won out over the toon, as (at least in the Mad Doctor's mind) animatronics don't sing; only toons do. Thus, when Mickey wins the final battle against him using paint, it makes the Doc a toon again, not only convincing him that this is the way heroes behave but also leading to his singing again.[40] After all, for the Mad Doctor, he is alive and a toon, and thus has his happy ending, as all good characters in Disney musicals should.

Conclusion

While the third part of Spector's planned *Epic Mickey* trilogy (which promised to have a particularly heavy musical presence) was never completed, the first two nevertheless form a unit to comment musically on Disneyland and the Disney musical. Many Americans and Disney fans around the world would like to see the Disney corporation as a shining example of conservative but mainstream American values and in perfect control of their environment. *Epic Mickey* and *Epic Mickey 2*, however, intimate that this is not always the case. *Epic Mickey* presents Wasteland as a dystopian version of Disneyland not only visually but musically as well. In *Epic Mickey 2*, the Mad Doctor wants so much to be a toon again that he does everything in his power to become so—including breaking into song, just as any princess (and many a villain) in a classic Disney musical animated film would. While both games pay homage to their Disney roots and heritage (and their associated values), that spotless image is no longer quite as clean and thus perhaps portrays the world a little bit more realistically.

Notes

1. Mike Snider, "Mickey Fan Lays Waste to Magic Kingdom; Designer Warren Spector Deconstructs Disney for Game," *USA Today*, November 23, 2010, 2D. Oswald the Lucky Rabbit was a star for Disney before Mickey Mouse was created; in fact, Mickey was created to replace Oswald once Disney lost the rights to Oswald.
2. Disney has since brought back many of these characters, both in its shows and as greetable characters in Disneyland. In fact, Oswald and his girlfriend Ortensia (a cat) were the featured characters for Disney California Adventure's Lunar New Year Festival in 2023.
3. Spector has indicated that his original plan was to make an *Epic Mickey* trilogy, with the final entry covering areas outside of Wasteland and having even more singing. According to industry reports, however, this seems unlikely to materialize, as the rights are still owned by the now-defunct software company Junction Point. See Mitch Vogel, "Warren Spector Reminisces about the Development of the Epic Mickey Series," Nintendo Life, May 3, 2015, https://www.nintendolife.com/news/2015/05/warren_spector_reminisces_about_the_development_of_the_epic_mickey_series; Emily Gera, "'Epic Mickey 2' Is Just the First Step in Warren Spector's Foray into Musical Games," Polygon, August 17, 2012, https://www.polygon.com/gaming/2012/8/17/3249664/epic-mickey-2-is-just-the-first-step-in-warren-spectors-foray-into.

4. To note a few examples: For employees (known as "cast members") at the Disney theme parks in the United States, this was literally true, in that they were not allowed to have facial hair for most of the parks' existence; mustaches were not allowed until 2000, and beards were banned until 2012. The television show *Walt Disney's Disneyland* and its successors (as well as the *Mickey Mouse Club*) worked not only to make money for the company and keep it in the public eye but also to purposefully connect Disney with what Walt considered to be typical (white) Middle American values. Many critics and scholars have described in some detail Disney's philosophy of making the studio's work in that vein.
5. See Frank Pallotta, "Disney Park Employees Have a New Dress Code," CNN, April 15, 2021, https://www.cnn.com/2021/04/15/media/disney-parks-diversity-inclusion/index.html; Jim Korkis, "Walt Disney World Chronicles: The Disney Look," AllEars, January 5, 2016, https://allears.net/walt-disney-world-chronicles-the-disney-look/.
6. See Lisa Scoggin, "The Foreign and the Other in the Music of Mulan (1998)," *American Music* 39, no. 2 (Summer 2021): 196–211.
7. See, for example, *Enchanted*, *Tangled*, and *Phineas and Ferb*. For more on the changes in recent Disney works, see Eve Benhamou's chapter in this volume. For more information on postmodernism in animation (as well as music in animation specifically), see Lisa Scoggin, *The Music of Animaniacs: Postmodern Nostalgia in a Cartoon World* (Hillsdale, NY: Pendragon, 2016), especially chapter 2.
8. In case there was any doubt, the game is indeed sanctioned by Disney; the company thought it might rejuvenate the character of Mickey Mouse and bring in more merchandise sales, especially in the United States. Brooks Barnes, "Taking a Risk with an Icon, Disney Gives Mickey an Attitude," *International Herald Tribune*, November 6, 2009, Finance, 1.
9. Seth Schiesel, "Mickey Moves to Another Screen," *New York Times*, December 14, 2010, C1.
10. Warren Spector, the primary force behind the game, has noted that he wanted to use the slightly naughtier version of Mickey that people see in the early sound shorts rather than the tamer version of Mickey seen later. See Chris Morris, "Mouse Morph," *Variety*, November 3, 2009, News, 1.
11. "*Epic Mickey*'s Warren Spector: 'Adults Are the Ones Who Have Blinders On," IGN, October 9, 2010, https://web.archive.org/web/20101212204705/http://wii.ign.com/articles/112/1126943p1.html. Earlier versions of the game also included visual changes in the character where Mickey would become more ratlike and thus uglier (à la the video game *Fable*) but were discarded by the final product. Austin Grossman with Warren Spector, *The Art of Disney Epic Mickey* (New York: Disney Editions, 2011), 22. (These changes were discarded late enough that they were in press releases as late as 2009; see, for example, Barnes, "Taking a Risk.") For more on the role of Mickey as "arbiter" in this game, see Andrew Powell, "What Is Real? Diegetic Spaces in *Epic Mickey*," in *The Intersection of Animation, Video Games, and Music: Making Movement Sing*, ed. Lisa Scoggin and Dana Plank (New York: Routledge, 2023), 3–16.
12. Author interview with Jim Dooley, March 24, 2012.
13. Toontown was extensively renovated in Disneyland starting in March 2022 and reopened in March 2023, with some changes to the overall layout and structure. See Kelsey Lynch, "Mickey's Toontown at Disneyland Park to Be Reimagined with New Experiences, More Play and Interactivity for Young Families in 2023," Disney Parks Blog, November 15, 2021, https://disneyparks.disney.go.com/blog/2021/11/mickeys-toontown-at-disneyland-park-to-be-reimagined-with-new-experiences-and-more-play-and-interactivity-for-young-families-in-2023/. Other rides in the park (e.g., the Carousel of Progress in Disneyland) have also been modified or closed since then.

14. A platformer is an action game in which the main character runs, jumps, and often (though not always) shoots their way through levels in order to progress. Ostensibly, they were so named because of the need to jump from platform to platform. Examples include *Donkey Kong*, *Super Mario Bros.*, and (more recently) *Cuphead*.
15. Grossman, *The Art of Epic Mickey*, 143–144.
16. While fairly precise correlation between the visuals and sounds/music can happen in video-game play, I maintain that the functionality of the game version of mickey-mousing—what Tim Summers calls "dynamizing play" (Tim Summers, *Understanding Video Game Music* [Cambridge: Cambridge University Press, 2016], 199)—is different from the animated version, as one is informed by player actions, while the other is bound up entirely with the creators. (For more on the connections and differences between film music and video-game music, Summers's book is an excellent resource, particularly chapter 6, "Hollywood Film Music and Game Music.") Note that the music is also dependent on the action here. For example, whenever the enemy Blotlings are within a certain range, the music changes to a general enemy music that overrides the background music until the enemies are dealt with in some fashion.
17. Instruments listed in this chapter are approximations, as most of the music is synthesized using sampled instruments.
18. Descriptions of the music from Disneyland are based on recordings made during visits to the park by the author February 29–March 2, 2012, and official Disney recordings, particularly *Disneyland Resort: Official Album* (Walt Disney Records, 2008), which was released during the game's production. Descriptions of the rides are based on visits to the park by the author in 2012, on February 26, 2022, and on January 7, 2023, as well as the Yesterland website (Werner Weiss, "Yesterland," https://www.yesterland.com/) and Jeff Kurtti, *Disneyland: From Once upon a Time to Happily Ever After* (New York: Disney Editions, 2010).
19. Interestingly, the "Bunny Children" in this level—nonplayer characters here who are presumably Oswald's kids—watch televisions that are showing *Steamboat Willie*, complete with the music from that film.
20. Ride listings are current as of January 2023.
21. Not all theaters were wired for sound at the initial release of *Steamboat Willie*, so Disney (and other animation studios around the same time that were creating sound cartoons) continued to include visual demarcations of sound, including musical notes and lines around the mouth for speech or yelling.
22. The segment shows a sketch of Mickey as Steamboat Willie whistling "Steamboat Bill," thus suggesting historical and nostalgic connections for the associated Disney creation. Nostalgia and a sense of history have been a strong part of the Disney product, especially in recent years (as shown by this and the various anniversary celebrations, among other things).
23. Dooley noted in an interview with the author (March 24, 2012) that "The Sorcerer's Apprentice" is the only precomposed music in *Epic Mickey* (despite the use of other themes that are woven into other works).
24. For more on the music that typically accompanied silent cartoons, see Edith Lang and George West, "Animated Cartoons and Slap-Stick Comedy," in *The Cartoon Music Book*, ed. Daniel Goldmark and Yuval Taylor (Chicago: A Capella, 2002), 17–19; originally published in *Musical Accompaniment of Moving Pictures: A Practical Manual for Pianists and Organists* (Boston: Boston Music Company, 1920). In the DVD collection *Walt Disney*

Treasures: The Adventures of Oswald the Lucky Rabbit (Walt Disney Home Entertainment, 2007), newly composed music by Robert Israel uses snippets of *Meistersinger*, too, though not quite in the same way (and also on theater organ).

25. Grossman, *The Art of Epic Mickey*, 66. Mary Blair is perhaps best known for her work on the art design in the It's a Small World ride.
26. The Blotlings are villains scattered throughout *Epic Mickey* that are essentially minions of the Blot, the primary villain of the game (though they can be turned to Mickey's side).
27. Gus the Gremlin is one of the many gremlins in both *Epic Mickey* and its sequel. They specialize in handling all things mechanical. Disney's gremlins stem from an abandoned project with Roald Dahl, and as such, they qualify as forgotten characters. For more details, see Reed Milnes, "'The Gremlins' and a Tale of Two Storytellers," Walt Disney Family Museum, August 19, 2011, https://www.waltdisney.org/blog/gremlins-and-tale-two-storytellers.
28. Interview with the author, March 24, 2012.
29. Ibid.
30. Interestingly, several of the "forgotten" characters here may now be seen in some of the more nostalgic works of Disney over the past ten years as of this writing, as some of them have been brought back in newer Disney projects such as the short *Get a Horse!* (2013) or the Walt Disney World/Disneyland ride Mickey & Minnie's Runaway Railway.
31. Note that neither the games *Epic Mickey* and *Epic Mickey 2* themselves nor any of the materials surrounding the games that the author has encountered as of this writing consider the historical baggage of Mickey Mouse concerning minstrelsy, race, class, or money (other than in-game money and collectibles). That the game does not address this, however, should not be surprising, given the dearth of similar considerations in most other games based on older cartoons (e.g., *Kingdom Hearts* and *Cuphead*). For more on minstrelsy and animation, see especially Nicolas Sammond, *Birth of an Industry: Blackface Minstrelsy and the Rise of American Animation* (Durham, NC: Duke University Press, 2015). For more on how race may play a role (inadvertently or not) in such video games (particularly *Cuphead*) and their music, see Lisa Scoggin, "The Pseudo-1930s World of *Cuphead*," in *The Intersection of Animation, Video Games, and Music: Making Movement Sing*, ed. Lisa Scoggin and Dana Plank (New York: Routledge, 2023), 62–75.
32. For a description of how mumbles and mumble mode work in *Lego Star Wars: The Skywalker Saga*, see George Foster, "*Lego Star Wars* Fans Are Split on *The Skywalker Saga*'s Mumble Mode," The Gamer, January 23, 2022, https://www.thegamer.com/lego-star-wars-mumble-mode/.
33. Some of the spaces (such as the area under Mean Street) may be considered as parallel to the inner workings behind the scenes of Disneyland, while others (such as Disney Gulch) may be considered as parallel to sections of Disney California Adventure. Unlike the first game, though, the music in these does not relate to the actual park.
34. Andy Green, "Warren Spector Hints at Epic Mickey 3," Nintendo Life, December 16, 2012, https://www.nintendolife.com/news/2012/12/warren_spector_hints_at_epic_mickey_3. As indicated by this article, Spector was expecting to create *Epic Mickey 3*, in which there would be even more singing, but *Epic Mickey 2* sold poorly, and Spector's studio Junction Point closed a few months after the game's release. For more details, see Michael McWhertor, "Epic Mickey Developer Junction Point Closes (Update)," Polygon, January 29, 2013, https://www.polygon.com/2013/1/29/3925960/disney-epic-mickey-developer-junction-point-closes.

35. Jordyn Taylor, "How Video Game 'Disney Epic Mickey 2: The Power of 2' Is Like a Musical," *Backstage*, August 16, 2019, https://www.backstage.com/magazine/article/video-game-disney-epic-mickey-power-like-musical-50658/.
36. "*Epic Mickey 2: The Power of Music* Trailer," Gameplanet, https://www.youtube.com/watch?v=MEoZZwf-6CY. They claim that this is the first musical video game, though that has not been verified by the author. Songs in a role-playing game are generally limited to cutscenes or are used as background music, however, because of the player's agency.
37. The Mad Doctor is not only a forgotten Disney character but also one of the villains in *Epic Mickey* and the primary villain in *Epic Mickey 2* (though this is not apparent at the beginning of the latter).
38. There is no need technically for the game to focus on the Doc for singing. Spoken parts do not take up more disc space. Several of the voice actors in the game have shown off their singing talents elsewhere (e.g., MacNeille and Welker in *Animaniacs*), so the voice talent was not an issue. (See Scoggin, *The Music of Animaniacs*, for details.) It could have been a time issue, either for writing songs or for recording them, or a money issue (though money did not seem to be a strong factor in production values), but that is not certain. In addition, matching artwork style to the music does not work, as the artwork style changes regularly between the 3D sections and the Mary Blair–style sections.
39. "*Epic Mickey 2: The Power of Music* Trailer."
40. Interestingly, when Mickey defeats him using paint thinner, the Doc is destroyed, and no such moral is stated.

Bibliography

Barnes, Brooks. "Taking a Risk with an Icon, Disney Gives Mickey an Attitude." *International Herald Tribune*, November 6, 2009, Finance, 1.

Disneyland Resort: Official Album. Walt Disney Records, 2008.

"*Epic Mickey*'s Warren Spector: 'Adults Are the Ones Who Have Blinders On.'" IGN, October 9, 2010. https://www.ign.com/articles/2010/10/10/epic-mickeys-warren-spector-adults-are-the-ones-who-have-the-blinders-on.

"*Epic Mickey 2: The Power of Music* Trailer." Gameplanet. https://www.youtube.com/watch?v=MEoZZwf-6CY.

Foster, George. "*Lego Star Wars* Fans Are Split on *The Skywalker Saga*'s Mumble Mode." *The Gamer*, January 23, 2022. https://www.thegamer.com/lego-star-wars-mumble-mode/.

Gera, Emily. "'Epic Mickey 2' Is Just the First Step in Warren Spector's Foray into Musical Games." Polygon, August 17, 2012. https://www.polygon.com/gaming/2012/8/17/3249664/epic-mickey-2-is-just-the-first-step-in-warren-spectors-foray-into.

Green, Andy. "Warren Spector Hints at Epic Mickey 3." Nintendo Life, December 16, 2012. https://www.nintendolife.com/news/2012/12/warren_spector_hints_at_epic_mickey_3.

Grossman, Austin, with Warren Spector. *The Art of Disney Epic Mickey*. New York: Disney Editions, 2011.

Korkis, Jim. "Walt Disney World Chronicles: The Disney Look." AllEars, January 5, 2016. https://allears.net/walt-disney-world-chronicles-the-disney-look/.

Kurtti, Jeff. *Disneyland: From Once upon a Time to Happily Ever After*. New York: Disney Editions, 2010.

Lang, Edith, and George West. "Animated Cartoons and Slap-Stick Comedy." In *The Cartoon Music* Book, edited by Daniel Goldmark and Yuval Taylor, 17–19. Chicago: A Capella, 2002. Originally published in *Musical Accompaniment of Moving Pictures: A Practical Manual for Pianists and Organists*. Boston: Boston Music Company, 1920.

Lynch, Kelsey. "Mickey's Toontown at Disneyland Park to Be Reimagined with New Experiences, More Play and Interactivity for Young Families in 2023." Disney Parks Blog, November 15, 2021. https://disneyparks.disney.go.com/blog/2021/11/mickeys-toontown-at-disneyland-park-to-be-reimagined-with-new-experiences-and-more-play-and-interactivity-for-young-families-in-2023/.

McWhertor, Michael. "Epic Mickey Developer Junction Point Closes (Update)." Polygon, January 29, 2013. https://www.polygon.com/2013/1/29/3925960/disney-epic-mickey-developer-junction-point-closes.

Milnes, Reed. "'The Gremlins' and a Tale of Two Storytellers." Walt Disney Family Museum, August 19, 2011. https://www.waltdisney.org/blog/gremlins-and-tale-two-storytellers.

Morris, Chris. "Mouse Morph." *Variety*, November 3, 2009, News, 1.

Pallotta, Frank. "Disney Park Employees Have a New Dress Code." CNN, April 15, 2021. https://www.cnn.com/2021/04/15/media/disney-parks-diversity-inclusion/index.html.

Powell, Andrew. "What Is Real? Diegetic Spaces in *Epic Mickey*." In *The Intersection of Animation, Video Games, and Music: Making Movement Sing*, edited by Lisa Scoggin and Dana Plank, 3–16. New York: Routledge, 2023.

Sammond, Nicolas. *Birth of an Industry: Blackface Minstrelsy and the Rise of American Animation*. Durham, NC: Duke University Press, 2015.

Schiesel, Seth. "Mickey Moves to Another Screen." *New York Times*, December 14, 2010, C1.

Scoggin, Lisa. "The Foreign and the Other in the Music of *Mulan* (1998)." *American Music* 39, no. 2 (Summer 2021): 196–211.

Scoggin, Lisa. *The Music of Animaniacs: Postmodern Nostalgia in a Cartoon World*. Hillsdale, NY: Pendragon, 2016.

Scoggin, Lisa. "The Pseudo-1930s World of *Cuphead*." In *The Intersection of Animation, Video Games, and Music: Making Movement Sing*, edited by Lisa Scoggin and Dana Plank, 62–75. New York: Routledge, 2023.

Snider, Mike. "Mickey Fan Lays Waste to Magic Kingdom; Designer Warren Spector Deconstructs Disney for Game." *USA Today*, November 23, 2010, 2D.

Summers, Tim. *Understanding Video Game Music*. Cambridge: Cambridge University Press, 2016.

Taylor, Jordyn. "How Video Game 'Disney Epic Mickey 2: The Power of 2' Is Like a Musical." *Backstage*, August 16, 2019. https://www.backstage.com/magazine/article/video-game-disney-epic-mickey-power-like-musical-50658/.

Vogel, Mitch Vogel. "Warren Spector Reminisces about the Development of the Epic Mickey Series." Nintendo Life, May 3, 2015. https://www.nintendolife.com/news/2015/05/warren_spector_reminisces_about_the_development_of_the_epic_mickey_series.

Walt Disney Treasures: The Adventures of Oswald the Lucky Rabbit. Walt Disney Home Entertainment, 2007.

Weiss, Werner. "Yesterland." https://www.yesterland.com/.

CHAPTER 15

THE *JUNGLE BOOK* VULTURES AND GENERATIONAL LISTENING

ELIZABETH RANDELL UPTON

WALT Disney's *The Jungle Book*, released in 1967, features several enduringly popular characters: lovable Baloo the bear, voiced by comic and bandleader Phil Harris; orangutan King Louis, the "swinging" king of the monkeys, voiced by jazz bandleader and entertainer Louis Prima; and the silkily menacing Shere Khan the tiger, voiced by film actor George Sanders, whose threat to kill Mowgli, the "man cub" raised by wolves, sets the film's plot in motion. Bagheera the panther, voiced by British actor Sebastian Cabot, volunteers to take the reluctant Mowgli to a nearby Man Village, and their adventures as they journey through the jungle make up the bulk of the film.

One episode of the film features animal characters who are far less well remembered and beloved than the others. After escaping from King Louis, Bagheera and Baloo try to convince Mowgli that he will never be safe living in the jungle. Mowgli, feeling betrayed by Baloo, whom he calls Papa Bear, runs away from his animal guardians. Eventually, a dejected Mowgli comes across a quartet of vultures in a bleak and desolate landscape, a setting that can be seen as reflecting Mowgli's own mood. The vultures tell Mowgli that even if he feels rejected and friendless, *they* will be his friends, "to the bitter end" (a dark joke about carrion eaters that went right over my head as a child); they promise, in lush barbershop harmonies, to keep Mowgli "safe in the jungle forever more," because "that's what friends are for."[1]

The vultures are peculiar, in that their appearance does not match the style of the song they sing. Three of the four vultures have Beatles-esque "mop-top" haircuts à la 1963–1964 (the fourth Vulture, more typically vulture-like, appears bald), and while the four speak with a variety of British accents, one of them does sound distinctly Liverpudlian. But instead of singing Beatles-like rock-and-roll music or music in some other 1960s pop style, they perform as a barbershop quartet, a genre of American music dating back to the early 1900s. This makes no sense: why include a sight gag of characters who look like the meteoric hit Beatles for a singing quartet but then not gesture toward their own musical style?

Urban legends claiming that the Beatles were actually asked to perform the vultures' vocals seem to date back to an interview with composer Richard M. Sherman, published in the British newspaper *The Telegraph* in 2016.[2] In the most recently published book on *The Jungle Book*, animator Andreas Deja implies that any discussion of the Beatles' participation came from the Disney side, without stating whether or not the band or its manager, Brian Epstein, was approached: "During the production of the film, Beatlemania was in full swing. Walt originally considered having the Beatles—or a Beatles-like group—voice the vultures and perform songs for *The Jungle Book*, but the idea was ultimately abandoned. Milt Kahl, Eric Larson, and John Lounsbery worked on the animation of the vultures, who retained their original Beatles-inspired mop-top design and vocal accents."[3]

From a twenty-first-century perspective, the decision to have the Beatles-esque vultures sing as a barbershop quartet seems odd, as nowadays barbershop singing is not particularly associated with the 1960s. Reconstructing the likely sequence of creative decisions involving the vultures' look and the style of their song shows how the mismatch came to be, including elements such as what Walt Disney and his creative team knew about the Beatles around 1964, what they understood rock and roll to be, and how they judged the lasting centrality of older styles of American popular music, based on their own experiences. Ultimately, this clash of styles must not have seemed to be a problem to the creative team.

The people in charge of creating *The Jungle Book*—the story men,[4] director, directing animators, and songwriters—were born over a span of almost thirty years from the very beginning of the twentieth century, but they break into two distinct cohorts. The first group is headed by Walt Disney himself, born in 1901, with the three credited story men just five to eight years younger, born between 1906 and 1909.[5] Also born in 1909 was the director, Woolie Reitherman (1909–1985) and one of the four directing animators, Milt Kahl (1909–1987). The three other directing animators, John Lounsbery, Frank Thomas, and Ollie Johnston, were born in 1911 and 1912, ten and eleven years younger than Walt Disney.[6] Bill Peet (1915–2002), whose initial story development for the film would be rejected by Disney, was the youngest of this group of top creatives. This means that during the development of the film, Disney and the story men were in their early sixties, and the director and directing animators were in their fifties.

The songwriters, brothers Robert B. Sherman (1925–2012) and Richard M. Sherman (1928–2024), were in their thirties, a full generation younger than Disney, and their father, Al Sherman (1897–1973), a successful Tin Pan Alley songwriter in the 1920s and 1930s, was close to Walt Disney in age.[7] But their perspectives on American popular song were not limited to the music of their own lifetimes. As songwriters, the Sherman brothers were stylistic chameleons, unusually talented at writing songs in a wide variety of styles.[8] By the time the Shermans were added to the *Jungle Book* team, they had written songs for eight Disney films, set in a variety of historical eras, most notably *Mary Poppins* (1964), for which they won two Academy Awards in 1965.[9] For *The Jungle Book*, they wrote songs that employ a wide range of musical styles—nineteenth-century exoticism ("Trust in Me," "My Own Home"), marching-band music ("Colonel Hathi's March"), barbershop ("That's What Friends Are For"), and 1920s New Orleans–style jazz ("I Wanna Be Like You")—dating from different periods of American popular music. This mix of styles and their coexistence in a single film must have seemed appropriate to the creative artists who planned *The Jungle Book*.[10]

Almost sixty years later, the vultures' combination of Beatles wigs and barbershop quartets seems incomprehensible, a juxtaposition of two unrelated elements from twentieth-century popular music chosen seemingly at random. But to the *Jungle Book* creative team, replacing a planned rock-and-roll number with a barbershop quartet suggests that the two styles must have been perceived by them as equivalent, with each style equally appropriate for the proposed scene. Barbershop quartets were popular when Walt Disney and most of his creative team were young, so the substitution of barbershop for what could be seen as the current fad in music would represent—to them—a more broad-based, timeless, popular music than the potentially flash-in-the-pan rock and roll.

Replacing the older view that meaning resides in the works themselves, reader-response criticism posits that the meaning of an artwork is constructed in the mind of the reader/viewer/listener.[11] The idea of interpretive communities recognizes that more than one person at a time can derive the same (or similar) meaning from a work.[12] Brian Upton shows how play spaces, in which play occurs, are structured by constraints—the rules of a game, the words of a text, the notes in a score, and even the cultural conditions under which reception occurs. People who share cultural constraints can form interpretive communities.[13] What I am calling generational listening highlights the constraint of age cohorts, people born within the same decade or two decades, on the interpretation of music. Barbershop quartets were current when Walt Disney and much of the *Jungle Book* design team were children, and later revivals kept their memories fresh while introducing younger people to the genre. By the twenty-first century, barbershop had faded in general cultural significance. Meanwhile, the Beatles, who could have been dismissed as an ephemeral fad in 1963–1964, have only grown in importance, both culturally and aesthetically. The balance between what once could have been seen as equivalent forms of popular music has realigned, leaving twenty-first-century viewers and listeners with a different interpretation.

Where Did the "Mop-Top" Vultures Come From?

According to Deja, work on *The Jungle Book* started in 1962.[14] Veteran Disney sketch artist and story man Peet had proposed adapting Rudyard Kipling's 1894 book to Walt Disney, who approved the idea.[15] However, Peet's initial story development, delivered in April 1963, was rejected by Walt Disney as "too dark."[16] Instead, a new story team was assembled, and in a meeting held in 1964 or 1965, Disney told them and the songwriters *not* to read the Kipling books, so as to avoid the ponderous and dark themes he had rejected.[17] The new story team used Peet's character designs but simplified his dramatic plot to its bare essence—the story of Mowgli's journey from the jungle to the Man Village, with episodes featuring the different animal characters—focusing less on plot elements and much more on character and character interactions.[18]

Peet's story treatment included an original (i.e., non-Kipling) character, Ishtar, a vulture who served as a messenger among the animals in the jungle. Peet had also invented a nearsighted rhinoceros.[19] The new story team kept the rhinoceros, named Rocky, and multiplied the vulture to a group—eventually a quartet—of vultures. For their sequence, the vultures were shown encouraging Mowgli to pick a fight with Rocky; what went without saying was that the vultures needed Rocky to kill Mowgli so that they could then eat his corpse. Work on this sequence got as far as the creation of full storyboards and recording the voice actors; a selection of the storyboards fitted to the recorded dialogue can be seen in an "extra" DVD video. As the narration puts it:

> Walt and the story team kept striving for more personality for the vultures, who evolved from typically scruffy vultures into the four Liverpudlian mop-tops inspired by British Invasion bands of the time.... Walt initially suggested that the vultures sing their song in the style of the Beatles.[20]

In their final designs, one of the vultures, Buzzie, retains Ishtar's original scruffy "bald" look, while the other three vultures look as if they are wearing Beatles wigs in three different colors: one blond (Flaps), one auburn (Dizzy), and the last dark brown (Ziggy).[21]

In 1962, when Peet's story development for *The Jungle Book* began, the Beatles were unknown outside small clubs in Liverpool and in Hamburg, Germany.[22] They exploded into mass popularity in Great Britain in 1963 with the release of their fourth Parlophone (EMI) single, "She Loves You," in August.[23] The British press coined the term "Beatlemania"—which first appeared in the London tabloid newspaper the *Daily Mail* in October 1963—to describe the crowds of screaming fans in and outside concert venues. Their fifth single, "I Want to Hold Your Hand," went to number one in the US in December, and in February 1964, more than a third of the US population, 73 million American viewers in 23 million households, saw the Beatles make their US debut in the first of three appearances on the CBS variety program *The Ed Sullivan Show*.[24] While Beatlemania in the UK was the subject of a video report by CBS News London correspondent Alexander Kendrick, broadcast on *CBS Morning News with Mike Wallace* on November 22, 1963,[25] it is more likely that Walt Disney and his story team first learned of the Beatles with their February 1964 US visit and the media frenzy it inspired.[26] The Beatles' Liverpool accents and deadpan attitudes in interviews could have been experienced via television and radio, even as press interviews with the group invariably focused on superficial, nonmusical topics.[27] Adding these details to the character design and voice work for the *Jungle Book* vultures would have read clearly to audiences as referring to the Beatles, in the same way that simply presenting a quartet of similar-in-appearance characters could irresistibly have suggested a Beatles reference to the story team post–February 1964.[28]

THE PLANNED SCENE FEATURING ROCKY THE RHINOCEROS AND THE VULTURES

It is possible to speculate about the process that lay behind the creative decisions involved in shaping the sequence featuring Rocky and the vultures. First, Peet's rhinoceros character was likely named Rocky for the alliteration with "Rhino." To adults in the early 1960s, the name Rocky irresistibly suggested the boxer Rocky Graziano (1919–1990), retired since 1952 but a famous and newsworthy champion in the postwar '40s. Planning Rocky the Rhino to be a pugnacious prizefighter fits with known rhinoceros attributes, such as having poor eyesight and being quick to attack.[29] But Rocky's name could also have suggested the new subgenre of popular music, rock and roll, to the story team in 1964, prompting the suggestion that the scene feature a "rock" song, sung by four vultures, while basing them visually on the hottest new musical group, the Beatles.

As first storyboarded by the new story team, the scene with Rocky and the vultures began with the vultures goading Mowgli into challenging Rocky, whom he has never met, to a fight. Mowgli, moping, isn't interested, but Rocky charges anyway. The "fight" begins with the sound of a bell, as in a boxing match, produced by the slapstick gag of one vulture hitting another on the head with a stick. Mowgli dodges Rocky's attacks, and the rhinoceros smashes into a rock, breaking his horn. He sobs, and Mowgli consoles him. The vultures, astonished, offer to make Mowgli an honorary vulture, but Mowgli, again, isn't interested, and he tells the vultures that he has no friends. This cues the vultures' song, "We're Your Friends," with Rocky participating, singing solo lines at important points. In contrast with the final version of the song, these lyrics play with the image of a prizefight and then list five different kinds of animals the vultures are fond of, leaving unspecified why these scavengers might be "fond" of different animals.

The song "We're Your Friends" and its scene as planned feature a number of Disney-esque elements: wordplay, funny voices, a proposed friendship (though perhaps of an exploitative sort), and the child-friendly naming of many animals. Nevertheless, compared with the various episodes included in the final film, the story design for Rocky's scene seems unfocused and overlong. Indeed, in a story meeting in January 1966, Walt Disney said, "[T]here are too many action sequences in a row. The monkeys, the vultures, and Rocky are all ugly. There's no balance. Maybe we could drop Rocky."[30] Dropping Rocky meant not only altering the whole sequence but also revising the song to be sung by the vultures alone. It was probably at this point that someone, perhaps Walt Disney himself, made the decision to recast the song stylistically, shifting from the initial rock-and-roll style to some other musical style. Deja notes that Walt Disney expressed concerns that the rock style would make the film seem "dated" by the time it was released, perhaps because there was concern that the Beatles wouldn't retain their white-hot popularity.[31] But this change didn't trigger a redesign of the vultures; if in the future the Beatles were no longer the hottest musical act, then it wouldn't matter that the vultures retained their mop-top hairstyles, because few people in the audience would care. Disney and his team had no way to predict that by the time the film was released in 1967, the Beatles would have become even more famous and popular than they had been in 1964 or even that they (and their music) would still be famous in the twenty-first century, almost sixty years later.

Rock and Roll and the Sherman Brothers

Before comparing the two versions of the vultures' song, I want to explore what the two musical styles could have meant to listeners from different generations during development and production of *The Jungle Book*, as well as what particular musical features the Sherman brothers thought would signal each of the two styles to a general film audience. First, what was rock and roll understood to be in the late 1950s and early 1960s?[32] The music's style was developed from that of earlier swing bands as played by Black performers; it came to white audiences' attention only when white artists, especially Elvis Presley, began covering the songs and performance styles of Black artists. Since rock and roll's emergence into mass consciousness in 1955, it was seen as particularly appealing to young people—teenagers—while not taken very seriously as a genre by older people.[33] At this point, there was no way to predict what would happen in the later 1960s, that rock would become the dominant genre of American and British popular music, in part because of the massive size of the "baby-boomer" audience who loved it.[34] Before the Beatles, rock and roll was viewed by adults as a novelty genre, something ephemeral that would be popular for a while and then fade in interest, replaced by whatever the next new thing turned out to be; indeed, this was Walt Disney's own view, as expressed in the January 1966 meeting. Disney, by then in his early sixties, had seen different musical styles and genres come and go, and sometimes come back in revival, during his own lifetime.

The Sherman brothers worked as staff songwriters at the Disney studios from the summer of 1960 until the spring of 1968 (Robert was thirty-five to forty-three and Richard was thirty-two to forty during this time), but their initial work for Disney was writing what were then described as rock-and-roll songs for Mouseketeer Annette Funicello.[35] In December 1958, Funicello's first recording of a Sherman brothers song, "Tall Paul," charted, selling more than four hundred thousand copies, and the Sherman brothers were asked to write more songs for her.[36] Between 1959 and 1965, thirteen LPs starring Funicello, with thirty-six new songs by the Shermans, were released on the new

Disney label Buena Vista Records.[37] Writing songs for Funicello meant the Sherman brothers, themselves at least fifteen years older than her teenage audience, were of necessity aware of the younger audience and their tastes in popular music.

Richard Sherman describes how he felt he and his brother were viewed by other musicians at Disney:

> When we first came on staff, the established composers and arrangers at Disney referred to us as "the rock-and-roll guys." We were politely tolerated but felt like outsiders. No doubt this was due to our success with songs like "Tall Paul" and "You're Sixteen." Our first recording session on the lot was for Hayley Mills' performance of "Let's Get Together." The heavy rock rhythm pattern must have sounded like blasphemy to more traditional sensibilities.[38]

Based on their success writing for Funicello, the Shermans were then asked to write three songs for a live-action Disney feature film, *The Parent Trap* (1961).[39] This assignment allowed the Shermans to demonstrate their unusual facility for writing songs in different popular musical styles.[40] For the rock-and-roll song, "Let's Get Together," they used characteristics of rock-and-roll music that would be recognizable as such by a film audience made up of adults of all ages as well as teenagers and children. "Let's Get Together" reveals what the Sherman brothers thought would register as rock and roll to a mixed-age audience, as well as hinting at the kind of music they identified as rock.[41] A few years later, the Sherman brothers would draw on their experience writing "Let's Get Together" when it came time to write a rock-and-roll song for *The Jungle Book* vultures.

"Let's Get Together" is based on the standard three-chord, twelve-bar blues form but with two deviations from the model.[42] First, the verse is fourteen bars long, rather than the eponymous twelve; the two extra bars are added as an extension in the last line, so that instead of the expected cadential chord progression V–IV–I, we hear V–IV–V–IV–I.[43] (See tables 15.1 and 15.2.) The third row of table 15.2 shows the formal adjustment: the progression V–IV is repeated before returning to the tonic I. The fourteenth bar uses the V chord when followed by a repeat of the verse and I for the end of the song.

Second, the Shermans add a contrasting eight-bar bridge section, as in the standard Tin Pan Alley thirty-two-bar song form, before the final repeat of the fourteen-bar verse.[44] In a normative blues song, the twelve-bar pattern would be repeated for however many verses the composer wants. Adding an eight-bar bridge produces the form AABA, with A representing the verses and B representing the bridge. With three verses

Table 15.1. Standard twelve-bar blues chord progression.

I	I	I	I
IV	IV	I	I
V	IV	I	I

Table 15.2. Chord progression for "Let's Get Together."

I	I	I	I
IV	IV	I	I
V	IV	V	IV
I	V or I		

and the bridge, the total length of the song is fifty bars. These two formal changes show that while the Shermans were aware of the twelve-bar blues tradition, they overwrote that knowledge with their sense of what made a popular song work, drawing on the then-dominant Tin Pan Alley song tradition.

The instrumentation for the song is limited, matching the amateur ethos of the scene. A prominent piano part, "played" on-screen by one of the twins, plays repeated eighth-note chords à la Jerry Lee Lewis, accompanied by a rhythm section of electric guitar, electric bass, and drums.[45]

The Two Versions of the Vultures' Song

The "rock and roll" version of the vultures' song doesn't quote or allude to particular recordings, nor does it use a stereotypical song form or chord progressions; rather, it signals its stylistic participation through tempo, instrumentation, and the rhythmic "yeah yeah" responses at the ends of the first two lines of each verse. The demo for "We're Your Friends" presents the song performed by minimal forces: lead and harmony vocals, prominent drums, tambourine, and a twangy guitar that mostly doubles the vocal melody. The stripped-down instrumentation in the demo matches the rhythm section used in *The Parent Trap* for "Let's Get Together," guitar and drums, but without using the prominent piano part of "Let's Get Together." The similarity between the two songs' instrumentation suggests that any finished version of "We're Your Friends" would probably have used the instrumentation as heard in the demo. By noticing the instrumental sounds, teen (and perhaps adult) audiences for *The Jungle Book* would have been able to identify their new favorite genre, rock-and-roll-inflected popular song, and would immediately have connected the vultures' "Beatles" hairstyles and English accents with the then-current rock-and-roll nature of the song.

The first version of the song begins with the vultures chanting (rather than singing) "We're your friends" over a tom-tom drum. The vultures sing the first line, Rocky sings the second, and the vultures alone finish the intro. A snare drum introduces the verse, with the guitar entering along with the voices. The verse's structure can be heard as four lines, punctuated in the middle of each line with either tambourine (the first verse) or sung "yeah yeahs" (the second verse), or, alternatively, as eight short lines ending with the rhythmic punctuation (except for the third line, sung by one solo vulture, which has tom-tom punctuation only at the end of the line). The fourth line of the first verse is chanted by the vultures, while in the second verse, the fourth line is chanted by Rocky. In combination, the rhythmic punctuation and shorter line lengths signals rock-and-roll style.

The verse melody is simple and repetitive: each of the first two lines outlines a triad, while the chords oscillate between I and vi. Two voices sing the melody in harmony in parallel thirds (compare the Beatles' "All My Loving," in which a double-tracked Paul McCartney sings parallel-thirds harmony with himself for the third verse, or the bridge of "I Want to Hold Your Hand," with melody and harmony sung by McCartney and Lennon together).[46] The third, solo, line begins with the 5-to-1 ascending melody, repeating the 1 pitch, descending stepwise down to 5 and then going back up to 1, over the chord progression I–iii–IV–IV#, and the fourth line finishes up 5–1–2–7–1 over the chords I–V–I. These aren't stereotypical rock-and-roll harmonic patterns; rather, the quatrain's musical setting uses basic pop tonality. Coupled with the lyrics, the simple melody and simple harmonic language represent early-'60s rock and roll, if not the specific sounds and innovations introduced to American audiences by the Beatles in 1964.

THE BARBERSHOP REARRANGEMENT OF THE VULTURES' SONG

When the decision was made to eliminate Rocky the Rhino and to change the song style to that of a barbershop quartet, the musical alteration was straightforward and uncomplicated. The song retained its melody and many of the original words, but the overt allusions to prizefighting and the lists of animals liked by the vultures were eliminated, in favor of emphasizing the vultures' general friendliness. The verses are performed a cappella, while in the bridge, an unseen guitar, strumming chords on each beat, accompanies the vocals.

Each line in the verses begins with a solo vulture (Flaps) echoed by the other vultures, and these echoes are arranged with "swipes," characteristic barbershop-style shifting chromatic harmonies.[47] The swipes replace the rhythmic punctuation of the first version, and the slower tempo enhances hearing the lyrics as the shorter half-lines rather than four longer lines. Compared with the earlier rock-and-roll version, the new tempo is distinctly slower, with rubato, here a slowing tempo, on the chromatic harmony echoes. After four short lines, the next two units (corresponding to the third line of the earlier four-line verse) are sung without interruption by three of the vultures; the fourth vulture joins the others for the line "That's what friends are for." The verse ends with all four vultures singing another couplet, echoing the previous two lines. The bridge section has a faster tempo than the verses, more similar to the tempo of the rock-and-roll version; the staccato rhythmic guitar strumming on the beat also sounds more like rock and roll, for a last hint of the original conception for the song.

What Might Barbershop Have Meant to Walt Disney?

It is not documented who suggested that the vultures sing their song in barbershop style, but the ways the story is told by various people who were there suggests that even if the idea hadn't been Walt's, the firm adoption of the change was his decision. Rather than rewriting the vultures' song from scratch, this practical move replaced one style of music arranged for a group of four male singers with a different style of music that would also be sung by a quartet of male voices. Barbershop, an American musical tradition of close-harmony a cappella singing, employs an invariable arrangement of voices, with the melody sung by the "lead" tenor, another tenor singing higher pitches, a bass singing the bass line, and a baritone filling in the chordal harmony; the vocal ranges from highest to lowest are thus tenor, lead, baritone, bass. Coincidentally, this is the same lineup of voices later used by most doo-wop singing groups, and an astute listener to contemporary popular music in the late 1950s or early 1960s could have perceived that connection, perhaps even understanding doo-wop as a new twist on barbershop.[48]

Barbershop singing has its roots in the nineteenth century, with musical antecedents a mixture of German and Austrian Romantic harmony, Protestant hymn singing, and the minstrel-show tradition; its "golden age" is seen as beginning in the 1880s.[49] The repertoire included older nineteenth-century songs by composers including Stephen Foster, as well as songs by the then-new Tin Pan Alley composers, and the style itself could be heard sung by professionals in the staged variety shows of vaudeville, as well as sung by amateurs in a wide range of venues. A revival of barbershop as a genre steeped in nostalgia for the pre–World War I, turn-of-the-century world began in the 1920s and flourished in the 1930s.[50] Gage Averill writes: "The barbershop revival was born from this confluence of conservative reactions to changes in the physical, social and cultural landscape of America. It was a quest to reconstruct a space of privilege for white American middle-class males based on nostalgia for unchallenged and exclusive sociability and camaraderie located in the adolescent memories of middle-aged men."[51] By the 1960s, listeners were again reminded of traditional barbershop singing by the 1957 Broadway musical *The Music Man* (filmed by Warner Bros. in 1962), set in 1912 in the same kind of Midwestern town celebrated at Disneyland (opened in 1955) on Main Street USA.[52] To Americans like Walt Disney, born at the start of the century, barbershop could have felt like a constant presence throughout their lives, rather than a style that died and was later revived.

Walt Disney included barbershop quartets in several of his projects in the 1950s. When planning a set of miniature "Americana" exhibits that would lead ultimately to the animatronic figures shown at Disneyland, the third display was a barbershop quartet.[53] In 1957, the Mellomen, a vocal quartet featured in several 1950s Disney projects, recorded an album, *Meet Me Down on Main Street*, for Disneyland Records, including performances of a dozen barbershop standards.[54] Two years later, in 1959, performances by a live quartet, called the Dapper Dans, were added to Main Street USA at Disneyland (with multiple changes of personnel); another iteration of the Dapper Dans has performed at Walt Disney World since its opening in 1971.[55]

To Walt Disney, as well as to the older members of the *Jungle Book* creative team, barbershop singing would have suggested the world of his childhood, a nostalgic view of the turn of the last century, currently on display on Main Street USA at Disneyland. But due to decades of revivals, the style was also current in 1960s musical experience. Nowadays, the association, via costume and repertoire, between barbershop and the period around 1900 cements barbershop as a musical style from the past, but in the 1960s, the style could be understood as still a living one by people who first heard the repertoire as new popular music when they were children. When the vultures' song was changed from rock and roll to barbershop, the change wouldn't have been seen as anachronistic.

Conclusions

The same music heard for the first time as an adult will register differently from hearing it for the first time as a child or teenager. To children, all the music they hear exists as an undifferentiated stylistic mélange. By the time they're teenagers, they become aware of new music as new—something that hadn't existed before that moment. Many consumers stick with "their" music—the music they knew as teenagers—for the rest of their lives; while they will continue to experience new music as they age, they are still likely to judge it by the standards set by the baseline musical preferences formed in their teenage years.

Creative artists born in three different decades worked together to create *The Jungle Book*. Not surprisingly, the largest group of the men who worked on the film, nineteen artists, belonged to the same generational cohort as Walt Disney himself, born between 1900 and 1920. For the people connected with the music of the film, Walt Disney and his cohort would have heard Tin Pan Alley songs and barbershop quartets as children or teens; in contrast, the Sherman brothers, born in the 1920s, would only know barbershop in revival, and they would have first heard rock and roll when they were already professional songwriters in their thirties. The youngest audience members, children in 1967, would not remember barbershop at all, while their parents, born in the 1920s and 1930s, could have recognized the style from later revivals. For the oldest men working on the film, barbershop would have continued to seem relevant from their lifelong experiences with the style and its echoes in later harmony quartet singing, including doo-wop. And so to them, the decision to have the vultures sing barbershop wouldn't have seemed out of place.

People of different ages experiencing the same music differently highlights a drawback to the standard presentation of the history of popular music in America as a discrete set of styles, one consecutively following the other. People continue to like the music they grew up with long after it was new. Instead of being seen as a linear progression, music history is better understood as an overlapping conglomeration of styles, as is well demonstrated by the Beatles-esque vultures singing barbershop in 1967 in *The Jungle Book*.[56]

NOTES

1. "That's What Friends Are For," words and music by Richard M. and Robert B. Sherman.
2. The Sherman brothers' idea was to have the Beatles sing the song. But it didn't happen—either due, according to lore, to scheduling problems, or because a grumpy John Lennon declined. "Yes, the second part of it is true," Sherman fires back. "We thought it would be great to have the Beatles do it. And we wrote a quartet for them to do it. We attempted even to [write the song] in a rock style. And with the Beatles, John was running the show at the time, and he said [dismissively] 'I don't wanna do an animated film.'" Craig McLean, "*The Jungle Book*: The Making of Disney's Most Troubled Film," *The Telegraph*, July 30, 2013. This story is unlikely to be completely true, because Lennon was demonstrably *not* "running the show" in the early 1960s. The Beatles' manager, Brian Epstein, was, and Epstein was fully committed to making the most of his group's astonishing popularity. The Beatles even approved a Saturday-morning cartoon series loosely based on their first film, *A Hard Day's Night* (1964), originally broadcast from 1965 to 1967. Mitchell Axelrod, *Beatletoons: The Real Story behind the Cartoon Beatles* (Pickens, SC: Wynn Pub, 1996). The image of "grumpy John" dates to the period immediately after the Beatles broke up in 1970, as exposed in his long December 1970 *Rolling Stone* interview, published in the magazine in January and February 1971 and later that year as a book: Jann S. Wenner, *Lennon Remembers* (New York: Straight Arrow, 1971; 2nd ed. London: Verso).
3. Andreas Deja, *Walt Disney's* The Jungle Book: *Making a Masterpiece* (San Francisco: Walt Disney Family Foundation, 2022), 145.
4. Unlike live-action films, Disney's animated films weren't based on written scripts. Instead, "story men," the writers and artists in the Story Department, planned sequences and created storyboards—individual sketches for unfolding action that were pinned up on a large corkboard—in a process developed at the Disney studio in the 1930s. "Story boards are four-by-eight-foot panels, and a continuity of sketches is pushpinned onto the boards to show the main phases of the action and the personalities and attitudes of the characters as a plan for the animation." Bill Peet, *Bill Peet: An Autobiography* (Boston: Houghton Mifflin, 1989), 96. The full storyboard would then be critiqued by Walt Disney and the other story men. Disney himself usually determined a film's overall story, with others designing individual sequences for Disney's approval. Disney "directors" didn't work with actors but rather supervised the artistic process from storyboards to animated film; the "actors" were the characters as drawn by the animators. See Frank Thomas and Ollie Johnston, *The Illusion of Life: Disney Animation* (New York: Disney Editions), 1981, especially 80–84, 366–391.
5. Larry Clemons (1906–1988), Ralph Wright (1908–1983), and Ken Anderson (1909–1993). Walt Disney would die on December 15, 1966, when *The Jungle Book* was "only half finished." Deja, *Walt Disney's* The Jungle Book, 169. The full cast and crew credited for *The Jungle Book* can be found on IMDB: https://www.imdb.com/title/tt0061852/fullcredits?ref_=tt_ov_wr_sm.
6. John Lounsbery (1911–1976), Frank Thomas (1912–2004), and Ollie Johnston (1912–2008). Kahl was responsible for animating Bagheera, Kaa, and Shere Khan; Lounsbery animated the elephants; Johnston animated Baloo and the girl at the end of the film; and Thomas

animated Mowgli, with Thomas and Johnston collaborating on the many scenes of Baloo and Mowgli interacting. Kahl, Lounsbery, and Thomas animated King Louie and the monkeys, and Hal King (1913–1986) animated the wolves. Deja, *Walt Disney's* The Jungle Book, 33, 59, 75, 101, 145, 159.

7. Robert B. Sherman and Richard M. Sherman, *Walt's Time: From Before to Beyond*, ed. Bruce Gordon, David Mumford, and Jeff Kurtti (Santa Clarita, CA: Camphor Tree, 1998), 88–105.
8. Their compositional virtuosity is directly highlighted in the short film *A Symposium of Popular Songs* (Walt Disney Productions, 1962), which surveyed American popular music styles from ragtime to early rock and roll.
9. The Sherman brothers won Oscars for Music (Song) ("Chim Chim Cher-ee") and for Music (Music Score, substantially original). *Mary Poppins* won three other Academy Awards as well: Film Editing, Special Visual Effects, and Best Actress (Julie Andrews). https://www.oscars.org/oscars/ceremonies/1965.
10. Terry Gilkyson (1916–1999) wrote "The Bear Necessities," the only survivor of a set of songs he wrote to accompany Peet's initial story treatment. When Peet's treatment was rejected, Gilkyson's songs apart from this one were dropped, and the Sherman brothers were brought to the project. Demos for the other Gilkyson songs can be heard on *Walt Disney's The Jungle Book: 40th Anniversary Edition* (Walt Disney Studios Home Entertainment, 2007), disc 1, "Deleted Songs." "The Bear Necessities," like "I Wanna Be Like You," was also arranged as 1920s New Orleans–style jazz.
11. On reader-response criticism, see Lois Tyson, *Critical Theory Today: A User-Friendly Guide*, 4th ed. (Oxford: Routledge, 2023), 149–181.
12. The idea of interpretive communities, popularized by Stanley Fish, is part of what's called social reader-response criticism; see Stanley Fish, *Is There a Text in This Class? The Authority of Interpretive Communities* (Cambridge, MA: Harvard University Press, 1980), especially 147–174, 303–321.
13. Brian Upton's exploration of the mechanics of play focuses specifically on video games and literature, but I have found it to be applicable to the experience of listening to music as well. Brian Upton, *The Aesthetic of Play* (Cambridge, MA: MIT Press, 2015), especially 238–240; Elizabeth Randell Upton, *Music and Performance in the Later Middle Ages* (New York: Palgrave Macmillan, 2013), 97–129.
14. Deja, *Walt Disney's* The Jungle Book, 9. In dating particular moments in the development process, I am constrained by what materials the Disney company has made available. Deja's mention here of the year 1962 is the first time this information about the start of production has appeared in print.
15. "After completing the story boards on *The Sword in the Stone* and getting all the voices recorded and ready for animation, I talked Walt into getting the rights to Rudyard Kipling's *Jungle Book*. 'A great chance to develop some good animal characters' was my pitch, and he agreed. I read and reread the Kipling stories until they were well in my mind, then I spent a couple of months writing a script." Peet, *Bill Peet: An Autobiography*, 173. *The Sword in the Stone* was released in December 1963. John Canemaker repeated Peet's claim: "Then it was actually Bill Peet who proposed *The Jungle Book* to Walt Disney," *Walt Disney's The Jungle Book*, disc 2, 3:05.
16. Peet's story treatment is dated April 23, 1963; Wolfgang Reithermann's memo suggesting changes to Peet is dated January 20, 1964. Charles Solomon, "The Last Hurrah," in *The Walt Disney Film Archives: The Animated Movies 1921–1968*, ed. Daniel Kothenschulte (Cologne: Taschen, 2020), 477. After an acrimonious meeting nine days later, on January 29, 1964, Peet quit his job at the studio. Peet, *Bill Peet: An Autobiography*, 180.

17. In a video presentation, "*The Jungle Book*—Exclusive Richard Sherman Interview, Empire Magazine," posted to YouTube on August 12, 2013, Richard Sherman said, "My brother Bob and I were called to a meeting. We had no idea there was a previous version being written, and we came to this meeting. First thing he [Walt Disney] said to us that morning was 'OK fellas, how many of you people have read Rudyard Kipling's *The Jungle Book*?' And not one of us raised our hands, we hadn't. And he said, 'Good. I'm going to tell you the story; I don't want you to read the book, I want you to listen to the way I'm going to tell it.' . . . [A]t the end of this thing, he said, 'Now remember, take the serious, take the scary, take the mysterious, murky stories, and make them fun! Turn them on their ear and make them fun.'" In the bonus feature "The Bare Necessities: The Making of *The Jungle Book*," Richard Sherman said, "Bob and I had been staff writers at the studio for approximately five years by that time. And one day Walt called us in and said, 'I don't like the way *Jungle Book* is going.'" The Sherman brothers began work as staff writers in the summer of 1960, so a *Jungle Book* story meeting "approximately five years" later could mean late 1964 or 1965.
18. "Disney's Kipling: Walt's Magic Touch on a Literary Classic," a video on disc 2 of the 40th Anniversary Edition, demonstrates the adaptation process, showing examples of what Kipling wrote, how Peet adapted Kipling, and how Walt Disney and the new story team edited Peet's version.
19. "Peet also added some characters, including Ishtar the vulture, a nearsighted rhinoceros, and the orangutan king of the monkeys." Solomon, "The Last Hurrah," 477. See also Thomas and Johnston, *The Illusion of Life*, 377–379.
20. "The Lost Character: Rocky the Rhino," video extra on disc 1 of the 40th Anniversary Edition. It is disingenuous to ascribe the "mop-tops" to "British Invasion bands" in general, as the hairstyle was introduced to English and American audiences by the Beatles themselves and then adopted in imitation of the Beatles. On the source of the Beatles' haircuts, see Mark Lewisohn, *Tune In: The Beatles, All These Years*, Vol. 1 (New York: Crown Archetype, 2013), 421, 487, 489; Jonathan Gould, *Can't Buy Me Love: The Beatles, Britain, and America* (New York: Three Rivers, 2007), 78–89. On the British invasion in general, see Annie J. Randall, "British Invasion," Grove Music Online, 2013, https://doi.org/10.1093/gmo/9781561592630.article.A2234548.
21. "The Beatles wig was such a popular item that the Lowell Toy Corporation couldn't produce them fast enough, although their factories were manufacturing them at a rate of over 24,000 a day." Peter Brown and Steven Gaines, *The Love You Make: An Insider's Story of the Beatles* (New York: McGraw Hill, 1983; reissued New American Library, 2002), 117.
22. The best single-volume book about their lives and careers remains Gould, *Can't Buy Me Love*. For an exhaustive guide to the Beatles' careers as performers and recording artists, see Mark Lewisohn, *The Complete Beatles Chronicle: The Definitive Day-by-Day Guide to the Beatles' Entire Career* (London: Hamlyn, 1992; Chicago: Chicago Review Press, 2010). Lewisohn is currently writing the most extensively sourced history of the band; his first volume, *Tune In: The Beatles: All These Years*, covers the nascent Beatles' lives through the end of December 1962, after the release of their first single, "Love Me Do" in October 1962.
23. Gould, *Can't Buy Me Love*, 157–160.
24. On the Beatles' first visit to the US, see ibid., 1–6; The Beatles, *The Beatles Anthology* (San Francisco: Chronicle, 2000), 116–123; Albert and David Maysles, dirs., *The Beatles: The First U.S. Visit* (MPI Home Video, 1990; re-edit of the 16mm documentary *What's Happening! The Beatles in the U.S.A.*, first shown on CBS TV November 13, 1964).

25. A planned second broadcast on the *CBS Evening News with Walter Cronkite* was preempted by coverage of the assassination of President John F. Kennedy. https://www.cbsnews.com/news/cbs-news-reports-on-the-beatles-in-1963/.
26. See Michael Frontani, "The Beatles and Their Fans: Image and the Media, October 1963–February 1964," in *Fandom and the Beatles: The Act You've Known for All These Years*, ed. Kenneth Womack and Kit O'Toole (New York: Oxford University Press, 2021), 55–80.
27. For transcripts of Beatles interviews, see "The Beatles Interview Database," www.beatlesinterviews.org.
28. Concept art by Ken Anderson (1909–1993) shows five vultures, with different names and a variety of body types and "hair." Deja, *Walt Disney's* The Jungle Book, 148. The final designs for the four vultures present them more similarly shaped, with identical feather "clothes": white neck ruffs, dark gray outer wings, and light gray body and leg feathers. See Deja, *Walt Disney's* The Jungle Book, 149–151.
29. "Black rhinoceroses have a sort of attack-first-and-ask-questions-later attitude. When a rhino catches the scent of a human or anything else unfamiliar, it is likely to charge. Rhinos can't see well, so they sometimes charge objects like trees and rocks, mistaking them as threats. But rhinos have keen senses of smell and hearing." "Black Rhinoceros," National Geographic Kids, https://kids.nationalgeographic.com/animals/mammals/facts/black-rhino. Rocky is represented as an Indian rhinoceros, with folds of skin that look like armor plates, rather than the smaller (African) black rhino, but the behavior of the two species is similar.
30. "The Lost Character."
31. The vultures were "originally intended to sing a rock-and-roll rendition of 'That's What Friends Are For'—initially called 'We're your friends'—but Walt concluded that a contemporary rock song would give the film a short shelf life." Deja, *Walt Disney's* The Jungle Book, 145. This concern echoes, unknowingly, the judgment of Decca Records, which rejected the Beatles in early 1962, saying "guitar groups are on the way out." The Beatles, *The Beatles Anthology* (San Francisco: Chronicle Books, 2000), 67.
32. For an overview of the history of rock and roll including discussion of its styles, see Mickey Vallee, "Rock and Roll," Grove Music Online, 2014, https://doi.org/10.1093/gmo/9781561592630.article.A2257196. On the emergence of rock and roll in the mid-1950s, see Richard Aquila, *That Old-Time Rock & Roll: A Chronicle of an Era, 1954–63* (Urbana: University of Illinois Press, 2000), especially chap. 2, "Rock Styles."
33. "By 1955, it was clear that a new musical trend centered in the social worlds of teenagers had taken solid shape.... Black voices, unvarnished for mainstream tastes and disseminated for the most part by small regional labels, were moving beyond their intended markets, filtering into the broader culture through their popular appeal in the vastly numerous audience of white teenagers." Albin J. Zak III, *I Don't Sound Like Nobody: Remaking Music in 1950s America* (Ann Arbor: University of Michigan Press, 2010), 43.
34. For a sociological discussion of the role of rock music in the lives of the "baby boomers," see Joseph A. Kotarba, *Baby Boomer Rock 'n' Roll Fans: The Music Never Ends* (Lanham, MD: Scarecrow, 2013).
35. Walt Disney invited the Sherman brothers to work full-time for his studio in August 1960, after they delivered their first songs for *Mary Poppins*. Sherman and Sherman, *Walt's Time*, 9, 40. On the Sherman Brothers, see also James Bohn, *Music in Disney's Animated Features:* Snow White and the Seven Dwarfs *to* The Jungle Book (Jackson: University Press of Mississippi, 2017), 175–202.

36. On Disneyland Records, see Tim Hollis and Greg Ehrbar, *Mouse Tracks: The Story of Walt Disney Records* (Jackson: University Press of Mississippi, 2006); Jimmy Johnson, "The Disneyland Records Story," *Billboard*, March 27, 1971, D2; Jimmy Johnson, *Inside the Whimsy Works: My Life with Walt Disney Productions* (Jackson: University Press of Mississippi, 2014), 91. On Funicello, see Lorraine Santoli, *The Official Mickey Mouse Club Book* (New York: Disney Editions, 1995), 151–160; Alexandra M. Apolloni, "Funicello, Annette," Grove Music Online, 2013.

37. "In a series of concept albums for Annette, we wrote Hawaiian songs, Italian songs, and every kind of dance rhythm song we could think of. We would write four or five originals, and Tutti Camerata would then choose seven or eight classics of that genre to complete each album." Sherman and Sherman, *Walt's Time*, 133. See also Hollis and Ehrbar, *Mouse Tracks*, 50–51.

38. Sherman and Sherman, *Walt's Time*, 26. As performed by rockabilly singer Johnny Burnette, "You're Sixteen" reached number eight on the *Billboard* Hot 100 in December 1960. Ringo Starr's recording of the song, his fifth single after the breakup of the Beatles, would hit number one in January 1974.

39. In a 2002 interview, Richard Sherman explained, "By the late 50s we were writing a lot of rockers. We wrote song after song for Annette, and one day Walt said 'Who are those fellas who are writing those fun songs for Annette, I want to meet them.'" *The Parent Trap* (Vault Disney Collection, 2002), disc 2, special features: "The Sherman Brothers."

40. The other two songs were the title song, "The Parent Trap," and a ballad, "For Now, for Always." Richard Sherman described the title song as reflecting popular music for adults: a "simple, little, easy swinging kind of a song, the way Sinatra was singing in those days, with that thumb-snapping bit and everything." About "For Now, for Always," Richard Sherman explained, "that's the style of ballad that was being sung in 1946," when the fictional parents would have been dating. Ibid. On Sinatra in this period, see Elijah Wald, *How the Beatles Destroyed Rock 'n' Roll: An Alternative History of American Popular Music* (New York: Oxford University Press, 2011), 184–198, especially 189–191.

41. Richard Sherman explained: "'Let's Get Together' was written as a contemporary rocker, I mean, it was just the two little girls, as if the two girls had written it. The way we did it, we kept it very simple, and very typical [for a] rock-and-roll-type song of that time." *The Parent Trap*, disc 2, special features: "The Sherman Brothers."

42. On twelve-bar blues, see Elijah Wald, "Blues," Grove Music Online, 2012, https://doi.org/10.1093/gmo/9781561592630.article.A2223858. On the blues progression, see Barry Kernfeld and Allan F. Moore, "Blues Progression," Grove Music Online, 2001, https://doi.org/10.1093/gmo/9781561592630.article.41276. Kernfeld and Moore cite "Rock around the Clock" (1954) as presenting the blues progression's "simplest form." A rare Beatles song that uses twelve-bar blues chords in its verse is "Can't Buy Me Love" (1964).

43. The Roman numerals here stand for the relationship between chords in a tonal piece of music. I represents the tonic, the key of the song, while IV and V represent triads based on the fourth and fifth notes of the scale for that key. In the tables, each cell represents one bar of music.

44. In twentieth-century popular song, a bridge is a musical section that contrasts with the repeated verse. In a prototypical example of thirty-two-bar song form, Harold Arlen and Yip Harburg's "Over the Rainbow" from *The Wizard of Oz* (1939), the bridge section is the part that starts, "One day I'll wish upon a star." On "Over the Rainbow," see Walter Frisch, *Arlen & Harburg's Over the Rainbow* (New York: Oxford University Press, 2017).

45. Richard Sherman himself played the repeated right-hand piano chords in his interview on the 2002 DVD release of *The Parent Trap*, suggesting that this element was present from the start; it is likely that the other instrumental parts were arranged by Franklin Marks, listed in the film's credits as "orchestrator."
46. "All My Loving" was first released on the Beatles' second UK album, *With the Beatles* (1963). In the US, "All My Loving" closed the first side of the album *Meet the Beatles!* (1964), the first album released by EMI's US subsidiary, Capitol Records. "I Want to Hold Your Hand" was the Beatles' first number one single in the US, topping the *Billboard* Hot 100 chart on February 1, 1964, where it would remain for seven weeks. "I Want to Hold Your Hand" opened *Meet the Beatles!* American audiences watched the Beatles perform both songs and three others in their first appearance on *The Ed Sullivan Show* on February 9, 1964. The Beatles learned this style of harmony from the Everly Brothers' hit recordings in the late 1950s and early 1960s.
47. Gage Averill, "Bell Tones and Ringing Chords: Sense and Sensation in Barbershop Harmony," *World of Music* 41, no. 1 (1999): 37–51. "One of the favorite arranging devices in barbershop harmony is the 'swipe,' in which three of the singers change their notes while the fourth holds his original note. When sung in succession, swipes can produce a dramatically unfolding chord sequence" (44).
48. See David Sanjek, "Doo-wop," Grove Music Online (print 2013, online 2014); David Goldblatt, "Nonsense in Public Places: Songs of Black Vocal Rhythm and Blues or Doo-Wop," *Journal of Aesthetics and Art Criticism* 71, no. 1 (Winter 2013): 101–110.
49. Gage Averill, *Four Parts, No Waiting: A Social History of American Barbershop Harmony* (New York: Oxford University Press, 2003), 21–48. See also Frédéric Döhl, "From Harmonic Style to Genre: The Early History (1890s–1940s) of the Uniquely American Musical Term Barbershop," *American Music* 32, no. 2 (Summer 2014): 123–171. "The current models that chart the birth of barbershop harmony are diverse and often contradictory with regard to categories such as race, gender, regional context, social environment, amateur or professional, impromptu or composed-arranged, and highbrow or lowbrow. There is just one point of near mutual consent in this field: the date by which this genre was first fully established and enjoyed its classic or 'golden age' is supposed to have been around 1900" (123–124). Döhl includes extensive bibliography for barbershop scholarship in his first five footnotes (156–158).
50. Averill, *Four Parts, No Waiting*, 87–114. Averill associates the barbershop revivals of the 1930s with a wave of cultural neo-Victorianism (88–91).
51. The Society for the Preservation and Encouragement of Barber Shop Quartet Singing in America (SPEBSQSA), now called the Barbershop Harmony Society, founded in 1938 in Tulsa, Oklahoma, now recognizes the Black musicking in what had long been an all-white endeavor, "a uniquely American close harmony musical art form whose roots lie in African-American improvisation and European harmony traditions." https://www.barbershop.org/about. The prominent acknowledgment of Black American roots dates to the 1990s and later.
52. A 1955 guidebook describes Main Street: "The nostalgic charm of 1890 comes to life again in this accurate reproduction of Main Street in a typical American town." *The Story of Disneyland, with a Complete Guide to Fantasyland, Tomorrowland, Adventureland, Frontierland, Main Street U.S.A.* (Anaheim, CA: Disneyland, 1955), 5. On Main Street USA and Walt Disney's own past, see Robert Neuman, "Disneyland's Main Street, USA, and Its Sources in Hollywood, USA," *Journal of American Culture* 31, no. 1 (March 2008):

83–97; Elizabeth Randell Upton, "Nostalgia for a Past Futurism: The Main Street Electrical Parade," *American Music* 39, no. 2 (Summer 2021): 169–181.

53. Michael Barrier, *The Animated Man: A Life of Walt Disney* (Berkeley: University of California Press, 2007), 230–231.

54. On the Mellomen, see Hollis and Ehrbar, *Mouse Tracks*, 85–86. Probably the most recognizable member of the Mellomen is bass Thurl Ravenscroft, the longtime voice of Tony the Tiger as well as the (uncredited) soloist singing "You're a Mean One, Mr. Grinch" in the 1966 animated TV Special *How the Grinch Stole Christmas*, directed by Chuck Jones. Melloman Bill Lee sang in many Disney features of the 1950s and '60s, including providing Shere Khan's line at the end of the vultures' song in *The Jungle Book*; he also can be heard dubbing Christopher Plummer's singing voice in *The Sound of Music* (1965). The Mellomen can be heard painting the roses red in *Alice in Wonderland* (1951), yowling as a quartet of dogs backing up Peggy Lee at the dog pound in *Lady and the Tramp* (1955), joining Colonel Hathi's Dawn Patrol of elephants in *The Jungle Book*, and singing "Yo Ho (A Pirate's Life for Me)" in the Disneyland attraction Pirates of the Caribbean (1967) and "Grim Grinning Ghosts" in the Haunted Mansion (1969; the singers' faces are visible animating a set of busts in the graveyard), among many others.

55. Chris Strodder, *The Disneyland Encyclopedia*, 3rd ed. (Santa Monica, CA: Santa Monica Press, 2017), 136–137.

56. On the historiography of music, see Annette Kreutziger-Herr, "Music, Historiography of," in Encyclopedia of Early Modern History Online, ed. Graeme Dunphy and Andrew Gow (2015), http://dx.doi.org/10.1163/2352-0272_emho_COM_024405. On popular music historiography, see Steve Waksman., "Reconstructing the Past," in *The Routledge Companion to Popular Music History and Heritage*, ed. Sarah Baker, Catherine Strong, Lauren Istvandity, and Zelmarie Cantillon (London: Routledge, 2018), 55–66, https://www.routledgehandbooks.com/doi/10.4324/9781315299310-6.

CHAPTER 16

THAT'S INTEGRATION! DIGITAL VFX TECHNOLOGIES AND THE DISNEY RENAISSANCE MUSICALS (1989–1999)

CHRISTOPHER HOLLIDAY

BEGINNING with the release of *The Little Mermaid* (1989), the successive Disney animated films *The Rescuers Down Under* (1990), *Beauty and the Beast* (1991), *Aladdin* (1992), *The Lion King* (1994), *Pocahontas* (1995), *The Hunchback of Notre Dame* (1996), *Hercules* (1997), *Mulan* (1998), and *Tarzan* (1999) have collectively been understood as marking the "Disney Renaissance" era of the studio's animation output. Multiple hagiographic accounts of the Disney corporation have typically identified this commercially profitable and critically lauded ten-year period of its feature animation unit as an industrial and aesthetic phase of creativity and recovery, one that was sharpened by the company's otherwise unfavorable reputation in the years immediately after Walt Disney's death on December 15, 1966. Following the exodus of longtime Disney animators Don Bluth, Gary Goldman, and John Pomeroy in 1979 during the production of *The Fox and the Hound* (1981), the late 1970s and early 1980s were "tumultuous years for the Disney studio, with changes of management and philosophy taking their toll on every department."[1] Yet the release of *The Little Mermaid* in October 1989—that took $84.4 million at the US box office—provided Disney with a moment of much-needed security that played out as much through its increased industrial stability as through a newfound economic prosperity. Indeed, the repeated framing of the Disney Renaissance by another name, the "Eisner era," has achieved the aim of attributing the upturn in the company's fortunes and creative direction to Michael Eisner, the chief executive officer of the Walt Disney Company from September 22, 1984, to September 20, 2005, and his management team of Frank Wells, Jeffrey Katzenberg, and Helene Hahn.[2]

Alongside the behind-the-scenes contributions of these key personnel, however, the Disney Renaissance has also been championed as a run of feature films between 1989 and 1999 that were marked by an increased quality in narrative, characterization, and artistic standards. Sean Wilson argues that the Disney Renaissance constituted a "wave of glossy, slickly produced and exuberantly scored Disney animated blockbusters that restored the studio's credibility."[3] It is due to their sophisticated stories, pristine animated illusionism, and expansive engagement with musicality that the Disney Renaissance features are commonly aligned with the earlier "Classic Disney" phase of production—also known as "Disney-Formalism"—in which Disney first institutionalized its aesthetic principles and pictorial sensibilities into something resembling a patterned formula.[4]

Despite an assumed degree of precision with which the Renaissance era of Disney animation has been conceptualized as "the Studio's second most significant phase" after the golden age of the 1930s and 1940s, a fuzziness still persists as to the exact terms of its aesthetic restoration and the market forces that shaped Hollywood animation in this transitional moment of production.[5] Chris Pallant suggests that "there remains a lack of critical engagement with the period" that has resulted in a "fragmented foundation when approaching the period as a whole."[6] This chapter seeks to examine the discourses of revitalization and renewal typically attached to the Disney Renaissance through the convergence of two stylistic principles that have largely defined the era's impact on Disney's internal history and the direction of US commercial animation more broadly: the influence of Broadway-style musical numbers on the arrangement of sound and image and the industrial and aesthetic incorporation of computer graphics into an otherwise cel-animated style. Disney's well-documented structural and stylistic involvement with the conventions of the Broadway musical during its Renaissance has regularly accounted for its prestige and coherency as a set of popular animated films, while equally separating the late 1980s and early 1990s from both the "Classic Disney" era and the studio's previous audiovisual explorations into the creative synchrony of sound and animated image embodied by the Silly Symphonies (1929–1939) series of musical shorts. Ryan Bunch argues that while "Disney animated features have always included songs ... since the so-called Disney Renaissance of the late 1980s and 1990s, Disney's animated features have both modelled their songs and forms on the contemporary Broadway musical and influenced it in turn."[7] However, it was also during the successful Disney Renaissance era that digital image processing was likewise solidified as part of Disney's hand-drawn workflow, with digital ink-and-paint systems, computer-generated imagery (CGI), and specially designed software (such as the Computer Animation Production System or CAPS, Faux Plane, and Deep Canvas programs) used not just in several standout action-oriented sequences (chases, fights, explosions) but ultimately to provide the specific formal conditions for the era's range of spectacular and highly creative musical performances.

The numbers "Belle," "Be Our Guest," and "Beauty and the Beast" (*Beauty and the Beast*); "A Whole New World" (*Aladdin*); "Just Around the Riverbend" (*Pocahontas*); "Out There" and "Topsy Turvy" (*The Hunchback of Notre Dame*); "Go the Distance" (*Hercules*); "I'll Make a Man out of You" (*Mulan*); and "Son of Man" and "Two Worlds"

(*Tarzan*) all register a mode of musical presentation clearly powered by the possibilities of computer graphics, which in turn positions the Disney Renaissance as symptomatic of the acceleration of digital visual effects (VFX) technologies occurring simultaneously across mainstream Hollywood cinema. Furthermore, it is this increasing technological hybridity of the Disney Renaissance musicals that ultimately evokes one of the defining notes of the musical as a popular Hollywood genre. Writing on the Hollywood musical and its arrangement of "song, dance, and story," John Mueller argues that "integration" has become vital for understanding the generic identity and historical contingency of the musical.[8] Framed by concepts of narrative causality and textual unobtrusiveness, the "integration" of story with song qualifies the varied methods by which musical numbers can "take up the action and advance the plot by their content."[9] By focusing on an alternative industrial and stylistic "integration" of computer technologies with cel-animated elements in the production of specific Disney Renaissance songs, this chapter reconceptualizes the importance of the musical numbers to the technological trajectory of cartooning in Hollywood, framing this period of Disney animation as evidence of where (and how) the affordances of the digital would be made to coexist with cel-animated aesthetics.

The State of the Art

For a 1990 issue of the *Hollywood Reporter Magazine*, animation historian Charles Solomon compiled a brief five-page dossier titled "Animation: Special Report" on the state of the North American animation industry as it stood at the start of a new decade. The survey looked back at the preceding ten years as "the most exciting" since the golden age of the Hollywood cartoon, which had been crystallized by the particular successes of the Disney studio and the release of *Snow White and the Seven Dwarfs* (1937) that had established animation as an industrial art form and the feature-film format as a "prestigious (and potentially lucrative) area of animation."[10] Standing in contrast to this earlier classic phase of industrial stability, however, Solomon identified the 1980s as an altogether more chaotic and creative period of animation production replete with many "artistic and financial triumphs and failures," and he graphed the medium's initial fall through the poor commercial and critical reaction to several cel-animated features released earlier in the decade. This included the Warner Bros. compilation feature *Daffy Duck's Fantastic Island* (1983), the dark fantasy adventure film *Fire & Ice* (1983) from independent animator Ralph Bakshi, and John Korty and Charles Swenson's mixed-media *Twice upon a Time* (1983).[11] But as Solomon noted, the release of ex-Disney animator Bluth's *An American Tail* (1986) had signaled something of a potential turnaround for the US cartoon industry, setting a box-office record for an animated film that would itself be quickly usurped by both the filmmaker's next feature, *The Land Before Time* (1988), and, later, Disney's cel-animated film *Oliver & Company* (1988). As Solomon suggested in his closing remarks, "as a new decade begins ... American animation appears healthier than it has for at least 30 years," and the 1990s "should be an exciting time for that most flexible and protean of art forms, animation."[12]

Although the commercial and critical revival of Disney animation throughout the 1990s would fulfill something of Solomon's broader prediction (there is only a speculative comment regarding *The Little Mermaid* as "expected to set a new record"), his plotting of animation's mixed state of the art and possible future gives a clear sense of the fractured industrial conditions into which the Disney Renaissance would subsequently enter, if not the terms of the medium's potential Hollywood restoration.[13] There are hopeful references made in the dossier to the revitalization of television animation thanks to the name recognition of Disney, George Lucas, and Jim Henson (Matt Groening's *The Simpsons* would also begin in 1989), alongside the popularity of *Who Framed Roger Rabbit* (1988), which in its nostalgic reimaging of Classical Hollywood cartoons "proved that audiences would pay to see a sophisticated, contemporary animated film."[14] There are even suggestions that Bluth's emergent creative rivalry with Disney was potentially helping to fuel animation's growing vibrancy as a medium of commercial and creative opportunity.[15] However, a key element that Solomon anticipated could really drive the animated medium forward and help support Hollywood's resurgent cartoon market was the role of computer graphics as a "much-publicized and potentially innovative area" of animation's technological transformation.[16]

The animated musicals of the Disney Renaissance, then, clearly represent a point of convergence between two competing and complementary trends that would emphatically define popular Hollywood cinema of this era. These are films that, most directly, coincided with important shifts in the musical genre and the subsequent emergence of a "reconstructive musical" across late-1980s Hollywood.[17] Even though by the 1970s, the musical genre (in the broadest sense) had no longer existed as a regular production category in the same way it had in the studio era, Disney animation was historically one of the few places in Hollywood where the musical *was* able to survive, thanks to its regular roster of cel-animated features and calculated reissues of golden age properties. Yet the Disney Renaissance created a new cycle of animated films that would galvanize this latest return of the Hollywood musical, with the studio's new creative kinship with Broadway musical theater arriving at a time when the "classic show syntax" and basic narrative patterns "typical" of the genre were being reconstructed and restored.[18] Furthermore, the very attraction of Broadway's "executive personnel, talent, musical style, [and] narrative structure" for Disney feature animation in this period was central to the renewed status of the studio's animation division and wider corporate expansion (thanks to Eisner) into a multimedia conglomerate with diverse business interests and synergies that would generate economic capital.[19] However, no less vital to the animated look and style of the Disney Renaissance was the industrial and aesthetic impact of computer graphics of the kind that Solomon would predict as being "certain to remain one of the most innovative and exciting areas of animation during the '90s."[20] This was the era when CGI began to migrate from the margins to the mainstream, and throughout the '80s, it moved steadily from a specialized technique used in television commercials and for interstitials (logos, title sequences, digital VFX characters, or environments) to a greater involvement in the production of big-budget Hollywood feature films. Disney animation in its Renaissance era would ultimately be shaped by—and fully contribute to—this emergent integration of CGI within mainstream US film, particularly as studios and animation facilities became increasingly invested in the potential of computer graphics and digital visualization technologies.

Much like in the era of Classic Disney to which it is often compared, technology was a defining note of the industrial infrastructure and aesthetic style of the Disney Renaissance. Walt's long-standing desire to innovate had already served to mythologize his status as a uniquely American genius equivalent to George Gershwin, Irving Berlin, Thomas Edison, and Henry Ford (a reputation somewhat galvanized by his death from cancer at only age sixty-five). For J. P. Telotte, "investment in technology and technological culture" has always represented a cornerstone of the Disney multimedia enterprise, including the company's tentacular reach since the 1950s across "television, radio, the Internet, book and music publishing, theme parks, theatre, and the more amorphous leisure industry."[21] The studio's animated feature films have steadfastly remained part of this narrative of innovation, while initially evolving the broader animated medium through sophisticated and influential technological developments. However, if the golden age had counted the arrival of sound, the multiplane camera, and adoption of the three-strip Technicolor process (as well as cost-effective Xerox copying equipment in the 1960s) among its technological breakthroughs, then the Disney Renaissance's integration of cel- and computer-animated processes reflected the wider industrial and aesthetic adoption of computer graphics within postclassical (or New Hollywood) blockbuster cinema. Lisa Purse argues:

> The emergence and development of digital imaging technologies in mainstream filmmaking is perhaps the most familiar special effects narrative we now associate with the years 1981–1999, not least because key digital milestones appear in this period.... One could, therefore, characterize 1981–1999 as a "transitional period" in which digital imaging processes grow in prominence and technical sophistication.[22]

A similar time frame of technological "transition" is offered by Michele Pierson, who argues that the increasingly reflexive centralizing of the computer-generated image as a spectacular digital artifact between 1989 and 1995 bears out the intensified role played by digital technology within mainstream cinema's "entertainment experience."[23] For Pierson, this 1989–1995 period can be defined as the "wonder years" of VFX production in Hollywood, a moment when computer-generated effects were bracketed via exhibitionist techniques of display on-screen but also when the very application of digital effects technologies in high-concept blockbusters "became the focus of intense speculation: not only for cinema audiences, but also for the special effects industry itself."[24] The Disney Renaissance musicals ultimately sit in the crosshairs of these competing market forces, evidencing the conjunction of the returning "reconstructive musical" emerging across late-1980s Hollywood with this growing acceptance by mainstream US cinema of sophisticated digital image processing, including, of course, the industrial and aesthetic incorporation of CGI into feature-length cel animation. Indeed, Solomon argues that nowhere were these practices of integration more visible than at Disney, where "drawn and computer animation were [becoming] skillfully blended" thanks to a series of cel-animated films that tested the virtual production and rendering of digital characters and environments alongside established hand-drawn techniques.[25] The momentous release of Disney's first "in-house" and fully computer-animated film, *Chicken Little* (2005), as part of its animated feature-film canon—a loose remake of its 1943 short film directed by Clyde Geronimi—must therefore be viewed as the culmination of several important experiments made by the studio during its own internal "wonder years" to integrate digital VFX effectively and seamlessly into its Renaissance-era cel-animated features.

Disney's Wonder Years

Featuring a popular-music soundtrack (including original songs by Billy Joel, Bette Midler, and Huey Lewis), *Oliver & Company* was the first animated film to gross $100 million worldwide upon its initial theatrical release and was Disney's biggest animated box-office success in a decade. Coming after a run of four nonmusicals, *The Rescuers* (1977), *The Fox and the Hound*, *The Black Cauldron* (1985), and *The Great Mouse Detective* (1986), the 1988 musical—inspired by the 1838 Charles Dickens novel *Oliver Twist*—was equally the first film in the Disney animated canon to have a department created specifically for computer animation. This department would go on to house Disney's defining technological development that would shape the production of its animated films and involvement with digital techniques over the next ten years. Costing an initial $3.9 million, the Computer Animation Production System (CAPS) was developed in 1987 and, after trials at Epcot's Spaceship Earth theme park at Walt Disney World, was first implemented at Disney for the final scene of *The Little Mermaid* to digitally transfer hand-drawn images into a computer, giving greater potential for visual manipulation, enriching color palettes, and crafting three-dimensional environments. The mouse-and-mouse chase amid the whirring cogs of Big Ben during the climax of *The Great Mouse Detective* had already blended computer-generated backgrounds with hand-drawn characters in the hybrid 2D/3D production of the clocktower, though *The Black Cauldron* was the first Disney cel-animated feature to integrate digital VFX, "albeit on a small scale," into the rendering of individual bubbles, a levitating orb of light, and the cauldron.[26] However, rather than simply a "means to support traditional cel animation," CAPS was used throughout the Disney Renaissance largely as an economical replacement for the studio's cel-animated ink-and-paint processes.[27] It was able to reproduce the "sketchiness" of hand-drawn line quality familiar from the Xerox photography of *One Hundred and One Dalmatians* (1961) and could offer "transparent shading, blended colors, and other techniques not previously available."[28] Yet the technology's most substantial innovation was the simulation of camera movements afforded by the arrangement of digital cels, including the multilayering of shots within a digital environment among its sophisticated graphic operations.

In a 1994 issue of *Computer Graphics World* coinciding with the release of *The Lion King*, Barbara Robertson reflected on the workflow of Disney's still "secret" digital animation system despite the technology's Academy Award for scientific and technical achievement two years before. Robertson explained:

> Once a pencil test of the animation and layout for a new film are approved, the exposure sheet becomes digital; the inking and painting are done by artists coloring pencil sketches scanned into a computer; backgrounds, middle grounds, foregrounds, and other painted layers are scanned into the computer for digital compositing and special effects; and digital files are sent to a film recorder to create the movie.[29]

The integration of computer processing with CAPS capitalized on the mainstreaming of digital VFX within live-action cinema during these "wonder years" described by Pierson but also coincided with Disney's own corporate interests in computer animation, having signed a deal with Pixar Animation Studios in 1991 "to make and distribute at least one computer-generated animated movie."[30] It was also Pixar (initially as Lucasfilm's Computer Division) that had developed and supplied the software for the computerized "Disney Project" later renamed CAPS, and following Disney's purchase of the technology in a deal dated May 24, 1986, the system was given the primary goal "to digitize the conventional 2-dimensional cel animation process to reduce the cost of Disney-quality animation."[31] While Disney had initially sought to mystify the CAPS system following its extensive use in the Disney Renaissance's only nonmusical, *The Rescuers Down Under* (with Robertson's piece coming a full decade after the system's inception at the Computer Graphics Lab at the New York Institute of Technology), the studio's turn toward three-dimensional computer animation was nonetheless ultimately mobilized among the Hollywood trade press as a selling point throughout the era.

A 1986 edition of *American Cinematographer*, for example, was headed "Computer Graphics Aid Animation Rebirth" and explored the influence of special-effects technologies popularized by New Hollywood directors Lucas and Stephen Spielberg upon the revival of Disney animation, which could similarly now include animated images "literally drawn with computers."[32] Alongside its use of the computerized Automatic Camera Effects System (ACES)—a "motion-controlled tracking system" guiding the movement of the physical camera apparatus—*The Great Mouse Detective* was also celebrated for its "computer-assisted layouts and graphics" and "computerized images."[33] As Les Paul Robley notes in relation to the film's final Big Ben chase sequence between villain Ratigan and the hero Basil, "The computer drew vector lines of the moving gears on printout paper, which was then copied by machine onto clear acetate animation cels and painted in the normal fashion."[34] The increased presence of Disney's animated features among specialist VFX trade journals—such as *Starlog* and *Cinefantastique*, which both ran features on several of the Disney Renaissance films—likewise reflected an intensified cultural connoisseurship of digital technologies, as well as the studio's broader industrial shift toward digitally aided production beyond the successful CAPS system.[35]

FIGURE 16.1. Three-dimensional computer animation used for *The Lion King*'s wildebeest stampede. Screenshots by author.

In the same issue of *Computer Graphics World* in which Robertson extolled the virtues of CAPS, Gary Pfitzer had also discussed the kinetic wildebeest stampede that charges toward lion cub Simba and claims the life of his father, Mufasa, in *The Lion King*.[36] Eight hundred individual wildebeests were created for the two-and-a-half-minute scene using Softimage crowd-simulation software for the modeling, rigging, and animation (rendering was achieved via Pixar's proprietary RenderMan software, with compositing in CAPS), with the result a fully three-dimensional animated stampede. The computerized CAPS system certainly made it easier to integrate other animated elements into its digital exposure sheets (particularly three-dimensional computer animation), and the Softimage program multiplied individual wildebeests as they charged through the prideland's ravine, while the technique of cel shading (also known as toon shading) replicated the hand-drawn style in CGI as the herd moved in perspective through painted backgrounds (figure 16.1). Other sequences plotting the trajectory of three-dimensional computer animation throughout the Disney Renaissance were, perhaps expectedly, oriented toward action sequences designed to fully showcase the dynamic simulations afforded by computer technology. These include several wrecked ships, staircases, and carriages in *The Little Mermaid*; the lion's-head entrance to the Cave of Wonders rising from the Arabian sands in *Aladdin*; the elderly Grandmother Willow from *Pocahontas*; the roaring Parisian crowds in *The Hunchback of Notre Dame*; the battle sequence between Hercules and multiheaded monster Hydra in *Hercules* (figure 16.2); and the charge of the Chinese army in *Mulan*.

When taken together, these digital objects and environments stake out the rhetorical possibilities of computer animation for reorganizing animated space into three dimensions. Yet as the Disney Renaissance progressed, computer graphics moved

FIGURE 16.2. The monster Hydra in *Hercules*. Screenshots by author.

from simply rendering background action, scene enhancements, and individual props to becoming more readily involved with character animation that was otherwise still largely produced using hand-drawn methods. In a piece for *Cinefantastique* on *Aladdin*, Sheldon Teitelbaum identified the film's expressive Magic Carpet character as "the first marriage ... of computer graphics and character," as it was a digitized object that mixed cel-animated techniques with digital texture-mapping software.[37] Following the rendering of the digital monster Hydra for *Hercules*, as well as the film's use of "morphing" techniques taken from prominent films of the "wonder years" *The Abyss* (1989) and *Terminator II: Judgment Day* (1991), CGI was becoming openly championed in the Hollywood trade press and by the studio themselves as "an integral part of recent Disney's animated efforts."[38] But despite the expansion of digital VFX as a valuable creative tool embedded into Disney's production workflow, on-screen it was not just in action-oriented sequences of heightened narrative drama that the studio would adopt and explore the formal parameters of digital imaging processes. Rather, such technologies were also found in the musical sequences and extravagant Broadway-style numbers, which were utilized as a valuable testing ground to showcase the heightened expressivity of CGI via the glamour of song and dance.

Digitizing the Disney Musical

Computer technologies certainly came to play a progressively pivotal role throughout the Disney Renaissance era in the articulation of the Broadway-style musical number, which in its spectacular arrangement provided the ideal backdrop for highly creative explorations into the expressive capabilities of emergent computer graphics. Teitelbaum's piece on *Aladdin* had argued the film was essentially "Arabian Nights set to music with Robin Williams and computer animation," while his earlier examination of *Beauty and the Beast* similarly noted how the 1991 film combined "computer graphics techniques" with "a more expansive integration of music."[39] In her analysis of the casting of experienced musical-theater and Broadway singers such as Paige O'Hara and Jodi Benson in Disney's Renaissance features, Jennifer Fleeger also suggested that "the operatic voice, CAPS and the increasing use of computer-aided effects were justified as essential to a good 'show' by the Broadway voice."[40] These comments suggest the various ways in which the organization of specific musical numbers provided a crucial context for understanding how (and where) the Disney Renaissance would explore digital technologies and the vital role played by computer processing in putting on a "show." Bunch further hints at this potential interplay by noting that "the mode of adolescent desire expressed in these musical films is specific to their melding of musical theater singing and animation technology."[41] Such connections between musical performance and computer graphics are made immediately apparent in "Belle," the first number from *Beauty and the Beast* and a song in which the heroine expresses a degree of resistance to and dissatisfaction with her suffocating rural lifestyle.

Offset against the choral performance of the busy villagers, who sing of how Belle is "very different from the rest of us," the character's exceptionality and desire for freedom are articulated visually throughout the aesthetic realization of the "Belle" number, from the specific layering of background planes achieved via CAPS to the mobile camerawork also enabled by the technology. As the song begins, the young bibliophile moves purposively through the village and passes the busy local crowds going about their daily chores. Belle retains her position centrally in the frame throughout, and maneuvers effortlessly past the villagers' activities to show that she is well versed in their "same old" domestic routines. She even sings somewhat wistfully at the song's opening that every day in this "quiet village" is "like the one before," with "every morning just the same, since the morning that we came, to this poor, provincial town." Yet as *Beauty and the Beast*'s opening number reaches its conclusion, a new formal style and organization of space begin to express elements of her character's narrative and emotional desires. Belle's delivery of the line "There must be more than this provincial life" as she finally reaches the village square is accompanied by an unexpected swirling camera that rotates fully around the cel-animated figure. The shot's exuberant composition is further matched by Belle's more expressive physical movements, as she suddenly looks up from her book, gestures outward with her hands, and spins her body clockwise, all while the camera moves in the opposing direction (figure 16.3). The multiple planes of action layered and organized by CAPS therefore not only authentically convey the spatial arrangement of the town and its inhabitants in three dimensions but also help to provide a formal break in the sequence that is, like Belle herself, "very different" from its usual style to help visually signal her longing for something more. At the same time, the intrusive presence of

THAT'S INTEGRATION! 325

FIGURE 16.3. Belle wishes for "more than this provincial life" in *Beauty and the Beast*. Screenshots by author.

a streetlamp placed in the immediate foreground momentarily obscures the spectators' view of Belle and the action as it passes right to left in the shot, both grounding the performance in the authentic geography of the setting and hinting at the very discourses of constraint that frame her otherwise energetic movements.

For *Beauty and the Beast*'s later Busby Berkeley–inspired "Be Our Guest" number, sung by Broadway performers Jerry Orbach (Lumière) and Angela Lansbury (Mrs. Potts) to an enraptured Belle inside the Beast's castle, acetate cels were likewise

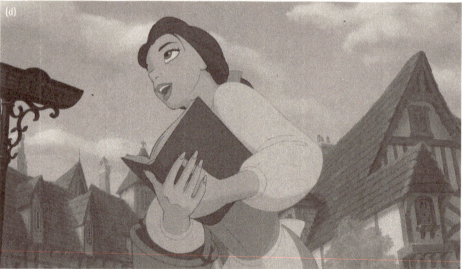

FIGURE 16.3. Continued

synthesized with computer animation, this time alongside Pixar's RenderMan software to create the anthropomorphized "dancing plates, forks, goblets, bubbles" that were all "created with computers."[42] The ornate geometry in motion, concentric circles, and symmetrical shaping typical of Berkeley's musical style (which would reappear in the ordering of crocodiles, giraffes, and antelope in "Just Can't Wait to Be King" from *The Lion King*) translated into the animated kaleidoscope of interweaving patterns produced by the dancing clusters of computerized cutlery. The signature digital VFX scene of the predominantly cel-animated *Beauty and the Beast* is equally a lavish musical number, albeit in the mold of Fred Astaire and Ginger Rogers's elegant duets (rather than the geometric patterns of activity popularized by Berkeley), yet similarly integrates cel- and computer-animated elements. Belle and the Beast's graceful dance in the castle ballroom involved hand-drawn characters and a three-dimensional color environment, with the ballroom first modeled as a digital wireframe inside a computer through which a mobile virtual camera plotting the figures' movements could be continually (re)positioned. Producer Don Hahn explains, "We did this with computer graphics techniques, building a set digitally and flying a camera around."[43] CGI supervisor Jim Hillin adds that the use of computer-generated color backgrounds via RenderMan in this sequence also "gives the advantage of sweeping camera moves and perspectives as well as theatrical lighting that would otherwise be impossible."[44] As Belle and the Beast begin their romantic waltz (synchronized to the lyric "as the sun will rise" sung by Lansbury/Mrs. Potts), the virtual camera suddenly soars away from the couple toward the gold-encrusted chandelier hanging above them.

The sequence then cuts from the ornate light fixture (created, like the ballroom, in CGI), with the camera now reversing its position to begin its dramatic descent. It circles clockwise back down toward the ballroom floor at a steep angle to mimic both Belle and the Beast's spiraling movements and the curvature of the ballroom's domed structure (figure 16.4). Such an expressive placing of the spectator formally registers the decadence of the Baroque design of the castle, which in its gilded features counterpoints the Romantic ideals of Belle's "provincial life" long since left behind. As the virtual camera glides smoothly around the dancing couple, the shot also keeps each character in correct graphic perspective as they swirl in circles as part of their elaborate routine. The complex process of layering of cel-animated characters over a fully CGI space and then compositing with CAPS was later switched for the musical performances of *The Lion King*. The stylistic influence of Elton John and Hans Zimmer certainly sets the 1994 film apart from other Disney Renaissance musical numbers written by lyricist Howard Ashman (who died during the production of *Aladdin*, his work completed by English lyricist Tim Rice) and composer Alan Menken, who together had strongly contributed to the "revival of Disney animation in the 1990s."[45] Yet *The Lion King* retains the kind of Berkeley-style kaleidoscopic dance sequences and composition of bodies that provide the context and opportunity for the creative arrangement of computer-generated components. As part of its digital design, the number "Be Prepared," sung by the villainous Scar (Jeremy Irons) incorporated the same copy-and-paste multiplication process as the film's computer-animated wildebeest stampede to duplicate hyenas as they marched in patterns against a cel-animated location. Requiring less randomized movements of digital objects than the chaotic and unpredictable stampede, the sequence used the Softimage computer program and its procedural calculations to arrange the parading hyenas in a more orderly fashion and enhance their cumulative threat through automatic, regimented action.

The sustained combination of computer-animation effects with cel animation in films such as *Beauty and the Beast* and *The Lion King* fully sharpens the idea that the musical genre, at least when considered within the industrial parameters of Hollywood, has always been a space of technology. As Rick Altman's history of the American musical

FIGURE 16.4. The digital ballroom in *Beauty and the Beast*. Screenshots by author.

"as the most complex art form ever devised" suggests, the musical "served as a testing ground for many of Hollywood's most important technical innovations (sound film itself, later developments in sound technology like the playback system, [and] special visual effects of numerous sorts)."[46] Hannah Lewis also argues that "technological intervention" has "always been present in film musicals," adding to sound elements such as "dubbing and post-synchronization" the value of editing that combines "multiple takes of a complex dance number."[47] While the economic and artistic benefits of "technological intervention" to the musical's style of spectacle is certainly matched by the Disney Renaissance's own negotiation of digital imagery, the particular interplay and

THAT'S INTEGRATION! 329

FIGURE 16.4. Continued

exchange between cel- and computer-animated elements during this period of Disney animation both intensifies and disrupts the Hollywood musical's long-standing investment in technological virtuosity and enhancement, which is often made notable by its absence. Indeed, contrary to the genre's application of audiovisual effects that build its exhibitionist mode of address, spectators are typically "never allowed to realize that musical entertainment is an industrial product and that putting on a show (or putting on a Hollywood musical) is a matter of a labor force producing a product for consumption."[48] As Jane Feuer notes, such processes of erasure hold because the Hollywood musical operates as "mass art which aspires to the conditions of folk art."[49] Technological intervention in the musical was consequently made "transparent to foreground the virtuosity of singing" during the classic era, aside from in the subset of self-reflexive "backstage musicals" and "Hollywood behind-the-scenes narratives" where the conspicuousness of the "world behind the camera" emphatically corrected any view that musicals were ever "born from spontaneous combustion."[50]

Despite the musical's desire to veil, disguise, and suspend the system of capitalist production through seemingly impromptu and improvisatory performances that bear little or no relation to the coordinated processes that construct them, the medium specificity and alternative rhetorical stakes of animation as an art form fundamentally complicate any ability for the (animated) musical to maintain this folk-narrative masquerade. Susan Smith argues that the musical's long-standing generic desire to "pass itself off as folk art" through the "illusion of spontaneity and improvisation" is ultimately "difficult to sustain against the specific conditions of the animated musical" given the graphic medium's defining unreality.[51] In the specific case of the stop-motion musical *The Nightmare Before Christmas* (1993), where the jerky movements and "blatantly stitched-together" quality of the puppet bodies further identify rather than efface the film's laborious "constructedness," Smith argues, the "utopian pleasures of this branch of the musical seem more plausibly rooted in a self-conscious delight in animation's capacity for bringing things to life."[52] The polished digital imagery of the Disney Renaissance musicals achieves a similar outcome, as the self-conscious presence of digital VFX further overwhelms the animated musical's already-constructed claims to folk art through the momentary combination and negotiation of competing image-making technologies and registers. By briefly projecting the audience into yet another space of modernity and pointing another finger at—and then back toward—animation's intrinsic ontology as a medium of convincing trompe l'oeil simulation, the "very different" computer-generated sequences draw extra attention to the constructedness of animation as a sophisticated technology of representation.

Diamonds in the Rough

Bracketed via formal networks of organization, the many musical numbers powered by digital imagery in the Disney Renaissance typically intervene in the cel-animated style to offer alternative computerized spaces of wonder, with their visible effects reflexively intensifying the animated spectacle of their digital engineering. As *Beauty and the Beast*'s virtuoso ballroom sequence in particular makes clear, the application of digital VFX within song-and-dance performance provides a clear formal interplay between computer-animated environments and hand-drawn character animation that certainly fits within long-standing traditions of "effects" cinema, including the defining visual exhibitionism of computer graphics in this "wonder years" phase of digital VFX production. The musical genre's own fundamental tension between regulation and extravagance has, of course, also been frequently understood through similar processes of comparison and disjuncture and how more spectacular performance styles are typically reserved for the exuberant display of the number as the genre's primary semantic element. Martha Shearer argues that several Classical Hollywood musical numbers (particularly those designed by Berkeley) were "divorced from any grounding in realist space and foreground their spatial impossibilities," with their abstract and "expansive" style offset against the restrained verisimilitude of the framing diegesis.[53] Seemingly at odds with the musical's obscuring of the technological mediation at work in its numbers, such discourses of reconciliation have been further challenged by instances where animated and nonanimated elements are made to playfully and impossibly perform together, obtaining their power through a visible mixed-media ontology rooted in the rhetorical performance of conflicting yet momentarily coexistent media. Gene Kelly's dance with MGM's Jerry Mouse in *Anchors Aweigh* (1945) or Kelly dancing with numerous animated figures in the "Sinbad the Sailor" number from the anthology film *Invitation to the Dance* (1956); the underwater synchronized routine in *Dangerous When Wet* (1953), in which Esther Williams swims with Tom and Jerry; the penguin routine in *Mary Poppins* (1964); the sequence from *Bedknobs and Broomsticks* (1971) that unfolds "at the bottom of the beautiful briny sea"; and the 1989 music video for "Opposites Attract" by Paula Abdul (where Abdul dances with cartoon character MC Skat Kat, inspired by the Kelly/Jerry performance in *Anchors Aweigh*) collectively play out the presentational dimension to the musical as much as the genre's investment in "spatial impossibilities" via the combination of live action with cartoon aesthetics.[54]

Such "patterns of meaning" can be firmly implicated in the wider generic tension in the musical rooted in an "integration" between "the main protagonists and the numbers (freedom) and . . . the conventional, reconciliatory plot strategies (inhibition)."[55] Yet such an exchange between two *animation* technologies in the realization of the Disney Renaissance musical numbers also fits neatly under what Mark Langer has described as the medium's potential for a "stylistic dialectic," a term he conceives through the specific aesthetic history of the Disney animated musical and its potential for moments of graphic incongruity in the interplay of sound and image. Langer discusses certain overlooked sequences within Disney's animated output that are marked by an anomalous graphic style, resulting in an interplay of registers that draws attention to "stylistically discontinuous" elements in the animation that contradict an otherwise "hyper-realist" visual agenda defined by pictorial believability and "modes of naturalism."[56] This "dialectic" is best exemplified by the "two-dimensional and artificial" pink elephants musical sequence in *Dumbo*, a scene that visually signifies an inebriated Dumbo and Timothy's subjective states through a reflexive shift in formal style.[57] As directed by Norman Ferguson, the expressive "counterstyle" of the pink elephants sequence incorporates colorful elephant silhouettes, transforming and duplicating bodies and shapes, inverted colors and patterns, optical rhythms, and surrealist configurations all set to pulsing orchestral music.[58] These moments of visual abstraction at once evoke early animation's own culture of quick change and rapidly metamorphosing drawings—exemplified by J. Stuart Blackton's *Humorous Phases of Funny Faces* (1906) and *Fantasmagorie* (1908) by French caricaturist Émile Cohl—as well as the impressionistic configurations familiar from experimental, nonnarrative, and visual music traditions popular in European animation of the 1920s and 1930s (figure 16.5). Within the trajectory of Disney feature animation, too, the pink elephants sequence strongly recalls the bold abstraction and visualization of music in *Fantasia* (1940), which began production in 1936 and was released the year before *Dumbo*. Yet aside from challenging the classic stylistic unity of Disney's golden age formula, this occasional cartoonal register of *Dumbo* (that Langer attributes to the East Coast influence of New York animators Raoul Barré, John Bray, Pat Sullivan, and the Van Beuren, Terrytoons, Fleischer, and Charles Mintz studios) anticipates the shifting ontological order and digital VFX of the Disney Renaissance. Computer graphics in Disney musicals of the 1980s and 1990s function as elemental moments of digital intervention and embellishment that, just like *Dumbo*'s pink elephants sequence, both disrupt and confirm the surrounding "hyperreality" but in their new digitally assisted expressiveness provide the Disney Renaissance with alternative formal strategies of presentation.

In the Disney Renaissance's mixed-media musicals, this "stylistic dialectic" of tone and register is a consequence of the hybrid aesthetic that combines cel and computer image-making forms to manipulate depth, dimension, and perspective within animated

FIGURE 16.5. *Dumbo*'s surrealist pink elephants parade sequence as an example of stylistic discontinuity in Disney's musical numbers. Screenshots by author.

THAT'S INTEGRATION! 333

FIGURE 16.5. Continued

FIGURE 16.5. Continued

environments. Indeed, Disney's thirty-seventh animated feature film, *Tarzan*, pioneered the studio's second major development in computer animation—the painting and rendering software system Deep Canvas—that as with the effects of the multiplane camera and the CAPS system, reinterpreted the concept of animated layout. David Whitley explains that the Deep Canvas technology "enables animators to model a sense [of] three-dimensional space on the screen that accurately adjusts perspective, lighting and contour as the camera moves through a particular environment."[59] As a computer-assisted tool designed to enhance the complexity of its moving backgrounds, the Deep Canvas system crafted dense foliage accented with exotic flora and fauna. Gray virtual cylinders were first constructed inside a computer to represent trunks and branches, with a preprogrammed virtual camera pathway plotted in multiple directions before any insertion of cel-animated characters and backgrounds. A stylus and digitizing tablet were then used to simulate the painterly style and brushstrokes of hand-drawn techniques, applied digitally to the computer-generated models to gradually build the film's convincing three-dimensional junglescape. The ten minutes of *Tarzan* created via the Deep Canvas design tool was targeted largely at the film's action sequences (particularly in the confrontation where Tarzan kills ferocious leopard Sabor) and to visually signify Tarzan's growing fluency with his environment. However, the technology was also mobilized in specific musical numbers, even though the film departed from the Disney Renaissance's defining Broadway style in favor of a soundtrack sung by Phil Collins, who acts as the film's narrator.

Coming twenty minutes into *Tarzan* and immediately preceding the chase sequence culminating in Sabor's death, the number "Son of Man" follows the young Tarzan's ascension to adulthood as he learns the ways of the wilderness. As Tarzan swings with increasing confidence through the lush virtual environment produced via the Deep Canvas system, his movements (inspired by US skateboarder Tony Hawk) are tracked seemingly in one long take by the virtual camera that follows him through the labyrinthine jungle as he acrobatically jumps, swings, glides, and pirouettes between the hanging vines and contorting branches (figure 16.6). The sequence is then repeated as the film's last shot, which also offers a reprise of the musical number "Two Worlds" as the film's recurring theme, though Tarzan now performs his acrobatic movements with love interest Jane, who has opted to stay with her father on the island. In this thirty-second climactic sequence, the cel-animated characters perform dizzying maneuvers and accelerate in motion through the virtual Deep Canvas environment, twisting under and around the canopy of digital leaves and trees that make up the computer-animated foreground. The stylistic framing of both Tarzan's journey to maturity and his romance with Jane (including her assimilation into jungle life via her perfect mirroring of Tarzan's athletic movements) as heightened moments of action illustrates how the application of digital technology sharpens—and, in the Disney Renaissance, strikingly narrows—the stylistic proximity between the musical and other popular genres. The formal relationship between the rhetoric of musicals and action-cinema aesthetics has, for example, resulted in the recognition of a "structural analogy between the action set-piece and the musical number."[60] Many of the digitally assisted musical sequences in *Tarzan*—as well

FIGURE 16.6. Tarzan swings through the sweeping 3D backgrounds as both boy and man during "Son of Man." Screenshots by author.

as the "I'll Make a Man out of You" number from *Mulan* depicting the soldiers' "boot camp" training—blur the distinction between action and musical cinemas thanks to the contribution of computer processing. Both "Son of Man" and "Two Worlds" solicit a mode of spectatorial address that invites audiences to marvel at the depth, dimension, and detail of the digitally composed shot within the creative organization of the musical number as a frenetic sequence of activity.

This connection between the Hollywood musical and action cinema is equally visible in the earlier Disney Renaissance numbers "A Whole New World" (*Aladdin*), "Just around the Riverbend" (*Pocahontas*), and "Out There" (*The Hunchback of Notre Dame*), which collectively hold cel and computer animation in rich creative tension via the spectacle of movement. In the songs, the protagonists—Aladdin, Jasmine, Pocahontas, and Quasimodo—travel through and across their respective animated worlds in ways that intensify their actions, and as "they begin to float, fly, and defy gravity," the Disney Renaissance's broader investment in the validation of adolescent desire, optimism, and jouissance becomes dramatically realized through digitally mediated production.[61] Furthermore, given the liberation of youthful characters "assisted by the technology of the magic carpet in 'A Whole New World'"—including first-person perspectives as Jasmine and Aladdin ride the digitally animated object—it comes as little surprise that the film's theatrical release in 1992 coincided with the development by Disney Imagineering of a "high-fidelity virtual reality (VR) attraction" for Disney's theme parks.[62] In this interactive digital simulation, guests could "fly a magic carpet through a virtual world," experiencing "synthetic characters and a narrative story line" all within a computer-generated location.[63] Such experiments with "using VR as a new medium to tell stories" translated back into the aesthetic of Disney's feature films, with digital technology in the musical sequences subsequently shaping the design of the three-dimensional environment as well as the cel-animated character's contact with the pictorial space.[64]

As with "Son of Man" from *Tarzan* (and even "Go the Distance" from *Hercules*, showing the fifteen-year-old hero traveling overland to Mount Olympus), *The Hunchback of Notre Dame*'s "Out There" provides another expressive treatment of space motivated by character mobility. It is a song that narratively marks the desire of imprisoned Quasimodo (voiced by Tom Hulce) to integrate into the society below. In comparison with the song's opening verses (performed by antagonist Claude Frollo [Tony Jay], who compels the bell-ringer to remain hidden in the bell tower), the latter stages of the number are marked by Quasimodo's dreams of acceptance accentuated by the sophisticated movement of the CAPS camerawork that supports his defining exceptionality via "gravity-defying feats of agility."[65] The verticality of Notre Dame is digitally enhanced as Quasimodo slides down its gutters and past the colonnade (figure 16.7), and he later hangs off the cathedral to draw attention to its architectural splendor and his own moment of weightlessness.

Earlier in the film, too, the extravagant and playfully unruly "Topsy Turvy" musical number reflects how musical performance was regularly used to test the creative limits of specific computer programs. Sung by Broadway actor Paul Kandel (as Roma leader Clopin Trouillefou), "Topsy Turvy" takes place in the bustling town square located in the shadow of Notre Dame and is part of the Feast of Fools celebration of alterity, subversion, and contradiction ("Everything is topsy turvy, at the Feast of Fools"). The film's digital production department, headed by CGI supervisor Kiran Joshi, developed the proprietary CROWD software system that could generate individual animated character templates and set the parameters of their movements. These digital puppets of varied genders and body types could then be duplicated and transformed (exchanging clothing, facial hair, accessories) to fill the streets of Paris with a lively horde

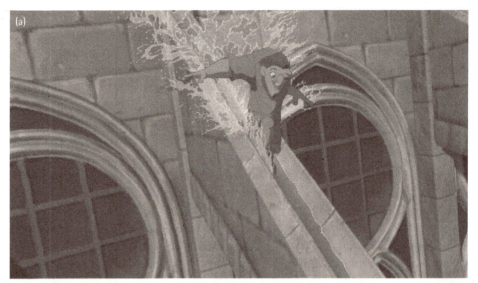

FIGURE 16.7. CAPS camerawork in "Out There" from *The Hunchback of Notre Dame*. Screenshots by author.

and, by extension, populate the cel-animated space with modified virtual elements. Anticipating the sophisticated computer-animated crowd-simulation programs such as MASSIVE and DENIZEN commonly used in postmillennial Hollywood blockbusters to render CGI swarms and armies (alongside the ATTILA and DYNASTY software developed for *Mulan*'s climactic crowd shot in the song "I'll Make a Man out of You"), *The Hunchback of Notre Dame*'s own expansive "digital multitude" was designed specifically to meet the demands of its large-scale "Topsy Turvy" musical number and convincingly

THAT'S INTEGRATION! 339

FIGURE 16.7. Continued

stage the spectacle of its performance.[66] Alongside the Deep Canvas software in *Tarzan*, and even the development of the Faux Plane shading technique for *Mulan* that made two-dimensional images appear three-dimensional in the rendering of the Great Wall of China and the Forbidden City, the generating of three-dimensional crowds using the CROWD program in *The Hunchback of Notre Dame* bears out how technological innovations found more than a welcome home in the Disney Renaissance's roster of musical numbers.[67]

Conclusion

In the years immediately following the Disney Renaissance, the studio's complex relationship with digital technology and computer graphics would largely be understood industrially through a series of business relationships and creative collaborations (notably with Pixar, which Disney purchased in May 2006 for $7.4 billion), rather than the kinds of integrated computer processes and expressive VFX imagery that would define the visual repertoire of the studio's Broadway-style musicals. This is because after the release of *Tarzan* and the sequel *Fantasia 2000* (1999), Disney quickly abandoned the musical format until the release of cel-animated *The Princess and the Frog* (2009) and shifted emphasis toward the action-adventure and science-fiction genres with *Dinosaur* (2000), *Atlantis: The Lost Empire* (2001), *Treasure Planet* (2002), and *Lilo & Stitch* (2002).[68] In moving away from the Broadway-musical template, Disney would also follow the pattern set by *Toy Story* (1995) and the emergence of the computer-animated feature film, which in the late 1990s and early 2000s were summarized as nothing more than "cyber-animated comedies with a few incidental songs."[69] Cel-animated films released in this same period would, by contrast, remain a space of cartoon music, with *Rover Dangerfield* (1991), *Rock-a-Doodle* (1991), *FernGully: The Last Rainforest* (1992), *Thumbelina* (1994), *Anastasia* (1997), *Cats Don't Dance* (1997), and *Quest for Camelot* (1998) all influenced by the Disney Renaissance template of American musical theater. Alongside other cel-/computer-animated hybrid films such as DreamWorks' *The Prince of Egypt* (1998), *The Iron Giant* (1999), and *Titan A.E.* (2000), computer-generated objects, virtual sets, and digital character animation became progressively cleaved from the conventions of the musical format and instead situated within new generic frames.

A closer look back at the short-lived Disney Renaissance phase ultimately reveals the extent to which musical numbers played a vital role in the studio's evolving digital history, with computer animation central to the aesthetic work and formal repertoire of its Broadway-style performances. The cycle of ten cel-animated films produced in this era combined sound and image in ways not seen since the Silly Symphonies, using computer animation to build on the musical's long-standing relationship to spectacle, utopia, and nostalgia in stylistic progressive ways. The Disney Renaissance films had also arrived at a time when other computer-animation facilities were diversifying their production portfolios through lucrative commissioned work with advertising agencies as a stepping stone to full feature-film production (Pixar's first computer-animated commercial was produced in 1989, the same year as *The Little Mermaid*).[70] By comparison, Disney was exploiting the Broadway design and musicality of its cel-animated features to investigate the nature of digital illustration and computer animation in late-1980s and early-1990s Hollywood, which was itself dominated by an exploration of computer-generated effects largely in relation to developments in the science-fiction genre. Until the recent production of CGI-heavy "live-action" remakes of Disney Renaissance animated films—such as *Beauty and the Beast* (2017), *Aladdin* (2019), *The*

Lion King (2019), and *Mulan* (2020)—Disney's animated musicals produced during its Renaissance stand as rare examples of the theatricality of musical performance being actively combined with computer graphics and digital VFX technologies. Dietmar Meinel suggests the experiments with digital imagery throughout the Disney Renaissance "prepared audiences for a computer-animated viewing experience" as CGI in mainstream Hollywood cinema moved headlong into the 1990s.[71] But these films also represented a unique era of Disney animation that mined and expanded the expressivity of musical numbers to test out the pristine visual illusionism of digital imagery and consolidate the creative possibilities of a set of technologies that would quickly come to envelop and define the future of popular US animation.

Notes

1. Leonard Maltin, *Of Mice and Magic: A History of American Animated Cartoons* (New York: Plume, 1987), 78.
2. Sean P. Griffin, *Tinker Belles and Evil Queens: The Walt Disney Company from the Inside Out* (New York: New York University Press, 2000), 133–181.
3. Sean Wilson, *The Sound of Cinema: Hollywood Film Music from the Silents to the Present* (Jefferson, NC: McFarland, 2022), 157.
4. Janet Wasko, *Understanding Disney: The Manufacture of Fantasy* (Cambridge: Polity, 2001); Chris Pallant, *Demystifying Disney: A History of Disney Feature Animation* (London: Bloomsbury, 2011), 89.
5. Pallant, *Demystifying Disney*, 110.
6. Ibid., 89.
7. Ryan Bunch, "'Love Is an Open Door': Revising and Repeating Disney's Musical Tropes in *Frozen*," in *Contemporary Musical Film*, ed. Kevin J. Donnelly and Beth Carroll (Edinburgh: Edinburgh University Press, 2017), 89.
8. John Mueller, "Fred Astaire and the Integrated Musical," *Cinema Journal* 24, no. 1 (Autumn 1984): 28.
9. Ibid., 30.
10. Charles Solomon, "Animation: Special Report," *Hollywood Reporter Magazine*, January 15, 1990 S3.
11. Ibid.
12. Ibid., S34.
13. Ibid., S4.
14. Ibid.
15. Ibid.
16. Ibid., S33.
17. Jane Feuer, *The Hollywood Musical*, 2nd ed. (Bloomington: Indiana University Press, 1993), 126.
18. Ibid., 130. Embodied most emphatically by the teen-focused narratives of *Grease* (1978), *Flashdance* (1983), *Footloose* (1984), *Dirty Dancing* (1987), and *Hairspray* (1988), such postmodern films restored the plot structure of Classical Hollywood while avoiding any "parodic or deconstructive" registers in their citation of studio-era musical conventions, while stylistically borrowing from MTV and music videos to reconfigure the genre for a new generation.

19. Jennifer Fleeger, *Mismatched Women: The Siren's Song through the Machine* (Oxford: Oxford University Press, 2014), 119.
20. Solomon, "Animation," S34.
21. J. P. Telotte, *The Mouse Machine: Disney and Technology* (Urbana: University of Illinois Press, 2008), 3.
22. Lisa Purse, "The New Hollywood, 1981–1999: Special/Visual Effects," in *Editing and Special/Visual Effects*, ed. Kristen Whissel and Charlie Keil (New Brunswick, NJ: Rutgers University Press, 2015), 142–143.
23. Michele Pierson, *Special Effects: Still in Search of Wonder* (New York: Columbia University Press, 2002), 93.
24. Ibid., 137.
25. Solomon, "Animation," S34.
26. Pallant, *Demystifying Disney*, 95.
27. Ibid., 96.
28. Krystina Madej and Newton Lee, *Disney Stories: Getting to Digital* (New York: Springer, 2012), 88.
29. Barbara Robertson, "Disney Lets CAPS out of the Bag," *Computer Graphics World*, July 1994, 58–59.
30. See https://www.pixar.com/our-story.
31. "Confidential—Disney Project: Executive Summary," AlvyRay.com, May 24, 1986, 1, http://alvyray.com/DigitalLight/CAPS_ExecSummary_AlvyToPixar_4May86.pdf.
32. Les Paul Robley, "Computer Graphics Aid Animation Rebirth," *American Cinematographer* 67, no. 10 (1986): 78.
33. Ibid., 74, 80.
34. Ibid., 79.
35. See Brian Lowry, "Animating 'The Black Cauldron,'" *Starlog Magazine*, August 1995, 65–67; Sheldon Teitelbaum, "Walt Disney's 'Beauty and the Beast,'" *Cinefantastique*, February 1992, 42–43; Sheldon Teitelbaum, "Disney's 'Aladdin,'" *Cinefantastique*, December 1992, 14–15; Allen Malmquist, "Pocahontas," *Cinefantastique*, August 1995, 14–15; Bill Warren, "The Hunchback of Notre Dame," *Starlog Magazine*, July 1996, 102–109; Mike Lyons, "Walt Disney's 'Hercules,'" *Cinefantastique*, June 1997, 14–25, 61; Kyle Counts, "Hercules," *Starlog Magazine*, May 1997, 32–36; Kyle Counts, "Lord of the Apes," *Starlog Magazine*, July 1999, 39–47.
36. Gary Pfitzer, "Wildebeests on the Run: Disney Engineers a Stampede for *The Lion King*," *Computer Graphics World*, July 1994, 52–54.
37. Teitelbaum, "Disney's 'Aladdin,'" 15.
38. Lyons, "Walt Disney's 'Hercules,'" 24–25.
39. Teitelbaum, "Disney's 'Aladdin,'" 14; Teitelbaum, "Walt Disney's 'Beauty and the Beast,'" 42–43.
40. Fleeger, *Mismatched Women*, 129.
41. Ryan Bunch, "Soaring into Song: Youth and Yearning in Animated Musicals of the Disney Renaissance," *American Music* 39, no. 2 (Summer 2021): 183.
42. Joe Tracy, "An Inside Look at the Original Beauty and the Beast," *Digital Media FX Magazine*, 2001, https://web.archive.org/web/20230130133856/ https://www.digitalmediafx.com/Beauty/Features/originalbeauty.html.
43. Teitelbaum, "Walt Disney's 'Beauty and the Beast,'" 43.
44. Tracy, "An Inside Look."

45. Tracey L. Mollet, *A Cultural History of the Disney Fairy Tale* (London: Palgrave Macmillan, 2020), 53.
46. Rick Altman, *The American Film Musical* (Bloomington: Indiana University Press, 1987), ix.
47. Hannah Lewis, "The Virtuosic Camera: Nostalgia, Technology, and the Contemporary Hollywood Musical," in *The Oxford Handbook of the Hollywood Musical*, ed. Dominic Broomfield-McHugh (Oxford: Oxford University Press, 2022), 568.
48. Feuer, *The Hollywood Musical*, 13.
49. Ibid., 3.
50. Lewis, "The Virtuosic Camera," 569; Feuer, *The Hollywood Musical*, 45.
51. Susan Smith, "The Animated Film Musical," in *The Oxford Handbook of the American Musical*, ed. Raymond Knapp, Mitchell Morris, and Stacy Wolf (New York: Oxford University Press, 2011), 172.
52. Ibid.
53. Martha Shearer, *New York City and the Hollywood Musical: Dancing in the Streets* (London: Palgrave Macmillan, 2016), 29–30.
54. Ibid., 30.
55. Martin Sutton, "Patterns of Meaning in the Musical," in *Genre: The Musical: A Reader*, ed. Rick Altman (London: Routledge, 1981), 191.
56. Mark Langer, "Regionalism in Disney Animation: Pink Elephants and *Dumbo*," *Film History* 4, no. 4 (1990): 312; Paul Wells, *Understanding Animation* (London: Routledge, 1998), 25–26.
57. Langer, "Regionalism," 312.
58. Ibid., 306.
59. David Whitley, *The Idea of Nature in Disney Animation* (Aldershot, UK: Ashgate, 2008), 123.
60. Yvonne Tasker, *The Hollywood Action and Adventure Film* (Oxford: Wiley-Blackwell, 2015), 48.
61. Bunch, "Soaring into Song," 182–184.
62. Ibid., 188.
63. Randy Pausch, Jon Snoddy, Roberta Taylor, Scott Watson, and Eric Haseltine, "Disney's Aladdin: First Steps Toward Storytelling in Virtual Reality," paper presented at SIGGRAPH '96, New Orleans, August 8, 1996, 193, https://dl.acm.org/doi/pdf/10.1145/237170.237257.
64. Ibid.
65. Bunch, "Soaring into Song," 191.
66. Kristen Whissel, "The Digital Multitude," *Cinema Journal* 49, no. 4: 90–110.
67. Ian Failes, "The CG side of the Animated 'Mulan,'" Befores & Afters, 2020, https://beforesandafters.com/2020/09/26/the-cg-side-of-the-animated-mulan/.
68. Barbara Robertson, "Staying Tooned," *Computer Graphics World*, July 2001, https://www.cgw.com/Publications/CGW/2001/Volume-24-Issue-7-July-2001-/Staying-Tooned.aspx.
69. Marc Miller, "Of Tunes and Toons: The Movie Musical in the 1990s," in *Film Genre 2000: New Critical Essays*, ed. Wheeler W. Dixon (Albany: State University of New York Press, 2000), 55.
70. Christopher Holliday, "'Movin' to a Different Beat': Commercial Pixar and the Simulated Ordinary," in *Animation and Advertising: Commerce, Persuasion and Appeal*, ed. Malcolm Cook and Kirsten Thompson (London: Palgrave Macmillan, 2020), 283–298.
71. Dietmar Meinel, *Pixar's America: The Re-animation of American Myths and Symbols* (London: Palgrave Macmillan, 2016), 7.

PART IV

CULTURE AND IDENTITY

CHAPTER 17

"THE DOORS OF PERCEPTION": ANIMATED COLOR, SURREALISM, AND THE LATIN AMERICAN DISNEY MUSICALS

KIRSTEN MOANA THOMPSON

Music has always played a significant role in classic American cel animation since the introduction of sound in the late 1920s. Many cartoon series that appeared in the 1930s, such as Merrie Melodies (Warner Bros), Happy Harmonies (MGM), and Silly Symphonies (Disney), reflect the importance of popular and classical melodies in animation as narrative structuring devices and as means for comedic expression.[1] From the operetta-like melodies in the Disney studio's first feature, *Snow White and the Seven Dwarfs* (1937) to the experimental concert feature *Fantasia* (1940)[2] and the fairy tales *Cinderella* (1950) and *Sleeping Beauty* (1959), songs and music have been key aesthetic components of the Disney feature film and have played a critical role as expressive devices for heterosexual and heteronormative romance.[3]

The American animated musical genre was influenced by the financial constraints of World War II, as well as broader changes in animation styles, and it allowed for a new direction in the Disney feature film. Challenging the perception of Disney's move to ever greater realism, this chapter examines several case-study sequences from Disney's *Saludos Amigos* (1943) and *The Three Caballeros* (1945), made in the early 1940s under wartime conditions, when Technicolor IV helped shape a far more experimental and surrealist style than previously seen in Disney. These features combined music and comedy with color in a stylistic shift whose aesthetic strategies had been foreshadowed by sequences in *Dumbo* (1941). With reference to the writings of Heinrich Klüver (*Mescal and Mechanisms of Hallucinations*) and Aldous Huxley (*The Doors of Perception; Heaven and Hell*) and their focus on specific color and pattern effects that are hallucinated by the viewer under the effects of drugs such as mescaline, I examine the ways in which color represents light in movement in cel animation through the simulation of prismatic, scintillating, or oscillating light effects that shared some of the formal techniques and abstraction of the avant-garde. More particularly, through recurrent patterns that overlap or bear remarkable similarity to Klüver's form constants, musical and color experimentation in the Latin American features created "color forms" and other aesthetic techniques that might be understood as manifestations of Huxley's "visionary perception."

Traditionally, animation has been defined as the frame-by-frame photography of two-dimensional or three-dimensional cels or objects that, when flipped or projected, create the illusion of movement. More recently, scholars have been debating how we understand the term "animation," moving beyond this more technical definition to suggest that animation might be an aesthetic form in which relationships between stillness and movement, between petrification and mobilization, are engaged.[4] My own work in examining Disneyland's and Disney World's nighttime fireworks and water shows (in which animation is projected onto mist and fountain jets) has suggested that cel animation is an aesthetic process in which structural relationships between the transparent, translucent, and opaque are staged and through which emotions and ideas around permanence and the ephemeral, the fixed and the fugitive, and the mortal and the fleeting coalesce.[5] In the Latin American features, animated color represents ephemeral light in abstract form and musical movement, as key aesthetic strategies not only to represent but also to produce visionary perception.

Present from cinema's inception, color was applied to celluloid through paints, stencils, or color baths in hand painting, tinting, toning, and stenciling, or it was produced through later additive or subtractive cinematographic processes such as Kinemacolor and Technicolor I–IV, processes that also informed animation.[6] Cinematic color favored particular genres: historical period pieces, costume dramas, fantasy and fairy tales, comedies, and the musical. The musical's long association with fantasy and utopia was complemented by the introduction of a new color process in the 1930s. Ted Eshbaugh Studios and Disney were both pioneers in the development of animation in Technicolor IV,[7] with Disney securing an exclusive contract to produce Technicolor IV cartoons from 1932 to 1934. From its first cartoon short in color (*Flowers and Trees*, 1932), the Disney studio would use the Silly Symphonies series as a training ground for experimentation and development as it geared up for the release of *Snow White* in 1937. The arrival of World War II altered studio production processes, with Disney shifting to government work producing training films for US troops and propaganda films for homefront audiences, as well as other wartime work.[8] Budgets were strained during the 1940s with the high costs of *Pinocchio* (1940) and the loss of some wartime European markets, and Disney shifted to issuing "package" features such as *Make Mine Music* (1946) and *Melody Time* (1948). These combined multiple cartoon shorts with musical soundtracks or songs with bridging transitions, assembling them into composite feature-length films that were quicker and cheaper to produce.

Disney, Realism, and Surrealism: Foundational Techniques in *Dumbo*

The Disney studio has long been known for its meticulous attention to constructing a form of "hyperrealism," or "the creation of a realistic image system which echoes the 'realism' of the live action film."[9] As part of the studio's development of its production process in the shift to features, Disney created an industrialized, highly specialized assembly line that built on the divisions of labor necessitated by a time-intensive art form, with directors, animators, in-betweeners, layout artists, background painters, ink-and-painters, color designers, and others. One of Walt Disney's innovative contributions to the animation industry was the creation of a new specialized team at the studio, the effects department, which created difficult-to-animate subjects such as atmosphere (rain, fog, mist, steam), water (ripples, waves, bubbles), and fire and light (candlelight, firelight, shadows).[10] For example, in the Mickey Mouse cartoon *The Worm Turns* (Wilfred Jackson, 1937), many of these detailed light, shadow, and water effects are used in a scene where Mickey is working on a potion in his laboratory late one night. Developed through the Silly Symphonies and Mickey Mouse shorts as preparation for its features, this effects work contributed to the studio's pioneering verisimilitude and came closer to a form of cinematographic realism than had previously seemed possible in American cel animation. This realist tendency dominated the studio style in the 1930s, with its "squash and stretch" attention to weight and volume replacing the zanier rubber-hose style of animation that had predominated in the 1920s at Disney and elsewhere.[11]

Nevertheless, within Disney's meticulous verisimilitude were periodic eruptions that used color in highly nonrealistic ways and reflected avant-garde influences; indeed, Salvador Dalí considered Walt Disney "an American surrealist."[12] Disney's more experimental directions and the musical genre (along with comedy) are closely connected. Indeed, the development of the American (live-action) musical was one that moved away from realism. As Thomas Schatz has observed, "As the musical genre evolved, it sacrificed plausibility for internal narrative logic, steadily strengthening its basis in fantasy and artifice."[13] Christopher Gullen rejoins: "As a genre, the musical is separated from other genres due to its intentional break with verisimilitude."[14] Musicals like the Disney Latin American films "with culminating production numbers," in Schatz's terms, feature "tensions between object and illusion, between social reality and utopia."[15] In the 1940s and '50s, Disney films were influenced by the mid-century modernist graphics of the United Productions of America (UPA) studio and the speed, self-reflexivity, and irreverence of new wisecracking characters like those introduced by Warner Bros. (Bugs

Bunny), Walter Lantz (Woody Woodpecker), and Tex Avery at MGM (the Woolfie series, Screwy Squirrel). A seminal musical example of these stylistic shifts in Disney animation are two sequences from *Dumbo* (1941), beginning with "Hiccups and Cure" and followed by the "Pink Elephants on Parade" song sequence (with music by Frank Churchill and Oliver Wallace, lyrics by Ned Washington).[16]

In "Hiccups and Cure," Dumbo the elephant and Timothy the mouse drink what they believe to be water but is actually alcohol, become intoxicated, and then hallucinate pink elephants that start to multiply (the "Pink Elephants on Parade" song sequence then begins). One of the most creatively inventive and wildly surrealist sequences in the Disney canon, the Pink Elephants sequence transitions are non sequiturs as one episodic section follows another, where pink elephants march and play trumpets or cymbals, belly dance, ice skate, water ski, toboggan, and dance the samba. Direction of the sequence was by Norm Ferguson, layout by Ken O'Connor, and principal animation by Howard Swift and Hicks Lokey, with several brief reaction shots by Freddie Moore and Harvey Toombs (Timothy the mouse) and John Lounsbery (Dumbo).[17]

Attracting critical attention for its hallucinatory properties,[18] the pink elephants sequence shifts rapidly from figural representation into pure abstraction, metamorphosis following metamorphosis. It begins with one balloon-like pink elephant who blows another from his trunk, each one in turn blowing forth another, as the elephants multiply. The sequence even self-reflexively draws attention to itself as an image by having the elephants march around the square frame, until they grow ever larger, swallow the screen, and explode, with the structure following a mad dream logic.[19] Then another sequence begins with flat images and outlines of the elephants chaotically layering the screen into a kind of cubist nightmare as we hear singing to a march-like beat, "Look out! Look out! Pink Elephants on parade! ... They're here! And there! Pink Elephants everywhere!!" The elephants swirl around an upside-down bed, which rotates right-side up to reveal a white elephant who seems to be dreaming this nightmare.

The next sequence features two white elephants (as if they were not yet colored in), who then metamorphose into what appear to be a male and a female worm (now in color), as we hear the following lyrics from the "Pink Elephants on Parade" song:

> I could stand the sight of worms
> And look at microscopic germs
> But technicolor pachyderms
> Is really too much for me!
> ... Pink elephants on parade![20]

As the camera pans, the worms turn out to be the trunks of two elephants, one blue with vertical red stripes, and one yellow with purple horizontal stripes, marching toward each other as we hear the lyrics, "Technicolor pachyderms is really too much for me" (figure 17.1). As they pass each other, they form a fused, multicolor plaid, two-headed elephant, which then stretches and explodes to form six cutout elephants, each with a different-colored pattern, marching in unison to the beat of the song. Color is used to

FIGURE 17.1. Technicolor pachyderms self-reflexively play with color and form.

either enhance or deny depth, acting as ground to the strange and void-like black field. Using wild patterns or designs to confuse the viewer's eye, the flat relief-like nature of the two-dimensional outline of each elephant is emphasized, each through different vertical (*palé*), horizontal (*fascé*), or diagonal (*barré*)[21] colored stripes. As Michel Pastoureau has shown in his research on stripes, the stripe resists palimpsestic readings and disrupts the relationship between figure and ground; it seems to "put in motion the medium in which it appears."[22] In an animated context, it is another example of the graphically self-reflexive. Suddenly, the sequence jump-cuts to pure abstraction, as the stripes and patterns shake into squiggles and dots of color to the percussive sound of maracas, the image synesthetically inviting us to hear color and see sound.

The sequence is highly self-reflexive, articulating an awareness of animation as a drawn medium, as drawings made up of lines, patterns, and colors, which produce the illusion of motion. As Mark Langer has suggested, those parts animated by Hicks Lokey in the first part of the sequence, in particular, "are more obviously drawings—the image of the initial pink elephant retains the lines of the pencil roughs." Following Langer, I name this tendency to foreground the formal and graphic features of the artform "self-reflexively cartoonal."[23]

Citing the famous composite techniques of Italian painter Giuseppe Arcimboldo (1526–1593), who made paintings of subjects through combinations of fruit, vegetables, fish, or flowers, the Pink Elephants sequence also shows a self-reflexive awareness of animation as visual art form within a longer visual tradition, as the sequence segues to a composite elephant made up of individual elephant heads marching toward the implied camera. We see a giant yellow elephant face eventually dominate and swallow the frame with its black pyramid-shaped eyes. These eyes then become pink pyramids (with purple shadows) that pulse to the beat of the Pink Elephants' march before shifting to a new musical style as an elephant-camel appears from behind the pyramid. To the swirl of a snake charmer's pipe, the camel metamorphoses into a cobra and then into an elephant belly dancer whose belly, in turn, becomes a circle and then blinks opens to become an eye, which finally fades out to black as the next sequence begins. These metamorphoses seem to be narrative non sequiturs, but nonetheless, they are linked graphically and formally to their antecedent and subsequent images through shape and movement.

With a trumpet fanfare, we shift again in musical styles, from the sinuous belly dance to a lush orchestral score playing a romantic theme (with flute, strings, and harp predominant) as we see two elephants, first ballet dancing, then ice skating, silhouetted against a stark black field. Black velvet was used by the animators as the background surface on which the cel drawings were arranged to avoid any reflection by lights; as layout artist Ken O'Connor noted, "There is nothing blacker than a piece of velvet with no light on it."[24] The effect of this background texture is to accentuate the abstract quality of the sequence and magnify the color contrast of the cels overlaid on the velvet. Hot-pink lines outline the tops of the elephant forms, as if they are spotlit, while dark green and light green lines suggest shadows. White lines against the black field indicate changing environmental surfaces, as one elephant starts paddling a canoe while the other becomes a fountain, then both shift to ice skating (with hot-pink outlines simulating rim lighting and blue lines for shadows) and then skiing, as they lyrically dance from background to foreground in a crisscross motion.

Finally, the sequence shifts in musical style yet again, to a samba, as the elephants dance in snow, turning from cold blue to red hot as the music warms them up, literally and figuratively. Against a fuchsia field, the now-orange elephants dance, a bolt of electricity uniting them. One elephant throws a bolt of lightning, which hits his partner on the head. Then with a flash, we cut to a wide shot of many elephants dancing (now pink again). In a series of quick alternating shots, we see black silhouettes against a hot-orange field, then pink elephants against a blue field, then black against a yellow-orange field, then pink against a black field, and black (with green eyes) against a pink field, alternating these color schemes ever faster as the multiplane camera tracks in and out. The effect of these rapid alternations between figure and ground colors is hallucinogenic. The alternation of color fields becomes so fast it is almost subliminal, as the elephants transform in breakneck fashion, becoming pink cars, a train, passengers on an amusement-park ride, waterskiers, and finally boaters, culminating in the inevitable explosion. The narrative has finally released us from its relentless forward movement. Soothingly, the elephant bubbles slowly float down, dissolving into the rosy clouds of dawn as the sequence ends.

I have gone into some detail here because a similar scene recurs in *The Three Caballeros*, with many of the same techniques and structures repeating. This form of recycling was common in a labor-intensive industry, particularly under the constraints of wartime production; gags that were used in one cartoon were frequently repeated in a later one. Balloon-like pink elephants are repeated with Donald as an elastic balloon in *The Three Caballeros*. Similarly, both *Saludos Amigos* and *The Three Caballeros* are characterized by densely edited alternating color fields, foregrounding characters abstracted against stark monochrome backgrounds, with explosions that act as abrupt, non sequitur transitions that "tunnel" into the next scene.

The Pink Elephants sequence places an ever-metamorphosing, pink-colored line (and pink-colored balloon) at the center of animated creation and movement, making color and music central to narratives of magic, intoxication, and the supernatural. These self-generating, fluidly transforming pink bubbles of intoxication act as deeply unsettling and voracious membranes that consume each other. It is a hallucinatory vision of expanding and contracting pneumatic exchange, and with this elasticity and its transgressive expansiveness always comes the threat of explosion—reiterating the palpable at the very moment of its disappearance under animation's relentless movement. The strategies in "Pink Elephants on Parade" foreshadow similar experimental aesthetic techniques in the Latin American features, and key to all three features was the perceptual, synesthetic, and affective role of color.

"The Doors of Perception": Color and Hallucination

In their writings on the hallucinatory effects of mescaline and LSD, British writer Aldous Huxley (*The Doors of Perception*; *Heaven and Hell*) and German American psychologist Heinrich Klüver (*Mescal and Mechanisms of Hallucinations*) each identified the key role that color played in psychedelic perception, particularly in shaping a strong sense of enchantment and ecstatic euphoria or dissociation, as well as a sense of psychological, and sometimes physical, transportation.

Aldous Huxley

Huxley was interested in mescaline, an alkaloid that produces hallucinogenic effects like those of LSD and psilocybin ("magic mushrooms"). Occurring naturally in some types of cactus, including Mexican peyote and the Peruvian San Pedro cactus, mescaline has long held a traditional role in Native American cultural rituals.[25] Examining secondary research on mescaline intoxication as well as his own experiences, Huxley observed that color perception was radically intensified, noting "how significant is the enormous heightening under mescalin of the perception of color! ... Mescalin raises all colors to a higher power and makes the percipient aware of innumerable fine shades of difference, to which, at ordinary times, he is completely blind."[26] For Huxley, mescaline produced an ecstatic metaphysical sensation of conceptual oneness with the world, through the perception of, and engagement with, intensely colorful hallucinations of strange, undulating forms. These metamorphosing hallucinations shared certain formal characteristics and perceptual effects, with Huxley pointing to luminosity, intense color, and a heightened sense of meaning as three key characteristics of visionary experience (a special form of the imagination). On one occasion, he described his books in this way:

> Like the flowers, they glowed, when I looked at them with brighter colors, a profounder significance. Red books, like rubies; emerald books; books bound in white jade; books of agate; of aquamarine, of yellow topaz; lapiz lazuli books whose color was so intense, so intrinsically meaningful, that they seemed to be on the point of leaving the shelves to thrust themselves insistently on my attention.[27]

In an essay, "Drugs That Shape Men's Minds," Huxley explored how mystics, ascetics, hermits, and other religious practitioners used sleep deprivation, fasting, altered breathing, and other techniques to produce biochemical changes in the body akin to the effects of mescaline and to alter consciousness and induce visions.[28] Like Johann Wolfgang von Goethe before him, Huxley suggested that ascetics, artists, and children all potentially share visionary perception, noting that art, in particular, can reproduce or, at the very least, echo this ecstatic state: "Whatever in nature or in a work of art, resembles one of those intensely significant, inwardly glowing objects encountered at the minds' antipodes, is capable of inducing, if only in a partial and attenuated form, the visionary experience."[29] But for everyone, visionary perception can also be triggered by special kinds of aesthetic objects, exemplified by the jewel, which is "self-luminous" and which exhibits a preternatural brilliance of color and significance, whose "colored, moving, living geometrical forms" typify a recurrent formal dimension of hallucinatory vision under the effects of mescaline.[30]

Heinrich Klüver

Like Huxley, Klüver's *Mescal and Mechanisms of Hallucinations* synthesized primary research of perceptual changes under the effects of mescaline, pointing to the intensity of color, as well as highlighting the colored gem as a luminous, overdetermined, and intensely chromatic hallucinatory figure:

> As I gazed every projecting angle, cornice, and even the face of the stones at their joinings were by degrees covered or hung with clusters of what seemed to be huge precious stones, but uncut, some being more like masses of transparent fruit. These were green, purple, red, and orange; never clear yellow and never blue.... [T]o give the faintest idea of the perfectly satisfying intensity and purity of these gorgeous colour-fruits is quite beyond my power. All the colours I have ever beheld are dull as compared to these. As I looked and it lasted long, the tower became of a fine mouse hue, and everywhere the vast pendant masses of emerald green, ruby reds, and orange began to drip a slow rain of colours.[31]

Similarly for Huxley, precious jewels were exemplary objects because of their rarity, luminosity, color, and preternatural significance and came closest to the geometrical forms synthesized by Klüver as recurrent features of the hallucinatory experience under mescaline.

In Technicolor IV cartoons of the 1930s and '40s, there is a recurring fascination with the *simulation* of prismatic and scintillating colored light through stuttering or blinking movement, where jewels are displayed in "treasure cave" sequences such as in the Fleischer Bros. Technicolor featurette *Aladdin and His Wonderful Lamp* (1939). In these cartoons, precious gems such as emeralds, rubies, and diamonds were a narrative device for product differentiation, foregrounding the spectacular saturation, striking contrast, and affective appeal of the colors made possible by the full color range of the new Technicolor process. Cartoons represent the glitter of the animated jewel as one that spatially saturates and subjectively blinds in hallucinatory fields of color. In *Aladdin*, Olive Oyl is a princess who receives several precious gems from Popeye, a diamond, an emerald, and a ruby whose luminous glowing inhabits space as sequential colors (white, green, and red, respectively) and requires Olive to don protective sunglasses, reiterating the interchangeability of light and color in animation. Certainly, the animated jewel cannot reproduce the complex ways in which light is reflected, refracted, and mirrored by the color and cut, polish, and brilliance of a real diamond. Here I am suggesting that the incremental shimmer and frame-by-frame control of speed, duration, and concentration of light of the animated jewel are instead an aesthetic trigger which produces a form of visionary perception through the flicker of light between screen and spectator.

Klüver's principal contribution to color theory is his identification of specific perceptual color patterns: rotating jewels, honeycombs, cobwebs, lightning, comets, explosions, tunnels, spirals, and other oscillating, scintillating, or kaleidoscopic color-shapes in movement, which frequently "repeated, combined, or elaborated into ornamental designs and mosaics of various kinds."[32] He grouped these patterns into four principal categories, which he called "form constants" and which included these principal figures: the grating/lattice/fretwork/honeycomb/filigree/chessboard, the tunnel/funnel/cone, the cobweb, and the spiral.[33] There is a nightmarish quality to these form constants in their monstrously relentless repetition of pattern. Animated artists have masterfully used repeated form constants to unsettle or disturb, as with the cobwebs or chess patterns in Ted Parmalee's animated adaptation of the 1843 Edgar Allan Poe tale *The Tell Tale Heart* (UPA, 1953) or the funnel of color that plunges us down with the Wicked Queen as she transforms into a murderous crone in Disney's *Snow White*.

Klüver observed that these form constants had certain repeated qualitative features; they featured all colors of the visible (human) spectrum, and they were bright, saturated, and highly symmetrical geometrical figures in the center of the perceptual field.[34] Further, hallucinated objects perceptually produced by mescaline had a peculiar flat or two-dimensional quality, and the color of these objects seemed to fluctuate somewhere between a flat surface color and what we might think of as cinematographic color, or color produced through light, as objects glowing from within. This underscores what I suggest is the cinematic, indeed *animated*, quality of the hallucinatory experience.

There are two additional interesting qualitative dimensions to note here in terms of their relationship to animation before we turn to the Disney features. First, Klüver identified a quality of multiplicity in hallucinations, which he called "polyopic," whereby subjects would hallucinate repeated chains of patterns following the form constants earlier mentioned, such as cobwebs, chessboards, funnels, and so on.[35] This attribute of repetition and multiplicity is also a structural feature of cel animation, which is built on multiple drawings, usually twelve drawings with incremental differences, each of which is then photographed twice, to produce one second of on-screen movement. Further, as a self-referential gesture that plays with the visual freedom of the drawing on which its form depends, animation frequently depicts characters who explode into multiple iterations or duplicates of themselves as visual gags. Such polyopic repetitions recur frequently with our three guest hosts in the Latin American features. For example, in the concluding bullfight sequence of *The Three Caballeros*, José Carioca explodes into multiple versions of himself as spectators in the ring, shouting "Olé!" as a comedic flourish on the beat. Like Dumbo's ever-metamorphosing elephants, these polyopic copies might be considered further examples of the self-reflexively cartoonal. Second, what Klüver called *presque vu* described chains of endless, ever-mutating kaleidoscopic patterns as having an incomplete, almost but not quite, unfinished quality to them; in his words, they "suggest an end which is not quite reached, or they lack the proper completion; they do not—to use a *Gestalt* psychological term—call forth a closure-experience."[36]

These form constants were often reproduced in the drug films and expanded cinema of the 1960s, such as *The Trip* (Roger Corman, 1967), *Psych Out* (Richard Rush, 1968), and *Easy Rider* (Dennis Hopper, 1969), which sought to induce a contact high or affectively altered consciousness in the viewer through representations of kaleidoscopes, lattices, pulsating images that tunnel in and out, moving objects with trails, saturated colors, strobing, flicker films, and other distortions of motion and speed that rhythmically contracted or jerked, each produced through a variety of cinematic techniques that included lighting and animation.[37] I argue that there are some preliminary structural affiliations between these abstract effects and cel animation of the 1940s, which shared an interest with those later filmmakers in producing retinal expansion. Unlike experimental film, narrative animation harnessed, yet contained, rapidly moving perceptual effects through the genres of comedy and the musical that made this fantasmatic play possible. Like "Pink Elephants on Parade," Disney's Latin American features used color, music, and sound for hallucinatory effect—in Huxley's terms, producing visionary experience.

THE LATIN AMERICAN FEATURES

Saludos Amigos (1943) and *The Three Caballeros* (1945) appeared as part of nine package films made by Disney between *Bambi* (1942) and *Cinderella* (1950).[38] Shaped by the financial constraints of the war and the cutoff European market, the Disney studio's two

Latin American features were sponsored by a branch of the State Department headed by Nelson Rockefeller, the Office of the Coordinator of Inter-American Affairs (CIAA), which was also known as the "Good Neighbor" policy. The CIAA's goal was to realign the loyalties of the Central and South American countries with the US at a time when Nazi Germany was deepening its influence there. Planned as a compilation of twelve one-reel cartoons with bridging material, to be produced and released in groups of four, Disney's sponsored Latin American features initially followed animator Bill Cottrell's suggestion that the animation would fall into two groups with either a musical or a comedic focus, with Cottrell, Lee Blair, and Jim Bodrero assigned to the musical and Ted Sears, Webb Smith, and Jack Miller to comedy.[39] In reality, the lines between the two groups blurred, and comedy was a constant. *Saludos Amigos* paired Donald Duck with a new character, José Carioca, a Brazilian parrot, and *The Three Caballeros* added a second new character, Panchito, a Mexican rooster. Together with Donald as the US representative and comedic fall guy, these three characters are narrative guides, taking the viewer on a journey through Central and South America, with a particular focus on Mexico, Brazil, and Argentina. A third feature focusing on Cuba, *Blame It on the Samba*, was planned but ultimately never produced. In August 1941, the Disney studio sent fifteen of its top animators, writers, and colorists, along with Walt Disney and several of his family members, on an extensive three-month trip to South and Central America. The trip would ultimately lay the groundwork for two features and many educational and propaganda cartoon shorts on topics ranging from the samba to malaria prevention.

The Latin American features are musical travelogues (sharing aspects of what Rick Altman calls the "fairy tale musical" and the "folk musical"),[40] in which color becomes a device for the hallucinatory and synesthetic expression of traditional music, song, and dance. As foreign-policy mechanisms for the development of regional alliances under the brand of friendship, these Disney films might also be considered as a form of what Arun Saldanha has called "psychedelic whiteness," or that which is grounded within a Western or settler colonialist sensibility, in which, to use Joanna Gosse's terms, "a spatiotemporal logic of infinite expansion" and "internal and external self-discovery" are linked to Western ideologies of primitivism and exoticism.[41]

Saludos Amigos

The inaugural feature, *Saludos Amigos*, is made up of four main sequences, with the first three introducing Peru ("Lake Titicaca"), Bolivia and Chile ("Pedro"), and Argentina ("Gaucho Goofy"), and concluding with Ary Barroso's enormously popular melody "Aquarela do Brasil" ("A Watercolor of Brazil"), also known in English as "Brazil." The song's samba rhythms (originally used for Carnival), are described by the film's narrator, Fred Shields, as a "musical picture of [Barroso's] native land." The rights to Barroso's "unofficial national anthem," along with several other Brazilian songs such as Barroso's "Os Quindins de Yayá" (for *The Three Caballeros*) and Zequinha de Abreu's "Tico-Tico no Fubá" (for *Saludos Amigos*) were secured by the Disney studio.[42] As J. B. Kaufman's research has shown, the popularity of the samba in the US in the 1940s was partly produced by the Good Neighbor policy. It was also enabled by a series of circumstances around a labor dispute between the American Society of Composers, Authors, and Publishers (ASCAP) and radio networks that led to a new company, Broadcast Music Incorporated (BMI), filling a boycott shortage on the airwaves with the back catalog of a music entrepreneur named Ralph Peer. The effects were ubiquitous: "Suddenly, Latin American music was everywhere on US airwaves."[43] Peer also owned the rights to "Aquarela do Brasil," and as a result, the song received extensive exposure in the States through Peer's licensing and Disney's film.

The musical sequence "Aquarela do Brasil" begins as a blank piece of paper, on which the animator brings the song and images of Rio to life with a paintbrush as we hear producer, composer, and performer Aloysio (Louis) Oliveira[44] sing the opening bars of Barroso's song, whose lyrics personify Brazil in explicitly racial and gendered terms. Indeed, as Kariann Goldschmitt has noted, the song's lyrics and discursive circulation in Brazil have much to do with Brazil's own nationalism, particularly its history of slavery and long-standing marginalization of Afro-Brazilians, in whose culture samba had its roots.[45] The song begins: "Meu Brasil Brasileiro / Mulato inzoneiro" ("Brazil! / My Brazilian Brazil / My good-looking mulatto"). As throughout the Latin American features, the narrative is highly self-reflexive about cel animation's formal genesis as a drawing that splashes to life through color, vertically following the downward pathway of the brush and drips of blue paint as the opening sketch of landscape on a blank sheet of paper fills with color (beautifully animated by Disney effects artist Joshua Meador). In other words, color is both animator and activator. As with "Pink Elephants on Parade," music and visual metamorphosis structure the narrative, with images and sounds constantly flowing, depicting what Goldschmitt describes as a clichéd "lush landscape."[46] Metamorphosis is a key formal attribute of animation, and here color's fluidity is transformational: splashes of red paint become tiger lily plants and then morph into singing red-lipsticked mouths, a splash of pink paint animates into two dancing flamingos, and a yellow clutch of bananas dissolves into the percussive clacking beaks of a group of toucans (accentuated by trumpets), all under the effects of the samba's beat.

To the rhythm of the carioca (a variant of the Brazilian samba), a bee bursts out of a flower and then transforms into Donald. If we look at frame-by-frame images of a split second of this sequence (see figure 17.2), we see the ways in which smears of pastel or paint color and distorted bodies metamorphose fluidly under the effects of the song, inviting a synesthetic connection of sound, color, and image simultaneously. In a sense, Donald is present, first in deconstructed form as pure frustrated affect, the buzz of the trapped bee, and then reconstructed as a duck by the cheerful musical power of the samba.

Donald Duck (Clarence Nash) and José Carioca (José Oliveira) meet for the first time and introduce themselves to each other. As the samba beat begins again, Barroso's "Aquarela" melody then segues into a faster, sharper musical sequence with de Abreu's "Tico-Tico," as Donald and José start to walk through the streets of Rio. As they walk

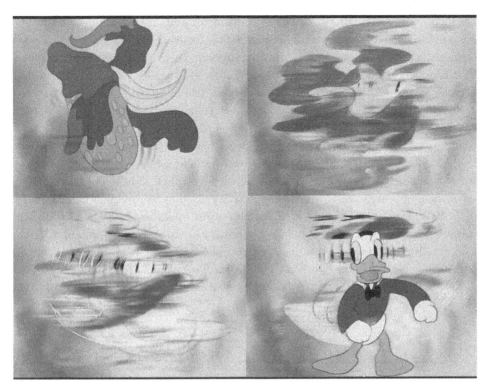

FIGURE 17.2. Color comes to life: smears of paint enlivened by the samba.

downward across a blank white field, the paintbrush fills in the steps, until they come to the famous wavy pavement mosaics of Rio de Janeiro.[47]

The colored smears and textured pastel shadings of the characters, as they move quickly to the musical beat, foreground their chromatic construction, using the colored line and drop as a signifier of speed and rhythm. Donald at first tries to follow the wavy mosaic lines of the pavements of Rio and quacks in frustration, as he finds it difficult. But then his tail feathers start beating with the syncopated rhythm of the samba, and he can follow the lines more easily. Rhythm is linked to the natural *and* the man-made world: it comes from the colorful flora and fauna (the beat of the toucans' beaks, the dance of the flamingos, and the buzz of the bee), and its design is curvilinear like the flow of the paintbrush that began the "Aquarela" sequence, leading us through the streets and musical life of Rio.

José and Donald come to a cafe where they sit and have a drink of cachaça, a Brazilian distilled alcoholic drink with strong effects (one of its many names is *bafo de tigre*, or "tiger breath"). When Donald drinks it, bells and whistles ring as red and green pupils in his eyes ping-pong back and forth; he breathes out fire, then starts hiccupping to a syncopated beat of the samba. José says, "Donald—now you have the spirit of the samba!" The paintbrush returns, dipping into the cachaça bottle, underscoring the connection between an intoxicating drug (alcohol) and the perceptual and affective intoxications of color. This leads us into the conclusion of the film, with a reprise of the refrain of "Aquarela do Brasil," as we cut from Donald and José to hot-pink background color fields, like those in *Dumbo*'s Pink Elephants sequence. As the music starts again, a paintbrush splashes in maracas, a *güiro*, tambourine, drums, and other traditional Brazilian percussion instruments in silhouetted close-up against a red field. With a clash of cymbals on the beat accompanied by the paintbrush splashing yellow paint, we cut to a silhouette of a woman dancing, in complementary colors foreshadowing the ultimate appearance of Aurora Miranda (Carmen Miranda's sister) in the film's sequel, *The Three Caballeros*. We see the woman joined by Donald (also in silhouette), now hot pink, and then the woman in stark blue against saturated yellow, suggesting the infectious and transformational properties of the samba, which align Donald and her into similar color schemes, now joined by dancing others. A series of lap dissolves follow canted images of the flashing lights of famous Rio nightclubs—the Copacabana, the Atlántico, and the Casino da Urca—as we zoom out to a wide shot of Rio and Sugar Loaf Mountain. As the song and the film conclude, the image reveals itself to be a painting on an easel, like the one that began the sequence. This association of color, flashing neon lights, and the modernity of the city would return in *The Three Caballeros* in "Baía" and "You Belong to My Heart."

THE THREE CABALLEROS

In the sequel feature, *The Three Caballeros* (production supervision and direction by Ferguson), our protagonists tour South and Central America through another series of episodic song-and-dance sequences. Each sequence is introduced through the framing device of Donald Duck unwrapping a series of presents, with the first being a film and a projector, followed by a series of popup books that name specific countries such as Mexico and Brazil. The Brazilian parrot, José Carioca, reappears to greet Donald, and midway through the film, a new rooster character, Panchito (voiced by Joaquin Garay and called Pancho Pistolas in Mexico), joins the others to form the eponymous three caballeros. But before Panchito arrives to introduce the Mexican sequence, Donald unwraps a popup book on Brazil (anthropomorphically dancing to a samba beat), in which a miniature José Carioca appears, extolling the beauty of the Brazilian region of Baía.

The Baía sequence introduces another Barroso song, "Na Baixa do Sapateiro" ("In the Shoemaker's Hollow"), performed by singer and composer Nestor Amaral (1913–1962), as well as "Vocé Já Foi à Ba(h)ía?" ("Have You Been to Baía?") with actor and composer Dorival Caymmi (1914–2008). Both Brazilian performers would come to the United States to perform with Carmen Miranda. The song sequence "Baía" begins with José pointing to a map of Brazil, in which the state is a small dot in pink. This pink dot on the map grows to become a large pink cloud, acting as an iris into the next shot, a fuchsia painting of Baía's capital, with its beautiful view over the bay, the light sparkling on the water as the camera pans and zooms and the song begins with a slow drumbeat.

Over the course of the song, we see images of the city of Salvador lap-dissolving into red and orange sunsets and pink pastel palettes of clouds and beautiful old churches. The overall effect is dreamlike, accentuated by the lyrics, which give prominence to the word "reverie":

> Oh, Baía
> When twilight is deep in the sky
> Baía
> Someone that I long to see
> Keeps haunting my reverie ...

As elsewhere in *The Three Caballeros*, the sequence showcases the extensive effects work by Meador of light on the surface of the bay scintillating by moonlight, with beads of water glistening on flowers and other details of light rippling and reflecting on water.

Disney's visual effects were exemplified by shots like these featuring shimmering, stuttering, or scintillating light, often dramatically motivated by starlight, magical fairies, fantastic jewels, or the glint of light reflected or refracted through bubbles, water, snowflakes, or ice, as seen in the Nutcracker sequence and many other scenes in *Fantasia*. Visual-effects artists created the hallucinatory sparkle of diamonds that bedazzles the vision of the easily bemused Dopey in *Snow White*, the radiating white lines of the Blue Fairy who first appears as a star over Geppetto's village in *Pinocchio* (1940), and the scintillating gradients of light cascading from Tinker Bell as she sprinkles fairy dust in *Peter Pan* (1953). To achieve these visual effects, multiple layers of partially opaque or transparent cels are stacked together and photographed. To produce the composite image of the scintillating glint of drops of water on orchids (see figure 17.3), star shapes are painted on separate cels that overlay the cels with orchids, along with the background painting of branches and sunset, to create the illusion of light sparkling on water. In each case, specialist effects artists simulated reflected, refracted, or radiating light through color by painstakingly painting oscillating lines, squiggles, or star shapes, which change in scale, color, or position from shot to shot, producing the illusion of movement.

Twinkling stars, sparkles, fairy dust, and other scintillating or radiating gradients of luminosity through animated fireworks, explosions, or glittering jewels are recurrent visual signifiers of what I call starburst animation, embodying the nature of change through their intervallic alternations of light and dark stimuli and manipulation of intensities of light over time. As Scottish animator Norman McLaren once said, "What happens between each frame is more important than what happens on each frame."[48] Like Times Square advertising, some of which was designed by animators,[49] starburst animation (with its on-off-on blinking process) is a form of visual stimulus that organizes our attention, affecting our bodies and our brains and creating a sensual experience. From the glittering North Star that shines above Pinocchio's village to the pixie dust of Tinker Bell, it also reminds us of the long hagiographic tradition in visual culture and Western art that signified light as the power of the deity, here transformed into Disney magic.

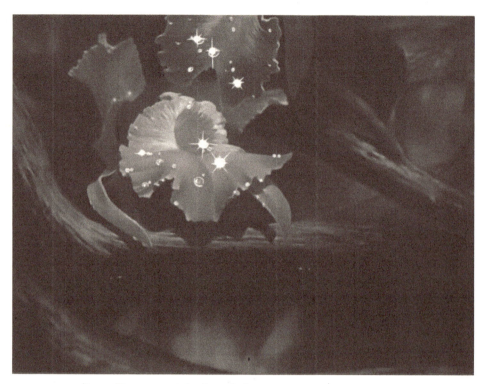

FIGURE 17.3. Dreamlike reverie and color as light in Baía.

Scintillation can refer to a flash of light produced in a phosphor by an ionizing event or as a rapid variation in the light of a celestial body produced by the turbulence in the earth's atmosphere. In a psychological study, researchers examined babies who licked plates with glossy finishes, speculating that the human fascination with light effects like glitter and sparkles has to do with an instinctual need to search for water.[50] An indication of the importance of scintillation as an aesthetic feature is glitter's contemporary ubiquity in consumer products and surfaces, which can be found everywhere from makeup to interior design. Glitter was first invented in the 1930s by shredding scrap metal into small pieces. Refined in the '60s, glitter's modern industrial counterparts are brands like Glitterex (first invented in 1963), in closely guarded top-secret proprietary formulas which involve evaporating and then rebonding hundreds of layers of aluminum onto Mylar or plastic film.[51]

Disney's innovative attention to glittering, twinkling light and color is part of a long-standing aesthetic in many of its films, evoked as it is in the studio's own logographic, in which Tinker Bell sprinkles fairy dust over the Magic Castle. Indeed, scintillating light and pixie dust are central to Disney's brand. Similarly, the Disney studio has also been a consistent innovator in color technologies in the film industry, from its pioneering Silly Symphonies cartoons in the 1930s, to its early adoption of color television in *The Wonderful World of Color* series in the '60s, to its technological innovations with fireworks, water fountains, and projected animation in more recent theme-park shows such as *World of Color* (2010–) or Epcot's *Harmonious* (2021–2023). An example that brings together Disney's fascination with both color and glitter is the recent creation of a textured surface called EARidescence which produces scintillating light effects in the eye of the viewer. Created to celebrate the fiftieth-anniversary year of Disney World that began in fall 2021, EARidescence would appear throughout the park as textured surfaces on statues and cast members' costumes, as well as on products marketed to consumers, or as projected light on the Magic Castle. As studio promotional literature excitedly reported, "each structure will glisten as if painted by 'magical moonbeams'—an illumination that doesn't just brighten the surfaces but surrounds the icon with a dimensional glow." Additionally, eight characters (Mickey, Minnie, Donald, Daisy, Pluto, Goofy, Chip, and Dale) received new EARidescent costumes in periwinkle, purple, and metallic blue, producing "the hint of a prismatic effect that underscores the sense that the costumes are not one color, but many."[52]

Here I'm suggesting that whether it is Disney's attention to producing iridescent scintillating light and color on cast members' costumes or the Disneyland castle or colorful light and water nighttime entertainment shows in its theme parks, the studio repeatedly and meticulously constructs an immersive glittering brand of magic that is designed to perceptually intoxicate. The simulation of prismatic, scintillating, or oscillating light effects shares much formally with the abstract techniques of avant-garde animators in producing visionary perception. More particularly, animators use recurrent patterns that overlap or bear remarkable formal similarity to Klüver's "form constants," especially through their specific qualitative features of saturated or glowing color, brightness, symmetricality, and flatness, as well as polyopia and *presque vu*, which I see as structurally key to much of animation.

So how did this long-standing studio commitment to scintillation appear in the Latin American features? In a Mexican nightlife sequence introduced to Donald and José by Panchito, we see them stand in front of a giant album, with a high-angle animated shot of Mexico City, its colored electrical signs and marquees blinking in the night. The photo album of Mexico that Donald unwraps functions as an interstitial transition into the next musical sequence, with a song called "You Belong to My Heart/Solamente Una Vez" performed by Mexican singer Dora Luz (1918–2018) with Donald. The night scene of Mexico City depicts a prominent star as Panchito says, "Even the sky is full of romantics." That star becomes larger and splits as the live-action head of Luz comes into view, overlaid with yellow lines that pulse and frame her face as her song begins. As the song proceeds, more scintillating lights blink around her, with Mexico City's neon lights now transforming into the blinking stars of the night sky (figure 17.4).

Starburst animation recalls the strange imagery of Georges Méliès's *A Trip to the Moon* (1903), as Donald sticks his head through a star and becomes a kind of celestial body—a shooting star—as he dances through the night sky, spraying scintillating lights and stars in his wake. He tosses stars around him as if they were flowers and dances, first on a cloud and then a crescent-shaped moon. Then we take a completely surrealist turn. The night sky becomes a series of giant guitars as Donald rubs his eyes in

FIGURE 17.4. Sexual reverie: a dance of scintillated light across the night sky.

puzzlement; then disembodied red lips appear and kiss Donald, causing him to turn bright red and metamorphose into a rocket in a sexual gag common in American animation in the 1940s. What ensues is a series of rapidly shifting non sequiturs as we saw in the *Dumbo* Pink Elephants sequence. Donald becomes a winged insect (probably a bee) and flies through a field of flowers; then the flowers and Donald turn into neon outlines against a black field as if the neon nightscape of Mexico City is the unconscious of his desire for Luz (whose name in Spanish and Portuguese means "light"), reiterating the conceptual and visual importance of natural and man-made light throughout this sequence. The saturated neon colors are intensified against the black background and act as markers of color's representational capacity to signify the light of both the urban and natural worlds. Now Luz has become a strange human–flower hybrid, a live-action photographic face framed by animated petals. As Donald's desire for Luz intensifies, the imagery increasingly takes an abstract turn, cross-modally inviting us to see sound and hear color. We saw this synesthetic crossing of sound, music, and color earlier in the first Mexican sequence, when José and Donald unwrap a Mexican present and start dancing to the ranchera "Ay! Jalisco, no te rajes" ("Jalisco, don't back down"), with the image as a Rorschach-like visualization of the soundtrack that becomes increasingly abstract, favoring bands of colors that match Donald's blue and white sailor suit, José's green and yellow design, and the oranges and reds of a serape blanket[53] (figure 17.5).

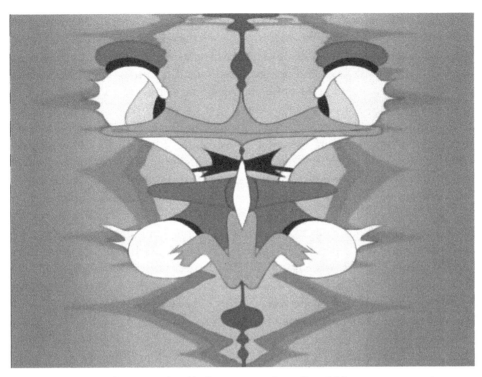

FIGURE 17.5. Synesthetic sound and hallucinatory color as Donald dances.

Donald and Luz are briefly interrupted by the appearance of José and Panchito singing "Three caballeros, three gay caballeros." When Luz-as-flower brings Donald into her embrace for a kiss, Panchito appears again, also turning into polyopic flowers, before spinning into a piñata, and the sequence explodes in tempo, in a quickly edited montage. Like the end of the Pink Elephants sequence, we see rapid shots that are themselves hybrid, a combination of live-action photography (a group of women seen on the beach of Rio) and animated (polyopic shots of Donald as cutout paper dolls), followed by layered composite shots of women falling vertically underwater and women on a flying carpet chased by Donald. Alternating color fields create lightning flashes, quickly abstracting the characters as colored cutouts, turning the live-action women into animated two-dimensional shapes. As in *Dumbo*, Donald jumps into a black void, and his splash produces another flat, symmetrical composite image: an animated flower in which live-action women are arranged in a circle, as if they were petals.

This sequence alludes to Busby Berkeley's famous techniques, which choreographed chorus lines of female performers into rapidly transforming geometrical shapes and patterns by shooting them from above, below, and through mirrors. The three caballeros now fuse with the women, becoming collage-like composites typical of the avant-garde of the 1920s—animated caballero heads with female legs and animated pink wings. After several more interludes with Mexican actress Carmen Molina (1920–1998) dancing the

Mexican Zandunga, with Donald swaying to the music as a giant flower, an overhead shot of the spinning Donald takes us spiral-like into the infamous "Dance of the Cacti."

The Three Caballeros' penultimate sequence features Molina dancing the traditional Mexican Jesusita with Donald and a giant row of cacti, seeming to self-consciously play with the very subject and form of hallucination, as rows of cacti metamorphose and grow ever larger in scale, with Donald also becoming polyopic rows of cutout cacti in profile form. The sequence is a filigreed fever dream of endless forms looping, stretching, and shrinking into a serape-like abstraction of sunset colors. Rows of green Donald cacti and purple cacti fan out diagonally to the left and right of Molina, centered in the background, in a symmetrical image. The cacti and the Donald cacti suddenly grow monstrously larger and larger, filling the frame in an endlessly looping form of multiplicity and *presque vu*, all to the march-like beat of the Jesusita dance. Interestingly, Huxley identified the cactus as a key hallucinatory figure of the desert, not the least because of its connection to peyote. He referred to an episode of Disney's live-action television documentary series, which featured a giant cactus, and described the photography as "a notable new form of popular visionary art," adding, "The immensely magnified cactus blossoms, into which, at the end of Disney's *The Living Desert*, the spectator finds himself sinking, come straight from the Other World."[54]

A jump cut and explosive graphic match introduce José, Panchito, and several straw cowboys on horses, who come marching out of the tunnel-like shape of a round trumpet's mouth, as we hear it announce with a loud fanfare the eponymous song sequence that will conclude the film. "The Three Caballeros" is staged as a musical bullfight, with Donald in the role of a mock wooden bull and José and Panchito as his tormentors. Panchito reminds us of color's central visual and dramatic role in the feature as he waves the traditional red cape at Donald the bull. "What's the matter with you? Are you color blind?" he mocks. José lights the firecrackers tied to Donald the bull's tail, and the sequence builds into an explosive finale of scintillating light, starburst animation, and explosive flashes, which periodically illuminate glimpses of Donald as a flat black outline inside the bull (see figure 17.6). Donald literally becomes a firecracker when Panchito jams one into his rear.

Donald escapes the wooden bull, and they charge at each other, as smears of pastel colors depicting speed recur as aesthetic strategy. The collision of Donald and the bull produces the final explosion, with split-second color-field alternations producing perceptual flashes of light as Donald shoots through the air and abseils down a rocket's sparkling trails. The flare of rockets, explosions, and shooting stars across the night sky is joined by fireworks, which spell out in a visual climax "The End" in English, Spanish, and Portuguese (as the colors of the American, Mexican, and Brazilian flags are represented in the words "The End/Fin/Fin," meticulously animated by George Rowley).[55] Like the Pink Elephants sequence, *The Three Caballeros* progressively builds in dramatic and musical tempo, with color acting as intoxicating narcotic. In David Batchelor's terms, we are caught in color's "intense gaze"[56] and recall Huxley's observation that popular cultural practices such as fireworks, pageantry, and theatrical spectacles were "vision inducing devices"—they were "visionary arts."[57] In other words, José, Panchito, and Donald are our avatars on a revelatory ride through color.

FIGURE 17.6. Explosions, firecrackers, and scintillating light as Huxley's "visionary art."

Conclusion

Neuropsychologist Daniel Stern has termed "vitality affects" those visual effects that are "surging, falling, fading, increasing, crescendo, explosion" and are key recurrent elements in animation, frequently represented through transformation, flux, and metamorphosis.[58] The Pink Elephants sequence in *Dumbo*, the "Aquarela do Brasil" in *Saludos Amigos*, and multiple musical sequences, including the eponymous musical climax in *The Three Caballeros*, demonstrate these vitality affects as produced by the perceptual phenomena of pulsating, transforming, abstract colored forms. From repeated polyopic forms to endless loops (*presque vu*), with explosions, tunnels, and spirals as transition devices, these sequences also feature extended examples of Klüver's form constants.

From color as glittering, stuttering light to enactments of Klüver's form constants, Disney animation of the 1940s developed visual stimuli that were important continuities of animation's earliest anarchic experimentalism. This aesthetic attention to the hallucinatory perceptual effects of color, in conjunction with the anarchic expressivity of the animated medium, suggested that the development of Disney effects animation and its meticulous attention to the scintillating effects of light, fire, and water need not always follow the studio's dominant verisimilitude that had been established by the late 1930s but rather enabled an alternative path of innovation and unconventionality that had always been present from animation's very beginnings.

Influenced by the self-reflexivity, zany characters, and modernist design of 1940s animation, *Saludos Amigos* and *The Three Caballeros* were a hallucinatory experiment, partly enabled by the low-budget freedom of wartime production conditions. Guided by Donald, José, and Panchito on a magical serape ride through the song, dance, and music of many different nations in Latin and Central America, has ultimately been a journey through color as euphoria—an explosive, chaotic, and hallucinatory ride through the doors of perception.

Notes

1. For more on the role of music and sound in cartoon shorts, see Daniel Goldmark. *Tunes for 'Toons: Music and the Hollywood Cartoon* (Los Angeles: University of California Press, 2005).
2. The Disney studio developed one of the earliest surround-sound technologies, Fantasound. Charles Solomon, "Fantastic 'Fantasia': Disney Channel Takes a Look at Walt's Great Experiment in Animation," *Los Angeles Times*, August 26, 1990, https://www.latimes.com/archives/la-xpm-1990-08-26-tv-552-story.html.
3. Select songs include "With a Smile and a Song," "I'm Wishing," "Whistle while You Work," "Some Day My Prince Will Come," "Heigh-Ho" (*Snow White*); "Sing, Sweet Nightingale," "A Dream Is a Wish Your Heart Makes," "Bibbidi-Bobbidi-Boo" (*Cinderella*); "Once upon A Dream" (*Sleeping Beauty*).
4. See Karen Beckman, ed., *Animating Film Theory* (Durham, NC: Duke University Press, 2014); Suzanne Buchan, ed., *Pervasive Animation* (New York: Routledge, 2013); Esther Leslie. "Animation's Petrified Unrest," in *Pervasive Animation*, ed. Suzanne Buchan (New York: Routledge, 2013), 73–93.
5. See Kirsten Moana Thompson, "Animating Ephemeral Surfaces: Transparency, Translucency and Disney's World of Color," *Refractory: A Journal of Entertainment Media* 24 (June 2014), https://webarchive.nla.gov.au/awa/20141116230413/http://pandora.nla.gov.au/pan/30981/20141117-0000/refractory.unimelb.edu.au/2014/08/06/thompson/index.html; Kirsten Moana Thompson, "Falling In(to) Color: Chromophilia and Tom Ford's *A Single Man*" *Moving Image* 15, no. 1 (Spring 2015): 62–84; Kirsten Moana Thompson, "Tattooed Light and Embodied Design: Intersectional Surfaces in *Moana*" in *Media Crossroads: Intersections of Space and Identity in Screen Cultures*, ed. Paula Massood, Angel Daniel Matos, and Pamela Robertson Wojcik (Durham, NC: Duke University Press, 2021), 250–261.
6. Most of the earliest cartoons in different cinematographic color processes are not extant, such as *In Gollywog Land* (Charles Urban, Kinemacolor, 1912) or *Thomas the Cat* (J. R. Bray, Brewster Color, 1920). For a more detailed account of animation's color history, see Jere Guldin, "Photographing Animated Motion Pictures in Early Color Film Processes," *Animatrix* 7, no.7 (1993): 20–30; Kirsten Moana Thompson, *Color, Visual Culture and American Animation 1895–1960* (forthcoming).
7. Ted Eshbaugh is now believed to have been the first to produce a Technicolor IV short (*The Snow Man*) for exhibition, but Disney was the first to theatrically exhibit a Technicolor

IV cartoon, and their rivalry was even evident in their joint appearances in Los Angeles Museum exhibition on animated cartoons in 1933–1934; see "Report of the Historical and Museum Committee," *Society of Motion Picture and Television Engineers* 22, no. 1 (January 1934): 13–16; Ted Eshbaugh, "Eshbaugh Cites Fifteen Years of Color Cartoons," *Motion Picture Herald*, March–April 1946, 46. For specific aesthetic and technological histories, the field of color studies is extensive, but in particular, see Richard Misek, *Chromatic Cinema: A History of Screen Color* (New York: Wiley-Blackwell), 2010; James Layton and David Pierce, *The Dawn of Technicolor, 1915–1935* (New York: George Eastman House, 2015); Joshua Yumibe, *Moving Color: On the History of Color in Mass Culture, Modernism, and Silent Cinema* (New Brunswick, NJ: Rutgers University Press, 2012).

8. Such as the production of wartime logos and insignias for military and civilian units; see David Lesjak, *Service with Character: The Disney Studio and World War II* (Los Angeles: Theme Park Press, 2014): 109–176.

9. Paul Wells appropriating Umberto Eco's concept of hyperrealism, in Paul Wells, *Understanding Animation* (New York: Routledge, 1998), 25.

10. Frank Thomas and Ollie Johnston, *The Illusion of Life: Disney Animation* (New York: Hyperion, 1981): 251–267.

11. Rubber-hose animation designed limbs as rubber hoses and torsos as balloons, with no attention to physical physiognomic accuracy. For an outline of "squash and stretch" and the other eleven principles of animation (anticipation; staging; straight-ahead and pose-to-pose; follow-through and overlapping; slow out and slow in; arcs; secondary action; timing; exaggeration; solid drawing; and appeal), see Thomas and Johnston, *The Illusion of Life*, 47–70. The twelve principles were dedicated to clearly conveying an action and making it appealing and realistic in its sense of weight, gravity, and movement through space.

12. Cited by Hank Hine, director of Fundació Gala-Salvador Dalí Museum in St. Petersburg, Florida, in Walt Disney Family Foundation, *Disney and Dali: Architects of the Imagination* (Los Angeles: Disney Editions, 2015), 11.

13. Thomas Schatz, *Hollywood Genres: Formulas, Filmmaking, and the Studio System* (New York: Random House, 1981), 186–220, 194.

14. Christopher Gullen, "Corporeal Modification in the Hollywood Musical," PhD diss. Wayne State University, 2012, 16.

15. Schatz, *Hollywood Genres*, 188.

16. See composite file made up of Dumbo Draft 2/24/41, Production No. 2006, Draft #1, pp. 1–4, and Dumbo Draft 21/29/4, Production No. 2006, Sequence 18, Draft "FINAL," pp 1–7, in John Canemaker Animation Collection, NYU Fales Library and Special Collections, Series 1 Subseries B, box 9, file 72. See also Dumbo Draft 1/29/41, Production No, 2006. Sequence 18, Draft 2, p. 1, in the Hans Peck A. Film L.A. Collection, May 12, 2010, https://afilmla.blogspot.com/search?q=pink+elephants.

17. I am indebted to Mark Langer, "Regionalism in Disney Animation: Pink Elephants and Dumbo," *Film History* 4, no. 4 (1990): 305–332, which first made me closely examine this sequence. Authorship of the sequence is not entirely certain and can only be reconciled with the Disney studio archival files, which are inaccessible to scholars. The Canemaker and Peck files contain multiple drafts, and Sequence 18 "Final Draft" in the Canemaker files does not list any authorial contributions to the sequence, although Sequence 17 of the same file does. Presumably, the final draft replaced the earlier drafts where authorial contributions had been assigned.

18. "When [Ward] Kimball was asked 'were you guys on drugs when doing this?' he answered, 'maybe Alca-Seltzer [sic] and Pepto-Bismol. We were just trained to think this way.'" Hans Peck, "Production 2006, Seq. 18, Pepto-Bismol Trip," A. Film L.A., June 15, 2006, https://afilmla.blogspot.com/search?q=pepto, but in an interview with Jim Korkis, he made a similar observation about the "candy colors" of the Pastoral Symphony sequence of *Fantasia* (1940): "Kids ask me if we were on some drugs when we made the picture and I say, 'No, we were just trained that way. We thought that way. The strongest drug we had was an occasional martini.'" Years later, Ward Kimball also acknowledged, "In the '60s, I experimented with mescaline and peyote and was involved with a study being run by UCLA at that time on the effects of those drugs." "Ward Kimball's Final Farewell," Hogan's Alley, no. 11, 2003, https://www.hoganmag.com/blog/ward-kimballs-final-farewell.
19. Mark Langer has argued that the animators who worked on the Pink Elephants sequence exemplified a New York style that "violated [West coast style] through its emphasis on the artificial quality of animation." Langer, "Regionalism in Disney Animation," 306.
20. "Pink Elephants on Parade" lyrics © Walt Disney Music Company, Bourne Co., Wonderland Music Company Inc.
21. The form of the diagonal stripe (right to left) is relatively rare compared with the more common left-to-right diagonal stripe (*bandé*) and had negative connotations. This form is used on the elephants as they split into marching outlines, each with a different pattern, and accentuate their menacing and nightmarish quality. Michel Pastoureau, *The Devil's Cloth: A History of Stripes and Striped Fabric* (New York: Columbia University Press), 1991, 28.
22. Ibid., 49–50. As a sartorial emblem of social structures in the Middle Ages, the stripe was also a marker of exclusion (the Jew), social inferiority (the servant), the ignominious (the criminal), and the infirm (the leper), as well as the exotic and the animal. The alternation of bright colors such as red, green, and yellow was particularly unseemly, but over the sixteenth to nineteenth centuries, there was an amelioration in meaning, shifting from the diabolical to the domestic and ludic, with stripes on recreational clothing and equipment, childhood toys, and equipment related to hygiene and athletics. See also ibid., 3, 7≠40, 63–92.
23. Ibid., 316.
24. Don Peri, ed., *Working with Walt; Interviews with Disney Artists* (Jackson: University Press of Mississippi, 2008), 186–187.
25. https://www.drugfoundation.org.nz/matters-of-substance/archive/matters-of-substance-november-2014/about-a-drug-mescaline/.
26. Huxley uses the variant spelling "mescalin" which I have preserved in his cited words. Aldous Huxley, *The Doors of Perception & Heaven and Hell* (New York: Harper, 2009 [1954]), 26–27.
27. Ibid., 19.
28. In ibid., 6–16. Essay originally published in *Collected Essays by Aldous Huxley* (New York: Harper), 1958.
29. Ibid., 105.
30. Ibid., 95–96, 103.
31. Heinrich Klüver, *Mescal and Mechanisms of Hallucinations* (Chicago: University of Chicago Press, 1970), 16.
32. Ibid., 66.
33. Ibid.
34. Ibid., 25–26.

35. Ibid., 72.
36. Ibid., 31. In some ways, one can think of the GIF as a new-media variant whose circular loop foregrounds this endless incompleteness by isolating and foregrounding animated detail.
37. These hallucinatory effects overlaid animation on live-action film to produce a hybrid form. For more on psychedelic cinema, see Andrew Derek Syder, "'Shaken out of the Ruts of Ordinary Perception': Vision, Culture and Technology in the Psychedelic Sixties," PhD diss., University of Southern California, 2009; Gene Youngblood, *Expanded Cinema, 50th Anniversary Edition* (New York: Fordham University Press, 2020). See also Bregt Lamaris, "Hallucinating Colors: Psychedelic Film, Technology, Aesthetics and Affect," *Cinéma & Cie* 19, no. 32 (Spring 2019): 85–97.
38. These package films were *Saludos Amigos* (1943), *Victory through Air Power* (1943), *The Three Caballeros* (1945), *Make Mine Music* (1946), *Song of the South* (1946), *Fun and Fancy Free* (1947), *Melody Time* (1948), *So Dear to My Heart* (1949), and *The Adventures of Ichabod and Mr. Toad* (1949). The two films that preceded *Bambi*—the concert feature *Fantasia* (1940) and *The Reluctant Dragon* (1941)—were also compilations of shorter cartoons, live-action material, and bridging material.
39. J. B. Kaufman, *South of the Border with Disney: Walt Disney and the Good Neighbor Program, 1941–1948* (New York: Disney Editions, 2009), 26, 71.
40. Rick Altman, *The Musical* (Bloomington: Indiana University Press, 1989); 129–199 for fairy-tale musical, 272–327 for folk musical.
41. Arun Saldanha's The concept of "psychedelic whiteness" is in Arun Saldanha, *Psychedelic White: God Trance and the Viscosity of Race* (Minneapolis: University of Minnesota Press, 2007, 8); Joanna Gosse, "'Altered States': Psychedelic Experimental Cinema as Border Crossing in Bruce Conner's *Looking For Mushrooms*," *Journal of Cinema and Media Studies* 61, no. 5 (2021–2022): 183–209, https://quod.lib.umich.edu/cgi/t/text/idx/j/jcms/18261332.0061.508/--altered-states-psychedelic-experimental-cinema-as-border?rgn=main;view=fulltext.
42. Kaufman, *South of the Border*, 89.
43. Ibid.
44. Aloysio (Louis) Oliveira (1914–1995) was a key figure in Brazilian musical culture. Bandleader of Bando da Lua, he also played a role in the introduction of Brazilian music to the international stage and, through that, in the career of Carmen Miranda. He also led Odeon and founded the Elenco record label and was a cultural consultant to Disney for the Brazilian section of *Saludos Amigos*. See no *Dicionário Cravo Albin da Música Popular Brasileira*, https://dicionariompb.com.br/.
45. Goldschmitt also notes that *Saludos Amigos* played a key role in the song's continued circulation in the US and Europe. Kariann Goldschmitt, "From Disney to Dystopia: Transforming 'Brazil' for a US Audience," in *The Routledge Companion to Screen Music and Sound*, ed. Miguel Mera, Ronald Sadoff, and Ben Winters (New York: Routledge, 2017), 363–374.
46. Ibid., 367. Goldschmitt suggests this landscape is "without people or civilization," but in fact, the musical sequence is a lengthy one whose reprise concludes with Donald, José, and a woman dancing with others as we see the nightclubs and hotels of Rio.
47. The painting was completed first and then run backward to make it seem as if the image was being painted in. Kaufman, *South of the Border*, 94n46.
48. Giannalberto Bendazzi, *Le film d'animation* (Paris: Pensée Sauvage, 1985), 178.

49. For example, Douglas Leigh's Epok advertising of the 1940s was animated by Otto Messmer (who also animated Felix the cat). For more on animation, advertising, and color, see Kirsten Moana Thompson, "Rainbow Ravine: Color and Animated Advertising in Times Square, 1891–1945," in *The Color Fantastic: Chromatic Worlds of Silent Cinema*, ed. Joshua Yumibe, Sarah Street, and Vicky Jackson (Amsterdam: Amsterdam University Press, 2018), 161–178; John Canemaker, "The Electric Felix Man," *Animation World*, November 1996, http://www.awn.com/mag/issue1.8/articles/canemaker1.8.html.
50. Caity Weaver, "What Is Glitter? A Strange Journey to the Glitter Factory," *New York Times*, December 21, 2018, https://www.nytimes.com/2018/12/21/style/glitter-factory.html
51. Ibid.
52. Bruce C. Steele, "A World of Magical Moments," *D23*, Fall 2021, 6, 7.
53. Panchito introduces the first Mexico sequence ("Piñata") to the music "Ay! Jalisco, no te rajes!" with English lyrics by Ray Gilbert.
54. Huxley, *The Doors of Perception & Heaven and Hell*, 168.
55. Kaufman, *South of the Border*, 231.
56. David Batchelor, *Chromophobia* (London: Reaktion, 2000), 34.
57. Huxley, *The Doors of Perception & Heaven and Hell*, 157.
58. Daniel Stern, "The Role of Feelings for an Interpersonal Self," in *The Perceived Self: Ecological and Interpersonal Sources of Self-Knowledge*, ed. Ulric Neisser (Cambridge: Cambridge University Press, 1993), 205–2015; Richard Grusin, *Premediation: Affect and Mediality After 9/11* (London: Palgrave Macmillan, 2010), 95.

Bibliography

Altman, Charles F. (Rick). *The American Film Musical*. Bloomington: Indiana University Press, 1989.

Batchelor, David. *Chromophobia*. London: Reaktion, 2000.

Beckman, Karen, ed. *Animating Film Theory*. Durham, NC: Duke University Press, 2014.

Bendazzi, Giannalberto. *Le film d'animation*. Paris: Pensée Sauvage, 1985.

Buchan, Suzanne, ed. *Pervasive Animation*. New York: Routledge, 2013.

Canemaker, John. "The Electric Felix Man." *Animation World*, November 1996. http://www.awn.com/mag/issue1.8/articles/canemaker1.8.html.

Eshbaugh, Ted. "Eshbaugh Cites Fifteen Years of Color Cartoons." *Motion Picture Herald*, March–April 1946, 46.

Gosse, Joanna. "'Altered States': Psychedelic Experimental Cinema as Border Crossing in Bruce Conner's *Looking for Mushrooms*." *Journal of Cinema and Media Studies* 61, no. 5 (2021–2022): 183–209. https://quod.lib.umich.edu/cgi/t/text/idx/j/jcms/18261332.0061.508/--altered-states-psychedelic-experimental-cinema-as-border?rgn=main;view=fulltext.

Goldmark, Daniel. *Tunes for 'Toons: Music and the Hollywood Cartoon*. Los Angeles: University of California Press, 2005.

Goldschmitt, Karian. "From Disney to Dystopia: Transforming 'Brazil' for a US Audience." In *The Routledge Companion to Screen Music and Sound*, edited by Miguel Mera, Ronald Sadoff and Ben Winters, 363–374. New York: Routledge, 2017.

Guldin, Jere. "Photographing Animated Motion Pictures in Early Color Film Processes." *Animatrix* 7, no. 7 (1993): 20–30.

Gullen, Christopher. "Corporeal Modification in the Hollywood Musical." PhD diss., Wayne State University, 2012.

Huxley, Aldous. *The Doors of Perception & Heaven and Hell*. New York: Harper, 2009 [1954].
Kaufman, J. B. *South of the Border with Disney: Walt Disney and the Good Neighbor Program, 1941–1948*. New York: Disney Editions, 2009.
Korkis, Jim. "Ward Kimball's Final Farewell." *Hogan's Alley*, no. 11, 2003. https://www.hoganmag.com/blog/ward-kimballs-final-farewell.
Klüver, Heinrich. *Mescal and Mechanisms of Hallucinations*. Chicago: University of Chicago Press, 1970.
Lamaris, Bregt. "Hallucinating Colors: Psychedelic Film, Technology, Aesthetics and Affect." *Cinéma & Cie* 19, no. 32 (Spring 2019): 85–97.
Langer, Mark. "Regionalism in Disney Animation: Pink Elephants and Dumbo." *Film History* 4, no. 4 (1990): 305–321.
Layton, James, and David Pierce. *The Dawn of Technicolor, 1915–1935* (New York: George Eastman House), 2015.
Lesjak, David. *Service with Character: The Disney Studio and World War II*. Los Angeles: Theme Park Press, 2014.
Leslie, Esther. "Animation's Petrified Unrest." In *Pervasive Animation*, edited by Suzanne Buchan, 73–93. New York: Routledge, 2013.
Misek, Richard. *Chromatic Cinema: A History of Screen Color*. New York: Wiley-Blackwell, 2010.
Pastoureau, Michel. *The Devil's Cloth: A History of Stripes and Striped Fabric*. New York: Columbia University Press, 1991.
Peri, Don, ed. *Working with Walt; Interviews with Disney Artists*. Jackson: University Press of Mississippi, 2008.
Schatz, Thomas. *Hollywood Genres: Formulas, Filmmaking, and the Studio System*. New York: Random House, 1981.
SMPTE. "Report of the Historical and Museum Committee." *Society of Motion Picture and Television Engineers* 22, no. 1 (January 1934): 13–16.
Solomon, Charles. "Fantastic 'Fantasia': Disney Channel Takes a Look at Walt's Great Experiment in Animation." *Los Angeles Times*, August 26, 1990. https://www.latimes.com/archives/la-xpm-1990-08-26-tv-552-story.html.
Steele, Bruce, C. "A World of Magical Moments." *D23*, Fall 2021, 4–11.
Stern, Daniel. "The Role of Feelings for an Interpersonal Self." In *The Perceived Self: Ecological and Interpersonal Sources of Self-Knowledge*, edited by Ulric Neisser, 205–215. Cambridge: Cambridge University Press, 1993.
Syder, Andrew Derek. "'Shaken out of the Ruts of Ordinary Perception': Vision, Culture and Technology in the Psychedelic Sixties." PhD diss., University of Southern California, 2009.
Thomas, Frank, and Ollie Johnston. *The Illusion of Life: Disney Animation*. New York: Hyperion, 1981.
Thompson, Kirsten Moana. "Animating Ephemeral Surfaces: Transparency, Translucency and Disney's World of Color." *Refractory: A Journal of Entertainment Media* 24 (June 2014). https://webarchive.nla.gov.au/awa/20141116230413/http://pandora.nla.gov.au/pan/30981/20141117-0000/refractory.unimelb.edu.au/2014/08/06/thompson/index.html.
Thompson, Kirsten Moana. *Color, Visual Culture and American Animation 1895–1960*. Forthcoming.
Thompson, Kirsten Moana. "Falling In(to) Color: Chromophilia and Tom Ford's *A Single Man*" *Moving Image* 15, no. 1 (Spring 2015): 62–84.
Thompson, Kirsten Moana. "Rainbow Ravine: Color and Animated Advertising in Times Square, 1891–1945." In *The Color Fantastic: Chromatic Worlds of Silent Cinema*, edited

by Joshua Yumibe, Sarah Street, and Vicky Jackson, 161–178. Amsterdam: Amsterdam University Press, 2018.

Thompson, Kirsten Moana. "Tattooed Light and Embodied Design: Intersectional Surfaces in *Moana*." In *Media Crossroads: Intersections of Space and Identity in Screen Cultures*, edited by Paula Massood, Angel Daniel Matos, and Pamela Robertson Wojcik, 250–261. Durham, NC: Duke University Press, 2021.

Walt Disney Family Foundation. *Disney and Dali: Architects of the Imagination*. Los Angeles: Disney Editions, 2015.

Weaver, Caity. "What Is Glitter? A Strange Journey to the Glitter Factory." *New York Times*, December 21, 2018. https://www.nytimes.com/2018/12/21/style/glitter-factory.html.

Wells, Paul. *Understanding Animation*. New York: Routledge, 1998.

Youngblood, Gene. *Expanded Cinema, 50th Anniversary Edition* (New York: Fordham University Press, 2020).

Yumibe, Joshua. *Moving Color: On the History of Color in Mass Culture, Modernism, and Silent Cinema*. New Brunswick, NJ: Rutgers University Press, 2012.

CHAPTER 18

DISNEY DIVAS

DEBORAH PAREDEZ AND STACY WOLF

THE Disney musical has long been synonymous with the Disney princess. Animated princess musicals from the "classic era," which were based on fairy tales—*Snow White* (1937), *Cinderella* (1950), and *Sleeping Beauty* (1959)—characterized the Disney princess for decades. Modeled after the carriage and choreography of a ballerina, the classic Disney princess is thin but curvy, graceful, beautiful, and white. Rebecca-Anne C. do Rozario describes "[t]he posture of the early princesses, with teenage girls going about their chores practically *en pointe*."[1] Elizabeth Bell writes that "the Disney apparatus buys into and then sells the twofold fantasy of little girls who want to grow up to be princesses *and* ballerinas."[2] The princess exhibits traits of innocence, patience, humility, generosity, and attachment to animals. The character of the classic Disney princess never changes, but her external circumstances do when the prince finds her and marries her.[3] These traits have become so defining of the Disney princess that the 2007 live-action Disney princess film *Enchanted* simultaneously pays homage to and lampoons these qualities as the source of its humor.

Just as the princess has been a key feature of the Disney animated musical, so has her nemesis and evil opposite, the witch, a romantically unattached older woman with a foreboding presence and ugly features that mark her as well past her prime. As in much of Western culture, good girls and bad women are defined in opposition to each other. The oppositional tension between the princess and the female villain drives the narrative of the classic Disney animated musicals. The Evil Queen hunts down and poisons Snow White; the Wicked Stepmother torments Cinderella; the vengeful fairy Maleficent curses Sleeping Beauty. Where the princess is young, passive, eventually married, preserving the status quo, and prone to self-sacrifice, the evil witch is old, active, single, disruptive to the social order, and self-interested. Not unlike the archetypal female villains in opera, melodrama, and European fairy tales, the classic Disney female villain regards the ingénue's beauty and goodness as threats to her quest for power and riches. Consumed by jealousy of the princess and the princess's ability to win the heart of the handsome prince, these wicked women seek to banish or destroy the princess but are ultimately punished for their actions.

Scholars and critics have classified the classic Disney antagonists variously as femme fatales, camp witches, and diva villains.[4] These villains share many characteristics with traditional divas: they are troublesome but compelling older women, embody both masculinity and femininity, possess a commanding presence, remain fiercely singular, and pursue power and delight in possessing it.[5] But, significantly, they don't sing. Only the sweet-voiced ingénue gets to sing in these classic Disney princess musicals. The evil witch, in contrast, expresses herself in shrieks, yells, wails, fierce commands, and shaky-voiced threats. Her exile from the music in a musical ensures that the audience will not sympathize with her or identify with her and thus prevents her from achieving full diva status. Within the logic of the musical, these villains are proto-divas who serve as the blueprint for the diva villain that emerges in the "Disney Renaissance" period and, later, the diva heroine of the twenty-first-century Disney princess musicals.

The diva, as we define her here, is an unapologetically fierce, over-the-top, gender-expansive, charismatic female character whose power is often associated with her vocal prowess. We draw our definition of the diva from the long-standing diva traditions in both opera and musical theater.[6] The label "diva," which can be traced back to "Casta Diva" ("chaste goddess"), an 1831 aria from Vincenzo Bellini's opera *Norma*, initially referred to virtuosic and temperamental female opera sopranos. By the late-twentieth century, though, "diva" was applied both to the larger-than-life, complicated female characters on stage and screen and the larger-than-life, complicated women who played them. As Imogen West-Knights observes, "Over the years, the opera diva gave way to the Hollywood talkies diva (Marlene Dietrich, Bette Davis); the soul music diva (Aretha Franklin, Nina Simone); the pop megastar diva (Rihanna, Lady Gaga); and many more iterations."[7] Musical-theater divas are figures, as Michelle Dvoskin writes, "who sing loudly, take up space (both narratively and physically) and demand attention."[8] Distinct from the ingénue, the diva in this context is often a woman of hard-fought accomplishment whose rafter-shaking belt in an eleven o'clock number asserts her triumph over struggle. The diva endures, and her remarkable resiliency is often showcased by her ability to sing louder or higher or longer than anyone else around her. She is distinctively singular—both in her skills as a performer and often in her romantic relationship status.

In contrast to the princess figure, the diva's difference is marked by her refusal to adhere to the status quo or the demands of propriety or gender conventions. Sometimes this means she is racialized and sexualized in troubling ways, her excess (of emotion or volume or body type) marked as Blackness (or other categories of nonwhite otherness) or as queer. Sometimes her "aggressiveness, dominance, and individualism is masculinizing," rendering her "exceptional in her defiance of traditional Western notions of femininity."[9] Other times, the diva's virtuosity or signature sense of glamor is celebrated as a way to bolster ideals of white femininity. Often, her distinctive singularity leads to a sense of narrative and emotional isolation for the diva and, simultaneously, to a fervent following of countless fans who worship her precisely because of her ability to sing powerfully within and beyond these confines. Within the genre of the musical, a diva often sings (at least one of) the most memorable and technically virtuosic songs in a performance form in which songs are the primary mode of character development, expression, and communication.

In this chapter, we chart four key moments in the development of the Disney diva. We begin with the diva villain Ursula in *The Little Mermaid* movie. In 1989, Ursula was a new kind of Disney villain, a featured character who sings one of the musical's most memorable songs. We then examine Belle in *Beauty and the Beast* (1991) as a character type we call the prindiva, a combination of princess and diva, a diva-esque princess. Over the history of her various figurations as an animated character, a Broadway star, and a live-action movie heroine, Belle is a Disney Renaissance princess who also integrates characteristics of a diva. (Later Disney princesses, such as Mulan, Moana, Merida, and Raya, also exhibit prindiva traits.) We then consider the 1998 Disney-produced, made-for-TV movie Rodgers and Hammerstein's *Cinderella*, which features a multiracial diva ensemble and reveals how diva traits can adhere to both good and bad female characters. Finally, we land on the diva heroine Elsa in the animated movie *Frozen* (2013). As we demonstrate, the Disney princess remains the central female type; even *Frozen*, which stars a diva, shores up the princess rather than supplanting her. Our examples are animated films, live-action films, a made-for-TV movie, plus the stage version of *Beauty and the Beast*. *Beauty* is our one example that includes discussion of the animated movie, the stage version, and later film versions, because Belle transforms into the prindiva from celluloid to stage. In our other examples, the characters we discuss are divas from the start.

Adding the category of diva expands potential analyses of Disney female characters.[10] Our typology—diva villain to prindiva to ensemble [of] divas to diva heroine—is also historical, as the connotation of diva changes from the 1980s to the early 2000s, and "diva" moves into the mainstream as a complimentary label.

Ursula: The Diva Villain

In 1984, under the newly installed leadership of Michael Eisner and Jeffrey Katzenberg, Walt Disney Productions decided to revive its flailing animation department. The studio returned to animation with a vengeance when it hired Howard Ashman, who brought Alan Menken on board; the team had written and gained acclaim for the off-Broadway musical *Little Shop of Horrors* (1982).[11] Ashman and Menken's first Disney film, *The Little Mermaid*, brought back the princess musical, which had been on a thirty-year hiatus since the release of *Sleeping Beauty* in 1959; the project "felt like the studio's last chance at a blockbuster."[12] The pair followed up with *Beauty and the Beast* (1991) and *Aladdin* (1992), creating a trio of musicals that revived Disney's presence as a major film studio and the animated film as a commercial and critical success. (Although the film does not revolve around her, Princess Jasmine in *Aladdin* is the first nonwhite animated Disney princess. While she possesses the same updated spunky spirit as Ariel and Belle, she sings only one song, the duet "A Whole New World," with Aladdin. This circumscribed role underlines the racial terms of the Disney animated princess and conveys a hesitancy to fully update her to include nonwhite princesses. Twenty-seven years after the release of its animated feature, Disney added a solo, "Speechless," for Jasmine in the 2019 live-action version, but the film's story and conflict remain focused on Aladdin, the Genie, and the villain, Jafar.)

Ashman and Menken brought knowledge of and experience with Broadway musical theater to animated movies, incorporating key features from the formally integrated musical-theater tradition. They wrote songs that develop characters, such as "I Want" songs, as well as songs that move the plot along and function as the requisite "tentpoles" of the musical's narrative.[13] Although, as Peter C. Kunze points out, "Disney had little hope" for what it saw as a "girls' film,"[14] in retrospect, the musical launched a new era: the "Disney Renaissance," marked by both its blockbuster success in the animation world and its introduction of a new kind of Disney princess. And with the new princess came a new villain.

As in the Disney princess musicals that preceded it (and the fairy tale on which it's based), *The Little Mermaid*'s central conflict revolves around an ingénue princess and the worldly female villain who, driven by jealousy, attempts to thwart or exploit the young girl's longings and romantic fulfillment. The princess this time around is Ariel, the teenage mermaid who yearns for escape from her undersea world. Like princesses before her, she befriends and is aided by animals and seeks romantic fulfillment. And yet she's distinctly updated from previous princesses, with her spunky and defiant attitude and her movement style characterized by acrobatic and athletic grace rather than the balletic grace of the princesses of yore.[15] Her voice is also updated. Where classic princesses such as Snow White sang with a youthful, soubrette soprano voice, Ariel's voice, as sung by Tony Award–winning actress Jodi Benson, is a lyrical soprano with a belt stronger relative to other singers at the time,[16] which Ashman coached her to restrain for the animation's intimacy.[17]

From the start of the musical, Ariel is fascinated with the human world and sings "Part of Your World." After she saves Prince Eric from a shipwreck, revives him with her singing, and falls in love-at-first-sight with him, she becomes even more determined to live on land. She visits Ursula the sea witch, who agrees to transform Ariel into a human for three days in exchange for her voice. During that time, Ariel must secure a true love's kiss from Eric; if she fails, Ariel will return to mermaid form and will forever belong to Ursula. Predictably, Ursula pulls out all the stops trying to thwart Ariel's plans, and the battle between good (princess) and evil (sea witch) ensues, until Ursula meets her demise and wedding bells ring for Ariel and Eric.

Ursula resembles early Disney wicked women in many ways: she's conniving, older, resolutely single, driven by envy toward the princess, obsessed with power, commanding in stature, and marked by physical difference and gender ambiguity. But as a sea witch who takes the form of a humorous and flamboyant inky-tentacled octopus with the upper body of a plus-size drag queen and sings an unforgettable musical number, Ursula departs from those types in a significant way: she is a fully fledged diva villain.

Ursula's diva persona is due in part to the origins of her character development. The directors and screenplay writers, Ron Clements and John Musker, initially created the role with the basso-voiced diva Bea Arthur in mind. Ashman had hoped soap-opera diva Joan Collins would sing the lyrics he penned. They finally settled on Broadway diva Elaine Stritch, and when she didn't work out, they hired the comedic stage and television actress Pat Carroll to voice the role.[18] "Unlike Stritch, Carroll was amenable to Ashman's direction, later admitting that she 'stole' his 'very sardonic, raunchy, low down approach' to the role."[19] Carroll fashioned the character of Ursula as a world-weary "ex-Shakespearean actress who now sold cars."[20] The origin story of these larger-than-life grand dames of the stage and screen serving as the models for Ursula reveals how diva-ness was baked into her character from the start.

Disney animators Rob Minkoff and Ruben Aquino also drew inspiration for Ursula's appearance and movement style from famous divas. Minkoff based Ursula's exaggerated voluptuousness, sexual voraciousness, vampy arrogance, dramatic eye makeup, and arched eyebrows on the drag queen Divine, who gained notoriety and a cult following for her roles in John Waters's films.[21] In fact, early design ideas for Ursula included a pink mohawk inspired by Divine's hairstyle in Waters's *Pink Flamingos*, though the mohawk was later discarded in favor of Ursula's signature shock of white hair.[22] Ursula's demeanor and delusions of grandeur were also based on the high theatricality of another legendary film diva. Animator Kathy Zielinski recalled, "I watched *Sunset Boulevard* with the character Norma Desmond, and I studied the way she would move and … it would inspire me when I tried to put some life into [Ursula]."[23] Given these influences, it's no surprise that Ursula is not just a diva but a deliciously campy one, performing her role with a knowing wink and utter delight in her devious ways. As do Rozario observes, "That Ursula has it in her power to be a stereotypical vixen and yet remains gloriously rapt in her larger-than-life guise is part of the particular parody: the *femme fatale* turned camp diva."[24] Ursula's campiness—her high theatricality, delightfully outrageous artifice, and sly irony—contributes to her queer appeal, given the long tradition of camp aesthetics and cultural practices among many queer communities.[25]

Ursula makes her entrance in the film as a shadowy figure in her undersea cave. We hear her gravelly, sardonic voice before we see her body, which emphasizes and foreshadows the importance of voice for this diva. Slowly, her body emerges from the darkness, first her hand reaching out to grab a shivering sea worm and then, notably, a close-up on her mouth—full red lips and sharp gleaming teeth—as she voraciously consumes her snack in the midst of an aggrieved monologue about her banishment from the sea king's palace. She is, as Susan Leonardi and Rebecca Pope have argued about representations of the diva, "the devouring diva, a diva dentata" who "can eat you up and swallow you down."[26] And when at last we are granted a glimpse of Ursula, she stretches her fleshy arm dramatically above her rotund and pouting face in a Norma Desmond–inspired pose and sighs, "Now look at me! Wasted away to practically nothing! Banished and exiled and practically starving!" After she delivers the line, her undulating, full-figured, tentacled body comes fully into view. This entrance—saturated with irony and histrionics—marks her as a campy, villainous diva.

Above all, what most secures Ursula's status as a diva is that she sings what has become a legendary song in a musical. She is, in fact, the first Disney villainess who is granted her own musical number. She vamps and shimmies and growls and purrs throughout her song, "Poor Unfortunate Souls," whose vamping chorus, tempo, and orchestration evoke Kurt Weill's cabaret ballad "Mack the Knife" from *The Threepenny Opera* (1928) and the sardonic delight of "Willkommen," the opening number from John Kander and Fred Ebb's musical *Cabaret* (1966).[27] And it's not just that she sings but that through her song, she persuades Ariel to relinquish her voice to Ursula in exchange for just three days of life as a human. Ursula's song and her ability to deliver it with such convincing flair make her Disney's first singing diva and inaugurate the very conflict that drives the rest of the story.

As a consummate diva, Ursula is obsessed with and values the virtuosic singing voice above all else and will do anything to possess it. And while the diva villain meets the same fate as the female/femme fatale villains before her, she and her unforgettable, over-the-top song encourage a sense of connection among audiences, especially those who disidentify with the heteronormative, wedding-bound princess. Most notably, Ursula invites queer readings and paves the way for future animated queer (or queerly read) villains such as Jafar and Scar.[28] As Kerry Mallan and Roderick McGillis argue, "an octopus in drag as a woman instructing a mermaid (with a pre-Madonna seashell bra) on the art of come-hither moves and heterosexual romance, invites the audience to look at the world queerly. Normality simply has no place."[29] The success of Ursula as a diva villain also inaugurated the practice of casting established Broadway divas as diva villains in Disney princess stories that followed, such as Bernadette Peters as the Wicked Stepmother in Disney's televised (and diva-packed) restaging of Rodgers and Hammerstein's *Cinderella* (1997) (discussed below) and Donna Murphy as the voice of Mother Gothel in *Tangled* (2010).

BEAUTY AND THE BEAST: FROM FEMINIST PRINCESS TO DUTIFUL DAUGHTER TO PRINDIVA

If Ursula embodies the diva villain and laminates diva-ness onto a central, singing Disney character, Belle—through her many versions from screen to stage and back again—infuses the second-generation princess with diva qualities. Like *The Little Mermaid*, *Beauty and the Beast*'s score was written by Ashman and Menken, but the screenplay was written by Linda Woolverton, the first woman to write an animated film for Disney and a fervent feminist. "They didn't know what they were dealing with when they brought me on," she said.[30] With Ashman's support, Woolverton fought to counter Disney's passive princesses, to create a female character "that isn't based on being kind and taking the hits but smiling all the way through it."[31] As one example of her battle with the producers, Woolverton recounted writing a scene with "Belle sticking pins into a map of all the places she wished to travel. By the time it got to storyboarding, Belle had been rewritten into a kitchen, decorating a cake."[32] Woolverton objected. The compromise? Belle would have her nose in a book while walking to make the animation more visually interesting. "I'd been through the women's movement in the '60s and '70s," Woolverton said, "and I definitely couldn't buy that this smart, attractive young girl, Belle, would be sitting around and waiting for her prince to come."[33] Woolverton consciously wrote a character with an "independent, open mind" who would be a positive role model for kids, especially girls.[34]

With Belle, Disney begins to incorporate elements of diva performance into the protagonist, thus changing the conventional connotations of "diva" from negative (e.g., temperamental, arrogant) to positive (e.g., strong, empowered). By analyzing Belle as what we call a prindiva, we value the qualities that make her unique, larger than life, and envoiced. As English media personality and self-described diva Gemma Collins said, "At the end of the day, a diva is just a woman who knows what she wants."[35]

When Belle first appears as an animated character in 1991, she defines the second-generation Disney princess, with a few hints of the prindiva to come in later versions of her. Voiced by Paige O'Hara and modeled on Sherri Stoner, a five-foot-two-inch, ninety-two-pound improv comedy performer, Belle is a white, thin, young woman with flowing brown hair worn in a no-nonsense ponytail, big brown eyes, and a heart-shaped face. According to Elizabeth Bell, though the figures of Belle (and Ariel, who is also based on Stoner's body) convey a teenage girl's energy and verve more than the earlier passive and pliable Disney heroines, their bodies "moved from the realm of classic dance aesthetics to popular conventions of cheesecake," intentionally titillating, slyly sexualized, and flirtatious; their movements "tease with the conventions of burlesque."[36] Her body is stronger than those of classic Disney princesses, but she is still drawn in a conventionally feminine way.

The defining Disney Renaissance princess, Belle at once embodies Disney's conservative values even as she expresses hints of a diva's girl-power feminism. In the animated movie, much about Belle is princess-like. First, her costumes resemble those of daughters and princesses-to-be of an earlier era. She wears a white blouse under a pale blue jumper and a white apron, which signifies her ties to the home, cooking, and cleaning. Later she trades this everyday dress for a yellow, silky, flowing ball gown, both confirming her princess identity and adding a new color to the Disney palette of princesses.[37] In addition, Belle's fantasies are conventionally heterosexual, even as they are tinged with adventurousness. In the opening scene with the bookseller, for example, she breathlessly chooses a book that is "my favorite! Far-off places, daring sword fights, magic spells, a prince in disguise!" Then, in the song's bridge, book in hand, she sings to the sheep that surround her, "Here's where she meets Prince Charming, but she won't discover that it's him 'til chapter three," foreshadowing her own future, which features some adventures and a matrimonial conclusion.

Like other princesses of her generation, Belle is what Amy Davis calls a "dutiful daughter,"[38] loyal, self-sacrificing, and subservient—hardly a diva. She cares for her clever, scatterbrained father, and her love for and protectiveness of him set her on her journey. She lands in the Beast's castle when she offers to take her father's place as the Beast's prisoner. Belle is manipulated by the household objects—cursed through no fault of their own and fearful of the Beast, whom they call "master"—through their hospitality ("Be Our Guest"), as they try to keep her there.[39] Belle later patiently teaches the Beast table manners and how to waltz, "civilizing" him as an exemplar of the "Cult of True Womanhood," "a collection of attitudes" that began in the nineteenth century and, as historian Jeanne Boydston explains, "associated 'true' womanhood with the home and family."[40] Women, it was believed, especially white middle-class women, "effortlessly directed their households and exerted a serene moral influence over their husbands and children."[41] As Patrick D. Murphy writes, "Belle will acculturate the Beast, saving him from his tragic fate through domestication." But, he wonders, "who really gets domesticated and whose nature is really transformed in the course of this film?"[42] Belle's adventurous spirit is quelled by marriage at the end of the movie.

When Belle falls in love with the Beast, she succumbs to Stockholm syndrome, having become attached to her captor. The end of the movie delivers Belle her prize in conservative, quintessentially Disney terms. The spell is broken, and the Beast's looks are restored to his "natural" and appropriate handsomeness.[43] She says, "It *is* you," and their kiss launches a flare that explodes into fireworks in the sky. As Murphy argues, because "the curse requires that someone love him, not that he love someone else," "the smart woman gets the prince not by dint of her intellect but by means of her self-sacrificing devotion and selfless love."[44] The objects return to their human forms, and the setting changes to the castle's ballroom. Belle and the Prince, predictably beautiful and heterosexual, recostumed in a gown and a suit, waltz around the room to the title song, and Chip, now a little boy, confirms that they'll live happily ever after (and that he doesn't have to sleep in the cupboard anymore). As Bell observes, the film fulfills Belle's "destiny as marriage/reward for the prince/beast," as she is "commodif[ied] in the marriage plot."[45] For the most part, then, Belle in the movie is too passive and conventional to qualify as a diva.

On the other hand, Belle differs from previous Disney princesses in ways that hint toward the diva. For example, the musical's opening number, "Belle"—which is an example of what Jane Feuer calls a "traveling song," one that takes a character across a town or through a landscape—stresses Belle's difference and singularity (both diva traits) in relation to mainstream society.[46] The song serves as Belle's "I Am/I Want" song, allowing her to express her diva-like disdain for the townspeople (including and especially Gaston), her love for books, and her desire to escape "this poor provincial town." Belle's mobility—that she moves through the town independently, greets people, and runs errands—distinguishes her from the princess who is trapped in a house, in a corner, in a castle, or in a coffin and links her with the mobile, self-motivated diva. Belle is out and about, alone and decisive. Susan Jeffords labels Belle "a Disney Feminist."[47] The number also marks Belle as the star, the object of curiosity, and a queer subject. The townspeople describe her as "odd," "strange," "most peculiar," and "a funny girl." "She doesn't quite fit in," they sing; still, they repeatedly note her beauty. Although Belle seems to be oblivious to their judgment, she absorbs it, since in the next scene, she echoes their words and asks her father, "Do you think I'm odd?" and tells him, "I don't fit in here." Later it's confirmed that she is the only young woman in the town who doesn't swoon over Gaston—singularly odd because she has no use for him and uniquely perceives what an oaf he is.

As the movie goes on, Belle continually reveals her distinctiveness, often transcending gender boundaries and suggesting the diva's refusal to remain within conventional, stereotypically passive femininity. She leaves the house alone to rescue her father; she's not afraid of the Beast (when he emerges from the shadows, she recoils more in disgust than in fear); she offers to trade herself for her father's freedom. She knows her mind and is stubborn. She refuses to have dinner with the Beast when he demands it; she explores the castle against his order; she herself decides when she's ready to spend time with him. Later Belle leaves the castle to save her father from being committed to an asylum, but she returns to the castle to rescue the Beast. Belle's agency not only upends the traditional princess narrative but also activates diva qualities noted by Kirsty Fairclough, "self-acceptance" and "empowerment,"[48] as she is the one who saves the Beast from the spell, both returning him to his handsome state and allowing the household items to "become human again." Belle's ascension in the story—she gets herself out of the town and raises her class status—carries class connotations, another link to the diva. As Kirby Farrell writes, "Belle achieves her preeminence by rejecting community for a fantasy of individual omnipotence."[49]

Belle's status as the only woman in *Beauty and the Beast* enables a more expansive performance of femininity. The musical eschews a female villain diva—whether a nonsinging evil queen or a cruel stepmother or the singing, scene-stealing Ursula—as Belle's counterpart. Rather, Belle is set with and against three men: Gaston, the embodiment of toxic masculinity, stupid, arrogant, and carelessly cruel, as the antagonist; the Beast, changeable from bad to good, as the hero; and her father, loving but hapless. But no other female characters in the musical offset Belle's femininity. The comically rendered household objects in the castle, including Mrs. Potts, Plumette, and Wardrobe, occupy other feminine roles—grandmother, flirt, opera singer (a traditional diva). Belle's singularity opens the potential for her to perform as both a princess and a diva.

Belle restores order to the castle, but given her adventures throughout the movie, it seems unlikely that she will remain happily contained there with only the Prince, a bevy of servants, and an ample library. Despite the movie's stereotypical and conventional fairy-tale (and musical-theater) ending—the couple waltzes, surrounded by the restabilized community—Belle challenges the image of the dutiful daughter/new Disney princess and begins to move toward a different type: the prindiva.

The movie of *Beauty and the Beast* was met with rapturous reviews, was the first full-length animated movie to be nominated for Best Picture at the Academy Awards, and solidified Disney's return to animation and the presence of a new female protagonist. According to Shearon Roberts, *Beauty and the Beast* (along with *Aladdin* and *Mulan*) "proved to Disney that a film with a female lead as strong as her male love interest could make money."[50] Critics, scholars, and Disney executives noted Belle's power as a woman and a new kind of princess. It would require a reconstruction of the character on the Broadway stage to bring Belle closer to being a prindiva.

Belle on Broadway

Like *The Little Mermaid*, *Beauty and the Beast* also proved the success of musical-theater conventions and the value of having musical-theater artists on the creative team.[51] Disney executives were already discussing moving "product" to Broadway, and when *New York Times* theater critic Frank Rich praised *Beauty and the Beast*'s soundtrack as "the best Broadway musical score of 1991," the move was inevitable.[52] Robert Jess Roth, who directed mini-musical stage versions of the movies at the Disney theme parks, was hired by the chair of Walt Disney Studios, Katzenberg, to "stage the movie."[53] But first, the eighty-minute movie needed to be expanded to two hours and twenty minutes, the length of a typical Broadway musical. Ashman had died in 1991 and was replaced by lyricist Tim Rice, who teamed with Menken to write several new songs, including "Home" for Belle and "If I Can't Love Her" for the Beast. Every ensemble number grew in length, and book writer Woolverton extended the book scenes that she'd written for the movie (and earned a Tony nomination). The designers imagined and built Disney's magic—previously achieved through animation—on the Broadway stage. Costume designer Ann-Hould Ward, who brought the household objects to life, won the one Tony for the show.[54]

Belle in the stage version resembles her animated counterpart in characterization, story arc, and costume. But the addition of a new song for Broadway expands Belle's role, giving her more time onstage alone and moving her character from dutiful daughter/princess to a prindiva. Susan Egan originated the role on Broadway, giving Belle comic verve. As Egan tells it, she hadn't seen the movie version when she auditioned. When she read the script, she found Belle "quirky," and Egan's funny choices and unique vocal style impressed the producers more than other actors who imitated O'Hara's delivery in the movie.[55] At the final callback, director Roth asked her to play Belle as "a straight ingénue," and he cast Egan once she proved that she could play both comedy and the ingénue's innocence and earnestness.[56] From the very creation of Broadway's Belle, her performance of femininity expanded beyond a typical ingénue's, suggesting the possibility of a diva performance.

Belle's ballad, "Home," is the musical's first diva number, which she sings during her first night in the castle, locked into her room (that is, her cell) after refusing to have dinner with the Beast. As she tries to decide how she will cope with her situation, Belle gathers her strength. Through direct lyrics and a simple, repetitive melody, the song grows in intensity and volume. The slow-tempo, standard AABA song opens with the main lyrical idea, phrased as a question: "Is this home?" She asks herself, "Is this where I should learn to be happy?" She knows that as much as she didn't feel "at home" in her town, this "cold and dark" place" is worse. She tries to sort out the difference between where her body resides ("Am I here for a day or forever?") and where her heart lives ("Far, far away"), as she realizes that even if she's physically trapped, she can control her emotions by imagining her heart—her true self—elsewhere. In the last verse, Belle dares the Beast to entrap her, "Build higher walls around me," as the melody rises, and "Change ev'ry lock and key," as it falls. In a circular melody, she asserts her own agency: "Nothing lasts, nothing holds / All of me." His place can't contain her. She concludes the song quietly, determined that no matter what physical limits he imposes, she can retain her emotional freedom and distance: "My heart's far, far away / Home and free." By the end of the song, Belle is resolved to maintain her emotional integrity even as a physical prisoner. Dan Rubins observes that "Home" resembles other Broadway diva ballads such as Fantine's "I Dreamed a Dream" from *Les Misérables* and Christine's "All I Ask of You" (among other songs) in *The Phantom of the Opera*, "the Disney princess absorbing the vocal heft of the European diva."[57]

The song alters who Belle is at a relatively early point in the show. Unlike in the film version, Belle onstage analyzes her situation and articulates her determination to maintain her autonomy. As Kate Bailey, curator of a 2023 exhibition on divas at the Victoria and Albert Museum, explains, being a diva is about "using your voice to do something useful."[58]

While the number itself makes Belle into a prindiva, the actual, live presence of a body onstage also contributes to her power and singularity. The audience witnesses the actor's physical, vocal, and emotional labor and sees and hears her breathe. They see the glitter in her eyes and the sweat on her brow, her belted performance of fabulousness. Solon Snider Sway explains that Egan's voice here sounds "heavier" than O'Hara's in the movie.[59] "There is pain to it, a richer quality, darker, and a distinctive tone," he observes. Egan "might be considered more of a spinto [here] like Verdi's Aida."[60]

Over the years, different women's physicality continually altered Belle, moving her toward prindiva-ness. In 1994, Egan, like the animated Belle, was thin and white, with brown hair. Critic John Lahr wrote, "Disney's Belle has spunk; and Susan Egan, who has a fine voice and a sweet, strong nature, is a perfect embodiment of the American ideal of decent self-sufficiency."[61] Brad Smith concurred: "Belle looks and acts like a cross between Snow White and Mary Poppins, the Disney ideal of unctuous femininity."[62] Later Belles on Broadway and on the national tour replicated the look, confirming Disney's mega-musical production dynamics.

Belle was transformed in 1998—the same year "diva" solidified its positive valence and presence in mainstream culture with the VH1 concert with Mariah Carey, Celine Dion, Gloria Estefan, Shania Twain, and the very definition of diva, Aretha Franklin—when R&B superstar and diva Toni Braxton took over the role. The casting, which took months to negotiate, helped both Disney and Braxton, as the show was experiencing lagging ticket sales and Disney had a reputation for conservative casting practices, and Braxton needed money (in spite of being a huge star, she filed for bankruptcy in January 1998).[63] Not only did Braxton make Belle Black—as the performer said, "You could say her character was like a big old glass of punch, and I had to spike her a little bit."[64]—but she overlaid the character with her star persona as a sex symbol and diva. In his article

"Toni Braxton, Disney, and Thermodynamics," Jason King observes that the word used most repeatedly to describe Braxton in the press before, during, and after her appearance as Belle is "sultry."[65] Costume designer Ward lowered the necklines and tightened the corsets to reveal more of Braxton's form.[66] King argues that Braxton's performance remade the show entirely: "Suddenly, Belle takes on the spunky, sassy attitude that is imagined to be the hallmark of young, hip, black, inner-city femininity."[67] Belle's new physicality as embodied by Braxton altered the character.

As part of Braxton's contract, Menken and Rice wrote a new song for her, "A Change in Me," which was so well received that it was permanently added to the show. Near the end of the musical, Belle explains to her father why and how she's fallen in love with the Beast. The eleven o'clock number gives Belle an additional, higher-stakes opportunity for self-expression. While "Home" reveals Belle's early determination to stay the course and be brave, "A Change in Me" underlines how she's grown. She sings, "For now I realize / That good can come from bad," admitting that she sees the world more flexibly. She's become optimistic—a different emotion for her from what she felt in the beginning and through most of the show. Belle sings, "For now I love the world I see / No change of heart / A change in me." The song synthesizes the Disney princess and the diva when Belle sings, "I feel / A truer life begin / And it's so good and real / It must come from within." The princess experiences what's "good and real," and the diva powerfully calls it up herself. The melody's simple lines and repetition allow for the performer's own vocal flourishes.

Braxton envoiced Belle as a prindiva. With musical roots in gospel and soul, Braxton incorporated a breathier, more improvisational style, and "some keys were adjusted to better suit her more dulcet and deep tones."[68] Composer Menken said, "She's got that wonderful, husky, beautiful vocal quality that's unlike any Belle we've had before."[69] In an interview, Braxton explained her technique: "My voice is very thick and rich, like a milkshake, and that tends to be sexy. But for Belle, who's like 16 or 19, you don't want her to come across that sexy, so I have to make my tone a little brighter."[70] Still, most spectators agreed that her Belle was indeed sexy. As a member of the audience, King writes, "As she approached the chorus of 'A Change in Me,' Braxton let loose a vocal wail that seemed to send a shuddering rush through to the back of the audience." He goes on, "During the number, her singing style decidedly transformed from standard Bel Canto musical theatre to the radio-ready, pop-soul sound she has become known for."[71] Rubins observes that Braxton's performance of "Home" seldom "deviate[s] from the melody."[72] In contrast, Menken and Rice wrote "A Change in Me" for an R&B performer, "presumably with the intention that she would deviate from the melody melismatically," and Braxton's version "features embellishments almost from beginning to end."[73]

Braxton's performance remade Belle into a prindiva. Reflecting on the casting, Pat Cerasaro writes that "the color-blind casting … opened the door for future actresses of perhaps less traditional fairy tale appearance to take on the title role." Braxton's "memorable debut … caused a sensation at the time," but what "initially could appear to be stunt-casting—putting a pop star in a famous role in a big family-friendly show turn[ed] out to be quite ingenious and inventive when seen played out in full."[74] Snider Sway argues that "Toni is totally singular in her approach to" the ballads.[75] He points out that numerous online fans say, "I hear a diva ... I don't hear Belle," while others say they do hear Belle rather than Braxton.[76] Although Braxton's stardom might have originally taken the character out of the show and overtaken the character with her star identity, a Black woman playing the role and in a different style ultimately changed Belle going forward. Later Belles, whatever their race and ethnicity, frequently imitate Braxton's slides and long-held notes.

Beauty beyond Broadway

Since Disney released the rights to *Beauty and the Beast* in 2004, and regional theaters, community theaters, and high schools across the US produce the show, many have attempted to replicate the original with a white, thin Belle with flowing hair, dressed in a pale blue pinafore and then a yellow ball gown.[77] Over the years, though, many women, girls, and nonbinary performers of different ages, races, ethnicities, and sizes have taken on the role in national and international tours, sit-down companies, regional theaters, community theaters, and high schools, expanding Belle's image beyond the physicality of the traditional Disney princess.

In a critically acclaimed 2022 production directed by Marcia Milgrom Dodge at the Olney Theatre Center in Maryland, for example, Jade Jones, a plus-size, nonbinary, queer Black performer, played Belle, at once building on the legacy of the role and performing Belle as a prindiva. Dodge reimagined the show's themes of "beauty" and "ugliness" and challenged conventional ideals of ability by casting Evan Ruggiero, a white tap dancer with a prosthetic leg (which he calls his "peg leg"), as the Beast. Jones's Belle was a prindiva from the start. Wearing in the first act what Jones called a "fierce" costume—bright blue overalls and red Dr. Martens boots—the actor moved with confident directness, ignoring the townspeople's looks and whispers.[78] Jones said, "In the text, you see how she dismisses Gaston and doesn't really give two shits about anybody else except her father.... She has a tough exterior. It's her protection of her father, protection of her family. She stands true to her values, the conviction she carries about what she believes is right."[79]

Jones's rendition of "Home" confirms that Belle is independent and strong from the beginning. As Rubins writes, Jones "opens up the melody through a series of riffs, embellishing the moments in which Belle most dramatically reflects on her imprisonment." He explains, "If the melody itself is a constraint, a series of rules to follow, a prison of sorts itself, riffing is an act of liberation, an expression of the personal, internal potential for freedom." Rubins argues that "by allowing Belle to riff in Act 1, Jones demonstrates vocally from the start that [Belle] is a character who is willing to free herself and break the rules." More than that, Jones's "stylistic choices [are] most closely rooted in Black vocal traditions, [so] that liberatory act becomes explicitly tied to race and identity as well." Jones's performance of "Change in Me" hews more closely to the melody (than Braxton's, for example), but Jones still "imbues the song with a purposeful force in her rich vocal tone that, far from diluting Belle's expression of freedom, suggests a renewed clarity."[80]

When Belle's costume changes to a flowing gown in Act 2, she wears pink and not yellow, again defying Disney's norm. As reviewer Celia Wren wrote in the *Washington Post*, "Jade Jones's superb performance raises Belle to a new level, ... her Belle exudes complexity and realness, without sacrificing comic pizazz."[81] Another reviewer concurred: "Jones' voice is as powerful and sweet as any Broadway diva, and she wins us over quickly in the opening number 'Belle.' Despite the fact that Jones does not fit the stereotype of an 18th century French provincial girl, we have no problem believing that men find her irresistible."[82] Overall, then, Belle emerges "as a self-liberated, self-aware figure,"[83] or, we would argue, a prindiva.

From Belle's first appearance on the stage in 1994 to Jones's extraordinary portrayal of her twenty-seven years later, the character became a combination of Disney princess and what Fairclough describes as the diva: "They exist as figures to admire, due to the ways in which they amplify self-acceptance, empowerment and celebrate individuality."[84]

Beauty Returns to the Screen

In 2017, Disney released a new live-action version of *Beauty and the Beast*, which starred Emma Watson and Dan Stevens. It adds a backstory in which Belle is also an inventor, and Watson's star persona as Hermione-grown-up, a feminist, activist, gives Belle spunk and agency.[85] Yet this version, because it is a remake of the 1991 movie and not the 1994 stage version, moves Belle away from prindiva-ness and instead revives the feminist princess. Rebecca Weidman-Winter sees Watson's Belle as a woman "of integrity and intelligence" who is "often stepping outside of roles prescribed to her by society." She is "resourceful and independent" and "redefin[es] the role of a princess." For Weidman-Winter, "the film offers a glimpse of how realism and feminism can coexist within the imaginary world of a fairy tale."[86] But by returning to the original movie as source, compared with the stage production, this version feels as if it shrank Belle's role by cutting both diva numbers, "Home" (though its melody underscores the scene in which Belle enters her room, in this version a gorgeous princess bedroom, which eliminates the physical unpleasantness of her entrapment) and "A Change in Me," leaving her without a solo. Although this version might be more self-reflexively "feminist," it features a Belle whose diva traits are diminished.

In 2022, R&B singer H.E.R. starred in *Beauty and the Beast: A 30th Anniversary Celebration*, which combined live musical performances and excerpts from the animated movie, hosted and narrated by Rita Moreno. H.E.R. said, "There's a strength in

Belle, you see it in the movie, but I think I'm really trying to bring that out and show women they can be anything they want to be. Of course, nobody's ever seen a Black and Filipino Belle, so it's really cool that young Filipino Black girls get to see a Disney princess that looks like them."[87] Because of her background as a singer, her star identity as a diva, and her awareness of her status as a role model, H.E.R. performs Belle as a prindiva.

Cinderella's Ensemble of Divas

In 1997 (a year before Braxton played Belle), divas in Disney musicals became more prominent with the release of *Cinderella*, an updated, multiracial, made-for-TV version of the Richard Rodgers and Oscar Hammerstein II classic.[88] In this production, all of the women are divas. Disney's first *Cinderella* animated (literally) the images of the originary princess as prim and passive and the evil stepmother, as we noted, as an early (nonsinging) diva. The Fairy Godmother was drawn as jolly and rotund, and her song, "Bibbity Bobbity Boo," suggested a kind and ditzy older woman whose magical powers exceeded her intelligence.[89] Rodgers and Hammerstein's live television production in 1957, replete with a formally integrated Broadway-style score, drew more than 100 million viewers (possibly more than the Super Bowl that year)[90] and introduced Julie Andrews to a mass audience. Her Cinderella presented more spunk than Disney's animated character, and the Fairy Godmother was played by an elegant Edie Adams. The TV musical was remade again in 1964 with Leslie Ann Warren—dark-haired, wide-and-limpid-eyed, and whiny—and Celeste Holm as the Fairy Godmother. The 1964 version belied anxieties about the women's liberation movement by overcompensating; this *Cinderella* expanded the Prince's role (played by Stuart Damon) and gave him the first "I Am/I Want" song in the show, "Loneliness of Evening" (written for and then cut from the 1949 show *South Pacific*). But none of these *Cinderellas* presaged the diva parade that would arrive in 1997.

In the early 1990s, pop superstar and diva Whitney Houston bought the rights to the Rodgers and Hammerstein property, and she teamed with producer Debra Martin Chase, the first Black woman to collaborate with a major film studio, who worked for Disney at the time. Chase, who also produced *The Princess Diaries*, brokered the deal for Disney for a new version of the musical for the *Wonderful World of Disney* telecast. Directed by Robert Iscove and choreographed by Rob Marshall, the teleplay cost $12 million (the most expensive TV movie then to date) and broke records when 60 million people watched it—31 percent of the viewing audience—and the home video sold 1 million copies in the first week. New generations of viewers grew up on this multiracial diva version of *Cinderella*. In 2022, Disney+ celebrated its twenty-fifth anniversary and released the show for streaming.

Originally, Houston planned to play the title role, but she later decided to tap teen icon and pop singer Brandy Norwood to take on the lead, casting herself as a new kind of Fairy Godmother: gorgeous, sexy, effervescent, and Black. To capitalize on Houston's stardom, librettist Robert L. Freeman expanded the Fairy Godmother's role. The show begins and ends with her appearance, opening with her flying above the castle, which echoes Disney's branding of Tinker Bell's twinkling flight at the beginning of all Disney shows, as she sings "Impossible." The show concludes with her singing an added finale, "There's Music in You," floating above the town as the newlyweds' carriage rides to the castle. As producer Chase said, "We needed a sensational song... to really end the movie with a huge bang."[91] Houston's performance was simply fabulous—the very definition of diva.

While the role of the fairy godmother seems diva-ready, Chase and Houston cast every other female role in the musical with a diva performer; thus, every female *character* became a diva. Norwood transformed Cinderella—previously played by prim, white performers—into a Black girl, showing, as she said, "a culture that was beautiful"[92] and becoming a role model for generations of girls. Norwood's Cinderella is an alto; not only did musical director Paul Bogaev transpose the score, but he also coached Norwood to infuse the classic Broadway songs with her own pop, gospel, and R&B style, prompting performer Billy Porter to claim, "Because of the quality of her voice, it's a completely different story."[93] Norwood's Cinderella is an earnest diva.

The role of the Stepmother went to Bernadette Peters, a major Broadway diva who originated the role of Dot in Stephen Sondheim's *Sunday in the Park with George* and the Witch in *Into the Woods*. Peters plays the Stepmother as observant and smart; she recognizes Cinderella at the ball. Hers is the comic diva—edgy, sarcastic, bitchy, conniving, and mean. She performs with fierce pizzazz, crowned by another musical number added to the show, "Falling in Love with Love," retrieved from the Richard Rodgers and Lorenz Hart catalog to give the star more visibility. The Stepmother leads the song with the Stepsisters, played by Veanne Cox and Natalie Deselle, who are less evil than ridiculous; framed by Peters and in scenes with Norwood, they emerge as silly, slapstick diva wannabes.

The Queen, embodied in 1957 and 1964 by demure white women—Dorothy Stickney and Ginger Rogers, respectively—was played by Black comedian Whoopi Goldberg, who wore velvet and ermine and a knowing smirk. Although Goldberg didn't possess Houston's glamor, Brandy's pop appeal, or Peters's Broadway bona fides, she had starring roles in the movies *The Color Purple* (1985), *Ghost* (1990), and *Sister Act* (1992) and was a celebrity diva, too. As Mia Mask puts it, "Goldberg is Hollywood's unruly woman. She is sometimes described as too fat, too funny, too noisy, and too rebellious."[94] In this *Cinderella*, Queen Constantina initiates "The Prince Is Giving a Ball" and sings a verse of "Do I Love You Because You're Beautiful?"; the Queen gets to sing. Goldberg's Queen, wearing real Harry Winston jewelry, which the diva actor demanded,[95] is wry and sardonic.

The ensemble of divas in *Cinderella* occupied a range of diva types. This production expanded the template for divas in Disney musicals and defied conventional expectations of the classic *Cinderella* with agency, self-confidence, and fabulousness.

Frozen: The Diva Heroine

By the end of the first decade of the twenty-first century, Disney's animated films had added Mother Gothel from *Tangled* (2010) to its roster of diva villains and had updated its princesses such as Mulan (1998), Tiana from *The Princess and the Frog* (2009), and Rapunzel from *Tangled* with qualities of the prindiva modeled by Belle. But its most popular diva would ultimately ascend the throne as neither a wicked witch nor a girl-powered princess. Enter Elsa, the tortured, ballad-belting queen of Arendelle, voiced by stage diva Idina Menzel in *Frozen*. Elsa marked a notable departure from Disney's approach to animated divas; for the first time in forever (to quote the duet Elsa sings with her sister Anna), the diva joined the princess as a protagonist in a Disney princess film. And yet even as the conventional diva villain is transformed into a diva heroine with Elsa, she doesn't ultimately supplant the princess but rather continues to secure the princess's status as a foil to the diva figure.

As with other Disney princess films, *Frozen* is an adaptation of a classic fairy tale. The film is loosely based on Hans Christian Andersen's *The Snow Queen*, and early in its development, it adopted the original story's portrayal of the titular queen as the antagonist. Menzel recalls, "When I first came on, they had made her this blue character with spiky hair. It seemed like she was just your quintessential evil queen."[96] It was for this character that the songwriters, Robert Lopez and Kristen Anderson-Lopez, set out to write her solo, as Anderson-Lopez recounts: "At the time, Elsa was a villain.... So we were still writing a villain song. And we started getting into the headspace of what you'd feel like if you were that isolated.... And once we started writing from the reality of that, we found that we had something to say."[97] The result was a pop-influenced anthem that captured and sympathized with the complex interiority of a young woman embracing her "curse" and coming into her full powers. When they shared the demo of their now-famous song, "Let It Go," with the rest of the production team, the screenwriter, Jennifer Lee, responded by saying, "Oh God, I have to rewrite the entire movie again."[98]

The plot resulting from Lee's final revisions revolves around Elsa and Anna, who are sisters and princesses of Arendelle. Elsa, the older sister, was born with cryokinesis, or magical ice-making powers. After Elsa accidentally injures Anna when they are children, their father consults with a troll, who encourages the family to protect Elsa against the potential dangers of her burgeoning power. Elsa's father responds by hiding her away in a locked room, covering her magic-wielding hands with gloves, and instructing her to "Conceal it. Don't feel it." As a result, both girls grow up with a deep sense of isolation, estranged from each other and from the outside world.

Elsa is a princess for all of ten minutes in the film. After her parents die at sea, she ascends as queen. On Elsa's coronation day, both girls emerge from their isolation, and Anna promptly falls in love-at-first-sight with Hans, a prince from a neighboring kingdom. Upon discovering Anna's impulsive wish to marry Hans, Elsa loses control of her temper and her powers, accidentally freezing the kingdom as she flees, abandoning the throne. Unaware that she has left behind a frozen kingdom, Elsa ascends a snow-covered mountain, singing the anthem, "Let It Go," the song's swells propelling her transformation from a tortured young woman afraid of her powers into a queen who delights in unleashing them. Anna sets out to find Elsa and eventually risks her own life to save Elsa's at the hands of Hans, who, in a twist on Disney's traditional storylines, has revealed himself as the story's true villain. The sisters are reunited, securing their reigns as queen and princess of Arendelle and as the central couple in the film. Sisterly love above romantic love prevails.

Disney's deviation in *Frozen* from its usual princess film formula (the queen is a heroine; Prince Charming is evil; a bond between sisters rather than a wedding is celebrated at the end) paid off in unprecedented measures. In the decade since its release, *Frozen* has grossed more than $1 billion in ticket sales, earned more than $400 million in home-video sales, won Academy Awards for Best Animated Feature Film and Best Original Song, and spawned a behind-the-scenes documentary, two animated shorts, a Broadway musical, and a feature-length sequel. As of this writing in 2024, it remains among Disney's highest-earning animated films, eclipsed only by *Frozen II* and *The Lion King* remake.[99]

Frozen also spurred an avalanche of popular and critical responses that focused largely on Elsa. She's hailed as a feminist triumph and a queer icon; she's regarded as a postfeminist problem and as the latest version of the virgin/villain dichotomy. She's a campy witch; she's the apotheosis of girl power; she's an affirming model for disability rights. What most can agree on is that the girl can sing.[100] (Interestingly, "Let It Go" is Elsa's only solo, which may suggest an ambivalence about letting the diva heroine showcase too much vocal power lest she completely destabilize the princess's secure status as Disney's long-reigning protagonist.) The proliferation and passionate conviction of such divergent assessments of Elsa arise precisely because of her diva status. Like all divas, Elsa sustains—delightfully, frustratingly—contradictions. This superpower is a large part of the diva's appeal and the threat she poses to the status quo. As such, divas like Elsa elicit strong and often polarizing opinions and affiliations, all of which are often equally persuasive and deeply felt among her fans and critics alike.

Beyond her ability to embody and provoke juxtapositions, Elsa possesses a variety of recognizable diva qualities. As mentioned earlier, she originated as an evil queen, or as what Mark Helmsing has identified as the diva villain pervasive in Disney princess films.[101] While Elsa may have transformed from nemesis to heroine, strands of the diva villain DNA remain. This origin story suggests that in some ways, Elsa was destined to be a diva. And like the diva villains who have fraught relationships with the normative worlds surrounding them, Elsa invites queer readings and affiliations. Her particular narrative journey resonates with and affirms the life journeys of many queer fans: she moves from a youth who was forced to hide—"closeted"—behind locked doors because of powers she was born with to a queen who owns her difference and the power it brings as she sings a spectacular "coming out" song. She is a diva who lets go of conventional roles and a life of repressed self-expression and, like many solitary queens before her, emerges as a queer figure—or at least a figure beloved among queer audiences.

Part of Elsa's queer appeal is her lack of engagement with heterosexual romance. The diva belongs to no one and is thus available to everyone. Throughout the movie, Elsa, like many traditional divas before her, is and remains resolutely single. She has no romantic attachments or any apparent interest in seeking them out in a world where heterosexual romance is the only option. As Hans observes when he reveals why he chose to pursue/dupe Anna in his quest to seize power: "As heir, Elsa was preferable, of course. But no one was getting anywhere with her." Elsa, as a diva, is remote and unattainable and worldly-wise, her (vocal) powers setting her apart and propelling her narrative through a path of singularity rather than the marriage plot.

In fact, despite her connection with her sister at the beginning and end of the story, Elsa spends most of the movie alone in spaces—a locked room in her childhood castle, her ice palace, a prison cell—sealed off from the rest of the world. When Anna finds Elsa in her ice castle and pleads with her to return to Arendelle, Elsa responds, "I belong here. Alone.... Yes, I'm alone. But I'm alone and free." Her powers make her singular and special but ultimately contribute to her isolation. Power is a blessing and a curse for the diva. Her ability to summon her own power to build herself a castle or hit a high note or make her own way in treacherous conditions lends itself easily to liberal feminist readings of Elsa as a model of female empowerment. But even as she and Anna are "sisters doing it for themselves," Elsa, like all divas, has a vexed relationship to a larger sisterhood of other women. She is unapologetically on her own, just as uninterested in a shared feminine community as she is in heterosexual romance. This is due in part to the narrative constraints that often ensure that there is only ever room for one diva in the story. Elsa sings, "A kingdom of isolation / And it looks like I'm the queen." The diva's emphasis on singularity and self-reliance can thus support the claim that a diva like Elsa is a manifestation of postfeminist ideals that valorize individuality and self-improvement over an attention to community formation and structural solutions. Elsa's diva powers are freighted with these contradictions.

Elsa's diva status is further secured by the fact that established diva performer Menzel voices the role. Menzel brings her star text and her recognizable powerhouse singing voice to Elsa, imbuing her with a diva aura. In particular, as Liske Potgieger and Zelda Potgieger observe, "The grain of Menzel's well-known voice provides a distinctive intertextual association between the character and Elsa and those of other theatrical and filmic characters for which Menzel has gained considerable recognition."[102] All actors, Marvin Carlson reminds us, certainly haunt each new performance with the roles they played before.[103] But when a diva performs a character, she not only haunts the part with her past performances but often plays both the character and *herself* in the role, her larger-than-life persona invariably showing through or never fully contained within the limits of characterization. This is literally true for Elsa, as the animators based her mannerisms and general carriage on Menzel's movements and posture.[104] Elsa is shaped by Menzel's towering diva persona and is haunted most notably by Menzel's previous role as Elphaba, another iconic character who began as a villain but was transformed into a protagonist who sings several soaring numbers in the Broadway musical *Wicked* (2003). *Frozen* follows *Wicked*'s departure from musical genre conventions by featuring two young women as the central couple and casting Menzel as the misunderstood heroine who seeks freedom in isolation and who quite literally rises above her obstacles—Elphaba ascends toward the theater's rafters, and Elsa climbs the mountain—through song.

Above all, Elsa triumphs as a diva because she belts the most memorable song in the musical. "Let It Go" is the most successful breakout song in the history of Disney princess films, launching a global sing-along phenomenon, reaching number five in the *Billboard* Hot 100, and garnering an Oscar and a Grammy. In *Frozen*, Elsa's musical solo is the very engine that drives her transformation into a diva heroine and, in this way, shares qualities with the Broadway musical's song of female assertion that closes the first act. Whether read as a feminist anthem or a "coming out" song or an embrace of her disability-as-superpower, "Let It Go" fits within the musical genre's conventions of powerful "I can do it" songs that often end Act 1, such as "Coming Up Roses" from *Gypsy* and "Defying Gravity" from *Wicked*. It also stands out from the film's other numbers in its style, effect, and relationship with the audience. These key distinctions highlight Elsa's diva status and her difference and isolation from the other characters.

Unlike the other songs in *Frozen*, "Let It Go" sounds very much like a pop song with its shift from a minor-key piano intro to a swelling major-key anthem. As Bunch notes, "the pop style of the music, with its exhilarating groove and motoric rhythm, gives the sequence a feeling of inevitability rather than the expectant yearning of the Broadway-style 'I Want' song."[105] The song requires a singer who can move across a great range and can sail through its giant swells. Although both Elsa and Anna sing songs in pop registers, Elsa's singing voice has the depth and darkness of a mezzo belter in contrast to the light, lyric soprano voice of Anna and the Disney princesses from whom she descends. Menzel's capacious voice in Elsa's signature song of self-assertion and transformation reveals how the diva's vocal power *is* her superpower or is, at least, the very source that fuels it.

As her song builds with bold orchestrations and key changes through various sections, Elsa increasingly owns and displays her ice-making powers.[106] Co-songwriter Robert Lopez notes that the song's unique sound was deliberate, and while it uses the same chords as others in the score, "we modulate into it from the verse in F minor to the pre-chorus in E-flat major to the chorus, which is in A-flat major. We deny that A-flat major chord for a very long time, and when it arrives on the downbeat of the chorus, it's so welcome." The effect: "It helps tell Elsa's story of a lifetime of self-denial, leading to this one moment of truth as she finds herself."[107] During the songwriting process, the song was raised from D to E-flat at Menzel's request, allowing her to showcase the high range of her belt and also conveying a younger sensibility. She said that a half step higher "sounds a little bit more innocent in my voice, a little younger I think … a little bit more vulnerable."[108] (This key change also renders Menzel's voice more vulnerable in live performances if ever she fails to hit the highest note—a testament to the towering ambitions and public risks that divas take which showcase both their extraordinary abilities and all-too-human frailties.) Elsa's vocal power is the engine that drives her superpower and her increasing ability to proclaim that power with pride. The more she belts, the more she builds: intricate snow flurries, an adorable snowman, a sparkling staircase on which she traipses across an abyss, and a dazzling ice castle in which she seeks shelter. And at the song's pinnacle, when her transformation is complete, she uses her magic to design a new costume for herself. Gone is the somber, long-sleeved princess dress and tidily upswept hair, and in its place is a makeover more befitting a diva: she lets down her hair and strides toward the camera in high-heeled pumps and a glittering silver evening gown with a slit up the thigh as she sings, "that perfect girl is gone." She is singing and building a world unto and for herself. She is, like all divas, sui generis.

And as with other divas, she is also singing directly to us. A diva performance is often characterized by its full-frontal stance, no matter what character she may be playing or addressing in a scene. In this way, the diva suggests with a wink to the audience that she is always aware that the stage or the narrative can't fully contain her power or her focus. In a move uncommon for a Disney princess film, "Let It Go" ends abruptly without a sense of musical resolution and with a close-up on Elsa looking directly into the camera as she proclaims her final line, before turning away and slamming the door on us all. Elsa breaks the fourth wall with her diva vamp and invites us to cheer her on no matter what damage she's wrought on the town below.

For all the ways Elsa commands the screen and the story as a diva heroine, her function in the film is ultimately to stabilize the role of her sisterly counterpart, the Disney princess. Musically, Anna directs her opening solo, "Do You Want to Build a Snowman," longingly toward Elsa, establishing Anna as a character who will spend the story in relation to others. Elsa, in contrast, sings "Let It Go" to herself (and to the film's audience) and spends much of the film alone. Anna sings "Love Is an Open Door" with Hans; Elsa slams the door on us in "Let It Go." The duet that Elsa and Anna share and reprise, "For the First Time in Forever," actually serves to foreground distance rather than intimacy between the two sisters, with each of them conveying divergent emotional states and, as Bunch notes, singing in counterpoint.[109]

Their countenances and temperaments are also set in contrast to each other. Elsa is regal and reserved; Anna is goofy and boisterous. And above all, Elsa's diva powers impose the very obstacles that Anna must face on a journey that leads her toward familiar Disney princess narrative markers: an act of supreme feminine sacrifice and eventual true love with Sven, whom she meets along the way. Elsa and Anna may be the central couple in *Frozen*, but their relationship is still shaped by the vestiges of the dynamic between the evil queen and the long-suffering princess featured in previous Disney films. Ultimately, the diva heroine's power in the film, impressive as it is, is circumscribed by the fact that Elsa only sings one solo, which helps keep the princess firmly in place as a beloved protagonist.

Charting the development and different iterations of the diva in Disney princess stories reveals how Disney frequently turned to and adapted the diva role as a way of updating its princess franchise while still preserving the princess role as a central protagonist. Even so, the diva finds a way to triumph. For example, as much as *Frozen* may try to secure the princess's reign through Anna's recognizable and relatable personality and storyline, Elsa's costumes and dolls outsell Anna merchandise, and fans across the world post videos of themselves belting "Let It Go." Fans may relate to Princess Anna, but they aspire to be Queen Elsa, which should come as no surprise, since a diva always exceeds the narrative bounds in which she's placed. And it is in that space of excess where fans converge to assert themselves in newfound ways, to rise above the world that would see them fall, to slam some doors, to let it go.[110]

Notes

1. Rebecca-Anne C. do Rozario, "The Princess and the Magic Kingdom: Beyond Nostalgia, the Function of the Disney Princess," *Women's Studies in Communication* 27, no. 1 (Spring 2004): 46.
2. Elizabeth Bell, "Somatexts at the Disney Shop: Constructing the Pentimentos of Women's Animated Roles," in *From Mouse to Mermaid: The Politics of Film, Gender, and Culture*, ed. Elizabeth Bell, Lynda Haas, and Laura Sells (Bloomington: Indiana University Press, 1995), 111.
3. See Amy M. Davis, *Good Girls and Wicked Witches: Women in Disney's Feature Animation* (Eastleigh, UK: John Libbey, 2006).
4. Lisa Duffy, "From the Evil Queen to Elsa: Camp Witches in Disney Films," *Frames Cinema Journal*, https://framescinemajournal.com/article/from-the-evil-queen-to-elsa-camp-witches-in-disney-films/; Mark Helmsing, "'This Is No Ordinary Apple!': Learning to Fail Spectacularly from the Queer Pedagogies of Disney's Diva Villains," in *Disney, Culture, and Curriculum*, ed. Jennifer A. Sandlin and Julie C. Garlin (New York: Routledge, 2016), 59–72. See also Bell, "Somatexts."
5. According to Bell ("Somatexts," 115–118), these early animated Disney villains were modeled after Marlene Dietrich and Greta Garbo.
6. For more on divas in opera and musical theater, see John Clum, *Something for the Boys: Musical Theater and Gay Culture* (New York: Palgrave Macmillan, 2001); Wayne Koestenbaum, *The Queen's Throat: Opera, Homosexuality, and the Mystery of Desire* (New York: Poseidon, 1993; reprinted Da Capo, 2001); Susan J. Leonardi and Rebecca A. Pope, *The Diva's Mouth: Body, Voice, Prima Donna Politics* (New Brunswick, NJ: Rutgers University Press, 1996); Deborah Paredez, "Diva Relations in *The Color Purple*, the 2015 Broadway Revival," in *Gender, Sex, and Sexuality in Musical Theatre: He/She/They Could Have Danced All Night*, ed. Kelly Kessler (Chicago: University of Chicago Press, 2023), 205–225; Stacy Wolf, "*Wicked* Divas, Musical Theater, and Internet Girl Fans," *Camera Obscura* 22, no. 65 (2007): 39–71.
7. Imogen West-Knights, "Just What Is a Diva? Fabulous, for Starters," *New York Times*, July 3, 2023, C1.
8. Michelle Dvoskin, "Embracing Excess: The Queer Feminist Power of Musical Theatre Diva Roles," in *Gender, Sex, and Sexuality in Musical Theatre: He/She/They Could Have Danced All Night*, ed. Kelly Kessler (Chicago: University of Chicago Press, 2023), 178.
9. Peter C. Kunze, personal communication, July 13, 2023.
10. Our examination of divas in Disney musicals is neither comprehensive nor rigid. We offer this brief exploration to expand interpretations of Disney women beyond the princess—a term that Disney initiated and defined. Other studies might consider, for example, the Queen in *Alice in Wonderland* or Mary Poppins, whose "coloratura bit in 'A Spoonful of

Sugar' is traditional diva semiotics," as Dominic Broomfield-McHugh observes. Walt Disney's well-known conservatism, plus the hegemony of white male creators (perhaps) limited the types of women characters and the terms through which they might be analyzed in the classic period. Thanks to volume editor Dominic Broomfield-McHugh for his helpful query and observation about Mary Poppins.

11. The Broadway musical *Smile* was also an important precursor to *The Little Mermaid*, and Ashman and Menken cast one of its leads, Jodi Benson, as the voice of Ariel. Thanks to Liza Gennaro and Doug Reside for this information.
12. Nicole Pasulka and Brian Ferree, "Unearthing the Sea Witch," Hazlitt, January 14, 2016, https://hazlitt.net/longreads/unearthing-sea-witch.
13. Peter C. Kunze, *Staging a Comeback: Broadway, Hollywood, and the Disney Renaissance* (New Brunswick, NJ: Rutgers University Press, 2023), 79. Kunze chronicles how the infusion of musical-theater talent helped turn Disney's fortunes around and notes that the particular formula for the integrated musical was a key to this success.
14. Kunze, personal communication.
15. See do Rozario, "The Princess and the Magic Kingdom," 46.
16. Solon Snider Sway, interview, June 13, 2023; November 17, 2023.
17. Kunze, personal communication.
18. Kunze, *Staging a Comeback*, 81.
19. Ibid., 81–82.
20. "Pat Carroll, Emmy Winner and Voice of Ursula, Dies at 95," NPR, August 1, 2022, https://www.npr.org/2022/08/01/1114830647/pat-carroll-died.
21. Pasulka and Ferree, "Unearthing the Sea Witch."
22. Jim Collins, Hilary Radner, and Ava Preacher Collins, *Film Theory Goes to the Movies: Cultural Analysis of Contemporary Film* (London: Routledge, 2012), 286.
23. "The Making of The Little Mermaid," Disney Channel [1989], October 26, 2016, https://www.youtube.com/watch?v=IuHR5ZOWp-U.
24. Do Rozario, "The Princess and the Magic Kingdom," 44–45.
25. For more on camp in relation to queer cultural practices, see, for example, Moe Meyers, ed., *The Politics and Poetics of Camp* (London: Routledge, 1994); Fabio Cleto, ed., *Camp: Queer Aesthetics and the Performing Subject* (Ann Arbor: University of Michigan Press, 1999).
26. Leonardi and Pope, *The Diva's Mouth*, 199.
27. See Kunze, *Staging a Comeback*, 79.
28. Will Letts, "Camp Disney: Consuming Queer Subjectivities, Commodifying the Normative," in *Disney, Culture, and Curriculum*, ed. Jennifer Sandlin and Julie Garlen Maudlin (New York: Routledge, 2016), 148–160.
29. Kerry Mallan and Roderick McGillis, "Between a Frock and a Hard Place: Camp Aesthetics and Children's Culture," *Canadian Review of American Studies* 35, no. 1 (2005): 14–15.
30. Eliza Berman, "How *Beauty and the Beast*'s Screenwriter Shaped Disney's First Feminist Princess," *Time*, May 23, 2016, https://time.com/4344654/beauty-and-the-beast-linda-woolverton/.
31. Ibid.
32. Ibid.
33. Joe McGovern, "*Beauty and the Beast*, *Alice* screenwriter Linda Woolverton Remembers a Belle Battle," *Entertainment Weekly*, May 26, 2016, https://ew.com/article/2016/05/26/linda-woolverton-alice-belle-disney-heroines/.

34. Ibid.
35. West-Knights, "Just What Is a Diva?," C5.
36. Bell, "Somatexts," 114.
37. Thanks to Jessica Sternfeld for pointing out the requisite ball-gown color array.
38. See Davis, *Good Girls and Wicked Witches*.
39. See Linda Coates, Shelly Bonnah, and Cathy Richardson, "*Beauty and the Beast*: Misrepresentation and Social Responses in Fairy-Tale Romance and Redemption," *International Journal of Child, Youth and Family Studies* 10, no. 1 (2019): 119–136, https://doi.org/10.18357/ijcyfs101201918809.
40. Jeanne Boydston, "Cult of True Womanhood," PBS, n.d., https://www.pbs.org/kenburns/not-for-ourselves-alone/cult-of-true-womanhood.
41. Ibid.
42. Patrick D. Murphy, "'The Whole Wide World Was Scrubbed Clean': The Androcentric Animation of Denatured Disney," in *From Mouse to Mermaid: The Politics of Film, Gender, and Culture*, ed. Elizabeth Bell, Lynda Haas, and Laura Sells. (Bloomington: Indiana University Press, 1995), 133.
43. On Disney's conservative disability politics, see, for example, Katherine E. Smith, "'It's a Pity and a Sin': Images of Disability, Trauma and Subverted Power in Disney's Beauty and the Beast," *Word and Text* 8 (2018): 111–128.
44. Murphy, "'The Whole Wide World,'" 134.
45. Bell, "Somatexts," 114.
46. See Jane Feuer, *The Hollywood Musical* (Bloomington: Indiana University Press, 1982).
47. Susan Jeffords, "The Curse of Masculinity: Disney's *Beauty and the Beast*," in *From Mouse to Mermaid: The Politics of Film, Gender, and Culture*, ed. Elizabeth Bell, Lynda Haas, and Laura Sells. (Bloomington: Indiana University Press, 1995), 170.
48. West-Knights, "Just What Is a Diva?," C5.
49. Kirby Farrell, "Beauty and the Beast of L.A.," *Massachusetts Review*, 34, no. 2 (Summer 1993): 317. See also Jason King, "Toni Braxton, Disney, and Thermodynamics," *Drama Review* 46, no. 3 (Fall 2002): 54.
50. Sara Bahr, "'Lilo & Stitch' at 20: Disney Mold Breaker," *New York Times*, June 22, 2022, C3.
51. See Kunze, *Staging a Comeback*, 113.
52. Eden Hildebrand, "Beauty and the Beast," in *50 Key Stage Musicals*, ed. Robert W. Schneider and Shannon Agnew (New York: Routledge, 2022), 216.
53. Kunze, *Staging a Comeback*, 126.
54. On the importance of Disney's arrival on Broadway, see, for example, Steve Nelson, "Broadway and the Beast: Disney Comes to Times Square," *TDR* 39, no. 2 (Summer 1995): 71–85; Elizabeth L. Wollman, "The Economic Development of the 'New' Times Square and Its Impact on the Broadway Musical," *American Music* 20, no. 4 (Winter 2002): 445–447; Amy S. Osatinski, *Disney Theatrical Productions: Producing Broadway Musicals the Disney Way* (New York: Routledge, 2019).
55. Timothy Callaway, "Susan Egan: Belle, Meg, Glamour and Goop—Part 1," The Mouse Castle, July 29, 2012, http://www.themousecastle.com/2012/07/susan-egan-belle-meg-glamour-and-goop.html; Jesse North, "Susan Egan on Her Dirt-Catching Days as a Disney Princess and Humble Motherhood," Stage Rush, October 25, 2011, http://www.stage-rush.com/2011/10/susan-egan-disney-beauty-and-the-beast-secret-of-happiness-interview/.
56. North, "Susan Egan."
57. Dan Rubins, personal communication, June 14, 2023.

58. West-Knights, "Just What Is a Diva?," C1.
59. Snider Sway, interview, November 17, 2023. He also notes the importance of the musical director, Michael Kosarin, in shaping Egan's interpretation and performance of the song.
60. Snider Sway, interview, June 13, 2023.
61. John Lahr, "The Shock of the Neutral," *The New Yorker*, May 2, 1994, 102.
62. Brad Smith, "'Beauty's' Production Values Are Skin Deep," *Denver Business Journal*, July 25, 1997, 26A.
63. Chuck Philips, "Toni Braxton Files for Chapter 7," *Los Angeles Times*, January 31, 1998, https://www.latimes.com/archives/la-xpm-1998-jan-31-fi-13915-story.html.
64. "Toni Braxton Makes Broadway Debut as Belle in Disney's 'Beauty and the Beast,'" *Jet* 94, no. 22 (October 26, 1998), 34. Thanks to Steven Knowlton for locating this quote.
65. King, "Toni Braxton, Disney, and Thermodynamics," 54.
66. Ibid., 71; Tornquist, "Braxton Adds 'Chocolate Syrup.'"
67. King, "Toni Braxton," 71.
68. Pat Cerasaro, "Flash Friday: Toni Braxton Back on Broadway," Broadway World, September 27, 2013, https://www.broadwayworld.com/article/FLASH-FRIDAY-Toni-Braxton-Back-On-Broadway-20130927.
69. Tornquist, "Braxton Adds 'Chocolate Syrup.'"
70. Ibid.
71. King, "Toni Braxton," 62.
72. Rubins, personal communication, June 14, 2023.
73. Ibid.
74. Cerasaro, "Flash Friday."
75. Snider Sway, interview, June 13, 2023.
76. Snider Sway, interview, November 11, 2023.
77. As of this writing in March 2024, Disney has suspended licensing for professional and amateur (including high school) productions after December 2024 as it prepares for an international tour of the show. See https://www.mtishows.com/disneys-beauty-and-the-beast.
78. See Alissa Klusky, "Designer Focus: Belle's Journey through Her Costumes," Olney Theatre Center, November 11, 2021, https://www.olneytheatre.org/about-us/blog/designer-focus-belles-journey-through-her-costumes.
79. Leah Putnam, "Jade Jones Finds Their Fairytale in Beauty and the Beast as Belle," *Playbill*, December 20, 2022, https://playbill.com/article/jade-jones-finds-their-fairytale-in-beauty-and-the-beasts-belle.
80. Rubins, personal communication.
81. Celia Wren, "Olney's 'Beauty and the Beast' Succeeds with a Belle Who Brings Complexity to the Role," *Washington Post*, November 14, 2021, https://www.washingtonpost.com/entertainment/theater_dance/beauty-and-the-beast-olney-theatre/2021/11/14/b08c3c90-431f-11ec-a3aa-0255edc02eb7_story.html.
82. Susan Brall, "Theatre Review: 'Disney's Beauty and the Beast' at Olney Theatre Center," MD Theatre Guide, November 14, 2021, https://mdtheatreguide.com/2022/11/theatre-review-disneys-beauty-and-the-beast-at-olney-theatre-center-2/.
83. Rubins, personal communication.
84. West-Knights, "Just What Is a Diva?," C5.
85. See Yohana Desta, "Emma Watson Gave *Beauty and the Beast* a Fresh Feminist Twist," *Vanity Fair*, November 3, 2016, https://www.vanityfair.com/hollywood/2016/11/emma-watson-beauty-and-the-beast-spin.

86. Rebecca Weidman-Winter, "Belle: Beyond the Classic Story for the Modern Audience," in *Recasting the Disney Princess in an Era of New Media and Social Movements*, ed. Shearon Roberts (New York: Lexington, 2020), 201.
87. Pallavi Bhadu, "Here's How to Watch 'Beauty and the Beast: A 30th Celebration,'" Popsugar, December 16, 2022, https://www.popsugar.com/entertainment/her-beauty-and-the-beast-special-48901721.
88. Some of this material appears differently contextualized in Jordan Ealey and Stacy Wolf, "*Cinderella*," in *The Oxford Companion to Rodgers and Hammerstein*, ed. William Everett (New York: Oxford University Press, forthcoming).
89. See Davis, *Good Girls and Wicked Witches*, on the three types of women in classic Disney movies.
90. James Hibberd, "Did 'Cinderella' Ratings Outdraw the Super Bowl?" *Hollywood Reporter*, November 30, 2010, https://www.hollywoodreporter.com/tv/tv-news/cinderella-ratings-outdraw-super-bowl-53101/.
91. "*Cinderella*: The Reunion," *20/20*, ABC, August 23, 2022.
92. Ibid.
93. Ibid.
94. Mia Mask, "Whoopi Goldberg's Unflinching Rise to the Top," *Tell Me More*, NPR, March 3, 2010, https://www.npr.org/templates/story/story.php?storyId=124051053.
95. Christian Allaire, "Why *Cinderella*, Starring Whitney Houston and Brandy, Is One of Disney's Bests," *Vogue*, February 10, 2021, https://www.vogue.com/article/cinderella-disney-whitney-houston-brandy.
96. *The Story of* Frozen: *Making a Disney Animated Classic*, ABC, September 4, 2014, https://vimeo.com/518432681.
97. Ibid.
98. Ibid.
99. Kunze, personal communication.
100. For examples of arguments for Elsa as a feminist, see Michelle Law, "Sisters Doin' It for Themselves: *Frozen* and the Evolution of the Disney Heroine," *Screen Education* 74 (2014): 16–25; Esben Myren-Svelstad, "The Witch in the Closet: Disney's *Frozen* as Adaptation and Its Potential for Queer and Feminist Readings," *Scandinavian Studies* 94, no. 1 (2022): 1–23; Sarah Whitfield, "'For the First Time in Forever': Locating *Frozen* as a Feminist Disney Musical," in *The Disney Musical on Stage and Screen: Critical Approaches from 'Snow White' to 'Frozen,'* ed. George Rodosthenous (London: Bloomsbury, 2017), 215–228. On Elsa as a queer icon, see Ryan Bunch, "'Love Is an Open Door': Revising and Repeating Disney's Musical Tropes in *Frozen*," in *Contemporary Musical Film*, ed. Kevin J. Donnelly (Edinburgh: Edinburgh University Press, 2017), 89–103; Auba Llompart and Lydia Brugué, "The Snow Queer? Female Characterization in Walt Disney's *Frozen*," *Adaptation* 13, no. 1 (2019): 98–112. On Elsa as postfeminist, see Michael Macaluso, "The Postfeminist Princess: Public Discourse and Disney's Curricular Guide to Feminism," in *Disney, Culture and Curriculum*, ed. Jennifer A. Sandlin and Julie C. Garlen (New York: Routledge, 2016), 73–86 ; Maja Rudloff, "(Post)Feminist Paradoxes: The Sensibilities of Gender Representation in Disney's *Frozen*," *Outskirts* 35 (2016): 1–20. On Elsa as virgin/villain, see Liske Potgieter and Zelda Potgieter, "Deconstructing Disney's Divas: A Critique of the Singing Princess as Filmic Trope," *Acta Academica* 48, no. 2 (2016): 48–75. On Elsa as part of the Disney tradition of camp witches, see Duffy, "From the Evil Queen to Elsa." On Elsa in relation to girl power, see Hannah Robbins, "'I Can't Be What You

Expect of Me': Power, Palatability, and Shame in *Frozen: The Broadway Musical*," *Arts (Basel)* 9, no. 1 (2020): 39. On Elsa in relation to disability studies, see Ann Schmiesing, "Disability," in *The Routledge Companion to Media and Fairy-Tale Cultures*, ed. Pauline Greenhill, Jill Terry Rudy, Naomi Hamer, and Lauren Bose (New York: Routledge, 2018), 91–99.

101. Helmsing, "'This Is No Ordinary Apple!'"
102. Potgieger and Potgieger, "Deconstructing Disney's Divas," 69.
103. Marvin Carlson, *The Haunted Stage: Theatre as Memory Machine* (Ann Arbor: University of Michigan Press, 2001).
104. *The Story of* Frozen.
105. Bunch, "'Love Is an Open Door,'" 97.
106. Snider Sway, interview, June 13, 2023.
107. Rebecca Milzoff, "How Picnic-Table Belting Led to an Iconic Disney Hit: Writers Bobby Lopez & Kristen Anderson-Lopez on the 'Let It Go' Chorus," *Billboard*, April 26, 2017, https://www.billboard.com/music/pop/idina-menzel-let-it-go-frozen-songwriters-chorus-interview-7775309/.
108. "Idina Menzel Asked for Major Change to 'Let It Go' while Recording It," CNN, January 23, 2023, https://www.youtube.com/watch?v=mF4jd9cCnms.
109. Bunch, "'Love Is an Open Door,'" 95.
110. Abundant thanks to Solon Snider Sway for his generous engagement with our work, especially his insights about music and the voice; to the Musical Theatre Forum for reading a draft of the *Beauty and the Beast* section; to Peter Kunze for reading the whole draft and offering important corrections and valuable refinements; and to Angela Libo Tan for her help with the bibliography and notes.

Bibliography

Allaire, Christian. "Why *Cinderella*, Starring Whitney Houston and Brandy, Is One of Disney's Bests." *Vogue*, February 10, 2021. https://www.vogue.com/article/cinderella-disney-whitney-houston-brandy.

Bahr, Sara. "'Lilo & Stitch' at 20: Disney Mold Breaker." *New York Times*, June 22, 2022, C3.

Bell, Elizabeth. "Somatexts at the Disney Shop: Constructing the Pentimentos of Women's Animated Roles." In *From Mouse to Mermaid: The Politics of Film, Gender, and Culture*, edited by Elizabeth Bell, Lynda Haas, and Laura Sells, 107–124. Bloomington: Indiana University Press, 1995.

Berman, Eliza. "How *Beauty and the Beast*'s Screenwriter Shaped Disney's First Feminist Princess." *Time*, May 23, 2016. https://time.com/4344654/beauty-and-the-beast-linda-woolverton/.

Bhadu, Pallavi. "Here's How to Watch 'Beauty and the Beast: A 30th Celebration." Popsugar, December 16, 2022. https://www.popsugar.com/entertainment/her-beauty-and-the-beast-special-48901721.

Boydston, Jeanne. "Cult of True Womanhood." PBS, n.d. https://www.pbs.org/kenburns/not-for-ourselves-alone/cult-of-true-womanhood.

Brall, Susan. "Theatre Review: 'Disney's Beauty and the Beast' at Olney Theatre Center." MD Theatre Guide, November 14, 2021. https://mdtheatreguide.com/2022/11/theatre-review-disneys-beauty-and-the-beast-at-olney-theatre-center-2/.

Bunch, Ryan. "'Love Is an Open Door': Revising and Repeating Disney's Musical Tropes in *Frozen*." In *Contemporary Musical Film*, edited by Kevin J. Donnelly, 89–103. Edinburgh: Edinburgh University Press, 2017.

Callaway, Timothy. "Susan Egan: Belle, Meg, Glamour and Goop—Part 1." The Mouse Castle, July 29, 2012. http://www.themousecastle.com/2012/07/susan-egan-belle-meg-glamour-and-goop.html.

Carlson, Marvin. *The Haunted Stage: Theatre as Memory Machine*. Ann Arbor: University of Michigan Press, 2001.

Cerasaro, Pat. "Flash Friday: Toni Braxton Back on Broadway." Broadway World, September 27, 2013. https://www.broadwayworld.com/article/FLASH-FRIDAY-Toni-Braxton-Back-On-Broadway-20130927.

"*Cinderella*: The Reunion." 20/20. ABC, August 23, 2022.

Cleto, Fabio, ed. *Camp: Queer Aesthetics and the Performing Subject*. Ann Arbor: University of Michigan Press, 1999.

Clum, John. *Something for the Boys: Musical Theater and Gay Culture*. New York: Palgrave Macmillan, 2001.

Coates, Linda, Shelly Bonnah, and Cathy Richardson. "*Beauty and the Beast*: Misrepresentation and Social Responses in Fairy-Tale Romance and Redemption." *International Journal of Child, Youth and Family Studies* 10, no. 1 (2019): 119–137. https://doi.org/10.18357/ijcyfs101201918809.

Collins, Jim, Hilary Radner, and Ava Preacher Collins. *Film Theory Goes to the Movies: Cultural Analysis of Contemporary Film*. London: Routledge, 2012.

Davis, Amy M. *Good Girls and Wicked Witches: Women in Disney's Feature Animation*. Eastleigh, UK: John Libbey, 2006.

Desta, Yohana. "Emma Watson Gave *Beauty and the Beast* a Fresh Feminist Twist." *Vanity Fair*, November 3, 2016. https://www.vanityfair.com/hollywood/2016/11/emma-watson-beauty-and-the-beast-spin.

Do Rozario, Rebecca-Anne C. "The Princess and the Magic Kingdom: Beyond Nostalgia, the Function of the Disney Princess." *Women's Studies in Communication* 27, no. 1 (Spring 2004): 34–59.

Duffy, Lisa. "From the Evil Queen to Elsa: Camp Witches in Disney Films." *Frames Cinema Journal*. https://framescinemajournal.com/article/from-the-evil-queen-to-elsa-camp-witches-in-disney-films/.

Dvoskin, Michelle. "Embracing Excess: The Queer Feminist Power of Musical Theatre Diva Roles." In *Gender, Sex, and Sexuality in Musical Theatre: He/She/They Could Have Danced All Night*, edited by Kelly Kessler, 209–224 Chicago: University of Chicago Press, 2023.

Ealey, Jordan, and Stacy Wolf. "*Cinderella*." In *The Oxford Companion to Rodgers and Hammerstein*, edited by William Everett. New York: Oxford University Press, forthcoming.

Farrell, Kirby. "Beauty and the Beast of L.A." *Massachusetts Review* 34, no. 2 (Summer 1993): 312–320.

Feuer, Jane. *The Hollywood Musical*. Bloomington: Indiana University Press, 1982.

Helmsing, Mark. "'This Is No Ordinary Apple!': Learning to Fail Spectacularly from the Queer Pedagogies of Disney's Diva Villains." In *Disney, Culture, and Curriculum*, edited by Jennifer A. Sandlin and Julie C. Garlin, 59–72. New York: Routledge, 2016.

Hibberd, James. "Did 'Cinderella' Ratings Outdraw the Super Bowl?" *Hollywood Reporter*, November 30, 2010. https://www.hollywoodreporter.com/tv/tv-news/cinderella-ratings-outdraw-super-bowl-53101/.

Hildebrand, Eden. "Beauty and the Beast." In *50 Key Stage Musicals*, edited by Robert W. Schneider and Shannon Agnew, 216–220. New York: Routledge, 2022.
"Idina Menzel Asked for Major Change to 'Let It Go' while Recording It." CNN, January 23, 2023. https://www.youtube.com/watch?v=mF4jd9cCnms.
Jeffords, Susan. "The Curse of Masculinity: Disney's *Beauty and the Beast*." In *From Mouse to Mermaid: The Politics of Film, Gender, and Culture*, edited by Elizabeth Bell, Lynda Haas, and Laura Sells, 161–172. Bloomington: Indiana University Press, 1995.
King, Jason. "Toni Braxton, Disney, and Thermodynamics." *Drama Review* 46, no. 3 (Fall 2002): 54–81.
Klusky, Alissa. "Designer Focus: Belle's Journey through Her Costumes." Olney Theater Centre, November 11, 2021. https://www.olneytheatre.org/about-us/blog/designer-focus-belles-journey-through-her-costumes.
Koestenbaum, Wayne. *The Queen's Throat: Opera, Homosexuality, and the Mystery of Desire*. New York: Poseidon, 1993; reprinted Da Capo, 2001.
Kunze, Peter C. *Staging a Comeback: Broadway, Hollywood, and the Disney Renaissance*. New Brunswick, NJ: Rutgers University Press, 2023.
Lahr, John. "The Shock of the Neutral." *The New Yorker*, May 2, 1994, 102.
Law, Michelle. "Sisters Doin' It for Themselves: *Frozen* and the Evolution of the Disney Heroine." *Screen Education* 74 (2014): 16–25.
Leonardi, Susan J., and Rebecca L. Pope. *The Diva's Mouth: Body, Voice, Prima Donna Politics*. New Brunswick, NJ: Rutgers University Press, 1996.
Letts, Will. "Camp Disney: Consuming Queer Subjectivities, Commodifying the Normative." In *Disney, Culture, and Curriculum*, edited by Jennifer Sandlin and Julie Garlen Maudlin, 148–160. New York: Routledge, 2016.
Llompart, Auba, and Lydia Brugué. "The Snow Queer? Female Characterization in Walt Disney's *Frozen*." *Adaptation* 13, no. 1 (2019): 98–112.
Macaluso, Michael. "The Postfeminist Princess: Public Discourse and Disney's Curricular Guide to Feminism." In *Disney, Culture and Curriculum*, edited by Jennifer A. Sandlin and Julie C. Garlen, 73–86. New York: Routledge, 2016.
"The Making of the Little Mermaid." Disney Channel [1989], October 22, 2016. https://www.youtube.com/watch?v=IuHR5ZOWp-U.
Mallan, Kerry, and Roderick McGillis. "Between a Frock and a Hard Place: Camp Aesthetics and Children's Culture." *Canadian Review of American Studies* 35, no. 1 (2005): 1–19.
Mask, Mia. "Whoopi Goldberg's Unflinching Rise To The Top." *Tell Me More*. NPR, March 3, 2010. https://www.npr.org/templates/story/story.php?storyId=124051053.
McGovern, Joe. "*Beauty and the Beast, Alice* screenwriter Linda Woolverton Remembers a Belle Battle." Entertainment Weekly, May 26, 2016. https://ew.com/article/2016/05/26/linda-woolverton-alice-belle-disney-heroines/.
Meyers, Moe, ed. *The Politics and Poetics of Camp*. London: Routledge, 1994.
Milzoff, Rebecca. "How Picnic-Table Belting Led to an Iconic Disney Hit: Writers Bobby Lopez & Kristen Anderson-Lopez on the 'Let It Go' Chorus." *Billboard*, April 26, 2017. https://www.billboard.com/music/pop/idina-menzel-let-it-go-frozen-songwriters-chorus-interview-7775309/.
Murphy, Patrick D. "'The Whole Wide World Was Scrubbed Clean': The Androcentric Animation of Denatured Disney." In *From Mouse to Mermaid: The Politics of Film, Gender, and Culture*, edited by Elizabeth Bell, Lynda Haas, and Laura Sells, 125–136. Bloomington: Indiana University Press, 1995.

Myren-Svelstad, Esben. "The Witch in the Closet: Disney's *Frozen* as Adaptation and Its Potential for Queer and Feminist Readings." *Scandinavian Studies* 94, no. 1 (2022): 1–23.

Nelson, Steve. "Broadway and the Beast: Disney Comes to Times Square." *TDR* 39, no. 2 (Summer 1995): 71–85.

North, Jesse. "Susan Egan on Her Dirt-Catching Days as a Disney Princess and Humble Motherhood." Stage Rush, October 25, 2011. http://www.stage-rush.com/2011/10/susan-egan-disney-beauty-and-the-beast-secret-of-happiness-interview/.

Osatinski, Amy S. *Disney Theatrical Productions: Producing Broadway Musicals the Disney Way*. New York: Routledge, 2019.

Paredez, Deborah. "Diva Relations in *The Color Purple*, the 2015 Broadway Revival." In *Gender, Sex, and Sexuality in Musical Theatre: He/She/They Could Have Danced All Night*, edited by Kelly Kessler, 205–225. Chicago: University of Chicago Press, 2023.

Pasulka, Nicole, and Brian Ferree. "Unearthing the Sea Witch." Hazlitt, January 14, 2016. https://hazlitt.net/longreads/unearthing-sea-witch.

"Pat Carroll, Emmy Winner and Voice of Ursula, Dies at 95." NPR, August 1, 2022. https://www.npr.org/2022/08/01/1114830647/pat-carroll-died.

Philips, Chuck. "Toni Braxton Files for Chapter 7." *Los Angeles Times*, January 31, 1998. https://www.latimes.com/archives/la-xpm-1998-jan-31-fi-13915-story.html.

Potgieter, Liske, and Zelda Potgieter. "Deconstructing Disney's Divas: A Critique of the Singing Princess as Filmic Trope." *Acta Academica* 48, no. 2 (2016): 48–75.

Putnam, Leah. "Jade Jones Finds Their Fairytale in Beauty and the Beast as Belle." *Playbill*, December 20, 2022. https://playbill.com/article/jade-jones-finds-their-fairytale-in-beauty-and-the-beasts-belle.

Robbins, Hannah. "'I Can't Be What You Expect of Me': Power, Palatability, and Shame in *Frozen: The Broadway Musical*." *Arts (Basel)* 9, no. 1 (2020): 39.

Rudloff, Maja. "(Post)Feminist Paradoxes: The Sensibilities of Gender Representation in Disney's *Frozen*." *Outskirts* 35 (2016): 1–20.

Schmiesing, Ann. "Disability." In *The Routledge Companion to Media and Fairy-Tale Cultures*, edited by Pauline Greenhill, Jill Terry Rudy, Naomi Hamer, and Lauren Bose, 91–99. New York: Routledge, 2018.

Smith, Brad. "'Beauty's' Production Values Are Skin Deep." *Denver Business Journal*, July 25, 1997, 26A.

Smith, Katherine E. "'It's a Pity and a Sin': Images of Disability, Trauma and Subverted Power in Disney's Beauty and the Beast." *Word and Text* 8 (2018): 111–128.

The Story of Frozen: Making a Disney Animated Classic. ABC, September 4, 2014. https://vimeo.com/518432681.

"Toni Braxton Makes Broadway Debut as Belle in Disney's 'Beauty and the Beast.'" *Jet* 94, no. 22 (October 26, 1998): 34–38.

Weidman-Winter, Rebecca. "Belle: Beyond the Classic Story for the Modern Audience." In *Recasting the Disney Princess in an Era of New Media and Social Movements*, edited by Shearon Roberts, 199–209. New York: Lexington, 2020.

West-Knights, Imogen. "Just What Is a Diva? Fabulous, for Starters." *New York Times*, July 3, 2023, C1–C5.

Whitfield, Sarah. "'For the First Time in Forever': Locating *Frozen* as a Feminist Disney Musical." In *The Disney Musical on Stage and Screen: Critical Approaches from 'Snow White' to 'Frozen,'* edited by George Rodosthenous, 215–228. London: Bloomsbury, 2017.

Wolf, Stacy. "*Wicked* Divas, Musical Theater, and Internet Girl Fans." *Camera Obscura* 22, no. 65 (2007): 39–71.

Wollman, Elizabeth L. "The Economic Development of the 'New' Times Square and Its Impact on the Broadway Musical." *American Music* 20, no. 4 (Winter 2002): 445–447.

Wren, Celia. "Olney's 'Beauty and the Beast' Succeeds with a Belle Who Brings Complexity to the Role." *Washington Post*, November 14, 2021. https://www.washingtonpost.com/entertainment/theater_dance/beauty-and-the-beast-olney-theatre/2021/11/14/b08c3c90-431f-11ec-a3aa-0255edc02eb7_story.html.

CHAPTER 19

NEGOTIABLE DIVERSITY: HOW THE *FROZEN* FRANCHISE DISNEYFIED SÁMI MUSIC AND CULTURE

MIHAELA MIHAILOVA

Frozen's History of Sámi Cultural Appropriation

SHORTLY after its release, Disney's hit musical feature *Frozen* (2013) was met with criticism from Indigenous groups for its unauthorized and largely unacknowledged incorporation of elements from the customs of the Sámi, a culturally and linguistically diverse group of Finno-Ugric peoples whose homeland spans territories in present-day Norway, Sweden, Finland, and Russia.[1] In this chapter, I examine the studio's attempt at course correction in *Frozen II* (2019), a direct sequel which introduces an Indigenous group, the Northuldra people, modeled after the Sámi with the input of a Sámi advisory board. My analysis reflects on the film's creative and ideological approaches toward representing Sámi art forms, spiritual beliefs, and cultural references in its soundtrack, character design, and narrative. Through a combination of close analysis, examination of production materials, and investigation of scholarly and critical responses to the film, I conclude that *Frozen II* exhibits consistent patterns of reliance on generalized, Anglo-American concepts and symbols of Indigeneity. Despite gesturing toward a culturally informed, methodical approach to Indigenous representation in mainstream animation, the feature largely obscures the specificity of Sámi life and customs, frequently sacrificing accuracy and avoiding cultural nuance in favor of the well-established rules of traditional Disney filmmaking.

The Sámi are the only ethnic group in the European Union to be recognized as an aboriginal people. The principal language in Sápmi (the Sámi homeland) is North Sámi, but it is not understandable to speakers of the other Sámi languages. At present, Sámi in Finland, Sweden, and Norway are represented by their respective *sámediggi*, parliaments that have advisory powers in these countries' state governments.[2] Historically, since the mid-twentieth century, "Sámi discourses on indigeneity have emphasized transnational Sámi cooperation, traditional subsistence models such as reindeer herding, maintenance of Sámi languages, and revival of *joik*."[3]

Frozen drew on Sámi heritage in various ways, including in its references to reindeer husbandry, the character Kristoff's clothes, which bear an evident resemblance to Sámi reindeer herder outfits, and the opening song, "Vuelie," which features *joiking*[4] and borrows its name from the South Sámi word for this vocal tradition.[5] The absence of Sámi characters from the story and Sámi staff from the production, combined with the lack of acknowledgment of this Indigenous group's impact on the look and sound of *Frozen* (save for passing mentions in behind-the-scenes accounts of the costume-design process), inspired a discussion about "non-Indigenous filmmakers yet again appropriating, twisting, and profiting off Indigenous culture."[6]

Kristoff, who is voiced by white American actor Jonathan Groff, is not coded as an Indigenous person either visually or narratively. The design of his facial features does not set him apart from other characters, and even though the plot leans into his affinity for reindeer herding, the practice itself is showcased without any mention of its historical importance to Sámi societies. In the foreword to *The Art of Frozen*, co-directors Chris Buck and Jennifer Lee describe him simply as an "ice-harvesting, mountain man," even though, in the next sentence, they point out that "the design of his heavy tunic, pants, and shoes grew out of researching the Sámi people, an ancient, Indigenous group that still lives in the arctic area."[7] In the same volume of production trivia, the film's art director, Michael Giaimo, refers to Kristoff as a "rustic character" whose "rough-hewn appearance had to contrast with the courtly elegance of Anna and Hans." To achieve this, Giaimo's team "riffed on the traditional costumes of the Sámi people, and used some folk art motifs in his sash."[8] Generic descriptions such as "mountain man" preclude any direct association between the character and the Sámi as a specific Indigenous group, while the suggestion that Sámi clothing was used as visual shorthand for rural, unrefined living evokes stereotypical associations of Indigeneity with nature, particularly in contrast with civilization. In that sense, Disney admits to drawing (on) Sámi clothes for the sake of characterization and stylistic distinctiveness, while simultaneously erasing the Sámi community from *Frozen*'s fantasy version of Norway. Additionally, Kristoff's outfit has been criticized for its many cultural inaccuracies, drawing attention to Disney's inconsiderate treatment of Sámi clothing customs and the resulting "badly put-together mishmash of Sámi inspired garbs" that "failed to understand [the] many unwritten rules and messages that [Sámi] traditional clothes actually do convey."[9]

The song "Vuelie," arguably one of *Frozen*'s most recognizable melodies aside from the mega-hit "Let It Go," is similarly incorporated into the film without a single nod to the Indigenous origins of its distinct choral sound. The hauntingly beautiful chant, which plays over the production-studio sequence with Disney's famous castle and is reprised at the end of the film, is "never accompanied by a clear referent to Sámi culture."[10] As "Vuelie" becomes the soundtrack to which the Disney logo is unveiled, the decontextualization of *joik* allows the studio to harness the expressive melodic potential of Sámi music while visually tying it to (and thereby ideologically subsuming it under) its own brand.

FROZEN II AND THE PROMISE OF COLLABORATION

Leaders of the Sámi community responded to *Frozen*'s negligent approach to appropriation and its disregard for Sámi cultural specificity by taking the initiative to advocate for more authentic and culturally informed representation in the successful franchise's inevitable second installment. In a move that has been hailed as creating a blueprint for Indigenous people fighting for accountability and transparency from media corporations, the Sámi parliaments of Norway, Sweden, and Finland, along with the Saami Council (a nongovernmental organization of the Sámi people), reached out to Disney with an offer to consult on cultural matters during the production of *Frozen II*, leading to a collaboration between the studio and an advisory group, *verddet* (a Sámi word meaning "friends" or "partners").[11] The *verddet* included Sámi playwrights, artists, historians, politicians, and elders, all tasked with the goal of offering guidance to the animation team on "how to accurately and respectfully portray Sámi culture, history, and society."[12]

While Disney has relied on cultural advisory groups for several of its most recent features, including *Moana* (2016) and *Raya and the Last Dragon* (2021), the production of *Frozen II* introduced a significant legal element to this practice: a signed written agreement between Walt Disney Animation Studios and the Sámi people, as represented by the political institutions mentioned above, formalizing the filmmakers' "wish to show respect to the Sámi people and their concerns."[13] As part of this agreement, Disney committed to dubbing *Frozen II* in the most commonly spoken Sámi language and to "participating in cross-learning initiatives that contribute to Indigenous communities in Scandinavia."[14]

This marks the first time the House of Mouse has publicly taken on contractual obligations relating to its depiction of marginalized groups. Both parties leaned into the promotional potential of this historic deal, resulting in the release of a ceremonial, nonconfidential version of the contract to the press. The document, signed by *Frozen II*'s producer Peter del Vecho, declares Disney's "desire to collaborate with the Sámi in an effort to ensure that the content of *Frozen 2* is culturally sensitive, appropriate and respectful of the Sámi and their culture." While the contract has widely been received as an expression of goodwill and progressive values on the part of Disney, Aili Keskitalo, who was Sámi parliament president during the negotiations, has described it as "the result of several people's strategic and hard work over many years and not something Disney did just to be nice."[15]

Some Sámi sources on the *verddet*'s work on *Frozen II* position it as a mutually beneficial creative partnership. For instance, Christina Henriksen, vice president of the Saami Council, describes it as a "win-win" situation in which "Disney gets credit for working with the Sámi, and the Sámi get an opportunity to expose their culture, without having to be worried about how it would be portrayed."[16] Anne Lájla Utsi, managing director at the International Sámi Film Institute and member of the advisory council, describes it as a collaboration the *verddet* is "truly proud of."[17] Most notably, in a pointed critique of his nation-state's treatment of the Sámi, Sámi parliament director Rune Fjellheim states that it was "much easier to relate to, and negotiate with, Walt Disney Animation Studios than to fight many power structures that ignore Sámis in Norwegian society, including an indifferent Norwegian media industry, where Sámis are either exotified, trivialized or scandalized."[18]

The key outcome of the agreement was *Frozen II*'s depiction of the Northuldra, an Indigenous group coded as Disney's animated version of the Sámi through direct references to Sámi outfits, lifestyle, and cultural customs. The group is introduced as reindeer herders who "live in wooden tents that resemble the Sámi *lavvo* as well as in *goadit* (turf huts), wear clothes similar to the *gákti* (Sámi traditional [clothes]), and welcome Elsa and Anna and their companions with a *joik*."[19] The sequel reveals that Elsa and Anna's mother, Iduna, was a member of this community, a significant and unanticipated twist on established *Frozen* lore whose ramifications will be discussed in more detail below. The recognizable allusions to Sámi traditions, as well as the importance of the two sisters' Indigenous heritage to the plot and to their character arcs (particularly Elsa's), reveal the impact of the advisory council's involvement on the film's approach to Sámi representation. However, evidently even a direct collaboration with the *verddet* could not eliminate stereotypical notions of Indigenous mysticism; the Northuldra inhabit a magical realm, unimaginatively named the Enchanted Forest, and are cast as guardians of nature's magic via the deep connection they share with the elemental spirits of wind, fire, water, and earth. The link *Frozen II* draws between Indigeneity and magic is so unambiguous that Elsa's magical powers have now been retroactively framed as having come from her native lineage.

Keeping in perspective the unprecedented nature of Disney's contract with the Sámi, its undeniable PR value to the studio, and the uneven results I've begun sketching out, I will devote the rest of the chapter to an in-depth exploration of the impact of Disney's commitment to culturally sensitive Indigenous representation on the form and content of *Frozen II*. I will focus on the Northuldra, showing how their portrayal draws on certain aspects of Sámi customs and practices while heavily leaning into a generalized Anglo-American vision of Indigeneity that fits comfortably within the broader Disney brand and the particular style of the *Frozen* franchise.

JOIKING: A BRIEF HISTORY

The *joik* tradition has played a central role in *Frozen*'s sonic world-building since the original feature film, and *Frozen II* continues to draw on its unique musical characteristics while also indirectly referencing the practice of *joiking* a person in a pivotal scene. For this reason, I will begin my close analysis by briefly summarizing the history and cultural significance of *joik*, before I move on to the specific manifestation of this unique art form in *Frozen II*. Music historian Nils Grinde summarizes the distinguishing characteristics of this singing style:

> The word *joik* is a transitive verb as well as a noun: a Sami "joiks" his neighbor, his sweetheart, the world, the northern lights, and so on. The *joik* is a means of communicating with everything that is important in the life and circumstances of the Sami people. A *joik* is rarely associated with a coherent, descriptive text. There are catch words, hints—just enough to give the listeners who know the *joik* the appropriate associations.... The rhythm is also sometimes varied in accordance with the content of the *joik*—for example, to depict a reindeer at rest or in motion.[20]

From a musicology perspective, the structure of most *joik* is deceptively simple: pentatonic melodies consisting of short phrases, the most common patterns being ABAC and ABCB. However, as Grinde has noted, "the absence of a concluding cadence ... shows that the melody can and should be repeated as long as one wishes."[21] This opens up the potential for gracefully flowing, almost hypnotic rhythms—a potential used effectively in *Frozen*'s signature *joik* chant.

Veli-Pekka Lehtola, a professor of Sámi culture and member of the *verddet*, has pointed out that the suppression of *joiking*, which extended to both spiritual and secular variants, played a key role in Christian and nationalistic colonial efforts to erase Sámi identity and "break down the Sámi belief system and world-view."[22] Indeed, prohibitions against *joik* performance, which was often associated with shamanism, date back to the late seventeenth century, and the church's "negative perceptions of *joik* ... extended to the 1970s under the influence of Laestadianism, a nineteenth-century Christian revivalist movement in northern Scandinavia."[23] As a result, by the mid-twentieth century, *joik* traditions were almost completely lost in some parts of Sápmi, until Nils-Aslak Valkeapää's public performances, which began in 1966, breathed new life into the form.[24] The decades that followed marked a major revitalization of the tradition, with *joik* once again taking an important role in Sámi cultural life while also spreading to an international audience. This is partially due to governmental support coming from ministries of tourism and education,[25] as well as to the domestic and international success of artists such as Mari Boine, Sara Marielle Gaup, Adjágas, and Frode Fjellheim from Norway; Sofia Jannok from Sweden; and Wimme Saari and Ulla Pirttijärvi from Finland.[26]

Contemporary *joik* has entered popular music genres and has been shaped by them in turn. Tina Ramnarine reports that "cross-genre performance includes joik-inspired popular music, and joik elements in Sámi symphonies, rap, and rock. Increasingly, joik is appearing in the mainstream popular music scene within the Nordic countries and beyond." As *joik*'s gradual permeation into the musical mainstream suggests, *Frozen*'s use of its signature sound was neither random nor unprecedented but rather informed by contemporary musical trends in the Scandinavian region.[27]

In addition to expanding the cultural reach of Sámi Indigenous sound, *joik* has also been instrumental in establishing Sámi ties to other Indigenous communities around the world and affirming a sense of belonging built partially on global solidarity among native peoples. Musicologists have noted that *joik* shares "many of its basic features with similar products of other sub-polar peoples, from the inhabitants of Siberia to the Native Americans and Eskimos of North America."[28] Valkeapää, pioneering Sámi activist, writer, and musician, who performed a *joik* at the inaugural meeting of the World Council of Indigenous People in Port Alberni, Canada, in 1975, recalls that *joik* "acted as a sort of common language."[29]

In other words, *joik* has emerged as a symbol of Sámi indigenous identity both within the borders of Sápmi and beyond. In that sense, its (mis)use in the *Frozen* franchise is deeply politically loaded; both its decontextualized inclusion as a sonic introduction to the world in the first feature and its partial reinscription within Indigenous spaces in the sequel carry significant weight for Sámi viewers and can offer crucial clues regarding Disney's approach toward Indigenous soundscapes.

"Vuelie": A *Joik* by Any Other Name

"Vuelie," the melodic chant *Frozen* opens with, was composed by Frode Fjellheim, a South Sámi musician from Norway, and performed by Cantus, a famous Norwegian all-female choir made up of nonprofessional singers.[30] The track is an arrangement of an earlier composition by Fjellheim, "Eatnemen Vuelie."[31] It is likely that Disney reached out to Fjellheim because of his well-established international reputation as a *joiker* specialized in arranging "age-old yoiks from his ancestors in a modern musical language"; his band Transjoik (formerly known as the Frode Fjellheim Jazz Yoik Ensemble) had already won acclaim for taking *joik* "into the direction of improvisation and jazz, achieving through tempo and voices a state of hypnotic trance."[32]

Fjellheim describes his original composition as a "mix between a yoik-inspired melody and a hymn floating on top of that." The lyrics for this hymn, originally called "Deilig er jorden" ("Wonderful Is the Earth"), were written by Danish poet Bernhard Severin Ingemann in 1850. According to Fjellheim, "in English-speaking countries the same folk tune is known as 'Fairest Lord Jesus.'"[33] For *Frozen*, Disney requested a new version, "without the hymn part." To adapt his tune to the needs of the studio, Fjellheim worked with film composer Christophe Beck. The end result kept all the original *joik*-inspired parts (including the recognizable repetition of syllables with no linguistic meaning in "Vuelie") and most of the Sámi musician's original arrangement, with a melody co-written with Beck. Fjellheim's vision involved the marriage of two distinct vocal styles: "the deep 'chant-like' yoik, combined with a more classical vocal style."[34]

When asked if he agreed that it was "very satisfying to see how Disney gave attention to making this film sound authentic," Fjellheim responded that "Disney should perhaps answer this themselves—whether the goal was to have something 'authentic'—or just some relevant inspiration for making this animated movie."[35] Although diplomatic in its tone, the musician's comment implicitly questions the studio's motivation for including his work while also challenging the embrace of facile interpretations of "authenticity" in relation to *Frozen*'s use of "Vuelie." Fjellheim is justified in underplaying any potential claim to a musicologically informed approach to Indigenous representation vis-à-vis his music's recognizable *joik* features; after all, it is the composition's quality as a memorably melodic opening tune, rather than its cultural importance as a Sámi chant, that the film's soundscape foregrounds and capitalizes on. Furthermore, any appeal to the authenticity of "Vuelie" as a *joik* would have to contend with the composition's aforementioned musical hybridity, which is a level of specificity that neither *Frozen* itself nor its production paratexts have reached in their treatment of Fjellheim's work.

Despite all the cultural sensitivity training that went into the production of *Frozen II*, there is little indication that the franchise's revisiting of "Vuelie" was informed by a deeper understanding of the distinct nature of *joik* and its importance to the track or the narrative. This is particularly evident in interviews with returning composer Christophe Beck, who refers to "Vuelie" as the "Hey Na Na music." In conversation with *Forbes*, Beck describes the thought process behind scoring a key Northuldra scene featuring a reprise of the song:

> It's a very wondrous and magical moment where the forest people see the blue sky for the first time. For that, we went back to Frode [Fjellheim] and Cantus and created a new piece with the same singing style as the 'Hey Na Na' music, which is a singing style called joiking. It's a kind of Northern European yodel and we made a new piece, what could be called Chapter 2 of 'Hey Na Na' for that moment. And I think that was really one of the biggest challenges in terms of how to incorporate some of the Scandinavian elements that were there in the first film in the second film without it feeling redundant while still introducing new material.[36]

This statement and the attitude it reflects shed light on several problematic aspects of the treatment of Sámi music in *Frozen II*'s publicity campaign. The label "Hey Na Na music," presumably a reference to the dominant syllable heard in the chant, sounds pointedly dismissive and condescending, especially coming from a fellow musician collaborating with Fjellheim for the second time. Moreover, while Beck references *joik*, he completely erases the Sámi from the narrative of the soundtrack's creation by calling their signature art form a "Northern European yodel" and a "Scandinavian element." This Eurocentric view decontextualizes *joik*, obscures its status as an Indigenous musical form, and privileges geographic markers (Northern Europe, Scandinavia) over cultural specificity. The failure of *Frozen II*'s lead composer to correctly attribute *joiking* to the Indigenous groups who perform it (one of which Fjellheim himself belongs to) directly undermines Disney's claims to respectful and careful stewardship of Sámi heritage. While Beck may not necessarily speak for his employer, his interviews have nevertheless misrepresented or outright concealed a pivotal aspect of the role of Indigenous art in *Frozen,* and his flippant nickname for "Vuelie" hints at a likely disconnect between the studio's official stance on Sámi representation and key creatives' actual level of understanding and sensitivity toward the issue.

While tracing the adaptation journey of "Vuelie" and considering representative paratexts such as the *Forbes* interview provides important context for *joik*'s entry and positioning in the Disney canon, analyzing the composition's sonic presence and narrative framing in *Frozen II* further complicates Disney's claims of cultural inclusivity and authenticity. The key scene that not only showcases the film's new rendition of "Vuelie" but attempts to present a culturally appropriate context for its performance occurs as Elsa and Anna are formally welcomed into the Northuldra community in the middle of a clearing in the Enchanted Forest. After the sisters announce that their mother was Northuldra, a mystical wind picks up and swirls around them, and the film's Indigenous characters begin singing "Vuelie" as they form a spiral-like structure by linking their bodies arm to shoulder. At the center of the spiral, elder Yelana offers her hands to the girls and says, "We are called Northuldra. We are the people of the Sun." Given that some Sámi epic songs trace the group's ancestry back to the sun, this line is a direct nod to the Northuldra's real-world models.[37] The scene reads like an induction into Northuldran/Sámi society, which corresponds to one of the cultural functions of *joik*. As Harald Gaski, scholar of Sámi literature and culture, has explained, "traditionally the giving of a yoik to a person was like a naming process; by receiving her or his own yoik, an adolescent would be reckoned as a whole member of the local society. The ideology of yoik is thus communal, with a yoik linking the individual to a collective."[38]

Disney's inclusion of "Vuelie" in this scene offers a surface-level approximation of this custom without any explicit reference to it or any explanation of its meaning to the film's Indigenous group. While the narrative progression of the scene ties the *joik* to the Northuldra's acceptance of the sisters as members of their society, no further information is communicated to the viewer regarding the nature or significance of this vocal performance. Additionally, attempting to present this scene as a naming ritual is complicated by earlier uses of "Vuelie" across the franchise, particularly as background music not connected to either sister until this very moment.

Elsa and Anna's entry into the collective is likewise an unconvincing portrayal of an important induction ritual, undermining the film's attempt at paying homage to the social roles of *joiking* even more. Notably, "the girls step into their Northuldra identities and are immediately accepted, despite having no prior awareness of or connection to that part of their heritage. For that matter, Iduna seems to have at least partly disavowed her home culture."[39] Indeed, despite Elsa and Anna's mother severing ties with her roots, resulting in her children's ignorance of Northuldran life, and the fact that the two sisters have made no concrete steps toward genuine integration (as they only just discovered their true origin), the Northuldra embrace them unanimously and ceremoniously.

Neither the colonial trauma inflicted on the community by their grandfather nor the cultural betrayal of their mother appears to factor into the sisters' ability to instantaneously claim their perceived birthright. This stereotypical fantasy of an Indigenous community willing to overlook multiple injustices perpetuated against them in order to enlist the protection of a benevolent, powerful prodigal son (or daughter, as it were) diminishes the gravity of induction rituals and the distinct meaning and ideology behind the performance of *joik* at such an event. Ultimately, then, "Vuelie" is stripped of most of its cultural specificity and becomes background music to an emotional but largely unearned Disney moment presenting Indigenous–colonial reconciliation as a simple, straightforward matter.

Animation scholar Jacqueline Ristola has commended Disney's inclusion of "Vuelie" in this scene, arguing that "giving this song directly to the Northuldra helps address criticism of the previous film, placing the beautiful voices directly into indigenous visual representation."[40] However, this line of reasoning, while correct in pinpointing Disney's likely motivation for this particular soundscape choice, ends up highlighting another problem with this scene's approach to Indigenous representation: the "beautiful voices" of the Cantus choir are not, in fact, Sámi. This is another instance of the slippage between "Sámi" and "Scandinavian" (also evident in Beck's *Forbes* interview) that appears to occasionally destabilize the foundations of Disney's mandate to honor and showcase Sámi expression in *Frozen II*.

"Generalized Indigeneity"

Disney's attempt to draw on *joik*'s cultural associations and expressive power without properly contextualizing it or incorporating it into a fitting narrative development is a symptom of a broader, systemic flaw in *Frozen II*'s representational strategies. Trude Fonneland has argued that despite Disney's collaboration with the Sámi, the film remains "an American story, where the local materialities, knowledge, and traditions are moved to and shaped by a global setting to appeal to a global audience."[41] Tuija Huuki and Kata Kyrölä have pointed out that "in the production process, Anglo-American views of 'generalized' indigeneity sometimes risked overshadowing Sámi specificity."[42] Drawing on the concept of generalized Indigeneity, I examine *Frozen II*'s visual depictions of Sámi culture, highlighting connections with issues already discussed in relation to the film's soundscape, while also revealing additional trends evident in Disney's animation of the Northuldra's lifestyle, environments, and beliefs.

The first indication that the studio is sacrificing accuracy in the name of depicting a more conventionally "legible" image of Indigeneity appears in the Northuldra characters' design. Sámi people tend to appear white to outside observers; in his recollection of the first meeting of the World Council of Indigenous Peoples, Valkeapää writes the following: "we met for the first time at the meeting at Port Alberni, and the meeting was by no means an easy affair.... The fact that Samis have a light skin, and some of us are quite blond, certainly had no positive associations for people who had learned to equate a white skin with colonialism and the terrible assaults on people which accompanied it."[43] In a 1993 article, Gaski refers to the Sámi as the "White Indians of Scandinavia."[44] As they are meant to represent the Sámi, the Northuldra should thus resemble the Norwegian-inspired characters in the film in terms of complexion. Instead, most of them (with the notable exception of Iduna) are easily distinguishable from Elsa and Anna. Compared with the two princesses, Northuldra characters such as Honeymaren have darker skin and hair and noses that are noticeably broader at the base. Additionally, their eyes are smaller and more elongated, and their cheekbones appear higher and more pronounced. In fact, the Northuldra community appears to be modeled after conventional representations of North American Indigenous peoples, including characters from Disney's own expansive library. They share their earth-toned outfits and sensible footwear with *Peter Pan*'s Tiger Lily and their fur-trimmed fashion with *Brother Bear 2*'s Nita and Atka. Yelana comes from a lineage of dignified, gray-haired Indigenous elders, such as Kekata (*Pocahontas*, 1995) and Grandmother (the *Gargoyles* TV series, 1995).

This visual othering of the Northuldra did not remain unnoticed by critics; in response to it, Erik Kain asks, "why does every member of the Northuldra look somewhat Native American or maybe Inuit, but then [Elsa and Anna's] mom is just completely white?"[45] While many American journalists such as Kain erroneously accused Disney of not giving Anna or Elsa "any physical signs of being part mixed-race,"[46] it is the *other* Northuldra who are misrepresented by being designed with features that correspond to Anglo-American ideas about Indigeneity, rather than to the lived reality of Sámi peoples. To further complicate matters and reveal the self-contradictions and inconsistencies in Disney's attempt to center Indigeneity through a storyline about reclaiming one's heritage, there are pronounced differences between the Enchanted Forest Northuldra and the royal Northuldra. Queen Iduna, who was born to Northuldran parents, bears no resemblance to the rest of her group, except for her dark hair. Instead, her facial features and skin are exact copies of Anna and Elsa's, complete with enormous blue eyes, a thin upturned nose, and thin eyebrows (in contrast to the thick eyebrows of the forest group). This is likely the unavoidable outcome of Disney's decision to retcon her background for the sequel; there are clear indications that Iduna's character wasn't originally meant to be Indigenous, including concept art by Cory Loftis, which shows her as a classic Disney princess sporting Cinderella's signature updo, elegantly posed for a portrait in the style of European aristocracy.[47] The result of reintroducing Iduna and her progeny as Northuldra while retaining their *Frozen* designs is to confirm the film's visual association of royalty with features commonly attributed to a broad, ahistorical vision of Europeanness rooted in Disney canon, now opposed to a generalized vision of Indigeneity that does not represent the Sámi truthfully but reduces them to stereotypical notions of (magical) forest-dwelling natives easily digestible by audiences familiar with the Disney canon.

The production team's approach to Northuldra styling and costumes raises further questions about Disney's success in animating a "culturally appropriate, sensitive, and respectful" reflection of Sámi culture. For example, Nick Orsi, a visual development artist on *Frozen II*, has shared that Yelana, the leader of the Northuldra, wears her hair "in a style that resembles a crown, which gives her a regal bearing that is our nod to her status as an elder."[48] While this design choice was apparently an attempt to honor this Indigenous woman's role in her society, it reflects a Eurocentric understanding of royalty and its symbols, rather than a vision informed by Sámi social structures and status markers. On a broader level, Anne Kalvig has pointed out that the community is "depicted as a people wearing brown and beige clothes, contrasting their real life typical use (concerning traditional clothes) of bright colors like red, blue and yellow." She suggests that the *Frozen II* team may have sacrificed accuracy in order to visually enhance the contrast between the people of Arendelle and the Northuldra or to have the latter "fit into possible mainstream representation and iconography of 'the indigenous' as typically 'earth colored.'"[49]

Production texts about the making of this film lend further credence to the notion that Northuldra costumes were envisioned as representative of generalized Indigeneity rather than the specificity of Sámi clothing. For instance, character model supervisor Chad Stubblefield describes the Northuldra as people "very much connected with nature," explaining that "they spend much of their time living and working outdoors and have adapted to thrive in all conditions. We wanted their look to reflect that."[50]

In addition to leaning into stereotypes of Indigenous people's lifestyles as inextricably linked to nature, this description makes no mention of the Sámi as a source of inspiration. Indeed, Disney had originally designed Northuldra outfits "drawing from the clothing traditions of various Arctic Indigenous peoples, including the Sámi but also, for instance, the Nenets inhabiting Russia's Far North." It was not until the *verddet* intervened that Disney redesigned the costumes to resemble Sámi *gákti* more, reflecting the cultural significance of the garment, which is traditionally handmade, "and the processes of making it and wearing it are considered important markers of a Sámi belonging and identity, connectedness to ancestors, location and land." Notably, however, *verddet* member Lehtola has mentioned that the advisory council did not get all the changes they wanted, ending up "satisfied enough."[51] While one can only guess the nature and extent of the unmet redesign requests, the contrast between Lehtola's suggestive phrasing and producer del Vecho's choice to highlight the final costumes for Honeymaren, Ryder, and Yelana as the product of Disney's successful partnership with the Sámi people[52] hint at a mismatch in the two parties' criteria for evaluating the results of their collaboration.

Sámi landscapes—in the sense of both art and geography—are also conspicuously absent from the film. The environment of the Northuldra does not have a distinct style, nor does it appear to show any Sámi art influences. In fact, the film's production team has discussed the importance of creating a sequel that "follow[s] the established design rules for the world and characters, and maintain[s] the visual style and sensibility of the first film." In particular, this involved ensuring that "all the new characters and environments look like they belong in the *Frozen* world."[53] However, the studio still made room for references to classic Disney artists, including Eyvind Earle and Mary Blair, as well as a range of European fine artists, "such as [Henri] Rousseau and Toulouse-Lautrec, as well as Norwegian illustrator Gerhard Munthe, German-American painter Albert Bierstadt, and several Russian painters who depict forests in all types of weather."[54] In the context of this long list, the absence of Sámi art inspiration becomes even more conspicuous, and the need to maintain stylistic consistency no longer sounds like a convincing justification.

"A NATURE BLEND": THE VAGUE SPIRITUALITY OF *FROZEN II*

Another aspect of Sámi representation in *Frozen II* that merits scrutiny is the film's replacement of Sámi religious symbols and practices with a relatively vague, nature-based belief system based on the four elements, indiscriminately intermixed with borrowings from Scandinavian mythology. Fonneland observes that the Northuldra religion, as described by *Frozen II*'s directors, is "an indistinct form of spirituality; a spirituality embedded in indigenous ways of life and thinking, and with a focus on concepts such as holism, environmental protection, feminism, ancestral anchorage, and nature worship."[55] All of these concepts, which either are secular or have secular counterparts, inscribe the film in a "religious neutral environment," while at the same time allowing Disney to envision the Northuldra as a society "located in a mythical past of indigenous traditions and ceremonies that serves as a part of the 'seasoning' of the ... narrative."[56]

Kalvig reports that "in real life, the majority of Sámi people (or people living in Sámi areas, as ethnic identity is not counted in religious belonging statistics) belong to various Christian denominations, including the Norwegian Church."[57] While the absence of Christian practices in the film likely stems from their incompatibility with Disney's depiction of nature-based spirituality and from the studio's traditional avoidance of overt Christian references, Indigenous Sámi forms of spirituality and worship are likewise erased. As Fonneland points out, "the film is stripped of the goavvdis (Sámi ritual drums), the [sieidi] (Sámi sacrificial stones), as well as the noaidi (Sámi religious specialist), which are the most well-known markers of the ethnic religion of the Sámi indigenous population."[58] While Huuki and Kyrölä have argued that the four large boulders featured in the film are meant to be *sieidi*, "sacred sites of ritual and offering,"[59] they are neither described as such nor given any corresponding role in the narrative.

Echoing *Frozen II*'s refusal to fully embrace the distinctiveness of Sámi music, appearance, and costume, its approach to Indigenous religion follows a similar pattern of reliance on generalized, globally legible concepts. At the same time, any meaningful connection to traditional Sámi cosmologies is further undermined by the production team's decision to introduce cultural references borrowed from Scandinavian folklore and tie them to the elements that the Northuldra share a bond with. Co-director Buck's description of the inspiration behind the different elements represented in *Frozen*

II reveals a liberal approach toward appropriating iconographies and tales from the broader Scandinavian region: "the Water Spirit is inspired by Old Norse myths. A wind spirit appears in some Scandinavian folk tales. There are myths about the giant boulders left over from the ice age that are scattered throughout Scandinavian forests and are said to have been thrown by rock trolls.... All of these elemental creatures come from the folktales, myths, and legends of the region."[60] The Fire Spirit manifests as a salamander because "in some European folklore, the salamander is connected to fire."[61]

The film presents Elsa's connection to these elements as inextricably related to her Northuldra heritage; it is because of her Indigenous roots that she is capable of fully embracing her magic and becoming the fifth element. This aspect of the narrative directly contradicts Disney's commitment to honoring Sámi culture in two ways. First, it replaces Indigenous beliefs and symbols with European folklore from the same region, tying the film's Indigenous group to colonial iconographies. Second, it leans into "problematic aspects of Sámi peoples representing themselves/being represented as having a default connection with nature." As Trine Kvidal-Røvik and Ashley Cordes have pointed out, such depictions have significant political ramifications, since they can "radically [limit] the possibilities for Sámi self-identification in the modern world."[62]

In addition to obscuring Sámi belief systems and practices in favor of a generic cosmology inspired by an amalgamation of Scandinavian folklore, *Frozen II* erases the multiplicity of subcultures within Sámi communities by affirming one specific Sámi archetype as representative of the entire group. Kvidal-Røvik and Cordes note that "the symbolism connected to the Sámi in the film (the reindeer, the lavvus, the gákti) are the main symbols used over and over again in tourism and media images, reinforcing the reindeer herding Sámis as the 'real' Sámi, while the diversity within Sámi cultures and communities remains invisible."[63] Fonneland concurs, criticizing Disney's decision to link the Northuldra exclusively to a single Sámi practice, reindeer husbandry, a representational choice that "can be said to provide a univocal understanding of Sámi identity and ... can be seen as a constructed 'myth of origin' that both simplifies the past and excludes contradictory voices."[64] In addition to perpetuating an exclusionist ideology, Disney's overreliance on reindeer herding as a visual and narrative shorthand also leads to stilted, stereotypical characterization of Northuldra individuals. For example, Bill Schwab, art director for characters, frames Ryder's bond with Kristoff in the following terms: "Ryder has a deep connection to reindeer, just like Kristoff, so they're fast friends."[65] Reindeer are not only the core aspect of Sámi identity, as presented in Disney, they are also an easy substitute for authentic character development.

What is more, the film's implicit endorsement of reindeer herders as the "true" Sámi comes hand in hand with Disney's dubbing policy, which similarly privileges a particular group (speakers of North Sámi) while disregarding the linguistic diversity of the community. As Kvidal-Røvik and Cordes explain, choosing only one of the Sámi languages, which is "most pervasive because of colonial politics," ends up "presenting North Sámi as the 'real' Sámi."[66] In other words, Disney's Sámi-inspired representation of Indigenous life and customs simultaneously erases much of the distinctiveness of their culture while deemphasizing multiplicity and diversity within their community.

Through a combination of close reading of the film itself, a study of its production paratexts, and a synthesis of the various critical readings referenced above, the following trends emerge in Disney's depiction of Sámi communities and their beliefs. First, Sámi cosmologies and spiritual practices and their corresponding iconographies are only partially referenced, and their specificity is further undermined via the film's haphazard interweaving of Scandinavian mythological elements. As a result, the spiritual life of *Frozen II*'s Northuldra is neither adequately representative of nor sufficiently informative about the diverse and complex Indigenous belief systems and traditions they purportedly allude to. Second, certain Sámi groups are privileged over others through narrative and visual design (reindeer-herding communities) and through dubbing practices (North Sámi speakers). The choice to perpetuate a politically fraught myth of the "true" Sámi not only contributes to the erasure of communities historically marginalized *within* this particular Indigenous group but also obscures, especially for an international audience, the historical and social processes that have shaped Sámi diversity.

THE DAM CONFLICT: SÁMI HISTORY MEETS AMERICAN REPARATIONS DISCOURSE

There is a major plot point in *Frozen II* that has been read as a reference to the Alta dam conflict, an important political controversy in twentieth-century Sámi history. The connection between the two actually predates the *verddet*'s involvement in the film's production, but the group's members "deeply appreciated" it.[67] The seeds of *Frozen II*'s dam conflict are sown by Anna and Elsa's grandfather King Runeard, who, under the pretense of neighborly goodwill, builds the Northuldra a dam. In reality, however, the dam is designed to reduce the Northuldra's resources as part of the king's larger plot to eliminate the Indigenous group, whom he fears and despises. Shortly after the Northuldra recognize the dam's harmful potential, Runeard murders their leader and instigates warfare, which angers the forest spirits, causing them to trap both the Arendellian army and the Northuldrans within a wall of fog. After all this comes to light, Anna decides to right the wrongs of her ancestor by destroying the dam, even though she knows this will catastrophically flood Arendelle. Meanwhile, Elsa discovers that she is the fifth element, who is destined to unite people and wield the magic of nature, and she manages to divert the flow of water, saving Arendelle from her sister's dramatic act of atonement. In the end, Elsa abdicates the throne in favor of Anna and joins the Northuldra as their shaman, having restored peace between the two communities.

This plot development shares significant similarities with an important event in twentieth-century Sámi history: the Norwegian government's plan, first announced in 1968, to build a dam and a hydroelectric power plant on Sámi ancestral land. As the project endangered the largest Sámi reindeer-herding system and threatened to flood

Sámi communities, it inspired a major political uprising.[68] Even though the dam was eventually built and the government stifled Sámi protests, political theorist Aslak-Antti Oksanen believes that this conflict "transformed the notion of pan-Sámi national solidarity from a utopian ideal held by the Sámi cultural and political elite, to one shared by the mass Sámi population."[69] Political discourse surrounding the project also led to impactful policy changes, after the Norwegian Sámi Rights Committee appointed during the uprising produced a report in 1984 "recommending the creation of a Sámi representative assembly, a constitutional Sámi rights article and a Sámi Language Act making Sámi an official language while mandating arrangements for Sámi language education." All of these recommendations were codified into Norway's legal system within six years, marking an important step for Sámi rights in the country.[70]

While the parallel between *Frozen II*'s dam storyline and these real-world events was apparently accidental, it could have become an opportunity for the film to delve deeper into Sámi history and politics, particularly since Arendelle is inspired by Norway. Instead, the narrative pursues analogies with US history, starting with the bloody conflict between Runeard's forces and the Northuldra. As scholars have noted, *Frozen II*'s depiction of warfare between colonial forces and the Indigenous population reflects the history of North America's native communities, rather than that of the Sámi. In fact, the Sámi "did not experience war, but their colonization began in the seventeenth century through Christian missionary work, exploration in the name of science, and forced land transfers. In the nineteenth century, exploitative colonialism in the Sápmi region gradually turned into settler colonialism with the aim of complete cultural assimilation and replacement, but without literal genocide."[71] Yet again, Disney has sacrificed a distinct aspect of the Sámi's past in the name of a generalized depiction of Indigenous history.

Bringing the North American political allegory to its conclusion, the plot also frames Anna's decision to break the dam in terms that directly evoke topical Anglo-American political debates around decolonization and racial justice. After performing an emotional musical number about choosing to do "the next right thing," Anna declares that "Arendelle has no future until we make this right. King Runeard betrayed everyone." She explicitly presents the act of breaking the dam as atonement for the king's colonial policies and the harm they have caused the Northuldra and the forest. Notably, "making this right" involves accepting that Arendelle's destruction is a fair price to pay for the sins of its rulers. While Anna's chosen social justice method is to sink structures of oppression rather than incinerating them (a common metaphor in the North American context), her actions echo the spirit of US radical left-wing calls to fully dismantle, rather than attempt to reform, racist institutions. This discourse is exemplified by Edwin Mayorga, Lekey Leidecker, and Daniel Orr de Gutiérrez's piece on US higher education, in which the authors conclude that higher education is "not only incompatible, but irredeemably incommensurable with decolonization," and to address this, "we should burn it down and start anew."[72] Another representative piece, collectively penned by *Abolition Journal* staff, concludes that "abolition as a praxis and vision must contend with how to burn down all of the mechanics of contemporary governance, to cooperatively dismantle the state as such, before promoting alternative social systems and political worlds."[73] Thus, in the North American context, the dam scene may certainly appear to tap into this particular approach to activism.

Perhaps unsurprisingly, *Washington Post* reviewer Priya Satia received *Frozen II* as "a movie that calls on heirs of colonialism to question ... national myths about the past and atone for the ugly truth they cover up." The same review suggests that "the movie's contemplation of reparations for historical wrongs is a call for a new kind of public ethics, one that asks us to extend the values we teach our children to our politics."[74] *Slate*'s Inkoo Kang reads the film in the context of North American politics as well, criticizing it for "framing reparations in this zero-sum way." As she puts it, "we have so few fictional portrayals of what postcolonial restitution looks like that we should be careful of how we depict it, especially as reparations for descendants of American slaves has become an unlikely 2020 talking point."[75]

While blowing up the dam is certainly a drastic measure, its radical potential is ultimately undermined by Elsa's miraculous intervention, which saves Arendelle from the powerful wave about to sweep it off the map. Ristola, who otherwise praises the film for doing a "remarkable job of confronting colonialism and demonstrating the material conditions for reparations," was left unimpressed by this twist, pointing out that "a braver choice would certainly be to have the kingdom destroyed, and as it is rebuilt, connections between the Northudra and the Arendelle are rebuilt as well."[76] Norwegian scholars Kvidal-Røvik and Cordes, who, unlike their North American counterparts, read this conflict through the lens of Sámi politics, have also taken issue with the lack of consequences for Arendelle and the film's conclusion, which asserts that all the trauma inflicted on Northuldra society can be erased by a single gesture of goodwill on behalf of Arendelle's royal family. As they point out, this ending "can be read as a settler-move-to-innocence re-presenting the facade that problems between Sámi and non-Indigenous peoples are all resolved. This is a representational and narrative problem Disney has not fixed, where they consistently recycle tropes of racial reconciliation or perpetuate that Indigenous peoples are colonizers' helping hand—something that traces back to Disney's *Pocahontas*."[77]

It is interesting to note that *Frozen II*'s production accounts reveal that in a scrapped version of the story, Arendelle's castle was going to be washed away in the flood following the dam's destruction and then rebuilt "as a combination of the Northuldra and Arendellian styles."[78] While maintaining the royal seat of power and its corresponding political institution is hardly a radical gesture, this could have been a small step toward world-building that reflects the cultural traditions of both communities, potentially signaling Anna and Elsa's willingness to openly represent and honor their Northuldran heritage. By deciding against even this token gesture, Disney affirms its commitment to the status quo by maintaining visual consistency with the original *Frozen* and keeping the Indigenous community on the periphery—geographically, politically, and representationally.

Conclusion: *Frozen II*'s Impact

Despite the shortcomings of certain aspects of Sámi representation in *Frozen II*, Sámi communities across Scandinavia praised the film nearly unanimously. Norwegian scholars report that all over Norway, "activities around the film itself also provide[d] important arenas to show and engage indigenous presence." For instance, opening-night screenings turned into cultural celebrations, with Sámi viewers attending in traditional clothes and Sámi games (such as lasso throwing) being played.[79] The Sámi Film Institute shared the poster for the North Sámi–language version, *Jikŋon 2*, on its Facebook page, accompanied by the following comment: "This collaboration is groundbreaking in so many ways and a good example of how companies can collaborate with Indigenous peoples in a truly respectful way."[80]

However, some of the positive Sámi reviews appear to come with a significant caveat: they foreground the cultural importance of the dub. Former Sámi Parliament president Keskitalo pointed to viewer interest in *Jikŋon 2* as "evidence that there is an audience who is starving for Sámi language films." Echoing this, "many Sámis and Sámi institutions praised the film because of the difference they think it will have for language recognition and visibility."[81] In other words, it is not necessarily the film's content but the dubbed version's success as a film in a Sámi language long suppressed by local governments that evoked Indigenous pride and was seen as cause for celebration. It is telling that when asked by a Sámi talk-show host if the film provides an accurate portrayal of Sámi peoples, Keskitalo responded that "Sámis will see recognizable elements, especially with language, although it should be in several Sámi languages."[82]

Keskitalo's tactful phrasing hints at the key shortcoming of Disney's interpretation of its agreement with the Sámi. In *Frozen II*, Sámi culture permeates all aspects of the world, but it ultimately does so entirely on Disney's terms, without disrupting the company's established brand (either visually or ideologically). While Indigenous forms of expression enrich the soundtrack, art design, and narrative, they are never allowed to emerge as a distinct storytelling language. Instead, Disney maintains its long-standing policy of approaching cultural references as additional ingredients to be sprinkled liberally but largely superficially across a product meant for global consumption and largely representative of Anglo-American values and politics. As producer del Vecho put it, "The Sámi culture has a unique history. We are very interested in different angles, so we can try to make films that appeal universally. That is why we are here."[83]

In their seminal study of Disney's global cultural impact, Henry Giroux and Grace Pollock write that "a contradiction emerges between the reality of Disney's cutthroat commercial ethos and the Disney image, whereby the company presents itself as the paragon of virtue and childlike innocence.... Such contradictions should not be taken as grounds for dismissing Disney as a cultural force but instead should be exposed and used for the potential spaces of resistance they provide and for the imaginative possibilities they might offer."[84] Indeed, Disney's work with the *verddet* has, to a certain extent, opened up a space of Indigenous resistance and possibilities by bringing international awareness to various aspects of Sámi culture. However, as Kvidal-Røvik and Cordes have pointed out, while "inclusion and consultation with indigenous communities for Disney films is an important step, perhaps the least Disney could do, ... inclusion is not decolonization."[85]

In the end, this is a film with Indigenous people but not about them. Indigenous perspectives are never centered, nor are Indigenous voices heard (unless they are singing to welcome Disney princesses into their ranks). There is no meaningful role for the Northuldra outside of their relationship with Anna and Elsa, no room for them to exist by and *for* themselves. In *Frozen II*, Disney tries to sell presence as representation and reap the ideological dividends. Rather than a blueprint for a sensitive and informed approach to depicting Indigeneity in animation, the studio's execution of its agreement with the Sámi is, at best, a rough draft.

Notes

1. Tina K. Ramnarine, "Sonic Images of the Sacred in Sámi Cinema," *Interventions* 15, no. 2 (2013): 240.
2. Veli-Pekka Lehtola, *The Sámi People: Traditions in Transition*, trans. Linna Weber Müller-Wille (Fairbanks: University of Alaska Press, 2004), 9–10.
3. Ramnarine, "Sonic Images," 240.
4. A variant spelling of this term is *yoik*. While both versions appear in scholarly and popular sources, I will use *joik* in my own analysis, while preserving each citation's original spelling.
5. Jérémie Noyer, "Composer Frode Fjellheim on *Frozen*'s Native Spirit," Animated Views, March 18, 2014, https://animatedviews.com/2014/composer-frode-fjellheim-on-frozens-native-spirit/.
6. Tuija Huuki and Kata Kyrölä, "'Show Yourself': Indigenous Ethics, Sámi Cosmologies and Decolonial Queer Pedagogies of *Frozen 2*," *Gender and Education* 35, no. 2 (2022): 3.
7. Chris Buck and Jennifer Lee, foreword to Charles Solomon, *The Art of Frozen* (San Francisco: Chronicle, 2013), 7.
8. Charles Solomon, *The Art of Frozen* (San Francisco: Chronicle, 2013), 34.
9. Johan MacGuinne, Tumblr, January 19, 2014, https://selchieproductions.tumblr.com/post/73866006709/same-anon-here-i-know-you-did-a-comparison-way.
10. Alyssa Christine Magee Lowery, "Buying the Blueprints: Investing Emotionally and Materially in the Icy Ideologies of Disney's *Frozen* Films," PhD diss., Ohio State University, 2020, 41.
11. Radheyan Simonpillai, "Disney Signed a Contract with Indigenous People before Making *Frozen II*," NOW Toronto, November 19, 2019, https://nowtoronto.com/movies/news-features/disney-frozen-2-indigenous-culture-sami
12. Trine Kvidal-Røvik and Ashley Cordes, "Into the Unknown [Amas Mu Vuordá]? Listening to Indigenous Voices on the Meanings of Disney's *Frozen 2* [Jikŋon 2]," *Journal of International and Intercultural Communication* 15, no. 1 (2022): 24.
13. Simonpillai, "Disney Signed a Contract."
14. Ibid.
15. Kvidal-Røvik and Cordes, "Into the Unknown," 24.

16. Kevin McGwin, "How a Collaboration with Disney Shaped the Way Sámi Cultural Details Were Portrayed in *Frozen 2*," *Arctic Today*, February 3, 2020, https://www.arctictoday.com/how-a-collaboration-with-disney-shaped-the-way-sami-cultural-details-were-portrayed-in-frozen-2/.
17. Simonpillai, "Disney Signed a Contract."
18. Kvidal-Røvik and Cordes, "Into the Unknown," 26.
19. Trude Fonneland, "Religion-Making in the Disney Feature Film, *Frozen II*: Indigenous Religion and Dynamics of Agency," *Religions* 11 (2020): 5.
20. Nils Grinde, *A History of Norwegian Music*, trans. William H. Halverson and Leland B. Sateren (Lincoln: University of Nebraska Press, 1991), 110.
21. Ibid., 111.
22. Lehtola, *The Sámi People*, 106.
23. Ramnarine, "Sonic Images," 241.
24. Lehtola, *The Sámi People*, 106.
25. Neil Kent, *The Sámi Peoples of the North: A Social and Cultural History* (London: Hurst, 2018), 240.
26. Simon Broughton, "If Our Memory Fails Us, We Exist No More," *Finnish Music Quarterly*, April 26, 2019, https://fmq.fi/articles/if-our-memory-fails-us-we-exist-no-more.
27. Tina K. Ramnarine, "Frozen through Nordic Frames," *Puls Journal for Ethnomusicology and Ethnochoreology* 1 (2016): 25.
28. Grinde, *A History of Norwegian Music*, 110.
29. Nils-Aslak Valkeapää, *Greetings from Lapland: The Sami—Europe's Forgotten People*, trans. Beverley Wahl (London: Zed, 1983), 115.
30. Laura Biemmi, "All-Female Vocal Stars of 'Frozen' Talk New Release," Cut Common, July 17, 2017, https://www.cutcommonmag.com/all-female-vocal-stars-of-frozen-talk-new-release/.
31. Noyer, "Composer Frode Fjellheim."
32. Lehtola, *The Sámi People*, 111.
33. Noyer, "Composer Frode Fjellheim."
34. Ibid.
35. Ibid.
36. Josh Weiss, "'Frozen 2': How Christophe Beck Carved a More Mature Score out of the Ice for Disney's Sequel," *Forbes*, December 2, 2019, https://www.forbes.com/sites/joshweiss/2019/12/02/frozen-ii-how-christophe-beck-carved-a-more-mature-score-out-of-the-ice-for-disneys-sequel/?sh=ba5062d71adc.
37. Harald Gaski, "The Sami People: The 'White Indians' of Scandinavia," *American Indian Culture and Research Journal* 17, no. 1 (1993): 126.
38. Harald Gaski, "The Secretive Text: Yoik Lyrics as Literature and Tradition," *Nordlit* 5 (1999): 16.
39. Lowery, "Buying the Blueprints," 55–56.
40. Jacqueline Ristola, "'Frozen II' and the Material Necessity of Decolonization," Animation Studies 2.0, January 13, 2020, https://blog.animationstudies.org/?p=3431.
41. Fonneland, "Religion-Making," 8.
42. Huuki and Kyrölä, "'Show Yourself,'" 5.
43. Valkeapää, *Greetings from Lapland*, 113.
44. Gaski, "The Sami People."

45. Erik Kain, "'Frozen 2' Review: The 5 Biggest Problems with Disney's Disappointing Sequel," *Forbes*, December 8, 2019, https://www.forbes.com/sites/erikkain/2019/12/02/the-5-biggest-problems-with-frozen-2/?sh=6a06fba33261.
46. Ibid.
47. Solomon, *The Art of Frozen*, 12.
48. Jessica Julius, *The Art of Frozen II* (San Francisco: Chronicle, 2019), 92.
49. Anne Kalvig, "Nature and Magic as Representation of 'The Sami': Sami Shamanistic Material in Popular Culture," *Religions* 11 (2020): 9.
50. Julius, *The Art of Frozen II*, 95.
51. Huuki and Kyrölä, "'Show Yourself,'" 8.
52. Julius, *The Art of Frozen II*, 94.
53. Ibid., 8.
54. Ibid., 9.
55. Fonneland, "Religion-Making," 8.
56. Ibid., 7.
57. Kalvig, "Nature and Magic," 12.
58. Fonneland, "Religion-Making," 8.
59. Huuki and Kyrölä, "'Show Yourself,'" 9.
60. Julius, *The Art of Frozen II*, 11.
61. Ibid., 108.
62. Kvidal-Røvik and Cordes, "Into the Unknown," 20.
63. Ibid., 28.
64. Fonneland, "Religion-Making," 6.
65. Julius, *The Art of Frozen II*, 94.
66. Kvidal-Røvik and Cordes, "Into the Unknown," 28.
67. Huuki and Kyrölä, "'Show Yourself,'" 10.
68. Ibid., 10.
69. Aslak-Antti Oksanen, "The Rise of Indigenous (Pluri-)Nationalism: The Case of the Sámi People," *Sociology* 54, no. 6 (2020): 1148.
70. Ibid., 1150.
71. Huuki and Kyrölä, "'Show Yourself,'" 5.
72. Edwin Mayorga, Lekey Leidecker, and Daniel Orr de Gutiérrez, "Burn It Down: The Incommensurability of the University and Decolonization," *Journal of Critical Thought and Praxis* 8, no. 1 (2019): 87.
73. Abolition Collective, "Burn It Down: Abolition, Insurgent Political Praxis, and the Destruction of Decency," *Abolition Journal*, April 22, 2018, https://abolitionjournal.org/burn-it-down/.
74. Priya Satia, "Frozen II Isn't Just a Cartoon. It's a Brilliant Critique of Imperialism," *Washington Post*, December 5, 2019, https://www.washingtonpost.com/outlook/2019/12/05/kids-love-anna-elsa-frozen-iis-lesson-is-adults/.
75. Inkoo Kang, "*Frozen 2*'s Bizarre Storyline about Reparations, Explained," *Slate*, November 21, 2019, https://slate.com/culture/2019/11/frozen-2-reparations-northuldra-twist-ending-spoilers.html.
76. Ristola, "'Frozen II' and the Material Necessity of Decolonialization."
77. Kvidal-Røvik and Cordes, "Into the Unknown," 28.
78. Julius, *The Art of Frozen II*, 18.
79. Kvidal-Røvik and Cordes, "Into the Unknown," 23.

80. Ibid., 22.
81. Ibid., 23.
82. Ibid., 25.
83. Fonneland, "Religion-Making," 8.
84. Henry Giroux and Grace Pollock, *The Mouse That Roared: Disney and the End of Innocence* (Plymouth, UK: Rowman & Littlefield, 2010), 27.
85. Kvidal-Røvik and Cordes, "Into the Unknown," 30.

CHAPTER 20

TELEVISION GIRLHOODS, THE MUSICAL: DIVERSITY, IMPERFECTION, AND EMBEDDED FAN PRACTICES IN DISNEY CHANNEL'S *DESCENDANTS*

MORGAN GENEVIEVE BLUE

In May 2022, Disney Branded Television announced the production of a fourth installment in its popular *Descendants* (2015, 2017, 2019) musical-movie franchise, which would extend its story world to "the hostile unincorporated territory of Wonderland."[1] Like previous iterations, the fourth movie would introduce new songs and revisit some familiar Disney classics, but unlike the previous three, *Descendants: The Rise of Red* (initially titled *The Pocketwatch*), directed by Jennifer Phang, would premiere on Disney+ rather than on Disney Channel, centering two new girl protagonists. Interviewed for Deadline, Jennifer Rogers Doyle, a Disney senior vice president, revealed, "The fan engagement and high demand for extensions of *Descendants* continues because viewers have a very special relationship with the core characters and not just because they love the way they look, but because they are relevant, heroic figures, and soon, they'll be invited to meet 'Red' and 'Chloe.'"[2]

While I appreciate the ungendered nature of Doyle's characterization of *Descendants* viewers, Disney Channel ratings identify the majority as girls,[3] and many researchers have argued that Disney television plays a significant role in girls' everyday lives.[4] As such, we might interpret Doyle's comments as an appeal to viewers' (and parents' or guardians') interests in feminine (if not feminist) empowerment. Her reference to the characters' "look" here might allude to the increased representation of performers of color in the franchise or the movies' use of popular trends in its costuming and the recreation of these wardrobes as licensed apparel for young consumers. As I'll explore below, both are applicable. With previous *Descendants* premieres pulling in upward of 10 million viewers apiece in their first three days and their soundtracks being certified gold and topping the *Billboard* Soundtracks and Children's Albums charts, *The Rise of Red* had an impressive legacy to live up to.[5] The ratings successes of this musical franchise and its Disney Channel predecessors *High School Musical* (2006, 2007, 2008)[6] and *The Cheetah Girls* (2003, 2006, 2008), among others, indicates a large audience for television musicals among feminine and feminized youth, which demands scholarly and critical attention. My aim here is to explore how girl audiences might be interpellated by Disney Channel's *Descendants* franchise and how the musicals generate girlhood discourses.

Until recently, scholarly attention to musicals has largely ignored television. In 2011, Robynn J. Stilwell noted that the television musical had "been left out of the discussion almost entirely."[7] This chapter and Kelly Kessler's chapter in this volume help to address the exclusion of television from musical-theater scholarship, as will the forthcoming *Oxford Handbook of the Television Musical*. Television musicals demand our attention because they have played a significant role in the popularization of musical theater on and beyond the screen at multiple points in television history.[8]

For Disney, the popularity of the early 2000s musicals mentioned previously opened the door for additional successful Disney Channel Original Movie musical franchises, including *Camp Rock* (2008, 2010), *Teen Beach Movie* (2013, 2015), *Descendants*, and *Zombies* (2018, 2020, 2022). The ongoing popularity of *High School Musical*, evident in licensing for school productions and spin-offs such as *High School Musical the Musical the Series* on Disney+ (2019–2023), has rendered the children's television musical impossible to ignore and much loved by many.

As I have explored elsewhere, Disney Channel envisions its audience as a female and feminized child and preteen, "tween," consumer market.[9] It targets that audience in large part by developing live-action multicamera sitcoms starring girl performers and by promoting those performers and their characters through lifestyle marketing and music recording.[10] Recognizing the Disney television musical as another significant force in the production and circulation of girlhood discourses, it behooves scholars of both Disney media and musicals, as well as childhood and youth researchers, to explore the meaning(s) and identities represented in and through these texts.

Although much has been written about Disney's musical fairy-tale films, there has been limited scholarly attention to Disney television musicals. A few scholars have provided critical perspectives on issues of identity and representation in Disney Channel musicals, including Dominic Symonds (2017) and Angharad N. Valdivia (2008, 2011). Others, including Natalie Coulter (2012), Katalin Lustyik (2013), Anna Potter (2012), and Tyler Bickford (2012), locate *High School Musical* as an enduring property with significant strategic relevance for the Walt Disney Company across multiple industry contexts. Still others, most notably Shiri Reznik and Dafna Lemish (2011), Nancy Jennings (2014), Ingvild Sorrensen (2014), and Cynthia Maurer (2018), have taken an ethnographic approach to explore Disney television's functions among audiences, specifically with regard to how girls negotiate messages about friendship and romance in Disney series and movies.

Jennings finds that girls use their favorite Disney Channel and Nickelodeon characters to build a sense of community and explore self-expression, which aligns with common themes in Disney's television musicals.[11] Reznik and Lemish argue that the girls in their study interpret *High School Musical*'s depictions of teen romance in various ways depending on their cultural contexts and use the franchise to exercise their "melodramatic imagination."[12] Ien Ang theorizes identification with melodramatic television characters as especially gratifying for viewers whose identities are most constrained by social norms. For these viewers, many of whom are women, such engagement with fantasy can provide recognition of "the weighty pressure of reality on one's subjectivity, one's wishes, one's desires," as well as "room to indulge in [sentimental and melancholic] feelings."[13] Girl audiences, then, may come to Disney media in search of fantastical and melodramatic modes of femininity through which they might process their own feelings, identifications, and experiences. As Stacy Wolf argues, "the representation and performance of gender and sexuality function as building blocks as basic to the form as song, dance, script, or design."[14] The musical for Disney Channel is constrained by reliance on television production technologies as well as being gendered to cater to Disney's real and imagined girl audiences. In addition to seeking melodramatic identification, those audiences also demand original (or newly adapted) narratives, on-trend music, and fashion-forward costuming in stories that feature familiar young and youthful performers.

A Royal Prep School to the Rescue

Disney Channel programs of recent decades frequently narrativize sanitized and simplified versions of high school life and teenage relationships for preteen and family audiences, building on common social issues of belonging and becoming. As Coulter describes them, Disney's "soft" teen media "showcase the zany hijinks of musical teens as they navigate the trials and tribulations of high school clique culture."[15] Given the social stratification and identity struggles commonly used to illustrate teenage life in the US and frequently reified on Disney Channel, the themes of belonging and becoming seem inexhaustible, if overused. Yet *Descendants*' ensemble cast and themes of teamwork, friendship, and unity might push beyond the neoliberal logics of so much other Disney media, which frequently privilege individual choice and empowerment rhetoric over collaboration and structural change.

The original premise of the *Descendants* franchise is that the teenage children of exiled fairy-tale villains Maleficent (Kristin Chenoweth), the Evil Queen (Kathy Najimy), Cruella de Vil (Wendy Raquel Robinson), and Jafar (Maz Jobrani) are invited to leave their homes on the Isle of the Lost and live in Auradon among fairy-tale royalty, including Cinderella's Fairy Godmother (Melanie Paxson) and Queen Belle (Keegan Connor Tracy) and King Adam/Beast (Dan Payne) and their children, who attend Auradon Prep boarding school. Having been unceremoniously selected by Prince

Ben (son of Belle and the Beast), Mal (played by Dove Cameron) and her three friends escape their toxic parents and their exile. Their new school is a converted fairy-tale castle and constitutes the center of nearly all activity in Auradon—the scene for royal proclamations, extravagant parties, and celebratory performances.

In stark contrast to Auradon, the Isle of the Lost is presented as an industrial scrap heap, whose inhabitants are deprived of basic necessities and are (or have become) bitter, competitive, and conniving. Yet the villain kids or self-titled "VKs," Mal, Evie (Sofia Carson), Carlos (Cameron Boyce), and Jay (Booboo Stewart), demonstrate devotion to their home and one another as they dance and sing through streets and warehouses. Each of these four VKs represents a new branch of a villain family tree, and their costumes and personalities demonstrate that heritage. Although the stories unfold in different ways and foreground various characters (e.g., Ursula's daughter Uma [China Anne McClain], Aurora's daughter Audrey [Sarah Jeffery], and Hades [Cheyenne Jackson] as Mal's dad), each of the initial three *Descendants* musicals stems from Mal's struggles to break from her mother's evil ways and unite her Isle and Auradon identities. The fantastical, fairy-tale aspect of the trilogy arguably pulls the narrative away from typical representations of high school drama and positions its teen characters as accomplished young adults with significant authority in their worlds.[16]

Despite the movie's ensemble cast, Mal is foregrounded as the primary protagonist across all three movies. She provides voice-over narration and exposition at the outset of the first movie and teases a sequel at the end.[17] The *Descendants* title sequence establishes the movie as a modern twist on Disney's traditional fairy tale(s), starting with the image of a leatherbound book embossed with a title graphic. This is a direct reference to the storytelling aspect of Disney's early fairy-tale films, many of which begin in this way. Here, though, the book shares its perch on a table with a familiar accoutrement of modern feminine performativity: two bottles of fingernail polish in rebellious shades of neon purple and green. The book opens to reveal not an ornate title page as in earlier fairy-tale adaptations but the glossy screen of an electronic tablet. Purple-nailed fingers swipe upward to "turn" pages and pinch the screen to pull a gleaming castle up into relief, as the narration begins, "Once upon a time..."

Mal narrates an origin story, beginning with Belle marrying "her Beast" (symbolized by a towering wedding cake, which Mal swipes through and topples). Instead of taking a honeymoon, "Beast united all the kingdoms and got himself elected president of the United States of Auradon." A map briefly presents the various locales of the kingdom, and Mal describes how the king "rounded up ... basically all the really interesting people and booted them off to the Isle of the Lost." She describes the Isle as "My hood. No magic, no Wi-Fi, and no way out." She doesn't call it a prison, but it's clearly a trap, an exile, and a punishment that has reverberated through generations and which only optimistic youth—represented by Prince Ben and eventually Mal, too—can repair. In a sense, the three movies constitute a Disneyfied, tween-centric, immigration or post-incarceration story, choreographed and vocalized, in large part, through Mal's white, cis, heteronormative girlhood.

If the United States of Auradon is an allusion to the United States of America, the Isle of the Lost might hark back to the historical use of penal colonies by multiple nations of the West, including Great Britain's use of North America and Australia to divert convicted and incarcerated persons and perhaps institutions like the US island prison of Alcatraz. But the experience of life on the Isle is presented not as incarceration per se. As a colony with limited resources and cut off from the Auradon mainland and popular consciousness, the Isle might also suggest life on one of the US's many claimed island territories. In this fantastical version, the VKs lack access to basic necessities such as sunlight, agricultural produce, and education, and their status as "other" and outsider aligns them with "at-risk" youth discourses. If "at-risk" youth discourse is predominantly applied to youths of color and people living in poverty, the Isle distills such socioeconomic disadvantages down to being (or choosing to be) "evil." As Anita Harris argues, "structural disadvantage is ... reworked as at-risk, such that young women, their families, and communities can be held responsible for outcomes that are socioeconomic in nature."[18] Isle residents are free to make the best of their limited resources, albeit contained to a single location and without access to magic. By the end of the *Descendants* trilogy, Mal and friends have removed the barrier that entraps Isle residents and have revealed a bridge between the two lands, inviting the other villain kids to come to Auradon.

Although Mal's narration introduces the story, the first face we see in the initial *Descendants* movie is that of Prince Ben (played by Mitchell Hope) as his tailor fits him for a new suit. Belle and the Beast (in human form) enter, and Ben explains that he would like to offer asylum to the children of the Isle of the Lost. As the first family introduced in the movie, and perhaps despite their royalty and the Beast's potential for animal transformation, these three represent the narrative's normative nuclear family. They live in abundance and treat one another with kindness and love. They are also phenotypically white and wear the colors popularized by the *Beauty and the Beast* films, yellow and blue, a motif repeated in Auradon Prep's sports and marching-band uniforms so that all of Auradon might be dressed in, and united by, their image. Prince Ben has selected the first four kids he would like to welcome to Auradon, and when the king and queen ask who their parents are, the mention of Maleficent enrages them. They eventually admit that the villains' children are, of course, "innocent" and don't deserve their imprisonment. And now, finally, with the blessing of the king, we get to meet those "children" (they are teenagers) and enjoy the first choreographed musical performance of the hour.

The villain kids' anthem, "Rotten to the Core," introduces the four main characters as they dance and parkour through the dilapidated cityscape of the Isle of the Lost, committing (what on Auradon might be) petty crimes along the way. Mal is foregrounded first, painting colorful graffiti—her tag being a royal crest of sorts made from "Long LIVE/EVIL"—but the other three characters are given more detailed treatments, glimpses into their personalities and strengths as they explore an outdoor market. Evie sings that "I never got no love" and later describes herself as a "flirt" as she gazes at a (male) vendor and passes through his array of scarves, linking her to heteronormative romance and to textile work and fashion; Jay charms and steals his way through vendor stalls, showcasing his athleticism and collecting gold items for his father to sell; Carlos reveals his mischievous, puppy-like nature and talent for dance as he bounds under and over obstacles, playfully taunting bystanders. They join in the street with other Isle residents for a dance-mob finale.

In Disney's behind-the-scenes rehearsal footage available on the *Descendants* DVD and shared on YouTube, one member of the choreography team reveals that the dance was largely inspired by 1970s punk, because it's "aggressive and it's dirty and it's gritty."[19] As the introductory performance, she wanted it to be "the one piece that you can just let loose and really go for it."[20] Carson comments on the "hairography," and Cameron mentions the sweat they generate and the "animalistic" aspect of immersing herself in the performance. The music provides an electronic-dance-pop backdrop, which might contradict the grittiness of the choreography. But the mostly spoken vocals add a slightly ominous layer. With a chorus sung by Cameron and Carson, the actors' voices, while recognizable, are audibly tuned to correspond to the music. This, of course, is common practice for recording artists, but as I argue below, incongruities between the actors' abilities and the various demands of each performance might serve a productive function for Disney Channel viewers.

THE DISNEY CHANNEL ORIGINAL MOVIE, BUT MAKE IT A MUSICAL

As with any Disney production, the role of the corporation in Disney Channel's musicals cannot be overstated. As David Savran writes regarding Disney Theatrical on Broadway, corporations are "the true Broadway stars in the twenty-first century. They are the bestowers of identity, community, and the magical power of the franchise."[21] Certainly, the additional constraints of being produced for television and Disney Channel's close relation to Disney Music Group position television musicals directly in conversation with the goals of the larger Walt Disney Company. Former CEO Bob Chapek claimed that the company's goals for 2022 were "storytelling excellence, innovation, and a relentless focus on our audience."[22] Although in its Broadway productions Disney tends to eschew recognizable performers and directors to better exalt its intellectual property,[23] the constant call for new programming that appeals to young audiences means that Disney's television musicals take the opposite tack. The Disney Channel musicals discussed here rely instead on the familiar faces and voices of Disney Channel stars and on experienced directors, such as Kenny Ortega, who can lend their credentials by training and advising Disney performers and promoting the musical as quality family fare.

Across the conglomerate's many divisions, issues of representation and diversity have been increasingly important for the past few decades, but only recently have they been centered by upper-level executives. As Diana Leon-Boys notes, Chapek, whose brief tenure as Disney CEO ended in 2022, pledged in 2020 to focus on greater diversity and inclusion. Disney's subsequent "2021 Corporate Social Responsibility Report," according to Leon-Boys, easily aligns with "'woke' Disney" discourse by centering diversity and inclusion throughout.[24] Yet, because Disney Channel largely idealizes a normative, feminized consumer tween audience, it continues to produce representations of postfeminist and color-blind girlhoods, privileging whiteness, thinness, and material wealth.[25] Turning an antiracist, feminist critical lens toward Disney's *Descendants* provides an opportunity to better understand how normative girlhood discourses continue to structure Disney Channel franchises even as Disney invests in greater diversity.

The *Descendants* franchise speaks to the Walt Disney Company's efforts to simultaneously shore up and rejuvenate its early texts and characters, particularly through attention to diversity, inclusion, and feminine empowerment. *Descendants* easily repurposes for Disney Channel audiences the central conceit of the popular ABC series *Once upon a Time* (2011–2018), which mines Disney versions (among others) of fairy tales and myths to unite iconic characters in a single story world. *Descendants* and its sequels can also be understood as the television version of Disney's successful formula of producing live-action remakes and prequels for theatrical release, as evident in its growing list of such films, including *101 Dalmatians* (1996), *Cinderella* (2015), *Beauty and the Beast* (2017), *Aladdin* (2019), *Mulan* (2020), *Cruella* (2021), and *The Little Mermaid* (2023). Also worth noting are Disney's live-action extensions of *Sleeping Beauty* in *Maleficent* (2014) and *Maleficent 2: Mistress of Evil* (2019), which help cement Maleficent's iconicity for new audiences and center the villain's story.

Positioned within a landscape of series and interstitials (the advertisements, network promotions, and short videos in between programs) that routinely foreground diegetic music and/or performance,[26] Disney Channel Original Movies can use the musical format to connect television audiences, performers, and licensing efforts to other mediated worlds, in excess of the intertextual and cross-cultural references baked into the music and the choreography. The original *Descendants* trilogy, in particular, banks on intertextuality and embedded fan practices as strategies for trans-media franchise expansion. *Descendants* revives and reprises characters and themes from iconic Walt Disney Studios animated musicals. including *Snow White and the Seven Dwarfs* (1937), *Cinderella* (1950), *One Hundred and One Dalmatians* (1961), *The Little Mermaid* (1989), *Beauty and the Beast* (1991), and *Aladdin* (1992), among others. Instead of centering Disney's princess characters, however, *Descendants* revisits these films' villain characters, creating new links between Disney's television offerings, musical performance, and its library of feature films. *Descendants* director Ortega is well known for his Disney choreography and director roles, including for *Cheetah Girls 2* (2006), the *High School Musical* movies, and *Newsies* (1992), along with related music videos and making-of shorts. Commenting on *Descendants*, he references the historical significance of its characters and his role in the franchise: "I felt a great sense of responsibility—these are major Disney heritage characters. They aren't just given to anyone."[27] Ortega's influence helps position the Disney Channel musical in conversation with Disney's fairy-tale history and Broadway history.

The casting of Chenoweth as *Descendants*' Maleficent also calls Broadway to mind due to her fame as Galinda/Glinda the Good alongside Idina Menzel's "Wicked Witch" Elphaba in one of the longest-running musicals on Broadway, *Wicked* (2003–). Chenoweth provides a suitably campy and feminine musical villain while lending her Broadway credentials and vocal strength to the introductory *Descendants* movie. Indeed, although she nearly disappears from the narrative later in the movie, Chenoweth's Maleficent performs the movie's first "I Want" song, "Evil Like Me." She appears to her daughter Mal as an all-too-real hallucination—her wax-museum likeness comes to life to manipulate Mal. Maleficent tries to persuade Mal to want what her mother wants: to use magic, to gain power, to "be evil." She sings and dances around Mal, and we sense that Maleficent sings *on behalf of* Mal. Chenoweth gives a virtuosic performance that blends musical styles and incorporates multiple character voices into a single song. This song proves a deft use of Chenoweth's talents in proximity to Cameron and at a powerful moment early in the narrative.

Mal's/Cameron's role as a spectator, as a fan, and as an aspiring diva becomes palpable here. She gazes, even grins, at Maleficent/Chenoweth, awed by her and eager to join in. While some *Descendants* viewers, perhaps especially teen or adult viewers, will have been drawn in by the presence of *Wicked* diva Chenoweth,[28] most young viewers of the premiere were likely more familiar with Emmy Award–winning Disney Channel star Cameron of *Liv & Maddie* (2013–2017) fame. Elsewhere, I have argued that in her *Liv & Maddie* roles, Cameron's pop vocals and hyperfeminine performances become queer technologies.[29] Cameron's lack of virtuosity in *Descendants*, exhibited by her straight performance style, lack of dance experience, and limited vocal power, also emphasizes the artifice of her performances and locates her as decidedly an *aspiring* diva. In this way, she can speak powerfully to young viewers as they sing along. As the primary protagonist of the movie(s), leader among the villain kids, and eventually the franchise's queen of Auradon, Cameron *could* be *Descendants*' reigning diva. However, the franchise's ensemble musical form encourages multiple diva identifications.

Evie, daughter of *Snow White*'s Evil Queen, is Mal's devoted best friend, confidant, voice of reason, and conscience. Seemingly brainwashed by her mother on the Isle, whose evil is here distilled into simple vanity, Evie comes to Auradon seeking only a handsome and wealthy prince to marry. But she quickly discovers self-fulfillment through building a fashion-design business supported by her new friends and acquaintances. *Wicked*, Wolf argues, is structured by two women's evolving homosocial relationship rather than by heterosexual romance.[30] Like *Wicked*, *Descendants* is primarily structured by friendships—Evie's with Mal and the bonds they share with friends Jay and Carlos. In addition to the many ensemble performances throughout the trilogy, in *Descendants 2*, Evie and Mal perform "Space Between," in which they pledge their undying friendship over a montage of their most intimate moments. Although several of the musical performances in the trilogy also offer nods to fan practices of shipping (the creation of new, often queer or nonconforming character relationships through fan fiction and video editing),[31] as I'll discuss more below, the characters, Evie included, are nearly all paired into heteroromantic couples by the end of the first movie, and romantic subplots also structure sequels and spin-off media.

Evie's "I Want" song doesn't occur until the third movie, in which she must kiss Doug (Dopey's son, played by Zachary Gibson) for the first time, to save his life. Evie, though not exactly representing Latinidad in character, is played by Colombian American actor and singer Carson. Frequent reminders that she has prioritized her friendships (and her fashion-design business) over romance might help counteract harmful tropes of hypersexuality or hyperfertility in representations of Latina girls.[32] Evie's narrative arc is demonstrated in her evolution from her performance of the "flirt" in the introductory cast performance, "Rotten to the Core," to her hesitancy over a first kiss in "One Kiss," in which she sings, "Does he love me? Or does he not?" with friends Mal and Uma providing backing vocals and spying from the doorway. Although Evie's dance might be viewed as sexually suggestive in some moments, it becomes abruptly clumsy and comical when she tries to dance with Doug while he sleeps. As she dances with Doug, who is phenotypically white and a privileged citizen of Auradon, Evie literally carries him, sleeping, on her back. Her performance offers both a fantasy of romantic love and a touch of silly physical comedy, which might be a comfort for young Disney Channel viewers. As I explore below, Evie also brings fan practices, American dream mythos, and neoliberal economic principles into view via her portrayal of entrepreneurial femininity.

As the two primary girl characters of the franchise, Evie and Mal together provide a model of supportive girlfriendship[33] and avoid common tropes of girlhood competitiveness and postfeminist individualism, at the risk of introducing other problematic tropes.

The Power of Imperfect Girlhood

As the narrator and as a leader among her friend group, Mal's presence can easily uphold neoliberal notions of self-empowered girlhood where the girl is constructed as "the ideal citizen, ambassadress, or savior/leader of her nation ... to counter the perceived threats of globalization and migration."[34] Mal's mother is presented as the ultimate leader of the villains, juxtaposed against her more mild-tempered sidekicks. Mal's ruling evil heritage, along with her malleable whiteness, presents an escape from her "at-risk" existence on the Isle of the Lost. And when given proximity to wealth and citizenship (here royalty and sovereignty) in Auradon, Mal is able to find her individuality and her sense of community by overcoming her need for her mother's approval and rejecting her mother's self-serving motives. While Maleficent (Chenoweth) performs Mal's initial "I Want" song, Mal finds her voice soon after, in "If Only," when she sings about falling in love with Ben. Mal's motivation might seem to be her romance with Ben, but ultimately, Mal is positioned as a leader, first on the Isle, then among her displaced friend group, and finally for all as she unites the Isle with Auradon.

Solo performances, such as the characters' "I Want" songs, as well as many of the cast performances and duets, are produced as music-video-ready interludes that move their narratives forward and engage audiences across multiple platforms. For instance, the DisneyMusic Channel on YouTube features "official music videos" of Cameron's performances of "My Once upon a Time" from *Descendants 3*, when she sings about her mistakes, and a cover of Christina Aguilera's "Genie in a Bottle" (1999) from the spin-off series *Descendants: Wicked World* (2015–2017).[35] Cameron's duets with

Carson, Chenoweth, McClain, and Jackson also appear in the Disney YouTube lineup. Cameron's and Carson's solo and duet performances are juxtaposed with montages of previous *Descendants* scenes between the duet partners or between the singer and a friend or love interest. This approach makes each performance easily extractable from the larger movie, requiring no further editing or postproduction attention prior to being circulated for promotions.

The use of montage encourages viewers' melodramatic identifications, both within the narrative by revisiting previous scenes and apart from the narrative through online access to the music videos.[36] The movies can thus generate nostalgia for the franchise from the first viewing. This built-in nostalgia and repetition of intimate moments also can encourage young viewers to imagine a variety of cross-cultural, romantic, heterosocial, and homosocial relationships between characters. This might be understood as the franchise taking up the resistant fan practices of shipping and vidding (re-editing or creating videos to alter stories and characterizations).[37] The movies model these practices in some ways but also depoliticize them by presenting already "re-edited" videos that emphasize the movies' canonical relationships. Of course, fans continue to engage in shipping and vidding practices using these texts.[38] Nonetheless, Disney's ready-made approach, apparent in its music videos as well as elsewhere,[39] might also discourage viewers' creativity when it comes to reinterpreting these aspirational narratives.

As in the case of film musicals, one benefit of the television musical is its use of prerecorded music, which can allow performers to focus on the physicality of acting and dance. Unlike film musicals, made-for-TV movie musicals must work as promotional texts for their network and therefore can be constrained by the network's aesthetics, audiences, and available talent. Relying not on live performances but instead on lip-syncing also means it can be noticeable when a performer is not able to generate congruity. Carson's and Cameron's lip-syncing efforts are notably incongruous in their solo performances. Cameron's Mal mouths multiple, overlapping vocal parts in "If Only," and both performers attend more to dramatic facial expression than to singing verisimilitude. There is a visible lack of lung power behind their pantomimes, and the further incorporation of speech affects calls attention to performativity. In these moments, the characters might be seen as "unfinished" in the sense Heather Warren-Crow uses the term. And this can have particularly compelling results for audiences, by "[facilitating] greater participation."[40] Applying Peter Lunenfeld's concept of "the aesthetic of unfinish," Warren-Crow argues that "'unfinished' has a number of connotations that resonate with familiar understandings of childhood, and especially, girlhood—such as unbuilt, unrealized, unresolved, and incomplete."[41]

The musical's reliance on direct address, along with the incongruities of lip-syncing, might challenge audiences' suspension of disbelief. In her performances of "If Only" and "Rotten to the Core," in particular, Cameron provides Mal with the affect of pronouncing words that begin with M through a mischievous grin that exposes her top teeth as if to bite her tongue. This affect marks her performances as distinctly hers while also opening to interpretation the lyrics and the performance itself. Although the voice is hers, she is clearly *not* singing here. But the mask provided by heavily produced, catchy, prerecorded music also makes these performances clear invitations for viewers to bring their own personalities and mannerisms to the songs, to perform alongside (or over) the stars, to know the stars through their characters within and beyond the text, and to practice their Disney fandom through music. Whether intentional or not, such an appearance of "unfinish" creates space for imperfection and personality. As performers, Cameron and Carson might thus resemble aspiring divas passing as Disney fans, as girls in the audience.

GIRL HOODS AS POST-RACIAL FANTASYLANDS

As a unifying force and ambiguously racialized girl of color in *Descendants*, Carson's Evie also represents the reworking of past narratives and characterizations that overtly privilege upper-class, white, thin, domestic femininity, to instead demonstrate the Disney company's broad claims of attention to diversity and inclusion. Evie resists stereotypical imagery and challenges neoliberal girlhood discourses, even as she represents their successful navigation both on the Isle of the Lost and in Auradon. Both places might be understood as postfeminist, post-racial fantasylands where structural differences are offloaded onto individual characters and their "evil" deeds. Leon-Boys analyzes representations of Latinidad and girlhood in Disney media and at Disney theme parks and argues, "By providing images that are ambiguously brown, Disney takes a flexible approach to representation that is not limited to Latinidad."[42] Her concept of "flexible Latinidad" provides an excellent framework for understanding how girls of color can function as the link(s) between ethnic ambiguity and ethnic specificity in Disney media. In the case of *Descendants*, where cultural differences that span story worlds, continents, and centuries are collapsed to be recognizable to a narrowly defined contemporary audience, the ambiguous Brown girl body provides enough ethnic specificity to be identified as "not white" but is denied cultural specificities beyond the distinctions between Isle and Auradon lives.

Writing about *Cheetah Girls* character Chanel, Valdivia finds that the Latina "plays the bridge whether in terms of class, language and nation, and girlfriend solidarity."[43] *Descendants*' Evie represents Latina girlhood in close proximity to whiteness, preventing reliance on overused Black-best-friend tropes, even after the *Descendants 2* entrance of Ursula's daughter Uma, who is played by Black actor McClain and whose performances are more overtly inflected by Black musical and movement traditions.[44] Evie gains representational space for US Latinidad but might also "replace or displace Blackness from the mainstream."[45] In *Descendants*, there is no overt cultural distinction to be made between girls' languages or accented speech within the diegesis. However, fans who view Disney Channel content on YouTube will hear Carson speak Spanish as she gives a behind-the-scenes tour on the set of *Descendants 3*.[46] And her character's sense of national identity, while likely distinct from that of those who live in Auradon, is also bound to Auradon by a colonial relationship. While she may not function in as stark a way as other "bridge" characters, Evie arguably extends that trajectory of representation.

Although *Descendants* creates a more racially diverse and inclusive fairy-tale world, it continues to be structured by whiteness in some ways. Auradon is this fairy tale's land of promise, a present-day pastel fantasy of privilege and security and joy, built by othering and imprisoning its "evil" population, or, as Mal describes them, "all the really interesting people." In addition to the ways in which Mal's desire for assimilation and the fairy-tale tropes of heteronormative romance might represent the franchise's centering of whiteness, whiteness also provides a structuring presence via Disney's attempts to attend to aspects of diversity and inclusion. The cast is racially and ethnically diverse, and many of the characters seem to be cast in a color-blind manner such that historically white-appearing characters are played by actors of color but with little attention to the differences in experience and positionality such changes might imply. This creates a sense of what Kristen J. Warner has called "visible invisibility," wherein a network books "racially ambiguous actors in non-racially specific roles."[47]

Such practice is not particularly new, nor is it exclusive to Disney Channel, but its use in *Descendants* suggests a return to earlier efforts at diversity in representation that centered on tokenism and multiculturalism. As Mary C. Beltrán has argued in relation to Hollywood cinema, "An emphasis on actors with an 'is she or isn't she?' off-white look can be said to erase ethnic difference and deny the nation's and the film industry's history of racial discrimination."[48] *Descendants* characters do not comment on racial or ethnic differences, beyond maintaining that residents of the Isle are not like the residents of Auradon, due to their parentage. Royal and villain kids' backstories are glossed over, their interracial heritage unexplored, but several of the primary performers and many of the chorus and background performers are phenotypically brown, aligning easily with the generally post-racial perspective of the movie. Just as Disney media continue to reproduce the fetishization of youth and femininity, so do they fetishize racially mixed and ethnically ambiguous bodies.[49]

While Carson's Evie can represent flexible Latina girlhood and allows the narrative to sidestep the Black-best-friend trope, her friends Jay and Carlos, as well as Auradon kid and sometime-villain Audrey, might represent multiracial ambiguity. These key characters are played by multiracial actors Stewart, Boyce, and Jeffery, each of whom presents as phenotypically *not* exactly Black or white. Stilwell has argued, "In an era when ... Disney has been seen as perpetuating racial and ethnic stereotypes in its animated films, it seems a positive step to present a multiracial cast as 'natural.'"[50] Even so, Disney's "race-blind casting" demands further critical attention.

Similar to Valdivia's conceptualization of the Disney Latina bridge figure is Ralina Joseph's argument that "the exceptional multiracial figure is scripted to dismiss the 'black voice' so much that it erases blackness entirely."[51] By representing difference for its own sake (rather than for the sake of the narrative or as part of a nuanced characterization), these multiracial performers can manifest the Disney corporation's diversity efforts through the creation of multiracial (not multi*cultural*) fantasylands. The franchise's reliance on bodies and voices of color in culturally nonspecific roles also aligns with both Warner's arguments about the "plastic representation"[52] of color-blind television casting and Warren-Crow's theorization of girlhood as plastic and applicable to any body or image.[53] Plasticity is evident here both in the trilogy's use of racial and ethnic ambiguities and in its routine presentation of girlhood as unfinished, malleable, and produced relationally, whether through diegetic pairings or fan practices of shipping and bounding (more on this below). In this way, *Descendants* looks racially diverse but speaks a language of aspirational whiteness.

EMBEDDED DISNEY FANDOM AND EVIE'S ENTREPRENEURIAL FEMININITY

In addition to the ways in which the franchise invites viewers to envision themselves as performers, the milieu, environs, and musical influences of *Descendants* also reproduce Disney fan practices of bounding and crafting. Bounding is the fan practice of creating "stylish outfits that capture the essence of fictional characters or media, without directly evoking the characters."[54] As Kelsey Borresen points out, bounding was originally popularized by Disney fans as "Disneybounding."[55] Related to this practice, fans also use their crafting skills to create unlicensed apparel and accessories to sell to other fans. In *Descendants*, original costumes create clear-cut color stories to distinguish the characters, their families, and their communities. This is not unique to *Descendants* or even Disney media, although it is also readily apparent across Disney Channel, including in *High School Musical* and *Zombies*. Here, though, the costumes and color stories are built on a relation to non–Disney Channel characters, referencing the VKs' villainous parents who originate in Disney's oldest fairy-tale adaptations. In nearly every aspect, the kids' wardrobes actively rejuvenate those historic Disney characters and their films while also producing their own modernized styles for viewers to replicate or reference. In a sense, the VKs and their Auradon counterparts participate in the fan practice of Disneybounding by working Disney references into their everyday attire in ways that avoid direct textual reference or licensed merchandise. Rebecca Williams explains that Disneybounding "involves the piecing together of mass-market clothing items and accessories to reflect the style or color palette of a specific Disney character, film, or theme park attraction."[56]

Disney licenses merchandise for *Descendants* fans just as it has with many other franchises, including marketing signature ready-to-wear outfits that resemble the characters' wardrobes. Target stores sell *Descendants* clothing lines, for example, that range from graphic T-shirts to everyday outfits to Halloween costumes. While many of the offerings center around Mal's dark purple and black color palette, there have also been multiple offerings featuring Uma or referencing her green and aqua wardrobe and some based on Evie's red and blue wardrobe. Disney Stores have offered character dolls and a range of clothing, including multiple iterations of faux-leather moto-style jackets referencing Mal's, Evie's, and Uma's various looks.[57] Of particular interest here is the work this apparel does within the narrative and the larger Disney universe. When viewed as bounding, wearing it represents a resistant fan practice, elsewhere employed to circumvent the corporation's licensing constraints and cosplay bans,[58] now embedded in a Disney narrative without which its characters would be unrecognizable.

Related to this, Evie pursues her talent for fashion design throughout the trilogy—she creates special-occasion gowns and suits that reflect the personal style of each wearer, using her newfound Auradon resources. This is reminiscent of the domestic femininity taken up by Snow White as she mends clothing for her housemates.[59] In Evie's case, sewing skill is subsumed by the larger entrepreneurial enterprise of designing, constructing, and delivering garments that adhere to the narrative's Disneybounding aesthetic, a business she grows, which provides her with authority and autonomy. She conducts fittings first in her school dorm room and later develops her own label, Evie's 4 Hearts, in her own cottage ostensibly purchased with money from the business and where she resides and rehomes other villain kids. Tellingly, her solo performances are sung and choreographed in her studio spaces, scattered with textiles and sewing equipment.

Evie benefits from the neoliberal logics of entrepreneurial femininity even in the fantasy world of Auradon, where wealth, health, and happiness are accessible to all. As Brooke Erin Duffy and Emily Hund argue, entrepreneurial femininity is one manifestation of postfeminism in which individual choice renders invisible labor and economic investment in order to produce the self through career success.[60] Evie does not struggle with belonging in Auradon. Indeed, from the moment she sets foot in Auradon, she is enamored with its opulence, and she swiftly finds her niche as the school's, and by extension the kingdom's, dressmaker. She not only takes refuge here from the Isle, but she also builds a new life that takes advantage of the wealth of resources in Auradon, and she appoints herself ambassador to other talented children trapped on the Isle.

In the sequels, Evie mentors other girls from the Isle who show creative promise but lack economic resources. As Harris has found with regard to the significance of consumer citizenship in "can-do" girlhood discourse, "Both economic independence and ambassadorial status are best realized in entrepreneurship and entrepreneurship is best realized in the making and marketing of disposable lifestyle commodities to be purchased by other young women."[61] Evie's easy integration into Auradon results from her entrepreneurial skills and talent for fashion design, recognized by her new peers. This acceptance facilitates her successful relation to her new life of access and abundance. Beyond the display of American dream mythos, her entrepreneurial acumen and creative reputation, as well as her peacemaking efforts among her friends, make her a unifying force for the communities of Auradon and the Isle of the Lost. Evie thus also can represent an optimistic model of social and economic integration out of imperialist exile—a challenge to the perceived threat of migration.

Seeing the fan practices of bounding and crafting embedded in *Descendants*' characterizations, and especially exemplified by Evie, can encourage viewers to engage in these practices using their own skills and resources, and it can also work as lifestyle branding for licensed *Descendants* clothing and costumes. This may not constitute a new strategy on Disney's part, since fashion licensing has long been an aspect of Disney Channel marketing.[62] However, it adds another dimension to the intertextual nature of the *Descendants* franchise and targets Disney fans more directly than have previous musical franchises from the network.[63]

Queer Time for Normative Subjects

The populations of Auradon and the Isle, hailing from disparate fairy-tale adaptations as they do, are so diverse that to envision them in a single story world means collapsing time and place and culture. Aside from their socioeconomic, ethnic, and racial differences, decades (even centuries) also separate the characters, in their respective narrative contexts and in their emergence within the Disney oeuvre.[64] What unites them here is the intergenerational connection fabricated by the *Descendants* premise. In a sense, the franchise queers time by crafting its narratives on a foundation that can only work through what Elizabeth Freeman calls "queer hypersociability."[65] By collapsing time, the franchise insists on universalizing temporal identifications and their subjects, glossing over or ignoring differences between individuals and groups to craft them all as subjects of a familiar (Disneyfied) contemporary moment.

While the narrative reifies the heteronormative relations of its phenotypically white royalty (i.e., Belle, the Beast, Prince Ben, and eventually Mal), it also shrouds in mystery its villains' life trajectories and suggests a variety of kinship patterns not always aligned with "the middle-class Anglo-American norm of the monogamous nuclear household."[66] The four original VKs are introduced as simultaneously being raised in single-parent families and living communally with one another. As exiles, they all exist outside the labor logics of Auradon. In "Rotten to the Core," the VKs perform their identities as rebellious youth making their way in a world not beholden to Auradon's norms. Following Jack Halberstam's theorization, we might consider as queer subjects those who "live outside of reproductive and familial time as well as on the edges of logics of labor and production,"[67] such as the people of the Isle and, perhaps, some families of Auradon, whose kinship patterns rely on adoption and guardianship and whose youths live in community with friends at school.

Yet as the VKs search for belonging in Auradon and try to make space there for more kids from the Isle, the movie reveals its heteronormative structure, perhaps as a reaction to the queer potential of "radical girlness"[68] that it might otherwise produce. As multiple scholars have argued, girlhood is characterized by liminality, as a transitory identity.[69] Whitney Monaghan explores how queerness has also been routinely represented this way in commercial media. She argues that representations of queer girlhoods can "eschew the logic of forward-moving, linear, and teleological temporality, offering a new way of thinking about queerness, girlhood, and growing up."[70] Seemingly in avoidance of this, *Descendants* drives toward normativity in nearly every instance, refashioning (or abandoning, in the case of the villains who don't reappear) its queer subjects. In Mal's case, her duets with Maleficent in *Descendants* and later with her father, Hades, in *Descendants 3*, demonstrate her complicated relationships with her estranged parents and the supposed damage done by their failure to conform.

Heteronormative relations are centralized in her performance of the rock-derived "Do What You Gotta Do" with Hades, for example, when Hades expresses to Mal, "you're stronger with those Daddy issues." The line is a nod to adult audiences that gives the performance a sexualized aspect as the pair dance together in Hades's darkened underground lair. The performance reproduces compulsory heterosexuality through its caricature of toxic masculinity, attempting to recuperate potentially queer characters toward heteronormativity. In addition to the ongoing romance between Mal and Ben, who marry in a spin-off, nearly every other VK and Auradon kid is also part of a seemingly heteroromantic pair at some point in the trilogy. Notable exceptions to this include the pairing of Jay and Gil (Gaston's son, played by Dylan Playfair), who bashfully realize they have common interests in *Descendants 3* and decide to "take a gap year" together, and Evie, who, although loyal to Doug, prioritizes career and friendships. My point is not to suggest that queer identificatory potential might be limited to these characters or to specific narrative sequences. I mean to point to some of the trilogy's queer aspects, while demonstrating that the franchise, like much Disney media, remains largely structured by heteronormative identification.

Conclusion

In an era of pronounced attention to diversity and inclusion in mainstream culture, Disney Channel could create high-impact properties that reconfigure its past narratives and characters to acknowledge, if not also represent, the diversity of its audiences. *Descendants* attempts to do this and perhaps sometimes even succeeds. *Descendants* uses girlhood discourses in conjunction with contemporary music and dance to re-Disneyfy its oldest properties for its imagined early-twenty-first-century tween consumer audience. Relying on intertextual references that span many of Disney's most well-known musical fairy-tale adaptations, this franchise collapses history and disregards its characters' sociohistorical significance. It reworks famous Disney musical numbers such as "Be Our Guest" from *Beauty and the Beast* and "Dig a Little Deeper" from *The Princess and the Frog*, sung by characters Disneybounding a variety of Disney properties. The franchise also capitalizes on the unfinished aesthetic of imperfection, endemic to plastic images of girlhood.

By embedding feminized and resistant fan practices within its narratives and musical numbers, *Descendants* can speak to a multitude of Disney fandoms while also co-opting fan practice toward commercial purposes. By casting actors of color, in a color-blind fashion, franchise creators can target audiences of color and provide a form of diverse representation for the network and its parent company. Finally, *Descendants* appeals to the melodramatic imagination by revealing the overwhelming pressure of gendered expectations in hetero-patriarchal cultures, generating prescriptive moments of nostalgia, and offering glimpses of escape. These made-for-TV movie musicals ultimately present a racially and ethnically diverse cast of feminized, ostensibly heteronormative characters longing to live in a patriarchal world that privileges whiteness and wealth. How *Descendants* and its sequels telegraph all this—through intertextual reappropriation, embedded fan practices, and plastic representations of girlhood—is what makes this television musical franchise a rich site for study and a significant property in the Disney media oeuvre.

Notes

1. Denise Petski, "*Descendants* Sequel *The Pocketwatch* Movie Greenlighted by Disney+; Jennifer Phang to Direct," Deadline, May 10, 2022, https://deadline.com/2022/05/descendants-sequel-the-pocketwatch-movie-disney-plus-1235020234/.
2. Ibid.
3. The Walt Disney Company corporate website reports its impressive viewership numbers for the *Descendants* premieres specifically among "Kids 6–11," "Tweens 9–14," "Girls 6–11," and "Girls 9–14" ("Boys" are not mentioned). See https://thewaltdisneycompany.com/disney-channels-descendants-3-is-highest-rated-telecast-among-kids-and-tweens-in-two-years/.
4. See, for instance, Shiri Reznik and Dafna Lemish, "Falling in Love with *High School Musical*: Girls' Talk about Romantic Perceptions," in *Mediated Girlhoods: New Explorations of Girls' Media Culture*, ed. Mary Celeste Kearney (New York: Peter Lang, 2011), 151–170; Nancy A. Jennings, *Tween Girls and Their Mediated Friends* (New York: Peter Lang, 2014); Diana Leon-Boys, *Elena, Princesa of the Periphery: Disney's Flexible Latina Girl* (New Brunswick, NJ: Rutgers University Press, 2023); Cynthia Maurer, "Tween Girls' Use of Television to Navigate Friendship," *Girlhood Studies* 11, no. 1 (Spring 2018): 25–42.
5. Rick Porter, "*Descendants 3* Scores Big Ratings for Disney Channel," *Hollywood Reporter*, August 7, 2019, https://www.hollywoodreporter.com/tv/tv-news/descendants-3-scores-big-ratings-disney-channel-1230053/. Upon its release in July 2024, *The Rise of Red* broke a Disney+ record, with 6.7 million views. For more on its ratings, see Loree Seitz, "'Descendants: The Rise of Red' Becomes Disney+'s Most-Watched Live Action Original Movie Since 'Hocus Pocus 2' with 33 Million Views," *The Wrap*, October 16, 2024, https://www.thewrap.com/descendants-the-rise-of-red-disney-plus-ratings/.
6. Note that *High School Musical 3: Senior Year* (2008) premiered in theaters rather than on television.
7. Robynn J. Stilwell, "The Television Musical," in *The Oxford Handbook of the American Musical*, ed. Raymond Knapp, Mitchell Morris, and Stacy Wolf (New York: Oxford University Press, 2011), 152.
8. For more on the emergence of the television musical, see Kelly Kessler, *Broadway in the Box: Television's Lasting Love Affair with the Musical* (New York: Oxford University Press, 2020).
9. Morgan Genevieve Blue, *Girlhood on Disney Channel: Branding, Celebrity, and Femininity* (New York: Routledge, 2017).
10. Ibid.

11. Jennings, *Tween Girls*.
12. Ien Ang, *Watching Dallas: Soap Opera and the Melodramatic Imagination* (New York: Routledge, 1982) cited in Reznik and Lemish, "Falling in Love."
13. Ien Ang, "Melodramatic Identifications: Television Fiction and Women's Fantasy," in *Feminist Television Criticism: A Reader*, 2nd ed., ed. Charlotte Brunsdon and Lynn Spigel (New York: Open University Press, 2008), 243.
14. Stacy Wolf, "Gender and Sexuality," in *The Oxford Handbook of the American Musical*, ed. Raymond Knapp, Mitchell Morris, and Stacy Wolf (New York: Oxford University Press, 2011), 210. While Wolf writes specifically about gender and sexuality, an intersectional perspective reveals that gender and sexuality are always/already also structuring and structured by multiple identities and discourses, including those related to race, socioeconomic status, ethnicity, nationality, and ability. For more on intersectionality, see Kimberlé Crenshaw, "Mapping the Margins: Intersectionality, Identity Politics, and Violence against Women of Color," *Stanford Law Review* 43, no. 6 (July 1991): 1241–1299.
15. Natalie Coulter, "From Toddlers to Teens: The Colonization of Childhood the Disney Way," *Jeunesse* 4, no. 1 (2012): 147.
16. This might be most apparent in Mal's quick assumption of the role of queen-to-be (and wife- and mother-to-be) and Evie's somewhat sudden home and business ownership.
17. This is in contrast to *High School Musical*'s masculine point of view via Troy (Zac Efron).
18. Anita Harris, *Future Girl: Young Women in the Twenty-First Century* (New York: Routledge, 2004), 59.
19. Mark Samuels, one of the *Descendants* choreographers, shared the DVD bonus footage on YouTube. See "The Descendants—Behind the Scenes—Dance Rehearsal," January 6, 2017, https://www.youtube.com/watch?v=gdK0YT_rLAM.
20. Ibid.
21. David Savran, "Class and Culture," in *The Oxford Handbook of the American Musical*, ed. Raymond Knapp, Mitchell Morris, and Stacy Wolf (New York: Oxford University Press, 2011), 247.
22. Jennifer Maas, "Disney CEO Bob Chapek Reveals 2022 Goals in Staff Memo to 'Set the Stage for Our Second Century,'" *Variety*, January 10, 2022, https://variety.com/2022/biz/news/disney-bob-chapek-2022-goals-1235150476/.
23. Savran, "Class and Culture," 247.
24. Leon-Boys, *Elena*, 127.
25. See, for example, Blue, *Girlhood on Disney Channel*; Leon-Boys, *Elena*; Diana Leon-Boys and Angharad N. Valdivia, "The Location of U.S. Latinidad: *Stuck in the Middle*, Disney, and the In-Between Ethnicity," *Journal of Children and Media* 15, no. 2 (2021): 218–232; Angharad N. Valdivia, "Mixed Race on the Disney Channel: From *Johnnie Tsunami* through *Lizzie McGuire* and Ending with *The Cheetah Girls*," in *Mixed Race Hollywood*, ed. Mary C. Beltrán and Camilla Fojas (New York: New York University Press, 2008), 269–289; Angharad N. Valdivia, "This Tween Bridge over My Latina Girl Back: The U.S. Mainstream Negotiates Ethnicity," in *Mediated Girlhoods: New Explorations of Girls' Media Culture*, ed. Mary Celeste Kearney (New York: Peter Lang, 2011), 93–109.
26. Blue, *Girlhood on Disney Channel*.
27. Patrick Ryan, "Disney Waves Wand Again with *Descendants*," *USA Today*, July 29, 2015, https://www.usatoday.com/story/life/tv/2015/07/29/descendants-disney-channel-original-movie/30802413/.

28. Chenoweth has also appeared in or voiced a multitude of other media, including Disney's popular straight-to-DVD *Tinker Bell* adventures and Fox's musical series *Glee* (2009–2015), which can be read as a grown-up twist on the *High School Musical* narrative, although its creators claim it did not influence them.
29. Morgan Genevieve Blue, "Performing Pop Girlhood on Disney Channel," in *Voicing Girlhood in Popular Music: Performance, Authority,* Authenticity, ed. Jacqueline Warwick and Alison Adrian (New York: Routledge, 2019), 171–190.
30. Stacy Wolf, "*Wicked* Divas, Musical Theatre, and Internet Girl Fans," *Camera Obscura* 22, no. 2 (2007): 39–71.
31. Fanlore.org defines shipping as "the act of supporting or wishing for a particular romantic relationship—that is, a het (different-sex), slash (male/male), femslash (female/female), or poly (three or more partners) ship—by discussing it, writing meta about it, or creating other types of fanworks exploring it." https://fanlore.org/wiki/Shipping.
32. Leon-Boys and Valdivia, "The Location of U.S. Latinidad."
33. Alison Winch, *Girlfriends and Postfeminist Sisterhood* (New York: Palgrave Macmillan, 2013).
34. Harris, *Future Girl*, 88.
35. McClain makes a powerful entrance singing "What's My Name" in *Descendants 2* and in *Descendants 3* with her cover of "Dig a Little Deeper" (Randy Newman). Also in *Descendants 3*, Jeffery performs "Queen of Mean" as Aurora. Carson and Jeffery also have made solo music videos featuring original footage and remixes of *Descendants* songs. For example, see Jeffery's remix of "Queen of Mean" on the DisneyMusicVEVO YouTube channel, https://www.youtube.com/watch?v=hq63uQZqBnM.
36. Ang, "Melodramatic Identifications"; Reznick and Lemish, "Falling in Love."
37. For more on vidding, see Francesca Coppa, *Vidding: A History* (Ann Arbor: University of Michigan Press, 2022).
38. *Descendants* fan fiction can be found at Archive of Our Own, https://archiveofourown.org/tags/Descendants%20(Disney%20Movies)/works; FanFiction.net, https://www.fanfiction.net/movie/Descendants-2015/; WattPad.com, https://www.wattpad.com/stories/descendants, among other sites.
39. Morgan Genevieve Blue, "D-Signed for Girls: Disney Channel and Tween Fashion," *Film, Fashion & Consumption* 2, no. 1 (March 2013): 55–75.
40. Heather Warren-Crow, *Girlhood and the Plastic Image* (Hanover, NH: Dartmouth College Press, 2014), 58.
41. Ibid., 57.
42. Leon-Boys, *Elena*, 34.
43. Valdivia, "This Tween Bridge," 101.
44. McClain's Uma performs the gospel-inspired tune "Dig a Little Deeper," originally performed by Jenifer Lewis and the Pinnacle Gospel Choir in Disney's *The Princess and the Frog*.
45. Valdivia, "This Tween Bridge," 106.
46. This video, "On Set with Sofia Carson in Spanish!," is available on Disney's *Descendants* YouTube channel, https://www.youtube.com/watch?v=FqsmhSma_g8.
47. Kristen J. Warner, *The Cultural Politics of Colorblind TV Casting* (New York: Routledge, 2018), 101.
48. Mary C. Beltrán, "The New Hollywood Racelessness: Only the Fast, Furious, and Multiracial Will Survive," *Cinema Journal* 44, no. 2 (Winter 2005): 63.

49. While the *Descendants* movies employ many performers of color, few of the characters are adapted from Disney characters of color. Hailing from *Aladdin*'s orientalist Arabian milieu, Jafar is one of the few *Descendants* characters to originate from a nonwhite role. Characters whose parents represent other Disney film characters of color include Lonnie, Mulan's daughter, and Celia (Jadah Marie), daughter of Dr. Facilier from *The Princess and the Frog*.
50. Stilwell, "The Television Musical," 166n7.
51. Ralina L. Joseph, *Transcending Blackness: From the New Millennium Mulatta to the Exceptional Multiracial* (Durham, NC: Duke University Press, 2013), 22.
52. Warner, *The Cultural Politics of Colorblind TV Casting*.
53. Warren-Crow, *Girlhood and the Plastic Image*. For example, in *Descendants 2*, Carlos pleads for inclusion when Evie and Mal are "always going off in a huddle whispering your girl talk stuff or whatever and Jay and I are tired of it ... we're your family too. We've been through a lot." Tenets often pathologized as feminization, then, as well as Carlos's proximity to girls and girlhoods, quashes any hint of toxic masculinity and allows for a more nuanced portrayal of boyhood.
54. Lauren Boumaroun, "Flying under the Radar: Culture and Community in the Unlicensed Geek Fashion Industry," in *Sartorial Fandom: Fashion, Beauty Culture, and Identity*, ed. Elizabeth Affuso and Suzanne Scott (Ann Arbor: University of Michigan Press, 2023), 86.
55. Kelsey Borresen, "'Disneybounding' Is the Dress-Up Trend Creative Fans Are Obsessed With," HuffPost, November 15, 2017, https://www.huffpost.com/entry/disneybounding-ideas-for-disney-lovers_n_59e5185ce4b02a215b325a30.
56. Rebecca Williams, "Disneybounding and Beyond: Fandom, Cosplay, and Embodiment in Themed Spaces," in *Sartorial Fandom: Fashion, Beauty Culture, and Identity*, ed. Elizabeth Affuso and Suzanne Scott (Ann Arbor: University of Michigan Press, 2023), 205.
57. Nicole Mancini, "Disney Descendants Line Brings Teenage Sons and Daughters of Villains to Life," WDWinfo.com, July 27, 2015, https://www.wdwinfo.com/entertainment-2/disney-descendants-line-brings-teenage-sons-daughters-of-villains-to-life/.
58. Williams, "Disneybounding and Beyond."
59. Related examples of domestic feminization include Cinderella and her animal friends, who sew a dress for the ball, and Aurora's proximity to the cursed spinning wheel in *Sleeping Beauty*.
60. Brooke Erin Duffy and Emily Hund, "'Having It All' on Social Media: Entrepreneurial Femininity and Self-Branding among Fashion Bloggers," *Social Media + Society* (July–December 2015): 1–11.
61. Harris, *Future Girl*, 94.
62. Blue, "D-Signed for Girls."
63. This *Descendants* apparel includes dresses labeled "cosplay costumes" as distinct from Halloween costumes, as well as character shirts and hybrid cosplay/promotional garments such as a dress with a colored tulle skirt that matches those that Evie and Mal wear but adds images of the characters. A few garments also include Jay and Carlos, and DisneyShop.com advertises a few T-shirts aimed at boys.
64. This franchise is not the only one to bring together fairy-tale characters from disparate worlds. Other examples of this include Stephen Sondheim's long-running Broadway production *Into the Woods* (1987), which Disney adapted to film in 2014, as well as Disney's *Shrek* (2001), ABC's *Once upon a Time* (2011–2018), NBC's *Grimm* (2011–2018), and Netflix's animated series *Ever After High* (2013–2017).

65. Elizabeth Freeman, *Beside You in Time: Sense Methods and Queer Sociability* (Durham, NC: Duke University Press, 2019), 17.
66. Ibid., 35.
67. Jack Halberstam, *In a Queer Time and Place: Transgender Bodies, Subcultural Lives* (New York: New York University Press, 2005), 10.
68. Whitney Monaghan, *Queer Girls, Temporality, and Screen Media: Not Just a "Phase"* (London: Palgrave, 2016).
69. See for example, Catherine Driscoll, *Girls: Feminine Adolescence in Popular Culture and Cultural Theory* (New York: Columbia University Press, 2002); Susan Driver, *Queer Girls and Popular Culture: Reading, Resisting, and Creating Media* (New York: Peter Lang, 2007); Harris, *Future Girl*.
70. Monaghan, *Queer Girls*, 161.

Bibliography

Ang, Ien. "Melodramatic Identifications: Television Fiction and Women's Fantasy." In *Feminist Television Criticism: A Reader*, 2nd ed., edited by Charlotte Brunsdon and Lynn Spigel, 235–236. New York: Open University Press, 2008.

Ang, Ien. *Watching Dallas: Soap Opera and the Melodramatic Imagination*. New York: Routledge, 1982.

Beltrán, Mary C. "The New Hollywood Racelessness: Only the Fast, Furious, and Multiracial Will Survive." *Cinema Journal* 44, no. 2 (Winter 2005): 50–67.

Bickford, Tyler. "The New 'Tween' Music Industry: The Disney Channel, Kidz Bop, and an Emerging Childhood Counterpublic." *Popular Music* 13, no. 3 (2012): 417–436.

Blue, Morgan Genevieve. "D-Signed for Girls: Disney Channel and Tween Fashion." *Film, Fashion & Consumption* 2, no. 1 (March 2013): 55–75.

Blue, Morgan Genevieve. *Girlhood on Disney Channel: Branding, Celebrity, and Femininity*. New York: Routledge, 2017.

Blue, Morgan Genevieve. "Performing Pop Girlhood on Disney Channel." In *Voicing Girlhood in Popular Music: Performance, Authority, Authenticity*, edited by Jacqueline Warwick and Alison Adrian, 171–190. New York: Routledge, 2019.

Borresen, Kelsey. "'Disneybounding' Is the Dress-Up Trend Creative Fans Are Obsessed With." HuffPost, November 15, 2017. https://www.huffpost.com/entry/dis neybounding-ideas-for-disney-lovers_n_59e5185ce4b02a215b325a30.

Boumaroun, Lauren. "Flying under the Radar: Culture and Community in the Unlicensed Geek Fashion Industry." In *Sartorial Fandom: Fashion, Beauty Culture, and Identity*, edited by Elizabeth Affuso and Suzanne Scott, 84–98. Ann Arbor: University of Michigan Press, 2023.

Coppa, Francesca. *Vidding: A History*. Ann Arbor: University of Michigan Press, 2022.

Coulter, Natalie. "From Toddlers to Teens: The Colonization of Childhood the Disney Way." *Jeunesse: Young People, Texts, Cultures* 4, no. 1 (2012): 146–158.

Crenshaw, Kimberlé. "Mapping the Margins: Intersectionality, Identity Politics, and Violence against Women of Color." *Stanford Law Review* 43, no. 6 (July 1991): 1241–1299.

Driscoll, Catherine. *Girls: Feminine Adolescence in Popular Culture and Cultural Theory*. New York: Columbia University Press, 2002.

Driver, Susan. *Queer Girls and Popular Culture: Reading, Resisting, and Creating Media*. New York: Peter Lang, 2007.

Duffy, Brooke Erin, and Emily Hund. "'Having It All' on Social Media: Entrepreneurial Femininity and Self-Branding among Fashion Bloggers." *Social Media + Society* (July–December 2015): 1–11.

Freeman, Elizabeth. *Beside You in Time: Sense Methods and Queer Sociability*. Durham, NC: Duke University Press, 2019.

Halberstam, Jack. *In a Queer Time and Place: Transgender Bodies, Subcultural Lives*. New York: New York University Press, 2005.

Harris, Anita. *Future Girl: Young Women in the Twenty-First Century*. New York: Routledge, 2004.

Jennings, Nancy A. *Tween Girls and Their Mediated Friends*. New York: Peter Lang, 2014.

Joseph, Ralina L. *Transcending Blackness: From the New Millennium Mulatta to the Exceptional Multiracial*. Durham, NC: Duke University Press, 2013.

Kessler, Kelly. *Broadway in the Box: Television's Lasting Love Affair with the Musical*. New York: Oxford University Press, 2020.

Leon-Boys, Diana. *Elena, Princesa of the Periphery: Disney's Flexible Latina Girl*. New Brunswick, NJ: Rutgers University Press, 2023.

Leon-Boys, Diana, and Valdivia, Angharad N. "The Location of U.S. Latinidad: *Stuck in the Middle*, Disney, and the In-Between Ethnicity." *Journal of Children and Media* 15, no. 2 (2021): 218–232.

Lustyik, Katalin. "Disney's *High School Musical*: Music Makes the World Go 'Round.'" *Interactions: Studies in Communication & Culture* 4, no. 3 (2013): 239–253.

Maas, Jennifer. "Disney CEO Bob Chapek Reveals 2022 Goals in Staff Memo to 'Set the Stage for Our Second Century.'" *Variety*, January 10, 2022. https://variety.com/2022/biz/news/disney-bob-chapek-2022-goals-1235150476/.

Mancini, Nicole. "Disney Descendants Line Brings Teenage Sons and Daughters of Villains to Life." WDWinfo.com, July 27, 2015. https://www.wdwinfo.com/entertainment-2/disney-descendants-line-brings-teenage-sons-daughters-of-villains-to-life/.

Maurer, Cynthia. "Tween Girls' Use of Television to Navigate Friendship." *Girlhood Studies* 11, no. 1 (Spring 2018): 25–42.

Monaghan, Whitney. *Queer Girls, Temporality, and Screen Media: Not Just a "Phase."* London: Palgrave, 2016.

Ortega, Kenny, dir. *Descendants*. Disney Channel; Bad Angels Productions; 5678 Productions, 2015.

Ortega, Kenny, dir. *Descendants 2*. Disney Channel; Bad Angels Productions; 5678 Productions, 2017.

Ortega, Kenny, dir. *Descendants 3*. Disney Channel; Bad Angels Productions; 5678 Productions, 2019.

Phang, Jennifer, dir. *Descendants: The Rise of Red*. Disney+; Disney Branded Television; GWave Productions, 2024.

Petski, Denise. "*Descendants* Sequel *The Pocketwatch* Movie Greenlighted by Disney+; Jennifer Phang to Direct." Deadline, May 10, 2022. https://deadline.com/2022/05/descendants-sequel-the-pocketwatch-movie-disney-plus-1235020234/.

Porter, Rick. "*Descendants 3* Scores Big Ratings for Disney Channel." *Hollywood Reporter*, August 7, 2019. https://www.hollywoodreporter.com/tv/tv-news/descendants-3-scores-big-ratings-disney-channel-1230053/.

Potter, Anna. "It's a Small World after All: New Media Constellations and Disney's Rising Star—the Global Success of *High School Musical*." *International Journal of Cultural Studies* 15, no. 2 (2012): 117–130.

Reznik, Shiri, and Dafna Lemish. "Falling in Love with *High School Musical*: Girls' Talk about Romantic Perceptions." In *Mediated Girlhoods: New Explorations of Girls' Media Culture*, edited by Mary Celeste Kearney, 151–170. New York: Peter Lang, 2011.

Ryan, Patrick. "Disney Waves Wand Again with *Descendants*." *USA Today*, July 29, 2015. https://www.usatoday.com/story/life/tv/2015/07/29/descendants-disney-channel-original-movie/30802413/.

Savran, David. 2011. "Class and Culture." In *The Oxford Handbook of the American Musical*, edited by Raymond Knapp, Mitchell Morris, and Stacy Wolf, 239–250. New York: Oxford University Press, 2011.

Seitz, Loree. "'Descendants: The Rise of Red' Becomes Disney+'s Most-Watched Live Action Original Movie Since 'Hocus Pocus 2' with 33 Million Views." *The Wrap*, October 16, 2024. https://www.thewrap.com/descendants-the-rise-of-red-disney-plus-ratings/.

Sorrensen, Ingvild Kvale. "Domesticating the Disney Tween Machine: Norwegian Tweens Enacting Age and Everyday Life." PhD diss., Norwegian University of Science and Technology, 2014.

Stilwell, Robynn J. "The Television Musical." In *The Oxford Handbook of the American Musical*, edited by Raymond Knapp, Mitchell Morris, and Stacy Wolf, 152–166. New York: Oxford University Press, 2011.

Symonds, Dominic. "'We're All in This Together': Being Girls and Boys in *High School Musical* (2006)." In *The Disney Musical on Stage and Screen: Critical Approaches from* Snow White *to* Frozen, edited by George Rodosthenous, 169–184. New York: Bloomsbury, 2017.

Valdivia, Angharad N. "Mixed Race on the Disney Channel: From *Johnnie Tsunami* through *Lizzie McGuire* and Ending with *The Cheetah Girls*." In *Mixed Race Hollywood*, edited by Mary C. Beltrán and Camilla Fojas, 269–289. New York: New York University Press, 2008.

Valdivia, Angharad N. "This Tween Bridge over My Latina Girl Back: The U.S. Mainstream Negotiates Ethnicity." In *Mediated Girlhoods: New Explorations of Girls' Media Culture*, edited by Mary Celeste Kearney, 93–109. New York: Peter Lang, 2011.

Warner, Kristen J. *The Cultural Politics of Colorblind TV Casting*. New York: Routledge, 2018.

Warren-Crow, Heather. *Girlhood and the Plastic Image*. Hanover, NH: Dartmouth College Press, 2014.

Williams, Rebecca. "Disneybounding and Beyond: Fandom, Cosplay, and Embodiment in Themed Spaces." In *Sartorial Fandom: Fashion, Beauty Culture, and Identity*, edited by Elizabeth Affuso and Suzanne Scott, 205–218. Ann Arbor: University of Michigan Press, 2023.

Winch, Alison. *Girlfriends and Postfeminist Sisterhood*. New York: Palgrave Macmillan, 2013.

Wolf, Stacy. "Gender and Sexuality." In *The Oxford Handbook of the American Musical*, edited by Raymond Knapp, Mitchell Morris, and Stacy Wolf, 210–224. New York: Oxford University Press, 2011.

Wolf, Stacy. "*Wicked* Divas, Musical Theatre, and Internet Girl Fans." *Camera Obscura* 22, no. 2 (2007): 39–71.

CHAPTER 21

IMAGINEERING *CON SABROSURA*: CULTURAL IMAGINEERING AND LATINIDAD IN THE TWENTY-FIRST-CENTURY DISNEY MUSICAL

JACQUELINE AVILA AND
JUAN FERNANDO VELÁSQUEZ OSPINA

IN 1990, Disney Enterprises Inc. trademarked a word that would become a central concept for shaping the company's research and development departments: "Imagineering." Conflating "imagination" and "engineering," Imagineering became the core principle in designing amusement parks, merchandise, and other projects, including the stories and films created at Walt Disney Studios. At the heart of Disney Imagineering is the idea of "Making the Impossible Possible: Where innovation and storytelling combine to bring Disney stories, characters and worlds to life."[1] However, as exemplified by the contradictory and sometimes troublesome experiences with ethnic representations in films such as *Aladdin* (1991), *Pocahontas* (1995), and *Mulan* (1998), Imagineering's logic also carried a profound contradiction. Although it aimed to set new technological and artistic standards to secure Disney's position as the leading animation company in the twentieth and twenty-first centuries, Imagineering did not necessarily question or challenge the company's long-standing tradition of representational strategies.

Such a contradiction put Walt Disney Studios under considerable scrutiny at the turn of the twenty-first century, particularly concerning the ethnic, racial, and cultural representations in its films and television and streaming-media serials. Repeatedly accused of cultural appropriation, stereotyping, and whitewashing, Disney and its subsidiary Pixar Animation Studios have attempted to rectify these practices to repair their corporate reputation by extending the scope of Imagineering to the cultural sphere. As a result, since the 2010s, the company has reshaped the production process to include teams of advisers who are familiar with the cultural and musical intricacies of the Black and Indigenous people of color (BIPOC), non-Anglo-American (NAA), and non–Western European (NWE) people and cultures represented in animated films and serials, triggering a process that we describe as Cultural Imagineering. This process extended to the construction of Latinx and Latin American voices, musics, cultures, and identities on- and off-screen.

The on-screen representation of Latinx and Latin American communities in Disney films and serials has had an intriguing and complicated history. Except for some animated movies produced during the 1940s, the studio only referred to this geographical region, its people, and its cultures sporadically in films and serials, often as secondary characters who added some picturesque effect to the plot. However, the increasing significance of Latinx and Latin American consumers in the cinematic market has triggered a renewed interest on the part of the company to include characters and storylines that engage these communities with Disney and Pixar products.[2] This chapter examines the history and the construction of Latinx and Latin American characters and cultures as represented in Disney animated features. We present a three-part analysis that considers how Disney and Pixar studios constructed cinematic Latinx and Latin American identities using specific images, narratives, and music that negotiated—and at times contested—preexisting stereotypes, working under the parameters embraced by Cultural Imagineering.

Macaws, Llamas, Music, and Dance: Disney's Pan-American Dream

During the mid-1930s, the rising of totalitarian regimes in Europe concerned many politicians in Washington. They feared the threat that southern neighbors following the example of Germany and Italy could pose to the US and its interests. Moreover, Franklin Delano Roosevelt's government also recognized that a successful recovery from the damage that the Great Depression had done to the US economy and its social fabric demanded reassessing capitalism and securing new and profitable markets for American products under a "New Deal."[3] The result was a "Good Neighbor" policy that promoted a new Pan-American order through a series of actions designed to reinforce the role of the US as the leading power in the region while presenting its Latin American counterparts as nations that, despite any cultural differences, shared the goals and agreed on the ideological principles embraced by the US. However, the numerous US interventions and invasions of Latin American and Caribbean countries between the second half of the nineteenth century and the first two decades of the twentieth century created distrust, discredit, and hatred toward this country in the region.[4] In response to this challenge, Roosevelt's administration created the Office for Coordination of Commercial and Cultural Relations between the American Republics in 1940. In 1941, this agency became the Office of the Coordinator of Inter-American Affairs (CIAA), headed by Nelson Rockefeller.[5]

Hence, besides contributing to the "stabilization of Latin American economies," the CIAA's aim was to design and implement plans and activities that undermined the impact of the "Axis' incursions into the hemisphere, particularly in the commercial and cultural spheres."[6] To do so, the CIAA established ties with the US cultural industry to develop products promoting the Good Neighbor policy.[7] The film industry was crucial for this endeavor due to cinema's strategic value as a medium that conveyed messages to broad audiences, despite differences in social class, cultural background, gender, race, ethnicity, and age.[8] Thus, Rockefeller created the CIAA Film Division, directed by John Hay Whitney, to reach the companies controlling the US cinematic market. In 1942, Whitney persuaded the studios in the US to hire Latin Americans and to produce movies that placed Latin America in a favorable light. Moreover, Whitney traveled throughout the Americas, establishing a system of information and communication with partners and promoters that could collaborate with producing, circulating, and promoting films sponsored by CIAA.[9] Meanwhile, the 1941 animators' strike and World War II had a detrimental impact on Disney's profits, making the company eager to work with CIAA.[10]

Then the company assembled a team of fifteen studio employees, two employees' wives (one of them was Walt Disney's wife, Lilian Disney), and Walt Disney himself. Among the employees was Charles Frederick Wolcott, general musical director at Disney. As explained in the opening of *Saludos Amigos* (1942), this team, known as "El Grupo," left the US on August 13, 1941, on a three-month "goodwill tour" that began in Brazil and Argentina. Then El Grupo split into two teams that visited Chile and Peru.[11] This selection of South American countries was planned beforehand. The countries of the Southern Cone were more distant from the US than their Central American or Caribbean counterparts, and diplomatic reports suggested that they were prone to become allies of the Axis, as a significant diaspora of Germans, Japanese, and Italians and their descendants resided there.[12] Moreover, the US military industry depended on raw materials such as Brazilian rubber or Chilean copper. Therefore, the members of El Grupo became cultural diplomats who attempted to accomplish two goals: first, to promote the US among Latin American local authorities while establishing cultural and commercial ties with Latin American artists and institutions, and second, to produce animated films for audiences in the US and Latin America that presented a positive image of the region, using a collection of the impressions, colors, landscapes, traditions, and cultures they interacted with during the goodwill tour.

This second aspect of El Grupo's mission was attuned to the previous extractivist logic that characterized Latin American and Caribbean "expeditions" of employees of US companies, who collected cultural objects that later became commodities salable in a transnational market.[13] El Grupo's missions relied on a series of actors in the US and

Latin America with different skills who connected Disney's team and local diplomats, politicians, entrepreneurs, and musicians. Ultimately, the interactions among these actors produced an audiovisual presentation of the "exotic and diverse friends in the South," reflecting US audience expectations. This was also inspired by a negotiation between El Grupo's gaze as travelers coming from a neocolonial power and the stereotypes of Latinness in vogue in Hollywood.[14]

The final result was a series of three films: *South of the Border with Disney* (1941), *Saludos Amigos* (1942), and *The Three Caballeros* (1945). The first movie, *South of the Border with Disney*, provides the audience with the historical background regarding the trips. Presented as a travelogue that shows Walt Disney and his team working from a hotel room, looking at storyboards, and discussing themes and topics to include in the films. We see and hear the beginnings of the animated characters and locations that would later be featured in *Saludos Amigos* and *The Three Caballeros*, in particular the pencil sketches of José (or Joe) Carioca, "the fast-talking, cigar-smoking, umbrella-toting parrot from Rio."[15] The film presents an almost educational insider look into the workings (the construction of the identities, the synthesis of live-action movement with animation) of the succeeding films.

As Julianne Burton-Carvajal astutely points out, *Saludos Amigos* follows the travel outline of its predecessor, but the animated characters take a centralized role, isolated in four short vignettes that move through varying locations of South America: (1) Donald Duck's visit to Bolivia's Lake Titicaca, which combines live action and animation; (2) the little Chilean plane Pedro, who delivers mail through a massive rainstorm in the Andes; (3) Goofy as a transplanted Texan cowboy turned Argentine gaucho; and (4) Joe Carioca in "Aquarela do Brasil" ("Watercolor of Brazil"), who introduces Donald Duck to samba, cachaca, and Rio nightlife.[16] This last segment is a synthesis of animation with two prominent songs: Ary Barroso's "Brazil" and a samba by Zequinha de Abreu. The images of the Brazilian landscape, with vibrant colors, synchronized movements, and camera shots, shape some of the first representations of a Brazilian cultural identity within this trilogy.

Representations of the Argentinian gaucho in *Saludos Amigos* also illustrate that Disney adapted color, sound, and movements that bounced between what the US audiences would perceive as both familiar and exotic. As mentioned before, Texan cowboy Goofy becomes a gaucho when transplanted to the Pampa.[17] The following scenes introduce visually and aurally the gaucho's traditional costumes and some "gaucho dances." Three activities developed in Argentina informed El Grupo's animated representation of the gaucho: first, a visit to illustrator Florencio Molina Campos (1891–1959), a painter known for his typical scenes of the Pampa; second, the music and dances that Andrés Chazarreta (1876–1970) and the members of the Arte Nativo folkloric dance company performed for the members of El Grupo on the Alvear Palace Hotel's terrace;[18] and finally, an *asado* in an Argentinian *estancia*. Although an *asado* could resemble a barbecue in some aspects, in Argentina, it is a tradition closely related to the gaucho culture and became essential to Argentina's national identity. It is as much about friends and family coming together as the beef, vegetables, and *provoleta* grilled over coal. Meanwhile, the *estancia* is a large estate often used for raising livestock that Argentinians associate with the Pampa and gaucho culture.

This film describes cosmopolitan Buenos Aires as the "third largest city in the Western hemisphere." However, rather than introducing the "modern tango" that was so popular in the Argentinian capital, the members of El Grupo turned to the gaucho, a central figure in narratives of Argentine-ness during the nineteenth and early twentieth centuries.[19] As a result, *Saludos Amigos* introduced a sonic representation of Argentina articulated around "Yo soy la blanca paloma," a song from the *género triste*, and three "country dances of the Argentine, the same old tunes that the parents [of contemporary Argentinians] had danced": the Chacarera, the Malambo, and the Pala Pala.[20] According to the film, these dances represented traditional values and picturesque traditions while resembling US "square dances." However, Goofy dances the Chacarera following the steps of the bunny hug, an "animal dance" that is thought to have originated in California during the ragtime era. As pointed out by Juan Carlos Poveda Vieira, this mixture of music that introduced Latin American features and animated choreographies that presented dances in vogue in the US mirrors the visions of the Pan-American dream supporting the Good Neighbor policy.[21] From this standpoint, although El Grupo's goodwill tour produced an audiovisual narrative of Latin America that seemed to look for similarities between the south and the north of the hemisphere, the cinematic product set a representation that intertwined images and symbols that audiences in the US related with "exotic and primitive others" and romantic notions of folklore used by local actors and institutions to produce, perform, and reproduce representations of belonging and nationhood.

The Three Caballeros concludes the trilogy and El Grupo's sojourn to Latin America. In his essay on the film, Eric A. Galm indicates that "this film provides an excellent opportunity for the exploration of identity construction and cultural misrepresentation by Hollywood projects,"[22] with Donald Duck acting as a cultural outsider who gains access through his own interlocutors, "Joe" Carioca (reprising his role from *Saludos Amigos*) and the gun-toting macho rooster Panchito from Mexico. In the film, Donald receives a special surprise package, with the tag reading, "From your friends in Latin America."[23] Inside the package are various gifts from different parts of Latin America. The first is a projector and a home movie labeled *Aves Raras* ("Strange Birds"), which details the adventures of the penguin Pablo, who travels from Antarctica to the Galapagos Islands in search of warmer weather, and another is the story of the Little Gauchito who traps a flying donkey and wins a race in Uruguay. These sections feature a narrator and orchestral underscoring designed to highlight the actions taking place on-screen. The most musically concentrated sections occur after, when the storylines move to the Bahia region of Brazil and to various cities in Mexico, including Mexico City, Pátzcuaro, Veracruz, Acapulco, and the Isthmus of Tehuantepec. The movement through these regions features culturally problematic representations that are accompanied by music.

Donald is first transported to Brazil. Galm points out that this vignette is set in the northeastern city of Salvador, Bahia, a location that Walt Disney himself and his research group never visited during their sojourn. Instead, Walt Disney and his team spent their time in Rio de Janeiro, studying and learning about the cultural practices and the flora and fauna of that region. As a result, Rio came to represent, as Galm notes, the "entire construction of Brazil." Other geographic locations of Brazil were not the only significant absences; Galm illustrates that this section is devoid of specific cultural and racial representations. Since the colonial period, the Bahia region maintained "a strong presence of African descendants," which the Disney film virtually ignores or avoids.[24] Instead, what is included is a reinterpretation of the music, culture, and practices of Afro-Brazilians through a whitewashed filter.

According to Galm, Disney's portrayal of Bahia was fairly confined to one figure: the *bahiana*, "an Afro-Brazilian woman whose traditional attire includes a white hoopdress, head wrap and expensive *pano da costa* shawl."[25] The *bahiana* is a national representation of the African roots and cultures of Brazil. However, in the film, this portrait was confined to the figure of Aurora Miranda (1915–2005), sister of the Portuguese-born Brazilian actress Carmen Miranda (1909–1955). In the film, Aurora Miranda plays the live-action character Iaiá, who engages with the animated characters, selling cookies and performing a version of Barroso's 1941 song "Os quindins de Iaiá" ("Iaiá's Sweets"). Galm asserts that the audience soon becomes aware that she is selling more than cookies. In the film, she comes down the street, singing in a high soprano voice the street vendor's song, and Donald falls immediately in love with her and tries to win her over by moving through a series of macho behaviors, including jealousy, competitiveness, and desire. During her performance, a group of male percussionists surround her and sing "'*cumé, cumé, cumé*' (eat 'em)."[26] The sequence is quite suggestive through the interactions of Iaiá with the percussionists and the growing jealousy of Donald. Galm observes that while Disney kept the song in Portuguese to create an air of authenticity, Disney only utilized the first verse of the song and omits the second verse, which describes the "people, places and things that can be found in Bahia."[27] The performance by Iaiá in this vignette transforms her as the exotic ambassador for US audiences into the "essences of Africa in Bahía."[28] However, as Galm reveals, any presence of African culture is completely erased and replaced by light-skinned performers who fulfill Anglo-American (and, by extension, Disney's) expectations of exoticism.

Disney delves further into exoticist stereotypes as the film shifts to Mexico and takes on the Mexican national symbol of masculinity, the charro, reinterpreting it as the gun-wielding rooster named Panchito. In this section, Disney features the *canción ranchera* "¡Ay, Jalisco no te rajes!" ("Ay, Jalisco Don't Back Slide!"), composed by Manuel Esperón with lyrics by Ernesto Cortazar. Made popular in Mexican cinema during the *época de oro* (golden age, roughly 1931–1952) as the title song for the *comedia ranchera* (ranch comedy) by the same name, this film and its song became the star vehicle for the actor and singing charro Jorge Negrete (1911–1953). After starring in this film, Negrete was positioned as the definitive representation of the charro, and "¡Ay, Jalisco no te rajes!" became the theme song of his exploits. Unlike with the music in the Brazil section of *The Three Caballeros*, the music department revised the lyrics for "¡Ay, Jalisco no te rajes!"

and focused the topic not on the utopian-esque qualities of the Mexican state of Jalisco but on the masculine solidarity of the film's three principal characters:

> We're three happy chappies
> With snappy serapes
> You'll find us beneath our sombreros
> We're brave and we'll say so.[29]

Instead of the glorification of Jalisco, the lyrics provide references to Mexican culture and words manipulated to fit a specific idea or image of Mexico shaped by Disney, such as the mispronunciation of "serape" in order to rhyme with "chappie."

Donald's foray into Mexico includes flying over parts of the country on a magic serape with Joe Carioca and Panchito, visiting Pátzcuaro, Veracruz, and Acapulco. While the three characters are moving through these locations with ease, the music changes to feature regional performances in Veracruz, which includes the *huapango* and *son jarocho*. The *huapango* is a fast-paced couples dance and a musical genre that feature violinists, harp, and guitar. The *son jarocho* features string instruments, such as violin, *guitarra de son*, and harp and also a singer singing *coplas*. These performances feature a *son* ensemble consisting of guitars, *guitarron*, harp, and vocalists, with dancers *zapateando* (tap-dancing) on a *tarima* (wooden platform). This section offers the most genuine performances of the Veracruz *son* tradition. These brief attempts at authenticity transition to the section's primary focus: the beach of Acapulco. Here the camera fixates on women in bathing suits, swimming and sunbathing. During this sequence, Donald jumps off the serape and begins to run after the women in a heated frenzy. The final section of Mexico takes place in Mexico City and showcases the vibrant nightlife of the metropolis accompanied by the strains of Mexican singer Dora Luz performing "You Belong to My Heart," a revised version of *bolerista* Agustín Lara's romantic "Solamente una vez":

> You belong to my heart
> Now and forever
> And our love had its start
> Not long ago.

Unlike the songs in the Brazilian section, several of the songs in the Mexico section are translated into English, creating more of an intimate connection with the Anglo-American audience.

Both *Saludos Amigos* and *The Three Caballeros* made a considerable impact on the construction of the visual and aural representations of Latin Americans on the big screen. The sizable focus on male protagonists while women were objectified, constructed as both exoticized and sexualized figures, would have ramifications during the rest of the twentieth century. From this standpoint, El Grupo set a series of standards for representing Latin American cultures and traditions that combined color, sound, and difference that simultaneously satisfied the expectations of audiences in the US and echoed the sense of timelessness and self-exoticization that characterized notions of cultural uniqueness and national identity, which were embraced by different actors and institutions across Latin America.

WORKING TOWARD POSITIVE REPRESENTATIONS AT THE TURN OF THE TWENTY-FIRST CENTURY

After the film trilogy by El Grupo, the presence of Latin American characters in Disney's products languished for several decades, albeit with some minor references in other films during the 1980s and 1990s. Actor and comedian Cheech Marin played a secondary role in the 1988 animated feature *Oliver & Company*, in which an orphaned tabby kitten is separated from his family and makes friends with a group of stray dogs in New York City. Marin voices the character of Tito, a spunky chihuahua who sports a bandana and speaks with a thick Chicano accent, crossing the language barriers between English and Spanish. The film features the musical stylings of Billy Joel for the theme song "Why Should I Worry?"

During the late 1990s, the talking chihuahua was a fairly common representation of Latin/a/o/x identity, not just with Disney but also in US popular media. The pseudo-Mexican fast-food chain Taco Bell featured a talking chihuahua in its advertising, and other Disney features, such as the live-action *Beverly Hills Chihuahua* (2008), which portrayed varying social constructions, from the privileged and pampered chihuahua Chloe voiced by Drew Barrymore to the working-class chihuahua Papi voiced by George Lopez. In this film, Chloe is lost while on vacation in Mexico and receives help from other dogs in order to get back home. Her adventure is accompanied by an eclectic soundtrack, including songs by Los Pericos, Ricardo Montaner, Los Lonely Boys, Banda Sinaloense, and others.

Back in the realm of animated features, Disney continued a trend—albeit a small trend—of diversifying heroines. This included Middle Eastern (Jasmine), East Asian (Mulan), and Native American (Pocahontas) main characters. However, critics and audiences heavily criticized these representations for exhibiting anglicized voices, facial features, demeaning stereotypes, and problematic narratives. *Sofia the First* (2012–2018) was the Disney Channel and Disney Junior's first attempt to introduce a Latina princess into the princess club. First featured in the film *Sofia the First: Once upon a Princess*, Sofia became the protagonist of her own show, which takes place after her mother Queen Miranda marries King Roland II of the fictitious land of Enchancia. Sofia becomes a princess virtually overnight and is instantly enrolled at the Royal Preparatory Academy, where she receives guidance on how to be a princess from the three fairies from *Sleeping Beauty*—Flora, Fauna, and Merryweather. The show includes adventure narratives and strategically placed musical numbers that operate more like the Disney musical format of the past.

In terms of the portrayal of a Latina identity, *Sofia the First* has become a source of controversy. During a press tour in October 2012, a Disney executive identified Sofia as Latina, affirming that Disney was "committed to diverse, multicultural, and inclusive storytelling" and that *Sofia the First* features a range of characters that represent this approach.[30] This, however, brought a sense of confusion, as Sofia was portrayed as a blue-eyed, white-presenting princess, which aligned more with a decidedly Hispanic heritage rather than Latina.[31] While the construction of Sofia instigated questions regarding adequate representation, the character of Queen Miranda was decidedly identified as Latina because of her darker complexion, and Sofia's fictional homeland of Galdiz supposedly featured "Latin influences."[32] Musically speaking, the theme song for the series is a pop-infused number that, much like other theme songs for Disney serials, provides the young audience with a quick overview of the main character's background and her goals for the future. Throughout the series, the music follows in this particular pattern of pop songs but sometimes includes musical references to other cultures and communities. For instance, in episode 12, season 3, the show introduces a new princess, Lani, who is described as a native princess from the tropical island kingdom of Hakado and has a darker complexion. Princess Lani teaches Sofia through song that she may not look like a typical princess, but through her good deeds and actions, she is a princess. Lani's music, which includes percussion, such as bongos, and acoustic guitars, shapes her otherness in comparison with Sofia.

After *Sofia the First*, Disney organized a team of cultural advisers from nationally recognized Latinx arts organizations, a Latin music consultant, and a women- and Latinx-led writers' room.[33] As a result, *Elena of Avalor* (2016–2020) was well received as the series introduced Latinx-looking characters and relatable representations of Latin America, such as the Teotihuacan-inspired scenery, the mythical beasts, the locally specific flower on Elena's head, and the magical elements based on Indigenous traditions. Moreover, many of the episodes' storylines build on legends from the non-anglophone parts of the American continent. According to Mathew Sandoval, Disney made legitimate attempts to infuse *Elena of Avalor* with Latinidad. He states:

> The main characters were voiced by an all-Latinx cast of actors. Much of the production crew were Latinx. *Elena of Avalor*'s theme song is sung by Guatemalan singer-songwriter Gaby Moreno. Each episode of the show features musical traditions and genres from across Latin America—salsa, mariachi, merengue, banda, and bossa nova, to name a few. Elena's costumes were designed by Brazilian fashion designer Layanna Aguilar. Many of the plot devices used in the show's seventy-seven episodes incorporate elements of mythology and folklore drawn from across Latin America.[34]

Although the production team of *Elena of Avalor* endeavored to "get it right" in terms of cultural representation, Sandoval notes that the show was mainly geared to a non-Latinx audience, as the production team and the show took great pains to explain those cultural elements that would be considered foreign to the audience. For instance, in his study on the construction of Día de Muertos in the show, Sandoval points out that in order to shy away from even mentioning death, the episode's writers opted for other ways to insinuate the word and the concept, resorting to euphemisms such as "passed away," "gone," "no longer here," and "not with us anymore."[35] This became a way for Disney to make the material more consumable to Anglo-American audiences.

This approach, however, did not transition to Pixar's next project. During the 2010s, Pixar began production on a new storyline centered around the Mexican holiday of Día de Muertos (Day of the Dead), a period that takes place from the evening of October 31 to November 2. During these days, those celebrating remember their departed loved ones, creating altars in their homes, churches, and/or cemeteries adorned with photos, their favorite foods, candles, and *calacas de azucar* (sugar skulls). This new film would be a drastic departure from other films produced by Disney and Pixar, one that would maintain a specific cultural relevance to (and from) Mexico and the Mexican-American community. The end result was *Coco*.

Coco tells the story of a young boy named Miguel Rivera, from the fictional town of Santa Cecilia (named after the Catholic patron saint of musicians), whose dream is to be a famous mariachi performer like his favorite actor-singer Ernesto de la Cruz. He keeps his musical talents and ambitions a secret because the family's deceased matriarch, Mamá Imeda, has forbidden music (both listening to it and performing) after she and her daughter Coco were abandoned by her musician husband. Determined to follow his dream, Miguel prepares for a musical competition during Día de Muertos but is magically transported to the Land of the Dead. While there, he is reunited with deceased family members, who also discourage him from performing music. Miguel eventually joins forces with the *calaca* Héctor, who is trying to cross over the bridge into the Land of the Living before he is forgotten forever.

The cultural-identity politics, specifically the construction of Mexicanidad (the cultural identity of the Mexican people), have been discussed in Jacqueline Avila's article "*Memorias de Oro*: Music, Memory, and *Mexicanidad* in Pixar's *Coco*." In it, Avila argues that *Coco* has become a significant cinematic and musical marker of Mexicanidad during a period of social and political angst in the United States.[36] *Coco* experienced backlash due to Disney's attempts to register the copyright of "Dia de los Muertos," a traditional Mexican festivity deeply entangled in notions of national pride and belonging. Notwithstanding, the company responded by stopping its plan while establishing a culturally sensitive team to guide the production. The newly formed production and creative team traveled to Mexico and visited several cities that boasted prominent Día de Muertos celebrations, including Mexico City, Guanajuato, Morelia, and Pátzcuaro. While conducting research on these culturally significant spaces and places, the research team also concentrated on music, particularly with the help of Camilo Lara, DJ, music producer, and founder of the Electronic Dance Music (EDM) project Instituto Mexicano del Sonido (Mexican Institute of Sound). Because music and musical performance are central components in the narrative, creating the appropriate soundscape became a crucial task. With Lara's help, the research team collected samples of several genres, including "Northern Mexico's *banda* tradition, Veracruz's *son jarocho*, and romantic boleros performed by trios."[37] Examples of these practices make momentary sonic appearances in the film, coloring the soundscapes of Santa Cecilia and the Land of the Dead.

Intriguingly, the music performed by the characters is not explicitly taken from the traditions mentioned. As previously mentioned, *Saludos Amigos* and *The Three Caballeros* featured arrangements of already performed and known songs (and melodies) from their respective regions and cultures. For *Coco*, new songs were composed for the film that were incorporated into the storyline to highlight specific events or to showcase the musical stylings of the characters. These songs incorporate some elements of Mexican styles and genres, but ultimately, the songs provide audiences with a Pixarization (or even a Cultural Imagineering) of Mexican music, falling back to complicated orchestral arrangements that follow patterns of the Hollywood film musical. Although the performed music moves through this filter, the placement of the music adheres closely to the Mexican musical-film genre of the *época de oro*, the *comedia ranchera*, "where musicality is a significant narrative and structural focus."[38] As Avila mentions, the *comedia ranchera* is typically set in the countryside in a utopian space, such as a hacienda or *rancho*, and features the singing charro, one of the most significant figures of Mexican cultural identity. The charro performs in designated spaces and at times that would appear to be "normal and logical" for the story. The narrative structure and character development of *Coco* closely follow this structure, acting as a cultural bridge from one musical and cinematic practice to another.

The focus on Mexican cinema's *época de oro* also relates to other musical performances. There are several songs in the film that have symbolized an important connection to the formation of a Mexican identity performed by the male charro characters of the story. Building on the influence and importance of Mexico's *época de oro*, the character of Ernesto de la Cruz mirrors a conflation of screen legends Pedro Infante and Jorge Negrete, two actors who were lovingly and nostalgically known in the Mexican cinema for their performances as singing charros with rich, velvety voices.

"Remember Me" is the most-performed song of the film, taken up by Ernesto de la Cruz, Héctor, and Miguel at different points in the narrative. As a result, the song takes on different iterations, arrangements, and meanings. The first time the audience is introduced to the song, it is performed as a flashy stage number with several groups of mariachi and backup singers (figure 21.1).

Although the lyrics of the song indicate longing, the arrangement and the performance emphasize a curated musical number much like the Hollywood musicals of the 1930s by Busby Berkeley. The second performance of the song is more intimate and sincere. Héctor, it is revealed, is the song's original composer, and he intended the song to be a lullaby for his daughter Coco, Miguel's great-great-grandmother. In a flashback, he performs this lullaby on his acoustic guitar and sings with tenderness, encapsulating the emotion of the song's lyrics.

> Remember me
> Though I have to say goodbye,
> Remember me
> Don't let it make you cry.

THE DISNEY MUSICAL AND LATINIDAD   461

FIGURE 21.1. Ernesto de la Cruz singing "Remember Me."

In this scene, Little Coco, his intended audience, watches and listens attentively before joining him in the last stanza. In the third iteration of the song, Coco is once again the intended audience for the performance of the lullaby, but this time it is performed by Miguel in an effort to help her remember her father. The progression of the song through these different performances by three different generations of charros "construct[s] a bridge of musical practice" that relies on memory and nostalgia.[39] The survival of the song from the period of Ernesto de la Cruz's fame, or the *época de oro*, to the supposed contemporary time of Miguel as the second generation who loves this song comments on the generations of Mexican American and Latinx audiences living in the US who grew up watching and listening to these culturally important films.

While the film consists of originally composed music, the song list also features arrangements of existing and culturally significant songs. One of the most culturally relevant is "La Llorona" ("The Weeping Woman"), a *son istmeño*, a regional song form from the Isthmus of Tehuantepec that features guitar and *requinto*. The *son*'s melody makes several sonic appearances in the film. Based on a popular legend, "La Llorona" tells the story of a woman who drowns her children after her lover abandoned her. Her ghost wanders the countryside, crying out for her children. This song and the story hold a significant space in Mexico and on the US–Mexico border, serving as a cautionary tale, in particular for misbehaving children. Indeed, La Llorona has become a "monster" from childhoods that span generations on both sides of the border and, by extension, Latin America.

The inclusion of "La Llorona" in the film is significant for its recognition of the importance of the song and its place in Día de Muertos. A full performance takes place at the end of the film. The once anti-music matriarch Mamá Imeda finds herself trapped onstage, attempting to outrun Ernesto de la Cruz, who turns out to be Héctor's murderer. To buy time, she begins to sing "La Llorona," at first alone, then accompanied by Héctor and a full orchestra. Surprisingly, the song is introduced not as a melancholy, dark lament but as an upbeat dance number, taking away the somber and mournful feel of the song. Rather than change the lyrics, which was the procedure in the past as evidenced in *The Three Caballeros*, the composers and music directors opted to change the music. Although the lyrics still convey the drama of the story, the music reflects otherwise.

The music and representation of Mexican identity in *Coco* convey the attempts by Disney and Pixar to provide for audiences a culturally relevant film that did not focus on exoticism and stereotypes, as the previous films did, but concentrated on a representation in which Mexico and those who identified as Mexican or Mexican American were the dominant sources of research and influence. This Cultural Imagineering strategy proved to be successful with audiences and critics alike and became the go-to model for future film projects, especially the 2021 feature *Encanto*.

WE DID TALK ABOUT BRUNO: DIVERSITY, COLOMBIANNESS, AND LATINIDAD

Encanto's production team collaborated with a group of cultural advisers to feasibly introduce Colombian characters, cultural features, and traditions to new audiences in Latin America and the US. Still, the filmmakers faced the same challenge El Grupo did decades ago: how to convey a story that could present a vast geography with different peoples and cultures. In *Coco* and *Elena of Avalor*, the decision was to portray some familiar elements and representations associated with Mexico as representations of Latin America. Unsurprisingly, *Encanto* followed this approach. Thus, instead of an extensive view that connected a series of sketches resembling a travelogue proposed by El Grupo, Disney's Cultural Imagineering took a synecdochal approach, interchanging a part for a whole, as suggested in a talk by its director, Jared Bush:

> Latin America is enormous. Where do we set it? ... Where in Latin America can we talk about perspectives and different points of view and bring in as much of Latin America as we can without making it a sort of fantasy place? We wanted, actually, to set [the story] in a real place, and we kept coming back to Colombia because it is such a crossroads of Latin America. Well, naturally, you know, [there are] many different cultures and dance, music, food, architecture, and magical realism. It is all in Colombia. So all signs kept on pointing us there.[40]

Several reasons could explain why *Encanto* was set in Colombia, a country never portrayed in Disney's movies or serials before. However, Bush's words suggest that chief among them was the notion that Colombia's diversity summarizes Latin American geographic, biological, ethnic, and cultural diversity. Besides, Bush's approach to diversity as a marker of Colombianness echoed official narratives of Colombianness introduced in the 1990s as a consequence of two sociopolitical and sociocultural changes. First, the 1991 constitution recognized the country as a multicultural nation, opening the space for the recognition of the rights of minorities such as Indigenous and Afro-Colombians and the design and implementation of cultural policies that finally acknowledged the needs and realities of these communities. Second, multiculturality added a new layer of meaning to preexisting discourses emphasizing geographical and biological diversity, offering an alternative narrative of pride, belonging, and nationhood in a period marked

FIGURE 21.2. Procolombia's website (https://colombia.travel/en) promotes the country as a tourist destination (February 5, 2023).

by the harmful impact of the war on drugs and the negative stereotypes it produced, which associated Colombia with criminality and violence.

Articulating new notions of Colombianness around diversity is a process that became preeminent in the promotion of the country as a prime tourist destination after the FARC guerrilla group and the local government signed a peace agreement in 2016.[41] As illustrated on the website of Procolombia (figure 21.2), the governmental agency that promotes Colombia abroad, the Colombian institutions had produced and reproduced a narrative that intertwines diversity and self-exoticization to attract tourists from the Global North. As exemplified by *Cocreation, Connection, and Conservation* (2022), Procolombia's handbook for cultural tourist guides, this agency extended the scope of its offer beyond the realm of landscapes and biodiversity that prevailed in the 2000s and early 2010s, introducing cultural diversity as a central feature in a touristic "Colombian experience" that immerses visitors in the country that inspired Gabriel García Márquez's magic realism.[42]

The striking similarities between Bush's statement cited earlier and Procolombia's description of Colombian culture suggest that official discourses and narratives connecting diversity and Colombianness informed Disney's approach to Colombia in *Encanto*.[43] Procolombia insists that García Márquez's magic realism, a close relationship between culture and territory, biodiversity, and cultural diversity characterized the country:

> The territory we inhabit and its biodiversity give rise to many manifestations of Colombian culture that are reflected in our rhythms, traditions, languages, handicrafts, culinary customs, and, not least, in the work of Nobel Prize winner, Gabriel García Márquez, according to UNESCO, one of the most widely translated authors in history and the creator of magical realism.[44]

From this standpoint, Disney's Cultural Imagineering combined representations of Colombianness produced for international audiences and information gathered through expeditions and work with consultants, creating a timeless representation of a multicultural society that commodifies cultural objects as exotic qualities representing difference. In 2018, following the model established by El Grupo in the 1940s, a Disney team traveled to Colombia for two weeks of fieldwork to collect ideas and materials necessary for *Encanto*'s production in locations such as Cartagena, Bogotá, and Barichara. The members of this team were directors Jared Bush and Byron Howard, the composer Lin-Manuel Miranda and his father Luis, the producer Yvett Merino, and Tom MacDougall, president of Walt Disney Music. Like their predecessors, *Encanto*'s team relied on a network of artists and experts in different aspects of Colombian culture, to grasp elements palatable for different audiences yet recognizable as expressions of cultural, geographic, and natural idiosyncrasies identifiable as Colombian.[45]

This network of local consultants, headed by Natalie Osma and Juan Rendon, who previously collaborated with Bush and Howard on *Zootopia* (2016), was crucial for shaping *Encanto*. Osma and Rendon coordinated a visit to the Gabriel García Márquez Foundation in Cartagena. They also put together the Colombian Cultural Trust, selecting architects who showed them the materials and characteristics of traditional Colombian architecture, chefs who talked about food, artisan groups who showed them their crafts, and specialists in Afro-Colombian cultures. Finally, the filmmakers met with botanists to talk about Colombian biodiversity.[46]

The experiences of *Encanto*'s team and those of El Grupo had significant similarities. Lin-Manuel Miranda traveled with the production team to immerse himself in a different musical culture during the production of *Encanto*. As he explained in an interview for CNÑ, CNN's network for Hispanic audiences, Miranda listened to music in different Colombian locations, including live music in dance clubs in Colombian cities such as Bogotá and Cartagena and private concerts of traditional string ensembles of *tiple* and guitar in Barichara, a town in the Colombian northeast.[47] Miranda's creative process entailed an expedition to collect sounds and images as Wolcott did in Argentina and Brazil seventy years before. Still, there is a crucial difference between Wolcott and Miranda. Wolcott had to rely on music scores and recordings to grasp some ideas of Latin American music's sounds. Meanwhile, Miranda's ideas of Colombian sonic diversity also came from the works of Colombian musicians who had a prominent presence in the transnational Latino music industry and, in some cases, were active in the US record industry in Miami:

> All I knew about Colombia, other than having a lot of Colombian friends, was the diversity of its music. There is an amazing salsa singer and songwriter named Joe Arroyo; there is Carlos Vives, who is a global figure and you heard in the movie; and then, I went to high school growing up on brunette-era Shakira [singing] rock en español.[48]

The prominent presence of Vives and Shakira as sonic referents of Colombianness for Miranda deserves further attention (Vives himself sang "Colombia Mi Encanto" for the film). As Maria Elena Cepeda has insightfully explained, the number of Colombians exiled to southern Florida grew in the 1990s and 2000s due to the war on drugs and the confrontation between the guerrillas and the Colombian army.[49] Colombian migration to the Miami area transformed Colombian musicians into active participants in the city's Latino music industry, fostering the construction of a transnational US Colombian identity imbricated within the so-called Latin boom. The relationship between the sonic representations of Colombia and those stemming from the Latinx music industry shaped *Encanto*'s soundtrack, as exemplified by the presence of Colombian artists who followed Vives's example and successfully integrated within the US music industry, such as Sebastián Yatra and Maluma.

From this standpoint, Miranda's journey to Colombia informed his notion of Colombian music. However, the sonic representations of Colombianness resulting from a transnational Latinx market established in the US also shaped Miranda's music. The final result was a combination of fieldwork experience and preestablished notions of sonic Colombianness as a form of sonic Latinidad that enriched Miranda's musical style, introduced to Disney's musicals in *Moana* but successfully developed and tested on Broadway in musicals such as *In the Heights* (2008) and *Hamilton* (2015). Thus, this complex process of resignification involved collecting, remembering, transforming, and adapting these sonic expressions of Colombian Latinidad to formulas and sonorities that the composer developed to negotiate sonic representations of difference with the institution of Broadway and its historic (mis)representation of "people of color."[50] This creative approach was so successful that it made *Encanto* the first film to sweep the visual-media categories at the 2023 Grammy Awards, while Miranda's ensemble song "We Don't Talk about Bruno" beat out works from Beyoncé, Taylor Swift, Lady Gaga, Angélique Kidjo, and Billie Eilish.[51]

References to magic realism also were central for establishing representations of Colombia that balanced the locally constructed notions of Colombianness and a transnational standard of Latinidad shaped by the US cultural industry. Magic realism also connected the plot. Taking place in the mountains of Colombia, the film centers on the Madrigals, a multigenerational family whose members received magical gifts when El Milagro, a magic candle, appeared after Abuelo Pedro, the patriarch of the family, sacrificed himself to save his wife and three children. Besides providing magic powers to the Madrigals, El Milagro also brought a house, the casita, that came alive, offering a refuge for the family and other people.

However, El Milagro is fragile. Mirabel, one of the youngest members of the Madrigal family, did not receive her gift during her initiation rite. This mystery turned into misfortune when her uncle Bruno, gifted with premonition, disappeared that same night. As a result, Mirabel became a tolerated outcast within the family, and her relationship with Abuela Alma went awry. Later Mirabel finds Bruno hidden between the walls of the casita and persuades him to help her understand a vision that shows her with the casita crumbling behind her back. Bruno's new vision shows that reconciliation between Mirabel and her sister, Isabela, would save El Milagro. Following the vision, Mirabel mends the relationship, only to face an angry and displeased Abuela Alma, who confronts her. The ensuing argument ends with the casita falling apart and Mirabel leaving Encanto. Abuela Alma finds Mirabel at the river shore. The two reconcile, and Bruno joins them. Then they return to rebuild the casita with the help of friends and neighbors. Suddenly, the magic returns.

Hence, magic realism introduces a mixture between reality and fantasy to the plot, making possible the multiple references to different regional Colombian cultures and ethnic backgrounds. For example, in the film's opening, Mirabel introduces her family to three children: one Afro-Colombian girl, a blond girl, and a mestizo boy. The Madrigal family also reinforces such a narrative: Mirabel's grandmother and mother are mestizos, her sister Isabela has Indigenous features, her father and aunt Pepa are white, and her uncle Félix and her cousin Antonio are Afro. However, this diverse picture also relies on cultural references: her uncle Félix wears traditional costumes from the Pacific region, her aunt Pepa's clothes resemble those of a Caribbean *palenquera*, and Mirabel wears a traditional dress from Santander in the Andes. Finally, an image in this scene puts together three musicians playing an accordion (associated with the Caribbean Vallenato), a *cununo* (a drum used in the marimba ensembles in the South Pacific), and a *tiple* (a traditional plucked string instrument from the Andes), reinforcing the idea that Encanto is a town that reunites Colombia's geographical, cultural, and ethnic diversity into a single place (figure 21.3). Therefore, the film reinscribes, from a multicultural perspective, a traditional narrative that portrays Colombia as a mestizo nation that results from the peaceful coexistence of three main racial groups—Hispanic (white), Indigenous, and Afro—in a complex geographical framework.[52]

Magic realism also transforms the Madrigal family's history into a means for introducing complex and possibly problematic aspects of Colombian history within the plot by opening the space for a Macondian narrative. Such a narrative, which Ana Maria

FIGURE 21.3. Introducing *Encanto*'s Madrigals.

FIGURE 21.4. The rising of El Milagro.

Ochoa defines as the "Latin-Americanist celebration of magical realism," represents violence poetically through fiction, establishing a metaphor for the contradictions and conflicts within Colombian society. As a result, the Macondian narrative sets up "mirror images of identity" where the contradictions and excesses acquire an aesthetic value that makes them tolerable, even picturesque.[53] An example is the representation of Abuelo Pedro's death after shielding his family and neighbors from armed riders, a reference to the Colombian conflict and its painful and traumatic consequences, which ends with the raising of El Milagro when a shining yellow butterfly, a reference to García Márquez's magic realism, appears in the candle that a young Abuela Alma was carrying when she was running away from the armed men with Abuelo Pedro (figure 21.4).

Meanwhile, Yatra sings "Dos Oruguitas" by Miranda. The simple and calm music and lyrics of this song contrast with the references to the Colombian internal conflict and its victims, conveying the feelings in a crucial turn in Abuela Alma's history that normal dialogue could not do. This discordance between image and music reinforces the idea that love and resilience prevail over death and pain, suggesting that Colombian history is not about violence but about transformation, change, forgiveness, and hope.

Ay oruguitas,	Oh caterpillars,
no se aguanten más	don't hold each other any longer
hay que crecer aparte y volver	you must grow apart and return
hacia adelante seguirás	that is the way forward
vienen milagros, vienen crisálidas	miracles are coming, chrysalises are coming
hay que partir,	you must part,
y construir su propio futuro	and construct your own future

This depiction of Colombia contrasts with other portrayals of the country by productions such as Netflix's *Narcos*, which dig into the country's recent past to create antiheroes and histories that present Colombia as a failed state, violent and ruled by drug lords and outlaws. By introducing alternative and positive audiovisual representations of Colombianness inspired by approaches that echoed institutional discourses while following the suggestions made by cultural advisers, *Encanto* continued Disney movies' approach to positive representations of Latin America and Latin American people introduced in *Coco*. Colombians valued this new audiovisual representation of the country and acknowledged its international impact. *Encanto* was well received and celebrated by Colombian audiences and members of the Colombian diaspora. This positive reception even opened the doors for questionable commodification processes of Disney's Colombianness in Colombia. For example, in 2021, *Encanto* was the central theme of the traditional Christmas lights in Medellín, the second-most-populous Colombian city. However, before installing and turning on the lights, the Medellín municipality paid around $174,536 (US) to Disney for the image rights.[54]

Another layer of meaning connecting representations of Colombianness and Latinidad is the extended family's central role in *Encanto*'s plot. The Madrigals are a multigenerational family; grandma, uncles, aunts, mothers, fathers, cousins, sons, daughters, and siblings coexist in the casita, sharing the table, talking to one another, and sharing secrets. Even Bruno, the family's outcast, painted his dishes on his hideout's dinner table; thus, he could see his mother, sisters, brothers-in-law, and nephews sharing meals at the main dinner table (figure 21.5). Centering the history of a family with such characteristics facilitates the introduction of the representations of ethnic diversity mentioned before as well as opportunities to develop each character's history in a way that sets the multiple tensions connecting those histories. Following Mirabel, the

FIGURE 21.5. Mirabel looks at Bruno's dinner-table hideout.

audience discovers individual frustrations, traumas, and misunderstandings, as well as love, forgiveness, and redemption. In addition, extended multigenerational families are often considered cultural markers of Latinx and Latin American people within the US, as exemplified by successful sitcoms such as *Jane the Virgin* (2014–2019), *One Day at a Time* (2017–2020), and *Gentefied* (2020–2021).

However, portraying the subtle intricacies characterizing interpersonal relations and inner dynamics of an extended multigenerational Latino family requires a deep level of cultural intimacy that fieldwork cannot supply, nor can it be developed from conversations with a team of cultural advisers. To overcome such a challenge, *Encanto*'s team relied on La Familia, a group of Latinx Disney employees: Yvett Merino (producer), Jorge Ruiz Cano (animation), Rebecca Perez Stodolny (animation), and Juan Pablo Reyes (creative executive of development). Merino explained, in an interview for Rise Up Animation (2022),[55] that the film directors wanted to put together a group of people of Latinx descent to "just talk about family and life" once a month. This group later played a central role in terms of cultural advice. Indeed, as Merino pointed out, La Familia "read every script written by Jared [Bush] and Charice Castro Smith," providing feedback. These conversations became crucial for the production of *Encanto*, as they introduced personal stories that helped the directors learn about the singular dynamics and relations that many Latinx people experience within their families in their daily lives. Therefore, La Familia served as an additional cultural trust for *Encanto*, bringing into account the singularities of the Latinx experience in the US.

From this standpoint, building trust with members of the Latinx minority at Disney was as crucial for establishing a community that contributed to the creation and production of *Encanto* as were the dialogues and international insight provided by the Colombian Cultural Trust. Therefore, demographic changes and cooperative policies favoring diversity not only have transformed Disney's and Pixar's staff, but they also allowed a new negotiation between the representation of the Madrigals as an extended multigenerational family whose experiences were relatable both for Colombians and for Latinx people in the US. The consequent reterritorialization of Colombianness through the commodification of diversity in *Encanto* shows the search for such a balance. *Encanto*'s success relied on Disney's Imagineering response to the singularities of representing Colombia and Colombians in terms that fit within the expectations of difference or relatability expected by Latinx audiences in the US.

Conclusion

In the fall of 2023, the Disney Channel and Disney+ streaming service introduced a new animated series that focuses on Latinx representation and the Latinx experience, relying again on the extended family as marker of Latinidad. *Primos* (*Cousins*) tells the story of Tater Ramirez Humphrey, who is a young girl in Hacienda Hills (Earthquake Heights as a fake name for Los Angeles) attempting to make her summer fantastic but whose life is interrupted when her twelve cousins move in. Disney had dropped the theme song video for the series in early June, which is about fifty seconds long and introduces the audience to Tater and her cousins, with the repetitive tag "¡Oye! ¡Primos!" ("Hey, Cousins!"). This short video has become a center of controversy and criticism of racist representation. Posters on social media have commented on the stereotype of "multiple family members living under one roof," the incorrect phrasing of the tagline, which should be the plural form "¡Oigan! ¡Primos!," the use of the yellow filter to represent a Latino neighborhood, and the questionable names given to the cousins (the name of the youngest cousin, Cuquita, is slang for "vagina" in some parts of Latin America; Cuquita's name was later changed to Lucita). Disney pulled the video from its social media and website and streamed the series beginning June 25, 2024, for only one season. Although the series is based on the experiences of Mexican American creator Natasha Kline, who grew up in a multicultural household in Los Angeles, the show has still been met with considerable hostility online. At what point can an acceptable representation be achieved? Is it possible to engulf the myriad experiences, histories, and cultures that coexist in Latin America and the Caribbean in a series of well-intended generalizations?

The pursuit of new audiovisual representations of Latinx and Latin American people by Disney's Cultural Imagineering illustrates the challenges involved in producing animated films and series relatable to the experiences and expectations of changing audiences in the twentieth-first century. In addition to the interest in bringing cultural advisers and experts to extend the scope of the production process, the rise of Cultural Imagineering also shows the impact that new multicultural consumers and their sensibilities have on an increasingly globalized animated industry. However, the analysis presented in this chapter also suggests that Cultural Imagineering introduces a complex series of ruptures and continuities within conceptual approaches that have shaped how animators, designers, editors, writers, and musicians have responded to the challenge of representing difference in animated media.

The rise of Cultural Imagineering in the twentieth-first century fostered a process that negotiated preexisting audiovisual narrative strategies with the increasing importance of Latinx and Latin American audiences as consumers of Disney's and Pixar's products, driving a reconfiguration of the representations of Latinx and Latin American characters in Disney's animated films and serials. However, Cultural Imagineering is also a result of a long hemispheric history that can be traced back to the era of the Good Neighbor policy. As a result, Cultural Imagineering also inherited a long-standing tradition that represented Latin America and Latin American people by exoticizing diversity and difference to draw audiences in the US. While El Grupo appealed to stereotypes well established within Hollywood's cinematic industry in the 1940s to represent Latin American cultures and people, Cultural Imagineering has introduced new forms of representing Latin America, informed not only by cultural advisers but also by Disney's insiders who identified themselves as Latinx. Therefore, rather than reproducing an outsider's gaze, *Coco*'s and *Encanto*'s production teams incorporated Latinx and Latin American gazes to blur the boundaries separating local notions of nationhood and belonging from a US Latinx identity, aiming to produce films appealing to audiences in Latin America and the US. Ultimately, such an analysis suggests that the treatment of Latinx and Latin American characters and music in Disney's Cultural Imagineering is both a response to shifting demographics within the US and a cooperative effort to produce more feasible and culturally acceptable representations of a vast region whose cultural and ethnic diversity has challenged Disney's animators, musicians, and editors for several decades.

Notes

1. Walt Disney Imagineering, https://sites.disney.com/waltdisneyimagineering/.
2. According to the 2020 US Census, slightly more than half (51.1 percent) of the total US population growth between 2010 and 2020 came from growth in the Hispanic or Latino population. This is the second-fastest-growing nonwhite community after Asian Americans. For further information, see https://www.census.gov/library/stories/2021/08/improved-race-ethnicity-measures-reveal-united-states-population-much-more-multiracial.html.
3. See Frederick B. Pike, *FDR's Good Neighbor Policy: Sixty Years of Gentle Chaos* (Austin: University of Texas Press, 1995).
4. The conflicts between the US and its southern neighbors began in 1845 with the annexation of Texas and continued after the victory in the Mexican-American War in 1848. After the Civil War, the US turned its interest to Central America and the Caribbean, fostering a long list of invasions and interventions that included countries and territories such as Colombia-Panama (1903), Cuba (1898, 1906, 1912, 1917), Dominican Republic (1916), Guatemala (1903), Haiti (1915), Honduras (1924), Mexico (1914, 1916), Nicaragua (1909, 1912, 1925, 1926), and Puerto Rico (1898). See Alan McPherson, *A Short History of U.S. Interventions in Latin America and the Caribbean* (Chichester: Wiley-Blackwell, 2016).
5. The Office of Coordinator of Inter-American Affairs in the Executive Office of the President was formally established and enacted by US Executive Order 8840 on July 30, 1941.
6. Gisela Cramer and Ursula Prutsch, "Nelson A. Rockefeller's Office of Inter-American Affairs (1940–1946) and Record Group 229," *Hispanic American Historical Review* 86, no. 4 (2006): 786.
7. See Andrea Matallana, *Nelson Rockefeller y la diplomacia del arte en América Latina* (Buenos Aires: Universidad de Buenos Aires Press, 2021).
8. See Rolf Giesen, *Nazi Propaganda Films: A History and Filmography* (Jefferson, NC: McFarland, 2003).
9. See András Lénárt, "América Latina según Whitney y Disney: El cine interamericano de la política de Buena Vecindad en los años 1930 y 40," *Acta Hispanica* 23 (2018): 55–67.
10. See Jake Friedman, *The Disney Revolt: The Great Labor War of Animation's Golden Age* (Chicago: Chicago Review, 2022).
11. The documentary *Walt & El Grupo* by Theodore Thomas (Walt Disney Studios, 2008) presents this tour in further detail.
12. For example, between 1880 and 1930, more than 2 million Italian citizens migrated to Argentina; this is the second-largest Italian diaspora in the hemisphere after the US. Meanwhile, 42 percent of the immigrants who settled in Brazil between 1870 and 1920 were Italians. Brazil also has the largest Japanese population outside Japan. See Anna Rosa Campagnano, *Italianos: História e memória de uma comunidade* (São Paulo: Companhia Editora Nacional, 2006).

13. An example is the Victor Talking Machine's scouts, who traveled across South America and the Caribbean between 1905 and 1926, recording matrixes of Latin American music that were later sent to New Jersey to be pressed and sold as "ethnic records." See Sergio Sergio Ospina Romero, "Fonógrafos ambulantes: Las expediciones de la Victor Talking Machine Company por América Latina, 1905–1926," in *Del archivo al playlist: Historias, nostalgias y tecnologías*, ed. Liliana Moreno (Mendoza: IASPM-AL, 2020), 81–89 and Sergio Ospina Romero, *La Conquista discográfica de América Latina (1903–1926)* (Buenos Aires: Gourment Musical, 2024).
14. Dale Adams, "Saludos Amigos: Hollywood and FDR's Good Neighbor Policy," *Quarterly Review of Film and Video* 24, no. 3 (2007): 294.
15. Julianne Burton-Carvajal, "Surprise Package: Looking Southward with Disney," in *Disney Discourse: Producing the Magic Kingdom*, ed. Eric Smoodin (New York: Taylor & Francis, 1994), 134.
16. Ibid.
17. The pampas are grassy plains located in South America, particularly prominent in Argentina, Brazil, and Uruguay.
18. By 1941, Chazarreta was a celebrated folklorist in his country, recognized for his pioneering research of northern Argentinian folk music, the songs he collected and recorded, and his role as founder and director of the Companía de Arte Nativo. This company was the first folkloric troupe to successfully tour Argentina performing traditional music and dances.
19. After the Argentine writer José Hernández published his epic poem *El gaucho Martín Fierro* in 1879, the gaucho, a cowboy who lived in the Argentinian planes (or pampas), became a figure representing values such as freedom, honor, simplicity, musicality, and patriotism. Thus, the gaucho increasingly became associated with a form of patriarchal Argentine-ness celebrated in the production of many Argentine artists, including Alberto Ginastera's ballet *La estancia*.
20. Carol Hess, "Walt Disney's *Saludos Amigos*: Hollywood and the Propaganda of Authenticity," in *The Tide Was Always High: The Music of Latin America in Los Angeles*, ed. Josh Kun (Oakland: University of California Press, 2017), 116.
21. Juan Carlos Poveda Vieira, "Music and Propaganda in Two Animated Films Produced by Disney during the Second World War," *Revista Musical Chilena* 75, no. 236 (2021): 132.
22. Eric A. Galm, "*Baianas, Malandros*, and Samba: Listening to Brazil through Donald Duck's Ears," in *Global Soundtracks: Worlds of Film Music*, ed. Mark Slobin (Middleton, CT: Wesleyan University Press, 2008), 258.
23. These friends include the three animated characters Donald Duck, Joe Carioca, and Panchito and three live-action actresses and singers, Aurora Miranda, Carmen Molina, and Dora Luz. See Burton-Carvajal, "Surprise Package," 136.
24. Galm, "*Baianas, Malandros*, and Samba," 259.
25. Ibid., 262.
26. Ibid., 267.
27. Ibid., 269.
28. Ibid., 275.
29. Lyrics from the film. Also included in Burton-Carvajal, "Surprise Package."
30. Cindy Rodriguez, "Backlash for Disney's First Latina Princess," CNN Edition, October 19, 2012, http://edition.cnn.com/2012/10/19/showbiz/disneys-first-latina-princess/index.html.

31. For further information about this debate, see ibid.; Christopher Zara, "Sofia, the Blue-Eyed 'Hispanic' Princess, Sparks Controversy; Disney Denies Character's 'Latina' Heritage," *International Business Times*, October 23, 2012, https://www.ibtimes.com/sofia-blue-eyed-hispanic-princess-sparks-controversy-disney-denies-characters-latina-heritage-852530.
32. Emily Rome, "'Sofia the First': Disney's First Hispanic Princess?," *Entertainment Weekly*, October 16, 2012, https://ew.com/article/2012/10/16/disney-princess-sofia-the-first-latina/.
33. See Mercedes Milligan, "'Elena of Avalor' Takes Disney Channel Throne July 22," *Animation Magazine*, June 10, 2016, https://www.animationmagazine.net/2016/06/elena-of-avalor-takes-disney-channel-throne-july-22/.
34. Mathew Sandoval, "Unholy Holiday: Día de Muertos in Disney's *Elena of Avalor*," in *Latinx TV in the Twentieth Century*, ed. Frederick Luis Aldama (Tucson: University of Arizona Press, 2022), 162.
35. Ibid., 163.
36. As Avila notes, the premiere of this film came after Donald Trump announced his candidacy for president and ignited outrage by calling Mexicans "thieves, drug dealers, and rapists" in a press conference. This event caused shock waves across the US and in Mexico. See Jacqueline Avila, "*Memorias de Oro*: Music, Nostalgia, and *Mexicanidad* in Pixar's *Coco* (2017)," *Americas: A Hemispheric Music Journal* 29 (2020): 4.
37. Ibid.
38. Ibid., 6.
39. Ibid., 12.
40. "Charla ENCANTO con Lin-Manuel Miranda & el Director Jared Bush," TheMovieReport.com, December 22, 2021, https://www.youtube.com/watch?v=3CL2OKVpOkY&t=751s.
41. By 2016, the Fuerzas Armadas Revolucionarias de Colombia (FARC) was the oldest and biggest Latin American guerrilla movement. Although founded in 1966, its origins could be traced to 1949, when organized peasant self-defense groups appeared in response to aggressions and attacks by the conservative police and the Colombian army. During the 1960s, under the leadership of Jacobo Arenas and Manuel Marulanda (known as "Tirofijo"), these groups embraced communism and anti-imperialism. In the following decades, FARC guerrillas spread throughout the country, employing various military tactics and more unconventional methods including terrorism while participating in drug traffic. By 2015, the last official census showed that this guerrilla group had 5,765 men distributed at sixty-six to seventy fronts and structures across Colombia. See Mario Aguilera, ed., *Guerrilla y oblación civil: Trayectoria de las FARC 1949–2013* (Bogotá: Centro de Memoria Histórica, 2013).
42. The manual *Cocreation, Connection, Conservation* was conceived as an illustrated and research-based repository of stories about Colombia's cultural history, complemented by a fifty-chapter podcast series. The manual is available at https://guiacultura.colombia.travel/en/handbook.
43. These similarities were so evident that Flavia Santoro, the director of Procolombia in 2021, affirmed in an interview: "*Encanto* has been a great promotional opportunity for the country. As several international media indicate, it was the most-watched animated film in the United States in 2021. Therefore, hundreds of Colombian peculiarities such as customs, folklore, and [cultural] richness have had a unique showcase to reach thousands of viewers thanks to Disney's tremendous outreach." See https://www.larepublica.co/economia/encanto-ha-sido-una-gran-oportunidad-de-promocion-del-pais-a-nivel-internacional-3279923.

44. Procolombia, *Cocreation, Connection, and Conservation: An Illustrated Handbook for Cultural Tourism Guides in Colombia* (Bogotá: Punto Aparte Editores, 2022), 4.
45. Laura Zornoza, "'Encanto' May Be Accurate, but Can It Carry a Whole Country?," *New York Times*, March 11, 2022, https://www.nytimes.com/2022/03/11/movies/encanto-colombia.html.
46. Osma and Rendon are the founders of Figmento Inc., an independent production company that produces premium content directed to the Latino market, ranging from documentaries to animation and films. In addition to Disney, this company has produced content for companies such as HBO, Amazon Prime Video, Netflix, Univision, Televisa, and Televisión Española Internacional.
47. "Lin-Manuel Miranda y su inmersión en Colombia para la música de 'Encanto,'" CNÑ, February 2022, https://www.youtube.com/watch?v=rg0xjwrb5PM.
48. "ENCANTO Talk with Lin-Manuel Miranda & Director Jared Bush," TheMovieReport.com, December 22, 2021, https://www.youtube.com/watch?v=3CL2OKVpOkY&t=751s.
49. Maria Elena Cepeda, *Musical ImagiNation: U.S.-Colombian Identity and the Latin Music Boom* (New York: New York University Press., 2020).
50. See Elena Machado, "Blackout on Broadway: Affiliation and Audience in *In the Heights* and *Hamilton*," *Studies in Musical Theatre* 12, no. 2 (2018): 181–197.
51. Jessica Lipsky, "'Encanto' Sweeps the 2023 GRAMMYs: Disney's Animated Smash Wins 3 Categories," Grammy Awards News, February 6, 2023, https://www.grammy.com/news/encanto-sweeps-2023-grammys-visual-media-categories-we-dont-talk-about-bruno-lin-manuel-miranda-germaine-franco.
52. As in other Latin American countries, Colombian urban elites molded and promoted paradoxical national identity upon the ideology of *mestizaje*, a nation-building discourse that claimed that cultural mixing of Indigenous and Hispanic people was the essence of the Colombian nation, while privileged whiteness was the standard for measuring the degree of civilization that enabled the participation in power structures, citizenship, and rights. Therefore, *mestizaje* was an ideology that was inclusive in theory but exclusionist in practice and perpetuated forms of colonial control over the subalterns that reinforced the hegemonic position of the "white" urban elites, especially those from Andean cities, over other social classes and ethnic groups. See Ronald Stutzman, "El Mestizaje: An All-Inclusive Ideology of Exclusion," in *Cultural Transformation and Ethnicity in Modern Ecuador*, ed. Norman E. Whitten Jr. (Urbana: University of Illinois Press, 1981), 59–75.
53. Ana María Ochoa, "García Márquez, Macondismo and the Soundscapes of Vallenato," *Popular Music* 24, no. 2 (2005): 212.
54. This scandalous amount sparked intense debates in the city and the country. While some politicians and members of civil society denounced this expense as unnecessary in the period of hardship that followed the Covid-19 pandemic, Daniel Quintero, Medellín's mayor at that time, and some of his allies at the municipal council affirmed that it was an investment that would be repaid with the income from the flocks of tourists visiting the city to enjoy the Christmas lights. See https://www.elespectador.com/colombia/medellin/alumbrados-de-medellin-entre-criticas-y-aplausos/; https://www.infobae.com/america/colombia/2022/10/13/asi-sera-el-polemico-alumbrado-navideno-de-medellin-inspirado-en-los-personajes-de-encanto/.
55. See "Encanto's La Familia," Rise Up Animation, February 22, 2022, https://www.youtube.com/watch?v=gMG3qhBt_Ug.

PART V
DISNEY THEATRICAL

CHAPTER 22

BEFORE *THE BEAST*: ENTERTAINMENT CONGLOMERATES ON BROADWAY IN THE 1980S

ELIZABETH L. WOLLMAN

THE 1980s saw a series of extensive political, technological, economic, and legal shifts that together exerted unprecedented influence on America's mass-entertainment industries. The volatility of the 1980s—during which entertainment companies scrambled to adapt to sweeping federal deregulation policies, a slew of new technologies, a trend for vertical and horizontal integration toward conglomeration in response to global expansion, and an urgent need to cater to ever-growing international audiences—resulted in the transformation of American popular entertainment.[1] While mass-mediated entertainments were most immediately transformed by the turbulence of the 1980s, the commercial theater industry was influenced, too; the changes that took place during the 1980s culminated in the Walt Disney Company's arrival on Broadway as a theater manager and producer in the early 1990s.

Most scholarship about Disney's presence on Broadway centers on the company's aesthetic imprint on the genre, usually beginning with its commercially successful if critically tepid stage musical version of *Beauty and the Beast* in 1994.[2] Arts scholarship that considers the business side of Broadway's transformation during the 1990s tends to treat Disney's arrival on Broadway as a foregone conclusion but does not delve into the shifts in entertainment culture or the many ventures into commercial theater production attempted by entertainment conglomerates during the 1980s, which led Disney to Times Square in the first place.[3]

The dearth of scholarship on the ways mass entertainment's shifts in the 1980s helped lead to Disney's Broadway debut in 1994 is understandable. Mass-entertainment companies, after all, were actively experiencing the most spectacular (and thus the most newsworthy) transitions, while the relatively tiny and analog commercial theater industry remained relatively stable and unaffected by comparison. Coverage in the trades and the popular press invariably emphasized the frequent mergers, acquisitions, takeovers, and bankruptcies that occurred as competing media conglomerates raced to master and capitalize on fast-developing technologies including home video, cable television, pay channels, satellite delivery, and early gaming platforms. The fact that many of these companies were simultaneously attempting to devise new, mutually beneficial relationships with the theater industry tended to be treated as far less remarkable than the many larger shifts taking place across the mediated entertainment landscape.

Further, the commercial theater was struggling during the 1980s with a number of crises that, at least at the time, could easily be interpreted as wholly unrelated to the shifts taking place in the world of mass entertainment. At the dawn of that decade, New York City's financial crisis was no longer a threat, but the theater industry remained preoccupied by the tourist-alienating squalor of Times Square, climbing costs of theatrical production, a series of critically and commercially disappointing seasons, and declining ticket sales.[4] While they had been circulating for a while, four different studies that had been released in the mid- to late 1960s, all of which argued that the commercial theater would be unable to sustain itself economically without significant transformations, continued to loom.[5] Finally, even as American mass entertainment and Broadway have long been mutually interdependent, cross-industrial scholarship that sheds light on relationships between the theater and film, television, radio, and popular music has been deficient until fairly recently.[6]

Attempts by mass-entertainment companies, including Disney, to make inroads on Broadway in the 1980s might have been obscured at the time, but Disney's arrival in 1994 relates back to the industrial shifts that took place across that decade. In the mid-1980s, Disney was but one of many rapidly conglomerating entertainment companies to attempt to benefit from new partnerships with Broadway personnel. While none of the models pioneered by companies such as 20th Century Fox, Paramount, or Warner Bros. proved as slickly branded, packaged, ready-made, and lucrative as Disney's would, the Mouse would not have landed on Broadway without them. This chapter, which aims to clarify the ways the changes impacting mass entertainment in the 1980s led to Disney's arrival on Broadway in 1994, ends where Disney Theatrical begins.

Broadway and Mass Entertainment before the 1980s

In her book *Broadway in the Box*, Kelly Kessler points out that even as they are often studied, historicized, and written about as separate entities, "different media and performance platforms have *always* enjoyed blurred borders," which have helped them accommodate what fandom scholar Henry Jenkins describes as "'the migratory behavior of media audiences who will go almost anywhere in search of the kinds of entertainment experiences they want.'"[7] From their inception, most American mass-entertainment companies devised ways to make steady streams of income through professional partnerships formed with representatives from the commercial theater.

Numerous film companies—the earliest of which were, after all, established by theater people who retained their connections to Broadway long after "going Hollywood"—regularly financed Broadway stage productions that might become hit films, usually in exchange for the first rights of refusal.[8] The music industry consolidated in New York City in the early twentieth century due in part to the mutually beneficial relationship it had developed with Broadway, but long after the sheet music heyday, the theater continued to make plenty of money for the music industry in the form of show music catalogs, Broadway cast and compilation albums, commercial jingles, middle-of-the-road and specialty radio stations, themed radio shows, and various other segments of the "nostalgia folio market."[9] And from its infancy in the mid-1940s, television looked frequently to Broadway's artists, productions, and music as it built its own identity.[10]

Yet Broadway's relationships with mass-entertainment companies have simultaneously been viewed with anxiety and defensiveness by members of the theater industry itself—as well as by gatekeepers such as journalists, scholars, historians, and fans—since such relationships are widely interpreted as being more beneficial to the entertainment companies themselves than to the health and wellbeing of the American theater.[11] Kessler points out that even at the dawn of broadcasting in the 1920s, Broadway "entered into a love/hate relationship" with it that arguably continues at present; theater personnel have a long history of gobbling up the exposure to wider audiences that new technologies grant their productions, even as they simultaneously fret that "free over-the-air access" will inevitably cause the decline of live audiences and the eventual death of the theater.[12]

The treatment of playwrights, composers, and lyricists has only added to the theater industry's anxieties when it comes to relationships with larger and more far-reaching entertainment industries. While such creative artists are typically granted relatively active involvement and control in theater making, they are widely understood to be stripped of such centralized roles, along with much in the way of recognition, once they move beyond the stage.[13] As a result, relationships Broadway has developed with mass-entertainment companies, lucrative as they are, tend to get painted as detrimental to the artistic integrity of the stage and thus a necessary evil at best.

As early as 1932, for example, *New York Times* theater critic Brooks Atkinson warned of the perils he saw in Broadway producers' then-regular practice of accepting seed money from Hollywood in exchange for first dibs on the rights to productions that might translate well to film. Claiming to be no enemy of the new medium, Atkinson nevertheless accused the film industry of ignoring art and prioritizing "merchantable entertainment" that, while diverting in its own right, was ultimately "designed chiefly to keep the industry going" and therefore detrimental to the theater:

> Hollywood cannot be isolated for condemnation. Every one [sic] makes mistakes in show business. But when money is easy to get, producers go ahead with plays they

would not risk putting on in more penurious circumstances, hoping that screen rights will pull them out of the red-ink hole. I suspect that easy Hollywood backing brings out the worst in theatre men.[14]

For as long as mass-entertainment companies have acted as Broadway financiers, the love/hate relationship Kessler describes has gone both ways. Broadcasting companies love hit Broadway productions and the revenue streams that come with synergizing them. Even so, for as long as the theater has mistrusted media companies, media companies have perceived the theater industry as frustratingly clubby, old-fashioned, and deeply wary of corporate "'carpetbaggers ... out to take control of Broadway ... for their own purposes.'"[15]

This mutual tension, born of the fact that "Broadway and Hollywood were in competition with one another even as they did business together,"[16] had set in long before the media explosion and conglomerations of the 1980s. Because of such tensions—which were often exacerbated in the press and in many theater histories—mass-entertainment companies with a history of conducting business on Broadway tend to have done so quietly, by serving as literal silent investors or engaging in other kinds of secretive financial agreements, but little more, for the better part of the twentieth century.

Yet Broadway properties became increasingly desirable as entertainment companies began to integrate vertically and horizontally—that is, to absorb related (and often competing) businesses and to acquire companies that operate above or below them in the supply chain. As such companies conglomerated in the last decades of the twentieth century, most embraced the concept of synergy.[17] Beginning in the late 1970s and continuing through the 1980s, several American entertainment companies began building past the long-established practice of simply bankrolling Broadway shows in the new hope of gaining more creative control over properties that could be repeatedly sold to audiences across multiple platforms. By the mid-1980s, Disney joined other, larger entertainment companies such as 20th Century Fox, Paramount, and Warner Bros. in fresh attempts to forge new, untried connections and approaches to Broadway. While these early forays were often moderately successful at best, most were also far subtler than the model Disney landed on when it established a presence in the commercial theater in the 1990s.

THE 1980S: DEREGULATION DRAMA AND CABLE CONFUSION

While technological and global shifts, along with industrial deregulation, had begun in earlier years, much of the volatility of the American entertainment market in the late twentieth century resulted from policies prioritized by President Ronald Reagan and his administration. Until the early 1970s, a strict series of federal rules and regulations had largely prevented the kinds of vertical and horizontal integration that have since resulted in the creation of international multimedia conglomerates. While trends toward industrial deregulation began during the Gerald Ford and Jimmy Carter presidencies, Reagan took full advantage of the swell of "anti-government sentiment that had increased throughout the 1970s," and that had helped sweep him into office in a landslide election, by even more dramatically "eliminating the use of antitrust enforcement as a means of regulating business" in the US.[18]

When it came to broadcasting, Reagan believed that government regulations stifled the "creativity, ingenuity [and] diversity of programing" and in the worst cases allowed "the government to intrude into sensitive First Amendment areas to the detriment of the public and broadcasters alike." Reagan argued that the deregulation of broadcasting would result in more varied programming across all platforms and that "more reliance on marketplace forces and less on the heavy hand of government regulation and control" would better serve audiences.[19]

Despite concerns about the monopolies that would result from such sweeping deregulation, the Reagan administration took a "laissez-faire approach to mergers and acquisitions" and to the rapid growth of international conglomerates. While numerous barriers to vertical integration remained on the books through Reagan's presidency, virtually "*no* vertical mergers were challenged in any industry" during his eight years in office. A result in the entertainment world was that "barriers between media industries began to break down," resulting in a decade-long scramble among entertainment companies that entered into hot competition with one another as they grew in as many directions as they could:

> Film studios combined with broadcast networks (Fox), production/distribution entities reunited with exhibition outlets (Universal, Paramount, Warner Bros.), and film companies merged with cable properties (Warner Bros., MCA/Universal, Columbia), thereby creating innovative alliances across formerly distinct industrial boundaries. It was a time of intense merger activity in film and television, and all of it took place with the blessing of the Department of Justice. By 1996, most of the major film studios and broadcast networks had become part of global conglomerates that encompassed some of the largest players in media and entertainment.[20]

Even prior to the restructuring that occurred during the Reagan era, Hollywood had begun to embrace new technologies and to look toward global expansion as a means of recouping growing production costs.[21] Broadway's own precarious situation in the 1970s—as the purveyor of increasingly expensive live entertainment situated in an infamously run-down neighborhood in a cash-starved metropolis—was hardly lost on mass-entertainment companies. Nor was a significant spike in the commercial reach of cast albums from hit musicals such as *A Chorus Line* (1975), *The Wiz* (1975), and *Annie* (1977). The rapid growth of cable and home video during the 1970s spurred an urgent need for new and varied programming that might reach larger, more diversified audiences. High-ranking executives of mass-entertainment industries, increasingly convinced that "the substance and direction of American musical theater [was] up for grabs," began actively rethinking their approaches to Broadway.[22]

At first, "the path to fully integrated empires of entertainment ... wound through the cable industry, via the film studios."[23] Cable was introduced to the US in 1948 as a means of improving reception in rural or mountainous regions. Cable operators quickly figured out how to pick up broadcast signals from increasingly great distances, which transformed cable from a means of boosting local television signals into a provider of new programming. As cable's reach grew in the 1950s and '60s, local stations began to complain about having to compete with broadcasters far from the communities they were meant to serve. In the mid-1960s, the FCC responded by restricting the reach of broadcasting signals and slowing the expansion of cable systems into major marketplaces.[24]

Cable restrictions remained in place until 1972, after which they were gradually loosened; in the Reagan era, so, too, were rules restricting the cross-ownership of broadcasting systems. Yet even before such barriers were lifted, Hollywood had begun selling movies to burgeoning cable companies and forming divisions devoted to releasing films on videotape. Cable's groundbreaking adaptation of satellite communications technology, the successful launch of Home Box Office (HBO) in November 1972, and the subsequent shift toward vertical and horizontal integration made the deregulation of cable television something of a linchpin in the larger telecommunications deregulation package that was created in the 1980s.[25]

As media-entertainment industries grew in power, size, and reach, and as the commercial theater center of the US continued to signal a need for its own significant transitions, numerous entertainment companies—not only film studios but also cable companies, television stations, and record labels—began approaching Broadway with fresh ways of doing cross-industrial business. The efforts of entertainment conglomerates, combined with the theater industry's need to remain viable in a world that increasingly prioritized mass-mediated entertainment, eventually resulted in Times Square's redevelopment, the commercial theater industry's globalization, and Disney's entry into Broadway and global theatrical production.

Cross-Industrial Inroads in the Late 1970s and the 1980s

Through much of the 1970s, as cross-industrial collaboration became increasingly possible for all parties, mass entertainment's involvement on Broadway remained stuck in the same old approaches. Making financial contributions to promising plays or musicals in exchange for first dibs on film or television production rights was seen by all parties as minimally invasive on the creative front and not especially financially risky for growing conglomerates.[26] Yet as corporations adapted to the synergy model, many began to increase their terms of investment, from right of first refusal to agreements that granted companies access to more aspects of the same property.

For example, 20th Century Fox served as chief investor of the hit 1975 musical *The Wiz* in exchange for first options on that property's subsequent film, publishing, and album rights. In exchange, Fox took a more active role as overseer of *The Wiz* during its creative development and signaled a willingness to gamble more on the show as it made its way from out-of-town tryouts to Broadway. While 20th Century Fox's initial investment was $750,000, the company spent an additional $200,000 to keep *The Wiz* open and another $100,000 on a hasty advertising blitz when slow word of mouth and a lack of advance ticket sales initially prompted closing notices the morning after its Broadway opening.[27] These efforts paid off: once it connected with audiences, *The Wiz* became one of Broadway's highest-grossing shows of the season and recouped 20th Century Fox's swollen investment within a year.[28]

Other entertainment companies began to recognize the logic of looking more frequently to Broadway and of investing more startup money in exchange for more control over more aspects of promising properties there. The increase in activity on Broadway is striking: there were five Broadway productions financed by mass-entertainment companies in the 1978–1979 season (*Dancin'*, *Comin' Uptown*, and *Sugar Babies* were supported by Columbia; *Platinum* was bankrolled, rehearsed, costumed, and lit by Paramount; and *The Best Little Whorehouse in Texas* was purchased, financed, and produced by employees and affiliates of Universal). By the 1982–1983 season, fourteen different Broadway productions had conglomerate backing. *Cats*, a paradigm-shifting production in its own right, arrived on Broadway with support from ABC, the (now-defunct) conglomerate MetroMedia, and the mogul David Geffen, who had recently been fired as vice president at Warner Bros. and had established Geffen Records.[29]

Still, devising cross-industrial approaches that moved beyond the corporate-angel model continued to be challenging for stubborn, deeply rooted reasons: Broadway remained highly distrustful of mass-entertainment companies, and many such companies continued to demonstrate a lack of understanding not only about the ways theater gets made, but also of the ways theater artists are centralized and honored in the process. Meanwhile, critics continued to air their anxieties about the dangers of media companies' increasing involvement in theatrical production.[30] On the one hand, there was no shortage of intrigue among producers and theater owners about the potential for cross-industrial partnerships with media conglomerates. "You almost have to get film money or forget the project," one producer mused at the time. "It's reached the point now where you have to look for 50% of your financing from a combination of investments from the theatre owner, a record firm and a film company.... Otherwise you have so many producers and coproducers (supplying the financing) that the billing looks like a bad wedding invitation."[31] On the other hand, however, wariness in the theater world persisted about the possibility of money-hungry outsiders sweeping en masse onto Broadway with no regard to the theater industry's own artistic interests, culture, personnel, or best practices.[32]

The resultant map of cross-industrial arrangements, agreements, and partnerships that were forged between the late 1970s and the early 1990s is dizzyingly complicated and ultimately filled with more false starts, dead ends, and failures than mutually beneficial triumphs. As the cable market grew during the early 1980s, and early companies such as HBO and Showtime began featuring film musicals and stage productions in their lineups, announcements of new partnerships between cable startups, Broadway producers, and theater owners made frequent headlines in the trades, usually only to quietly fizzle out years or even months later. In December 1979, ABC's new video wing announced a partnership with the Shubert Organization and the film director Robert Altman "to restage Broadway, Off Broadway and regional theater productions for video..., pay-cable, cassette and videodisk markets," which never materialized.[33] A similarly fruitless agreement between RKO and the Nederlander Organization, announced in January 1982, promised to "broadcast Broadway shows to cable subscribers."[34] Yet even in this "honeymoon stage, the marriage of cable and theater ... underscored basic differences between mounting productions for the stage and for the home screen," a conundrum that remained unresolved by the time both agreements dissolved.[35] As Kessler points out, arts-related cable television was "an incredibly expensive and marginally lucrative game of trial and error—often just error" in the early 1980s.[36]

Some conglomerates attempted to make it on Broadway by barging in without much in the way of assistance from or communication with the theater industry itself. In rare cases, projects produced under this model proved successful but did not result in a lasting presence in the commercial theater thereafter. One of the first corporations to announce this sort of departure from the angel model was Universal, under its former moniker MCA/Universal. Universal enjoyed initial success on Broadway in 1978 with *The Best Little Whorehouse in Texas*. The Hollywood agent Stevie Phillips saw an early workshop of that musical and convinced Universal head Ned Tannen to finance it, with Phillips as the sole producer.[37] Universal secured all future stage, motion-picture, television, publishing, recording, and merchandising rights[38] and gave handsome lump sums to composer-lyricist Carol Hall and book writers Larry L. King and Peter Masterson.

Whorehouse was a commercial success, but Universal's iron control of the property and its subsequent life in mediated entertainment alienated members of the theater industry. The production drew particular ire from the Dramatists Guild, which was denied the opportunity to represent the show's creative team.[39] Universal hastily made Phillips a vice president in charge of securing more theatrical properties for it; with remarkable foresight, Phillips described the desire to mine "some of Universal's old properties, especially old comedies that we can contemporize and musicalize into new properties" openly hoped that Universal would eventually establish its own internal theater division with her at its head.[40] Yet Phillips was unsuccessful in securing other commercially viable theater properties, and Universal was unable to establish much of a lasting theater footprint until the turn of the millennium.

Warner Bros. and Paramount, on the other hand, had more success with their late-twentieth-century forays into the commercial theater and have remained active there to date. Both companies proceeded more cautiously than Universal did and, despite numerous stops and starts, slowly developed partnerships with experienced theater people in the late 1970s and the '80s. Both companies also established offices in New York City, which allowed executives to familiarize themselves with the culture and practices of the theater industry. Such partnerships were not expensive to maintain, and most of them granted theater makers freedom and control over the projects they instigated.

In July 1978, *Variety* announced Warner Bros. as the first entertainment conglomerate to establish its own "separate division specifically devoted to longterm investment in the legitimate theatre."[41] Warner Bros. initially created a joint venture with Regency Communications, an independent producing company formed by producing partners Irwin Meyer and Stephen R. Friedman. Owners of the 46th Street Theater, where *Whorehouse* was running at the time, Meyer and Friedman had enjoyed recent success as co-producers of the hit musical *Annie*. While Warner Bros. and Regency announced a "formal, long-range contract," the agreement was nevertheless viewed by both parties as highly flexible; it allowed executives at Warner Bros. to serve as active participants in "the planning and execution of any projects," even as Meyer and Friedman would retain creative control.[42]

This partnership didn't last. Warner Bros. terminated its contract with Meyer and Friedman in June 1979 after losing $300,000 on the Cy Coleman musical *Home Again, Home Again*, which closed out of town in Toronto, and the Ira Levin comedy *Break a Leg*, which closed on opening night at the Palace.[43] But Warner Bros. continued to hone a relationship with Tony Award–winning producer Claire Nichtern, who had served as director of creative affairs at Regency. Nichtern was named the first president of Warner Bros.' theater division, Warner Theater Productions, when it was created in 1979 as a New York–based extension of the company's Burbank headquarters.[44]

Under Nichtern, who had been working in New York theater for more than twenty-five years when she became president, Warner Theater Productions introduced some small but significant changes to corporate dealings with the American theater. Nichtern persuaded Warner Bros. to invest not just in Broadway properties, but in ones that might appear in off-Broadway houses or in the regions. Theater, not the mass media, was made central to the mission of Warner Theater Productions; this made the fledgling division unique

> not only in its extent, but in the nature of its interest. The company [didn't] see Broadway solely as a laboratory in which to develop film and tv material. Nichtern [was] given a free hand to select projects which [made] theatrical sense and [wasn't] under a mandate to back only shows with obvious potential for other media.[45]

In the words of one vice president, "looking at theatrical investment strictly from a film or television point of view often means that you make bad theatrical investments."[46] Paramount made it clear that it was not interested in making some of the same mistakes its competitors had.

Because the theater division remained independent under Warner Bros.' ever-expanding umbrella, Nichtern was under less pressure to adapt to the ways of

Hollywood. Her involvement with individual shows was flexible and varied. Sometimes she merely met with a playwright or optioned a script; at other times, she became more directly involved, as when she served as line producer for an early, successful option, Beth Henley's Pulitzer Prize–winning play *Crimes of the Heart* (1981). The gradual, flexible approach to theater making, as well as the tactic of hiring people from within the theater world, paid off quickly for Warner Bros., which by December 1981 had become the most actively involved film corporation in the theater industry.[47] Warner Bros. continues to have an active presence in the commercial theater to date.[48]

Paramount got off to a rockier start. Like Universal with *The Best Little Whorehouse in Texas*, Paramount initially attempted to break into the commercial theater by optioning, developing, and designing a property and then opening it on Broadway without much in the way of the theater industry's help or support.[49] But Paramount's first effort, *Platinum* (1978), which was largely constructed in Hollywood, ran only a month on Broadway and lost the company's entire investment. Paramount next put up the full capitalization for the Garry Marshall and Jerry Belson comedy *The Roast*, which closed on Broadway after only four regular performances in May 1980.

Paramount had better success once it took the Warner Bros. approach. Its own new theater division, Paramount Theater Productions, was announced with an initial, undisclosed eight-figure budget in February 1982.[50] While the head of the new division, former head of East Coast production Dan Sherkow, was less experienced in the theater industry than Nichtern was, his offices were headquartered in New York City, and coverage about the new division made clear his desire to learn on the ground, whether by "seeking advice from legit contacts about which social functions and restaurants to attend," finding out "how to get into the gossip columns,"[51] or reinforcing the fact that his new division was not getting involved in theater primarily to generate content "for Paramount's many electronic entertainment outlets," even as it retained "first refusal on media rights—cable, feature film, video cassette—for all its stage productions."[52]

Paramount Theater Productions co-produced the 1982 Broadway premiere of John Pielmeier's 1979 play *Agnes of God*, financed the first workshop of the musical *Nine*, and co-sponsored a pioneering program with the Apollo Group to develop, produce, and stage theatrical productions in Chicago.[53] Paramount's Gershwin musical *My One and Only*, which starred Tommy Tune and Twiggy and was initially to be directed by Peter Sellars, received disastrous out-of-town reviews; the musical was restructured on the road and doctored during previews by artists with both Broadway and film experience, including Peter Stone, Michael Bennett, Mike Nichols, and Tune himself, at significant cost to the company. Their interventions paid off when the musical opened on Broadway for a commercially successful two-year run in 1983. Depicted in the press during its pre-Broadway woes as a "revealing guide to the pressures and pitfalls of that await anyone rash enough to become involved in producing a multimillion dollar musical,"[54] *My One and Only* recouped its $3.75 million investment by the following season,[55] embarked on several national tours during the 1980s, and premiered in London's West End in 2002.[56] Perhaps more important, the production reflected new approaches to commercial theater making that drew money, creative input, and talent from a widening pool of cross-industrial players in a rapidly metamorphosing, cross-fertilizing entertainment marketplace.

Disney's First Dip

While it has made up for lost time, Disney in the early 1980s was a relatively small company that struggled as much with the development and direction of its own content as it did to make sense of and absorb the many delivery systems that had rapidly become available. A report on Disney's "high-risk venture" into the new world of cable in 1984 identified internal struggles over the company's image, on which it could no longer rely but beyond which it could not figure out how to build. "Disney is the only motion-picture company whose name defines its product," Steve Knoll wrote for the *New York Times*. Disney had cornered the market on "wholesome family fare emphasizing positive values and flights of imagination,"[57] but amid the tumultuous transitions taking place during the '80s, the company no longer believed that such fare would be enough for increasingly global audiences.

Faced with new competition following the 1979 defection of more than half its animators, Disney leadership grew increasingly concerned that even the company's most loyal fans would no longer be enough to keep it viable at the box office. As live-action film failures such as *The Black Hole* (1979) and *The Devil and Max Devlin* (1981) eclipsed Disney's triumphs, the company slid from a 7 percent share of the American box office in 1976 to 4 percent by 1981.[58] A series of internal shuffles, resignations, and rudderless leadership left the company scrambling to figure out how to adapt to the needs of changing audiences while retaining hold on the Disney brand and avoiding hostile takeovers or corporate mergers.[59] It is during this brief period of relative rootlessness that Disney first delved into the theater world. Disney's earliest forays were some of the smallest, most gradual, most flexible agreements an entertainment conglomerate would strike with theater representatives at the time.

In June 1981, several entertainment trades announced that Disney had entered into an "extensive arrangement" with the seasoned Broadway producing team of Elizabeth I. McCann and Nelle Nugent. Under the terms of the three-year trial agreement, Disney would look for material with which to make "more mature films and expand its vistas" while McCann and Nugent would hone their own portfolios in the changing marketplace.[60] This contract was, in some respects, similar to the Warner Bros. and Paramount agreements in that McCann and Nugent, like Nichtern and Sherkow, were under no pressure to select theatrical content specifically for its potential as a mediated property. Also, the producing partners were free to pursue their own projects while under contract.

But in other ways, the agreement was looser and more porous than those forged by other corporations, especially in its centering of creative content, regardless of medium. As Disney's vice president of creative development at the time explained, Disney was hesitant to rush into any new market "full bore, because 'all the ancillary markets everyone is talking about are not yet ready to absorb the product.'"[61] But under its arrangement with McCann and Nugent, one party could simply alert the other about interesting content: "if it's a screen idea, Disney has first right of refusal. If the project is live theatrical, McCann and Nugent will try it out in a workshop format with Disney first before taking it to Broadway if they like it." With this loose arrangement, Disney took initial steps into theatrical production, while Nugent and McCann dipped just as gradually into film and television production.[62]

When the deal was announced, Nugent and McCann noted that they had been approached by many other studios but had chosen Disney even though that company had not offered them more money than any other. The producers explained that they chose Disney because it struck them as "more open to off-the-wall ideas" and had "a continuity of people and outlook" that felt refreshingly free of bureaucracy.[63] McCann, too, was especially blunt about what remained an overriding concern at a time when film companies were cropping up all over Broadway: "One of the reasons we decided to go with Disney was … because it was founded by a creative person and they have much more understanding and a sympathetic attitude than some of the motion picture companies who come to Broadway and try to rape the authors."[64]

Disney did not back a single commercial production during the three-year agreement with McCann and Nugent, though it did finance workshops for two plays the producers brought to its attention.[65] Disney chose to pass on further support of Larry Atlas's 1983 courtroom drama *Total Abandon*, because that play's theme of child abuse was determined to be a poor fit for the company.[66] Arthur Giron's play *Becoming Memories*, about several generations of life in small-town America, was a better fit for the company, but McCann, Nugent, and Disney all parted ways with that property following a workshop, also in the spring of 1983.[67]

All three parties went their separate ways once their three-year agreement elapsed. McCann, who discovered that she disliked producing for television and film, returned full-time to theatrical production.[68] Nugent also remained active in the theater but continued to produce for television as well; in the late '80s, she joined Dick Clark Productions to develop TV movies and series.[69] Disney financed just one commercial production in New York during the 1980s: in May 1989, it partnered with several independent producers and the John F. Kennedy Center for the Performing Arts to bring Bill Irwin's silent film- and media-influenced "rumination on life in New York," *Largely New York*, to Broadway for a four-month run. Afterward, Disney's involvement in commercial theater in New York dropped off completely, if temporarily.

The efforts by growing media conglomerates to forge new paths on Broadway in the 1980s were eclipsed by larger, more lucrative shifts in the media landscape. Arguably, the partnerships such companies forged with producers such as McCann, Nugent, and Nichtern did not depart enough from old models to be especially newsworthy on their own. Gender assumptions didn't help matters; for her enormous contributions to the theater and the connections she forged with mass entertainment, Nichtern—one of very few female producers in New York during the 1960s and early '70s—was regularly profiled in the press as a bored if "tall, comely and stately looking" housewife whose husband granted her permission to enter the workforce.[70] Journalism had changed enough by the early 1980s that McCann and Nugent were spared quite as much in the way of sexist assumptions, though the biggest profile of them to run at the time explains that they were first known in the theater industry as "the girls" and were eventually redubbed "the ladies" as their producing work grew in reputation.[71]

Yet beyond gender assumptions, the partnerships formed between Broadway and larger entertainment conglomerates were gradual, halting, and certainly depicted as less interesting than the highly lauded actions of the many "[f]ree-spirited entrepreneurs," all of them men, whose aggressive empire-building through the 1980s were frequently described as "[stunning] the establishment" with what were interpreted as rampant displays of individualism that reinforced the American dream.[72] Individual up-and-comers who became unprecedentedly wealthy and powerful through the 1980s were painted in the press as risk-taking, iconoclastic, creative visionaries. Such "great man narratives," communications scholar Peter Kunze points out, tend to "neglect industrial context, the collaborative nature of [mass entertainment], and the organization of labor throughout production," even as they also help put names, faces, and "a clear and limited focus, period, and narrative" to what are otherwise enormously detailed, complicated shifts taking place across a vast, anonymous, and comparatively flavorless business world.[73]

In the 1980s, then, focus was often trained on individual executives such as broadcaster Ted Turner, credited for turning a single Atlanta-based television station into a media empire; moguls David Geffen and Robert Stigwood, lauded for expanding beyond the music industry into film, television, publishing, and theater; theater impresario Cameron Mackintosh, whose publicity and marketing savvy helped him work his way from a producer of modest British road shows to a purveyor of mega-musicals with international appeal; and the film producer and distributor Garth Drabinsky, whose reinvention as a Broadway impresario was tarnished when his company, Livent, declared bankruptcy in 1998. Regardless of their backgrounds, the men who became business tycoons in the 1980s were described with flash, bravura, drive, and the kind of mystique that did not translate easily to broader corporate shifts—or to the myriad, comparatively anonymous executives who set them in motion.

Disney on Broadway, Redux

The events that took place in mass entertainment during the 1980s led directly to Broadway's "own globalization tale," which was set in motion with the cross-industrial experiments detailed above and which culminated in the redevelopment of Times Square in the 1990s.[74] Disney's second coming on Broadway is often treated as such, although its centering as a transformative force that somehow magically arrived, Mary Poppins–like, to rescue a long-suffering neighborhood and its long-suffering entertainments has been vastly overstated by many journalists, historians, scholars, and Disney itself.[75]

Other studies have offered detailed examinations of the economic, technical, cultural, and aesthetic innovations that helped spur the creation of Disney Theatrical Productions in 1993,[76] but in brief, Disney's struggles to remain "focused on product as opposed to delivery systems" while retaining control of its brand and avoiding hostile takeover in the early 1980s were assuaged when the company was revamped mid-decade by three seasoned new leaders, all of whom had recently overseen the vertical and horizontal expansion of other, larger entertainment conglomerates: Frank Wells was vice chairman of Warner Bros., Michael Eisner was president and CEO of Paramount Studios (where he had overseen Paramount's work on *Platinum*), and Jeffrey Katzenberg was president of production under Eisner at Paramount before the three became heads of Disney in 1984.[77]

Under this triumvirate, Disney doubled down on tactics that had allowed it to behave "like a bona-fide media conglomerate" since at least the 1950s: "developing intellectual property, branding, and synergy ... cross-promoting film properties, television series, music, and theme parks."[78] This renewed embrace of what Disney had honed over decades in the first place resulted in new prosperity for the company as it grew and expanded beyond Walt Disney Studios. By the time the company entered another period of flux in the mid-1990s following the untimely death of Wells and the ouster of Katzenberg, it had grown large enough to establish itself on Broadway and acquire ABC.[79]

For its widely touted successes, however, Disney's arrival on Broadway was hardly sudden; while its renovation of the New Amsterdam was certainly newsworthy, its overall approach to Broadway was not otherwise especially novel. Disney's "grand entrance," then, without question an important linchpin in Times Square's redevelopment, was hardly the "catalyst" that single-handedly transformed the neighborhood.[80] Nor was the production model Disney honed on Broadway especially new by the time the company arrived. Because it has long been so closely connected to "the changing motivations and capacities of capital, the recent progress of digital technologies, and the constant movement between Fordist and 'post-Fordist' moments of production in neoliberal times," Broadway's march toward globalization extends further back into the past than much contemporary writing on the subject suggests.[81]

Even immediately prior to Disney's arrival on Broadway, contemporary approaches to "theatrical Fordism" were being actively refined by producers such as Andrew Lloyd Webber, Mackintosh, and Livent. These entities helped nudge corporate interest past the financier role toward the end of the millennium. By applying vertical-integration strategies and synergy in order to exert more control over more aspects of the production process, while simultaneously "emulating Hollywood-sized global marketing campaigns for their shows," the British producers and Livent honed an approach that Disney could simply build on, given its size, reach, and resources.[82]

Kunze unpacks and historicizes the vagueness of the term "Disney Renaissance," the periodization of which, he notes, varies widely among scholars depending on field, lens, and perspective.[83] Disney's arrival on Broadway has long been treated as a crucial aspect of said "Renaissance," which is often seen to begin around 1989 with the release of the film *The Little Mermaid* and which tends to prioritize animation over other aspects of Disney's empire.[84] Yet a number of vitally important ingredients fell into place for Disney during the 1980s, even at some of its low points, which enabled its expansion to Broadway in the 1990s.

As noted above, the company's forays into commercial theater extend back far earlier than February 1994, which is when news broke that Disney had agreed to "rehabilitate and reopen the landmark New Amsterdam Theater ... as a major push to reinvigorate the long-stalled effort to revitalize 42nd Street in mid-Manhattan."[85] The mid-1980s was also the period in which Disney's new leaders, all former heads of conglomerates that had previously cultivated new relationships with commercial theater, recruited playwright and lyricist Howard Ashman, who with composer Alan Menken would be responsible for *The Little Mermaid, Beauty and the Beast* (1991), and *Aladdin* (1992).

The contributions by these creatives are often seen to result in Disney's "triumphant return" to animation and then its expansion to Broadway—even as the company had never departed from or stopped being widely lauded for its animated films.[86] This trajectory, however, simplistic and ahistorical though it is, makes good linear sense: in the mid-1980s, two dedicated musical-theater creators devised beloved animated films for Disney that delivered "all the panache of a Broadway show without any of the foot-dragging nonsense."[87] Yet Disney's 1994 arrival on Broadway was the result not only of significant shifts in the entertainment world but also the transformation of New York City's real estate market, the city's transition to a leisure economy, the willingness of a Republican governor and mayor to negotiate with an entertainment conglomerate, a dash of cronyism, and extraordinarily fortuitous timing.

For the better part of two decades, the renovation of Times Square was centered around the construction of large office towers along Forty-Second Street, which "public officials and real estate developers had insisted were the necessary first step to renewal."[88] When the city's commercial real estate market collapsed, a renewed interest in focusing on the neighborhood's theaters helped quell opposition to the long-stalled project.[89] Coincidentally, Eisner, a native New Yorker with powerful connections to the city, happened to be the childhood friend of architect Robert A. M. Stern, who oversaw most of the design guidelines for the Times Square redevelopment project, and Marian S. Heiskell, chair of the New 42nd Street, the nonprofit organization overseeing the renovation of the theaters there. These factors made Disney increasingly attractive to New York City, which revitalized a decades-long plan to redevelop Times Square as a new tourist mecca; Heiskell apparently tried repeatedly to interest Eisner in Broadway once he arrived at Disney in 1984.[90]

Disney was involved in several other "expansionist strategies" across its three divisions (resorts and theme parks, films and broadcasting, and merchandise), but most sparked "intense environmental issues or high-profile political battles" and thus a slew of hotly negative press. At around the time Disney began to seriously ponder a presence on Broadway, it was also planning Disney's America, a theme park near the

Manassas National Battlefield Park in Virginia, and two waterfront parks in Southern California, none of which made it past the development stages. The unsuccessful launch of Euro Disney only contributed to bad publicity about the company. At least some of the public memory for these failed ventures "dissolved in an orgy of press coverage and media hype" when the deal between Disney and the City and State of New York was announced.[91]

Of course, there was also plenty of concern expressed when the City and State of New York finalized their "sweetheart deal" with Disney, which granted the company numerous concessions, including "a low-risk means of buying a Broadway platform and testing the market for urban entertainment" by restoring the New Amsterdam. The deal initially seemed as if it would benefit Disney more than it would the theater industry:

> To the city and state's direct $26-million capital investment made in the form of a subsidized 30-year loan, Disney had agreed to put in $8 million in equity and advance an additional $5.4 million in the form of a loan to the public entities. After accounting for a 20-percent federal historic tax credit for the cost of rehabilitation, its net investment in the deal, less than $3 million, would amount to a tiny fraction (less than 8 percent) of what the renovation finally cost—$38.6 million, including the production oriented scope items on Disney's tab.[92]

Such a move thus raised the hackles of many people in the theater industry, where negative reactions to the deal were initially plentiful. Executives at the Nederlander, Shubert, and Jujamcyn organizations, which together operate the majority of theaters in Times Square, were enraged to learn of "Disney's privileged position" as a theater manager, even as they eventually agreed to work with and not protest the newcomer.[93] Concerns about Times Square being transformed into a theme park and about the possibility that Broadway's theaters would soon be overrun with musicalized versions of animated films were frequently aired in the press and in theater circles. And the arrival of Disney contributed to the growing anxieties of independent producers, who were already scrambling to compete as conglomerates arrived on Broadway; many fretted that it would be virtually impossible to compete with a huge, beloved, and brilliantly branded entity like Disney.[94]

On the other hand, concerns about the treatment of theater's creative teams were, for once, comparatively muted, Disney, after all, arrived on Broadway with its own ready-made material, and so age-old concerns about Hollywood players "raping" Broadway creatives were eclipsed by still-extant anxieties about the ways a rialto saturated with musicalized film adaptations might work to limit performers' freedom of interpretation and expression. The enormous critical and commercial success of *The Lion King* helped tamp some concerns, as did the naming of Peter Schneider and Thomas Schumacher as heads of Disney Theatrical Productions. Both men had deep roots in the theater and, according to *Lion King* director Julie Taymor, were as comfortable, respectful of, serious about, and familiar with Broadway as "any New York producer."[95]

Despite these many concerns, however, there was an understanding by the 1990s that Times Square and the industry it housed had to change with the times. Even Frank

Rich grudgingly threw his support behind Disney's arrival, noting that for all its "expansionist" tendencies, the company was "exactly what is needed on 42nd Street ... if Times Square is ever again to be the crossroads of the world." Rich was especially eager for Disney to "attract more tenants to the other dark theaters on the street and more customers to the other struggling theaters throughout the Broadway district." Of course, in the same op-ed, Rich opined about how nice it would be if Disney worked to "shake up both the management and labor status quos in the New York theater" in order to "stop the spiral that is leading to the $75 ticket."[96] Disney, a money-making conglomerate that is infamously concerned about its own bottom line, most certainly didn't do that. Then again, two out of three ain't bad.

Conclusion

The biggest hit musicals on Broadway—ones that come along only every few decades and hit as hard as *Oklahoma!*, *A Chorus Line*, or *Hamilton* did—are generally understood to reflect an exceedingly rare combination of "exceptional writing, casting, staging, and packaging" and serendipitous timing, all of which can make a production seem more groundbreaking than it actually is.[97] If producers could bottle such a rare, precious combination of assets, after all, every Broadway show would be a *Hamilton*, just as every Broadway theater owner or producer would be a Disney.

Times Square's redevelopment, deemed necessary for the city and its theater district to keep up with changing, rapidly globalizing times, benefited from Disney's arrival—as it did from the entertainment corporations that preceded it and that continue to produce and finance productions alongside it. Concerns that such entities would swallow Broadway up have been assuaged, especially since a number of nonprofit theater companies have moved into the neighborhood as producers and theater owners in the first decades of the twenty-first century. And Disney's brand, its renovation of the New Amsterdam, its ABC studios, and its family-friendly image have ensured that the neighborhood, once viewed by the middle classes as a grotty, alienating hellhole, is now deemed approachable enough for tourists to wander wide-eyed through the streets, as they might at Disney theme parks the world over. Disney and Broadway have surely helped each other by bringing each other into their synergistic webs.

Disney has, from its inception, made a practice of bottling and selling excitement, joy, and wholesome fun for people of all ages across the world in a way no other conglomerate has. As a conglomerate with a unique and deeply ingrained brand, Disney forged strong, lasting ties to Broadway and its musicals and has remained actively involved in theatrical production in the three decades since it first agreed to restore the New Amsterdam. Disney's mission of remaining true to content, creativity, and its own brand is, after all, why this book is about Disney musicals—not those by Paramount, 20th Century Fox, Universal, or Warner Bros. Perhaps that's magic enough.

Notes

1. Jennifer Holt, *Empires of Entertainment: Media Industries and the Politics of Deregulation, 1980–1996* (New Brunswick, NJ: Rutgers University Press, 2011), 1–3.
2. See, for example, George Rodosthenous, ed., *The Disney Musical on Stage and Screen: Critical Approaches from Snow White to Frozen* (London: Bloomsbury, 2017).
3. See, for example, Amy Osatinski, *Disney Theatrical Productions: Producing Broadway Musicals the Disney Way* (New York: Routledge, 2019); Elizabeth L. Wollman, "The Economic Development of the 'New' Times Square and Its Impact on the Broadway Musical," *American Music* 20, no. 4 (2002): 445–465.
4. Carol Lawson, "Broadway: Paramount Plans to Put Millions Into Stage Productions," *New York Times*, February 5, 1982, C2.
5. Robert McLaughlin, *Broadway and Hollywood: A History of Economic Interaction* (New York: Arno, 1974), i–iii. McLaughlin is referring here to the findings of the Rockefeller Panel Report, *The Performing Arts: Problems and Prospects: Rockefeller Panel Report on the Future of Theatre, Dance, Music in America*, Rockefeller Brothers Fund (New York: McGraw Hill, 1965); William J. Baumol and William G. Bowen, *Performing Arts, the Economic Dilemma: A Study of Problems Common to Theater, Opera, Music, and Dance* (New York: Twentieth Century Fund, 1966); Thomas Gale Moore, *The Economics of the American Theatre* (Durham, NC: Duke University Press, 1968); Jack Poggi, *Theatre in America: The Impact of Economic Forces, 1870–1967* (Ithaca, NY: Cornell University Press, 1968).
6. Peter Kunze, "Belles Are Singing: Broadway, Hollywood, and the Failed *Gone with the Wind* Musical," *Historical Journal of Film, Radio and Television* 38 no. 4 (2018): 787. For recent cross-industrial studies that center the commercial stage, see Raymond Knapp and Jessica Sternfeld, eds., *The Oxford Handbook of the Television Musical* (New York: Oxford University Press, forthcoming); Peter Kunze, *Staging a Comeback: Broadway, Hollywood, and the Disney Renaissance* (New Brunswick, NJ: Rutgers University Press, 2023); Kelly Kessler, *Broadway in the Box: Television's Lasting Love Affair with the Musical* (New York: Oxford University Press, 2020).
7. Henry Jenkins, *Convergence Culture: Where Old and New Media Collide* (New York: New York University Press, 2006), 2.
8. Alfred L. Bernheim, *The Business of the Theatre: An Economic History of the American Theatre, 1750–1932* (New York: Benjamin Blom, 1932). Bernheim notes, for example, that as early as the mid-1920s, William Fox, founder of the Fox Film Corporation, had forged "an agreement with certain legitimate producers which had for its purpose the production of stage plays not for their own sake but to serve as feeders for the movies" (90).
9. Irv Lichtman, "Show Publishing: Millions Change Hands for Revival-Rich Catalogs," *Billboard*, January 29, 1983, B17.
10. Kessler, *Broadway in the Box*, 13.
11. Kunze, "Belles Are Singing," 802.
12. Kessler, *Broadway in the Box*, 4.
13. Marilyn Stasio, "Broadway's Newest Angel: Hollywood," *New York Magazine*, December 4, 1978, 71.
14. Brooks Atkinson, "Hollywood Dough: A Theatre Financed by the Screen Raises Several Questions," *New York Times*, November 10, 1935, X1.
15. Stasio, "Broadway's Newest Angel," 74.

16. Jonathan Burston, "Recombinant Broadway." *Continuum: Journal of Media & Cultural Studies* 23, no. 2 (April 2009): 160.
17. Holt, *Empires of Entertainment*, 3.
18. Jennifer Holt, "In Deregulation We Trust: The Synergy of Politics and Industry in Reagan-Era Hollywood," *Film Quarterly* 55, no. 2 (Winter 2001): 25–26.
19. Ronald Reagan, letter to Sol Taishoff, June 16, 1967. Reprinted in *Broadcasting Magazine*, November 10, 1980, 27.
20. Holt, *Empires of Entertainment*, 3.
21. Holt, "In Deregulation We Trust," 26.
22. Ed Ochs, "Broadway Around the World: A *Billboard* Special Report," *Billboard Magazine*, January 29, 1983, B1–39. Quote here is from p. B1.
23. Holt, *Empires of Entertainment*, 22.
24. See 1940s (https://syndeoinstitute.org/wp-content/uploads/2022/10/CableTimelineFall2015.pdf).
25. Adam M. Zaretsky, "I Want My MTV . . . and My CNN and My ESPN and My TBS and . . .: The Cable TV Industry and Regulation," *Regional Economist*, July 1995, http://research.stlouisfed.org/publications/regional/95/07/CableTV.pdf.
26. Richard Hummler, "Pix Are Now Biggest B'way Angels: Early Stakes Insure Later Film Rights," *Variety*, January 18, 1980, 1.
27. "'The Wiz' Becomes Wizard of B'way, SRO, Top Grosser," *Variety*, February 26, 1975, 57.
28. "Fox Not Filming Its Own 'Wiz': Ken Harper's 18-Month Option; Sees an 'Everybody Appeal,'" *Variety*, February 11, 1976, 36.
29. Sandra Salmans, "Broadway Lures the Corporate Angel," *New York Times*, October 31, 1982, H1.
30. See, for example, Frank Rich, "Stage View: What Ails Today's Broadway Musical?," *New York Times*, November 14, 1982, H1.
31. Hummler, "Pix Are Now Biggest Broadway Angels," 112.
32. Stasio, "Broadway's Newest Angel," 71.
33. Peter Funt, "Broadcasters Are Switching to 'Narrowcasting,'". *New York Times*, December 16, 1979, D43.
34. C. Gerald Fraser, "New Cable Signs Stage Shows," *New York Times*, January 13, 1982, C24.
35. John Duka, "Cable TV Turns Hungrily to the Theater," *New York Times*, January 27, 1982, 1.
36. Kessler, *Broadway in the Box*, 31.
37. Richard Hummler, "'Little Whorehouse' to Recoup $800,000 Cost Next February," *Variety*, November 29, 1978, 98.
38. Stasio, "Broadway's Newest Angel," 72.
39. Hummler, "'Little Whorehouse,'" 99.
40. Stasio, "Broadway's Newest Angel," 72.
41. Stephen Klain, "Warners and Regency Jointly Tread B'way Legit Boards," *Variety*, July 5, 1978, 3.
42. "Major Film Company Sets Up Broadway Show Investment Group," *Show Business*, July 13, 1978, 22.
43. "Regency Communications 'Interested' in Allied Pic Library," *Variety*, June 13, 1979, 6.
44. "Claire Nichtern Reshifts to Warner Legit Firm," *Variety*, May 23, 1979, 97.
45. Ibid.
46. Richard Hummler, "Warners: Active Broadway Angel Now Involved in 10 Legit Productions," *Variety*, December 16, 1981, 1, 78.

47. Ibid., 1.
48. The list of productions Warner Bros. has produced on Broadway or the road is too long to give here, but the company has seen its share of hits and misses with relatively recent shows such as *Lestat* (2006), *Elf* (2010), *The Bridges of Madison County* (2014), *The Curious Incident of the Dog in the Night-Time* (2014), *Charlie and the Chocolate Factory* (2017), and *Beetlejuice* (2019).
49. Stasio, "Broadway's Newest Angel," 71.
50. Lawson, "Broadway: Paramount Plans," C2.
51. "Par Following WB in Legit Backing: 'Agnes' as Starter," *Variety*, February 10, 1982, 115.
52. Lawson, "Broadway: Paramount Plans," C2.
53. "Chi Theatre Project Sets 3-Wk. Studio Runs for 9 Untried Scripts," *Variety*, April 6, 1983, 81.
54. Don Shewey, "How 'My One and Only' Came to Broadway," *New York Times*, May 1, 1983, H1.
55. "7 Payoff Shows ('Cage' Soon) Brightened '83–'84 B'way Season," *Variety*, June 6, 1984, 81.
56. Whether as Paramount Theater Productions or in its later iteration as Paramount Pictures Corporation, the company remains active on Broadway and beyond, with a roster of productions including *Shirley Valentine* (1989), *Grand Hotel* (1989), *Seven Guitars* (1996), *A Funny Thing Happened on the Way to the Forum* (1996), *Saturday Night Fever* (1999), *Mean Girls* (2018), *Head over Heels* (2018), and *Almost Famous* (2022).
57. Steve Knoll, "The Disney Channel Has an Expensive First Year," *New York Times*, April 29, 1984, H28.
58. Bart Mills, "Disney Looks for a Happy Ending to Its Grim Fairy Tale," *American Film*, July–August 1982, 52. Mills's article adds that Disney hoped the much-anticipated *Tron* (1982) would help reverse the trend of live-action failures, but that film failed at the box office before eventually becoming something of a cult hit in subsequent decades.
59. David Barton, "Disney Pacts McCann-Nugent of Legit: Projects to Avoid Bubble Gum Plots," *Variety*, June 24, 1981, 35.
60. Ralph Kaminsky, "Disney Signs Screen, TV, Stage Deal with New York Producers," *Entertainment Industry Magazine*, July 6, 1981, 59.
61. Barton, "Disney Pacts," 35.
62. "Disney Prods. Join with B'way for Future Projects," *Back Stage*, June 26, 1981, 56.
63. Mills, "Disney Looks for a Happy Ending," 56.
64. Barton, "Disney Pacts," 35.
65. Private workshops, now far more typical in the development of theater properties, were relatively novel at the time but had by the early 1980s been eagerly embraced by the theater industry as a cost-saving and "creatively beneficial" means of developing new works prior to production. See Richard Hummler, "New Legit Incubators: Private Workshops," *Variety*, November 11, 1981, 83.
66. McCann and Nugent brought *Total Abandon* to Broadway on their own; it closed on opening night in April 1983.
67. Aljean Harmetz, "Disney Backs Second Stage Production," *New York Times*, April 1, 1983, C8
68. Adrienne Onafri, "Women Who Made Theater History: Producer Nelle Nugent," *Broadway World*, March 19, 2005, https://www.broadwayworld.com/article/Women-Who-Made-Theater-History-Producer-Nelle-Nugent-20050319.
69. "Tony Winner Nugent Joins Clark Team," *Back Stage*, January 13, 1989, 3A.
70. John G. Houser, "A Woman Producer Likes Her 'Family,'" *Los Angeles Herald-Examiner*, March 6, 1966, n.p. In the 1970s, coverage of Nichtern inevitably focuses on her marriages, divorces, children, looks, domestic talents, and "maternal" behavior. See also Louis Calta,

"Claire Nichtern Upsets the Odds," *New York Times*, January 1, 1965, 10; Beverley Wilson, "For and about Women: Producer's a 'Luv' and Just 'Mama' to the Cast," *Miami Herald*, August 20, 1965, n.p.; Rebecca Morehouse, "Producer Is Now 'playing moment' in and out of Theater," *Long Island Press*, July 30, 1972, n.p.

71. Elin, Schoen, "Presenting McCann & Nugent," *New York Times*, February 1, 1981, SM9.
72. Leslie Wayne, "An Annual Report on 1984," *New York Times*, December 23, 1984, F4.
73. Kunze, *Staging a Comeback*, 17.
74. Burston, "Recombinant Broadway," 161.
75. Lynne B. Sagalyn, *Times Square Roulette: Remaking the City Icon* (Cambridge, MA: MIT Press, 2001), 343.
76. See especially Holt, *Empires of Entertainment*; Kunze, *Staging a Comeback*; Sagalyn, *Times Square Roulette*.
77. Holt, *Empires of Entertainment*, 156.
78. Ibid., 155–156.
79. Kunze, *Staging a Comeback*.
80. Osatinski, *Disney Theatrical Productions*, 2.
81. Burston, "Recombinant Broadway," 161.
82. Ibid., 162.
83. Kunze, *Staging a Comeback*.
84. Ibid.
85. Douglas Martin, "Disney Seals Times Square Theatre Deal," *New York Times*, February 3, 1994, B1.
86. Kunze, *Staging a Comeback*.
87. Janet Maslin, "A Beauty or a Beast? Contrasting Film and Musical," *New York Times*, April 23, 1994, 16.
88. Paul Goldberger, "The New Times Square: Magic That Surprised the Magicians," *New York Times*, October 15, 1996, C11.
89. Sagalyn, *Times Square Roulette*, 340.
90. Alan Finder, "A Prince Charming? Disney and the City Find Each Other," *New York Times*, June 10, 1995, 21.
91. Sagalyn, *Times Square Roulette*, 341–343.
92. Ibid., 348.
93. Alex Witchel, "Is Disney the Newest Broadway Baby?," *New York Times*, April 17, 1994, H1.
94. Peter Marks, "Broadway's Producers: A Struggling, Changing Breed," *New York Times*, April 7, 1996, H1.
95. Barry Singer, "Just Two Animated Characters, Indeed," *New York Times*, October 4, 1996, AR7.
96. Frank Rich, "Journal: Mickey Does 42nd Street," *New York Times*, January 16, 1994, E17.
97. Elizabeth Wollman, "From *The Black Crook* to *Hamilton*: A History of Hot Tickets on Broadway," in *Historians on* Hamilton: *How a Blockbuster Musical Is Restaging America's Past*, ed. Renee C. Romano and Claire Bond Potter (New Brunswick, NJ: 2018), 188.

CHAPTER 23

BRANDING, DEMOGRAPHICS, AND THE DISNEY BROADWAY PLAYBOOK

DEAN ADAMS

When the Walt Disney Company opened its first Broadway musical, *Beauty and the Beast*, in 1994, it began an "all-in" approach to entering a new marketplace, much as it would in introducing Disney+ to the streaming industry almost three decades later. The business strategies of Disney Theatrical Productions, the theater-producing arm of the company that is part of the Disney Theatrical Group, have helped inspire the look and feel of Times Square and, arguably, the content of Broadway shows. But have its "family-friendly" productions changed the demographics of Broadway audiences or the business strategies by which shows are produced? Are there significant advantages that Disney Theatrical has over other Broadway producers?

There is no question that musicals produced by Disney Theatrical have been successful since 1994. By the end of 2022, Disney Theatrical had twenty-eight productions running in eleven countries around the world. Disney's ten Broadway titles have been seen by more than 210 million theater-goers worldwide.[1] Only Cameron Mackintosh, producer of *Cats*, *Les Misérables*, and *Miss Saigon*, can claim higher total Broadway attendance or more gross revenue as a producing entity.[2] By the fall of 2022, fifteen North American national tours have been produced by Disney Theatrical (four *Beauty and the Beast*, three *The Lion King*, two *Mary Poppins*, two *Aladdin*, one *Frozen*, one *Newsies*, one *Aida*, and one *High School Musical*).[3] For comparison, Mackintosh produced thirteen national tours during the same period. Nearly 40 percent of patrons who attend a current Disney Theatrical production are seeing their first Broadway show, and 75 percent of the audience at any given performance is older than eighteen.[4] This success and production of similar shows that followed from other corporate producers such as *Shrek the Musical* (which lost money) led to complaints of the "corporatization" of Broadway in the 1990s.[5]

The Lion King stage musical's worldwide gross is the highest of any in box-office history (this is the musical's ticket sales only and does not include receipts from *The Lion King* films, home-entertainment sales, merchandise, record sales, or other ancillary streams). It exceeds the gross of the top three movies of all time combined. This is equivalent to the total theatrical attendance of all ten films of J. K. Rowling's *Wizarding World* franchise, all six films of the *Jurassic Park* franchise, and all ten films of *The Fast and the Furious* franchise.[6]

Theater owners in the early 1990s asked theatrical unions to boycott Disney's presence because of its "privileged position."[7] Instead of Disney productions upending other productions, however, all boats were raised: Broadway attendance has increased 55 percent from the 1993–1994 season when *Beauty and the Beast* opened to the 2018–2019 season, and Broadway revenue has increased from $8.12 million to $14.77 million.[8] Still, while there has been growing acceptance of Disney on Broadway, and in particular of *The Lion King*'s success, there remains grumbling about the advantages Disney has as a producer. Broadway producer Thomas Viertel notes on marketing capabilities, for example, that while Disney "has borrowed from us ... it has basically been a one-way street. The synergy involved when you own a television network, several cable networks, a half-dozen theme parks and all that stuff is unimaginable from our perspective. We really can't do what they do."[9]

Disney did not invent the "family-friendly"[10] musical, nor was it the first to produce one. The golden age of musicals featured many shows that grandparents, parents, and children could enjoy together: *The Music Man* (1957, followed by the film in 1962), *Cinderella* (written for television by Richard Rodgers and Oscar Hammerstein II in 1957), *Peter Pan* (1954 on Broadway followed by three live television versions in the early 1960s), and *You're a Good Man, Charlie Brown* (off-Broadway in 1967 followed by a brief stint on Broadway in 1971). Disney had its own success with the live-action 1964 film *Mary Poppins*, but it did not own the rights to the intellectual property beyond what it had licensed for the film and would not be able to produce it on the stage until decades later.

One of the most successful family-friendly Broadway musicals in the late twentieth century was *Annie* (1977), which ran for six years and played 2,377 performances on Broadway. The film rights were sold in 1977 for a then-record $9.5 million.[11] *Annie* created a blueprint that Disney would later follow: it was based on a familiar comic strip, it appeals to adults as well as children, and it utilizes familiar stories, characters, and themes. The 1977 production won seven Tony Awards, including Best Musical. It also had four national tours running simultaneously during the Broadway run, something then repeated with the mega-musicals of the 1980s and was what Disney would later do for *Beauty and the Beast* and *The Lion King*.[12]

The Walt Disney Company has been making full-length animated movies featuring popular songs since 1937 with *Snow White and the Seven Dwarfs*, but the use of music in the stories wasn't structured in the same way as a typical Broadway musical. Disney's animated films run roughly ninety minutes in one act, while Broadway musicals are often constructed with two acts and are two and a half hours long or longer. When Howard

Ashman became involved with developing *A Little Mermaid* and *Beauty and the Beast*, first as animated features and then as Broadway shows, he brought his extensive book and lyric writing, as well as his theatrical directing work to help translate Disney's film library to a Broadway musical structure.

Transforming the Animated Library

The "Disney Renaissance" of animated films, from 1989's *The Little Mermaid* through 1999's *Tarzan*, reflected the use of traditional musical-theater rules for storytelling and character development thanks to Ashman's work during this period on *Beauty and the Beast*, *The Little Mermaid*, and *Aladdin*. Peter Schneider, who had years of experience in the theater, took over Disney's feature animated division in 1985 and helped to revitalize the unit by employing theater composers and writers such as Ashman, Alan Menken, and Tim Rice. The success of the animated *Beauty and the Beast* and Frank Rich's now-famous comment on how it was the year's best Broadway score—just not on Broadway—led to company president Michael Eisner greenlighting Disney's first Broadway production of its own intellectual property: "We are not Stephen Sondheim, or Cameron Mackintosh, or Rodgers and Hammerstein. If we try to be, we will be second rate, and we will fail. We are Disney, and that is an asset. It doesn't mean we can't deal with challenging topics, but we must do it our own way, the best we can, and hope that audiences respond."[13] While the reported $15 million project would be a gamble for independent producers, the production was only one segment of a lucrative property with multiple income streams (film, theme-park shows, merchandising). To hedge their bets in meeting audience expectations of the production, the director and design team, hired from Disney's theme parks, were told to make the show as close as possible to the original animated film.[14]

The resulting success of *Beast* on Broadway allowed for less literal or theme-park conceptualization for shows that followed such as *The Lion King*. Thomas Schumacher, a skilled theater producer who had also headed Disney's animation division after Schneider and worked on such features as *The Rescuers Down Under*, knew and could reach a wealth of theatrical talent such as Julie Taymor. As Schumacher remembers:

> *Beauty and the Beast* came out of the theme parks. Three months after it opened, *The Lion King* opened as a film, and Michael Eisner then said to Peter [Schneider] and me, "Why don't you take over *Beauty and the Beast* and start a real theatre department for Disney, and you guys can do that on the weekends and fly into New York when you need to?" Michael Eisner then said, "Let's put *Lion King* onstage." I said, "That's the worst idea ever."[15]

Eisner insisted on *Lion King* moving forward, which resulted in Schumacher taking a risk with Taymor, the antithesis of a theme-park director. It turned out to be one of the best artistic and business decisions Schumacher could make, and it reflected the willingness of a former theater producer and artistic director to take a risk removed from the corporate parent. The Disney Theatrical Group eventually became a full-time business within the Walt Disney Studios division of the company, and it currently employs more than one hundred theater professionals who are housed above the New Amsterdam Theatre in New York City. Disney Theatrical's track record of success relies in part on the selection of material from Disney's enormous catalog, the hiring of top musical-theater artists, and adherence to traditional musical-theater construction. Schumacher, longtime president of Disney Theatrical, notes:

> The titles we've chosen are a very select few from a very large catalog of titles. Most things are not worthy of what the theater can do best, particularly when you are doing movies that are about special effects, movies that are about fantasy characters that have fantasy behaviors that are impossible to recreate or movies that are built on scale issues, like *Toy Story*—it works because there are giant people and little, tiny toys. I always look for what would be enhanced by being told in the theater, what about it is classical enough that calls for what the theater wants to do, and also which ones utilize their music in a way that is most theatrical. People often say, "Oh, you are just taking movies and making them into musicals," and it is true that there has been a lot of that in our industry going back to the last fifty–sixty years, but we are taking *musicals* and reinventing them for the stage.... We only control our IP [intellectual property].[16]

The intellectual property is owned in perpetuity by the company, unlike many Broadway musicals that are controlled by the initial producers for only a set period. *Beauty and the Beast*, for example, can be remounted on Broadway at Disney's discretion without renegotiating first-class rights from the original creators.

Schumacher's team of Broadway professionals was willing to innovate in other ways as well. After the success of *Lion King*, negotiations with the Berlin Theatre in 1999 for a *Lion King* production fell through, and a production of *The Hunchback of Notre Dame (Der Glöckner von Notre Dame)* was offered instead. Developing a Broadway musical for production without a Broadway run was a first for Disney and a first for the Berlin Theatre (now Theater am Potsdamer Platz), which had previously only presented Broadway tours. The success of the production, which ran for three years, allowed Disney to continue developing it for licensing on the US stage. Meanwhile, *Elton John and Tim Rice's Aida*, originally intended as an animated feature, was developed as a live-action musical in the late 1990s using the Alliance Theatre in Atlanta and the Cadillac Palace in Chicago for development. Opening on Broadway in 2000, it became the third successful Disney Theatrical production and ran for more than 1,800 performances.[17]

Tarzan (2006) and *The Little Mermaid* (2008) both failed to recoup their capitalization costs on Broadway, but Disney was expanding into other production models, including a coproduction of *Mary Poppins* with Mackintosh (opening first in London in 2004 and then on Broadway in 2006), nonmusical productions such as *Peter and the Starcatcher* (2012), and direct-to-licensing shows such as *Freaky Friday* (2016) and *High*

School Musical On Stage! (2007). On Broadway, *Aladdin* transformed its animated source material into a kind of "Genie's Follies" and became a hit in 2014, and *Frozen* (2018), while not as successful, was enjoying moderate success before closing during the Covid pandemic in 2020. Of the nine Disney fully produced Broadway shows, six recouped their original investment, a 66 percent success rate.[18] Typically, only 20 percent of Broadway musicals recoup their capitalization costs.[19]

In fiscal year 2022, the Walt Disney Company earned $83.745 billion in revenue. Of that amount, approximately $600 million came from the Disney Theatrical Group's Broadway productions (not including touring and international productions which could easily double this amount).[20] While this represents less than 1 percent of the company's total revenue, it is substantially larger than most other theater producing companies. The nonprofit Public Theater, for example, which has co-produced the Broadway transfers *A Chorus Line, Cats,* and *Hamilton,* had revenue of $88 million in 2018, including its *Hamilton* royalty.[21] Disney Theatrical self-funds its new Broadway productions without co-producers (except for *Mary Poppins*) and "always returns money to the company each year," according to Schumacher. The unit's small size and its successful track record have meant that it can operate with some autonomy from Disney's corporate office while utilizing the marketing and research resources of the large company. While a new attraction at Disney World might cost well over $100 million to build and require extensive oversight by large teams of designers and builders as well as approval of the CEO and CFO, Disney Theatrical's new theater productions are nurtured within the unit and funded with the profits of existing successes such as *The Lion King* and *Aladdin*.

Disney Theatrical doesn't have to finance a show's capitalization in the way other Broadway producers do because it doesn't have to raise money from investors. Because of the early and ongoing successes of *Beauty and the Beast* and *The Lion King*, it also doesn't have to ask Disney for money beyond what the unit earns, even though every production is approved by the corporate office.[22] Yet Disney Theatrical is similar to other units of the company in that its branding, marketing, and demographic research are part of a larger synergistic company effort. Within the theatrical arm, the exploration of multiple creative properties matches up with a notable flexibility of the organization's business strategy, creating a significant presence in Broadway, regional, international, and licensing markets.[23] Disney Theatrical can fund the long-term development of several projects simultaneously by a number of artistic teams throughout the country. This is a significant innovation on Broadway, as most individual producers could not afford to subsidize several shows in development, thus not earning income, at the same time.[24] Disney Theatrical's independent entrepreneurship makes the company impervious to the clashing demands of co-producers with conflicting priorities and creative visions, but it also bears the full impact of a success or failure. In many ways, it has become the impresario of days past, when producers such as David Merrick would sometimes buy out other investors and "go it alone."[25]

Demographics

Disney has extensive experience with broad demographic appeal. Its theme parks, particularly Walt Disney World in Orlando, Florida, seek to attract families as well as a wide swath of demographic categories. According to the Broadway League, Broadway audiences in 2018–2019 were split among locals (35 percent) and tourists (65 percent).[26] Similarly, 70 percent of attendees at Disney World are non-Florida residents.[27] While Disney is notoriously secretive about its park businesses, several independent studies have shown that it is adults, not kids, who are the prominent demographic at the theme parks.[28] However, the target income demographic has historically been different. The Disney parks experience is targeted to middle-income families: people who earn between $50,000 and $74,999 a year want to visit Disney parks the most.[29] Those in the highest income group, between $150,000 and $200,000 a year, were the least likely to want to visit a Disney park in the coming year.[30] However, on Broadway, the average yearly income of a theater-goer in 2019 was $261,000,[31] far exceeding the income of the middle-class family targeted by the Disney theme parks.

In both cases, a Disney experience on Broadway or in the parks is expensive, and it is marketed as an event that many families might experience only once, if at all. There are, however, ways for families to buy affordable tickets to Broadway shows (discussed below).

Disney arrived on Broadway at the right time. In 1980, prior to the success of such mega-musicals as *Cats* (1982), *Phantom of the Opera* (1986), and *Les Misérables* (1987), Broadway producers relied on an audience that was primarily from the New York metro area. The 1980 audience was 41 percent tourist and 59 percent from the New York metro area.[32] After the revitalization of Times Square in the 1990s, supported in part by Disney's investment in the New Amsterdam Theatre which encouraged other corporations to follow, tourist attendance began to increase: by 2000, Broadway attendance was 56 percent tourist and 45 percent New York metro, and by 2018, tourists accounted for 65 percent of the audience and New York metro accounted for only 35 percent.[33] This "flipping" of Broadway demographics has allowed for longer-running shows as the audience is refreshed with each new wave of tourists. As a global brand, Disney has an advantage in terms of name recognition for tourists who might not be familiar with most Broadway titles.

Unlike other Broadway shows that might market T-shirts or cast albums for ancillary income, Disney has many more levers to pull for its intellectual property, including theme-park and cruise-line performances; streaming (Disney+, Hulu) or network television shows (ABC); merchandise of all kinds, including jewelry, genie lamps, stuffed toys (whether sold in Disney Stores or at other retailers); and conventionally released theatrical films. Because Disney owns the intellectual property of its Broadway shows, it can also license them for schools and amateur and professional theater companies.

The cross-pollination across the many Disney platforms keeps the Disney show's brand in front of consumers. While the Broadway audience may skew wealthy, female, and middle-aged, 45 percent of the Disney+ user base is younger than eighteen.[34] Access to much of the Disney library of animated and live-action films through Disney+ streaming has replaced the theatrical film rerelease cycle and the VHS release strategies of the 1980s, 1990s, and early 2000s. Seventy-seven percent of Disney+ subscribers earn less than $100,000 per year,[35] in stark contrast to the Broadway audience income of $260,000.[36] Both the animated (1994) and live-action (2019) versions of *The Lion King* are available to stream on Disney+ exclusively, along with *The Lion King Sing-Along*, *The Lion King 1½*, *The Lion King 2: Simba's Pride*, and three seasons of *The Lion Guard*.

In addition to the exploitation of successful material such as *The Lion King*, Disney has the advantage of mining a wide range of data across its many platforms regarding what properties might be considered for a Broadway-musical treatment. Schumacher notes, "We're discovering . . . that one of the most popular things on Disney+ are parents in their thirties or forties watching some old Disney Channel material—and sharing it with their kids. And twenty-year-olds are watching the Disney Channel shows of their childhood. Nostalgia is very powerful, and it cuts through all levels of our culture."[37] Disney enjoys the loyalty that customers throughout the world feel for the brand itself as well as its catalog.

Disney Theatrical's long-running production of *Aladdin* (2014) at the New Amsterdam Theatre has similarly blanketed exposure. Disney+ has both the animated (1992) and the live-action (2019) theatrical features as well as *The Return of Jafar* (1994) and *Aladdin and the King of Thieves* (1996). The latest Disney cruise ship, the *Treasure*, "has been designed with adventure in mind. It will be a Triton-class ship featuring characters from *Aladdin*, one of the entertainment company's classic films."[38] Other ships such as the *Disney Wish* feature a reimagined stage adaptation of *Disney's Aladdin—A Musical Spectacular*. This show was originally presented at Disney's California Adventure from 2003 to 2016.[39] Unlike typical theme-park shows that run for twenty minutes, *Spectacular* is a forty-five-minute reduction of the *Aladdin* Broadway show. The success of the Broadway show relies on broad audience exposure to the story, and the number of connections each audience member may bring. From 2001 to 2009, theme-park and cruise-line productions were supervised by Anne Hamburger, a noted producer in New York's avant-garde world. Like Taymor, she brought years of theatrical expertise to Disney's ancillary theatrical productions.[40]

The all-important *New York Times* review by Charles Isherwood for *Aladdin* was somewhat stronger ("defied my dour expectations") than Ben Brantley's skewering of *The Little Mermaid* ("Loved the shoes. Loathed the show"). Like *Lion King*, the reimagining of *Aladdin* in a more theatrical context, in this case a Ziegfeld-like extravaganza appropriate for its New Amsterdam Theatre venue, provides something for both Disney and musical-theater fans. Those fans span multiple generations. Since only 30 percent of ticket purchasers for Disney Broadway shows include a child in the group, each production is geared toward reaching a very diverse age range.[41] Speaking particularly of *Aladdin*, Schumacher elaborates on the company strategy in reaching a wide audience: "we produced the stage version twenty-two years after the film version was made, and an entire generation grew up loving that property. If you were twelve when you saw it, you're thirty-four now, right? You're coming. So the theater's full of these kind of Brooklyn hipsters that are coming, but if you're the forty-five to sixty-five crowd, you're coming because we're the closest thing to the Ziegfeld Follies you're ever going to see, and this big, spectacular show that's very grown-up and interesting. We produced a show that anyone can come to."[42]

Disney Theatrical further maximizes revenue through multiple income streams, including tours, international productions, licensing amateur and professional productions of its catalog through Music Theatre International (MTI), and merchandising. Sales of merchandise are through multiple outlets: online, at the theater, and at Disney Stores and other retail outlets.

Even though Disney is a publicly traded company that must be transparent about its finances through its board to its shareholders, information on individual theatrical production budgets and development costs is remarkably opaque. Disney Theatrical Group's financial information is folded into Walt Disney Studios' financials. Disney Theatrical does provide the Broadway League with data on income and participates in the Broadway League's survey data on Broadway productions and tours, so income and audience demographics can be compared across the Disney Broadway years beginning with *Beauty and the Beast* in 1994.

With 40 percent of the audience members for a Disney production seeing a Broadway show for the first time, there has arguably been a lift in Broadway attendance because of Disney's shows.[43] Before *Beauty and the Beast* opened in 1994, Broadway struggled to keep its theaters open. The 1990–1991 Broadway season saw only twenty-eight new productions, four of which were singing artists in concert, a comic act, and a magic show. There were twelve new plays and seven new musicals, and the rest were revivals.[44] Business has improved on Broadway since Disney launched *Beauty and the Beast*. All forty-three Broadway theaters were booked solidly in 2019, and many shows were waiting for theaters to become available. In the 2018–2019 season, thirty-nine new and thirty-two continuing productions meant that many new shows were queuing for a theater.

Broadway attendance has risen about 55 percent from 1993 to 2019,[45] and the Broadway audience is supporting a wide spectrum of unconventional musicals that have included *Fun Home*, *Avenue Q*, *A Gentleman's Guide to Love and Murder*, and *The Band's Visit*. Despite the concern that Disney's presence would affect the diversity of Broadway content and casting, the opposite has been true.

The slow return of Broadway production after the Covid pandemic reduced the number of productions again. Disney was the first Broadway producer to make a decision, in May 2020 at the height of the pandemic, to close the Broadway production of *Frozen*[46] and instead focus on the national tour and international productions. Disney's two anchor shows—*The Lion King* and *Aladdin*—resumed strong business in the 2022–2023 season. According to the Broadway League, *Lion King* did not have a weekly gross less than $1.5 million between May 2022 and March 2023, and *Aladdin* had a weekly gross of at least $1 million except for two weeks.[47]

Disney leverages its exclusive use of the New Amsterdam Theatre (through a ninety-nine-year lease) by booking its own Broadway shows; since the 1990s renovation, these have been *King David* (a limited-run Alan Menken/Tim Rice oratorio that opened the venue in 1997), *The Lion King, Mary Poppins*, and *Aladdin*. Outside of the New Amsterdam, Disney must compete for theaters to book its productions like every other Broadway producer. The largest theater owners—the Shubert Organization (seventeen theaters), the Nederlander Organization (nine theaters), and Jujamycn Theaters (five theaters)—often have a producing financial interest in shows themselves to keep their theaters booked with successful productions. To date, Disney Theatrical has used the New Amsterdam, The St. James (Jujamycn Theaters), and Nederlander Theatres for its Broadway shows. While members of the Nederlander family are independent Broadway producers, the organization itself does not often fund or develop Broadway productions for its theaters, making it an ideal partner for Disney.[48]

Having the right-sized theater to maintain a show's run is imperative, and Disney has successfully transferred shows from one theater to another to maintain a longer run. In 1999, Disney moved *Beauty and the Beast* from the Palace Theatre to the Lunt-Fontanne, both Nederlander theaters, to make room for the opening of *Aida* at the Palace.[49] Disney Theatrical took advantage of the Actors' Equity rule that requires a six-week time lapse between closing a production at one theater and reopening in another with a revised, smaller version of *Beast*. *Variety* reported that the downsized production would save $4.8 million in expenses with a reduced cast size and production values.[50] The "new" production featured a cast size of thirty-two, down from the original thirty-nine.[51] With 265 fewer seats and lower operating costs, Disney Theatrical was able to keep the show running for an additional eight years while using the New Amsterdam and the Palace to launch new, larger shows. Disney's Schneider stated in 1999, "We're not out there saying simpler, smaller, cheaper. We're saying it's a move to the Lunt-Fontanne to keep it running longer."[52] However, when *The Lion King* moved from the New Amsterdam to the Minskoff in June 2006 to make room for *Mary Poppins*, there was a one-week transfer period and no reductions in cast or production, and the number of seats remained almost the same. This has added many additional years to the run.

TICKET PRICING

Making a Broadway musical is expensive. Musicals are handmade (scenery, costumes, and other design elements), and running a show is labor-intensive. Capitalization and weekly operating budgets in the last few decades have escalated rapidly. As Schumacher points out, "the first thing people do is bemoan the cost of labor. And there are issues regarding labor that I think will ultimately get in the way of producing. But theater rents are high, marketing costs are very high, and production costs are *really* high. When you think of the ratio of ticket prices to operating expenses, it's dramatically different today than it was for *Oklahoma!* in 1943."[53]

When *Beauty and the Beast* opened in 1994, tickets were competitively priced among other musicals that year, ranging from $20 to $65. Tickets for children were not discounted, and only ages four and above were allowed in the theater. During the first week of *The Lion King* performances in 1997, the most expensive ticket sold for $75. Twenty years later, in April 2017, the highest-priced ticket sold at $225.[54] That same month, just down the street, *The Book of Mormon* was selling tickets for $477, and *Hamilton* VIP tickets topped out at $849.[55] As of 2014, Disney made an intentional (and unusual) decision to limit ticket prices to $227. Lowest-price tickets are in the range of $80 to $90 range as of 2023, and digital tickets sold by lottery are as low as $35.[56] "Doing so makes *The Lion King* relatively affordable for large groups and families, lessens the chance of buyer's remorse leading to bad word of mouth and offers room to raise prices over the long term."[57] David Shrader, executive vice president and managing director of Disney Theatrical until 2014 stated in that year, "We're never going to be the top price. We're never going to have the highest VIP price. We're never going to have the highest orchestra price. We're not in this for tomorrow afternoon. We're in it for however many years we've got. We're trying to be moderate."[58]

Like going to a theme park, seeing a Broadway show will be an infrequent event for most families. The company positions both as "events" that will create lasting memories, and who can put a price on that? Since 1971, the price of an entrance ticket to the Magic Kingdom at Walt Disney World has roughly equaled the price of a Broadway musical ticket and, as with Broadway, has far exceeded the cost of inflation. A ticket for entry to Walt Disney World's Magic Kingdom in 1971 was $3.50, with an additional cost for ticket booklets for rides.[59] When adjusting for inflation, that would equal about $25.65 in 2022. Instead, tickets for one Disney World park admission in 2022 range from $109 to $159 per day, while an average Broadway-musical ticket can cost $100 to well over $200 dollars. Figure 23.1 illustrates the parallel price increases between Broadway and Disney World.

Aside from a few blockbuster shows in the early part of their runs (such as *Hamilton*) or high-demand limited-run shows with stars such as Hugh Jackman (*The Music Man*), most Broadway shows do not sell out months in advance. According to Schumacher:

> [E]verything changed on 9/11 in terms of ticket buying. Prior to what happened in New York on 9/11, people were willing to buy tickets a year [to a] year and a half out. *Lion King* was sold out for a year and then three and four months into the next year. Sold out clean. Today no one has an advance ticket sale that's like that. Advance numbers just don't match what they used to match, even if you adjust for inflation, because people buy in the short term. So now, with the exception of a few colossal hits, you can always kind of score a ticket.[60]

Because of buyers' preference for purchasing tickets much later, the Disney company uses science over intuition to set ticket prices. Dynamic pricing, or flexible pricing that

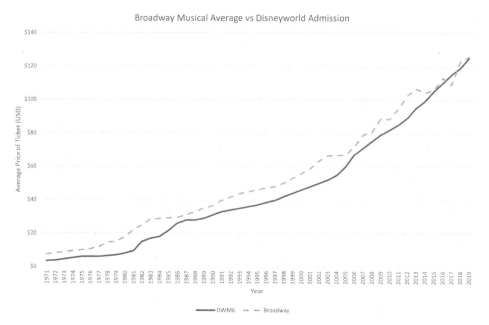

FIGURE 23.1. A comparison of the average price of a Broadway-musical ticket and the price of a single one-day admission at the Magic Kingdom at Walt Disney World.

reflects demand and time of year, is one way to achieve maximum income from a restricted supply or inventory. Airlines have used dynamic pricing ever since they were deregulated in 1978 and no longer had to seek government approval for fares. The dynamic-pricing strategies are most effective when two factors are present: the product expires at some point in time (hotel rooms, cruise-line berths, live entertainment tickets), and capacity is fixed well in advance.

While a theoretically unlimited audience can view a broadcast or streaming show, the Minskoff Theatre, where *The Lion King* plays, is limited to 1,696 tickets for each performance. Union rules restrict the number of performances generally to eight per week; therefore, the total weekly capacity for *The Lion King* is 13,568 seats. In 2011, Disney became an innovator in creating a computer algorithm, like those used by the hotel and airline industries, to adjust top prices for its shows on a weekly basis. Prior to this, producers of non-Disney Broadway shows did a version of dynamic pricing for holiday high-demand weeks and "shoulder" weeks which historically don't sell well, but Disney has the advantage of sophisticated management-science experts in its corporate office to fine-tune pricing daily for each seat on a weekly basis.[61]

Other theater producers now utilize dynamic ticket pricing, but none has the advantage of the analytic team at Disney, overseen by Mark Shafer, senior vice president of revenue and profit management at Disney Parks and Resorts. Shafer supervises a team of more than 120 analysts who work on business analytics, largely on pricing, sales, marketing, and revenue-management topics. While the group is based within the parks and resorts group, it supports projects across Disney business lines, including the parks and resorts, television networks (ABC, Disney Network, ESPN), the cruise line, and

Disney Theatrical Productions.[62] While the rest of the industry may have caught up with utilizing dynamic-pricing technology and strategy, no other producer has the advantage of Disney's analytics team.

Thanks to this dynamic pricing, *The Lion King* still routinely has a higher weekly gross revenue than its closest long-term competitor, *Wicked*, even though its regular prices ($75–$125 for *Lion King* versus $105–$175 for *Wicked*) and premium ticket prices ($199 for *Lion King* versus $275 for *Wicked*) are lower and the show has been running longer. For 2022, *Lion King* grossed $94 million over 673,349 seats sold, while *Wicked* grossed $85 million over 686,348 seats sold.[63] Disney maintains a $140 average ticket price with fewer seats sold for *Lion King* versus a $124 average ticket price for *Wicked*.[64] A recent study for the 2017–2020 period illustrated that while *The Lion King* and *Aladdin* adjusted prices weekly, *The Book of Mormon* and *Wicked* almost never do.[65] More than a decade after its introduction, Disney's dynamic-pricing strategy continues to be more effective than those of its competitors.

Branding and Marketing

Disney Theatrical enjoys the resources of the Walt Disney Company's enormous marketing arm which can carefully target its key demographic, yet it also utilizes some of the same marketing firms that promote other Broadway shows. Like those of the Mackintosh musicals of the 1980s, the logos for Disney Theatrical shows are bold and iconic. The *Beauty and the Beast* rose and Beast illustration and the *Lion King* lion graphic are two of the most recognized marketing images on Broadway. But Disney does not rely on the power of its intellectual property and iconography alone. Like all Broadway producers, Disney pays for traditional Broadway signage and *New York Times* advertising, and it has increasingly relied on the "impressions" that potential ticket buyers experience through social media, theme parks, cruise productions, and linear and streaming television. For the original presale of *The Lion King*, customers were offered a free watch for purchasing four or more tickets, but there was no internet marketing. That soon changed.

Disney Theatrical ventured into virtual reality in 2015, producing a 360-degree video of *The Lion King*'s "Pride Rock" opening number.[66] The experiment marked the first time a musical number was captured in virtual reality in a Broadway theater. For *Frozen*, Disney released ten major pieces of related video content in the show's first nine months, a strategy that attracted more than 30 million views across Facebook, YouTube, and Instagram.[67] Andrew Flatt, Disney Theatrical's senior vice president of strategy and revenue, believes that social media is an important part of the equation: "upwards of twenty-eight million people have seen our *Frozen* Tony Awards performance somewhere online. That twenty-eight million has opened up a substantial retargeting pool for us to be able to, in turn, go back and serve advertising that they can then click through to purchase to see the show."[68]

Additional online content includes highlights and complete performances of cruise-line and theme-park shows that are professionally produced by Disney. A one-hour theatrical production of *Disney Cruise Lines Frozen: A Musical Spectacular* is available in its entirety on the Disney Parks YouTube channel.[69] While it was not produced by Disney Theatrical, many of the designs and production values echo the Broadway show, and the additional exposure to a live performance might encourage audiences to see the full-length show on Broadway or on tour.

To producer Viertel's point that other producers "can't do what Disney does," Disney Theatrical's marketing utilizes other company-owned outlets, including ABC, Disney+, and even ESPN. The recent *Backstage with Disney on Broadway: Celebrating 20 Years* on ABC featured interviews and scenes from eight Disney Theatrical Productions musicals. When Broadway began to reopen in the fall of 2022, cast members from the theatrical presentations of *Aladdin*, *The Lion King*, and *Frozen* appeared on *The View* on ABC to sing a medley of classic songs from their respective shows. *ESPN Sport Science* has done multiple features utilizing cast members from Disney shows: ESPN Sport Science *Meets* Aladdin*: The Genie Marathon* and ESPN Sport Science *Meets* The Lion King*: Stamina*. Disney+ features such specials as *Disney's Broadway Hits at Royal Albert Hall* as well as a complete Disney Theatrical production of *Disney Newsies* filmed at the Hollywood Pantages Theatre in September 2016.

Merchandising

> You can judge the world of theatre by how the merchandising goes.
> —Thomas Schumacher

Given that Broadway and touring audiences are almost 70 percent women,[70] it follows that merchandising at Broadway and touring shows would be aimed at women. While Disney had licensed products since the days of Walt Disney, it became more aggressive about selling its own products in the 1980s with the expansion of the Disney Stores. Often placed in malls, the Disney Stores reflected the brand by creating a "Disney experience" that included showing movies at the back of the store, a backstage-like setting, "cast members" in costume who would greet customers, and merchandise that would appeal to children, adults, and collectors in discrete areas of the store.[71]

By 2021, with the demise of shopping malls, Disney looked at replacing stand-alone stores with "mini-stores" (typically 750 square feet) within existing retail stores, and opened more than one hundred "Disney Stores at Target."[72] Few of the original Disney Stores exist today, although New York's "World of Disney" Manhattan store moved from Fifth Avenue to Broadway in 2010 to become the flagship Disney Store. This provides a nearby retail anchor for Disney's Broadway shows. The two-floor Disney Store in Times Square has abundant Broadway-show merchandise, with items ranging from princess clothing to *Aladdin* figurines.

Using Disney Store knowledge, Disney Theatrical created mini-stores in its Broadway theaters (particularly the New Amsterdam) where Disney-themed items would be sold. During *Beauty and the Beast*, Disney opened merchandise booths on every level of the theater to give it maximum exposure in the relatively small Palace Theatre.[73] Some items, such as the Tricksters from *The Lion King*, were "exclusively" sold in these shops as well as in Disney Stores and at Disney World, sometimes for premium prices. Other items are now sold in the Playbill Store, indexed by show and ranging in price from $9 to $60. Playbill, the publisher of programs for Broadway shows, has an extensive online presence, including a "store" for Broadway merchandise as part of the continued transformation of traditional in-person retail to online. Disney is the only Broadway producer with its own section of the Playbill store.[74]

Unlike other Broadway producers that use third-party retailers that pay the producers a royalty of 15 percent to 20 percent of goods sold, Disney runs its own merchandising operation and keeps all the profits. It also controls the selection and manufacturing of its merchandise, ensuring quality of the products. The Trickster beanbag dolls based on Taymor's designs from *The Lion King* were originally manufactured by the Canasa Trading Company in Indonesia. This company was acquired by Disney in 1997.[75] This kind of synergy is part of Disney's business strategy that does not require a Broadway production to make a profit. Rather, according to Schumacher, "if you break even on Broadway, you're feeling OK. You set up Broadway as the marketing point for the rest of the world."[76] This applies both to merchandise and to future theatrical productions.

Disney sold almost ten thousand dollars' worth of *Beauty and the Beast* memorabilia at the first New York preview alone.[77] A *Beauty and the Beast* boutique opened at Bloomingdale's during the early run of the show.[78] A single rose with a medallion with the show title *Beauty and the Beast* was the highest-grossing merchandising item during the show's run,[79] and a sturdy parrot-head umbrella retailing for forty dollars became a bestseller for *Mary Poppins*,[80] confirmation that merchandising was not just focused on children. "Merchandising has gotten more sophisticated," according to David Schrader, former managing director and chief financial officer of Disney Theatrical. "Sellers are paying more attention and getting a little smarter, and the consumer seems to be more accepting of it."[81] While no sales figures for Disney's Broadway merchandise are available, its competition *Wicked* reported $100 million in merchandising sales in its first five years.[82]

For *Aladdin*, Disney hired StyleWorks Creative to expand its merchandise base through expanded use of the logo and show graphics. The result was an expansion of the merchandise available, in this case through the Playbill Store, of ornaments, shoes, and other merchandising items.[83] When purchasing a ticket to *Aladdin* through Ticketmaster, customers are routed to an *Aladdin* merchandise page where items can be added to the cart before purchasing.

Licensing

The Walt Disney Company is the largest licensor of intellectual property in the world, with $56.2 billion in 2022.[84] From the earliest history of the company, it has used and synergized its creative content over a wide swath of commercial outlets. While many of its source materials utilize public-domain works by such authors as Hans Christian Andersen and the Brothers Grimm, its visual interpretations and storytelling are fiercely protected by copyrights and are exploited in multiple media.

When such Broadway shows as *The Little Mermaid* and *Tarzan* fail to recoup their Broadway investment, the afterlife of the secondary licensing markets and tours and resident productions—both domestic and international—more than make up the difference in capitalization costs. When these ancillary revenue streams are taken into consideration, no Disney Theatrical production has ever lost money.

Since 2004, there have been more than 125,000 Disney-licensed theater productions around the US and Canada with more than 500,000 performances. More than 150 million people have engaged with a licensed show, either in the cast and crew or in the audience.[85] That represents 45 percent of the US population. In 2017 alone, more than 16 million people in the US and Canada engaged with a licensed show either in the cast and crew or in the audience versus the 13.8 million who attended a Broadway show. More than 123,000 individual theaters in the US alone have licensed a production of *Beauty and the Beast*, including professional, community, and school productions.[86] This saturation of Disney-created theater gives it an advantage in name recognition for tourists selecting a Broadway show when they visit New York City.

Disney Theatrical Licensing is Disney Theatrical Group's show-licensing arm, which licenses its shows for performance by professional companies, amateur groups, and local school and community theaters via MTI. This is not limited to Disney Theatrical's Broadway titles. In October 2016, *Freaky Friday* premiered as a licensed professional theatrical production at Signature Theatre in Virginia without any plans for a Broadway run. This was followed by a Disney Channel and Disney Theatrical Productions television adaptation of the stage musical in August 2018. *Pinocchio*, produced by the Royal National Theatre, London, in 2017 and using songs from the 1940 animated film, was "presented by special arrangement" with Disney Theatrical Productions. This followed an earlier rendition of the Carlo Coldoni *Pinocchio* story titled *Disney's My Son Pinocchio: Geppetto's Musical Tale*, with music and lyrics by Stephen Schwartz that was first an ABC television production in 2000, then was adapted into a stage musical first performed in 2006, and now is available for professional and amateur licensing. Other titles in development such as *The Jungle Book* (Goodman Theatre, 2013) and *Hercules* (Paper Mill Playhouse, 2023; West End, 2025) provide valuable research for Disney Theatrical in terms of what shows might eventually be developed for Broadway.

Newsies is one such success story. Originally planned by Disney as a direct-to-licensing musical version of the 1992 film, the Paper Mill Playhouse production in the fall of 2011 was intended to test out the material and give it some exposure before adding it to the licensing catalog. The audience response and the critical response were so strong that Schumacher arranged a twelve-week limited run at the Nederlander Theatre on Broadway in March 2012. Twelve weeks turned into two and a half years followed by a successful national tour.[87] While other Broadway producers have pre-Broadway tryouts, Disney has the scale (and pockets) to develop material and productions in multiple locations and formats simultaneously.

Disney also licenses special versions of Broadway shows for performance by younger children, such as *Aladdin JR.*, *The Lion King JR.*, *Mulan JR.*, and *Mary Poppins JR.* As of July 2022, there are thirty-seven Disney titles available for license (fifteen full-length, ten JR., and seven KIDS).[88] JR. titles are sixty-minute reductions designed for middle-school production; KIDS versions are thirty minutes marketed to elementary schools. Middle and elementary school students can perform shortened versions of current Disney Theatrical Broadway titles, making students more likely to want to see the full-length professional Broadway or touring productions. This is a significant change from the traditional Broadway licensing model which does not offer shows for professional or amateur productions until the Broadway and first-class tours have completed their runs. Of the seventy-one titles in the MTI JR. and KIDS catalog, only Disney licenses titles that are currently running on Broadway.

Licensed Disney Theatrical productions through MTI are provided copious material from Disney, including ideas for choreography and ways of economically producing the show with casts of various ages and ways to produce the shows on a tight budget. The *Aladdin JR.* packet, for example, includes four ways of staging the magic carpet ride.[89] The quality of the materials published through MTI is also much higher than that of competitors that send rental packages with errors or poorly printed materials because the scores have been edited for tours or the licensed versions merge multiple productions without the original artists' supervision. Disney protects its brand by supervising the creation of its licensed materials in the same painstaking process it uses for its Broadway shows. The resulting materials not only give explicit instructions for teachers on how to stage and produce a show, but they also provide information on how to accommodate flexible and larger casts in schools.

Conclusion

Given the extensive reach Disney has through movies, recordings, television (ABC, ESPN), streaming (Disney+), theme parks, school licensing, cruise ships, and Disney Stores, Disney Theatrical's Broadway titles have lives well beyond their initial Broadway runs. *Aladdin*, first released as an animated feature in 1992, was followed by a live-action release in 2019, theme-park shows (*Aladdin: A Musical Spectacular*, 2003–2016), and amateur licensing for elementary school and middle school students (*Aladdin KIDS* and *Aladdin JR.*, respectively). The 2014 Broadway production ranks with *The Lion King* and *Beauty and the Beast* as one of its most successful productions, with more than $542 million in gross sales as of 2023.[90]

The success of Disney animated "Renaissance" titles *Beauty and the Beast*, *The Lion King*, and *Aladdin* have more than made up for the failures of *Tarzan* and *The Little Mermaid*, particularly when the international, professional, and school-licensed productions through MTI are considered. While the $35 million *Frozen* was not doing the same business as *Lion King* or *Aladdin*, it saw total attendance of more than 1.3 million and grossed more than $150 million. It was closed during the Covid pandemic as attempting to open three Disney shows after the pandemic "would become untenable."[91] The sets and costumes have been used for tours and international productions, so the capitalization costs could be amortized over time as touring productions resumed after the pandemic.[92]

Other film studios have attempted to replicate Disney's success by using their film libraries as sources for Broadway musicals, notably Warner Bros. (*The Color Purple*), Universal Theatrical Group (*Billy Elliot the Musical, Back to the Future: The Musical*) and its subsidiary DreamWorks Theatrical (*Shrek*), and Paramount Pictures (*Mean Girls, Almost Famous*). But none of these productions has rivaled Disney's success,[93] and most are co-produced with other Broadway investors. None of the film studios has Broadway theatrical offices or infrastructure like Disney Theatrical Productions. In many ways, Disney Theatrical operates as its own theater company that develops works at a variety of levels for a wide spectrum of audiences.

As a part of the 2019 acquisition of 20st Century Fox by the Walt Disney Company, the Disney Theatrical Group inherited Fox Stage Productions under the new Buena Vista Theatrical banner, which licenses Fox titles for stage adaptations, including the Broadway and touring productions of *Moulin Rouge! The Musical* and *Mrs. Doubtfire*. This gives Disney an opportunity to expand its titles using the Fox film catalog, and it also allows for more adult content under a different moniker. A similar strategy was employed by the Disney film studio in the 1980s when Disney created the Touchstone Films banner to allow more adult content in such films as *Splash* and *Down and Out in Beverly Hills* (the company's first R-rated film).

The four-year gap between the openings of *Aladdin* in 2014 and *Frozen* in 2018 is a further reflection that Disney productions on Broadway will be only one component of a much larger business strategy. While several Broadway productions are in development, Disney continues to use regional theaters such as Paper Mill Playhouse (*Hercules* in 2023) and international productions to test-drive emerging work, and it doesn't hesitate to bypass Broadway and directly license its titles to amateur and professional companies (*High School Musical*). A musical in development from the 20th Century Fox catalog, *The Greatest Showman*, was announced in August 2024 by Disney. Recoupment may involve long-term thinking about how much tours, international productions, or MTI licensing will help with the bottom line. Neither *The Little Mermaid* nor *Tarzan* had US tours, so more pressure was on recoupment through international and MTI licensing.

The Broadway audience has become incrementally younger over the last decade, which will help Disney shows. But Disney doesn't look at "family-friendly" as a specific metric for choosing shows. Schumacher asks his team, "Can you get it so grandma wants to come? Can you get it to be a great date night? *Beauty and the Beast* was a great date night show, which people have forgotten."[94] Beginning in the fall of 2024, Disney Theatrical Group is now led by a group of three, including Schumacher (chief creative officer) and Andrew Flatt and Anne Quart (executive vice presidents), who will jointly run the day-to-day operations.[95] With a huge catalog and a willingness to take creative chances with Disney intellectual properties, Schumacher and Disney Theatrical have showed a remarkable flexibility in business strategy. "If you don't mix up the portfolio, it can cannibalize your ability to market and position your own shows. I don't think our business model should ever be: There's just one model."[96] As of 2024, Disney Theatrical has produced three of the fifteen longest-running Broadway musicals, an impressive feat for a division that is only thirty-one-years old. On Broadway and beyond, Disney is in it for the long haul.

Notes

1. Production and attendance statistics courtesy of Disney Theatrical Productions, July 2022.
2. Peter Marks, "Cameron Mackintosh: The Showman Must Go On," *Washington Post*, March 19, 2017, E10.
3. Attendance numbers, number of productions, and touring statistics courtesy of Disney Theatrical Productions, July 2022.
4. Survey results courtesy of Disney Theatrical Productions, July 2022.
5. Elizabeth Wollman, "The Economic Development of the 'New' Times Square and Its Impact on the Broadway Musical," *American Music* 20, no. 4 (2002): 445–465.
6. For film grosses, I am using IMDB.com; for Broadway, the Broadway League reports.
7. Alex Witchel, "Is Disney the Newest Broadway Baby?," *New York Times*, April 17, 1994, H1.
8. Broadway League survey data. Since the Covid pandemic substantially affected Broadway attendance and income, I am using 2018–2019 Broadway League reporting for industry demographics and income statistics.
9. Wollman, "The Economic Development of the 'New' Times Square," 456.
10. While there is no technical definition for "family-friendly," I am referring to audiences that include children as young as six, since children younger than that will probably not be able to sit through a full-length musical.
11. A. H. Weller, "9.5 Million for Filming 'Annie,'" *New York Times*, December 30, 1977, C26.
12. "'Annie' Production History," Broadway World, https://www.broadwayworld.com/shows/backstage.php?showid=3205.
13. Michael Eisner with Tony Schwartz, *Work in Progress* (New York: Random House, 1998), 255.
14. Steve Nelson, "Broadway and the Beast: Disney Comes to Times Square," *Drama Review* 39, no. 2 (1995): 72.
15. Ken Davenport, *The Producer's Perspective Podcast*, no. 206, https://kendavenport.com/episode-206-thomas-schumacher/.
16. Ibid.
17. Campbell Robertson and Brooks Barnes, "Disney Wonders if a Mermaid Can Follow a Trail Blazed by a Lion," *New York Times*, December 20, 2007, E1.
18. *Tarzan* and *A Little Mermaid* did not recoup their capitalization costs; it is unclear whether *Frozen* did.
19. Ken Davenport, "What Is the Broadway Recoupment Rate over the Last Five Years?," https://kendavenport.com/what-is-the-broadway-musical-recoupment-rate-over-the-last-5-years-part-i/.

20. Because Disney's annual report doesn't break down Disney Theatrical's earnings separately, I have relied on Zippia and a calculation based on the public information provided by the Broadway League on weekly box-office grosses.
21. New York Shakespeare Festival IRS Form 990, 2018.
22. Davenport, *The Producer's Perspective Podcast*, no. 206.
23. Gordon Cox, "Disney Looks beyond the Magic Kingdom for Broadway Prospects," *Variety*, November 22, 2013.
24. Stephen Adler, *On Broadway: Arts and Commerce* (Carbondale: Southern Illinois Press, 2004), 15.
25. Michael Kantor, dir., *Broadway: The American Musical* (PBS, 2003), ep. 6, "Putting It Together."
26. Broadway League, "The Demographics of the Broadway Audience 2018–19," November 2019, https://www.broadwayleague.com/research/order-research-reports/.
27. Antonia Cheatam, "Measuring Travel Behavior Demographics at Walt Disney World," https://www.streetlightdata.com/measuring-travel-behavior-by-demographics-disney-world/?type=blog/.
28. Thomas Bywater, "Disney Adults: Visitors without Children Have Become Disney Parks' Largest Demographic," *New Zealand Herald*, June 26, 2022, https://www.nzherald.co.nz/travel/disney-adults-visitors-without-children-become-disney-parks-largest-demographic/IT2ST7K7J5C66YV37PL5M7IY3M/.
29. Ibid.
30. The two surveys used here are Streetlight Data, https://www.streetlightdata.com/measuring-travel-behavior-by-demographics-disney-world/?type=blog/, and the survey of 1,154 people in the Disney with Dave's Daughters blog, https://disneywithdavesdaughters.com/disney-world-visitor-statistics/. While the two surveys are consistent with each other and with Disney's annual report, a larger sample size is needed.
31. Broadway League, "The Demographics of the Broadway Audience 2018–19," https://www.broadwayleague.com/research/order-research-reports/.
32. Karen Hauser, "The Demographics of the Broadway Audience 2008–9," September 2009, https://www.broadwayleague.com/research/order-research-reports/.
33. Broadway League, "The Demographics of the Broadway Audience 2018–19."
34. Daniel Ruby, "Disney Users (2022)—Latest Facts and Figures," Demandsage, October 29, 2022, https://www.demandsage.com/disney-users/.
35. Ibid.
36. Ibid.
37. Davenport, *The Producer's Perspective Podcast*, no. 206.
38. Hayley Skirka, "Disney Cruise Line Launches New 'Aladdin'-Inspired Mega-Ship 'Disney Treasure,'" National News, September 12, 2022, https://www.thenationalnews.com/travel/2022/09/12/disney-cruise-line-unveils-new-aladdin-inspired-mega-ship-disney-treasure/.
39. Cole Geryak, "Disney Extinct Attractions: Disney's Aladdin—A Musical Spectacular," Laughing Place, September 29, 2016, https://www.laughingplace.com/w/blogs/disney-extinct-attractions/2016/09/29/disney-extinct-attractions-disneys-aladdin-musical-spectacular/.
40. Adler, *On Broadway*, 101.
41. Ibid.
42. John Horn, "Disney's Tom Schumacher on the Massive Success of The Lion King and How Broadway Has Changed Over 20 Years," *Vulture*, November 20, 2014, https://www.vulture.com/2014/11/disneys-theatrical-head-on-broadways-changes.html.

43. Joel Lyons, "Disney on Broadway Celebrates 25th Anniversary with a Magical Mashup," *GMA* Online, April 12, 2022, https://www.goodmorningamerica.com/culture/story/disney-broadway-celebrates-25th-anniversary-magical-mashup-62341305.
44. Frederick M. Winship, "Broadway May Be Sick, but It Mints Money," UPI Archives, June 4, 1991, https://www.upi.com/Archives/1991/06/04/Broadway-may-be-sick-but-it-mints-money/8184676008000/.
45. Broadway League data.
46. Michael Paulson, "Disney Closes 'Frozen' on Broadway, Citing Pandemic," *New York Times*, May 14, 2020.
47. https://www.broadwayleague.com/research/grosses-broadway-nyc.
48. Internet Broadway Database, https://www.ibdb.com/broadway-organization/the-nederlander-organization-72149.
49. "'Beauty' Moving from the Palace to the Fontanne," *New York Times*, July 14, 1999, E3.
50. Claude Brodesser, "Beauty Makeover Awakens Equity Ire," *Variety*, May 3, 1999, 89.
51. Based on a comparison of the Palace and Lunt-Fontanne *Playbill* cast lists.
52. Robin Pogrebin, "Downsizing the Broadway Musical," *New York Times*, September 19, 1999. *Gale Academic OneFile*, link.gale.com/apps/doc/A150955584/AONE?u=char69915&sid=sitemap&xid=c40ca561.
53. Davenport, *The Producer's Perspective Podcast*, no. 206.
54. Michael Paulson, "Broadway's High Prices for Tickets Fuel Boom," *New York Times*, May 24, 2017, C1.
55. Patrick Healy, "Ticket Pricing Puts 'Lion King' atop Broadway's Circle of Life," *New York Times*, March 17, 2014, A1.
56. https://www.tdf.org/shows/1601/The-Lion-King.
57. Healy, "Ticket Pricing."
58. Mark Kennedy, "'The Lion King' Earns Record Box Office," *Seattle Times*, September 22, 2014, https://www.seattletimes.com/nation-world/the-lion-king-earns-record-box-office/.
59. https://allears.net/walt-disney-world/wdw-planning/wdw-ticket-history/.
60. Davenport, *The Producer's Perspective Podcast*, no. 206.
61. Healy, "Ticket Pricing."
62. Robert Phillips, "Why "'The Lion King' Roars So Loud: Business Analytics at Disney," Columbia Business School, December 12, 2013, https://www8.gsb.columbia.edu/bizanalytics/content/why-%E2%80%9C-lion-king%E2%80%9D-roars-so-loud-business-analytics-disney.
63. https://www.broadwayworld.com/grossesbyyear.cfm?year=2022.
64. Ibid.
65. Kyle D. S. Maclean and Fredrik Odegaard, "Revenue Implications of Celebrities on Broadway Theatre," *Journal of Revenue and Pricing Management*, June 17, 2022. While the article focuses on revenue-management impacts of celebrities and Tony Awards, it also illustrates the results of different dynamic-pricing strategies.
66. https://www.youtube.com/watch?v=7T57kzGQGto.
67. Christopher Zara, "For Disney Theatrical, Video Fuels the Broadway Star," *Fast Company*, August 15, 2018, https://www.fastcompany.com/90217610/for-disney-theatrical-video-fuels-the-broadway-star.
68. Ibid.
69. https://www.youtube.com/watch?v=BgL3vp8bEKo&t=3210s.
70. Broadway League, "The Demographics of the Broadway Audience 2018–19."

71. An excellent history of Disney Stores and its experiential concept can be found in Eisner and Schwartz, *Work in Progress*, 240–248.
72. Kelly Tyko, "Target to Add More Than 100 Disney Store Locations by the End of 2021," *USA Today*, August 23, 2021, https://www.usatoday.com/story/money/shopping/2021/08/23/target-disney-store-expansion-holiday-shopping-toy-list/8214032002/.
73. Mitch Weiss and Perri Gaffney, *The Business of Broadway: An Insider's Guide to Working, Producing, and Investing in the World's Greatest Theatre Community* (New York: Allworth, 2017), 78.
74. https://playbillstore.com/collections/disney-on-broadway.
75. State of New York, Tax Appeals Tribunal, In the Matter of the Petition of Disney Enterprises, https://www.dta.ny.gov/pdf/archive/Decisions/818378.dec.pdf.
76. D. Cox and G. Evans, "B'way Rules Rewritten to Heed 'Lion's' Roar," *Variety*, December 22, 1997–January 4, 1998, 78.
77. Witchel, "Is Disney the Newest Broadway Baby?"
78. Ibid.
79. Davenport, *The Producer's Perspective Podcast*, no. 206.
80. Gordon Cox, "Tuners Trumpet Their Trinkets," *Variety*, January 1, 2007, 37–38.
81. Ibid.
82. Robert Simonson, "A Wicked Success: Broadway's Favorite Witch Turns Five," *Playbill*, October 8, 2008, https://playbill.com/article/a-wicked-success-broadways-favorite-witches-turn-five-com-154697.
83. https://styleworkscreative.com/portfolio/aladdin-on-broadway-key-art-merchandising/.
84. https://www.licensingsource.net/disney-holds-firm-as-worlds-leading-licensor/.
85. Broadway League data, https://www.broadwayleague.com/research/grosses-broadway-nyc/.
86. Courtesy of Disney Theatrical Productions, July 2022.
87. The MTI Performance Guide provides a complete history: https://issuu.com/mtivault/docs/newsies_performance_guide.
88. Full-length shows for licensing: *Aida, Aladdin Dual Language Version, Beauty and the Beast, Freaky Friday, High School Musical, High School Musical 2, The Hunchback of Notre Dame, The Little Mermaid, Mary Poppins, My Son Pinocchio: Geppetto's Musical Tale, Newsies, Peter and the Starcatcher, Shakespeare in Love, Tarzan*. Sixty-minute/JR. shows: *Aladdin JR., Beauty and the Beast JR., Finding Nemo JR., Frozen JR., High School Musical JR., The Lion King JR., The Little Mermaid JR., Mary Poppins JR., Moana JR., My Son Pinocchio JR., Newsies JR*. Thirty-minute/KIDS versions: *101 Dalmatians KIDS, Disney Aladdin KIDS, The Aristocats KIDS, Finding Nemo KIDS, Frozen KIDS, The Jungle Book KIDS, The Lion King KIDS, Winnie the Pooh KIDS*.
89. Stacy Wolf's excellent observations and research on Disney JR. and KIDS shows describes the positive effects of these licensing packets. Stacy Wolf, "Not Only on Broadway: Disney JR. and Disney KIDS across the US," in *The Disney Musical on Stage and Screen: Critical Approached from "Snow White" to "Frozen,"* ed. George Rodosthenous (New York: Bloomsbury, 2017), 138.
90. Broadway League, "The Demographics of the Broadway Audience 2018–19."
91. Greg Evans, "Disney's 'Frozen' Becomes Broadway's First Long-Running Coronavirus Casualty: Producers Announce Permanent Closing," *Deadline*, May 14, 2020, https://deadline.com/2020/05/disneys-frozen-becomes-broadways-first-long-running-coronavirus-casualty-producers-announce-permanent-closing-1202934944/.

92. Michael Paulson, "Frozen Is Broadway's First Pandemic Victim, but More Disney Is on the Way," *New York Times*, May 15, 2020, A10.
93. *Billy Elliot* came closest, with Broadway gross of $183 million and 1,312 performances, according to Broadway League data, but it is still only a fraction of Disney's top three.
94. "Disney on Broadway Celebrates 25th Anniversary with Beauty and the Beast Revival," IHeartRadio Broadway, https://www.youtube.com/watch?v=VlVFSa3QSto.
95. Michael Paulson, "Disney's Thomas Schumacher Takes on New Broadway Role," *New York Times*, September 28, 2023, https://www.proquest.com/blogs-podcasts-websites/disney-s-thomas-schumacher-takes-on-new-broadway/docview/2869616645/se-2.
96. Gordon Cox, "Disney Looks beyond the Magic Kingdom for Broadway Prospects," *Variety*, November 22, 2013, https://variety.com/2013/legit/news/disney-looks-beyond-the-magic-kingdom-for-broadway-prospects-1200866092/.

CHAPTER 24

WE'RE ALL IN THIS TOGETHER: DISNEY THEATRICAL IN PARTNERSHIP

AMY S. OSATINSKI

Disney Theatrical, the theatrical arm of the Walt Disney Company, has been producing live stage musicals on Broadway since 1994 and touring and producing productions internationally since 1995. The company's process for many international and some domestic productions has been to work in partnership with other artists and organizations. Although Disney is famous for having an iron grip on its intellectual property, there have been times when it made the most sense, whether for artistic, financial, or legal reasons, for Disney Theatrical to work with others to make theatrical magic.

In the early days of its foray onto the stage, Disney relied solely on its own people to craft stage adaptations of its films. For the 1994 production of *Beauty and the Beast*, Michael Eisner, then chairman and CEO of Disney, decided to utilize Disney's own people, pulled from other divisions, rather than hire established Broadway artists, explaining that "Walt Disney World alone puts on more live theater than all of Broadway."[1] While Eisner's decision did allow Disney to produce *Beauty* without any partners, shutting out the Broadway establishment may also have contributed to the perception that the company was a corporate intruder primed to destroy the artistic legitimacy of the Broadway musical.[2] Although time would prove this sentiment untrue, it would take decades for a Disney musical to be evaluated solely on its merits and not its connection to the Mouse. Wisely, when it came time to open its first production overseas, Disney decided to do it in partnership. This was the first in a long line of collaborations that would help Disney Theatrical become a dominant force in commercial theater domestically and globally.

This chapter explores the many ways Disney Theatrical has worked in partnerships since 1995 to create and produce live productions, both within the US and abroad, in order to show how working in tandem with other theater organizations has allowed Disney Theatrical to extend the reach of its live productions globally and innovate artistically. It covers a variety of partnerships from 1995 to 2014, illuminating how the company was able to become one of the leading producers of live Broadway-style musicals around the world in less than three decades.

International Partnerships

From the very beginning, Disney Theatrical was determined to open international productions of its Broadway-musical offerings. Since the company broke its first leg on the Great White Way, international partnerships have been part of the Disney-on-Broadway plan and the Disney Theatrical process. Just over a year after the first Disney Theatrical production, *Beauty and the Beast*, opened on Broadway, the first international partnership was forged to produce the property overseas. On July 8, 1995, *Disney's Beauty and the Beast* opened at the Princess Theatre in Melbourne, Australia, in partnership with Kevin Jacobsen Promotions and Michael Edgley International. The Australian production was the first in a long line of international productions of Disney properties that were produced in partnership with other organizations around the world.[3]

While in a few markets, such as the UK and recently Australia, Disney Theatrical works on its own to mount resident productions and tours of its properties, it is more common that it partners with a local company to mount international productions, particularly in countries where the primary language is not English. Although each partnership, each production, and each country is different, there are some standard procedures that the company follows. For example, for each partnership, Disney draws up practical guidelines with its international collaborators, determining who gets what, who is responsible for what, and who recoups their investment first.[4] Additionally, it is standard for Disney to send its creative teams to supervise and mount the production in partnership with the local producer. Disney also provides all the merchandise so that the products associated with any given title are uniform internationally.[5] In markets where the production will be performed in a language other than English, the partner is most often in charge of the translation, with Disney providing feedback during the translation process.

This model provides Disney with several benefits. First, by keeping control of the merchandise and having creative teams present for the rehearsal and production process, Disney can ensure that all official productions[6] adhere to the stringent Disney brand standard. But by enlisting a local company to translate, cast, rehearse, and run the production, Disney does not have to hire personnel in every location a show opens and does not have to do research in-house to ensure that the production will be appropriate for the community in which it plays. By partnering, Disney also passes a portion of the risk for each production to its partners, since both Disney and the producing partner invest and reap the rewards or suffer the losses for the collaborative production.

Since 1995, Disney has produced in partnership in dozens of countries and with dozens of partner organizations; however, two companies in particular have been prolific partners for Disney productions overseas: the Shiki Company in Japan and Stage Entertainment in Europe.

The Shiki Company

The Shiki Company was founded in Tokyo in 1953 and is currently one of the largest theatrical groups in Japan. The company began with the goal of producing French theater for Japanese audiences. However, in 1973, Shiki produced a Japanese-language version of Andrew Lloyd Webber's *Jesus Christ Superstar*, which was very successful and followed by productions of many Western musicals in the 1980s.[7] Every year, the Shiki Company stages both imported and domestic productions in more than three thousand performances for more than 3 million patrons. Shiki has multiple international partnerships, and through these partnerships, it is able to bring in productions from the US and the UK and adapt them for Japanese audiences quickly. In addition to Disney titles, Shiki has also produced *Phantom of the Opera*, *Cats*, *Mamma Mia!*, and *Wicked* (among many others) for Japanese audiences.[8]

The partnership with Disney began in 1995 with the first Asian production of *Beauty and the Beast*. It opened in Tokyo and then toured to Osaka. Shiki has produced multiple productions of *Beauty and the Beast* which include productions or tour stops in Fukuoka, Nagoya, Sapporo, Kyoto, Hiroshima, Shizuoka, and Sendai, in addition to return trips to Tokyo.[9] In 2022, Shiki again partnered with Disney to open a new full-length production of *Beauty and the Beast* at Tokyo Disney as a part of several new *Beauty and the Beast*–themed attractions, including the much-anticipated Enchanted Tale of Beauty and the Beast ride, which features Disney's state-of-the-art trackless ride technology.[10]

However, the Disney–Shiki partnership didn't end with *Beauty and the Beast*. In fact, the most profitable and prolific production, *The Lion King*, was developed a few years later. The Japanese production of *The Lion King*, which opened in 1998, was the first international production of the title, premiering only a year after the original opened on Broadway. Shiki was interested in creating a new iteration, rather than just translating the existing version into Japanese. In their article for "Embodying Animal, Racial, Theatrical, and Commercial Power in *The Lion King*," scholars Ken Cerniglia and Aubrey Lynch II note:

> Like every foreign producer, Japan's Shiki Company really wanted its own version of *The Lion King*. The company also demanded a completely Japanese cast. Disney was worried that the unique south African sound would be lost, but many of the sounds necessary to produce the south African lyrics ended up being easier for Japanese singers than most Western performers. In addition, Julie [Taymor's] vocabulary as

a director, which stems from her years working in Indonesia and includes Javanese and Balinese puppetry, masks, and movement, was often more easily embraced by the Japanese, who have similar performance traditions. *The Lion King* is not the same show in Japan as in other locations around the world, but it works in its context and, in some respects, resonates more.[11]

The Japanese production of *The Lion King* is an excellent example of why Disney's partnership model works so well internationally. By partnering with Shiki to create a new version of the property that is specific to Japanese audiences, Disney was able to capitalize on a whole new market for the production and the story. A testament to the quality of the production, it is still running as of this writing, having played for twenty-four years, almost as long as *The Lion King* has played on Broadway. *Beauty and the Beast* and *The Lion King* were just the first of many titles that Disney and Shiki created for Japan.

Shiki is an ideal partner for Disney Theatrical because it not only produces musicals but also owns theaters around Japan. This means that through one partnership, Disney can have multiple productions, or multiple versions of the same production, running in various cities around Japan at once. As of January 2023, Shiki owns four theaters in Tokyo and one each in Nagoya, Kyoto, Sapporo, and Osaka. Also as of January 2023, there are four Disney–Shiki productions running, *The Hunchback of Notre Dame*, *Frozen*, and *Aladdin* in Tokyo and *The Little Mermaid* in Sapporo. In addition to the productions running in Shiki-owned theaters, as mentioned above, Shiki partnered with Disney to open a permanent production of *Beauty and the Beast* in the Maihama Amphitheater at Tokyo Disney, which is planned as a permanent production and features a refreshed script and new technical elements[12] from the original Shiki Japanese-language production of the property.[13] Shiki is but one of several partners that Disney Theatrical works with in Asia, but the Disney–Shiki model has provided a template for many of the company's partnerships around the world.

Stage Entertainment

Stage Entertainment is a European production company that was founded in 1998 by Dutch television and theater producer Joop van den Ende. Like Shiki, Stage Entertainment both produces original works and partners with other producers to mount foreign productions. Additionally, the company, also like Shiki, owns and manages theaters across Europe to house its productions. Stage Entertainment has produced a variety of non-Disney Broadway musicals in Europe through partnerships with other producers.

Disney and Stage Entertainment signed a partnership agreement in 2000 which led to the first production, a German-language version of *The Lion King*, *Der König der Löwen*, which opened in December 2001 in Hamburg and at the time of this writing is still running. With the success of the German version, several more productions of the property opened across Europe, including an English-language production in Scheveningen, Netherlands, from 2004 to 2006, and a French version, *Le Roi Lion*, which ran in Paris from 2007 to 2010 and then returned to Paris in September 2021 and is still running at the time of this writing. There is also a Spanish version, *El Rey León*, which opened in Madrid in 2011 and is also still running at the time of this writing. Since the Disney–Stage Entertainment partnership found success with *The Lion King*, a string of other Disney–Stage Entertainment productions sprang up, including *Aida*, which opened in Scheveningen in 2003 and later moved to Essen, Germany, and then eventually toured Germany. In 2005, *Beauty and the Beast* opened in the Netherlands and eventually took up residence in thirteen European cities in five different languages: English, German, Italian, Spanish, and Russian.[14]

However, the Stage Entertainment partnership didn't just produce Disney's successful Broadway musicals, but it also produced those that found less success in the US, including 2006's box-office bomb, *Tarzan*. The musical, which was based on the 1999 Disney animated feature, which in turn was based on the 1912 novel by Edgar Rice Burroughs, never recouped its investment while running on Broadway and was the first Disney musical on Broadway that didn't hit that mark.[15] There are many reasons for *Tarzan*'s failure on Broadway, but one possible reason was a mismatch between Broadway audience expectations and what the show delivered. However, when the Disney–Stage Entertainment production opened in the Netherlands in 2007, it was a huge hit and ran sold-out for more than two years, selling more tickets than *The Lion King*. Adjustments were made to the production, particularly to make it more immersive (as was the initial vision for the Broadway iteration, but due to the constraints of the Richard Rodgers Theatre, that plan had to be scaled back).[16] But those adjustments were only one tiny piece of the European production's success.

There are several factors that led *Tarzan* to triumph in Europe even though it flopped in the US. Quoted in Cerniglia's chapter "Tarzan Swings onto Disney's Broadway," Jeff Lee, the production's associate director, surmised that the show was popular in Europe for three reasons: "Phil Collins, Disney, and a European aesthetic appreciation of design and presentation not shared by traditional [US] musical-theatre audiences."[17] That aesthetic may have contributed to the show's inability to recoup on Broadway in two ways. First was its cost. Tarzan was expensive, which meant that even though it ran for almost five hundred performances, it still lost money. Next, the abstract nature of the design was not what American audiences expected, particularly from a screen-to-stage Disney musical. Broadway musicals are often viewed as more serious entertainments, and the show's circus-like aesthetics, a product of its original conception as a traveling tent show, were mismatched with the expectations of a Broadway audience, which was less foreign to European audiences given the wider variety of entertainments that are regularly produced there.[18] It is not uncommon for unconventional shows that are less successful in the US to have long runs in Germany; take, for example, the long-running production of *Starlight Express*, a show about a steam engine with big dreams that has been playing in Bochum since 1988. *Starlight Express* baffled US critics and was panned by most. Frank Rich of the *New York Times* called the show a "confusing jamboree of piercing noise, routine roller-skating, misogyny and Orwellian special effects" and noted that "the high-tech scenic environment, designed by John Napier, is something to see, if only at intermission."[19] Like *Tarzan*, *Starlight Express* found only modest success in the US but is a huge hit in Germany.

In addition to Collins's popularity and *Tarzan*'s aesthetics, by 2007, the Disney–Stage Entertainment productions in Europe were widely popular and very visible, which may also have contributed to the property's longevity. *Tarzan* played multiple venues in Germany—Hamburg (2008), Stuttgart (2013), and Oberhausen (2016)—spending years in each city. By around 2016, the European iterations of the production brought in enough money (even split between the two producers) for the property to pay back its investment and for Disney to start turning a profit from the title.[20] Additionally, the musical was scheduled to open a new production in Stuttgart in November 2023, a testament to its popularity and success in Germany.

At the time of this writing, Stage Entertainment has eight productions of Disney musicals running: *The Lion King* in Paris, Hamburg, and Madrid; *Aida* in Scheveningen; *Tarzan* in Stuttgart; *Aladdin* in Stuttgart and Scheveningen; and *Frozen* in Hamburg. Additionally, there is a production of *Sister Act* in Milan, for which Disney is a producer in name only. The partnership between Stage Entertainment and Disney Theatrical, like the Shiki partnership, has allowed Disney to produce musicals across Europe with less risk, as both the profit and the risk are spread between the two companies. The partnership also leverages Stage Entertainment's knowledge of the local cultural and performance landscape, helping Disney to program titles that are likely to bring in audiences, allowing even floundering properties to find new life and new profits abroad.

Development Partnerships

In addition to its partnerships overseas, which allow Disney Theatrical to open international versions of its properties, Disney Theatrical has also made a habit of partnering to develop theatrical productions that are aimed at Broadway or domestic licensing in the US. Although the international partnerships were a part of the Disney process from the beginning, the first development partnerships were forged in the twenty-first century. While Disney Theatrical has most often produced its stage musicals on its own with its own teams, there have been several instances in which it has partnered with other organizations to create musicals destined for Broadway and elsewhere. Each of these partnerships was for a different reason, and for each, Disney Theatrical had a different level of involvement. Additionally, Disney Theatrical has partnered with other theater companies to develop its in-house productions outside of New York, and it has even partnered with other divisions within the Walt Disney Company to bring a property to Broadway.

Mary Poppins (London 2004, Broadway 2006)

Mary Poppins had a very long road to her first Broadway bow, one that was filled with conflict and ultimately required the cooperation of other powerhouse producers.[21] That journey began before Poppins appeared in the now-iconic 1964 film. For many years, Walt Disney really wanted to make a film of the popular book series *Mary Poppins*. However, the book's author, P. L. Travers, was skeptical of her character being "Disneyfied." But after many years of negotiations, Disney and Travers came to an agreement, and in 1964, *Mary Poppins* the film opened to audience delight and critical acclaim. Although the film was a huge hit and is still wildly popular and beloved by many children and families across the world, Travers was never satisfied with the adaptation. In her book *Mary Poppins She Wrote: The Life of P. L. Travers*, Valerie Lawson writes:

> Pamela [Travers] told her London publisher that although the film received a rave reaction, it contained little of the essence of her books. The film was "Disney through and through, spectacular, colourful, gorgeous but all wrapped around mediocrity of thought, poor glimmerings of understanding," and over-simplification. In short, it was truly a Hollywood movie that would make a fortune, although it was the best thing that Disney had ever done, for [Travers], the finished product was simply sad.[22]

Because of Travers's disdain for the final product, Disney's plan to develop a sequel a year after the initial film's release was sidelined. The company would try again in the 1980s and again would be rebuffed.[23] Eventually, almost twenty years after Travers's death, Disney would make the sequel, but the path to a stage production was more complicated, as it took more than just permission from Travers or her estate.

Enter Sir Cameron Mackintosh. Best known for producing a wave of British musicals that crossed the pond in the 1980s and changed the landscape of Broadway, Mackintosh was a huge fan of *Mary Poppins* and had always wanted to turn it into a stage show. In the 1970s, a young Mackintosh approached Travers about obtaining the stage rights to the character, and although Travers had always wanted Poppins to appear onstage, Mackintosh's initial request was denied. However, years later, Mackintosh tried again. In 1993, he visited Travers and brought a gift of a cherry tree.[24] This time, Travers granted him the rights. Before he left, Mackintosh made another request. He believed that the songs from the Disney film were essential to the success of a stage production, as audiences would expect it to include the now-iconic tunes. Despite Travers's feelings about the film, Mackintosh was able to persuade her to allow him to use the songs in the stage adaptation.[25] Now all he needed was to persuade Disney to let him have the rights to the music.

In the meantime, Disney Theatrical had also been discussing a stage adaptation of the property. As quoted in Brian Sibley and Michael Lassell's book, *Mary Poppins, Anything Can Happen if You Let It*, Thomas Schumacher, the president of Disney Theatrical, shared that from the time Eisner became CEO of Disney in the 1980s, he had been talking about a sequel to *Mary Poppins*. Once the stage version of *Beauty and the Beast* opened its out-of-town tryout in Houston in 1993, Eisner started talking about putting *Mary Poppins* onstage.[26] However, even though Travers's death in 1996 meant that her ire for Disney would no longer be an obstacle, the fact that Disney did not hold the stage rights to the property was. Schumacher explained, "What it came down to was that Disney and Cameron [Mackintosh] were working on parallel tracks to figure out how to make a viable stage production out of *Mary Poppins*. What Cameron fundamentally wanted was autonomy and the music from the show. What we fundamentally wanted were Cameron's theatrical rights."[27] Neither side would get what it wanted, as neither side was willing to give up its claim to the property, so it looked as if the stage adaptation would never happen.

However, several events occurred that led to the first stage adaptation Disney would develop and produce in partnership. First, as Travers had recently died and her estate was aware of her desire for Mackintosh to turn the story into a musical, Mackintosh had the estate's blessing.[28] Next, although Eisner and Mackintosh had never been able to reach an agreement about a possible collaboration on the property, Eisner wasn't in charge anymore; Schumacher was. By chance, Schumacher met Mackintosh at a party, and although the two never discussed *Poppins* or a possible collaboration, it became clear to Mackintosh that Schumacher was a kindred spirit and a true man of the theater, something that Mackintosh could not say about Eisner. Finally, in 2001, the two men would officially meet to strike a deal that led to a common vision for a production of *Mary Poppins* and a partnership to produce it, a first for Disney Theatrical.[29]

This partnership not only led to a Broadway production for *Poppins*, but it also allowed Disney Theatrical to develop the musical in London, where it is significantly cheaper to mount a new production. In addition to a smaller price tag, developing the title across the pond also kept it out of the eye line of the New York critics, who had targeted Disney's properties for destruction for years. On the other hand, a successful production in London could generate the positive energy needed to propel the property to success in New York, as had happened for Mackintosh on many previous occasions. To Mackintosh's tried-and-true formula, Disney contributed the idea of an out-of-town tryout, a practice that was not always used by Mackintosh. *Mary Poppins* took her first bow in Bristol, one hundred miles to the west of the West End, in September 2004. With a positive reception in Bristol, the production opened in London on December 15, 2004, and eventually on Broadway on October 14, 2006.

Disney's first production-development partnership was forged by necessity, as neither entity was willing to give up its claim to the property. However, the partnership paid off, leading to financially successful runs in both London and New York.[30] However, when the show finally reached Broadway, like many of Disney's Broadway offerings, *Mary Poppins* was not a hit with the critics. For example, in his review, *New York Times* critic Ben Brantley called the show "rather tedious" and said that the "megamusical is ultimately less concerned with inexplicable magic than with practical psychology."[31] Despite lackluster reviews, *Mary Poppins* would fly on Broadway for seven years and closed not because of weak sales or a lack of interest but to make way for another Disney property, 2014's *Aladdin*.[32]

Peter and the Starcatcher (Broadway 2012)

When it opened on Broadway in 2012, *Peter and the Starcatcher* became one of Disney's best-reviewed and most-awarded projects. It was also unique in the fact that it was a play rather than a musical, as *Peter and the Starcatcher* does contain music but is categorized as a play with music rather than a musical. However, instead of using the model that up to that point had led multiple musicals to Broadway openings, Disney decided not to advertise its involvement in the project as it was in development. In his chapter "Dramaturgical Leadership and the Politics of Appeal in Commercial Theatre," former Disney Theatrical resident dramaturg and literary manager Cerniglia explains:

> Disney Theatrical's president and producer Thomas Schumacher made the prudent decision to keep "Disney" off the show's title and its leadership low-profile. Due to the power of the Disney brand and the huge target of sometimes unwarranted criticism that our theatrical ventures had become, at least in New York, it seemed better to let Disney's first play stand on its own and the Broadway credentials of its billed creators—[Rick] Elice *(Jersey Boys)*, [Roger] Rees *(Nicholas Nickleby)*, and [Alex] Timbers *(Bloody Bloody Andrew Jackson)*—draw ticket buyers downtown to New York Theatre Workshop in the spring of 2011.[33]

Although Disney was involved financially and creatively in the project, the choice not to broadcast that involvement paid off, as the play quickly transferred to Broadway and earned nine Tony Award nominations, winning five, including Best Scenic, Costume, Lighting, and Sound Design, sweeping the design categories.[34] The production would become the longest-running play of its season and embarked on a national tour, a rarity for nonmusical productions in the US. Throughout the successful run, Disney, though named as a collaborator, stayed quiet, declining to put "Disney" in the title or on any of the marketing materials. Rather, it remained one of the many producers listed in the fine print despite its active role in the development of the production.

In addition to the lack of Disney branding, the play was also different in that it had multiple productions at multiple theaters during its development process. These collaborative productions happened at the Williamstown Theatre Festival, La Jolla Playhouse, and the New York Theatre Workshop. Although part of Disney's standard practice was to have an out-of-town tryout for each property and occasionally shows had been workshopped at theaters far from New York City, workshops of this nature in the five-year run-up to a Broadway opening were not always part of the Disney Theatrical process.

The play's journey to the stage began in the early 2005, when Schumacher was given an advance draft of Dave Barry and Ridley Pearson's novel *Peter and the Starcatchers*. Schumacher was taken with the book, seeing its potential for both stage and screen, and optioned it for both.[35] In 2007, dramaturg Cerniglia and directors Timbers and Rees began the process of adapting the book. The trio found common ground in their desire to craft an adaptation that was "cheeky, irreverent, anachronistic, and modern, like

Dave and Ridley's book, but also celebrated the classical richness of language that J. M. Barrie infused in his original 1904 play."[36] Eventually, Elice, joined the team, and the first iteration of the play was mounted at the Williamstown Theatre Festival in June 2007. Cerniglia said: "[At Williamstown] we tested our 'poor theatre' staging concept in a log cabin with fifteen acting apprentices, attempting to tell the story using only minimal props, actors' bodies, and words."[37] Many of the discoveries made in the initial workshop ended up in the final product, including props, staging, and "having a sexy, athletic company tell an 'old-fashioned' story in a fresh irreverent way."[38]

After the concept for the production was proven at Williamstown, the team, along with some new collaborators, mounted a staging lab in New York City followed by a workshop production in partnership with the La Jolla Playhouse in early 2009. The decision to go to La Jolla for the next stage of development was made because Disney "wasn't set up to produce this type of play solo," and therefore, a partner who was built to produce a production like *Peter and the Starcatcher* was needed.[39] La Jolla had its own space, its own shops, and its own personnel and regularly produced workshops of plays of many sizes. That combined with the theater's "Page to Stage" project, which was dedicated to producing titles adapted from literature, made La Jolla an ideal partner.

After the La Jolla workshop, the show went through a series of rewrites and landed in an open slot in the New York Theatre Workshop's 2010–2011 season, the first that was available at the storied theater. Again, the show was adjusted in partnership with the theater. Budget and space constraints led to a streamlining of the ensemble, and rewrites continued to further hone the dramatic structure and characters. When the show opened its New York premiere, it quickly sold out and was extended as long as the theater was available.[40] It was at this point, once it was clear that the show had the potential to be a commercial hit, that Schumacher made the wise decision that "it was in the show's best interest if Disney remained supportively behind [the show], just as it had been at every step of the process," rather than branding the show as a Disney property.[41]

The Broadway production of *Peter and the Starcatcher* opened in April 2012 and ran for more than nine months and three hundred performances, a significant achievement for a nonmusical production on Broadway. *Starcatcher* is a well-written play that was given an imaginative production and was deserving of all the praise and attention it received. However, it is likely that the conversation surrounding the play, particularly during the development process, would have been vastly different if it had been branded as a Disney property. As Disney Theatrical grew up in the second decade of the twenty-first century, the company found creative ways to ensure that its properties in partnership would be judged on their merits rather than their connection to the Mouse.

Newsies (2012)

Newsies, which opened on Broadway in March 2012, was a surprise hit and recouped its initial investment faster than any other Disney Theatrical production before it.[42] The production is based on the 1992 film *Newsies*, which was a box-office disaster. The film cost an estimated $15 million to make and only grossed $2.8 million.[43] However, despite its lack of success at the box office, the film amassed thousands of fans in the 1990s and early 2000s. In a 2011 interview, composer Alan Menken said:

> We became aware over the years, ever since the movie just sort of crash-landed at the box office, that a whole generation had quietly adopted this as their own. And it was everybody's sort of secret pleasure. And, at a certain point, that secret pleasure began to surface and there were pirated production of the movie. And it became apparent that this was going to happen. And if we weren't going to write it, somebody was going to write it. And we should be the ones to do it.[44]

For many children who grew up in the late 1990s and early 2000s, *Newsies* was an important fixture in their childhood. As quoted in Cerniglia's book *Newsies: Stories of the Unlikely Hit*, Noni White, the film's co-screenwriter, reports, "Whenever Bob [Tzudiker] and I are asked to speak at colleges, people tell us that we wrote their favorite movie. The people that *Newsies* reached, it touched deeply."[45] Because there was clearly a market for a stage adaptation, particularly among high school and college students, Disney set out to create a script for licensing. The decision was made to send the title straight to licensing, rather than a large-scale production, because although the cult status of the film meant a built-in market for a stage show, *Newsies* was still a gamble. In addition to the fact that the story was simplistic and some of the music and lyrics were less than stellar, the film was also far different from any other film successfully adapted for the stage by Disney.[46] Other than *Aida*, whose source material was outside the Disney catalog, on Broadway, Disney Theatrical had previously worked only in the genre of fantasy drawn from animated features. However, the decision to turn the film into a stage production did come on the heels of the well-received stage adaptation of *High School Musical*, another Disney live-action feature. Like *High School Musical*, *Newsies* was not destined for Broadway, so the question of its commercial viability rested on educational and regional theaters, rather than the Great White Way.[47]

Disney made several attempts at adapting the script. However, eventually, everyone agreed that *Newsies* was not working as a stage show, and the idea was shelved."[48] Cerniglia credits Harvey Fierstein with putting the property on its path to triumph. In Cerniglia's *Newsies: The Broadway Adventure*, Fierstein recalls how he came to write the book for *Newsies*, having noticed a *Newsies* poster on the wall of Menken's studio and asking him to let him "take a whack at it."[49] Fierstein's outside perspective and experienced hand were exactly what the project needed, and his entrance is what set *Newsies* on its course toward a winning Broadway run. In addition to Fierstein's script, composer Menken and lyricist Jack Feldman returned to revisit the score and made adjustments to the existing songs and contributed new songs.[50]

With the script and score ready, Disney moved into a pilot production, which is a standard practice for all shows that Disney releases for licensing. Because the company is extremely careful about everything it puts out, no property is released for licensing without first having a pilot production at a professional theater. This model had been employed in 2007 with the licensed version of *High School Musical*, so Disney approached the Paper Mill Playhouse in Millburn, New Jersey, about producing the pilot for *Newsies*. The plan was to make sure that it worked and to perhaps snag some publicity in the process.[51] Cerniglia notes:

> We didn't really know [if it would work] for sure until we tried, so we said, "Let's do a pilot production, let's hire Broadway-caliber people, do it right, don't spend any money on it, but let's just see how it goes." Paper Mill out in New Jersey put in some money, we put in some money, not a lot because, again, this wasn't going to come to Broadway and be a big hit and recoup its investment in a year and start to make a profit. We were, like, "We can't spend that much money on it because licensing is a much longer recoup period and high schools doing it is not going to give these huge royalty checks." We just wanted to make a good show; that was totally the intention.[52]

Cerniglia alludes to the financial pressure felt by Disney Theatrical in developing *Newsies*, or any other show, for licensing. A balance had to be struck between spending the necessary funds to ensure a quality product that was up to Disney's stringent brand standards and not spending so much money that it would take an inordinate amount of time to recoup its investment. *Newsies* also came at a time when Disney had to be exceptionally careful, as its last two Broadway offerings were not financially successful; 2006's *Tarzan* and 2008's *The Little Mermaid* both lost money while on Broadway.

For the pilot production, Paper Mill utilized Broadway talent. Jeff Calhoun, whose Broadway directing credits include *Bonnie and Clyde*, *Brooklyn*, and Deaf West's production of *Big River*, was brought in to direct the show. And Christopher Gattelli, whose Broadway credits include *Woman on the Verge of a Nervous Breakdown*, *13*, and *South Pacific*, was brought in to choreograph. In addition, high-caliber performers were cast to bring the characters to life onstage. This co-production between Disney Theatrical and Paper Mill was never intended to last longer than its New Jersey run; however, in the development process, a decision was made that would change the course of *Newsies*' future onstage. In the design process, extra money was spent on the set with the intention of making it able to tour or to be rented to regional theaters that produced the show. This meant that the entire production could quickly and easily be disassembled and then reassembled somewhere else. Although the team did not know it at the time, creating a mobile set that could be loaded in quickly at almost any theater would heavily influence the decision to bring the show to Broadway the next year.[53]

Success in New Jersey was not guaranteed. Disney was optimistic that the millennials who had grown up with the film would jump at the chance to see it onstage, but would the property have a wider appeal? Fortunately, the answer was yes. *Newsies*' story and characters spoke across multiple generations, which was necessary to sustain a Broadway run.[54] The timing of the production was also advantageous, as it coincided with the Occupy Wall Street movement. On September 17, 2011, just two days after *Newsies* opened at the Paper Mill Playhouse, protesters marched into Liberty Square in Lower Manhattan protesting the widening gap between the rich and the poor.[55] As news coverage of Occupy Wall Street grew, the story and themes of *Newsies* seemed more and more relevant, despite its historic setting. *Newsies* is fundamentally an underdog story, of "David" triumphing against "Goliath," and in the wake of the Great Recession, that was a story that theater-goers in the US could get excited about.

Newsies was closely tied to the zeitgeist of late 2011, which may account for some of its success; however, the Paper Mill production of the show was also very good. In his *New York Times* review, David Rooney admits he doesn't like the film but then goes on to praise many aspects of the stage adaptation. He lauds Menken and Feldman's music and lyrics, calling them "buoyant" and "rousing." He also applauds the choreography and direction and the strong cast. He states that *Newsies* "slathers on the sentiment. But it does so in an honorable Disney tradition that connects with the embattled kid in all of us."[56] The show may be solidly Disney, with its optimistic characters and happy, deus ex machina ending, but the show is good, and Rooney makes sure to point that out.

With the positive reviews from the critics, the positive reception from the older subscription base at the Paper Mill, and the clamor of all the millennial fans on the internet, Disney decided to move the production to Broadway. After only sixteen previews, *Newsies* opened on Broadway at the Nederlander Theatre on March 29, 2012. The show was originally scheduled for a limited run, meant to kick off either a tour or licensing, but the response was overwhelming.[57] Cerniglia explains:

> [We] went to the decision, you know, "Well, maybe we can open run it and just see," and it ended up being our quickest recouping show, because it was cheaper. We had a small house, the ticket [inventory] was tight initially, [so] we could actually sell it. Then we recouped and the attitude was, "Well, people love it," there was a lot of affection for it. We were developing marketing around social media; it's a fan-fueled thing. And then other people were, like, "It got eight Tony nominations, it won for Best Score, oh, it's legitimized all of a sudden." [It wasn't] just this one-off thing, it's a real Broadway show! So then we kept it going as long as we could. What was supposed to be 100 performances ended up being 1,005.[58]

Eventually, *Newsies* would go on tour and would become available for licensing, leading to productions all around the US. During the 2021–2022 school year, *Newsies* was the ninth most-produced musical in US high schools.[59] *Newsies* also opened in London in November 2022 and is still running at the time of this writing. By listening to the fans and shifting the production model, Disney was able not only to produce a high-quality show but also to make a lot of money in the process.

Hercules (2019)

In February 2019, the Public Theater announced that it would be partnering with Disney to adapt the 1997 animated feature *Hercules* as a part of the theater's Public Works program at the end of its summer 2019 Shakespeare in the Park season.[60] The Public Works program is "a national and international initiative of The Public Theater that seeks to engage the people of New York by making them creators and not just spectators.... Public Works deliberately blurs the line between professional artists and community members, creating theater that is not only *for* the people but *by* and *of* the people as well."[61] For its 2019 offering, Public Works partnered with Disney to stage an adaptation of the 1997 animated film. The film was moderately successful, stymied by its release in a summer full of blockbuster offerings. But despite its forgettable box-office performance, it is beloved by many millennials, perhaps due to the fact that it was the first Disney franchise to appear as a toy in McDonald's Happy Meals. The film also featured an excellent score by Menken and employed technical innovations in its animation.[62] As with all Public Works projects, the *Hercules* stage adaptation featured a cast of both professional actors and local amateur actors. The production was the sixth title adapted by Public Works[63] and was chosen to appeal to program participants, drawing from the five boroughs of New York, and not all participants were familiar with "traditional" theatrical titles. Lear deBessonet, the director of the Public Works program and the production, noted that she had been thinking about doing a Disney title since the beginning of the program and that she "saw buried in [*Hercules*] these elements that subvert a traditional narrative of what a hero is, and what strength is ... the thing we externally celebrate as being heroic is not real strength—there's a much deeper journey."[64]

Many were surprised by the partnership, as it is unlike Disney to give up creative control. However, the Public Works program is in line with Disney brand values and presented an opportunity for the development of a Disney title in a way that could avoid critical scrutiny. Allowing a nonprofit entity to develop a Disney title as part of a community-based program that could later be produced commercially by Disney was smart. The stakes were low, as the production was a collaboration between theater professionals and amateurs, and the primary focus was on the community's experience of the production rather than the production itself. Any critic who would attack the property or Disney would seem out of touch with the purpose of the program, and therefore, Disney could escape the critical ire that was standard procedure for its productions. Additionally, the Public Works production served as a workshop for a commercial iteration of the title.

In March 2013, the title was staged with a professional company at the Papermill Playhouse in New Jersey, the same theater that piloted *Newsies* in 2012. Although the Papermill production of *Hercules* generated a great deal of buzz, the critical reception was lackluster. Juan Ramirez of the *New York Times* noted, "Everything from plot points to character beats unfold with little significance or cohesion, and the whole production feels under-rehearsed, underwhelming, and unimportant."[65] Roma Torre of *New York Stage Review* commented that despite "clever puppet designs and direction, there's no way [director James Ortiz] could match the on-screen excitement of watching Hercules battle those marauding Titans."[66]

Although the Papermill production was not the runaway hit that Disney hoped for, *Hercules* hasn't finished his theatrical labors. In February 2023, shortly before the show opened in New Jersey, Disney and Stage Entertainment announced that a production of

Hercules would open in Hamburg, Germany, in spring 2024.[67] The announcement also stated that the title will later become available for licensing but gave no indication of when. Once it does, like the other titles from the Disney Theatrical catalogue, *Hercules* will likely become a staple of educational and community theater around the United States.

Ratatouille: The TikTok Musical (2021)

Another example of Disney's willingness to partner with nonprofit and charitable organizations is the 2021 digital production of *Ratatouille*. Based on the 2007 Disney-Pixar film of the same name, *Ratatouille: The TikTok Musical* was streamed more than 350,000 times and raised more than $2 million for the Actors Fund (now called the Entertainment Community Fund), more than any other single fundraiser in the organization's history.[68] The Actors Fund is a New York–based charity that supports workers in the entertainment industry. During the 2020 Covid pandemic, when the industry was shut down for an unprecedented amount of time and most artists were out of work, the fund provided much-needed support.

The musical began as a single video on TikTok, a social-media platform that allows users to generate video content and share it with a network of friends and strangers. A user's video feed is populated by an algorithm that determines what a user will like based on other videos they have viewed. The first musical *Ratatouille* video, "Ode to Remy" was created by Emily Jacobsen, a twenty-six-year-old schoolteacher, and featured images of Remy the Rat, the main character in the film, singing a silly but very catchy song composed by Jacobsen. Jacobsen sang the tune in a tiny rat voice to celebrate the fact that the Ratatouille ride would soon be opening at Epcot in Disney World. Through the algorithm, Jacobsen's video was seen and shared by TikTok celebrity Brittany Broski, better known as Kombucha Girl, and then viewed by more than a million users. When the video went viral, it set off a collaborative online effort to create a *Ratatouille* musical that included contributions in the form of songs, choreography, costumes, and marketing materials from a variety of amateurs and professionals. These collaborators from around the world contributed TikToks to the musical's canon, delighting social media and receiving coverage on major US news outlets including NBC and ABC.[69]

Ratatouille: The TikTok Musical was quickly created during the pandemic, and eventually, the idea of actually creating a digital production of the musical picked up steam online. Soon after, that idea would reach the ears of people in the theater industry who could make it happen, and a digital production of the musical began to coalesce. In "How *Ratatouille: The TikTok Musical* Came to Be (and Yes, Disney's Okay with It)," Helen Shaw writes that it was simply "a matter of phone calls" to secure the rights.[70] Shaw explains, "The spark was first struck by producers Jeremy O. Harris, the extremely online writer-producer, and Greg Nobile of the theatrical production company Seaview.... Nobile called Tom Schumacher, the president of Disney Theatrical, over Thanksgiving. Tom said, 'That's a good idea. I think Disney can free up the rights ... let's try to do it. I'll clear the path.'"[71] And clear it he did. Schumacher agreed to let the production happen as long as it was for charity (the Actors Fund) and limited to only a few performances.

Again, although many were surprised that Disney would allow the production, the circumstances surrounding the creation of *Ratatouille: The TikTok Musical* made blessing the production a savvy choice and one that was not unprecedented. By 2020, Disney had partnered with several other companies to develop titles for licensing, and the production was for a good cause. Like the Public Works production of *Hercules*, the Actors Fund event could engender goodwill for the company and possibly lead to a viable script for licensing. The production also demonstrated an alternative model for creating commercial musicals and illuminated a growing connection between musical theater and social media. At the time of this writing, there have not been any plans announced for a future for *Ratatouille: The TikTok Musical*, but it did receive positive reviews in multiple publications, including the *Washington Post*, the *Los Angeles Times*, and the *New York Times*.

Aladdin (2014)

In addition to partnering with other organizations to develop properties, Disney Theatrical has also partnered with other divisions within the Walt Disney Company. Disney Theatrical is a part of the studio division and is entirely separate from the Disney Parks Division, which also produces live shows. On several occasions, Disney Theatrical has partnered with the Parks Division for properties that would end up on Broadway. A notable example is 2014's *Aladdin*, which started its journey to Broadway at Disney's California Adventure theme park in 2002.

Anne Hamburger, a former artistic director for several theater companies, was named head of entertainment for Disney theme parks in 2002. Her first major project was a stage version of *Aladdin* for Disney's California Adventure.[72] Hamburger's theme-park version was a forty-minute adaptation, and in its conception, there was no Broadway development plan attached to the production. It was planned and executed to be an attraction at the park. However, the team for the show was full of theater artists, and the final product felt like a Broadway-style musical.[73] When the decision was made to adapt *Aladdin* for Broadway, Disney looked to the production in California. Because of its high quality and theatrical sensibility, rather than starting from scratch, Disney Theatrical decided to expand the theme-park production, saving time and money in the process.

To prepare the title for Broadway, Disney did not simply lift the show from California Adventure and open it on Forty-Second Street; there was a lengthy development process. After several unsuccessful Disney Theatrical productions in the early 2000s, most notably *Tarzan* and *The Little Mermaid*, the company was more cautious in the 2010s about how it developed titles for Broadway. Although out-of-town tryouts were standard for most Disney musicals, Disney began to spend more time and attention testing the productions before bringing them to Broadway or releasing them for licensing. *Aladdin* received productions at several regional theaters before the decision was made to bring it to Broadway. The show was workshopped at the 5th Avenue Theatre in Seattle, the Tuacahn Amphitheatre[74] in Ivins, Utah, and the Muny in St. Louis. With the feedback received in these multiple pilot productions, the show was adjusted before coming to New York. For example, in early iterations of the production, the Genie wore blue body paint to make the character look like his animated counterpart; through workshopping, the smart decision was made to cut the paint. After productions at multiple theaters, *Aladdin* had its official pre-Broadway tryout in Toronto in 2013. The show parked at the Ed Mirvish Theatre for three months before moving into the New Amsterdam Theatre on Broadway in February 2014.

By the time *Aladdin* arrived in New York, the production was ready not only for a Broadway audience but also for Broadway critics. Even Charles Isherwood, a critic at the *New York Times* who often skewered Disney productions, admitted that the production "defied my dour expectations."[75] By extending the development period and visiting multiple theaters in multiple cities to test and hone the production, Disney was able to craft a musical that was ready for intense scrutiny, and *Aladdin* found both critical and financial success. Although the version that would open on Broadway in 2014 was vastly different from the one that played at Disney's California Adventure, the bones of the production came from the theme-park adaptation.[76] By working across divisions, Disney Theatrical ended up with a successful production that at the time of this writing has had more than three thousand performances and is still playing on Broadway.

Conclusion

As Disney Theatrical "grew up" in the twenty-first century, so did its partnering practices. Schumacher was consistently savvy in his decision-making about how Disney would be involved in producing in partnership both for Disney titles and for other projects leading to multiple artistically and financially fruitful collaborations. Disney Theatrical has always remained flexible in its production practices, looking to innovate and improve the way it brings properties to the stage. One of those innovations in the twenty-first century was the introduction of development partnerships. Disney no longer did it all itself but rather leveraged strategically selected partners to aid it in crafting the highest-quality productions before opening them on Broadway or elsewhere.

With the early financial success Disney Theatrical found in its first Broadway outing, *Beauty and the Beast*, it would have been easy for the company to simply repeat the same process for future production. However, the model the company has employed to develop productions for Broadway and beyond has continued to shift. By keeping its production processes nimble and being willing to try new things and take new risks, Disney has had enormous success with live stage musicals. Disney never had to take on any partners to succeed on Broadway, but the decision to work in partnership has grown the company's reach and its successes exponentially. The willingness of Disney Theatrical's leadership to do what was best for each production, each property, and each country has made it one of the leading producers of Broadway-style musicals around the world in less than three decades.

Notes

1. Michael Kantor, dir., *Broadway: The American Musical*, (PBS, 2004).
2. One only needs to look at the coverage of both the renovation of the New Amsterdam Theatre and the development of *Beauty and the Beast* to see how the company was consistently vilified in this period.
3. It should be noted that contemporary productions in Australia are no longer produced in partnership but rather are managed in-house by Disney Theatrical.
4. Ken Cerniglia, interview by author, New York, May 26, 2015.
5. Amy S. Osatinski, *Disney Theatrical Productions: Producing Broadway Musicals the Disney Way* (New York: Routledge, 2019), 171.
6. Disney also licenses productions. In these productions, another company pays for the rights to perform the property and produces the show on its own. Disney Theatrical is not in any way involved with the production other than providing the materials to produce the show (scripts, scores, etc.) for a fee.
7. Osatinski, *Disney Theatrical Productions*, 173.
8. Shiki Theatre Company, https://www.shiki.jp/en/.
9. Memorandum by Disney Theatrical Productions, "DTP Opening and Closing Nights," 2012.
10. This technology has been used for several other high-profile attractions around the world, including Remy's Ratatouille Adventure and both Disneyland Paris and Epcot at Walt Disney World and at Disney's Hollywood Studios for the Star Wars Rise of the Resistance ride.
11. Kenneth Cerniglia and Aubrey Lynch II, "Embodying Animal, Racial, Theatrical, and Commercial Power in *The Lion King*," *Dance Research Journal* 43, no. 1 (2011): 3–9, https://doi.org/10.1017/S0149767710000234.
12. Many of the adjustments were based on the production at Shanghai Disney Resort, which ran from 2018 to 2020.
13. Stephi Wild, "Permanent Production of *Beauty and the Beast* Is Coming to Tokyo Disney," BroadwayWorld, December 10, 2021, https://www.broadwayworld.com/japan/article/Permanent-Production-of-BEAUTY-AND-THE-BEAST-is-Coming-to-Tokyo-Disney-20211210.
14. Osatinski, *Disney Theatrical Productions*, 172–173.
15. Cerniglia, interview.
16. Cerniglia, interview.
17. Kenneth Cerniglia, "Tarzan Swings onto Disney's Broadway," in *Global Perspectives on Tarzan: From King of the Jungle to International Icon*, ed. Annette Wannamaker and Michelle Abate (New York: Routledge, 2012), 55.
18. Cerniglia, interview.
19. Frank Rich, "Stage: Andrew Lloyd Webber's 'Starlight Express,'" *New York Times*, March 16, 1987, C17, https://timesmachine.nytimes.com/timesmachine/1987/03/16/483387.html?pageNumber=49.

20. Cerniglia, interview.
21. Although *Mary Poppins* originally opened in London, the production was planned for Broadway from the beginning, rather than opened overseas in partnership after a Broadway run; therefore, it is being classified as a domestic partnership.
22. Valerie Lawson, *Mary Poppins, She Wrote: The Life of P. L. Travers* (New York: Simon & Schuster, 2006), 274.
23. Tim Barlass, "The Reason Mary Poppins Almost Didn't Return," *Sydney Morning Herald*, December 20, 2018, https://www.smh.com.au/entertainment/movies/the-reason-mary-poppins-almost-didn-t-return-20181217-p50mre.html.
24. Osatinski, *Disney Theatrical Productions*, 160.
25. Brian Sibley and Michael Lassell, *Mary Poppins: Anything Can Happen if You Let It* (New York: Disney Editions, 2007), 58.
26. Ibid.
27. Ibid.
28. Ibid., 60.
29. Ibid., 58.
30. Cerniglia, interview.
31. Ben Brantley, "Meddler on the Roof," *New York Times*, November 17, 2006, https://www.nytimes.com/2006/11/17/theater/reviews/17popp.html.
32. Cerniglia, interview.
33. Ken Cerniglia, "Dramaturgical Leadership and the Politics of Appeal in Commercial Theatre," in *The Routledge Companion to Dramaturgy*, ed. Magda Romanska (London: Routledge, 2016), 230–231.
34. Ibid., 230.
35. Kenneth Cerniglia, "Production History," in *Peter and the Starcatcher: The Annotated Script of the Broadway Play*, by Rick Elice, Ridley Pearson, and Dave Barry (New York: Disney Editions, 2012), viii.
36. Ibid.
37. Ibid., ix.
38. Ibid.
39. Ibid., x.
40. Ibid., ix–xiii.
41. Ibid., xiii.
42. Cerniglia, interview.
43. Newsies (1992), Internet Movie Database, https://www.imdb.com/title/tt0104990/.
44. DanceOn, "Alan Menken Interview—Disney—Newsies the Musical," October 14, 2011, https://www.youtube.com/watch?v=10-C2kAJeD0, 01:55.
45. Ken Cerniglia, ed., *Newsies: Stories of the Unlikely Broadway Hit* (New York: Disney-Hyperion, 2014), 27.
46. Cerniglia, interview.
47. Cerniglia, interview.
48. Cerniglia, *Newsies*, 43.
49. Ibid.
50. For more details about the changes made for the stage production, see Osatinski, *Disney Theatrical Productions*, 127–156.
51. Cerniglia, interview.
52. Ibid.

53. Cerniglia, *Newsies*, 52–69.
54. Cerniglia, interview.
55. Jaime Lalinde et al., "Revolution Number 99," *Vanity Fair*, January 10, 2012, https://www.vanityfair.com/news/2012/02/occupy-wall-street-201202.
56. David Rooney, "Newsboy Strike? Sing All about It," *New York Times*, September 27, 2011, C5, https://www.nytimes.com/2011/09/28/theater/reviews/newsies-the-musical-review.html.
57. Cerniglia, interview.
58. Ibid.
59. Logan Cullwell-Block, "The 10 Most-Produced High School Plays and Musicals of 2021–2022," *Playbill*, June 7, 2022, https://playbill.com/article/the-10-most-produced-high-school-plays-and-musicals-of-2021-2022.
60. "Public Theater to Premiere 'Hercules' Musical," *American Theatre*, February 6, 2019, https://www.americantheatre.org/2019/02/06/public-theater-to-premiere-hercules-musical/.
61. "Hercules," The Public Theater, https://publictheater.org/hercules/.
62. Carlos Aguilar, "'Hercules' Was a Box Office Bust—and the Real Savior of Disney's '90s-Era Renaissance," IndieWire, August 6, 2022, https://www.indiewire.com/features/general/hercules-disney-90s-animated-renaissance-1234751827/.
63. The six productions are *The Tempest* (2013), *The Winter's Tale* (2014), *The Odyssey* (2015), *Twelfth Night* (2016), and *Hercules* (2019). At the time of this writing, Public Works was scheduled to present *As You Like It* in summer 2023.
64. Michael Paulson, "An Unexpected Hero Will Visit Central Park: Here Comes Hercules," *New York Times*, February 9, 2019, C3, https://www.nytimes.com/2019/02/06/theater/an-unexpected-hero-will-visit-central-park-here-comes-hercules.html.
65. Alan Henry, "Review Roundup: Disney's HERCULES Musical Opens at Paper Mill Playhouse," BroadwayWorld, March 2, 2023, https://www.broadwayworld.com/article/Review-Roundup-Disneys-HERCULES-Musical-Opens-at-Paper-Mill-Playhouse-20230302.
66. Ibid.
67. "Disney's HERCULES Musical Will Open in Hamburg Next Year," BroadwayWorld, February 27, 2024, https://www.broadwayworld.com/article/Disneys-HERCULES-Musical-Will-Open-In-Hamburg-Next-Year-20230227.
68. Helen Shaw, "How *Ratatouille: The TikTok Musical* Came to Be (and Yes, Disney's Okay with It)," Vulture, December 31, 2020, https://www.vulture.com/2020/12/how-ratatouille-the-tiktok-musical-came-to-be.html.
69. Alyssa Bereznak, "Anyone Can Cook: The Oral History of 'Ratatouille: The Musical,'" The Ringer, December 31, 2020, https://www.theringer.com/movies/2020/12/31/22206943/ratatouille-musical-oral-history-tiktok-trend-making-of.
70. Shaw, "How *Ratatouille: The TikTok Musical* Came to Be."
71. Ibid.
72. Amy S. Osatinski, "Disney Theatrical Productions: Anything Can Happen if You Let It," in *The Palgrave Handbook of Musical Theatre Producers*, ed. Laura MacDonald and William A. Everett (New York: Palgrave Macmillan, 2017), 423.
73. Cerniglia, interview.
74. The Tuacahn is a frequent choice for testing out new material, as the theater's remote location makes the productions unlikely to be covered by national press. The theater also has a very specific audience base whose members love Disney and will attend anything the brand brings into the theater.

75. Charles Isherwood, "Sly Alchemy from That Lamp," *New York Times*, March 21, 2014, C1, https://www.nytimes.com/2014/03/21/theater/aladdin-tweaks-the-disney-formula-with-breezy-insouciance.html?partner=rss&emc=rss&_r=1.
76. Cerniglia, interview.

Bibliography

Aguilar, Carlos. "'Hercules' Was a Box Office Bust—and the Real Savior of Disney's '90s-Era Renaissance." IndieWire, August 6, 2022. https://www.indiewire.com/features/general/hercules-disney-90s-animated-renaissance-1234751827/.

Barlass, Tim. "The Reason Mary Poppins Almost Didn't Return." *Sydney Morning Herald*, December 20, 2018. https://www.smh.com.au/entertainment/movies/the-reason-mary-poppins-almost-didn-t-return-20181217-p50mre.html.

Bereznak, Alyssa. "Anyone Can Cook: The Oral History of 'Ratatouille: The Musical.'" The Ringer, December 31, 2020. https://www.theringer.com/movies/2020/12/31/22206943/ratatouille-musical-oral-history-tiktok-trend-making-of.

Brantley, Ben. "Meddler on the Roof." *New York Times*, November 17, 2006. https://www.nytimes.com/2006/11/17/theater/reviews/17popp.html.

Cerniglia, Ken. "Dramaturgical Leadership and the Politics of Appeal in Commercial Theatre." In *The Routledge Companion to Dramaturgy*, edited by Magda Romanska, 230–235. London: Routledge, 2016. https://thetheatretimes.com/dramaturgical-leadership-politics-appeal-commercial-theatre/.

Cerniglia, Ken, ed. *Newsies: Stories of the Unlikely Broadway Hit*. New York: Disney-Hyperion, 2014.

Cerniglia, Ken. "Production History." In *Peter and the Starcatcher: The Annotated Script of the Broadway Play*, by Rick Elice, Ridley Pearson, and Dave Barry, viii–xiii. New York: Disney Editions, 2012.

Cerniglia, Kenneth. "Tarzan Swings onto Disney's Broadway." In *Global Perspectives on Tarzan: From King of the Jungle to International Icon*, edited by Annette Wannamaker and Michelle Abate, 51–66. New York: Routledge, 2012.

Cerniglia, Kenneth, and Aubrey Lynch II. "Embodying Animal, Racial, Theatrical, and Commercial Power in *The Lion King*." *Dance Research Journal* 43, no. 1 (2011): 3–9. https://doi.org/10.1017/S0149767710000234.

Cullwell-Block, Logan. "The 10 Most-Produced High School Plays and Musicals of 2021–2022." *Playbill*, June 7, 2022. https://playbill.com/article/the-10-most-produced-high-school-plays-and-musicals-of-2021-2022.

DanceOn. "Alan Menken Interview—Disney—Newsies the Musical," October 14, 2011. https://www.youtube.com/watch?v=1o-C2kAJeDo.

"Disney's HERCULES Musical Will Open in Hamburg Next Year." BroadwayWorld, February 27, 2024. https://www.broadwayworld.com/article/Disneys-HERCULES-Musical-Will-Open-In-Hamburg-Next-Year-20230227.

Henry, Alan. "Review Roundup: Disney's HERCULES Musical Opens at Paper Mill Playhouse." BroadwayWorld, March 2, 2023. https://www.broadwayworld.com/article/Review-Roundup-Disneys-HERCULES-Musical-Opens-at-Paper-Mill-Playhouse-20230302.

"Hercules." The Public Theater. https://publictheater.org/hercules/.

Isherwood, Charles. "Sly Alchemy from That Lamp." *New York Times*, March 21, 2014, C1. https://www.nytimes.com/2014/03/21/theater/aladdin-tweaks-the-disney-formula-with-breezy-insouciance.html?partner=rss&emc=rss&_r=1.

Kantor, Michael, dir. *Broadway: The American Musical*. PBS, 2004.

Lalinde, Jaime, Rebecca Sacks, Mark Guidicci, Elizabeth Nicholas, and Max Chafkin. "Revolution Number 99." *Vanity Fair*, January 10, 2012. https://www.vanityfair.com/news/2012/02/occupy-wall-street-201202.

Lawson, Valerie. *Mary Poppins, She Wrote: The Life of P. L. Travers*. New York: Simon & Schuster, 2006.

Newsies (1992). Internet Movie Database. https://www.imdb.com/title/tt0104990/.

Osatinski, Amy S. "Disney Theatrical Productions: Anything Can Happen if You Let It." In *The Palgrave Handbook of Musical Theatre Producers*, edited by Laura MacDonald and William A. Everett, 413–426. New York: Palgrave Macmillan, 2017.

Osatinski, Amy S. *Disney Theatrical Productions: Producing Broadway Musicals the Disney Way*. New York: Routledge, 2019.

Paulson, Michael. "An Unexpected Hero Will Visit Central Park: Here Comes Hercules." *New York Times*, February 9, 2019, C3. https://www.nytimes.com/2019/02/06/theater/an-unexpected-hero-will-visit-central-park-here-comes-hercules.html.

"Public Theater to Premiere 'Hercules' Musical." *American Theatre*, February 6, 2019. https://www.americantheatre.org/2019/02/06/public-theater-to-premiere-hercules-musical/.

Rich, Frank. "Stage: Andrew Lloyd Webber's 'Starlight Express.'" *New York Times*, March 16, 1987, C17. https://timesmachine.nytimes.com/timesmachine/1987/03/16/483387.html?pageNumber=49.

Rooney, David. "Newsboy Strike? Sing All about It." *New York Times*, September 27, 2011, C5. https://www.nytimes.com/2011/09/28/theater/reviews/newsies-the-musical-review.html.

Shaw, Helen. "How *Ratatouille: The TikTok Musical* Came to Be (and Yes, Disney's Okay with It)." *Vulture*, December 31, 2020. https://www.vulture.com/2020/12/how-ratatouille-the-tiktok-musical-came-to-be.html.

Sibley, Brian, and Michael Lassell. *Mary Poppins: Anything Can Happen if You Let It*. New York: Disney Editions, 2007.

Wild, Stephi. "Permanent Production of *Beauty and the Beast* Is Coming to Tokyo Disney." BroadwayWorld, December 10, 2021. https://www.broadwayworld.com/japan/article/Permanent-Production-of-BEAUTY-AND-THE-BEAST-is-Coming-to-Tokyo-Disney-20211210.

CHAPTER 25

AN ETHNOGRAPHIC AND CRITICAL APPROACH TO DISNEY MUSICALS IN US K–12 SCHOOLS

SAMMY GROB AND STACY WOLF

Disney, Broadway, and Schools

Every kid in America recognizes Disney characters and knows Disney stories. The company's diversified network of theme parks, films, TV shows, musicals, and merchandise has defined and continues to shape the American zeitgeist. Through this lateral media monopoly on children's imaginations, as Henry Giroux describes it, Disney as a "cultural institution that fiercely protects its legendary status as purveyor of innocence and moral virtue."[1] According to former executive Michael Ovitz, "Disney isn't a company as much as it is a nation-state with its own ideas and attitudes, and you have to adjust to them."[2]

Capitalizing on its historic success in films and theme parks, in 1994, Disney struck a deal with the City of New York to renovate and operate a multidecade lease on the New Amsterdam Theatre (which currently houses *The Lion King*). This deal catalyzed a period of massive commercial investment and urban cleanup—dubbed the Disneyfication of Times Square—that persists to this day.[3] Beginning with *Beauty and the Beast* in 1994, the Disney Theatrical Group—the theatrical producing arm of the Disney corporation—has mounted more than a dozen Broadway shows. Four of its musicals, as of 2024, are among the longest-running productions of all time: *The Lion King* (no. 3, still running), *Beauty and the Beast* (no. 10), *Aladdin* (no. 19, still running), and *Mary Poppins* (no. 23).[4] As Disney Theatrical Group president Thomas Schumacher bragged in 2018, "We are the new songbook of Broadway."[5]

Ten years after *Beauty and the Beast*'s debut, Disney partnered with Music Theatre International (MTI) to license the show—and, subsequently, the rest of its theatrical catalog—for amateur productions. The creative and commercial synergy that followed reshaped the entire educational musical-theater landscape: since the 2010s, Disney musicals have ranked as some of the most frequently produced shows in US middle and high schools.[6] As of 2018, a reported 38 percent of the North American population had engaged with more than 90,000 live productions of licensed Disney titles—either as part of the cast, crew, or audience.[7] Ken Cerniglia, who was Disney Theatrical Group's literary manager and dramaturg from 2003 to 2019, writes that these licensed musicals allow "young Disney fans [to] engage beloved characters, stories, and songs not just as passive movie consumers or theme park guests, but with theatrical agency, owning their personal experience over weeks of rehearsal and performance."[8]

As the "gateway art" for many American youth, Disney shapes the developing tastes, expectations, and perspectives of children. The company emphasized the theatrical fusion of entertainment and education during its burgeoning stages: "[Walt] Disney himself was extremely informed about current thought on child development, and he required that his employees also be versed in the field."[9] In a world where business conglomerates act as media-entertainment producers (e.g., streaming companies such as Amazon Prime and Apple TV) and younger people are inundated with social technology (e.g., TikTok, Instagram), the decades-old warnings of Giroux—perhaps Disney's fiercest cultural critic—are more pressing than ever. "Media culture ... has become a substantial, if not the primary, educational force in regulating [consumers'] meanings, values, and tastes," Giroux writes, so one must critically investigate the influence of giant media corporations.[10] Although "people mediate what they see, buy, wear, and consume and bring different meanings to the texts and products that companies like Disney produce," he continues, when scholars examine cultural politics, we must not merely recognize Disney's power but "investigate both its limits and its strengths, particularly in dealing with [children]."[11] In this chapter, we follow Giroux's lead to examine the possibilities and problems of Disney's musical theater in schools.

Talking to Teachers and Students

Being in a school musical can provide a uniquely holistic socio-emotional and creative learning experience. Beyond providing opportunities for students to develop performance skills, participation in school shows is associated with improvements across cognitive domains related to personal development, such as emotional regulation, self-confidence, empathy, risk-taking, problem-solving, perseverance, self-discipline, collaboration, and relationship development.[12] Additionally, as James Leve and Donelle Ruwe write, musical theater is a "teaching tool" that plays "an important role in how children negotiate identity and achieve self-realization."[13] Rehearsals provide a space for kids to escape the challenges of everyday life and pretend to be someone (or something) else.

The ethnographic approach we employed for some of our research for this chapter aimed to include on-the-ground perspectives of individuals who create and are directly affected by musicals in educational settings.[14] As part of our research, we interviewed twenty teachers and sixty students (mostly in groups) at seventeen middle and high schools across the US who participated in a Disney musical at their school during the 2021–2022 academic year.[15] We asked teachers about their decision to produce a Disney show, their past experiences with Disney musicals, and what they felt that they, their students, and the school community took away from the process. We asked students to reflect on their participation in Disney shows and their thoughts on Disney's iconic influence.

While teachers often talked about the significance of the process in making the show, students often reflected on what it meant to be role models—even celebrities—for younger audience members. One middle school performer from Iowa said, "After the shows, we would go out of the theater and the kids could meet us and get our autographs. That was one of my favorite parts as well because some kid would just walk up to you and tell you that you were their favorite character and it just warms your heart." Another added, "Those kids think we are the real characters and I think there is something so special about being able to take on a role and put on a show that these kids are going to remember for the rest of their lives." Indeed, students recalled the influence that seeing musicals had on them. Another student from the same school said, "I know that when I was younger and went to these musical productions, I will remember them forever [and] how amazing it was to see those older kids take on the roles of characters that I knew and loved and be able to just see all the amazing work that is put into a production come to life." These interviews confirm the resonant power of musical-theater participation for youth of all ages.

Although these fairy-tale stories may seem innocuous and "just for fun," Samuel Grob describes how "the spectacular artifice of [musical theater]—its escapist, campy pleasures of epic emotions, larger-than-life characters, and suddenly breaking into song and dance—gives the art form a delightful, beguiling sheen that masks its political messaging."[16] As kids play characters—and younger audiences watch—what representations are embodied? What ideas are communicated and learned? Our goal—spurred by Giroux's call to action—is to critically assess Disney's achievements, messaging, and massive influence in the educational musical-theater scene.

Licensing and Musical Theatre International

Although many audience members may overlook "produced with permission by" in small print on a program, in fact, licensors are powerful players in the amateur-theater ecosystem.[17] For artists, the licensor—Musical Theatre International (MTI) for Disney properties—buys the rights to a show and guarantees that the creative authors (e.g., composers, lyricists, librettists, etc.) are compensated for their labor. Residuals from amateur licensing potentially provide a long-term revenue stream for artists, especially lucrative in comparison with the 80 percent of musicals that do not financially recoup their investment on Broadway. *The Little Mermaid*, for example, failed financially on Broadway in 2008–2009 but was adapted into a JR. version (2010) and a revised full-length version (2012) and has since become one of MTI's most popular titles.[18] Moreover, amateur productions provide a "second life" for a show in the public consciousness, beyond its original Broadway run and/or national tours. Licensors also protect the show as intellectual and artistic property by ensuring that productions present the script and score as written. Directors are forbidden to cut lines or songs, officially change the gender of characters, or introduce a whole new concept to a show—though teachers often do.[19]

Before Disney shows entered the distributional market, MTI had been a successful licensing company for professional and amateur productions since the 1950s, selling shows to regional and community theaters, summer camps, and high schools. Beginning in 1996, MTI launched its "Broadway JR." and "Broadway KIDS" catalogs—a groundbreaking licensing model for sixty- and thirty-minute adaptations of Broadway musicals that are accessible to and producible by elementary and middle schools—which currently dominate the educational theater industry.[20] In addition to being shorter, the JR. and KIDS versions of shows feature streamlined plots, less violence and "adult themes," more named featured characters to give ensemble members individual roles, and an expandable chorus to accommodate larger casts.[21] As the Disney Theatrical Group created shows "aimed at the same target audience, children and families," its musicals were the perfect product for the educational market.[22]

Beginning in 2004 with full-length titles (most popular with high schools) and in 2008 with JR./KIDS titles (most popular with middle and elementary schools, respectively), Disney's partnership with MTI provided yet another avenue for the media giant to connect with the K–12 student population and profoundly transformed the standard repertoire for school musicals. By 2019 alone, according to MTI's director of marketing Jason Cocovinis, MTI had licensed more than one hundred thousand productions of Disney titles around the world since the partnership began in 2003.[23] By 2023, the MTI-Disney catalog included thirty-five shows.[24]

As documented by the Educational Theatre Association's (EdTA) annual survey of school shows, by the end of the 2000s, *Beauty and the Beast* had become the decade's sixth most-popular high school musical; in the 2010s, it became the most-produced high school musical, with *The Little Mermaid* as the fifth most-produced show of that decade.[25] In the 2021–2022 academic year, *Newsies* joined the two shows in the top ten list of full-length musicals, and in the 2022–2023 season, *Beauty and the Beast* and *The Little Mermaid* tied for fifth place.[26] EdTA started tracking "short musicals" in 2021–2022, and by 2022–2023, *Frozen JR.* had ranked first for both years, while other Disney titles represented nearly half of the top ten most-produced titles of the school year.[27]

While MTI oversees the distribution of Disney's scripts, scores, and other educational resources, Disney moved its adaptation process in-house a few years after the JR./KIDS catalog was launched, expanding its education department and eventually creating entire curricula built around its shows.[28] In addition to having been effectively "field-tested" by preceding film versions, Disney Theatrical Productions (the producing subsidiary of Disney Theatrical Group) workshops "pilot" productions of JR. titles with reputable schools and arts-education organizations before officially releasing them to the public. Schumacher speaks of the efficient adaptability of Disney stories: "We can reduce shows down, make them singable, make them producible, and make it possible."[29]

Capitalism Meets Art Meets Identity

From our perspective, the jury's out on an ultimate judgment of Disney's cultural and educational interventions. We're critical of Disney's rapacious appetite for money, the creation of multimedia franchises around Disney products, and the exploitation and colonization of young minds and bodies. At the same time, we admire Disney's efforts toward access and inclusion for musical-theater participation and its ability to reach huge swaths of the US population through its comprehensive educational-licensing approach. Whether exploitative or progressive, Disney's school-licensing arm is a unique, savvy, and well-oiled machine, created and improved through years of research and development. As Stacy Wolf summarizes her ambivalence about the Disney Musicals in Schools program: "Whatever my skepticism about global corporate capitalism or my frustration with Disney's parade of princesses, I suspect that any chance of a racially, ethnically, and socioeconomically diverse musical theatre is here, enabled by the organizational machinery, the adaptable repertoire, and the money of one of the richest corporations that owns Broadway."[30]

Because Disney wants every school in the US to be able to stage its musicals, its show licensing allows considerable flexibility in casting according to gender and race. Well aware of the predominance of girls who participate in school musicals, Disney historically allowed directors to cast any role with any actor, as long as the character's original gender remained in the script; in this way, educators can fill the musicals' expansive ensemble casts with girls.[31] Still, in most shows, the leading male character—typically involved in a romance plot with the leading female—is presumably played by a boy, which maintains the performance of heterosexuality.

As more schools produced JR. and KIDS shows over the years and identity-based learning became more prevalent in K–12 schools, Disney realized that this tacit "cross-gender" casting policy wasn't sufficient. Thus, "attempting to address the canon's gender imbalance," Disney "identified characters that could be considered *gender neutral*," including many animal characters.[32] The company rewrote dialogue to eliminate pronouns and developed more shows "to include gender diversity."[33] And yet this strategy didn't provide opportunities for kids to play characters whose gender explicitly aligned with theirs. Building on previous practices, Disney endorsed a "*gender-flexible* strategy": "Rather than erase gender from character to increase casting access, particularly with performers very much interested in gender but rejecting old-fashioned roles," Cerniglia explains, "we decided to preserve the original gender in character descriptions and open a *very small* window to script changes."[34] If a character's gender was not "relevant to the plot," schools might adjust "personal pronouns to align with the gender of the actor."[35]

Teachers also must navigate the racialization of Disney characters. While the racial and ethnic coding of, for example, the characters in *Aladdin*, *The Little Mermaid*, and *The Lion King* is baked into the shows' stories, musical styles, and settings, none of the characters in these shows (or any other Disney musical) is described with racial specificity. This ambiguity results in a double-edged sword when it comes to casting. On the one hand, casting a performer whose visible identity does not match the canonical casting of the seminal film or original Broadway production may lead to performances that promote negative stereotypes (particularly when it comes to systemic power imbalances, such as white actors portraying characters with African American racial coding). This concern is particularly critical given Disney's checkered history of orientalism and racial othering in its films.[36] On the other hand, Disney is committed to providing opportunities for young people of any identity to engage in its work, no matter the specific cultural context. On the company's official licensing page for *Moana JR.*, it writes:

> As with all Disney shows, we encourage casting that represents your community. Your production will benefit from a cast that includes a variety of races, genders, abilities, and body types, so approach your casting process with care and an open mind. We believe that musicals allow young people to engage with stories, characters, cultures, and communities they might not otherwise be exposed to and that all young people should have the opportunity to engage with every story.[37]

While teachers' concerns about racial representation through casting and show material may be salient factors when they produce shows for their communities, many teachers may perceive the racial coding in Disney shows so subliminal (in contrast to shows with characters and plots explicitly related to race, such as *West Side Story* and *Hairspray*) as to be nonexistent or, at least, irrelevant to casting. In an EdTA forum discussion titled "When Shows Require Diversity but the School Is Not Diverse," one teacher at a small rural school reported: "We have stuck with mostly MTI Disney shows because we have always been able to cast these shows."[38] For many, Disney titles offer a helpfully neutral show choice that avoids complications related to identity.

In the early 2020s, Disney has demonstrated its commitment to casting flexibility and nontraditional representation, for example, by casting Black performers as the title characters in the UK tour of *Beauty and the Beast* (2021–2022) and Ariel in *The Little Mermaid* live-action film (2023). Moreover, Disney continues to produce animated musical film properties (which are often adapted into stage versions) that showcase cultural traditions, languages, and identities outside of traditional white and Western stories, such as *Moana* (2016), *Coco* (2017), and *Encanto* (2021).

Why Are Disney Shows So Appealing?

What sets Disney musicals apart from other school-friendly shows, and why do arts educators license them? Three intertwined factors are at play: support for teachers, "family-friendly" content, and familiarity.

Support for Teachers

Disney musicals offer unparalleled support to educators in terms of content, story form, formatting of materials, production resources, and curricular guides.[39] Cerniglia writes that Disney's substantial R&D budget means that it can prioritize "the core dramaturgical practice that leads creative development and the careful curation of appeal."[40] Teachers can count on Disney shows' emotionally vibrant, tuneful, and entertaining songs, their well-structured plots, their large and expandable ensemble casts, and their potential for gender flexibility in featured roles. As one teacher from Michigan told us, "From a directorial standpoint, what I like about Disney shows is that they give a really well-rounded theater experience ... acting, vocals, but also costuming, tech, set.... It really gives every student a challenge and something to build and be proud of."

Cerniglia and Lisa Mitchell, director of education for Disney Theatrical Productions, explain that the company "has carefully constructed its KIDS and JR. shows to align developmentally and academically with key phases of student development."[41] One of the teachers we interviewed, who directed *Newsies* at a school in Pennsylvania, concurred and described her experience: "I've found with the kids as they transition from middle school to high school, they have that craving to explore the adult world in a safe way ... finding a safe space to explore like an adult issue feels very satisfying for them."

The librettos and scores distributed to schools and amateur groups are created with all levels of theatrical and musical ability in mind. One music director extolled Disney Theatrical for being "superior in their music materials. Not only are their scores easy to read, but they give very specific cue lines, instrumentation information, and there are very few discrepancies between the score and the actors' vocal books (which is a big problem with other shows)."[42] He went on, "Their orchestrations are precise and full, and really know how to get that 'Disney' sound even from a condensed group."[43]

In addition, Disney produces a slew of resources—both free and for purchase or rental—that aim to ensure that teachers of varying theater experience can direct a successful Disney show. When organizations license a Disney show, they receive a "Director's Guide" (for JR. and KIDS titles, a "ShowKit"), which offers extensive instructions—from how to run auditions to how to set up a rehearsal schedule to how to build a set. Director's Guides also include details about vocal range, characterization, and ideas to expand a cast, since schools typically have more children who want to be in a show than the number of named roles. Disney, in partnership with MTI, produces a huge array of supplementary production materials, from scenic projection backdrops to fully orchestrated music tracks to be used during performances. Finally, MTI runs a robust website with answers to questions about producing a show and a well-used hotline of amateur-licensing representatives who take around two thousand calls a day.[44] This kind of assistance for typically overworked teachers—many of whom are not trained theater professionals—offers a strong incentive for schools to select Disney titles.

In addition to supporting established educational theater programs, in 2010, Disney launched Disney Musicals in Schools, an ambitious philanthropic program to grow sustainable musical-theater programs in underserved public elementary schools that lack musical-theater education.[45] In cities across the US and the UK, Disney hires local teaching artists to mentor and collaborate with first-time teacher-directors to put on one of Disney's KIDS shows, providing free scripts and fully orchestrated recorded music. At the end of the school year, all the kids and their teachers gather for a big event at the local performing-arts center, and kids from each school perform a song as their "professional debut." As of 2023, the program has served more than five hundred schools, fifteen hundred teachers, and sixty thousand students.[46]

Family-Friendly Content

When teachers select shows for their schools, Grob writes, they often seek "a safe choice: a musical that doesn't offend or annoy too many people, appeals to a sense of rosy nostalgia, comfortably communicates an easy moral, and sends you home with a lovely song stuck in your head and a smile on your face."[47] Indeed, the liberal and humanist themes of Disney shows—goodwill and generosity, embracing difference and individuality, acceptance and community solidarity, and so on—typically align with the values that schools seek to espouse. "Disney shows are safe," said a teacher from Minnesota. She explained that after a student-led production of *Mamma Mia!* garnered "complaints from the community about the adult themes," she learned "to be careful about picking a show." Conservative principals and school boards have canceled productions that include LGBTQ+ characters or depictions of violence that they deem offensive or inappropriate for their community—such as *Rent*, *Les Misérables*, and *Sweeney Todd*.[48] Indeed, the EdTA's 2022–2023 survey revealed that 85 percent of the 2,300 teachers surveyed are "at least somewhat concerned about censorship," and 67 percent said that "'censorship concerns' are influencing their selections for next year."[49] In contrast, Disney shows are rarely axed.[50]

Disney stories also fuel a self-perpetuating cycle of transgenerational appeal, by which there is a vicarious incentive for adults to share their beloved childhood tastes with their own children. It's no surprise, then, that Disney Theatrical markets shows to adults as well as kids; after all, parents are the ones who buy tickets for their kids to see Disney musicals and movies, whether in theaters or via a subscription to the Disney+ streaming service. Relatedly, "family-friendly" can operate as a dog whistle for the conservatism of older (yet still popular) Disney musicals—perpetuating white-supremacist, cis-heteronormative, exoticizing, and misogynistic character representations in more subtle, yet salient, ways.

Familiarity

In the industry of educational musical theater, name recognition is grade A cultural capital. Especially when a theater program relies on ticket sales to sustain itself, the popularity of a show's title can be an overriding factor to guarantee "butts in seats." Disney shows are much more recognizable than most Broadway musicals because of their associated multimedia franchising. Both teachers and students agree that a known show garners more enthusiasm from audiences and participants. Disney "sells well," according to a Minnesota teacher. A teacher from Pennsylvania explained that there are a lot of good shows, "but the kids don't know" them. The teacher went on, "When you announce that you're doing *Beauty and the Beast*, the kids are immediately on board because they know the show and they're still excited." As a Minnesota high school student said, "When you do more obscure shows, people who are kind of borderline usually don't come out unless you talk to them." The student went on to explain the draw of a more recognizable show, "which is how I came out [to audition], and I started doing all this theater stuff." Once rehearsals begin, a known show is also easier to learn. A New York high school student found that rehearsing a Disney show "definitely is a quicker process [because] there is that familiarity that's already built in."

Yet the ubiquity of the Disney product both helps and hinders teacher-directors' and students' creativity. On the other hand, some students feel pressure to replicate the movie because, as one from Pennsylvania said, "Disney shows are more iconic, so you want to make sure you do it right." Students were aware that they were playing well-known characters in a well-known show. Some teachers, too, worried that the audience expected a live school production of a Disney musical to replicate the movie. Disney shows are "much more labor-intensive," according to a teacher from another school in Pennsylvania. "You have kids dressed as animals. You have inevitably one dance number after another after another. And it's a lot." Still, like most teachers in the early 2020s, she and her co-instructor chose a Disney show because "we wanted something that would sell tickets because …we needed to rebuild" following the Covid pandemic. She accepted the intense "level of detail" and demands of these shows as simply "Disney being Disney."

CASE STUDIES OF SHOWS

To assess what "Disney being Disney" means, we offer a critical analysis of the politics of representation in select Disney musicals.[51] We chose to study several theatrical adaptations of Disney films created during different periods of the company's history. *Beauty and the Beast* (1991 movie, 1994 stage musical) is a touchstone of the "Disney Renaissance," a period that began in the mid-1980s and saw the revitalization of the company's animation department through blockbuster films such as *The Little Mermaid* and *Aladdin* (all three created by musical-theater writers Howard Ashman and Alan Menken. These shows rely on traditional musical-theater storytelling conventions and have introduced a new kind of liberal feminist princess who is smarter, feistier, and more self-directed than the passive first-generation heroines of Disney's initial releases in the mid-1900s: *Snow White*, *Sleeping Beauty*, and *Cinderella*.[52] Our analysis emphasizes gender and considers how representations of female characters in more contemporary shows of the twenty-first century (*Newsies*, *Frozen*, *Moana JR.*) both "repeat and revise" tropes of past Disney narratives.[53]

Beauty and the Beast

Based on the hit 1991 film, which was ironically praised by *New York Times* theater critic Frank Rich as "the best Broadway musical score" of the season,[54] *Beauty and the Beast* marked Disney's first commercial venture on Broadway, in 1994. After a successful Broadway run and national tour, the show has maintained its pop-culture relevance through a 2017 live-action film remake, a 2021–2023 UK tour, and a 2022 televised concert celebrating the original movie's thirtieth anniversary. Since MTI released the licensing rights in 2004, the full-length and 2008 JR. versions have consistently ranked among the most-produced school musicals.[55]

While *Beauty* is an appealing choice for educators because of its story's popularity, this familiarity produces ambivalence: especially as the original Broadway producers aimed to "put the movie onstage," schools may feel pressure to appease traditional audience expectations and replicate the movie through their staging.[56] Teachers putting on the show said they wondered, "Do you have to be creative in a Disney show or do you have to follow [the movie]?" and "Does the audience want to come and see the cartoon?" Some feared families would be "disappointed if it doesn't look like the expectation," leading one school to rent Belle's iconic yellow ball gown from a professional theater. While innovative interpretations of Disney musicals may be less logistically feasible or well received within a school community, they are still possible. In fact, MTI and Disney curated a "Reimagining Disney Classics" virtual town hall in 2022 to discuss edits in the licensed libretto and to showcase reconceived regional productions, including productions with immersive staging and Latin American instrumentation.[57]

Students, too, articulated the contradiction between creativity and conformity. "There's an expectation that you have to ... make [the character] yours," said one high school performer from Minnesota, "but also make it be the character that everyone knows and loves." Other students who performed in *Beauty* noted the pleasure—and powerful influence—of embodying roles that younger children know and love. The student who played Belle at the same high school in Minnesota said she would meet "a lot of small children or little girls" after performances who "came dressed up like Belle. One time, a little girl asked, 'Do you think Gaston will marry me?'" The high schooler, "trying to be Belle still," replied, "*I'm* not gonna marry him!" Unlike performing in an original devised show or a more obscure musical, students must navigate the character's iconic presence and how fully alive it appears for little kids.

Educators and students have also found liberation in the text's ambiguity. While the castle appliances might be read as gender-coded, one high school teacher in Pennsylvania felt that the objects "kind of transcend gender." This interpretation allowed her rehearsal process to become a "safe space" for nonbinary or transgender students and others who were still "exploring their gender identities." Relatedly, teacher-directors might welcome the musical's primary message of individual acceptance. As one Pennsylvania teacher told us, "We respect the theme of the show, that beauty is found within, and we wanted to give it voice."[58] Belle, trapped as a prisoner in the Beast's castle, eventually befriends and then loves him as she comes to perceive a gentle soul beneath his frightful exterior. Because of Belle's attention and affection, the Beast's cruelty toward her and his disregard for the servant-objects give way to kindness and generosity. Another message of the musical, then, is that with love, a person can change to become kind and empathetic. The story values emotional connection and empathy, which schools and teachers want to encourage.

Yet *Beauty* represents the theme of appearances versus behavior in contradictory ways. On the one hand, Belle's appearance reflects her character: she is beautiful—as the townspeople sing in the opening number, "Now it's no wonder that her name means 'Beauty' / Her looks have got no parallel"—and she is a kind, smart, and generous person. Gaston, in contrast, presents a handsome exterior (which even Belle observes to her father) but is despicable, egocentric, and—as one middle school teacher described him—the "poster boy for toxic masculinity." Gaston's chauvinistic behavior toward Belle may be played for laughs within the frame of his cartoonish villainy, but his harassing misogyny still carries negative connotations that may be hard to perform and watch.

Similarly, the musical both reinforces and subverts negative stereotypes of disability, the age-old assumption that one's appearance reflects one's interiority. In the first part of the musical, the Beast's ugly appearance mirrors his internal nastiness; in fact, the enchantress transformed him into a monster precisely because he coldly refused to welcome her into his home. As the show proceeds, the Beast transforms from abusive, anguished, and cruel at the outset of his relationship with Belle to generous, kind, and romantic—while still retaining his ugly appearance. When Belle admits that she loves the Beast and the spell is broken, he reverts to his true visage as a handsome prince, which reinforces the idea that his true self is handsome. So while the musical asks spectators to contemplate the relationship between appearance and behavior, it doesn't undo those conventional, normalizing associations.

As a princess of the Disney Renaissance, Belle is, in many ways, an appealing character for a student to embody. She is good-hearted but not idealized, bookish and smart, and unfazed at being different from everyone else. She's judgmental about her "poor provincial town"—as is the musical itself—but still polite to everyone she meets. Belle is loyal to her father and sacrifices herself for him. She can be stubborn, as when she refuses to succumb to the Beast's pressures to join him for dinner until she is ready or when she explores the forbidden west wing. One New York teacher praised *Beauty* as one of the first Disney stories "where a woman is not saved by anyone, simply enhanced by the love she offers the Beast." The teacher continued, "Although I deeply love the classic stories of *Cinderella* and *Snow White*, I appreciate how contemporary Belle's story is. I respect that she's assertive but gentle and that she knows what she likes and isn't swayed or influenced to change." The teacher went on, "What matters to her is her dad and her books, and she already knows who she is before she goes into the Beast's castle. 'I like her spunk,' as Mrs. Potts says."

Still, feminist critics are divided in their assessment of the narrative's gender politics.[59] Indeed, the movie and musical's writer Linda Woolverton sought to create the character of Belle as "a woman of the 90s," which juxtaposes ambivalently in the context of contemporary productions.[60] On the one hand, Belle's intelligence, determination, and strength distinguish her from the passive and dependent classic Disney princesses. Her initial ambition is not for romance but to escape the confines of her town for "adventure in the great, wide somewhere," an affinity she shares with both Disney Renaissance–era (e.g., Ariel) and contemporary (e.g., Moana) heroines. Rebecca Weidman-Winter sees Belle as being "resourceful and independent," having "integrity and intelligence," and "often stepping outside the roles prescribed for her by society."[61]

For other feminist scholars, Belle's virtues of patience and kindness reinforce negative stereotypes that idealize girls and women as caretakers. Her "spunk" and "feistiness"—words almost exclusively used to condescendingly describe strong women—represent a form of agency that has been circumscribed by paternalism. Belle's bravery is a little subversive but not substantively disruptive to sexist conventions. Allison Craven argues that Belle's temporary escape from the castle "is no doubt imagined by Disney as a positive virtue of 'feistiness,'" but "her reward ... is recapture and romance with the Beast."[62] Other scholars, including psychologists, and many fans point out that Belle suffers from Stockholm syndrome when she becomes attached to, falls in love with, and defends her captor.[63] The household objects are slaves who defend their "master's" abusive behavior and manipulate Belle to persuade her to fall in love with the Beast. The Beast gets to sing a beautiful and heart-wrenching solo to soliloquize his self-hatred and self-pity in his struggle to love Belle in "If I Can't Love Her": "No pain could be deeper / No life could be cheaper / No point anymore, if I can't love her." Thus, through the empathetic storytelling tools of musical theater and misrepresentations by beloved "social responders" such as Lumiere, Mrs. Potts, and Cogsworth, *Beauty* absolves the Beast's negative stereotypical masculine behaviors, which in some ways are as toxic as Gaston's.

Belle is ultimately a teacher and a mother figure, whose purpose in the musical is to save, change, and love the Beast. In this way, she replicates the (again) stereotypical, self-abnegating role of many classic long-suffering heroines in operas who redeem men, as in *Rigoletto*, *Madama Butterfly*, and *La Traviata* and in musicals including *Carousel* and *Camelot*.[64] In spite of her expressed desires at the beginning of the musical to expand herself, Belle's heroism, intelligence, and curiosity function to serve the arcs of her two most cherished men: her father and the Beast. Moreover, however we interpret Belle's agency, the musical ends—as many do—with a celebration of heteronormative matrimony. Belle settles to be a housewife with books, and in "a tale as old as time,"

Beauty furthers the "family values" that Disney musicals prize. In terms of featured female characters, the doting comic coterie of women fawning after Gaston have been renamed from "Silly Girls" to "Les Filles de La Ville" in official licensing, a substantial but ultimately surface change (the actual characters and dialogue have not been altered), reflecting the company's changing attitudes on gender.[65] Whereas stage adaptations of Disney movies (e.g., *The Little Mermaid*) aimed to revise parts of the story to empower female characters, *Beauty* as a school musical maintains the same "consumer feminism"—a performance of "feistiness" accompanied by a reduction in actual agency and power—in its faithful reproduction of the traditional source material.[66]

Newsies

Newsies became increasingly popular as a school musical just before and after the Covid pandemic, especially for teacher-directors who had already programmed the rest of the Disney repertoire. *Newsies* is the only Disney show developed specifically for high school licensing and is among the few Disney narratives based on neither a classic fairy tale nor an animated film.[67] The musical—an adaptation of Disney's own 1992 live-action movie—is based on the actual 1899 newsboys' strike in New York City.

Many of the characters in *Newsies* are of similar age to the students playing them; as one New Jersey student said, "We're kids playing kids." *Newsies* embeds both a coming-of-age and a romance narrative within its story of class struggle. These aspects make the show, according to one New York high school teacher, "relatable to the current audience" and resonant with its performers.

Newsies is at once an outlier in the Disney catalog and completely emblematic of its norms. Formally, the show relies on traditional conventions of musical theater and Disney Renaissance narratives: a protagonist with integrity who is both an underdog and an outsider, a chorus that performs numerous anthemic production numbers, and a heterosexual enemies-to-lovers arc between the male main character and a female love interest. (The Jack/Katherine romance is remade into a platonic friendship in the JR. version.) In contrast to the spectacular stage magic and extravagant clothes of most Disney shows, *Newsies*' minimal sets and working-class costumes make it easier to produce. Adapted from a historical live-action film, *Newsies* doesn't require "putting the cartoon on the stage," according to one Illinois high school teacher. For other well-known Disney musicals, the teacher felt obligated to reproduce the source material, whereas the less frequently produced *Newsies* allowed for "a little more artistic interpretation."

Should a teacher be interested and the community open to it, the musical invites conversations about power, privilege, and political activism. As Marah Gubar argues, "*Newsies* suggests that ordinary Americans need to get involved and take action on their own behalf."[68] For some schools, *Newsies*' support of resistance, human rights, fair labor practices, and effective protest offers a message that aligns with a community's values. A high school educator from New York felt *Newsies* spoke to the current political moment (in 2022) when her students mounted the show. "Our students have really grown up in the era of the Trump presidency to Covid and George Floyd," she said, "and I just felt like there was a lot of restlessness that hadn't necessarily been directed into something specifically.... I wanted our students to feel empowered to ... spill whatever protesting spirit was within them." She noticed parallels between the show's narrative and causes that her students had been actively protesting, such as gun violence. Other educators valued the show's historical dimension and appreciated how embodying real-life figures gave students an opportunity, as one said, to learn about "the difficulty ... of the haves and have nots at the time."

Some students interpreted the musical in slightly less political and more abstractly humanist ways—a typical Disney "you can do it" call to action. One middle schooler from Mississippi described the meaning of the show as "whatever your goals may be, they may sound tough, but with a little elbow grease and hope, you can achieve them ... you just need to work hard and have a little bit of luck to really get where you want to be." A castmate added that the show was about "doing something that feels impossible or when you have people telling you that you can't do something and then you work for it and do it anyway. These kids have all been through so much but they don't just let someone privileged and greedy get what they want." One Pennsylvania high schooler said, "A bunch of scrappy little kids can still do stuff.... There's a bunch of parts of the show where they falter, and they think, maybe we can't do this, but there's always someone there to back them up." *Newsies* is not so subversively revolutionary as to betray Disney's trademark "family-friendly" liberal messaging that goodness prevails. It offers a critique of a powerful media company—the newspaper barons of New York—packaged inside a show that is nonetheless—perhaps ironically—produced and licensed by one of the world's largest media companies.

In terms of casting and gender, *Newsies* departs from other Disney shows—and the often-favored school musicals with majority-female roles—because it is dominated by male characters, with a boy frequently cast as the lead (Jack) to sustain the heterosexual romance.[69] Only two significant female characters inhabit *Newsies*' theatrical world. Budding journalist and daughter of publisher Joseph Pulitzer, Katherine Plumber—she invents a pen name to avoid association with her famous father—is a nominal leading character and a slightly more complex take on a Disney Renaissance princess. She is supported by a powerful father and ultimately falls in love with a man, yet she is neither a maiden-in-waiting like Cinderella nor a dutiful daughter like Belle.[70] Katherine's determination, savvy, and intelligence echo those traits in Ariel and Mulan. In the anthem "Watch What Happens," she expresses her insecurities as a journalist, her career ambitions, and her justice-seeking desire to speak truth to power, and the song's tunefulness and infectious energy assure the audience that she will succeed.

The other significant supporting female role is Medda Larkin, the vaudeville performer and theater owner who shelters and supports the newsies during their protests. Medda, a longtime friend and mother figure to Jack, encourages him in her jazzy solo "That's Rich." (For *Newsies JR.*, Menken and Feldman wrote "Just a Pretty Face," which Cerniglia describes as "a new empowering feminist song," replacing "That's Rich" with a less sexualized song.)[71] Although the script doesn't specify Medda's race, the character is historically based on a Black person and typically portrayed in professional productions by a Black performer, and the role features musical stylings and African American Vernacular English phrasings that racially code the role.[72] Medda at once offers a star turn for a girl and reinforces tired tropes of Black women as show-stopping performers and caretaker figures.

The character of Crutchie might trouble some teachers from a disability perspective. On the one hand, it's rare to see a featured character with a disability in a musical; Crutchie plays a key role in the story and sings numerous solos. He's a good-hearted and generous character with energy and pluck. On the other hand, Crutchie's purpose in the musical—from his very first line—is to suffer so that Jack can draw him into the Refuge and save him. In addition, in a musical that prioritizes movement, mobility, and dance, Crutchie can't participate fully in the show's most valued mode of storytelling. In an effort to offset this stereotypical representation of a person with a disability, Disney's production handbook includes several pages of dramaturgical analysis, historical insights, and personal perspectives from a disabled actor on performing disability onstage.[73]

Despite the male-dominant cast, most featured male roles in *Newsies* can be played by female or nonbinary students. MTI's official production handbook, which covers production logistics and provides extensive historical research, offers costuming ideas and specific line/lyric changes to support some of these gender-flexible roles and a mixed-gender chorus, such as cutting "boys" and "fellas" or changing those labels to "kids."[74]

Gender flexibility can offer liberating and supportive experiences for performers. A Pennsylvania high school teacher felt *Newsies* allowed her to "create a safe space where students can just be themselves." The girl who played Crutchie in that production said, "I liked playing a boy. Every day. It gave me gender euphoria. It's been a little validating that I didn't have to switch Crutchie's gender."

Different localities manage the politics of gender and performance in different ways. Some teacher-directors honor the historical fact that female newsies existed, which the production handbook notes. "We dressed our girls and we didn't make them play boys ... to portray the way it was," one teacher from Massachusetts said. Others made the same choice, although not for historical accuracy. "I know my conservative community," said one Mississippi teacher, "and having boys play girls or girls play boys would be met with a lot of backlash and criticism." For some educators, *Newsies*' message transcended gender. A teacher from Delaware told us, "We just asked them to create a character, and we kind of emphasized that gender doesn't really matter in this story. This is a story about kids and ... people seeking power and trying to make change. And that's not a story of gender. Any gender can do that." Support for gender-flexible casting allows *Newsies* to be interpreted in both gender-blind and gender-conscious ways.

Moana JR.

While *Beauty and the Beast* and *Newsies* remain popular produced titles in both full-length and JR. versions, Disney properties based on newer movies have expanded the JR. catalog. These shows reveal Disney's economic awareness of the limitless capacity for school musicals and cultural awareness of the value of diverse stories and richer, more self-empowered, and less heterosexualized roles for girls and nonbinary kids.

Moana JR., based on the wildly successful 2016 animated feature film, was EdTA's fifth most-produced "short musical" of the 2021–2022 school year.[75] At one high school in North Carolina, where voting on the selection of the annual musical and choosing a Disney JR. title are traditions, theater students voted to produce *Moana JR.* in 2022. "High school students like to do shows for children," explained the teacher-director. She also noted that they had a strong senior male performer of color who could play Maui.

Moana JR. draws upon Oceanic and Polynesian cultural traditions and showcases Disney's efforts to include non-Western stories, diverse representation, and authentic perspectives in its shows. Written and adapted for the stage by a diverse team of composers and writers, the project was developed in collaboration with an "Oceanic Trust": "a group of anthropologists, cultural practitioners, historians, linguists, and choreographers from the Pacific Islands."[76] Performers sing in Samoan and Tokelau, and the ShowKit for directors provides guides to the lyrics' pronunciation and meaning. Despite these efforts, some have criticized the piece for its practice of cultural appropriation and colonialist reframing within traditional Western musical-theater idioms.[77]

Secondary schools that produce *Moana JR.* have an opportunity to learn about and grapple with respecting cultural traditions that may be outside of their own. On a practical level, teaching a new language may be hard—especially on top of producing a musical. One North Carolina teacher said, "It was difficult. They had to learn a foreign language. That was challenging." The adults talked about doing "some research on the tribal dances." The teachers at another North Carolina school struggled to understand the use of tattoos on Maui, which the ShowKit warns against using: "Maui's tattoos, which are an important part of the Disney animated film, have been removed from this adaptation so that this character's integrity remains intact across all productions.[78] ... Tattoos are an earned, sacred part of Pacific Islander culture and should not be worn by any non-Pacific Islander as part of a costume; *under no circumstances* should your actor wear any tattoos."[79] They suggest, "Keep it island casual for this charismatic shapeshifter, dressing him in a black or green shirt and tan shorts with sandals. Accessorize him with a necklace or belt made of bits and pieces of found materials such as shells and leaves."[80] The teacher explained that the costumes they rented were marked with tattoos. "I wasn't sure about the interpretation of that, but we decided that because we saw so many on YouTube that had the tattoos, we just thought the Maui costume came with the tattoos." Although they were worried about being disrespectful to the culture, they decided that the warning was about applying tattoos to the actor's skin and used the costume.

At one school in North Carolina, producing *Moana JR.* caused more conflict than the teachers anticipated. The school has a "diverse" population, and as one teacher said, "We cast whoever is the best for the part." A white girl played Moana, and all of the supporting roles were played by kids of color. The girl "got crap from people online about being white," the teacher told us. The adults got "questions about why was she not a person of color, but our crab and the grandmother and Maori were people of color." A school that elects to produce *Moana JR.* may encounter difficult dynamics and conversations regarding race and casting.

Unlike previous Disney princesses, Moana is respected and explicitly consulted for guidance as chief-to-be by her family and community. Her femininity is transgressive and nuanced, at once excitedly yearning ("How Far I'll Go"), intimidatingly scary ("Warrior Face"), and bravely vulnerable. Her final "confrontation" doesn't involve heroically defeating the villain Te Ka but requires her to use intuition, emotional intelligence, and care to rescue the lost god Te Fiti through the power of love. The subversion of Moana's femininity mirrors the skewering of masculinity in Maui, whose machismo is framed as comical, fragile, and a liability to Moana's mission.[81] As is clear to young students, Moana is a more independent and progressive Disney princess than her predecessors. In a small study of girls and boys ages five to eight, psychologists Paula Hamilton and Rhyannon Dynes found that "both boys and girls valued the more active traits portrayed by the contemporary princesses," and a few chose Moana as their favorite.[82]

Moana JR. explores the struggle between one's responsibility to societal expectations and validation of individual desire, which schools and teachers also deal with. The show champions the value of a young woman enacting her goals despite (and outside of) patriarchal expectations. Indeed, her desire is not for marriage (there is no heterosexual romance in the plot) or obedience to her father but to explore in order to save her community. Additionally, it is Moana's grandmother—the family member closest to Moana, who receives far more stage time than either of Moana's parents—who supports and catalyzes her granddaughter's journey. Moana is able to complete her dangerous mission (which her father disapproves of) through wayfaring, a skill she learned from her ancestors who developed the navigation tool. *Moana*'s representation of family as outside the nuclear family unit and contingent on cultural heritage complicates and transcends Disney's traditional reliance on patriarchal tropes. In this way, the show offers a more progressive representation of family for a "family-friendly" musical.

Moana is by no means a perfectly progressive step for Disney musicals. Despite Disney's pursuit of authenticity, Sotirios Mouzakis asserts that "Moana is yet another white, masculine creation of a cultural hybrid, despite the partially feminist message the film tries to convey through a female heroic character."[83] Moreover, Tēvita Ka'ili questions whether the establishment of Disney's "Oceanic Trust" "serves to promote a better understanding of the region's many cultures and thus to silence/appease critics, or if it is merely a cleverly orchestrated publicity stunt to legitimize the latest instance of cultural appropriation."[84] These critiques point to future trends in the politics of representation in corporate-created musicals and "how far they'll go" in showcasing "authenticity."

Frozen

Frozen is one of Disney's most commercially successful and far-reaching contemporary franchises. Loosely based on Hans Christian Andersen's "The Snow Queen," *Frozen* began as a 2013 blockbuster movie, receiving Oscars for Animated Feature and Original

Song, "Let It Go." Featuring a female co-composer and lyricist (Kristen Anderson-Lopez) and the Disney studio's first female director (Jennifer Lee, who also penned the book for the film and stage versions), *Frozen* brings a fresh perspective to an art form and industry that have historically valued female performers but sidelined female authors. As of this writing in March 2024, *Frozen* and *Frozen II* are the third- and second-highest-grossing animated films of all time—behind Disney's 2019 live-action remake of *The Lion King*. It was made into a Broadway musical (2018–2020), which went on a national tour, was adapted and licensed as *Frozen JR.* (2018), and was developed into a ride and a live sing-along show at Disney World. In 2022, Disney Theatrical licensed the full-length stage version through the "United States of Frozen"—a nationwide competition in which fifty high schools were chosen to produce the first production of *Frozen* in their respective states.[85] In the EdTA's 2021–2022 survey, *Frozen JR.* topped the list of the most-produced "short musicals."[86]

In a breakthrough departure from past Disney-princess narratives, *Frozen* focuses on the relationship between sisters Anna and Elsa. Moreover, heterosexual romance is subverted: Elsa isn't interested or ultimately engaged with a romantic partner, and the duplicitous Hans tries to charm and manipulate Anna toward his own selfish ambitions. While in the full-length stage version Kristoff and Anna's romance is furthered through love soliloquies and a "happy-ever-after" engagement, the film and JR. versions portray their platonic friendship and, by the finale, offer no clear indication of a romantic future.[87]

Frozen has been heralded as one of Disney's most feminist musicals, disrupting earlier conventions of female characters. As Susanne R. Hackett writes, Elsa "represent[s] all of the complexities of a woman with power, both in her capacity to lead and her capacity to love."[88] Her dichotomy with Anna showcases the ambivalence of sisterhood, a broad spectrum of womanhood, and the importance of female solidarity in the larger fight against the oppression of women. In "Let It Go," as Lynda Haas and Shaina Trapedo write, "Elsa departs from her princess predecessors by rejecting the fairy tale notion that the best way to achieve a 'happy ending' is by trying to please everyone"; she values self-acceptance instead.[89] Unsurprisingly, then, young girls who are in the process of self-actualization are clamoring to perform in *Frozen JR.*, and young female performers see themselves as similar to Anna and Elsa. One student said, "So I was able to get Elsa's personality and I knew how to act like her already." Another added, "I already act—not in a bad way—but I have some of the same characteristics. That's why I was cast for the role, because I have a more sassy attitude."

Other scholars critique *Frozen* as troublingly postfeminist. Michael Macaluso, for example, observes that Elsa's "transformation" sequence is unlike, for example, Ariel's trading her fins for human legs but "simply represents a glamorous makeover."[90] Macaluso writes, "While she can let go of her fear, inhibition, and depression, her liberation is also tied to a postfeminist vision of femininity and sexuality, as depicted by her new wardrobe and hairdo."[91] Macaluso analyzes Reddit and fan websites to demonstrate how fully a postfeminist perspective has been embraced by spectators, even self-named feminists. While Elsa and Anna in *Frozen* may be a vast improvement over early

Disney princesses, they still embody a white, neoliberal form of individual, apolitical empowerment.

Disney in Schools and Theatrical Agency

Frozen's success as a "feminist" film and theatrical title is both ironically and, according to Sarah Whitfield, intentionally related to the movie's "turning to the Broadway musical for a model that supports more comprehensive character development and permits women characters to enact the resolution to their own dramatic conflict."[92] Such is the complicated "double duty" of Broadway—and, by extension, Disney—musicals, according to Wolf: "to promote conservative values *and* to provide empowering representations of women" and other marginalized identities "sometimes simultaneously."[93]

Many of the teachers and students we spoke to emphasized the challenges as well as the pleasure and fulfillment of restarting theater after the pandemic. Especially in a post-Covid landscape rife with mental-health challenges, arts education provides essential opportunities for socio-emotional growth. A teacher in Minnesota who directed *Beauty and the Beast* said, "Coming off of Covid, I wanted to involve a lot of kids." For the production, they "bumped up the costumes and the set for the show" and rented the costumes from a dinner theater. One student at this school said, "I really liked being in the musical with people I was in a musical with before.... I really enjoyed the practices because ... it's all of a bunch of people who just want to continue to grow and become better at their part." Another added, "I made so many friends, new friends I didn't think I'd be friends with at all." Disney's power in the educational market has held through the Covid pandemic, with its shows remaining well represented on the list of most-produced shows in 2022–2023.[94] Cerniglia notes that during the pandemic, "amateur and school theatres—supported by [Disney's] digital resources yet unencumbered by the financial, regulatory, and organizational obstacles of their professional counterparts—were the first to return to live, in-person musical theatre performance in every market, generating much-needed income for a battered industry."[95]

As Cerniglia writes, "For the first time in history [through the amateur licensing of Disney musicals], young Disney fans would engage beloved characters, stories, and songs not just as passive movie consumers or theme park guests, but with theatrical agency, owning their personal experience over weeks of rehearsal and performance."[96] Disney, for its part, maintains a two-pronged approach that is at once economically lucrative and artistically, educationally, and politically forward-thinking. While the organization has made strides in flexible casting, authentic cultural representation, and nuanced study guides, we hope that Disney school musicals can be fun and fulfilling for all kids while also conveying messages of inclusion and empowerment for marginalized identities.[97]

Notes

1. Henry A. Giroux, *The Mouse That Roared: Disney and the End of Innocence* (Lanham, MD: Rowman & Littlefield, 2010), 86.
2. Ibid., 26.
3. See Elizabeth L. Wollman, "The Economic Development of the 'New' Times Square and Its Impact on the Broadway Musical," *American Music* 20, no. 4 (Winter 2002): 445–447.
4. James Miller, "Longest-Running Shows on Broadway," *Playbill*, March 13, 2023, https://playbill.com/article/long-runs-on-broadway-com-109864.
5. Ruthie Fierberg, "How Disney Shows Are Changing the Landscape of the American Musical Theatre," *Playbill*, August 10, 2018, https://playbill.com/article/how-disney-shows-are-changing-the-landscape-of-the-american-musical-theatre.
6. Elissa Nadworny, "The Most Popular High School Plays and Musicals," NPR, July 30, 2020, https://www.npr.org/sections/ed/2019/07/31/427138970/the-most-popular-high-school-plays-and-musicals.
7. Fierberg, "How Disney Shows Are Changing the Landscape."
8. Kenneth J. Cerniglia, "'We're All in This Together': Student and Amateur Musical Theatre Performances," in *The Routledge Companion to Musical Theatre*, ed. Laura MacDonald and Ryan Donovan (New York: Routledge, 2022), 453.
9. Nicholas Sammond, *Babes in Tomorrowland: Walt Disney and the Making of the American Child, 1930–1960* (Durham, NC: Duke University Press, 2005), 15.
10. Giroux, *The Mouse That Roared*, 2–3.
11. Ibid., 7.
12. See, for example, Rob Horowitz, "Evaluation of the Broadway Junior–ArtsConnection Program in Three New York City Public Schools," New York City Department of Education, 2001; Carol Shokhoff, "Three Broadway Junior Case Studies," New York City Department of Education, 2009. Cited in Joshua Streeter, "Broadway Junior: Musical Theatre for Young Performers," Master's thesis, University of Texas at Austin, 2016, 65–67. https://repositories.lib.utexas.edu/server/api/core/bitstreams/a0c860e2-93c2-462d-a2ba-75a424b20552/content. Horowitz and Shokhoff examine the Broadway Jr. program within the New York City Public School system, with a focus on social-emotional growth and impacts on school culture. Also see Kary Thomas Haddad, "'This Is How It Feels': The Lived Experience of High School Musical Theater," DMA diss., Boston University, 2018, https://search.proquest.com/docview/2024228267/abstract/C6F639F4A41E46C0PQ/1; Ryan John, "Part of It All: The High School Musical as a Community of Practice," *Visions of Research in Music Education* 24 (2014): 29; Reed W. Larson and Jane R. Brown, "Emotional Development in Adolescence: What Can Be Learned from a High School Theater Program?," *Child Development* 78, no. 4 (2007): 1083–1099, https://doi.org/10.1111/j.1467-8624.2007.01054; Ric Lynn Watkins, "The Musical Theater Experience and the Extent to Which It Affects High School Students," PhD diss., University of Illinois at Urbana-Champaign, 2005, https://search.proquest.com/docview/305001887/abstract/C718971B450F4D35PQ/1; Nevine A. Yassa, "High School Involvement in Creative Drama," *Research in Drama Education* 4, no. 1 (1999): 37–49, https://doi.org/10.1080/1356978990040104; Debra Jo Davey, "Musical Theatre in Secondary Education: Teacher Preparation, Responsibilities, and Attitudes," DMA diss., Arizona State University, 2010.
13. James Leve and Donelle Ruwe, "Introduction," in *Children, Childhood, and Musical Theater*, ed. James Leve and Donelle Ruwe (London: Routledge, 2020), 14.

14. The quotes have been edited for grammar and clarity. We identify schools by state, students by age, and teachers and students by gender.
15. Many thanks to Elliot Lee for locating schools that produced Disney musicals before, during, and shortly after the Covid pandemic and for helping to conduct the interviews and analyze the transcripts.
16. Samuel Grob, "Just for Fun? The Politics of Representation and Critical Education in High School Musical Theater," BA thesis, Yale University, 2021, 9.
17. See Stacy Wolf, *Beyond Broadway: The Pleasure and Promise of Musical Theatre across America* (New York: Oxford University Press, 2020), 18–23.
18. For a firsthand account of the development of *The Little Mermaid*, see Cerniglia, "'We're All in This Together,'" 455–457. Also see Amy S. Osatinski, *Disney Theatrical Productions: Producing Broadway Musicals the Disney Way* (New York: Routledge, 2019), 48.
19. As verified by teacher sources close to the authors—as well as productions that the authors have attended—educators have created small additional roles, cut certain scenes and songs, changed a character's gender (even when gender flexibility is not explicitly permitted), and made other adjustments to the licensed material. Anecdotally, adaptations are a normal practice in educational theater.
20. Music Theatre International, "Broadway Junior," https://www.mtishows.com/broadway-junior.
21. See Wolf, *Beyond Broadway*; Joshua Rashon Streeter, "Broadway Junior: Musical Theatre for Youth Performers," MFA thesis, University of Texas at Austin, 2016.
22. Osatinski, *Disney Theatrical Productions*, 15.
23. Ibid., 176.
24. Music Theatre International, "Produce Your Very Own Disney Show!," https://www.mtishows.com/disney-shows.
25. Nadworny, "The Most Popular High School Plays and Musicals."
26. See "84th Annual Play Survey Reveals Most Popular Plays & Musicals," Educational Theatre Association, June 6, 2022, https://schooltheatre.org/84th-annual-play-survey-reveals-most-popular-plays-musicals/. The 2021–2022 list included *Frozen JR.* (no. 1), *The Lion King JR.* (no. 3), *High School Musical JR.* (no. 5, tie), *Moana JR.* (no. 5, tie), *The Little Mermaid JR.* (no. 9). For 2022–2023, see "Play Survey Reveals 2023's Most Popular High School Shows," Educational Theatre Association, June 5, 2023, https://schooltheatre.org/2023-play-survey-reveals-most-popular-high-school-shows/. The 2022–2023 list included *Frozen JR.* (no. 1), *Newsies JR.* (no. 3), *High School Musical JR.* (no. 6), *The Little Mermaid JR.* (no. 7), *The Lion King* (no. 10, tie).
27. "84th Annual Play Survey"; "Play Survey Reveals."
28. Cerniglia, "'We're All in This Together,'" 453–454. Also see Disney *The Lion King*, "Educational Materials," https://lionking.com/education/.
29. Fierberg, "How Disney Shows Are Changing the Landscape."
30. Wolf, *Beyond Broadway*, 276.
31. Cerniglia, "'We're All in This Together,'" 458.
32. Ibid.; emphasis in original.
33. Ibid.
34. Ibid.; emphasis in original.
35. Ibid.
36. For example, see Johnson Cheu, ed., *Diversity in Disney Films: Critical Essays on Race, Ethnicity, Gender, Sexuality and Disability* (Jefferson, NC: McFarland, 2013); Kutsuzawa Kiyomi, "Disney's Pocahontas: Reproduction of Gender, Orientalism, and the Strategic

Construction of Racial Harmony in the Disney Empire," *Asian Journal of Women's Studies* 6, no. 4 (2000): 39–65; Celeste Lacroix, "Images of Animated Others: The Orientalization of Disney's Cartoon Heroines from *The Little Mermaid* to *The Hunchback of Notre Dame*," *Popular Communication* 2, no. 4 (2004): 213–229.

37. "Disney *Moana JR.*," Disney Theatrical Licensing, https://disneytheatricallicensing.com/show/moana-jr/.
38. Erika Trahan, commenter, "When Shows Require Diversity but the School Is Not Diverse," Educational Theatre Association, January 19, 2019, https://community.schooltheatre.org/communities/community-home/digestviewer/viewthread?GroupId=133&MID=15389.
39. For a detailed insider account of the development of Disney activities for kids, see Ken Cerniglia, "Dramaturgical Leadership and the Politics of Appeal in Commercial Theatre," in *The Routledge Companion to Dramaturgy*, ed. Magda Romanska (New York: Routledge, 2014), 230–235; Cerniglia, "'We're All in This Together.'" Also see Osatinski, *Disney Theatrical Productions*.
40. Cerniglia, "Dramaturgical Leadership," 231–232.
41. Ken Cerniglia and Lisa Mitchell, "The Business of Children in Disney's Theatre," in *Entertaining Children: The Participation of Youth in the Entertainment Industry*, ed. Gillian Arrighi and Victor Emeljanow (New York: Palgrave Macmillan, 2014), 139.
42. Osatinski, *Disney Theatrical Productions*, 17.
43. Ibid.
44. Wolf, *Beyond Broadway*, 22.
45. See Ibid., 249–277.
46. https://disneymusicalsinschools.com/about.
47. Grob, "Just for Fun?," 8.
48. Arts educator, advocate, and writer Howard Sherman covers the censorship of school musicals on his website (hesherman.com). For specific examples of the shows mentioned here, see Maddie Hanna, "Central Bucks Students Say District Killed Production of Musical 'Rent,'" *Philadelphia Inquirer*, April 16, 2022, https://www.inquirer.com/education/central-bucks-west-rent-musical-lgbtq-censorship-20220416.html; Hannah Natanson, "The Culture War's Latest Casualty: The High School Musical," *Washington Post*, May 2, 2023, https://www.washingtonpost.com/education/2023/05/02/banned-school-plays-musical-theater-censorship/; Logan Culwell-Block, "Ohio High School Reverses on *25th Annual Putnam County Spelling Bee* Cancellation," *Playbill*, February 9, 2023, https://playbill.com/article/ohio-high-school-reverses-on-25th-annual-putnam-county-spelling-bee-cancellation; Dave Jordan, "Students Speak on Columbia High School Play Being Postponed Due to Concerns over Its Content," WITN, December 7, 2022, https://www.witn.com/2022/12/08/columbia-high-school-play-postponed-due-concerns-over-its-content/.
49. Elizabeth Blair, "These Were the Most Frequently Performed Plays and Musicals in High Schools This Year," NPR, June 5, 2023, https://www.npr.org/2023/06/05/1179417838/most-popular-high-school-musical-play-2022-2023#:~:text=More%20than%202%2C300%20public%20and,top%20spot%20among%20short%20musicals. Also see "Play Survey Reveals"; Michael Paulson. "It's Getting Hard to Stage a School Play without Political Drama," *New York Times*, July 4, 2023, https://www.nytimes.com/2023/07/04/theater/school-plays-politics.html.
50. As a rare exception, in Ithaca, New York, a show was canceled because of student objections. A high school director cast a white girl as Esmeralda in *The Hunchback of Notre Dame*. Because so few roles in musicals explicitly call for a woman of color, and Esmeralda is identified as a "gypsy" (or Roma), students protested, and the production was canceled.

See Sopan Deb, "Casting Controversy Derailed a High School Play. Then Came the Threats," *New York Times*, February 8, 2018, https://www.nytimes.com/2018/02/08/theater/hunchback-of-notre-dame-ithaca-high-school.html.
51. For more in-depth and intersectional analysis of other Disney shows and popular school musicals, see Grob, "Just for Fun?"
52. See Peter C. Kunze, *Staging a Comeback: Broadway, Hollywood, and the Disney Renaissance* (New Brunswick, NJ: Rutgers University Press, 2023).
53. Ryan Bunch, "'Love Is an Open Door': Revising and Repeating Disney's Musical Tropes in *Frozen*," in *Contemporary Musical Film*, ed. K. J. Donnelly and Beth Carroll (Edinburgh: Edinburgh University Press, 2017), 89–104.
54. Frank Rich, "Throw Away Those Scripts. Some of the Greatest Moments Were Wordless," *New York Times*, December 29, 1991, https://www.nytimes.com/1991/12/29/theater/year-arts-theater-1991-throw-away-those-scripts-some-greatest-moments-were.html.
55. See database in Nadworny, "The Most Popular High School Plays and Musicals."
56. Michael Goldstein, "Broadway's New Beast," *New York Magazine*, March 14, 1994, 43.
57. "Reimagining Disney Classics: *Beauty and the Beast*," Music Theatre International, September 26, 2022, https://www.mtishows.com/reimagining-disney-classics-beauty-and-the-beast-2.
58. See Rebecca Warner, "The Beauty and the Beast Trope in Modern Musical Theatre," *Studies in Musical Theatre* 9, no. 1 (March 2015): 31–51.
59. See, for example, Linda Coates, Shelly Bonnah, and Cathy Richardson, "*Beauty and the Beast*: Misrepresentation and Social Responses in Fairy-Tale Romance and Redemption," *International Journal of Child, Youth and Family Studies* 10, no. 1 (February 2019): 119–137, https://doi.org/10.18357/ijcyfs101201918809; Allison Craven, "Beauty and the Belles: Discourses of Feminism and Femininity in Disneyland," *European Journal of Women's Studies* 9, no. 2 (May 2002): 123–142, https://doi.org/10.1177/1350682002009002806; June Cummins, "Romancing the Plot: The Real Beast of Disney's *Beauty and the Beast*," *Children's Literature Association Quarterly* 20, no. 1 (1995): 22–28, https://doi.org/10.1353/chq.0.0872; Sharon D. Downey, "Feminine Empowerment in Disney's *Beauty and the Beast*," *Women's Studies in Communication* 19, no. 2 (July 1996): 185–212, https://doi.org/10.1080/07491409.1996.11089812; Susan Z. Swan, "Gothic Drama in Disney's *Beauty and the Beast*: Subverting Traditional Romance by Transcending the Animal-Human Paradox," *Critical Studies in Mass Communication* 16, no. 3 (September 1999): 350–369, https://doi.org/10.1080/15295039909367100.
60. Elaine Dutka, "Ms. Beauty and the Beast: Writer of Disney Hit Explains Her 'Woman of the '90s,'" *Los Angeles Times*, January 19, 1992, https://www.latimes.com/archives/la-xpm-1992-01-19-ca-544-story.html.
61. Rebecca Weidman-Winter, "Belle: Beyond the Classic Story for a Modern Audience," in *Recasting the Disney Princess in an Era of New Media and Social Movements*, ed. Shearon Roberts (New York: Lexington, 2020), 201.
62. Craven, "Beauty and the Belles," 135.
63. See Coates, Bonnah, and Richardson, "*Beauty and the Beast*." For a counterpoint, see Constance Grady, "Is *Beauty and the Beast* 'a Tale as Old as Stockholm Syndrome'? Depends How You Read It," Vox, March 23, 2017, https://www.vox.com/culture/2017/3/23/15000768/beauty-and-the-beast-feminist-stockholm-syndrome.
64. On this theme in opera, see Catherine Clement, *Opera, or the Undoing of Women*, trans. Betsy Wing (Minneapolis: University of Minnesota Press, 1988).

65. "Disney's *Beauty and the Beast*," Music Theatre International, https://www.mtishows.com/disneys-beauty-and-the-beast.
66. Craven, "Beauty and the Belles," 127; Grob, "Just for Fun?" On Doug Wright's dramaturgical revisions to *The Little Mermaid* Broadway production, see Michael Lassell, *The Little Mermaid: From the Deep Blue Sea to the Great White Way* (New York: Disney Editions, 2008); Michael Lassell, "Disney's *Beauty and the Beast*," in *Disney on Broadway*, ed. Michael Lassell (New York: Disney Editions, 2002), 16–57.
67. Osatinski, *Disney Theatrical Productions*, 129. On the history of *Newsies* and its surprising success on the professional stage, see Kenneth Cerniglia, ed., *Newsies: Stories of the Unlikely Broadway Hit* (New York: Disney Editions, 2013); Cerniglia, "Dramaturgical Leadership," 230–235; Osatinski, *Disney Theatrical Productions*, 127–156.
68. Marah Gubar, "Urchins Unite: *Newsies* as an Antidote to *Annie*," in *Children, Childhood, and Musical Theatre*, ed. James Leve and Donelle Ruwe (New York: Routledge, 2020), 156.
69. See Aaron C. Thomas, "Dancing toward Masculinity: *Newsies*, Gender and Desire," in *The Disney Musical on Stage and Screen*, ed. George Rodosthenous (New York: Bloomsbury, 2017), 155–168.
70. See Amy M. Davis, *Good Girls and Wicked Witches: Women in Disney's Feature Animation* (Bloomington: Indiana University Press, 2006).
71. Cerniglia, "'We're All in This Together,'" 459.
72. Capathia Jenkins originated the role on Broadway. See Dan Dinero, "A Big Black Lady Stops the Show: Black Women, Performances of Excess, and the Power of Saying No," *Studies in Musical Theatre* 6, no. 1 (2012): 29–41.
73. Julie Haverkate, ed., *Newsies Production Handbook*, 18–21, https://issuu.com/mtivault/docs/newsies_production_handbook.
74. Ibid., 26–27.
75. "84th Annual Play Survey."
76. "Disney's *Moana JR*.," Music Theatre International, https://www.mtishows.com/disneys-moana-jr. Also see Cerniglia, "'We're All in This Together,'" 460. The collaborators included Lin-Manuel Miranda, Opetaia Foa'i, Mark Mancina, Susan Soon He Stanton, and Ian Weinberger.
77. See Jenny Banh, "*Moana*: Daughter of the Chief and Polynesian (in)Visibility," in *Recasting the Disney Princess*, ed. Shearon Roberts (Lanham, MD: Lexington, 2020), 129–146; Robin Armstrong, "Time to Face the Music: Musical Colonization and Appropriation in Disney's *Moana*," *Social Sciences* 7, no. 7 (2018): 1–9; Ida Yoshinaga, "Disney's *Moana*, the Colonial Screenplay, and Indigenous Labor Extraction in Hollywood Fantasy Films," *Narrative Culture* 6, no. 2 (2019): 188–215, muse.jhu.edu/article/741296.
78. Music Theater International, "*Moana JR*. ShowKit." https://www.mtishows.com/sites/default/files/moana_jr.-_a_note_on_culture.pdf.
79. Ibid.; emphasis in original.
80. Ibid.
81. Madeline Streiff and Lauren Dundes, "From Shapeshifter to Lava Monster: Gender Stereotypes in Disney's *Moana*," *Social Sciences* 6, no. 3 (2017): 91.
82. Paula Hamilton and Rhyannon Dynes, "From 'Tiaras and Twirls' to 'Action and Adventure': Eliciting Children's Gendered Perceptions of Disney Characters through Participatory Visual Methodology," *International Journal of Early Years Education* 31, no. 2 (2023): 482, 489.
83. Sotirios Mouzakis, "Princess of a Different Kingdom: Cultural Imperialism, Female Heroism, and the Global Performance of Walt Disney's *Mulan* and *Moana*," in *Heroism*

as a Global Phenomenon in Contemporary Culture, ed. Barbara Korte, Simon Wendt, and Nicole Falkenhayner (London: Routledge, 2019), 74.
84. Tēvita Ka'ili, "Goddess Hina: The Missing Heroine from Disney's *Moana*," Huffington Post, December 6, 2016, www.huffingtonpost.com/entry/goddess-hina-the-missing-heroine-fromdisney%CA%BCs-moana_us_5839f343e4b0a79f7433b6e5.
85. Logan Culwell-Block, "See Which 51 U.S. High Schools Will Be the 1st to Produce Disney's *Frozen*," Playbill, September 9, 2022, https://playbill.com/article/see-which-51-u-s-high-schools-will-be-the-1st-to-produce-disneys-frozen.
86. "Play Survey Reveals."
87. The story takes a different direction in *Frozen II*.
88. Susanne R. Hackett, "'Let It Go' as Radical Mantra: Subverting the Princess Narrative in *Frozen*," in *Recasting the Disney Princess in an Era of New Media and Social Movements*, ed. Shearon Roberts (Lanham: Lexington, 2020), 222.
89. Lynda Haas and Shaina Trapedo, "Disney Corporation," in *The Routledge Companion to Media and Fairy-Tale Cultures*, ed. Pauline Greenhill et al. (London: Routledge, 2018), 184.
90. Michael Macaluso, "The Postfeminist Princess: Public Discourse and Disney's Curricular Guide to Feminism," in *Disney, Culture, and Curriculum*, ed. Jennifer A. Sandlin and Julie C. Garlin (London: Routledge, 2016), 75.
91. Ibid.
92. Sarah Whitfield, "'For the First Time in Forever': Locating *Frozen* as a Feminist Disney Musical," in *The Disney Musical on Stage and Screen: Critical Approaches from "Snow White" to "Frozen,"* ed. George Rodosthenous (New York: Bloomsbury Methuen Drama, 2017), 233.
93. Stacy Wolf, "Hamilton's Women," *Studies in Musical Theatre* 12, no. 2 (2018): 167–180.
94. "Play Survey Reveals."
95. Cerniglia, "'We're All in This Together,'" 454.
96. Ibid., 453.
97. Many thanks to Angela Libo Tan for her excellent help in editing this chapter.

Bibliography

Armstrong, Robin. "Time to Face the Music: Musical Colonization and Appropriation in Disney's *Moana*." *Social Sciences* 7, no. 7 (2018): 1–9.
Banh, Jenny. "*Moana*: Daughter of the Chief and Polynesian (in)Visibility." In *Recasting the Disney Princess*, edited by Shearon Roberts, 129–146. Lanham, MD: Lexington, 2020.
Blair, Elizabeth. "These Were the Most Frequently Performed Plays and Musicals in High Schools This Year." NPR, June 5, 2023. https://www.npr.org/2023/06/05/1179417838/most-popular-high-school-musical-play-2022-2023#:~:text=More%20than%202%2C300%20public%20and,top%20spot%20among%20short%20musicals.
"Broadway Junior." Music Theatre International. https://www.mtishows.com/broadway-junior.
Bunch, Ryan. "'Love Is an Open Door': Revising and Repeating Disney's Musical Tropes in *Frozen*." In *Contemporary Musical Film*, edited by K. J. Donnelly and Beth Carroll, 89–104. Edinburgh: Edinburgh University Press, 2017.
Cerniglia, Ken. "Dramaturgical Leadership and the Politics of Appeal in Commercial Theatre." In *The Routledge Companion to Dramaturgy*, ed. Magda Romanska, 230–235. New York: Routledge, 2014.

Cerniglia, Kenneth, ed. *Newsies: Stories of the Unlikely Broadway Hit*. New York: Disney Editions, 2013.
Cerniglia, Kenneth J. "'We're All in This Together': Student and Amateur Musical Theatre Performances." In *The Routledge Companion to Musical Theatre*, edited by Laura MacDonald and Ryan Donovan, 450–464. New York: Routledge, 2022.
Cerniglia, Ken, and Lisa Mitchell. "The Business of Children in Disney's Theater." In *Entertaining Children: The Participation of Youth in the Entertainment Industry*, edited by Gillian Arrighi and Victor Emeljanow, 129–145. New York: Palgrave Macmillan, 2014.
Cheu, Johnson, ed. *Diversity in Disney Films: Critical Essays on Race, Ethnicity, Gender, Sexuality and Disability*. Jefferson, NC: McFarland, 2013.
Clement, Catherine. *Opera, or the Undoing of Women*. Translated by Betsy Wing. Minneapolis: University of Minnesota Press, 1988.
Coates, Linda, Shelly Bonnah, and Cathy Richardson. "*Beauty and the Beast*: Misrepresentation and Social Responses in Fairy-Tale Romance and Redemption." *International Journal of Child, Youth and Family Studies* 10, no. 1 (February 2019): 119–137. https://doi.org/10.18357/ijcyfs101201918809.
Craven, Allison. "Beauty and the Belles: Discourses of Feminism and Femininity in Disneyland." *European Journal of Women's Studies* 9, no. 2 (May 2002): 123–142. https://doi.org/10.1177/1350682002009002806.
Culwell-Block, Logan. "Ohio High School Reverses on *25th Annual Putnam County Spelling Bee* Cancellation." *Playbill*, February 9, 2023. https://playbill.com/article/ohio-high-school-reverses-on-25th-annual-putnam-county-spelling-bee-cancellation.
Culwell-Block, Logan. "See Which 51 U.S. High Schools Will Be the 1st to Produce Disney's *Frozen*." Playbill, September 9, 2022. https://playbill.com/article/see-which-51-u-s-high-schools-will-be-the-1st-to-produce-disneys-frozen.
Cummins, June. "Romancing the Plot: The Real Beast of Disney's *Beauty and the Beast*." *Children's Literature Association Quarterly* 20, no. 1 (1995): 22–28. https://doi.org/10.1353/chq.0.0872.
Davey, Debra Jo. "Musical Theatre in Secondary Education: Teacher Preparation, Responsibilities, and Attitudes." DMA diss., Arizona State University, 2010.
Davis, Amy M. *Good Girls and Wicked Witches: Women in Disney's Feature Animation*. Bloomington: Indiana University Press, 2006.
Deb, Sopan. "Casting Controversy Derailed a High School Play. Then Came the Threats." *New York Times*, February 8, 2018. https://www.nytimes.com/2018/02/08/theater/hunchback-of-notre-dame-ithaca-high-school.html.
Dinero, Dan. "A Big Black Lady Stops the Show: Black Women, Performances of Excess, and the Power of Saying No." *Studies in Musical Theatre* 6, no. 1 (2012): 29–41.
"Disney *Moana JR*." Disney Theatrical Licensing. Disney https://disneytheatricallicensing.com/show/moana-jr/.
"Disney's *Beauty and the Beast*." Music Theatre International. https://www.mtishows.com/disneys-beauty-and-the-beast.
"Disney's *Moana JR*." Music Theater International. https://www.mtishows.com/disneys-moana-jr.
Downey, Sharon D. "Feminine Empowerment in Disney's *Beauty and the Beast*." *Women's Studies in Communication* 19, no. 2 (July 1996): 185–212. https://doi.org/10.1080/07491409.1996.11089812.

Dutka, Elaine. "Ms. Beauty and the Beast: Writer of Disney Hit Explains Her 'Woman of the '90s.'" *Los Angeles Times*, January 19, 1992. https://www.latimes.com/archives/la-xpm-1992-01-19-ca-544-story.html.

"Educational Materials." Disney *The Lion King*. https://lionking.com/education/.

"84th Annual Play Survey Reveals Most Popular Plays & Musicals." Educational Theatre Association, June 6, 2022. https://schooltheatre.org/84th-annual-play-survey-reveals-most-popular-plays-musicals/.

Fierberg, Ruthie. "How Disney Shows Are Changing the Landscape of the American Musical Theatre." *Playbill*, August 10, 2018. https://playbill.com/article/how-disney-shows-are-changing-the-landscape-of-the-american-musical-theatre.

Giroux, Henry A. *The Mouse That Roared: Disney and the End of Innocence*. Lanham, MD: Rowman & Littlefield, 2010.

Goldstein, Michael. "Broadway's New Beast." *New York Magazine*, March 14, 1994, 40–45.

Grady, Constance. "Is *Beauty and the Beast* 'a Tale as Old as Stockholm Syndrome'? Depends How You Read It." *Vox*, March 23, 2017. https://www.vox.com/culture/2017/3/23/15000768/beauty-and-the-beast-feminist-stockholm-syndrome.

Grob, Samuel. "Just for Fun? The Politics of Representation and Critical Education in High School Musical Theater." BA thesis, Yale University, 2021. https://educationstudies.yale.edu/sites/default/files/files/Sammy_Grob_FinalCapstone.pdf.

Gubar, Marah. "Urchins Unite: *Newsies* as an Antidote to Annie." In *Children, Childhood, and Musical Theatre*, edited by James Leve and Donelle Ruwe, 138–163. New York: Routledge, 2020.

Haas, Lynda, and Shaina Trapedo. "Disney Corporation." In *The Routledge Companion to Media and Fairy-Tale Cultures*, edited by Pauline Greenhill, Jill Terry Rudy, Naomi Hamer, and Lauren Bosc, 178–187. London: Routledge, 2018.

Hackett, Susanne R. "'Let It Go' as Radical Mantra: Subverting the Princess Narrative in *Frozen*." In *Recasting the Disney Princess in an Era of New Media and Social Movements*, edited by Shearon Roberts, 211–226. Lanham, MD: Lexington, 2020.

Haddad, Kary Thomas. "'This Is How It Feels': The Lived Experience of High School Musical Theater." DMA diss., Boston University, 2018. https://search.proquest.com/docview/2024228267/abstract/C6F639F4A41E46C0PQ/1.

Hamilton, Paula, and Rhyannon Dynes. "From 'Tiaras and Twirls' to 'Action and Adventure': Eliciting Children's Gendered Perceptions of Disney Characters through Participatory Visual Methodology." *International Journal of Early Years Education* 31, no. 2 (2023): 482–501.

Hanna, Maddie. "Central Bucks Students Say District Killed Production of Musical 'Rent.'" *Philadelphia Inquirer*, April 16, 2022. https://www.inquirer.com/education/central-bucks-west-rent-musical-lgbtq-censorship-20220416.html.

Haverkate, Julie, ed. *Newsies Production Handbook*. https://issuu.com/mtivault/docs/newsies_production_handbook.

Horowitz, Rob. "Evaluation of the Broadway Junior–ArtsConnection Program in Three New York City Public Schools." New York City Department of Education, 2001.

John, Ryan. "Part of It All: The High School Musical as a Community of Practice." *Visions of Research in Music Education* 24 (2014): 29.

Jordan, Dave. "Students Speak on Columbia High School Play Being Postponed Due to Concerns over Its Content." WITN, December 7, 2022. https://www.witn.com/2022/12/08/columbia-high-school-play-postponed-due-concerns-over-its-content/.

Ka'ili, Tēvita. "Goddess Hina: The Missing Heroine from Disney's *Moana*." Huffington Post, December 6, 2016. www.huffingtonpost.com/entry/goddess-hina-the-missing-heroine-fromdisney%CA%BCs-moana_us_5839f343e4b0a79f7433b6e5.

Kiyomi, Kutsuzawa. "Disney's Pocahontas: Reproduction of Gender, Orientalism, and the Strategic Construction of Racial Harmony in the Disney Empire." *Asian Journal of Women's Studies* 6, no. 4 (2000): 39–65.

Kunze, Peter C. *Staging a Comeback: Broadway, Hollywood, and the Disney Renaissance*. New Brunswick, NJ: Rutgers University Press, 2023.

Lacroix, Celeste. "Images of Animated Others: The Orientalization of Disney's Cartoon Heroines from *The Little Mermaid* to *The Hunchback of Notre Dame*." *Popular Communication* 2, no. 4 (2004): 213–229.

Larson, Reed W., and Jane R. Brown. "Emotional Development in Adolescence: What Can Be Learned from a High School Theater Program?" *Child Development* 78, no. 4 (2007): 1083–1099. http://www.jstor.org/stable/4620691.

Lassell, Michael. "Disney's *Beauty and the Beast*." In *Disney on Broadway*, edited by Michael Lassell, 16–57. New York: Disney Editions, 2002.

Lassell, Michael. *The Little Mermaid: From the Deep Blue Sea to the Great White Way*. New York: Disney Editions, 2008.

Leve, James, and Donelle Ruwe. "Introduction." In *Children, Childhood, and Musical Theater*, edited by James Leve and Donelle Ruwe, 1–19. London: Routledge, 2020.

Macaluso, Michael. "The Postfeminist Princess: Public Discourse and Disney's Curricular Guide to Feminism." In *Disney, Culture, and Curriculum*, ed. Jennifer A. Sandlin and Julie C. Garlin, 73–85. London: Routledge, 2016.

Miller, James. "Longest-Running Shows on Broadway." Playbill, March 13, 2023. https://playbill.com/article/long-runs-on-broadway-com-109864.

Mouzakis, Sotirios. "Princess of a Different Kingdom: Cultural Imperialism, Female Heroism, and the Global Performance of Walt Disney's *Mulan* and *Moana*." In *Heroism as a Global Phenomenon in Contemporary Culture*, edited by Barbara Korte, Simon Wendt, and Nicole Falkenhayner, 61–80. London: Routledge, 2019. Music Theater International. "*Moana JR*. ShowKit." https://www.mtishows.com/sites/default/files/moana_jr.-_a_note_on_culture.pdf.

Nadworny, Elissa. "The Most Popular High School Plays and Musicals." NPR, July 30, 2020. https://www.npr.org/sections/ed/2019/07/31/427138970/the-most-popular-high-school-plays-and-musicals.

Natanson, Hannah. "The Culture War's Latest Casualty: The High School Musical." *Washington Post*, May 2, 2023. https://www.washingtonpost.com/education/2023/05/02/banned-school-plays-musical-theater-censorship/.

Osatinski, Amy S. *Disney Theatrical Productions: Producing Broadway Musicals the Disney Way*. New York: Routledge, 2019.

Paulson, Michael. "It's Getting Hard to Stage a School Play without Political Drama." *New York Times*, July 4, 2023. https://www.nytimes.com/2023/07/04/theater/school-plays-politics.html.

"Play Survey Reveals 2023's Most Popular High School Shows." Educational Theatre Association, 5 June 2023. https://schooltheatre.org/2023-play-survey-reveals-most-popular-high-school-shows/.

"Produce Your Very Own Disney Show!" Music Theatre International. https://www.mtishows.com/disney-shows.

"Reimagining Disney Classics: *Beauty and the Beast*." Music Theatre International, September 26, 2022. https://www.mtishows.com/reimagining-disney-classics-beauty-and-the-beast-2.

Rich, Frank. "Throw Away Those Scripts. Some of the Greatest Moments Were Wordless." *New York Times*, December 29, 1991. https://www.nytimes.com/1991/12/29/theater/year-arts-theater-1991-throw-away-those-scripts-some-greatest-moments-were.html.

Sammond, Nicholas. *Babes in Tomorrowland: Walt Disney and the Making of the American Child, 1930–1960*. Durham, NC: Duke University Press, 2005.

Shokhoff, Carol. "Three Broadway Junior Case Studies." New York City Department of Education, 2009.

Streeter, Joshua Rashon. "Broadway Junior: Musical Theatre for Youth Performers." MFA thesis, University of Texas at Austin, 2016.

Streiff, Madeline, and Lauren Dundes. "From Shapeshifter to Lava Monster: Gender Stereotypes in Disney's *Moana*." *Social Sciences* 6, no. 3 (2017): 91.

Swan, Susan Z. "Gothic Drama in Disney's *Beauty and the Beast*: Subverting Traditional Romance by Transcending the Animal-Human Paradox." *Critical Studies in Mass Communication* 16, no. 3 (September 1999): 350–369. https://doi.org/10.1080/15295039909367100.

Thomas, Aaron C. "Dancing toward Masculinity: *Newsies*, Gender and Desire." In *The Disney Musical on Stage and Screen*, edited by George Rodosthenous, 155–168. New York: Bloomsbury, 2017.

Trahan, Erika (commenter). "When Shows Require Diversity but the School Is Not Diverse." Educational Theatre Association, January 19, 2019. https://community.schooltheatre.org/communities/community-home/digestviewer/viewthread?GroupId=133&MID=15389.

Warner, Rebecca. "The Beauty and the Beast Trope in Modern Musical Theatre." *Studies in Musical Theatre* 9, no. 1 (March 2015): 31–51.

Watkins, Ric Lynn. "The Musical Theater Experience and the Extent to Which It Affects High School Students." PhD diss., University of Illinois at Urbana-Champaign, 2005, https://search.proquest.com/docview/305001887/abstract/C718971B450F4D35PQ/1.

Weidman-Winter, Rebecca. "Belle: Beyond the Classic Story for a Modern Audience." In *Recasting the Disney Princess in an Era of New Media and Social Movements*, edited by Shearon Roberts, 119–210. New York: Lexington, 2020.

Whitfield, Sarah. "'For the First Time in Forever': Locating *Frozen* as a Feminist Disney Musical." In *The Disney Musical on Stage and Screen: Critical Approaches from "Snow White" to "Frozen,"* edited by George Rodosthenous, 221–238. New York: Bloomsbury Methuen Drama, 2017.

Wolf, Stacy. *Beyond Broadway: The Pleasure and Promise of Musical Theater across America*. New York: Oxford University Press, 2020.

Wolf, Stacy. "*Hamilton's* Women." *Studies in Musical Theatre* 12, no. 2 (2018): 167–180.

Wollman, Elizabeth L. "The Economic Development of the 'New' Times Square and Its Impact on the Broadway Musical." *American Music* 20, no. 4 (Winter 2002): 445–465.

Yassa, Nevine A. "High School Involvement in Creative Drama." *Research in Drama Education* 4, no. 1 (1999): 37–49. https://doi.org/10.1080/1356978990040104.

Yoshinaga, Ida. "Disney's *Moana*, the Colonial Screenplay, and Indigenous Labor Extraction in Hollywood Fantasy Films." *Narrative Culture* 6, no. 2 (2019): 188–215. muse.jhu.edu/article/741296.

CHAPTER 26

"THERE MAY BE SOMETHING THERE THAT WASN'T THERE BEFORE": NEW SONGS IN DISNEY'S BROADWAY MUSICALS

ALEX BÁDUE

In an article from December 1991, theater critic Frank Rich reminisced and re-evaluated "the year in the arts" and concluded that the best Broadway score of the year had been that for Disney's animated film *Beauty and the Beast*, "the hit that got away."[1] Certainly, not only that film but the entire Disney animation "Renaissance" of the late 1980s through the 1990s relied on and owed its success to musical theater structure and the dramatic functions of songs. For *The Little Mermaid* (1989), *Beauty and Beast*, and *Aladdin* (1992), the studio hired composer Alan Menken and lyricist Howard Ashman, whose musical theater backgrounds included off-Broadway works (including the hit *Little Shop of Horrors* in 1982) and who approached animated films as they did stage musicals. Menken confirms, "From the beginning, when writing the score for [*Beauty and the Beast*] ... Howard Ashman and I structured it as a stage musical. We wanted each song to push the plot forward. Our characters sing about their thoughts and feelings, telling the story. It's entirely musical theater."[2]

In the middle of that Renaissance, Disney spread its wings to Broadway and founded Disney Theatrical Productions in New York City. The stage version of *Beauty and the Beast* opened on Broadway in April 1994, two months before *The Lion King* opened in movie theaters. For this new endeavor, creative teams had to expand the plots, characters, and scores of the original films. Animation in particular poses the challenge of turning cartoons into live musical theater. Casey Nicholaw, director of *Aladdin* on Broadway, validates this, saying that in the process of adapting the film for the stage, "we had to shift the emphasis from the visual effects to the singing and dancing, from an adventure story to a classic Broadway musical comedy. We got rid of the animals and added more songs."[3] While the adaptation process differs for each Disney Broadway musical and with varying degrees of success, all of them transformed a film musical (not all of which are animations) into a two-act Broadway musical and introduced new songs that oblige the new versions of the plots to comply with musical theater aesthetics. As Thomas Schumacher, who headed Disney Theatrical when *The Little Mermaid* was adapted to Broadway, put it, "the stage version is not just the translation of a film to the stage, it's a translation of a film musical back to the stage."[4]

This chapter demonstrates the dramatic functions that new songs in Disney's Broadway musicals acquire and the character development that they promote when film musicals are adapted to stage productions. New songs expose characters' personality traits or backstories, give them an opportunity to sing about their dreams and aspirations for the future, and explore their growth and changes after they have gotten what they wanted. Characters who do not sing in the films get songs in the Broadway versions; characters who do sing in the films acquire at least one additional song that deepens their dramatic journey in ways not seen in the films. New songs replace events that can be animated but not staged (such as Ariel and Flounder being persecuted by a shark). While these new songs fulfill these dramatic functions, they also facilitate the task of adapting a film to the stage, because they expand the plot substantially, enough for an eighty-to-ninety-minute film to become a two-act book musical. These new songs change the structure and some of the content of the original film musicals, but they do not eliminate the essence of the plots and characters with which audiences identify, resulting in a theatrical experience that adheres to Disney's commercial drive to provide (and sell) different means to enjoy (and consume) its products.

I analyze the new songs based on three categories: new songs for the protagonists, new songs for the villains, and new songs that enhance characterization of supporting female characters. Representative cases come from Disney stage musicals that played on Broadway from *Beauty and the Beast* to *Frozen* (2018), including *The Lion King* (1997), *Tarzan* (2006), *Mary Poppins* (2006), *The Little Mermaid* (2008), *Newsies* (2012), and *Aladdin* (2014).[5] The chapter does not include all of the new songs composed for these musicals but focuses on the ones that concern or inform the main plots and characters. This chapter also does not concern songs from the original films that remained in the stage version but went through significant modification in lyrics ("Arabian Nights"), were placed in a different part of the plot ("Santa Fe," "Let It Go"), were inserted into a sequence different from the film ("Supercalifragilisticexpialidocious"), or featured new dance breaks ("Be Our Guest," "Gaston," "Under the Sea").

New Songs for the Protagonists

While Disney's musical films are in some ways structured like a Broadway musical and character development happens through songs, their Broadway counterparts were expanded with songs that amplify the protagonists' emotional journey and explore dramatic situations that do not occur in the film, or if they do, they do not happen in song.

The new songs for the protagonists fulfill three specific dramatic functions. First, a key moment in a musical is the "I Am" or "I Want" number, a song that functions as an inner monologue through which characters sing about themselves and/or their aspirations and establish essential aspects of their personalities and backstories that the rest of the plot will develop. These numbers often appear early in the first act. While Disney's Broadway musicals maintain the "I Am" and/or "I Want" numbers from the films ("Part of Your World," "Belle," "One Jump Ahead," "I Just Can't Wait to Be King," "Santa Fe"), the stage musicals contain additional songs that articulate how the protagonists come to terms with their identities and dreams. Second, the stage musicals include a number in the second act that allows the protagonists to sing about their life after they have attained what they wanted. This is a considerable difference from the films, whose second half rarely features the protagonists singing new music. Third, some new songs in Disney's Broadway musicals fulfill the dramatic function of the eleven o'clock number. The protagonist of a musical often sings this number toward the end of their journey, before the denouement. The character reflects on how far they have gone, and by the end of the song, they have decided which action to take toward the resolution of their conflict.[6] In the process of turning films into stage shows, the creative teams of Disney Broadway musicals identified these key moments for the protagonists to sing, and new songs were added to the narratives, expanding characterization in ways that enlarge the action and dialogue of the films.

Beauty and the Beast

Both Belle and the Beast receive new songs in Act I that function as interior monologues. Belle sings "Home" after she agrees to replace her father in the Beast's castle. She understands her fears and starts off on a journey beyond her village. In the film, she finds herself alone in her new room but does not break into song. In the stage version, she sings about her happy home in the past and wonders if the same can be found in the palace. The song expands the theme of home and family touched on in the film but not in song. "Home" also becomes another song for Mrs. Potts, who sings a reprise to Belle in order to encourage the heroine to see the castle as more than an overwhelming building. It is, after all, the home of everyone there. Mrs. Potts consoles Belle by singing the same melody, revealing herself to be a helper in Belle's journey, a role that other objects in the castle will assume later in the plot.

In the film, the Beast sings only a verse of "Something There," but in the musical, he acquires his own songs. He first has a brief solo, "How Long Must This Go On?," after Belle refuses to eat with him. The Beast reflects on the fact that he is paying for past carelessness and now has to deal with rejection. He sees himself as "an object of revulsion and derision." It is his "I Am" song, as he recognizes his own plight. The ballad "If I Can't Love Her" also gives the Beast a musical voice that the character lacked in the film. The Beast confronts his reality and condition, which in the film occurs through some of his facial expressions but not dialogue or song. A combination of music from the prologue and new music, the song reveals the human beneath the bestial skin. After scolding Belle for almost touching the rose, which forces her to run away from the castle, the Beast—in the course of the song— realizes his mistake, feels ashamed, tries to cope with his monstrosity, and admits that if he does not learn to love her, he will remain a beast forever. This is a crucial scene and song for both Belle and the Beast, and the song brings the first act to an end. In the words of composer Menken, the "song was put in specifically for the act break of a Broadway show."[7] He continues, "as the Act One curtain falls, if we've done our job correctly, the audience is left with a cliff-hanger. It all seems hopeless, for the Beast has driven Belle away, and yet there is still a glimmer of hope."[8] Linda Woolverton, who wrote both the film's screenplay and the musical's book, confirms that the song was crucial for rewriting the Beast's character. According to her, "When I first heard Alan Menken play the song, I knew that I had to make sure the Beast evolved naturally into a character who could sing such an emotional powerful song."[9] She made changes to the character's language in the spoken dialogue and added personality traits and stage directions that highlight the fact that the Beast is ultimately a man.[10]

Both Belle and the Beast have numbers in the second act that allow them to sing about their lives after they have attained what they wanted. The Beast reprises "If I Can't Love Her" when he allows Belle to go back to her father. Lyricist Tim Rice added a twist to the Beast's lyrics, as he now sings, "no point anymore, if she can't love me." This is a subtle way to reveal that the Beast has fallen in love with Belle but believes it is unrequited love. Despite the crescendo in the music as the Beast sings the reprise, he ends the song in a low pitch and without holding it, reinforcing his hopelessness. The Beast surrenders himself to his fate in song, which did not happen in the film. In her "I Want" song, "Belle (Reprise)," Belle wants "much more than this provincial life," an "adventure in the great wide somewhere," and "someone who understands." After she meets and learns to love the Beast, she ponders how much the experience changed her. In the first four years of *Beauty and the Beast* on Broadway, Belle only sang about this change in a portion of "Something There" that is identical to the film. In 1998, the character received a brand-new song, "A Change in Me," in which she reunites with her father and expresses how finding a home in the castle and living with the Beast have made her grow.[11] "A Change in Me" functions as Belle's eleven o'clock number and fleshes out this iconic Disney princess in ways not seen in any other film in which she appears, and the changes for Broadway were intentional. In the animated film, Belle is fierce, "a heroine for the nineties—not just beautiful and virtuous, but also smart and strong-willed, unafraid to challenge the Beast."[12] Woolverton has said about adapting Belle to the stage, "We felt strongly about making her an intelligent woman—woman, not girl—who could be accepted as a good role model.... At the same time, she has to have the qualities of a fairy-tale heroine."[13]

The Lion King

Simba does not receive a new number in Act I, but in Act II he gets to a point in his journey when he needs answers about his past. After a conversation with Timon and

Pumbaa about what the stars represent, Simba remembers that his father once told him that the stars are kings of the past looking down (this, in turn, is presented in a new song for Mufasa in Act I, "They Live in You"). After Timon and Pumbaa laugh at that idea, Simba needs a moment alone. He leaves his friends and gazes at the stars. In the film, the dust and leaves that fly away when he lies down travel through the savanna until they reach Rafiki, who realizes that Simba is alive. In the stage musical, the dust and leaves are replaced with a new song, "Endless Night" (which also reaches Rafiki). Simba addresses the stars, hoping that his father can hear him. He asks for the guidance that Mufasa promised to Simba when he was a cub. Similar to "A Change in Me," "Endless Night" dramatizes the protagonist interrogating himself after realizing that he has grown. The stage version of *The Lion King* thus provides a strong contrast between the naive dreams of young Simba in his "I Want" song, "I Just Can't Wait to Be King," with the harsh reality of growing up and understanding how the past affects who we become as adults. Despite the song's importance to Simba's journey, "Endless Night" is not the musical's eleven o'clock number. This is "He Lives in You (Reprise)," sung by Rafiki. During this number, Simba sees Mufasa and learns the lesson that he has to face his past.

Tarzan

New musical numbers with similar dramatic functions to those observed in *Beauty and the Beast* and *The Lion King* also occur in the stage version of *Tarzan*, but this musical should be framed with a special caveat. The 1999 film was not a traditional animated musical because the characters do not sing. With the exception of Kala's brief "You'll Be in My Heart" and Terk's "Trashin' the Camp" (both of which appear in the stage version), the other songs were all sung by Phil Collins (who also wrote them) as a disembodied narrative voice that comments on or describes the action. All songs from the film were adapted into conventional book numbers for Broadway (sung by the main characters), and Collins wrote new songs for the stage.[14] "I Need to Know" is Tarzan's "I Am"/"I Want" song. It occurs when the protagonist is still a child and tries to understand his identity as he realizes that he does not look like the others in his community and that the difference causes pain to everyone involved.[15] "Everything That I Am" is Tarzan's eleven o'clock number, sung after he identifies with other humans. Adult Tarzan sees his younger self, who reprises "I Need to Know," and then sings about being torn between life with the apes and his newfound humanity. The song is a microcosm of the character's journey in the musical. He starts the number asking questions that connect to his "I Am" song: "I got to know where I came from, I got to know the reason why I'm here." Toward the end of the song, Tarzan concludes that he is a man, and his questions become assertions: "I know where I belong, I know where I came from … the future is clear for me to see, to be the man I'm meant to be."[16] These two solo songs explore Tarzan's sense of belonging, and how he sees the family he acquires by growing up with the gorillas versus the one he discovers after he meets other humans, and the tensions between the two.

Mary Poppins

The screen-to-stage adaptations of *Mary Poppins* resulted in an "I Am" song for the protagonist. In the 1964 film, Mary's first song is "A Spoonful of Sugar," and her quirky personality is introduced in spoken dialogue with Mr. Banks, Jane, and Michael. After she "measures" the kids' personalities, she does her own, and the tape measure indicates "Mary Poppins, practically perfect in every way." Richard and Robert Sherman, who wrote the songs for the film, initially wrote a song titled "Practically Perfect" for Mary to sing in that moment. However, the music for that song was later adapted into "Sister Suffragette," as a means to convince Glynis Johns to play Mrs. Banks, leaving the film without an "I Am" song.[17] Composer George Stiles and lyricist Anthony Drewe found that spot to be ideal for a song in the stage musical and wrote their own version of "Practically Perfect," which captures Mary's essence and shows that her character is "spit-spot spic and span." Mary literally describes who she is: "Both prim and proper and never too stern, / well-educated yet willing to learn."[18] While the film's Mary Poppins exudes self-confidence through magic tricks and admiring herself in mirrors, her stage counterpart adds a new song to showcase similar personality traits that define the protagonist.

The Little Mermaid

While "Home" in *Beauty and the Beast* comes after Belle's "I Am"/"I Want" number, in the stage version of *The Little Mermaid*, the new number for Ariel in Act I precedes "Part of Your World." Ariel sings her first solo song, "The World Above," upon her first entrance onstage, before she even speaks. The number replaces the scene in the film in which Ariel and Flounder escape from a shark. Now Ariel swims and sings about how comfortable she is above water. This adds to her characterization in a way that does not happen in the film. Book writer Doug Wright wanted "to make it clear that Ariel's longing is not so much for the prince, but for a world in which she feels truly realized on her own terms, and it's important that she voice those aspirations before she even meets a prince."[19] She expresses her "fish-out-of-water" situation in the lyrics, "It's like my life was wrong and somehow, now, at last I'm in my own skin, up here in the world above."[20] The song introduces Ariel singing about her desire to be part of that world, and how much of an outsider she is in her own.

Like Belle, Ariel has a number in the second act in which she sings about her life after she has attained what she wanted. In "Beyond My Wildest Dreams," Ariel is finally a human and part of the world she always dreamed about. She now gets to express her excitement in song. The number is literally a sung inner monologue, since Ariel does not have her voice and the other characters cannot hear her. It also voices the servants of the castle, who wonder about Ariel. "The World Above" and "Beyond My Wildest Dreams" expand Ariel's character in song in ways not seen in the film and support intentional changes made to the protagonist for the stage adaptation. Ariel now takes matters into her own hands, and as director Francesca Zambello stated, Ariel's "ambitions are bigger than any one man.... She creates her own dilemma and resolves it."[21] Wright confirms, claiming that changes for Ariel parallel those made for Prince Eric: "I wanted to make sure that Ariel, when she falls for Prince Eric, is captivated by more than just a pretty face. We made him an outsider in his own world, too; instead of ascending to the throne as expected, he wants to break free and sail the high seas. He's no more at home on land than Ariel is 'under the sea.' So they are both strangers in the worlds they inhabit.... And in Ariel's final confrontation with Ursula, we felt she should save herself, not be rescued by a male figure."[22]

The Little Mermaid features an eleven o'clock number that adds complexity to the protagonists thanks to its format as a quartet. "If Only" is a series of interior monologues by Ariel, Prince Eric, Sebastian, and Triton that coalesce into one song. Ariel knows that she has a deadline and is about to lose everything, Eric does not know that Ariel is the girl he saw on the beach with the beautiful voice, Sebastian wishes he could make Ariel's dream come true without Ursula's curse, and Triton realizes that Ariel has been missing for days and wishes she would come back so he can change his ways and try to understand her. By the end of the quartet, the characters all know that they have to take some initiative in order to get what they want. Menken made creative choices to connect the characters musically in the quartet. The aquatic characters (Ariel, Sebastian, and Triton) sing the same music throughout, while Eric reuses music from his earlier song "Her Voice." Toward the end of the number, however, Eric sings to the melody of "Part of Your World," providing a musical subtext of the connection he feels with Ariel. A quartet in the eleven o'clock slot amplifies what we learn about each character's thoughts and conveys the actions that they have to take toward the musical's denouement.

Aladdin

Aladdin gets an additional number in Act I that develops the protagonist beyond his "I Am" song, "One Jump Ahead." The added song, "Proud of Your Boy," which immediately follows the reprise of "One Jump Ahead," function as his "I Want" song. In spoken dialogue earlier in the act, Aladdin has revealed that his mother passed away two months earlier, and now he is trying to change his ways and not steal anymore. "Proud of Your Boy" exposes Aladdin's insecurities and the fact that his mother was a big presence in his life. It clarifies Aladdin's intentions in ways that differ from the film. When Aladdin meets the Genie and learns about the three wishes, he does not want to just impress Jasmine but also to make his mother proud and redeem his mischievous past. Aladdin's mother was a character in early versions of the film, and the song was initially written as the film's main ballad (by Menken and Ashman). After Ashman died, the mother and the song were both cut, which led to Menken and Rice writing a new ballad, "A Whole New World."[23] "Proud of Your Boy" was restored for the stage musical even if the mother was not, and Aladdin sings it in memory of her. Similar to Ariel's "The World Above," "Proud of Your Boy" offers an additional window into the protagonist's yearnings before he embarks on the journey that changes his life. Aladdin reprises the song as the eleven o'clock number, when he considers the dilemma of whether to "tell the truth, lose the princess; keep the princess, live a lie." He concludes that he will make his mother proud by telling Jasmine the truth about his real identity.

Frozen

The stage version of *Frozen* includes a greater number of new songs than the stage adaptations discussed above because its plot includes two protagonists who change and grow, Elsa and Anna. "Do You Want to Build a Snowman?" and "For the First Time in Forever" develop Anna's character the same way as in the film. She wants to reconnect with her sister, understand why Elsa keeps her distance, and experience life beyond the palace. The stage musical develops their journeys and relationship with five additional songs: "A Little Bit of You," "Dangerous to Dream," "I Can't Lose You," "Monster," and "True Love." "A Little Bit of You" is a duet for young Elsa and Anna while they play in the bedroom. They build Olaf, and Elsa hurts Anna, which is a spoken scene in the film. The princesses sing the same melody, representing their sisterhood and bond. Later in Act I, "A Little Bit of You" is revealed to be diegetic: Anna and Kristoff hear it sung in the mountain (by Olaf, immediately before he enters), and Anna says, "I know that song. How do I know that song?," symbolizing the fact that Anna had not entirely forgotten the memory of building Olaf with Elsa.

"Dangerous to Dream" complicates the "I Am" and "I Want" expressions of both sisters. Elsa sings this song as an inner monologue during her coronation. She balances the conflict of knowing who she is (not a monster because of her power, which she has learned to control) and how she is perceived as queen and Anna's big sister. Elsa wishes to tell Anna the truth and "make choices of [her] own," but she has to be careful. She is also happy that she has delivered what she promised to her father (to conceal, not feel, and become queen). "Dangerous to Dream" develops how Elsa does not know how to handle her fears, which occurs in the film but not in song, and it offers Elsa a song between the two numbers through which Anna's character is developed in Act I (and in the film), "For the First Time in Forever" and "Love Is an Open Door." Considering that in the stage version "Let It Go" is moved to later in the plot and occupies the Act I finale, "For the First in Forever" is Anna's "I Want" song, "Dangerous to Dream" is Elsa's "I Want" song, and "Let It Go" becomes Elsa's song of self-recognition and growth.

The second act of *Frozen* as it was performed on Broadway furthers the characterization of the two protagonists in song, especially if compared with the second half of the film. The duet "I Can't Lose You" was added to the musical during the Broadway run in February 2020, replacing the reprise of "For the First Time in Forever." The song occurs in the scene when Anna arrives at Elsa's hideaway castle and tries to convince Elsa that they do not have to live apart. Elsa, however, having just found the depth of her own power, wants to be alone, which she sees as a way of protecting Anna. "I Can't Lose You" is a sung dialogue that keeps the conversational aspect of "For the First Time in

Forever (Reprise)." As in "A Little Bit of You," Elsa and Anna sing the same melody. Sarah Whitfield writes that in the film, Elsa and Anna "at no point sing together in unison or in harmony, and [this] functions as a way to express conflict."[24] "I Can't Lose You" delivers what Whitfield hoped a potential Broadway adaptation would do: introduce a song "in which two women in the same place sing together to and with one another about something other than a boy."[25]

In the film, neither Elsa nor Anna sings after the reprise of "For the First Time in Forever," but in the stage version, two numbers in Act II provide moments of reflection for both princesses. "Monster" is Elsa's when she questions herself, her journey, and her identity. The number fulfills the dramatic convention of an eleven o'clock number. Elsa fights the notion that she is the monster people say she is because of her inability to control her power. She considers whether to keep hiding or embrace the identity she discovered during "Let It Go," which leads to her decision to surrender to Hans and ignite the musical's denouement. "True Love" is Anna's moment after she finds out about Hans's true goals and is left alone to freeze (before Olaf arrives to help her). She meditates on how her lonely childhood drove her to rush into an engagement with Hans. The ballad "True Love" is Anna's first and only solo number; until then, she only sings in duets. However, "True Love" became associated with Patti Murin, who originated Anna on Broadway, and the song was cut after Murin left the Broadway production in February 2020.

New Songs for the Villains

Not only do the protagonists get additional songs in Disney's Broadway musicals, but the villains do, too. These new songs provide more depth to the characters and context for their evil schemes. The new songs provide additional background information about the villains that we do not see in the films. The songs shed light on the roots of their evilness and how it changes throughout the plot. Even some of the musical styles that the composers chose for the villains' new songs indicate aspects of their characters that we do not get in their film counterparts. The only exception is Clayton in *Tarzan*, who remained without a song in the stage adaptation.

Gaston in *Beauty and the Beast* appears in three songs in the film—"Belle," "Gaston," and "The Mob Song"—which is more than any villain in any other Disney film. In the stage version, he sings all of these plus two additional songs, "Me" and "Maison des Lunes." The former appears in his first scene alone with Belle early in the first act. It starts out as a solo (as he envisions their married life), but it turns into a duet when Belle joins the singing and dialogues in song with Gaston's preposterous points. "Maison des Lunes" occurs in a Dickensian scene that allows another singing opportunity for Lefou and one for Monsieur D'Arque. With Gaston, they plan to have Belle's father sent to an insane asylum. Book writer Woolverton emphasizes that one of the questions that *Beauty and the Beast* posits is who actually is a beast: "The Beast is someone with a beastly exterior and a human interior.... In contrast, Gaston has a handsome exterior and a beastly interior. As the story evolves, the two switch places—the Beast becomes more human, and Gaston's beastly nature is revealed."[26] Although this occurs in both the film and the Broadway musical, the addition of songs for Gaston drives the point home. In "Me," he uses his good looks and charm to seduce Belle. In "Maison des Lunes," his "beastly interior" gains more prominence than when he first concocted the plan in "Gaston (Reprise)" and reveals his true evilness, which culminates with the intention to kill the Beast in "The Mob Song." He thus becomes a rounded villainous character.

In the film *The Lion King*, there was going to be a reprise of Scar's "Be Prepared" when the villain takes over the kingdom, but it was eventually cut. For that reason, the spot in the plot for a song already existed when the stage adaptation was done, and the creative team added "The Madness of King Scar." The new king sings about the changes in the land after his ascension and betrays his paranoia about being compared with Mufasa. He also makes advances toward Nala to have an heir, which leads to her being expelled from Pride Rock. As Thomas S. Hischak and Mark A. Robinson write about the song, "The stream-of-consciousness number alternates between buffoonish comedy and cold-blooded evil."[27] The song went through some cuts in 2010, when the creative team made the show a little shorter.[28] Because the singing that remains is done by the hyenas and not Scar, the new song is more about plot—life in Pride Rock during Scar's reign—than enhancing a villain through song.

Julian Fellowes's book for *Mary Poppins* features a backstory for understanding Mr. Banks, his childhood, and the distance he felt from his parents, which is exacerbated when the nanny he had as a child, Miss Andrew, returns. The character comes from P. L. Travers's books and was added to plot of the musical because the story did not have a villain.[29] She sings "Brimstone and Treacle" early in Act II, in her scene with the children (after Mary Poppins leaves at the end of Act I). The song provides a contrast between the nannies, which, in turn, reveals contrasts between Mr. Banks and his own children. Miss Andrew's elixir to discipline the children, made with "brimstone and treacle and carbolic soap," is the opposite of Mary's "spoonful of sugar."[30] In fact, when Mary returns, she reprises the song to confront Miss Andrew and juxtaposes the theme from "A Spoonful of Sugar" against Miss Andrew's "Brimstone and Treacle." Since *Mary Poppins* is about Mr. Banks's journey (he is, after all, the character who has a change of heart in the eleven o'clock number, "A Man Has Dreams [Reprise]"), it is a coherent choice that the villain of the story is connected to his backstory.

Similar to "Me" in *Beauty and the Beast*, Ursula's "I Want the Good Times Back" in *The Little Mermaid* is a new song that precedes the one the villain has in the film. Ursula now has her own "I Am"/"I Want" song, since "I Want the Good Times Back" provides her with a backstory. Inspired by early drafts of the film's script, Wright's book for the musical made Ursula and Triton siblings. Both inherited the ocean from their father, Poseidon, but when Ursula proved to be cruel and employed black magic, Triton took her half of the ocean from her. Now she seeks revenge. She tells this story at the beginning of "I Want the Good Times Back," and in the song's bridge, she, Flotsam, and Jetsam come up with the plan to get revenge through Triton's daughter Ariel. When Flotsam distinguishes Ariel as the daughter "with the beautiful voice," Ursula sings, "which she takes for granted. A woman doesn't know how precious her voice is until she's been silenced. Ha! Perhaps we could teach them both a lesson," implying that Ursula, too, has been silenced by Triton.[31] The song is performed in vaudeville style, with a syllabic, slow-tempo opening verse that introduces her backstory followed by a tuneful chorus in soft-shoe music (with fermatas in pickup measures and the bass emphasizing the first and third beats of the quadruple meter). Not only does this musical style add humor to the villain, but it also contrasts with the musical styles found in other songs of *The Little Mermaid*, depicting the past (here represented by vaudevillian music) as the "good times" for Ursula. The song thus establishes Ursula's personality and goals before "Poor Unfortunate Souls," and she reprises it in the second act when she sends Flotsam and Jetsam to block Ariel and Eric's kiss. After the Broadway run ended, however, the musical went through some rewriting, and the song was replaced with a new one that accomplishes a similar dramatic function, "Daddy's Little Angel," which is at the time of this writing how the musical is licensed.

The villain of *Newsies* is Joseph Pulitzer, publisher of the newspaper *New York World*. Guided by greed and chances to improve the newspaper's revenue, he increases the cost of the paper for the newsboys, who have to buy the papers and sell them for a higher price to make a profit. This happens early on in both the film and the stage versions of *Newsies* and leads to the strike that forms the bulk of the musical's plot. Pulitzer's decision does not occur in song in the film, but it does in the stage musical, and the creative team came up with two different songs for the scene. The first was "The News Is Getting Better," used during the musical's run at Paper Mill Playhouse in 2011. Menken chose ragtime, a popular form of music and a racialized music genre from the turn of the twentieth century (when the action of the musical takes place), to depict the carelessness with which Pulitzer makes his decision and the fact that he celebrates his success before even implementing the raise in cost for the newsboys. For the Broadway run, the song was replaced with "The Bottom Line," which fulfills the same dramatic function but with a more moderate swing instead of ragtime. In both songs, Pulitzer is aware of the burden he is causing for the boys and admits it is a cruel move, but the changes in musical style and tempo (in addition to changes in the lyrics) make Pulitzer's intention less celebratory and more malevolent.

The villain in the film *Aladdin*, Jafar, sang only a brief reprise of "Prince Ali" in the final confrontation scene, when he reveals that Prince Ali and Aladdin are the same person. While this was maintained in the stage version, the creative team included a new song in Act I for Jafar and his sidekick, Iago (no longer a parrot in the stage version but a human). Initially, Jafar and Iago sang "Why Me," a song that Menken and Rice wrote for the film and which was restored in earlier performances of the musical. For the Broadway production, they replaced "Why Me" with the new "Diamond in the Rough." The song occurs in the scene when Jafar persuades Aladdin to enter the Cave of Wonders. The title "Diamond in the Rough" refers to the condition that must be met to enter the cave and the reason Jafar chooses Aladdin. Jafar and Iago mention both Aladdin's mother and Princess Jasmine, successfully convincing Aladdin that this is a chance for him to prove himself. This creates an effective dramatic link to two other new songs, "Proud of Your Boy" (discussed above) and "A Million Miles Away" (discussed below). As in previous musicals, Menken finds a different musical style to portray the villain in music. Similar to Ursula's soft-shoe and Pulitzer's ragtime, Jafar and Iago sing a tango with flamenco castanets in the accompaniment, which, in addition to providing humor to the scene, adds to their sinister, tempting, and even seducing goals.

In *Frozen*, the new song for the villain is "Hans of the Southern Isles," through which Prince Hans introduces himself to Anna. He induces her (and the audience) to believe that they are alike. Just as she is a princess who has lived a sheltered life, he is "someone even more embarrassing to be," a prince who is overshadowed by his twelve brothers and comes from a small place no one hears or sings about. The dramatic action is similar to that in the film: spectators are led to believe that he is the Prince Charming for Princess Anna. In the stage musical, this is articulated through a musical theater convention that tricks the audience: "Hans of the Southern Isles" functions as an "I Am" song early in Act I that sets a noble purpose that the character supposedly achieves by the end of the story (his true intentions are not revealed until late in Act II). Thus, Anna is persuaded to marry Hans not just because of what they sing in "Love Is an Open Door" but also because of what he sings in this purposefully deceiving ballad. He reprises "Hans of the Southern Isles" later in the act, when he assures the people of Arendelle that he truly loves Anna and can lead the kingdom in the absence of the queen and the princess. He is successful in his persuasion because the people reprise his melody as he prepares to go find Anna. Assuming that most audience members would be familiar with the film, they know that Hans is the villain of the story, and the song and its reprise become an "I Want" song through which Hans manipulates Anna and the people of Arendelle to get what he wants: power. Using musical theater conventions of the "I Am" number and singing the same music to indicate agreement, the stage version of *Frozen* masks Hans's villainy in an innovative way compared with the film's spoken dialogue.

New Songs for Supporting Female Characters

The new songs in Disney's Broadway musicals have also become means for the creative teams to revisit supporting female characters who were not developed in the films beyond their connection to male characters and turn them into more three-dimensional characters than their filmic counterparts. These include Rafiki (who was a male character in the film), Nala, and the lionesses in *The Lion King*; Mrs. Banks in *Mary Poppins*; Katherine in *Newsies*; and Jasmine in *Aladdin*. *Tarzan*—the only one of these musicals that flopped on Broadway—failed to accomplish changes in that regard, as exemplified by the new songs for Kala and Jane.[32]

The Lion King was directed by a woman, Julie Taymor, who purposefully enhanced the presence of female characters in the Broadway musical. It was clear for Taymor and the creative team that the plot was short on female characters, and those who did exist (especially Nala and Sarabi) needed development. This was combined with the fact that "Circle of Life" was not sung by any character and Taymor did not want the song to be sung offstage by a disembodied voice. Taymor's solution was to turn Rafiki into a female and from animal to human. This solved the singing in the opening number and added a female character to the plot. The musical's Rafiki is a *sangoma*, a South African shaman, and a storyteller.[33] She sings both the opening chant "Nants Ingonyama Bagithi Baba" and "Circle of Life." In addition, the actress who originated Rafiki on Broadway, Tsidii Le Loka, contributed a small but important portion of the score. Taymor believed that there should be a musical moment to mourn the death of Mufasa and the presumed death of Simba, and the result is the number "Rafiki Mourns."

The lionesses were also expanded in the stage musical in ways that surpass their characterization in the film. Taymor said, "I thought women were missing gravely from the story. The lionesses are really the ones who go out and get the food and run the show."[34] "The Lioness Hunt" is not a song but a dance number (choreographed by Garth Fagan). With music by Lebo M, the number occurs early in Act I and presents the lionesses as crucial to the dynamics of both Pride Rock and the savanna ecosystem. The number is demanding on the performers, who dance impressive body movements with masks on top of their heads. Of all the lionesses, adult Nala gains more depth and character development, especially with the song "Shadowland." Unlike in the film, Nala does not leave Pride Rock to look for food, but she goes because Scar makes lecherous advances toward her (as we saw in "The Madness of King Scar").[35] Taymor determined that Nala needed a number in Act II and chose the track "Lea Halalela" ("Holy Land"), originally sung in Setswana and written by Lebo M, Hans Zimmer, and Mark Mancina, from the recording *Rhythm of the Pride Lands* (1995), which became Nala's "Shadowland." She now expresses her pain at having witnessed the changes in the land since Scar became king, and she starts off on her own journey. Taymor wanted this number to pair with Simba's "Endless Night."[36] She believed that "[t]hese two ballads offered an opportunity to reveal the inner workings of Nala's and Simba's hearts and minds as well as helping to forward their stories."[37]

In *Mary Poppins*, Winifred Banks's drama comes from her struggle to accept what her husband expects of her. Richard Eyre, who directed the original London and Broadway productions, realized that Mrs. Banks should be expanded: "By the second or third of our sessions, I began to feel strongly that Winifred was very underrepresented and just by my saying that, everybody's views shifted and they started to contribute ideas of how Winifred's story should be presented in parallel with George's story."[38] According to book writer Fellowes, Travers's books do not provide much material to help expand the character.[39] Walt Disney himself had tackled the issue by making Winifred a comic character involved in the suffragette movement. For the stage adaptation, as Eyre explains, "Winifred Banks has to find that she actually wants the role of being wife and mother, that it will fulfill her, and that she will do it well. It is only when Mr. Banks is completely down that she discovers her strength, only when he starts to suffer and he needs her that she comes up to the challenge. That seemed to us to be a message that would speak to an audience today more than belittling her by making her a figure of fun."[40] Mrs. Banks sings in some of the new songs ("Cherry Tree Lane" and "Anything Can Happen") but also has her own number, "Being Mrs. Banks," which is her "I Am"/"I Want" monologue. She used to be an actress and now sings about her ideals and aspirations as she struggles to adjust to her new role as housewife in an upper-class home. She confirms her role as supportive housewife in the second-act reprise, which she sings to Mr. Banks when he confesses to having financial issues.

In *Newsies*, Katherine Plumber is a new character, one of only four female characters in the show. She is a composite of two characters from the film, Sarah Jacobs (Jack's love interest) and the *New York Sun* reporter Bryan Denton. This idea is credited to Harvey Fierstein's new book for the musical.[41] Katherine is Jack's love interest, but she fights for her voice to be heard and her skills as a journalist to be appreciated. As Isabel Cervantes writes, "Compared to Sarah Jacobs, whose character simplifies down to just caring about her younger brother Les and being generally nice, Katherine is witty and bold, with goals centered in trying to push the boundaries for what was expected of women at the time."[42] The new character also has her new song. In early readings of the musical, she had a song titled "The Story of My Life," which was then replaced with "Watch What Happens."[43] The song's fast tempo and witty rhymes depict Katherine as ambitious to make a name for herself, funny, and resourceful. She also sings a new love duet with Jack, "Something to Believe In." Chris Montan, the musical's executive music producer, pointed out the musical variety that Katherine brought to the score of *Newsies*: "As good as it was, the trouble with the film score was that it was a little bit too monochromatic. You know, "The World Will Know," "Seize the Day," ... all the big anthem songs. We needed to vary it for the stage, and I think a lot of what we added, like Pulitzer's song and Katherine's song and the love song, just changed the balance of the score so that it wasn't just anthems."[44] In the process of adapting the film to the stage, Fierstein, Menken and lyricist Jack Feldman made room for more character-driven songs than in the film, enhancing the characterization of Katherine.[45]

In the stage version of *Aladdin*, new songs developed Princess Jasmine's character, who in the film only sang the duet "A Whole New World." As Krystal Ghisyawan writes, "The 1992 animated film's depiction of Jasmine reiterated gender stereotypes of the region. She is an exoticized sexual 'other' and an oppressed other."[46] In the same trend of "Shadowland," "Being Mrs. Banks," and "Watch What Happens," Jasmine receives her own new song, "These Palace Walls," in the musical's first act. Jasmine had a song in the film that was ultimately cut, "Call Me a Princess" (by Menken and Ashman). It was used in earlier productions of the stage adaptation but was also cut before the musical reached Broadway. The new "These Palace Walls" allows Jasmine to sing about being forced to marry. Like Belle and Ariel, Jasmine has her "I Want" song to dream of a place beyond where she lives and what it takes to get there (although by the end of the musical, she is back in the palace to marry the man she chooses, Aladdin). Jasmine also has a new duet with Aladdin, "A Million Miles Away." They sing it when they first meet and express desires to live beyond the world they know. In the duet, Jasmine knows Aladdin's true identity, but he does not know hers, which is the opposite of the case in "A Whole New World," when he knows her true identity and she does not know his. "A Million Miles Away" follows a similar dramatic setting created for Eric and Ariel in the stage version of *The Little Mermaid*. It establishes that both Aladdin and Jasmine are unhappy and would rather live in the other's world.[47]

Kala and Jane in *Tarzan* do not follow the same pattern observed in these other supporting female characters. They are not expanded from their animated counterparts and lack independent voices in song. Kala sings "You'll Be in My Heart" when she adopts baby Tarzan at the beginning of the musical, and she sings a longer portion of the song than the character does in the film (which is partly sung by Collins commenting on the action). The longer singing in the musical, however, does not add to her character development or maternal instincts toward the baby human. The other new songs in which Kala participates are duets with her husband and leader of the gorilla tribe, Kerchak. "No Other Way" is technically a number for Kerchak, in which he insists that Tarzan is not one of them and must be banished. Kala tries to argue, but she never sings and, instead, interjects spoken lines into his singing. The moment when she makes the decision to leave with Tarzan occurs in spoken dialogue with underscoring. While this sung/spoken dialogue may be a subtext of the characters' different opinions, it prevents Kala from breaking into song to express herself. "Sure as Sun Turns to Moon" is constructed as a sung dialogue, in which Kala does sing with Kerchak. The number reveals that they love each other but that because of their differences regarding Tarzan, they cannot be together. They reprise the song when Kerchak is dying. With no other solo song for Kala, these make her journey entirely subservient to those of the male characters (Kerchak and Tarzan).

Jane gets more new songs than Kala, but her character journey remains strictly connected to Tarzan's. She has her "I Am" song in Act I, "Waiting for This Moment." Unlike Belle, Ariel, Jasmine, and Elsa, who all sing about a different place where they wish to go, Jane finds herself already in that place from her first entrance in the story. The number makes it clear that she feels at home in the jungle, finally encountering the flora that she studies. The song does not reveal anything about Jane other than this excitement. The moment is more efficient in stagecraft and visual spectacle than in dramatic development. As critic David Rooney pointed out, "One of the show's most elaborate visual sequences accompanies Jane's song 'Waiting for This Moment,' in which she wanders wide-eyed among undulating giant orchids as a ravishing moth flies overhead."[48] The Act I finale, "Different," mirrors the structure of "No Other Way." Jane's world has changed now that she has met Tarzan, but she does not sing in the number. She speaks her lines as Tarzan sings about how feels now that he has found someone new in the jungle. As in "No Other Way," the sung/spoken dialogue can represent the differences between Jane's and Tarzan's worlds, but it also prevents Jane from expressing herself more in song.

In Act II, Jane sings only in duets. "Like No Man I've Ever Seen" is a duet between Jane and her father about Tarzan, in which she finally explains in song the differences that she does not get to sing about in "Different." The song, however, serves more for the father to realize that his daughter is falling for Tarzan than for Jane to express her feelings. "For the

First Time" is Jane and Tarzan's love duet. She sings that "my world is changing," but the number confirms everything we have already learned about her feelings for Tarzan and fails to add anything new to her characterization.[49] Thus, Jane is a character who aligns more with early musical comedy female characters whose dramatic arc is not complete without men (her father and Tarzan) than the other supporting female characters Disney has brought to Broadway. Considering that the creative team of *Tarzan* reversed what Taymor did with Rafiki and turned Terk, a female character in the film, into a male character onstage, the musical falls short of enlarging female characters.

CONCLUSION

New songs from Disney's Broadway musicals open classic Disney films to new possibilities to employ the marriage of music and narrative that defines both the stage and film musical. They bring additional opportunities for the protagonists and villains to express themselves and ponder over their journeys in song. They allow characters who did not sing in the film to sing and be developed through song. They enhance the characterization of supporting characters. In the process of expanding the films into conventional Broadway musicals with enough music for a few hours in the theater, these new songs enliven protagonists and subplots. Although the levels of success vary depending on the musical, the new songs add "something there that wasn't there before" and create a variation of the film with enough to make it innovative.

The Disney company often reimagines its products for profit. The franchises of the titles discussed in this chapter comprise of not just film (including live-action remakes) and Broadway musicals, but also toys, accessories, as well as presence in theme parks, Disney on Ice, Disney channel, Disney+, and Disney Cruise. The Broadway versions of these titles and the new songs exemplify how Disney reinvents these titles' franchises in order to ensure that customers and fans leave the theater satisfied after experiencing something "new." The songs discussed in this chapter do some of the heavy lifting in this process by connecting with audiences on an emotional level and establishing new creative and engaging touchpoints with them. There is enough to remind the audience of what attracted them in the first place (to revisit characters and reexperience songs like "Beauty and the Beast," "Under the Sea," "A Whole New World," and "Let It Go") and simultaneously make the musicals sound fresh. Disney's Broadway musicals continue Disney's intention to create a seamless consumer experience that keeps film spectators and theater audiences coming back.

NOTES

1. Frank Rich, "Throw Away Those Scripts. Some of the Greatest Moments Were Wordless," *New York Times*, December 29, 1991, https://www.nytimes.com/1991/12/29/theater/year-arts-theater-1991-throw-away-those-scripts-some-greatest-moments-were.html.

2. Donald Frantz, *Beauty and the Beast: A Celebration of the Broadway Musical* (New York: Roundtable, 1995), 143–144.
3. Geoffrey Himes, "What Do Broadway's 'Aladdin,' 'Mean Girls,' and 'Book of Mormon' Have in Common? Director Casey Nicholaw," *Washington Post*, July 24, 2019, https://www.washingtonpost.com/goingoutguide/theater-dance/what-do-broadways-aladdin-mean-girls-and-book-of-mormon-have-in-common-director-casey-nicholaw/2019/07/22/52d3f226-ac6f-11e9-bc5c-e73b603e7f38_story.html.
4. Michael Lassell, *The Little Mermaid: From the Deep Blue Sea to the Great White Way* (New York: Disney Editions, 2009), 35.
5. These years refer to the musicals' Broadway openings.
6. The term "eleven o'clock number" originated when Broadway musicals started at eight thirty p.m., and such numbers occurred around eleven p.m.
7. Ashley Lee, "*Beauty and the Beast* Composer Alan Menken on Rediscovering Lost Lyrics and Why He's 'Shutting Up' about That Gay Character," *Hollywood Reporter*, March 14, 2017, https://www.hollywoodreporter.com/movies/movie-features/beauty-beast-new-songs-composer-alan-menken-lost-lyrics-gay-character-985602/.
8. Alan Menken, "Foreword," in Frantz, *Beauty and the Beast*, 13.
9. Frantz, *Beauty and the* Beast, 96, 98.
10. Ibid., 98.
11. "A Change in Me" was written for Toni Braxton when she played Belle in 1998.
12. Frantz, *Beauty and the Beast*, 137.
13. Ibid., 85–87.
14. For more on the screen-to-stage adaptation of *Tarzan*, see Kenneth Cerniglia, "Tarzan Swings onto Disney's Broadway," in *Global Perspectives on Tarzan: From King of the Jungle to International Icon*, ed. Michelle Ann Abate and Annette Wannamaker (New York: Routledge, 2012), 41–58.
15. "I Need to Know" is a new arrangement of "Leaving Home," which Collins wrote and sang on the soundtrack of the film *Tarzan II* (2005). Thomas S. Hischak and Mark A. Robinson, *The Disney Song Encyclopedia* (Lanham, MD: Scarecrow, 2009), 87.
16. Transcribed from the original Broadway cast recording. Walt Disney Records, 2006.
17. Brian Sibley and Michael Lassell, *Mary Poppins: Anything Can Happen if You Let It; The Story behind the Journey from Books to Broadway* (New York: Disney Editions, 2007), 63.
18. Transcribed from the original London cast recording. Walt Disney Records, 2005.
19. Lassell, *The Little Mermaid*, 37.
20. Transcribed from the original Broadway cast recording. Lyrics by Glenn Slater. Walt Disney Records, 2008.
21. Lassell, *The Little Mermaid*, 66.
22. Arnold Wayne Jones, "Doug Wright Talks How to Adapt 'The Little Mermaid' for Stage," Backstage, March 11, 2016, https://www.backstage.com/magazine/article/doug-wright-talks-adapt-little-mermaid-stage-8198/.
23. Lior Phillips, "'Songs Are Like Love': *Aladdin* Songwriters Look Back on 'A Whole New World,'" Grammys, May 21, 2019, https://www.grammy.com/news/songs-are-love-aladdin-songwriters-look-back-whole-new-world.
24. Sarah Whitfield, "'For the First Time in Forever': Locating *Frozen* as a Feminist Disney Musical," in *The Disney Musical on Stage and Screen*, ed. George Rodosthenous (London: Bloomsbury, 2017), 225.
25. Ibid., 233.
26. Frantz, *Beauty and the Beast*, 105.

27. Hischak and Robinson, *The Disney Song Encyclopedia*, 126.
28. Michael Lassell, *The Lion King: Twenty Years on Broadway and around the World* (New York: Disney Editions, 2017), 99, 127.
29. Sibley and Lassell, *Mary Poppins*, 75.
30. Transcribed from the original London cast recording.
31. Transcribed from the original Broadway cast recording.
32. Olaf in *Frozen* was played by a woman during the musical's Broadway run. I do not include Olaf in this discussion because my focus is on female characters and not characters that allow for gender bending.
33. Lassell, *The Lion King*, 29.
34. Michael Riedel, "How *The Lion King* Became a $9 Billion Broadway Smash," *Vanity Fair*, October 16, 2020, https://www.vanityfair.com/hollywood/2020/10/how-the-lion-king-became-a-dollar9-billion-broadway-smash.
35. This was also in early scripts of the film and was later cut.
36. Lassell, *The Lion King*, 128. The music of "Shadowland" also occurs as underscoring in the film.
37. Julie Taymor, *The Lion King: Pride Rock on Broadway* (New York: Disney Editions, 2017), 32.
38. Sibley and Lassell, *Mary Poppins*, 79.
39. Ibid.
40. Ibid.
41. Amy S. Osatinski, *Disney Theatrical Productions: Producing Broadway Musicals the Disney Way* (New York: Routledge, 2019), 136.
42. Isabel Cervantes, "How Disney's 'Newsies' Went from Box Office Flop to Broadway Blockbuster," Collider, November 30, 2021, https://collider.com/how-disney-newsies-became-a-broadway-success-explained.
43. Kenneth Cerniglia, ed., *Newsies: Stories of the Unlikely Broadway Hit* (New York: Disney Editions, 2013), 47.
44. Ibid. Aaron C. Thomas contextualizes the role that Katherine assumes in a male-dominated plot (especially her inclusion in "King of New York," which in the film is sung by the boys only). He also discusses the other female character missing in my discussion here, music-hall performer and proprietor Medda Larkin. See Aaron C. Thomas, "Dancing toward Masculinity: *Newsies*, Gender, and Desire," in *The Disney Musical on Stage and Screen*, ed. George Rodosthenous (London: Bloomsbury, 2017), 155–168.
45. The song "Letter from the Refuge" for Crutchie, the disabled newsboy who is put in a juvenile detention center, marks another example of a character-driven song in *Newsies*. The song was added to the musical after the Broadway run.
46. Krystal Ghisyawan, "A Whole New Worldview: Gender Norms, Islamophobia, and Orientalism," in *Recasting the Disney Princess in an Era of New Media and Social Movements*, ed. Shearon Roberts (Lanham, MD: Lexington, 2020), 186.
47. For more on gender in *Aladdin* (both the film and the stage musical), see Sam Baltimore, "Ashman's *Aladdin* Archive: Queer Orientalism in the Disney Renaissance," in *The Disney Musical on Stage and Screen*, ed. George Rodosthenous (London: Bloomsbury, 2017), 205–220. Baltimore points out that in the musical, Jasmine "is given a trio of supportive servants to form a musical and romantic parallel for Aladdin's boy band [Babkak, Omar, and Kasim]. The servants are nameless and function only as backup singers for Jasmine's new song."
48. David Rooney, "Tarzan," *Variety*, May 10, 2006, https://variety.com/2006/legit/markets-festivals/tarzan-2-1200516354/.

49. Jane also sings a new portion of "Stranger Like Me," which is a song from the film. She confirms what she sings in "Waiting for This Moment," which is that the jungle has everything she needs: the flowers that she studies and the man she falls in love with.

Bibliography

Baltimore, Sam. "Ashman's *Aladdin* Archive: Queer Orientalism in the Disney Renaissance." In *The Disney Musical on Stage and Screen: Critical Approaches from "Snow White" to "Frozen,"* edited by George Rodosthenous, 205–220. London: Bloomsbury, 2017.

Cerniglia, Kenneth, ed. *Newsies: Stories of the Unlikely Broadway Hit*. New York: Disney Editions, 2013.

Cerniglia, Kenneth. "Tarzan Swings onto Disney's Broadway." In *Global Perspectives on Tarzan: From King of the Jungle to International Icon*, edited by Michelle Ann Abate and Annette Wannamaker, 41–58. New York: Routledge, 2012.

Cervantes, Isabel. "How Disney's 'Newsies' Went from Box Office Flop to Broadway Blockbuster." Collider, November 30, 2021. https://collider.com/how-disney-newsies-became-a-broadway-success-explained.

Frantz, Donald. *Beauty and the Beast: A Celebration of the Broadway Musical*. New York: Roundtable, 1995.

Ghisyawan, Krystal. "A Whole New Worldview: Gender Norms, Islamophobia, and Orientalism." In *Recasting the Disney Princess in an Era of New Media and Social Movements*, edited by Shearon Roberts, 181–198. Lanham, MD: Lexington, 2020.

Himes, Geoffrey. "What Do Broadway's 'Aladdin,' 'Mean Girls,' and 'Book of Mormon' Have in Common? Director Casey Nicholaw," *Washington Post*, July 24, 2019. https://www.washingtonpost.com/goingoutguide/theater-dance/what-do-broadways-aladdin-mean-girls-and-book-of-mormon-have-in-common-director-casey-nicholaw/2019/07/22/52d3f226-ac6f-11e9-bc5c-e73b603e7f38_story.html.

Hischak, Thomas S., and Mark A. Robinson. *The Disney Song Encyclopedia*. Lanham, MD: Scarecrow, 2009.

Jones, Arnold Wayne. "Doug Wright Talks How to Adapt 'The Little Mermaid' for Stage." Backstage, March 11, 2016. https://www.backstage.com/magazine/article/doug-wright-talks-adapt-little-mermaid-stage-8198/.

Lassell, Michael. *The Lion King: Twenty Years on Broadway and around the World*. New York: Disney Editions, 2017.

Lassell, Michael. *The Little Mermaid: From the Deep Blue Sea to the Great White Way*. New York: Disney Editions, 2009.

Lee, Ashley. "*Beauty and the Beast* Composer Alan Menken on Rediscovering Lost Lyrics and Why He's 'Shutting Up' about That Gay Character." *Hollywood Reporter*, March 14, 2017. https://www.hollywoodreporter.com/movies/movie-features/beauty-beast-new-songs-composer-alan-menken-lost-lyrics-gay-character-985602/.

Osatinski, Amy S. *Disney Theatrical Productions: Producing Broadway Musicals the Disney Way*. New York: Routledge, 2019.

Phillips, Lior. "'Songs Are Like Love': *Aladdin* Songwriters Look Back on 'A Whole New World.'" Grammys, May 21, 2019. https://www.grammy.com/news/songs-are-love-aladdin-songwriters-look-back-whole-new-world.

Rich, Frank. "Throw Away Those Scripts. Some of the Greatest Moments Were Wordless." *New York Times*, December 29, 1991. https://www.nytimes.com/1991/12/29/theater/year-arts-theater-1991-throw-away-those-scripts-some-greatest-moments-were.html.

Riedel, Michael. "How *The Lion King* Became a $9 Billion Broadway Smash." *Vanity Fair*, October 16, 2020. https://www.vanityfair.com/hollywood/2020/10/how-the-lion-king-became-a-dollar9-billion-broadway-smash.

Rooney, David. "Tarzan." *Variety*, May 10, 2006. https://variety.com/2006/legit/markets-festivals/tarzan-2-1200516354/.

Sibley, Brian, and Michael Lassell. *Mary Poppins: Anything Can Happen if You Let It: The Story behind the Journey from Books to Broadway*. New York: Disney Editions, 2007.

Taymor, Julie. *The Lion King: Pride Rock on Broadway*. New York: Disney Editions, 2017.

Thomas, Aaron C. "Dancing toward Masculinity: *Newsies*, Gender, and Desire." In *The Disney Musical on Stage and Screen: Critical Approaches from "Snow White" to "Frozen,"* edited by George Rodosthenous, 155–168. London: Bloomsbury, 2017.

Whitfield, Sarah. "'For the First Time in Forever': Locating *Frozen* as a Feminist Disney Musical." In *The Disney Musical on Stage and Screen: Critical Approaches from "Snow White" to "Frozen,"* edited by George Rodosthenous, 221–238. London: Bloomsbury, 2017.

CHAPTER 27

FINDING NEMO: THE MUSICAL: WHEN THEATER IS A THEME-PARK ATTRACTION

JENNIFER A. KOKAI AND TOM ROBSON

LOCATED in the eastern portion of Disney's Animal Kingdom, at the border between the overtly fictionalized "DinoLand U.S.A." and the overtly genericized "Asia" area, sits the Theater in the Wild, a fifteen-hundred-seat space that has housed theatrical productions through most of the life span of Walt Disney World's fourth theme park. First opened in 1998 as the home for the short-lived *Journey into the Jungle Book* show, which gave way in 1999 to a seven-year run of *Tarzan Rocks!*, the Theater in the Wild has been home since 2007 to singing versions of Marlin, Nemo, Dory, and the characters from Pixar's *Finding Nemo*. While there are no formal critical reviews of musicals in theme parks, the audience response to all of these shows has been decidedly mixed, with the strongest consensus being feelings about the seats (it is widely agreed that they are uncomfortable).

This chapter is an examination of what it means for a musical-theater production to be an attraction at a theme park. How are audience expectations shaped by positioning a musical in a blistering-hot Florida park between roller coasters, as opposed to housing it in a Broadway theater in New York? The chapter focuses primarily on *Finding Nemo: The Musical*, which ran from 2007 until the Covid shutdowns of all Disney parks in 2020. Disney originally poured a great deal of money and resources into this production, with press around the original *Finding Nemo: The Musical* trumpeting a team of elite theatrical artists. The initial investment indicates that Disney thought musicals could be a marquee attraction, or what is referred to in parks parlance as an "E ticket." These are the most-beloved attractions with the longest wait times. However, audiences disagreed with this classification, largely rejecting the musicals, which led to the parks radically reshaping the latest show with a non-publicized, non-theater-specific production team. In this chapter, we ask why this disconnect occurred, using the production as a case study to examine the dramaturgical similarities (and differences) between a roller coaster and a show about a lost puppet fish, the audience demographics for Walt Disney

World and Broadway theater, and the audience expectations for each. Ultimately, we argue that the *Finding Nemo*[1] show demonstrates that rather than simply being a Disney musical housed at a park, there are fundamental aesthetic differences between successful park-based musicals and theater-housed shows and that they should be considered two separate genres of Disney musicals.

FINDING NEMO: THE MUSICAL

Disney's involvement in musical theater has always been contentious, even in traditional theater spaces and approaches. In her book *Disney Theatrical Productions*, Amy S. Osatinski recounts the frosty reception Disney received upon its initial entry into producing live musicals on Broadway, pointing to the extensive criticism the company received from both the mainstream theater press and scholarly writers. She summarizes this resistance by saying, "Disney Theatrical's musicals are often dismissed as commercial theatre that contains no artistic merit and is undeserving of scholastic praise or discussion outside of its perceived flaws."[2] If this is the critical response to the lavish productions of *The Lion King*, *Beauty and the Beast*, and the like, these same critics give theme-park shows such as *Finding Nemo: The Musical* even less regard, generally opting to ignore them entirely.

Finding Nemo: The Musical presented a condensed version of the plot of the 2003 Pixar film on which it is based. In *Finding Nemo*, clownfish Marlin becomes separated from his young son Nemo, who sought adventure on his own in rebellion against his overprotective father. Following Nemo's capture by an oblivious dentist (Pablo Sherman, DDS), who intends to give the orange and white bundle of adorableness to his fish-killer terror of a daughter, Darla, Marlin confronts his fears and sets off across the ocean to rescue his son. Aided by the forgetful blue tang fish Dory and the wise surfer-dude sea turtle Crush, Marlin arrives in Sydney, Australia, to find his son. Meanwhile, Nemo, with the collaboration of the "Tank Gang" of fellow fish captives in Dr. Sherman's dentist office, stages a prison break and reunites with his dad. The musical removes many scenes for the sake of time. For example, the stage show features no encounter with a whale. Other popular scenes from the movie receive a fresh coat of paint when adapted for the musical stage, as Bruce the shark's motto, "Fish are friends, not food," transforms into a soft-shoe dance number, the 150-year-old sea turtle Crush now presents his philosophy of "Go with the flow" as an uptempo surfer-rock anthem, complete with multiple requisite musical-theater modulations up, and Marlin and Dory's harrowing journey through the jellyfish forest offers further clarity to a moment only implied in the movie, as the musical stages Dory being stung, where the movie leaves that act off-screen.

The musical features songs written exclusively for the stage by composers Robert Lopez and Kristen Anderson-Lopez, who have extensive experience composing for stage and screen. Robert Lopez's Broadway credits include *Avenue Q* and *The Book of Mormon*, while Kristen Anderson-Lopez was the creator of the Broadway musical *In*

Transit. Together, they most notably composed the songs for Disney's animated *Frozen* and for its subsequent sequel and stage adaptation. Given that every character who appears onstage in the musical is an animal, the musical features human actors operating puppets while singing, with puppets designed by Michael Curry, designer of puppets for Disney Theatrical's most successful enterprise, *The Lion King* on Broadway. The production was directed by Peter Brosius, most famous as the artistic director for the Tony Award–winning Children's Theatre Company of Minneapolis.

A musical watched in a theme park has different comparison points from one watched in a Broadway or major regional theater. Should Disney have opened *Finding Nemo: The Musical* on Broadway in 2007 instead of in Animal Kingdom, it would have been judged in comparison with previous Disney musicals such as *The Lion King*, *Beauty and the Beast*, and *Tarzan* or other musicals from that year such as *Legally Blonde*, *Young Frankenstein*, or *The Pirate Queen*. Those comparisons would have been made based on traditional theater aesthetic values such as strength of performance, quality of writing, or impressiveness of design.

Within the theme-park space, however, tourists evaluate *Finding Nemo: The Musical* on a completely different scale. *Nemo* is certainly less active than many other theme-park attractions. Most of the rides at Animal Kingdom permit tourists to insert themselves into the narrative, casting them as explorers (DINOSAUR, Expedition: Everest) or scientists (Avatar: Flight of Passage), encouraging them to visually hunt for difficult-to-spot animals on the Kilimanjaro Safaris expedition, or even exhorting them to sing and dance along at Animal Kingdom's most popular stage show, *The Festival of the Lion King*. *Nemo*, conversely, mirrors the overwhelmingly passive audience experience of mainstream commercial theater. Such passivity is de rigueur for a Broadway house, but when contrasted with the heavy engagement that the tourist-as-actor brings to the theme-park space, it can often lead to cries of "boring."

While there is zero official critical reception for this production, there is ample information online from guests about their opinions, which seem decidedly mixed and indeed perhaps dependent upon knowledge of theater traditions. Guests at Disney fan site AllEars.net give it a 7.5 out of 10 rating, with only 69 percent recommending it.[3] Some guests seemed startled by the Bunraku-style puppets, stating, "I didn't like the Finding Nemo show. Felt like seeing the people who work the puppets was really distracting." Given its theme-park location, many guests assume it is not even a live performance, with threads arguing over whether or not the show is lip-synced (it isn't; performers are all singing live, although some of the ensemble work is supplemented by prerecorded tracks). Guests report dissatisfaction with the fact that they did not know the songs in advance and so could not sing along (as the movie was not a musical).

Aesthetically, *Finding Nemo* was in line with the prevailing approach to Disney musicals. Alex Bádue and Rebecca S. Schorsch argue that "Disney stage musicals celebrate American culture and enterprise, and they combine this legacy with technological aesthetics and commercial tactics that originated in British megamusicals."[4] Key hallmarks of the British mega-musical style for them include standardization of performance choices by "demanding literal reproduction" in how lines are delivered and songs are sung, prioritizing a consistent and universal artistic experience for audiences over innovation or artistry. Similarly, Bádue and Schorsch note that the musicals include a great deal of spectacle and visual effects, and we would argue that the stage effects also largely seek to replicate cinematic approaches over more transparently theatrical ones, using complicated technological approaches to change Elsa's dress or transform the Beast from monster to man instead of a simpler but more obvious strategy. Likewise, the vocal choices seek to simply replicate the movies as faithfully as possible, a "bright youthfulness" in style with "light pop scoops, controlled or vibrato-free tone, and unstressed vocal slides, as well as an easy, neutral delivery."[5]

The most vocally demanding role in the show belongs to the performer playing Crush, whose "Go with the Flow" song generally steals the show. The song features an expansive range that continually climbs throughout, requiring the actor to mix between chest and head voice, often within the same word (for example, on the line "Let us see how Squirt does flying solo," the word "solo" is sung on three ascending notes, and performers often make the flip from chest to head for the final note). The Crush performer must sustain a high C during the challenging song and reach a momentary D during the chorus. It is also not uncommon for Crush to seek alternatives to fully singing some of the highest notes, such as the word "keep" in the line "Sit back and keep it mellow." In one recorded performance reviewed for this chapter, the clearly talented actor produces little vowel sound in the short-duration word "keep," making sure the audience gets the consonants for understanding but preserving his voice. Such vocally demanding songs are unsurprising coming from the songwriters behind the challenging-even-for-Idina-Menzel "Let It Go" from *Frozen*. Adding to the difficulty of the song, because of the attempts to recreate cinematic effects, the actor playing Crush must "Go with the Flow" while kneeling on the back of a vigorously moving turtle puppet the size of a small monster truck, with the physical requirements to safely ride the turtle impeding some standard singer techniques to draw full breath into the body (see figure 27.1).

While it seems unfair or even unreasonable to ask a performer to belt top notes while navigating around another performer on a ladder on a moving giant turtle, given that nearly all of the Disney musicals are based on well-known movies, this cinematic replication approach makes sense. These aesthetic choices all contribute to making nostalgia a key element of these musicals. Audiences might feel disappointed and betrayed if the stage version differed too greatly from the movie they know and love. This is evident in the casting controversy over Halle Bailey as Ariel in the live-action *Little Mermaid* movie, where some white audience members felt betrayed when the actress didn't match their memories of the white character in the movie as precisely as possible, despite the fact that the movie was first released thirty-three years ago and a stage version (the Broadway production was one of Disney's rare economic flops) has existed since 2007. Although Bailey conforms to the "Disney style" of singing as described by Bádue and Schorsch, in the trailer she departs from faithful reproduction to add an extra vocal run to the music, a vocal hallmark of Bailey's contemporary R&B background, which no doubt exacerbates the racially driven concerns of the vocal online complainers. While *Finding Nemo: The Musical* did not have these issues with faithful reproduction of the

FIGURE 27.1. The actor playing Crush navigates singing a difficult solo while balancing on a giant turtle puppet. Photo credit: Eric Means.

original sound, since it was not originally a musical, the tension between stage adaptation and absolute fidelity is apparent.

Osatinski's book focuses (as the title makes clear) on the production elements of Disney musicals and not the artistic elements. Within her argument, however, Osatinski notes that Mary Zimmerman's *The Jungle Book* is "not a typical Disney musical," so its variances are helpful in illuminating what is.[6] While Osatinski does not expand upon this thought in her book, reviews indicate that Zimmerman sought to include Indian approaches to deconstruct some of the colonialism of the source material (both Rudyard Kipling's book and the Disney movie based on it). Joshua Williams writes in his review of "Christopher Gattelli's dance numbers, which he developed in consultation with prominent bharatanatyam choreographer Hema Rajagopalan." Williams found them a positive, albeit slight, contribution.[7] Meanwhile, the *Chicago Tribune* notes that it feels more like "a play with music than a musical." While this is a somewhat arbitrary distinction that often serves to shore up classism in theater (often, it is formally adventurous or content that focuses on underrepresented experiences that is labeled "a play with music"), the author adds, "There is no song list in the program, not much for Mowgli to sing, no big Tony-coaxing number in Act 2 for any of the actors."[8] And if Zimmerman's work rejected traditional musical-theater expectations to allow for a more diverse approach, Emily Clark and colleagues argue that was also not successful. They believe that ultimately, "in staging *The Jungle Book* Disney and Zimmerman capitalize upon white supremacy by carefully producing and delimiting acceptable Orientalist and minstrel 'pleasures' and simultaneously disavowing institutional and structural racism."[9]

Osatinski's thorough analysis of *The Lion King* solidifies what qualities made *The Jungle Book* atypical, especially as one reason *The Jungle Book* was not transferred to Broadway or toured was that it was perceived to occupy the same niche as the already successful *The Lion King*. Osatinski writes that "DTP [Disney Theatrical Productions] did not want *The Lion King* to look or feel like a theme-park ride and hired [director Julie] Taymor for her avant-garde sensibilities."[10] This serves to turn most of the elements that define a "Disney musical" on their head—the set is intentionally not "realistic," and the music brings together pop songs from Elton John and Tim Rice, the white English composers of the songs from the original movie, with additional music from African composers such as Lebo M, who had also contributed music to the original movie score. In opposition to cinematic approaches that would seek to faithfully recreate the nonhuman animals, Taymor drew upon Asian puppetry conventions to create puppets with designer Curry that intentionally and consistently show the human actor. Osatinski quotes Taymor's argument that "In the theatre you can expect more from your audiences, they know they are in a theatre."[11] While scholars may be critical of exactly how much more was expected of audiences, we want to highlight this notion that one can "expect more" of an audience in the theater, as audience response is a key way we see musicals at the theme parks as a separate genre from musicals hosted in traditional theater spaces. Specifically, the expectations in these shows are linked to the visual language, primarily the representation of nonhuman animals through puppetry forms.

Much has been made of the Asian influences on Taymor's approach to puppetry in *The Lion King* (although Curry does not reference it at all in the interview described below, and Taymor claims she designed the aesthetics of the puppets and Curry did the mechanics). In an interview with Richard Schechner, both Taymor and Schechner use a variety of references to Asian puppetry forms, including Indonesian puppets, Japanese shadow puppets, and several forms of Japanese three-dimensional puppets such as Bunraku and Awaji, the latter forms being similar three-person puppets, with Awaji traditionally performed outdoors and so involving larger puppets.[12] What these forms all have in common is that the intended audience is adults or family but not specifically children, toward whom Western puppetry has so often been directed, and that the skill of the visible puppeteer is as much a part of the show as the stories told by the puppets themselves. Maurya Wickstrom quotes Taymor reflecting on this in the *Lion King* Stagebill: "Audiences relish the artifice behind the theater. When we see a person actually manipulating an inanimate object like a puppet and making it come alive, the duality moves us. Hidden special effects can lack humanity, but when the human spirit visibly animates an object, we experience a special, almost life-giving connection."[13] Taymor speaks to Schechner of the process she used to convince Disney executives that this was the correct aesthetic choice and says that Disney's then CEO Michael Eisner ultimately told her: "Let's do all the puppet stuff. Because it is definitely more risky, but the payoff is bigger."[14]

Dassia N. Posner describes the work that Taymor and Curry's puppetry do as a performance where "the audience is embraced as a co-creator of visual meaning and is made a participant in a celebration of belief (rather than a suspension of disbelief)." While Posner notes that we (presumably meaning both audiences and theater scholars) "remain, to date, more adept at analyzing the *stories* those illusions and faces tell than we are at investigating the productive tensions of theatre's 'mutually exclusive possibilities,'" she offers an array of other things that we might take into consideration, including "rhythm, tempo, dynamics ... different levels of movement ... the dramaturgies of material objects in performance ... and especially in puppet theatre, the interplay between liveness and objectness."[15] Both the guest feedback and the revised musical version of *Finding Nemo* that opened in 2022 indicate that for a musical as a theme-park attraction, guests frequently declined the invitation to co-create the event and construct the visual meaning and would have preferred an experience that allowed them to simply focus on a retelling of a beloved story.

While Taymor claims artistic responsibility for *The Lion King*'s puppetry, Curry echoes the assumed differences between Broadway audiences and his work at the parks, which includes the *Finding Nemo* musical and the now-defunct evening show *Rivers of Light*. Interviewer Skye Strauss notes that he speaks of "a distinct gap between theme park work and the license that comes with a Broadway production where the work is expected to take on a new level of sophistication." When working with feature animation in a parks environment, he always begins with "what's called 'on model' references," and Curry says that he "tries to change them only as much as I have to make them useable on stage" as he is aware this is the first time some park guests may ever have been to the theater.[16] Perhaps the key word here is "useable," as despite Curry's acknowledgment of the difference in audiences for a Broadway musical and a theme-park musical, the puppets in *Nemo* differ greatly from other puppets in the park's shows and indicate that how the show was conceived dramaturgically—what the puppets were supposed to do—might more closely resemble theatrical genre expectations than is tenable for a park attraction.

In *Finding Nemo: The Musical*, the puppets work in a similar fashion to those of *The Lion King*'s Broadway production, using a variety of mechanics but always with actors visible.[17] Dory, Nemo, and Marlin, all main characters, are one-person puppets operated through buttons on a stick that move their eyes and mouths. The puppeteers, fully visible at all times and also acting with their face and bodies, wear costumes that echo the colors of the fish they play. This is in contrast to the puppeteers of minor fish, who are clothed in blue unitards representing the sea but also still performing facially alongside their puppets. There are hand puppets that represent a school of fish, kite puppets that are flown off tall sticks, and puppets operated by more than one person mounted on top of bicycle-like contraptions. In a video interview with the puppeteers, the actor playing Marlin notes, "A lot of people in the audience will say, 'You know, at the beginning I didn't know what to do, I didn't know who to watch, if I should watch the actor or if I should watch the puppet.' Then they'll say, 'By the end of the show it all just made sense, it all just automatically started working where I was watching both and the whole story happened as if it were one.'"[18]

As an example of this audience confusion, roughly one-third of the way into the show, Marlin and Dory encounter three seemingly ferocious sharks: Bruce, Anchor, and Chum. Despite their initial terror, the heroes quickly discover that these characters are a support group for sharks attempting to stop eating other marine animals. The three sharks begin singing "Fish Are Friends, Not Food," a song that begins as a gentle soft-shoe sung in three-part harmony. In this number, the performer playing Bruce actually hands off the front of the Bruce puppet to an auxiliary puppeteer to do some choreography leading to a moment where the human Bruce and the puppet Bruce (whose mouth is still moving) appear to be dueting. This is the cognitive work that Taymor and Curry say the theater makes space for and theme parks do not; however, this moment could be semiotically confusing even for seasoned theater attendees. Further exacerbating this confusion, while the sharks explain their worldview, Marlin and Dory argue over the reappearance of the fateful mask containing the information "P Sherman 42 Wallaby Way, Sydney," which will lead them to Nemo. In this struggle, Marlin accidentally strikes Dory in the face with the mask, leading her to bleed and sending the sharks into a frenzy. While retaining the same melody, the song quickly morphs into an up-tempo rocker, as Bruce and friends hungrily pursue the smaller (and tastier) fish heroes. Unfortunately, conveying exactly what happens in this moment to an audience proves more challenging onstage than it does on-screen.

While filmed animation has the advantage of close-ups and careful editing, stage presentation has only the ability to show what can transpire within the physical bounds of the stage. Following the "clunk" of contact between Dory and the mask, an ensemble member twirling a red ribbon—signifying blood—spins from behind the Dory puppet and across the stage, encountering the sharks. Unfortunately, this ribbon dancer must perform the choreography simultaneously with a dialogue scene between Marlin and Dory. The speaking characters remain illuminated in bright light stage right, while the dancer twirls toward the left side of the stage, which is dimmer and bathed in red. As audience members, we find ourselves with attention fixed on the brighter portion of the stage—which also happens to be where characters are speaking. As a result, it is quite easy for an audience not to track what specifically causes the shark attack. Without preexisting knowledge of the *Nemo* movie, this moment could be confusing.[19]

While we could assume classism or elitism is at play in the artists' claims about the differences in genre between theater and theme park, their appraisal is borne out by contrasting the puppetry approach in *Finding Nemo* and the theatrical musical *The Lion King* with the approach taken in *The Festival of the Lion King* and the respective popularity of each. *The Festival of the Lion King* is a wildly popular performance at Disney's Florida Animal Kingdom Park. In contrast to the puppets used in the Broadway play, the *Festival* generally uses large stationary automated puppets on parade floats to represent the characters from the film, such as Simba and Pumbaa. It uses a few performers in mascot-style costumes, such as for Timon (creating a significant scale issue that is mitigated by having the actor playing Timon avoid the Pumbaa float), and human performers with gestural half-hearted costumes as birds or monkeys. Essentially, the puppets are asked to do very little. Aesthetics and affect take a backseat to a vaudeville/English music hall approach to the material. There are audience sing-alongs of the popular film songs, acrobatics, fire breathing, and aerial performances. There is no discernible plot, other than a manufactured competition among audience members for which of the griot figures' sections of the audience will prevail in volume. Unlike Taymor's belief that you can ask more of your audience in the theatre, the *Festival* uses intentionally cartoony puppets for the major *Lion King* characters and the park's aesthetic approach to meet-and-greet characters and performers in its other choices. That this show is incredibly popular and that both shows Curry worked on, the original *Finding Nemo* and *Rivers of Light*, frequently left audiences dissatisfied indicate the gap between the aesthetic expectations for a park attraction and for a traditional musical.[20]

Opportunity Costs

While audiences complained about aesthetic choices like puppetry and logistical issues like the comfort of the seats, the largest source of audience negativity seems to come from the musical's status as one attraction in a theme park with many competing attractions included in the same ticket price and the underestimation by Disney of how guests would esteem the attraction. Prior to closing at the outset of the 2020 Covid pandemic, *Finding Nemo: The Musical* lasted roughly forty minutes in performance, making it the longest show inside one of Walt Disney World's four theme parks. While some guests welcomed the chance to sit down in air conditioning, away from the sometimes challenging central Florida elements, others measured the show not as a "free" Broadway play but rather in comparison with what they could be doing with that time. *Nemo*'s forty-minute runtime represents the same time commitment as the combined attraction experiences of Kilimanjaro Safaris, Avatar: Flight of Passage, Na'vi River Journey, Expedition: Everest, DINOSAUR, and TriceraTop Spin. Many guests leaving negative reviews of *Finding Nemo* on online review boards cite the length as a primary complaint. Consider the following examples from the reviews on popular Disney fan site AllEars.net:

> The worst show ever takes so long it is so boring and you'll pass out (Koko).
> This is a cute musical production but too long (Anonymous).
> Great production values and performers, just too long (EeyoreSkipper).
> I like Finding Nemo the movie but this show is long and boring and the music is not my favorite (SarahA).

Though none of these reviews explicitly uses the term "opportunity cost," that is the subtext of their comments. Suggesting that an attraction in a theme park takes "too long" implies a loss of ability to do something else, an inherent comparison between the time invested in one event and theoretical time invested in another.

Susanne Becken and Jude Wilson discuss the concept of the "travel budget," a conceptual tool "common in travel behaviour research," in which "tourists seek to allocate their money, time, and 'travel capacity' among competing uses."[21] Tourists expect to financially budget for a Disney theme-park vacation but do not always consider as deeply the need for the creation of what Douglas G. Pearce termed a "time-budget."[22] While experienced Disney guests understand the finite nature of time within the park environment and are often able to plan accordingly, new park-goers can at times become overwhelmed by the options available to them—and the time investment required for each. Travel blogs regularly advise first-timers to prepare for this; for example, DisneyTouristBlog states directly that "Everything takes longer than you'll expect." Other sites remind guests that they won't be able to do everything; The Frugal South states directly that "Trying to do too much is the #1 way people ruin their Disney vacation." Despite these warnings, most experienced park-goers can easily spot the newbies rushing from place to place, dragging recalcitrant children (or adults) desperately in need of a nap. These travelers push themselves beyond their physical and emotional limits in an effort to wring every last second of magic out of their costly trip, and to them, sitting still for a prolonged period results in the visualization of minutes ticking off their park clock.

Daniel S. Hamermesh documents compelling research on why American tourists in particular feel such pressure in relation to time on vacation. He writes, "The scarcity of time is obvious. What is important and novel in the developed world is that time is increasingly *relatively* scarce." He establishes that compared with other developed nations, Americans work more hours per year and have "markedly lower" amounts of leisure time and paid vacation than citizens of other developed nations."[23] This contributes to Americans feeling a constant leisure-time crunch, attempting to cram more into smaller chunks. This explains why some guests would blanch at investing the time required to watch the relatively lengthy original iteration of *Finding Nemo*. Philip L. Pearce, building on Becken and Wilson's research, shows that for tourists, "Using time well was pivotal to a good day, but frustration and annoyance prevailed when the time allocated ... left the tourists with no time to explore the destination they had reached."[24] Sitting in a darkened theater provides some tourists with too much inactive time, emphasizing the loss of opportunity elsewhere in their day.

Examining decades of research into boredom reveals several interrelated elements that could further explain these audience members' rejection of the *Nemo* musical. Peter Toohey calls boredom "an emotion which produces feelings of being constrained or confined by some unavoidable and distastefully predictable circumstance and, as a result, a feeling of being distanced from one's surroundings and the normal flow of time."[25] Richard Farmer and Norman D. Sundberg attribute boredom to "*an environment that is perceived as static*, with the actor remaining largely disconnected from the processes that comprise his or her environment."[26] Wendell O'Brien theorizes boredom as a combination of the seemingly oppositional forces of weariness and restlessness, describing the feeling as "I lack energy, interest, and patience to attend to what is at hand; but I do have energy to burn, and I long for something else to burn it on."[27] Finally, Jim Davies and Mark Fortney, while describing their theory that boredom emerges due to the individual having an excess of mental resources (or, as they term them, "mentons"), assert that "Boredom occurs when there is a surplus of unused mentons. The feeling of boredom is your mind pushing to find new challenges."[28]

Taken together, these theories explain why many audience members would find a forty-minute musical that exists inside a bustling theme park to be unengaging, contrary to Disney's expectations that it would be a marquee attraction. As we have written elsewhere, one of the great pleasures of theme-park attendance is its expansive space.[29] Guests at Disney's Animal Kingdom explore walking trails where they can see and engage with animals, enjoy highly physical rides that deliver thrills, and are faced with constant active choices as they perform their role of "tourist" within the theme-park space, with constantly shifting creative roles. Conversely, *Finding Nemo: The Musical* constrained tourists into the much more passive role of "audience" within a traditional theater space, bounded by a roof and walls. Effectively, *Nemo* functions as a play-within-a-play, a piece of highly conventional theater dropped into a massive immersive performance. The park trains the tourist to perform with a significant degree of agency, then asks them to reject that emancipated state in order to watch a heavily scripted and noninteractive retelling of a familiar movie in which they have no specified imaginative part.

Throughout a park day, tourists perform significant mental labor, assembling stimuli, making choices, balancing the needs and desires of their group. This, of course, also combines with the significant physical labor of walking miles in the often-challenging central Florida heat. But for forty minutes, these same tourists are expected to sit quietly and passively, absorbing a story that neither requires nor requests participation. Returning to Davies and Fortney's menton theory, "Boredom, essentially, is dissatisfaction with how challenging an environment is."[30] Guests expect their park experience to challenge them, yet *Finding Nemo* does the opposite.

We use "challenge" here in the sense of mental processes, not in the sense of taxing an audience's experience with daring artistic work. Ironically, *Nemo* has the potential to create boredom both by asking too little of its audience and by asking too much. Davies and Fortney say that when engaging with art, the viewer is looking for "the sweet spot between familiarity and incongruity."[31] Based on some audience-member responses, *Finding Nemo: The Musical* has perhaps too much incongruity. The unconventional (for American audiences) performance style of highly elaborate puppets being controlled by visible puppeteers pushes spectators to consider visual storytelling in a different way. None of the other live performances at Walt Disney World featuring recognizable characters from movies utilizes this sort of puppetry so heavily, meaning that audience members must learn to read theater images in a new way in real time in the middle of an otherwise difficult day. The task may simply be too difficult for some spectators, creating a sense of boredom akin to a student sitting in a class where they don't quite understand the subject.

Naturally, human beings are not monolithic and may have different acceptable levels of familiarity and incongruity. Often the role of the artist is to determine what the potential audience wants and/or needs, which raises the question of who the traditional audiences are for each genre and how we might compare their experience prioritizations. An analysis of demographic data of both Broadway and theme parks finds interesting connective threads. In the last full season prior to the Covid pandemic, 2018–2019, 65 percent of Broadway tickets were sold to tourists, marking New York's theater district as one of the biggest tourism draws in the city.[32] The regular complaints about the "Disneyfication" of Times Square and New York's theater district that emerged in the late-1990s and beyond make the connection between commercial theater and theme parks even more explicit. During that same season of 2018–2019, the average cost of a Broadway theater ticket was $145.60 (according to the Broadway League). In 2022, the price of a one-day, one-park ticket to Walt Disney World ranged between $109 and $159, putting it roughly on par with the Broadway ticket.

Although the costs of the experiences are in the neighborhood of equivalent, the economic status of the patrons is not. According to the same Broadway League data, the average annual household income for a Broadway theater-goer is $261,000. Finding an exact comparable data point for Walt Disney World specifically proves elusive, but two reports provide enough context to get close. First, writer Terry Roen of *Theme Park Tribune* cites a study that the average annual household income for a theme-park visitor across the United States is $86,000,[33] while Drew Harwell in the *Washington Post* cites a study that the average annual household income of a tourist to Orlando is $93,000.[34] Taken together, we see a rough idea that despite nearly identical experience pricing, the Broadway tourist has an average annual household income of more than twice that of the Disney theme-park tourist. So while both spaces and experiences rely heavily on tourist interest, they reach significantly different classes of tourists.

THE DRAMATURGY OF ROLLER COASTERS

Although it might seem ludicrous, at this point, we are going to compare a musical to a roller coaster. J. Meredith Neil argues that "the roller coaster has long held in the American mind an unambiguous emblematic status ... the roller coaster symbolizes the amusement park."[35] The expectation that theme/amusement parks have at least one roller coaster is so strong that guests have long criticized Epcot for lacking any, the Motley Fool noting in an article about the then-forthcoming, now-opened Guardians of the Galaxy ride: "We can start with the obvious attraction of a roller coaster in a park that lacks this kind of thrill ride. Epcot is the only major theme park in Central Florida that doesn't have a coaster, and that distinction will be toast next month."[36] *Finding Nemo* was originally sandwiched between two: Expedition Everest and Primeval Whirl.

Despite the very different perceptions, we argue that at their roots, a roller coaster and a musical are actually attempting to do very similar things and, more important, that Disney anticipated audiences would view them equivalently. A traditional Aristotelian plot, which *Finding Nemo* has, is marked by beginning at a place of stasis, rising action to a climax, and then descending action to a denouement. The intention is to create a swell of feelings, or affective engagement, that results in a catharsis purgation of pity and fear. Traditional roller coasters utilize a similar structure, leaving on a relatively horizontal path, ascending up a steep hill, and then rushing through a series of twists, drops, and plot points until reaching a new stasis and depositing the audience at the end. Neil stresses the curvilinear nature of roller-coaster design is crucial—"it symbolizes relaxation and pleasure while straight lines have sober and business-like overtones"[37]—and similarly, contemporary audiences expect a musical plotted with reversals and recognitions, plot twists and the unexpected, which differentiates it as leisure media in opposition to a scholarly argument. Likewise, while coasters may not necessarily evoke pity, they certainly generate strong emotions, including potentially fear or jeopardy en route to a rider returning to emotional equilibrium on solid ground. Designers of both play around with the plot structures, musicals occasionally starting in media res and roller coasters occasionally shooting you off at sixty miles per hour like the Aerosmith Rock 'n Roller Coaster, but at the end of the day, most of them are working with the same set of tools and the same affective intentions.

The largest difference between the two is that a musical attempts to create catharsis strictly through empathy. We watch the Nemo and Marlin puppets encounter dangers like sharks and jellyfish as our avatars, but unlike in Flight of Passage, we do not experience their thrills within our bodies. Elsewhere, we have argued that nearly all attractions at Disney are ones that center individual interior guest experiences—it is about you and what you feel. Disney parks generally map to highly immersive theater practices. Josephine Machon has identified qualities such as "in its own world, awareness of space and place, scenography, sound, duration of experience, hybridized approaches, bodies, and audience" as things that can be evaluated on a scale when determining how immersive an experience is.[38] By creating a traditional musical-theater performance, which generates affect as you decenter yourself and focus on the experience of another, immersivity is minimized. Audiences are asked to silence and still their own bodies, to step out of space and place, to ignore the lack of meaningful scenography in the standard theater house. It is this incongruity in approach that we argue is what alienates theme-park guests from *Finding Nemo* and leaves them disappointed or even avoiding the theater in favor of something more "fun."

Finding Nemo: The Big Blue ... and Beyond!

Finding Nemo: The Musical played its final performance in Animal Kingdom on March 15, 2020. The next day, Walt Disney World closed all four of its theme parks due to the rampaging Covid pandemic.[39] Animal Kingdom reopened just less than four months later, on July 11.[40] Although the gate was open, the theater remained closed. Neither *Nemo* nor *The Festival of the Lion King* reopened during the height of the pandemic.[41] Prior to the arrival of vaccines, and in a period when the Actors' Equity Association was justifiably concerned about exposing its members to a life-threatening disease that could be easily spread, it was medically imprudent to attempt a return to the stage.[42]

Soon the company would announce a replacement for *Finding Nemo: The Musical*, one that would make use of the elaborate (and expensive) puppets designed for *Nemo*. In a November 20, 2021, post on the official Disney Parks Blog, Shawn Slater announced that the name of the new show would be *Finding Nemo: The Big Blue . . . and Beyond!* The show would be set during the timeline of popular sequel movie *Finding Dory* and would utilize the "tank gang" of fish from Dr. Sherman's office, now relocated from Australia to California, as a frame device. Slater's post said, "They tell the story of Nemo and how they all got there, incorporating many of the beloved songs and production numbers from the original show." This revised production played its first performance on June 12, 2022. Notably, unlike the press for the first *Nemo* show, these announcements did not mention the artistic team at all, and it took a fair amount of digging to determine that they were all full-time Disney Live Entertainment employees who specialize in creating theme-park entertainment and not theatrical productions.[43]

While repurposing many of the puppets and songs from *Finding Nemo*, *The Big Blue and Beyond* is decidedly a different experience.[44] Notably, the attraction no longer identifies itself as a musical in its title, although, of course, it still features nearly start-to-finish singing. It also bears a far shorter runtime than its predecessor, clocking it at a lean twenty-five minutes, compared with *Finding Nemo*'s forty. We noted that the longest time between an entrance or exit onstage was one minute and forty-nine seconds. Finally, the cast of unionized actors has slightly shrunk, from eighteen down to fourteen. Featuring a heavily revised book, reportedly by Sara Wordsworth and James Silson, who are employed full-time by Disney to design spectacles for the parks, and with significantly revised staging by Silson, *The Big Blue and Beyond*'s changes are notable from the moment the house opens.

In the original show, an opening projection and voice-over welcomed audiences with a projection of the show's title and the spoken line "We are proud to present . . . *Finding Nemo: The Musical*." The new opening has a projection that tells the audience they are at the "Marine Life Institute" (a fictional aquarium from the movie's sequel, *Finding Dory*). The pre-show offers a variety of actual scientific facts about science while animated fish silhouettes float by. It explicitly addresses the audience as "ocean explorers" or "marine life explorers," giving them a role to play beyond that of audience member. This approach also seeks to urge guests to further action, encouraging those who want to know more about preserving ocean creatures to "start by visiting your local library." The pre-show safety announcement also carefully specifies that what audiences are at is "the open ocean exhibit," *not* a musical.

Where the original show followed the *Finding Nemo* movie plot as a linear narrative, the new show adds a framing device with the tank fish telling the story of *Finding Nemo*.

Essentially, this is borrowing the framing model of things like the Hollywood Studios attraction *For the First Time in Forever: A Frozen Sing-Along Celebration*, which provides narrators who tell us the story of *Frozen* and can skip large chunks of exposition or plot using narrated interstitial talks. This means that the staged moments that we argued were previously unclear are now straightforwardly told to the audience. Additionally, the scenery now highlights an enormous LED screen that provides cartoon backdrops of the ocean flora or the skyline of Sydney. This change to a more animated style parallels the changes made at the Living Seas pavilion in Epcot, where a previous tour of actual aquarium fish was reconfigured to minimize fish and highlight cartoon projections from *Nemo*. Jennifer Kokai has argued elsewhere that the overlay of *Nemo* elements and cartoon projections emphasized affective connections with *Nemo* characters over the actual oceans and the flora and fauna that live there.[45] Likewise, the LED screen seems to be working to emphasize affective relationships with the animated movie over the experience of live theater as attempts were made to clarify scenes we had identified as confusing to audiences in the previous version, notably both the nosebleed and the bombs in the sharks' scene, which are given additional scenic elements and exposition in the dialogue. It is interesting that the actor playing Bruce still hands off his puppet while singing—not all overtly theatrical choices have been eliminated.

This framing and narrative device also means that the production avoids total blackouts at any point, which in videos of the first iteration frequently left audiences sitting in confused silence for periods of time before starting to clap. Many of the changes do serve to make the story more accessible to those who might not intimately know the film and to keep the action moving, both preventing boredom and eliminating theatrical conventions that this audience might not be familiar with. The use of narrators gives the audience a role in terms of being visitors to the ocean aquarium and having a direct acknowledgment and relationship with the narrators who break the fourth wall. The closing voice-over directly thanks the audience—still in the role of visiting the Marine Life Institute—and gives them a direct action: "if Nemo's story has inspired you to expand your knowledge of marine life and the world around you, you can also connect with nature by exploring the local beach or spending time watching wildlife on the shore. Remember our friends in the big blue world are counting on all of us to make a positive conservation impact." This narration, again, gives an explicit way for audiences to interpret and connect to the material of the show.

These changes demonstrate that there are specific generic conventions for a Disney theme-park musical that differ from a Disney musical writ large, which perhaps allow for a larger scope of artistic approaches than the parks do with their extreme opportunity-cost calculations. A theme-park musical needs to be brief, to be high-speed, to give the audience a specific role and a direct relationship with an actor/character (if not just actual participation), to be narratively straightforward (if it contains a narrative at all), to be generally faithful to the cinematic and vocal choices of the original, and to avoid strenuous cognitive tasks and semiotic interpretations that theater audiences seek out in their staging choices.

Conclusion

On September 15, 2022, Disney Parks performer Rob Lott posted an image on his personal Instagram account that was simply white text on a black background. It read: "Attractions bring them in the first time. Entertainment is what brings them back again and again." With these words, Lott—a good friend of one of this essay's authors—landed on one of the fundamental tensions between a piece of traditional musical theater and the theme-park environment. As this chapter has established, many spectators of *Finding Nemo: The Musical* found it to be boring and questioned its place within the bustle of Disney's Animal Kingdom. Yet to many repeat park-goers, *Nemo* was a must-watch. For first-time Disney tourists, *Nemo* violated their expectations for what a Disney day should be, whereas park veterans grew to savor the slower experience of a theme-park musical. This reflects the major divide in parks guests—first-timers versus veterans, best exemplified by the Annual Passholder. Since the reopening of the parks after their Covid shutdowns—and the accompanying rise of Bob Chapek to the position of Disney CEO—Disney has taken significant steps to reduce the number of repeat park-goers on their properties (it is not possible at this moment to see if newly reinstalled CEO Bob Iger will undo any of these strategies). The cost of an annual pass has risen substantially, and the number of annual passes and types sold has been restricted. One can't help but wonder whether the reduction in length of the *Nemo* musical that has occurred at the same time is part of a deliberate strategy to appeal primarily to nonregular guests, as opposed to serving those veterans who come at least once a year, if not more often.

Can-Seng Ooi reminds us that in the tourism sector, "People have different experiences even if they are doing the same thing in the same place."[46] For Ooi, expectations heavily dictate how a tourist will respond to a product, location, event, or activity. This provides one possible explanation for why *Nemo* often appealed to repeat visitors: having previously seen the performance, they knew what to expect, how much time to expect it to take, and what trade-offs they were making with the rest of their day. To keep guests' minds from wandering during the show, Disney might wish to consider Marc Wittman's research into the relation among embodiment, emotion, and the perception of time: "The association between duration reproduction performance and increasing neural activation in the insular cortex on the one hand and body functions and body experience on the other hand points to the notion that subjective time is strongly embodied."[47] As Philip Pearce explains, "It is not simply watching emotionally stirring episodes or stimuli that matters in reducing time estimates, but individuals have to be engaged with those emotions for the estimates to be reduced."[48] In other words, the more actively engaged the tourist is with the activity, the less their perceived loss of time will be. As Ooi says, "The right environment, props and cues will make people *interact* with the product at a deeper level, and these people will thus feel that the product has been personalized to suit them. Their experiences will be more satisfying."[49]

Finding Nemo: The Musical asked audience members to build an empathetic connection to Marlin as in a traditional piece of theater—or film. We followed him on an emotional journey, not just a literal one. As he traversed the ocean in search of his son, he also grew as a character, learning things about both his son and himself. Dramaturgically, *Finding Nemo: The Musical* mirrored the movie's arc of Marlin accepting that his son *can* in fact do things on his own and must be allowed to do so.

Finding Nemo: The Big Blue ... and Beyond!—again, notably not labeled as a musical—dispatches with all of this. We no longer see the initial trauma of Coral's death at the jaws of a shark that creates Marlin's overprotective behavior. We also see far fewer struggles for Marlin on his journey across the ocean, otherwise known as the traditional obstacles and complications that constitute Aristotelian rising action, most consequentially Dory's near-death experience in the jellyfish forest. As a result, we no longer experience a character arc for Marlin. We simply see the retelling of a plot.

We've subtitled this chapter "When Theatre Is a Theme-Park Attraction," and the transition between *Finding Nemo: The Musical* and *Finding Nemo: The Big Blue ... and Beyond!* reveals the significant differences. The addition of the frame story and the reduction in both number and development of dramatic episodes, coupled with the sprint-like speed at which *The Big Blue and Beyond* careens from story snapshot to story snapshot, reduces the musical into something entirely different from a stage musical, but not for the theme-park guest. We also compared the dramaturgical structure of a musical with that of a roller coaster, which may have been correct for *Finding Nemo: The Musical*, but its successor instead mirrors something else: the classic theme-park dark ride. In a Disney dark ride, the tourist boards a vehicle and travels through a series of scenes designed to tell a visual story. For Suzanne Rahn, "A Disney dark ride is conceived much like a cinematic or theatrical production," and it makes use of storyboards in the telling (or retelling) of its story.[50] On the Walt Disney World property, the closest comparison to *The Big Blue and Beyond* is actually the Magic Kingdom attraction Ariel's Adventures under the Sea, an Omnimover ride-through of the story of *The Little Mermaid*. In Ariel's Adventures, tourists board a "clamshell" vehicle and are greeted by the voice of Scuttle the seagull, who begins narrating Ariel's story, clearly establishing it as an event that occurred in the past and has since been resolved—much like Gill does in *The Big Blue and Beyond*. The clamshell continues moving through iconic scenes from the animated classic, each accompanied by songs from the film. An audio animatronic Ariel sings "Part of Your World" while examining her gadgets and gizmos, a cavalcade of sea creatures dance to the tune of Sebastian's "Under the Sea," and a highly complex audio animatronic Ursula musically celebrates the "Poor Unfortunate Souls" she "helps," building to Ariel and Prince Eric staring into each other's eyes while Sebastian urges the Prince to "Kiss the Girl," all culminating in a celebration scene complete with fireworks. The ride distills the movie down to iconic images and catchy tunes, dispatching with much by way of nuance and complication but never ceasing to present its audience with engaging spectacle and song.

Dark rides by their nature offer entertainment to tourists who might wish to skip higher-intensity rides like roller coasters, are aimed at the entire family regardless of age, and typically do not generate the sort of extreme wait times more commonly associated with the more elaborate "E ticket" attractions. While most dark rides might not generate as much fervid enthusiasm as something like Space Mountain, they offer a pleasant experience for the entire party, with comparatively shorter lines, and they absorb large quantities of tourists at once. *The Big Blue and Beyond* thus combines both the function and the storytelling of a dark ride, transplanting them to a theater venue—with deeply uncomfortable benches. This change, and the positive audience reception of it, demonstrates that while theatrical musicals and theme-park musicals may share the same building blocks and the same talented performer base, the generic conventions, aesthetic desires, and general regard of the idea of a Broadway musical on the part of the audience are widely divergent.

Notes

1. For purposes of clarity, throughout this chapter, we refer to the 2007–2020 *Finding Nemo: The Musical* show with either that full name or a shortened *Finding Nemo* or just *Nemo*. In 2022, Disney opened a heavily revised version known as *Finding Nemo: The Big Blue ... and Beyond*. When referring to that production, we will use either its full title or the shortened *The Big Blue and Beyond*.
2. Amy S. Osatinski, *Disney Theatrical Productions: Producing Broadway Musicals the Disney Way* (New York: Routledge, 2019), 11.
3. We conducted our research into fan reactions and ratings for *Finding Nemo: The Musical* prior to the opening of the revised show in 2022. Since the new show has opened, ratings sites have not distinguished between reviews and ratings for the old show versus the new one, simply aggregating them all into one listing, making data comparison between the two iterations tricky. Still, we are confident that the rating noted here reflects only fan response to the original show.
4. Alex Bádue and Rebecca S. Schorsch, "Animated Broadway: Disney and Musical Theater in the 1990s and Early 2000s," *American Music* 39, no. 2 (2021): 213, muse.jhu.edu/article/803313.
5. Ibid., 220.
6. Osatinski, *Disney Theatrical Productions*, 16.
7. Joshua Williams, "Review of *The Jungle Book* Directed by Mary Zimmerman," *Theatre Journal* 66, no. 2 (2014): 276–278, http://www.jstor.org/stable/24580318.
8. Chris Jones, "'The Jungle Book' at the Goodman Theatre," *Chicago Tribune*, December 24, 2018, https://www.chicagotribune.com/2013/07/01/the-jungle-book-at-the-goodman-theatre-3/.
9. Emily Clark et al., "'I Wanna Be Like You': Negotiating Race, Racism and Orientalism in *The Jungle Book* on Stage," in *The Disney Musical on Stage and Screen: Critical Approaches from 'Snow White' to 'Frozen'*, ed. George Rodosthenous (London: Bloomsbury, 2017), 185.
10. Osatinski, *Disney Theatrical Productions*, 79.
11. Ibid., 83.
12. Richard Schechner, "Julie Taymor: From Jacques Lecoq to *The Lion King*," *The Drama Review* 43, no. 3 (1999): 36–55, https://doi.org/10.1162/105420499760347315.
13. Maurya Wickstrom, "*The Lion King*, Mimesis, and Disney's Magical Capitalism," in *Rethinking Disney: Private Control, Public Dimensions*, ed. Mike Budd and Max H. Kirsch (Middletown, CT: Wesleyan University Press), 99–121.

14. Schechner, "Julie Taymor," 44.
15. Dassia N. Posner, "The Dramaturg(ies) of Puppetry and Visual Theatre," in *The Routledge Companion to Dramaturgy*, ed. Magda Romanska (London: Routledge, 2014), 339–340.
16. Skye Strauss, "Know the Value of Your Ideas: An Interview with Michael Curry," in *Theatre Artisans and Their Craft*, ed. Rafael Jaen, Holly Poe Durbin, and Christin Essin (New York: Routledge, 2019), 165.
17. All descriptions of *Finding Nemo: The Musical* are based on the authors' personal observations and memories of seeing the show in person multiple times over several years, confirmed through watching videos recorded by audience members and posted to YouTube, primarily "Finding Nemo—The Musical 4K," Steve's Theme Park Shows, March 27, 2018, https://www.youtube.com/watch?v=nTXm4eqisJU&t=606s.
18. "Meet the Puppeteers at 'Finding Nemo—The Musical,' Walt Disney World," Disney Parks, August 23, 2012, https://www.youtube.com/watch?v=EBHSIeBWsUw.
19. As evidence that it was confusing, this entire sequence was reworked for *The Big Blue and Beyond* yet still is difficult to follow.
20. See Tom Robson, "Haunted Waters: The Elimination of Liveness in Disney's *Rivers of Light*," in *Fan Phenomena: Disney*, ed. Sabrina Mittermeier (Bristol, UK: Intellect, 2022), 142–155.
21. Susanne Becken and Jude Wilson, "Trip Planning and Decision Making of Self-Drive Tourists—A Quasi-Experimental Approach." *Journal of Travel & Tourism Marketing* 20, nos. 3–4 (2006): 59.
22. Douglas G. Pearce, "Tourist Time-Budget," *Annals of Tourism Research* 15, no. 1 (1988): 106.
23. Daniel S. Hamermesh, "Not Enough Time?," *American Economist* 59, no. 2 (Fall 2014): 119–122; emphasis in original.
24. Philip L. Pearce, "Tourists' Perception of Time: Directions for Design," *Annals of Tourism Research* 83 (2020): 4.
25. Peter Toohey, *Boredom: A Lively History* (New Haven, CT: Yale University Press, 2011), 45.
26. Richard Farmer and Norman D. Sundberg, "Boredom Proneness—The Development and Correlates of a New Scale," *Journal of Personality Assessment* 50, no. 1 (1986): 15; emphasis in original.
27. Wendell O'Brien, "Boredom," *Analysis* 74, no. 2 (April 2014): 239.
28. Jim Davies and Mark Fortney, "The Menton Theory of Engagement and Boredom," First Annual Conference on Advances in Cognitive Systems, Poster Collection, 2012, 134.
29. Jennifer A. Kokai and Tom Robson, "Immersive Performance and Transgression at the Disney Theme Park," in *Enveloping Worlds: Toward a Discourse of Immersive Performance*, ed. E. B. Hunter and Scott Magelssen (Ann Arbor, MI: University of Michigan Press, 2025), 148–162.
30. Davies and Fortney, "The Menton Theory," 131.
31. Ibid., 136.
32. For more on the relationship between Broadway, aesthetics, and tourism, see, for example, Susan Bennett, "Theatre/Tourism," *Theatre Journal* 57, no. 3 (2005): 407–428; David Savran, "Middlebrow Anxiety," in *A Queer Sort of Materialism: Recontextualizing American Theatre*, ed. David Savran (Ann Arbor: University of Michigan Press, 2003), 3–55.
33. Terry Roen, "Theme Park Demographics Changing: Higher Incomes and More Millennials," Theme Park Tribune, April 24, 2017, https://www.themeparktribune.com/theme-park-demographics-changing-higher-incomes-and-more-millennials/.

34. Drew Harwell, "How Theme Parks Like Disney World Left the Middle Class Behind," *Washington Post*, June 12, 2015, https://www.washingtonpost.com/news/business/wp/2015/06/12/how-theme-parks-like-disney-world-left-the-middle-class-behind/.
35. J. Meredith Neil, "The Roller Coaster: Architectural Symbol and Sign," *Journal of Popular Culture* 15, no. 1 (Summer 1981): 108.
36. Rick Munarriz, "Disney World's New Roller Coaster Is Bigger Than You Think," The Motley Fool, April 5, 2022, https://www.fool.com/investing/2022/04/05/disney-worlds-new-roller-coaster-is-bigger-than-yo/.
37. Neil, "The Roller Coaster," 108.
38. Josephine Machon, *Immersive Theatres: Intimacy and Immediacy in Contemporary Performance* (New York: Palgrave Macmillan, 2013), 93–100.
39. Carlye Wisel, "Disney World and Disneyland Closed Indefinitely amid Covid-19 Fears," Vox, March 31, 2020, https://www.vox.com/the-goods/2020/3/12/21177375/disney-coronavirus-covid-19-theme-parks-disneyworld-disneyland.
40. "Walt Disney World Reopens in Florida amid Covid-19 Surge," BBC, July 11, 2020, https://www.bbc.com/news/world-us-canada-53371336.
41. "Walt Disney World Resort Reopening Information and Updates," DIS, n.d., https://www.wdwinfo.com/disney-world/reopening-information-updates.htm.
42. For more on the changed experience of a Disney park during this period, see Jennifer A. Kokai and Tom Robson, "Disney during Covid-19: The Tourist and the Actor's Nightmare," *Journal of Themed Experience and Attractions Studies* 2, no. 1 (2022): 17–20.
43. The new director does have extensive work in puppetry, and that was noticeable in the more sophisticated ways puppets were moved throughout the new version.
44. We watched two performances of the live production of *The Big Blue and Beyond* together at Disney's Animal Kingdom at eleven a.m. and twelve p.m. on Friday, January 6, 2023.
45. See Jennifer A. Kokai, "The Nemofication of Nature," in *Performance and the Disney Theme Park Experience: The Tourist as Actor*, ed. Jennifer A. Kokai and Tom Robson (London: Palgrave, 2019), 87–106.
46. Can-Seng Ooi, "A Theory of Tourism Experiences: The Management of Attention," in *Experiencescapes: Tourism, Culture and Economy*, ed. Tom O'Dell and Peter Billing (Copenhagen: Copenhagen Business School Press, 2005), 52.
47. Marc Wittman, "The Inner Sense of Time: How the Brain Creates a Representation of Duration," *Nature Reviews: Neuroscience* 14 (March 2013): 222.
48. P. Pearce, "Tourists' Perception of Time," 2.
49. Ooi, "A Theory of Tourism Experiences," 54; emphasis added.
50. Suzanne Rahn, "The Dark Ride of Snow White: Narrative Strategies at Disneyland," in *Disneyland and Culture: Essays on the Parks and Their Influence*, ed. Kathy Merlock Jackson and Mark I. West (Jefferson, NC: McFarland, 2011), 88.

Bibliography

Bádue, Alex, and Rebecca S. Schorsch. "Animated Broadway: Disney and Musical Theater in the 1990s and Early 2000s." *American Music* 39, no. 2 (2021): 212–225. muse.jhu.edu/article/803313.

Becken, Susanne, and Jude Wilson. "Trip Planning and Decision Making of Self-Drive Tourists—A Quasi-Experimental Approach." *Journal of Travel & Tourism Marketing* 20, nos. 3-4 (2006): 47–62.

Bennett, Susan. "Theatre/Tourism." *Theatre Journal* 57, no. 3 (2005): 407–428.
"The Broadway League Reveals 'The Demographics of the Broadway Audience' for 2018–2019 Season." Broadway League, January 13, 2019. https://www.broadwayleague.com/press/press-releases/the-broadway-league-reveals-the-demographics-of-the-broadway-audience-for-2018-2019-season/.
Clark, Emily, Donatella Galella, Stefanie A. Jones, and Catherine Young. "'I Wanna Be Like You': Negotiating Race, Racism and Orientalism in *The Jungle Book* on Stage." In *The Disney Musical on Stage and Screen: Critical Approaches from 'Snow White' to 'Frozen'*, edited by George Rodosthenous, 185–203. London: Bloomsbury, 2017.
Davies, Jim, and Mark Fortney. "The Menton Theory of Engagement and Boredom." First Annual Conference on Advances in Cognitive Systems. Poster Collection, 2012, 131–143.
Farmer, Richard, and Norman D. Sundberg. "Boredom Proneness—The Development and Correlates of a New Scale." *Journal of Personality Assessment* 50, no. 1 (1986): 4–17.
"Finding Nemo—The Musical 4K." Steve's Theme Park Shows, March 27, 2018. https://www.youtube.com/watch?v=nTXm4eqisJU&t=606s.
Hamermesh, Daniel S. "Not Enough Time?" *American Economist* 59, no. 2 (Fall 2014): 119–127.
Harwell, Drew. "How Theme Parks Like Disney World Left the Middle Class Behind." *Washington Post*, June 12, 2015. https://www.washingtonpost.com/news/business/wp/2015/06/12/how-theme-parks-like-disney-world-left-the-middle-class-behind/.Jones, Chris. "'The Jungle Book' at the Goodman Theatre." *Chicago Tribune*, December 24, 2018. https://www.chicagotribune.com/2013/07/01/the-jungle-book-at-the-goodman-theatre-3/.
Kokai, Jennifer A. "The Nemofication of Nature." In *Performance and the Disney Theme Park Experience: The Tourist as Actor*, edited by Jennifer A. Kokai and Tom Robson, 86–107. London: Palgrave, 2019.
Kokai, Jennifer A., and Tom Robson. "Disney during Covid-19: The Tourist and the Actor's Nightmare." *Journal of Themed Experience and Attractions Studies* 2, no. 1 (2022): 17–20.
Kokai, Jennifer A., and Tom Robson. "Immersive Performance and Transgression at the Disney Theme Park." In *Enveloping Worlds: Toward a Discourse of Immersive Performance*, edited by E. B. Hunter and Scott Magelssen, 148–162. Ann Arbor: University of Michigan Press, 2025.
Kokai, Jennifer A., and Tom Robson. *Performance and the Disney Theme Park Experience: The Actor as Tourist*. London: Palgrave, 2019.
Machon, Josephine. *Immersive Theatres: Intimacy and Immediacy in Contemporary Performance*. New York: Palgrave Macmillan, 2013.
"Meet the Puppeteers at 'Finding Nemo—The Musical,' Walt Disney World." Disney Parks, August 23, 2012. https://www.youtube.com/watch?v=EBHSIeBWsUw.
Munarriz, Rick. "Disney World's New Roller Coaster Is Bigger Than You Think." The Motley Fool, April 5, 2022. https://www.fool.com/investing/2022/04/05/disney-worlds-new-roller-coaster-is-bigger-than-yo/.
Neil, J. Meredith. "The Roller Coaster: Architectural Symbol and Sign." *Journal of Popular Culture* 15, no. 1 (Summer 1981): 108.
O'Brien, Wendell. "Boredom." *Analysis* 74, no. 2 (April 2014): 236–244.
Ooi, Can-Seng. "A Theory of Tourism Experiences: The Management of Attention." In *Experiencescapes: Tourism, Culture and Economy*, edited by Tom O'Dell and Peter Billing, 51–68. Copenhagen: Copenhagen Business School Press, 2005.
Osatinski, Amy S. *Disney Theatrical Productions: Producing Broadway Musicals the Disney Way*. New York: Routledge, 2019.
Pearce, Douglas G. "Tourist Time-Budget." *Annals of Tourism Research* 15, no. 1 (1988): 106–121.

Pearce, Philip L. "Tourists' Perception of Time: Directions for Design." *Annals of Tourism Research* 83 (2020): 1–9.

Posner, Dassia N. "The Dramaturg(ies) of Puppetry and Visual Theatre." In *The Routledge Companion to Dramaturgy*, edited by Magda Romanska, 369–375. London: Routledge, 2014.

Rahn, Suzanne. "The Dark Ride of Snow White: Narrative Strategies at Disneyland." In *Disneyland and Culture: Essays on the Parks and Their Influence*, edited by Kathy Merlock Jackson and Mark I. West, 87–100. Jefferson, NC: McFarland, 2011.

Robson, Tom. "Haunted Waters: The Elimination of Liveness in Disney's *Rivers of Light*." In *Fan Phenomena: Disney*, edited by Sabrina Mittermeier, 142–155. Bristol, UK: Intellect, 2022.

Roen, Terry. "Theme Park Demographics Changing: Higher Incomes and More Millennials." Theme Park Tribune, April 24, 2017. https://www.themeparktribune.com/theme-park-demographics-changing-higher-incomes-and-more-millennials/.

Savran, David. "Middlebrow Anxiety." In *A Queer Sort of Materialism: Recontextualizing American Theatre*, edited by David Savran, 3–55. Ann Arbor: University of Michigan Press, 2003.

Schechner, Richard. "Julie Taymor: From Jacques Lecoq to *The Lion King*." *The Drama Review* 43, no. 3 (1999): 36–55. https://doi.org/10.1162/105420499760347315.

Strauss, Skye. "Know the Value of Your Ideas: An Interview with Michael Curry." In *Theatre Artisans and Their Craft*, edited by Rafael Jaen, Holly Poe Durbin, and Christin Essin, 159–170. New York: Routledge, 2019.

Toohey, Peter. *Boredom: A Lively History*. New Haven, CT: Yale University Press, 2011.

"Walt Disney World Reopens in Florida amid Covid-19 Surge." BBC, July 11, 2020. https://www.bbc.com/news/world-us-canada-53371336.

"Walt Disney World Resort Reopening Information and Updates." DIS, n.d. https://www.wdwinfo.com/disney-world/reopening-information-updates.htm.

Wickstrom, Maurya. "*The Lion King*, Mimesis, and Disney's Magical Capitalism." In *Rethinking Disney: Private Control, Public Dimensions*, edited by Mike Budd and Max H. Kirsch, 99–121. Middletown, CT: Wesleyan University Press, 2005.

Williams, Joshua. "Review of *The Jungle Book* Directed by Mary Zimmerman." *Theatre Journal* 66, no. 2 (2014): 276–278. http://www.jstor.org/stable/24580318.

Wisel, Carlye. "Disney World and Disneyland Closed Indefinitely amid Covid-19 Fears." Vox, March 31, 2020. https://www.vox.com/the-goods/2020/3/12/21177375/disney-coronavirus-covid-19-theme-parks-disneyworld-disneyland.

Wittman, Marc. "The Inner Sense of Time: How the Brain Creates a Representation of Duration." *Nature Reviews: Neuroscience* 14 (March 2013): 217–223.

Index

For the benefit of digital users, indexed terms that span two pages (e.g., 52–53) may, on occasion, appear on only one of those pages.

Tables and figures are indicated by an italic *t* and *f* following the page number.

ABC, 209–10, 215–18, 219–20, 221–25, 483, 484, 490, 493, 510
Abdul, Paula, 330–31
Abreu, Zequinha de, 357–59, 453
Abyss, The, 322–23
ACES. *See* Automatic Camera Effects System
Adams, Edie, 389
Adams, James Truslow, 63
ADC. *See* American-Arab Anti-Discrimination Committee
Adelquist, Hal, 90
"A-E-I-O-U," 163–64
AFTRA. *See* American Federation of Television and Radio Artists
Agnes of God, 486–87
Aguilar, Layanna, 458
Aida, 501, 506, 523–24, 525, 530
Aladdin (1992), 101–2, 194, 202, 203–4, 450, 513, 581–82
    Ashman and Menken songs for, 377–78, 491, 500, 550–51, 571, 577–78
    computer animation in, 322–24, 336–37
    orientalism of, 101, 102–5, 109, 112
Aladdin (2019), 105–8, 119, 188, 204–5, 340–41, 377–78
    Arabian Nights narratives, rebuilding Agrabah and, 108–16
    Bollywood and, 110–11, 113–16
    "I Want" song in, 188–90, 194–97
    orientalism of, 109, 112–14, 117–18
    racial ambiguity, casting controversies and, 116–18
    romantic song in, 202, 203–4

Aladdin (theatrical musical), 104–5, 177, 501–2, 504–6, 511, 513–14, 523, 525, 571–72
    development partnerships and, 535–36
    Disney theme parks and, 535–36
    new songs in, 577–78, 581–82, 584–85
Aladdin, Jelani, 209–10
Aladdin and His Wonderful Lamp, 355
Aladdin and the King of Thieves, 504
Aladdin JR., 513
Aladdin: The Return of Jafar, 134–35, 504
Alaimo, Stacy, 257–58
Alexander, Jason, 222
Alice Chops the Suey, 51–52
Alice Comedies, 40, 43–45, 47–48, 50–52, 53, 55, 56, 151
Alice Gets in Dutch, 43–45
Alice Gets Stung, 44–45
Alice Helps the Romance, 43–44, 51
Alice in Wonderland (1951), 233–34, 260–62
    as adaptation, 150–57, 158, 166
    songs of, 150–51, 157–65, 166
    songwriting teams for, 149–51, 166
    on television, 216–17, 218–19, 221, 224
    vaudeville and, 154, 156, 158–59, 162–64, 165, 166
Alice in Wonderland (Carroll), 152–53, 159
Alice's Circus Daze, 43–44, 51–52
Alice's Egg Plant, 50–51
Alice's Mysterious Mystery, 44
Alice Solves the Puzzle, 44–45
Alice's Spooky Adventure, 47
Alice's Wild West Show, 55
Alice's Wonderland, 43–44, 47–48, 150
Alice the Fire Fighter, 45, 47

Alice the Jailbird, 44–45
Alice the Peacemaker, 44–45, 47
Alice the Piper, 45
Alice the Whaler, 43–44, 45
"All Alone," 6
Allan, Robin, 24
"All I Ask of You," 384–85
"All I Need Is an Angel," 213–14
"All in the Golden Afternoon," 159, 160
"All I Want," 85, 86, 89
"All My Loving," 305
"All Star," 200–1
All Wet, 47
"Almost There," 189–90
"Aloha E Komo Mai," 138
"Aloha 'Oe," 133
Altman, Rick, 52, 66–67, 197, 327–30
Altman, Robert, 484
Alvin and the Chipmunks, 262
Amaral, Nestor, 360–61
American-Arab Anti-Discrimination Committee (ADC), 102
American Cinematographer, 321
American dream, 62–63, 64–65, 67, 70
American Federation of Television and Radio Artists (AFTRA), 238–39
American in Paris, An, 32
American Society of Composers, Authors, and Publishers (ASCAP), 357–58
American Tail, An, 317–18
AMPTP. *See* Association of Motion Picture and Television Producers
Anchors Aweigh, 330–31
Andersen, Hans Christian, 391, 558–59
Anderson, Christopher, 216, 219
Anderson-Lopez, Kristen, 201–2, 391, 592–93
Andrews, Julie, 173, 175–77, 183–84, 222
Ang, Ien, 429
animals, 255–73
Ān líng yǔ shǐ dí qí, 126
Annie, 222, 223, 485, 499
"Anything Can Happen," 583–84
"Aquarela do Brasil," 357–60, 367, 453
Aquino, Ruben, 379
"Arabian Nights," 111–12
Arabian Nights narratives, 108–16
Arcimboldo, Giuseppe, 351–52

Armstrong, Harry, 55
Arroyo, Joe, 464
ASCAP. *See* American Society of Composers, Authors, and Publishers
Ashman, Howard, 104–5, 327, 377–78, 379, 380–81, 384, 491, 499–500, 550–51, 571, 577–78, 584–85
Association of Motion Picture and Television Producers (AMPTP), 238–39
Astaire, Fred, 9, 63–64, 66–67, 325–27
Atkinson, Brooks, 479–80
Atlantis: The Lost Empire, 91–92, 340
Atlas, Larry, 488
Auberjonois, René, 222
Automatic Camera Effects System (ACES), 321
Averill, Gage, 306
Avery, Tex, 30, 349–50
Avila, Jacqueline, 459–60
"Ay! Jalisco, no te rajes," 363–64, 455–56

Babbitt, Art, 23–24
Babington, Bruce, 67–68
backstage musicals, 33–34, 65–68, 191–92, 193, 327–30
Backstage with Disney on Broadway: Celebrating 20 Years, 510
Badshah, 115–16
Bádue, Alex, 593–95
"Baía," 359–61, 362f
Bailey, Halle, 594–95
Bailey, Kate, 385, 594–95
Bailin, Marc, 244–45
Baker, Dee Bradley, 137
Bakshi, Ralph, 317–18
"Ballad of Davy Crockett, The," 220
Baltimore, Sam, 104–5
Bambi, 17–18, 20–25, 31–32, 34, 129, 164, 219, 256
effacing technology, 30–35
music and, 25–30
nonhuman animals in, 258, 269
Snow White and the Seven Dwarfs and, 20, 22–23, 25, 26, 29, 30–31, 258
World War II and, 24, 36
Band Concert, The, 8–9
barbershop, 297–99, 305, 306–8, 313n.49, 313n.51

Barnyard Concert, The, 6
Barrie, J. M., 528–29
Barrier, Michael, 23, 24, 83–84
Barroso, Ary, 357–59, 360–61, 453, 455
Barry, Dave, 528–29
Bart, Roger, 209–10
Baskett, James, 83, 85, 86–87, 88
Batchelder, Daniel, 274n.14, 274n.16
Bates, Kathy, 222
Bayless, Martha, 113–14
Bean, Kellie, 194
Beatles, the, 297–98, 299, 300–2, 304, 305, 307–8, 308n.2
Beaumont, Kathryn, 151
Beauty and the Beast (1991), 67, 68–69, 70, 104–5, 109, 110, 172, 192, 194, 202–3, 279–80
　Ashman and Menken songs for, 377–78, 380–81, 491, 499–500, 550–51, 571
　computer animation in, 323–31, 325f, 328f
　Descendants and, 431, 442
　in Disney Renaissance, 550–51, 552–53, 571–72
　princess in, 377, 380–84, 552–53, 574
Beauty and the Beast (2017), 188, 194–95, 202–5, 340–41, 388–89, 431
Beauty and the Beast (theatrical musical), 177, 222–23, 384–87, 477, 498, 499, 501, 502, 507, 514–15, 520, 536–37, 542, 571–72
　beyond Broadway, 387–88
　demographics and, 505, 506
　Disney theme parks and, 500
　international partnerships and international productions, 521, 522
　licensing, 512, 513–14
　merchandising, 510–11
　new songs in, 573–74, 579–81
　school performances of, 543, 545, 550–56, 560
　Shiki Company production of, 522, 523
　Stage Entertainment production of, 523–24
"Beauty and the Beast," 188–89, 197, 198–99, 202–3, 204–5
Beauty and the Beast: A 30th Anniversary Celebration, 225, 388–89
Beck, Christophe, 411–13, 414
Becken, Susanne, 600

Becoming Memories, 488
Bedknobs and Broomsticks, 150, 176, 183–84, 330–31
"Being Mrs. Banks," 583–85
Bell, Elizabeth, 375, 381, 382
"Bella Notte," 234, 236, 246–47
Belle, Regina, 114
"Belle," 192, 194, 323–25, 382–83, 388, 579–80
"Belle (Reprise)," 574
Bellini, Vincenzo, 376
Belson, Jerry, 486
Beltrán, Mary C., 438
Benedict, Ed, 6
Benson, Jodi, 224, 246, 323–24, 378
"Be Our Guest," 68–69, 203–4, 325–27, 382, 442
"Be Prepared," 327
Berkeley, Busby, 9, 325–27, 330–31, 365–66, 460
Berlin, Irving, 6, 319
Best Little Whorehouse in Texas, The, 484, 485, 486
Beverly Hills Chihuahua, 457
"Beware the Jabberwock," 157–58
Beynon, George, 53–54
"Beyond My Wildest Dreams," 576–77
"Beyond the Laughing Sky," 161–62
"Bibbity Bobbity Boo," 389
Bickford, Tyler, 428
Big Bad Wolf, The, 184
Big Hero 6, 187
Bishop, Henry, 42–43
Black and Tan, 80–81
Black artists, in Hollywood, 77–78
Black Cauldron, The, 320
blackface minstrelsy, 51, 82, 83, 93n.23
Black Hole, The, 487
Blackness, 77–78, 79, 80–81, 83, 84, 87, 93n.21, 104–6, 376–77, 437–38
Blackton, J. Stuart, 331–32
Black Widow, 231–32
Blair, Lee, 356–57
Blair, Mary, 285, 416–17
Blame It on the Samba, 356–57
Blasband, David, 240, 241, 244
Bloodsworth-Lugo, Mary K., 102
Blue Rhythm, 6
Blunt, Emily, 180, 182

Bluth, Don, 315–16, 317–18
BMI. *See* Broadcast Music Incorporated
Bodrero, Jim, 356–57
Bogaev, Paul, 390
Bohanon, Margaret, 51
"Bohemian Rhapsody," 201–2
Bohn, James, 32, 128–29
Bollywood, 110–11, 113–16
Bonhomme, Bérénice, 203
Book of Mormon, The, 507, 509
Bordwell, David, 63–64
Borresen, Kelsey, 439
"Bottom Line, The," 581
Boydston, Jeanne, 382
Bradford, Clare, 194
Brandy, 222, 390
Brantley, Ben, 504–5, 527
Brave, 107
Braxton, Toni, 385–88, 389
"Brazil," 453
Break a Leg, 485
Brecht, Bertolt, 31
Breen, Joseph, 87–88
Brer Rabbit, 84–85, 218–19
Bright Lights, 51–52, 56
"Brimstone and Treacle," 580
Broadcast Music Incorporated (BMI), 357–58
Broadway, 480–87
    mass entertainment and, 477–80, 482–83, 488–90
Broadway, Disney and, 477–78, 480, 487–93
    branding and marketing, 509–10
    demographics, 503–6
    family-friendly musicals and, 499
    licensing, 511–14
    merchandising, 510–11
    New Amsterdam Theater, 177, 491, 492, 493, 503, 504–5, 506, 510–11, 542
    schools and, 542–43
    ticket pricing, 506–9, 508f
    Times Square redevelopment, 482, 489–90, 491–93, 498, 503, 542, 601–2
    transformation of animated library, 500–2
    Walt Disney World and, 502, 503, 507, 508f, 520, 602
    See also Disney Theatrical

Broadway-style musical numbers, 316, 318–19, 323–24, 325–27, 340–41, 378, 389, 394, 491, 571
Brode, Douglas, 173–74
Broken Toys, 11–12
Brosius, Peter, 592–93
Broski, Brittany, 534
Brother Bear 2, 414–15
brownface, 110–11, 116, 118
Bryson, Peabo, 114
Buck, Chris, 269, 407, 417–18
Buena Vista Home Video, 245, 247
Buena Vista Television, 223
Buena Vista Theatrical, 514
Building a Building, 7
Bukatman, Scott, 47–48
Bunch, Ryan, 268–69, 316, 394, 395
Burke, Joseph F. "Sonny," 234–35, 236, 237f, 238
Burroughs, Edgar Rice, 524
Burton-Carvajal, Julianne, 453
Bush, Jared, 462–63, 464, 469
Busse, Henry, 49–50
Byrne, Eleanor, 103

Cabaret, 380
Cabot, Sebastian, 297
Calhoun, Jeff, 531
"Call Me a Princess," 584–85
Calloway, Cab, 82, 83
Cameron, Dove, 429–30, 432, 433–34, 435–37
Campos, Florencio Molina, 453–54
Camp Rock, 428
Candland, Paul, 140
"Can You Feel the Love Tonight," 198–99
"Can You Imagine That," 180–81
Capra, Frank, 93n.21
CAPS. *See* Computer Animation Production System
Care, Ross, 7–8, 27, 28, 29
Carey, Drew, 222
Carlson, Marvin, 393–94
Carman, Emily, 232
Carnegie, Dale, 65–66
Carrere, Tia, 132–33, 137–38
Carroll, Lewis, 149, 150–53, 154, 155–58, 159, 160, 163–64, 166
Carroll, Pat, 379

Carson, Sofia, 430, 432, 434–38
Caselotti, Adriana, 191–92, 248
"Casey Junior," 81
Castro Smith, Charice, 469
Cats, 483, 502, 503
"Caucus Race, The," 163, 165
Caymmi, Dorival, 360–61
Cepeda, Maria Elena, 464–65
Cerasaro, Pat, 386–87
Cerniglia, Ken, 522–23, 524–25, 528–29, 530–31, 532, 543, 546–47, 548, 555–56, 560
Cervantes, Isabel, 584
CGI. *See* computer-generated imagery
"Change in Me, A," 386, 387–88, 574
Chapek, Bob, 432–33, 606
Charley on the Farm, 47
Chase, Daveigh, 137
Chase, Debra Martin, 389–90
Chazarreta, Andrés, 453–54
Cheetah Girls, The, 427–28, 437–38
Cheetah Girls 2, 433
Cheng, Emily, 131–32, 138–39
Chenoweth, Kristin, 222, 429–30, 433–34, 435
"Cherry Tree Lane," 583–84
Chicken Little, 319–20
Chip and Dale, 260–62
"Chipmunk Song, The," 262
Chocolate Soldier, The, 50
Chorus Line, A, 493, 502
Chouinard Art Institute, 22, 24
Churchill, Frank, 6–9, 11–12, 13, 14, 15–16, 17–18, 18n.10
    Alice in Wonderland songs by Osborne and, 149, 155
    Bambi score by Plumb and, 25, 27, 32
    Bambi songs by Morey and, 20, 28–29
    Dumbo songs by Wallace and Washington and, 81, 349–50
CIAA. *See* Coordinator of Inter-American Affairs
Cinderalla (1997), 222, 223, 377, 380, 389–90, 499
Cinderella (1950), 67, 69–70, 110, 197, 199, 218–19, 233–34, 249, 256–57, 260–63, 347, 375, 389, 550–51
Cinderella (2015), 194–95, 202
"Circle of Life," 583

Clark, Emily, 104–5, 595–96
Clarke, Savile, 152
Clements, Ron, 379
Clock Store, The, 6
Coben, Cy, 150
Coco, 225, 459–62, 468, 470–71, 547
Cocovinis, Jason, 545
Cohen, Harvey, 63–64
Cohl, Émile, 331–32
Coldoni, Carlo, 512
Coleman, Cy, 485
Collins, Arthur, 283
Collins, Gemma, 381
Collins, Phil, 200–1, 332–35, 524–25, 575
"Colombia Mi Encanto," 464–65
Colombianness, 462–69
Colonna, Jerry, 156
color, 352–67, 359*f*, 362*f*, 365*f*, 366, 367–68
"coming out" songs, 392, 394
"Coming Up Roses," 394
Computer Animation Production System (CAPS), 320, 321–22, 323–25, 327, 332–35, 337, 338*f*
computer-generated imagery (CGI) and computer animation, 316, 318–21, 322*f*, 322–31, 325*f*, 328*f*, 337–39, 340–41. *See also* digital visual effects
Computer Graphics World, 321, 322
Confrey, Zez, 8–9
Conlon, Jud, 160–61
Connelly, Marc, 78, 79–80
Conner, William, 239–40
Cookie Carnival, The, 11
Cooper, Bud, 49–50
Coordinator of Inter-American Affairs (CIAA), 356–57, 451–52
Copyright Act of 1909, 243
Copyright Extension Act in 1998, 241
Cordes, Ashley, 418, 421, 422–23
Cortazar, Ernesto, 455–56
Costa, Mary, 249
Cottrell, Bill, 8–9, 356–57
Coulter, Natalie, 428, 429
"Cover Is Not the Book, A," 180–81
COVID-19 pandemic, 231, 501–2, 505–6, 534–35, 550, 554–55, 560, 591–92, 599, 601–2

Cox, Veanne, 390
Crafton, Donald, 41, 44–45, 51–52, 56
Craig, Tony, 135–36
Cravalho, Auli'i, 213
Craven, Allison, 553
Crenshaw, Kimberlé, 117
Crimes of the Heart, 485–86
Crommett, Julie Ann, 116–18
Crowther, Bosley, 86–87
Cruella, 225
cultural appropriation, 112, 114, 406–8, 450–51, 557, 558
Cultural Imagineering, 450–51, 460, 462, 464, 470–71
Cummings, Jim, 288
Curry, Michael, 592–93, 596–97, 598–99

Daboo, Jerri, 116
"Daddy's Little Angel," 580–81
Daffy Duck's Fantastic Island, 317–18
Dalí, Salvador, 349–50
Daly, Ann, 245–47
Damon, Stuart, 389
"Dance of the Cacti," 365–66
"Dangerous to Dream," 578
Dangerous When Wet, 330–31
Daniel, Eliot, 85, 233–34
Dapper Dans, the, 306–7
Darby, Ken, 86
Darlington, Marion, 32, 256
Darwin, Charles, 153–54
Dateline: Disneyland, 220
David, Karen, 117–18
David, Mack, 149–50, 156–57
Davies, Jim, 600–1
Davis, Amy, 194, 382
Davis, Lou, 49–50
Davy Crockett, 218–20
"Dawn on the Meadow," 25
Day, Maurice "Jake," 24
deBessonet, Lear, 532–33
DeBlois, Dean, 125, 128, 129–30, 131–32, 133–35, 136, 139
Decca Records, 234, 235, 242
Deep Canvas, 332–36, 337–39
"Defying Gravity," 394
"Deilig er jorden," 411–12

Deja, Andreas, 103–4, 298, 299–300, 301–2
DeLuca, John, 180
del Vecho, Peter, 408–9, 416, 422
DeMello, Margo, 256
De Paur, Leonard, 89
Descendants, 106, 427–28, 429–32, 433–43
Descendants 2, 434, 437–38
Descendants 3, 435–36, 437–38, 441–42
Descendants: Wicked World, 435–36
Deselle, Natalie, 390
Deutsch, Alvin, 240–41
Devil and Max Devlin, The, 487
"Devil in Disguise," 128–29
DeVoll, Cal, 50–51
"Diamond in the Rough," 581–82
Dickens, Charles, 320
"Different," 585–86
"Dig a Little Deeper," 442
digital visual effects (VFX), 316–17, 318–20, 321, 322–23, 325–27, 330–32, 340–41
Dinosaur, 340
direct-to-television (DTV) sequels, 134–38
Diskin, Ben, 141–42
Disney+, 55, 143, 183–84, 209–10, 224–25, 231, 427, 428, 469–70, 504, 549
Disney, Lilian, 452
Disney, Roy, 14, 176–77, 216–17, 220, 224–25, 246–47
Disney, Walt
   on *Alice in Wonderland*, 151, 154, 155–56, 158–59, 165, 166
   American dream and, 64
   Babbitt and, 23–24
   Bambi and, 24–25
   barbershop and, 306–7
   on the Beatles, 298, 300–2
   branding of animated films in name of, 33, 34
   on Churchill, 18n.10
   conservationism and environmentalism of, 255–56, 258–59, 273
   Dalí and, 349–50
   death of, 175–77, 181–82, 315–16
   Dumbo and, 23
   effects department created by, 349
   Fantasia and, 23
   in El Grupo, 452, 454–55
   on innovation, 319

Johnson, H., and, 77
on *The Jungle Book*, 298, 299–302, 308n.4, 309n.15, 310n.17
Lady and the Tramp, Lee, P., and, 233, 234–35, 236, 244, 246–47
Latin American features and, 356–57
at Laugh-O-Gram Studio, 43–44
on *Mary Poppins*, 173, 174, 179, 181–82, 184, 526, 583–84
on merchandising, 216–17
on Mickey Mouse, 40–41
on "Minnie's Yoo Hoo," 5, 6
multifaceted public persona of, 35
on "The Silly Song," 14
Snow White and the Seven Dwarfs and, 12–13, 64, 68
Song of the South and, 84, 87
on sophisticated craftsmanship in late 1930s films, 12–13
in *South of the Border with Disney*, 453
Steamboat Willie and, 3–4
on story and character in animated cartoons, 48
surrealism and, 349–50
television and, 216, 217, 218–19, 220, 224–25
on *The Three Little Pigs*, 184
on Uncle Remus stories, 84
on "Who's Afraid of the Big Bad Wolf," 8
Disneybounding, 439, 440, 442
Disney Channel, 217–18, 221, 223, 427–29, 432–33, 434–35, 437–38, 440–41, 442, 469–70, 504, 512
Disney Character Voices International, 127, 141–42
Disney Cruise Lines Frozen: A Musical Spectacular, 509–10
Disney cruise ships, 504
Disneyformalism, 315–16
Disney formula, 188–89, 198–99, 204–5
Disney Imagineering, 336–37
Disneyland, 175–76, 179–80, 217–20, 224–25, 238, 277–87, 280t, 282f, 288, 291, 306–7, 348, 362–63
Disney Music Group, 432
Disney Renaissance era, 101–2, 315–17, 318–41, 376, 378, 381, 490–91, 500, 513–14, 550–51, 552–53, 554, 571–72

Disney's Aladdin—A Musical Spectacular, 504
Disney's My Son Pinocchio: Geppetto's Musical Tale, 512
Disney Stores, 439–40, 505, 510
Disney theatrical musicals, in schools, 542–44
Beauty and the Beast, case study, 551–54
capitalism, art, identity and, 546–47
case studies of shows, 550–60
Disney Musicals in Schools program, 546, 549
familiarity of, 550
family-friendly content of, 549
Frozen, case study, 558–60
gender and, 546–47, 552, 553, 555–56, 558
JR. and KIDS versions, 544–47, 548–49, 551, 554, 555–59
Moana JR., case study, 556–58
MTI and, 544–46, 547, 548–49, 551, 556
Newsies, case study of, 554–56
race and, 546–47, 555–56, 557
support for teachers, 548–49
theatrical agency and, 560
Disney theatrical musicals, new songs in, 572, 586
Aladdin, 577–78, 581–82, 584–85
Beauty and the Beast, 573–74, 579–81
Frozen, 578–79, 582
"I Am" songs, 572–74, 575–76, 577–78, 580–81, 582, 583–84, 585
"I Want" songs, 572–73, 574, 575, 576, 577–78, 580–81, 582, 583–85
The Lion King, 574–75, 580, 582–83
The Little Mermaid, 576–77, 580–81, 584–85
Mary Poppins, 576, 580, 582, 583–84
Newsies, 581, 584
for protagonists, 572–79
for supporting female characters, 582–86
Tarzan, 575, 579, 582, 585–86
for villains, 579–82
Disney Theatrical, 172, 209–10, 432, 498, 542–43, 545, 546, 592, 596
branding and marketing, 490, 509–10, 528, 533, 549
demographics and, 504, 505, 506
development partnerships, 525–36
JR. and KIDS versions of theatrical musicals, 513, 544–47, 548–49, 551, 554, 555–59

Disney Theatrical (*cont.*)
   licensing, 512, 513, 514, 525, 530–31, 532, 535–36, 543, 544–46, 548–49, 551, 558–59
   merchandising, 510–11, 521
   music materials for schools, 548
   partnerships of, 520–37, 543, 544–46, 548–49
   Schumacher at, 492, 500–1, 502, 504–5, 506–7, 510, 511, 512–13, 514–15, 526–27, 528, 529, 534–35, 536, 542, 546, 571–72
   Shiki Company partnership, 522–23
   Stage Entertainment partnership, 523–25
   Team Disney and, 176–77
   transformation of animated library for theatrical productions, 500–1, 502, 571–72
Disney theme-park shows, 336–37, 500–1, 535–36, 591–605, 606–8
divas, 376–84, 387, 388–90, 391–96
Divine, 379
Dodd, Jimmie, 90
Dodge, Marcia Milgrom, 387
"Do I Love You Because You're Beautiful?," 390
Donald Duck, 9–10, 219, 260–62, 352–53, 356–57, 358–60, 363–66, 364*f*, 365*f*, 367*f*, 368, 453, 454–55
Dooley, James, 278–79, 280, 281, 282, 285–86, 288, 289–90
doo-wop, 306, 307
do Rozario, Rebecca-Anne C., 375, 379
"Dos Oruguitas," 467–68
"Do What You Gotta Do," 442
"Do You Want to Build a Snowman," 395
Drabinsky, Garth, 489
Drake, Philip, 232
"Dream Is a Wish Your Heart Makes, A," 67
DreamWorks Theatrical, 514
Drewe, Anthony, 576
Dreyfuss, Richard, 223
DTV. *See* direct-to-television
Dumbo, 17, 23, 129, 219, 233–34, 269
   Hall Johnson Choir and, 77–78, 81–84
   "Pink Elephants on Parade" sequence in, 81, 331–32, 332*f*, 349–53, 351*f*, 356, 358, 359–60, 363–65, 367
   surrealism in, 347–48, 349–53
Dyer, Richard, 63–64, 189
Dynes, Rhyannon, 558

EARidescence, 362–63
Earle, Eyvind, 416–17
Easy Rider, 356
"Eatnemen Vuelie," 411
Ebb, Fred, 380
Edelman, Susan, 246
Edison, Thomas, 319
Educational Theatre Association (EdTA), 545, 547, 549, 557, 558–59
Edwards, Cliff, 16–17, 83, 84
Egan, Susan, 384, 385
Eisner, Michael, 125–26, 134–35, 176–77, 179, 240, 241, 315–16, 318–19, 377–78, 490, 491, 500, 520, 526–27, 596
Elena of Avalor, 458–59, 462
Elice, Rick, 528–29
Eliot, Marc, 24–25
Elyas, Sadeen, 62–63
Encanto, 462–69, 466*f*, 467*f*, 468*f*, 470–71, 473n.43, 547
Enchanted, 192–93, 197–99, 201–2, 204–5, 375
"Endless Night," 574–75, 583
Epic Mickey, 277–87, 279*f*, 280*t*, 282*f*, 284*f*, 286*f*, 288, 291
Epic Mickey 2: The Power of Two, 277, 287–91, 288*t*, 289*f*
época de oro, 455–56, 460, 461
Epstein, Brian, 298
Esperón, Manuel, 455–56
Evans, Peter William, 67–68
"Everything That I Am," 575
"Evil Like Me," 433–34
Eyre, Richard, 177

Fagan, Garth, 583
Fain, Sammy, 150, 158, 159, 160–65, 166
Fairclough, Kirsty, 383, 388
"Fairy Godmother Song," 200–1
"Falling in Love with Love," 390
Familia, La, 469
Fanning, Dakota, 137
Fantasia, 23, 30–31, 81, 219, 249, 278, 283, 284*f*, 287, 331–32, 347, 361, 370n.18
Fantasia 2000, 340
Fantasmagorie, 331–32
Farid-ul-Haq, 117–18
Farmer, Richard, 600–1

Farrell, Kirby, 383
"Feed the Birds," 173, 174, 180–81, 183
Feldman, Jack, 530, 532, 555–56, 584
Felix Outwits Cupid, 54
Felix Strikes It Rich, 47
Felix the Cat cartoons, 47, 50, 52–54
Fellowes, Julian, 177–78, 580
female villains, 375–76, 377–80, 383, 392, 395
feminism, 108, 175, 182–83, 193–94, 202, 268, 269, 380–84, 388, 394, 432–33, 550–51, 553, 559, 560
Ferguson, Norman, 331–32, 350, 360
Festival of the Lion King, The, 593, 598–99, 603–4
Festspielhaus, 31
Feuer, Jane, 33–34, 192, 327–30, 382–83
Fiddling Around, 6
"Fidelity Fiduciary Bank," 173, 174, 182–83
Fierstein, Harvey, 212, 530, 584
Finding Dory, 604
Finding Nemo, 281–82, 591, 604–5
Finding Nemo: The Big Blue . . . and Beyond!, 603–5, 607–8
Finding Nemo: The Musical, 591–604, 595f, 606–7
Fine, Sidney, 233–34
Fire & Ice, 317–18
"Fish Are Friends, Not Food," 598
Fisk Jubilee Singers, 92n.2
Fjellheim, Frode, 411–13
Fjellheim, Rune, 409
Flatt, Andrew, 509
Fleeger, Jennifer, 191–92, 323–24
Fleischer Bros., 355
Flowers and Trees, 348–49
Floyd, George, 554–55
Flying Mouse, The, 11–12
Follow the Fleet, 66–67
Fonneland, Trude, 414, 417, 418
Ford, Henry, 319
form constants, 347–48, 355–56, 363, 367–68
"For the First Time," 585–86
"For the First Time in Forever," 395, 578–79
"For the First Time in Forever (Reprise)," 578–79
For the First Time in Forever: A Frozen Sing-Along Celebration, 604–5

Fortmueller, Kate, 232, 238–39
Fortney, Mark, 600–1
Foster, Michael Dylan, 141
Foster, Norman, 218–19
Foster, Stephen, 306
Four Musicians of Bremen, The, 43–44
Fox and the Hound, The, 223, 315–16, 320
Fox Chase, The, 44–45
Freaky Friday, 501–2, 512
Freeman, Elizabeth, 441
Freeman, Robert L., 389–90
Friedman, Stephen R., 485
"Friend Like Me," 114–15, 203–4
Frozen, 70, 107, 109, 180, 187, 189–90, 193–94, 198–99, 200–1, 558–59, 579, 592–93, 594
  diva in, 377, 391–96
  joik in, 407–8, 410–14
  Sámi culture and, 406, 407–8, 410–14
  voicing nonhuman animals in, 256–57, 268–72, 271f
Frozen (theatrical musical), 501–2, 505–6, 509, 513–14, 523, 525, 558–60, 578–79, 582
Frozen II, 110, 188–89, 198–202, 204–5, 224–25, 268, 392, 558–59
  joik in, 409, 410, 411–14
  Sámi culture and, 406, 407, 408–9, 410, 411–21, 422–23
Frozen JR., 545, 558–59
Funicello, Annette, 90, 302–3
Funny Little Bunnies, 9

Gad, Josh, 269
Galella, Donatella, 118
Gallagher, Peter, 212
Galm, Eric A., 454–55
Gannaway, Robert "Bobs," 135–36
Garay, Joaquin, 360
Garber, Victor, 222
Garcia, Desirée, 70
García Márquez, Gabriel, 463, 464, 466–67
Gargoyles, 414–15
Gaski, Harald, 413, 414–15
"Gaston," 579–80
Gattelli, Christopher, 531, 595–96
Gavin, James, 238, 244
Geffen, David, 483, 489
"Genie in a Bottle," 435–36

Genz, Stéphanie, 193–94
George, Gil, 233–34
Geppetto, 222, 223
Gerard, Richard H., 55
Geronimi, Clyde, 319–20
Gershwin, George, 32, 94n.34, 257–58, 319, 486–87
Gesamtkunstwerk, 31, 33
Ghisyawan, Krystal, 584–85
Giaimo, Michael, 407
Gilbert, Ray, 233–34
Gill, Florence, 9–10
Giron, Arthur, 488
Giroux, Henry, 422–23, 542, 543, 544
"Give a Little Whistle," 16
Goethe, Johann Wolfgang von, 354
Goldberg, Whoopi, 222, 390
Gold Diggers of 1933, 64, 67–68, 69
Goldenson, Leonard, 217
Goldman, Gary, 315–16
Goldmark, Daniel, 41, 55
Goldschmitt, Kariann, 358
"Good Neighbor" policy, 356–58, 451–52, 454, 470–71
Goofy, 10–11, 219, 453–54
Gorilla Mystery, The, 6
Gosse, Joanna, 357
"Go the Distance," 337
"Go with the Flow," 594
Grasshopper and the Ants, 9, 10–11, 13
Graziano, Rocky, 301
Grease Live!, 211–14, 215–16, 224
Great Depression, 36, 63, 64–65, 66–68, 69, 70, 182, 451–52
Great Mouse Detective, The, 320, 321
Greene, Ward, 233
Green Pastures, 78, 79–80, 93n.21
Grieg, Edvard, 4–5
Grier, Katherine, 270
Grinde, Nils, 410
Grob, Samuel, 544, 549
Groening, Matt, 318
Groff, Jonathan, 201–2, 270, 407
Grossman, Austin, 279–80
Grupo, El, 452–55, 456–57, 462, 464, 470–71
Gubar, Marah, 554–55
Guiliano, Edward, 152

Gulf Wars, 103, 106
Gullen, Christopher, 349–50
Gypsy, 394

Haas, Lynda, 559
Hackett, Susanne R., 559
"Had I Known," 233–34
Hahn, Don, 325–27
Hahn, Helene, 315–16
Hairspray Live!, 211–12, 213–14
Hairston, Jester, 89
Halberstam, Jack, 441
Hall, Carol, 484
Hall, David S., 149, 154
Hall, Juanita, 89
Hallelujah, I'm a Bum, 9
Hall Johnson Choir, 77–92, 93n.21, 95n.57
hallucination, color and, 352, 353–56, 357, 365f, 366, 367–68
Hamburger, Anne, 504, 535
Hamermesh, Daniel S., 600
Hamilton, 465, 493, 502, 507
Hamilton, Hamish, 212–13, 224, 225
Hamilton, Paula, 558
Hammerstein, Oscar, II, 9, 33, 389
Hammond, Mark, 138
Hanks, Tom, 179–80
"Hans of the Southern Isles," 582
Happy Harmonies, 347
"Happy Working Song," 192–93
Haraway, Donna, 269
Harline, Leigh, 8–12, 13, 16–18
Harmon, Francis, 88
Harris, Anita, 430–31, 440
Harris, Jeremy O., 534–35
Harris, Joel Chandler, 84
Harris, Phil, 297
Hart, Lorenz, 9, 390
Harwell, Drew, 602
Haughton, Hugh, 153, 163
Haydn, Richard, 163–64
Heath, Hy, 85
"Heigh Ho," 14, 68
Heiskell, Marian S., 491
"He Lives in You (Reprise)," 574–75
Helmsing, Mark, 392

"Help Me Harvest Corn," 9–10
"Help Me Plant My Corn," 9–10
Henderson, Charles, 27
Henley, Beth, 485–86
Henriksen, Christina, 409
Henson, Jim, 318
H.E.R., 388–89
Hercules (1997), 102, 194, 322–23, 323f, 337
Hercules (theatrical musical), 209–10, 512, 532–34, 535
"Her Voice," 577
"He's a Tramp," 234, 236
High School Musical, 68–69, 427–29, 433, 439, 501–2, 530–31
High School Musical the Musical the Series, 428
Hiller, Jeff, 209–10
Hilliard, Bob, 150, 158, 159, 160–65, 166
Hillin, Jim, 325–27
Himelstein, Mike, 288
Hischak, Thomas S., 580
H.M.S. Pinafore, 162–63
Hoffman, Al, 149–50, 156–57
Holliday, Christopher, 62–63
Hollywood musicals, 62–65, 66–68, 69, 70, 325–31, 336–37, 460
Holm, Celeste, 389
"Home," 384–85, 386, 387–88, 573
Home Again, Home Again, 485
"Home Sweet Home," 42–43, 48–49, 54–55, 56
Hoʻomalu, Mark Kaliʻi, 128–29, 133
Horn, Alan, 179
Horne, Lena, 91
"Hot Lips," 49–50, 54
Hour in Wonderland, An, 216–17
Houston, Whitney, 222, 389–90
Howard, Byron, 464
"How Does She Know," 199
"How Doth the Busy Little Bee" (Watts), 163–64
"How Do You Do and Shake Hands," 158–59
"How Long Must This Go On?," 573–74
Huemer, Dick, 83–84
hula, 132, 139
Humorous Phases of Funny Faces, 331–32
Hunchback of Notre Dame, The, 199, 221–22, 322, 336–39, 338f

Hunchback of Notre Dame, The (theatrical musical), 501, 523
Hungry Hoboes, 44–45
Husbands, Lilly, 203–4
Hussein, Saddam, 103
Hutcheon, Linda, 151, 153–54, 156
Huuki, Tuija, 414, 417
Huxley, Aldous, 347–48, 353–55, 356, 366, 367f
hyperrealism and hyperreality, 24–25, 32, 188, 331–32, 349

"I Am" songs, 572–74, 575–76, 577–78, 580–81, 582, 583–84, 585
"I Bring You a Song," 27
"I Can't Lose You," 578–79
"I Dreamed a Dream," 384–85
"If I Can't Love Her," 384, 553, 573–74
"If I Were a Bird," 11–12
"If Only," 435, 436–37, 577
Iger, Bob, 179, 606
"I Just Can't Wait to Be King," 574–75
"I'll Make a Man out of You," 335–36, 337–39
"I Love to Laugh," 180–81
Imagineering, 450–51
    Cultural Imagineering, 450–51, 460, 462, 464, 469, 470–71
"I'm Free as the Breeze," 233–34
"I'm Late," 162, 163
"I'm Odd," 158
"Impossible," 389–90
"I'm Wishing," 14, 15, 64–65
"In a World of My Own," 161–62
"I Need to Know," 575
Infante, Pedro, 460
Ingemann, Bernhard Severin, 411–12
"In the Good Old Summertime," 6
In the Heights, 465
Invitation to the Dance, 330–31
Irwin, Bill, 488
Iscove, Robert, 389
"I 198–99, See the Light,"
Isherwood, Charles, 504–5, 536
Ishizuka, Tomoko, 140
Islamophobia, 103
"It's a Small World," 281
"It's Crazy to Be Sane," 155, 156
"I've Got a Dream," 70, 197–98

INDEX

"I've Got No Strings," 16, 222
"I Want" songs, 64–65, 108, 161, 188–89, 197, 378, 382–83, 389, 394, 433–36
   in *Aladdin* (2019), 188–90, 194–97
   in Disney theatrical musicals, 572–73, 574, 575, 576, 577–78, 580–81, 582, 583–85
   liberating fantasy of, restaging, 189–97
   in *Ralph Breaks the Internet*, 189–93, 194, 199, 204–5
"I Want the Good Times Back," 580–81
"I Want to Hold Your Hand," 300–1
Iwerks, Ub, 3–4
"I Won't Say (I'm In Love)," 194

"Jabberwocky" (Carroll), 152–53, 157–58
Jackson, Eugene, 82–83, 94n.29
Jackson, Gemma, 112–14
Jackson, Wilfred, 3–4, 6
Jacobs, Lea, 41
Jacobsen, Emily, 534
jazz, 82–83, 84
Jeffords, Susan, 382–83
Jenkins, Henry, 478–79
Jennings, Nancy, 428–29
Jepsen, Carly Rae, 213–14
Jess-Cooke, Carolyn, 188
Jesus Christ Superstar, 211–12, 522
Jikŋon 2, 422
Jim Crow South, 87
"Jim Dear," 234
Jiminy Cricket, 16, 83, 218
Jobs, Steve, 179
Johansson, Scarlett, 231–32
John, Elton, 200–1, 327, 596
Johns, Glynis, 576
Johnson, Hall, 77–78, 94n.34
   Hall Johnson Choir, 77–92, 93n.21, 95n.57
Johnson, Mindy, 260–62
Johnston, Ollie, 298
joik and *joiking*, 407–8, 409, 410–14
"Jolly Holiday," 180–81, 285
Jones, Jade, 387–88
Jones, Wathea Sims, 90
Joshi, Kiran, 337–39
Journey into the Jungle Book, 591

Jungle Book, The (1967), 249, 256, 260–62, 297–99, 302, 303, 307, 310n.17
   the Beatles and, 298, 299, 300–2, 304, 305, 307–8, 308n.2
   Disney, W., and, 298, 299–302, 308n.4, 309n.15, 310n.17
   "We're Your Friends" in, 301–2, 304–5
Jungle Book, The (theatrical musical), 104–5, 512, 595–96
Jungle Rhythm, 18n.4, 285, 287
"Just a Pretty Face," 555–56
"Just around the Riverbend," 336–37
"Just Can't Wait to Be King," 325–27

Kahl, Milt, 298
Ka'ili, Tēvita, 558
Kain, Erik, 415
Kalvig, Anne, 415–16, 417
Kandel, Paul, 337–39
Kander, John, 380
Kang, Inkoo, 421
Kaplan, Martin, 176–77
Kapoor, Raj, 215–16, 225
Karnival Kid, The, 5
Katzenberg, Jeffrey, 176–77, 315–16, 377–78, 384, 490
Kaufman, J. B., 48, 357–58
Kelly, Gene, 330–31
Kendrick, Alexander, 300–1
Kern, Jerome, 9
Keskitalo, Aili, 408–9, 422
Kessler, Kelly, 428, 478–79, 480, 484
Khomeini (Ayatollah), 103
Khosla, Proma, 114–15
Kimball, Ward, 82–84, 151, 156, 370n.18
Kinemacolor, 348–49
King, C. Richard, 102
King, Jason, 385–86
King, Larry L., 484
King's Men, the, 81, 86
Kipling, Rudyard, 299–300, 309n.15, 595–96
"Kiss the Girl," 213, 214, 263–65, 264f, 607
"Kitten on the Keys," 8–9
Klein, Norman, 41
Kline, Natasha, 469–70
Klüver, Heinrich, 347–48, 353, 354–56, 363, 367–68
Knoll, Steve, 487

Kokai, Jennifer, 604–5
Korty, John, 317–18
Krause, Bernie, 258
Krippendorf's Tribe, 223
Kunze, Peter C., 111, 378, 489, 490–91
Kvidal-Røvik, Trine, 418, 421, 422–23
Kyrölä, Kata, 414, 417

LaBash, Michael, 136–37
Lachs, Stephen, 244–45
Lacroix, Celeste, 194
"Lady," 233–34
Lady and the Tramp, 218, 219–20, 224–25, 231–32, 233–36, 235f, 237f, 238–48, 260–62
"Lady and the Tramp," 233–34, 241
Lahr, John, 385
"La La Lu," 234
Lamarre, Thomas, 142
Land Before Time, The, 317–18
Lane, John T., 86–87
Lang, Edith, 53–54
Lange, Henry, 49–50
Lange, Johnny, 85
Langer, Mark, 331–32, 351–52
Lansbury, Angela, 183–84, 325–27
Lantz, Walter, 349–50
Lara, Agustín, 456
Lara, Camilo, 459–60
Larson, Eric, 235, 298
Lassell, Michael, 177–78, 526–27
Latinidad, 434–35, 437–38, 462–69
Latinx and Latin American communities, representations in Disney films and serials, 450–71
Laugh-O-Grams, 43–44, 64
Lavin, Jack, 234–35
Lawson, Valerie, 526
"Lea Halalela," 583
Lebo M, 583, 596
Lee, Jason Scott, 133, 137–38
Lee, Jeff, 524–25
Lee, Jennifer, 269, 391, 407
Lee, Peggy, 231–36, 235f, 237f, 238–49
Lee v. The Walt Disney Company, 240–48
"Legend of Davy Crockett, The," 218–19
Lehtola, Veli-Pekka, 410, 416
Leidecker, Lekey, 420–21

Lemish, Dafna, 428–29
Lennon, John, 308n.2
Leonardi, Susan, 379
Leon-Boys, Diana, 432–33, 437
Leondis, Tony, 136–37
Leroy & Stitch, 135–36, 137, 138, 140
Lessing, Gunther, 234–35
Lester, Catherine, 128
"Let It Go," 180, 187, 196–97, 391–92, 394–96, 407–8, 558–59, 578, 579, 594
"Let's Face the Music and Dance," 66–67
"Let's Get Together," 303, 304, 304t
"Let's Go Fly a Kite," 180–81
"Let's Sing a Gay Little Spring Song," 28–29
"Let the Rain Pour Down," 85–86
Leve, James, 543
Levin, Ira, 485
Lewis, Bert, 6, 11–12
Lewis, Hannah, 327–30
Lewis, Jerry Lee, 304
"Life I Lead, The," 174
"Like No Man I've Ever Seen," 585–86
Lili'uokalani, 133
Lilo & Stitch (2002), 125–27, 128–33, 134–39, 140–42, 143, 340
Lilo & Stitch 2: Stitch Has a Glitch, 136–37, 139
Lilo & Stitch: The Series, 126, 135–36, 137–39, 141–42
Lin, Dan, 112
"Lioness Hunt, The," 583
Lion King, The (1994), 101, 104–5, 198–99, 256, 392, 504
  branding and merchandising, 172
  computer animation in, 321, 322, 322f, 325–30
Lion King, The (2019), 172, 187, 340–41, 558–59
Lion King, The (theatrical musical), 222–23, 499, 501, 502, 504–6, 507, 508, 509, 571–72
  branding and marketing, 172, 509
  Disney theme parks and, 500–1
  licensing, 513–14
  merchandising, 172, 510–11
  new songs in, 574–75, 580, 582–83
  puppetry in, 592–93, 596–97, 598–99
  Shiki Company production of, 522–23
  Stage Entertainment production of, 523–24, 525
  Taymor and, 492, 500–1, 511, 583, 585–86, 596–97, 598–99

"Little April Shower," 26–27, 28–29
"Little Bit of You, A," 578–79
Little Mermaid, The (1989), 68–70, 104–5, 172, 189–91, 193, 194, 199, 224, 246, 268–69, 322
    Ashman and Menken songs for, 377–78, 380–81, 491, 499–500, 550–51, 571
    Disney Renaissance era and, 101, 315–16, 318, 490–91, 550–51
    diva villain in, 377–80
    in *The Little Mermaid Live!*, 212–13, 213f
    princess in, 378
    voicing nonhuman animals in, 256–57, 263–68, 264f, 266f
Little Mermaid, The (2023), 547, 594–95
Little Mermaid, The (theatrical musical), 212–13, 501–2, 512, 513–14, 523, 531, 535–36, 544–45, 553–54, 576–77, 580–81, 584–85
Little Mermaid, The (theme park show), 607
Little Mermaid Live!, The, 210, 211, 212–16, 213f, 214f, 215f, 217–18, 221–22, 223–25
Little Shop of Horrors, 377–78, 571
live television musicals, 210–16
Living Desert, The, 366
Livingston, Jerry, 149–50, 156–57
Liv & Maddie, 434
"Llorona, La," 461
Locke, Alain, 79
Loftis, Cory, 415
Lokey, Hicks, 350, 351
"Loneliness of Evening," 389
Lonesome Ghosts, 219
"Looking for Romance (I Bring You a Song)," 28–29
"Look Out for Mr. Stork," 81
Lopez, Robert, 391, 394–95, 592–93
"Lost in the Woods," 188–89, 198–202, 204–5
Lott, Rob, 606
Louis-Dreyfus, Julia, 222
Lounsbery, John, 298, 350
"Love Is an Open Door," 198–99, 395, 578, 582
"Love Is a Song," 20, 26, 28–29
Love Me Tonight, 9
Lucas, George, 318, 321
Lugo-Lugo, Carmen, 102
Lullaby Land, 9

Lumenick, Lou, 179–80
Lunenfeld, Peter, 436
Lustyik, Katalin, 428
Luz, Dora, 363–65, 364f, 456
Lynch, Aubrey, II, 522–23

"Ma Belle Evangeline," 197
Macaluso, Michael, 559–60
MacDonald, Jimmy, 260–62
MacDougall, Tom, 464
Machon, Josephine, 603
Mackintosh, Cameron, 177, 179, 184, 489, 490, 498, 501–2, 509, 526–27
"Mack the Knife," 380
Macleod, Dianne Sachko, 103–4
Macnab, Geoffrey, 179–80
MacNeille, Tress, 288
Mad Doctor, The, 279–80
"Madness of King Scar, The," 580, 583
magic realism, 463, 465, 466–67
"Maison des Lunes," 579–80
Make Mine Music, 348–49
Maleficent, 110, 194–95, 202, 433
Maleficent 2: Mistress of Evil, 433
Malik, Zayn, 114
Mallan, Kerry, 380
Malotte, Al, 11–12
Mamma Mia!, 549
Mamoulian, Rouben, 33
Mancina, Mark, 583
"Man Has Dreams, A," 174
"Man Has Dreams, A (Reprise)," 580
Manufacturing and Production Organization (MAPO), 175–76, 177
Marcel, Kelly, 179
"March of the Cards," 165
"March of the Dwarfs," 4–5
Marin, Cheech, 246, 457
Marshall, Garry, 486
Marshall, Rob, 180, 389
Martin, Mary, 210–11
Mary Poppins (1964), 150, 173–76, 179, 180–82, 183–84, 285, 298–99, 330–31, 499, 526, 576, 583–84
Mary Poppins (theatrical musical), 177–78, 184, 499, 501–2, 506, 511, 526–27, 576, 580, 582, 583–84

Mary Poppins brand and franchise, 172–73, 175–78, 179–84, 511
Mary Poppins Comes Back, 176–77
Mary Poppins Returns, 180–83
Mask, Mia, 390
Mason, James, 218
Masterson, Peter, 484
Maurer, Cynthia, 428
Mayorga, Edwin, 420–21
McCann, Elizabeth I., 487–89
McClain, China Anne, 437–38
McDaniel, Hattie, 85, 88
McDonald, Audra, 222
McGillis, Roderick, 380
McLaren, Norman, 361
McQuillan, Martin, 103
"Me," 579–81
Meador, Joshua, 358, 361
"Mean Papa, Turn in Your Key (You Don't Live Here No More)," 50–51
Meet Me Down on Main Street, 306–7
Meinel, Dietmar, 340–41
Méliès, Georges, 363–64
Mellomen, the, 165, 306–7
Melody Time, 348–49
Menken, Alan, 189–90, 194–95, 200–1, 386, 529–30, 573–74, 577, 581–82
  Ashman and, 104–5, 327, 377–78, 380–81, 384, 491, 500, 550–51, 571, 577–78, 584–85
  Feldman and, 530, 532, 555–56, 584
Menzel, Idina, 391, 393–95, 433–34, 594
Merino, Yvett, 464, 469
Meron, Neil, 210
Merrick, David, 502
Merrie Melodies, 347
Merritt, Russell, 6, 48
Messmer, Otto, 47
"Meu Brasil Brasileiro / Mulato inzoneiro," 358
Mexicanidad, 459–60
Meyer, Irwin, 485
MGM, 349–50
Michele, Lea, 212
Mickey Mouse
  in *Building a Building*, 7
  Disney, W., on, 40–41
  in *Epic Mickey*, 277–80, 279f, 281, 282f, 283–87, 284f

  in *Epic Mickey 2*, 287, 290–91
  in *Fantasia*, 219
  in *The Karnival Kid*, 5
  MacDonald voicing, 260–62
  in *Mickey's Follies*, 5
  The Opry House, 4
  in *Plane Crazy*, 219
  in *Puppy Love*, 8
  in *Steamboat Willie*, 3–4, 56
  in *The Worm Turns*, 349
Mickey Mouse Club, 55, 89
Mickey Mouse Club, The (MMC), 90–91, 281
mickey-mousing, 21–22, 25–28, 29, 31–32, 41, 165, 193, 274n.16, 285
Mickey's Follies, 5, 6, 13–14
Mickey's Nightmare, 56
Mickey's Once upon a Christmas, 223
Miller, Bob, 50–51
Miller, Jack, 356–57
"Million Miles Away, A," 581–82, 584–85
Mills, Hayley, 303
Mills, Mara, 262
Minkoff, Rob, 379
Minnie Mouse, 3–4, 7, 8
"Minnie's Yoo Hoo," 5, 6, 18n.3, 18n.4
Miranda, Aurora, 359–60, 455
Miranda, Carmen, 360–61, 455
Miranda, Lin-Manuel, 464–65, 467
Misérables, Les, 384–85, 503
Mitchell, Lisa, 548
MMC. *See* Mickey Mouse Club, The
Moana, 102, 110–11, 131–32, 190, 408, 465, 547
Moana JR., 547, 556–58
"Mob Song, The," 579–80
Molina, Carmen, 365–66
Mollet, Tracey, 194–95, 202
Monaghan, Whitney, 441–42
"Monster," 578, 579
Montan, Chris, 584
Montgomery, Colleen, 131–32
Moore, Freddie, 350
Moore, Mandy, 191–92
Moreno, Gaby, 458
Moreno, Rita, 388–89
Morét, Villa, 5
Morey, Larry, 12, 13, 14, 15, 20, 26, 28–29
Morgan-Ellis, Esther, 54–55

Morrill, Sharon, 137
Morton, Alicia, 222
Mother Goose Goes to Hollywood, 82
"Mouse Song, The," 262
Mouzakis, Sotirios, 558
MTI. *See* Music Theatre International
Mueller, John, 316–17
Mulan, 102, 108, 110–11, 134, 223, 225, 277–78, 322, 335–36, 337–39, 391, 450
Mulan (2020), 340–41
multiculturalism, 101–2, 112, 114, 116–17, 438–39, 458, 462–63, 464, 466
Mundy, Rachel, 257
Murin, Patti, 579
Murphy, Donna, 380
Murphy, Patrick D., 382
Music Land, 8–9
Music Man, The, 306, 499, 507
Music Theatre International (MTI), 505, 512, 513–14, 543, 544–46, 547, 548–49, 551, 556
Musker, John, 379
My Fair Lady, 175–76, 181–82
"My Once upon a Time," 435–36
My One and Only, 486–87
"Mysterious Fathoms Below," 215f

NAACP, 85–88, 89–90
"Na Baixa do Sapateiro," 360–61
"Nants Ingonyama Bagithi Baba," 583
Neale, Steve, 190
Negrete, Jorge, 455–56, 460
Neil, J. Meredith, 602–3
neoliberalism, 429, 434–35, 437, 440, 490, 559–60
Nesset, Deborah, 241
"Never Gonna Dance," 64
New Amsterdam Theater, 177, 491, 492, 493, 503, 504–5, 506, 510–11, 542
New Deal, 67–68, 451–52
Newman, Thomas, 180
New Negro movement, 79
Newsies (1992), 529–30
Newsies (theatrical musical), 512–13, 529–32, 533, 545, 548, 554–56, 581, 582, 584
"News Is Getting Better, The," 581
Nicholaw, Casey, 571–72
Nichtern, Claire, 485–86, 487, 488–89

Nickelodeon, 429
Nightmare before Christmas, The, 330
Nine, 486–87
Nobile, Greg, 534–35
"No Other Way," 585
Norma, 376
Norwood, Brandy, 389–90
Novis, Donald, 28–29
"Nowhere to Go but Up," 180–81, 183–84
Nugent, Nelle, 487–89

O'Brien, Wendell, 600–1
Occupy Wall Street, 531–32
Oceanic Story Trust, 110–11, 557, 558
Ochoa, Ana Maria, 466–67
O'Connell, Katie, 246
O'Connor, Ken, 350, 352
Odedra, Kaushal, 118
Oh, What a Knight, 43–44, 283–85
O'Hara, Paige, 323–24, 381, 384, 385
Oh Teacher, 50
"Oh Teacher Teacher: Let Me Do the Teaching Awhile," 50
Oklahoma!, 33, 493, 506–7
Oksanen, Aslak-Antti, 419–20
"Old Father William," 158–59, 162
"Old Trusty," 234
Olin, Spencer, 234–35
Oliveira, Aloysio (Louis), 358
Oliver & Company, 246, 317–18, 320, 457
Oliver Twist, 223
O'Malley, J. Pat, 158–59
"Once upon a Dream," 67, 197, 218, 280, 283
Once upon a Time, 106, 117–18, 433
One Hundred and One Dalmatians, 320
"One Jump Ahead," 108, 577–78
"One Jump Ahead (reprise)," 108
"One Kiss," 434–35
"One Song," 14–15
On Ice, 10–11
Ooi, Can-Seng, 606
Opper, Frederick Burr, 49
"Opposites Attract," 330–31
Opry House, The, 4, 56
Orbach, Jerry, 325–27
orientalism, 101, 102–5, 109, 112–14, 117–18, 163–64, 595–96

Orr, Christopher, 181–82
Orr de Gutiérrez, Daniel, 420–21
Orsi, Nick, 415–16
Ortega, Kenny, 432, 433
Ortiz, James, 533
Osatinski, Amy S., 592, 595–96
Osborne, Ted, 149, 155
Osma, Natalie, 464
Oswald the Lucky Rabbit cartoons, 40, 41–52, 42f, 47f, 54, 56
　Epic Mickey 2 and, 288–89, 290–91
　Epic Mickey and, 277–78, 279–80, 282, 283–86, 287
"Out There," 336–37, 338f
"Over the Rainbow," 64–65
Ovitz, Michael, 542
Ozzie of the Mounted, 47

"Painting the Roses Red," 165
Pallant, Chris, 62–63, 125, 134–35, 316
Paper Mill Playhouse, 512–13, 514, 530–32, 533–34, 581
Papiano, Neil, 241, 245
Paramount, 484–85, 486–87, 514
Paramount Decision, 1948, 216–17
Parent Trap, The, 277–78, 303, 304
Parker, Fess, 218–19, 220
Parmalee, Ted, 355
"Part of Your World," 190–91, 194, 213, 378, 576, 577, 607
Passion, The, 212
Pastoureau, Michel, 350–51
patriarchy, 174, 183, 190–91, 194, 195, 196–97, 442–43, 558
Paul, Gene de, 149–50, 157–58
Payne, John Howard, 42–43
PCA. *See* Production Code Administration
"Peace on Earth," 234
Pearce, Douglas G., 600
Pearce, Philip, 606
Pearce, Philip L., 600
Pearson, Ridley, 528–29
Peer, Ralph, 357–58
Peet, Bill, 298, 299–301, 309n.15
Peggy Lee v. Walt Disney Productions, 232
Penner, Ed, 233–34, 236
Perea, Katia, 135–36

Perez Stodolny, Rebecca, 469
Perkins, Al, 149, 154
Peter and the Starcatcher, 501–2, 528–29
Peter Pan, 150, 161–62, 218–19, 233–34, 260–62, 361, 414–15
Peter Pan (live television musical), 210–11, 499
Peter Pan (theatrical musical), 499
Peter Pan Live!, 211, 213–14
Peters, Bernadette, 222, 380, 390
Pfitzer, Gary, 322
Phang, Jennifer, 427
Phantom of the Opera, The, 384–85, 503
Philadelphia Orchestra, 249
Phillips, Graham, 213
Phillips, Stevie, 484
Picnic, The, 6
Pielmeier, John, 486–87
Pierce, Todd James, 82
Pierson, Michele, 319–20, 321
"Pig and Pepper," 150–51, 154
"Pink Elephants on Parade" song and sequence, 81, 331–32, 332f, 349–53, 351f, 356, 358, 359–60, 363–65, 367
Pink Flamingos, 379
Pinocchio, 16–18, 22–23, 81, 83, 218, 222, 256, 348–49, 361
Pinocchio (theatrical musical), 512
Pixar Animation Studios, 321, 322, 325–27, 340–41, 450–51, 459, 460, 462, 469, 470–71
"Place Called Slaughter Race, A," 188–91, 192–94, 199, 204–5
"Place Where Lost Things Go, The," 180–81, 183
Plane Crazy, 41, 219, 278
Platinum, 486
"Playing the Game," 178
Plumb, Edward, 25, 27, 32
Pluto, 219
Pocahontas, 322, 336–37, 414–15, 421, 450
Pocketwatch, The, 427–28
Pollock, Grace, 422–23
polyopic repetitions, 356, 363, 365, 366, 367
Pomeroy, John, 315–16
Poor Papa, 43–44, 47–48, 49, 49f, 54, 56
"Poor Papa (He's Got Nothin' at All)," 49, 52

"Poor Unfortunate Souls," 213, 214f, 380, 580–81, 607
Pope, Rebecca, 379
Porgy and Bess, 83–84, 95n.56
Porter, Billy, 390
Posner, Dassia N., 597
postfeminism, 188–90, 193–95, 196–97, 198–99, 432–33, 435, 559–60
Potgieger, Liske, 393–94
Potgieger, Zelda, 393–94
Potter, Anna, 428
"Practically Perfect," 576
Practical Pig, The, 184
Presley, Elvis, 128–29, 139, 302
presque vu, 356, 363, 366, 367
Prez, Josquin des, 257–58
Prima, Gia, 249
Primos, 469–70
"Prince Ali," 114–15, 581–82
"Prince Is Giving a Ball, The," 390
Princess and the Frog, The, 67, 102, 105, 189–90, 197, 340, 391, 442
princesses, 375–77, 378, 380–84, 387, 388, 391, 395–96, 415, 550–51, 552–53, 559–60, 574
prindiva, 377, 380–84, 387, 388–89
Procolombia, 463, 463f, 473n.43
Production Code Administration (PCA), 87
"Proud of Your Boy," 577–78, 581–82
Psych Out, 356
Public Theater's Public Works program, 532–33, 535
Puppy Love, 8
"Puppy Love," 8
Purse, Lisa, 319

Quayle, Dick, 50
Queen, 201–2
Queen Latifah, 213, 214
"Quindins de Yayá, Os," 357–58, 455

racism, 77–78, 102, 103, 213–14, 420–21, 595–96
Radcliffe, E. B., 24
"Rafiki Mourns," 583
Rahn, Suzanne, 607
Rajagopalan, Hema, 595–96
Ralph Breaks the Internet, 188, 189–93, 194, 197–98, 199, 200, 204–5

Ramirez, Juan, 533
Ramnarine, Tina, 410–11
Rapee, Erno, 53–54
Ratatouille: The TikTok Musical, 534–35
Raya and the Last Dragon, 187, 408
Raye, Don, 149–50, 157–58
Reagan, John J., 241
Reagan, Ronald, 239, 480–82
realism, surrealism and, 349–53
"Red Hot Mama," 49–50
Rees, Roger, 528–29
Regency Communications, 485
"Reindeer(s) Are Better Than People," 199, 270, 271f, 272
Reitherman, Woolie, 298
"Remember Me," 460, 461f
RenderMan software, 322, 325–27
Rendon, Juan, 464
Rent Live!, 212, 213–14
Rescuers, The, 320
Rescuers Down Under, The, 188, 321, 500
residual compensation, 238–49
Reyes, Juan Pablo, 469
Reznik, Shiri, 428–29
Rhythm of the Pride Lands, 583
Rice, Tim, 327, 384, 386, 500, 574, 581–82, 596
Rich, Frank, 384, 492–93, 500, 524–25, 551, 571
Rinaldi, Joe, 236
Ristola, Jacqueline, 414
Ritchie, Guy, 108, 110–11, 112, 115–16
Rival Romeos, 4, 45–47, 47f, 49–50, 51, 54
Rivers of Light, 598–99
Roast, The, 486
Robber Kitten, The, 11
Roberts, Shearon, 383–84
Robertson, Barbara, 321, 322
Robinson, Cédric, 85–86
Robinson, Mark A., 580
Robley, Les Paul, 321
rock and roll, 298, 299, 301–5, 303t, 304t, 307
Rockefeller, Nelson, 356–57, 451–52
Rocky Horror Picture Show, The: Let's Do the Time Warp Again, 212
Rodgers, Richard, 9, 33, 389, 390
Rodgers and Hammerstein's Cinderella, 222, 223, 377, 380, 389–90, 499
Roen, Terry, 602

Rogers, Ginger, 9, 63–64, 66–67, 325–27, 390
Rogers, James Bradley, 33–34
Rogers Doyle, Jennifer, 427
Romy and Michele's High School Reunion, 223
Ronell, Ann, 7
Rooney, David, 532, 585
Rooney, Mickey, 239–40, 242
Roosevelt, Franklin Delano, 63, 64–65, 66, 67–68, 451–52
Rose, Billy, 49
Rose, Fred, 49–50
Roth, Robert Jess, 384
"Rotten to the Core," 431, 434–35, 436–37, 441
"Row, Row, Row Your Boat," 163
Rowley, George, 366
"Royal Doulton Music Hall, The," 180–81
Rubins, Dan, 384–85, 386, 387–88
Ruddell, Caroline, 203–4
Ruggiero, Evan, 387
Ruiz Cano, Jorge, 469
Run, Little Chillun, 80
Russell, Dave, 54–55
Ruwe, Donelle, 543

"Sab Sahi Hai Bro," 115–16
SAG. *See* Screen Actors Guild
"Sailor's Hornpipe," 163
St. Louis Blues, 80–81
Saldanha, Arun, 357
Salisbury, Mark, 156
Saludos Amigos, 84, 347–48, 349–50, 352–53, 356–60, 359f, 367, 368, 452, 453–54, 456–57, 460
Sámi people and culture
　Frozen and, 406, 407–8, 410–14
　Frozen II and, 406, 407, 408–9, 410, 411–21, 422–23
　joik and, 407–8, 409, 410–14
Sammond, Nicholas, 47–48, 51
Samuel, Lawrence R., 63
Sanders, Chris, 125, 128, 129–35, 136, 137–39, 142
Sanders, George, 297
Sandoval, Mathew, 458–59
San Filippo, Maria, 202
Santa's Workshop, 7
Santoro, Flavia, 473n.43

Satia, Priya, 421
Saving Mr. Banks, 179–80, 181–82, 183
Savran, David, 432
Schatz, Thomas, 349–50
Schechner, Richard, 596
Schneider, Peter, 492, 500, 506
Schorsch, Rebecca S., 593–95
Schrader, David, 511
Schreiber, Michele, 202
Schroeder, Russell, 233–34
Schumacher, Thomas, 492, 500–1, 502, 504–5, 506–7, 510, 511, 512–13, 514–15, 526–27, 528, 529, 534–35, 536, 542, 546, 571–72
Schwab, Bill, 418
Schwartz, Stephen, 222, 512
scintillation, 361–64, 364f, 366, 367–68, 367f
Scott, A. O., 129–30
Scott, Naomi, 116–17
Screen Actors Guild (SAG), 232, 238–39, 246, 249
Screen Cartoonists Guild, 23–24
Seal Island, 219–20
Sears, Ted, 150, 162, 163–64, 356–57
"Second Star to the Right, The," 161–62
"Seize the Day," 584
Sellars, Peter, 486–87
sequels and remakes, 188, 189–205, 209–10, 340–41, 433
"Shadowland," 583, 584–85
Shafer, Mark, 508–9
Shaggy, 213, 214
Shaiman, Marc, 180, 183
Shakira, 464–65
Sharpsteen, Ben, 83–84, 218–20
Shaw, Helen, 534–35
Shearer, Martha, 330–31
"She Loves You," 300–1
Sherkow, Dan, 486, 487
Sherman, Al, 298–99
Sherman, Richard M., 173, 174, 176, 177, 184, 298–99, 302–4, 308n.2, 310n.17, 576
Sherman, Robert B., 173, 174, 176, 177, 184, 298–99, 302–4, 308n.2, 310n.17, 576
Shiki Company, 522–23, 525
Show Boat, 9
"Show Yourself," 201–2
Shrader, David, 507

Shrek, 200–1
Shrek 2, 200–1
Shrek franchise, 188, 200–1
Shrek the Musical, 498
"Siamese Cat Song, The," 234, 236, 237f
Sibley, Brian, 158–59, 176–78, 526–27
silent-era Disney cartoons, 40–55, 47f, 56
"Silly Song, The," 14
Silly Symphonies, 3, 4, 6, 7, 8–12, 22, 64, 285, 316, 340–41, 347, 348–49, 362–63
Silson, James, 604
Silverman, Sarah, 191–92
Silvestri, Alan, 128–29
Simpson, Eugene Thamon, 77, 78, 80, 89, 90–91, 95nn.56–57
Simpsons, The, 318
"Singing ('Cause He Wants to Sing)," 234
Sister Act, 525
"Sister Suffragette," 182–83, 576
Skeleton Dance, The, 4–5, 6, 13–14
Sky Scrappers, 44–45
Slater, Shawn, 604
Sleeping Beauty, 67, 197, 218, 249, 280, 283, 347, 375, 377–78, 457–58, 550–51
"Slow but Sure," 11
Slyfield, Sam, 83–84
Smash Mouth, 200–1
Smith, Brad, 385
Smith, Clara, 50–51
Smith, Matthew Wilson, 31
Smith, Paul J., 13
Smith, Russell, 134
Smith, Susan, 330
Smith, Webb, 356–57
Smith, Will, 105–6, 111–12, 114
Smoodin, Eric, 35
Snider Sway, Solon, 385, 386–87
Snow White and the Seven Dwarfs, 3, 12–15, 16–17, 22, 36, 48, 81, 164, 172, 317–18, 347, 348–49, 499–500, 550–51
  American dream and, 62–63, 64–65, 67, 70
  Bambi and, 20, 22–23, 25, 26, 29, 30–31, 258
  Caselotti and Stockwell seeking residual compensation for, 248
  "Cinderella" narrative of, 64–66
  collectivism in, 67–70
  color and visual effects in, 355, 361
  Disney, W., and, 12–13, 64, 68
  fairy tales and, 64–67, 68, 70, 375
  Hall Johnson Choir and, 93n.21
  "Heigh Ho" in, 14, 68
  "I'm Wishing" in, 14, 15, 64–65
  "Someday My Prince Will Come" in, 13–14, 15, 16–17, 64–65, 66, 161, 248
  sound design of, nonhuman animals and, 258–60, 261f
  voicing nonhuman animals in, 256–57, 258
  on *Walt Disney's Disneyland*, 219
  "Whistle while You Work" in, 14, 15, 65, 67, 68–69, 256
  "With a Smile and a Song" in, 14, 260, 261f
"So Close," 198–99
Sofia the First: Once upon a Princess, 457–58
"Solamente una vez," 456
Solomon, Charles, 317–20
"Somebody Rubbed Out My Robin," 11
"Someday My Prince Will Come," 13–14, 15, 16–17, 64–65, 66, 161, 248
"Something There," 573–74
"Something to Believe In," 584
Sondheim, Stephen, 390
"Song of the Roustabouts," 81, 86
Song of the South, 77–78, 84–90, 218–19
Son of Man, 78
"Son of Man," 335–36, 336f, 337
Sorrensen, Ingvild, 428
"So This Is Love," 197
Sound of Music Live!, The, 210–11, 213–14, 224
South of the Border with Disney, 453
Space Jam, 223
"Speak Roughly to Your Little Boy," 156
Spector, Warren, 277, 278–79, 285–86, 288, 291
"Speechless," 188–90, 194–97, 204–5, 377–78
"Speechless (Part 2)," 107, 108
Spielberg, Stephen, 321
Spiner, Brent, 222
"Spoonful of Sugar, A," 177, 180–81, 576, 580
Sportsmen Quartet, the, 81
Sprites and Sprouts, 90–91
Stage Entertainment, 523–25, 533–34
Staiger, Janet, 63–64
Stalling, Carl, 4–5, 6, 11–12, 17–18, 55
Stanley, Helene, 218
Starlight Express, 524–25

Star Wars, 281–82
"Stay Awake," 174
"Steamboat Bill," 283
Steamboat Willie, 3–4, 20, 21–22, 36, 40–41, 46, 56, 282, 283, 287
"Step in Time," 180–81
Stern, Daniel, 367
Stern, Robert A. M., 491
Sterne, Jonathan, 262
Stevens, Dan, 388
Stevenson, Robert, 176
Stickney, Dorothy, 390
Stigwood, Robert, 489
Stiles, George, 576
Stilwell, Robynn J., 428, 438
Stitch!, 126–27, 135–36, 138, 140–42, 143
Stitch and Ai, 126–27, 140, 141–42, 143
Stockwell, Harry, 248
Stoddard, Guy, 50
Stokowski, Leopold, 23, 249
Stoner, Sherri, 381
"Story of My Life, The," 584
Straus, Oscar, 50
Strauss, Skye, 597
Strike, Joe, 137
Stubblefield, Chad, 416
Sullivan, Pat, 47
Summers, Sam, 200–1
Sundberg, Norman D., 600–1
Sunset Boulevard, 379
"Supercalifragilisticexpialidocious," 173–74, 180–81
"Sure as Sun Turns to Moon," 585
surrealism, 347–48, 349–53
"Suspicious Minds," 128
Swank-Haviland, Norma, 260–62
Sweet, Joshua Strongbear, 91–92
"(You're the Flower of My Heart,) Sweet Adeline," 55
Swenson, Charles, 317–18
Swift, Howard, 350
Swing Time, 64
Symonds, Dominic, 428
synchronization, audiovisual, 21–22, 26, 41

"Tall Paul," 302–3
Tall Timber, 43–44, 47

Tally, Robert T., Jr., 109
Tangled, 68, 69–70, 107, 189–90, 191–92, 193–94, 197–99, 200–2, 380, 391
Tannen, Ned, 484
Tarzan (1999), 332–36, 336f, 337–40
Tarzan (theatrical musical), 501–2, 512, 513–14, 524–25, 531, 535–36, 575, 579, 582, 585–86
Tarzan Rocks!, 591
Tasker, Yvonne, 198–99, 202
Taymor, Julie, 492, 500–1, 511, 583, 585–86, 596–97, 598–99
Team Disney, 125–26, 176–77, 179
Technicolor, 319, 350–51, 351f
Technicolor IV, 347–49, 355
Ted Eshbaugh Studios, 348–49
Teen Beach Movie, 428
Teitelbaum, Sheldon, 322–24
television, 216–17, 223–25
    Disney, W., and, 216, 217, 218–19, 220, 224–25
    Disneyland, *Walt Disney's Disneyland* and, 217–20, 221
    The Wonderful World of Disney on, 210, 221–22, 223, 389
television musicals, 427–29, 432–35, 436, 442–43
    live, 210–16
Tell Tale Heart, The, 355
Telotte, J. P., 319
"Temper, Temper," 178
Tenniel, John, 153, 163–64
Terminator II: Judgment Day, 322–23
"That Fellow's a Friend Of Man," 234
"That's How You Know," 197–98
"That's Rich," 555–56
"There's Music in You," 389–90
"These Palace Walls," 584–85
"They Live in You," 574–75
Thomas, Frank, 151, 298
Thompson, Bill, 163
Thompson, Emma, 179–80
Thompson, Kristin, 63–64
Three Caballeros, The, 84, 347–48, 349–50, 352–53, 356–57, 359–67, 362f, 364f, 365f, 367, 367f, 368, 453, 454–56, 460, 461
"Three Caballeros, The," 366

"Three Cheers for Anything," 17
Three Little Pigs, 7–8, 9–10, 13–14, 64, 184
Three Little Wolves, 184
Threepenny Opera, The, 380
Through the Looking-Glass (Carroll), 152–53, 156–57, 159
Through the Mirror, 278
"Tico-Tico no Fubá," 357–59
Tiger Town, 221
Timbers, Alex, 528–29
Times Square redevelopment, Disney in, 482, 489–90, 491–93, 498, 503, 542, 601–2
Tin Pan Alley, 149–50, 298–99, 303–4, 306, 307
Tiomkin, Dmitri, 93n.21
Tomlinson, David, 176
Toohey, Peter, 600–1
Toombs, Harvey, 350
Top Hat, 66–67
"Topsy Turvy," 337–39
Torre, Roma, 533
Tortoise and the Hare, The, 11
Total Abandon, 488
Touchdown Mickey, 18n.4
Touchstone Pictures, 223, 514
Toy Story, 221–22, 340, 501
Transjoik, 411
Trapedo, Shaina, 559
"Trashin' the Camp," 575
Travers, P. L., 174, 176–77, 178–79, 181–82, 184, 526–27, 583–84
Treasure Planet, 340
Trip, The, 356
"Trip a Little Light Fantastic," 180–81
Trip to the Moon, A, 363–64
"True Love," 578, 579
Trump, Donald, 554–55
Tucker, Sophie, 49–50
"Tulou Tagaloa," 190
Tune, Tommy, 486–87
"Turkey in the Straw," 3–4, 56
Turner, Ted, 489
"Turning Turtle," 180–81
"Turn On the Old Music Box," 17
Tuton, Marc, 180
"'Twas Brillig," 149–50, 157–58, 160
20th Century Fox and 21st Century Fox, 483, 514

20,000 Leagues under the Sea, 218, 219–20
Twiggy, 486–87
"Two Worlds," 335–36

"Ugg-a-Wugg," 213–14
Ugly Duckling, The, 64
"Unbirthday Song, The," 149–50, 156–57, 158–59, 165
Uncle Remus and Uncle Remus stories, 84–87, 218–19
"Uncle Remus Said," 85
Uncle Tom's Crabbin', 47
"Under the Sea," 68–69, 193, 214, 215f, 265–68, 607
United Productions of America (UPA), 349–50
Universal, 484–85, 486
Universal Theatrical Group, 514
UPA. *See* United Productions of America
Upton, Brian, 299
Usher, 222
Utsi, Anne Lájla, 409

Valdivia, Angharad, 117, 428, 437–39
Valkeapää, Nils-Aslak, 410, 411, 414–15
Vandersommers, Dan, 257
Van Dyke, Dick, 182
Vanishing Prairie, 219–20
"Very Good Advice," 164–65
VFX. *See* digital visual effects
Vieira, Juan Carlos Poveda, 454
Viertel, Thomas, 499, 510
Vining, Iris Ethel, 50, 52–53, 54, 55
virtual reality (VR), 336–37
visionary experience and perception, 347–48, 353–54, 355, 356, 363
Vives, Carlos, 464–65
"Você Já Foi à Bahía?," 360–61
VR. *See* virtual reality
"Vuelie," 190, 407–8, 411–14

Wagner, Harry, 52–53
Wagner, Richard, 30–31, 33, 283–85
"Waiting for This Moment," 585
Wallace, Oliver, 81, 83–84, 150, 162, 163–64, 233–34, 349–50
"Walrus and the Carpenter, The," 158–59, 160, 162

Walt Disney Animation Florida, 134
Walt Disney Japan, 140
Walt Disney's Disneyland, 217–20, 221, 224–25, 236, 237f, 244
Walt Disney World, 175–76, 277–78, 279–80, 320, 348, 362–63, 502, 503, 507, 508f, 520, 591–92, 599–602, 603–4, 607
War Activities Committee, of motion-picture industry, 87–88
Ward, Ann-Hould, 384, 385–86
Ward, Zhavia, 114
Warfield, William, 79
Warner, Kristen J., 438–39
Warner Bros., 349–50, 484–86, 487, 514
Warren, Leslie Ann, 389
Warren-Crow, Heather, 436, 438–39
Washington, Ned, 16–17, 81, 83–84, 349–50
Wasko, Janet, 62–63, 125–26
"Watch What Happens," 555, 584–85
Waters, John, 379
Watson, Emma, 388
Watts, Isaac, 163–64
Watts, Steven, 35–36
Weaver, Sylvester "Pat," 210–11
Webber, Andrew Lloyd, 490, 522
WED Enterprises, 175–76
"We Don't Talk about Bruno," 465
Weidman-Winter, Rebecca, 388, 553
Weill, Kurt, 380
Welker, Frank, 270, 288
Wells, Frank, 176–77, 315–16, 490
Wells, Gilbert, 49–50
Wells, Paul, 24, 33–34, 105–6
"We're All in This Together," 68–69
"We're Gonna Get Out of the Dumps," 11–12
"We're Your Friends," 301–2, 304–5
West, George, 53–54
West-Knights, Imogen, 376
WGA. *See* Writers Guild of America
"What Is a Baby?," 234
"When I'm Older," 201–2
"When I 81–83, 84, See an Elephant Fly,"
"When You Wish upon a Star," 16–17, 81, 218
"Whistle while You Work," 14, 15, 65, 67, 68–69, 256
White, Noni, 530

whiteness, 102, 357, 432–33, 435, 437–39, 441, 442–43, 474n.52
Whitfield, Sarah, 560, 578–79
Whitley, David, 24–25, 29, 332–35
Whitney, John Hay, 452
Who Framed Roger Rabbit, 318
Who Killed Cock Robin?, 11
"Whole New World, A," 114, 188–89, 194, 198–99, 202, 203–5, 336–37, 377–78, 577–78, 584–85
"Whole New World (End Title), A," 114
"Who'll Buy a Box Lunch?," 7
"Who's Afraid of the Big Bad Wolf?," 7–8, 9, 10–11, 13–14, 17, 64
"Why Me," 581–82
Wicked, 393–94, 433–34, 509, 511
Wickstrom, Maurya, 596
Williams, Esther, 330–31
Williams, Joshua, 595–96
Williams, Robin, 105, 111–12, 323–24
"Willkommen," 380
"Will You Love Me Tonight," 11
Wilson, Jude, 600
Winfield, Jess, 135–36, 141–42
Winkler, Margaret, 48
Winnie the Pooh, 223, 260–62
Wise, Christopher, 103
Wise Little Hen, The, 9–10
"With a Smile and a Song," 14, 260, 261f
Wittman, Marc, 606
Wittman, Scott, 180, 183
Wittmer, Micah, 79
Wiz, The, 483
Wizard of Oz, The, 64–65
Wiz Live!, The, 211, 213–14
Wolcott, Charles, 32, 452, 464
Wolf, Stacy, 429, 444n.14, 546, 560
Wonderful World of Color, The, 362–63
Wonderful World of Disney, The, 210, 221–22, 223, 389
Wood, Elijah, 223
Woodland Café, 82
Woods, Harry, 49
Woodward, Agnes, 256
Woolverton, Linda, 380–81, 384, 553, 573–74, 579–80
Wordsworth, Sara, 604

"Work Song, The," 256
"Work Song, The (Cinderelly, Cinderelly)," 262
Works Progress Administration (WPA), 77–78, 80, 90–91
"World Above, The," 576–78
"World of Aladdin," 112
"World Owes Me a Living, The," 9, 10–11, 13–14
World War II, 24, 36, 87–88, 233, 347–48, 452
"World Will Know, The," 584
Worm Turns, The, 349
WPA. *See* Works Progress Administration
Wreck-It Ralph, 188–89, 190, 193–94
Wren, Celia, 388
Wright, Cobina, 78
Wright, Doug, 576–77, 580–81
Writers Guild of America (WGA), 239, 249
Writing, Samuel E., 265
Wrubel, Allie, 233–34
Wynn, Ed, 156

Yi-Fu Tuan, 109
yōkai, 140–41
"Yo soy la blanca paloma," 454
"You Belong to My Heart," 359–60, 363, 456
"You'll Be in My Heart," 575, 585
You're a Good Man, Charlie Brown, 499
"You're Nothin' but a Nothin'," 11–12
"You're Sixteen," 303

Zadan, Craig, 210
Zaldy, 214
Zambello, Francesca, 576–77
Zamecnik, J. S., 51–52
Zielinski, Kathy, 379
Zimmer, Hans, 327, 583
Zimmerman, Mary, 595–96
Zombies, 439
Zootopia, 187–88, 464
Zulager, William, 244